MW00846208

Principles of Cognition

Principles of Cognition
Finding Minds

Eduardo Mercado III

University at Buffalo, The State University of New York

Princeton University Press   Princeton and Oxford

Copyright © 2024 by Princeton University Press

Princeton University Press is committed to the protection of copyright and the intellectual property our authors entrust to us. Copyright promotes the progress and integrity of knowledge. Thank you for supporting free speech and the global exchange of ideas by purchasing an authorized edition of this book. If you wish to reproduce or distribute any part of it in any form, please obtain permission.

Requests for permission to reproduce material from this work should be sent to permissions@press.princeton.edu

Published by Princeton University Press

41 William Street, Princeton, New Jersey 08540

99 Banbury Road, Oxford OX2 6JX

press.princeton.edu

All Rights Reserved

Library of Congress Cataloging-in-Publication Data

Names: Mercado, Eduardo, author.
Title: Principles of cognition : finding minds / Eduardo Mercado III.
Description: Princeton : Princeton University Press, [2024] | Includes bibliographical references and index.
Identifiers: LCCN 2023045160 (print) | LCCN 2023045161 (ebook) | ISBN 9780691225043 (paperback ; alk. paper) | ISBN 9780691225050 (ebook)
Subjects: LCSH: Cognition.
Classification: LCC BF311 .M4475 2024 (print) | LCC BF311 (ebook) | DDC 53—dc23/eng/20240124
LC record available at https://lccn.loc.gov/2023045160
LC ebook record available at https://lccn.loc.gov/2023045161

British Library Cataloging-in-Publication Data is available

Editorial: Sydney Carroll and Johannah Walkowicz
Production Editorial: Terri O'Prey
Text Design: Wanda España
Cover Design: Wanda España
Production: Jacqueline Poirier

Cover art by Brandon Lillibridge

This book has been composed in Minion 3 Display and Rustica

Printed in China

10 9 8 7 6 5 4 3 2 1

In memory of Akeakamai, Hiapo, Phoenix, and Elele
minds worth knowing

Brief Contents

Contents

| **Chapter 2** | **Mechanisms of Mind** | **35** |

Preface

On page two of *The Principles of Psychology*, published in 1890, William James notes the following:

"Any particular cognition, for example, or recollection, is accounted for on the soul-theory by being referred to the spiritual faculties of Cognition or of Memory. These faculties themselves are thought to be the absolute properties of the soul…there is something grotesque and irrational in the supposition that the soul is equipped with elementary powers of such an ingeniously intricate sort. Why *should* our memory cling more easily to the near than the remote? Why should it lose its grasp of proper sooner than abstract names? Such peculiarities seem quite fantastic; and might…be the precise opposites of what they are."

James then proceeds, over the following 1000+ pages, to do his best to make some sense of the many peculiarities associated with the operations of minds.

James was invited to write *Principles*, widely acknowledged as the first textbook devoted to psychology, by the publisher Henry Holt in 1878. After spending twelve years working on the book, James described it to his publisher as "a loathsome, distended, tumefied, bloated, dropsical mass, testifying…that there is no such thing as a *science* of psychology, and 2nd, that W. J. is an incapable." A couple of years after finishing *Principles*, James created an abridged version, *Psychology: The Briefer Course,* which he described as "more directly available for classroom use." My aim in writing this textbook was to build on the legacy of William James by providing a modern, comprehensive overview of what psychologists currently know about the nature of cognition.

Critics of this book suggested that attempting to "update James" was a mistake, noting that James's ideas about minds were outdated and more focused on consciousness than cognitive psychology. A different book written by Ulric Neisser called *Cognitive Psychology,* that was published more than seventy years after *Principles,* was offered as a better starting point, because many regard it as the first textbook on cognition. I invite the reader to compare and consider the table of contents for each of these seminal textbooks, summarized here:

Cognitive Psychology by Neisser	*Briefer Course* by James
1. The cognitive approach	2.–6. Sensation in general: Sight, hearing, touch, motion
2. Iconic storage and verbal coding	7.–9. Structure and functions of the brain and neural activity
3. Pattern recognition	13. Attention
4. Focal attention and figural synthesis	14. Conception
5. Words as visual patterns	15. Discrimination
6. Visual memory	16. Association
7. Speech perception	17. Sense of time
8. Echoic memory and auditory attention	18. Memory
9. Active verbal memory	19. Imagination
10. Sentences	20. Perception
11. A cognitive approach to memory and thought	21. Perception of space
	22. Reasoning
	23. Consciousness and movement
	24. Emotion

To my mind, the topics covered by James provide the more modern and comprehensive overview of the fields of cognitive psychology and cognitive neuroscience. James reviewed studies of imagery, concept formation, reasoning, and conscious awareness, topics that are at the core of current cognition research. James also closely considered the mechanisms of attention, learning, perception, and memory. While Neisser's textbook was groundbreaking and helped solidify a resurgence of scientific interest in cognitive processes, James's *Principles* and its abridged cousin established cognitive processes and their neural substrates as the foundation of psychological science.

It's fair to assume that James's century old ideas about cognition have not stood the test of time given that thousands of experimental studies of cognitive processes have been performed since he wrote *Principles*. Fair but false. Precursors to modern theories of embodied cognition, cognitive plasticity, multimodal perception, and dynamic processes in cognitive development, are evident throughout James's textbook, along with descriptions of memory and concept formation that are similar to modern interpretations. Considering cognition from a Jamesian perspective is not simply a historical exercise. It is an attempt to come to grips with those aspects of cognition that are most scientifically challenging: understanding how cognition works, the role of awareness in mental processes, and the factors that determine what it is possible for an individual to know. Modern cognitive research has not resolved the origins or principles of the cognitive "peculiarities" noted by James. If anything, those peculiarities have metastasized. The strength of James's approach is that he addresses these cognitive conundrums head-on, even when he recognizes that the odds are low that his analyses will reveal the truth of the matter.

In my attempt to take up James's baton, I have deviated from the status quo textbook structure that is today the mainstay of cognitive psychology courses around the world. Some topics that typically span several chapters in other textbooks have been compressed into a single chapter in this one, while other topics that are seldom mentioned in other textbooks are discussed in detail here. Like *Briefer Course*, there are hundreds of pages of text that I have not included for the sake of making the material manageable. If you're expecting that reading this textbook will provide you with a thorough understanding of all things cognitive, then sadly you will be disappointed. Like *Principles*, which James described as "mainly a mass of descriptive details," this textbook, like most textbooks and despite my best efforts to keep things concise, probably contains more details than you need to know. However, they are a means to an end. Similar to taking vitamins, where you don't need to retain every vitamin and mineral they offer in order to gain health benefits, you don't need to memorize every last detail included in this book to gain insights into the science of cognition.

I began my cognitive psychology career attempting to train dolphins to learn concepts about shapes and actions, which they eventually did learn. This hands-on experience was both exciting and confusing yet taught me an incredible amount about cognition and minds. Throughout this book, I've attempted to not only capture some of this excitement, but to also not shy away from the inevitable confusion we face when confronting a non-human mind (as well as a human mind). Confusion is not your enemy when trying to understand cognition—or when trying to understand anything really—but complacency, boredom, and certainty will most likely do you in. I've tried to avoid this.

I've ordered chapters in this book mostly following the standard orthodoxy, but in my opinion this order is not the best way to teach cognitive psychology to undergraduates. Consequently, I've tried to make the book as reconfigurable as possible so that the intrepid reader/instructor can use the chapters in almost any order. I did not want to repeat James's mistake of writing a textbook that he could not use for his own classes. I personally favor the original organization used by James, which starts with brain function, then shifts to "habit" (a topic covered using slightly different jargon in Chapter 7 of this book), followed by consciousness and attention, concept formation, memory, and finally perception and reasoning. If any reader is curious why I (and James) think this order is preferable, feel free to contact me at emiii@buffalo.edu. To my knowledge, no one has ever conducted an experiment to measure the effect that teaching cognitive topics in different orders has on understanding or enlightenment, so it's possible that whatever way you chose to read or use the book will be the optimal way.

Each chapter attempts to combine the old and the new, including pointers to some of the newest theories and findings, along with descriptions of classic conceptualizations. Some topics are emphasized because there are new and interesting findings from the field of neuroscience which can clarify the cognitive processes involved. Other topics are mentioned because it is possible to study them experimentally in non-human animals, or because they have some societal implications that I thought were worth highlighting. If some of your favorite topics or findings are missing, join the club! There are tons of intriguing scientific data and ideas relevant to better understanding cognition. This book is only intended as a starting point for those interested in knowing more.

In *Principles*, James noted that centuries may pass before scientists get a handle on "cognitions, reasonings, decisions, and the like." So far, his predicted timeline has proven to be accurate. Although much more is now known about cognitive processes and their underlying mechanisms than was known in the 1800s, many of the dominant ideas about memory, attention, and thought today are not substantially different from those proposed by Aristotle over two thousand years ago. How likely is it that Aristotle got things wrong in thinking that all matter is a combination of earth, air, fire, and water, but was spot on in his explanations of how minds work? Are the models and mechanisms described throughout this text a leap forward or a scientific sidestep? You will have to judge for yourself, turning the tools of mentality against themselves, questioning both your understanding of the relevant data and others' explanations of what cognition is and the principles of mental function.

ACKNOWLEDGMENTS

I am grateful to the team at Princeton University Press for taking on the challenge of crafting a textbook on cognitive psychology designed to rock the boat. The editor that transformed the original idea for this book from proposal to project was not a member of that team, however. Jane Potter was the first editor to buy into the idea that a Jamesian frame could provide a new way of synthesizing findings from studies of brains and cognition that goes beyond human neuroimaging research. Her endorsement and encouragement made this book possible. Sydney Carroll took up Jane's torch (twice) and kept the project chugging along, despite COVID-related complications. Two developmental editors worked their way through multiple versions of chapters: Kerry O'Neill and Danna Lockwood. I am particularly grateful to Danna who spent many hours working out details of figures and photos, in addition to the work she did correcting my prose. Jan Troutt was given the unenviable task of trying to make sense of my artistic misdirection to create the broad range of images appearing throughout this book. The book took six years to progress from one chapter to twelve (half the time it took James!), and I'm guessing everyone on the team was more than ready to send it to the printer by the end.

If you think six years is a long time to work on a book, then you will be horrified to learn that the book was originally conceived, organized, and sketched out more than a decade earlier than the completion of the first chapter, during my time as a Fellow at the Center for Advanced Study in the Behavioral Sciences at Stanford (CASBS). The support I received at CASBS, from center staff as well as the other fellows I interacted during my idyllic time there, was invaluable to building the momentum required to integrate the broad range of topics studied by cognitive psychologists. I also am indebted to Martha Daniel Newell, whose support for the Newell Visiting Scholar program at Georgia College & State University made it possible for me to test out my approach to integrating human and animal cognition research within a course called "Mammalian Minds."

Numerous undergraduate and graduate students have left their marks on the contents of this book through their comments and questions in class and responses to earlier drafts of chapters. Karen Chow provided extensive suggestions and critiques on the social cognition chapter (Chapter 11); she continues to be skeptical. Aria Wiseblatt offered numerous questions and specific suggestions for corrections on multiple chapters. Finally, Sydney Emley, my first and finest undergraduate teaching assistant, helped collect feedback from many students about what aspects of the cognitive topics were most and least appreciated.

Several colleagues have both directly and indirectly influenced the form and flavor of this book. Mark Gluck (Rutgers-Newark) and Catherine Myers (Rutgers-New Jersey Medical School), who I have collaborated with on textbook writing for a quarter century, have shaped my thinking on learning, plasticity, cognitive neuroscience, computational modeling, and applied cognitive psychology. Many of the pedagogical strategies inculcated within and between chapters are the progeny of my experiences writing on cognitive topics with them. Paulo Carvalho (Carnegie Mellon University) provided useful feedback on earlier versions of the book, especially in relation to how cognitive theories are incorporated into chapters. Ava Brent (Columbia University) helped tremendously with finding illustrations, refining figures, corralling definitions, and motivating me to keep moving forward.

Reviewers who provided feedback on specific chapters include Scott Murray (University of Washington), Chris McNorgan (University at Buffalo, SUNY), James Magnuson (University of Connecticut), Tom Palmeri (Vanderbilt University), Paul Meyer (University at Buffalo, SUNY), and Julia Hyland Bruno (New Jersey Institute of Technology). Additional reviewers also provided thoughtful feedback: Martin van den Berg (California State University, Chico), Steven Neese (Cornell College), Kevin Autry (California State Polytechnic University, Pomona), Dale Dagenbach (Wake Forest University), Jessica Engelbrecht (The New School for Social Research), Robert J. Hines (University of Arkansas, Little Rock), Justin Hulbert (Bard College), Alexandra Morrison (California State University, Sacramento), Donald Tellinghuisen (Calvin University), and Molly Zimmerman (Fordham University).

Finally, a word of thanks to my family members. My mother, Donna Mercado, continually supported my academic efforts, even when they involved wacky ideas like moving to Hawaii to explore how dolphins think. My wife, Itzel Orduña, has constantly had to pick up the slack on the many days I spent staring at my laptop trying to solve some new textbook-related riddle. Fiora (aka Amalia) critically and brutally assessed artwork and examples throughout the book, while Iam assisted with Powerpoint edits and cat herding.

Beginnings

Humans have probably studied minds informally for as long as minds have been around. Psychological laboratories, in contrast, only began popping up at universities in the nineteenth century. One of the first psychology labs was established by a professor at Harvard named William James (1842–1910). James used his lab mainly for teaching demonstrations as part of the first known psychology course ever offered.

William James started off his career as a painter but quickly switched over to chemistry, then physiology, and finally ended up in medical school. Dissatisfied with medicine, he briefly followed in the footsteps of Darwin by joining an expedition to the Amazon as a naturalist, where he quickly discovered a deep dislike of jungles. After a period in Europe, supposedly spent studying the physiology of nervous systems, James ultimately got a position at Harvard as an instructor teaching comparative physiology. Soon afterward, the first course in psychology and its associated laboratory were born.

From Physiologist to Cognitive Psychologist

James started studying medicine mainly because his father told him to, and he chose physiology as a focus to avoid having to deal with doctors and patients. He became intrigued, however, by the emerging research experiments relating sensations to neural circuits being developed in Germany. James's first course on psychology was called "The Relations between Physiology and Psychology," reflecting his early interest in linking brain mechanisms to mental processes. In fact, the main focus of this course was on the new experimental methods that German researchers developed to study "physiological psychology" and "psychophysics."

The starting point for psychology in the United States was thus based on experimental studies of sensation, perception, and the relationship between mental experiences and biological mechanisms. James's interests in psychology quickly shifted from understanding the mechanisms of mentality to identifying fundamental principles that described how all minds function. James attempted to explain these principles in what is widely regarded as the first textbook on psychology, a lengthy text entitled *The Principles of Psychology*. The first principle James identified was, "the phenomena of habit in living beings are due to the plasticity of the organic materials of which their bodies are composed" (James, 1890, v.1, p. 105). In other words, James claimed that the things people and other animals do and think on a regular basis are the result of physical changes in their nervous system that have accumulated throughout their lives. Those changes not only affect how you might walk and talk but also how you see the world and understand it.

In the first volume of *Principles*, James lays out how neural plasticity and habits affect consciousness of the self, attention, conceptual thought, the perception of time, learning, and memory. His second volume extends these ideas to explain imagination, spatial perception, production of voluntary actions, emotions, and reasoning. In attempting to understand and explain how minds work, James quickly identified many of the core processes that are now the focus of cognitive research around the world.

Cognition and Consciousness

Ironically, paternal attempts to lead James toward a practical life in the field of medicine ultimately led him to pursue a career that by the standards of that time was probably even less respectable than a career as a painter. James's interest in mental states quickly expanded into personal explorations of spiritualism and transcendent psychedelic states (often pharmaceutically induced). James famously rejected the idea that cognition could be understood mechanistically and instead argued that psychology should be the science of mental states, especially consciously experienced "streams of thought." That is not to say that James disregarded the role of the brain. The second chapter of *Principles* is an extended discussion of brain function. And, as noted earlier, James considered human "habits" to be the direct result of changes to peoples' brains. Nevertheless, from the Jamesian perspective, neural circuits serve mainly as channels that guide the ways in which your conscious states tend to flow, they do not determine what you think or the kinds of cognitions that might arise from those states.

As you'll see in the next several chapters, cognition continues to be central to our understanding of minds and behavior, forming the core of what distinguishes psychology as a scientific field. Modern cognitive research, however, tends to focus less on the experiential elements of thought that James thought were critical and more on the collection, organization, and manipulation of information. It has only been in the last decade that cognitive scientists have begun to give James's "first principle" the consideration it deserves. If your everyday activities and thought patterns are the cumulative outcomes of physical changes in your neural pathways that have been building up since the time you were born, then what does it mean to say that your brain (or mind) is like a biological computer or information processor? Because computers do NOT change their hardware based on how they are used. And so far, computers appear to experience nothing. What really makes something cognitive? Are behavioral, neural, or experiential properties critical? Or is storage and manipulation of information key? Following the path blazed by James, the next three chapters argue that behavior, brains, and consciousness are all fundamental components of cognition and to truly understand minds one needs to experimentally explore how all three change over time.

1 The Science of Minds

Max4e Photo via Shutterstock

The final tally: Watson with $77,147 and everyone else in the competition, combined, with $45,600. So ended humankind's reign as master of the television quiz show *Jeopardy!* (**Figure 1.1**)

Contestants on *Jeopardy!* must supply answers, in question form, that match specific clues from a wide range of categories, including pop culture, history, and science. To qualify for the show, people have to pass a screening quiz and do well in practice games. Successful contestants have a phenomenal ability to rapidly retrieve answers that match the clues.

IBM's Watson, a system that originally included a room-sized supercomputer, was developed to compete on *Jeopardy!* and win. The more impressive part of Watson's performance on *Jeopardy!*, however, was its ability to use spoken sentences to construct appropriate questions to the clues. Some of the clues involved puns, allusions, or obscure references, making them challenging for many people, never mind a machine, to answer.

Watson differs from most apps in that it improves over time through a kind of trial-and-error learning; it's not simply following predefined programs. According to its makers and marketers, Watson is the first cognitive computer.

But what does it mean to say that a computer is cognitive? What would a computer have to do to qualify as cognitive? In general, the kinds of things a computer needs to do to be called cognitive are the same things a person might do that other people would consider cognitive—things like responding appropriately to spoken sentences, recognizing familiar individuals, making reasonable decisions, solving problems in clever ways, remembering things that they've been told, and so on. In short, a cognitive computer should behave somewhat like a human.

This seems like a straightforward criterion until you try to decide which specific computer behaviors should be compared to human behaviors. Animatronic robots at Disneyland *act* a lot like humans, but you probably wouldn't say that they *think* like humans. Digital personal assistants like

FIGURE 1.1. Watson. IBM's Watson computer system dominated human champions on the game show *Jeopardy!* What do the superior abilities of machines, at least when playing mind games, tell us about cognition?

Siri can answer your questions and follow your instructions. Does that mean Siri knows, perceives, or understands anything about you or what you are trying to achieve? Probably not. Did IBM's Watson need to know anything about people or the world to beat its human competitors? Or was it simply Siri with a bigger library of facts?

Watson shares many of the qualities that are associated with cognition, but not all of them. First, the system responded to natural sentences and produced answers comparable to those produced by the other contestants. Watson's behavior, therefore, mimicked the behavior of the contestants, whom everyone would agree are thinkers. Second, the sentences Watson produced were mostly correct responses. This is what raises Watson above the level of a talking doll. Watson's sentences are intelligent, in that they demonstrate Watson's ability to solve problems by flexibly accessing and conveying facts. If you heard Watson competing and weren't aware of its digital nature, you'd probably be convinced that "he" was just as cognitive as any other contestant.

One quality that distinguishes Watson from other *Jeopardy!* contestants is that Watson doesn't want to win. Fundamentally, Watson does not understand what winning is all about. Watson cannot appreciate the pressure of competition, the uncertainty of other contestants, or the implications of the outcome of the contest.

Most people don't have access to the piles of facts that Watson does, but they do know what it's like to watch people compete and can even imagine what it's like to be a contestant. This kind of awareness is what makes watching game shows entertaining. It's also what makes knowing that Lincoln was president of the United States (a fact) different from knowing that you have never been the president (a personal memory).

There are some exceptional individuals who are able to recall massive amounts of details about past events (LePort et al., 2017), somewhat like Watson. When people with this ability attend a sporting event, they can answer questions about details of the game years after the event, including the date it happened, what the weather was like, and who made critical plays. This impressive recall ability is called **highly superior autobiographical memory (HSAM)**, and it is not limited to sports—detailed memories of many meals, lines from movies, clothes worn, and emotions felt are also available. People with highly superior autobiographical memory describe memory retrieval as reliving a previous moment in time. You might experience something similar if you think back to some of the most notable events of your life.

Your ability to remember notable events and the feelings of familiarity that they spark are essential components of cognition. Watson lacks any ability to do this. Calling Watson cognitive is like saying a puppet is funny. Puppets are funny only to the extent that their puppeteers make them look and act funny. Puppies, on the other hand, are often funny without the help of handlers.

What makes puppies funny, at least partly, is the way they actively explore the world. But what exactly are playful puppies doing? Are they forming personal memories of playing with your shoe that they will recall the next time they see you? If they were, how would you be able to tell? If a puppy learns to recognize you and seems to have fun playing with you, does this mean that the puppy thinks about you? Which is more cognitive: a computerized *Jeopardy!* champion or a playful puppy? Or maybe both are cognition-less?

Cognition, which enables people to contemplate, converse, question, realize, reflect, remember, solve problems, think, and understand, seems self-evident yet it's enigmatic. Lacking cognition, people become little more than bodies. At its peak, cognition enables geniuses to reshape planets.

This book is about the scientific study of cognition, including how studies are carried out and what such studies have revealed. People have been interested in the nature and capacities of minds long before scientists came on the scene, but it has only been in the last century that researchers have begun to pinpoint the mechanisms that make minds tick. As you read this chapter, you will gain a better sense of the types of questions that cognitive psychologists have answered and the types that they have yet to answer—questions like, "What would it take to give Watson a mind or to show that it has one?"

COGNITION: IT'S WHAT YOU THINK

SNEAK PEEK: Psychologists develop models to better understand how cognition works. By looking at how well different models predict and explain what individuals notice, remember, and think, researchers can change the ways that future generations think about thinking.

Psychology is often described as the study of mind and behavior—two topics that are different yet undoubtedly linked. The connection between mind and behavior is apparent from the way people talk about them. For instance, people whose behavior is abnormal are described as having mental disorders, which implies that their minds aren't working right. Similarly, actions that seem foolish or pointless often are described as "mindless." While behavior mainly refers to those things you do with your body—or physical activities that you could record yourself doing—the concept of mind is trickier to define.

Right now, you're reading, and you could record yourself doing it, so it's a behavior. But while you're reading, you might also be thinking about other things, such as what you're planning on doing later. That's not going to show up in the video. Also, while you are reading, you might come across an unfamiliar acronym like HSAM. Feelings of uncertainty are not going to show up in the video either.

These kinds of hidden mental actions and events probably seem just as real to you as reading, even if no one else can verify that they're happening. It seems reasonable to say that if physical activities are what your body does then mental activities must be what some hidden part of your body does.

Mind is what many people in Western societies call that hidden part, and cognition refers to a particular kind of mental activity, sort of like how "sports" refers to certain kinds of physical activities. Just as the prowess of an athlete depends on that athlete's body, the genius of a thinker depends on that thinker's mind. But since no one has ever seen a mind, it's difficult to know what properties of it would even contribute to genius.

When athletes perform, they exercise a range of skills—running, hitting, catching, aiming—that when combined together might be called competing. When thinkers perform, they similarly engage in various mental skills—perceiving, knowing, understanding, recognizing. This kind of mental performance is referred to as cognizing.

When you **cognize**, you are consciously aware of ongoing events, both internal and external. A process is considered to be cognitive when it involves an act of cognizing, just like a sporting event is competitive when it involves athletes competing.

Cognizing may seem a lot like thinking. But thinking usually involves some effort to achieve a goal (see Chapter 10), while cognizing does not necessarily require any effort. You pretty much just have to be awake and taking in your experiences.

Because mental activities are unobservable to everyone other than the person performing them (and sometimes to the person who is cognizing, too), it's often difficult to know when or how minds actually matter. Is mindless behavior ever really mind-free? How much control do minds have over behavior, and what is it about minds that enable them to cognize? In attempting to answer such questions, cognitive psychologists rely heavily on models of minds.

Models of Minds

Imagine a kindergartner asks you what a mind is. Assuming you don't go with the classic "I don't know," you might attempt to explain to the child what a mind is by using various examples. Of course, your explanation might lead to a never-ending stream of follow-up questions, but in the best-case scenario, you will manage to come up with answers that satisfy the child's curiosity.

In answering the question, you're providing the child with a conceptual model, or simplified description, of how to think about a mind. People have come up with all kinds of conceptual models of minds. One of the most influential of these is the model popularized by the French philosopher René Descartes (1596–1650) (**Figure 1.2**).

In Descartes's model, your mind (or, as Descartes called it, your soul) is not part of the physical world, and so it does not follow the same rules as objects in the world, including your body (Descartes, 1644/1984; 1662/1972). This division between body and mind maps smoothly onto the difference between physical (public) and mental (private) activities. Moreover, it offers the possibility of mental immortality, making the model intuitively appealing. From a scientific per-

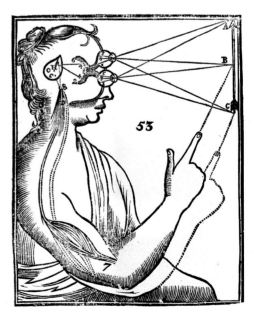

FIGURE 1.2. Descartes' model of how minds work. Descartes viewed minds as spiritually based controllers of bodies. He modeled bodily actions as a kind of hydraulics in which external events release fluids in the brain that trigger the release of other fluids that control muscles. The mind influenced these processes remotely from a spiritual world—the eyes react, but the mind sees. (Photo 12/Alamy Stock Photo)

spective, however, Descartes' model doesn't explain much about why minds work the way they do nor does it provide many insights into how one might heal a mind that has become "disordered" (Urban, 2018).

Associationist Models

While Descartes focused on the unique capacities of minds, such as their ability to think, other philosophers pointed out that the kinds of thinking performed by minds seemed to depend a lot on experience (Locke, 1693). They noted that scholars who grew up in different countries often used different languages, writing systems, and explanations for how minds work. Most thoughts, ideas, and concepts that you have are a consequence of memories you've formed from past experiences, and many of your mental activities depend on your ability to make connections between current events and past experiences.

For example, if most apples you've seen are red, you'll tend to link the color red to apples. If you draw an apple, describe one, or imagine eating one, it will likely be a red one. Everything you know and understand about apples comes from past encounters you've had with them, including what you've read about them. Since apples are not the only things that are red, this color will also be linked to other objects you've experienced. In **associationist models** of mind, cumulative experiences shape how you think.

One of the more influential associationist models was proposed in the late 1800s by the American psychophilosopher William James (1842–1910) (**Figure 1.3**). James proposed that the links between memories and ideas are literally physical connections in your brain and that these associative connections form gradually, becoming stronger over time. In other words, James thought that the organization of your thoughts directly corresponds to the structural organization of observable, physical connections inside your head (James, 1890; 1962). This associationist model implies that most thoughts, ideas, and concepts that you have are a consequence of memories you've formed from past experiences

James's approach carried models of mind from the domain of religion and philosophy into the world of science. In principle, since physical connections in the brain are observable, those connections can be compared with how people think about things. Many modern models of minds argue that "minds are brains" or that "minds are what brains do," which seems similar to what James claimed. However, James actually ridiculed the idea that minds are brains; instead, he felt that mental states

FIGURE 1.3. William James. (A) American mind modeler and explorer of conscious cognition. James was the first psychologist to champion the idea that mental contents are a function of physical links between brain cells that make it possible for experiences to guide thought processes. (B) In James' associationist model, your mental activities are like a set of falling dominos; ongoing events knock over the first "mental domino," which then triggers the retrieval of associated memories (shown here as connected circles). Modern associationist models are descendants of James's ideas. (A MS Am 1092 (1185), Houghton Library, Harvard University; B after Hurwitz 2016.)

(A)

(B)

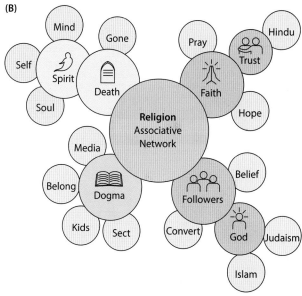

FIGURE 1.4. A computational model of letter recognition. Early computer models portrayed perception and identification of letters as a process of recognizing simple features followed by recognition of combinations of those simple features.

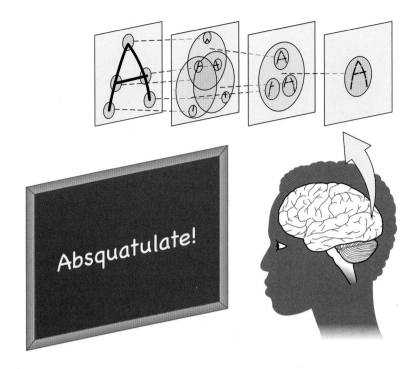

followed different laws from those that determine physical reactions within brains. He particularly emphasized purposeful action, willpower, and consciousness as key features of minds (Marchetti, 2021).

Modern examples of associationist models appear several times throughout this book—anytime you see the word "network," "connections," or "learning," you should immediately think, "Here comes another associationist model."

Minds as Machines

When Descartes split minds from bodies, he described bodies as biological machines. He argued that humans were the only creatures with bodies that also housed a mind; all other animals were deemed mindless machines.

James took the opposite position, claiming that every organism that could move probably had a mind, even going so far as to suggest that the minds of the most capable nonhuman animals were cognitively superior to those of the least capable humans.

It was only a matter of time before someone suggested a third possibility: that minds *are* machines (Putnam, 1960). If you think that this third option seems counterintuitive, you may be surprised to learn that this is the most popular model among all modern scientists.

The mind-as-machine model is commonly called the **computational theory of mind**. It proposes that brains are biological computers and that minds are information processing systems (like IBM's Watson) (**Figure 1.4**). From this perspective, cognition is computation (Minsky, 1986). In the terminology of computers, brains are the hardware, cognitive processes and consciousness are the software, and together they make up a mind.

The computational theory of mind began gaining steam in the 1960s, about the same time that computers started becoming useful tools and neuroscience began to take off as a scientific field (Fodor & Pylyshyn, 1988). Part of the appeal of this model was that one could use computers to simulate mental activities, creating the first physical (electronic) models of minds (Oliveira, 2022). These simulations included computer programs specifically designed to behave like humans—**artificial intelligence (AI)**—the forerunners to today's chatbots and automated customer services.

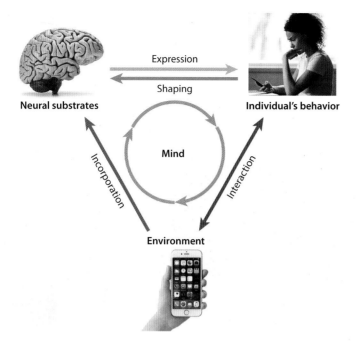

FIGURE 1.5. Expanding the concept of mind. While most mind models lodge your mind inside your brain, the extended mind thesis claims that your mind includes elements of the world outside your head, including objects you interact with to augment your cognitive activities and your own actions. (After Lux et al., 2021, brain: DNY59, student: Fizkes, phone: Prykhodov)

External Elements of Minds

In the last few decades, there has been a mini-rebellion against the computational theory of mind, based on the idea that how minds operate is tightly linked to the bodies and environments within which they function—unlike most computers (Clark & Chalmers, 1998; Menary, 2010).

This newest model of mind, sometimes called the **extended mind thesis**, proposes that minds are not something trapped inside your head; instead, minds encompass any tools that you use to support your thought processes, including written notes, computers, smartphones, and even your own body (**Figure 1.5**). Have you ever talked to yourself when no one else was around, sung in the shower, or pulled your hair in frustration? The extended mind thesis suggests that such behavior is not a sign of mild derangement but may actually support or enhance certain mental processes (Ongaro et al., 2022).

Minds are many-splendored entities: souls, brains, associations, machines, and more. Like ancient astronomers, cognitive psychologists are able to explore and describe patterns in the movements of minds without necessarily having a complete grasp of what the patterns mean or even what it is that they're seeing move.

Cognitive processes are the constellations in these patterns—scientific mind maps of associated phenomena given weighty labels like "attention," "language," and "memory." As you read through this text, you may discover new ways of thinking about minds and cognition, expanding not only your understanding of what cognition is but also your ability to judge the pros and cons of different claims about how your mind works. An important step toward both goals is to get a better handle on why cognitive psychologists are obsessed with models.

Why Models Matter

Models of cognitive processes—all the operations of your mind that enable you to cognize—come in two basic flavors: quantitative and qualitative. Quantitative models are based on quantities, represented as numbers, and on techniques for combining or comparing those quantities, like equations. The most common quantitative models used by cognitive psychologists are computational models—basically, computer simulations of cognitive processes (Farrell & Lewandowsky, 2018). Most other models are qualitative, meaning that they focus on describing the qualities of a cognitive process, usually through diagrams and/or stories. Both quantitative and qualitative models are abstractions that try to capture some essential elements of what cognizing involves and how cognitive processes work (**Figure 1.6**).

(A) Data to be explained

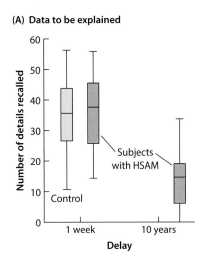

(B) Qualitative model

(C) Quantitative model

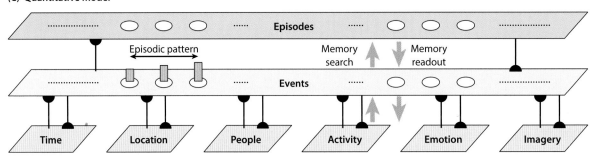

FIGURE 1.6. Modeling variations in autobiographical memory. (A) Behavioral studies show that a subset of adults (subjects with highly superior autobiographical memory) can recall details of personal episodes after a decade. (B) Qualitative models often explain this unique ability as an almost limitless capacity for mentally replaying past episodes. (C) A quantitative model of variations in autobiographical memory must specify numerically what information people store from their experiences, how each event is represented (in this example as an episodic pattern), and how specific episodes from the past are found and reactivated. In this model, verbal questions about a past date would trigger an episodic pattern, after which a memory search would be initiated to locate a past episode that best matches that pattern, making recall of additional details possible. (A after Wang et al., 2016; B bubble: shironosov; square: martin-dm; C after LePort et al., 2016.)

Here's a qualitative model of highly superior autobiographical memory: "People with highly superior autobiographical memory are more likely to recall details of personal episodes many years after they happened. Most people store memories of notable events and can recall those events years later. People with highly superior autobiographical memory process memories the same way as everyone else but perceive every day of their life as highly notable. Why? Because the part of their brain that detects cross-day similarities is dysfunctional, such that every day seems special."

This qualitative model explains a unique cognitive ability—highly superior autobiographical memory—as an extension of the usual memory mechanisms that most people possess caused by a brain disorder. You could potentially create a quantitative model of highly superior autobiographical memory that is similar to this qualitative model. The quantitative version might be a computational model that includes a special computer subroutine devoted to storing highly notable inputs, which has lost the ability to discriminate notable events from everyday events.

Putting Models to the Test

Is the qualitative model of highly superior autobiographical memory described in the previous section correct? Probably not, but that's okay because a model doesn't need to be correct to be useful (Marr, 1982; Warren, 2012).

A better question might be, does this model allow scientists to accurately predict phenomena that they would be unable to predict otherwise? For instance, the model predicts that if you could watch the brain of a person with highly superior autobiographical memory recalling a random day in their life, you might see the same sort of activity that happens when they are recalling a historically relevant day. And if you compared brain activity in people with highly superior autobiographical memory to activity in people with more mundane memory capacities recalling a historical event, then the model predicts that their brains should be doing basically the same thing.

These predictions are testable. If it turns out that the predictions are accurate, then you understand more about how memory works than you did before. If they are inaccurate, you may still have learned something from the experiment that you didn't know, which could help you to develop a more useful model.

Refining models is a never-ending process in cognitive psychology (and in most other sciences). Even the best models can't predict and explain everything. In some cases, the models that perform best are so complicated that they are not much easier to understand than the cognitive process they were built to explain. In other cases, there may be two or more models using different explanations of what's happening that seem to work equally well. The models of cognition presented in this textbook include some of the latest and greatest, as well as some older models that have proven to be particularly useful. You should think of these models as formalized hypotheses—testable explanations for a phenomenon—rather than as facts to memorize. The models provide ways of thinking about cognition that have proven useful to those scientists that have thought the most about cognitive processes, and they can give you a head start in your quest to know more about how minds work (O'Reilly, 2006; O'Reilly et al., 2010).

Confusingly, models of cognition are often called theories, and different researchers have used the two terms in ambiguous ways. For the purposes of this book, you can think of theories of cognition as impressive models or sets of models that are meant to explain how cognition works.

Human Mind, Animal Mind: Comparisons across Species

When psychologists talk about "the mind," they usually have one particular class of minds in mind: those of adult humans. While Descartes argued that these were the only kinds of minds there are, other scientists, including Charles Darwin (1809–1882), begged to differ (Darwin, 1871). It would be ridiculous to argue that only adult humans have physical bodies (including brains), so the fact that people find it reasonable to argue that humans are the only organisms with minds reveals a conceptual divide between how people think about physical acts of the body versus mental acts of the mind. This divide also relates to the persistent feeling people have that humans aren't really animals. Even scientists who confidently claim that human brains generate minds often hesitate to claim that other animals' brains can do the same.

Margaret Washburn (1871–1939) was a pioneering psychologist who argued that lots of animals other than humans have minds (**Figure 1.7**); she was also the first woman to get a Ph.D. in psychology and the first woman psychologist to be elected into the National Academy of Sciences, one of the highest honors any scientist can receive. In the early 1900s, she published a classic textbook called *The Animal Mind*, which catalogued experimental and physiological evidence that she felt supported her (and Darwin's) claims that minds were less rare in nature than people assumed (Washburn, 1926).

You may be wondering what sort of evidence Washburn used to try and convince other scientists that nonhuman animals have minds. Some evidence was based on physiological comparisons showing few major structural differences across vertebrate brains. Most of the evidence, however, revealed how similarly nonhuman animals and humans behaved when faced with various cognitive tasks (Andrews, 2020).

(A)

(B)

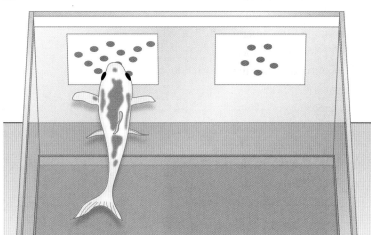

FIGURE 1.7. Margaret Washburn. (A) Champion of experimental studies of animal minds and mega-pioneer. (B) She explored many cognitive processes in various species, including visual perception in fish. (A The Drs. Nicholas and Dorothy Cummings Center for the History of Psychology, The University of Akron)

Self-Reflection versus Experimental Observation

Interestingly, Washburn's doctoral training focused on introspective approaches (described later in this Chapter) that require reporting on one's own mental activity. This was once the dominant approach to studying cognition, which makes some sense given that the only thinking you can directly observe is your own. Even then, there is no guarantee that your impressions are accurate (Boring, 1953; Danziger, 1980).

If animals other than humans think about their experiences, we don't yet have a way to detect it. However, by using the same tests that researchers use to examine peoples' perceptions, it's possible to show that many other animals respond to sensory differences in ways that are comparable to humans (Stebbins, 1970) (Chapter 4 describes several such perceptual studies).

Given these similarities, you would have about as much evidence for claiming that nonhuman animals can perceive sensory differences as for claiming that humans do. You might think that the fact that people can tell you, "I'm perceiving a difference," provides stronger evidence that they're consciously aware of a difference, but you ultimately have no way of verifying this. You could probably train a parrot to say something similar while performing the same kind of task.

Reasoning versus Instinct

Of course, being able to tell things apart is not a particularly impressive cognitive act compared to something like figuring out that the earth is orbiting the sun. For many, acts of reasoning are what make cognition in humans radically different from mental activity in other animals (Penn & Povinelli, 2007).

The kind of rational thought that people engage in when solving problems or making decisions (see Chapter 10) definitely goes beyond merely perceiving what the world is like. But whether rational thinking involves cognitive processes that are unique to humans is still up for debate (Beran et al., 2016; Laland & Seed, 2021).

For a long time, researchers thought that humans were the only animals that could solve problems by constructing and using tools, but now there is evidence that many other animals do this (Goodall, 1964; Shaw, 2021). Scientists also assumed that nonhuman animals were driven by instincts while human behavior was more rational (as suggested by Descartes). However, observations of dolphin, bonobo (a type of ape), and even ant behavior (**Figure 1.8**) have revealed creativity and insight in performing actions and solving problems (Olmstead & Kuhlmeier, 2015) (see Chapter 9).

Realistically, how frequently do you reason in any given week? When you decide what to have for lunch, do you do it by considering all the potential consequences? Or do you think, "What do I want for lunch?" Or maybe you just look at a list of options and choose one that looks good. Just because it's possible for humans to logically consider the outcomes of multiple actions before choosing one, doesn't mean they normally do it.

Memory-based action selection can account for many of your daily "choices," like what you do first when you wake up, when you go to a store, or what time you go to bed. These "normal things that people do," are learned actions that depend on memory abilities rather than on instincts or reasoning. Chapters 5, 7, and 8 will reveal the many ways that memories affect behavior and cognition in all animals, including humans.

Language and Thought

The one feature of human cognition that is most often noted as being the difference that makes humans different from other animals is language (Adler, 1967; Chomsky, 1959). As far as anyone can tell, no animals other than humans naturally use language.

Many nonhuman animals communicate using sounds and other signals (see Chapter 12), but none seem to communicate using symbols in the way that humans do (Fitch, 2020). The use of symbols is heavily emphasized in educational contexts, so it's not surprising that thinking and cognition would be closely linked to language. This does not imply, however, that one needs language to cognize. It simply means that at least part of human cognizing typically involves associating arbitrary symbols with perceived events, especially if one wants to demonstrate a certain level of intelligence to others.

That being said, there are many cognitive skills that do seem to benefit from the capacity to produce and comprehend language, and much of the evidence that people perceive, know, and understand what is happening comes from their use of language (Gentner & Goldin-Meadow, 2003). So, it's not too surprising that ideas about language and thinking are tightly linked. This is perhaps most clear in standardized tests of individual differences in cognition, which depend heavily on a person's ability to answer questions. The following section considers what such tests have revealed about the relationship between intelligence and cognitive abilities.

FIGURE 1.8. Ant de soleil. Ants show sophisticated abilities to socially coordinate their actions, creating complex structures customized to solve specific foraging and navigation problems that they encounter. Is their ability to do this innate? And if so, then why does it take people years of specialized training to perform similar feats? (frank60 via Shutterstock)

SIGHT BITES

 Conceptual models of minds describe cognitive processes in terms of associations, computations, and more, providing a way for cognitive psychologists to test the usefulness of different proposals.

 Researchers are always refining existing models of cognitive processes based on experimental tests of model predictions.

 Comprehensive approaches to studying cognition depend on developing methods that can be applied to both humans and other animals.

INTELLIGENCE: KNOWING HOW TO THINK

SNEAK PEEK: Individual differences in cognitive abilities separate the duds from the brainiacs. More than just brains and cognitive capacities determine how people perform on intelligence tests, however. What are the factors that make some minds excel and others fail?

The idea that humans possess cognitive abilities that are superior to those of all other animals has a long history rooted in religious beliefs. However, even humans vary greatly in their abilities to solve problems, gain new knowledge, and critically evaluate information (Worrell et al., 2019).

Cognitive psychologists historically have given less attention to individual differences in cognitive ability than to identifying general principles that apply to cognitive processes in most people. Sometimes, though, it is the exceptional mind that provides the clue that sheds light on typical cognitive processes.

For instance, studies of mnemonists (people with exceptional memorization abilities) have clarified the important roles skill learning and imagery can play in memory retrieval (Luria, 1968), and research with chess champions has revealed just how closely their exceptional problem-solving abilities apply to chess (Charness et al., 2005). Interviews with famous scientists and artists can potentially reveal aspects of their thought processes that differ from the norm, and studies of individuals with exceptional abilities (like people with highly superior autobiographical memory or amnesia) can lead to new ways of thinking about cognitive processing (Lubinksi & Benbow, 2021; Simonton, 2009).

Geniuses, whose ideas and accomplishments seem to exceed those of all their peers, are particularly intriguing because they highlight how little is known about the factors that contribute to lower or higher levels of intellectual ability, not to mention what levels of cognition are even possible.

Geniuses: Domestic and Wild

The defining quality of a genius is that other people judge that individual to be exceptional to an extreme degree (**Figure 1.9**). This quality can vary depending on who the judges are and when they make their decision.

Genius is often viewed as the high end of a continuum of smartness that begins with idiocy. People who aren't geniuses often assume that geniuses are born with hyper-capable brains that give them special abilities, like a seven-foot basketball player who benefits from their height advantage.

People who have been called geniuses, however, often attribute their successes to qualities that tend to be associated with mental disorders, such as extreme perseverance and disinterest in typical social activities and norms. Yet, people who persevere and don't attract public attention are unlikely to be classified as geniuses, regardless of their cognitive capacities. Since not all people with unique brain power are recognized by the public at large, the qualities that are often possessed by geniuses may actually be more widespread than they seem.

Nature versus Nurture versus Computational Power

The origins of individual differences in cognitive capacities have been hotly debated for centuries—this is a key element of the nature versus nurture debate regarding whether genetics or experience more strongly determines how individuals act and what they can achieve (Plomin & von Stumm, 2018; Sternberg, 2020).

In the field of cognitive psychology, the question of whether DNA or practice makes perfect has been studied most extensively using strategic games like chess in which there are quantifiable differences in performance that can be compared to the amount and quality of a player's training (Howard,

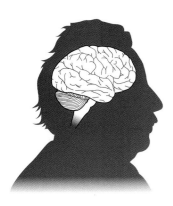

FIGURE 1.9. Origins of intelligence. Exceptional minds are often assumed to come from exceptional brains. Why might measures of brain structure be less reliable indicators of above-average cognitive abilities than behavioral tests?

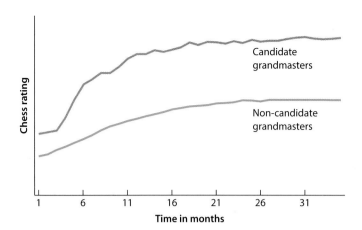

FIGURE 1.10. Practice in chess doesn't always make perfect. Chess competitors who started out performing better in tournaments and who ultimately became grandmasters benefitted more from practice than other chess experts, suggesting that their initial talents strongly determined their ultimate chess rating, a numerical indicator of their performance in tournaments. (After Howard, 2009.)

2009). One thing that studies of chess players make clear is that the best players in the world usually aren't also Nobel laureates, math wizards, musical savants, or world-class poker players—their brilliance is often limited to selecting winning chess strategies. If good genes are what enable grandmasters to excel at chess, then the relevant genes are not genes for "smartness."

As in sports, exceptional cognizing requires exceptional specialization. Training experiences play a key role in how highly a chess player is likely to be ranked (Ericsson et al., 2009); starting intensive training at a young age can make a big difference. But chess experts with thousands of hours more practice are still often defeated by younger, less experienced players—an outcome which seems to point toward talent (nature) winning the day (Blanch, 2020) (**Figure 1.10**).

And then there are current artificially intelligent chess engines (chess-playing software), the best of which are so proficient that they have never lost a match to any human. Their only competition now is other computer programs. Like Watson, artificially intelligent chess programs mimic the behavior of human chess experts and are essentially computational models of chess-related problem-solving. Several factors determine how good a chess program is, including its processing power, its database of chess positions, and the rules it uses to sort through possible moves. Could similar factors determine your cognitive capacities?

Potential Differences

A notable feature of top-ten chess experts is that they are almost always males of European or Asian descent. Only one woman has ever competed in a world chess championship, and it is rare that more than one woman is in the top 100 players.

The skewed distribution of chess champions cuts to the heart of whether nature versus nurture is determining cognitive abilities. Are there no women at the top because of genetic differences (nature)? Or is this a cultural artifact related to social norms in the countries where chess is most popular (nurture)?

Women are about five inches shorter than men, based on worldwide averages, a difference that is mostly coming from the nature side of the equation. Could chess-playing ability be like height? Or, maybe, it's like strength, which also differs between men and women, but depends much more on experience? So far, no male-specific chess genes have been identified and debate rages on about what specific cognitive abilities grandmasters have that give them an edge.

The problem is that, unlike height and strength, the cognitive processes that contribute to chess-playing finesse are invisible, making any side-by-side comparisons dicey. This is true not just for chess players but for all behaving organisms. The hidden nature of mental actions makes it tricky to know what is varying cognitively between individuals, much less how capacities and potential are varying.

It may be hard to say for sure what it is about an individual that makes them cognitively exceptional, but it is undeniable that some thinkers stand out (Sternberg, 2018). In the earliest studies of problem-solving by chimpanzees, it was one chimpanzee in particular, named Sultan, that consistently led the pack in discovering the steps required to reach high-hanging fruit (Köhler, 1925). It was one parrot, named Alex, that convinced researchers that they had been underestimating the cognitive capacities of birds (Pepperberg, 2013). And it was one dog, named Chaser, that showed that dogs can learn thousands of spoken words (Pilley & Reid, 2011).

Like human geniuses, it is difficult to know how exceptional such animal stars truly are. One thing these unique cases do tell us is that even the most sophisticated cognitive abilities can vary considerably across individuals, and even within an individual, as they develop. Identifying ways to measure variations in mental processes has been a key challenge throughout the history of cognitive research.

Measuring Intelligence

At the core of all measures of cognitive competence, or intelligence, are tests. The tests vary in terms of whether they probe what an individual knows versus what that individual can figure out, but they all serve the same goal of ranking an individual's performance relative to that of other test takers (Spearman, 1904; Horn, 1968).

The basic idea is that tests convert unobservable mental abilities into observable behavior. Most current tests of intelligence assess a broad range of verbal, perceptual, reasoning, and memory abilities (**Figure 1.11**). The results of multiple tests aren't always consistent, however, making it hard to know which mental abilities determine a person's score on different tests. Much of the debate about intelligence tests revolves around their validity—are the highest scorers really the most cognitively competent (Haier, 2016)?

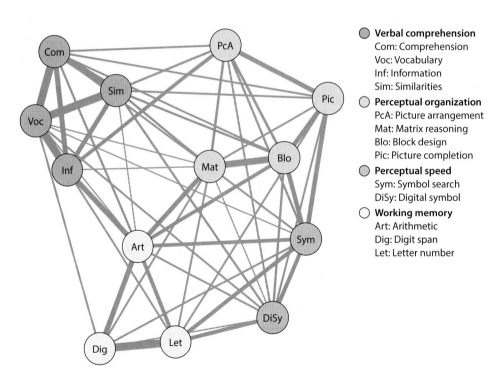

FIGURE 1.11. A quantitative model of intelligence. Intelligence tests use the accuracy of answers to various questions to compare individuals' performance. This makes it possible to assess not only how well a person performs in different areas but also how overall performance relates to specific strengths and weaknesses. Analyses of people's performance on intelligence tests have revealed that a person's ability to succeed on certain tasks is most predictive of their performance on related tasks. For example, your vocabulary size does a good job of predicting your ability to comprehend language (indicated here by a thick gray line). In contrast, vocabulary size is not a great predictor of your ability to arrange pictures (PcA) into a meaningful story (indicated by a thin gray line). (After Van Der Maas et al., 2017.)

Potential Biases

One of the main complaints about intelligence tests is that they can be culturally biased. A culturally biased test assumes that all test-takers have similar background knowledge and experiences so that test-takers are unlikely to be confused by the questions. This would not be the case, however, if the test includes questions that cover unfamiliar topics, or questions that are written in an unfamiliar language.

The concern is that intelligence tests may unfairly rank individuals based on factors other than their actual intellectual abilities, especially in cases where entire racial, ethnic, socioeconomic, or gender groups show lower-than-average scores (Reynolds et al., 2021). Systematic differences in test scores also are seen across generations, with average scores continuously increasing over time (called the Flynn effect; Flynn, 2000).

Such changes are consistent with the idea that systematic differences in experience or environmental conditions may affect people's scores on intelligence tests. For example, increases in health or educational support may improve cognitive performance, and cultural emphasis on particular cognitive skills like reading and mathematical skills can also affect performance.

Another common critique is that intelligence tests don't really reveal what an individual's future potential is. For instance, one long-term study of children classified as geniuses found that although many of them achieved success later in life, most lived relatively unexceptional lives (Terman, 1940). Also, some children who did not make the cut to be included in the study ended up becoming Nobel laureates, suggesting that performance on intelligence tests was not a great predictor of who would accomplish the most intellectually.

On the other hand, measures of intelligence are currently some of the best predictors of later success in college and in job performance (Deary et al., 2010), suggesting that intelligence tests do capture some differences in cognitive ability that can affect future performance.

Correlates of Intelligence

Interest in measuring intelligence was originally driven by practical problems related to sorting students and soldiers (Wasserman, 2018). Specifically, the goal was to weed out the people who were unlikely to get much out of school or training in complex military skills before effort was put into trying to teach them.

From this perspective, intelligence tests provide clues about the kinds of cognitive skills a person is likely to be able to learn. If intelligence were like height, then it would be relatively simple to predict what levels a person might reach in their lifetime. But unlike height, most cognitive abilities of adults depend on learned skills: language use, writing, reading, decision-making, and problem-solving.

The ease with which a person learns such sophisticated skills depends on even more basic perceptual and memory abilities, most notably **working memory** (Baddeley, 2012), which relates to the capacity to store, temporarily maintain, and manipulate recent thoughts in mind (see Chapter 8) (**Figure 1.12**), like when a server remembers what each customer ordered once the food is ready. Measures of working memory are highly correlated with measures of intelligence—people with exceptional working memory capacity are often highly intelligent (Conway et al., 2003).

Why working memory and intelligence are so closely linked remains mysterious. But the fact that one's capacity to remember the recent past is in some way connected to their overall cognitive competence suggests that understanding more about how working memory works could be important to understanding why differences in cognitive capacity arise. Recent studies suggest that the link may have less to do with retention and more to do with attention (Draheim et al., 2022). Specifically, your capacity to control where your attention is directed during performance of both working memory tasks and intelligence tests may affect how you perform on both.

FIGURE 1.12. A qualitative model of working memory. Working memory refers to the ways in which you can keep certain ideas or images in mind for a short period of time and manipulate them to perform cognitive tasks or control attention. A person's capacity to do this is predictive of how well they will perform on intelligence tests.

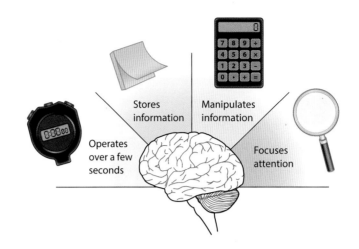

WEIRD, TRUE, FREAKY

Working Memory Wizard

Tests of intelligence typically consist of a series of specially designed problems of varying difficulty. In general, the more questions a person can answer correctly in such tests, the higher the person's intelligence score will be. Measures of working memory capacity, in contrast, focus on how long a person can keep information in mind before it fades away. As mentioned previously, working memory measures are surprisingly good at predicting the results of intelligence tests (Conway et al., 2003). Some researchers have pointed to the relationship between working memory and intelligence as evidence that working memory is important for performing many cognitive tasks and that lower working memory capacity makes such tasks more difficult.

At the same time that American psychologists were gathering evidence linking working memory to intelligence scores, a unique research study in Japan called the Ai Project was developing new computerized techniques for testing cognition in chimpanzees. One of the tasks chimpanzees were trained to perform involved remembering where the numbers one through nine appeared on a screen. They

were tasked with touching the places on the screen where each number appeared in sequential order after the numbers were covered with squares (Inoue & Matsuzawa, 2007).

All chimpanzees were able to learn this task, but one chimpanzee in particular, named Ayumu, was way better than the other chimpanzees (see figure). Ayumu consistently remembered about 80% of number positions, even when the screen only displayed the numbers for 200 milliseconds. For comparison, college students identified about 20% of numbers when tested on the same working memory task.

Could it be that some chimpanzees have working memory capacities exceeding those of humans? Might working memory in chimpanzees also be correlated with intelligence, and if so, would that make Ayumu a chimp genius? The researchers studying Ayumu suggested another possibility: that Ayumu used eidetic imagery to perform the task.

Eidetic imagery, more commonly referred to as photographic memory, involves mentally retaining a detailed image of a perceived event for relatively long periods. It has been reported in some young children (Giray et al., 1976).

Another possibility, however, is that extensive training on a working memory task can dramatically increase an individual's working memory capacity. In fact, two undergraduate students at the University of California, Santa Cruz, who practiced the same number memory task, were able to remember more than 90% of the numbers after extensive training (Cook & Wilson, 2010).

The students did not report using eidetic imagery, so it seems that Ayumu didn't need a photographic memory to achieve his amazing memory abilities. Even so, his abilities highlight the fact that scientists are just beginning to discover the extent to which basic cognitive capacities can vary across genetically similar individuals.

Ayumu uses a touch screen to select numbers in order and can do so even when the numbers are rapidly covered. (BBC)

SIGHT BITES

 Individuals vary greatly in their cognitive abilities. The origins of individual differences in mental capacities continue to be debated.

 Intelligence tests map mental performance onto observable behavior, but variations in scores can be driven by factors other than cognitive abilities.

 Intelligence measures provide clues about the kinds of cognitive tasks a person is likely to be able to perform well.

BEHAVIOR: ACTIVITIES, ABILITIES, AND THEIR ORIGINS

SNEAK PEEK: The main evidence of cognitive processes comes from what individuals do, both in the lab and in the wild. Evolutionary forces provide the building blocks that experience shapes to construct knowledge and cognitive abilities.

When you think about why people you know or encounter behave the way they do, you might point to their character, personality, or general intelligence. You might also blame a person's bad behavior on clueless parenting or peer pressure. When it comes to explaining your own behavior, however, you're more likely to provide reasons why your actions made sense given the circumstances, even if those reasons suggest there was no reason, like "I panicked."

This kind of postgame analysis, both of other peoples' actions and your own, depends on your ability to put yourself in someone else's shoes—to evaluate what cognitive and noncognitive processes are controlling the actions. Thinking about why your friend refuses to pet dogs, or about why you might notice this, or even about how dogs view such non-petters, involves a peculiar kind of cognitive process called **metacognition** (Beran et al., 2012; Dunlosky & Metcalfe, 2009) (see Chapter 8).

When you are contemplating cognition (like now), you are thinking about the origins of actions and thoughts. This process is key to understanding cognition and how it relates to mental and physical activity. In particular, identifying which actions and thoughts are driven more by innate mechanisms (nature) versus specific experiences (nurture) is fundamental to developing an accurate picture of how different cognitive processes work.

Innate versus Learned Abilities

Debates about how much of human cognition is innate versus acquired through experience have been around for a long time. At one extreme, **nativists** claim that experiences are shaped by the innate properties of the human mind and brain, which effectively determine what percepts and thoughts are like. On the other side, **empiricists** have argued that pretty much everything that humans perceive and know comes from experience.

Researchers studying the behavior of our furry and feathered friends have similarly argued either that most animals' actions are effectively pre-programmed reactions to environmental conditions (as

"No amount of culture would seem capable of modifying a man's GENERAL retentiveness…All improvement of memory consists then, in the improvement of one's habitual methods of recording facts."
—James, 1890, p 667

suggested by Descartes), or that they are more often habits shaped by an individual's specific experiences (Pavlov, 1927; Thorndike, 1932, 1949; Watson, 1924) (see Chapter 7 for a complete discussion). The modern take on this debate is that genes and the environment interact to determine cognitive mechanisms and behavioral tendencies (Carey & Gelman, 1991). But there is still no agreement on how specifically biological mechanisms relate to things like emotional responses, thoughts, consciousness, or intelligence (Berent, 2021; Carruthers, 2005), which is why it is not yet possible to tell a baby genius from a baby serial killer.

Talents versus Skills

Consider William James's paradoxical quotation above about memory abilities. James thought that a person's ability to store memories was determined by his or her ability to reorganize connections between neurons. He considered this ability to be a built-in feature of brains—so, innate. At the same time, he recognized that an individual's ability to remember things could definitely improve over time, which is why a server who has worked at a restaurant a long time is less likely to forget people's orders than a server who has been working for only a few weeks.

A person might be born with faster, better, stronger mechanisms for storing memories—they could be mnemonically talented. However, without sufficient training, they might still perform worse in memory tests than someone with less impressive memory-storing capacities.

So, which do you think is the case for people with highly superior autobiographical memory or for *Jeopardy!* champions? Do they possess unique brain qualities for storing memories? Or have they acquired exceptional skills for storing memories of personal episodes or facts? What about birds that retrieve thousands of seeds during the winter that they buried months earlier? In all of these cases, observations of behavior alone cannot definitively reveal whether innate or acquired cognitive mechanisms are the source of exceptional memory abilities.

One way to tease apart which aspects of cognition are "built-in" is by exploring which behavioral abilities can be shaped through selective breeding (Tryon, 1940). For instance, years of selective breeding has led to dog breeds that are better able to assist humans in the herding of sheep than others. Recent attempts to breed tame foxes revealed that tamer foxes showed greater capacity to interpret human gestures (Hare et al., 2005) (see Chapter 11). Brain imaging showed that selective breeding for tameness caused several brain regions that are known to contribute to cognitive capacity to enlarge (Hecht et al. 2021) (**Figure 1.13**).

When it comes to human cognition, however, assessing the innateness of cognitive abilities requires a bit more finesse than simply putting potential lovers together in cages.

(A)

(B)

FIGURE 1.13. Shaping cognition across generations. Selective breeding of silver foxes based on their tameness quickly leads to a host of changes to their brains (A) and behavior (B). Not only do they become less aggressive, but they also show increased vocal communication and an enhanced ability to interpret human intentions. (A from Hecht et al., 2021, *J Neurosci* © 2021 by the Society for Neuroscience [CC-BY-4.0], B ressormat via Shutterstock)

Cognitive Scaffolding

Language abilities are the star of the nativist versus empiricist debate because they are clearly acquired through experience but are only naturally learned by humans (Chater & Christiansen, 2018). This has led some to argue that there must be some innate feature of human brains that makes language learning possible (Chomsky, 1975; Pinker, 1994) (see Chapters 2 and 12).

The social environments within which humans develop are unique among animals. It takes a comparatively long time for children to develop into self-sufficient adults, which provides extensive opportunities for children to learn from others (Bruner, 1965; Pozuelos et al., 2019). Psychologists like Lev Vygotsky (1896–1934) argued that human-specific cultural scaffolding, basically social support and traditions, guides language development. Guidance from peers and parents has shaped your self-directed speech, ultimately determining the kinds of thoughts that direct your actions and reasoning (Vygotsky & Cole, 1978). In this scenario, learned language abilities may fundamentally alter your mental activities.

The idea that your environment and learning experiences can profoundly shape how you think is a focal feature of the extended mind thesis described earlier. Recall that this model of mind claims that many of your daily cognitive processes depend on tools like smartphones, textbooks, or your own body to function.

Like James's views on memory capacity, advocates of the extended mind thesis would argue that your general mentality is innate, because your mind is an extension of the properties of your body, but that you can still progress up the cognitive ladder by acquiring new cognitive tools and learning how to use them—which is why you're reading this book!

Evolutionary Constraints on Activities

When empiricists claim that people's cognitive acts are a consequence of their experiences, they are adopting a version of the computational theory of mind discussed earlier. For an empiricist, learning new cognitive skills, like the ability to add or to speak in sentences, is like installing a new app, while performing these skills is like running the app.

From this perspective, just like not all apps run on all computers, not all cognitive processes will happen in all brains. The abilities of people with highly superior autobiographical memory imply that they are engaging memory "apps" that differ in some way from those available to most people. Similarly, the ability of humans to recall past episodes in their lives seems to differ from the kinds of memories sea turtles use to guide them to their birthplaces years later (Allen & Fortin, 2013; Tulving, 2002).

Experiences affect physical and mental actions by creating memories that determine what an individual can do or know. The sorts of memories resulting from specific experiences can vary considerably depending on the age and species of the individual. When it comes to cognition, it's important to remember that similar labels don't always imply similar cognitive processes. For example, there are many shades of memory, a topic covered more fully in Chapter 8.

Continuity in Cognition

Different species behave differently, but the systems that enable them to behave are generally quite similar. Many animals' activities cluster into categories that are recognizable across species, including actions related to foraging, mating, navigating, communicating, exploring, socializing, sleeping, etcetera (Shettleworth, 2010).

People have long debated about what cognitive processes different species share and about which kinds of behavior require the most or least cognition (de Waal, 2010; Premack, 2007). Charles Darwin was the first to argue on scientific grounds that there should be continuity between the mental abilities of humans and other animals (Darwin, 1871). Darwin's "mental continuity" hypothe-

FIGURE 1.14. Beluga bubblebatics. Beluga in aquaria sometimes learn to make and manipulate bubble rings, transforming them in creative ways. Once one beluga figures out how to do this, others soon pick up the trick. What might such creativity tell us about beluga minds? (Allen Creative I Steve Allen/Alamy Stock Photo)

sis suggests that any mental process that occurs in humans is likely to be present in some other animals either to a greater or lesser degree.

This does not mean that the mental actions of nonhumans are the same as those of humans. Just as there are many ways that animals use their bodies to move around in the world, there could be many ways that they mentally control and experience such movements.

Observing how birds, bees, and bats fly ultimately made it possible for humans to understand the mechanisms of flight. Darwin thought that by studying mental processes in other animals, we might similarly gain new ways of understanding how all minds work (Angell, 1909) (**Figure 1.14**).

Biological Predispositions

A major reason why animals have such varied ways of traveling is that they have become specialists at moving in their specific natural environments (Alexander, 2003). Evolutionary psychologists argue that the same forces have shaped cognitive processes (Bolhuis et al., 2011; Cosmides & Tooby, 1997; Workman & Reader, 2021). For example, animals that often navigate in the dark might depend on specialized perceptual processes that enable them to recognize objects from their echoes, and animals that rely heavily on social coordination might develop specialized systems for communicating (like language).

You'll hopefully recognize that this view is a kind of nativism. The basic idea is that if there is some cognitive process that naturally comes easily to you, then it's probably because evolutionary forces have adapted the way that human cognition works to make that process more effective and efficient. In other words, those processes are adaptations—evolved solutions to problems.

So, if humans find learning language easy, and other animals don't, then it must be, according to evolutionary psychologists, because humans evolved some specialized language processing abilities. If some kinds of birds are really good at remembering where they've hidden seeds months ago, then it must be because they evolved some specialized memory abilities (Branch et al., 2022), and so on. From this perspective, it is important to consider the conditions within which cognitive processes evolved when attempting to understand why they work the way they do.

Social Cognition

When considering the evolutionary origins of cognition, there are piles of problems that seem likely to be major drivers of cognitive adaptations (Fuchs, 2017). They're basically the same kinds of problems you've likely encountered in your daily life—deciding where to go and when, finding your way there and back, navigating social encounters with others, maintaining your health and appearance, and so on. These kinds of problems may not seem to require any kind of Watson-like intelligence to solve, but their prevalence means that the problems can strongly affect how organisms evolve.

Problems related to social interactions, in particular, have attracted lots of scientific attention, not only because of their importance in daily life but also because many of the most mysterious cognitive processes (language use, imitation, musicality) are closely tied to such interactions (De Jaeger et al., 2010; Micheal et al., 2016).

Social cognition research focuses on these kinds of cognitive processes, which are often viewed as the most sophisticated and specialized components of cognition (**Figure 1.15**). Chapters 11 and 12 delve into whether the kinds of cognitive processes that make social interactions possible are really so special, or whether they depend on the same basic mechanisms as other less social actions.

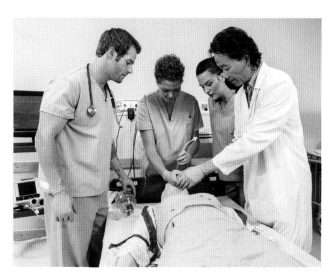

FIGURE 1.15. Social learning. Many complex skills that adults learn are taught or coached by experts who have previously learned them. Does this kind of learning through guidance require any specialized cognitive abilities, or would some kind of generic problem-solving process be good enough? (Tyler Olson via Shutterstock)

Motivation

Natural history may explain your innate tendencies to behave in certain ways, but if someone asked you to explain why you made a specific decision, like why you chose to take a certain class, you are probably more likely to mention factors such as your interest in the topic or your desire to sleep late rather than your parents' genes. The ongoing internal states that lead you to act in certain ways, either physically or mentally, are collectively referred to as **motivation**. These sorts of drives may seem separate from the kinds of processes you might typically think of as being cognitive, but they can strongly affect how you think, especially when you are trying to make decisions (Braem & Egner, 2018; Westbrook et al., 2020; Yee & Braver, 2018) (discussed further in Chapter 3).

For instance, many of the biases that can derail rational thought relate to motivational factors (Botvinick & Braver, 2015) (see Chapter 10). For example, people working together in committees notoriously make poor decisions, in part because individuals feel pressure to find solutions by a specific deadline and because of social drives to not be the odd person out. Motivational factors also can lead people to behave in ways that are irrational and even against their own beliefs, as in the infamous Milgram experiment in which participants showed a surprising willingness to electrocute random people for no reason other than that they were told to do so.

Cognitive Control

Closely related to the motivation to do things is **volition**, a cognitive process that enables you to consciously choose when and how to act (Haggard, 2019). Most cognitive acts, including recalling, deciding, problem-solving, and thinking, appear to be controlled in ways that imply the existence of a controller (Hammond, 1972; Miller, 2000). In cognitive psychology, processes that provide cognitive control are sometimes called **executive functions** (Posner et al., 2004).

Some people (like Descartes) would argue that it's motivation and volition in particular that differentiate people from machines like Watson. Volition is a tricky topic, however. Plenty of man-made control systems can perform sophisticated actions, such as flying a plane. Those systems do not need volition to choose or decide actions in the way that people seem to; autopilots do not "go with their guts." Modern discussions of cognitive control have shifted from using terms like voluntary (dependent on volition) and involuntary (independent of volition) to describing processes as either explicit or implicit to avoid messy questions about the nature of volition and where it comes from (Braver, 2012; Munakata et al., 2012).

Many psychological disorders involve degraded cognitive control. For instance, people suffering from major depression often have problems with initiating goal-directed actions and with shifting

FIGURE 1.16. Cognitive pathways to recovery. (A) Qualitative models describing how mechanisms of cognitive control like attentional control are related to physiological measures like EEG (see Chapter 2) can be used to develop new techniques for diagnosing psychological disorders, as well as for evaluating novel therapeutic interventions such as neurofeedback (B) that is coordinated with cognitive training. Knowing what processes to redirect and when provides powerful tools for treating disorders that are more precise, dynamic, and customizable than current approaches. (B © 2023 Neuroelectrics. All rights reserved.)

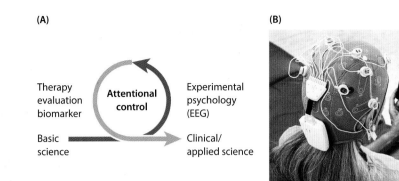

(A) (B)

attention away from negative thoughts (Dotson et al., 2020; Grahek et al., 2019). Findings from cognitive psychology not only can provide insights into why certain emotional states interfere with cognitive control but also can guide the development of interventions to overcome such limitations (**Figure 1.16**).

Information Seeking

The motivational force most closely tied to cognition and cognitive psychology research is curiosity. As soon as toddlers get a handle on communicating, the questions begin to fly.

Such acts of information seeking are another sign of metacognition in that they reveal that toddlers are, in some sense, aware of their ignorance. Exploratory actions provoked by novel objects, situations, or problems provide the clearest evidence of internal states that lead explorers to behave in the ways they do (Sobel & Kushnir, 2013).

Much of the learning that drives cognitive development is thought to come from curiosity—ignorance may be bliss, but it's still rewarding to be in the know (Hacques et al., 2021; Köster et al., 2020). Curiosity also drives your attention, which determines what you perceive (see Chapter 4), and ultimately what you know. If you're curious about how cognition works, you will be more likely to buy and read a book about cognition, more likely to not zone out while reading it, and more likely to be able to recall specific theories and experiments described in the book.

Curiosity can also lead to creativity (see Chapter 9) as you attempt to invent or discover new solutions to problems or new ways of experiencing the world. Curiosity lies at the heart of all scientific efforts to understand behavior and mental processes (Chu & Schulz, 2019; Gruber & Fandakova, 2021). If you're curious about exactly how scientists have attempted to understand these processes, then read on!

SIGHT BITES

 Cognition is shaped by evolutionary, environmental, and experiential forces—nature plus nurture—as are the behavioral markers of cognitive processes.

 Experiences affect physical and mental actions by creating memories that determine what an individual can do or know.

 Many cognitive acts, including recalling, deciding, problem-solving, and thinking imply voluntary control of cognition by a motivated controller.

SCIENTIFIC APPROACHES TO UNDERSTANDING COGNITION

SNEAK PEEK: Researchers seek to understand the nature of cognition by observing actions in various contexts and by conducting experiments to test the predictions of models.

People have studied minds and behavior for millennia. However, most early efforts relied on intuition, reflection, and reasoning rather than on the systematic collection of objective measurements, and so would not be considered scientific.

There are two main ways that scientists attempt to understand mechanisms of behavior and cognition: (1) through detailed observations and (2) through behavioral experiments. At first, psychological studies of minds emphasized observations over experiments, but in the last century, experimental approaches have taken over, especially in studies of cognition. The following sections cover a brief history of mind research, describing the basic methods that have led to modern ideas about what cognition is and how it works.

Ethology: Observing Natural Cognition

The starting point for what psychologists understand about cognition is folk psychology, also known as common sense or what your grandmother could have told you. It's a mix of authority, personal experiences, and secondhand reports that provides the foundation for scientific studies of cognition (Stich & Ravenscroft, 1994).

Darwin's early claims about the continuity of cognition across species relied heavily on folk psychology—his own observations of animal behavior as well as anecdotal stories that were passed on to him. Anecdotal evidence generally comes from unplanned observations of surprising or unique situations. For example, if you saw a squirrel in a park opening a soda can with its teeth, that would be anecdotal evidence that squirrels can solve the problem of how to open cans.

If you ever people-watch in an airport, you might also learn something about how cognition operates (or doesn't) in natural contexts (Kingstone, 2020). Such observations would only be considered scientifically relevant if you collected detailed measurements of actions that could potentially answer a specific question (Eibl-Eibesfeldt, 1979), such as, "Are people with less hair more likely to misplace their carry-on luggage?" Typically, that question would either confirm or refute a belief or suspicion you have about how and why people behave the way they do, such as "Older people have a shorter memory span."

Ethology is a scientific approach to studying behavior that involves systematically cataloguing the actions of individuals or groups in naturalistic contexts (Dhein, 2021; Tinbergen, 1972). You've probably heard about Konrad Lorenz (1903–1989), the European scientist who studied the natural tendency of certain birds to become attached to individuals they see soon after hatching (called imprinting) (**Figure 1.17**). Lorenz was an early ethologist who collected observations of animal behavior in many different contexts to try and better understand why they behave the way they do (Lorenz, 1978).

Ethologists tend to focus on studying natural actions performed by their subjects, such as those associated with mating, feeding, or social communication (Goodall, 1964). Observations of animals using tools (Seed & Byrne, 2010) and performing innovative actions (Arbilly & Laland, 2017) have increased researchers' interest in understanding how learning and experience contribute to an individual's ability to solve complex problems.

An advantage of the ethological approach is that, like evolutionary psychology, it considers how organisms behave in their natural environments, and attempts to relate behavior to the natural contexts within which the behavior evolved (Roth & Jornet, 2013; Sebanz et al., 2008).

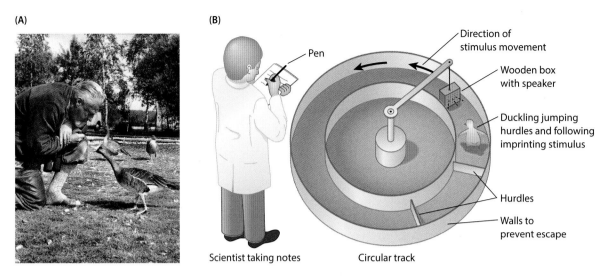

FIGURE 1.17. An ethological approach to understanding behavior. (A) Konrad Lorenz, shown here practicing his observational techniques, imprinted geese on himself to gain a better understanding of how the memories of young animals can shape their behavior toward specific individuals throughout their lives. (B) Later, more controlled experiments revealed the conditions necessary for imprinting to occur, like movement of a nearby object. (A dpa picture alliance/Alamy Stock Photo, B after Cardoso & Sabbatini, 2001.)

A limitation of this approach, however, is that ethologists are often at the mercy of their subjects with respect to what they can potentially study. For instance, if you attempt to conduct an ethological study of turtles in ponds, you might not observe much other than that they sometimes sit on logs and stick their heads above the surface when swimming. Such observations may reveal little about any cognitive processes that contribute to their actions.

People Watching

Ethology might seem less useful for understanding cognition in people, since if you want to know why a person is behaving in a specific way, you could just ask them. But there are many actions that people perform without noticing why or how they're acting. Plus, people's explanations for their actions may not be accurate.

Modern techniques for recording human behavior often use the same methods developed by ethologists. One method is studying how people's eyes move (called eye-tracking) as they read, look at a picture, or watch a movie (Hessels & Hooge, 2019; Lewis & Krupenye, 2022). This method can provide important insights into what features people focus on as they interpret visual scenes or recognize words (Just & Carpenter, 1976; Merkley & Ansari, 2010) (see Chapter 4).

Measuring movements, including those made while a person speaks or gestures, can reveal interactions between cognitive processes that contribute to the planning and execution of actions (Cienki, 2022; Özçalişkan & Goldin-Meadow, 2005). And technologies with the capacity to track changes within a person's body/brain as they perform different physical and mental actions (see Chapter 2) can identify hidden physical mechanisms of cognitive processing (Banich & Compton, 2018; Eagleman & Downar, 2015; Gazzaniga, 2009).

Careful scientific observation of the dynamics of natural behavior, including cognitive acts and the intricacies of functioning brains, provides an important supplement to the more casual observations that ground common sense interpretations of how minds work.

Behaviorism: Experimental Studies of Learning and Performance

Around the same time that Lorenz was swimming in European ponds with geese to try and understand what makes them tick, psychologists in the United States were stuffing other birds (pigeons) in boxes in an effort to reveal the secrets of how learning works (Skinner, 1938).

Unlike the ethologists, who emphasized the innate tendencies of different species that had evolved over millions of years, behaviorists were more interested in the effects of the recent past on changes in an individual's behavior—in other words, the role of nurture and specifically learning on behavior (Hull, 1943; Thorndike, 1932; Watson, 1924).

American behaviorists such as B. F. Skinner (1904–1990) emphasized the role of learning in behavioral change. Like ethologists, behaviorists were keenly interested in observing animal behavior. But unlike ethologists, behaviorists felt that more could be learned from looking at how animals behaved when placed in highly controlled scenarios than from simply watching how they behave in their daily lives (Skinner, 1953).

By controlling conditions in laboratory experiments, behaviorists gained insights into the factors that most strongly motivated animals to change their behavior and discovered new ways to reveal what animals other than humans perceive about the world. Behaviorists also discovered that many of the "rules of learning" operate in the same way for different species, presenting the possibility that one could reveal new facts about human learning by conducting experiments with nonhuman animals.

Looking at Learning

Behaviorist research is often associated with training rats to repeatedly press a lever for food. It may seem odd that psychologists would spend thousands of hours teaching rats to work vending machines in the hopes of understanding human behavior. However, behaviorists adopted a common scientific tactic of trying to understand a complex phenomenon by breaking it down into its most basic elements (an approach known as **reductionism**). By exploring which variables could lead to basic behavioral changes—increases or decreases in a simple action—behaviorists wanted to identify principles of behavior that would be likely to apply to most animals (including humans) and to many different kinds of actions.

Behaviorists considered the specific animals and tasks used in experiments to be less critical than how precisely experimental variables were controlled and measured. This way of thinking stemmed from an understanding that any set of principles should apply to all species and tasks. Psychologists conducted experiments mainly with small animals performing simple tasks because these methods were practical and worked well.

The rise of the modern field of cognitive psychology began, in part, as a response to limitations in the behaviorists' approach to studying complex human actions such as having a conversation (Chomsky, 1959), or thinking about possible solutions to problems (Miller, 2003). In shifting to experiments on humans, cognitive psychologists gradually turned from exploring how individuals learn toward measuring how they perform when faced with various tasks (Neisser, 1967).

The distinction between learning versus performance is an important one for behaviorists, because how an individual behaves only reveals an incomplete picture of what they have learned. For instance, someone observing your behavior while you are reading this book would gain little insight into what you are learning from reading it because what you are learning is hidden from observers.

Behaviorists call this latent learning because the evidence that any learning occurred has yet to show up in your performance. An American behaviorist named Edward Tolman (1886–1959) championed the idea that latent learning was happening all the time and that hidden memories played a major role in guiding behavior (**Figure 1.18**). Tolman developed several ingenious tasks to show that rats running through mazes knew more about the spatial layout of the mazes than researchers could guess just from watching them run (Tolman, 1925, 1932).

(A)   (B)

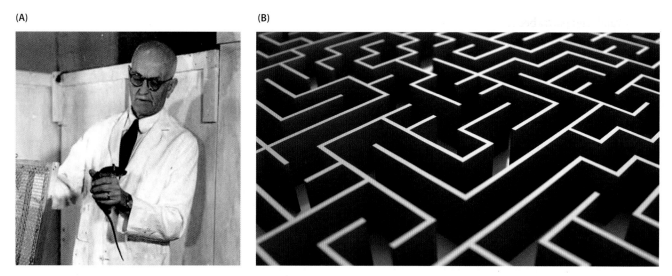

FIGURE 1.18. Amazing rats. Edward Tolman (A) explored what rats know about mazes (B) they are familiar with. He argued that rats gradually learn about the spatial layout of mazes in much the same way that humans do. (A from Berkely News. © 2023 UC Regents. All rights reserved; B James A Isbell via Shutterstock)

Cognitive Psychology: Drawing Inferences about Mental Processes

Like behaviorists, cognitive psychologists rely heavily on controlled behavioral experiments in their attempts to understand behavior (Gigirenzer, 1991; Glenberg, 2013). But rather than measuring how animals' behavior changes when they are rewarded or punished, cognitive psychologists focus more on measuring how people perform in tasks carefully designed to engage specific cognitive processes (Glaser, 1981; Roediger, 1980).

While ethologists and behaviorists differed in emphasizing either innate reactions (nature) or learned behavior (nurture), both groups agreed that the key to understanding the mechanisms of behavior was to carefully measure the actions of animals in different contexts. They also agreed that attempting to measure unobservable events that were happening inside an individual's head or mind was scientifically a waste of time. It's perhaps not surprising then that there has historically been some tension between ethologists, behaviorists, and cognitive psychologists (Lehrman, 1953; Mackenzie, 1977; Watrin & Darwich, 2012).

The earliest psychological laboratories often focused on experimental studies of cognitive processes like perception and memory. Many consider the German professor Wilhelm Wundt's (1832–1920) studies of attention and perception to represent the birth of experimental psychology as an academic field (Wundt sounds like "Voont"). Wundt trained researchers to make objective reports on their inner experiences while performing tightly controlled experimental tasks (Wundt, 1912), a kind of self-report he called **introspection** (the same approach Margaret Washburn used for her dissertation research).

People are sometimes described as introspective when they actively contemplate why things are the way they are or how they feel about ongoing events. Wundt's introspection differs, however, from just thinking about what it feels like to perform a cognitive task like reading or remembering. Wundt would probably argue that his trained observers were making judgments more like those that professional chefs make when judging entries at a cooking contest. In comparison, he might view your untrained observations of your own mental states as more comparable to those of a six-year-old describing a hamburger she ate at a fast-food restaurant.

Introspection hasn't been widely used in the last century as an experimental method for studying cognitive processes. This is partly because it's difficult to establish whether such observations are reliable or valid, and partly because it's hard to train observers to improve their reports when you don't know what they're observing (Gonzalez-Castillo et al., 2021).

Using introspection as a method for studying mental processes in nonhumans is even more problematic. This may explain why scientists who focused on studying animals historically considered attempts to understand animal behavior by studying mental processes to be a lost cause.

Self-reports remain part of some cognitive studies, however, such as when participants are instructed to "think aloud" as they solve a problem (Ericsson & Fox, 2011; van Someren et al., 1994), or to say whether they're certain they recently experienced an item in a memory test (Tulving, 1985).

Experimental Methods

Modern cognitive psychologists continue to use a subset of the experimental methods initially pioneered by Wundt, including measuring how long it takes people to respond to perceived and recognized events (Wenger & Townsend, 2000). Now, however, researchers focus more on analyzing patterns of performance that groups of participants consistently produce to try and figure out what's happening inside people's heads.

Developmental psychologist Jean Piaget (1896–1980), for example, constructed a variety of different tasks that could be presented to children to reveal how their responses to these tasks changed as they got older (**Figure 1.19**). Based on the specific kinds of errors that children made at certain ages, Piaget concluded that children pass through multiple developmental stages in which they cognize in specific ways (Piaget, 1952).

Piaget argued that just as infants first learn to crawl, then to walk, and finally to run, they also first learn to recognize objects and act on them, then to talk about those objects and actions, and finally to think about them. The key advantage of Piaget's approach over more introspective and observational methods is that researchers can quantitatively measure the reliability with which children make such errors (Baillargeon et al., 2011; Gelam & Gallistel, 1978).

You can still question, of course, whether the children made errors for the reasons that Piaget claimed they did (Spelke & Newport, 1998; Wynn, 1992). A behaviorist might argue that Piaget's explanations are no better than a fairy tale, since no one can ever really know what is going on inside a child's head. Perhaps Piaget would have countered that a potentially inaccurate hypothesis about how a child's understanding of the world guides his or her actions is preferable to the behaviorist assumption that it's impossible to know anything about what children understand.

FIGURE 1.19. Cognition revealed by children's errors. (A) Jean Piaget developed tasks to explore how children understand the world. (B) Young children often draw odd shapes when asked to copy a triangle. This suggests that they may think of triangles as something like squares with extra pointy parts. (A Bill Anderson/Science Photo Library)

(A)

(B)

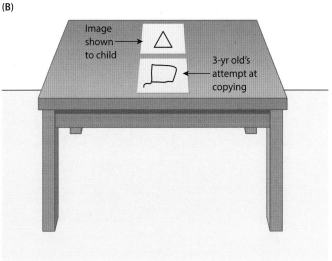

Image shown to child

3-yr old's attempt at copying

FIGURE 1.20. Where cognitive psychology came from. The history of cognitive research is a history of scientific methods and different ways of thinking about mental processes. Each new approach, from Descartes' skeptical self-reflection to Piaget's developmental construction of minds, yielded insights and raised intriguing questions. What are the biggest differences between these early approaches to understanding why people act and think the way they do? (Konrad B,ik/Alamy Stock Photo)

Constructing Minds

Latent Learning

Ethological Observations

Comparative Cognition

Brain–Experience Connections

Introspection

Skeptical Self-Reflection

The goal of cognitive research is not just to understand how cognition works, but to get a better handle on the kinds of approaches that are most likely to lead to such an understanding. Making progress in cognitive psychology is not about collecting more observations, but about collecting the kinds of observations that reveal where our current thinking has gone wrong (Neisser, 1967; Shepard, 1968).

Some of the experimental methods used in cognitive research that you'll learn about in this book may seem a bit ridiculous given the complexity of the processes being investigated. Can cognitive psychologists really understand how language works by having undergraduates press a button as fast as they can whenever a word is presented?

Other brain-based methods like magnetoencephalography (see Chapter 2) may seem so science-fictional that it's hard to even grasp what it is that cognitive psychologists are observing. Regardless of which methods are used, their value comes not from how fancy they are, but from what questions they can help cognitive psychologists answer.

Every method has its strengths and weaknesses, as does every approach to scientifically studying minds and behavior (**Figure 1.20**). In considering what current evidence reveals about cognition, it's important to always keep in mind that the case is not yet closed—there are many cognitive mysteries yet to be solved.

Current Practices of Cognitive Psychologists

In the early days of scientific research, there were few guidelines about how researchers should conduct studies of cognitive processes. Self-studies were common.

In the 1600s, Isaac Newton (1643–1727) investigated color vision by shoving a long sewing needle into his eye socket, which he reported caused him to see colored circles (Newton, 1972). Hermann Ebbinghaus (1850–1909) spent several years memorizing lists of nonsense words in the late 1800s so that he could later test his ability to recall and relearn the lists (Ebbinghaus, 1885/1964).

Modern cognitive psychologists rarely go to such extremes in exploring cognitive processes. More typically, they recruit a bunch of undergraduates (usually students in psychology courses) and

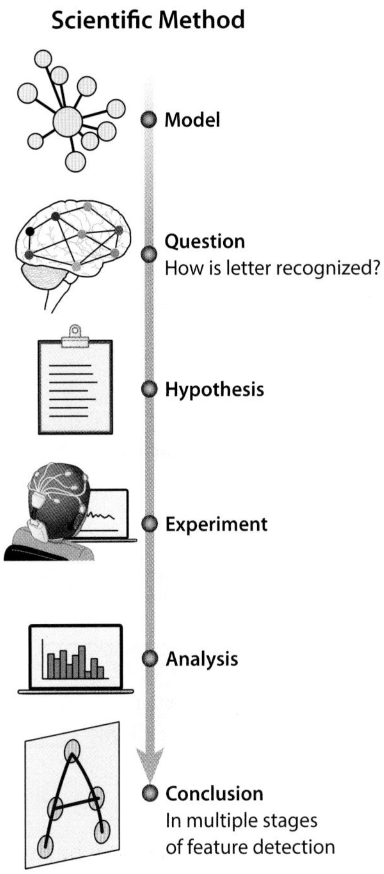

Scientific Method

Model

Question
How is letter recognized?

Hypothesis

Experiment

Analysis

Conclusion
In multiple stages
of feature detection

FIGURE 1.21. Where cognitive psychology has arrived. Modern cognitive studies focus heavily on scientific experiments of undergraduates performing computerized tasks. Cognitive psychologists use statistical analyses to evaluate whether participants perform in the ways that current theoretical models predict. Results of these analyses help researchers formulate new and better models of cognitive processes.

then have them perform various tasks on a computer. This allows for more rapid testing of a large number of individuals and for more precise control of experimental conditions.

By randomly assigning participants to different experimental groups, researchers can better assess whether certain manipulations are having the expected effect. This approach also can reduce the chances that an experimenter's or participant's expectations are influencing the results of the experiment.

Modern experimental designs make use of numerous techniques (including statistical analyses) to try and avoid pitfalls that can mislead researchers about what is really going on, most of which were discovered the hard way (Gelman & Goldin-Meadow, 2003; Nosek & Hardwicke, 2022; Tomasello & Call, 2011). These techniques can make cognitive psychology experiments seem a bit convoluted, but there is a method to the madness (**Figure 1.21**).

On the downside, there is some concern that attempts to increase the efficiency and accuracy of observations from cognitive experiments may lead to evidence that doesn't really apply to everyday cognition (Griffiths & Tennebaum, 2006; Lobo et al., 2018). Specifically, cognitive researchers might develop models that do a good job of predicting how undergraduate students perform when using computers in a laboratory, but that doesn't work so well when applied to individuals cognizing in a store or their home (Henrich et al., 2010).

Before the 1960s, there were few, if any, psychologists who would have described themselves as cognitive psychologists. Textbooks focusing exclusively on cognition only began to gain prominence in the late sixties, most notably *Cognitive Psychology*, by Ulric Neisser (1928–2012), which spawned decades of studies of cognition from an information processing perspective (Neisser, 1967). Since that time, interest in cognitive research has expanded rapidly. Ideas and findings from cognitive research have become integrated with neuroscience, social psychology, developmental psychology, and clinical psychology to change the ways that people think about human minds and about how they might be best understood.

SIGHT BITES

 Ethological and behaviorist approaches to studying cognition and behavior focus on detailed observations of an individual's actions in either naturalistic or training-related contexts, respectively.

 Like behaviorists, cognitive psychologists focus heavily on laboratory experiments. But unlike behaviorism, cognitive experiments emphasize performance over learning and mental processes over recently learned responses.

CLOSURE

Good explanations can be satisfying, even when they're wrong. Cognitive psychologists try to come up with good explanations of how minds work, even though it's hard to pin down exactly what minds are. Whatever minds are, they seem to be at the root of many intelligent (and not-so-intelligent) actions.

You probably have strong intuitions about what your mind is responsible for, which is why you might describe someone who makes a bad decision as thoughtless or mindless. And you might hesitate to describe an artificially intelligent system like Watson as having a mind or interests, despite its *Jeopardy*-winning actions. Cognitive researchers attempt to build on such intuitions by describing more precisely and objectively how minds cognize and how thinking can go wrong.

Thomas Edison (1847–1931) once said that genius is one percent inspiration and ninety-nine percent perspiration. Cognitive psychologists have bought into this idea, developing thousands of models, both computational and conceptual, and conducting hundreds of thousands of experiments, all to move a bit closer to understanding the hidden processes that go on inside people's heads.

As you read through this book, you'll gain glimpses of the many ways in which cognitive psychologists have attacked the problem of understanding the relationship between minds and cognition. You'll discover why some kinds of mental actions (like seeing) are easy and others (like remembering events from the distant past) are hard, and how experiences can shape an individual's cognitive abilities.

You will also hopefully gain new insights into the various ways in which an increased understanding of cognition can contribute to ongoing efforts to prevent and treat psychological distress and the development of new strategies for overcoming the kinds of cognitive limitations that exacerbate ongoing societal problems. And best of all, you might learn some useful new truths about how your own mind works, which may help you enhance your own suite of cognitive skills!

COGNITIVE LINGO

artificial intelligence
associationist model
cognition
cognize
computational theory of mind
empiricist

executive function
extended mind thesis
highly superior autobiographical memory (HSAM)
introspection
metacognition

motivation
nativist
reductionism
volition
working memory

CHAPTER SUMMARY

Cognition: It's What You Think
Models of mental activity describe cognition as involving associations, computations, movements, and conscious control of thoughts. Studies of humans and other animals provide a way to test out scientific models.

Intelligence: Knowing How to Think
Cognitive capacities vary across development, individuals, and different species. Some differences in intellectual ability relate to what one has learned while others are a consequence of how one cognizes. Measures of intelligence provide ways of quantifying these differences and predicting performance on cognitive tasks.

Behavior: Activities, Abilities, and Their Origins
The mental and physical actions that people perform are shaped by dynamic interactions between evolutionary processes and individual experiences. Experiences create memories that determine what an individual can think, know, or do. Some of the most impressive cognitive processes, including thinking, problem-solving, and decision-making, are those that can be actively controlled.

Scientific Approaches to Understanding Cognition
Behavioral observations provide the foundation for all scientific studies of cognition. Experimental approaches can clarify observations in naturalistic situations by establishing predictable associations between controlled events. Modern cognitive research explores behavioral patterns through tightly controlled (often computerized) experiments.

REVIEW EXERCISES

Cognition: It's What You Think
• Describe the relationship between cognition and minds.
• Define the computational theory of mind and compare this model with the extended mind thesis.

Intelligence: Knowing How to Think
• Provide examples of how genius might be a result of either nature or nurture.
• Explain how an intelligence test might be biased.
• How is working memory related to intelligence?

Behavior: Activities, Abilities, and Their Origins
• Summarize the key differences between empiricists and nativists.
• Define and provide examples of cognitive scaffolding.
• What is volition and how is it related to explicit and implicit cognitive processes?

Scientific Approaches to Understanding Cognition
• How are behaviorist approaches different from cognitive psychology? How are they similar?
• Explain how computers contribute to modern experiments on cognition.

CRITICAL THINKING QUESTIONS

1. IBM's Watson is currently being developed to assist healthcare providers and social workers. How might reliance on artificially intelligent systems change the way that doctors, counselors, and patients think? Which models of minds are best suited to predict what cognition will be like in a future where computers solve most problems more effectively than humans?

2. Geniuses are usually identified based on either their accomplishments or scores on intelligence tests. Neither approach is currently an option for identifying nonhuman geniuses. What other approaches might be used to identify the most intelligent members of different species?

3. Nativists argue that language learning capacities are built-in features of human brains. What sorts of evidence might support this claim or provide reasons to reject it?

4. The computational theory of mind suggests that brains perform computations and that minds are like software running on neural hardware. How might this model explain species differences in memory abilities?

5. Many experiments in cognitive psychology involve testing groups of undergraduates on computerized tasks. What are some possible limitations of testing conceptual models of minds in this way?

2 Mechanisms of Mind

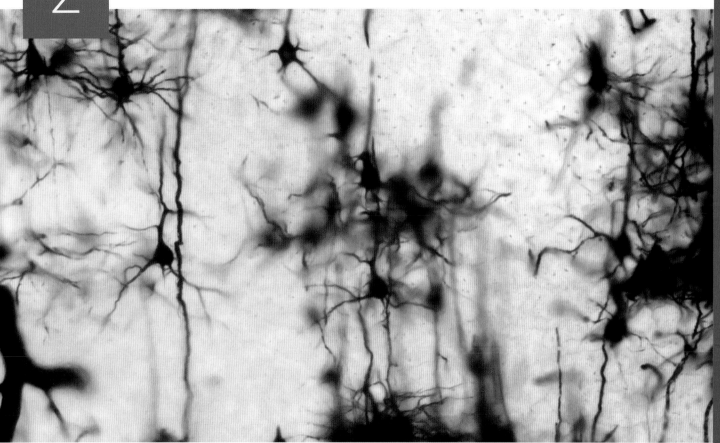

Alexandros Lavdas/Alamy Stock Photo

Over fifteen languages are at Christopher Taylor's disposal. Yet, he cannot find his way to the local grocery store and back. Christopher is both a polyglot and a savant, despite (or because of) his brain damage (Smith et al., 2011). His mental age is estimated to be comparable to that of a nine-year-old (Christopher is an adult), but how many nine-year-olds do you know who can read and translate fifteen languages?

What to make of a rarity like Christopher? What do his remarkable language-learning abilities reveal about how cognition works? First, he is clearly doing something different from people who aren't multi-lingual, presumably because his brain is functioning differently. But how differently, and why, remains a mystery.

Say you have a neighbor whose car has a stereo system rivaling that of a dance club's, and that the car also tends to backfire, leak oil, and not start. You would probably conclude that how a car runs is not really critical to how its stereo sounds. In the same way, some psychologists look at Christopher Taylor and think: "Aha! Genius-level language capacities combined with low-level intelligence. The mechanisms for language must be separate from those of other cognitive abilities!"

It may seem intuitive that you could be exceptional at one kind of cognitive task and dismal at another. Most people have mental tasks they struggle with. But why that would be the case is not obvious from most psychological theories of how minds work. Why would remembering the meaning of words be easier or harder than remembering spoken directions about how to get to a store? Why would learning a new language, which toddlers seem to do effortlessly, be harder than learning a new sport once you are an adult? Why would learning a new language be relatively easy for some individuals (like Christopher) and effectively impossible for others, particularly nonhumans?

Most scientists agree that the answer to all of these questions is that your brain determines the abilities you have. If you can't learn fifteen languages easily, it's because your brain is not up to the

FIGURE 2.1. Setting the stage. (A) Genetic variations produce size differences that can strongly limit a person's physical potential. (B) Genetic variations also produce brain differences that affect what cognitive skills people can ace. Those cognitive differences are better hidden, but like height, ultimately reflect differences in physical structure. (A Everett Collection via Shutterstock; B both images © The Granger Collection Ltd d/b/a GRANGER Historical Picture Archive)

(A)

(B)

task. You might then wonder, why can't all brains do this if some can? The answer to why all brains do not have the same capacities comes down to differences in how they are structured (**Figure 2.1**). And how brains are structured is mainly controlled by genes—genes are what make dog brains differ from human brains.

Genes set the stage for cognition by influencing brain structure and function, but they do not determine what brains ultimately do. In principle, a person could be born, live a long life, and die, without ever doing much of anything physically or cognitively (think extended coma), regardless of how their brain is structured. Christopher Taylor could have been put into an institution at a young age (his brain injury occurred either before or during birth), and as a result, never had the opportunity to learn any languages. Genes and brains are dynamic and their activity is strongly influenced by environmental events. Your experiences early in life, in particular, can strongly affect the kinds of cognitive feats you are likely to be able to achieve.

For most of the past century, studies of cognition have focused on people's behavior, especially their words and actions, in response to various tasks and puzzles. Less attention was given to how differences in brains or genes might affect cognition because it was not possible to directly observe those differences or their consequences, at least not in people.

Today, it is possible to measure variations in how organisms' brains are structured, to understand what determines that structure, and to discover how structural variations relate to differences in cognitive function. Physical measurements of brains and genetic manipulations are revealing new clues about the processes that make cognition possible.

INHERITING COGNITIVE MECHANISMS

SNEAK PEEK: Finding out how genes affect cognition requires either modifying what genes are present and active, controlling the experiences of genetically identical individuals, or correlating genetic differences with behavioral variations. Genes can affect cognitive processes in ways more complex than determining the presence or absence of cognitive ability.

Every family has standouts—some more than others. Wolfgang Amadeus Mozart had an older sister, nicknamed Nannerl, who would have been the musical superstar in almost any other family. The noted psychologist William James had a brother, Henry, who is considered one of the great American novelists of all time. The tendency for certain families to have more than their fair share of intellectual standouts prompted Francis Galton (a cousin of Charles Darwin) to conduct a detailed analysis of this phenomenon (Galton, 1869).

Galton found evidence that some families churned out high achievers at higher rates than others, a finding that modern genetics research supports (Deary et al., 2022; Plomin et al., 2018). The idea that certain "bloodlines" are superior to others (such as those of royal families) has been around for a long time, but it has only been in the last century that scientists have begun to nail down how abilities might be passed from one generation to the next through the study of **heredity**, the genetic transmission of traits.

The nature versus nurture debate discussed in Chapter 1 is all about the extent to which genes affect what minds are like (Diamond, 1988; Toga & Thompson, 2005). If any of your cognitive capacities are innate, then by definition you either inherited them or something about the genes you inherited was altered in transit. The same goes for any instinctual actions you might find yourself performing.

Along similar lines, if people have any cognitive abilities that other animals do not, then an obvious explanation for why this might be is that people evolved cognitive mechanisms that other animals did not (Bishop, 2009). Heredity is a driving mechanism of evolution, which is currently the only known natural process than can create cognitive species.

In the field of cognitive psychology, there has been a lot of debate about which aspects of cognition are inherited (nature) and which mechanisms or capacities (if any) are learned (nurture). Much of the argument has centered on whether certain cognitive abilities (like language and the ability to solve complex problems) function independently of others and which abilities are critical to intellectual prowess.

Modular Minds

Virtues such as wisdom, justice, courage, and temperance are often associated with moral actions, good decision-making, and self-control. It might seem that virtues are qualities that are only distantly related to cognitive mechanisms like memory or thinking. However, not only are such abstract qualities central to what many people view as the essence of human minds, but they also form the foundation for thinking about cognition as consisting of sets of abilities, qualities, or parts.

Mental Faculties versus Mental Organs

The Greek philosopher Aristotle (384–322 BCE) popularized the view that minds can be viewed as a family of mental forces, each playing a specific role (Barnes, 1971). Aristotle's analysis of minds applied to all animate organisms and some inanimate ones (plants). He did not view all organisms' minds as equal, however (Mesaros, 2014). In Aristotle's view, only animals have the faculty of perception and only humans possess the capacity to know things or to think (**Figure 2.2**).

Aristotle split mental processes into two basic functional chunks—perception and intellect—one of which is animalistic and largely automatic while the other rests on reason, goals, intent, and deliberate actions. He also identified imagination (including memory recall) as a separate faculty that was present in all animals, as well as a faculty for desire, which motivates most actions and thinking. Notice that none of these faculties can be directly observed—they are hypothetical mechanisms or explanations for how minds might work.

Aristotle was aware of heredity and even proposed that a father's traits were passed on to his children through semen (Bos, 2009). He convinced many subsequent researchers that mental activities depend on multiple independent faculties that work together as a sort of mental team to produce what we currently think of as cognition. This idea has proven to be particularly influential in

FIGURE 2.2. Aristotelian faculties of minds. All lifeforms share the innate faculty of growth and reproduction, but according to Aristotle, only animals are also born with the faculty of perception. Aristotle proposed that one animal in particular goes a step beyond perception and is born possessing the mental faculty of intellect. (The Print Collector/Alamy Stock Photo)

brain-based theories of cognitive abilities, although Aristotle himself thought that brains contributed nothing to mental faculties (Gross, 1995).

Franz Gall (1758–1828), in contrast to Aristotle, proposed that mental abilities came from specific parts of a person's brain (Zola-Morgan, 1995). Gall's proposal rests on several assumptions that are still widely held by psychologists: (1) brains are the source of minds; (2) the mind consists of a group of separate brain regions, or "organs," that serve specific intellectual functions; (3) the particular brain region that is associated with a specific mental function is the same in all humans; and (4) the size of a brain region is related to its functional capacities (like a muscle).

Gall proposed more mental abilities than Aristotle, including such obscure gems as "adhesiveness," and "philoprogenitiveness." Notably missing from Gall's list of twenty-seven "mental organs" are organs for perception, memory, reasoning, imagination, attention, and desire—the Aristotelian mental faculties. Unlike Aristotle, Gall thought that splitting the mind into faculties like perception, memory, and intellect made no sense. How could a person be good at remembering gossip, but not math facts, if both abilities depend on the same memory faculty? Like Aristotle, Gall assumed that most mental functions were present in all animals. The eight he deemed unique to humans were wisdom, poetical talent, obstinance, kindness, the ability to imitate, and the senses of metaphysics, satire, and God.

The idea that each cognitive ability, whether it be the capacity to compose music or read a book, depends on one or more innately specialized brain regions is referred to as **domain specificity** (Laland & Seed, 2021; Leslie & Thaiss, 1992). In Gall's model of mental organs, the division of labor across your brain is similar to the division of labor across the rest of your body. Just as you have limbs for locomoting and lungs for breathing, you have specialized brain tissue for either remembering words or staying honest.

For most of the history of experimental psychology, researchers paid little attention to either Gall's or Aristotle's ideas about mental abilities and the inheritability of cognitive capacity. Then, in the 1950s, there was a "cognitive revolution" that revived Gall's proposal that there is a special mental organ for language without which people's ability to produce and comprehend speech would not exist (Griffiths, 2015; Lyons, 1978; Miller, 2003).

Cognitive Modules

The increased emphasis on cognitive studies of mental processes in the fifties and sixties was driven by several different factors. The computational theory of mind, in particular, encouraged researchers

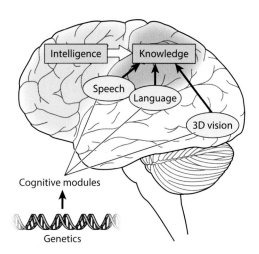

FIGURE 2.3. A modular model of mind. This qualitative model, developed by Mike Anderson (1992), includes genetically-determined, domain-specific cognitive modules (ovals) and more general mechanisms (shaded regions) that work together to make cognition possible. How might specialized modules for speech and language be different from a module for 3-D vision? (After Anderson, 1992.)

to think of mental faculties as processing inputs like a computer (see Chapter 1) (Churchland & Sejnowski, 1992). The different parts of a computer are like Gall's mental organs in that each has a specific function (discussed in Chapter 8). Interacting computer parts can perform tasks that none of the individual parts could accomplish alone.

One way to think about cognitive psychology is as an attempt to map out the unobservable parts of people's minds that make cognition possible. Language quickly was held up as a prime example of a specialized cognitive faculty that was made possible by a unique mental organ. American language researcher Noam Chomsky (born in 1928) did not claim that the language faculty was located in a specific brain region, but he did argue that humans' ability to learn languages was a genetically transmitted trait (Chomsky, 2002, 2017).

The philosopher Jerry Fodor (1935–2017) extended Chomsky's proposal to include a variety of other mental faculties, which he described as **cognitive modules** (Fodor, 1983). Cognitive modules differ from the mental faculties described by Aristotle in that they are thought to automatically perform specific kinds of computations (Coltheart, 1999). **Figure 2.3** illustrates a qualitative model of cognition that includes domain-specific cognitive modules (Anderson, 1992), presumed to be constructed through genetic mechanisms to perform specialized cognitive functions. Such models can potentially be used to explain cases like Christopher Taylor's, in which language learning skills are exceptional despite low intelligence, because they include a specialized language module that is mostly independent from intelligence (Carruthers, 2002), and that, in principle, could remain functional even when other cognitive modules are damaged.

Many psychological models of cognitive processes assume that specialized, inheritable modules work together with more general mental faculties (such as "memory") to collectively store and process information. An issue that most of these models don't address is where specific cognitive modules or abilities come from and how differences in modules determine which cognitive capacities an individual has.

Evolving New Minds

Cognitive modules are widely assumed to be present in all animals. But which modules are present in each species is less clear. The fact that mechanisms of physical activity are highly similar across vertebrates led Charles Darwin (1809–1882) to argue that mental activities, and the faculties that made them possible, were probably just as similar (Darwin, 1859). The belief that human minds are fundamentally different from those of other animals has a long history (Carruthers, 2013), however, predating psychological research and strongly shaping how psychologists think about cognition (**Figure 2.4**).

FIGURE 2.4. Ranking minds.
Ordering images of primate brains from smallest to largest suggests a chain of intellectual development from the primordial monkey to the hyper-advanced hominid. Why might such brain sorting misrepresent how evolution has shaped cognition? (After Sousa et al., 2017.)

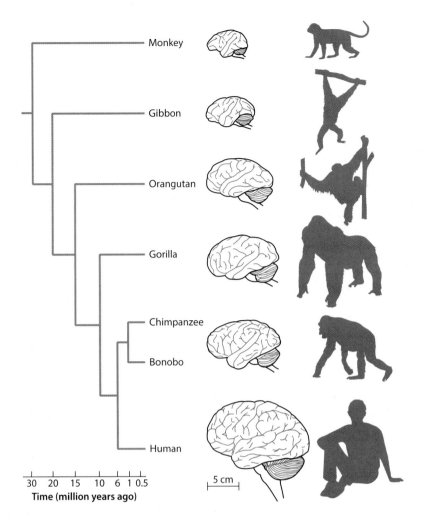

Breeding Intelligence

In the early twentieth century, American psychologists Edward Tolman (1886–1959) and Robert Tryon (1901–1967) attempted to breed rats that could quickly master mazes. They began by testing lots of rats and then breeding the best performers ("maze-bright rats") with each other. The worst performers ("maze-dull rats") were also paired together (a consolation prize?). Tolman and Tryon repeated this strategy for multiple generations of rats. The experiment worked spectacularly, with the later generations of maze-bright rats acing the tests (Innis, 1992; Tryon, 1940).

Only, it turned out that the maze-bright rats were not rat geniuses. When tested on tasks other than the specific maze used to sort the rats, the maze-bright rats didn't perform any better than the maze-dull rats. Efforts to breed brighter animals are still ongoing, although the emphasis now is on fish and invertebrates (Leung & Waddell, 2004; Petrazzini et al., 2020).

Around the same time that Tolman was trying to enhance rat minds, there were also attempts to breed smarter humans. **Eugenics**, selective breeding with the goal of improving humans, was a big enterprise in the United States (Rutherford, 2021a, 2021b). The movement was partly sparked by Galton's findings, noted earlier, that overachievers were often relatives and Galton is often credited with inventing eugenics. But he became inspired to advocate selectively breeding humans to improve the human race after reading the theories of his cousin, Darwin (Gillham, 2009), so it could be argued that eugenics was a family effort.

Rather than selecting breeding partners, American eugenicists used intelligence tests to identify "unfit" humans and then sterilized them, with the goal of increasing the proportion of "brights." These attempts to genetically increase the average intelligence of U.S. citizens were the inspiration for the more extreme approaches adopted in Nazi Germany. Eugenics became notorious because many people were involuntarily sterilized (in the United States) and because Hitler murdered mass numbers of people in his attempts to breed a "master race."

Tolman and Tryon's studies with rats showed that breeding brightness is easier said than done. But why? Why can't cognitive abilities be enhanced by artificial selection in the same way that farmers increased the size and sweetness of corn? If natural selection can ramp up cognitive capacities, why can't artificial selection? The short answer seems to be that the genetic mechanisms that determine cognitive abilities are more complicated than the ones that control corn kernel size and taste (Bludau et al., 2019; Day & Sweatt, 2011). This hasn't stopped scientists from trying to get a better handle on which genes are important for cognition, though.

There are three main ways that researchers are currently investigating how genes control cognitive capacity: (1) by analyzing the heritability of cognitive abilities, (2) by mapping the genes that are correlated with cognitive capacities, and (3) by attempting to control variations in cognitive ability through genetic engineering.

Heritability of Aptitudes

Heritability is a quantitative measure that estimates how much genetic variation contributes to variations in traits or performances seen within a group. It's possible to calculate such estimates for any measurable characteristic of an organism, including behavior.

High heritability does not imply that your current cognitive abilities are genetically determined or that your genes are more important than your environment in determining cognitive capacity. Imagine that all the humans alive today had been raised isolated in cardboard boxes. Same genes, different intellectual outcomes.

At some level, the heritability of certain traits, such as height, hair color, or skin color, is obviously high. Because variations in cognitive abilities are less directly observable, the degree to which they are heritable is less obvious. Consequently, specialized experimental methods have been developed to determine the extent to which different cognitive capacities are heritable.

Twins

The classic ways of estimating heritability focus heavily on identical twins. Since identical twins share nearly all their biological blueprints, most of the differences between them can be assigned to some cause other than genetic variation.

Typically, similarities in identical twins would be compared to similarities in fraternal twins, who are less genetically similar. Behavioral and physical features that identical twins share more frequently than fraternal twins do (like facial dimensions) would be considered higher in heritability.

The heritability of many cognitive abilities is about the same as height. Intelligence (as measured with written tests) has gotten the most attention because performance on intelligence tests consistently shows high heritability (Plomin & Deary, 2015). Findings on the heritability of intelligence have generated a lot of controversy because of differences in intelligence measures that are found across racial groups (Greenspan, 2022). Much of the controversy focuses on what such differences mean, the validity of intelligence tests, and the social implications of such differences.

You might expect that as people go through life, their unique experiences would increasingly affect how they think and behave. Counterintuitively, the heritability of intelligence actually increases with age, reaching a peak when people are in their late teens (Bouchard, 2013). This trend suggests that when young people are trying to "find their way in the world," they might actually be finding the way of their parents' genes.

Similarities between identical twins provide compelling evidence of the power that genes can have in shaping cognitive capacities (Hewitt, 2020), but they are less useful for understanding exactly how genes affect cognition in any given individual. To answer the "how" question, researchers need to conduct experiments that involve more actively controlling genes.

FIGURE 2.5. Genetically revealed cognition.
Through genetic engineering, it is now possible to directly observe the activity of every neuron in a fish's brain as it perceives and reacts to ongoing events, including during social interactions and the performance of cognitive tasks. (© Dr Kate Turner. Wilson Lab UCL)

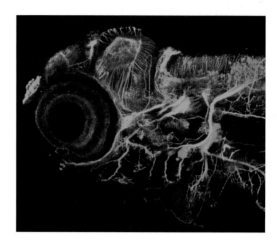

Genetic Engineering

Selective breeding experiments with nonhuman animals provide a way of exploring the effects of mixing different sets of genes, and twin studies make it possible to observe the degree to which genetic similarities lead to similarities in cognition and behavior. These scientific approaches, though powerful, are limited to naturally occurring genetic combinations. **Genetic engineering**, artificially removing, adding, and replacing specific genes, provides new and provocative ways of exploring how genes affect the cognitive abilities of an organism (Lowenstein & Castro, 2001; Park & Silva, 2019; Sun et al., 2020).

Early studies of genetically modified animals focused on exploring the effects that different changes had on learning and memory. For instance, mice and flies were genetically modified to learn certain tasks slower or faster than normal (Glanzman, 2005; Tang et al., 1999). More recent studies have focused on genetically modifying animals to make their internal processes more observable and controllable (Bernstein et al., 2011). For instance, by introducing genes from florescent jellyfish into the brains of rats, mice, and fish, researchers can increase the visibility of brain activity and structure (discussed later in this chapter) (**Figure 2.5**). The newest genetic engineering techniques make it possible to turn genes on or off in real time (Adesnik & Abdeladim, 2021).

In principle, results from genetic engineering studies suggest that it might one day be possible for people to modify their intellects like they currently can modify their hair color or facial features (El-Shamayleh & Horwitz, 2019). This might also mean that parents would have new options for molding the minds of their children (for better or worse). Although the prospect of custom-designed minds is a bit mind-boggling, in some ways this is already happening. People with substance use disorders incrementally change the way they perceive and think about the world. Children medicated to modify their behavior during development may also experience systematic changes in their cognitive abilities. Protracted use of drugs changes the genetic landscape within the user's brain in ways that alter cognitive capacity—a case of unintended genetic engineering (Hamilton & Nestler, 2019).

Individuals, such as Christopher Taylor, who have large cognitive deficits in areas other than language, could potentially benefit from genetic alterations early in development (typically referred to as gene therapy) (Ingusci et al., 2019). On the other hand, modifying minds to "normalize" them might make them less than what they might have been otherwise.

Savants

Many historically impressive intellects were possessed by people who would likely be diagnosed with mental disorders today. Amadeus Mozart, Isaac Newton, and Marie Curie were all oddballs. Some successful inventors such as Leonardo Da Vinci and Henry Ford suffered from reading disorders that may have indirectly contributed to their success. In such cases, modifying genes early on might have had unforeseen costs.

Modern day savants, people with exceptional abilities in one or more cognitive domains and below-average skills in others, may provide evidence of innate modules for complex cognitive skills like language, music, or mathematics (Smith et al., 2011). However, there are cases, both in humans and in other animals, in which brain damage that degrades performance in some tasks actually enhances performance in others (Treffert, 2010). For example, a few rare individuals have discovered that after experiencing a traumatic brain injury, they have rapidly and effortlessly acquired impressive musical, mathematical, or artistic skills (Treffert & Ries, 2021).

These cases suggest that there may be competition between different cognitive mechanisms for resources, or that interactions between mechanisms may limit certain kinds of cognition (Kapur, 1996). Consequently, attempts to genetically enhance specific cognitive abilities might have unintended, negative consequences for other abilities.

Are Genes Relevant to Understanding Cognition?

Recall from Chapter 1 that nativist theories of cognition assume that individuals are born with a genetic blueprint that determines their general cognitive capacity, as well as any specific cognitive strengths or weaknesses. From this perspective, understanding cognition includes identifying the mechanisms that determine how different aspects of cognitive abilities are constructed and interact.

Some psychologists assume instead that cognitive processes can be understood independently of underlying mechanisms. This view was popularized by British neuroscientist David Marr (1945–1980), who advocated analyzing cognitive processes as if they were computer programs (Marr, 1982).

First, you can analyze what the function of a specific process is. Marr described this as the computational level—basically a description of what's happening and why (**Figure 2.6**). This would be like playing around with a new app to see how it works and then giving a review of it. The computational theory of mind (discussed in Chapter 1), which equates cognitive processes with computations, focuses heavily on the computational level of analysis (Churchland & Sejnowski, 1992). Second, you can analyze how a process works by examining how it operates. Marr called this the representational level of analysis, which is similar to figuring out how a programmer made an app work. Finally, there is the implementational level of analysis, which focuses more on what is happening at the nuts and bolts level, like what happens electronically in your phone when you use an app.

Within Marr's framework, it's reasonable to ignore genetic mechanisms if all you want to know is what cognitive processes are doing. Taking apart your phone will tell you little about how any of the apps on your phone work and it could be that knowing more about what genes do will shed little light on how cognition works.

Consider though if Gall had been right about how brains are organized. Then, it might be possible to determine how many cognitive modules exist and how those modules interconnect and even which species possess which modules just by visually examining a person's brain. In that case, understanding basic mechanisms could give you lots of clues about how cognitive processes work.

FIGURE 2.6. Levels of Marr. Language use can be explained at multiple levels. Explanations at the computational level focus on why people talk—the goals of conversation, the properties and content of sentences, and the function of communication. Explanations at the representational level emphasize sequential cognitive processes that take place when people converse, including the visual recognition that someone is directing speech toward you, the auditory recognition that they are speaking a language you understand, and the recall and understanding of what the words being said mean. The implementational level tries to account for what is physically happening in the brain during a conversation, specifically focusing on how brains respond to sensed speech and how brain activity triggered by these sensations makes conversations possible.

Computational Level
People converse to exchange information.

Representational Level
Individuals recognize the meaning of words.

Implementational Level
Brains respond to sound waves.

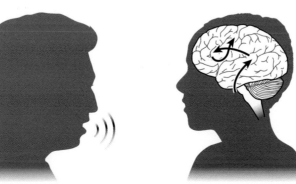

We know now that many of Gall's assumptions were inaccurate. We may learn later that Marr's assumption that cognitive processes can be understood independently of underlying mechanisms is faulty as well. Correlational studies in humans strongly suggest that genes can affect how cognitive processes operate (Hariri et al., 2003; Papassotiropoulos & de Quervain, 2011). The most straightforward way that genes can control cognition is by shaping brain structure and function, qualities that philosophers and scientists linked to mental capacities long before Gall proposed that variations in cognitive capacities come from differences in the sizes of specialized brain modules.

SIGHT BITES

One way that genes might affect cognition is by determining the number and qualities of domain-specific cognitive modules an individual has.

Natural and artificial selection of genes can affect an organism's cognitive capacities in complex ways.

Experimental studies of twins, savants, and genetically engineered animals can reveal the effects of genes on cognitive abilities.

DIVERSE BRAINS IN ACTION

SNEAK PEEK: The physical features of brains partly determine how cognitive abilities vary across different individuals. Synaptic connections, in particular, strongly affect how activity spreads within the brain as well as how brain regions interact during cognitive acts.

There's no question that differences in cognition are related to differences in brains—differences in size, organization, activity patterns, and more. There are many questions about which variations in brains matter most and about whether knowing more about the details of brain structure and function can clarify how cognitive processes work.

Historically, cognitive psychologists gave little attention to what brains do as people perceive, remember, and think. Partly, this was because researchers initially had no way of observing brains in action. But psychologists also had reasons to think that focusing on brains might not be the best way to make progress.

When people first tried to figure out how to fly, they spent a lot of time observing how birds flew. Ultimately, knowing details about feathers and flapping proved less useful than experiments with featherless, flap-free wings. The key to understanding flight came from identifying key principles rather than from precise biological measurements of natural mechanisms.

It's possible that cognitive psychology might follow a similar path. Or it could be that **cognitive neuroscience**, which involves studying brain function in order to better understand cognition, might reveal critical clues that psychologists would not have discovered using other methods. New technologies can sometimes reveal evidence that challenges scientists' assumptions about how things work (**Figure 2.7**). The following sections sketch out neuroscientific methods and findings that psychologists currently use to study cognition, emphasizing methods discussed in more detail in later chapters.

(A)

(B)

(C)

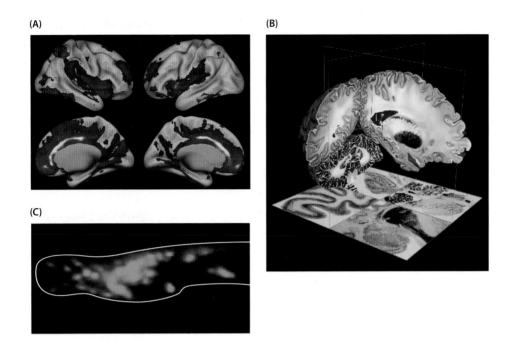

FIGURE 2.7. Seeing brains.
Modern techniques provide high-resolution images of brain structure. Whether brains are viewed in two-dimensional images (A), or in three-dimensional images (B), the cerebral cortex stands out in humans because of its curvy structure and large size. (C) Movies of the activity of individual neurons in small worms provide a way to observe brain function in much greater detail than is possible in humans. (A from Lee et al. *Front Behav Neurosci* © 2020 Lee, Kim and Tak [CC BY]; B from "BigBrain" [The McGill Centre for Integrative Neuroscience]. Reproduced with permission by Jülich Research Centre [Germany] and McGill University [Canada]; C from Nguyen et al., 2016.)

Brain Qualities

You probably don't get a chance to see, hear, or feel your brain very often, if ever. Seeing your own brain is a bit like finding out you have a famous relative; there's a connection to you, but somehow the connection doesn't seem quite real. Certainly, the idea that "you" are somehow a side effect of interactions between blobs of cells in your head is a bit bizarre.

Gall argued that not only were people's mental abilities a result of their brain structure, but that their virtues, vices, and talents were a direct consequence of how large specific bits of their brains were. If this sounds a bit far-fetched, you might be surprised to know that this idea is still prominent in theories of brain function. Human intellect, in particular, is often attributed to extra-large brain regions in specific locations (Gray & Thompson, 2004). Before considering further whether this idea is sense or nonsense, you need to know your way around a brain.

Brain Basics

Brains are the command centers of nervous systems. Your **nervous system** consists of specialized tissues that continuously work to maintain all of your organs so that you stay alive. All animals that have skeletons have a brain, but the physical and functional features of their brains are just as varied as their bodies.

The part of the brain that you are likely most familiar with—the iconic wrinkly gray, cauliflower-like blob—is the **cerebral cortex**. The cerebral cortex has been the main focus of cognitive neuroscience research for centuries.

Because of its size, neuroscientists have given names to different sections of the cerebral cortex (cortical brain regions). The left and right sides, or hemispheres, are mostly symmetric, like your face. Tissue in each hemisphere is classified as different "lobes" (like an earlobe, but in your head) based on their location. Ideally, these would be called the front lobe, the back lobe, and so on, but no. The lobe "**o**ut back" is the **occipital lobe**, the lobe at the "**p**eak" is the **parietal lobe**, the lobe by your "**t**emple" and closest to your dimple is the **temporal lobe**, and as a consolation prize, the lobe in the "**f**ront" is called the **frontal lobe** (Figure 2.8).

Sitting underneath the occipital lobe is what looks to be a mini-brain called the **cerebellum**. The cerebellum and other non-cortical regions were once thought to contribute little to cognition, but that assumption has been debunked over the last few decades. Actually, prior to Gall, most researchers

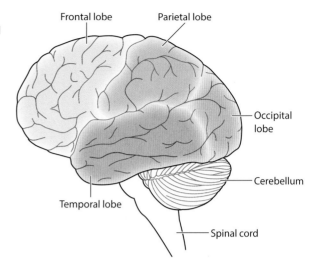

FIGURE 2.8. Four lobes. The major lobes of the cerebral cortex are defined in terms of where they are located: back/top or bottom/front. The smaller, uncolored blob beneath the temporal and occipital lobes is the cerebellum, considered to be a "subcortical" region because it is beneath the cerebral cortex.

thought that the cerebral cortex contributed little to cognition. So, the general lesson is that when it comes to brains, don't discount what you don't understand.

Does Size Matter?

You may have wondered while reading this chapter why Gall was so convinced that the size of brain regions determined a person's abilities. After all, plenty of other body parts vary in size without obviously affecting function. People with large eyes don't see better than people with small eyes and people with small hands don't have a reduced ability to feel things.

Gall's reasoning came partly from considering the brains of different animals. Animals with smaller brains, like fish, seemed less clever than animals with relatively larger brains, like cats. Bigger didn't necessarily mean better, however. Gall assigned negative qualities, such as "murderous," to some brain regions. In fact, people started calling psychiatrists "shrinks" because of the belief that some mental disorders resulted from oversized brain regions related to vices, and that the way to overcome mental and moral deficits was to somehow shrink those regions.

Over time, researchers focused less on the absolute size of cortical regions and more on their size relative to body size or to other brain regions, emphasizing species (like humans) where the size of cortical regions seemed disproportionately large given their body size. This switch was sparked in part by the fact that elephants and whales possess larger brains than humans. Modern research suggests, however, that Gall might have been on the right track after all in trying to predict capacity from volume. Performance on intelligence tests is predicted, at least in part, by the absolute size of certain regions in a person's frontal lobes (Gray & Thompson, 2004). The relationship between cortical size and capacity has grown murkier with the discovery that comparably sized brain regions can contain vastly different numbers of cells (Jardim-Messeder et al., 2017). Such complications have led some researchers to focus more on the details of brains and particularly on variations in cortical connectivity (Thivierge & Marcus, 2007; Triki et al., 2022).

Cortical Complexity

Your cerebral cortex gets its wrinkled appearance from being squashed into a tight space. Imagine stuffing a t-shirt into a water bottle. The brain of an animal with a small cerebral cortex looks as smooth as a beach ball.

If you could iron out your cerebral cortex, you would discover that it's pretty thin, as thin as a dime in some spots, which is about the same thickness as your skin. Assuming you had a microscope handy, you might also discover that the structure of your cortical tissue is pretty uniform. And if you compared a cat's cerebral cortex to yours, you would find that the structure of that cortical tissue is pretty similar to yours.

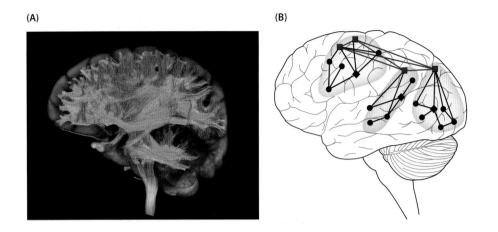

(A) (B)

FIGURE 2.9. Visualizing connections. (A) Images of physical pathways between different regions of the cerebral cortex reveal complex ways in which different regions can interact. (B) Functional interactions between brain regions can also be monitored to create maps of how different cortical regions work together during the performance of different cognitive tasks. (A Image Source Trading Ltd via Shutterstock; B after Bortoletto et al., 2015.)

So, how could different parts of your cerebral cortex be specialized for different cognitive processes if your cortex looks basically the same all over? One possibility is that what you can do cognitively depends on how your cortical regions are interconnected. Having more cerebral cortex provides more options for connecting different regions to each other and to subcortical brain regions. Maps of these cortical connections are called **connectomes** (Goulas et al., 2019; Xu et al., 2022) (**Figure 2.9**).

Different regions in the cerebral cortex can also show subtle differences in their structure that might affect their function. Maps of these structural variations are similar in size and distribution to the kinds of functional maps that Gall proposed. Animals with larger brains generally show a greater diversity of regions and have more connections, so both properties might contribute to differences in cognitive abilities.

Figuring Out the Functions of Brain Regions

If you accept that brains are biological machines that somehow make cognition possible, then the basic question facing you is this: "How do brains do it?" You have already read one possible explanation—the nativist story—which is that different brain regions have evolved to perform different cognitive functions, much like other organ systems have evolved to perform specific biological functions.

There was a time when people didn't know what any internal organs did. Researchers had to figure out how organs functioned one by one through a process of problem-solving in which they disassembled working systems to figure out how their parts functioned. This tactic has proven to be trickier in the case of brains. Despite thousands of cognitive neuroscience studies, there is still uncertainty about how brains make cognition possible. The following section illustrates the difficulty by considering what has been discovered about what your brain does when you listen to speech.

Speech Processing

At one level speech is just like any other sound. You usually hear speech when air vibrations infiltrate your eardrums. However, you may also hear speech if you are dreaming or hallucinating, in which case neither sound nor your eardrums are the source of your experiences. Regardless of whether sound is hitting your ear or your ear is squashed against a pillow, it is your brain that is "making you hear." You can also talk to yourself, either out loud or in your head, in which case you are making yourself hear. Unlike hearing someone else speak, you have control over the sentences you yourself produce, which makes the process of hearing yourself talk a bit different.

Modern technology has made it possible to watch what your brain is doing in these various scenarios, which has made a few features of speech processing clearer (Fridriksson et al., 2016; Jääskeläinen et al., 2021). First, when you hear speech, your brain does more than when you hear most other sounds. Second, for most people, the left and right hemispheres respond differently to speech, with

FIGURE 2.10. Speech in the brain. (A) Regions in your left and right temporal lobes change their activity whenever you hear a sound; each region is called an auditory cortex. (B) If you recognize the sound as speech, then a broader set of regions is activated, with more lateralization of activity. In many people, the left hemisphere (B, left) shows more complex patterns of activity in response to speech than the right. (A, B after Eagleman & Downar, 2016.)

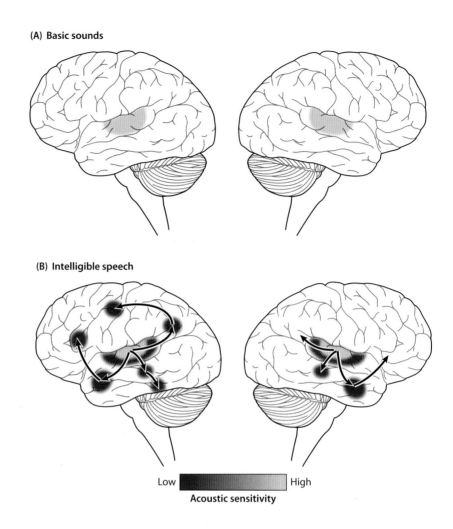

(A) Basic sounds

(B) Intelligible speech

Low [   ] High
Acoustic sensitivity

the left hemisphere typically showing more distributed activity, meaning that many cortical regions change what they do as you process speech (**Figure 2.10**) (Mesgarani et al., 2014). Finally, if you see how your brain responds to a sentence today, there is a good chance that you would see it responding in the same way to that sentence next week.

Tracking Activation

Attempting to understand what brains are doing by tinkering with them (or finding ones that have been accidentally altered) is a powerful method of exploring how cortical regions function. You usually don't get to see what a brain is doing before or after the alteration, however. Only during the last century has it become possible to observe brains in action. The earliest successes came in the form of electrical measurements.

Studies of electrical "brain waves" (repetitive patterns of brain activity) started in the 1920s and are still going strong (Biasiucci et al., 2019). An **electroencephalogram (EEG)** is recorded by placing electrodes on the scalp in order to measure changes in electrical activity in a brain. The waves of activity revealed by EEGs have been correlated with perceptual, attentional, and memory processes, meaning that researchers can use EEGs to predict what people will or won't perceive, notice, or remember. EEG recordings are obviously related to ongoing brain activity, but you don't need to know specifically how changes in waves arise to gain insights about cognition from measuring such electrical oscillations.

More recent advances in monitoring brain activity focus on measuring magnetic fluctuations coming from a person's brain. Magnetoencephalography (MEG) reveals correlations with cognitive processes similar to those seen using EEGs; however, MEGs also show where specific brain "waves"

(A)

(B)

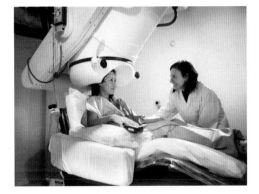

(C)

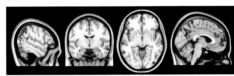

FIGURE 2.11. Observing brain activity.
(A) Electrodes on a person's scalp can be used to record electroencephalograms (EEGs) that reveal continuous changes in electrical activity generated by neurons. (B) Magnetoencephalography (MEG) makes it possible to record similar changes in magnetic fields generated by neural activity. (C) Magnetic resonance imaging (MRI) can reveal both the structural properties of brains as well as changes in brain activity during task performance (fMRI), shown here as red blobs. (A Microgen via Shutterstock; B Image Source Trading Ltd via Shutterstock; C from Mazzoni et al., 2019. *Cortex* 120 © 2019 Published by Elsevier Ltd.)

are coming from (Gross et al., 2013). How EEG and MEG recordings have been used to explore cognition is discussed in more detail in Chapters 3, 4, and 9.

Psychologists can now also monitor other biological processes that are indirectly related to brain activity, such as how blood is used throughout the brain. **Functional magnetic resonance imaging (fMRI)** tracks which brain regions are working the hardest during cognitive task performance. This makes it possible to create images, like the one in Figure 2.10, that relate activity in specific regions to different cognitive tasks. Chapters 3 through 12 all contain examples of the ways in which fMRI and other magnetic resonance measures have been used in cognitive research, and the specific ways in which cortical and subcortical activity correlates with different cognitive processes.

Tracking brain activity, either directly or indirectly, can provide new clues about what happens when people remember or think (Williams et al., 2018), but knowing where activity occurs in your brain is not enough to fully understand how cognition works. The fact that a brain region does not "work harder" during a specific cognitive task does not mean that it is not important for that task and many different tasks can lead to similar changes in brain activity.

Observations of brain activation have revealed important information about the chain of events that occur in brains when people perceive, act, and think (**Figure 2.11**). To really know how brains make cognition possible though requires a more complete understanding of how the various circuits within brains work. Understanding these circuits requires digging a bit deeper into the details of what brains are like and what neurons do.

Neural Circuits

The cell types within brains have been around for a long time. The "star" cells of the brain, **neurons**, appeared in invertebrates more than 500 million years ago. Neurons continuously receive and transmit electrical impulses within nervous systems. The key elements of neurons that make them distinctive—axons and dendrites—come in many different shapes and sizes, but they function pretty much the same in all nervous systems.

Dendrites are rootlike structures that extend out from a neuron. They provide the main interface between neurons. Like roots, dendrites gradually grow out into their surroundings as they

FIGURE 2.12. Parts of a neuron. (A) Neurons are cells. Like all cells, they have a nucleus at their core (in the cell body). Tendrils of tissue, called dendrites, extend from the cell body. Dendrites are roughly analogous to "roots" that pull in particles from their surroundings. A separate extension, the axon, leads to terminal branches ending in axon terminals that spew out chemicals—the neural equivalent of sap, pollen, leaves, and so on. (B) Transmission of information between neurons can be mathematically modeled as a process of totaling "votes" from inputs (in_1, in_2, in_n) and passing the message on to other neurons when sufficient inputs vote to do so.

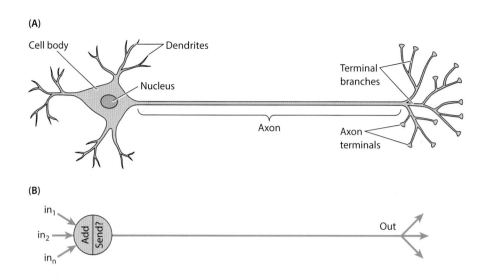

develop and collect chemicals. Unlike roots, which physically transport the nutrients they collect, dendrites convert collected chemicals into electrical signals. These signals travel to the "stump" of a neuron—its cell body—where the nucleus is located (**Figure 2.12**).

Most neurons have one to one hundred dendrites. In some cases, a single dendrite can respond to hundreds of thousands of chemicals at the same time. Dendrites are a lot more complicated than they look. Many researchers consider dendrites to be the foundation of all cognitive abilities (more on that in a bit). To understand why dendrites and neurons have caused such a fuss among scientists, you need to know how neurons contribute to brain activity.

What Brain Activity Is

Most of what scientists call brain activity is whatever neurons do. There is plenty going on in your brain beyond this. Fluids and gases are moving around. Other cells in the brain called **glia** are doing all kinds of interesting things—such as determining when connections between neurons are strengthened—that researchers are only now beginning to discover.

Some of what neurons do is considered to be more cognitively relevant than other neural processes, with the most hallowed aspect being the transmission of electrochemical signals within neural circuits. Specifically, neurons have the ability to generate brief electrical pulses called action potentials, or spikes.

Like EEG signals, changes in the spiking actions of individual neurons (called firing) can be correlated with cognitive processes such as perception. Unlike the kinds of "waves" measured in EEG, however, spikes are all-or-nothing events: either they happen or they don't. Consequently, correlations between neural firing and behavior tend to be simpler than in fMRI or EEG studies. A neuron can produce spikes faster, slower, or in specific patterns, sort of like a percussionist playing a drum.

Neurons in brain regions that respond strongly to sensory inputs fire the most when certain images are seen or sounds are heard, responding selectively to those images. Such neurons are often called **feature detectors.** Feature detecting neurons seem to operate something like a smoke detector in that they are activated by the presence of a specific stimulus (**Figure 2.13**). The computational model of letter recognition illustrated in Figure 1.4 uses multiple layers of feature detectors (detecting various combinations of line segments) to explain how you are able to identify the letters you are looking at right now, essentially explaining a cognitive process you have acquired in terms of things that neurons are known to do. Many associationist models of cognition (introduced in Chapter 1) are basically networks of interconnected feature detectors, including all connectionist models (discussed in Chapters 4 and 5).

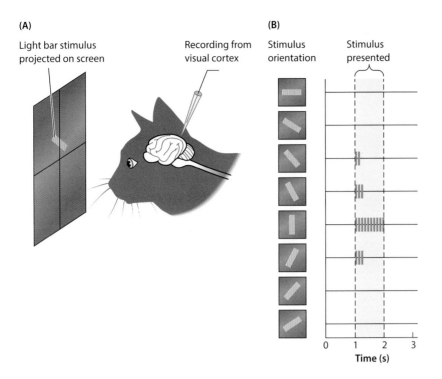

(A)
Light bar stimulus projected on screen
Recording from visual cortex

(B)
Stimulus orientation
Stimulus presented

Time (s)

FIGURE 2.13. Visual feature detectors in cats. (A) Recordings collected from neurons in cats revealed that neurons in visual cortex responded strongly to light bars. (B) Not all light bars are equally effective at triggering activity in a specific cortical neuron, however. In this example, the vertical bar provokes the strongest reaction, as indicated by the number of spikes triggered by that orientation (each vertical line corresponds to one spike). Because the neuron responds a lot to one specific light bar orientation, it effectively signals when a vertical bar is present—the feature this neuron detects is the vertical orientation of the stimulus. (A, B after Purves, 2021.)

Networks of Neurons

If your brain consisted of neurons each performing their own little spiking drum solos, it's unlikely that you would be able to think or that there would even be a "you."

All current theories assume that interactions between firing neurons are what make cognition possible. The main factors that determine how neurons interact are the connections between them, their tendency to produce spikes, and what is happening in the world around you and in your body.

Sets of neurons that interact during the performance of a particular function (including all cognitive functions) are referred to as populations or **networks** of neurons. Tracking interactions between neurons is tricky because every neuron is indirectly connected to every other neuron, with some being more closely connected than others.

A close connection isn't simply determined by the distance between two neurons in your brain. Rather, it depends mainly on where one neuron's **axon** terminals end relative to other neurons' dendrites. An axon is the main output of a neuron. Axon terminals act like a sprinkler system that spews out chemicals, called neurotransmitters, whenever the neuron fires (**Figure 2.14**).

Technically, most neurons are not physically connected to any other neurons, and instead, are only functionally connected, such that activity in one neuron affects activity in other neurons. The space between the axon of one neuron and the dendrite of another is called a **synapse**. These spaces facilitate interactions between neurons and are the main connections between neurons.

Synaptic Connections and Neural Interactions

Synapses are not the sort of thing you run into in daily life. When they were first described by the Spanish neuroanatomist Ramón y Cajal (pronounced "Ramoan E Cahall"), most neuroscientists did not take his observations seriously. Everyone believed that neurons were physically connected, like a fishnet or spider web (De Carlo & Borrell, 2007).

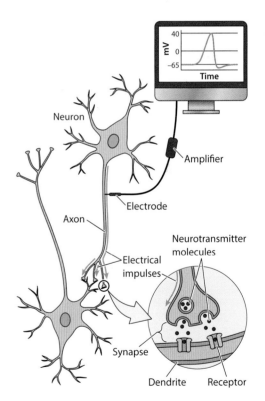

Neuron

Amplifier

Electrode

Axon

Neurotransmitter molecules

Electrical impulses

Synapse

Dendrite   Receptor

FIGURE 2.14. Missing links between neurons. Neurons interact with other neurons by releasing chemicals (neurotransmitters) from the ends of their axons whenever a spike happens. Some of these chemicals are captured by receptors on dendrites and converted into small electrical changes. The spaces in which these toss-and-catch chemical actions take place are called synapses.

FIGURE 2.15. Ramón y Cajal.
(A) Spanish conqueror of synaptic connections, Cajal could not see synapses, but he did spot their bases: dendritic spines—shown as tiny "thorns" in (B), a drawing of neurons made by Cajal. (A ©Iberfoto/Bridgeman Images; B BIOSPHOTO/Alamy Stock Photo)

(A)

(B)

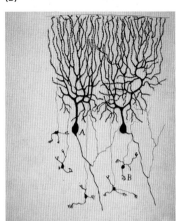

Cajal was unable to directly observe synapses because they are extremely tiny, but he could see (using a microscope and stained brain tissue) that neurons were individual cells, with axons that were not physically connected to other neurons (Glickstein, 2006). He also described small "thorns" on the dendrites, which he called **dendritic spines**, structures that are intimately related to synapses (**Figure 2.15**).

Cajal figured out that electrical transmission is mostly in one direction, from dendrites to the axon terminals, which means that neurons are influencing the firing of other neurons through synaptic connections with minimal information about what those neurons are doing. Synaptic transmission occurs when neurotransmitters are released from the axon of one neuron and detected and collected by other neurons. You can think of this as like a one-way conversation in which the first neuron says, "I'm firing more now, pass it on."

One of the surprising features of brains is that such seemingly simple interactions within neural populations can lead to the huge variety of physical and mental actions that brains control. It is still a mystery how neural interactions might generate percepts and thoughts, but it's clear that cognitive capacity must be related to the structural and functional properties of neural circuits. Currently, most hypotheses about how neural circuits can lead to cognition focus on how multiple stages of neural firing can increase the complexity of activity patterns that neurons can detect.

SIGHT BITES

The size, complexity, and connectivity of the cerebral cortex all contribute to variations in cognitive ability.

Speech processing triggers neural activity that is often lateralized and spread across multiple neural circuits.

Synaptic connections between the dendrites and axons of neurons form many of the links within large networks of interacting neurons.

HOW EXPERIENCE CHANGES BRAINS

SNEAK PEEK: Early experiences can play a key role in shaping how circuits within an individual's brain develop. How cognitive skills are practiced can also determine what percepts, thoughts, and memories are possible.

It's natural to think that variations in brains are like other variations in bodies—mostly determined by a grand genetic plan. The physical architecture of your height and hands determines what you can reach and grab without assistance, just like the length and strength of a horse's legs constrain how fast it can run.

Recall that genetic variations are the foundation of nativist theories of cognition. According to nativists, you are a natural-born thinker, and how you think is determined by how your parents' genes built your brain.

Though attractive, this scenario ignores a few key facts. First, networks of neurons are defined by their synaptic connections, and the locations of synapses are not included in the genetic plan. There are simply too many of them. Second, unlike most body parts, you can remove mass amounts of brain tissue without causing major losses in mental functions.

This second fact, in particular, caught the attention of a Canadian psychologist named Donald Hebb (1904–1985). He observed that removing the entire frontal lobe from a man with a genius-level IQ (160) had no effect on the man's mental capacities, and that removing half of the brain of a woman with above-average intelligence also had no measurable effect on her intellectual abilities (Brown, 2020; Hebb, 1949). Hebb wondered how that was possible.

There is currently no computer you can buy that will keep humming along normally if you rip out half its components. If minds are like machines (see Chapter 1), or "what brains do," then how are minds able to maintain function when half the parts are removed? Something about the way brains work is very different from how computers and other machines work. Hebb suggested that the key difference is how neurons come to be connected in the first place. He proposed that it was not genes that were building networks of neurons with cognitive functionality, but experience.

Developmental Processes

One of the cornerstones of the 1950s "cognitive revolution," and of the belief that cognitive modules exist, came from Chomsky's claim that language abilities were too complicated for children to learn from experience—that the ability to develop language skills must be innate (Pléh, 2019). If the neural interactions that make language possible are not genetically specified, as suggested by Hebb, or if language processes are not representative of other cognitive processes, then understanding how cognitive processes develop may be important for understanding how cognition works.

Where Cognition Comes From

Chapter 1 introduces Jean Piaget, the French psychologist who proposed that children construct their thought processes by interacting with the world. Hebb's ideas are similar to Piaget's, except that Hebb focused more on how people's perception changed through repeated experiences.

Psychologists who study development have conducted numerous experiments and observational studies to try and nail down when young children gain specific perceptual, attentional, and memory capacities. Abilities that show up soon after birth are viewed as more likely to be innate, while those that show up gradually, or later in development, are more likely to be shaped by learning (Oakes & Rakison, 2020; Spelke, 1998).

In some cases, children appear to start out with cognitive abilities that they gradually lose as they get older. For instance, young infants initially can distinguish speech sounds in many different languages from around the world, but as they gain more experience with speech, they lose this ability (Zhao & Kuhl, 2022). Such changes suggest that cognitive processes in children are not simply unripe versions of adult cognition. Children's cognitive abilities may serve as scaffolds for the development of adult abilities or they may be specialized for the specific circumstances faced by younger humans.

Better understanding of how cognition works makes it easier to develop appropriate interventions when cognitive development goes wrong. Consider the case of premature infants. Being born early is often associated with cognitive deficits. Neuroimaging studies suggest that part of the problem may be disorganized connections within neural networks caused by brain systems being exposed to the world before they are ready (Fischi-Gomez et al., 2015).

Children typically show a greater capacity to compensate for brain injuries than adults, so why don't premature infants quickly overcome their difficulties? One reason may be that there are certain periods during development when experience can rapidly change neural circuits in ways that are difficult to reverse.

Sensitive Periods and Lost Senses

Brain plasticity is the brain's ability to change its structure or function. The strongest evidence of brain plasticity comes from studies of animals that have been deprived of certain sensory experiences, either by deafening or blinding them soon after birth or by raising them in Alice-in-Wonderland-like environments that differ greatly from the norm.

Experiments with animals conducted in the fifties and sixties showed that manipulating developing brains by controlling external conditions can permanently change how animals see or hear the world (Hubel & Wiesel, 1970; Voss, 2013). But it matters how old an animal is when it gets this treatment. Some forms of sensory deprivation or alteration that produce large behavioral effects can have no effect at all if they are applied just a few weeks later in development, depending on how old the animal was during the treatment.

A **sensitive period** is a window of time during which neural circuits are especially plastic, with connections between neurons being strongly determined by sensory and social inputs (Knudsen, 2004). A "window" opens and closes at certain stages in development in ways that are not at all obvious from the outside. Right now, scientists don't know how many sensitive periods there are, how many different circuits are affected by them, or even what kinds of experiences are most likely to cause problems during sensitive periods.

The cognitive process most often associated with sensitive periods in humans is language (Ruben, 1999). Children who are deprived of language experiences at early ages can have lifelong language deficits, and children who learn a second language after a certain age are more likely to speak with an accent. In some cases, subtle changes in auditory processing that occur early in life can derail language learning forever after (Tallal et al., 1996).

"Plasticity, then, in the wide sense of the word means the possession of a structure weak enough to yield to an influence, but strong enough not to yield all at once... Organic matter, especially nervous tissue, seems endowed with a very extraordinary degree of plasticity of this sort."
—James, 1890, p 105

It is difficult to study sensitive periods in children for ethical reasons (Gabard-Durnam & McLaughlin, 2020). Studies of other species can be critical for understanding how sensitive periods work, just as they were for discovering that sensitive periods exist (Bateson, 2000). Cross-species comparisons have revealed that one effect of early experiences is to regulate the number, strength, and locations of synapses (Nordeen & Nordeen, 2004). The effects of sensitive periods on communicative learning have been explored most extensively in birds that learn how to sing from their elders (Daou & Margoliash, 2021) (**Figure 2.16**). As Chapter 1 notes, early experimental studies of imprinting in birds have strongly affected current ideas about how social factors during sensitive periods scaffold cognitive development (see also Chapter 11).

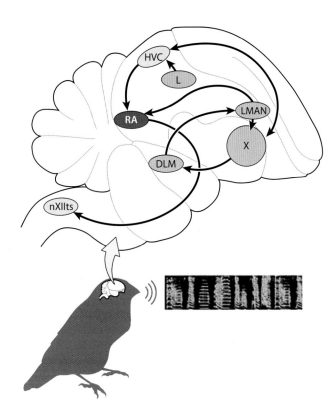

FIGURE 2.16. Anatomy of learned vocal control in a songbird.
Neural pathways in bird brains that make singing possible have been mapped out in detail in some species. The brain regions labeled HVC, RA, and nXIIts control movements of vocal output, while areas labeled LMAN, DLM, and X contribute to the learning of songs. Region L processes incoming sounds. Coordination of all these regions makes it possible for birds to produce complex sound streams (shown here as a set of yellow-green voice prints on the black rectangle). Detailed knowledge of song-learning circuits makes it possible for researchers to closely monitor changes in specific circuits during development and to precisely control what young birds experience as they learn to sing. These methods have made it possible to identify how early perceptual and social experiences during sensitive periods influence an individual's singing skills later in life. (After Daou & Margoliash, 2021. *Neurobiol Learn Mem* 180. © 2021 Elsevier Inc. All rights reserved.)

Structural Changes

Nativists suggest that people come into the world with a standard set of cognitive processes and that experiences provide opportunities to use those processes. In contrast, Hebb and James argued that babies come into the world with brains that are more like a pile of Legos, with experience constructing minds over time. One way to evaluate these competing views of where cognitive processes come from is to compare the brains of individuals that grew up in different conditions to see if their neural circuits are structured differently.

Enriched Environments, Dendrites, and Learning

Hebb was one of the first scientists to find that raising animals in different environments can affect their cognitive capacities. He discovered this accidentally after he gave some young rats from his lab to his grandchildren to keep as pets. Later, he tested the rats on various memory tasks and found that they performed better than any of the rats in his lab (Brown & Milner, 2003).

Other researchers developed a grandchild-less version of Hebb's procedure and reached similar conclusions (Nilsson et al., 1999). Rats raised in "rat playgrounds," referred to as enriched environments, performed better on a number of cognitive tasks than rats that grew up in standard cages (**Figure 2.17**). Additionally, neuroanatomical measurements of cortical circuits in the luckier rats showed that their dendrites had more branches and more synapses (Diamond, 1988). Findings from behavioral and neural studies of enriched rats are consistent with the idea that different experiences can affect the complexity of neural circuitry and increase cognitive capacities.

This doesn't tell you much about whether there are any differences in the cognitive "tools" that enriched rats develop relative to impoverished rats, though. It is possible that enriched rats are simply healthier and happier. Having more connections could mean that enriched rats' cortical circuits are in some way superior, but it's also possible that their experiences led to more varied and complex memories, which could also affect the number of connections within cortical networks (see Chapter 8).

FIGURE 2.17. Enriching rats.
(A) The impoverished housing conditions experienced by laboratory rats were initially thought to have little effect on their brains or behavior.
(B) Rats raised in environments with more opportunities for exercise and social interactions, however, showed enhanced performance on cognitive tasks and increases in the complexity of neural structure, making researchers more aware of the importance of living conditions on cognitive abilities. (A, B after Myers & DeWall, 2016, *Neurobiology of Learning and Memory*, 180. © 2021 Elsevier Inc.)

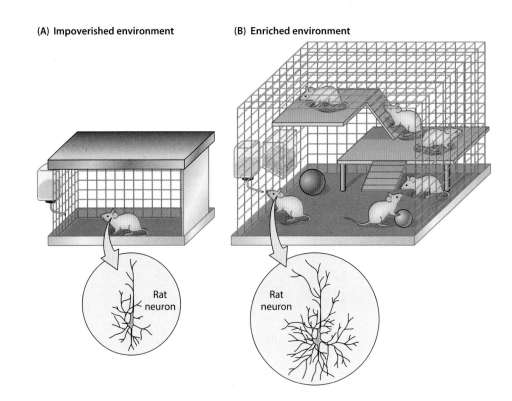

(A) Impoverished environment   (B) Enriched environment

Rat neuron

Rat neuron

Structural changes in the cerebral cortex not only play a key role in cognitive development of children but also make it possible for injured adults to regain lost cognitive functions.

Restoring Control and Repairing Circuits

On occasion, people have accidents or conditions that lead to brain damage. As observed by Hebb, this doesn't necessarily cause cognitive problems, but there are many cases where cognitive functions are lost. When this happens, there are usually focused attempts to help these individuals regain function. Sometimes rehabilitation works, and sometimes not.

Understanding the factors that drive brain plasticity can potentially be useful in restoring cognitive function (Su & Xu, 2020). For example, a person who has lost the ability to control part of the body can benefit from having control or sensations temporarily taken away from other body parts (Kwakkel et al., 2015). Reducing a person's ability to use one limb can help them regain function in another (**Figure 2.18**). Paradoxically, additional loss of function amplifies plasticity and facilitates incremental changes in a person's ability to control their movements in new ways (see Chapter 9).

FIGURE 2.18. Mitt-driven plasticity. Constraining the use of a functional hand can help individuals regain control of finger movements lost after a brain injury, in part because it forces the use of the less functional fingers. Individuals are more likely to show gradual improvement when they have no choice but to use the affected fingers, an effect that shows up in standardized measures of motor control. (Graph after Taub et al., 2011; image: CIMT)

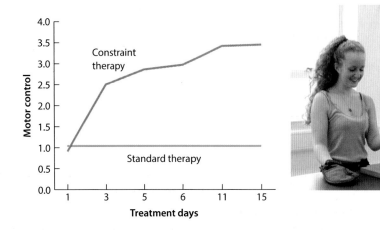

WEIRD, TRUE, FREAKY

Surprise! Most of Your Brain Is Missing

Each year, about twenty thousand adults living in the United States are diagnosed with brain tumors. Often, the symptoms that lead to the discovery of a tumor include changes in perception or judgment and memory problems. These cognitive changes come about as the tumor eventually derails neural circuits and reduces their blood supply.

Tumors can grow quite large, however, before they have any noticeable effect on the way you cognize. Brains will sometimes put up with a lot before they start breaking down functionally. As noted by Hebb, cognition can proceed even when your brain is not fully intact. In fact, a few people with surprisingly large regions of their brains missing have been living seemingly normal lives without knowing that anything was amiss in their heads. In one case, a French man with a job and family was found to be missing most of his brain (see figure). His skull was mostly filled with fluid (Feuillet et al., 2007).

In another case, a twenty-year-old student pursuing an advanced degree in mathematics was randomly found to be missing more than 90% of his brain without showing any cognitive problems (Lewin, 1980). People missing their en-

tire frontal lobe or cerebellum have lived much of their lives before the deficit was discovered (Yu et al., 2015).

Given that most people don't get their brains scanned for the fun of it, there are presumably many more people wandering around with unsuspected cavities inside their skulls, not to mention people, like those observed by Hebb, who know they have holes, but do just fine.

So, just how much brain do you need in order to have the typical cognitive capacities of a human? Oddly, there does not seem to be a magic amount. Sometimes removing large amounts of brain tissue has less of an impact than removing smaller amounts of tissue, and in some cases removing tissue can actually enhance cognitive function!

The resilience of brain function despite massive loss of tissue raises important questions about how cognitive processes can be preserved when most of the brain regions normally involved are no longer present. It's the mystery that Hebb spent his career trying to solve. His answer was that brain plasticity makes it possible for many different neural pathways to achieve similar functions.

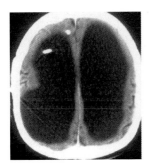 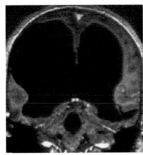 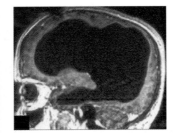

MRI images of an abnormal brain. This forty-four-year-old man, who came in complaining of weakness in his left leg, was found to be missing more than 80% of his brain. (From Feuillet et al., 2007.)

Similarly, a partly damaged brain region can sometimes cause more problems than if that same region were completely removed. This is because disruptive connections can wreak more havoc than no connections at all (Pulsifer et al., 2004).

In some cases, it is even possible to cognitively rehabilitate people without brain damage. For example, cognitive training programs have proven to be effective in treating children with attention deficit disorder and adults with schizophrenia (Fisher et al., 2015). Computerized repetitive practice programs that adapt to an individual's performance can lead to improvements in a person's attention and memory (Genevsky et al., 2010). Gaining a greater understanding of how training changes neural interactions can not only benefit people with injury-related cognitive difficulties but can also help people deal with (or avoid) cognitive decline (Nguyen et al., 2019).

Functional Changes

Neuroimaging technologies like those shown in Figure 2.11 have revealed that experience can change brain structure and function either during development or after extensive practice. Although neural circuits change in many ways as you learn, not all changes will affect what you can do cognitively.

Some experiences benefit multiple cognitive processes, while others only affect the specific skill being practiced or have no effect at all on cognition. Understanding how experience changes cogni-

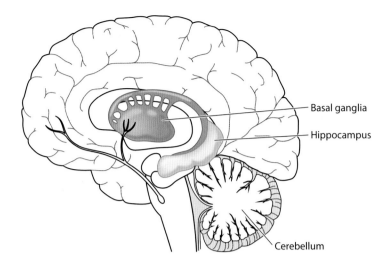

tive capacities is key to understanding cognition more generally (see Chapters 5 and 7). Becoming an expert at chess does not make you an expert at all strategy games, but it definitely can change how you perceive, attend, and think about chess. The cognitive skills that you've developed throughout your life go far beyond any built-in cognitive modules you may have been born with.

Becoming an Expert

When you spend time training on a particular cognitive skill, several interesting things happen. As your performance improves, activity in your brain changes. The changes are not simply increases or decreases in the size of a particular region of your cerebral cortex, as Gall might have predicted. Instead, activity in some regions may initially increase then decrease, while others may decrease and then increase depending on your level of expertise. And many of the neural circuits that change are not in your cerebral cortex, but beneath it in subcortical regions.

Three subcortical regions that often change as people learn new cognitive skills are the hippocampus, the basal ganglia, and the cerebellum (**Figure 2.19**). Each of these brain regions seems to contribute to the development of expertise in different ways that will be revealed throughout this text.

Hippocampal processing is often associated with spatial cognition and certain kinds of memory-related tasks (see Chapters 6 and 8). The basal ganglia seem to be more involved in tasks that integrate sensations and actions (see Chapter 7), like musical skills, and the cerebellum contributes to learning skills from observing others (see Chapter 11). Cerebellar changes are also associated with improvements in reading ability, and damage to this region degrades multiple cognitive processes, including attention and memory.

For the past century, many researchers have looked to the cerebral cortex for answers about what makes human cognition possible and exceptional. Observations of structural changes associated with cognitive training make it clear that many different brain regions, including non-cortical circuits, are involved and that different regions can play different roles at various stages of learning (Groussard et al., 2014; Poldrack et al., 2001). Nowhere is this more apparent than in studies of memory capacity.

Memory Training

Mnemonics are tactics that you can use to increase your ability to recall specific facts or events. Some work better than others and most require some practice before they can be used effectively (Smith et al., 2009). Mnemonics have been around for a long time, pre-Aristotle.

Before writing became popular, mnemonics were the main tools people used to keep track of facts and stories. Some Greek philosophers were opposed to written text because they felt it weak-

(A) Untrained children

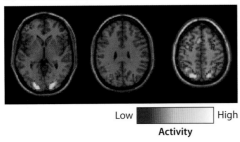

Low [ ] High
Activity

(B) Memory-trained children

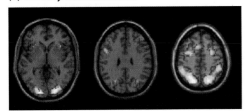

FIGURE 2.20. Training brains to remember. Extensive practice on memory tasks not only changes a child's memory capacity but also changes activity in the brain regions that are linked to the performance of memory tasks. (A) fMRI images from children performing a working memory task (see Chapters 1 and 8) reveal cortical areas that consistently show increased activity during performance of the task (depicted as colored blobs). The three images here show average increases across three different "slices" of a brain (the smaller the scan, the closer it is to the top of the skull), with brighter regions indicating bigger increases in cortical activity. In this control group of children (who did not receive memory training), the biggest increases in activity were seen in the occipital (lower blobs) and frontal lobes. (B) Children trained for five years to perform mental calculations using an imagined abacus showed larger increases in cortical activity than untrained children while performing the same working memory task (blobs are larger and brighter), as well as increases in brain regions not activated in untrained children (new blobs evident in middle scan). (A, B from Wang et al., *J Neurosci* 2019. © 2019 by the authors [CC-BY-4.0])

ened memory abilities (McCoy, 2009). In a way, this might be similar to what Google and Alexa are doing today.

How do mnemonics work? They seem to work by recruiting brain regions that normally would not contribute to routine memory processes (Dresler et al., 2019). For instance, the method of loci, or the mind palace technique, incorporates visual imagery and spatial processing as a way to cue unrelated memories for specific information. Teaching the elderly to use such mnemonics can be an effective way of fending off age-related memory loss (Singer et al., 2003). Children's memories can also be improved through practice, which appears to both engage additional brain regions and boost activity in regions normally engaged during memory processing (Wang et al., 2019) (**Figure 2.20**).

The capacity of individuals to modify their cognitive abilities through practice is called **cognitive plasticity**. Many researchers argue that early humans began to change their cognitive capacities when they started to learn languages and construct tools (Dunbar, 2012). The social transmission of such cognitive skills across generations is a major factor contributing to the enhanced intellectual capacities present in modern humans (see Chapters 11 and 12), and the foundation for modern educational programs.

Academic Interventions

Without cognitive plasticity, there would be little point in attending school, given that the purpose of school is to promote learning. Students can learn lots of things at school, including athletic and social skills, but the main criteria used to evaluate schools are assessments of cognitive skills in reading, writing, math, and so on. None of these skills are innate; instead, they all depend on experiences that change cognitive processes.

Obviously, individual differences in cognitive abilities and cognitive plasticity will interact with the effectiveness of sending youngsters to institutions to learn cognitive skills. Basic measures of cognitive processes in young children are highly predictive of their academic progress (Finn et al., 2014). Time spent in school is also predictive of performance on intelligence tests.

Surprisingly, almost nothing is known about how cognitive plasticity varies as a student progresses through school or about how cognitive plasticity relates to brain plasticity (Mercado, 2008). Given what is known about sensitive periods, it seems likely that there are periods when attempts to change an individual's cognitive abilities are more (or less) likely to be successful. It also helps if you are awake.

SIGHT BITES

Sensitive periods are stages of development during which specific experiences (or lack of experiences) can have big effects on what neural circuits can do.

Early experiences can affect the complexity of connections within neural circuits, suggesting that these connections are naturally plastic.

Changes in cognitive skills that occur as the result of training, such as the use of mnemonics, provide evidence of cognitive plasticity.

USING ANIMAL MODELS TO STUDY COGNITION

SNEAK PEEK: Comparing neural structure and activity across different species of animals, including humans, can reveal important clues about how cognitive processes work as well as new ways of repairing or enhancing cognition.

Before the cognitive revolution in the fifties and sixties, many psychological experiments focused on learning processes in rats and pigeons (see Chapter 1). The assumption underlying this behaviorist approach was that everything learned from studies of lab animals would also apply to people. After the cognitive revolution, many experimenters turned to studies of undergraduates. Many cognitive psychologists assumed that the best (or at least most efficient) way to understand cognition was to study college students.

Modern cognitive psychology experiments traditionally involve giving undergraduates instructions before having them spend time performing a cognitive task. Sometimes, nonnative speakers are excluded from experiments to avoid the possibility that they won't understand the instructions. There is no way to include nonhumans in such experiments.

This does not mean you can't test cognition in nonhumans though. Researchers have developed numerous ingenious experimental methods that make it possible to test the same cognitive skills in both humans and nonhumans. A major advantage of such tasks is that they introduce new ways of observing and manipulating cognitive performances genetically, neurally, and behaviorally.

Comparing Cognitive Effects of Brain Changes

Approaches used to link brain damage to cognitive deficits in humans can also be used in other animals, with the advantage that the location and type of damage can be more precisely controlled and measured in nonhumans. In some cases, it is even possible to repeatedly turn specific brain regions on or off at different stages of performance!

Early on, researchers created brain lesions to challenge Gall's proposal that cognitive abilities were localized in specific brain regions. The French researcher Jean Flourens (1794–1867), for example, removed brain tissue from rabbits and pigeons to test whether damage to different regions led to different deficits (Tizard, 1959). He agreed with Gall that the cerebral cortex made cognition possible, but found that regardless of which part he damaged, there were similar effects on performance.

Similarly, the American psychologist Karl Lashley (1890–1958) found that the location of cortical damage was less relevant to predicting effects on rats' memories of mazes than was the size of the lesion (Lashley, 1950). Such findings reinforced the idea that more cerebral cortex is better when it comes to cognition and increased skepticism about cognitive functions happening in predictable locations within a brain.

Someone like Descartes who believed that humans are special might have argued that findings from studies of rabbits and rats are not relevant because people's cognitive abilities are on a higher level. So, how similar is cognition in undergraduates and rodents?

Shared Capacities

Cognitive processes are unobservable, even in humans, so there is no way to show definitively that two people use the same processes. There are good reasons, however, to believe that many people do possess similar minds. Those reasons include evidence from performance on cognitive tasks and evidence of similar brain activity happening when different individuals perform the same task.

It's relatively simple to show experimentally that animals can perceive differences between sights, sounds, and other sensory events, and that they can recognize and attend to objects (see Chapter 4). Techniques for testing memory, problem-solving, imagination, and thinking in nonhumans are a bit more challenging but still possible (Andrews, 2020).

The main issue here is that most cognitive tasks used to test undergraduates depend on language. All memory capacities other than those that require verbal reports have been demonstrated in several species. Tasks that reveal thought processes in nonhumans (see Chapter 10) are less common and more controversial.

Animal models are nonhuman species that have been studied to try and answer scientific or medical questions, like the songbirds used to study sensitive periods described above. In psychology, animal models typically are selected either based on their behavioral similarity to humans, such as a shared capacity to discriminate different speech sounds, or based on similarities in how their brains react to changes. For example, damage to the hippocampus can impair spatial memories in both humans and rats (Burgess et al., 2002).

The relevance of data collected from studies of animal models depends on the validity of the comparisons being made (**Figure 2.21**). For instance, you may have seen videos of dogs appearing to say "I love you" to their owners. Studying this phenomenon in dogs is unlikely to shed much light on human speech or romantic feelings because similarities between the dogs' vocalizations and human speech are superficial and not driven by comparable cognitive processes (see Chapter 12).

Animal models are used extensively in studies of mental disorders that affect cognition like schizophrenia, autism, and attention deficit disorder. In those contexts, the animal models are considered to provide valid comparisons when experiments conducted with the models predict the effects of pharmacological or behavioral treatments on cognitive performance (Bale et al., 2019).

Animal Models of Developmental Processes

Studies with animals other than humans are particularly important in brain-based investigations of cognition, because not only can nonhuman animals' brains be studied in much greater detail, but sometimes animal models can be designed to test specific relationships between brains, behavior, and cognition (Wintler et al., 2020).

Animal models are also being engineered to have enhanced cognitive capacities, such as the ability to retain memories for longer periods (Lee, 2014; Xing et al., 2021). It's not yet known if all cognitive capacities can be genetically enhanced or what limits there are on increasing certain capacities. Currently, the only way researchers have of potentially answering such questions is by conducting experiments with animal models.

FIGURE 2.21. Peas in a pod.
Studies of cognition in young children and nonhumans often share methods, since verbal instructions are not an option. What might a nativist predict about findings from neural and behavioral comparisons between toddlers and apes? (Trinity Mirror/Mirrorpix/Alamy Stock Photo)

FIGURE 2.22. Constructing models of autism spectrum disorder.
Studies of chromosomal alterations associated with autism make it possible to genetically engineer rodents with similar alterations. The brains of animal models of autism can be monitored and modified much more flexibly than is feasible in children. This provides an extremely powerful setup for testing hypotheses about how autism affects cognitive processes as well as for testing potential treatments. (After Takumi, 2015.)

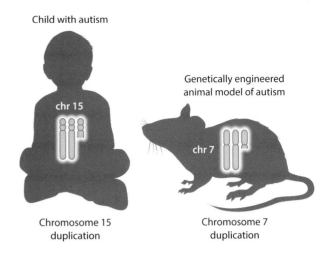

Researchers have genetically engineered animal models so that they show deficits similar to those of children with developmental disorders (Crawley, 2012). For example, there are now multiple mouse models of developmental disorders such as autism spectrum disorder (Chung et al., 2022) (**Figure 2.22**). By producing animals with deficits that mimic those that naturally occur in children, researchers hope to identify new strategies for treating or preventing this disorder.

Technologically, it is already possible to alter genes in humans and affect their cognitive abilities, but without knowing more about how differences in neural circuits affect cognition, making such changes is risky.

Cognitive Prosthetics

Beyond providing a way to conduct cognitive experiments that are unethical to conduct on humans, animal models provide unique opportunities to test new interfaces between biology and technology.

Brain-computer interfaces (BCIs), in which computers monitor brain activity, are a major focus of technologies designed to move beyond finger swiping and tapping. Recall from Chapter 1 that the extended mind thesis proposes that people can use physical tools such as notes or smartphones to boost mental processing. BCIs take this idea to the next level by making it possible for computers to use brain activity to control digital systems.

Early experiments with monkeys provided the first demonstrations that a monkey could learn to control the movements of a robot arm simply by thinking about doing this (Velliste et al., 2008). Researchers implanted electrodes into the monkey's motor cortex, a region of cerebral cortex that produces movements when electrically stimulated. Computers monitored activity in the motor cortex and then moved a robot arm in different ways based on ongoing patterns of neural activity.

The monkeys gradually learned through trial and error to use the arm to gain rewards, even though monkeys have no way of feeling what their cortex is doing (just like you!). Similar BCI technology was later implemented in paralyzed humans who also learned to control robotic arms by thinking about how they wanted the arms to move (Collinger et al., 2014) (**Figure 2.23**).

Various **cognitive prosthetics,** devices that replace or augment cognitive processes, are currently being developed, many of which are being tested in animal models before being tried out on people (Anderson et al., 2010; Moxon et al., 2020). So, if you are ever able to control your smartphone with your mind, you will probably have mice or monkeys to thank for this ability.

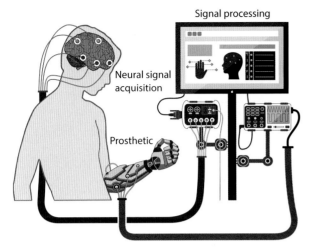

Signal processing

Neural signal
acquisition

Prosthetic

FIGURE 2.23. Mind over matter. Research with monkeys showed that they could learn to control a robotic arm using a BCI interface by thinking about what they wanted the arm to do. Similar technologies have enabled humans to mentally control novel prosthetic appendages. What brain regions would you suspect are critical for learning to be a cyborg? (After Portillo-Lara et al., 2021. *APL Bioengineering*, 5; licensed under a [CC BY] license.)

What Distinguishes Brains from Minds?

This chapter has revealed several ways in which knowing more about what brains do can potentially provide insights into cognition. It may seem obvious that your mental abilities depend on how neural circuits in your head function. This "fact" comes from thousands of years of debates and experimental observations.

Chapter 1 reviewed past models of minds as associations, machines, souls, and more. The proposal that minds are "what brains do" can be viewed as a special case of the mind-as-machine model, where the "machine" consists of neural circuits. But what do brains do that counts as cognitive?

Brains as Biocomputers

With their dendritic inputs, central processing cell bodies, and outputting axons, it's easy to think of neurons as surveying the reports of dendrites and then giving a thumbs-up or thumbs-down on whether those reports justify sending a signal to other neurons. This process can be modeled as a kind of calculation or computation. And if neurons are calculating, then what brains do must be something like computing. Computing brains would then give birth to computational minds (Churchland & Sejnowski, 1992).

Different brain regions clearly show some functional specializations, however, which means that not all neurons are computing in the same way. Neurons engaged in processing speech presumably are specialized for speech-related computations, just like computations within video game consoles are specialized for making the games run smoothly.

If brains function like computers, then linking brain functions to mental activity is just a more detailed version of building a computational theory of mind, as described in Chapter 1. The only difference is that the kinds of computations that can be included in this model must be ones that can be computed by networks of neurons. When minds are simply what brains do, then you end up with lots of kinds of minds, because there are lots of different brains within and across species doing lots of different things.

Worm Minds

Charles Darwin's final book, *The Formation of Vegetable Mould, through the Action of Worms with Observations of Their Habits*, describes his attempts to discover "how far the worms acted consciously and how much mental power they displayed" (Darwin, 1881, p. 3). Based on several years of observations and experiments, he concluded that the inner life of a worm was a cognitive world (Crist, 2002).

Modern scientists are less likely to claim that either consciousness or cognitive processes are present in worms. Why? Worms have brains, sensory systems, and the ability to move and learn from their actions. If minds are what brains do, then Darwin's conclusions about worm minds should be widely embraced.

The connectomes of some worms are known—every neuron and every connection between those neurons has been described in detail (Schafer, 2018). And yet, scientists still are unable to determine if worms perceive, feel, or remember anything (see Chapter 3). In short, there is not yet a way to reliably identify the mental capacities of any neural networks. There are tens of millions of interconnected neurons in your gut that perform computations (Gershon, 1999). What's preventing those piles of neurons from being cognitive?

Any explanations of cognition that ignore what actually happens in individuals are unlikely to be complete or accurate. The ultimate goal of cognitive psychologists is to construct the best explanations of cognitive phenomena possible. Considering the behavior, brains, and experiences of many different individuals and species provides wider opportunities for identifying the best explanations of cognition in all its varied forms.

SIGHT BITES

 When similar brain structures are engaged by similar cognitive processes across species, comparative studies can be particularly informative.

 Animal models provide new ways to experimentally investigate cognitive deficits and technological enhancement of cognitive abilities.

 Brains are often described as organs whose actions constitute minds, a portrayal that fits well with computational theories of minds.

CLOSURE

What does it take to learn fifteen languages? Or one language? It may be satisfying to think that humans are able to learn languages because we are neurally advanced—the highest link on the great chain of brainy beings (Pinker, 1994). However, polyglots are rare and there is no smoking cortex that reveals what the human-unique language learning circuit proposed by Chomsky actually is or where it might be.

There are genes that are known to affect language abilities (see Chapter 12), but those same genes affect lots of other abilities as well, not all of which are related to cognition. Whatever differences exist in human brains that make it easy for toddlers to learn language skills, there is no guarantee that those differences are an evolutionary advance. Similar to Christopher Taylor, unique language learning skills might have come with a cognitive cost. Human perception of odors is pathetic in comparison to olfaction in most mammals. Perhaps there are other cognitive capacities humans lost which freed up brain space for language processing circuits.

What psychologists know so far is that people naturally master a few cognitive skills that other animals do not and that language skills, in particular, seem to boost learning and performance of many other cognitive skills. Animals other than humans may similarly have cognitive skills that humans normally don't.

In some respects, cognitive psychology is still in its infancy as a scientific field. Only in the last few decades have advanced techniques for exploring genetic and neural contributions to mental processes become available. In other ways, cognitive psychology seems to be nearing its expiration date as a scientific approach, at least in terms of explaining perception and thought processes as boxes connected by arrows.

Most subfields of psychology, including social psychology, clinical psychology, and educational psychology, have bought into the idea that cognitive processes rule the (mental) world. For these subfields, understanding cognitive mechanisms is more of a pragmatic and therapeutic issue than a way to scientifically explain what minds are like.

When considering the cognitive abilities of an individual, how they develop over time and how they can go wrong, details about how brain functions help or hinder cognitive development and plasticity take center stage. At what point might medications be needed to "fix" attentional processes or to avoid memory decline? What preventative steps might be taken to decrease the chances that someone needs such medications?

The following chapters highlight some of the newest findings from genetics and neuroscience on mechanisms of cognition as well as current gaps in knowledge. You don't need to be a neuroscientist or a geneticist to take advantage of the breakthroughs that these fields are making in the study of cognitive mechanisms. But you do need to be willing to put some effort into understanding the basics of these fields if you want a better grasp on what's happening inside your head.

COGNITIVE LINGO

animal model
axon
brain-computer interface (BCI)
brain plasticity
cerebellum
cerebral cortex
cognitive module
cognitive neuroscience
cognitive plasticity
cognitive prosthetic
connectome

dendrite
dendritic spine
domain specificity
electroencephalogram (EEG)
eugenics
feature detector
frontal lobe
functional magnetic resonance imaging (fMRI)
genetic engineering
glia

heredity
heritability
mnemonic
nervous system
network
neuron
occipital lobe
parietal lobe
sensitive period
synapse
temporal lobe

CHAPTER SUMMARY

Inheriting Cognitive Mechanisms
Genetic variations contribute to cognitive capacity in complex ways. Changing the genetic profile of an individual can change brain development in ways that can potentially determine the number and qualities of domain-specific circuits.

Diverse Brains in Action
Diversity in the size of cortical regions and the complexity of connections within and between regions may determine what is cognitively possible. Neurons and regions that are connected form large networks that become active during cognitive processing.

How Experience Changes Brains
During sensitive periods of development, experiences can shape the strength of connections within brain networks. Similarly, repeated experiences throughout life can enhance or degrade cognitive skills by changing how brain circuits function.

Using Animal Models to Study Cognition
Animal models make it possible to experimentally study cognitive mechanisms in ways that are difficult or impossible to achieve in humans. Mental processes are often described as a product of brain function, but it is not yet known exactly how variations in brain activity or structure relate to variations in cognition across different animals.

REVIEW EXERCISES

Inheriting Cognitive Mechanisms
- Explain how domain specificity relates to the functions of cognitive modules.
- Describe the relationship between cognition and minds.
- Describe the three different levels of analysis of cognitive processing proposed by Marr and their implications for studies of cognition.

Diverse Brains in Action
- Provide examples of how cognitive neuroscientists might study speech processing.
- Explain the role of dendritic spines in networks of neurons and how they may relate to cognitive capacity.

How Experience Changes Brains
- Summarize the evidence for sensitive periods during development.
- Explain how enriched environments can affect brains.
- What is cognitive plasticity and how does it relate to mnemonics?

Using Animal Models to Study Cognition
- What role have animal models played in the development of cognitive prosthetics?
- How is the computational theory of mind related to the idea that minds are "what brains do"?

CRITICAL THINKING QUESTIONS

1. Savants are notable for possessing advanced cognitive skills in one intellectual domain while showing below-average abilities in many other intellectual tasks. What kinds of evidence might be collected to determine whether the abilities of savants are acquired or inherited?

2. Many have claimed that humans possess unique neural circuits or mental faculties that give them cognitive abilities that other species don't have. Some, like Darwin, suggest that many animals possess the same abilities as humans, just to a lesser degree. Which view better fits with the structural organization seen in brains?

3. Efforts are currently being made to map out connectomes of brains. What do theories of brain plasticity suggest about similarities and differences in the connectomes of individuals who grew up in different historical periods?

4. BCIs involve monitoring and interpreting brain activity, something that brains do naturally. How might studies of neural mechanisms of perception or memory be useful for developing new approaches to BCI?

5. Animals have shown some ability to learn to recognize speech. How might cognitive neuroscience techniques be used to clarify whether nonhumans recognize words in ways that are more similar to speech processing by toddlers or by nonnative speakers?

3 Conscious Cognitive Processes

Kaleb Starr/Alamy Stock Photo

Right now, you are in control. You are pointing your head at these words and making whatever eye and hand movements are necessary to get from one line of text to the next. But what if one of your hands suddenly started moving in ways that prevented you from reading, such as covering most of the words? Not just randomly flailing around in distracting ways, but like an obnoxious bully systematically preventing you from achieving your goal?

The idea that your own hand might interfere with tasks that you are voluntarily choosing to do might seem nonsensical. However, this is similar to the situation faced by people suffering from **alien hand syndrome**, a condition in which a person's hand seems to have an agenda that differs from the one reported by its owner (Hassan & Josephs, 2016). In extreme cases, a person's hand may even move in ways that are aggressive, leading to self-injuries or injuries to others. The hand may also "sneakily" perform actions that its owner does not appear to notice.

When you think about your own actions, you might intuitively divide them into things that you do on purpose and things you do involuntarily or accidentally. Subjectively, voluntary acts probably seem to be guided by your thoughts and intentions, while involuntary actions do not. Patients with alien hand syndrome watch their hand performing actions that don't look accidental. For example, the alien hand might unzip a coat zipper that the patient had just zipped up with the other hand; patients often describe the problematic hand as having a "mind of its own." So, are the odd actions of a person's "alien hand" involuntary? Or are they being controlled by some other agent? Could there be two minds in one body?

Chapter 1 reviewed various ways of thinking about and studying cognitive processes and Chapter 2 described some basic mechanisms of behavior and cognition, but neither chapter directly addressed the issue of how you get from thinking about doing something to actually doing it. What exactly is the difference between hand movements (or thoughts) that a person produces "on purpose" versus movements that just happen?

Relatively few cognitive psychologists have attempted to answer this question. Instead, they have left philosophers, religious scholars, or legal experts to struggle with the issue of who controls which actions. A premeditated killing (murder) is considered to be much worse than an accidental killing (involuntary manslaughter) because one act is considered more voluntary than the other. But if you are judged to be insane, then even a meticulously planned execution can be treated as involuntary. And if you are justifiably enraged by an extremely undesirable situation, then any killing you do would be legally classified as voluntary, even if your subjective impression was that you were "blinded by rage" and lost all control of your actions.

It is possible to scientifically study how thoughts or actions are controlled without necessarily specifying the controller. You can also study the effects of experience and genes on behavior, as well as the neural mechanisms associated with remembering or thinking, without focusing on whether those cognitive processes "just happened" or were purposely performed. However, this approach seems to skip over what is arguably one of the most intriguing aspects of cognition: the subjective experiences you have while deciding, reading, remembering, or thinking.

The intentional, conscious, voluntary components of cognition are key to what makes intelligence admired more than stupidity. A person's abilities to discover novel solutions to problems, invent things that never existed before, and change the way that people think are why cognitive processing is valued more than reflexive behavior. An artist's ability to evoke emotional states in situations where nothing is really happening—you're standing in front of paper and paint or sitting in a movie theater—is part of what differentiates the cognitive capacities of humans from those of other species.

Your conscious, subjective impressions of contemplating, feeling, hearing, and seeing provide the most compelling evidence you have that cognition happens and matters, even if you cannot directly observe thoughts (**Figure 3.1**). Voluntary control of thoughts and actions feels different, like you are doing something because you want to, or need to, in order to achieve some goal. Sometimes those goals relate to mental states you hope to attain—feelings of joy, pride, satisfaction, and so on—in which case, your mental states provide the motivation that drives your thoughts and actions.

So, while it may be scientifically simpler to avoid addressing how conscious awareness and volition relate to cognitive processes, it's questionable whether any understanding of cognition can be complete without taking these phenomena into account. Luckily, modern scientific approaches are providing new ways of exploring links between conscious mental states and behavior that may ultimately move researchers closer to a more complete understanding of what happens mentally when you are awake, aware, and choosing what to do or think about next. By the end of this chapter, you should have a clearer awareness of how conscious and unconscious cognitive processes interact.

FIGURE 3.1. Hidden forces. Magnetic fields are naturally invisible, only becoming evident through their effects on the movements of certain materials. Despite their invisibility, magnetic fields can be objectively measured and studied. Consciousness is similarly invisible and thought by most to affect the movements and thoughts of at least some organisms. However, identifying ways of objectively measuring and scientifically studying consciousness continues to be a challenge. (Phil Degginger/Alamy Stock Photo)

THE SCIENCE OF CONSCIOUSNESS

SNEAK PEEK: Minds without consciousness are no minds at all. But what is the link between consciousness and cognition? How can psychologists study consciousness if they cannot directly observe conscious states?

Psychological research in the United States started with attempts to understand consciousness. In fact, William James, the first American professor to teach a course in psychology, defined psychology as, "*the description and explanation of states of consciousness as such*. By states of consciousness are meant such things as sensations, desires, emotions, cognitions, reasonings, decision, volitions, and the like" (James, 1890, p. 15). Modern cognitive research continues to focus on many of these topics, but usually without emphasizing or acknowledging that the "things" being studied are associated with states of consciousness.

Scientific studies of consciousness emphasize two aspects: (1) when consciousness is present or absent and (2) what roles it plays when it is present. An organism may be classified as **conscious** if it is alert, awake, and capable of responding to sensed events. Alternatively, some researchers argue that organisms are only truly conscious if they recognize that they are alert, awake, and alive (see Chapters 8 and 11).

Scientists have used several approaches to try and understand conscious processes. One approach involves examining the brain activity of individuals as their alertness fluctuates. Researchers have also attempted to understand consciousness by studying cognition that happens unconsciously. The idea behind this second approach is that if conscious states are important for cognition, then they probably do something that unconscious processes cannot. The strengths and weaknesses of these two approaches are considered in the following sections.

Signs of Consciousness

Just as researchers rely on precise measurements to draw conclusions about cognitive processes that they cannot directly observe, they also use replicable measures to assess when an individual is conscious. Much of the evidence for consciousness comes from people's actions. However, visible movements are not a reliable predictor of when conscious states are present or absent.

Levels of Consciousness

For many years, researchers thought of consciousness as operating like a light switch: either it's on or off. Sure, someone might be more or less alert depending on how sleep-deprived they are, but such variations were considered to be comparable to the brightness of a candle flame. The flame might get dimmer and sputter a bit before going out, but the flame fundamentally is either present or absent. You are either aware or not.

Sleep studies have changed this view. "Being asleep" could mean several different things in terms of what is happening in people's heads and minds (**Figure 3.2**). Dreams do not quite fit the idea that consciousness is either on or off because objectively a dreamer acts unconscious, but awakened dreamers reported awareness of events happening within a dream world. Hypnosis and meditation can also lead to psychological states with qualities of both consciousness and unconsciousness.

The variety of mental states has led researchers to distinguish levels of consciousness using exotic labels like states of vigilance, coma, mindful, subconscious, preconscious, nonconscious, subliminal, wakeful, vegetative state, nirvana, and so on (Dehaene et al., 2006).

This explosion of terminology has led psychologists to view consciousness as a mix of mental states rather than as an all-or-nothing quality of minds (Birch et al., 2020). Even so, many researchers still describe transitions between these states as a kind of threshold crossing—from minimally conscious

FIGURE 3.2. Stages of sleep.
Recordings of electrical activity in the brain (A) reveal cycling through several different stages during the night (B), some of which are quite similar to awake activity. Subjective experiences can occur during multiple stages. (A Antonio Guillem/Alamy Stock Photo, B after Louie, 2020, under CC BY 4.0 license.)

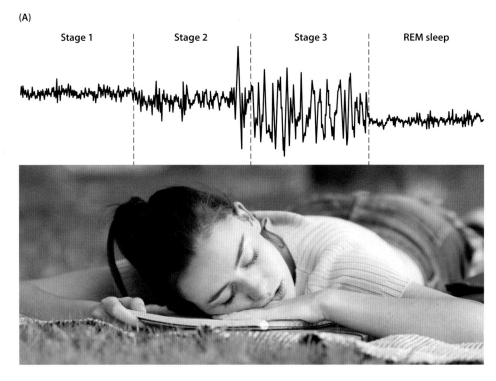

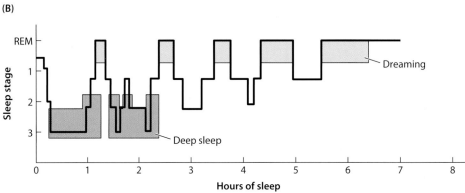

to conscious, unconscious to hibernating, sober to drunk, and unresponsive to responsive. Identifying the conditions associated with such transitions has been key to scientific studies of links between consciousness and cognitive processes.

Altering Conscious States

Humans have discovered many ways to alter conscious states. Some of these techniques relate to regulating emotions or arousal levels (for example, amusement parks or psychotherapy), while other techniques, such as anesthetics, are used to more dramatically shift consciousness. Some traditions, such as Buddhism and yoga, focus on raising consciousness to new levels.

Contemplation has always held a special place in people's thinking about experience. For ancient Greeks, contemplation was the path to knowing the good, a belief that is also apparent in many religious and spiritualist traditions. Ritualized contemplation is often touted as a means of gaining mental clarity, emotional stability, well-being, and many other desirable outcomes. Using techniques of controlled breathing patterns, body positions, and distraction suppression, you can shape your awareness in ways that are otherwise difficult to achieve.

Mindfulness is one approach to channeling awareness that has become a kind of movement in the United States (Gill et al., 2020); mindfulness-based stress reduction programs are rapidly popping up in schools, prisons, businesses, governmental organizations, and hospitals. Mindfulness at its core involves voluntarily controlling what you attend to, with "now" typically being the main target.

Simply attending to one thing (say this word) instead of something else (this emoji 👍) may seem like an odd way of improving your mental health or gaining insights. There is experimental evidence, however, that controlling awareness, and mindfulness in particular, can have psychological benefits (Chiesa et al., 2011). It is less clear if those benefits are greater than those you might get from other techniques for altering awareness, such as taking regular naps.

Mindfulness requires voluntary control of mental and physical acts geared toward achieving a specific mental state. Other altered states of consciousness happen more naturally. For instance, flow states, sometimes referred to as being "in the zone," happen when you are fully engaged in an activity and feel a kind of joy to be doing what you are doing (Csikszentmihalyi, 1996). In some ways, flow states are the opposite of mindfulness in that your awareness of "now" gets pushed to the background—you may lose track of time or your sense of your surroundings.

Flow is sometimes described as a merging of action and awareness combined with the loss of a sense of self (Sinnett et al., 2020). It is generally viewed as boosting performance beyond what would normally be possible through the voluntary control of actions. Flow does seem more likely to occur during challenging tasks (versus, say, brushing your teeth) and in individuals who have gained expertise in performing that task.

Neural Correlates of Consciousness

Medical conditions that lead to atypical mental states have driven much of the modern research into detecting when an individual is aware. When two-way communication is impossible, brain activity provides the only evidence of conscious awareness.

In recent studies, hospitalized patients who were nonresponsive and unable to communicate were neuroimaged while being given various instructions (Berlingeri et al., 2019). For instance, they might be told to imagine certain scenarios such as playing a particular sport or navigating through a familiar neighborhood. By comparing the brain activity of these patients to those of conscious individuals performing the same task, researchers were able to identify a subset of patients whose brain activity matched that of conscious participants. Those patients apparently understood the instructions and followed them despite their physical nonresponsiveness. They were conscious but trapped in nonresponsive bodies, a condition described as **locked-in syndrome** (Monti et al., 2010).

Given that a conscious mind can be trapped in a body with no way of directly revealing its presence, might there be minds hidden within your own body that you have yet to detect? This scenario may seem far-fetched, but you have about 100 million neurons embedded within your digestive system (Mayer, 2011). That's more neurons than there are in a mouse's brain. Could the disobedient hand of a patient with alien hand syndrome provide evidence of a previously locked-in consciousness that accidentally gained some capacity to interact with the world (Uddin, 2011)? How would you know if your gut is conscious?

To answer such questions, scientists have attempted to find neural processes that are consistently associated with conscious states (Koch et al., 2016). The search for **neural correlates of consciousness**, the minimal conditions or structures that can produce conscious states, has led to several new insights about when and how awareness contributes to cognition.

Cortical Contributions to Conscious States

The most studied neural correlates of consciousness relate to activity in the cerebral cortex. Emphasis on cortical activity has partly been driven by a belief that conscious deliberation requires sophisticated neural circuitry. Studies showing decreases in cortical activity when people are anesthetized are also a factor. Given that changes in cortical activity are also strongly associated with cognitive

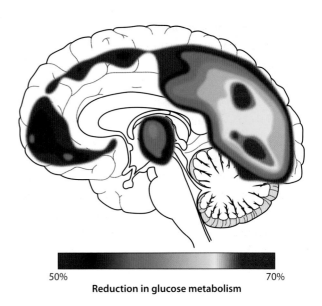

FIGURE 3.3. Cortical activity correlated with being conscious. Multiple regions across the cerebral cortex show diminished activity when a person loses consciousness under anesthesia, with decreases of as much as 70% (red) in some areas. (After Eagleman & Downar, 2016.)

50%   70%

Reduction in glucose metabolism

processing (see Chapter 2), it seems natural to conclude that conscious states and cognitive processing are tightly linked (**Figure 3.3**).

Not all regions of the cerebral cortex are closely associated with consciousness, however. Large chunks of cortex can be removed or damaged without having any noticeable effect on a person's conscious states. In contrast, damage to other much smaller cortical regions can dramatically change what a person consciously perceives (see Chapter 4).

Neural activity in the prefrontal, parietal, and occipital cortices, in particular, seems to be most closely associated with transitions between conscious and unconscious states (de Graaf et al., 2012). More activity is seen in these brain regions when people are consciously monitoring ongoing events.

One popular way of measuring cortical correlates of awareness is to monitor brain activity while individuals alternate between being aware of an object versus being unaware of it. Such tasks can be used with both humans and nonhumans, making it possible to monitor the activity of individual neurons as well as broader brain regions during transitions. For instance, in binocular rivalry studies in which different images are presented to each eye, participants can report on when they transition from seeing one of the presented objects to not seeing it (Tong et al., 2006). By monitoring what neurons in different regions are doing when an object pops into awareness, researchers can get a better sense of how and where neural activity changes when someone suddenly becomes aware of something that was there all along.

Subcortical Contributions to Consciousness

The strong correlations between cortical activity and conscious states might lead you to think that cortical circuits are the seat of consciousness. However, it's activity in subcortical regions that seems to more strongly determine when someone is or isn't conscious (Afrasiabi et al., 2021).

Damage to subcortical brain regions is much more likely to leave you in a coma or vegetative state than is damage to any cortical region. And it's the neurons in your brainstem that control levels of consciousness across the day-night cycle, mainly by adjusting the balance of neurochemicals distributed throughout your brain. Neurons in your subcortical regions fire in characteristic patterns when you are awake versus asleep. These predictable patterns of subcortical activity determine how your cerebral cortex reacts to external events and when such events lead to percepts (MacDonald et al., 2015).

The importance of subcortical regions to ongoing conscious processing has led some researchers to propose that interactions between different brain regions may be key to understanding how consciousness works. For instance, sets of neurons fire synchronously at specific rates whenever individuals actively attempt to remember recent events (Rizzuto et al., 2003).

One way of thinking about the different roles that the cerebral cortex and subcortical brain regions play in consciousness is that subcortical activity is necessary for there to be any consciousness, but cortical activity is necessary for conscious states to have the distinctive qualities associated with feeling, hearing, seeing, and so on.

Identifying neural correlates of consciousness provides a way for scientists to avoid some of the problems associated with using self-reports to understand the relationship between consciousness and cognition (discussed in Chapter 1). But one issue that such studies have not resolved is why you experience anything at all. If minds operate like computers, then brains should be able to process information fine without consciousness. From this perspective, cognitive processes could be mostly, and maybe entirely, unconscious. Implicit cognition refers to all such unconscious cognitive processes.

Implicit Cognition

Not too long ago, women giving birth in hospitals were routinely treated with a drug that induced "twilight sleep." The drug didn't make women unconscious to the pain of childbirth; instead, it effectively erased their memories of giving birth. If something as monumental as an excruciating birth can be wiped from your conscious experience, what else might you be missing from your past experiences? Might such lost memories still be able to affect your conscious thoughts? Mechanisms that affect your cognitive performance without your awareness, referred to as **implicit cognition**, are particularly tricky to study since by definition they are processes that you would not notice in your everyday life. The question of whether unconscious processes might influence **explicit cognition**, conscious thoughts, and experiences is one of the oldest in psychological research (Solms, 1997).

Sigmund Freud (1856–1939) popularized the idea that people's conscious thoughts and actions could be strongly affected by unconscious mental processes (Freud, 1920). From the Freudian perspective, the unconscious elements of a person's mind are just as important as the conscious elements for determining what a person thinks or does (**Figure 3.4**).

In the Freudian model, explicit cognition is just the tip of the iceberg when it comes to understanding a person's mind (Solms, 2004). The various levels of processing hypothesized by Freud are essentially metaphorical. His explicit processes basically end up being anything that is verbalizable, while the implicit ones include anything that a person fails to voluntarily mention.

Modern cognitive research supports the idea that unconscious processes can affect the way you think, remember, and perceive the world (Schacter et al., 1993; Teachman et al., 2019). Implicit cognitive processes are prominent in studies of creativity and insight in problem-solving (see Chapter 9)

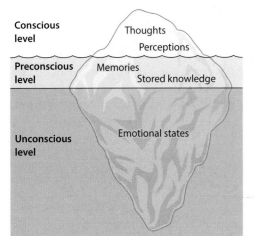

FIGURE 3.4. Freud's model of the human mind. Freud popularized the idea that subjective impressions of thoughts (explicit cognition, shown here as the conscious level) played a relatively minor role in determining how people think and behave relative to implicit cognitive processes (the preconscious and unconscious levels).

and in memory research (see Chapters 7 and 8). When you talk to a friend, the processes that enable you to generate sentences are almost entirely unconscious (see Chapter 12).

Interactions between unconscious and conscious cognitive processes are especially critical for theories of attention and perception (Crick & Koch, 1990) (see Chapter 4). How do unconscious processes like sensory receptor activity give rise to conscious percepts, and what role do conscious awareness and interests play in determining which sensations register?

Implicit cognitive processes are typically revealed when a person behaves in a predictable or appropriate way while at the same time claiming to have no subjective awareness that they are behaving that way or why. For instance, a person may report not being aware of some aspect of a scene before them, but then act as if they do perceive that aspect.

Blindsight

One of the most famous examples of individuals apparently lacking subjective awareness, but nevertheless responding as if they were aware, is blindsight. **Blindsight** is a condition, usually caused by brain injury, in which a person reports having extensive blind spots but sometimes acts as if they can actually see fine (Weiskrantz, 2004) (**Figure 3.5**).

Researchers first identified this phenomenon by having people with blindsight make guesses about where objects that they reported being unable to see were located. For people with vision, this test is equivalent to being asked to close one's eyes and then report on the number of fingers someone holds up. In the case of individuals with blindsight, though, their guesses are so accurate that it seems as if they must either be lying about being blind or are somehow "peeking." People with blindsight can also navigate around unseen objects (Weiskrantz, 2004) and correctly identify their shapes (Trevethan et al., 2007).

Psychologists have discovered techniques for temporarily disrupting vision in ways that simulate blindsight (Boyer et al., 2005). Experiments on simulated blindsight show that visual pathways all the way through to the visual cortex can become active without necessarily producing a conscious experience of seeing—early visual processing is mainly unconscious with consciousness coming online a bit later in cortical processing.

FIGURE 3.5. Knowing without seeing. Patients with cortical damage report seeing nothing in certain regions of their visual field, yet can accurately answer some questions about what is present in those regions despite their lack of awareness. (After De Gelder, 2010.)

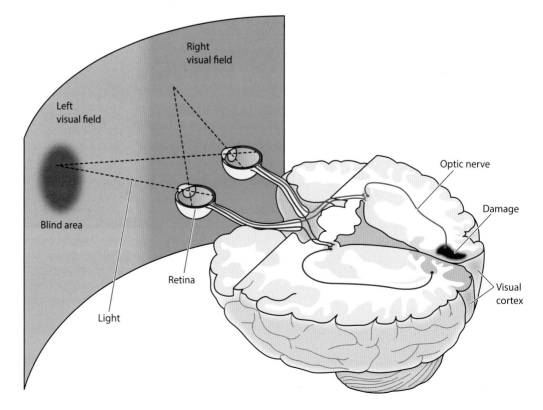

The same neural circuits are engaged during both conscious vision and unconscious blindsight. The difference between consciously seeing and unconsciously processing visual inputs relates more to the kinds of activity occurring within the cortical networks and when that activity occurs rather than some kind of specialized awareness-generating neurons (Hurme et al., 2017). Further evidence of shared mechanisms underlying both implicit and explicit cognition comes from studies of visual perception in special conditions.

Subliminal Perception

In perceptual tasks, implicit processing is sometimes referred to as **subliminal perception**. Psychologists study subliminal visual perception by briefly flashing a picture, followed by a blotchy black-and-white image (like a QR code), and then flashing a third image. Unlike people with blindsight, people viewing such rapidly changing displays report seeing pictures, but usually they are unable to say what the first image in the series was.

Evidence that participants subliminally perceive the first picture comes from how they describe the third image, which varies depending on what was shown in the first image. For example, if the first image was a smiling emoji, participants may be more likely to describe the third image using positive terms than people who were first shown a frowning emoji (Coll et al., 2019; Monahan et al., 2000).

Subliminal perception research has a somewhat shady past because of early reports that advertisers were using subliminal messages to influence customers. Backmasking, or recording a message backwards and adding it to music, was thought by some to be a subliminal way of warping the minds of teenagers. Less devious marketers have sold thousands of self-help products that claim to boost abilities (such as confidence, memory, or self-control) by embedding subliminal messages in recordings or by simply repeating the messages continuously in the background while a person is sleeping.

Surprisingly, some of these techniques actually can change a person's behavior. They only seem to work, though, when the person explicitly knows what the supposed effect of the hidden message is. Even if there were no subliminal messages hidden in a recording, the nonexistent messages could produce the same effect if the person believed such messages were present (Greenwald et al., 1991). So, parents urging their kids not to listen to "devil music" may have unintentionally transformed harmless songs into sin generators.

Priming

Previously experienced events do not need to be subliminal to unconsciously affect later cognitive processes. **Priming** happens when a person's forgotten perception of an earlier event affects how the person perceives or interprets a subsequent event (Schachter & Buckner, 1998). In visual perception, seeing or hearing particular scenes or sentences can increase the likelihood that a person interprets an ambiguous image in a particular way (Goolkasian & Woodberry, 2010). For example, after seeing a scary movie, you might be more likely to interpret a scratching sound near a window as someone or something trying to get inside.

Priming can be demonstrated using lots of different methods. One popular technique involves having participants complete a word fragment, like CON____. Right now, your likelihood of completing this fragment with "SCIOUS" is much higher than it would be for someone who hasn't been reading this chapter. You've recently read the word conscious multiple times, and so have been primed to fill in the blank in a certain way.

When you are accused of having your mind in the gutter, it's usually because you've been primed to interpret ambiguous statements a certain way. For instance, what is made of rubber, handed out at some schools, and used to prevent mistakes? If you did not answer "erasers," it is probably because of your earlier experience seeing "CON___" followed by the phrase "mind in the gutter" or the word "rubber."

WEIRD, TRUE, FREAKY

Surgery under Hypnosis

One of the more impressive cases of unconscious processing influencing cognition is seen in hypnosis (Lynn et al., 2020). The hypnotist guides a person into a distinctive mental state, during which the hypnotist can give the person verbal cues that trigger specific actions. Post-hypnosis, subjects may report no memory of what happened while they were hypnotized and show little awareness when they respond in specific ways to the cues the hypnotist provided.

Scientific studies of hypnosis have played an important part in the development of cognitive research. William James argued that hypnosis provided a window into hidden links between conscious and unconscious thought and provided a possible explanation for how something like alien hand syndrome might happen. Nobel Prize winner Santiago Ramón y Cajal (see Chapter 2) conducted experiments on hypnosis in both humans and nonhumans in an effort to clarify the neural origins of consciousness. Cajal hypnotized his wife while she was giving birth, enabling her to go through labor with apparently minimal pain. He reported that she was surprised when told that the baby had been born (Stefanidou et al., 2007).

Cajal's hypnosis of his wife during childbirth may seem like the sort of crazy home-brew experiment that only a Nobel Prize-winning scientist could pull off without getting arrested. In the last decade, however, physicians in Europe have gone one step further by using hypnosis in place of anesthesia during surgeries (see figure). In an evaluation of

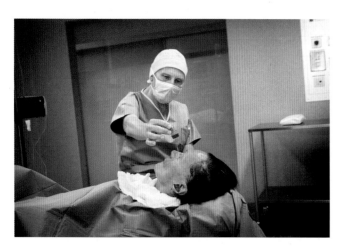

A surgeon brings a patient out of hypnosis after completing his surgery. (BSIP SA/Alamy Stock Photo)

150 surgeries performed on cancer patients using hypnosis in place of anesthesia, 99% of the cases resulted in successful surgeries with minimal reports of discomfort (Berlière et al., 2018).

In most hypnosis-based surgeries, hypnosis is combined with painkillers and sedatives, but the patient remains conscious throughout the procedure. This approach, called hypnosedation, avoids the side effects associated with general anesthesia and also appears to speed recovery, a benefit that Cajal also noted in his wife, post-birth (Faymonville et al., 1999).

A hospital in Belgium has used hypnosedation in over 12,000 surgeries since 1992 (Goldhill, 2018). In general, hypnosedation requires more preparation than does the use of general anesthesia because patients need to be experienced in undergoing hypnosis, a process that can take a month or more.

There are large individual differences in susceptibility to hypnosis, so not all patients are equally likely to be able to successfully suppress the pain associated with surgery or childbirth by being put into a hypnotic state. This is partly why hypnosedation hasn't caught on in U.S. hospitals; it requires a greater time commitment and doesn't always work. Drugs, in contrast, do not require any patient training and work on almost all patients.

Hypnosis is not the only technique being developed to reduce pain by behaviorally altering states of consciousness. Some researchers are attempting to develop internet-based cognitive behavioral therapies to treat patients suffering from chronic pain (Alberts et al., 2018).

Such approaches could be viewed as the weaponization of placebo effects, essentially using mental manipulations to suppress or counteract physiological problems. As suggested by findings that laughter or service dogs can actually be an effective component of medical treatments (Vagnoli et al., 2015), new methods of modulating explicit and implicit thought processes may prove to be an increasingly important tool in clinical interventions.

Priming is typically viewed as evidence of an implicit memory process affecting memory retrieval (see Chapter 7), sort of like how hints can help guide you to an answer. The main difference between priming and a hint is that with priming you don't need to be able to consciously recall the hint for it to affect what you later recognize or recall.

In fact, some evidence suggests that priming effects can happen more than a decade after the initial experience (Mitchell et al., 2018). This means that how you are interpreting this paragraph now could be the result of past implicit learning (see Chapter 7). Beyond just your knowledge of what the words mean, experiences that formed your beliefs about what the effects of reading textbook chapters should be, as well as similarities between the sentences in this book and sentences you have previously heard or read, may all be influencing what you think this paragraph means (see Chapter 12).

SIGHT BITES

Understanding variations in conscious states and how they coordinate with unconscious processes to determine mental activity and behavior is central to understanding cognition.

Cortical and subcortical activity determines your conscious states, but there is currently no definitive neural correlate that shows when an organism is aware.

Implicit (unconscious) cognitive processes can affect the way you think, remember, and perceive the world just as much as explicit cognitive processes.

VOLUNTARY CONTROL OF THOUGHTS AND ACTIONS

SNEAK PEEK: Evidence of minds comes from the acts of their owners. What determines which acts you choose? How do you control what you do and when did you start choosing? Is your body simply a biological machine with consciousness playing the role of a thoughtful puppeteer?

Every cognitive process that you can think of likely has an implicit component. There are implicit memories, implicit reasoning, tacit knowledge, implicit learning, subliminal perceptual processes, and so on. When you engage in actions automatically without really thinking about it, those reactions or "habits" are often controlled by implicit cognitive processes (James, 1890). Because implicit processes are not consciously accessible, there is no straightforward way for you to tell how much of your own cognitive processing is explicit versus implicit.

"All consciousness is motor… every possible feeling produces a movement, and that movement is a movement of the entire organism."
—James, 1890, p 372

Given that you can do so much unconsciously, what do you gain from any cognitive process being conscious? It's possible that your conscious experiences don't really have any purpose or function. They could just be a side effect of neural activity. On the other hand, whenever you explain why you do what you do, you're likely to mention explicit reasons. For instance, if you remember an assignment you forgot, you may quickly change your plans. In such situations, your conscious states seem to guide your thoughts and actions. You react to imagined futures that exist only in your mind and make decisions based on your subjective impressions. But what actually happens when you decide to do something?

Because implicit processes contribute to cognition both effortlessly and automatically, they are sometimes associated with reflexive or intuitive reactions to ongoing events (discussed later in the Emotion and Cognition section). Explicit cognition, in contrast, seems to require effort and attention to the task at hand as well as awareness that there is a task at hand. Conscious states happen when you are cognitively engaged, and you are most cognitively engaged when you are trying to do something.

Initiating Actions

Subjectively, you may have the impression that you decide to act, either slowly or quickly, after which you perform one selected mental or physical action. Consciousness seems to be key to this kind of process—awareness of what is happening now and what could be happening later provide the "reasons" for selecting a particular plan of action or for waiting until later to decide.

A particular action can be implemented in lots of different ways. So choosing what you will do often does not determine exactly how you will do it. Traditionally, cognitive psychologists have focused on understanding what processes contribute to action selection and on the role consciousness plays in action selection, giving less attention to the details of how movements are performed (see Chapter 10). Some modern theories instead argue that it's not really possible to understand action selection without considering the kinds of physical movements an individual can perform. Despite the differences in these approaches, most theories agree that for an action to be voluntarily controlled, there needs to be a controller.

Chains of Command

Perhaps the most intuitive way of thinking about voluntary actions is in terms of a **hierarchical model** in which instructions are delivered from a "commander" that directs movements or thoughts of multiple underlings, which in turn control different minion subsystems that ultimately get things done (**Figure 3.6**). This is exactly the kind of soul-steered automaton that René Descartes argued is what makes humans human.

Hierarchical models of action initiation are a type of information processing model in which an observer monitors external events and mental states to select an action and then sends commands to perform the actions (Balleine & Dezfouli, 2019). In these models, control of behavior depends on **top-down processing**. For Descartes, the "top," or source of instructions, was the soul. Psychologists now often point to a hypothetical central executive system as a possible commander (see Chapters 8 and 10).

Beyond the memories for what actions are possible and which situations suggest specific actions, hierarchical models of voluntary action generally include some mechanisms for sorting through memories to identify potential plans of action, mechanisms for choosing and implementing the most

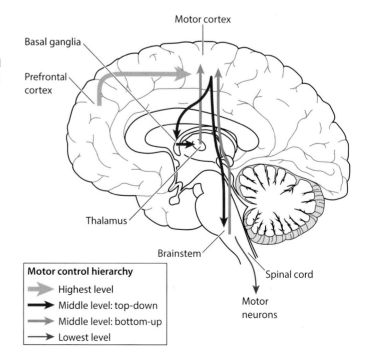

FIGURE 3.6. A hierarchical model of action control. In this model, instructions from the highest level are delivered to other brain regions (cortical and subcortical) that implement the action plan with different levels of detail and precision, ultimately generating specific movements through activation of motor neurons in the spinal cord (the lowest level in the hierarchy).

Motor cortex

Basal ganglia

Prefrontal cortex

Thalamus

Brainstem

Spinal cord

Motor neurons

Motor control hierarchy
Highest level
Middle level: top-down
Middle level: bottom-up
Lowest level

appropriate option, and mechanisms for monitoring whether the action performed led to a desired or expected outcome (the "highest level of control" in Figure 3.6). Although this process is sometimes described as involving a chain of command from a top cortical executive to lowly muscle fibers, the various mechanisms are usually all operating in parallel rather than like falling dominos.

Impressions of Control

William James argued that people's conscious experiences of controlling actions mainly were the result of them imagining the perceptual outcomes of those actions. In other words, when you feel you are doing something "on purpose," it's because you've mentally simulated the consequences of your actions just before performing them. In that case, the conscious state that you experience when you choose what to do could be something more like an impression of what is about to happen than a command that determines what will happen.

Consider again the paradoxical nature of alien hand syndrome: two sets of limb movements in the same person, both of which seem purposeful, but only one of which is reported to be voluntary. Is each arm being controlled by a "mind of its own?" Can unconscious, involuntary movements be actions if they are counterproductive to other ongoing consciously controlled actions? Is it possible that the movements of neither arm are actually under conscious control, and that the mover's subjective impressions of control are misinterpretations of what is happening?

You might think, "When I start moving, it is because I choose to." But some evidence from neuroscientific studies challenges that interpretation. Presumably, if you as conscious commander are initiating your movements, then you should consciously decide to start moving before neurons in your motor control circuits start firing, right? You can actually check that by monitoring the timing of electrical activity in your brain before, during, and after you decide to start moving.

If you stare at a clock and note the instant you choose to start moving, and then compare this to the timing of events happening in your brain, you will likely discover that motor activity associated with your movements starts happening about one second before you "choose" to begin (Libet et al., 1983).

This mismatch between subjective impressions of action initiation and neural activation has been studied extensively in laboratories using a task in which participants are instructed to press a button multiple times, whenever they want. The changes in brain activity that precede voluntary acts like button presses are called the **readiness potential** (**Figure 3.7**). In some cases, a readiness potential may begin as much as ten seconds before a person subjectively perceives that they have chosen to perform an action (Soon et al., 2008). How can your brain start executing an action before you consciously choose to perform it?

It is possible to create an illusion of control by simply instructing participants to judge how much control they have over lights that come on when they press buttons (Gino et al., 2011). Even in cases where the specific lights that come on are totally independent of which buttons are pressed, participants often report that they have some control over which lights come on. Do you believe that pressing the "Walk" button at a crosswalk really makes the traffic lights change faster? In casinos, gamblers often roll dice harder when they need higher numbers, suggesting that they believe that how they roll the dice partly determines the outcome. People are clearly biased in their subjective impressions of which outcomes and actions they can voluntarily control.

Let's assume that your impressions of your ability to choose your actions are a consequence of your actions and thoughts rather than a cause. Would this mean that the hierarchical model of action planning and execution is wrong? Not necessarily. The hierarchical model does not specifically require that conscious cognitive processes are the source of action instructions, it just suggests that there is a leader at the top to the chain of command. The head of the hierarchy could, in principle, be an implicit cognitive process.

FIGURE 3.7. The readiness potential. Recordings of electrical activity from a person's scalp (EEG) can be used to track what is happening in the brain when that person decides to press a button. Electrical activity associated with initiating a button press typically begins before a person indicates that they have decided to press it. (After Libet et al., 1983.)

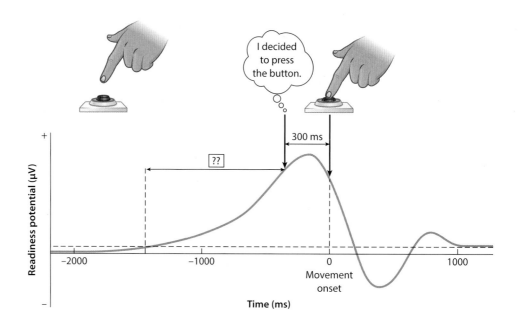

Control Systems

For much of the history of psychological research, the assumption has been that neural systems specialized for voluntarily controlling actions and thoughts were mostly independent of each other. Specifically, circuitry used for controlling movements was considered to be relatively primitive and similar across many organisms, while thinking was considered to be a highly advanced form of consciously controlled cognition that depends on specialized circuits present only in adult humans. Recently, however, it has become clear that many of the neural systems that make the control of actions possible are involved in controlling both physical and cognitive acts (Geranmayeh et al., 2014; Van Overwalle et al., 2020).

The cerebellum (see Chapter 2), which is present in all vertebrates, was initially considered to mainly control the timing and performance of motor skills. Later studies revealed that the cerebellum also regulates various cognitive and emotional processes, interacting directly with most brain regions that are engaged by such processes (**Figure 3.8**). Cerebellar damage impairs language abilities, mental arithmetic, memory retention over short intervals, and planning abilities, depending on the extent of the damage (Schmahmann, 2019). Cerebellar damage also disrupts social cognitive skills (see Chapter 11) such as attributing emotional states to others (Pierce et al., 2022).

Cortical circuits engaged during motor control and maintenance of memory are often located in different regions of cortex, but the structural circuits within each of those regions are highly similar, further suggesting that similar kinds of processing are suitable for controlling both thought processes and action generation. Understanding voluntary control of actions may be directly relevant to understanding voluntary control of thinking and memory recall (Leisman et al., 2016).

Maintaining Control

Hierarchical models of voluntary action planning and production describe this process as an organized flow of information down a chain of command. The model assumes that your action selector is calling the shots about what you do when.

Many of your actions require little supervision, however, like when you sit in a chair and stare at a screen. In fact, some actions seem to be under external control, such as when drivers involuntarily stare while passing an accident. And experts can rapidly perform impressive cognitive feats "without even thinking about it." For example, champions at mental calculation can rapidly figure out the cubed root of a number like 61,629,875 in their head in less than thirty seconds. Experts gain the ca-

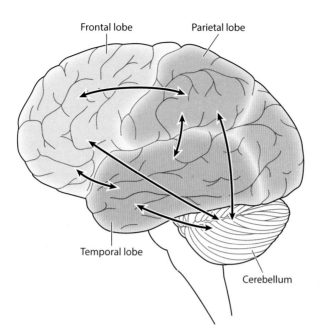

Frontal lobe   Parietal lobe

Temporal lobe

Cerebellum

FIGURE 3.8. Cerebellar connections to the cortex. Neural circuits in the cerebellum project throughout multiple cortical regions in ways that suggest that the cerebellum is involved in cognitive, motor, and emotional processing.

pacity to rapidly and flexibly control their thoughts and actions through learning and practice (see Chapter 7). Accumulated experiences gradually shape how experts act and react, overriding the responses that they might have selected as a novice.

Reflexes and Habits

In the early 1900s, the dominant theories of how organisms control their actions postulated that organisms control their actions through combinations of reflexes (Molnár & Brown, 2010; Windholz, 1986). These theories are built on Descartes's portrayal of behavioral control as machinelike, with an external sensory event, or "stimulus," triggering a specific set of movements, the response. From this perspective, the ultimate controller of actions is not some supervisory controller heading a hierarchical chain of command, but incoming sensations leading to predetermined reactions.

William James argued that repeated experiences performing certain actions, including mental acts, produced habits—basically routines that you perform by default. He described habits as being like ruts in the brain that made future repetitions of those actions both easier and more likely. In other words, James viewed most cognitive capacities and observable behavior as arising from the kinds of brain plasticity mechanisms described in Chapter 2.

James's theory of habits not only provided an explanation for why individuals behave in predictable ways as adults but also for how people organize percepts, form concepts, and reason. He also proposed that as mental and behavioral habits grow in strength, conscious awareness of those acts decreases. Put another way, he felt that cognitive processes gradually shift from being explicit to implicit with increases in proficiency. You might have once had to consciously think about amounts when asked, "how many is two plus two?" but now the answer probably pops into your head with little or no conscious effort.

Competing Controllers

Although many of the actions you habitually choose to perform may seem natural and almost inevitable, there are hidden battles for control going on inside your head that you do not consciously perceive. Dual process models of cognitive control (discussed in Chapter 10) pit implicit, automatic processes against explicit, voluntary processes.

One side effect of these competitions is that when either sensory or motor processes become impaired, a person's ability to control thoughts and actions degrades and explicit cognitive processes begin losing the competition for control.

Perhaps the clearest case of different processes competing for control of your actions occurs when multiple events demand your attention at the same time. Say you are in a movie theater watching a thriller when you suddenly discover that the jumbo soda was a mistake. Your auditory and visual sensations are telling you to stay put while your internal sensations are telling you to head toward a restroom. Laboratory studies of the cognitive costs of multitasking and divided attention are a core component of cognitive research (see Chapter 4).

Disorders like alien hand syndrome, described at the beginning of this chapter, also reveal the presence of competing controllers of actions. Surgical operations in which the two brain hemispheres are separated can lead to alien hand syndrome. Split-brain individuals (discussed in Chapter 12) are an extreme case of competing control that highlights hidden control mechanisms that can be trickier to discover in adults with intact brains (Volz & Gazzaniga, 2017). For instance, one of the major hazards faced by older adults is falling. Falls occur for many reasons, but one is that maintaining balance demands greater attentional resources; when competing demands (such as talking, thinking, and so on) deplete those resources, the likelihood of a fall rapidly increases (Silbert et al., 2008). The increasing attentional demands of controlling actions can come at a time of cognitive decline, further taxing cognitive resources.

One way that older individuals compensate for this is by slowing down their actions (Paraskevoudi et al., 2018). This does not entirely solve the problem, because slower action sequences can increase the effects of distractions. To a certain extent, what is happening after a certain age is that well-learned action options—familiar thought patterns or motor habits—are becoming dysfunctional, requiring the learning of new strategies and actions. For very old individuals, daily life effectively involves more cognitive multitasking. The situation is similar to what young children face daily, except probably more frustrating since motor and cognitive abilities that were once effortless have become more difficult.

Developing Cognitive Systems

The range of mental and physical actions you can perform changes dramatically across your lifespan. Hierarchical models of action control explain such changes as coming from the addition of new memories, like adding files and software to a computer. Reflex-based models, alternatively, explain changing skill sets as resulting from adjustments to neural connections that make new patterns of responding possible.

Both approaches provide an explanation for how new actions and thought processes can be acquired, but neither really explains why actions develop in predictable stages, or when consciousness is relevant. They also have little to say about rapid transitions in capabilities, such as when an infant transitions from crawling to walking or when an insect that loses a few legs immediately switches to new locomotion patterns.

Coordinating Actions

Hierarchical and reflex-based models describe the planning and performance of actions as a predictable chain reaction triggered by either instructions or sensed stimuli. **Dynamic systems** theory, instead, portrays action selection and production as a more interactive process in which physiological activity and environmental conditions lead to certain movement patterns, without requiring a specific trigger or command (Thelen & Smith, 1994).

Like the reflex-based models of responses favored by behaviorists, dynamic systems theories of action control emphasize changes in responses that occur over time. However, rather than assuming that changes come from modifications to links within a chain of stimulus processing, dynamic systems models focus on changing circumstances in the environment or in an individual's body (Spencer et al., 2012).

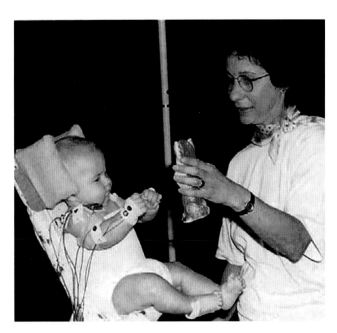

FIGURE 3.9. Esther Thelen.
Thelen explored how infants moved in different contexts to test the predictions of dynamic systems theory. (The IU Digital Library Program and Indiana University Office of University Archives and Records Management)

Studies of motor control development in humans have provided much of the motivation for considering alternative models of action control. Infants' rhythmic movements, in particular, have gotten a lot of attention in the last few decades. Esther Thelen (1941–2004) was one of the first to show that thinking of infants' actions as the outputs of dynamic systems could explain otherwise confusing findings (**Figure 3.9**). For example, movement patterns that infants rarely perform naturally can "magically" appear when an infant is suspended in water or supported by an adult and placed on a treadmill (Thelen & Ulrich, 1991). Rhythmic movements seem to be driven not just by neural firing but also by the physical flexibility and gravitational constraints on limb movements (Thelen & Ulrich, 1991).

Self-Organizing Development

Dynamic systems models describe the patterns that arise from interactions between control mechanisms and new conditions as **emergent patterns**. Babies' rhythmic movements are said to emerge or **self-organize** based on interactions between physical limitations on movements as well as patterns of coordinated activity across muscles. Self-organization of movements can lead to complex action patterns even when the mover has no specific goal in mind, as is presumably the case when infants rhythmically kick, wave, or babble (Quartz, 1999).

From the perspective of dynamic systems theories, changes in action patterns across the life span do not necessarily mean that an individual is learning new combinations of reflexes or acquiring new motor programs and planning abilities. Instead, changes in actions might just happen because of changes in muscle strength, body size, or the relative novelty and attractiveness of sensed scenes.

One familiar self-organizing process in nature is snowflake formation. Snowflakes take shape as super-cold water drops collide and freeze in clumps while falling. Without any guidance, the droplets combine into complex geometric patterns. Similarly, birds flying in flocks will rapidly synchronize their movements in ways that make it seem like their flight patterns have been choreographed in advance, but the patterns simply emerge from their independent interactions and reactions—there is no leader bird and no single trigger that guides the actions of the flock.

Dynamic systems theories explain the coordinated motor acts of individual humans as the result of "flocks" of interacting neural circuits, muscle reactions, and environmental conditions. Given that cognitive processes depend on neural circuits that overlap with those involved in motor control, it seems likely that cognition might work in ways that are similar to the interactive coordination of muscles (Bressler & Kelso, 2001).

From the perspective of dynamic systems theory, your ability to control your actions and thoughts, either through conscious efforts or through engrained habits, arises from all of the elements of your body, brain, and environment interacting (Cocchi et al., 2013). Consequently, subtle shifts in any of these elements can potentially lead to dramatic changes in behavior and mental states.

Learning How to Walk and Talk

Dynamic systems can generate complex action patterns without any learning, as is seen in flock formation by birds. But dynamic systems with the capacity to learn can enable a system to streamline operations.

Experiments in robotics have provided new insights into control systems that have the capacity to adapt over time. Simulations of moving robots with adaptive connections in control circuits spontaneously develop forward locomotion and rhythmic gaits, even when there is no specific goal or action plan (Der & Martius, 2015). The patterns that emerge depend on the shape of the robot's body and the physical features of the surface it is moving on.

If the coordination of limbs for locomotion is an emergent phenomenon, then might more complex actions and thoughts similarly emerge from reactions to internally and externally driven sensations (**Figure 3.10**)? Might your ability to talk about when and where you walk be less under your conscious control than you might think?

Language development is typically thought of as a cumulative process of acquiring speech production, reception, and interpretation capacities. Theories of conversational sentence production, like other models of action generation, generally start with some high-level idea creation and a

FIGURE 3.10. Newly re-legged.
Learning to walk with leg extensions as an adult highlights the challenges of balance and coordination faced by young children. In what ways might the mechanisms that enable adults to walk on stilts differ from the processes that enable children to first learn to walk? (JurgaR)

delivery process that guides the coordination of word selection, ordering, and physical speech production (see Chapter 12).

Toddlers possess less attentional, memory, and problem-solving abilities than adults, all of which predicts that learning a skill as complex as language should be much more difficult for them. Adding multiple languages into the mix should make learning even harder. Some view the relative ease of language learning by youngsters as evidence of innate, implicit language learning mechanisms (see Chapter 12).

From the perspective of dynamic systems, however, no such genetically endowed language competencies are necessary. Instead, the construction of words and sentences is viewed as a behavioral pattern that emerges from interactions between simpler internal and external events, much like the ability to dance (Hiver et al., 2021).

As with other dynamic systems, language development often progresses in jumps and starts. Some word forms may be used for relatively short periods before being discarded. As new forms emerge, those forms can become seeds for further emergent patterns of speech production. Like snowflakes, the specific forms that learning trajectories take may vary considerably from one person to the next, even though all the individuals are progressing and end up in similar overall configurations.

One implication of dynamic systems models of language learning, or the acquisition of other complex cognitive skills, is that the initial conditions of pattern formation can have a persistent effect on later learning. Just as the geometry at the core of a snowflake strongly constrains how later structures will develop, initial conditions during language learning have ripple effects throughout a person's life.

Toddlers exposed to multiple languages simultaneously may benefit from the fact that their neural circuits are not predisposed to organize different languages in a specific way, facilitating self-organizing processes that can accommodate multiple languages at the same time. Language learning by toddlers may thus be more effective than in adults because there are less habitual responses interacting with incoming sensations (de Bot et al., 2007).

Overall, dynamics systems models highlight the close interactions between implicit and explicit cognitive processes and question the assumption of dual process models that conscious and unconscious processes are in a constant battle for mental control. The remaining two sections of this chapter consider more closely how interacting voluntary and involuntary processes contribute to your conscious impressions of cognitive phenomena.

SIGHT BITES

In hierarchical models of the voluntary control of actions and thoughts, a command center selects action plans and delivers them to other systems for implementation.

Reflex-based explanations of behavior emphasize the role of learning in shifting functional connections between existing action control circuits.

Dynamic systems theories describe action selection and production as a self-organizing process that occurs when your body, brain, and environment interact.

EMOTION AND COGNITION

SNEAK PEEK: What is the connection between what you think, what you do, and what you feel? Emotions can shape your thoughts and vice versa, whether you are consciously aware of these internal interactions or not.

The very notion of emotion is closely tied to conscious feelings. Emotion is grammatically and conceptually an extension of motion, specifically the motion associated with the feeling of physical movements. Emotions can be defined in terms of both their conscious elements and their physical correlates, each of which can potentially interact with cognitive processing.

Traditionally, cognitive psychologists have treated emotions in one of two ways, either (1) as just another type of information that can be represented, remembered, and reflected upon (Bower, 1981), or (2) as a separate class of mental states that operate in parallel to more rational thought processes (Lazarus, 1991). Neuroscientists, in contrast, tend to describe **emotions** as a combination of neurophysiological processes, behavior, and subjective feelings but emphasize the observable processes over the experiences (Celeghin et al., 2017; Panksepp, 2003) (**Figure 3.11**).

Emotions often seem to arise reflexively but do so in response to events that are clearly driven by thought processes. For instance, someone who is told that a friend has unexpectedly died is likely to show an extreme reaction, not because of some immediate threat to their safety, but because of their understanding of what that death implies. Emotions are notable in that they are sometimes easier to recognize in others than in oneself, despite their status as a subjective mental state.

Expressing Emotions

Most studies of emotion focus on six emotions that researchers consider to be distinct and universal across human cultures: anger, disgust, fear, happiness, sadness, and surprise. Recent research suggests a more complex spectrum of emotional states, however, including triumph, sympathy, sexual desire,

FIGURE 3.11. Emotions as neurophysiological processes. (A) Your emotional reactions are associated with increased activity in multiple cortical regions as well as in subcortical regions like the amygdala, which is located beneath the temporal lobe. (B) How activity varies in these regions depends on your understanding of what you are witnessing. For example, witnessing an accidental dousing activates different regions from witnessing a purposeful one. (B top: Rommel Canlas via Shutterstock, bottom: Andrey_Popov via Shutterstock)

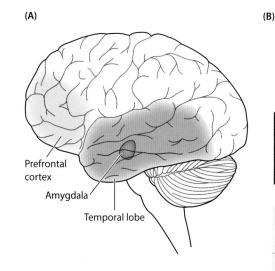

(A)

Prefrontal cortex

Amygdala

Temporal lobe

(B)

Accidental harm

Intentional harm

satisfaction, sadness, romance, nostalgia, joy, interest, horror, fear, excitement, envy, entrancement, empathetic pain, disgust, craving, confusion, calmness, boredom, awkwardness, awe, anxiety, amusement, aesthetic appreciation, adoration, and admiration (Cowen & Keltner, 2017).

Some emotional states share closer ties with cognitive processing than others. Confusion and surprise, for instance, are most likely to occur when recognition or strategic processes fail. Satisfaction and triumph are most common when goals have been achieved. And nostalgia depends on memories of experiences from long ago. Aesthetic appreciation of a musical performance also typically requires some familiarity with the type of music being performed. Unlike memory, perception, and thinking, each emotional state is marked by distinctive physical signs of what's happening mentally.

Emotional Triggers and Emotional Reactions

Situations that evoke emotions generally progress in three stages. First, ongoing events are evaluated and interpreted, a process that depends heavily on attention, perception, and memory. Depending on how this evaluative process goes, an individual may then either maintain their current emotional state or begin transitioning to a new state. In stage three, such transitions can lead to both physical reactions and shifts in an individual's consciously experienced feelings.

How these different stages interact over time has been a point of debate for over a century, with some arguing that physical reactions often precede conscious awareness of an emotion (James, 1890) and others arguing that conscious feelings and reflexive reactions to triggers are processed in parallel by separate systems (Cannon, 1931). Dual process models tend to associate emotions with impulsive or reflexive processes that lead people to make poor choices (Evans & Stanovich, 2013).

Actions and expressions triggered by emotions provide clues about an individual's emotional state. Because emotions are themselves triggered by interpretations of ongoing events, the behavioral correlates of emotions also convey something about the individual's awareness and interpretation of what is happening in the world. Charles Darwin argued that different species experience similar emotions when faced with similarly dangerous or entertaining contexts (Hess & Thibault, 2009).

Of course, some species might also experience distinctive emotional states that no human has ever experienced—there's no way (yet) to know if a scared cat feels the same way as a scared human. Nevertheless, similarities in the neural processes activated across species during emotional situations provide at least some evidence that in sentient organisms there is likely to be some overlap in emotional states (**Figure 3.12**).

FIGURE 3.12. Common cues. Similar physical expressions provide evidence of potentially shared emotional states across species. What other evidence might further support the possibility of comparable emotional experiences? (©photomaru/Fotosearch LBRF/agefotostock)

The most extensively studied emotional reactions in humans are facial expressions, which are generally believed to provide the clearest physical indications of a person's emotional state. In addition to the more obvious smiles and frowns, researchers have discovered **facial microexpressions**, slight facial movements that are usually subliminal and that are correlated with a person attempting to hide that they are lying, afraid, or excited (Dong et al., 2021). These "tells" can enable expert poker players to detect when another player is bluffing and also make it possible for psychics to "read the minds" of customers or to seemingly speak with dead relatives.

The precision and ease with which an individual's emotional state can be recognized from subtle facial and physical movements suggest that emotional expressions are important to the function of emotions (Lin et al., 2022). In particular, the sharing of emotional states is a key component of social cognitive processes (see Chapter 11), including the coordination of interactions between individuals.

Empathy and Emotional Perception

Identifying others' emotional states by seeing and hearing them is a mostly automatic process. It seems like the kind of thing that could be accomplished without any conscious awareness or cognitive abilities. In fact, there are computer programs that can identify emotions fairly accurately simply by crunching numbers measured from images (Saxena et al., 2020).

Other seemingly automatic responses to emotional expressions, including feelings of admiration, empathy, romance, or sympathy, seem to require a bit more cognitive sophistication (Shamay-Tsoory, 2011). **Empathy** (see Chapter 11), in particular, appears to involve not only identifying the emotional state of another individual but also understanding what the subjective experience of that individual is like (or at least a feeling of understanding), as well as having some capacity to share that experience.

Perception of an emotional state in oneself or in another often triggers mental representations of possible future scenarios (Moustafa et al., 2018). Shared feelings of attraction during eye contact may evoke thoughts of kissing, while mutual disgust may suggest a quick exit in the near future. Detecting a look of terror in a stranger's face is likely to trigger an active search for the source of the threat. In this sense, perceived emotional expressions act as cues that guide future thoughts and actions.

Emotional Regulation

Cartoons often use debates between shoulder angels and devils to depict the types of decision-making processes that emotions can provoke. The angel advocates doing the right thing, while the devil encourages options that satisfy more selfish urges. The devilish options tend toward impulsive actions that lead to immediate gratification (take the money and run) without considering potential downsides to those options. The angel's alternatives often involve suppressing such desires and impulses and following culturally established norms for how to behave.

Both the shoulder devil and angel make their case by pointing to possible future emotional states that could become a reality: you can choose pleasure now and suffer for it later or be rewarded in the future for suffering now. The mental process that this caricature is meant to capture is **emotional regulation**, the controlled reaction to ongoing emotional states. Emotional regulation involves implicit processes of recognition and reaction, as well as consciously controlled action selection and suppression (Gyurak et al., 2011). For example, you might initially be startled by an event that shares some features with scary ones, like the classic jump scare in horror movies where a cat suddenly appears out of nowhere. A rapid involuntary fear reaction may be quickly suppressed by the recognition that the "scary" intruder is actually not so scary (**Figure 3.13**).

Cognitive behavioral therapy and other modern strategies for treating patients with mental health issues focus heavily on teaching patients to react to emotional states in less problematic ways. The basic premise of cognitive behavioral therapy is that how a person thinks about ongoing emotional experiences and reacts to those feelings and thoughts, can negatively or positively affect their mental health (Willner & Lindsay, 2016).

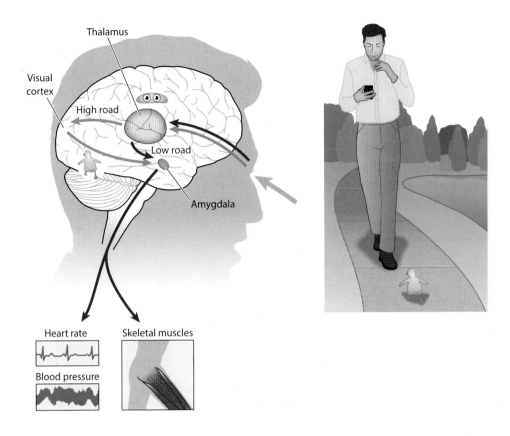

FIGURE 3.13. Ambush. Emotional reactions may occur quite rapidly when a potentially dangerous event is detected (the low road), but then be quickly suppressed when events are processed more fully and consciously (the high road). Both engage subcortical regions like the thalamus and amygdala, which lead to rapid physiological changes and motor responses. More nuanced interpretations and responses depend more on cortical processing.

The kinds of emotional distress that might lead someone to seek out psychological treatment could result from bad habits of emotional regulation. By training people to consciously combat such bad habits, clinicians hope to prime their patients' thought processes to help them voluntarily reduce emotional distress. Effectively, clinical psychologists who use cognitive behavioral therapy attempt to put angels on their clients' shoulders who will help them choose better responses to emotional states.

The Role of Emotion in Perception, Memory, and Decision-Making

Your everyday experiences are a mash-up of emotional and cognitive mental states. Many of your beliefs about how things are and how they should be are driven by how you feel when you contemplate those experiences. When you feel certain, you place greater trust in your beliefs. When new information contradicts those beliefs (say you discover you have cannibalistic relatives), then you are likely to become distraught.

Scientific attempts to understand interactions between emotions and cognition have often focused on brain regions that are specialized for one or the other mental process. For instance, unique cases like that of Phineas Gage, a railroad foreman who survived having his frontal lobes skewered by a massive iron spike, have been used to argue that some brain regions are particularly important for emotional regulation (Damasio et al., 1994). Gage's freak accident is said to have transformed him from a model citizen into a highly impulsive individual who was oblivious to anything other than his "animal passions"—an almost Jekyll-to-Hyde-type switch in personality. More recent studies have focused less on trying to locate where emotions happen in brains and more on the global effects that emotions can have on cognitive processing.

No aspect of cognition is immune to the effects of changing emotions. But specifically how and when various emotional states change cognitive processes is not entirely clear. Partly this is because the cognitive processes that determine what you experience are shaped by your emotional states.

Emotional Distortions of Perception

You probably think that whom you find attractive is a basic feature of who you are. But there is strong evidence that the ways you perceive others can change rapidly and involuntarily.

Consider the case of JX, a pediatrician who was caught performing sexually inappropriate actions toward a female kindergartner in his office with the door open. Prior to his arrest, he was highly respected. Surprisingly, JX showed no signs of recognizing that his actions were problematic, leading examiners to suspect potential brain damage. Sure enough, MRI images revealed a large tumor compressing parts of his brain (Sartori et al., 2016).

When the tumor was removed, JX's pedophilic urges disappeared, and his remorse for his actions emerged. The tumor was located in JX's frontal lobe, close to the region that Phineas Gage lost in his railroad accident. For JX, the kinds of aberrant emotions triggered by his interactions with children were a consequence of physical changes to his frontal lobes. These emotions dramatically changed how he perceived and thought about children.

Emotions shape your percepts in equally pervasive ways every day. If you are distracted or in a bad mood, the events you notice and consider significant may differ a lot from things you would normally perceive. If you are "jumpy," even harmless cues like someone touching your shoulder can cause you to shriek and possibly even attack the unlucky toucher. This sort of emotionally driven rush to judgment highlights the perceptual boost that sensory inputs get when they are on the emotional fast track. Enhanced or amplified perceptual processing of emotional events and stimuli can be seen in a wide range of perceptual tasks (Zadra & Clore, 2011). Even patients with blindsight, who claim not to see scenes of emotional events, can tell whether the unseen events are highly unpleasant (Gerbella et al., 2019), suggesting that emotional processing can occur even without perceptual awareness.

Interactions between cognitive and emotional processing cascade over time. Initial processing might be reflexive, implicit, and dependent on one's mood or current emotional state. This processing is followed by behavioral reactions, which can affect what is perceived, as when you look in the direction from which you hear a scream.

Conscious, explicit awareness of what is happening might kick in a bit later, counteracting or confirming initial impressions of what is actually happening. For instance, a scream followed by the sight of a person being attacked with water balloons might lead you to ignore future screams from that location or individual. Or if you recognize the attackers and realize that you may soon be the next victim then you might rapidly switch into fight-or-flight mode. In this scenario, not only will your strategic and attentional efforts rapidly shift gears, but depending on what happens next, a random aqua attack (or errant duckling) might turn into an episode that you recall and discuss many times in the future.

Memorable Episodes and Conditioned Emotional Responses

Perhaps the most extensively studied contributions of emotional states to cognitive processes relate to the effects of emotions on memory formation. From early traumatic experiences or highpoints in one's life to something as simple as a trip to the dentist, emotions seem to amplify memories in much the same way that they distort perception and demand attention (McGaugh, 2004).

If you feel nervous during dentist or doctor visits, you may have no vivid or accurate memory of when you first started feeling that way. Nevertheless, the feelings of apprehension triggered by such visits can be substantial. This type of implicit emotional learning or conditioning (see Chapter 7) is evident in a wide range of species and contexts (LeDoux, 2012). All organisms learn to predict important events based on emotions they experience during repeated events.

Emotional experiences not only determine much of what you learn, they also strongly affect what you are likely to explicitly remember. If you interview older relatives about events in their lives that they remember the best, they are likely to talk about things they did or saw between the ages of

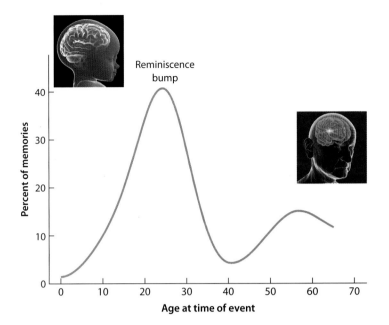

FIGURE 3.14. The reminiscence bump. People are generally more likely to recall episodes in their life in a specific age range, suggesting that forgetting is not simply a function of how old a memory (or brain) is and that twenty-year-olds have more fun. (Graph after Koppel & Rubin, 2016; images baby: jm1366; older person: Dr_Microbe)

ten and twenty-five years old. They are much less likely to mention episodes that occurred when they were between thirty and forty-five years old, even though those events happened more recently (**Figure 3.14**). This pattern of autobiographical recall, called a **reminiscence bump**, is thought to occur because your "first times" tend to be more emotionally distinctive (Rathbone et al., 2008). Situations that lead to extreme emotional reactions can lead to memory milestones, often referred to as flashbulb memories (see Chapter 8).

Memorable events can strongly affect your thoughts and planning processes. Your decisions about what to eat, where, and with whom are likely shaped by past meals you've enjoyed or hated (see Chapter 10). The emotional memories that lead you to prefer one option over another can be either explicit or implicit and tend to have cumulative effects. So, if you ever feel indecisive about where to head for lunch, you can blame both your implicitly learned preferences and your explicit memories of past episodes.

Decision-Making

The Greek philosopher Plato portrayed reason and emotion as two horses attempting to pull a chariot in different directions. Later thinkers morphed the actors in this metaphor: cognition became the chariot driver attempting to reign in the wild horses of passion. In the case of decision-making, selfish impulses, or fear of missing out (the main concerns of the shoulder devil) are the horses, while the cognitive charioteer might weigh costs versus benefits, put off acting while awaiting more information, or choose to follow moral rules (to avoid a shoulder-angel-induced guilt trip). Cognitive researchers have replaced chariots and horses with "dual processes," while preserving the essence of Plato's portrayal.

The problem with this kind of division of mental labor is that it assumes a clean split between two competing mental processes that are simultaneously attempting to determine the direction of future actions. Producing a list of pros and cons seems logical and rational. But what qualifies as a good or bad outcome depends almost entirely on a person's beliefs about whether specific outcomes are desirable, which depends strongly on emotional reactions. In other words, the consciously reflective processes that the chariot driver might use to steer emotional horses are themselves dependent on a second set of horses related to emotions.

When the pediatrician JX accosted a young girl in a place where anyone walking by would be able to see him, his tumor contributed to that decision by not only warping his ongoing emotional states but also by disengaging any kind of reasoning about what the future consequences of his actions might be. He did not feel that what he was doing was wrong and he did not imagine any bad outcomes.

In contrast, a person with an addiction might have the capacity to imagine in detail what bad outcomes might occur as a consequence of indulging but may end up taking the drug anyway. Where are the reins in this scenario? Some researchers suspect that dysfunctional interactions between frontal brain regions and the amygdala (see Chapter 2) may be contributing to addictions (Crews & Boettiger, 2009). Individuals with addiction make poorer decisions in cognitive tasks that require impulse control, behaving similarly to patients with frontal damage, like Phineas Gage and JX (Grant & Chamberlain, 2014).

The image of mental willpower overcoming "thoughtless" emotional reactions is a strong one, immortalized in the Jedi training of the *Star Wars* universe. But do emotional and cognitive processes really have this kind of wise-master-tempers-reckless-passions relationship? Neuroscientific evidence suggests not (see Chapters 8 and 11). Instead, it seems that interactions between emotional reactions and perception, thoughts, and plans are dynamic and coordinated, with emotional processes regulating cognition just as much as cognitive processes regulate emotions. At their core, emotion and cognition seem to be less like two horses fighting to pull a chariot forward and more like one horse coordinating its leg movements so that it can gallop fast without falling. Unfortunately, in some cases, this kind of coordinated control of mental states does not work out.

Resisting the Urge

Typically, emotion and cognition act in concert in ways that make life meaningful and understanding possible. It is not always the case, however, that such interactions lead to desirable outcomes. For example, musicians who experience performance anxiety often are highly accomplished and skillful. They know that they have put in the work and possess the necessary skills to perform musical pieces nearly flawlessly. Despite this, they experience strongly unpleasant emotional reactions whenever they perform in front of audiences. In some cases, their anxiety can become so great that they are no longer able to perform (Kenny, 2011).

In such cases, conscious knowledge of one's own skills is overcome by involuntary emotional reactions. Many current treatments for psychological disorders focus either on helping people to overcome emotional states that degrade their ability to function in daily life or on bolstering alternative emotions (like happiness or serenity) that might counteract those states. Understanding how cognitive processes interact with emotions can thus be key to developing effective interventions.

Obsessive-Compulsive Disorder and Uncontrollable Thoughts

You've probably experienced scenarios in which you got distracted and couldn't remember if you locked a door you intended to lock, or you may have second-guessed the wisdom of a decision multiple times after making it. Patients with obsessive-compulsive disorder (OCD) experience something similar, but more intensely and frequently.

The very name of this disorder reveals the tight link between emotion and cognition that characterizes it—obsession refers to a repetitive thought process while compulsion refers to a feeling that an action has to happen. The repetitive thoughts often relate to uncertainty about the future or dissatisfaction with the present. Recognition that such thoughts are problematic or pointless doesn't stop them from recurring.

Like an itch that you can't help scratching even when you know scratching will make it itch more, the action-emotion-thought cycle associated with obsessive-compulsive disorder is difficult to overcome. It's unclear what initially leads to the cyclical emotional and thought processes associated with

FIGURE 3.15. Herd mind.
On Black Friday, shoppers sometimes make decisions that differ from those they would normally make. What kinds of external stimuli might drive poor decision-making within such crowds? (Nelson Antoine via Shutterstock)

obsessive-compulsive disorder. Some suggest that a person with obsessive-compulsive disorder somehow experiences less conscious, voluntary control of actions, reducing their ability to suppress unwanted thoughts (Tolin et al., 2002). Others propose that implicit processes are the source of the problem, with habitual responses to uncomfortable states effectively taking control of action selection (Barahona-Correa et al., 2015). If explicit cognitive processes are competing with implicit processes, both scenarios may be happening. Current behavioral strategies for overcoming obsessive-compulsive disorder focus heavily on training patients to consciously choose not to give in to compulsions when anxious states arise.

Herd Mentality

Interactions between impulsive choices and uncontrollable thoughts and feelings of anxiety or compulsion are not only an issue for people with obsessive-compulsive disorder. They can potentially affect anyone. For instance, there is increasing scrutiny of fraternities on college campuses because of their potential for encouraging dangerous actions, particularly certain forms of hazing.

Hazing generally involves some sort of ritualized humiliation, suffering, or loss of control that is required to join a particular social group. The general view of why hazing is so prevalent is that the experience can form bonds between the hazers and their victims—a sort of staged empathetic event that promotes later helping behavior (see Chapter 11). Hazing also seems to increase the conformity of thinking across group members, which can further increase social cohesion.

Similar social influences on decision-making can be seen in the actions of crowds (**Figure 3.15**) and in people's online behavior. In one study that examined commenting behavior on websites, researchers found that when administrators randomly voted negatively or positively on an initial post, a positive rating increased the likelihood of future positive ratings by 25% on average (Muchnik et al., 2013). These kinds of socially induced cognitive biases are sometimes called **herding effects**.

Herding behavior, which occurs in larger groups of humans as well as other animals, seems to amplify irrational decision-making as well as the role of emotional states in thought processes. This is why large protests can transform into violent riots (Dezecache et al., 2021), and why panic within a large group can cause them to stampede and trample people to death.

Self-Regulated Learning

Emotions often have a bad rap in relation to cognition, being portrayed as something that you need to keep in check to think straight (remember Plato's horses). But emotions also can lead to transcendent cognitive acts. When a researcher has an epiphany, causing them to shout out "Eureka!" it is not because a brain has performed an additional computation in a series of computations, but because the researcher feels a surge of emotion triggered by a new idea.

Many of the cognitive capacities that are most admired in humans—mathematical abilities, chess playing, musical composition, novel writing—were achieved because of the emotional rewards individuals experienced while engaging in those activities. Experts often report that early feelings about an activity pushed them forward along their life path. Emotional experiences provide the foundation for the development of expertise and for cognitive development more generally.

Your beliefs about the benefits of education provide the foundation for how you react emotionally to learning experiences. If you believe that a task or course is simply a hoop you must jump through, you will be less likely to remember or apply the knowledge or skills that you "learned" during the experience (see Chapter 7). But if you are intrigued by a topic (an emotional response), then your capacity to rapidly and effectively learn new information or skills will be amplified.

Self-regulated learning, what most college students do outside of class to stay on track in their courses, depends on long-term regulation of emotional states to counteract boredom, frustration, and procrastination (Boekaerts, 1995). This requires that an individual be aware of emotional states and also monitor and strategically plan activities in a way that takes likely future emotional states into account. Self-regulated learning, therefore, requires metacognition, or the monitoring of one's own thought processes (see Chapters 1 and 8). So, your ability to develop effective learning strategies depends partly on your knowledge of how emotional states affect your cognitive processes.

SIGHT BITES

Actions and expressions triggered by emotions provide clues about ongoing mental processes that can guide observers' future thoughts and actions.

Interactions between emotion and cognition are dynamic, with both implicit and explicit processes constantly competing to influence action selection.

The cognitive processes that determine what you experience, what you learn, and how you think are shaped by your emotional states and vice versa.

AWARENESS AND THOUGHT

SNEAK PEEK: Your ideas about what your mind and other minds are like come from both your ongoing subjective impressions and your memories of past experiences. What would your thoughts be like without awareness? Are your impressions of what minds and cognition are like accurate?

You may be thinking, "What difference does it really make if actions and thoughts come from executive commanders, reflexes, dynamic interactions, or emotional impulses?" Identifying the sources of actions and thoughts can be useful for increasing desirable actions and for decreasing problematic ones, especially in situations where something mentally has gone awry.

People with thought disorders, often diagnosed as having schizophrenia or psychosis, produce sentences that are mostly understandable, but that may seem jumbled, oddly beorchestrated, I mean books are really purple. Rather than appearing self-organized and coherent, their speech seems almost self-disorganized.

Interestingly, people showing symptoms of a thought disorder often appear to be unaware that the speech they produce is odd or confusing. So, not only is their ability to converse impaired, but their ability to recognize that they are making mistakes also seems to be degraded. Schizophrenia, in particular, is notable because it affects the way a person thinks, feels, and acts, highlighting the close links between cognition, emotions, and the control of actions. And the symptoms of schizophrenia can occur intermittently, illustrating how a mind can temporarily slip into problematic thought patterns.

If people can be unaware of their own disorganized thinking, might they also be misinterpreting the minds of other individuals without realizing it? After all, you can access your own mind better than anyone else's. What exactly can you know about a mind that is not your own?

Recognizing Minds

It is natural to think that your mental experiences are comparable to those of your peers. You may also sometimes think that people who express ideas or act in ways that seem insane to you must have some kind of thought disorder. Murderers seem evil and deodorant testers seem wacky. The following sections consider where it is that your ideas about minds come from.

"No thought ever comes into direct sight of a thought in another personal consciousness than its own… It seems as if the elementary psychic fact were not thought or this thought or that thought, but my thought, every thought being owned."
—William James, 1890, p. 226

The Birth of Minds

The way you perceive minds now (including your own) is not the way you have always perceived them. Perceiving minds as things in the world is an instance of metacognition (see Chapter 8)—thinking about thinking or awareness of awareness. When you were a toddler, you likely didn't recognize that mental states exist, or realize that for such states to exist, something or someone must be experiencing them (**Figure 3.16**). For two-year-old you, cognition was not a thing.

Over time, you eventually started developing "is" or "isn't" categories with labels, like alive versus dead, awake versus asleep, and so on (see Chapter 5); all of those categories and labels fed into the

FIGURE 3.16. Self-discovery. Grasping that there are "others" distinctive from the self is a major cognitive milestone. Social categorization of this sort depends heavily on late-developing cortical regions, which may explain why it takes children so long to reach that point. (©CSP_goldenKB/ Fotosearch LBRF/agefotostock)

kinds of the situations you might verbally describe as someone thinking, knowing, or feeling. Those experiences also shaped your beliefs about your own mind and when the label "mind" made sense to use.

Psychologists argue that most people construct (or develop) ideas about what minds and mental states are like as they grow older. These include beliefs and feelings about necessary elements of minds and the assumption that minds are special relative to other objects. Psychologists also tend to assume that this process has a typical outcome that most people arrive at—the common-sense idea of the human mind that people use to identify individuals with mental problems.

Theory of Mind

Cognitive psychology research focuses more on understanding how minds work than on understanding how minds become able to recognize other minds. The approach is sort of like trying to figure out how software on a computer works without knowing how to reliably identify a computer. This is partly why so many cognitive studies focus on adults—researchers are generally more confident that adults have fully functional minds.

When you describe a person's acts or beliefs as being a consequence of what they know, you are basically assuming that their awareness of something about the world is leading them to select one action rather than another or to reach a particular conclusion. You are in some sense imagining what the person's mental experiences are like and how those mental experiences influence the person's thoughts and feelings. This kind of social imagery ability, typically referred to as theory of mind, is considered by some to be the foundation of social cognition (see Chapter 11). Social cognition includes the cognitive processes that contribute to social interactions (so basically all cognitive processes), with emphasis on skills that make successful interactions within groups possible.

The conscious, voluntary control of actions is thought to play a key role in social interactions. Deciding what to say, whom to say it to, when to remain silent, when to fake laugh, and when to nod as if interested all depend on recognizing and responding appropriately to the indirectly perceived mental states of others. Involuntary responses, such as empathetic reactions, laughter, and confused expressions, often provide clues that trigger (or dynamically interact with) ongoing actions. How individuals react to such cues and contexts can provide evidence of the sorts of atypical mental states that are likely to be diagnosed as disordered.

Consciousness in Infants and Nonhumans

Cognitive psychologists do not usually study rocks because rocks don't move themselves. Similarly, cognitive psychologists typically do not study sea urchins because of uncertainties about the mechanisms driving sea urchins' actions. Infants and pets are in more of a gray zone, with some researchers confident that consciousness and cognition are present and others reserving judgment about whether these groups experience the world and possess minds.

It is, nevertheless, possible to conduct cognitive experiments with rocks, sea urchins, and infants, and to use evidence from those experiments to draw conclusions about the kinds of internal processes that occur in subjects of such studies. Experimental findings from studies of learning and memory in flies, worms, spiders, and slime molds can provide useful clues to understanding human cognition, despite the fact that there is no way (yet) to determine how any experiences they might have compare to your own experiences.

Aside from the potential knowledge gained from studying mechanisms of behavior and consciousness in organisms other than adult humans, broadening the exploration of cognitive processes into contexts where their relevance is uncertain can potentially reveal conceptual mistakes and biases that may affect how you think about minds and cognition (**Figure 3.17**).

FIGURE 3.17. Faux consciousness. As artificial intelligence and robotics technologies improve, it will become increasingly difficult to distinguish consciously guided actions from unconscious acts. If behavior becomes unreliable as a way to make such distinctions, what other criteria might be used? (woman: ©Eurasia Press/Photononstop/agefotostock, robot: ©Cylonphoto/ZOONAR GMBH RM/agefotostock)

The Psychologist's Fallacy

All of the models and theories of cognitive processes discussed in this book run the risk of falling prey to what James called the **psychologist's fallacy**. This fallacy or conceptual error occurs when a researcher attributes some quality to a cognitive phenomenon (such as concepts, memories, or thoughts) based on personal impressions of the phenomenon. Often, those qualities include some combination of awareness, consciousness, feelings, or metacognition. Three cognitive processes that often trick researchers into committing the psychologist's fallacy are described below.

What Mental Images are Like

Recalled memories are often discussed as if their very reactivation inherently identifies them as being memories, when, in reality, reactivation simply implies that the same state that was present at some point in the past is present again. The sun "reactivates" its positions in the sky by repeating them each day or across years, but this does not imply either that the sun or its positions are memories or that there is any conscious awareness associated with those repeated states.

Memory researchers know that their own experiences of remembered events include an awareness that feels like the replaying of qualities of past experiences, and so they can easily fall prey to the psychologist's fallacy by assuming that retrieved representations usually or always include such feelings and actually involve mental replay (**Figure 3.18**).

Misimpressions of Thoughts

If you think about something like a pile of books, then you can easily go on to consider the properties of books (they have pages), the properties of piles (they can fall over), past times you have seen piles of books (say in libraries), and so on. This might give you the impression that your conscious thoughts of book piles contain within them a wide array of detailed subcomponents.

In this case, the psychologist's fallacy might lead you to think of "thoughts" as being something more complex than they really are because you as a person can do fancy things with them. It's as if you saw a hammer, imagined all the things a skilled carpenter could make with a hammer, and then afterwards treated hammers as if they included all the things that they can be used to make, while ignoring the role of the carpenter.

Language Mistakes

Consciousness and language are probably the two biggest sources of the psychologist's fallacy in cognitive psychology. Words and symbols can be used in so many different ways that they seem

FIGURE 3.18. Replay in recall? (A) Individuals with highly superior autobiographical memory (HSAM) recall much more than most about what has happened in the distant past. (B) They often describe their recall as a process in which past experiences replay in their minds. (C) However, they are as likely to recall events that never happened as people without HSAM, and to show similar patterns of brain activity when they falsely recall past episodes. Given that it is not possible for them to be replaying experiences they have never had, their impressions of what happens when they remember such events are not what actually happened. (A after LePort et al., 2015; B bubble: shironosov, square: martin-dm; C from Mazzoni et al., 2019)

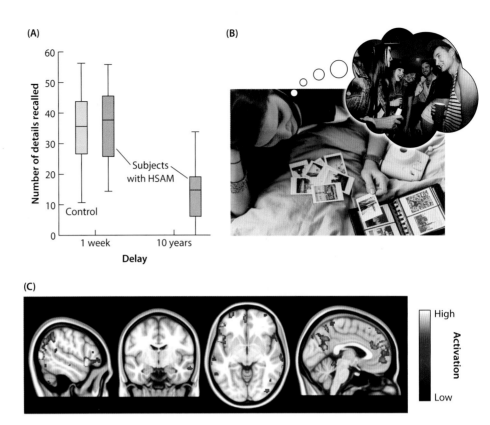

almost magical and, as a result, psychologists often describe cognitive processes that involve language as being much more sophisticated than other nonlinguistic processes (despite all neural evidence to the contrary). Consciousness, which sometimes seems to provide the foundation for voluntary acts, feelings, and deliberative thought, similarly can take on otherworldly qualities (like immortality).

You are naturally biased to expect your conscious processes to be more important in determining your actions than any implicit cognitive process. This bias is a **cognitive bias**, an unconscious tendency to mentally act in certain ways. The psychologist's fallacy happens because of a cognitive bias to generalize from personal experiences.

Cognitive biases tend to be associated with intuition, irrational decisions, gut feelings, or prejudices. They operate like mental habits, kicking in automatically whether you want them to or not. Cognitive biases can distort your worldview, but they can also make your life less confusing and frustrating. Chapter 10 discusses various cognitive biases that may affect how you think about cognition and how you make sense of the world.

Cognitive biases can influence behavior in any context, including during cognitive experiments. In behavioral studies, **expectancy effects** can occur when participants know or suspect what it is that an experimenter is attempting to show. Participants may unconsciously respond to the experimental task in ways that fit their expectations, skewing the results of the experiment. Implicit processes can also affect how an experimenter interacts with participants while preparing them for an experiment, which can further affect how participants respond, even when they have no clue what the experiment is about. In these cases, recognizing that others have minds accidentally changes thought processes in ways that can distort scientific results.

Your awareness of minds, both yours and others, biases how you think about cognition. There is a bit of a chicken-and-egg problem here, though, because it seems like a mind is necessary for there to be awareness of anything. From a scientific perspective, it's unclear exactly what your mind is aware of that you are calling consciousness, thoughts, and memories. You are clearly experiencing something, but how that "something" relates to cognition remains mysterious.

What It Is Like to Be Cognizant

Awareness, what James referred to as the "stream of consciousness," distinguishes people from computers, motion sensors, and snowflakes. Organized awareness—what you experience most of your adult life when awake or dreaming, including what you believe, know, perceive, recognize, and understand—is a result of your ability to cognize yourself and your environment. You cognize when you become aware of what is happening, when you stream consciousness. Selective awareness of ongoing events shapes your percepts and concepts. How your awareness changes over time in turn shapes the kinds of internal and external events you are most likely to attend to and care about (see Chapters 4–6).

Humans can usually say something about what they are cognizing, but how a person verbalizes an experience does not always accurately capture what they are experiencing or doing mentally. For instance, you might believe you are learning by watching a lecture, taking notes, or reading a textbook when you may simply be observing events without really understanding them. Like an individual with schizophrenia, you might be fully aware that you are listening during a lecture without having any awareness that you are failing to understand the relevance or meaning of the material being covered.

Comparing Conscious States

The subjective world of an organism, its **Umwelt** (sounds like "oom-velt"), includes both ongoing percepts as well as unconscious internal representations that guide actions (Allen, 2014) (**Figure 3.19**). *Umwelten* (more than one *Umwelt*) are thought to vary greatly across species and can also vary within an individual. The six-month-old you likely had different subjective experiences when encountering floors than the ones you have now. How you sense, process, organize, and interpret ongoing events (how you cognize) all contribute to the qualities of your perceptual awareness.

The concept of *Umwelten* is closely related to the idea of varying perspectives. You might not see things quite the same way I do. However, our differences in perspective are more like differences in opinions or values. Differences in *Umwelten* can be more extreme, like the way someone born blind and deaf might perceive and interact with the world compared to someone who can see and hear.

FIGURE 3.19. Exotic cognizance. The *Umwelt* of a bee includes percepts from light that humans cannot see, such as contrasting patterns on some flowers; the right image provides a bees-eye perspective on a flower that humans would perceive as being uniform in color (left image). What modalities in humans might provide percepts like those experienced by bees? (adrian davies/Alamy Stock Photo; inset: Denja1)

FIGURE 3.20. Tingling crunchiness. (A) Individuals who experience ASMR show strong emotional responses to innocuous events. (B) These heightened responses are associated with greater neural activity throughout the cortex. (A AndreyPopov; B from Lee et al., 2020. *Front Behav Neurosci* © 2020 Lee, Kim and Tak [CC BY].)

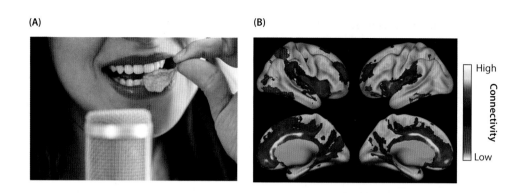

(A)   (B)

Across species, differences in subjective experiences tend to be associated with differences in how sensations are received. For example, the praying mantis has five eyes; three are simple and two are complex. Together, they generate thousands of separate images. The eyes of the praying mantis seem likely to produce visual experiences quite different from those you have.

Consistent with this prediction, mantises seem to only "see" things that are moving. This doesn't guarantee, however, that what mantises perceive differs radically from what you perceive when you see things move. Mantises might still experience distinct objects moving around in a three-dimensional world like you do. Alternatively, they might not experience anything at all, functioning as **automatons**, or machines that operate with no perceptual awareness.

One of the biggest issues with relating perceptual awareness, *Umwelten*, and conscious states to cognition is that it is difficult (some say impossible) to compare similarities and differences in these phenomena. Consider again the woman giving birth in a hospital a century ago. During the birth, she would likely have described her subjective experience as terrifying and torturous. Later on, she might claim that she had no such experience, that she was unconscious the whole time. Similarly, you may feel that you had no subjective experiences last night while you were sleeping, but if you had been woken up during certain stages of sleep, you likely would have reported experiencing all kinds of events in your "nonexistent" dreams.

Scientists agree that people can be more or less aware of what's happening around them and to them. There is less agreement about how consciousness might vary in nonhumans. **Sentient** beings are those that can feel pain, or more generally, any entity that is aware of the world, including oneself and others. Figuring out which organisms meet these criteria is tricky.

Currently, there are no agreed upon methods for reliably measuring variations in sentience. Even the self-reports of feelings by adults are often ambiguous. For instance, there is increasing interest in the autonomous sensory meridian response (ASMR), which people describe as something like a mild tingling with hints of euphoria (**Figure 3.20**). Only some people report experiencing this state, however, and those who don't may find it difficult to imagine what ASMR is actually like (Lee et al., 2020). Similarly, someone who experiences vivid imagery—thinking in pictures—might be skeptical that picture-less thinking is possible.

Qualia

Conscious states are felt states (Harnad, 2016). When you think, it feels like something. Your personal subjective experiences of what it is like to be conscious are your **qualia**. When you think about your thoughts and percepts, your qualia are likely to be what you think about. In cognitive research, however, there is less focus on qualia and more on processes that make thinking, remembering, and perceiving possible.

Qualia and cognitive processes can interact. Self-reports on conscious reflections, or thinking out loud, depend on verbal descriptions of qualia, as do reports of remembered experiences or of ongoing events. Consequently, researchers traditionally consider the capacity to verbally describe experiences to be the clearest evidence of both consciousness and sentience. That being said, there is no evidence that organisms lacking the ability to communicate about qualia are less likely to have subjective experiences. Infants are the poster children for speechless sentience. People often rely on their recognition of physical expressions to conclude that someone is cocky, confused, frustrated, or scared (an involuntary form of communication), but most don't doubt that someone might be experiencing any of those states without necessarily showing it.

The labels that people use to direct attention and awareness to subsets of perceived or imagined events give a strong sense of shared qualia. Evidence of phenomena like color-blindness provide good reasons to doubt that common labels always generate shared qualia, however. The potential for undetectable differences in experiences across individuals has often been pointed to as a major limitation of introspective methods and scientific studies of mental processes more generally. Less attention has been given to the fact that potential differences in subjective experiences within individuals are just as problematic. There is no way for you to objectively determine if any experiences you have had today match those you experienced in prior days.

Luckily, whether your qualia match those experienced by your friends or your past self doesn't really matter much in terms of developing and testing models of cognitive processes. What matters is how well the models predict and explain the actions of individuals. When an individual or group behaves in ways that differ systematically from typical patterns, as in individuals diagnosed with schizophrenia, then this justifies creating new models that can better account for these variations. This process of model revision is essentially how reports of phenomena like ASMR can lead to new cognitive experiments and theories.

Introspection Revisited

Psychological experiments were born through introspection. The regimented forms of inward gazing pioneered by Wilhem Wundt (see Chapter 1) were viewed by some as the key to experimentally exploring minds in ways that made it possible to objectively replicate psychological findings.

Introspection as an experimental approach involves focused contemplation of conscious experiences. In other words, you need to cognize what it's like to be aware. Cognizing one's own consciousness or cognition is a notoriously tricky business. The observation itself affects the thing/process being observed. If you contemplate what perceiving red is like, are you observing what your experience of red is like or are you observing what your experience of thinking about what experiencing red is like is like? Or are you experiencing what it's like to imagine contemplating redness?

It is not clear that conscious contemplation of qualia is the best path to new insights. When a solution to a difficult problem "hits you," it may seem as if the solution came from outside of your conscious awareness (see Chapter 9). When thinkers are doing their deepest thinking, they often engage in what appears to be purposeless fiddling, pacing, or posturing, which are all activities that generally seem designed to distract. These kinds of **displacement activities**—scratching your head, twirling a lock of hair, chewing on a pencil—may actually catalyze cognitive processing, however, by drawing your attention away from conscious thought processes (**Figure 3.21**).

Finally, it is entirely possible, and even likely, that introspection provides misleading impressions about what thinking, acting, and feeling are like. Students' judgments of what they have learned in a class are often not only inaccurate but also negatively correlated with later performance. Those most confident that they have learned a lot often perform the worst when their knowledge is tested.

Contemplating what your mind, consciousness, and cognition are like does not always require introspection. Reading texts on these topics, like what you're doing now, can trigger new experiences and thoughts about the nature of mental states without requiring that you consciously focus on what your own mental states and thoughts feel like. In fact, modern approaches to cognitive psychological research can be viewed as a socially self-organized attempt to do just that.

(A)

(B)

(C)

FIGURE 3.21. Displaced thoughts. (A) Rodan's *The Thinker* (shown here pitted against itself) is often viewed as a masterpiece of art that portrays an unobservable internal state. It also illustrates one of many possible displacement activities (the self-face-punch/elbow-to-the-knee combo). Others include the face squash (B) and cheek cradle (C). How might squashing a fist into your mouth enable you to produce better ideas? More generally, why do different face and arm combinations seem to reveal otherwise hidden states of consciousness, including emotional states? (A 3DSculptor; B FG Trade; C Sdart)

SIGHT BITES

 Scientific studies of conscious cognitive processes are always biased by personal preconceptions and are susceptible to many interpretational mistakes.

 Directing perceptual awareness on itself, or on the now, or on an engaging activity can potentially lead to unique mental states.

CLOSURE

Generally, people with alien hand syndrome are not happy about it. Aside from the fact that they are burdened with an extremity that they cannot control, the alien hand seems to proactively make its owner's life more difficult.

Imagine though, if an actual alien took control of your hand without your permission, but then used that hand in ways that made your life easier. The hand might serve as a personal assistant, making appointments or doing your taxes while you watch a movie and eat popcorn with your self-controlled hand. In that scenario, you might also be willing to hand over control of your other hand to the alien, since this would enable you to perform all kinds of useful actions without any effort or attention.

Effectively, you may already be living out this scenario. When you take a shower, do you really think you are consciously choosing how your limbs and body move beneath the water? When you place an order at a restaurant, are you choosing what sentences to speak or are the words just coming out? When you decide to make an important life decision based on your gut feeling or intuition, where is the decision really coming from?

Awareness of ongoing events lies at the center of almost everything you do that you are likely to consider cognitive. While engaging in most activities, the feelings you experience—boredom, familiarity, frustration, pride—provide the costs and benefits of continuing those activities as well as the triggers to switch to new activities.

The feeling of thinking and experiencing the world seems so core to what most people view as the essence of minds that you may be frustrated by studies of cognition that push such feelings aside and instead emphasize computer-based models of information processing and computational functions, or by experiments that attempt to explain minds based on how fast undergraduates press buttons while staring at computer screens.

Methods of investigating and theorizing about cognition have changed across the centuries, oscillating between a heavy emphasis on conscious elements and ignoring consciousness completely. Similarly, psychological researchers have varied in the attention they have given to "noncognitive" phenomena, such as emotional experiences and action control, when studying how cognitive processes work.

A basic premise underlying cognitive research is that what happens inside an individual's head is as important to understanding how that individual functions as the events happening on the outside. Given that conscious states are one of these inside things (or at least are commonly described in this way), understanding when and how consciousness is contributing to actions, emotions, and thoughts is an important part of understanding cognition.

As you read through the various experimental and theoretical findings discussed in the remainder of this book, you should always consider what is going on in the participants and experimenters that is not being directly emphasized or addressed. What kinds of experiences are happening and how are they contributing to performance? Are the participants entranced? Apathetic? Annoyed? Might that affect how they respond in different tasks? How much of what is being described relates to what participants are doing versus what experimenters imagine they could be doing? What implicit processes might be contributing to responses that neither participants nor experimenters are considering?

Understanding what cognition is and how it works is one of the greatest challenges facing psychologists today. If while thinking about cognition in yourself or others you experience feelings of doubt, unease, or a compulsion to check a digital device, then at least you can console yourself with the knowledge that your subjective impressions of ongoing events are only one piece of the cognitive puzzle. Other implicit processes that you have no awareness of may be just as important for creating a context from which new and better ideas about mental processes may emerge, altering your consciousness in surprising ways. If an inventor can come up with the idea for Velcro simply by wandering around in the weeds with his dog, who knows what sorts of revelations you might discover simply by sorting through social media sites or your sock drawer!

COGNITIVE LINGO

alien hand syndrome

automaton

blindsight

cognitive behavioral therapy

cognitive bias

conscious

displacement activity

dynamic system

emergent pattern

emotion

emotional regulation

empathy

expectancy effect

explicit cognition

facial microexpression

herding effect

hierarchical model

implicit cognition

locked-in syndrome

mindfulness

neural correlates of consciousness

priming

psychologist's fallacy

qualia

readiness potential

reminiscence bump

self-organize

self-regulated learning

sentient

subliminal perception

top-down processing

Umwelt

CHAPTER SUMMARY

The Science of Consciousness

Neural correlates of consciousness can distinguish different levels of consciousness but cannot reveal what a person experiences. Implicit processes can influence cognition as strongly as consciously controlled mental acts.

Voluntary Control of Thoughts and Actions

Volition is often modeled as a hierarchical process in which top-down processing controls ongoing mental and physical actions. Dual process models often contrast conscious controlled processes with more impulsive, emotionally-driven reactions. Dynamic systems instead describe volition as a more interactive process in which movements and thoughts self-organize. Learning can speed the selection and control of complex action sequences.

Emotion and Cognition

Emotional regulation can affect neurophysiological processes, behavior, thoughts, and feelings. Self-regulated learning often requires strategies for counteracting negative emotional states.

Awareness and Thought

Your ideas about the relationship between consciousness and cognition and their presence or absence in different organisms depend on your theory of mind as well as your cognizance of the mechanisms of actions.

REVIEW EXERCISES

The Science of Consciousness

• Provide examples of how the cerebral cortex relates to and supports consciousness.

• Outline how unconscious mental states affect cognition.

Voluntary Control of Thoughts and Actions

• Suggest ways in which dual process models relate to emotional regulation.

• How might top-down conscious processes affect the control of actions and thoughts?

Emotion and Cognition

• Define and provide examples of herding effects.

• Summarize the roles emotions play in perception, memory, and decision-making.

Awareness and Thought

• What is the psychologist's fallacy and why is it relevant to cognitive research?

• How does mindfulness differ from introspection?

• Explain how *Umwelten* relate to the subjective experiences of individuals.

CRITICAL THINKING QUESTIONS

1. Individuals who have a limb amputated often report experiencing a "phantom limb" that remains once the physical limb is gone. In some cases, they can feel chronic pain in the phantom limb. In what ways is this phenomenon similar to alien hand syndrome? What are some key differences?

2. Some people consider meditative gurus to be capable of achieving states of consciousness that are "higher" than what is normally possible. Some users of psychedelic drugs similarly claim to reach heightened states of consciousness. How might researchers objectively evaluate such claims?

3. Most experimental studies of brain circuitry associated with emotions have been conducted in rodents rather than humans. What are some possible ways of potentially establishing that two different species share a particular emotion?

4. Individuals with paraplegia can be trained to control the movements of robotic arms by thinking about where they want them to move while a computer monitors activity in their cerebral cortex. Which models of action control can explain this kind of artificial telekinesis?

5. Studies of theory of mind in young children often involve asking the children what they think a puppet or person might believe about where an object is located when it is moved while the puppet/person is not present. What are some strengths and weaknesses of this approach?

Perceiving Things

S pace. The final frontal tier. What the German philosopher Immanuel Kant (1724–1804) described as "not something objective and real, nor a substance, nor an accident, nor a relation; instead, it is subjective and ideal, and originates from the mind's nature in accord with a stable law as a scheme, as it were, for coordinating everything sensed externally" (Kant, 1900, v.2, p. 403). Coordinating everything sensed externally (and internally) is not just something you do in response to encountering or contemplating space, though. It is the foundation and starting point for all cognitive processes. For William James, it was also the starting point for understanding experience.

James viewed what you are experiencing now as the endpoint of a long process of discovery: "Experience, from the very first, presents us with concretized objects, vaguely continuous with the rest of the world which envelops them in space and time, and potentially divisible into inward elements and parts. These objects we break asunder and reunite. We must treat them in both ways for our knowledge of them to grow" (James, 1890, v.1, p. 487). From this view, he deduced what life must have been like for you, in the very beginning, when everything was still new. As James famously expressed it, "The baby, assailed by eyes, ears, nose, skin, and entrails at once, feels it all as one great blooming, buzzing confusion; and to the very end of life, our location of all things in one space is due to the fact that the original extents or bignesses of all the sensations which came to our notice at once, coalesced together into one and the same space" (James, 1890, v.1, p. 488).

What Is a Blooming, Buzzing Confusion Like?

The previous chapter separated being conscious (an awake and alert state) from the contents of consciousness (your experience of what that is like). The following three chapters explore the "stable laws" that generate those contents: sights, sounds, feelings, ideas, and states of confusion. On the one hand, James's claim that your experiences hot out of the womb differed drastically from your current experience of daily life seems trivially obvious. On the other hand, many people feel skeptical that a newborn would not be able to tell sights from sounds or sounds from a hand slapping their fanny. How might you figure out whether an infant's *Umwelt* is the spatial jumble that James imagined or something more like your current experience?

The approach that cognitive psychologists have adopted in attempting to answer such questions is to conduct highly controlled experiments, mostly in laboratories and usually with Westernized non-infants. Experimental studies of perception are arguably the cornerstone of all psychological research, starting with the psychophysical studies of Hermann von Helmholtz (1821–1894) who recruited one of his more famous students, Wilhelm Wundt (the first person to ever call himself a psychologist), as an assistant. Like James, Helmholtz viewed perception as an ability acquired through repeated experiences and he promoted the idea that percepts were best understood by considering their neural substrates. He fell squarely in the empiricist camp and spent much of his career arguing against the nativist position that perception is a built-in ability of brains. Also like James, he was very interested in discovering universal psychological principles that explain how perception happens.

Given the similarities in the perceptive perspectives of James and Helmholtz, you might expect that they would have been scientific allies. In fact, James was quite dismissive of Helmholtz's views on perception. At one point in the second volume of *Principles*, James suggests that "Helmholtz, though all the while without an articulate theory, makes the world think he has one" (James, 1890, v.2, p. 280).

Ouch! James's disdain might be set aside as the remnants of a quaint historical rivalry except for the fact that Helmholtz's basic proposals about how perception works match those endorsed by many modern cognitive and neuroscientific theories, which means that from James's perspective, modern theories of perception were a nonstarter. Why? One of the main problems James had with Helmholtz's "theory of perception" is that he felt it ignored differences in the experiential qualities of things like space and time. James tagged this kind of explanation of perception as an instance of the psychologist's fallacy—observers experience distinctive spatial and temporal qualities of perceived events and then automatically attribute those qualities to whatever neural activity occurs in reaction to the events perceived. Think about how computers provide you with information about the time of day or your location on a map. The computer represents both types of information as numbers, but there is nothing within those numbers that differentiates time from space (or that leads the computer to experience either). From the Jamesian perspective, what distinguishes you from a computer is that you experience time and space as qualities of the world that feel fundamentally different. James pointed to two cognitive processes that he felt were critical to your perceptual experiences but which Helmholtz largely ignored: attention and recognition.

Where Do the "Things" You Perceive Come From?

Cognitive psychologists often talk about perception as if it were a kind of cascading chain reaction triggered by energetic events colliding with sensory organs. James instead treated percepts as states of consciousness constructed by minds. "My experience is what I agree to attend to," claims James. "Only those items which I notice shape my mind—without selective interest, experience is an utter chaos. Interest alone gives accent and emphasis, light and shade, background and foreground—intelligible perspective, in a word…interest…makes experience more than it is made by it" (James, 1890, v.I, p. 402). From this perspective, your awareness and understanding of things in the world come from the ways in which you have learned to attend to events happening around and within you throughout your life. What you perceive is clearly shaped by your sensations, but only to the extent that you can mentally transform those sensations into some consistently organized form. Most of what you sense, you never attend to or perceive.

An important quality of perception that you probably rarely think much about is that percepts never repeat. Even if all the sensations in your body were reproduced identically (which never happens), they would still probably carry with them on the second round the feeling that this had all happened before, which would make that experience different from the first one. Your ability to recognize similarities across percepts while at the same recognizing qualities that make each experience unique underlies all your other cognitive abilities. Many of the principles of cognition identified to date relate to predicting what people will judge to be the same or different and the extent to which such judgments are learned versus inherent to human minds.

The next few chapters explore past and current theories of the mechanisms involved in perception, attention, recognition, and conception: the pillars of cognition and what grounds your experiences. Although tons of scientific data on these basic processes have been amassed since the days of James and Helmholtz, debates between nativists and empiricists (and within those camps) about the nature of percepts and concepts rage on. Frustratingly, the more psychologists and neuroscientists learn about the details of mental representations and experiential states, the more of a blooming, buzzing, confusion modern explanations of cognitive phenomena become. Nevertheless, there is no need (yet) to throw up your hands and stomp away in exasperation. Many secrets of mental function have been revealed through cognitive experiments—secrets that have made it possible for deaf individuals to hear, paralyzed individuals to walk, blind individuals to see, and adventurous individuals to add on a few new sensory modalities. Old ideas about the conceptual and existential roots of space and time are beginning to give way to more neurally grounded theories of spatiotemporal perception. Other old ideas about the plasticity of percepts are making a fresh new start. Much remains to be learned about the hows and whys of cognized experience. But progress has been made, and if your goal is to understand what minds are and how they work, then becoming aware of what others with similar goals have discovered so far is a good place to start. The next three chapters take up the torch lit by James and make the case that both perception and conception are best understood by viewing them through the lens of attentional processes and accumulated personal experiences.

4 Perception, Recognition, and Attention

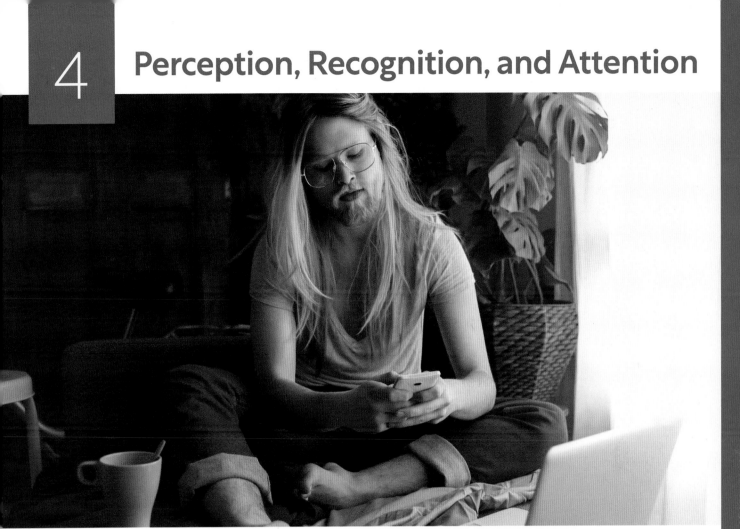

Westend61 GmbH/Alamy Stock Photo

Daniel Tammet sees and feels math. For him, colors, shapes, and emotions are as much a part of multiplying and dividing as amounts and equations are. Daniel has a unique form of **synesthesia**, a condition in which images, sounds, tastes, or touches trigger additional unrelated sensory experiences. About one in two thousand people have synesthesia, with women being six times more likely than men to have it (Baron-Cohen et al., 1996).

Daniel's synesthesia is particularly rare because it enables him to rapidly perform large calculations like $7 \times 7 \times 7$ (Baron-Cohen et al., 2007). According to Daniel, he doesn't use standard mathematical rules to solve such problems but instead waits for a visual scene to unfold in his head that he then uses to read out the answer to a particular math problem. He describes each sequence of numbers he sees or thinks about as a kind of dynamic landscape with unique colors, dimensions, movements, and moods (**Figure 4.1**).

Performing mathematical calculations by describing envisioned landscapes sounds almost like a magical ability. Your daily subjective experiences may seem relatively boring in comparison, but they are no less mystical. In everyday life, **percepts**, the mental consequences of sensations, feel like a given; they are part of what it means to be alive and awake. Your awareness of the world is grounded in percepts, including some that are internally driven, such as those you might experience while sleeping or when prodded by a neuroscientist armed with neurostimulating technology.

Psychologists often refer to externally provoked perception as **bottom-up processing**—your sense organs being at the bottom and your perceptual awareness being the ultimate outcome or top, somewhat like a fireworks display. All contributions to perception other than sensory contributions are collectively called top-down processing. What counts as the "top" often isn't specified, other than that it's relatively far from your sense organs. The gist of top-down processing is that your expectations,

111

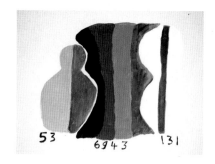

FIGURE 4.1. Math visions. Daniel Tammet's depiction of the images he experiences when given the multiplication problem 53×131. Each numeral triggers a complexly colored and shaped visual scene in his head. The product is a third image that emerges between the two original numbers. (© 2023 by Daniel Tammet. All Rights Reserved.)

recent and not-so-recent experiences, knowledge about the world, and general mental state shape how you perceive things (Press et al., 2020).

Somewhere in or near the top lies **attention**, a process or processes that strongly affect what you sense, perceive, and think. Many of the things you perceive are pretty mundane, but some are a bit less so and these are the ones your attention thrives on. Some sensations command attention. Others depend on attention to even be detected. Percepts that happen over and over can gradually escape attention until they effectively disappear. Or they can become increasingly annoying until it seems impossible to attend to anything else (Killingly & Lacherez, 2023).

Unlike perception, which mostly happens automatically, attention sometimes requires conscious effort. Mind-wandering seems in some ways more natural than trying to understand the arcane explanations of a lecturing (or textbook writing) professor. The exception is when the things you are attending to trigger extreme feelings, such as those that might occur if you pass by a car wreck so bad that there is no chance the driver survived. In that case, it can require mental effort (which is what exactly?) to pull one's attention away from the scene.

In Daniel Tammet's case, his unique subjective experiences of numbers and math seem to enable him to attend to subsets of his percepts and recognize them as solutions to math problems. If you were to see and feel the same visions that Daniel does when he calculates, the experiences would likely be meaningless to you, because you would not recognize the images as being numerically relevant.

Recognition, the matching of a current experience to a prior one, combined with a feeling of familiarity, is what makes percepts interpretable and attention worthwhile. Perception, attention, and recognition together are what cognizance is all about (**Figure 4.2**). These cognitive processes are how you become conscious of the world and everything in it. Without them, there is no thinking.

FIGURE 4.2. Cognizance during gaming. Attention determines perception, which triggers recognition that guides actions that direct attention. Cognizing while gaming determines success versus failure, and learning what to attend to is usually key to success. How do you think your percepts might have differed before you encountered video games? (Daisy-Daisy/Alamy Stock Photo)

Even though you may intuitively know that your present experiences are in some way a result of what you've experienced before (for instance, does the name Tammet ring a bell?), it's hard to wrap your head around the fact that the way you perceive things now is not the same way you perceived them a few years ago and additionally may not match the way your friends experience the world. Many people with synesthesia do not initially realize that their percepts differ from the norm. They just assume that how they see the world is how everyone sees it. Some may never discover their unique perspective. Similarly, you usually would not notice that most of what you perceive depends on what you recognize, which in turn depends on your specific interests. The way infants see, hear, touch, and taste gradually emerges based on what they sense more than once. All percepts are learned percepts.

The processes of perception, attention, and recognition enable you to know what is happening around you and how you can make things happen. What better place to start in your consideration of how cognition works?

BEHAVIORAL PROCESSES

If you are aware of something, it's because you have perceived it, so it's natural to think of perception as the gateway to cognition: the ultimate source of inputs that provides the foundation for cognitive processes. Most models of cognition portray perception in exactly this way. Before you can learn words, you need to perceive them. Before you can remember anything, you have to have experiences that you can recall. Perception feels so automatic and natural that it seems like the process should be as simple and basic as it gets. But this impression is misleading.

Understanding perception remains one of the greatest challenges faced by both scientists and philosophers. Consider visual perception (**Figure 4.3**). You know it depends on light hitting eyes. But then what happens? Modern psychological theories explain "seeing" as a process in which specialized cells in your retinas detect light patterns, triggering a cascade of neural reactions in your brain. Then, the magic happens and you see. According to this interpretation, light triggers seeing. The why and how of seeing is a bit less obvious.

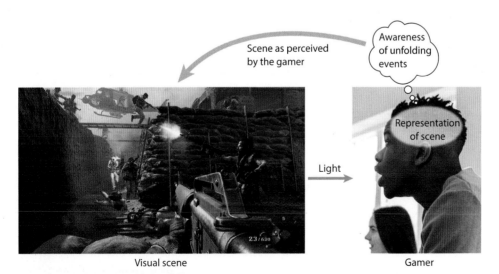

FIGURE 4.3. A conceptual model of seeing. When light from a display hits a person's retinas, activity produced by those retinas generates responses to light that ultimately lead to the awareness that something is happening in front of the viewer—the viewer perceives. (visual scene: pumkinpie/Alamy Stock Photo, gamer: Daisy-Daisy/Alamy Stock Photo)

Recognizing Objects, Agents, and Events

SNEAK PEEK: Early studies of perception attempted to discover principles that determine how people detect and interpret sensations. This perspective has since been supplemented with research on the specific functions that perceptual processes serve.

Figure 4.3 depicts visual perception while gaming as a process in which complex light patterns enable the player to see what's happening. Subjectively, the whole process seems to happen instantaneously, effortlessly, and in such a way that the gamer is likely to be highly confident that what he's seeing is what anyone looking at the screen would see—namely, what the screen is showing.

In this case, and in most other cases of perception, there is a strong feeling that what you perceive is what you get. In fact, if someone else playing the game reports seeing things differently, then player one is likely to conclude that the challenger is making a mistake or in denial. In 2015, a viral instance of this kind of perceptual dispute arose in response to "the dress," a photograph that some thought showed a white and gold dress (and others were sure did not).

According to the qualitative model of perception shown in Figure 4.3, there are two critical components of perception. One relates to **perceptual awareness**, or what it is like to perceive a game while playing it (see Chapter 3). To use the gamer as an example, perceptual awareness relates to the gamer's first-person experience or *Umwelt* during play. As Chapter 3 notes, psychologists have made little progress in clarifying the nature or functions of conscious states. The other component relates to perceptual representations of events, or how people internally represent the scenes that they perceive. Researchers have made more progress in understanding this component of perception, so perceptual representations will be the main focus of this chapter.

But what exactly is a perceptual representation? **Mental representations** are hypothetical substitutes for, or pointers to, concepts, memories, percepts, sensations, or thoughts that capture important aspects of experiences. If an original presentation includes the outcomes of visual sensations, then a "re-presentation" includes whatever mental states occur as a result of that event, independently of whether those states lead to perceptual awareness or not. So, if someone moved furniture around in your house while you were away, you might feel that something is different when you walk in (you are mentally representing the difference between your current and past experiences), but not be able to say exactly what is different. **Perceptual representations** would then be those mental representations that organize and preserve aspects of experienced events.

Perceptual Representations of Things and Beings

Perception without recognition is confusion. Some contemporary art has gotten so "out there" that there have been incidents where gallery janitors have stuffed exhibitions worth millions of dollars into garbage bags and tossed them into dumpsters. The janitors saw the "art" (composed of urinals, broken bottles, and pieces of chairs), but mistakenly recognized it as trash. Perceptual illusions can also lead to confusion—you can recognize that there are stairs in an M. C. Escher drawing but still be confused about where the stairs lead.

Recognition is a key element of perceiving. If you've ever used a microscope, you probably know that having the scope focused makes all the difference. Before the microscopic image comes into focus, you can see "something" through the lens, but you are likely seeing blurry blobs, not identifiable things.

Even when an image is not blurry, you might be able to perceive it without really seeing what's happening or what's there. Consider **Figure 4.4**. It may look to you like a bunch of blobs, but it is actually a photograph. Many people do not initially "see" the focal figure in this photo. Once they are told what to look for, however, their experience of the image can change dramatically: nothing becomes something.

FIGURE 4.4. Abstract art or pre-perceived object? Your perceptual awareness of this image can vary greatly depending on whether or not you recognize what is being shown in the image. Your sensations are the same whether you recognize the image or not. So, how does recognition change your perception? (From "Connecting art and the brain: an artist's perspective on visual indeterminacy" by Robert Pepperell. © 2011 Pepperell. Used with permission of the author and the University of Illinois Press.)

Recognizing Individuals

The moral of Figure 4.4 is that your percepts are strongly shaped by what you expect and what you expect is determined by what you have learned from past experiences. Sensations (bottom-up processing) may limit what you can potentially see, but top-down processing often determines what you will see. And if you were unable to recognize the image in Figure 4.4 without a hint, then that means that part of your "top" is me, your scholarly cognitive scaffolder.

Chapter 2 introduces the idea of cognitive modules, genetically constructed, domain-specific systems that make certain cognitive processes possible. Several researchers have argued that visual perception depends on several such modules, including modules for color perception, visual shape identification, and face and voice recognition (Fodor, 1983). Patients with certain kinds of brain damage lose the ability to recognize either faces or visual shapes (depending on the location of the damage), as you might expect if there were specialized modules devoted to these perceptual processes (Ayzenberg & Behrmann, 2022; Rossion, 2022).

Face recognition is often critical for social interactions, so it is intuitively plausible that mechanisms specialized for face processing might evolve. It was once thought that recognizing individuals by their faces was something only humans could do, but it's now known that at least some other animals can do this, including chimpanzees, birds, and some insects (Sheehan & Tibbetts, 2011). And other animals aren't limited to just using faces to identify individuals. Some apes can recognize specific individuals by viewing their rear ends (Kret & Tomonaga, 2016).

Most of the images that human infants perceive early in life include the faces of their parents (Smith & Slone, 2017). Possibly this intense early exposure, combined with a social need to learn about specific individuals, gives face recognition a head start relative to other kinds of visual perception in humans. Whether this means that face perception and recognition involve specialized, domain-specific processing (as described in Chapter 2) continues to be hotly debated, however (a debate discussed further in the Brain Substrates section of this chapter).

The ability to recognize an individual's identity from the sound of their voice is easier in certain respects than face recognition. For example, telling adults from children, men from women, and intoxicated individuals from sober ones only requires noticing differences in the pitch or intelligibility of speech. Infants appear to learn their mothers' voices while still in the womb, long before they ever see a face (Lee & Kisilevsky, 2014), suggesting voice recognition precedes face recognition.

Animals other than humans also use voice prints to recognize individuals (Aubin & Jouvetin, 2002). So, if cognitive modules are necessary for this ability, then they are not human-specific modules (**Figure 4.5**).

You no doubt can recognize familiar speakers from their voices. There are no voice cues that reliably identify individuals, however. This is why computers and phones don't use your voice as a pass-

FIGURE 4.5. Extreme voice recognition. Penguins learn to recognize the voices of family members and use them to home in on each other (Aubin et al., 2000). Which do you think is perceptually more challenging: recognizing a penguin's voice or recognizing a spoken word? (Mlenny)

word. Professional actors can disguise their voices so effectively that even their mothers might fail to recognize them on the phone. Similarly, visual recognition may break down when incoming images do not exactly match your expectations.

Illusions

People often perceive things that aren't happening, whether it's at magic shows, while seeing a ventriloquist perform, after taking drugs, or even just while dreaming. These phenomena convinced many philosophers early on that sensations and percepts were unreliable sources for gaining insights into the true nature of the world. Illusions are percepts that happen when sensations are misinterpreted, and hallucinations are spontaneously generated percepts.

There are so many cases in which percepts do not match what is really happening that it's reasonable to be skeptical about your perceptual experiences. How can you ever be sure that, like in the sci-fi movie *The Matrix*, your perceptions aren't totally misleading you?

Modern psychology has a different take on perceptual illusions, however. Cognitive psychologists use illusions to explore the mechanisms that make perception happen. By predicting when people will experience illusions and the factors that control the strength and nature of those illusions, scientists are beginning to better understand the nature and structure of perceptual representations (Gregory, 2009). From this perspective, illusions are not perceptual mistakes or lies about how nature really is but ways to open a mind's hood and observe how perception normally works. Features of sensory patterns that people frequently observe tend to determine how people perceptually represent images, including illusions (Purves et al., 2011).

One of the major conceptual frameworks guiding current studies of perception is the proposal that perceptual representations are formed through two main processes. One involves sorting sensations into sets of features that summarize patterns across sensations (Eimas & Miller, 1978). The other consists of sorting combinations of features to identify their sources (Wagemans et al., 2012). Researchers use **feature analysis models** of perception to determine what features and combinations of features are included within perceptual representations and how perceptual representations affect subjective experiences. Before reviewing some of the details of feature analysis models, however, it is worth considering a bit more closely the relationship between percepts and the external events that trigger them.

Perception seems simple because subjectively it just happens. Cars might also seem simple if all you ever do is get in them and ride around. Once you pop the hood, though, you discover the car's hidden complexity. In the case of perceptual representations, there's, unfortunately, no hood release. There is no way to actually perceive a perceptual representation. They might not exist at all (Gibson, 1986).

Nevertheless, if you assume that mental representations do determine what you perceive, you can experimentally identify a number of general rules about what the contents of perceptual representations are typically like. One rule is that perception favors experiences of probable things, specifically things that in the past have led to similar sensory combinations. Some sensations go together and others do not.

Sensations may be grouped because they are produced by particular sources (objects or agents, sometimes referred to as figures). Others may be more static, like the backdrop in a play (called the ground, as in the background). When playing a video game, the things that you control or interact with in the game are figures and the scenery is a ground. The room in which you're playing is another ground (a playground?).

In some cases, a ground can lead you to perceive figures that aren't sensed, like when you explore a creepy house or cave and see or hear things that aren't there, or when you view illusions like the Kanisza triangle that cause you to perceive **illusory contours** outlining objects that are not present (**Figure 4.6**).

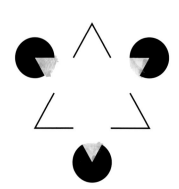

FIGURE 4.6. Kanisza triangle.
Where is the white triangle coming from?

FIGURE 4.7. Missing omissions. In change blindness studies, images are shown that differ in one specific feature and a participant's ability to detect the differences is measured. Most participants feel that they are seeing all of both images, yet find it difficult to spot the missing feature, until they do. (Both images Andrew Findlay/Alamy Stock Photo)

Perceiving Scenes

Sometimes people are unable to detect differences between percepts that should be way above their thresholds for detection, a phenomenon called **change blindness**. Check out **Figure 4.7**. It shows two images that look identical but they differ in a significant way that is easy to see once you detect it or are told where to look. Change blindness highlights the fact that, although you may feel as though you perceive all elements in your environment, in reality, you only perceive bits and pieces of what you sense (Jensen et al., 2011). It's the same sort of perceptual "filling in the blanks" that happens whenever you are awake—you don't notice the holes in light patterns caused by your blind spots and you don't see the rapid blurs caused by your eyes jumping around. Subjectively, your experience of seeing has no gaps, because your perceptual processes compensate for all the extra or missing sensations, or at least trick you into feeling that there are no missed or additional inputs.

PERCEPTUAL STABILITY. Change blindness shows that percepts tend to gloss over the details of sensations and emphasize stable features within perceived events. For instance, when you walk into a room, sensations of light reflecting from chairs are received by your retinas, leading you to see chairs. The specific sensations you have from chairs will change as you move around the room: images of the chairs will grow as you move closer to them, some parts of the chairs may be blocked by other objects or become visible as you walk by them, and the brightness of colors may fluctuate as your shadow falls on the chairs. Despite all these sensory variations, your perceptual representations will tend to give you the impression that the chairs are static, unchanging objects, that do not vary in shape, size, color, or intactness as you move through the room.

Perceptual constancy, the preservation of perceived qualities regardless of sensory fluctuations, suggests that perceptual representations do not simply collect separate sensations into a bundle, but instead transform the features that sensations reveal into a simpler, more mentally digestible form. This tendency works both ways in that identical sensations can generate very different percepts depending on the context. When you look at the diamonds marked A and B in **Figure 4.8**, you'd probably be willing to bet your life that they are different shades of gray. But they are actually identical.

The perceptual constancy of objects and agents includes **size constancy** (objects don't appear to grow as they get closer or shrink as they leave) and **shape constancy** (rotations are not a problem). In the case of size, you need some way to determine the distance to an object (which is why Dory thinks a whale is tiny in the movie *Finding Nemo*). In the case of shape, you need some way to figure out what

FIGURE 4.8. Perceptual constancy overrides sensations. The diamonds labeled A and B are exactly the same color, but your perceptual representations won't allow you to see them for what they are. Don't believe it? Cover everything in the image but A and B and watch the colors magically transform. (Edward H. Adelson [CC-BY-4.0])

angle you're viewing an object from to maintain a stable percept of shape. In both cases, you automatically account for the positions of the objects you are perceiving.

Despite perceptual constancy, there can be competing mental states associated with stable inputs (**Figure 4.9**). In such competitions, the winning state takes full control, at least for some time. As the upcoming discussion of multimodal percepts will soon reveal, such competitions are an important component of perception.

AUDITORY SCENE ANALYSIS. The figure-ground distinction formalizes the commonsense notion that things that are in your face are harder to ignore than things on the horizon. In most visual illustrations of figure versus ground, the figure is a more prominent object or agent (like a banana-obsessed woman) while the ground is less noticeable (like a checkerboard floor).

In scenes from daily life, things are more complicated. If you're at a (good) party, for instance, there's no end of things that could be perceived as figures. Interpreting such scenes visually is usually called seeing, while interpreting sounds coming from multiple places at once is called **auditory scene analysis** (Bregman, 1994). The fact that you can home in on one speaking voice in such chaos without too much trouble is known as the **cocktail party effect**. You can think of the cocktail party

FIGURE 4.9. Two views of the same sensations. Do you see a bearded man's face or a woman contemplating a dehydrated banana? How can you perceive both if the light hitting your retinas isn't changing? What you perceive in this image is not simply a function of what you sense, a fact that artists use to their advantage when creating such images. Percepts are always a consequence of both what you are sensing now and what you have experienced in the past. (Azoor Photo/Alamy Stock Photo)

effect as a case in which the figures (words or sentences produced by an individual) are voluntarily selected by the perceiver and everything else is designated as the ground or noise (Newman, 2005). Ideally, the ground should disappear from your perception as if you were wearing other-voice-cancelling headphones.

Any consistent series of sounds within an auditory scene is called an **auditory stream**. Like streams of water, the origins of auditory streams tend to be stable. Your ability to select from several simultaneous streams makes the cocktail party effect possible. In the case of party talk, perceptual constancy comes from your ability to selectively attend to individual speakers (interactions between perception and attention are discussed further in just a bit).

Surprisingly, your ability to separate figure from ground in such complex scenes may depend not just on your attentional prowess but also on your cultural background. For instance, individuals from East Asian cultures tend to be more aware of the relationship between figures and grounds than perceivers from Western cultures (Nisbett & Miyamoto, 2005). In other words, where you grew up partly determines what you can see and hear. The following section considers more closely some ways in which your development can shape your percepts.

Links between Perception and Action

Think about the world as perceived by babies. Initially, many of the most noticeable sensations are likely to relate to internal states: feelings of hunger, discomfort, or contentment. The relevant external events might be parents' facial movements, voices, and evasive nipples. Eventually, babies discover that some external events are more predictable and entertaining than others. They begin to act as if they are aware that the movements of their limbs are under their control and ultimately that those limbs can also control the movements and relative positions of other objects. The developmental psychologist Jean Piaget dubbed this the **sensorimotor stage** and considered it to be the foundation of cognitive development (Piaget, 1964).

"... all our trains of sensation and sensational imagery have their terms alternated and interpenetrated with motor processes, of most of which we practically are unconscious ... the distinction of sensory and motor cells has no fundamental significance."
—James, 1890, p 581

Babies sense and move well before they're born, so thinking of this as a post-womb "perceptual-action" stage might be closer to what babies are experiencing. Piaget's view was that a baby's actions determine its percepts rather than the other way around. So, a baby might stick its hand in its mouth and then perceive qualities associated with hands. Over time, the baby learns the kinds of percepts that specific actions are likely to produce. The baby gradually comes to construct perceptual representations through its interactions with the world (**Figure 4.10**).

This line of reasoning was picked up by the Canadian psychologist Donald Hebb (1904–1985), who argued that all percepts are constructed based on repeated experiences—you don't see a triangle as a coherent shape because that's how triangles are; you see triangles because you've encountered lots of triplet angles with lines oriented in ways that are predictably related to those angles. As a result, you've lumped all those things together as being one kind of thing that people call a triangle (Hebb, 1949). According to both Piaget and Hebb, you not only learned how to perceive during your early development (through your actions), you also learned what to perceive.

Where Percepts Come From

The Piagetian/Hebbian view that people learn how to perceive is the "nurture" view on where percepts come from. This view is sometimes called **constructivism** because the idea is that perceptual representations are built out of repeated experiences (Cohen et al., 2002).

The "nature" view, which proposes that percepts are built-in features of brains, suggests instead that percepts are just like sensations, except with neural activity taking the place of the more varied energy patterns encountered in the external world. This alternative view is called nativism (introduced in Chapter 1), and it argues that what you see is what you get. Nativists maintain that there is a one-to-one mapping between the world and percepts because evolutionary forces allow for no other alternative. Using this logic, all animals that share sensory systems should have comparable percepts.

FIGURE 4.10. Acting to perceive. Babies move and this leads to the discovery that there are things attached to them. Through repeated visual and tactile experiences, babies may learn that certain actions generate specific kinds of percepts. (©Picture Partners/easyFotostock/agefotosto)

Even from a nativist perspective, however, genetically endowed percepts might still be closely related to actions. For instance, percepts of objects might include their **affordances**—what the objects are good for: eating, throwing, sitting on, etcetera. In fact, J. J. Gibson (1904–1979), an American perceptual researcher, argued that the movements of observers were key to visually perceiving features, including affordances (Gibson, 1977).

Gibson felt that percepts were not summaries of sensations but were instead conscious discoveries made through active exploration. From this perspective, there are no perceptual representations hiding in your head, but rather mental states (percepts) that are a direct consequence of environmental variations revealed by your exploratory actions. The modern version of this idea is called enactivism (Noe, 2004). Enactivism portrays perceiving as a way of acting (like when you feel around in the dark), rather than as a way of mentally representing objects and events.

Active Perception

Auditory and visual scene analyses happen when you're observing events: a movie, TV, or team sports. You are the audience interpreting the scene as it unfolds before you. But what happens perceptually when you are a participant rather than an observer?

In humans, this kind of **active perception** has mainly been studied for tactile object recognition, where participants actively explore an object with their hands to recognize what it is (Lepora, 2016). Monitoring the actions people perform while they feel things with their fingers can provide clues about the kinds of cues they need to recognize an object. The key difference between active perception and observation is that in active perception the perceiver is generating the energy that drives the sensation, as when babies discover their hands by flailing. If you sent light beams out of your eyes to reveal what's in the world (as some Greek philosophers once thought people did), then seeing would be a kind of active perception.

Perhaps the best-studied case of active perception is echolocation, in which an individual "feels around in the dark" using sound. Echolocating animals precisely control the timing and acoustic properties of their vocal actions to generate echoes from objects and agents. The echoes are useful because of their relationships with the vocal acts that generate them. For instance, if an echolocating bat is getting closer to an insect, then the time between sound production to echo arrival will shorten (Jones, 2005).

Bats and dolphins use echolocation to catch moving prey that prefer not to be caught, so the dynamics of perception involve a lot of action. At the very least, the perception of echoes must be closely integrated with the movements and vocal acts of the echolocator to be interpretable as cues for adjusting ongoing vocal and navigational maneuvers. In such cases, perceiving is almost certainly a way of acting. Some blind humans have learned to navigate and recognize objects by clicking their tongues while listening for echoes; since they are making the clicks that produce the relevant auditory streams, they are actively perceiving auditory scenes (Thaler & Goodale, 2016).

Perception from Action

Intuitively, you might think that recognizing moving objects would be harder than recognizing static objects. In fact, in many cases, a moving object or agent is more quickly detected and recognized than a static one, like when a bird flies from one tree to another. You might not have perceived the bird at all before it started flying.

You can even recognize objects from motion alone, a phenomenon called **structure-from-motion**. This perceptual process is evolutionarily old and thought to be prevalent in most animals, including insects (Anderson & Bradley, 1998; Werner et al., 2016). To see how structure-from-motion works, bend a paperclip into a funky three-dimensional shape and hold it in front of a light source to make a shadow puppet. The actual shape of the bent clip puppet will probably not be obvious from its two-dimensional shadow. But if you start turning the clip, its three-dimensional shape will appear.

In laboratory experiments, randomly positioned dots are often placed on a transparent object (or simulated object) and rotated to reveal the three-dimensional shape of the object. Varying the number of dots, how long they appear, and the rate of rotation makes it easier or harder for people to recognize the shapes, enabling researchers to examine how these shapes are perceptually represented (Andersen & Bradley, 1998). Such experiments show that simultaneous tracking of multiple moving dots makes the reconstruction of object surfaces possible.

Perception of Action

Most animals, including humans, seem wired to use motion cues to guide perception. Researchers have studied **biological motion** perception by attaching ten to twenty lights on a person or animal (**Figure 4.11**) and then recording their movements in ways that only show the moving lights, called a **point-light display** (Jansson & Johansson, 1973). By comparing peoples' abilities to recognize objects from point-light displays to their perception of the same moving dots scrambled to random locations, researchers can see how dynamic relationships between moving features contribute to perception.

Point-light displays are **sparse representations** of agents because they consist of only a few elements. The dots themselves reveal little about the nature of an image when static. Individual moving dots in random locations also provide few clues about what figures or actions are present. Instead, multiple dots have to show coordinated movements to reveal what's happening. Observers can perceive a surprising amount of detail from point-light displays, including an agent's gender, weight, emotional state, and actions (Alaerts et al., 2011). Familiar animals are also recognizable from their movements in these displays (Pavlova et al., 2001).

Some studies suggest that people are better at identifying their own actions in point-light displays than those of other people (Sevdalis & Keller, 2010), which is weird because you don't usually

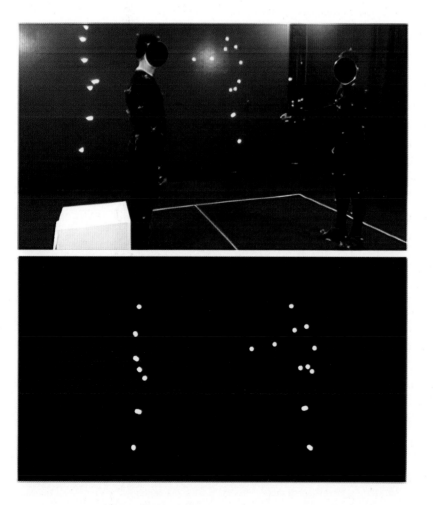

FIGURE 4.11. Point-light people. Sparse representations of moving humans consisting only of ten boring dots are sufficient for recognizing the mover's numerous qualities. (From Okruszek & Chrustowicz, 2020.)

watch yourself from a distance. This could mean that your ability to perform actions affects your ability to perceive them (Calvo-Merino et al., 2006).

Multimodal Action Perception

Most of your percepts are **multimodal** rather than unimodal, integrating sights, sounds, and actions. Modern studies of perceptual integration across modalities suggest that sensations that occur together in space, time, or both can actually boost reactions to modalities that are in synch (Stevenson et al., 2014). For instance, people often respond faster to synchronized visual and auditory sensations than to the same sights and sounds presented separately. Also, people are better able to understand speech when they can both see and hear the speaker's actions (Nahorna et al., 2012).

If you've experienced a situation where a video of a person speaking does not match what you hear, like in some dubbed foreign films, this can distort your perception of the speech. One of the clearest demonstrations of this is the McGurk effect, which was discovered by accident in a dubbed video. In the **McGurk effect**, matching the video of one speech sound with the audio recording of a different speech sound causes people watching the video to hear a third speech sound.

Another example of how synchronization can drive percepts is the rubber hand illusion. A person is positioned so that they cannot see one of their hands and a fake hand is placed in front of them. If the participant sees an experimenter stroking the fake hand with a paintbrush (triggering action perception), while at the same time stroking the person's hidden hand, the person will usually begin to experience the fake hand as being their own (Ehrsson et al., 2005).

This odd experiment has proven to have clinical value in that a similar technique can be used to treat people with phantom limb syndrome, a condition in which individuals retain sometimes painful percepts of limbs that have been amputated (see Figure 9.2). When a mirror image of an intact limb is made visible where an amputated limb would naturally be, patients begin to perceive this image of their intact limb as the phantom limb, making it possible for them to move their phantom limb in ways that relieve the pain (Foell et al., 2014). In this case, seeing their own actions enables them to feel those actions in a limb that does not exist.

Researchers are beginning to develop models of perception that incorporate multimodal representations as well as actions (Litwin, 2020; Olasagasti et al. 2015). Historically, however, most models of perception focus on explaining processing of simpler situations processed by passive observers.

Modeling Perception

Perception is a mental process that is hidden from scientific observers. Somewhat like magnetism, what's known about perception comes mainly from studies of its effects rather than from direct observation. At the core of debates between different theoretical explanations of perception is uncertainty about the sorts of details people mentally represent when they perceive events.

The most notable effects of perceiving are subjective impressions. By describing experiences, people can share impressions, making it possible to compare similarities and differences in the reports of different individuals. The earliest models of perception focused on describing principles of perception that predict peoples' experiences from physically measurable changes in external events (Helmholtz, 1878/1971).

Psychophysics

The German physicist Gustav Fechner (1801–1887) initiated the use of **psychophysical methods** to test how consistently people detect and discriminate different sensations or percepts (Heidelberger, 2004). Psychophysical methods relate internal experiences to external events. The external events that evoke reactions in your nervous system, referred to as **stimuli**, are distinct from behavioral **responses**, which are what you might do after detecting and recognizing a stimulus—responses provide indicators of your experiences.

PERCEPTUAL SENSITIVITIES. The minimum change in energy required for sensations to affect a perceptual representation is called the **absolute threshold**. This threshold has to be exceeded for you to detect that an external or internal event is happening. For some forms of energy, there is no absolute threshold of detection, which generally means that you don't have any sensory receptors capable of detecting that kind of energy. For instance, no matter how strong a magnetic field you are exposed to, you are not going to perceive it. Sharks, on the other hand, can detect even weak magnetic fields (Anderson et al., 2017).

When energy levels exceed your absolute threshold, you may perceive variations in levels as changes in intensity: brighter lights, louder sounds, harder hits. One of the first significant discoveries of psychophysical research was that there is a systematic relationship between changes in energy levels and changes in percepts that is similar across sensory modalities. One basic question addressed by psychophysics is how much energy needs to be added to the current level to produce a perceptual change. Initially, this change may be from perceiving nothing to perceiving something (at the absolute threshold). Later the change is from perceiving the same thing to perceiving more.

What psychophysicists discovered is that to produce a just noticeable change in one's perceptual experience, you must change the energy driving sensations by a fixed fraction of what was there before. This rule seems to apply to all modalities, with only the specific fraction changing for different senses. It also applies to all species that have been tested and so has been deemed a law of perception: Weber's law.

WEBER'S LAW. Weber's law states in a mathematically precise way that to increase the strength of a perceived event by a fixed amount, you always need to increase the input by a specific percentage. So, if you are holding a 1-pound weight in your hand and you want to add the smallest weight that would make you feel a difference, you might increase the total weight by 30% to 1.3 pounds. If you started off with a 10-pound weight, you would need to increase it by the same percentage (30% or 3 pounds) to feel the same difference. The specific percentage of change required to produce a **just noticeable difference (JND)** can vary somewhat from one person to the next, and even for a single person based on factors like their health, tiredness, age, and so on.

Because the difference is just noticeable, it will probably be detected in some tests, but not in others. To find a specific percentage of change, you would need to do several tests and then use statistics to select a value that best predicts a person's accuracy at detecting differences. The discovery of Weber's law was one of the most important findings in the history of cognitive psychology because it provided a clear example of a universal, quantitative principle that could predict variations in mental states across many different situations and individuals. It also turned out to be practically useful (Ross, 1995). For instance, tests of vision in eye exams build on techniques originally developed by psychophysicists.

COMPUTING LOCATIONS. Weber's Law quantitatively predicts how individuals will respond to specific stimuli and changes in those stimuli. It provides little insight, however, about what's happening internally as a person perceives.

Many percepts come from combining seemingly redundant sensations, such as the sensations coming from your two eyes and ears. Why bother sensing the same thing twice? Subtle differences between the patterns received by your two eyes make it possible for you to locate the origins of those sensations more precisely.

Redundant sensory cues within and across modalities make it possible for you to construct higher-resolution perceptual representations of objects and events, including three-dimensional representations. Natural selection has produced some species with many sensory organs (for example, spiders typically have eight or more eyes) because of the advantages gained from overlapping sensations (Snyder et al., 1977).

WEIRD, TRUE, FREAKY

Seeing Colors that Don't Exist

Psychophysical tests can be used to reveal individual differences in perception, such as when people lose their ability to hear higher pitches or are born unable to distinguish between certain colors. Color is an interesting case because people vary greatly in their ability to distinguish between colors. Which shades are easier or harder to discriminate also seems to vary depending on the culture and environment within which people grow up (Roberson et al., 2000).

Unlike intensity, color is not a specific quality of light but a perceptual quality attributed to certain properties of light based on sensitivities of the retina. There are many colors that most people can see (see figure), many colors that people could potentially see if they had the right kind of retinal responses, and then there are colors that people can see, but that are not visible—the so-called impossible or forbidden colors.

The visible colors you can see are a result of the properties of the photoreceptors in your eyeballs, specifically the cones. The number of different kinds of cones in your retinas determines how well you can resolve differences in light. The better resolution you have, the greater variety of colors you can potentially see.

If you were a butterfly, you might have a dozen or more different kinds of cones (Chen et al., 2016)—fifteen is the current record in butterflies. Then you'd see a truly impressive variety of colors and would be able to see all sorts of new colors, including kinds of light your eyes can't even detect, like ultraviolet. But you (probably) have a measly three types of cones, and there's a decent chance that not all three are fully functional, in which case you're "colorblind." Compared to butterflies, every human is colorblind.

There is a slight possibility, if you are female, that you have four kinds of cones. In the olden days, most mammals had four cones, and a few still do even now. Some research with monkeys and mice suggests that if you genetically engineer their retinas to include more cones, then you can increase the visible colors they can see (Neitz & Neitz, 2014). However, most people that have an extra kind of cone don't have a more detailed set of colors than triconers. Only a couple of women with four cones have been identified that do seem to have taken advantage of their extra cone type (Jameson et al., 2019), perceiving color differences that most people are unable to see.

Teasing apart differences in sensed light is important for color perception, but it's not how you see impossible colors, because your retinas are not what's doing the "seeing." What you perceive as color is determined by how your visual cortex responds to neural activity coming from your retina. So, what happens when your visual cortex detects activity patterns (supposedly) coming from your retinas that no light properties could ever generate in your cones? In some cases, you may see colors that do not exist, such as reddish-green or yellowish-blue (Billock & Tsou, 2010).

There are a few ways to make this happen. One is by creating color afterimages. You've probably experienced these in illusions where you stare at a colored image for a long time and then look at a white space where you can see the afterimage of the object you were staring at in opposing colors. Another method, which is a bit trickier and causes weirder percepts, involves staring at two colors side-by-side through a device that makes sure the image on your retina stays constant. Your brain's reactions to this abnormal scenario can cause the two colors to begin to perceptually blend in bizarre ways. Some synesthetes also report experiencing impossible colors when the physical color of a symbol does not match the internally generated color of that symbol, or when two synesthetically colored stimuli are physically close together or overlapping.

Variations in color perception result from both electromagnetic radiation (light) and brains responding to either detected differences in radiation or to changes in neural activity related to visual pathways. These variations highlight the fact that perceptual awareness is not just an automatic consequence of the way the world is—how you see the world now is not the only way it can be seen. Perhaps in the future, the "normal" palette of colors will become blasé and impossibly colored art (made possible through neurostimulation) will be the norm!

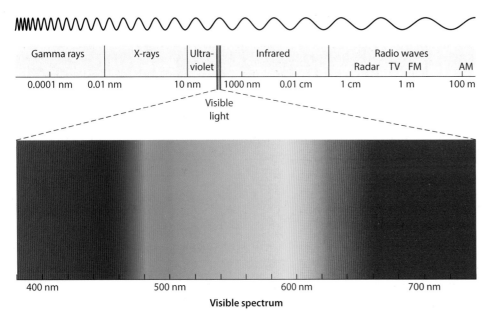

What do non-visible colors look like? (Peter Hermes Furian via Shutterstock)

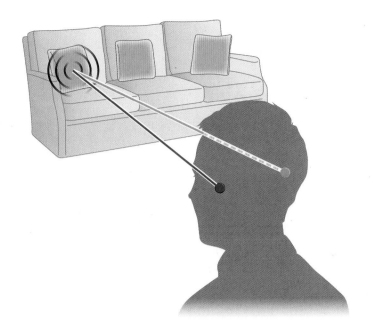

FIGURE 4.12. The duplex theory of sound localization. Perception of the source of a sound depends on detecting and combining differences between sensations from two ears. Sounds coming from a source on the left will reach the left ear first and will be slightly more intense than sounds that reach the right ear. These subtle differences in what are highly redundant sensations make it possible for you to rapidly perceive where a sound is coming from. Do you think having three ears would increase your auditory spatial acuity?

Since your eyes are forward-facing, you depend more on other modalities like hearing for monitoring events that aren't in front of you. Auditory perception of the locations of sound sources, like visual perception of objects, often involves comparing duplicate sensations.

In the early 1900s, Lord Rayleigh (1842–1919) proposed the **duplex theory of sound localization**, which argues that differences in the timing and intensity of sounds received at each ear are used to represent the direction from which a sound came (**Figure 4.12**). This theory mathematically predicts where a person will perceive a sound as coming from based on the time delay between sound reception at each ear as well as differences in the intensity of sensations from each ear (Macpherson & Middlebrooks, 2002). This theory ultimately led to the technology used in stereo headphones, which simulates sounds coming from out in the world rather than from two points on the sides of your head, a technology that continues to be refined in virtual reality headsets (Yost, 2017).

The duplex theory of sound localization was one of the first psychological models to suggest that neurons might perform computations on sensations to generate spatial percepts (Grothe et al., 2010). The idea that neural computations are important for constructing perceptual representations continues to be core to most models of perception. Note, however, that the duplex theory only considers the stimulus-driven, bottom-up aspect of auditory perception. Other approaches are needed to account for top-down mechanisms of perception.

Gestalts

Remember that photograph of a cow from Figure 4.4? The one where there's a white cow with black ears standing in front of a fence looking at the camera? If you did not realize until now that you were staring at a cow, then perhaps you can appreciate the power of labels as a top-down guide for organizing percepts. Naming an object or agent can narrow your expectations about what to perceive. Simplification eases recognition during perception.

This basic principle of perceptual simplification is the foundation of **Gestaltism**, an approach to understanding perception that originated in Germany (*gestalt* is a German word that roughly means "seeing the whole picture at once"). Gestaltism emphasizes the perception of form rather than the processing of sensations, as well as fundamental principles that make some forms stand out as figures rather than fade into the background. According to Gestaltism, when you finally do recognize the

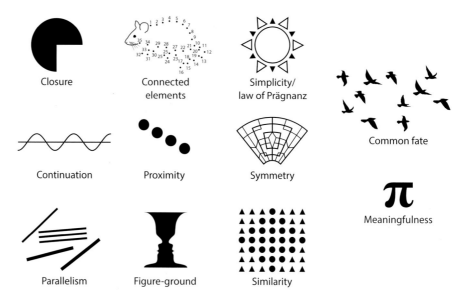

FIGURE 4.13. Gestalt principles of perception. People consistently group together certain features of visual images, leading them to perceive sets of features as objects. Properties of images that consistently lead to perceptual grouping have been labeled as different principles. For example, the proximity principle indicates that four circles arranged in a line are likely to be perceptually grouped together, and the principle of continuation predicts that the curvy line segments above will be perceived as a continuous line rather than as six separate curves. Why such principles arise in visual perception continues to be debated.

figure in Figure 4.4, your percept will emerge as a whole, all at once, before you even realize the specific features or qualities of the object (Wong, 2010).

Gestaltists have identified several "laws" or principles of perception that predict how organisms are likely to perceive scenes, most of which relate to how different visual stimuli are grouped together (**Figure 4.13**). For example, the law of closure states that when parts of a familiar shape are missing, perception will tend to fill them in (as with the Kanizsa triangle). Tracing a hidden or camouflaged object facilitates this process, making it easier to perceive. Familiar objects tend to be perceived as figures and providing a familiar label for an image effectively makes it more familiar. At least some of the Gestalt principles apply to monkeys (Agrillo et al., 2014) and pigeons (Lazareva et al., 2006), as well as to senses other than vision (Notter et al., 2019).

If you experienced the almost magical appearance of a cow in Figure 4.4, then you might be convinced that Gestalt principles are the way to go when modeling perception. These principles have only weakly influenced modern theories of perception, however, because like psychophysics, they describe phenomena without explaining them, and unlike psychophysics, they are qualitative rather than quantitative.

Pattern Recognition and Templates

Most modern models of perception are based on hypotheses about the contents of perceptual representations. Specifically, they've attempted to identify features of stimuli that mark certain patterns as being objects of interest.

Conventional models of **pattern recognition** assume that minds/brains automatically divide and conquer incoming sensations using suites of feature detectors (see Chapter 2). Feature detectors are like the round holes that block out square pegs—when a peg (feature) gets through a hole (feature detector), that component of a perceptual representation gets a mental check mark indicating that the peg is present. If enough of the right check marks are present, the pattern is recognized.

FEATURES AND CUES. One way to think about perceptual representations is as summaries of the properties that were present (or absent) in a perceived scene. A gamer's perceptual representation of a particular scene might include details like the number of characters on the screen, including their color, identity, location in the simulated environment, movements, and size. The representations might also include detailed qualities related to characters' facial features, the shapes of objects they're carrying or standing next to, the specific trajectories and speeds of their limbs, and so on.

All of these different qualities are **features** of the scene being perceived. Perceived features are often associated with consistent sets of sensations. **Sensory cues** are features that are particularly important for isolating specific objects or agents within a scene, such as when a friend simultaneously whistles and waves her arms to help you find them in a crowd.

Importantly, not all features in perceptual representations are directly sensed. In fact, many of the perceptual properties that you probably consider the most natural are not sensed; your impression that the world is three-dimensional, for instance. This quality comes from visual representations of **binocular cues** that are integrated across sensations from both of your eyes (Marr, 1982; Sakata et al., 2005).

The question of how features can be integrated into a unified perceptual awareness, called **perceptual binding**, either within or across modalities, is called the binding problem (Robertson, 2003). One way of viewing synesthesia is as an extreme case of people perceptually binding current sensations with self-generated perceptual representations triggered by those sensations. Emotional responses to particular musical styles might similarly involve automatic binding of auditory representations to triggered perceptual representations of emotional states (Peretz, 2010).

TEMPLATE THEORIES. Several theories of visual object recognition exist, most of which attempt to explain how you form perceptual representations and how you compare sensory patterns to memories of past percepts. Conventional models often assume that incoming features are compared with large sets of stored patterns that act like templates—it's tricky to know what perceptual templates might be like, but you can think of them as gold standards for comparison (Edelman & Poggio, 1991).

In the **template theory** of object recognition, perception is a contest of comparisons in which only one template can win (the one that is most similar to the sensed set of features). It's easy to imagine templates for two-dimensional shapes that could sort patterns like written letters (see Figure 1.4) because people have built toys that sort shapes. One limitation of this theory is that you would need to have lots of different templates to be able to find matches for all the possible things you might perceive (Palmeri & Cottrell, 2010).

An obvious solution to the too-many-templates problem is to imagine that you use templates of shape features rather than templates of the objects themselves. That way you only need templates for pieces, which could be as simple as small curves or line segments (edges). By combining relatively small sets of features in different configurations, you can create an unlimited number of shapes, as sketch artists do daily. The **recognition-by-components theory** of object recognition proposes that the components (templates) used to represent objects are simple three-dimensional shapes called geons (Biederman, 1987). By combining geons together, a wide variety of different object templates can be constructed (**Figure 4.14**).

Perhaps the biggest limitation of template theories is that they don't actually explain why perceptual representations lead to perceptual experiences. You can make toys that let kids sort objects using templates, but the toys on their own do nothing and perceive nothing. Similarly, without including an observer to interpret how shapes, features, or components are being sorted or constructed, template theories don't really explain object perception or recognition.

Template theories focus mainly on identifying figures within static images. These theories are less well suited for describing the perception of agents who tend not to sit still very long. Although

FIGURE 4.14. Identifying objects as collections of components. (A) Geons are three-dimensional shapes that can be easily distinguished from each other. (B) Many everyday objects can potentially be recognized as a combination of geons, as proposed by the recognition-by-components theory. (From Biederman, 1990.)

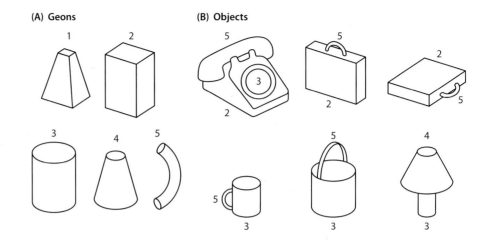

you can think of moving objects or people as sequences of still images—like those used to make movies and cartoons—there is little evidence that this is what happens perceptually. On the contrary, there is convincing evidence that the perception of static images may involve different mechanisms from those used during the perception of moving objects or agents (Chang et al., 2010).

DYNAMIC TEMPLATES OF ACTIONS. Perceptual templates are often portrayed as being something like mental descriptions or interpretations of stimuli that people use to guide their actions and decisions. As noted above, some researchers believe that perceptual representations may instead be more closely related to your actions. For instance, the **motor theory of speech perception** proposes that when you perceive spoken words, you represent them by recognizing the pattern of vocal actions you would have to reproduce to speak the same word (Liberman & Mattingly, 1985).

You can imagine that such representations of actions would be particularly useful to young children, since they could help them to imitate novel words that they hear others using (see Chapters 11 and 12). Perceptually representing sounds as vocal actions may seem odd, but the fact that you can imitate various novel sounds implies that you are able to represent sounds in this way at some level. One implication of the motor theory of speech perception is that even sensations registering through a single sensory modality may generate multimodal perceptual representations—playing speech over headphones does not mean that the speech will be represented in terms of auditory sensations or percepts alone.

Detecting and Recognizing Predictable Patterns

In ancient Rome, practitioners of haruspicy (haruspices) would remove and inspect the entrails of a chicken or sheep to gain insights regarding pressing dilemmas, like whether it would be a good idea to assault a neighbor. You might have qualms about making major life decisions based on the shapes of entrails, but for centuries this was a favored method of emperors.

Haruspices received extensive, highly specialized training to enable them to extract relevant information by poring over internal organs. The trick was to know where to look and what to look for to correctly interpret the signs within the mess. In the late 1800s, Hermann von Helmholtz (1821–1894) proposed that perception was a similar process in which an observer, faced with a massive flow of incoming sensory information, extracts from this mess percepts of objects (Helmholtz, 1878/1971). He described this process as a kind of implicit inference in which your mind collects evidence, weighs the evidence, and then reaches a verdict about what to perceive. According to Helmholtz, perception is just ordinary reasoning (see Chapter 10).

SIGNALS VERSUS NOISE. When haruspices are searching through innards for solutions, step one is to decide what's relevant and what's not. In this context, key organs like the liver constitute "the figure," while everything else is "the ground." The ground is like visual noise that the haruspices should ignore, while features of the liver are signs or signals that they must consider closely to divine an answer to their question. The signs provide the evidence that must be weighed.

Signal detection theory is a mathematical approach that can be used to describe how relevant evidence might be distinguished from irrelevant details. It considers two scenarios: one in which there is no figure, only ground, and another in which there is both figure and ground. From this perspective finding signs involves making decisions about whether a figure is present or not based on the current evidence (Ma, 2010).

Signal detection theory includes situations in which there is uncertainty. Imagine a celebrity walking up to you on a foggy night. There would likely be a short period where you might squint into the fog to try and verify that you're really seeing who you think you are. How long that period lasts might depend a lot on how likely you think it is that a celebrity would be coming up to you at all. Your inferences will then be affected not just by what you see but also by what you expect, which will in turn be affected by what you know.

BAYESIAN INFERENCE. Helmholtz's idea that percepts are the product of rapid reasoning is a qualitative model of how perception works. Recently, this idea has gained traction by being expressed in a more quantitative way, sometimes referred to as the Bayesian model of perception (Maloney & Zhang, 2010). The basic premise of Bayesian models of perception is that sensations alone are not sufficient for constructing a meaningful perceptual representation. Instead, what makes perception of the external world possible is prior knowledge about what is likely to be happening.

Given knowledge of what is likely to be perceived, the main perceptual problem for minds, according to Bayesian models, is to quickly select from those likely possibilities what is actually happening. And from the Bayesian perspective, the job of cognitive psychologists interested in understanding perception is to identify how brains do this (Chater et al., 2010). Just as skilled haruspices work their way through a sheep's innards to divine whether an emperor's aspirations are likely to work out in an uncertain world, a Bayesian model weighs all the available evidence to divine how to best perceive what's really happening.

Bayesian models place great emphasis on information that an observer has acquired (or inherited) about the nature of the world. In doing so, the models predict that perception will be largely determined by top-down processes and past learning, combined with an ability to detect sensible patterns within noisy backgrounds. The advantage of Bayesian models of perception over Helmholtz's original proposal is that they replace unobservable mental processes with precise mathematical formulas for calculating probabilities (Gershman & Niv, 2010).

A disadvantage of Bayesian models is that mathematical formulas generally do not have any experiences, and so do not really address why implicit decisions about probabilities should give rise to explicit experiences of things or agents, space or time, or any perceptual experiences at all. For Bayesian models, there are no *Umwelten* (see Chapter 3) and your interest in finding out more about what's out there in the world is perceptually irrelevant.

But aren't you the one choosing to stare at text right now? Choosing to focus in on a small region of space while many other would-be figures are streaming light directly into your eyes? Surely where you decide to concentrate your gaze is playing a major role in determining what you visually perceive. The following section considers how attention interacts with perception to shape both your experiences and actions.

SIGHT BITES

 Percepts are always a combination of what you are sensing now and what you have experienced in the past.

 Psychologists use psychophysical methods to determine what perceivers can and cannot detect and discriminate.

 Template theory focuses on finding sensations that fit specific patterns, while recognition-by-components theory is all about building objects from simpler parts.

Attention

SNEAK PEEK: Cognitive studies suggest that attention may operate in multiple stages that interact with perception and recognition. How attention can be voluntarily allocated depends on past learning experiences.

"Millions of items… are present to my senses which never properly enter my experience. Why? Because they have no interest for me. My experience is what I agree to attend to. Only those items which I notice shape my mind—without selective interest, experience is an utter chaos."
—James, 1890, p 402

There has probably been a time when you found yourself staring off into space, zoning out, oblivious to what is going on around you; hopefully not in the last few pages. You are not unconscious, but you are not conscious of anything in particular. Maybe you're bored or just out of it. Either way, your mental state is the polar opposite of focused. An unexpected or novel event can quickly free you from this mental limbo, causing you to direct your gaze toward the direction from which the surprising stimulus came.

This sort of reflexive engagement of attention is effortless. On the other hand, directing your attention to topics you're not really interested in for more than a few minutes can be quite difficult. Watching videos or listening to a concert: easy. Watching grass grow: not so much. These tasks involve similar kinds of perception, so why do some require more effort?

The general answer that psychologists have come up with is that attention is a limited resource. The idea is that, just like the amount of money in your bank account limits how much you can spend each day without going bankrupt, the way your mind works limits how much attention you can pay to ongoing events without having a mental breakdown. What exactly determines these attentional limits remains unknown.

Some researchers describe attentional resources as similar to renewable energy sources. Others suggest that limits on attention are more like those that affect traffic on a highway, with certain "bottlenecks" in processing leading to traffic jams and a fixed number of "cars" (figures) that can be handled at any time. Still others claim that the only limits are those set by the number of percepts a person can mentally juggle, implying that more highly skilled "jugglers" will have greater resources. For instance, Julius Caesar reportedly trained himself to read and write simultaneously. More recently, the savant Kim Peek learned to read the left and right pages of books at the same time.

Despite such exceptional attenders, the norm for most people is that even attending to one event stream can be a challenge. Having two people try to talk to you at the same time can quickly cause an understanding jam. Many psychological studies of attention have investigated limits on people's ability to attend to multiple objects or perceptual tasks at once and what those limits suggest about how attention works (Kristjánsson & Draschkow, 2021).

Selective Attention and Divided Attention

Listening to a single talker at a noisy party requires an active process of selecting one auditory stream among several to focus on (Lakatos et al., 2013). This favoring of a specific source of sensory patterns is called **selective attention**. Early experiments on selective attention to specific speakers involved using headphones with one person audible on the right headphone and a second person audible on the left (Cherry, 1953; Moray, 1959). In this **dichotic listening task**, participants are instructed to focus on one of the two speakers/ears (**Figure 4.15**). Later, they are asked questions about what the two people said.

Generally, participants are unable to tell researchers much about what the unattended speaker was talking about, just like you probably wouldn't notice other people's conversations while talking to a friend at a party. Some words, including a participant's name and swear words, do break through into perceptual awareness, however, even when participants actively focus on one talker. Presumably, if someone at a party began saying your name while cursing, it might catch your attention as well. Dichotic listening tasks are a bit different from what would happen in a party where all the sentences being spoken register at both ears, but dichotic listening tasks still highlight the fact that voluntary attention to one auditory stream can interfere with the processing of others.

Perceiving Words

In dichotic listening tasks, cursing presented to an unattended ear diverts attention away from what people are supposed to be listening to. A similar case of stolen attention occurs in a visual task called the Stroop test. In this test, you are shown lists of words and then instructed to name the font colors of each word. This task is perceptually trivial when either the words aren't color labels, or if the labels match the font colors. It's not super hard when there is a mismatch between the label and the font, like when the label is "red" but printed in the color blue, but it does take you a bit longer to say "blue".

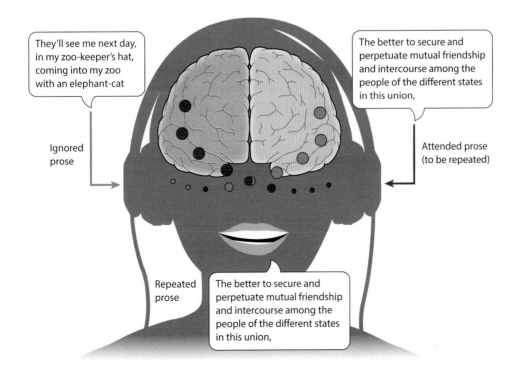

FIGURE 4.15. Dichotic listening. Tasks in which different speech recordings are presented to each ear and participants are instructed to focus on the voice in one ear have been used to investigate voluntary control of attention (selective attention) and cross-hemisphere interactions in speech processing.

Delayed color naming caused by label mismatch is called the **Stroop effect** (Macleod, 1991). Its discovery has had a surprisingly broad impact on psychological research (the original report of the effect has been cited over 24,000 times). One proposed explanation for the Stroop effect is that it's harder to selectively attend to the color of a figure than to spontaneously attend to the meaning of a word (Stroop, 1938). Your habit of reading words (happening right now) kicks in automatically, stealing attentional resources from the perceptual task you are supposed to be doing, which slows you down.

The color-naming task is often used to assess a person's capacity for selectively attending: the larger the Stroop effect, the lower the capacity. Many factors are known to affect attentional control measured in this way, including age, fatigue, emotional state, visual acuity, memory capacity, altitude, and brain integrity.

Does it seem weird to you that involuntarily attending to the meaning of written words is easier than voluntarily attending to a simple feature like color? After all, color is an intrinsic feature of almost everything you've seen your whole life. Plus, color vision evolved a while ago, while reading color labels is a specialized skill invented by humans that not all people can even do. Seeing colors is presumably perceptually easier than reading words, but the Stroop task requires you not just to see colors, but to *label* them. You are being asked to look at a figure that you recognize as being a word and then to say a word based on what you see. Your natural (learned) tendency will be to do what you've normally done in the past, rather than what you were recently instructed to do.

Labeling has a stronger effect on perception and attention than you might expect. For instance, it's easier to recognize a rapidly flashed word than to recognize isolated letters, a phenomenon called the **word superiority effect** (Reicher, 1969). If you glance at a road sign while driving, you can probably grasp its message in a second or less. If you saw the same sign with the letters scrambled, you'd be lucky if you could list more than a few letters that were on it.

Attending to meaningful wholes is easier than attending to components, and labels act like outlines for separating out complex sensory patterns that are more meaningful than others. This may be why when you first encounter someone you are extremely attracted to, one of the first things you attempt to discover is the person's name, and why an almost reflexive response to seeing some new gadget is to ask, "What's that?" Once you have a label, you not only can control other people's attention, you can also better control your own, especially when you are attempting to attend to more than one thing at a time.

Divided Attention

Divided attention, or perceptual multitasking, is probably the normal way that attention operates. Even in tasks like dichotic listening, there is no way you can detect your name being said by the voice you are supposed to be ignoring unless some part of you is not totally ignoring that voice. The predictable patterns of rapid eye movements and fixations revealed in eye-tracking experiments show that people are aware of certain features and objects within scenes even before their gaze settles on them.

Divided attention tasks used in experiments can reveal more systematically how people fare when asked to attend to multiple things at the same time. It turns out that, if the tasks are very different and involve different sensory modalities, then people don't have much of a problem (Herdman & Friedman, 1985). This finding suggests that there is not just one pool of attentional resources that has to be shared across all perceptual processes.

Also, the more experience you have with a task, the less it interferes with other tasks. So, if you are a professional juggler, you wouldn't find it hard to juggle while watching a tennis match. Or, if you were Julius Caesar, you'd have no problem reading and writing at the same time.

Even professionals can run into trouble, however, when labels get involved, such as when thoughts about the importance of what happens next in a game cause a professional athlete to choke. You might think that distractions of this sort are a failure of attention (or an attention deficit), but they are actually a natural component of perceptual multitasking—the same sort of process that might enable you to detect a rabid squirrel out of the corner of your eye right before it pounces on you, or to notice a "Free Hot Doughnuts" sign on a restaurant as you drive down a street.

Keeping Track of Objects

Attention naturally divides when expected events don't match perceived events. For instance, the sleight-of-hand that magicians use when performing tricks often depends on using distracting stimuli to produce perceptual illusions. Ventriloquists use the attention-grabbing effects of moving mouths to make it seem like their dummies can speak. These tricks work by directing a viewer's **spatial attention** to a particular location, especially a location where the viewer is likely to fixate (Macknick et al., 2008). When you shift your spatial attention, you are likely to point your eyes and ears in the direction you are attending to increase the clarity of sensations coming from that particular location.

Viewers can also attend to locations other than where their eyes are fixated, a type of attention known as **covert spatial attention**. Stimuli in the periphery of your perception are often quite effective at grabbing your attention, which is why feints are often effective. You can divide your attention across multiple spatial locations, an ability that comes in handy in some video games or if you are an air traffic controller. Studies of **multiple-object tracking** have shown that people can keep track of the movements of four to five moving objects at the same time (**Figure 4.16**), as long as the objects aren't moving too fast and aren't too close together (Cavanagh & Alvarez, 2005). In these tasks, people seem to be able to "target-lock" their attention on specific objects, known as **object-based attention**. Interestingly, a person is less likely to notice that features of moving objects are changing when they are tracking more objects, suggesting that monitoring where moving things are going can affect your ability to perceive what is happening.

You may be skeptical that watching things move might make you less able to perceive changes in objects or agents, but there are actually experiments demonstrating this effect. In one famous study, participants were instructed to track the movements of a basketball being passed between players. When doing so, many participants failed to notice a person dressed as a gorilla walking right through the middle of the players (Simons & Chabris, 1999). In another study, pedestrians who were stopped and asked for directions, and then interrupted by workers carrying a large object between them, often did not notice if the person who had originally asked for directions was replaced by a different person (Simons & Levin, 1998). This kind of obliviousness, called **inattentional blindness**, implies that even large changes that seemingly should be obvious can occur without an observer being perceptually aware of those changes.

An extreme form of inattentional blindness occurs in some people with brain damage who have **hemispatial neglect**. These individuals act as if they are unaware of anything existing in one-half of

FIGURE 4.16. Multiple-object tracking. Simultaneously tracking the movements of four or five objects is doable for many people, but that's about the limit for splitting attention across multiple objects. (pumkinpie/Alamy Stock Photo)

their environment (usually the left side), including half their own body (Buxbaum et al., 2004). In some cases, patients aren't just blind to one side but also may fail to hear, smell, or feel stimuli coming from that side. It's as if the patient were living an extreme version of a dichotic listening task. The unnerving aspect of inattentional blindness is that people experiencing it are oblivious to their blindness, which means that, in principle, you would have no way of knowing whether you are similarly oblivious to significant events that happen around you all the time (welcome to FOMO—fear of missing out—on steroids).

Watching the Road

Divided attention has become a hot topic in the public sphere due to the increasing number of accidents caused by phone use while driving. Texting in particular seems to lead to a sizeable number of crashes. Driving while distracted is nothing new, however. Ashtrays used to come standard in most vehicles and now cup holders and stereo systems are a given, all of which encourage drivers to do things other than driving while behind the wheel. Do you think texting is more problematic for your attentional processes than searching for a decent radio station? What about reading a text versus writing one? Both can muck up a person's ability to drive, mainly because drivers are less likely to notice key visual cues. But sending texts hurts performance more (Owens et al., 2011).

Texting doesn't seem the same as repeatedly closing your eyes for multiple seconds while driving, but perceptually it's not much different. You don't notice that you are missing visual cues (even if they are guys in gorilla costumes) and so you feel like everything is going smoothly, until you hit something. Typing a message as simple as "I'm on my way home," took drivers thirty-seven seconds on average—with drivers spending most of that time looking away from the road (Caird et al., 2014). Holding a phone can also interfere with perception and control of steering. It's not just visual attentional resources that are being divided by texting. It turns out that texting while driving is attentionally and perceptually more problematic than being drunk (Elvik, 2013), which is probably why texting drivers are increasing the number of traffic-related injuries and deaths.

Sustained Searching

The perceptual scenes faced by drivers are mainly visual, but occasionally sounds are important, too. For instance, you may hear emergency vehicles approaching before you see them. When you hear the familiar sirens, you may broaden your spatial attention in an attempt to identify where the sounds are coming from. In this scenario, you may divide your attention between the task of driving and the task of locating the emergency vehicles.

Searching for Targets

Visual search is a kind of voluntary attentional process in which you are actively attempting to experience a specific kind of percept. During a road emergency, the target percept is colored, flashing lights. In a grocery store, it might be a particular type of cereal. If you discover that someone deposited a box of the sought-after cereal in a display of bananas, the lonesome box will be much easier for you to spot than if you were searching for it through shelves full of similar cereal boxes. The similarity of the ground to the target figure makes finding a cereal box in a cereal aisle more perceptually difficult and attentionally challenging. It's why haystacks are a good place to hide needles.

If visually searching for known targets in perceptually similar backgrounds is tricky, then you might guess that searching for an unknown figure in a background that is highly similar is even harder. This kind of visual search task is what leads to the phenomenon of change blindness described earlier. It's like the opposite of what happens when there is a cereal box lying on a pile of bananas—the box pops out, but the change that you are blind to blends in. More generally, visual search experiments show that people are better at finding an extra feature in a visual scene than they are at finding something that's missing (Wolfe, 2021). The first can happen automatically, like when you spot a fly in your soup, but spotting something missing typically requires some active searching.

Whenever you are visually searching for a specific kind of target, say a speck of gold in a pan full of wet sand, or keys that seem to have magically disappeared, you have a specific expectation of what you want to perceive. Depending on the perceptual similarity between the sought-after object and the ground, this task ranges from trivial to impossible. William James described such desired target percepts as "pre-percepts." Researchers who study foraging in animals call them search images (Zentall, 2005). Scientists studying visual attention in adults sometimes refer to this process as **feature-based attention** to capture the idea that viewers are searching for images with certain qualities rather than for objects in particular places (**Figure 4.17**).

Paying Attention

Attention span is how long you can maintain your focus without becoming distracted or bored. In a visual search task, this might correspond to how long you are willing to keep looking before you give up. Individuals with a short attention span may be diagnosed with **attention deficit hyperactivity disorder (ADHD)**. ADHD is a developmental disorder associated not just with inattention but also with impulsivity and constant moving or fidgeting.

Tasks in which an individual is required to continuously search for specific targets over long periods, called vigilance tasks, provide one way of testing attention span. Vigilance tasks were originally developed to better understand the factors that determine how effective sentinels are over time (Thomson et al., 2016). When it comes to finding obvious targets, time on task makes little difference. In contrast, a person's ability to find targets near the threshold of detection usually deteriorates after less than an hour of active searching.

It's not clear what factors determine attention span. Dolphins can perform vigilance tasks in which they actively search for targets continuously using echolocation for 360 hours straight (15 days and nights) without showing any decline in performance (Branstetter et al., 2012). Dolphins have unique sleep mechanisms that allow them to remain conscious all day every day for their entire lives. The factors that enable dolphins to sustain attention for such long periods without getting bored or distracted are unknown. A better understanding of dolphins' attentional mechanisms could shed new light on how to increase attentional capacities in individuals with ADHD.

Now, some psychologists believe that attention is a process of repeatedly selecting sensory patterns (features) and combining them together to generate the percepts of objects, agents, and events that you experience when you're awake. Others think that attention enables you to voluntarily coordinate percepts and other mental representations (so that you can understand what you are perceiving). Attention could be some mix of these options and more. The following section reviews how researchers have gone beyond these general impressions to model attentional mechanisms in ways that can be empirically tested.

Models of Attention

The main goal of theoretical models of attention is to explain when, why, and how certain cognitive processes and mental states are favored over others. Another goal is to provide a simple explanation for everyday and experimental observations of behavior.

Early qualitative models characterized attention as a process of making one aspect of experience stand out in comparison to others (James, 1890). The process is sometimes described as an attentional spotlight, with attended experiences being the headliners on the stage of life (**Figure 4.18**). The spotlight metaphor highlights the fact that: (1) not all sensory patterns or ideas can be attended to at once (there is limited capacity), (2) the focus of attention can move around in space (selection is controllable), and (3) items in the spotlight of attention are clearer and easier to perceive than those that are not in the spotlight (attention boosts processing of some percepts while suppressing others).

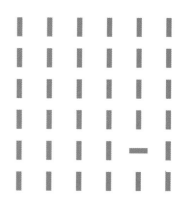

FIGURE 4.17. Pop out. Visually searching for a horizontal bar in an image full of vertical bars (requiring attention to relevant features) is not too difficult. Do you think that this is because the vertical lines bind together to form the ground while the horizontal line becomes the figure? Or could it have something to do with the specific features of the target?

(A)

(B)

FIGURE 4.18. Attentional spotlights old and new.
(A) Early theories of attention described this cognitive process as like focusing a spotlight beam on a subset of perceived features. (B) More modern theories similarly use the spotlight analogy, but no longer assume that there is a single beam or that all beams operate in the same way.
(A By matusciac; B Yuri_Arcurs)

Support for this model of attention comes from experimental studies showing that when participants are told to direct their attention to particular locations, they are faster at detecting objects in those locations, even when they don't move their eyes to fixate on the cued locations (Posner et al., 1978). In contrast, when participants are cued to attend in the wrong place, they are slower at detecting targets.

It's clear how an attentional spotlight might enhance perception and recognition of objects and agents, even if the specifics of what a mental "light" is are a bit hazy (Fernandez-Duque & Johnson, 1999). The model also is simple in that the main things you need to worry about are how bright the spotlight is and where it is pointed.

There are some complications, however. First, there's the issue of multi-object tracking. How can you keep track of four or more moving objects doing their own thing if you only have one spotlight to point at them? Modern versions of the attentional spotlight model account for this by either assuming that the spotlight can be split (a case of divided attention) or used to generate shapes that are more complex than an actual spotlight could produce (like doughnut shapes), or that there are multiple spotlights operating in parallel.

A trickier issue, faced by many models of attention, is: who's steering the attentional spotlight and adjusting its intensity? Put another way, who or what is controlling the mind's eye? In some cases, what is happening in the world seems to control the focus of your attention, like when you pass by a bad car wreck. Other times, it seems like you are calling the shots, like when you decide to watch a movie. Either way, attentional spotlight models provide no explanation for how you or the world might select an attentional focus or direct one or more beams onto your selected stars. That process is left for someone else to explain, which seems a bit like cheating given that spotlights without operators are just big lamps.

Selection Models

Theories developed to explain the results of dichotic listening tasks turned the attentional spotlight into something more like a gatekeeper or bouncer that lets a few select experiences into conscious awareness while keeping others out (Broadbent, 1958). In this framework, attention acts like a switch that participants can use to let in messages from one of their ears. Researchers have argued about how far percepts from both ears make it through mental security, with some psychologists arguing that unattended messages get booted very early in processing—**early-selection models**—and others claiming that percepts are interpreted before an attentional gatekeeper selects those that deserve to be brought into consciousness—**late-selection models**.

These different attentional models have been tested by asking participants to answer questions related to the sentences presented at each ear, the idea being that participants' answers would reveal how much information from the unattended ear was getting through. Such experiments uncovered evidence consistent with both early- and late-selection models, which was awkward.

Later studies of speech monitoring revealed that attention is compromised as the monitoring task increases in difficulty (Bookbinder & Osman, 1979). Specifically, when selectively attending to one speech stream requires more attention, then information from the unattended ear seems to get rejected pretty early. But when the speech monitoring task is easier, attention may be divided across both speech streams, such that more of the speech stream that participants are supposed to be rejecting makes it through to affect perception and recognition.

Note that the kinds of evidence used to evaluate attentional suppression of speech streams differ from the evidence used to evaluate attentional spotlight models. Tests of attentional spotlights emphasize where objects are detected and how quickly, while tests of input selection focus more on what participants perceive and how much an unattended stream interacts with the hearing and understanding of an attended stream (Posner & Dehaene, 1994). Attentional spotlight models say little about how simultaneously present objects or events compete for the spotlight, while early- and late-selection models are all about how attentional processes deal with the onslaught of possible percepts.

Feature Integration Theory

A third theoretical model that arose from visual perception experiments, called **feature integration theory**, proposed that attention wasn't so much turning away rejected percepts as it was combining sensed features into unified percepts of objects (Treisman & Gelade, 1980; Treisman, 1999). Feature integration theory assumes that qualities of visual inputs related to the color, intensity, or orientation of familiar figures are separately detected and then merged by attentional processes into a unified object percept. The new percept is then compared with stored templates of known objects. Recognition occurs when a match is found.

One piece of evidence supporting feature integration theory is that rapid displays of letters varying in color are sometimes reported as differing in color from what was actually presented, as if the letter colors had been incorrectly combined in participants' perceptual representations. Feature integration theory predicts such mistakes because it assumes that features are first detected and then combined, making it possible to accidentally combine features that weren't originally together. Incorrectly combined perceptual representations are called **illusory conjunctions**. They are most likely to occur when attention is overloaded and items are physically close together (Treisman & Schmidt, 1982).

Some psychologists interpret illusory conjunctions as evidence that features are not tightly linked to specific objects in the earliest stages of perception and that the integration of these features requires a second stage of processing. Some assume that errors in this second stage (visual feature binding) can produce illusory conjunctions (Quinlan, 2003). Illusory conjunctions are a surprising prediction of feature integration theory because most people would not expect that glancing at a red triangle next to a blue square would cause you to sometimes see a blue triangle.

A second source of evidence for feature integration theory came from visual search tasks in which participants viewed arrays of two-dimensional objects and performed a **conjunction search** whereby they had to either search for specific features (like a horizontal bar) or for combinations of features (like a red "T"). Measures of reaction times (RTs) revealed that feature searches were not affected by the number of items in the arrays (Treisman & Sato, 1990)—the target feature pops out like a cereal box in a banana pile.

For conjunction searches, larger arrays lead to slower reaction times. Feature integration theorists would suggest that these slower reaction times occur when participants have to voluntarily direct attention to each item in the array until they find the target combo. In other words, the theory proposes that feature searches are based on pure feature detection (stage one, attention-less processing) while conjunction searches require attending to whole objects (stage two, feature merging through focused attention).

This perceive-then-attend model of image processing has inspired hundreds of studies of visual processing and attention (Treisman, 1999). Unsurprisingly, findings from some of those experiments don't fit with the theory (Quinlan, 2003). For instance, some images that are conjunctions of features still pop out in arrays (like cereal on bananas). Similarities between the target and nontarget images seems to be more important than whether one is searching for a feature or a conjunction of features (Duncan & Humphreys, 1989). As new evidence has accumulated, feature integration theory has been modified to accommodate the findings. Alternative models have also been proposed to explain both how features are bound together and how attention affects visual search tasks (Wolfe, 2020).

Learning to Attend

Feature integration theory has two main claims that are featured in its name. First are the features, with different stimulus features (color, size, location) being independently processed. Second is the integration (perceptual binding), which is what attention is for, according to the theory (**Figure 4.19**).

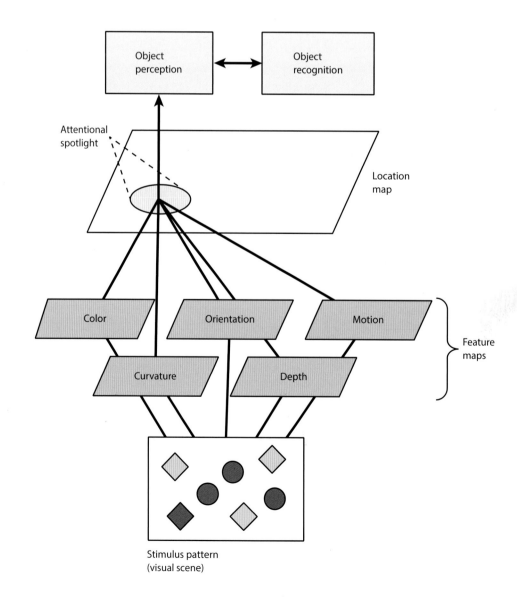

FIGURE 4.19. A model of perception and object recognition through attention. In feature integration theory, images are represented in terms of detected features (such as color and orientation) that are bound together through an attentional spotlight that locates the collection of features in space before they are bound together, perceived as an object, and then either recognized or not. The model was developed to explain and predict how long it takes for people to find different kinds of targets in visual search tasks. Conjunction searches (like when the green square shown here is the target) usually take a while because the green square does not pop out. (After Keebler et al., 2017.)

The first claim, which involves the independent processing of stimulus features, also shows up in early studies of selective attention in animal learning research (Krechevsky, 1932). Specifically, researchers proposed that when animals learned that some stimulus features were more behaviorally relevant than others, they were also learning to give greater weight to some features over others (Mackintosh, 1965). The animals were then thought to gradually associate the selected features with appropriate actions (see Chapter 7).

This model of selective attention differs from feature integration theory in that the salient, or more noteworthy, features of sensory patterns are never integrated into a unified representation. Additionally, learning theorists claimed that animals did not automatically or voluntarily select target features but instead gradually learned over time that some features are more important than others in certain situations or contexts (Castro et al., 2020). If you are looking for food, for instance, attending to the shape and location of objects might be more relevant. If you are competing for a mate, maybe the size of your competitors is what counts.

Models in which target features come to be considered more or less important over time are called **attentional reweighting** models. These models are like early-selection models in that there are detectors for each stimulus feature. But rather than having a psychologist in a lab tell you which features to focus on, you learn through trial and error which features are important (Leber et al., 2009). The main evidence of selective attention in animal learning experiments comes from changes in animals' responses over time rather than from changes in response times or self-reports of perceptual experiences.

Most traditional models of attention only consider a person's performance in the now—spotlights don't learn, they just shine on things. Psychologists are becoming more attentive to the importance of skills and flexibility in selective attention, however, and modern models of attention often include the role of learning when explaining attentional capacities (Kruschke, 2003).

At a minimum, the attentional resources you need to perform a specific perceptual task will vary depending on how much experience you have performing similar tasks. If you are a professional sock sorter, finding matching pairs of socks will be much easier for you than for most mortals. Expertise in sock matching probably won't help you spot gold dust in a pan, though. Recent experiences can also affect performance in visual search tasks, as occurs when foraging animals form search images for their prey du jour. Attentional models that account for context, learning across the lifespan, and recent experiences can get a bit complicated. So, I'll just let you imagine what those models are like.

All the models of attention described so far were developed more than forty years ago, but they provide the foundations for more recent models. For instance, current theories of how attention affects visual searching focus heavily on independently processed features and on the effects of task difficulty on attention (Wolfe, 2021). In cases where a target object pops out of a scene, most current theories propose that the role of attention is minimal and that the detection and representation of the identified target object is purely perceptual. It's only when multiple combinations of features have to be considered in parallel (a more difficult task) that voluntary attentional processes are thought to kick in (Shomstein et al., 2023). Attentional processes are also now closely linked to working memory and cognitive control (see Chapters 1 and 8).

Psychologists usually improve on earlier models by adjusting them so that the models better account for new findings, either by discarding assumptions that don't fit with what is known, or by adding new assumptions to account for possibilities that weren't considered in earlier versions of a model. One basic assumption that all current models of attention share is that pretty much every cognitive process depends on attention at some point. Although this chapter focuses on the role of attention in perception and object recognition, the same issues arise in every aspect of cognition, from whether you're trying to understand which memories are stored and retrieved (see Chapter 8) to what rules are followed when people solve problems or select actions (see Chapter 10).

SIGHT BITES

Attentional control determines what is perceived, but there is not just one pool of resources that is shared across all perceptual processes.

Voluntary attentional processes can make perception of specific figures easier, and in some cases are necessary for a figure to be perceived.

Perceive-then-attend models of image processing are beginning to include effects of learning on selective attention.

BRAIN SUBSTRATES

SNEAK PEEK: Perception depends on interactions between multiple stages of neural processing of stimulus features. Attention contributes to these interactions by enhancing a subset of neural responses and suppressing others.

Think again about how Daniel Tammet's synesthetic number percepts differ from the ways you experience numbers. Similar light patterns are entering his eyeballs when he sees a written numeral, but his perceptual representations of those symbols appear to include several subjective qualities not experienced by most people. What he perceives and recognizes as a number two differs from what you perceive and recognize as a two.

You may now be thinking, "It seems like his perceptual binding and perceptual representations differ from mine." But are those differences specific to numbers, and if so, why numbers? Number symbols are a relatively recent human invention (on an evolutionary time scale), so why might those symbols, in particular, be the ones that provoke odd perceptual experiences?

Possibly Daniel's lifelong love of numbers somehow contributed to his unique number percepts. Or perhaps his percepts are not really so different from yours and he just has a fanciful way of describing them. As Chapter 1 notes, it is often difficult to determine what differences in introspective reports really mean.

There are some behavioral tests psychologists now use to evaluate the validity of introspective reports of synesthetes. But more convincing evidence comes from measurements showing that their brains respond to sensory events differently from the brains of non-synesthetes (Nunn et al., 2002).

By watching brains do their thing as participants search for and recognize familiar objects, attend to specific locations in space, and see familiar and unfamiliar agents, researchers have gained new insights into how perception typically works and how attentional processes contribute to perceptual experiences. Such studies have been particularly important in investigations of the role that learning plays in attention, perception and recognition.

In Search of a Face Recognition Module

Chapter 2 introduces the concept of neural feature detectors, which refers to the fact that some neurons respond most strongly to a specific set of sensory patterns. Brain regions containing neurons that respond in this way are said to be selective to those features or tuned to specific sensory qualities.

Many cortical neurons are stimulus-selective, with neurons in different regions showing predictable selectivity for certain features in specific modalities—neurons in the auditory cortex tend to be tuned to features of sounds, and neurons in the visual cortex are tuned to features of sights.

Neural Selectivity for Faces

For most of the past century, researchers assumed that cortical feature detectors are built into brain structure and that specific regions of the cortex serve as dedicated perceptual modules with domain-specific functions (as described in Chapter 2). For instance, populations of neurons in the auditory cortex make it possible for you to hear (see Figure 2.10), and the auditory cortex is often thought of as a specialized part of the brain that facilitates hearing (a hearing module). The processing of sensations by the auditory cortex is domain-specific in that auditory neurons are for hearing rather than for seeing or tasting—its domain is "sounds" and its function is to process sounds.

Similarly, the visual cortex is for seeing, and some neurons in the visual cortex respond selectively to specific image features, including human faces. The fact that neurons in your brain respond to faces should not be surprising, given that you can see faces. But what is not so obvious is how you can see, and even recognize, a face just because a bunch of neurons fire whenever certain light patterns hit your retina. Many psychologists and neuroscientists believe that face recognition requires highly specialized **face-selective brain regions** that differ in function from all other types of visual pattern recognition mechanisms in your brain (Yovel, 2016).

Is face recognition really so biologically high-tech that you need specialized face perception and recognition modules to pull it off? There is both behavioral and neural evidence that face perception is pretty special. Most dramatically, there are patients with brain damage who lose the ability to recognize familiar faces, including their own, without losing the ability to recognize objects (Damasio et al., 1982).

Infants find faces to be super salient (Nelson, 2001), and as noted earlier, infants are often bombarded with caretakers' faces (Smith & Slone, 2017). Adults are horrible at recognizing upside-down faces—much worse than they are at identifying upside-down dogs or cars (Rhodes et al., 1993)—and some psychologists believe this is further evidence for the specialness of faces as visual stimuli.

Visually triggered neural activity flows from your eyes to the rearmost part of your brain before spreading out in multiple directions in your visual cortex (**Figure 4.20**). Brain imaging studies have identified specific face-selective brain regions in these visual pathways (Kanwisher et al., 1997), and

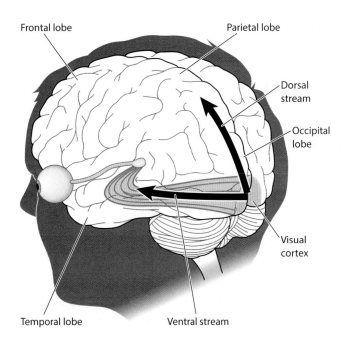

FIGURE 4.20. Visual pathways in your brain. Transduced sensations from your retinas can affect neural activity throughout your brain as neurons monitoring other neurons react. The earliest cortical responses to changing retinal activity are in the visual cortex, quickly followed by nearby neurons with activity spreading from there.

FIGURE 4.21. Face-selective brain regions. Activity in the ventral pathway of the visual cortex spreads to cortical regions in the temporal lobes that respond strongly to faces. These regions include the occipital face area, the fusiform face area, and the superior temporal sulcus. (Inset image: ARCHIVIO GBB/ Alamy Stock Photo)

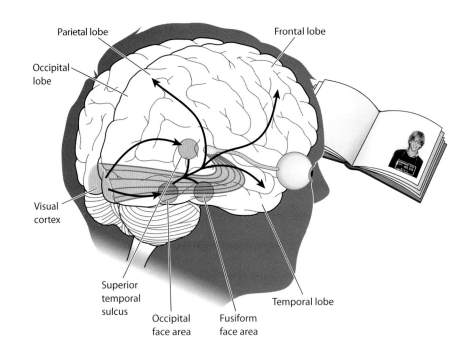

single-cell recordings from monkeys show that face-selective neurons are concentrated within these regions (Desimone, 1991).

Additionally, if you compare electrical signals that are recorded while you look at faces to those that are recorded while you look at other objects, you will see that cortical responses to faces are stronger than for many objects that you see (Eimer, 2000). Evidence like this has convinced many psychologists that human brains possess special face processing circuitry. On the other hand, researchers don't yet know what face-selective brain regions actually do. Some researchers suspect that these brain regions contribute to the perception of lots of complex images (Gauthier & Logothetis, 2000), not just faces, and comparable visual processing is happening in many animals (so not so specialized).

Brain imaging studies in humans and monkeys consistently show that certain brain regions respond more to faces than to other objects (**Figure 4.21**). When researchers disrupt neural activity in these regions, it can impair people's ability to discriminate between faces (Pitcher et al., 2007; Schalk et al., 2017). Furthermore, if there is damage to these regions, it can severely impair face recognition (Damasio et al., 1982). This finding is so consistent that some parts of the cortex are now called face areas, including the **fusiform face area** and the occipital face area.

Face-selective brain regions are positioned relatively late in visual processing pathways, implying that these regions are high up in the hierarchy (Chapter 2 reviews hierarchical processing of features), perhaps high enough to be considered part of the "top" in top-down processing. As Figure 4.21 reveals, face-selective neurons are present not just in the visual cortex, but in multiple cortical regions, including the prefrontal cortex. So, there are face-processing networks in your brain that are widely distributed and that function in parallel.

Face-selective brain regions are also activated when experts, such as dog show judges, make fine distinctions between complex visual images (Gauthier & Tarr, 2016). So, although the regions appear to be specialized in some way, they may not be limited to the specialized processing of faces. Such findings have led to extensive debates regarding the relative contributions of nature and nurture to face recognition.

Keep in mind that face-selective brain regions and neurons respond the most to faces, but they also respond to other visual patterns. The fact that you like one kind of orange more than other fruits doesn't mean that your ancestors evolved specialized systems specifically for tasting oranges, and the fact that some of your cortical neurons "like" faces more than other sensory patterns also does not mean that they are species-specialized face processing modules.

Processing Features of Faces

When you see a face, you don't just detect a face. That's probably the least of what is really involved; see 😧, detect face = trivial.

Even in basic qualitative models of face processing, there is a lot going on (**Figure 4.22**). You are going to see the location, orientation, and motions of a person's face, mouth, eyes, and eyebrows, even if you don't pay much attention to them. You may notice the age, attractiveness, gender, health, and race of the person, whether they are a human or a cartoon, and whether or not they are speaking in your general direction. Any of those perceptual experiences might depend on modules that are more or less specialized. And the processes shaping your face percepts might also be affected by voluntary attentional processes (such as when you're trying to tell when someone is lying), or involuntary attentional processes (such as when you can't help but notice that someone has a bloody nose).

The brain regions that enable you to recognize other people's emotional states from seeing their faces might be totally separate from the brain regions that you use to recognize who they are. But there might also be only one perceptual representation that you use for both things, which is probably what it would seem like subjectively if you saw one of your friends crying.

The neural processing that makes face recognition possible is not only precise but it's also quite quick. Within the first fifty milliseconds of a facial pattern hitting your retinas, you will perceive a face. Such ultrafast processing may seem so automatic that you might question whether it really counts as cognitive. Many psychologists have a similar impression. However, neural processes do not have to take a certain amount of time to be considered cognitive.

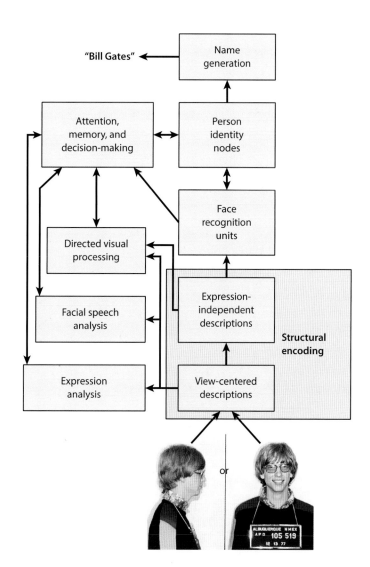

FIGURE 4.22. A qualitative model of face processing by your brain. In this assembly line model, an initial perceptual representation is formed that is view-dependent. Other modules then extract specialized information from this representation related to whether the person is talking, expressing an emotion, and/or is familiar. The results of these independent analyses are then evaluated by a "cognitive system" to figure out what's happening. The model assumes that most processing is bottom-up, except where double-headed arrows are shown, in which case something top-down is affecting processing. (After Bruce and Young, 1986, inset image ARCHIVIO GBB/Alamy Stock Photo)

FIGURE 4.23. Eye-tracked face. A heat map of fixations made by a person looking at this photo reveals that the individual fixated on the eyes and mouth. Given the colors overlaying the eyes and mouth, it is likely that your eyes produced a similar pattern of fixations when you first viewed this image. The one-two punches of color—with bright colors highlighting salient parts—are like eye magnets. The eye tracks might differ somewhat if the mouth were speaking, or if you were asked to judge the character of this person. (From Iskra & Tomc, 2016.)

You might be surprised at how much can happen mentally in less than a second. For example, when undergraduates viewed paired photos of unfamiliar politicians for 100 milliseconds, and were then asked to judge which politician was more competent, they selected election winners in about 70% of pairs (Ballew & Todorov, 2007). Intuitively, you might think (hope) that voters would base their decisions on candidates' records, statements, or promises rather than on a glance at the politician's face, but this may not be the case for many voters.

Even more disturbingly, after briefly viewing the faces of two prisoners, people are often able to predict which prisoner is on death row (Wilson & Rule, 2015). A few differences in the firing patterns of face-selective neurons in judges or jury members could determine whether a defendant lives or dies. So, rapidly formed face percepts can profoundly affect a person's thinking, even in situations where people should be carefully deliberating before making decisions (for further discussion of deliberation and decision-making, see Chapters 10 and 11).

When most people look at faces, their eyes move in predictable ways (**Figure 4.23**). Some facial features may be more attention-grabbing than others. Alternatively, it is possible that the process of face detection triggers habitual or innate eye movements. Either way, it seems likely that people fixate on eyes and mouths because those features, or facial locations, are useful for discriminating and recognizing faces, emotional expressions, speech patterns, and so on.

By recording from monkeys' cortical neurons as they scan visual scenes, researchers have found evidence that perceptual representations of objects are integrated across fixations and that selective neurons often begin firing even before an object is fixated on (Sheinberg & Logothetis, 2001). These findings suggest that fixations may reveal exploration of features that viewers have detected and possibly recognized.

Fixations provide clues about what feature patterns (objects or agents) a monkey or person finds salient or relevant; they also provide indications of which populations of neurons are likely to be engaged during the visual exploration of a scene. In the case of face recognition, undergraduates do well after only one or two fixations. However, people move their eyes in different ways depending on how they are judging a face, with different individuals defaulting to different patterns (Kanan et al., 2015). These individual differences suggest that different people might perceptually represent or explore faces in unique ways.

Models of Face Recognition

The idea that people internally analyze and represent sensory patterns in unique ways is a dominant theme in perceptual neuroscience. Today, psychologists commonly assume that there are multiple, separate systems for constructing perceptual representations to guide movements, navigate through space, recognize objects, track the movements of objects, and reproduce observed actions. Only some of these separate systems lead to conscious percepts, however, and all of them may operate differently for different senses.

A major reason why researchers are interested in perceptual binding is because this process seems to unify the efforts of these separate representational systems. One classic model of how this might work conceives of perception as a collaboration of demons. The Pandemonium model includes demons that record sensations, demons that detect specific features, and demons that recognize patterns and make decisions (Selfridge & Neisser, 1960). Demons that detect features "yell" at pattern demons, and pattern demons yell based on how many feature demons are yelling at them. Pattern demons that are yelling the loudest determine what you perceive (sometimes psychologists get bored and create demonic models as a result).

Sounds a bit crazy, but it's not so different from current brain-based models of face recognition. Just replace the word "demon" with "neural populations" and the word "yell" with "neural firing" and you are basically there. In the case of face recognition, the feature demons might be detecting edges and curves, and the pattern demons might be responding to feature sets for specific kinds of eyes, noses, and mouths (like Mr. Potato Head parts). The most active face pattern demons beat down the others, and whichever ones are left generate the face you perceive.

This kind of survival-of-the-fittest model of face perception is simple enough that you can simulate it. To do this, you just need to include multiple stages of feature detectors organized hierarchically, similar to the face-selective neurons found throughout the cerebral cortex.

In the first stage of image processing, you can automatically highlight features of scenes that observers typically fixate on to create a **saliency map**. The saliency map identifies regions of interest within a specific scene. For faces, this would tend to highlight the eyes and mouth. In the next stage, you can let the feature detectors respond to these regions and let the pattern detectors respond to the feature detectors, with both types of detectors competing for attentional resources (Itti & Koch, 2000). You could even include search images in the model that boost the responses of some feature detectors, and adjust the detectors based on how good a job they are doing. This is essentially the strategy that Google uses to process digital images of scenes.

Google has developed computer programs called **deep nets** (short for deep learning neural networks) to recognize objects and agents in digital photos. These programs work by searching for lots of different features and different patterns (**Figure 4.24**). These types of data-driven approaches to

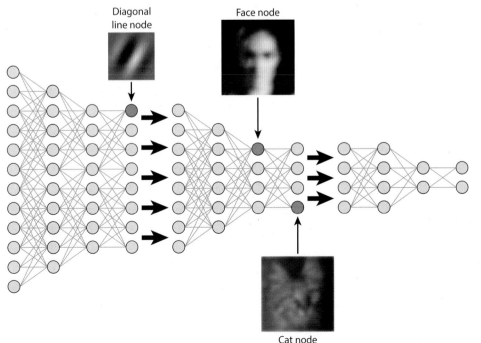

FIGURE 4.24. A programmable model of object and face recognition. Deep nets use multiple sets of feature detectors to automatically recognize what is shown in images. The networks are trained to detect objects like faces or cats through an extended trial-and-error process. The model is entirely bottom-up. Each set of feature detectors (shown here as columns of circles) learns to detect certain kinds of features. The farther along in the network you are, the more complex the features; this property is also seen in visual cortical pathways. The squares show image features that specific nodes (detectors) became selective for; effectively, the nodes are learned image templates. (From https://johnsmart .medium.com/your-personal-sim-pt-4 -deep-agents-understanding-natural -intelligence-7040ae074b71, images: face: Iconogeni, cat: Fotolotos)

Diagonal line node

Face node

Cat node

face recognition can sometimes lead to unintended consequences such as programs that are systematically biased against certain races or genders (Buolamwini & Gebru, 2018).

Some researchers believe that deep nets process visual scenes much like human brains (Kriegeskorte, 2015). But, as far as we know, none of Google's programs can see. Like most models of perception, the demons are in the details, and one detail in particular that has proven difficult for psychologists and neuroscientists to pin down is where and how the seeing is happening. At some point, researchers must deal with the fact that there is a perceiver experiencing the percept. One popular approach to dealing with this complication is to hand the job of consciously perceiving faces, objects, and everything else in the world over to attentional processes.

What Attentive Brains Look Like

When William James wrote, "My experience is what I agree to attend to," he wasn't being snarky. He was pointing out that much of perceptual awareness is self-selected. You could choose to close your eyes at any time or even permanently blind yourself. Perceptual awareness can also be researcher-selected. By tightly controlling participants' experiences in laboratory studies, cognitive psychologists are beginning to get a better sense of what happens internally when people attend to figures and features.

Monitoring Attentional Correlates

Fixations provide useful clues about where people are focusing their attention. But, as noted earlier, different people may fixate on images in different ways, which complicates studies of the general properties of attention. Researchers have addressed this issue by developing orienting tasks that control where and when participants look at targets independently of when they are attending to them (**Figure 4.25**). For instance, a participant may be asked to fixate on a + (plus sign) at the start of each trial, be given a cue indicating where a target will appear, and then be asked to respond as quickly as possible when they spot a target (Posner et al., 1978). The results from these trials indicate that knowing where to look directs attention to the right location even before a target appears. They also show that attending in the right place makes it easier to quickly detect a target's appearance, while attending in the wrong place delays the detection of the target.

Another simple task often used to study attention involves occasionally presenting a target stimulus within a repeating series of irrelevant stimuli. This task (called the oddball method) is similar to the task that animals face when foraging—most of the stuff they see is not food, but occasionally they spot something edible.

FIGURE 4.25. An orienting task used to study attention. In this task, cues signal where targets will occur and participants are asked to respond when they see the target. Participants have to continuously fixate on the plus sign, so their attention is directed left or right, but their eyes are always focused in the middle of the screen.

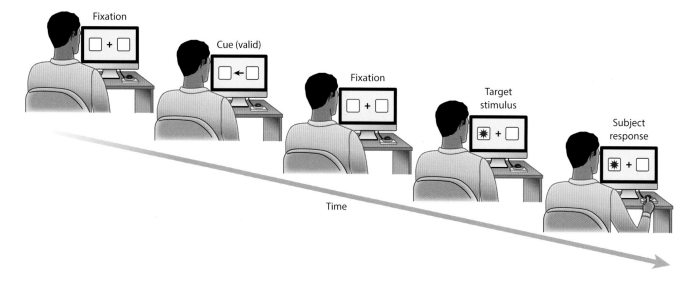

Fixation   Cue (valid)   Fixation   Target stimulus   Subject response

Time

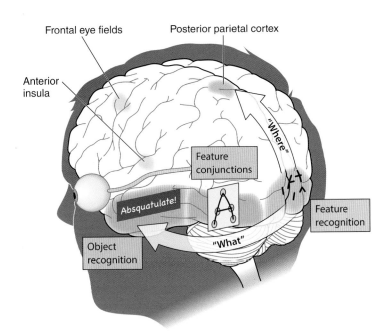

FIGURE 4.26. A division of labor in visual object monitoring and recognition. The ventral or lower pathway in the cerebral cortex (sometimes called the "what" pathway) is more strongly activated by tasks that involve object recognition, including word recognition. Activity in frontal eye fields, the posterior parietal cortex (the "where" pathway), and the anterior insula make up part of visual attentional networks. Attentional tasks affect processing in specific pathways depending on the task, rather than increasing activity in a single area.

Participants may be instructed to watch or listen for a certain kind of target, like in a vigilance task, or unexpected targets may be presented to trigger an involuntary attentional reaction. Researchers studying infant perception and attention often present unexpected targets to grab an infant's attention. As in foraging tasks, the idea is that individuals will respond more quickly to targets that they are expecting than to novel stimuli they are not expecting. Both orienting and oddball tasks are important for studying neural mechanisms of attention because it's possible to train and test both humans and nonhumans on highly similar tasks. You can't really observe attention in either task, but if you are doing the task yourself, you can at least monitor what your brain does when you subjectively feel like you are paying attention to visual or auditory stimuli.

Attentional Networks

By monitoring participants performing these simple attentional tasks, researchers have identified several "attention-selective" brain regions that are important for visual attentional processing (**Figure 4.26**). Brain imaging studies suggest that attention related to the locations of objects tends to increase activity in a different pathway compared to tasks that require participants to search for a particular target. This has led some researchers to propose that there are separate visual pathways: pathways that identify where objects are (the "where" pathway) and pathways that determine what objects are present (the "what" pathway) (see Figure 4.26). The face-selective brain regions mentioned earlier would be part of the "what" pathway because there doesn't seem to be a separate "who" pathway.

Attentional networks also seem to be somewhat different for each sensory modality. For instance, brain regions involved in monitoring visual stimuli differ somewhat from those engaged during auditory oddball tasks, and regions involved in tracking sound locations differ from those used in visual spatial attention. Overall, brain-imaging data suggest that attentional control mechanisms are much more complicated than psychologists might have hoped.

Attentional Modulation of Neural Activity: More Models

So, do different attention-related brain networks have anything in common? Well, one thing that seems to be consistent is that perceptual awareness of attended stimuli is always associated with broadly distributed activity across multiple cortical regions, even if is not always the same regions. Also, lesions in cortical regions associated with the earliest stages of sensory processing typically wipe

FIGURE 4.27. An electrophysiological marker of attention: the P300. In oddball tasks, infrequent targets that are detected lead to a large change in neural activity 300 milliseconds after the target (T) appears. The blue line is the neural response to the repeating stimulus (S). (After Polich, 2007)

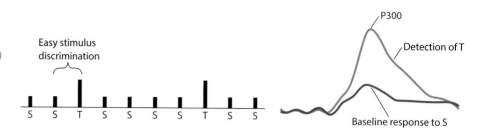

out perceptual awareness as well as the ability to voluntarily attend to sensations (consider the cases of blindsight discussed in Chapter 3 and hemispatial neglect described earlier in this chapter).

There is also some evidence that attention may increase the synchrony of neural firing in the cortical networks processing sensations that are the focus of attention (Fries et al., 2001). Could it be that the tie that perceptually binds sensed features is time-based? Might neurons that fire together bind perceptual features together?

One of the first discoveries of attention-related neural synchrony came from measuring electroencephalograms (EEGs) as people performed oddball tasks. Because stimuli are repeatedly presented during oddball tasks, it's possible to average neural activity across presentations to reveal neural responses that are consistently evoked by the oddball stimulus. Researchers found that the perception of attended stimuli was associated with a large change in cortical activity around 300 milliseconds after a target appeared (**Figure 4.27**). Such large changes only occur when many neurons fire in synchrony.

The size of this change in distributed neural activity, called the P300, depends on how much attention is engaged. The less attention, the smaller the P300. Note that the P300 happens relatively late in the perceptual process—you can recognize a face in less than 200 milliseconds and simpler stimuli in even less time. So, what's going on?

Some researchers think that when you detect and recognize an object or agent, your brain temporarily squashes (inhibits) the processing of everything other than that object and that the P300 is caused by this widespread inhibition of neural activity (Wood et al., 1980). The process would be like a faster version of love at first sight, as depicted in cartoons, where a soulmate captures one's complete attention and everything else becomes hazy. The P300, then, would be a sign that your brain automatically shut out everything else immediately after detecting a target.

Further evidence that attentional processes normally include a temporary shutdown comes from a phenomenon called attentional blink. **Attentional blink** occurs when a person fails to detect a salient target object that occurs between 200 and 500 milliseconds after a target was just detected (Shapiro et al., 1997). Experts at playing action video games show less of an attentional blink than non-gamers (Wong & Chang, 2018), leading some researchers to suggest that playing fast action video games may enhance attentional processes (Green & Bavelier, 2003). Don't be surprised if you start seeing this claim in commercials for new video games!

You might have guessed that synchronized neural responses would function to enhance object recognition rather than to inhibit the processing of unattended percepts. In the dichotic listening task, for example, attention is often described as highlighting speech coming into one ear, while speech at the other ear is ignored. But this may be the opposite of what happens in the brain.

It's possible that the cognitive part of dichotic listening involves suppressing percepts triggered by stimuli from the unattended ear. This interpretation doesn't really jibe with feature integration theory, however, which suggests that attention serves mainly to bind detected features together.

Given that attentional networks are so task-specific and spread out across the cortex, it's not obvious how they might bind features. However, the synchronous firing of a sparse population of neurons might amplify their effect on other neurons, even if those neurons are spread out all over the brain (**Figure 4.28**). Some researchers have found evidence that attention to visual targets increases

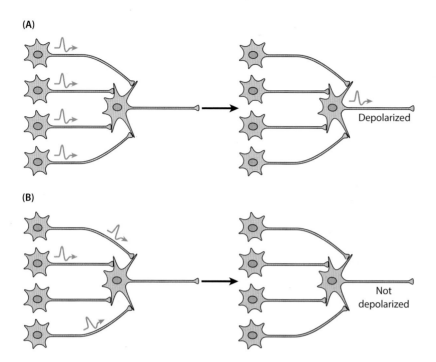

FIGURE 4.28. The power of synchrony. Neurons that fire at the same time (A) have a greater effect on other neurons than if their firing is uncoordinated (B). When incoming action potentials arrive together, they are more likely to depolarize the target neuron, leading it to produce an action potential. Attentional mechanisms can amplify the effects of a neural ensemble by increasing their synchrony. (A, B after Eagleman & Downar, 2016)

synchronous firing in visual pathways, as well as in frontal and parietal regions (Friese et al., 2016). So, attention might also enhance the perception of detected objects by increasing the odds that feature-detecting neurons fire simultaneously.

The attentional spotlight model assumes that attention doesn't so much change what is perceived as it amplifies sensory patterns to make percepts clearer or stronger. If you think of object perception and recognition as a process of detecting features or screaming demons, then you might think of attention as a mechanism that increases the sensitivity of the detectors or hands out megaphones to some demons.

Researchers who have recorded feature-selective neurons in animals performing orienting tasks where the feature is or isn't the focus of attention have found that attention does seem to amp up the responsiveness of those neurons to the target feature, but not to other features (Moran & Desimone, 1985). Some experiments show that weak stimuli, which wouldn't usually make a neuron fire, may be sufficient when those stimuli are the focus of attention (Reynolds & Chelazzi, 2004), consistent with the kind of highlighting proposed by the attentional spotlight model.

Scalp recordings of EEG signals show that large populations of cortical neurons are affected by attentional processes, but the recordings don't reveal much about what is happening in specific populations of neurons in the brain regions that contribute most to object perception and recognition. To observe such population activity, you need to record from multiple individual neurons (neural ensembles) at the same time.

Recording studies in monkeys show that attention not only affects firing in neurons that are detecting target features but also affects the firing of neurons that are not detecting anything (Cohen & Maunsell, 2009). In fact, the biggest attentional effects on firing were seen in ensembles of neurons that were not selective for target features—neural activity that would generally be regarded as noise.

The attentional control of background activity in the brain may be as important for enhancing perception as spotlighting a focal object or actor. Studying the brains of attenders makes it clear that many parallel processes are contributing to perceptual experiences that may not be apparent from either the subjective perspective of the attender or from experimental observations of their behavior.

SIGHT BITES

 Networks of face-selective neurons rapidly respond to faces, as well as other highly familiar, complex visual patterns.

 Models of face recognition use multiple stages of feature-selective nodes or specialized modules to explain how face recognition works.

 Attention changes activity in networks of cortical regions, the locations of which depend on the task and sensory modality.

 Attention-related changes in activity may affect perception by increasing neural synchrony, enhancing responses to attended stimuli, or inhibiting responses to nontargets.

APPLIED PERSPECTIVES

SNEAK PEEK: Your ability to attend to multiple tasks at the same time (or not) may not be what you think it is, and the ways that you currently perceive the world are not the only options.

Chapter 1 introduced you to highly superior autobiographical memory (HSAM), an ability possessed by a rare few who can report vivid details about relatively mundane events that they have experienced throughout their lives. There's a similarly impressive group of perceptual savants known as super-recognizers. Super-recognizers are people who are capable of recognizing the faces of many different individuals that they have only seen briefly once before (Russell et al., 2009). These are the kind of people you would probably want to have screening airports for terrorists.

Many people think that they are like super-recognizers, but they typically overestimate their face recognition abilities, especially for unfamiliar faces. Even people whose jobs require real-time face matching, like passport agents, are only about 70% accurate at catching mismatching faces (Papesh, 2018). So, if you have ever started talking with a "stranger" as if you knew them, you're not alone. If not, then maybe you are a super-recognizer!

People (and other animals) experience the world in unique ways that can be difficult to detect from their behavior or self-reports. Some people live their whole lives without realizing they are colorblind or blind in one eye. Most people believe that they perceive more of what's happening in the world than they really do and that how they perceive the world is the norm.

Overconfidence in one's perceptual and attentional abilities can cause significant problems, especially in situations where mismatches can kill (think texting drivers). New technologies, in particular, rarely account for the cognitive consequences of natural limits on perception or attention and could potentially derail cognitive processes in many users.

Media Multitasking

If there is one property of attention that psychologists agree on, it's that there is a limit on how many things one can attend to simultaneously. Cognitive psychologists might also agree that many people ignore this fact in their daily lives by taking on more tasks than their brain is built to handle.

College students, in particular, are notorious for **media multitasking**—using multiple information sources in parallel—both inside and outside of class (**Figure 4.29**). This includes activities like monitoring multiple windows on a laptop or scanning tweets while listening to a lecture. Multitasking in this way obviously depends on a person's ability to rapidly switch between tasks and/or divide their attention between tasks, which you might guess places high demands on attentional resources.

Recognizing different types of perceptual patterns may also be challenging when one is attempting to simultaneously monitor text on a phone, the speech patterns of a professor's lecture, and details of figures being projected on a large screen.

FIGURE 4.29. Media multitasking. Splitting your attention across multiple tasks while studying may guarantee that you are less bored, but it can also defeat the purpose of studying. But does media multitasking degrade your attention? Or does having attentional deficits or high impulsivity increase your desire to media multitask? (Estrada Anton via Shutterstock)

Heavy Media Multitasking

Initial comparisons between students who self-identify as heavy media multitaskers and students who multitask less suggested that students who frequently attempt to monitor multiple information sources tend to be more distracted by irrelevant stimuli and are in some cases less able to effectively switch between tasks (Ophir et al., 2009). More recent research found, however, that the relationship between media multitasking and distractibility is relatively weak or nonexistent (Wiradhany et al., 2020).

There is a subset of "supertasker" students who are able to perform multiple tasks in parallel without paying a price, but they are the exception. Additionally, there are some tasks where heavy media multitaskers actually perform better at task switching than other students (Alzahabi & Becker, 2013). Modern neuroimaging research looking at differences between the brain structure in heavy media multitaskers and other students found that heavy media use was associated with less gray matter (neural and glial cells) in the cortex (Loh & Kanai, 2014). It's not known whether these differences mean that people with certain brain features might be more likely to try to monitor multiple information sources or if doing this daily might somehow affect the structural features of students' brains.

Other research on the brains of people who practice Zen meditation (which could be viewed as the opposite of heavy media multitasking) has found that meditators don't show typical age-related losses in gray matter in the cortex. Research showed that meditators are also more likely to preserve attentional capacities (Pagnoni & Cekic, 2007), which is consistent with the idea that attentional practices may affect brain structure and function.

Multitasking Capacity

If attentional resources are limited, and you are trying to do multiple things at once, then it's not too surprising that you might have more problems than if you are only doing one thing at a time. But why might constant multitasking make you more distractible?

Think back to what attentional processes do to your brain. When you focus on certain percepts, you are not just enhancing responses to those objects and agents, you are also inhibiting responses to other possible objects. These inhibitory processes affect more neurons than those that are enhanced by attention.

Now, consider that when you are continuously switching between tasks, whole populations of neurons that were just being suppressed will need to come back online. To use a sports analogy, it's like repeatedly putting a player on the bench, and then back into the game, and then back on the bench, every minute or so for the whole game.

Such alternation between neural inhibition and excitation may lead to brain states that are difficult to keep stable (like rocking a boat). In contrast, meditation practices, which tend to keep a person's brain in a sustained, stable state, may make it easier for a person to voluntarily sustain attention in the face of external distractions.

Heavy media multitasking is positively correlated with students' assessments of how good a multitasker they are. However, in actual tests of multitasking, the students that media multitask the most are the worst at multitasking—there is actually a negative correlation.

It seems that part of what drives heavy media multitasking is an aversion to boredom rather than any talent at dividing attention. Metacognitive failures like this are not a sign of arrogance or cluelessness. They are, rather, typical of cognitive self-assessments (see Chapter 11). You could think of it as a kind of inattentional blindness in that the kinds of failures that media multitasking promote are much less salient than the rewards of keeping socially connected and being entertained.

Learning while Multitasking

Most college students report using electronic devices while in class or while studying. What sort of effect do you think this might have on students' learning and grades?

In terms of class performance, heavy media multitasking in classes is associated with lower grades (surprise). Interestingly, this is true even when the tasks being performed in parallel by students are all related to course content (van der Schuur et al., 2015), raising questions about whether high-tech classrooms may in some cases be counterproductive.

Experimental studies of learning and memory capacities in heavy media multitaskers suggest that, even in laboratory tasks that do not directly engage attentional processes, multitaskers may learn more slowly than other students (Edwards & Shin, 2017). Part of the problem seems to be that they are more likely to lose interest in the tasks more quickly (Ralph et al., 2014), suggesting that a reduced attention span might be either a consequence or cause of heavy media multitasking.

As mentioned earlier, some studies show that avid action video game players have a reduced attentional blink. Do you think that spending lots of time playing such games might counteract any attentional deficits caused by media multitasking?

It turns out that action video game playing doesn't affect all attentional processes equally (Cardoso-Leite & Bavelier, 2014). Experts at such games aren't any better than nonexperts at ignoring distracting stimuli. Given that heavy media multitaskers seem to be especially prone to distraction, it's unlikely that playing lots of action video games is going to fix the problem.

On the other hand, students that were trained in meditation practices (focusing on their breathing), showed improvements in sustained visual attention and perception (MacLean et al., 2010), so there probably are activities other than playing video games that can help students be less distractible.

You might be wondering why monitoring multiple media streams in parallel would be problematic, given that human brains seem to be designed for parallel processing. After all, a basic premise of modern perceptual theories is that sensory pathways are structured to sort sensory patterns in parallel and then choose subsets of those patterns to generate percepts of ongoing events. So, why can't you do this with multiple screens or parts of screens?

In part, the problem may come from the fact that much of what you do is driven by your goals. Implementing goals seems to be the opposite of perception in that a general goal gets broken down into increasingly detailed action sequences necessary to achieve the goal (**Figure 4.30**). If media multitasking involves trying to achieve multiple goals simultaneously, then any benefits you might gain from the parallel processing of sensations are probably offset by the "bottleneck" of goal execution.

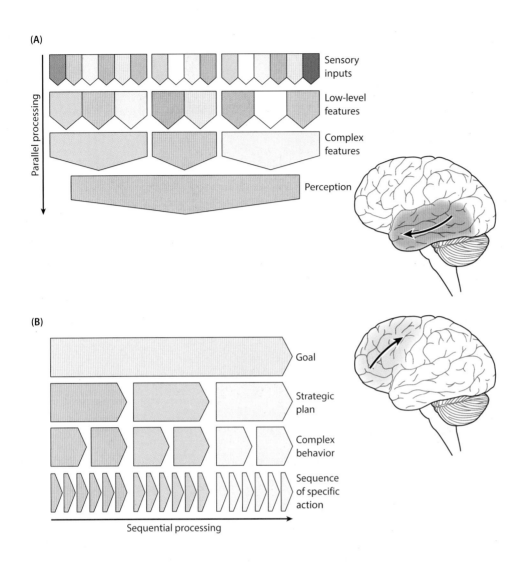

FIGURE 4.30. Parallel brain, serial processing. (A) Cortical processing in sensory pathways that drive perception is often viewed as a bottom-up process in which simpler features are analyzed in parallel before being joined together. For example, perception of a word occurs when neurons in the temporal lobe respond to sensory inputs that are combined over time as low-level auditory features and grouped based on familiar combinations of those complex speech features. (B) Voluntary control of a goal, however, seems to be more top-down in that a unified goal (arising from activity in frontal circuits) needs to be broken down into a sequence of actions that need to be completed to achieve the goal (a strategic plan) This strategic plan is coordinated across multiple body parts (producing complex behavior) through fine motor control leading to a specific sequence of movements. Multitasking involves multi-goals, so parallel pathways in your brain don't really make multitasking easier. (A, B after Eagleman & Downar, 2016)

Learning to See and Hear

In most organisms, the development of perception, attention, and object recognition abilities follows a predictable trajectory. For instance, a person's visual acuity may increase in the initial months after they are born and then later degrade until the person is forced to use lenses to recognize faces and objects clearly. The apparent inevitability of perceptual abilities tends to hide the role of learning in shaping how you perceive the world. Studies of kitten vision in the sixties revealed, however, that it's relatively easy to screw up perceptual development when one's sensory experiences aren't the norm (Hubel & Wiesel, 1979).

Sensitive Periods for Perceptual Development

Researchers found that temporarily blocking vision in one of a kitten's eyes for a few months after birth could degrade vision in that eye for the rest of the cat's life, even though the treatment had no effect on later sensory reception by that eye. Follow-up experiments showed that kittens raised only seeing vertical lines lost the ability to see horizontal lines (Blakemore et al., 1978)! As Chapter 2 notes, many mammals, including humans, go through sensitive periods, during which it is critical that sensory pathways are activated in certain ways for perception to develop normally.

You might think that blocking a kitten's vision in experiments is (1) mean and (2) pointless, since similar circumstances rarely occur in the real world. But there is a condition in about 4% of humans called amblyopia in which abnormal visual sensations transduced by one eye can degrade overall vision permanently.

You could have amblyopia and not even know it, since somewhat like colorblindness, the symptoms aren't always obvious, either externally or subjectively. Unlike colorblindness, however, the visual problems caused by amblyopia can be mostly avoided if it is detected early enough. That's because, as in the deprived kittens, the problems are caused by visual experiences within an early sensitive period (estimated to be between six weeks and six years after birth).

The best current treatment for amblyopia may surprise you. Rather than "fixing" the eye that's causing the problem, ophthalmologists instead block vision in the eye that's functioning normally by covering the eye several hours a day for two to three months (**Figure 4.31**).

In the case of amblyopia, sensory deprivation can lead to perceptual rehabilitation. The knowledge gained from studies of kittens has helped researchers understand why (and when) this nonintuitive treatment works.

Sensitive periods don't just affect how visual perception develops, they also affect how and what you hear. The effects are most obvious in speech perception. Before you were a one-year-old, you were able to perceive differences between most of the speech sounds produced in all the languages of the world (Kuhl, 2004). That includes about 600 consonants and 200 vowels (Chapter 12 describes how language learning progresses in greater detail).

By the time you were two, you had pretty much lost the ability to recognize any speech sounds apart from those that people in your family were frequently using. Assuming your first language is English, your brain likely keyed in on about forty distinct **phonemes**, which are variations in speech sounds that change the meanings of words. You learned to attend to and recognize this special subset of speech "objects" and to ignore other irrelevant (for you) speech variations.

As with amblyopia, early individual differences in auditory learning and perception can affect one's abilities throughout life—the best predictor of reading ability in school is phonemic awareness at an early age, shown by a child's ability to hear, recognize, and pull apart phonemes. In fact, some researchers believe that abnormal sensory experiences early in life contribute to several common developmental disorders that interfere with language skills and academic progress (Tallal & Gaab, 2006), and that treatments designed to counteract perceptual deficits can go a long way toward improving children's cognitive potential and performance (Merzenich et al., 1996).

Perceptual Upgrades

Increased recognition that people can overcome sensory deficits that they inherited or acquired has led to new technologies that can partially simulate natural sensations. The most successful of

FIGURE 4.31. Kitten-provided vision care. Children's early visual experiences can dramatically affect how they perceive the world for the rest of their lives. Understanding how early experiences shape perception can help people treat problems before they become problems. Treatments for amblyopia, such as patching the unaffected eye, take advantage of sensitive periods to redirect developmental trajectories. (MEDITERRANEAN)

these efforts so far are cochlear implants, electronic devices that stimulate the inner ear whenever sounds occur. Cochlear implants are most effective went they are installed at early ages. Children with cochlear implants gradually increase their ability to perceive sound variations over years (Fu & Galvin, 2007), highlighting the role that experience has on perception and the fact that listening requires skill.

Sound for someone hearing with a cochlear input is not the same as sound for someone who has never been deaf. If you replaced the typical person's auditory sensations with the sounds produced by a cochlear implant, the person would initially be unable to recognize any speech and that person's favorite music would sound distinctly unmusical. Eventually, the person would be able to recognize speech, but their musical experience would never be what it was.

Several companies are working toward developing retinal implants, but this has proven to be much trickier than transducing sounds through electrical stimulation (**Figure 4.32**). Technologies are also being developed that substitute touch sensors for visual stimuli, called sensory substitution. Can you imagine what it would be like to see with your tongue? The technology already exists to make this happen!

Sensory substitution shows just how flexible human perceptual systems are at processing sensory patterns. Researchers found that ferrets that had their visual pathways rerouted to the auditory cortex were still able to discriminate between images (Sharma et al., 2000). Not only can perceptual systems handle sensory patterns from other modalities but they also can handle novel patterns from "new" senses.

As discussed earlier in this chapter, some blind children teach themselves to echolocate by clicking their tongues—a perceptual ability not naturally used by humans. Might it be possible to develop technologies that would provide human echolocators with an even greater capacity to resolve and interpret echoes?

Studies with rats have shown that they quickly adapt to receiving sensations from implanted infrared sensors, enabling them to use infrared light to navigate (Thomson et al., 2017). Biohackers are already attempting to upgrade themselves to match the acquired infravision capabilities of rats. If rats can extend their visible spectrum, then it seems likely that humans might be able to extend their hearing to new sound frequencies, given the right kinds of implants.

It's easy to imagine how sensitive periods might affect perceptual development in babies. But you're no baby, so probably you are stuck with whatever perception you've got, right? Wrong. Researchers once thought that sensitive periods had an irrevocable expiration date after which brains were basically done developing. Turns out that this is just the default trajectory. It's now known that there are several ways of knocking your brain back into sensitive period mode (Hooks & Chen, 2007). This means that, in principle, you could radically change the way you feel, hear, and see the

FIGURE 4.32. New visions.
(A) Retinal implants can stimulate neurons directly to simulate transduction by the retina; however, the implants are unable to achieve the same resolution. (B) Transforming images into electrical signals makes it possible for blind people to "see" with their tongues. The sensations are something like having tiny, synchronized swimmers dance on your tongue while using tasers set to "mild" on it. What other kinds of sensory substitution do you think might work well as a way of perceiving light patterns? (A Equinox Graphics/Science Source, B from *BrainPort Vision Pro* © 2022 Wicab, Inc. WI, USA. All Rights Reserved)

(A)

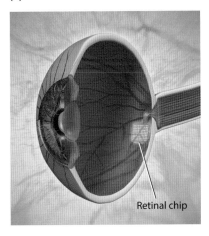

Retinal chip

(B)

world. Maybe you could even change your brain in ways that would let you perceive numbers like Daniel Tammet, although no one has a clue how you might go about doing that yet.

CLOSURE

Perceptual experiences are the foundation of all cognizing. They are the foundation of you. Some psychologists draw a distinction between perception and cognition because perception seems fundamentally different from thinking. Seeing a friend seems automatic and effortless, while thinking about what makes someone qualify as a friend seems more involved and somehow separate from any physical reality. Knowing that two gray diamonds like those in Figure 4.8 are identical doesn't stop you from seeing them as different shades—the seeing part of your mind doesn't seem to care what you know.

From this perspective, both perception and sensation are simply the outputs of modules that "higher-level" cognitive processes can consider, and top-down perceptual processes don't really exist (Firestone & Scholl, 2016). This interpretation is a revival of Descartes' model of mind described in Chapter 1, where "mind" means thought and everything else is biological machinery.

Now that you know a bit more about how attention and object recognition work, you can better appreciate that cognition-free perception is a rarity. How you cognize is a function of your past experiences and your current interests. Although it's true that you can't always control what you perceive or when you will or won't see a cow, you can be sure that when you do see cows, it's because you are attending to their recognizable cowness.

Attentional processes, in particular, seem to guide perception at every stage, from selecting where your eyes should fixate to controlling how your different cortical regions should coordinate their activity as you process objects within a scene. Attention and perception are so intertwined as to be almost inseparable.

Human echolocation is a good example of this connection between attention and perception. Most humans who aren't deaf can (in principle) hear the echoes that a blind child makes by clicking his tongue as he walks around a room or down the road—blind children do not have magical ears. However, most people do not hear these echoes, and even if they do detect them, they almost certainly do not perceive them as obstacles to avoid running into.

Echolocating children both hear and recognize these self-generated echoes because they pay attention to them. They are interested in being able to flexibly operate in the world and have gradually developed the ability to actively perceive the location of objects without needing to touch or see them. Daniel Tammet may have similarly learned to calculate products using his synesthetic multimodal percepts of numbers because of his interests in mathematics. He certainly was not born knowing what Arabic numerals are.

Perceptual awareness is one of the most compelling mental states you'll ever experience. The undeniable subjective qualities of perception are why "seeing is believing." What better evidence is there that you are reading right now than your own percepts of what's happening?

Psychologists are just beginning to understand the mechanisms that shape perception and limit attention, so there are likely many surprises yet to be discovered. New and improved sensory modalities and attentional control mechanisms may be just around the corner.

COGNITIVE LINGO

absolute threshold	attention span	biological motion
active perception	attentional blink	bottom-up processing
affordance	attentional reweighting	change blindness
attention deficit hyperactivity disorder (ADHD)	auditory scene analysis	cocktail party effect
	auditory stream	conjunction search
attention	binocular cue	constructivism

covert spatial attention

deep net

dichotic listening task

divided attention

duplex theory of sound localization

early-selection model

face-selective brain region

feature analysis model

feature-based attention

feature integration theory

feature

fusiform face area

Gestaltism

hemispatial neglect

illusory conjunction

illusory contour

inattentional blindness

just noticeable difference (JND)

late-selection model

McGurk effect

media multitasking

mental representation

motor theory of speech perception

multimodal

multiple-object tracking

object-based attention

pattern recognition

percepts

perceptual awareness

perceptual binding

perceptual constancy

perceptual representation

phoneme

point-light display

psychophysical method

recognition

recognition-by-components theory

response

saliency map

selective attention

sensorimotor stage

sensory cue

shape constancy

signal detection theory

size constancy

sparse representation

spatial attention

stimuli

Stroop effect

structure-from-motion

synesthesia

template theory

visual search

Weber's Law

word superiority effect

CHAPTER SUMMARY

Recognizing Objects, Agents, and Events

Percepts combine current sensations with past experiences to transform complex patterns into a coherent mental state. Psychophysical methods can reveal what perceivers detect and what they can tell apart. Theories of recognition emphasize pattern matching and feature detection.

Attention

How you recognize and label objects and events can dramatically affect how your attention is distributed across scenes. Voluntary attention can determine what you perceive as well as your capacity to keep track of multiple objects or events at the same time.

Brain Substrates

Some cortical regions show selective activity in response to complex images like faces, but evidence for specialized modules for perceiving certain kinds of objects is lacking. Attention seems to change cortical activity to both attended and ignored objects in multiple ways.

Applied Perspectives

Your capacity to divide your attention across multiple tasks may be less than it seems and attempting to divide your attention can make it harder to learn. How you perceive different events can vary a lot depending on how you develop during sensitive periods.

REVIEW EXERCISES

Recognizing Objects, Agents, and Events

- What is Weber's Law and how is it relevant to understanding perception?
- What are some of the key features of Gestaltism that are thought to affect visual recognition of shapes?
- What have studies of biological motion revealed about perceptual representations and processes of recognition?

Attention

- In what ways does selective attention differ from divided attention?
- How might one examine the role of covert spatial attention in a person's ability to play action video games?

Brain Substrates

- Why is the fusiform face area thought to be specialized for processing faces?
- What does the phenomenon of attentional blink suggest about how attention works?

Applied Perspectives

- Which theory of attention best explains the problems faced by people who are heavy media multitaskers?
- How has an understanding of sensitive periods been used to improve the perceptual processes of children?

CRITICAL THINKING QUESTIONS

1. Children are using electronic media at younger and younger ages. There are also increasing numbers of children being diagnosed with attention deficit hyperactivity disorder. How might you test the hypothesis that early exposure to electronics increases attention deficits in children?

2. When you were in the womb, you were repeatedly exposed to many sensations that you never experience now. How might you test whether you can still recognize sensory patterns from your in-womb experiences? Which of your sensory systems do you think would be most likely to have been shaped by those early experiences?

3. If playing action video games can increase some visual attentional capacities, then it seems likely that other things that people do for entertainment might also have similar effects. What sorts of activities might enhance auditory attention or tactile attention? How could you test for such effects?

4. Some patients with damage to part of their cortex lose the ability to recognize familiar voices. Such effects have often been interpreted as evidence that there is a specific module that is specialized for voice recognition. What other explanations can you come up with for why damage to a brain region might disrupt voice recognition but not word recognition?

5. Reports of synesthesia were once viewed skeptically because they were based on people's self-reports of their perceptual experiences. How might neural recordings be used to support such personal reports? Can you think of ways to test experimentally whether any nonhumans are synesthetes?

5 Categorization and Discrimination

mr-fox

Dr. Oliver Sacks led his patient, Dr. P, into his office. Dr. P's wife was concerned about her husband's vision, even though multiple ophthalmologists had assured her that his eyes were fine. The latest ophthalmologist had referred the patient to Dr. Sacks, who agreed to meet with the couple despite not being a vision expert.

After chatting with the couple, Dr. Sacks began running Dr. P through various tests. Dr. P engaged in conversation, showing no signs of confusion, dementia, or visual problems. On a hunch, Dr. Sacks asked Dr. P to describe the cover of a *National Geographic* magazine that showed a series of sand dunes. Dr. P described a river with a guesthouse nearby where people were dining. Dr. P seemed to think he had passed all of the tests and began preparing to leave. He reached out, grabbed his wife's head, and attempted to put her head on his own. He had mistaken his wife's head for his hat!

Later, Dr. Sacks visited Dr. P at his home to test Dr. P's ability to name different objects. Dr. P could name a cube and even a dodecahedron (a three-dimensional shape with twelve plane faces). He could name all the cards in a deck, including the joker, and recognized a cartoon picture of a cigar. Dr. P ran into problems describing scenes on a television, failing to identify what was happening, or even the sex of any character. He also couldn't identify his family members in photos. When shown a rose, Dr. P described it as "a convoluted red form with a linear green attachment" (Sacks, 1970, p. 12). When told to smell it, however, he immediately identified it as a rose. He described a glove as "a continuous surface infolded on itself," with "five outpouchings." When asked what it was, he suggested that it might be used as a container.

Dr. Sacks later learned that Dr. P's condition, called associative agnosia, had been described in several other people. In each case, the individual was able to see and describe detailed features of objects, and even point to named objects, but lacked the ability to name certain objects. In some cases, a person with associative agnosia only showed deficits for a specific subset of objects (Farah, 2004;

FIGURE 5.1. Surreal "faces." Artistic imagery can produce feelings of familiarity and recognition of describable parts (eyes, noses, and mouths) without giving a strong sense of how one might label or classify what is being seen, an experience that may be similar in some respects to the world experienced by people with associative agnosia. (© Successió Miró / Artists Rights Society (ARS), New York / ADAGP, Paris 2023; Philadelphia Museum of Art, Pennsylvania, PA, USA/The Louis E. Stern Collection, 1963/Bridgeman Images)

Warrington & Shallice, 1984). For instance, people have lost the ability to name pictures of living things but retained the ability to name household objects (Satori & Job, 1988). How is it that a person could lose the ability to recognize roosters but still be able to pick out toasters? How could a husband mistake his wife's head for a hat when his vision is unimpaired?

For most people, the act of recognizing, naming, and using things is so natural that it's hard to imagine what life would be like without this ability. Labeling familiar objects is one instance of **categorizing**, a cognitive act that involves sorting entities in the world. When people name objects, they are grouping their current percepts with similar percepts they have experienced in the past. Categorizing and naming require not only an ability to detect similarities but also the ability to discriminate. Without **discrimination**—the ability to distinguish percepts—categorization would be impossible (**Figure 5.1**). Understanding how and why people categorize their experiences has challenged both philosophers and psychologists for centuries. By the end of this chapter, you should be able to discriminate between several different kinds of categorization and appreciate why researchers have spent so much time trying to figure out how people categorize.

BEHAVIORAL PROCESSES

When Dr. P saw and described a rose, he was aware of the flower as a visual object, distinct from other objects in the room. The fact that he could name the flower once he smelled it shows that he also knew about roses and their qualities. Dr. P knew what a rose was and what roses were like, but he failed to link what he saw with what he knew. He had a concept of "rose," although for him the concept was not visually accessible.

A **category** is a set of things or events that share at least one characteristic. A **concept** is a mental representation that summarizes or tags percepts, categories, or relationships between them— basically, things you know about. Just as perception is what happens when you hear, see, and taste, conception is what happens when you consider, evaluate, and understand. When you cognize, you become aware that things are happening. When you "re"cognize, you perceive that something happening now has happened before. And, when you conceptualize, you identify and interpret things you are recognizing based on your understanding of how the world works. Categories and concepts enable you to organize everything you experience.

The Greek philosopher Plato, in his "Allegory of the Cave," describes prisoners in a cave who see only shadows cast on a wall from objects passing in front of a fire but never directly perceive the objects. The prisoners can categorize the images they see, but their concepts of what is going on may be far from the truth. For Plato, the real world consists of universal concepts or *Forms*, and the perceived, recognized, and categorized world provides only hints at reality.

A universal concept of doughnuts, for example, is not the shape of a doughnut that you have in your mouth; instead, "doughnutness" encompasses every doughnut that has ever existed or that ever will exist. Although Plato's claim that Forms are more real than the things you experience may seem a bit mystical, his proposal that concepts and categories are radically different kinds of things continues to influence debates about what happens when people categorize and conceptualize.

Kinds of Categories and Concepts

SNEAK PEEK: All categories are defined based on similarities between items within the categories. Those similarities can be physical, functional, or abstract. Distinctions between categories and concepts often relate to how items may be mentally compared.

A first step toward understanding how people categorize is to identify what they categorize. In most psychological studies of categorization, people are typically categorizing images, usually images of objects. You can view object categorization as a kind of object recognition (Goldstone et al., 2017). You see a doughnut, recognize it, and likely categorize it as "something sweet." You don't just see the doughnut—you see it as food.

Similar processes kick in if you hear someone speaking. When you hear someone's voice, you may recognize it, know who the speaker is, and understand what they are saying. In the case of speech, your ability to categorize sounds affects what you hear. For instance, if you grew up in Japan, you might categorize "r" and "l" sounds as falling within a single auditory category, because this distinction is not relevant to understanding Japanese speech. As a result, Japanese speakers often hear English syllables such as "la" and "ra" as being the same, and they find it very difficult to distinguish between them (Lively et al., 1993).

Categorizing involves more than just perceiving and recognizing, however. The kinds of concepts that Plato wrote about include things that can't be directly observed. The following sections describe some of the kinds of categories and concepts studied by cognitive psychologists.

Perceptual Categories

You continuously and automatically categorize sounds when listening to speech, just as you automatically categorize objects when looking at scenes. Categorization of this sort depends on **perceptual similarity**, which is the perceived overlap between two experiences.

Family Resemblance

Categories composed of perceptually similar items, or **perceptual categories**, are some of the first categories that infants use to organize their experiences. Two experiences with high perceptual similarity usually have many qualities in common. Those qualities can be thought of as features such as the presence or absence of hair, dimensions such as differences in size or color, or functions—what something does.

Perceptually similar objects and events share features and vary along similar dimensions. Many of the perceptual qualities that items within a category share are associated with specific labels, but it is also possible to create perceptual categories that vary in perceptual similarity, even when those categories do not correspond to differences in features or dimensions that can be easily labeled (**Figure 5.2**).

When things within a category are perceptually similar, they are said to share a **family resemblance** (Wittgenstein, 1953). Siblings tend to appear more similar than random non-siblings, and doughnuts tend to look, taste, and smell more like each other than they do non-doughnuts.

FIGURE 5.2. Sets of faces that vary along continuous, nameless perceptual dimensions. Faces numbered 1 through 4 were morphed to create sets of faces varying in perceptual similarity that could form the basis of one or more perceptual categories. Perceptual similarities between these images are like those caused by genetic overlap between family members, and items with categories that are perceptually similar are often described as showing family resemblances. (From Landy & Goldstone, 2005)

Dimension A

1

2

3

Dimension B

4

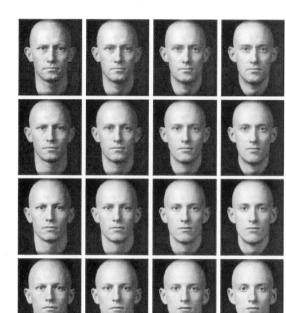

Naturalistic Categories

As noted earlier, some individuals with brain damage selectively lose the ability to categorize certain items, including living things. Living things share a number of qualities that nonliving things lack. So you might think that such people simply lost the ability to perceive certain visual features. But people like Dr. P are able to accurately describe objects they can't name. What stops them from using those perceived details to recognize and name objects?

Problems categorizing certain objects may arise because some things are just harder to categorize. When individuals lose the ability to perceptually categorize objects, more difficult categorization tasks deteriorate first and more noticeably. Perceptually similar objects (like living things) are typically harder to sort into different categories than are less similar items (like nonliving things). This is not just because people spend a lot of time indoors where they encounter relatively few living things because monkeys show the same pattern (Gaffan & Heywood, 1993). Both living and nonliving things can show family resemblances, but the perceptual similarities across nonliving things are more like those between distant cousins.

Psychologists consider categories that most adults use to be "naturalistic," regardless of whether the items within those categories occur in nature. The fact that you use many different naturalistic categories daily in ways that seem effortless does not mean, however, that all categories are equally easy to use. Many experimental studies of categorization focus on artificial categories (**Figure 5.3**) that vary in simpler ways than most naturalistic categories, making it easier to figure out the factors that can make categorization easier or harder.

Perfect Examples

While all items that fall within a category might qualify as members of that category, it is rarely the case that all category members are created equal. For instance, you might have a type of person that

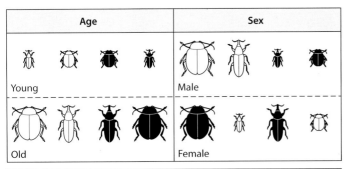

FIGURE 5.3. Six different ways of splitting eight objects into two categories. For each set of eight beetles, the top row shows one experimenter-defined category and the second row shows a second category. Categories that divide the beetles along a single dimension, such as size ("Age"), are easy to learn. Other ways of dividing up the beetles are typically harder to learn, even though all sets contain the same eight beetles, with the hardest categorization to learn being the one in which every feature matters ("Species"). (After Vigo et al., 2015)

you prefer dating, but it is unlikely that you'd be equally happy dating any person who fits that type. Nevertheless, over time your friends may start to recognize a pattern and be able to advise you about whether someone fits your type.

The best example or **prototype** for a category captures common qualities associated with many members of that category (Rosch & Mervis, 1975). The idea of prototypes is similar to Plato's proposed Forms. Your prototype of the category "roses" may consist of a flower having a certain shade of red, a certain shape, size, and smell, and so on. And yet, you may not have ever actually experienced a rose that possessed all of the features of this prototypical rose.

One way to think about category prototypes is as a sort of average of every example of a category that you have encountered. For example, Francis Galton, whom you learned about in Chapter 2, famously attempted to create prototypical images for various categories of "criminals" by overlapping photographic images of multiple criminals of each type (**Figure 5.4**). He hypothesized that the tendency to engage in specific criminal actions was inherited, and since facial features were also inherited, they could potentially be used to identify likely criminals (there is no modern evidence supporting Galton's hypotheses).

Like the morphed faces in Figure 5.2, Galton's composite photos do not show images of any humans that ever existed; instead, they highlight facial features that were common across a sample of convicted criminals. Notably, these "prototypical criminals" are instantly recognizable as being both humans and adult men; they might even remind you of some people you know. Prototypes of categories are quickly identified as being members of that category, and in some cases are judged to be better examples of a category than the actual members of the category (Mervis & Rosch, 1981; Posner et al., 1967).

FIGURE 5.4. Prototypical faces of murderers created by Francis Galton. Each image shows multiple photos superimposed, emphasizing facial features shared by multiple criminals. Galton theorized that the more a person resembles photographic "averages" of criminals, the more likely they are to actually be a criminal. (PAUL D STEWART/SCIENCE PHOTO LIBRARY)

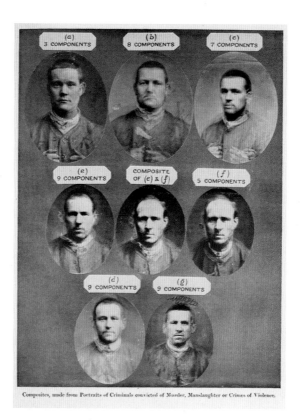

Perceptual tasks have been particularly important in experimental studies of categorization because the physical features of sensory stimuli can be controlled quite precisely and because animals can be tested using many of the same images and sounds used to test people.

Functional Categories

Perceptual categories are often viewed as a more primitive type of category than some other broader categories. Consider the following category: "things you can decorate walls with." This example is a functional category because it groups items together based on similarities in their function. Functional categories often include perceptually similar items; portraits are similar in shape, size, and color. But functional categories also may include perceptually dissimilar items—a preserved animal head is quite unlike a mirror.

Typicality and Equivalence Classes

A classic example of a functional categorization game is the game show called *Family Feud*. In this game, contestants attempt to reproduce popular answers given in response to somewhat random requests like "Name some things you might see hanging on a wall." In surveys, people typically give certain responses to such requests more often than others.

The goal of the game is to guess which answers people give most often. The fact that this game actually works shows that people often come up with similar category members when asked about a functional category. Psychologists have used this phenomenon to show that category members vary in their **typicality**—a measure of how likely people are to note an item as falling within a specific category (Collins & Qulillian, 1969; Rosch, 1975). "Clocks" might be a frequently mentioned wall decoration (having high typicality).

What members of the functional category "wall decorations" have in common is that their use is associated with a single specific outcome: dust collection. In this respect, all category members are equal, leading some researchers to refer to such functional categories as **equivalence classes** (Schusterman et al., 2000; Sidman, 1994). The key idea behind equivalence classes is that objects that are quite different can be categorized as being "the same thing" in some way. Skunks and deep holes

WEIRD, TRUE, FREAKY

The Uncanny Valley

Simulated humans, both digital and robotic, can be unnerving (see figure). Somewhat bizarrely, the capacity of a robot (a nonliving thing) to provoke discomfort increases as the robot becomes more similar to an actual human (a living thing), at least up to a certain point. The phenomenon was identified in the early seventies when it began to be referred to as the uncanny valley effect, but it has become an increasingly relevant issue with recent advances in robotics and computer-animated movies.

The "valley" refers to the dip in emotional reactions to simulated people that occurs just before the agents become highly perceptually similar to prototypical people (see graph). It's still a mystery why viewing humanoid images that are not typical might provoke shudders. There is some evidence that this effect also occurs for simulations of dogs (Yamada et al., 2013), but what other percepts might produce the effect is unclear. Interestingly, the uncanny valley effect also seems to be experienced by monkeys, who are frightened by knock-off Pixar animations of monkeys (Steckenfinger & Ghazanfar, 2009).

Researchers have attempted to identify the qualities of images, as well as the underlying cognitive mechanisms, that trigger the uncanny valley effect (Katsyri et al., 2015). Some researchers think that the effect relates to the image being miscategorized as that of a diseased or dead person, leading to involuntary reactions of disgust. While intuitively plausible, this explanation does not account for why the effect only happens for a small range of images near the boundary between living and nonliving.

Given that the uncanny valley effect is associated with category boundaries, some researchers have proposed that difficulties encountered while categorizing such images may contribute to the effect. Categorization difficulty is correlated with negative reactions when evaluating images, and there is evidence that deviations from categorical norms can heighten the effect. Not all distortions in visual appearance generate the effect. It seems most likely to happen when certain facial features are inconsistent with

Robots with humanoid features exemplify the uncanny valley effect, according to some viewers. Can you think of other examples? (REUTERS/Alamy Stock Photo)

other features; for example, the eyes might be disproportionately large (Katsyri et al., 2015). Reactions to disproportionate compositions suggest that peoples' fascination with atypical humans, such as those once exhibited in "freak shows," may be a similar phenomenon.

The uncanny valley effect may be related to the feeling that a person has when "something is not quite right," which is usually triggered by subtle differences in an otherwise familiar scenario. In extreme cases, such feelings can be a component of obsessive-compulsive disorder (OCD). If patients with OCD are more prone to showing the uncanny valley effect, then screenings of movies like *The Polar Express* might one day prove useful for identifying people at risk for developing OCD.

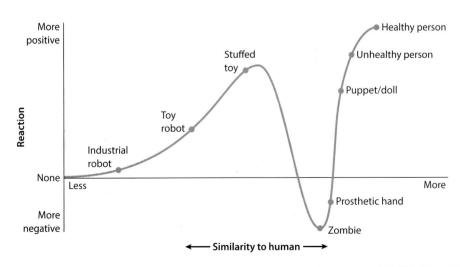

People often show negative emotional reactions to images that are perceptually similar to a typical person (zombie and prosthetic hand) but not quite the same. (After Mori, 1970 as cited in Mathur et al., 2020)

FIGURE 5.5. Items in the functional category "wall decorations." Some wall decorations are perceptually similar, but they need not be to qualify as wall decorations. How they are used is more important than how they look.

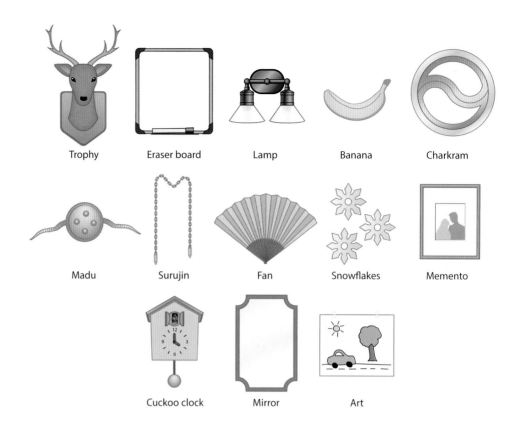

are equivalent in that they are both things you would not want to run into. Written words are equivalent to the spoken version of those words in that each conveys the same meaning.

It is tricky to study equivalence classes in humans because every individual may have somewhat different categories. For example, only people who have encountered a madu are likely to include it in a list of wall decorations. You would have to learn what a madu is to add it to your existing equivalence class of things people hang on walls (**Figure 5.5**).

Categorical Checklists

Let's say your goal is to determine whether someone qualifies as a celebrity. You might have a list of qualities that typify celebrities: have adoring fans, faces can be recognized by random people, likely to appear on a magazine cover. Using this kind of checklist you can sort out people that are celebrities.

In principle, you could use checklists to categorize lots of things. The more checks, the more likely an item qualifies as a member of a particular category. This approach also can be quite effective at ruling out large numbers of categories, which happens in the game *Twenty Questions*, where you try to identify what someone is thinking of by asking them questions with yes or no answers.

Functional categories depend more on past experiences than do perceptual categories. The more frequently you see (or read about) madus, the more likely it is that you will categorize madus as possible decorative devices. Similarly, the likelihood that you will classify someone as a celebrity depends on past episodes in which you heard those specific individuals mentioned or saw them in contexts where celebrities appear, such as in movies. The more major movies that feature Sherita Rankins, the more likely you are to consider her a celebrity. You collect more evidence, across multiple episodes, about how an agent or object should be categorized.

Exceptional Examples

In some cases, it might take many repetitions before an item makes it solidly into a category. You've probably encountered beans many times in your life, but you might not categorize them as fruits. If from now on, every time you see a bean you think, "I still can't believe beans are fruits," then eventually beans will become part of your fruit category, though you may always consider them a freak fruit. Importantly, every one of your past and future bean encounters can provide you with an additional exemplar of a bean-related experience.

Cognitive psychologists refer to a single piece of experienced evidence as an **exemplar**, a specific percept that falls into a particular category. If someone pokes you with a fork for ten minutes, that episode or person might become an exemplar that is part of your "people or situations to avoid" category. Now that you've seen a picture of a madu, your percept of the image gives you an exemplar that you can use to recognize and categorize madus when you see them in the future—your category of wall decorations has potentially expanded.

Abstract Concepts

Of all the categories and concepts that people use, the ones that seem to depend the least on percepts are typically held in the highest esteem. **Abstract concepts**, such as death, evil, life, love, and infinity seem to transcend specific sensations of objects and rise closest to the level of Plato's Forms. The term "abstract" often implies that the exemplars and categories associated with a concept are not limited to any particular sensory experience. For instance, the "sense of sameness" noted by William James as being the foundation of concepts can be triggered by odors, sights, sounds, or thoughts. In the case of categorization, abstractness implies that the criteria that identify category members can apply to many different kinds of items.

"…creatures extremely low in the intellectual scale may have conception. All that is required is that they should recognize the same experience again. A polyp would be a conceptual thinker if a feeling of 'Hollo! thingumbob again!' ever flitted through its mind. This sense of sameness is the very keel and backbone of our consciousness."
—James, 1890, p 462

Relational Categories

Abstract concepts are trickier to define in terms of shared features or dimensions. In part, this is because the "things" represented by an abstract concept are often relationships or comparisons between events rather than sensible properties of individual objects or agents. These kinds of abstract concepts are called **relational categories**. Relational categories tend to be dichotomous, meaning that items not in the category are members of an opposing category—think good and evil, dead or alive, symmetric or asymmetric, same or different.

Classifying pairs of objects as being the same might seem like a case of perceptual categorization, but what makes the task abstract is that *any* pair of objects can be classified as "same" or "different." Recent studies of young children's acquisition of symmetry concepts (recognizing that images can be split into equivalent parts) suggest that infants detect symmetry early in life but require more experience to be able to categorize images as symmetric (Hu & Zhang, 2019). Additionally, learning a general symmetry concept preceded the ability to classify more specific symmetrical relationships (**Figure 5.6**).

Relational categories can describe not only relationships between pairs of objects but also complex relationships between larger sets of items. For instance, you may have a category of "things you might do at a party" that includes activities such as eating food, talking to people, hitting donkeys filled with candy, and so on. This category could also be viewed as a functional category, but the fact that the common link between party activities is "having fun" (which is an abstract concept) combined with the fact that almost any activity might meet this criterion for some individuals (including getting into fights), moves this closer to the land of abstractness.

Who Categorizes?

In the last thirty years, many different species have shown the ability to categorize auditory, olfactory, and visual percepts (Smith et al., 2016). Most nonhuman animals do not classify objects or agents using words, but they can still treat different items as if they were equivalent.

Pigeons, for example, are able to sort images as being cats, cars, chairs, or flowers by pecking on specific keys associated with each category (Bhatt & Wasserman, 1989). These comparative findings, combined with evidence that newborns also show some capacity to perceptually sort images (Rakison & Poulin-Dubois, 2001), suggest that categorization abilities may make it possible for many organisms to flexibly organize ongoing experiences. Comparative and developmental

FIGURE 5.6. Varieties of symmetrical shapes. (A) In each set of four shapes, there is one shape that is not like the others in terms of its symmetry (indicated within ovals). Detecting the oddball in a set of translationally symmetric shapes is easier than detecting the oddball in a set of rotationally symmetric shapes. (B) Children gradually improve in their ability to detect symmetric oddballs from the age of four to six years old, with some types of symmetry being more obvious to them than others. (A, B after Hu & Zhang, 2019)

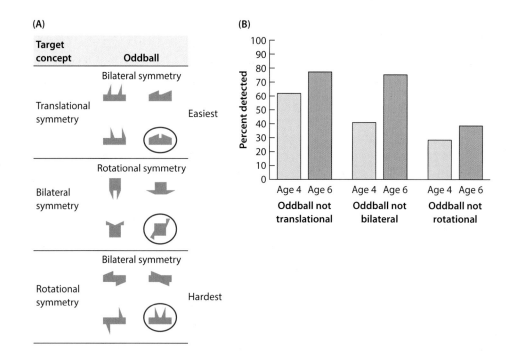

studies also show that although adults usually label categories, as well as the typical features and dimensions of items within a category, the ability to name items or their qualities is not a prerequisite for perceptual categorization.

The seeming sophistication of abstract concepts has led many researchers to claim that only humans can categorize objects or events in this way. This claim was weakened somewhat when researchers found that chimpanzees could classify pairs of objects as being the same or different and could even learn to classify pairs of such pairs as being the same or different (Premack, 1983). For instance, chimpanzees recognized that a pair of shoes was the same as a pair of bananas (they're both "twins") but different from an apple next to an orange. Other animals like birds and dolphins can also sort sets of objects (including ones they had never previously encountered) based on their sameness (Pepperberg, 2021).

Although nonhumans can learn relational categories, there are some differences in the ways that people use abstract categories that may depend more heavily on language skills (Penn & Povinelli, 2007). For example, the way that humans currently classify different cognitive processes seems to differ radically from the way that other species think about the minds of others.

SIGHT BITES

Members of a category that share a family resemblance are physically similar. Prototypes of perceptual categories are similar to most items in that category.

Members of functional categories can be physically similar, but they don't have to be. Every exemplar within a functional category can be different, as long it is associated in some way with other items in the category.

Abstract concepts, including relational categories, may include no physically similar members. They may instead capture relationships between groups of items.

Theories of Categorization

SNEAK PEEK: Cognitive psychologists are keenly interested in how people mentally represent and process concepts and categories. This has led to several competing models of how categorization works.

Given the many kinds of categories and concepts, you might expect that explanations for how people categorize and conceptualize would be equally diverse. There are many different proposals, but surprisingly, the differences between them relate more to the specific ways in which they describe mental representations of categories rather than to differences in the categories being represented.

Most theories focus on explaining how people assign items to categories, and most assume that when you categorize, you compare what you perceive to some internally stored standards. Current theories, often described using models (see Chapter 1), make varying claims about which standards you use when assigning items to categories and how you make comparisons. You can think of a model of categorization as a simplified theory of categorization—researchers often use models to try and predict how people will perform in specific categorization tasks.

Explaining Perceptual and Functional Categorization

There are currently three competing kinds of models that can predict many of the findings from past experimental studies of categorization: category-boundary models, exemplar models, and prototype models.

Category-Boundary Models

Category-boundary models of categorization suggest that what people compare when categorizing items is where each item falls relative to internally represented borders between categories. The category boundary is like a line in the sand that separates members of one category from those of other categories. In this model, how a person categorizes an item depends on the shape and orientation of the border between different categories (Ashby et al., 1998).

What makes this model unique is its emphasis on qualities that distinguish categories rather than on the similarities between items. As shown in **Figure 5.7**, category-boundary models explain categorization in terms of the locations of the "lines" that divide sets of items—the mentally represented dividing lines are what define different categories. So, although you can imagine that doughnuts might vary from super chocolatey to chocolate-free, there is some minimum level of

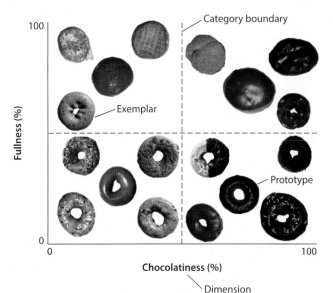

FIGURE 5.7. Features of different categorization models. Category-boundary models focus on how borders between categories (shown as dashed lines) are internally represented. The vertical line shows, for example, how chocolatey a doughnut needs to be to qualify as a member of the "chocolate doughnut" category. Exemplar models propose that current percepts are compared with many stored exemplars of past experiences (here, each doughnut photo serves as an exemplar), and prototype models suggest that current percepts are compared to a smaller number of representations that encapsulate the common features of most items in a category (the four central doughnuts in each quadrant show prototypical doughnuts from each category). Rule-based models focus more on representations of verbalizable dimensions. A rule for identifying a "filled doughnut" might be "doesn't have a hole." (Photos by Ava Brent)

chocolatiness required (the category boundary) before you will be likely to categorize a doughnut as "chocolate."

Category-boundary models predict that category members that are farther from a category boundary will be classified the quickest and most easily. The models explain why line drawings and cartoons are so immediately recognizable. Despite the fact that we would never come across cartoon images in the natural world, their simple lines and exaggerated features allow us to easily categorize them.

Exemplar Models

If you look around the room you are in, you'll see all kinds of items that you can easily categorize. Most likely, you've seen all of those items before, possibly many times. Given the repetition, you might imagine that simply recognizing things that you have seen before might give you some clues about how they should be classified. This is the basic assumption underlying exemplar models of categorization. **Exemplar models** propose that people categorize items by comparing them to representations of previously experienced items (Medin & Schafer, 1978), like when witnesses attempt to identify a criminal in a police lineup.

This might seem straightforward, but the tricky thing about exemplar models is that they claim that current percepts are compared to all existing representations of exemplars from multiple categories. How many exemplars is that? Good question; probably a lot.

In Figure 5.7, each different doughnut photo would count as an exemplar. Potentially, each visual image of every doughnut you have ever experienced in your life, from every angle and distance that you experienced it, could be an exemplar, and that's not including the possible variations in each doughnut's aroma or flavor.

The exhaustive scope of exemplar models is both a strength and a weakness. Sets of exemplars for categories may contain huge amounts of detailed information (Chapter 1 discusses individuals with prodigious memories for specific episodes). However, exemplar models do not specify which experiences will produce exemplars, or what details of an experience will be stored for use in future comparisons.

Unlike category-boundary models, exemplar models focus heavily on the features of all items within a category.

Prototype Models

In exemplar models of categorization, an item is judged to be a member of a particular category when it is sufficiently similar to one or more stored exemplars; categorization occurs when these similarities pass a certain threshold. When your current experience doesn't seem to match any category, then you might not have a clue what you're looking at (as might happen, for example, in some modern art exhibits; see Figure 5.1).

The idea that categorization involves searching for similarities between current percepts and stored representations of past experiences is also a key aspect of **prototype models** of categorization. Recall that a prototype for a category is an item that possesses most of the common qualities associated with members of that category.

The main difference between prototype models and exemplar models is that prototype models assume that current percepts are compared to stored prototypes of each category, rather than to specific instances of previously experienced members from each category (Osherson & Smith, 1981).

In Figure 5.7, prototypes for different categories of doughnuts might be the generic powdered, chocolate, or filled doughnuts shown in the center of each quadrant. Prototypes are often judged more quickly and accurately than other category members, and people tend to agree about which category members are most prototypical. Prototype models are particularly good at predicting how people categorize perceptual items that share a family resemblance. These models are not as good at

(A) Feature computation   **(B) Categorization process**

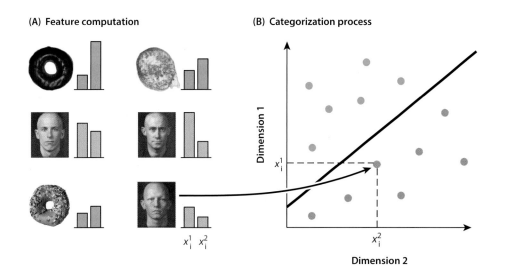

FIGURE 5.8. Quantifying the sorting of images. (A) The first step in many computational models of categorization is to replace complex images with numerical values that capture differences between those images. Here, each image is described using two values: x^1_i and x^2_i. (B) Once category items have been transformed into sets of numbers, differences between those sets can be represented spatially and researchers can focus on identifying different ways that those sets might be grouped and split into particular categories. Here, a line marks the boundaries between two categories. (A, B after Serre, 2016)

explaining how people recognize items in functional or relational categories or oddball items like rose-shaped doughnuts.

Computational models exist for category-boundary, exemplar, and prototype models of categorization and can be used to precisely compare and contrast their predictions (Richler & Palmeri, 2014; Rouder & Ratcliff, 2004). In computational models, objects or events are typically represented as sets of numbers and the process of categorization relates mainly to determining how those sets are divided and organized (**Figure 5.8**).

Modeling Meaning within Categories

The models described so far focus mainly on explaining how people categorize the percepts they experience in everyday life. Explanations that emphasize how people use and understand categories attempt to go beyond item sorting by modeling complex interactions between categories and concepts.

Rule-Based Models

Rule-based models explain categorization as a process of sorting items by testing whether they fulfill a specific set of conditions, almost as if your mind was playing a game of *Twenty Questions* for every item you encounter. In this model, your representation of items that fall into categories is a bit like a dictionary definition and a lot like a checklist of qualifications for category membership.

Biologists use this approach to determine the species of an animal and clinical psychologists use this process to diagnose mental disorders. The *Diagnostic and Statistical Manual of Mental Disorders*, commonly used by clinical psychologists, does not describe boundaries between disorders, background knowledge one must have to diagnose disorders, or case studies of patients. Instead, it provides lists of symptoms that can be used to categorize patients as being clinically depressed, addicted, stressed, and so on, depending on the severity and types of symptoms.

Rule-based models claim that analogous sets of internalized rules enable people to determine when what they are seeing fits into a category. Unsurprisingly, rule-based models do a good job of explaining how people sort items into rule-based categories (Nosofsky et al., 1994). They aren't so great at explaining how people successfully apply categories that cannot be easily specified using checklists, like "things you might do at a party" (Goldstone & Kersten, 2003).

Does painting a star on your forehead qualify as a "thing you might do at a party?" What set of internalized rules might correctly identify a banana as a wall decoration? Rule-based models tend to be linked to language competencies, because people are often able to report on the strategies or rules that they use to sort items. In Figure 5.7, dimension labels correspond to "rules" that a person might use to categorize different kinds of doughnuts.

Theory-Based Models

One of the most intuitive theories of categorization is the **theory-based model** of categorization, sometimes called the theory-theory (no joke). The premise of this model is that the way people categorize items depends a lot on their general understanding of ongoing events. For instance, most people would not include bananas in a list of wall decorations. If they recently visited someone whose walls were covered with bananabilia, however, then they might be more likely to include bananas in such a list.

The fact that people can rapidly adjust their categories in this way, independently of the physical qualities or past associations of items, suggests that their general understanding of events controls how they categorize objects and events (Murphy & Medin, 1985). Evidence supporting the theory-based model comes from experiments showing that people learn concepts more easily when they have relevant background knowledge (Pazzani, 1991; Spalding & Murphy, 1999).

The theory-based model of categorization works well for explaining the situation-dependent way people normally classify objects and events—you will categorize a frog leg on your plate in a French restaurant differently from one you see lying on the side of the road (these kinds of situational concepts are discussed in Chapter 11). A weakness of the theory-based model is that, although it predicts that people will categorize things differently based on their understanding of a situation, it doesn't offer much explanation as to how exactly people do this or any way to quantify the mechanisms involved.

Given all of these different theories of how categorization works (summarized in **Table 5.1**), you might be wondering why psychologists can't seem to figure out which model is the correct one. Actually, all the models are correct in the sense that they have all helped psychologists to understand more about categorization. And they are all incorrect in that they do not predict and explain all aspects of categorization.

Researchers can predict much more precisely how people will categorize things now than they could a century ago. There is no reason to think that categorization occurs in only one way, and many researchers believe that people categorize things differently depending on what they are categorizing, how much experience they have in categorizing similar things, and how refined their percepts of category members are. In fact, undergraduates categorize many items differently from either young children or older adults.

If you could test your much younger self on categorization tasks, you might be surprised at how differently you used to categorize basic things like foods and "fun things to do at parties." The following section explores the role of development and learning experiences on categorization and explains how understanding the ways that categories and concepts are formed can provide new clues about the underlying mechanisms that make categorizing and conceptualizing possible.

TABLE 5.1 Models of Categorization

Category-Boundary	People compare items by taking into account where each item falls relative to internally represented borders between categories
Exemplar	People categorize items by comparing current percepts to stored exemplars
Prototype	People categorize items by comparing current percepts to stored prototypes
Rule-Based	People sort items by testing whether they fulfill a specific set of conditions
Theory-Based	People apply concepts based on their general understanding of ongoing events

SIGHT BITES

 There are numerous theories and models of categorization, most of which attempt to explain how people compare current experiences to internal representations of category members, category boundaries, or rules.

 Just as there are multiple kinds of categories and concepts, there are multiple ways in which people may sort percepts and connect concepts.

Category Learning

SNEAK PEEK: Some species are born sorting percepts in predictable ways. Much of the categorizing you do, however, is based on categories you have learned throughout your life. Just as there are multiple kinds of categories, there are multiple ways that you can construct and use those categories.

So far, you've been introduced to some vocabulary that psychologists use to describe different kinds of categories, concepts, and models of categorization. You hopefully know a bit more about what categorization is and the kinds of categories studied by psychologists. Some categories are simple with a small number of predefined members. Some are much larger but still include predictable sets of items. And for some categories, like "party fun," there are few if any constraints. Now it's time to consider where categories and concepts come from.

Lumpers versus Splitters

There are two kinds of people: lumpers and splitters. Lumpers tend to focus on similarities, while splitters focus more on the qualities that make things distinct (Endersby, 2009). When splitters divide up the world, they end up with a larger number of smaller categories. Lumpers' categories are more big-picture and tend to be simpler.

In truth, everyone is both a lumper and a splitter. Nevertheless, in thinking about the origins of categories, it is useful to think about situations in which a person is more likely to lump things or split them.

First, consider the inputs. Step one in sorting the world involves dividing it up by sensing it through multiple sensory modalities: eyes, ears, nose, tongue, and touch receptors. But most people seem to naturally merge these sensations. William James famously suggested that in infants all experiences are lumped together into "one great blooming, buzzing confusion." He viewed human newborns as the ultimate lumpers. As an older human, you perceive the world as one unified world, not five separate ones. But unlike James's infant, you have no problem telling sights from sounds. Categorical labels have given you a way to split your lumps.

In the *Pyramid* series of game shows, contestants are given labels that identify a broad category of items, and then one contestant mimes or says various sentences to try and get a partner to name specific members of the category as quickly as possible. Given the category "smart phones," one player might say "little pictures you text" to try and coax their partner into saying "emojis." Contestants get points for every word their partner correctly guesses.

The key to racking up points in the game is for the clue-giver to choose movements, words, or phrases that make their partner blurt out correct labels. The *Pyramid* game works because people of similar ages often have learned similar categories. What makes the game fun is that few categories are identical across players, and mismatches (or lousy clues) can cause contestants to flail.

Experiments conducted in the early seventies examined a similar type of rapid category identification by having people name pictures as fast as possible (Rosch et al., 1976). The main finding from these studies was that many people labeled pictures similarly. For instance, people seeing the images in Figure 5.7 would likely blurt out "doughnuts." Few would label them as "food" or "pastries," although both would be accurate descriptions.

Basic level categories are what people typically call things (Collins & Quillian, 1969). They are what you think of first when describing pictures of objects, maybe because they were the words you heard or noticed when you first experienced the objects (**Figure 5.9**). Basic level categories are also the kind of labels that often show up in books for toddlers, labels that split large lumps of experiences into specific categories, like "birds" versus "fish."

Psychologists have also asked participants to judge whether words followed by pictures match. People perform this task more quickly when images were matched with basic level category labels, like "doughnut," than they did when labels are more general, like "food," or very specific, like "cruller."

Many people use basic level categories as their go-to labels. However, a person's experience determines what counts as "basic." If you've worked at a cupcakery, for instance, then the word "cupcake" is probably a more general label for you. If you (the cupcakery you) saw a picture of a cupcake, then you might be quicker to respond with a label like "Red Velvet" than "cupcake."

As you learn to make finer distinctions between items within categories, the ways that you interpret both the category and its members change: you turn into a splitter. As you become more familiar with certain features of the world, you don't just learn new ways of describing and categorizing things.

FIGURE 5.9. Levels of categories. Basic level categories such as dog, flower, plane, and shoe can be grouped into more abstract or "lumped" categories (superordinate categories like "natural"), and each contains more restricted categories (such as "black dogs") that split basic level categories into more precise subcategories. (From Iordan et al., 2015. *J Cog Neurosci*, 27. © 2015 by the Massachusetts Institute of Technology)

Rather, your ability to perceive objects and actions also changes, as does your ability to think about the things you perceive. Your understanding of the world (including yourself) depends on how you categorize your experiences. When you learn to categorize things in more refined ways, you effectively learn new ways to cognize.

Where Do Categories Come From?

Knowing when and how infants learn new categories is important for understanding how categorization works. William James (and later Jean Piaget) thought that infants learned how to categorize through their interactions with the world. Jerry Fodor (introduced in Chapter 2) argued, in contrast, that essentially all categories and concepts that humans possess are genetically pre-programmed (Fodor, 1998). He and other nativist researchers believed that learning experiences serve mainly to activate or tweak innate (inborn) categories (Lawrence & Margolis, 2002).

There is evidence of nonhuman animals showing genetic predispositions to sort events in specific ways. For instance, songbirds raised in isolation, who hear recordings of several species' songs during development, will learn only their own species' songs from listening to those recordings (Marler, 1997). Monkeys raised in a lab learn to fear rubber snakes faster than other potentially scary objects, and chickens produce alarm calls in response to the shadows of various raptors that they've never seen before. Even crickets seem to show categorical responses to tones depending on how similar those tones are to the calls produced by either potential mates or predatory bats (**Figure 5.10**). How such categorization abilities might be genetically determined remains a mystery.

Adults from different cultures categorize things somewhat similarly, and infants from different cultures categorize a wide range of items even more similarly (Kuhl et al., 1992). Some categories, such as how people classify emotional facial expressions, seem especially consistent across cultures.

Could many categories or concepts be inherited? Certainly, some show up at a very early age. It seems unlikely, though, that brains come pre-programmed to classify Pokémon. Most categories and concepts appear to be learned gradually. Children can quickly learn to sort hundreds of images from cartoons along multiple dimensions.

Children growing up in different cultures typically learn different ways of categorizing speech sounds (see Chapter 2), as well as different ways of assigning words to subsets of the objects in their surroundings. Although innate abilities to discriminate images and sounds undoubtedly affect how people categorize items, repeated experiences clearly shape these processes.

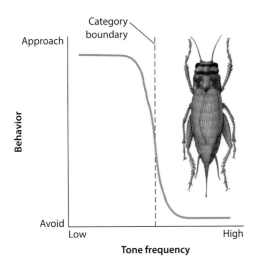

FIGURE 5.10. Categorical responses to tones by a cricket. Crickets show a dramatic shift in whether they approach or avoid tones of different frequencies based on how similar those tones are to sounds produced by either mates or predators, suggesting that these auditory categories are innate. (Image: Carlyn Iverson/Science Source; graph after Wyttenbach et al., 1996)

Learning Perceptual Categories

When children first learn to recognize words, they gradually begin responding to familiar speech sounds in cricket-like ways, treating some similar sounds as if they are quite different. This phenomenon, called **categorical perception**, happens in many different species, and so is likely an inherent (innate) feature of perceptual processing. However, the specific category boundaries that humans form for speech sounds depend on the languages they learn, showing that learning is key to determining which sounds a person hears as being "the same."

Categorizing Based on Acquired Associations

Early experiments on learning showed that repeated experiences could lead to predictable changes in how people responded to reliably correlated events. In one infamous study, American behaviorist John Watson (1878–1958) repeatedly tested an 11-month-old boy (known as Little Albert) by pairing a white rat with loud scary noises (Watson & Rayner, 1920). Eventually, Little Albert came to fear the white rat and cried when shown perceptually similar objects, including a Santa Claus mask and a rabbit (**Figure 5.11**). Watson concluded that Little Albert learned to fear various furry things after repeated exposures to the rat paired with scary sounds (this kind of experiment would not be allowed today due to ethical considerations).

One issue that you might have noticed when reading about Little Albert is that it is not clear whether Albert learned to fear items in the category "white furry things" or simply learned to hate fur. The second case only requires learning that fur predicts scary noises, which intuitively seems simpler than learning a new perceptual category.

Much of the history of research on category learning has focused on figuring out how to tell when categorization can be explained as a process of associating percepts, actions, and outcomes—called **associative learning**—versus learning to use specific rules, dimensions, or labels when sorting items (Shepard et al., 1961). The latter is often viewed as a "higher" form of learning thought to require more sophisticated cognitive abilities related to language, selective attention, and reasoning.

When a person's responses to novel objects or events are a consequence of associative-learning experiences with other similar events, the process is called **stimulus generalization**. For instance, Little Albert generalized from his scary experiences with a rat to other stimuli that were perceptually similar to the rat. The factors that determine how you generalize associations you have learned will be covered in detail in Chapter 7.

FIGURE 5.11. Conditioning categorical responses. Little Albert learned to associate white rats with fear and generalized this learning to other furry and/or white objects. (Photograph by John B Watson)

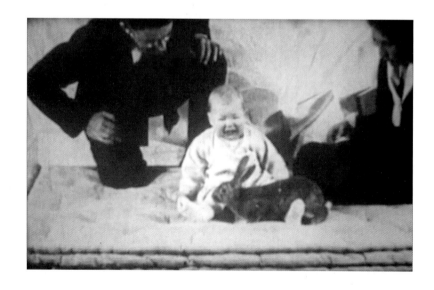

In most categorization tasks studied by psychologists, a person has to learn to produce one response, such as labeling an object or pressing a key, to multiple category members. Not all categories are equally easy to learn, and there is not a simple relationship between the number of items in a category and how hard it is to learn. Many categories that contain equal numbers of items vary greatly in how difficult they are to learn.

Researchers have used this fact to show that categories in which items are sorted based on common features (like perceptual similarities) are learned more quickly than when the same items are randomly assigned to different sets, which is referred to as assigning the objects to **pseudocategories** (Wasserman et al., 1988).

If category learning simply involved associating specific items with specific responses or outcomes, then individuals should learn pseudocategories as quickly as they learn categories of perceptually similar items. By varying the rules used to assign different items to different sets, researchers can systematically adjust the difficulty of category learning tasks to uncover new clues about what makes some categories harder to learn.

Categorizing Based on Recognized Rules and Dimensions

In one classic study of category learning, conducted in the early sixties, researchers tested participants' abilities to categorize two sets of shapes that varied along three dimensions (Shepard et al., 1961). For instance, items might be big or small, black or white, and squares or triangles (**Figure 5.12**).

When objects can be sorted along one of the dimensions, as occurs when all black items fall in one category and all white ones in the other, the task involves perceptual categorization. In all other cases, the two sets consist of pseudocategories. Because the items in each set can be described in terms of the presence or absence of particular features, the categories (and pseudocategories) in this study are rule-based. However, the number and complexity of rules that one would need to follow to place every item in its correct category vary depending on how the objects are divided.

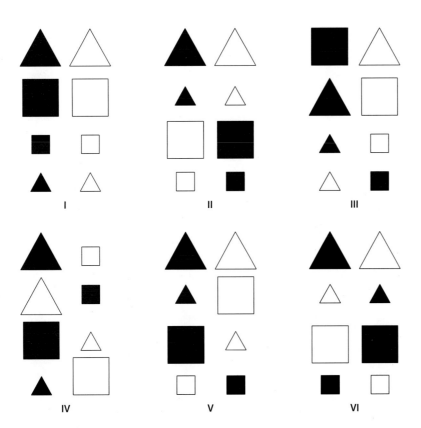

FIGURE 5.12. Learning different divisions. Eight images varying along three dimensions can be divided in half in many different ways, but all of those splits fall into six basic types. The simplest is to divide them using a single dimension (Type I). They can also be halved based on two dimensions (Type II) or using a rule with a single exception (Types III–V). For a Type VI split, there is no easy way out—you just have to memorize which items belong in each set. (From Shepard et al., 1961)

People learn the quickest when the categories can be split using one dimension (see Figure 5.11, Type I). Next quickest are tasks in which rules based on two dimensions work (see Figure 5.11, Type II). The slowest learning occurs for sets that require the most complex sets of rules (see Figure 5.11, Type VI). When participants are asked how they're choosing categories at the end of training, they often describe specific rules that they used to sort items.

People typically attend closely to dimensions and check for the presence or absence of different features along one or more dimensions when sorting such images. In such tasks, people often learn to categorize images by testing out different rules until they find ones that work most of the time. These experimental findings suggest that, in some cases, "learning" a new category may consist of searching through known ways of categorizing items until an appropriate category (or combination of categories) is discovered.

Given that people often use explicit rules to discover appropriate ways of categorizing images in the experiment just described, you might expect that animals without the ability to verbalize rules would have major problems learning these tasks. Monkeys do have more difficulty learning these artificial categories than humans do, but they can learn them. The versions of the task that are easiest and hardest for monkeys to learn are the same as those that are easiest and hardest for undergraduates (Smith et al., 2004). Monkeys seem to learn the intermediate tasks differently from students, however.

Interestingly, when young children and older adults were tested on these same category learning tasks, their difficulties learning the various types of categories were more similar to the pattern seen in monkeys than the pattern observed in undergraduates (Rabi & Minda, 2016). Adolescents with attention deficit hyperactivity disorder (ADHD) also showed the monkey-like patterns when learning different categories (Vigo et al., 2015).

The point here is not that your grandparents and some teenagers sort things like a monkey, but that there are multiple ways to learn different kinds of categories. Older individuals and many children can verbalize rules about categories just fine. Nevertheless, they seem to default to learning some categories by gradually associating items with responses or labels, rather than following explicit rules about which dimensions or features matter.

When an individual uses a particular category learning mechanism depends both on the individual and on the types of items within a category (Folstein et al., 2012). Some children with disorders like attention deficit hyperactivity disorder or autism spectrum disorder may learn categories in ways that differ from their parents or teachers (Church et al., 2010), which can cause problems when a student is either learning concepts more slowly than other students or is conceptualizing problems in ways that differ from the adults attempting to teach them.

Forming Complex Concepts

Much of the research discussed in this section so far has focused on understanding how people learn to categorize arbitrary sets of images—artificial functional categories. Most of the categories and concepts you learn in courses are more abstract and less random, however. So, it would be reasonable for you to question whether these laboratory findings are in any way relevant to how people naturally learn concepts and categories, such as those you are encountering in this chapter.

While there are no experiments examining how humans learn to categorize and conceptualize information presented within cognitive psychology textbooks, there are studies looking at how different training approaches affect students' abilities to generalize concepts involved in solving math problems (Braithwaite & Goldstone, 2015). These studies suggest that a student's background knowledge plays a large role in a person's likelihood of benefitting from problem-solving exemplars. Specifically, students with little prior background knowledge benefit most from being exposed to highly similar examples.

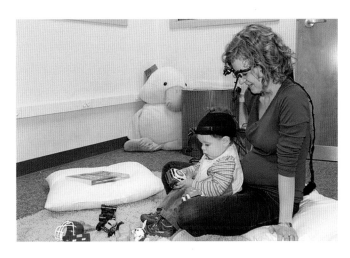

FIGURE 5.13. What it's like to be a categorizing baby. Head-mounted cameras enable researchers to collect the images experienced by babies as they learn to categorize objects and events. (From Yu, et al. 2021. *Proc Natl Acad Sci* 118: e2107019118. [CC BY-NC-ND 4.0])

If you are one of these students, then you would be more likely to generalize the concepts and categories presented in this chapter if all of the examples involved the same kinds of items, whether they were doughnuts or wall decorations. On the other hand, if you're a professor with extensive knowledge of cognitive processes, you will benefit more from a greater variety of exemplars.

Interestingly, most animals seem to be more like professors (and vice versa) in that they show a greater ability to learn and generalize abstract concepts when trained with a wide variety of items (Katz et al., 2007). Using many different items during training can also be beneficial when one is attempting to learn new perceptual categories, such as foreign speech sounds.

Given that novices who lack relevant background knowledge can learn more from repeated experiences with highly similar items, you might expect that young children would also benefit from such experiences. Recent studies confirm that the visual experiences of infants and toddlers do consist disproportionately of highly similar images (Clerkin et al., 2017).

By collecting video recordings using head-mounted cameras—basically, baby Go-Pros—researchers can gain a child's-eye perspective on the world (**Figure 5.13**). Infants' early visual experiences are dominated by the faces of a few individuals (usually parents) at close proximity, while toddlers' views consist mainly of a small set of objects that they manually manipulate while looking at them. The small number of different faces or objects viewed means that young children are experiencing many repeated instances of similar images.

Soon after children begin learning the names of different objects, they show a rapid increase in their ability to classify all kinds of objects, a phenomenon called **fast mapping**. Children are said to be fast mapping concepts when they can learn to identify which object a new word refers to after a single exposure (Carey & Bartlett, 1978).

Children usually gain this ability after two to three years' worth of visual and verbal experiences. There is some evidence that dogs also have the ability to fast map spoken words after learning the names of several different objects (Kaminski et al., 2004), suggesting that this may be a basic mechanism that many species use to learn new categories.

Hypothetically, as a child's background knowledge increases, exposure to more varied visual experiences can further expand their capacity to generalize learned concepts and categories. In extreme cases, a child may grow up to pursue categorizing or conceptualizing as a career, in which case their abilities to flexibly lump and split items in their area of interest would continue to expand. The following section describes how a person's ability to rapidly and accurately categorize items changes over time, even after a category or concept has been learned.

SIGHT BITES

 Basic level category labels are recognized and produced more rapidly than other category labels and are common across many individuals with similar experiences.

 Associative learning plays a key role in the formation of all kinds of categories, but recognition of relevant dimensions can make learning quicker and easier.

 Which experiences can help an individual learn new categories depends on the background knowledge that the individual already possesses.

Processes of Discrimination

SNEAK PEEK: Learning a new category is not just about learning what goes with what. It also involves representing objects, agents, and events in ways that highlight their distinctive properties.

Theories of categorization often focus on explaining how people sort items based on similar features, functions, or associations—the lumping part of categorization. What about the splitting? Discrimination of category members and of categories turns out to be just as crucial to the development of categorization abilities as the ability to recognize similarities.

Plato, in describing love as a kind of madness, identified two essential properties of categorical descriptions: (1) the principle of "perceiving and bringing together in one idea the scattered particulars," which involves listing all the qualities that justify classifying something as "love," and (2) the principle of "dividing things again by classes, where the natural joints are, and not trying to break any part, after the manner of a bad carver." The dividing up part (discrimination) is just as important as the grouping together of unique examples.

When participants learned the categories shown in Figure 5.12, they found it easiest to learn to categorize images that were divided along one specific dimension, probably because they could ignore all qualities of the images except for one. Chapter 4 describes this kind of restricted processing of perceptual qualities as selective attention. The only way a person can selectively attend to a particular dimension is if they can separate that dimension out from other perceivable features.

You probably can't imagine what it would be like to not notice the brightness, shape, or size of an image. But when you were much younger, you were oblivious to these dimensions. Children typically treat dimensions, like the brightness and size of a square, as if they were somehow merged together (Smith, 1989), which is partly why early education so heavily emphasizes sorting shapes, speech sounds, and quantities. This tendency toward lumping also shows up when children naturally learn categories; they first learn to group and name items that are physically similar. Categorization is not just about recognizing which items go together. Being able to tell things apart, to discriminate items, is just as critical.

Becoming a Perceptual Expert

As noted earlier, cupcake experts are less likely to say "a cupcake" when shown a picture of one than a novice would be and more likely to specify the type of cupcake. Studies of experts show that they are

(A) Stimuli examples

(B) Post-training discrimination

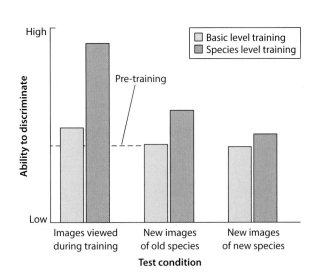

FIGURE 5.14. Effects of category refinement on the ability to classify images of birds. Training with basic level categories of birds (A) improved peoples' abilities to detect differences in familiar images, but not novel images (B). In contrast, training people to classify the same bird images as different species of owls or waterfowl improved their ability to distinguish between novel images of species they had observed during training (old species) as well as related bird species that were not presented during training (new species). (A [owls]: Robusta via Shutterstock, [geese]: HappyPictures via Shutterstock; B after Tanaka et al., 2005)

as fast at recognizing specific subcategories of objects that they know well as they are at matching basic level categories to those same items (Tanaka & Taylor, 1991).

You might think that experts are faster because they've memorized specific examples of many different objects. But they are also faster at discriminating unfamiliar objects that are similar to the ones they know about. **Perceptual expertise**, the ability to rapidly discriminate and recognize complex percepts (like images of cupcakes or wall decorations), usually develops over many repeated experiences in which similar objects or events are discriminated.

In one study examining perceptual expertise, researchers trained people to identify different categories of birds (different kinds of owls or different kinds of waterfowl), either focusing on basic level categories, like "owls," or more specific categories, like "Great Gray Owl" (Tanaka et al., 2005). Participants were tested on how quickly they classified two bird pictures as being from the same species, before and after a week of training.

Participants got better at performing this task for all species they had seen during training. When people were trained to make more subtle distinctions, say between screech owls and hawk owls, they improved not only at discriminating between those species but also at discriminating between other unfamiliar species (**Figure 5.14**). This didn't happen if they only learned to identify birds at a basic level, even though they were trained with all the same pictures of birds.

In other words, people that were trained to make more fine-grained distinctions, like those made by experts, were better at categorizing both novel and familiar images related to the birds they saw during training. Newly trained owl "experts" apparently noticed qualities that distinguish different kinds of owls just as cupcake experts may notice subtle differences between icing shades or patterns.

Learning to Perceive Differences

Perceptual experts become experts through a process of **perceptual learning**. Perceptual learning refers to relatively long-lasting changes in your ability to discriminate percepts gained through experience (Goldstone, 1998).

Perceptual learning occurs in many different species and across all ages. It sometimes occurs even without training. For example, if you've played cards a lot, then you may be more likely to notice differences in the face cards across decks. Animals that live in cages with small posters of shapes hanging on the walls learn to discriminate between those shapes faster than animals raised in cages without posters. The largest changes in perceptual abilities occur, however, when one is explicitly trained

FIGURE 5.15. Perceptual learning in medical diagnoses. A layperson inspecting an X-ray is less likely to detect subtle variations than a physician who has spent many years making such decisions. The right image includes annotations highlighting regions where bone cancer is indicated by subtle distinctions in shading. With the circles as guides, you may be able to identify these regions on the left image. (Both images reprinted from Seitz 2017. *Curr Biol 27*, with permission from Elsevier)

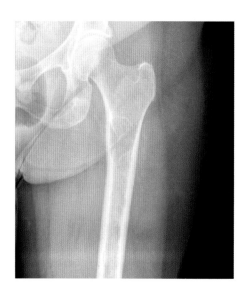 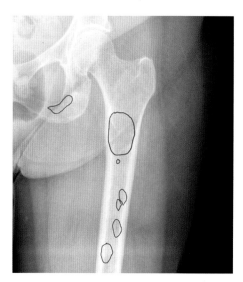

to make fine distinctions, such as the distinctions that piano tuners made before the invention of digital tuners or wine tasters make when comparing the qualities of different wines.

Often professionals who benefit from perceptual learning are unaware that their perceptual sensitivities are changing over time. For example, doctors are often required to review scans of patients' tissues to detect subtle variations that are signatures of a disease (**Figure 5.15**). Clinical psychologists may similarly become increasingly aware of mannerisms or self-descriptions that are signs of particular disorders.

Enhanced discrimination abilities may sometimes come with a hidden cost—the ways that you categorize and conceptualize the world not only help you to understand your experiences but they also can contribute to your misunderstandings. For instance, people are better at distinguishing between faces from races that they've frequently experienced (Shapiro & Penrod, 1986). A side effect of being good at discriminating familiar faces is that people rapidly categorize faces from unfamiliar races into one generic category (Valentine, 1991). Such involuntary lumping of "foreign" faces could contribute to racist stereotypes.

A similar trade-off happens in speech perception (see Chapter 2). As infants become better at discriminating speech sounds used in their native language, they lose the capacity to distinguish between speech sounds that are more common in foreign languages (Iverson & Kuhl, 2000). Learning your native language increases your ability to categorize familiar speech sounds while decreasing your ability to discriminate unfamiliar speech sounds from other languages.

Learning to sort things in one way can decrease your ability to sort them in other ways because of how you represent categories. The following section reviews clues from brain research about how categories are represented and how learning experiences can shape those representations.

SIGHT BITES

 Perceptual expertise can change the categories that operate like basic level categories and can help experts to make fine distinctions.

 Perceptual learning enables individuals to gradually refine how they categorize things, increasing their sensitivities to some qualities of percepts, while potentially decreasing sensitivity to others.

BRAIN SUBSTRATES

SNEAK PEEK: Multiple interacting brain regions contribute to your capacity to discriminate and classify events into familiar categories, including the prefrontal cortex, basal ganglia, and hippocampus. Modern neuroscientific theories attempt to describe how different regions work together to perform different categorization tasks.

When you form new categories or concepts, whether they are perceptual, functional, or abstract, something inside your head changes. When you become an expert at distinguishing different sights, sounds, or, tastes, your brain is also changing how it processes those sensations. By monitoring how brains change during category learning, scientists can gain a clearer picture of the complexity of the mechanisms involved in both categorization and discrimination.

How Categories Are Represented in Brains

Individuals with associative agnosia (like Dr. P) usually have damage to cortical regions that make it impossible for them to name objects. In some cases, people only lose the ability to label specific kinds of objects, such as household objects. These unique disabilities led researchers to propose that specific regions of the cerebral cortex were specialized for categorizing certain kinds of images and objects (Warrington & Shallice, 1984). This idea gained strength from neuroimaging studies showing selective activation of cortical regions when participants categorized tools versus natural objects or living versus nonliving things. The following sections describe a few of the ways in which your cortical neurons can contribute to your ability to categorize.

How Cortical Neurons Respond to Category Members

Seeing a brain region respond most to members of a specific category tells you that neurons in that region are detecting some qualities of the properties that are linked to the category (see Chapters 2 and 4). Cortical circuits, in particular, seem critical for successful categorization and have been a major focus of recent studies of the neural substrates of categorization.

Grandmother Cells

Many past theories of brain function assume that the circuits involved in recognizing and categorizing percepts and concepts are localized to specific regions of the cerebral cortex (see Chapter 2). An extreme version of this idea is known as the **grandmother cell hypothesis**. The grandmother cell hypothesis proposes that there is a neuron somewhere in your head that responds any time you perceive or think about your grandmother.

Chapter 4 describes how the responses of neurons in your visual cortex become more selective for abstract features at later stages of processing. You can imagine that if this sort of abstraction continued through later and later stages of cortical processing, you might eventually end up with neurons that respond to highly abstract inputs, like every scene you can envision your grandmother being in. Of course, there is nothing special about your grandmother relative to everything else in the world (except to people who know her). The general idea is that you have neurons in particular locations that respond selectively to inputs that define every category or concept that you possess.

Grandmother cells, if they exist, are **local representations** of people's concepts of their grandmothers in that a single neuron is located in one place. The idea that you have one neuron that responds to all things grandma might sound bizarre, but neurons that respond to the sounds and images of familiar people, such as celebrities have actually been observed in human brains (Quiroga et al., 2005; Rey et al., 2020; Viskontas et al., 2009).

FIGURE 5.16. Brain regions known to contribute to visual categorization. Cortical regions, such as the inferotemporal cortex and prefrontal cortex, interact with subcortical brain regions, such as the basal ganglia and the hippocampus, during the learning and use of visual categories. How your thalamus and visual cortex respond to visual activity largely determines what you are capable of seeing, but these other circuits strongly affect what you do see as well as how you describe your visual experiences.

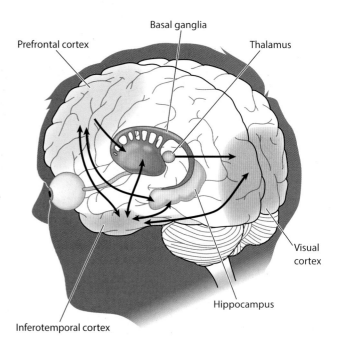

Category-Specific Neurons

Much of what is known about *how* cortical neurons represent categories comes from studies of monkeys. In monkeys, recordings collected from a part of the visual cortex called the **inferotemporal cortex** (**Figure 5.16**) show that neurons in this region respond most to specific complex shapes (Tanaka et al., 1991), including shapes that monkeys learned to categorize (Sigala & Logothetis, 2002). When monkeys were trained to categorize simple images, category learning increased the responses of neurons in the inferotemporal cortex to features of images that distinguished those categories (Sigala & Logothetis, 2002).

Neurons that respond selectively to items in a category, like those in the inferotemporal cortex, are called **category-specific neurons**. Unlike hypothetical grandmother cells, which might respond to any grandma-related sight, sound, or thought, category-specific neurons are actual neurons in the cerebral cortex that fire more to certain sets of perceptually similar images than to others.

Knowing that neurons in the inferotemporal cortex respond more to some sets of images than to others doesn't reveal much about how brains represent categories or the role that any given neuron plays in this cognitive process (Thomas & French, 2017). Neurons in the inferotemporal cortex might be storing exemplars, prototypes, or neither.

One way to get some clues about what category-specific neurons might be doing is to look at how their responses to category members vary. In one study that compared how neurons in the inferotemporal cortices of monkeys responded to different kinds of trees, category-specific neurons mainly responded to specific images that the monkeys had experienced during training (Vogels, 1999) and to specific parts of objects (Tanaka et al., 1991).

This kind of response is what you might expect if recent exemplars are being emphasized. The specificity of neurons in the inferotemporal cortex implies that groups of neurons are necessary to represent items within a category.

Changing How Cortical Neurons Respond to Category Members

The inferotemporal cortex is often described as the last level of processing in the visual cortex, with neurons in later stages of cortical processing responding to a broader range of sensory modalities. Until recently, most neuroscientists assumed that the response properties of neurons in the first stages of visual cortical processing were established early in development and that the features that people

(A)

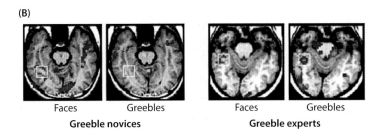

FIGURE 5.17. Cortical signs of perceptual expertise.
(A) People trained to make fine distinctions between abstract, humanoid shapes called Greebles gradually improve at classifying these shapes. (B) As their performance increases, cortical regions (indicated with white squares) that normally respond mainly to faces begin to also respond to Greebles, showing that: (1) these cortical regions are not limited to only including face-selective neurons, and (2) the formation of new shape categories leads to changes in how the visual cortex responds to various complex shapes within those categories. (A images courtesy of Michael J. Tarr; B from Gauthier et al., 1999. *Nat Neurosci* 2, reproduced with permission from SNCSC)

(B)

Faces   Greebles   Faces   Greebles
Greeble novices   **Greeble experts**

use to visually categorize objects were, for the most part, innately determined. Chapter 4 describes neuroscientific studies of regions in the cortex such as the fusiform face area that many scientists assumed were genetically programmed for specialized processing of species-relevant stimuli such as faces.

Researchers discovered, however, that it is possible not only to change how sensitive an adult's cortex is to basic features of images through training but also how sensitive it is to complex sets of features (Yin et al., 2014). Neuroimaging studies of adults who were trained to categorize images of three-dimensional shapes called Greebles (**Figure 5.17**) show changes in cortical regions including the fusiform face area (Gauthier et al., 1999).

Recording studies in various mammals show that neuronal responses in the auditory cortex can also become category-specific after animals are trained to sort complex sounds (Schreiner & Polley, 2014). The same kind of training can change how children categorize speech sounds (Tallal et al., 1996). These kinds of cortical changes make perceptual learning and the development of perceptual expertise possible.

If your cortical representations of category members are changing as you learn, then categorization may be a more dynamic and flexible process than was once thought. In fact, some developmental disorders may arise when, at an early age, perceptual categories form in ways that are abnormally rigid, derailing normal cognitive development (Mercado et al., 2020).

The Roles of Prefrontal Cortex

The clearest evidence of category-specific neurons in the cerebral cortex comes from recordings in the **prefrontal cortex (PFC)** (Miller et al., 2002), a region of the cerebral cortex near your forehead. PFC neurons in monkeys trained to categorize images show category-selective responses for exemplars from each category. Category-selective activation of subregions of the PFC also occurs in humans trained to perform perceptual categorization tasks (Zeithamova et al., 2019).

The inferotemporal cortex sends information to the PFC about recognized complex shapes and also receives signals from this region. Neuroimages of people trained to categorize different types of cars revealed that the PFC responded in different ways depending on how the cars were labeled (Jiang et al., 2007). In other words, how your prefrontal cortex reacts to your visual impressions of cars depends not just on what the images look like but also on the different categories you have learned to use to classify cars.

Researchers trained monkeys to categorize cat shapes, dog shapes, and cat-dog shapes (perceptual categories) and to choose matching or nonmatching shapes (abstract categories). Neuron responses in the PFC of these monkeys rapidly changed near category boundaries (Seger & Miller, 2010) (see Figure 5.7), sending shivers down the spines of category-boundary model fans.

The PFC is considered by many to be the brain region that controls and coordinates all other cognitive processes—not just categorization (Chapter 8 discusses this in detail). This global control is achieved by neurons in the PFC that send signals to multiple regions distributed throughout your brain.

Surprisingly, PFC damage does not consistently impair a person's cognitive ability (see Chapter 2) and seems to only hurt category learning when a person starts off using an ineffective strategy (Schnyer et al., 2009). People with PFC damage also run into trouble sorting items when they have to switch from using one rule to using another (Owen et al., 1993). So your PFC can affect how you categorize in many different ways.

Early studies of the neural substrates of categorization and concept learning focused heavily on identifying important cortical regions for categorizing based on assumptions about the modularity of cognitive processing (introduced in Chapter 2). More recent research paints a somewhat different picture, however, in which many different subcortical brain regions dynamically contribute to category learning and use, including parts of the hippocampus and basal ganglia.

Learning Implicit Categories

The **basal ganglia** are clusters of neurons deep inside the brain (see Figure 5.16). This region receives many different, highly processed sensory inputs and sends out signals that help to control movements. If your basal ganglia were damaged, you would have trouble learning new skills like catching popcorn in your ear.

You might not suspect that a brain region so deeply involved in the voluntary control of motor skills would contribute much to categorization. Few psychologists did either, until it was discovered that people with basal ganglia damage had problems learning certain types of perceptual categories.

Impaired Learning of Probabilistic Categories

Early evidence that the basal ganglia might be important for categorizing came from studies of individuals with Parkinson's disease. In Parkinson's disease, the basal ganglia gradually stop working. People with Parkinson's disease have problems learning visual categories that are probabilistic (Foerde & Shohamy, 2011).

In **probabilistic categories**, items in different categories tend to be linked to specific outcomes, but not 100% of the time. For instance, if you go to a party on a college campus, there is a good chance that pizza will be present, but that doesn't always happen. Parties at weddings are less likely to feature pizza, but it is still a possibility.

People with Parkinson's disease who were tested on their ability to learn through trial and error to predict in a computer game when it would be either rainy or sunny using cues similar to those shown in **Figure 5.18A** were greatly impaired relative to adults without Parkinson's. As training on a probabilistic category learning task progressed, individuals with Parkinson's had more difficulties (Foerde & Shohamy, 2011). They persisted in choosing items based on simple rules that don't always work. They slowly learned to categorize items, but not in the same way as people with functional basal ganglia.

People without Parkinson's disease start out trying to use simple rules just like the individuals with Parkinson's but eventually shift to better strategies. Neuroimaging studies show increased activity in the basal ganglia region during the later stages of probabilistic category learning (**Figure 5.18B**).

(A)

(B)

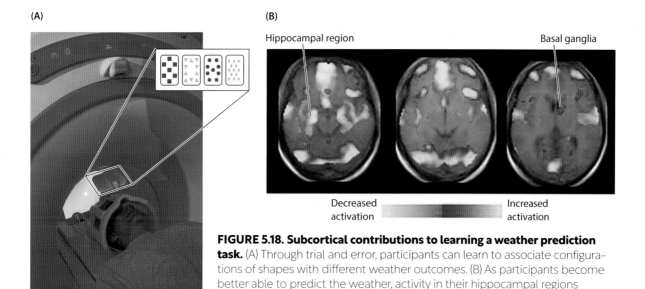

Hippocampal region

Basal ganglia

Decreased activation

Increased activation

FIGURE 5.18. Subcortical contributions to learning a weather prediction task. (A) Through trial and error, participants can learn to associate configurations of shapes with different weather outcomes. (B) As participants become better able to predict the weather, activity in their hippocampal regions decreases while activity in their basal ganglia increases. Activity in various cortical regions also increases as training progresses. (A BonkersAboutPictures/ Alamy Stock Photo, B after Poldrack et al., 2001 as cited in Gluck et al., 2016)

How active your basal ganglia will be during category learning varies depending on the kind of categorization task being learned (Seger & Peterson, 2013), showing that people may categorize in more than one way while learning probabilistic categories.

Information Integration

Interest in the role of the basal ganglia in categorization has steadily increased over the past decade. Today, some researchers argue that almost all forms of category learning may rely on processing in the basal ganglia (Ashby & Maddox, 2011; Ashby & Rosedahl, 2017).

The sensorimotor nature of basal ganglia function has led psychologists to view this brain region as essential for unconsciously learning categories. This kind of implicit (unintentional), trial-and-error type of category learning is probably what most children are doing when they sort things without paying much attention to specific dimensions (Piaget, 1952). Later in life, these "primitive" categories may be replaced with labeled categories.

The idea that some categories are organized based on perceptually merged dimensions or features ultimately led to the proposal that label-less perceptual categories depend on **information integration** (lumping dimensions), while rule-based categories, which can be verbally described, depend on consciously identified dimensions like color, shape, or size (splitting categories along a specific dimension).

Category learning that depends on information integration may rely more on the basal ganglia. Learning rule-based categories—like "ripe strawberries are red strawberries"—is thought to depend more on other brain regions, such as the prefrontal cortex and the hippocampus (discussed in the following section).

Categorizing with Distributed Networks

Like the basal ganglia, the brain region known as the **hippocampus** (see Figure 5.16) was originally thought to be primarily performing basic regulatory functions, such as regulating emotional responses to keep its owner alive. Only after an experimental surgery on an epileptic patient named Henry Molaison (H.M.), who had most of his hippocampus removed, did researchers begin to realize that the hippocampus might be important for cognition and concept formation (a discovery discussed more extensively in Chapter 8).

Studies of category learning by patients with hippocampal damage showed that although they could learn lots of categorization tasks, including probabilistic categorization tasks, they often had problems with functional categories and concepts (Marr, 1971; McClelland et al., 1995). This led researchers to suspect that two brain systems were interacting during category and concept learning: one that learned gradually, through trial and error, and another that learned more rapidly, by storing facts.

Complementary Mechanisms of Category Learning

In one version of this two-system model, the hippocampus is the fast system, quickly storing exemplars, while the cerebral cortex is the slow-poke system, gradually accumulating new concepts (Kumaran et al., 2016). James McClelland and colleagues described the two systems as **complementary learning systems** because together they stored knowledge more effectively (**Figure 5.19**).

Like the basal ganglia, the hippocampus receives inputs from several brain regions. Unlike the basal ganglia, outputs from the hippocampus feed back to the same cortical regions that are sending inputs to it. This is part of the reason why McClelland and others think that the hippocampus cooperates with the cerebral cortex to make categorization and conceptualization possible.

The complementary learning systems proposal highlights a common assumption about both categories and concepts, which is that concepts and categories are a kind of knowledge that is mentally stored, to be retrieved as needed. In this framework, knowledge gets into your head when you learn categories or form concepts, and categorizing simply involves using that knowledge.

Neuroscientists have pushed the idea of complementary learning systems further by proposing that the hippocampus actively trains cortical circuits by replaying previously experienced events in various forms (Wilson & McNaughton, 1994). So if you recently saw an actress in a movie, your hippocampus might transform that particular experience into a stream of repeating neural activity "echoes" of the experience that persist long after you've left the theater (especially when you're asleep).

Why might your cerebral cortex need to be trained by your hippocampus to store concepts or categories? Maybe because your existing concepts and categories are organized within tightly interwoven networks. Your "doughnut" category is related to your concepts of circles, sugar, food, things that can get stale, baked goods, cake doughnuts, things smaller than a bread box, and so on. For this

FIGURE 5.19.
Complementary learning systems in the brain.
Hippocampal processing may operate quickly to represent new exemplars and then may gradually help cortical circuits (blue arrows) integrate this new information with existing representations of background knowledge and concepts (black arrows). (After Kumaran et al., 2016)

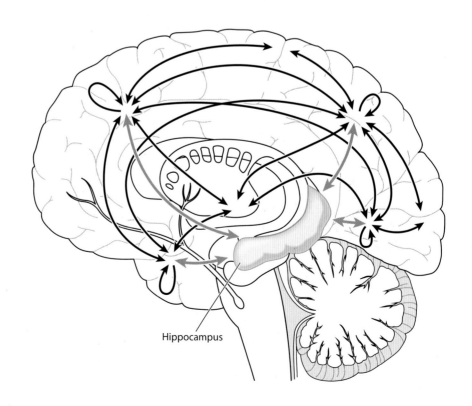

Hippocampus

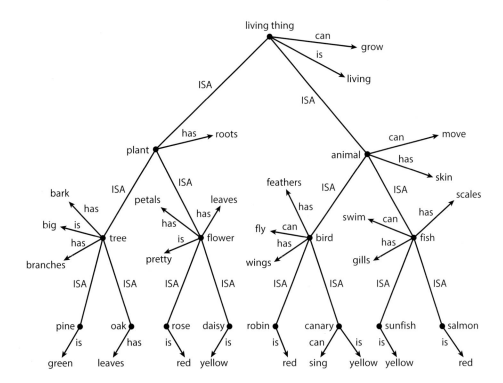

FIGURE 5.20. A network of concepts. Connections between concepts can be represented in graphs as links between labels for categories. This representation emphasizes qualities that all or many members of a category possess. For instance, most birds have feathers and wings and can fly. (From Rogers & McClelland, 2008)

reason, concepts and categories are often depicted as sets of connecting paths, like roads in a pre-planned community (**Figure 5.20**).

Within such networks, links between different concepts or category labels might reflect past associations, physical similarities, or relationships between items. If you've ever used online encyclopedias like Wikipedia, then you're familiar with this kind of linking of labeled information.

An entry for the word "doughnut" may include descriptions of the qualities of various types of doughnuts, the historical origins of doughnuts, recipes for doughnuts, the chemistry involved in making doughnuts, as well as images of doughnuts or what the word "doughnut" sounds like. Additionally, descriptions within the "doughnut" entry may be hyperlinked to entries for other words associated with doughnuts, such as desserts, coffee, cinnamon, Timbits (doughnut holes from the restaurant Tim Hortons), or Dutch settlers.

Networked entries in online encyclopedias, though interlinked, are independent of one another. Changing or adding an entry for a word to the network usually doesn't change the entries for other words.

Human concepts and categories, on the other hand, are not stored as files within your brain but as changes in the activity of millions of neurons and many millions of synapses (see Chapter 2). When representations are spread out across many separate neurons, they are called **distributed representations**. In networks of distributed representations, when you change one "entry," you can potentially change them all.

Distributed Representations of Categories and Concepts

The main difference between a distributed representation of a category in the cerebral cortex and a local representation is that distributed representations involve more neurons spread out over a larger area. If you think of a distributed representation as a web of interconnected neurons, then activity across the whole web would correspond to activation of a concept or category, not activity at a single point (like a grandmother cell) within the web.

Connectionist models can simulate the formation and application of distributed representations of categories and concepts within the cerebral cortex (McClelland et al., 1986), as well as interactions between the cerebral cortex and the hippocampus (Gluck & Myers, 1993). The connections within these models are analogous to the synaptic connections between neurons and can change over time to become either stronger or weaker as a category is being learned.

According to the complementary learning systems hypothesis, hippocampal replay of temporarily stored exemplars makes it possible for your brain to gradually add knowledge into your preexisting conceptual (cortical) networks. Connectionist models have been used to support the hypothesis that the hippocampus could facilitate the modification of representations that are distributed across many cortical neurons (see Figure 5.19). From this perspective, the main differences between perceptual categories, functional categories, and abstract concepts are the specific networks of item-representing neurons that are engaged during task performance.

With the hippocampus, basal ganglia, and cerebral cortex all contributing to categorization and concept formation, you may be starting to wonder whether there is any brain region that is not involved in these cognitive processes. And you would not be far from the truth, because many additional brain regions are involved in labeling category members and concepts (reviewed in Chapter 12).

SIGHT BITES

 The inferotemporal cortex contains category-specific neurons that may contribute to the representation of items within categories. Neurons in the PFC show strong changes in responding near the boundaries of categories.

 The basal ganglia contribute to the learning of probabilistic categories, especially when performance is gradually improving, and also to implicit category learning that involves information integration or the merging of stimulus features.

 Connectionist models can portray how the hippocampus helps to form categories and concepts by providing the cortex with distributed representations acquired through experience.

APPLIED PERSPECTIVES

SNEAK PEEK: Animals other than humans are able to discriminate and categorize events that humans cannot. People's limitations in terms of categorizing mundane objects can have life-or-death consequences.

Your capacity to categorize events affects your daily life, both in how you interact with the world and how you think about it. In some professions, this ability is more critical than in others. If your job is to diagnose illnesses, either physical or mental, you need to be able to recognize clusters of symptoms, patterns of data in X-rays, or side effects of different drugs to be able to sort patients and choose treatments. If you're a teacher, you need to be able to identify which concepts students understand and the kinds of experiences they need to help them form new concepts or refine their existing categories.

Knowing how concepts and categories can be learned and applied, and how perceptual representations are refined through experience, can have many practical implications. In some cases, it may be possible to train nonhuman animals to discriminate and sort things faster and better than humans can. For example, dolphins can find and recognize buried objects using echolocation better than any human or machine can. Studies showing that humans are not the only ones who can categorize objects and events have helped people realize that animals can help to solve some particularly tricky categorization problems.

Sorting Smells to Save Lives

When you think of jobs that require sorting, professional smeller might not make the cut as one of your basic level categories. People that smell for a living may test the allure of perfumes, the appeal of microwaveable meals, or the effectiveness of deodorants. However, there are many odor-related jobs that even humans are unwilling or unable to do, such as finding bodies, identifying suitcases containing illegal drugs, or even detecting mines. Also, there are some tasks that people hadn't previously realized could be performed by sorting odors.

Dog Detectives

One animal that you might guess would be better at discriminating, recognizing, or categorizing odors than humans is dogs. Dogs' sense of smell is about 10,000 to 100,000 times more sensitive to differences between odors than that of humans. They have about 50 times as many olfactory receptors and the brain regions that they use to process odor information are, proportionately, about 40 times larger than in humans.

Most people know that dogs can locate and track prey based on odor trails, an ability that likely contributed to their domestication. Later, people discovered that dogs could be trained to match the odor of a specific person to an odor trail left by that person, a skill that helps police searching for suspects or missing persons. The ability of dogs to match unique odors to other examples of those odors may require them to form an abstract concept of "sameness." The task is abstract in that the dogs learn to search for matches that vary over time rather than always search for one specific odor (like the smell of heroin). Dogs can also become experts at detecting broader perceptual categories of scents, like the smell of marijuana regardless of its form or strain. Police dogs have also been trained to locate buried bodies and certain kinds of explosives based on their smells.

In most of these jobs, dogs were trained to find odors that humans already knew existed. More recently, dogs have proven to also be capable of discriminating and perceptually categorizing smells that humans were oblivious to (**Figure 5.21**). For instance, dogs seem to be able to detect bladder and prostate cancer by smelling the urine of patients (Pirrone & Albertini, 2017) and ovarian cancer by smelling a patient's blood (Horvath et al., 2010).

At first, the discovery that dogs could smell cancers was met with disbelief, because scientists couldn't identify the specific odors that dogs were detecting. In the few studies of cancer sniffing dogs conducted so far, dogs are trained to discriminate samples in which cancer cells either are or are not present. No one knows whether dogs can discriminate smells associated with different cancers, what other diseases they might be able to identify by scent, or what concepts dogs might be able to form about odors.

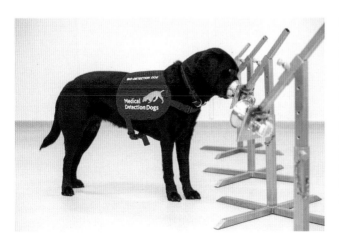

FIGURE 5.21. Cancer sniffers.
Dogs can recognize odors that neither humans nor machines have the ability to classify, including odors associated with certain types of cancer. How might one discover the ways in which dogs sort odors? Might teaching them the spoken names of different kinds of cancer increase their ability to make fine distinctions between cancer-related odors? (Abaca Press/Alamy Stock Photo)

Rescue Rats

Dogs are not the only animals with impressive odor discrimination abilities, and they may not even be the best at learning to detect and sort odors. Researchers in Africa recently started training giant pouched rats to screen patients for tuberculosis and found that the rats were catching cases that humans had missed!

Honeybees can categorize images and learn relational categories (Giurfa et al., 2001); they also have super sensitive odor receptors. And zebrafish brains respond to odors just like the category-specific neurons recorded in the prefrontal cortices of monkeys do (Niessing & Friedrich, 2010). Understanding how different neural systems affect an organism's talents at sorting smells should make it clearer which species are best suited for learning specific odor classification tasks.

Smelling out diseases is just one way in which expertise in odor sorting can be useful. In Tanzania, rats have been trained to help people find old buried land mines. The rats are placed in small harnesses and then allowed to search around areas where mines may have been buried. The rats are trained to scratch at locations where they smell the explosives that are within a land mine.

From these mine-detecting rats' performances alone, it is impossible to tell whether they are categorizing different smells as being scratch-worthy or not. In principle, they could perform this task simply by scratching whenever they detect the presence of a particular odor. However, given that rats can quickly learn to categorize complex sounds along multiple dimensions (Mercado et al., 2005), it seems likely that they might also learn to categorize a variety of odors when given the task of finding them.

Without knowing how categorization abilities vary across different species, it's hard to predict how well they might learn to categorize the kinds of things that humans are interested in sorting, and when they might do a better job. There is one perceptual categorization task, however, in which humans could definitely benefit from the help of animal assistants: scanning X-ray images of travelers' carry-on bags for weapons in airport security lines.

Spotting Threats in Baggage

The task of finding weapons inside suitcases seems simple at first glance. You learn what weapons look like in X-rays, form a functional category of "things that the Transportation Security Administration (TSA) doesn't want on a plane," and then search for those kinds of images.

In practice, however, this task appears to be nearly impossible for humans. Professional airport security screeners tested in the field with weapons that they had been specifically trained to detect missed more than 95% of them (Blake, 2017). How likely do you think it is that an airport screener would spot and classify something like a madu as a weapon?

Unless you work for the TSA, your category of "threats" likely differs dramatically from those of TSA agents. Their categories heavily emphasize smaller weapons. Their exemplars will mainly be two-dimensional images of weapons crammed in and under piles of other harmless objects. These are not the kinds of images that most people are going to see and think "deadly". Airport security screeners receive lots of training with these kinds of images, precisely because they need to learn to recognize the object qualities that would put an X-ray image into the functional category of "dangerous." (**Figure 5.22**)

Agents inspecting X-ray images must rapidly search through visual clutter while trying to match parts of the image to known perceptual categories of weapons—it's a high-stakes, real-world, visual search task of the kind described in Chapter 4. Weapons within a particular category, such as "guns," will show family resemblances, but other categories ("knives," "plastic explosives," etc.) will share few if any of the physical qualities that exemplify guns. Disassembled, disguised gun parts may also look very different from the prototype or exemplar of a gun.

FIGURE 5.22. Complicated categorization. Can you spot the weapon in this person's carry-on suitcase? (The correct answer is "No, I cannot.") Expert screeners routinely fail such tests. (PhonlamaiPhoto; overlay X-ray image: Anton Gvozdikov/Alamy Stock Photo)

Surprisingly few experiments have looked at what happens cognitively as TSA screeners perform this complex categorization task. Standardized tests are used to see how people perform when images of weapons are added to X-rays, or when testers attempt to sneak weapons through security. Screeners may gradually improve at detecting repeated weapon images as their experience increases (a sign of perceptual learning and increasing perceptual expertise) without necessarily getting better at finding other weapons hidden in luggage. When familiar or novel images of weapons are seen along with many other familiar and novel objects, performance can drop dramatically (Smith et al., 2005). In short, screeners fail to generalize from their past sorting experiences.

Given the difficulty of the task faced by airport security screeners, their poor performance in real-world tests, and the potential consequences of weapons being missed, what kinds of training regimens and perceptual experiences, if any, might be able to help the average TSA agent overcome these difficulties? Can systems that do more than simply present two-dimensional static images to screeners facilitate categorization? Perceptual experts often learn more specific labels and descriptions of the objects that they expertly discriminate. Would increasing the vocabulary screeners use to describe different elements of X-ray images enhance their ability to distinguish weapons from non-weapons in such images?

There are, of course, factors other than visual sorting prowess that can hurt a screener's performance—fatigue, boredom, and social distractions—all of the factors that make vigilance a challenge for non-dolphins (see Chapter 4). That being said, if the goal of airport security is to find potential killers in a group of nonviolent travelers by staring at X-ray images of luggage, then one would hope that all the cognitive factors that might make this easier (or that make it an impossible cognitive task) would be closely considered.

CLOSURE

Walk into any kindergarten classroom and you'll be surrounded by signs of categories and concepts: perceptual categories of shapes and colors, functional categories like the alphabet, and abstract concepts of quantities represented as numbers. Much of early education focuses on training children to identify and label categories, shaping the way that children cognize. As an adult, it may be hard for you to imagine what the world was like before you learned to categorize and conceptualize.

Some adults get to revisit this kindergarten world, unfortunately, when damage to their inferotemporal cortex or basal ganglia destroys their ability to categorize. Such deficits may be hidden from both the people with the damage and the people who know them. Recall how Dr. P's wife told Dr. Sacks that her husband had a "vision problem," not a "problem categorizing objects?" And how from Dr. P's perspective, he was simply starting to make odd mistakes? Although the origins of Dr. P's cognitive problems were never discovered, most experts would guess that either his inferotemporal cortex or connections between this region and his prefrontal cortex were damaged. What exactly Dr. P perceived when he saw his wife's head or a rose is unclear. His ability to identify a rose based on its odor shows that his concept of a rose was largely intact, despite his inability to name the flower based on his visual percepts.

The goal of this chapter was to help you learn new concepts of categorization and discrimination by introducing you to the different ways that cognitive psychologists measure and think about these processes. You've read about the different qualities, dimensions, and associations that people use to sort objects and agents, and you've read about some ways that genetics and learning affect how people categorize. You've also seen how practice, development, and experience can change peoples' categories over time.

Perception, attention, recognition, and categorization may seem simple because they require so little effort in everyday life. The more psychologists have studied these processes, however, the clearer it has become that these components of cognizing are far from simple. The ability to discriminate and categorize experiences and thoughts is vital for memory, language, problem-solving, and reasoning processes. Every experience you have is unique; sorting through and interpreting a continuous stream of changing conditions is a pervasive element of how you think and act. Your categories and concepts enable you to organize your experiences in memory, and the labels you've associated with your categories and concepts may enable you to reactive those memories at a later date.

Have you formed new concepts or categories while reading this chapter? Or, have you simply sorted the material that was presented into preexisting bins that you formed long ago or were perhaps born with? Probably the answer varies somewhat for every person that reads this text. What you can be sure of is that whatever you get out of this chapter will depend heavily on how you categorize and conceptualize its contents and that how you do this will reflect the skills and knowledge that you've learned throughout your life. With luck, your brain will replay elements of this chapter many times over, so that you can add its contents to your conceptual networks.

COGNITIVE LINGO

abstract concept	distributed representation	perceptual learning
associative learning	equivalence class	perceptual similarity
basal ganglia	exemplar	prefrontal cortex (PFC)
basic level category	exemplar model	probabilistic category
categorical perception	family resemblance	prototype
categorize	fast mapping	prototype model
category	grandmother cell hypothesis	pseudocategory
category-boundary model	hippocampus	relational category
category-specific neuron	inferotemporal cortex	rule-based category
complementary learning systems	information integration	rule-based model
concept	local representation	stimulus generalization
connectionist model	perceptual category	theory-based model
discrimination	perceptual expertise	typicality

CHAPTER SUMMARY

Kinds of Categories and Concepts

Different classes of categories vary depending on how much they relate to perceptual similarities between category members. Perceptual categories include highly similar items, while functional categories and abstract concepts may include perceptually dissimilar items.

Theories of Categorization

There are several competing models of how categorization works, including theory-based, rule-based, prototype, exemplar, and category-boundary models.

Category Learning

Some categories and concepts appear to be genetically predetermined, but many are acquired either through associative learning or recognition of variations along dimensions.

Processes of Discrimination

Your ability to distinguish different percepts and concepts can change with practice—category construction is not simply cumulative. Perceptual experts classify events differently from novices because of a lifetime of learning.

Brain Substrates

The various brain regions that contribute to categorization change over time as you gain perceptual expertise. Interactions between the hippocampus, basal ganglia, and prefrontal cortex are key.

Applied Perspectives

The limits of categorization and discrimination can vary considerably across species. Knowing more about the mechanisms that constrain categorization can potentially make it possible to overcome such constraints.

REVIEW EXERCISES

Kinds of Categories and Concepts

- What are some key differences between naturalistic categories and artificial categories?
- What evidence is there that nonhumans can form abstract concepts?

Theories of Categorization

- What are the main differences between exemplar models and prototype models of categorization?
- What advantages do rule-based models have compared to category-boundary models?

Category Learning

- What distinguishes category learning based on associations from category learning based on recognition of dimensions?
- What kinds of evidence suggest that some categories are innate?

Processes of Discrimination

- Give some examples of how perceptual learning has affected the kinds of distinctions you make each day.
- How might a perceptual expert who is famous for detecting art forgeries categorize paintings differently from you?

Brain Substrates

- How are complementary learning systems thought to contribute to concept learning?
- What are some naturalistic categorization tasks that a patient with Parkinson's disease might find difficult?

Applied Perspectives

- What kinds of categories are TSA agents likely learning during training?

CRITICAL THINKING QUESTIONS

1. Involvement of an evolutionarily old region like the basal ganglia in category learning is somewhat surprising, because categorization is often portrayed as a sophisticated cognitive ability. If subcortical brain regions involved in basic sensorimotor control and learning also contribute to categorization, then this raises new questions about what people are learning when they learn to categorize. Piaget proposed that children learn new categories by interacting with objects (Piaget, 1952). Could physically playing with objects affect how children categorize them, and if so, how might the basal ganglia contribute to this process?

2. The proposal that conscious, rule-based categorization is a more advanced cognitive process than unconscious, percept-based categorization that involves information integration is similar to Descartes's mind-body split discussed in Chapter 1. Both propose that the conscious use of concepts requires special, human-specific faculties, while the soulless sensorimotor responses performed by nonhumans sorting percepts are unconscious, involuntary, and brutish. What sorts of findings from

studies of animals or humans with brain damage might support this proposal?

3. It may seem odd to think of your hippocampus regurgitating previous experiences to alter how you represent concepts and categories. But if this can happen when you are awake and aware that it is happening—like when you can't stop thinking about someone you have a crush on—then it seems plausible that it might also happen unconsciously. Which theory of categorization is most consistent with the idea that hippocampal replays of past experiences contribute to the formation of categories?

4. The idea that different parts of your brain are specialized to categorize or conceptualize specific kinds of objects or agents is, to a certain extent, an extension of Gall's theory of mental organs (see Chapter 2). Cortical specializations have also been linked to claims that humans have evolved unique cognitive processes, including innately specified cortical circuits for processing facial features and expressions (Kanwisher, 2000). Which theory of categorization is most consistent with the idea that

different parts of the brain are specialized for different kinds of categorizing?

5. Might it be possible to train dogs or other animals to aid physicians in ways analogous to how they currently aid police officers? Could dogs screen individuals for specific disorders or health problems, or detect early stages of cancer in blood or urine samples that doctors or nurses could not possibly detect in a typical checkup?

6. Does the categorization of objects within more complex, naturalistic scenes follow the same rules as categorization in laboratory settings? Or, might the difficulty of discriminating and sorting objects in complex scenes require attentional or conceptual mechanisms beyond what people typically make use of in laboratory experiments?

6 Time, Space, and Number

Tetra Images, LLC/Alamy Stock Photo

The Play happened on November 20, 1982. The place: California Memorial Stadium in Berkeley, California. The score: 20 to 19 with four seconds left. Stanford had just scored a field goal to take the lead. Stanford players and fans, including members of the notorious Stanford band, began to celebrate. After one last kickoff, the band rushed onto the field. They had underestimated the time remaining in the game and overestimated the space the Berkeley football players would need to travel to score a goal.

The first Berkeley player touched the ball at about midfield. He made little progress before chunking the ball to a teammate. The second Berkeleyan fared even worse and decided to copy his predecessor by tossing the ball to yet another player. The third guy with the ball made it a total of five yards before finding himself surrounded by five eager Stanfordites. By this point, tossing back the ball had become a mini-tradition, and so he did. Berkeley player number four (jersey number 5), who coincidentally was the same player to catch the first desperation toss, made much better progress the second time around. By this point, all 144 members of the Stanford band had spilled onto the field. To be precise, they were in the end zone where Berkeley's players were heading.

The fifth Berkeley player to get the ball sprinted into the band, making it clean through about twenty instrumentalists before plowing into a lone trombonist to score the winning touchdown. Ironically, the band was playing their signature tune, "All Right Now," just as things were going all wrong for them.

It's easy to get caught up in a moment, especially when that moment is a once-in-a-lifetime event. It's much trickier to pin down what a moment is. Look it up, and you will find that it's defined as "a point in time." Look up "time," and you will probably find something like "the indefinite continued progress of existence." Indefinite, as in not clearly expressed or defined: vague. In the words of William James (1890, p. 608), "Let any one try…to notice or attend to the *present* moment of time.

197

One of the most baffling experiences occurs. Where is it, this present? It has melted in our grasp, fled ere we could touch it, gone in the instant of becoming." All cognizing takes place in time, but the only evidence anyone has of time is their perception of time—a cognitive product. This sort of circularity makes even physicists' heads spin.

Saying that cognizing takes place in time implies that there are places in time. But places are spaces—particular positions or points in space. While followers of Einstein may agree that time is space, such that specific times can be in specific places, most people would agree that time and space are perceptually different things. You are unlikely to confuse where you are with when you are.

Perceived space seems a lot more solid than perceived time. The world (including you) consists of structures of a certain height, width, depth, shape, and size that appear stable. However, percepts of time actually are more stable than percepts of space. Your percepts of your body and surroundings change imperceptibly every time your sensory organs move, which is most of the time. In fact, if a sensory input does not change, such as if you wear a contact lens with an image printed on it, then the spatial features of those inputs will gradually disappear. That's why you don't notice that there are "holes" in space caused by the blind spots in your retinas. Effectively, you are change-blind to these spatial variations (as discussed in Chapter 4), treating objects and places as if they have constant spatial qualities despite all the information your brain is receiving that indicates sensory scenes are rapidly changing.

The fundamental contributions of space and time perception to human cognition are self-evident. Yet, compared to sensory perception, relatively little progress has been made in understanding how these processes work. Researchers continue to debate basic issues such as the extent to which spatial and temporal percepts are innate or learned (de Hevia et al., 2014; Leibovich et al., 2017), and whether the representations underlying these percepts depend on amodal, abstract concepts or whether they are a consequence of reflexive responses to sensations and biological cycles (Borghi et al., 2017; Michel, 2021).

Psychological studies of number are similarly controversial, with some arguing that only humans possess the capacity to count, add, subtract, or divide (**Figure 6.1**), and others proposing that such abilities are basic abilities of most species that help them to navigate, solve problems, and make decisions (Carey & Barner, 2019; Leslie et al., 2008). As you will soon discover, the links between perception of time, space, and number are more intimate than scientists originally thought. It may be no accident that all the key features of "The Play" can be represented numerically, from the duration the play lasted, to the distance the players ran, to the rate at which the trombonist approached the ground after the scoring player trampled him.

Percepts of space, time, and number provide the foundation for much of the science of minds. They are the cognitive superstructure that grounds your daily interpretations of the events you experience as well as your thoughts and memories of the past and future. These percepts depend in

FIGURE 6.1. Ancient abstractions. Some of the earliest evidence of abstract concepts comes from symbolic representations of numbers (in this case Babylonian) that humans used to represent amounts, distances, and time periods. (Viacheslav Lopatin via Shutterstock)

surprising ways on your abilities to recognize, attend to, and respond to events and on your ability to categorize, conceptualize, and discriminate ongoing experiences, as this chapter will soon reveal.

BEHAVIORAL PROCESSES

Traditionally, psychologists and philosophers have leaned toward dividing mental experiences into either percepts or concepts, the latter being abstract and universal and somewhat independent of the raw details available in percepts. Subjective impressions of time, space, and number (or quantity) certainly seem to transcend sensations. For example, you can recognize two of almost anything and can recognize durations and shapes across modalities.

As far as psychologists know, time, space, and number are not forms of energy that sensory receptors can directly detect. And yet the first step of sensory transduction—the process of transforming energy into sensations—is to convert forms of energy into a common neural "code" that indicates when changes in energy were detected, where they were detected, and how much change occurred. Brains then proceed to transform these generic internal variations into forms that give rise to distinctive percepts.

Producing neural patterns that vary in time, space, and number is not the same thing as perceiving changes in time, space, or number. The hands on a watch move in ways that track temporal variations, but watches do not perceive time, just as rulers do not perceive space and calculators do not perceive numbers. The following sections explore what is known about the "something extra" that makes perception and conception of time, space, and number possible.

Timing and Time Perception

SNEAK PEEK: The processes that enable you to enter a revolving door differ from those that let you judge the time it takes to get to the other side. By looking at how well different models predict and explain temporal perception, researchers can clarify how time is mentally represented.

Stanford band members know a lot about time. They are a marching band after all and keeping time is what marching is all about. Musical performances also require attending to time, following rhythms, establishing and adjusting tempos, and sticking to a beat. The key to such coordination is perceiving precisely when certain repeating events are occurring and then timing actions to coincide with those events.

The process of adjusting your actions to match a temporal pattern, called **entrainment**, can occur at multiple time scales (Kaplan et al., 2020). People are more likely to run around semi-naked in the summer (entrainment to a seasonal cycle) and during the day (entrainment to a diurnal cycle). Many of your daily activity patterns are entrained to a diurnal cycle.

Actions entrained to exactly match the timing of events within a temporal pattern are **synchronized**. Marching musicians voluntarily synchronize their steps while audience members may involuntarily synchronize their feet to the beat. Production and perception of music, with its sometimes sophisticated rhythms, is perhaps the clearest example of auditory perceptual timing (Clayton, 2012; Lenc et al., 2021; Trainor et al., 2018).

Synchronizing Actions with External Events

Each school day across the United States, groups of children synchronously recite the Pledge of Allegiance. This is a feat that few, if any, other organisms can match. Many animals nevertheless naturally time their actions based on their observations (McCue et al., 2020), and most can learn to time them in specific ways based on experience (like Pavlov's dogs). Flocking birds can rapidly adjust their movements to maintain a tight configuration (O'Keeffe et al., 2017), but they do not flap their wings or vocalize in synchrony. No birds engage in the kind of customized, synchronized group display shown by pledging children (sadly, there are no *Happy Feet* penguins).

Predicting When to Act

It's easy to trigger simultaneous actions. All you need is a loud bang. It's much harder to get multiple individuals to synchronize their actions without an external cue. This is one of the main reasons that most large musical groups have a conductor. Synchronization seems to require not just entrainment but also temporally precise predictions—predictions that make it possible to respond proactively at a specific time, rather than reactively. Where do these temporal predictions come from?

Synchronization requires predicting *when* an upcoming event will occur. Generally, this prediction comes from past percepts of similar events. You can predict when a specific horse on a merry-go-round will reappear based on having seen it (and other horses) go by before. Hearing the beginning of a song sets the stage for you to predict when following notes, words, and drumbeats are likely to occur.

When listening to music, your auditory perception becomes entrained to ongoing sounds. Sensory receptors in your ears are literally firing to the beat (Todd & Lee, 2015). Current ideas about how you are able to pick up on when the next beat is going to happen assume that you rely on "mental merry-go-rounds," or **oscillators**, when you are timing repeating inputs (Doelling et al., 2019).

Circadian Rhythms

The strongest evidence of internal oscillators comes from studies of daily activity patterns. Many organisms that have been isolated from all cues about what time of day it is continue to sleep and wake up in predictable temporal cycles, called **circadian timing** (Hastings et al., 2019).

Without external cues, those cycles of activity gradually shift until they no longer match what is happening in the outside world, suggesting that something inside the individual is controlling sleep and wake times (**Figure 6.2**). In other words, brains are controlling the timing of sleep periods, just like the mechanics of a merry-go-round control when each horse will appear.

If your brain can make one mental merry-go-round, why not multiple carousels? The circuits controlling circadian timing are actually made up of multiple oscillators within your brain and throughout your internal organs (Reppert & Weaver, 2002). The rate at which these oscillators cycle is controlled by a looping sequence of genes affecting other genes. Each oscillator is basically a clock controlled by molecular interactions in which timing can be adjusted by external

FIGURE 6.2. Circadian timing in a cricket. Each row tracks the cricket's movements for one full day in chronological order, with black blocks indicating when the cricket was active (mainly when the lights were off). The bar up top shows the light-dark cycle the cricket experienced during the first eleven days of the experiment. On day twelve, the lights went out for good and the cricket's activity cycle began to shift to earlier and earlier times while remaining cyclical. (After Abe et al., 1997; image of cricket: Carlyn Iverson/Science Source)

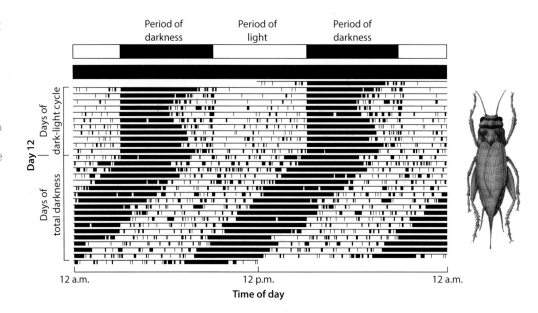

inputs (Patke et al., 2020). Like members of a marching band, these oscillators can only maintain synchrony with guidance from an internal conductor. This conductor is usually entrained to daylight.

In principle, with enough internal oscillators running at different rates, you could have "biological clocks" that can entrain to any regularly repeating input (Paton & Buonomano, 2018). For instance, the set of oscillators that best entrain to a specific input, say a popular country song, would provide a basis for predicting when the next twang is likely to occur, enabling you to synchronize your foot taps or cringes to the perceived beat. Most cognitive processes are affected by internal diurnal cycles, which is partly why you are more likely to retain material studied during times of the day when you feel refreshed than topics you've studied at 3 a.m.

Timing Intervals

Cognitive psychologists typically give little attention to synchronization, rhythm perception, or motor timing, in part because these processes appear to happen automatically. Other aspects of temporal perception that are more consciously accessible, such as perception of how much time has gone by, often steal the limelight from mere entrainment.

Subjective estimates of duration, or **interval timing**, are often verbalizable, making them easier to study in undergraduates. Historically, studies of interval timing have focused on shorter intervals, usually lasting less than a minute (Buhusi & Meck, 2005). Researchers prefer studying shorter intervals partly because neither experimenters nor experimentees are keen on multi-hour experiments—boredom leads to lousy data. Sometimes, researchers also distinguish interval timing from millisecond timing (Merchant et al., 2008), which is more likely to be unconscious and associated with conditioned responding (see Chapter 7). Perceiving the duration of temporal intervals is fundamental to many cognitive acts, including musical composition, speaking conversationally, and planning future activities.

Subjective Impressions of Passing Time

You can probably say how long you think it will take you to read the rest of this page, how long it took you to read the last two pages, and so on. You've likely experienced many informal tests of interval timing, such as when you are at a busy restaurant and deciding when you may need to wave your arms to get the attention of an employee. If so, you probably know that your estimate of how long you've waited for the check may vary depending on how eager you are to leave.

Your perception of duration is an aspect of your *Umwelt* (discussed in Chapter 3) that can fluctuate over time. The saying "time flies when you're having fun" captures the subjective essence of interval timing. Some intervals seem to go by quickly and others seem to drag on.

People tend to assume that the perception of time passing is the same for everyone. That is, until they end up behind an older driver moving down the road at a turtle's pace. Even then, it's hard to imagine that two people's subjective impressions of time might be quite different. From the elderly driver's perspective, he is the one driving normally, and the youngsters are the ones driving around at ridiculously fast speeds.

From a whale's or an elephant's perspective, humans may seem like manic monkeys and hummingbirds may be teleporters. From a fly's perspective, in contrast, humans are probably more like tree sloths. The perception of temporal intervals as being long or short is relative to the observer (**Figure 6.3**).

Psychophysical Studies of Time Perception

Because perceived intervals vary along a continuum (from short to long), duration perception can be analyzed psychophysically, just like percepts of pitch, brightness, or other sensory dimensions. One method that researchers use to evaluate how individuals perceive differences between intervals is the temporal bisection procedure (Killeen, 2023). In this task, individuals learn to make one response

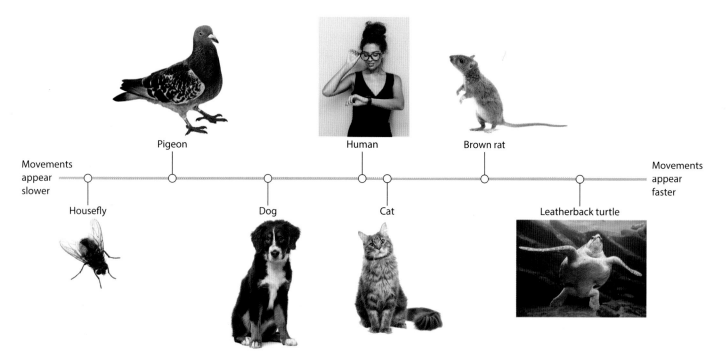

FIGURE 6.3. Different species, different time frames. Some animals perceive humans as moving in slow motion while others judge them to be quite frisky. Variations in perceived rates also can vary within species and across ages. (After Griffiths, 2014; Images housefly: irin-k via Shutterstock, pigeon: Altin Osmanaj via Shutterstock, dog: Eric Isselee via Shutterstock, human: Dean Drobot via Shutterstock, cat: Remark_Anna via Shutterstock, rat: Tenra, turtle: FourOaks)

(like a left button press) when they perceive a fixed, shorter duration interval, and a second response when they perceive a fixed, longer duration interval. For instance, you might be asked to say "short" when you hear a one-second tone and "long" when you hear a two-second tone. After learning this task, you might then be tested with a range of tones varying in duration from one to two seconds to see which ones you classify as long or short. This task can be used to establish your ability to discriminate between different durations and measure how similar you perceive different durations to be (Grondin, 2010).

Interestingly, although humans and rats can both learn the temporal bisection procedure, they differ in how they judge the similarity of shorter or longer intervals (Jozefowiez et al., 2018). The resolution of temporal intervals also varies within species depending on the sensory modality, the responses required in the task, and the motivation of the participant (Balci, 2015). It seems that what you're doing, and how much you like it, can change your perception of duration. Your mental representations of time vary in ways that a stopwatch does not.

Weber's Law in Duration Judgments

It's not just that brains are less precise timers than stopwatches. As with other perceptual abilities, your capacity to discriminate between different durations depends on what you are comparing. It's easier to discriminate 1 pound from 2 pounds than it is to tell 101 pounds from 102 pounds, and it's easier to distinguish 1 second from 2 seconds than to tell 101 seconds from 102. Interval timing seems to obey Weber's Law (see Chapter 4), which describes how much a perceived stimulus must change for that change to be just noticeable.

Experiments that test individuals' abilities to time a specific interval have revealed both how estimates of duration vary across trials and how absolute duration affects individuals' estimates (Gu et al., 2015). For instance, if individuals learn that any responses they make after a fixed duration are rewarded, then after many trials, they will begin timing their responses such that they respond the most at the specific time when a reward will be given, sort of like when shoppers rush a store on Black Friday (**Figure 6.4A**).

If no reward is given on a particular trial, then the individuals will persist in responding for a while after the reward normally would have arrived, just in case. Such wishful-thinking responses give an even clearer picture of subjects' abilities to judge the durations of specific intervals.

(A)

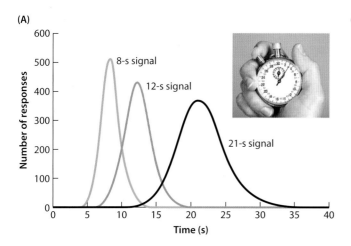

(B)

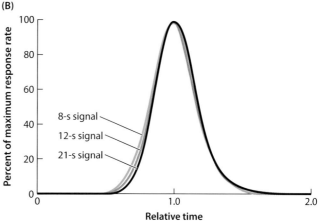

The Scalar Property and Behavioral Markers of Duration

As predicted by Weber's Law, longer intervals are not estimated as precisely as shorter intervals and your ability to resolve different durations decreases at a predictable rate as intervals grow longer (Lejeune & Wearden, 2006; Rakitin et al., 1998). In fact, if you were to divide all of your response times by the target duration that you were attempting to estimate, the relative accuracy of your duration estimates would be highly similar across different durations (**Figure 6.4B**). This property is known as the **scalar property** of timing (Gallistel & Gibbon, 2000).

The scalar property applies to "pure" estimates of duration but not to estimates in which people use learned strategies to time intervals, such as mentally reciting "One Mississippi, two Mississippi," and so on. The resulting difference in duration estimation accuracy highlights the fact that there is more than one way to time an interval. Humans may use different mechanisms compared to other animals and may use different mechanisms from each other. One person might visualize a watch ticking through seconds while someone else might move their fingers sequentially in specific patterns or hum a tune that lasts a known duration.

Behaviorists studying interval timing noticed that individuals often cycled through predictable sequences of actions while waiting to respond at a particular duration (Killeen & Fetterman, 1988). Imagine you are waiting for a bus. Initially, you might sit, then at some point, you stand up, begin pacing, or start looking down the street. Onlookers might interpret these actions as signs of impatience. Researchers instead suggested that such action sequences could serve as cues that tell you how long you have been waiting (De Kock et al., 2021). For example, if you are looking down the street and checking the time on your phone, then those are actions that can let you know that you have been waiting longer. This may seem like a weird way to judge time, but you can probably get some sense of how long people have been waiting in a line based on their actions and expressions. So presumably, those people's brains can also use those same cues too.

The Perceived "Present"

When you estimate differences in weight, brightness, or loudness, there are physical or energetic changes in the world that you perceptually assess. That's often not the case when you are judging duration. If you just sit and stare at this sentence for ten seconds, nothing physically will change. And yet, you will still perceive those ten seconds as being different from a one-second stare. There are various theories about what makes a person perceive ten seconds as being "more than" one second. Most suggest that gradual changes in neural processes (such as oscillators or decaying memory traces, discussed further in the Brain Substrates section of this chapter) drive temporal "sensations" (Gu et al., 2015; Killeen & Grondin, 2022). Others suggest that a perceived temporal interval is what you get when you attend to a sequence of conscious moments (chunks of experience) as a group—two moments is less than four, and so on (Block & Gruber, 2014; Matthews & Meck, 2016).

FIGURE 6.4. Accuracy at timing intervals. (A) Students required to make a response after a specific duration are more accurate at estimating 8 seconds than 12 seconds and more accurate for 12 seconds than for 20 seconds. (B) If you divide students' estimates of duration by the absolute duration being estimated, then the likelihood that participants will respond at a specific time before or after the "right time to respond" is essentially the same for all three durations. This phenomenon, which is closely related to Weber's law, is called the scalar property of timing. (A, B after Allman et al., 2014; replotted from Rakitin et al., 1998., inset image: kurhan via Shutterstock)

William James described these experienced moments as the "practically cognized present," by which he meant the recently experienced past (James, 1890). After all, brains do not respond instantaneously. Even the quickest percepts take time. Have fun trying to figure out how long time perception takes. What feels like the present seems to last a certain, relatively short, amount of time as well. But it's hard to tell how long the longest "now" lasts. Current estimates hover around 750 milliseconds for adult humans (Wittmann, 2011), but this can shrink or grow in certain circumstances, resulting in temporal illusions.

Temporal illusions are not like those visual illusions that you can stare at indefinitely without ever wrapping your head around what it is you're seeing. Temporal illusions typically last less than a second and change perception of time in relatively subtle ways, making events seem slightly shorter, longer, or more simultaneous than they otherwise would (Eagleman, 2008). For example, a flickering visual image that lasts only 600 milliseconds might appear to last 800 to 900 milliseconds depending on the flicker rate (Kanai et al., 2006), whereas the perceived duration of an unflickering version may be quite close to 600 milliseconds. Although temporal illusions might seem to just be time perception when it doesn't work right, studies of such illusions can provide new insights into the mechanisms of interval timing, as you will soon discover in the Time Warping section of this chapter.

Models of Time Tracking

At the core of most explanations of time perception is some type of **internal clock**, a biological mechanism that functions like a mechanical clock by repeatedly and reliably measuring out fixed intervals of time (Allman et al., 2014). In the case of interval timing, researchers typically model the fixed intervals as being relatively short, like those measured by the second hand of a watch. Also, there needs to be some mechanism that monitors what the internal clock is doing, a sort of internal watch watcher.

Early cognitive models of time perception were extensions of the computational theory of mind (see Chapter 1). They describe timing as a quantitative comparison between stored memories of standard times (like the presets on a microwave) with ongoing observations of an internal clock (Ivry & Schlerf, 2008) (**Figure 6.5**).

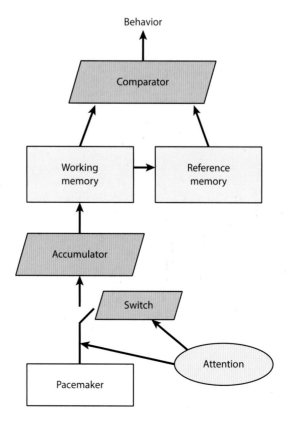

FIGURE 6.5. Model of interval timing. An internal pacemaker ticks off fixed, short-duration time intervals that are counted (like counting seconds on a watch). The pacemaker begins when the individual starts attending to the passage of time, triggering the storage of pacemaker outputs within an accumulator (like a stopwatch). The current count is stored in working memory and compared to the goal time (stored in reference memory). For instance, in a game of hide-and-seek, the reference memory would be the final number that triggers the "ready-or-not" mantra. By comparing the current tally to a goal state, an individual can decide when a certain amount of time has passed and react after a specific duration has passed. How working memories are compared to reference memories determines how the model predicts effects like the scalar property. (After Matthews & Meck, 2016)

Time Perception as Internal Clock Watching

The simplest models of time perception treat the internal clock like an internal stopwatch (van Rijn et al., 2014). All the remaining perceptual mechanisms work basically the same as they would for any sensory modality. From the perspective of this model, temporal illusions might occur if the internal clock was running faster or slower than normal or if attention started or stopped tracking the passage of time too early or too late. Subjective time also depends on clock speed in this model. So if a fly perceives time as happening in slow motion relative to a human's experience, then it must be because flies have sped-up internal clocks. A fly's internal clock might tick ten times or more for every one tick of a human's internal clock.

A limitation of standard internal clock models is that no one has discovered anything like a stopwatch in brains, much less a stopwatch monitor. This is not a major problem because you can replace this biologically implausible part of the internal clock model with groups of oscillators that oscillate at different rates—a bit like having a set of egg timers, each of which only dings after a specific duration. As mentioned earlier, there are biological mechanisms for tracking time with multiple oscillators, and there are biological mechanisms for entraining those oscillators to external events. The idea is similar for interval timing, except with shorter durations and different kinds of oscillators. Such models are often used to explain timing in musical perception or performance (McAuley & Jones, 2003).

Timing Events without a Clock

Most cognitive models of interval timing include an internal clock or pacemaker of some sort that is triggered by external events and compared to memories of durations represented as varying magnitudes or sizes (see Figure 6.5). In this framework, longer times correspond to larger magnitudes. This is not the only way that researchers have modeled time perception, however. An alternative approach is to assume that there are no internal representations of time comparable to those that exist for sensations. Instead, sequences of brain activity that last a certain duration may be used to time events (Karmarkar & Buonomano, 2007). These "no-clock" models work in basically the same way as the behaviorists' action-based explanation of timing (described earlier in the waiting for the bus example), except that the timing cues are neural patterns rather than motor acts like pacing or looking down the street for a bus.

Yet another view on time perception is that there are no abstract indicators of time, either clock-based or activity-driven, but that instead, each sensory modality has its own representations of time. For instance, an auditory representation of a phoneme might represent time as ordered changes in features that you can hear, while a visual representation of a flashing smiley face might simply encode the rate of change in the image. This sort of modality-specific timing can potentially account for why you can distinguish the durations of sounds more accurately than you can discriminate the durations of visual events (Roseboom et al., 2019).

Finally, some models of interval timing are simply circadian timing models, but on a shorter time scale (Addyman et al., 2016). Recall that circadian timing involves a kind of internal, eternal merry-go-round with a daily cycle; it never stops spinning. Unlike stopwatches, which can be stopped and restarted, circadian cycles rarely, if ever, reset. One way that a circadian timing mechanism could be used to time intervals is if the stage of a cycle is noted at the start and end of an interval and then used to calculate the difference. Have you ever checked a wall clock during a lecture to see how long the person has been droning on? It's basically the same idea.

Each of these models has different strengths and weaknesses. None of them alone can account for all that is currently known about time perception. Time perception differs from the kinds of sensory perception discussed in Chapter 4 in that it is not yet clear what sorts of events trigger awareness of moments or of time passing. It's not even clear whether the timing mechanisms that enable you to control your actions when catching a ball or writing a word are in any way related to those that enable you to perceive how long it takes you to do either of those things.

A final mystery about time perception is how exactly it relates to the perception of other abstract properties such as space and number. As the following section reveals, these three processes have a lot more in common than you might guess.

SIGHT BITES

 Synchronizing actions with external events requires you to predict specific times when events are likely to occur based on memories of regularities in past occurrences.

 Perception of duration and temporal patterns can vary across species, individuals, and situations.

 Judging the duration of an event (interval timing) may require processes that differ from recognizing when an event is likely to happen.

 Some theories of time perception assume that an internal clock makes it possible to estimate durations while others assume that interval timing can be achieved without an internal clock.

Spatial Cognition

SNEAK PEEK: Perception of space and navigation involve multiple modalities and memories for places. Models of spatial processing try to account for the many ways that dynamic inputs can be related to stable maps of locations.

"Primitively our space-experiences form a chaos, out of which we have no immediate faculty for extricating them. Objects of different sense-organs, experienced together, do not in the first instance appear either inside or alongside or far outside of each other, neither spatially continuous nor discontinuous, in any definite sense of these words ... throughout all this confusion we conceive of a world spread out in a perfectly fixed and orderly fashion, and we believe in its existence. The question is: How do this conception and this belief arise?"
—James, 1890, p 181

Space, like time, has a long history of confounding great minds. Early considerations of space focused less on what spatial perception is like, and more on where it came from and what exactly was being perceived. More recently, researchers have been focusing on the kinds of sensations that drive spatial percepts or actions, with much less emphasis on the origins of these percepts.

Spatial cognition generally refers to things an individual knows (or believes) about space, including awareness of properties like size, shape, distance, depth, position, and movement. Like time perception, there do not appear to be any dedicated "space sensors." Instead, spatial percepts seem to be constructed from sensations in multiple modalities, often involving comparisons between multiple sets of sensations, for instance by combining signals from both your eyes or ears.

Spatial percepts play a key role in movements because many actions are constrained by the position and location of your body. Much of the research on spatial cognition has focused specifically on strategies for navigating over larger spaces, however, rather than on mechanisms involved in more localized movements.

The following sections discuss spatial perception and navigation from multiple perspectives with an emphasis on those aspects of spatial processing that are linked to time perception. Unfortunately, there is insufficient space or time to review all the interesting findings on spatial cognition that cognitive psychologists have uncovered during the last century.

Spatial Perception and Action

If you were a black ghost knifefish, then whenever you electrified the water surrounding you, you would be able to check for disturbances in the force caused by small, edible crustaceans (Skeels et al., 2023). You would also be able to detect and localize nearby prey by feeling the electrical shifts they create on your skin. By moving your body up and down or back and forth, you would be able to gain additional clues as to where the lunch options are and what they are doing. For you (the fish you), space comes from electrical fluctuations, as it does for most vertebrates.

The main difference between you (the non-fish you) and electric fish, at least in terms of how you construct space, is that knifefish process electrical patterns coming from outside their bodies, whereas you use electrical patterns originating from neurons inside your brain. Also, when you feel objects in space, you are usually touching them.

The Feel of Space

Knowing where an object is by touching it requires not only feeling the object but also having some awareness of where the body part doing the touching is located. This, in turn, requires knowing something about the size and shape of your own body at the time of touching. You might be surprised to find out that your tactile representation of your body does not match your visual impressions of how your body appears spatially (Longo & Haggard, 2010). In fact, it is relatively simple to separate these two representations using a technique called the rubber hand illusion.

In the **rubber hand illusion**, a rubber hand is placed on a table in front of a person in a position where they could easily place their own hand (**Figure 6.6**). If the fake hand is then stroked while the person's real hand, which is out of sight of the person, is stroked in the same way, the person will begin to feel as though the rubber hand that they can see is actually their hand, effectively disowning their actual hand (Reimer et al., 2019). The person's real hand seems to vanish as visual information about what is happening relocates the participants' body map onto the table. The effect is similar to what happens when you see a ventriloquist's dummy talk (Alais & Burr, 2004), except that a teleported touch takes the place of a dislocated voice.

In the rubber hand illusion, two sensory modalities battle to decide where in space a person's hand really is. In more natural circumstances, however, different modalities are more likely to corroborate where things are located in the world (Lalanne & Lorenceau, 2004). Tactile and visual

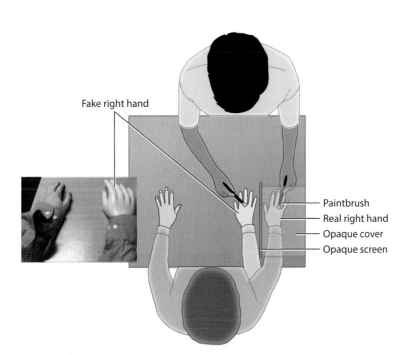

Fake right hand

Paintbrush
Real right hand
Opaque cover
Opaque screen

FIGURE 6.6. The rubber hand illusion. A rubber hand placed on a table can transform into "your hand" if it is visually consistent with where your hand could be and is visibly stroked in the same way that your real hand is being stroked out of view, illustrating cross-modal congruence of your body space. (From O'Dowd & Newell, 2020, *Neurosci Lett* 720, with permission from Elsevier)

sensations usually provide convergent spatial information for objects being touched. Auditory and visual cues that reveal the location of a sound-producing object are also usually consistent. The consistency of spatial cues across modalities, called cross-modal congruence, is an important component of localizing things in space (Spence, 2011). The rubber hand illusion only works when a person's hidden hand is stroked in the same way as the rubber hand, such that the tactile patterns match the visual patterns.

Spatial Representation

The multimodal nature of perceived space is clearly evident in a condition known as hemispatial neglect (Corbetta, 2014). People with hemispatial neglect, which is typically a symptom of brain damage, appear to be oblivious to everything on either their right or left side (almost always it's the left). Most obviously, they appear to be unaware of objects or events in their left visual field, as if they have a blind spot. However, the deficits are often not limited to things unseen.

A person may fail to put on the right sleeve of a jacket or to eat food from the right side of their plate, ignoring objects that could easily be seen by a head turn if the issue was simply a blind spot. Furthermore, the person may ignore people speaking to them from the left side as well as taps on the left arm, and they may shave only the right half of their body. If asked to draw an object, they often draw only its right side. When asked to imagine and describe a street they know well, they may describe only features from one side of the street. Dogs with hemispatial neglect will only eat food from the right side of their bowl, suggesting that odors from the left may also be ignored (Rossmeisl et al., 2007).

The broad range of problems that show up with hemispatial neglect suggests that patients with this disorder are no longer able to perceive space uniformly. There are differing views about why this is the case. Some researchers argue that the ability to attend to certain locations is lost, while others suggest that mental representations of space become distorted (Corbetta & Shulman, 2011). Either way, it's clear that individuals' spatial percepts are systematically messed up. For them, the world they are perceiving is normal, with inputs from multiple modalities seemingly confirming their atypical impressions.

Many psychological studies of spatial perception focus on identifying cues that people use to construct spatial representations. In the visual world, cues to features like depth come from eye movements, differences in the signals transduced by each eye, and properties of scenes that are associated with near and far distances, such as image size and clarity. For sound, differences in the timing across ears reveal the direction from which a sound came.

Knowing what sensory cues are important for constructing spatial percepts has made it possible to develop virtual reality (VR) systems that simulate variations in these cues. VR technologies not only make for some unique entertainment options but they can also be used to test how subtle variations in inputs change spatial perception.

One discovery from VR systems is that brains don't like it when movements in visual space don't match up with what the body says is happening spatially—a situation that leads to motion sickness (Chang et al., 2020). This discovery suggests that the vestibular system (mainly associated with balance and monitoring of orientation) plays a key role in validating audiovisual cues that signal dynamic changes in space, a fact that simulator rides use to full effect.

An individual's perception of motion links spatial perception to temporal judgments. In physics, motion is mathematically defined as changes in space over time. The idea that things move through space, and that doing so takes time, seems pretty intuitive for adults. But these are ultimately interpretations of perceptual experiences. Might these experiences be different for some individuals, such as children under the age of two?

Jean Piaget's studies of shape copying by young children, noted in Chapter 1, suggest that young children's notions of shape may differ significantly from what adults think of as shapes (Piaget & Inhelder, 1956). Children's copies of simple shapes such as triangles can be even more distorted than those produced by an individual with hemispatial neglect, although children's copies do not omit parts of the image.

Piaget argued that the systematic distortions in geometry present in children's drawings were not simply a result of gradually developing crayon control skills but instead revealed how children's conceptions of space gradually arise from their interactions with the world. More specifically, he proposed that how infants and toddlers perceive their movements in the world (including their drawing movements) determines how they conceptualize space.

Donald Hebb (introduced in Chapter 2) went one step further, arguing that initially young children do not perceive shapes, distances, or locations, and gradually they learn to perceive these properties of the world through their interactions with it (Hebb, 1949). From this perspective, much of what you refer to as space comes from mental representations that you acquired very early in your life, and how you cognize space is a direct consequence of how you perceived motion as a child.

This implies that if you had grown up in different circumstances, say as a bat, then how you cognize space and time might be very different (Nagel, 1974). Bats are nocturnal and so rely much less on vision. Their motions are much faster than yours and they operate much more freely in three dimensions. Their food also moves much faster than yours, again with three-dimensional freedom.

For bats to perceive prey at all, they have to precisely time not only their flight patterns but also their vocal production, since echolocation only happens if you make sounds that generate echoes. To know where trees, insects, or lampposts are located, bats use the time it takes echoes to arrive to judge their distance from such things. In this context, time literally becomes space. What is movement, space, or time like for a bat? What aspects of space might they be able to cognize that you cannot?

Changing Places

You might not be able to personally experience "bat space," but you can see what it's like to live in a different space. Prism glasses take incoming light and shift everything viewed to a different position, usually to the right or left, but some versions also flip the world upside down (Harris, 1965). If you put on such goggles, you will initially be disoriented because what you see does not match what you feel. If you perform a task like playing darts, your initial throws will likely be way off target. Once you get used to the visual shift, however, you can counteract the mismatch and may stop noticing it altogether. If you take off the glasses after this, you will become disoriented again as your systems recalibrate back to their original spatial organization of the world.

Surprisingly, the changes that make adaptation to a prism-shifted world possible are mainly kinesthetic, related to the feelings inside your limbs, rather than changes in visual space perception. Shifting your world with prism glasses could be little more than a party trick, except that wearing them can actually help people with hemispatial neglect to recover function (Serino et al., 2006).

Two processes are thought to make such space shifting possible: realignment of perception, in which new sensorimotor associations are quickly formed, and recalibration of movements, which is a more proactive response to the conscious recognition of a mismatch (Facchin et al., 2019). If recalibration is what is happening, then once the glasses are gone, everything should revert to normal. The strong after-effects that occur when the glasses are removed strongly suggest that the changes are not simply strategic.

Additional evidence of rapid spatial realignment comes from studies in which participants learned to hear with new ears. Your ability to localize sounds is partly based on the nooks and crannies in your outer ears. If these are modified, say by putting silicone molds shaped like a bat's ears over your own, this will temporarily interfere with your ability to perceive where sounds are coming from. If you continue wearing the ear molds, eventually your auditory localization abilities will return (Hofman et al., 1998).

Performing actions that highlight new spatial inaccuracies helps people to realign their auditory spatial maps (Carlile, 2014). Interestingly, taking off the ear molds does not lead to the sort of after-effects caused by wearing prism glasses for a long time—there's no performance drop. And once you

FIGURE 6.7. Growing up goggled. Owls that develop from a young age constantly wearing prism goggles will adjust how they perceive space to account for the fact that all incoming images are shifted relative to their actual positions. These kinds of spatial recalibration experiments make it possible for researchers to examine the mechanisms that contribute to flexible spatial processing. (Eric Knudsen)

have learned to hear with weird ears, you can put them back on sometime later without having to re-adjust to their oddities. It's like you have learned to hear through two pairs of ears!

Experiments with barn owls and ferrets have revealed several processes of perceptual plasticity that enable animals to adjust to new spatial reference frames during development and throughout adulthood (Fritz et al., 2007; Keuroghlian & Knudsen, 2007) (**Figure 6.7**). These findings are a bit surprising given the central place of space in organizing and coordinating perception across modalities.

Why is perceptual processing so accommodating of large changes in spatial properties? Possibly, this has something to do with the fact that one of the primary functions of spatial cognition is to guide locomotion, a task that has spawned a legion of sophisticated actions and unique natural strategies. From dancing bees to GPS-loving humans, there is a common need to move through environments that are sometimes unpredictable. The ability to flexibly construct spatial representations to meet novel needs may help organisms to make the best use of whatever terrain they encounter.

Spatial Navigation

Searching is a daily activity for most animals, whether it's searching for food, a mate, shelter, or enter-tainment. Searching means exploring and exploring usually means navigating new spaces and keep-ing track of not-so-new places. Because search behavior is rarely random, observations of search pat-terns during exploration and navigation can provide important clues about how animals represent space and how repeated experiences affect those representations. By controlling the conditions that individuals face while searching, experimenters can tease apart the various mechanisms that make spatial exploration and navigation work.

Orientation and Navigation

Two key elements of spatial navigation are controlled mobility and the ability to identify target loca-tions or objects. You need to be able to "get there" and to "know where" you are getting (Benhamou, 2010). Jellyfish are able to move throughout the ocean and collect prey while doing so, but it's ques-tionable whether they perceive space or control their movements. It's difficult to say if jellyfish are searching for anything. On the other hand, some evidence suggests that at least some jellyfish may be able to sense water currents and use those sensations to orient their movements (Fossette et al., 2015).

Spatial orientation, the process of monitoring and controlling one's movements in a particular direction (or positioning the body in a desired direction), distinguishes a curious mouse from a ca-reening pinball. This ability can vary considerably, from animals that migrate long distances in three-dimensional environments to absentminded professors who quickly get lost in a multilevel depart-ment store. Orientation can involve compass-like mechanisms as well as cues from most modalities. For many humans, visual cues reign supreme. But people born blind are still able to orient them-selves, so vision is not the only way to get where you want to go.

When you are exploring a place you have never been before, orientation becomes particularly important. If you can't keep track of where you are heading, there's a good chance you'll get lost. Thousands of people get lost in national parks each year and have to be located by rescue teams. Even

(A)

(B)

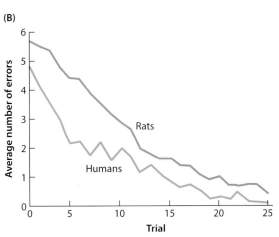

FIGURE 6.8. The first "rat maze." (A) The Hampton Court Maze, a hedge maze in the United Kingdom, provided the inspiration for early studies of spatial learning by rodents. (B) Observations of rats and humans learning to make their way through similarly complex mazes gave researchers new insights into the systematic ways that animals explore novel environments, as well as how their behavior changes as an environment becomes familiar. (A Sergi Nunez; B after Husband, 1929)

more get lost trying to find their way through an unfamiliar hospital. To reduce the number of people wandering around with confused expressions, humans came up with the idea of using maps and location markers. These spatial tools have proven critical not only for keeping people on track but also for thinking about how spaces may be mentally represented.

Mazes and Maps

Getting lost isn't always a bad thing. It can even be fun, which is presumably why humans began constructing environments for the sole purpose of making people become lost. One such structure, a hedge maze at the Hampton Court Palace in London, inspired a U.S. graduate student to construct a smaller version that rats could run through (**Figure 6.8**). His observations of rats exploring this mini maze sparked a century of experiments measuring maze navigation by rodents (Traetta, 2020).

Early descriptions of how rats behave when exploring mazes emphasized actions that, in humans, would be signs of confidence (leisurely running down an alley), uncertainty (hesitation at a choice point), or confusion (backtracking after reentering a dead-end path). Such interpretations were criticized because they anthropomorphized the rats, attributing humanlike qualities to them. This criticism led to more mechanistic explanations of rat behavior that focused on trial-and-error learning of turn sequences.

Later experiments by Edward Tolman (introduced in Chapter 1) showed that rats' actions in mazes were more flexible than would be expected if they were just learning to run through mazes like they were opening a combination lock. He proposed that rats instead constructed internal maps of mazes as they explored them. He referred to these internal maps as **cognitive maps**. Tolman didn't say what the maps were like or how rats accessed them while navigating. He simply argued that rats' navigational abilities showed that they had knowledge of the spatial relationships between locations in a familiar maze and could flexibly use that knowledge. The debate about whether cognitive maps exist (in rats, humans, or any other animal), and what such maps might be like if they do exist, has raged ever since.

Frames and Cues

Studies of spatial navigation have revealed two different ways that organisms represent where they are. Both involve using sensory cues. What distinguishes the two strategies is where the cues are coming from. When an organism determines where it is based on internally generated cues, such as kinesthetic percepts generated by its own actions or changes in orientation (vestibular cues), it's said to be using **idiothetic cues**. An organism may also use **allothetic cues**—external cues that are seen, heard, smelled, or touched.

Exploration is important for collecting both kinds of cues (Whishaw & Brooks, 1999), and both kinds of cues can be used to represent spatial information. Allothetic cues are more obvious to outside observers, and as such, they have been studied more extensively. Cognitive maps are thought to

(A) Landmarks

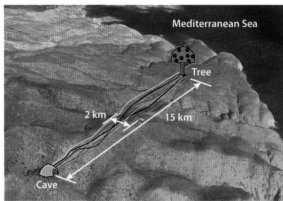

(B) Beaconing

(C) Route following

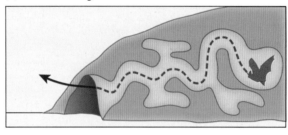

(D) Path integration

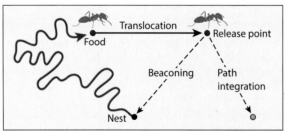

(E) Cognitive map

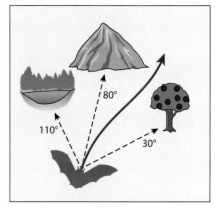

FIGURE 6.9. Potential navigation cues. Allothetic cues (sensed from the environment), such as landmarks (A) and beacons (B), may help bats navigate long distances. (A) Researchers can gain clues about the cues bats use by continuously tracking their flight paths as they navigate. (C) When external cues are not available, individuals may navigate using idiothetic cues (internally generated) by following memorized routes or keeping track of self-movements (referred to as path integration). (D) Researchers can get evidence that an individual is using idiothetic cues by "teleporting" them to a new location and then watching the paths they take from that location. (E) When animals can flexibly navigate an area in response to new conditions and goals, they may do so by using a cognitive map of that area. (A–E after Geva-Sagiv et al., 2015, *Nat Rev Neurosci* 16, with permission from SNCSC)

be constructed mainly from allothetic cues, the idea being that a person, ant, rat, or bat uses memories of how an environment appears to figure out how to get from point A to point B. If a person tells you how to get to the nearest ATM by telling you what to look for at each turn, they are drawing your attention to salient allothetic cues that you will likely encounter in your travels (**Figure 6.9**).

Spatial information organized in this way is referred to as an allocentric reference frame. Reference frames are systems for defining where things are. For instance, when you plot data in two dimensions, the *x*-axis and *y*-axis provide a reference frame for your plot. Since no one has ever seen a cognitive map, any proposed spatial reference frame is just a best guess.

In cases where an individual is depending mainly on idiothetic cues to navigate, spatial information is more of a personal history of things recently done, something like a mental retracing of steps than an actual map of environmental features. When spatial information is organized in terms of the position of the navigator's body, the reference frame is egocentric. Keeping track of where you are by continuously monitoring the movements you are making (through self-motion cues) is called **path integration**. Researchers who are skeptical about the existence of cognitive maps generally assume that navigation relies mainly on egocentric reference frames. If the directions you are given about how find to the nearest ATM are something like, "Walk for about ten minutes down this road, turn right, then walk straight five minutes, it'll be on your left," then you will be using a borrowed egocentric reference frame to get your cash.

Two kinds of allothetic cues stand out: landmarks and beacons. **Landmarks** include any stationary sources of information about where in space you are (see Figure 6.6A), and **beacons** (see Figure 6.6B) are stationary sources that tell you where you are going. If you are searching for a cash machine, a sign that says "ATM" would be a useful landmark, and the actual machine

WEIRD, TRUE, FREAKY

Celestial Dung Beetles

Dung beetles look to the sky as they rapidly roll their dung balls through space (see figure). Why to the sky? Because the external, allothetic cues that they use to tell they are going in the right direction are all far above them.

In certain respects, insects are more sophisticated navigators than humans are. Many have the ability to sense energy patterns such as magnetic fields and polarization gradients that people have no ability to perceive. Light from the sun or moon often provides insects with reliable indicators that they aren't running or flying around in circles.

Clouds can obscure the heavenly lights in some cases, however, and so many insects also make use of backup systems to avoid getting lost, including using local landmarks. Some wasps will scout out the area surrounding their underground burrows each time they leave and can become confused if the configuration of landmarks changes while they are gone. Insects can also navigate using path integration by monitoring their own movements through space, a strategy commonly used by explorer ants (see Figure 6.9D).

Dung beetles' navigational needs differ from other insects' in that their main goal is to get away with food (feces) quickly and efficiently. They do this by rolling the dung into a ball and then rapidly rolling it off in a random direction where they bury and eat it. This mainly serves to prevent other beetles from taking off with their freshly made dung ball. The roll sprint is less effective if the beetle ends up circling back toward the home dung pile, so they use external cues to maintain a straight course out.

Other fecal connoisseurs, like flies, use a combination of landmarks and self-motion cues to navigate, perhaps because of their increased mobility and minimal competition. Neuroscientists have recently created virtual reality environments for flies (no virtual feces yet) and are able to watch how hundreds of individual neurons respond as the flies navigate through simulated terrains (Seelig & Jayaraman, 2015). By controlling which cues are available during navigation, researchers can identify specific ways in which self-motion cues and landmarks affect neural activity, leading to the discovery that cues from one modality may sometimes override cues from other modalities.

Studies of fly navigation also revealed that when flies stop moving, and no cues are available, their neurons maintain activity patterns consistent with their last known orientation for at least thirty seconds, which may enable them to maintain a path even with no incoming navigational cues (in other words, based on their memories of where they were going before they stopped moving).

Experiments with dung beetles in planetariums revealed that when the Milky Way is visible, they use its position to guide their navigation (Dacke et al., 2013). So far, dung beetles are the only animals known to use this celestial cue as a way to guide their movements. Researchers noticed that before beetles began their sprint, they did a "dance" on top of the ball in which they spun around. During this dance, dung beetles appear to form the equivalent of a panoramic snapshot of the sky scene above them, which they then compare with what they see while run-rolling to make sure that they aren't turning (El Jundi et al., 2016). So beetles seem to depend on visual memory of a specific scene while sprinting. They're able to do this even when the space scene doesn't correspond to any observed in nature, showing that they are truly the kings of the manure pats.

Dung beetles are sensitive to the stars and use these cues to run away with their dung prizes. (AGAMI Photo Agency/Alamy Stock Photo)

would be a beacon. Predictable spatial configurations can also provide useful allothetic cues. For instance, if you are searching for water, the sloping sides of a valley might be a useful cue. Astronomical objects, like the North Star, can also serve as allothetic cues, despite the fact that they are not exactly stationary.

If you are navigating in an unfamiliar space, it's likely that you would be inspecting all kinds of environmental properties, both consciously and unconsciously, to increase your knowledge of what's where. In contrast, if you are traveling a familiar path, you may rely more on routine; it's how you can make it from your bed to the bathroom with your eyes closed. You may know what that path looks like, but you don't really need to see any landmarks or a beacon bowl to navigate successfully.

If you've walked a hiking trail (or sidewalk) many times before, you hardly need to pay any attention to where you are going to make it to your final destination. The predictable paths that rats took through familiar mazes are partly why early researchers thought rats were simply learning response chains rather than constructing spatial representations of maze layouts. Memories of how it feels to navigate a familiar space (idiothetic cues) can be as effective as street signs. Spatial exploration is not just a search for favored treasures, it is also a search for useful memories.

Spatial Learning and Memory

Exploring new terrain and forging new paths is often rewarding. Consider team sports. Invariably, they consist of people attempting to navigate through dynamic configurations of other people (including, occasionally, marching bands) to reach a specific goal location. Many video games require exploring virtual landscapes, searching through simulated buildings, and learning the layout of the land. Actions that lead to rewards inevitably lead to learning (see Chapter 7).

Not all spatial learning involves spatial navigation, however. Young infants depend on adults to navigate for them, yet they still learn about the qualities of their surroundings. One idiothetic cue that may be particularly important for spatial learning in infants is optic flow. **Optic flow** refers to patterns of motion that occur whenever a viewer moves through an environment. An infant being lugged through an apartment will sense expanding flow patterns when looking at objects that are getting nearer and contracting flow patterns for objects that are being left behind. Optic flow cues can thus reveal changes in the baby's distance from walls, furniture, a crib, and so on.

As babies learn to crawl and then walk, they will also gain active control over optic flow patterns as well as other idiothetic cues from their vestibular systems. Developmental psychologist Jean Piaget argued that youngsters initially learn about space within an egocentric reference frame, starting with places that are often nearby, and then gradually expand their range of spatial awareness. In the earliest stages, an infant's spatial percepts may focus on the nearness of environmental features, whether they are gummable, or if they ever move. Boundaries between body parts and surroundings may also be fuzzy.

Based on children's drawings, their performance on various tests of spatial ordering, and their explanations of their drawings, Piaget proposed a prolonged process of spatial learning lasting ten or more years, in which humans' spatial representations morph from locomotion-focused, egocentric reference frames to more allocentric, imagistic forms. He highlighted the fact that people's ability to reason about space (describing a scene from another person's perspective, for instance) lags far behind their ability to perceive space.

All of which simply means that the way you navigate now is a culmination of different ways that you have learned to navigate throughout your life and that there are multiple ways to solve the problem of getting from point A to point B. Laboratory experiments on spatial learning focus mainly on bare-bones spatial navigation tasks within small spaces. For instance, a person (or rat) might be trained to find their way from one or more starting points to a goal location a few feet away (**Figure 6.10A**).

Using simplified spatial search or navigation tasks speeds up learning and makes it easier to quantify how subjects' movements change as they learn. Mazes with multiple options similarly provide a way to test basic spatial memory abilities. For instance, by placing food in each arm of a radial arm maze (**Figure 6.10B**), researchers can observe how precisely animals keep track of where they have been.

(A)

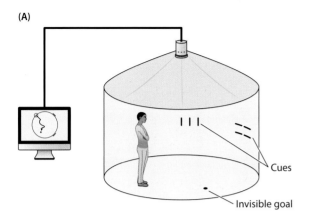
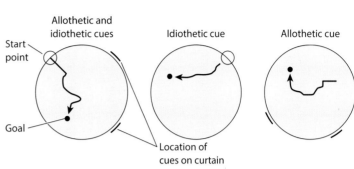

(B)

FIGURE 6.10. Testing spatial learning.
(A) Through trial and error, participants learn to move to an invisible spot in a circular arena. This task can be used to test spatial learning based on allothetic cues (images on curtains enclosing the arena) or idiothetic cues (having the person always start from the same location with no visible cues). (B) By placing food in each arm of a radial arm maze and recording how many times a subject enters each arm before all the food is gone, researchers can assess whether the subject is using spatial memories of which arms it has visited or simpler strategies, such as always turning to their right when exiting an arm. (A after Gazova et al., 2013; B Mauro Fermariello/Science Source)

Many different tasks have been developed to test spatial learning and memory in humans and other animals. These tasks have provided important clues about how individuals maintain memories over short intervals (see Chapter 8) and about how memory capacity varies across development as well as across species. Because these tests are usually nonverbal, they provide a powerful way of exploring the neural substrates of spatial processing, as detailed in the Brain Substrates section of this chapter.

Models of Spatiotemporal Processing

Models of space developed by physicists and philosophers attempt to explain what space is. Psychological models of space focus instead on trying to explain how we perceive, conceive, and act within space. One of the biggest challenges when theorizing about spatial perception and navigation is explaining how continuously changing inputs from multiple modalities and sensory receptors are merged into a stable, unified awareness of the spatial properties of the world. A common assumption of many models is that spatial processing depends on internal representations of the positions, sizes, and shapes of objects and their surroundings, as well as the relationships between them.

Spatial Representations

It's often convenient to think of space in visual terms, but individuals who are born blind usually develop sophisticated spatial abilities. So clearly, visual inputs are not required to represent space. In fact, no sensory modality seems to be a prerequisite for spatial processing. Inputs from all modalities have temporal and spatial properties. This has led some researchers to propose that spatial representations are abstract and amodal (not dependent on a specific modality).

The apparent abstractness of space is one way that it is similar to the concept of time—both are often described as abstract concepts (Borghi et al., 2017). If space is viewed as an abstract concept, then spatial representations would be similar to other abstract concepts described in Chapter 5.

Not everyone agrees that spatial representations are abstract, amodal, or conceptual, however. An alternative view is that spatial representations are multimodal and primarily contribute to perception and action. From this perspective, spatial representations serve to integrate inputs from sensory modalities, a process known as **multisensory integration**.

Some evidence that spatial representations are formed in ways that link modalities together comes from phenomena such as the ventriloquism effect, in which you believe a sound is coming from the wrong location because of what you see (Alais & Burr, 2004). This is why, when you watch a movie, it seems like the voices are coming from people on the screen, instead of from speakers located elsewhere.

As of yet, there is no agreement on what the contents of spatial representations actually are. As you will discover in the following subsection, there is even some debate about whether spatial representations exist at all.

Processing Spatial Cues

Most current models of spatial perception and navigation assume that two-dimensional sensory patterns from one or more modalities are analyzed to reconstruct where in three-dimensional space the sensations came from. These models treat spatial processing as analogous to analyzing the geometric features of a picture, in the case of vision and touch, or calculating the angle of arrival for sounds.

The models treat the world like a series of dioramas within which you search for specific spatial cues that tell you the shape, size, and layout of its parts. Space is like a container for the perceived objects. The problem of spatial perception and navigation mainly involves recognizing objects and places and linking them to the actions necessary to move around efficiently to achieve goals. More experience with particular scenes provides more opportunities to add details to spatial memories, which can be used to construct more complete cognitive maps.

Support for the idea that spatial processing is like an unconscious game of twenty questions about what is happening "out there" comes from illusions that fool you into seeing something that's not really there. For instance, the Ames room illusion (**Figure 6.11**) happens because your visual system expects certain visual cues to reveal the distance and size of objects and agents. Because of this expectation, when the cues are distorted, you perceive large differences in size, even when you know the people are the same size.

Some researchers have pointed to these persisting spatial illusions as evidence that the transformation of sensory cues into spatial percepts is an innate process—that spatial processes are imposed and primary rather than conceived.

Models of spatial processing that assume that spatial representations are built up by extracting information from sensory cues and then integrating those cues into a unified percept or concept align with the idea of cognitive maps. It's easy to imagine that as you visit new places corresponding spatial representations are added to your cognitive map of experienced space, like postcards collected on a road trip. And when you are looking through your set of postcards to see if you have been to a particular place before, it seems reasonable to think that you are making a judgment or inference (see Chapter 10) about whether the current scene is similar enough to past experiences to justify concluding that you are in a familiar place.

An alternative take on what happens when you perceive space, sometimes called the ecological approach, argues that you don't really need to construct representations of spatial properties or infer anything about the structure of perceived space. Instead what happens, according to this approach, is that organisms interact with their environment and in doing so detect patterns that make certain

(A)
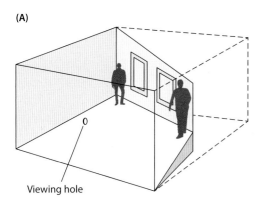
Viewing hole

(B)

FIGURE 6.11. The Ames Room. (A) Constructing an atypical room with an oddly slanted ceiling and floor creates an illusion of gigantism and dwarfism when viewed from the correct angle. (B) Cues that normally reveal size or distance instead lead to spatial distortion. (B Michael Doolittle/Alamy Stock Photo)

actions possible (Gibson, 1979). These interactions change the state of the perceiver's sensory organs as well as incoming energy patterns.

Some patterns of sensation will change faster than others depending on the structure of the environment, the energy available, and the movements of sensory receptors. The ones that change the least are called **invariant cues**. The ecological approach suggests that what you refer to as size, shape, landmarks, and locations—and even what you refer to as your own body—are different kinds of invariant cues that pop out perceptually as you move throughout the world.

Traditional models assume that spatial knowledge (such as cognitive maps) comes from examining the world and inferring spatial features like a hypersonic Sherlock Holmes. The ecological approach, instead, assumes that knowing about space is more of a process of learning to recognize and sort the different kinds of patterns that can occur when you move. From this perspective, spatial navigation is more about predicting what you will experience when your sensory organs move in specific ways than it is about your ability to track your position with a kind of mental GPS.

Integrating Space and Time

Historically, psychologists have studied spatial and temporal cognition separately. These two perceptual dimensions are, however, more closely related than they might as first seem. Ancient methods for measuring time were universally tied to spatial patterns: patterns in the movements of astronomical objects and in the movements of earth-bound entities, such as sand, water, and animals. More modern mechanical clocks also represent time spatially.

In contrast to humans who use changes in the world around them as indicators of time, some animals instead use changes in time to perceive their worlds. Rats, for example, move their whiskers in rhythmic patterns as they feel the spaces around them, while bats produce echolocation signals at precise rates such that any variation in the timing of echoes reveals the locations of moving prey (**Figure 6.12**). Many animals localize sound sources based on the time it takes for the signal to arrive at each ear. Durations naturally become positions and movements are fundamental to telling time.

Links between space and time also show up in language use. It seems natural to say that you've been "waiting a long time" or "looking forward to Friday," even though length and orientation are spatial properties. The use of spatial metaphors to describe intervals is seen across many cultures (Nunez & Cooperrider, 2013). This has led some researchers to argue that concepts of time are built on concepts of space (Winter et al., 2015).

One way that researchers have attempted to model the links between time and space is to expand on the idea of cognitive maps (Schiller et al., 2015). If you think of a cognitive map as not just a tool for navigating through space but as a guide for navigating through life, then including time in such maps is relatively straightforward. Just imagine the frames of a movie laid out spatially in a sequence and you can begin to get a feel for how "maps" of specific episodes might be organized. Your personal "timeline" then becomes an additional dimension within which your observations can be organized.

FIGURE 6.12. Time becomes space. (A) Bats time their echolocation signals so that they can intercept insects based on where they hear them. (B) Rats time their whisking (rhythmic sweeping of whiskers) while actively exploring to collect information about the spatial properties of the world around them. Once a rat discovers a surface and is attempting to discriminate or identify its properties, it switches to more rapid, focused whisking, rapidly collecting detailed spatial information, much like a bat in the final stage of attacking a nearby insect. (A, B after Geva-Sagiv et al., 2015)

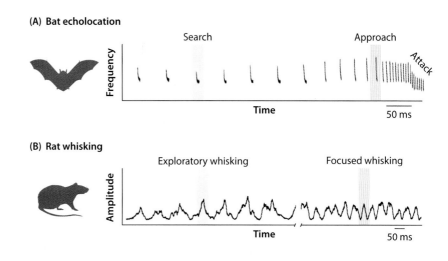

(A) Bat echolocation

(B) Rat whisking

SIGHT BITES

 The perception of locations, movement, shape, and size incorporates multiple modalities and changes over time based on what is experienced.

 The ability to orient and navigate through familiar and novel environments often depends on interpreting spatial cues and incorporating them into reference frames.

 Psychological models of spatial processing attempt to explain how constantly changing sensations are transformed into stable spatial representations.

 Spatial and temporal processing are linked both perceptually and linguistically in ways that suggest that they depend on overlapping representations.

Numerical Competence

SNEAK PEEK: How amounts are judged depends on the numbers present and one's capacity for symbolically representing different amounts. Time, space, and number can all be viewed as variations along a continuum of magnitudes.

Beyond detecting when and where things are happening in the world, perceptual systems are tuned in to detecting "how much" is happening. When nothing is happening, people tend to invent events to keep themselves entertained. When too much is happening, they may attempt to escape the chaos.

In between nothing and too much fall a wide range of intermediate amounts. Detecting when "enough" crosses over into "too much" or "not enough" is critical to deciding when to act and how. Still hungry after eating twenty chips? Maybe eating ten more will solve the problem. Attended school for fourteen years but still not eligible for the job you want? Maybe another two years will do the trick.

Amounts are often revealed by spatial or temporal judgments. Bigger stores typically contain more stuff and longer lines usually include more people. You can estimate how many people are in a line by knowing the wait time, and it usually takes a person with more items longer to make it through a checkout than someone with fewer items.

Bigger and longer does not always mean more, however. When it comes to judging amounts, quantities are king. Unlike time and space, number is clearly a human invention. Numbers shift the focus from "how much" (a lot) to "how many" (200).

Psychological studies of amount perception often focus on understanding how people recognize and process small numbers of items (fewer than twenty)—sometimes called "number sense" (Dehaene, 1997). Studies of mathematical cognition are less about number sense and more about reasoning and imagination (see Chapters 9 and 10). The following discussion considers what sorts of mechanisms make judging amounts possible and how those mechanisms relate to the perception of time and space.

"Number seems to signify primarily the strokes of our attention in discriminating things. These strokes remain in the memory in groups, large or small, and the groups can be compared"
—James, 1890, p 653

Assessing Quantities

If you ever think about quantities, numbers are likely to come up. Modern educational systems heavily emphasize using numbers as a way to label sets of items, and teaching kids to identify amounts by counting is standard operating procedure in most kindergarten classrooms. Counting is a cognitive skill that many children acquire through practice early on. But most kids know something about quantities long before they can count. Perceiving **numerosity**, or the approximate number of items, appears to be a basic mode of organizing inputs, one that humans capitalized on by inventing symbolic tools for representing specific amounts with numbers.

Perception of Numerosity

Evidence that numerosity is a primal property of perception comes from experiments in which individuals inspect images or scenes containing varying numbers of items and then show signs that they can tell which presentations contain more or fewer items (**Figure 6.13**). Perceptual estimates of quantities become less accurate when there are larger numbers of items—if two piles each contain lots of

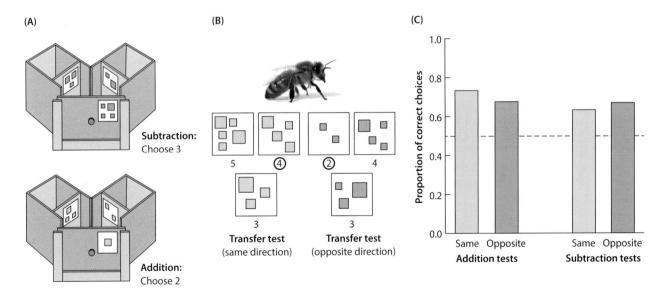

FIGURE 6.13. Numerosity discrimination by bees. Bees can be trained to control their flight paths based on the number of objects they see. (A) In a subtraction Y-maze, bees are rewarded if they fly to the image that is one less than the amount shown at the entrance to the maze. In an addition Y-maze, the same bees are trained to fly to the image that is one more than the entrance image. Whether a bee should add or subtract is indicated by the colors of the shapes (green=add). (B) After training, bees are tested on their responses to entrance image amounts that they had never seen before (sets of three) to see if they responded appropriately to novel amounts—correct responses are indicated by circles. The two alternatives could both be greater than the entrance image amount (change in amount is in the "same direction" for both alternatives), or one could be greater and the other smaller (changes in "opposite direction"). (C) Bees successfully solved new addition and subtraction problems, regardless of how alternatives changed. (A–C after Giufa, 2019, *Trends Cog Sci* 23, with permission from Elsevier; B image of bee: DanielPrudek)

items, then there needs to be a bigger difference in the total number of items in each pile before you will notice that one pile has more. Like interval timing, discrimination of numerosity follows Weber's law, which states that, to increase the strength of a sensed event by a fixed amount, you must increase the input by a relative amount.

Numerosity Perception or Numerosity Conception?

Infants and most animal species that have been tested show some ability to discriminate numerosity, even when other features, such as the overall size of a set, are taken into account. However, some studies on children suggest that numerosity discrimination can easily become distorted when spatial cues are varied. For instance, experiments by Piaget suggested that when a fixed number of items is spread out, children are likely to claim that the spread-out set contains more items than the same set of items squashed closer together. This finding is counterintuitive, given that simply spreading out items has no effect on their number.

Numbers refer to one amount and one amount only. The number of items persists regardless of how they are arranged, whether they are near or far, rotting or fresh, moving or not. So number is an invariant cue. But Piaget's experiments showed that children as old as five or six may ignore this cue in some contexts—amounts are sometimes less attention-grabbing than extent. Piaget suggested that this is because recognizing the invariant features of quantity, the abstractness and uniqueness of number, requires developing a concept of number. He argued that older children who have learned what numbers are about are not fooled by the rearrangement of items. Older children decide based on their concept of number rather than their percepts of the size of the set.

How then are infants and nonhumans able to discriminate numerosity? Are they born with an abstract concept of number preinstalled? Or might Piaget's experiments be misleading? Psychologists have tried to get to the bottom of this by testing individuals on their ability to recognize quantities across modalities. For instance, would an infant who had learned that three flashes mean it's about to be fun time quickly recognize that three beeps mean the same thing? If individuals recognize that "threeness" is a property that can be seen, heard, felt, and so on, then this would support the idea that representations of numerosity are abstract.

If perception of numerosity is abstract, then it shouldn't really matter what modality was used to perceive the amount—more should be more regardless of how it was detected. Several experiments do seem to show that numerosity perceived through sound or sight are linked, at least for smaller amounts (Feigenson et al., 2004).

One discovery made from studies of numerosity in young children is that small and large sets of items are processed differently. For instance, when given a choice between more or fewer crackers, one-year-olds are consistently greedy when three or fewer crackers are available. They seem oblivious to amounts, however, when more than three crackers are up for grabs (**Figure 6.14**).

Two Systems for Judging Numerosity

A possible explanation for why small numbers are judged differently from larger amounts is that the absolute number of a small set is perceivable while only the approximate number of larger sets registers perceptually. In other words, when only a few things are perceived, it's easier to tell exactly how many there are.

Chapter 4 describes how adults have a limited capacity to visually track multiple moving objects simultaneously, with a limit of around four or five. The crackers aren't moving when youngsters view them in numerosity discrimination experiments, but young children may still have problems keeping track of more than four or five of them. This may account for some of the difficulties one-year-olds have when assessing sets of four or more against smaller sets.

Based on findings from developmental and comparative experiments, psychologists have proposed that two different nonverbal systems exist for judging numerosity: an **object tracking system**, which automatically specifies the number of items in a small set based on how many items are being tracked, and an **approximate number system**, which estimates larger amounts based on

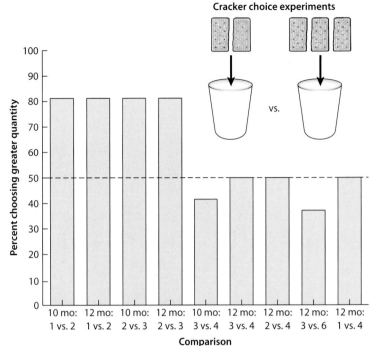

FIGURE 6.14. Discriminating the numerosity of crackers.
Young children reliably pick more crackers if the choices include only one, two, or three crackers, but when one of the choices includes more than three crackers, they choose randomly (dotted line). Discriminating one from four should be easier, suggesting that numerosity comparisons break down if sets above three are compared with smaller quantities. (Image: Nicola Katie; graph after Feigenson et al., 2014; adapted from Feigenson et al., 2002)

sensation patterns. Comparisons made using the approximate number system follow Weber's law while those made with the object tracking system do not. From this perspective, judging approximate numbers depends on pattern recognition while judging small, exact numbers depends on attentional mechanisms.

None of this explains what you're doing when you look at a bunch of bananas and think to yourself, "there are six." In that case, you have assigned a label to a specific amount, and it's generally assumed that you identified the quantity by counting. The seemingly simple process of counting has sparked debate for over a century, most of it relating to just how simple counting really is. Some researchers consider counting to be something that most animals, including invertebrates, do innately (Gallistel & Gelman, 2000), while others consider counting to be a hard-won conceptual skill that not even adult humans were capable of until relatively recently (Frank et al., 2008). It's also unclear whether your ability to count depends on the combined contributions of an object tracking system and a numerosity estimation system (van Marle et al., 2018).

Counting is the foundation for most mathematical skills that humans learn; it makes it possible for adults to accurately discriminate nineteen penguins from twenty. Consequently, you might guess that adding and subtracting—techniques that children usually only master after counting becomes a breeze—requires some pretty sophisticated reasoning abilities and number concepts. Surprisingly, this is not the case. Perceiving sums and differences does not depend on the symbolic tricks that humans have found for adding and subtracting, and it may not even require the ability to count.

Numerical Operations

It's tricky to tell if a nonverbal individual can add or subtract. One technique that experimenters use is essentially a magic trick (**Figure 6.15**). The idea is to create situations where an expected quantity does not match the observed quantity and to see if this provokes surprise. For example, if you saw three women go into a dressing room, one come out, and then you opened the door to find no women inside, you might be surprised. Individuals that show surprise in such situations were presumably expecting a different quantity than what they found.

A somewhat simpler approach is to add and remove items from opaque containers and then see if an individual is still able to select which contains more items (Beran & Beran, 2004). This task taxes

FIGURE 6.15. Detecting changes in numerosity. When nonverbal individuals detect anomalies in quantities, they often show signs of surprise, like staring at a scene intensely as if they cannot believe what they are seeing. For instance, a toddler that sees one toy hidden behind a screen (Steps 1 and 2), followed by a second toy moving behind that screen (Step 3), will tend to stare longer if lowering the screen reveals only a single toy (left test). Such responses can provide evidence that youngsters are tracking changes in amounts caused by adding or subtracting items. (After Feigenson et al., 2004, *Trends Cog Sci* 8, with permission from Elsevier)

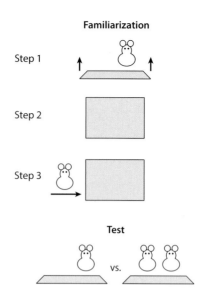

memory as well as numerical abilities, but when the task is doable, it provides good evidence that the individual can mentally keep track of a total amount even when some items are added or removed.

Putting Numbers in Order

In addition to identifying specific amounts, or specific individuals on a football team, numbers also provide information about relationships between amounts. Specifically, as amounts increase or decrease, the numbers associated with those amounts will change in a predefined sequence. This is why you can sort numbers from least to most and vice-versa.

Ordering numerosities implies both an ability to count and an ability to recognize which numbers are less than or greater than others. Ordering amounts appears to go beyond simply discriminating numerosity. Most evidence to date suggests that the ability to order quantities may be closely related to sequence learning (see Chapter 7) and the ability to appreciate that if A > B, and B > C, then A > C (see Chapter 10). Ranking items or outcomes using numbers may seem intuitive, but it depends more on learning than most of the other numerical abilities discussed in this section, as does using numbers to describe measurements.

Representing Amounts with Symbols

Representing numbers with verbal and written symbols enables people to think about quantities in ways that are not always obvious. For instance, there wasn't really a widely used symbol corresponding to the number zero until long after symbols for other numbers were common (Kaplan, 2000), and it was only after "nothing" was added to the arsenal of perceivable numbers that mathematics (and physics, and most other scientific fields) really began to gain steam.

Most of mathematics comes from culturally transmitted cognitive tools. Modern math is in many ways divorced from quantities and is more focused on predicting and understanding abstract patterns. While evolutionarily older processes for judging amounts may seem quaint by comparison, they could hold the key to understanding fundamental features of cognition.

Consider that space, time, and virtually every other scientifically studied dimension is now understood within the context of numbers: durations, distances, weights, energy, IQ: all are measured and stored numerically. Coincidence? Or is there something about numbers that makes them particularly well suited for mentally representing how the world works?

Links between Time, Space, and Number

The computational theory of mind, introduced in Chapter 1, views all cognitive processes as computations, including perception of time, space, and number. Computations require calculations and the only calculations that are not metaphorical involve numbers. No one really thinks that minds process numbers like a computer does, but many people think that spatial, temporal, and numerical processing involve something like extracting quantities from inputs and using representations of those quantities to calculate new quantities.

Case in point, the duplex theory of sound localization (see Chapter 4), proposes that you perceive the direction a sound is coming from by calculating the difference between when a sound arrives at each ear and then mapping that difference onto possible locations in space that might lead to this difference. You can calculate this difference yourself by putting little microphones in each ear and then comparing the signals they receive. The difference is zero when the sound is directly in front of you and it grows as a sound source moves either toward your left or right. Mathematically, the relationship is straightforward and so the idea is that your brain does something equivalent to that calculation, even if it is not using numbers to do it.

Magnitude as a Common Denominator

Some researchers have proposed that time, space, and number are all mentally represented in the same way to facilitate the kinds of computations that make it possible to link distance or direction to duration and other similarly useful calculations. These computations often involve judging differences between percepts—near versus far, short versus long, less versus more. The common element of these different dimensions of experience is that they all vary in magnitude. Magnitude in this context is similar to intensity or size in that magnitude can grow or shrink within some range.

Weber's law was originally developed to describe how a person's ability to distinguish differences in weight varies depending on how heavy the weights are. The weights you feel when making such comparisons are basically kinesthetic percepts of the force required to counteract gravity. Perceptual comparisons of weight depend on how you mentally represent variations in the pull of gravity.

Perceptual comparisons of duration, length, and number depend on how much is being compared in the same way as weights do—all follow the same rule that your sensitivity to differences decreases as the properties being compared grow (Weber's law). You can easily tell the difference between weights and time, however, so although both may be mentally represented as variations in magnitude, there must be some elements that uniquely mark them as particular kinds of experiences (**Figure 6.16**).

The common quality shared by weight, time, space, and number—magnitude—provides a link between these subjectively very different percepts. That link is often portrayed as a line starting at zero and ending at some large value never really reached: number lines, timelines, analog scales, and rulers all transform perceived variations of magnitude into spatial expanses along which quantities can be spaced out at equal intervals. At least in this respect, these different dimensions clearly show family resemblances of the sort described in Chapter 5. But it remains unclear what a mental magnitude representation actually is.

Besides sharing the property of being associated with growth and shrinkage, time, space, and number are also often described as being abstract concepts. Here, "abstract" mainly refers to the fact that the properties are independent of the modality through which they are perceived, although in fields such as mathematics and physics, the physical representations of these dimensions as symbols

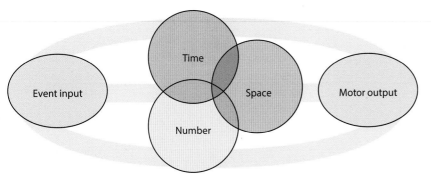

FIGURE 6.16. Overlap in representation of time, space, and number. Percepts of time, space, and number may overlap in terms of how they vary in magnitude while still preserving their unique qualities. Actions (motor output) may provide a link between these three perceptual domains in that each may determine how much, how far, and how long an individual will need to react in response to ongoing events. (After Walsh, 2003)

adds another level of abstractness. These concepts themselves develop within individuals and across generations. Consequently, any discussion of how a particular individual cognizes durations, places, or quantities needs to specify who is doing the cognizing and in what context. For instance, your experience of space right now likely differs greatly from what you perceived spatially while still in the womb.

Numbers as the Foundation of Modern Scientific Models

Modern science (including psychology) depends heavily on quantified representations of subjective experiences. In other words, it depends on numerical data. The main assumption driving this approach is that the relationships between numbers are analogous to the qualities of the world they designate. Mental representations of time, space, and number are thought to share this property. For instance, in the internal clock model described above, more time is represented as a larger sum of accumulated clock ticks. Whether this model accurately captures how you represent short intervals (or distances or amounts) depends on how similar your mental processing of temporal intervals is to collections of ticks.

One way to evaluate current psychological models of mental processing of time, space, and number is to see how well those models fit with what your brain is doing as you are perceiving durations, navigating through space, or judging numerosity. If your comparisons of intervals or amounts depend on a shared representation of magnitude, then you should see some neural evidence of this. If your concepts of time are built on your spatial representations, then this too should show up in your brain activity.

SIGHT BITES

The numerosity of objects, agents, and events is naturally perceived by many organisms.

Comparisons of quantities are thought to involve at least two different systems, neither of which requires any counting.

Ordering, counting, adding, and subtracting can be performed without symbols, but symbols greatly increase the range of feasible operations.

Time, space, and number can each be described as variations along a scale of different magnitudes, possibly because they are represented similarly.

BRAIN SUBSTRATES

SNEAK PEEK: Why does time fly when you're having fun? Are there other ways of distorting time perception? Some brain regions seem wired to process spatial and temporal information. But are they really specialized for those functions or might they be involved in many different kinds of cognitive processing?

Among Franz Gall's proposed list of twenty-seven mental faculties (see Chapter 2) were a "sense of locality" and a faculty called "arithmetic, counting, time." He assigned the spatial faculty to a region of cortex in the temporal lobe and the time/number faculty to a region in the prefrontal cortex. Although modern neuroscience has largely cast aside Gall's maps of cortically based mental faculties, researchers have retained the spirit of his efforts to map spatial and temporal processing to specific brain regions.

By monitoring activity in particular cortical and subcortical regions, researchers have shed new light on the complex processes underlying your ability to cognize spatial, temporal, and quantitative elements of the world. Researchers have also discovered new ways in which modulating brain activity in different regions can directly affect how an individual perceives time, space, or number.

Many of the advances made in identifying neural processes that contribute to spatial and temporal cognition have come from invasive studies of rodents but the principles that researchers have identified are relevant to understanding these cognitive processes in humans and other species as well.

Tracking Movements through Space

With thousands of rats running through mazes over the last century, you might expect that the first thing neuroscientists learned about spatial processing was gleaned from studies of rats traversing mazes. But no. The first major discovery was made by recording neural activity in rats wandering around on three one-foot-long boards joined together by a circular platform, all on table legs (called an elevated maze).

This may seem like a pretty pointless experiment, but an elevated maze can tell you a lot about how curious animals are, what strategies they use when exploring, how their behavior changes once they realize there is nowhere to go, etcetera. And, surprisingly, if you monitor the activity of certain neurons while a rat is wandering around on boards, you can actually tell where the rat is currently located based on which neurons are firing the most!

Spatially Tuned Neurons

The neurons that reveal a rat's location are found in several brain regions, most notably the hippocampus and the entorhinal cortex. The entorhinal cortex serves as a gateway between the rest of the cerebral cortex and the hippocampus (**Figure 6.17**). So you can think of these two brain regions as a sort of spatial processing team.

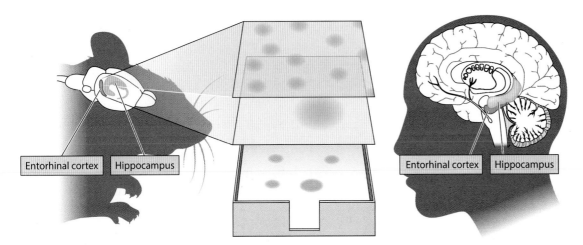

FIGURE 6.17. Brain regions linked to spatial processing. Recordings from neurons in the hippocampus and the entorhinal cortex reveal that some neurons fire more strongly when rats are in specific places (shown here as shaded circles indicating where in the box neurons in each area respond most strongly). These same regions are involved in spatial processing by humans, but less is known about whether neurons in humans respond to spatial features like neurons in rats. (After Karlén, 2014)

Place Cells

The first "spatial neurons" discovered in the hippocampus, called **place cells**, tended to fire whenever a rat arrived at a particular part of the maze—the researchers who made this discovery were awarded the Nobel Prize in 2014. Experiments in which the maze was rotated or altered revealed that place cells were firing mainly when external environmental features were sensed (Jeffery, 2007). This led researchers to suspect that populations of place cells might function as an allocentric representation of space and might even provide a sort of place database for a cognitive map (O'Keefe & Nadel, 1978).

Place cells are not specialized for detecting one particular place. They often respond in multiple environments and to more than one spot in a familiar environment—it would be more accurate to call them places cells. When an environment changes, the specific locations that trigger a particular place cell can also change (Smith & Mizumori, 2006). This means that place cells contribute to spatial processing in ways that are dissimilar to a GPS or physical map. Google maps are stable over time with each position assigned to one place. Your brain is doing something quite different.

Head Direction Cells

A second set of spatially sensitive neurons called head direction cells was discovered soon after place cells. Some of these neurons are in the hippocampus, but more are in the entorhinal cortex and other brain regions. Head direction cells are like place cells in that they fire most often when the rat is in a particular position. But in the case of head direction cells, it is the orientation of the head in three dimensions that triggers firing. In other words, head direction cells fire in response to the direction in which a rat's head is facing. The rat points its head up and one set of head direction cells fires. It points it to the left and a different set fires.

Head direction cells are not like little compasses that always use magnetic north as a reference; instead, they seem to align themselves with environmental features such as landmarks. Head direction cells, however, continue to track orientation even when the lights are turned out, suggesting that rats are using idiothetic cues to monitor their orientation in familiar environments.

Border and Grid Cells

Together, place cells and head direction cells provide a possible neural basis for identifying where you are and in what direction you are going. A third set of cells, called border cells, fire most when a rat is close to a particular environmental boundary such as the edge of a maze arm. These hippocampal neurons may be important for monitoring geometric properties of an environment.

Perhaps the most intriguing neurons with spatial sensitivities discovered so far are the so-called grid cells in the entorhinal cortex. Grid cells are like place cells that fire at many different places all spaced at equal distances from one another. Like cracks in a sidewalk, these regularly spaced firing hotspots provide an indirect way to represent distances between places. **Figure 6.18** summarizes the response properties of the four major classes of space-related neurons.

Beyond Cognitive Maps

As more exotic spatially tuned neurons are discovered, a new picture of spatial representation is beginning to emerge. Place cells, head direction cells, grid cells, and border cells were all observed in

FIGURE 6.18. Four types of spatial neurons. Red regions show where in a box each type of neuron responds most strongly. Place cells tend to respond most in a single location, while grid and border cells respond to multiple predictable locations Head direction cells can fire anywhere in a box, as long as the rat's head is pointed in the right direction (in this case, toward the lower right). (From Geva-Sagiv et al., 2015, *Nat Rev Neurosci* 16, reproduced with permission from SNCSC)

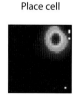
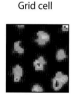
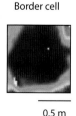
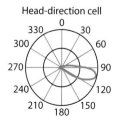

Place cell   Grid cell   Border cell   Head-direction cell

0.5 m

rats moving within small, simple enclosures in labs. Humans possess at least some comparable spatially selective neurons (Jacobs et al., 2013). If multiple modes of representing space are evident during the exploration of a box, it seems likely that even more ways of processing space might be used during the exploration and navigation of more naturalistic environments.

From this perspective, viewing spatial navigation as depending on a cognitive map or on an egocentric representation of a place is a bit simplistic. It seems likely that, instead, multiple systems are operating in parallel to represent the spatial features of the environment (and the body) at multiple levels of spatial and temporal resolution. Mentally using spatial representations to guide navigation may be more like selecting ingredients to add to a soup than like typing an address into Google Maps.

Some support for the idea that there are multiple parallel systems of spatial processing comes from neuropsychological studies of people with brain damage who are impaired at navigating. These people may show deficits in recognizing landmarks, recalling where recognized landmarks are located, or following a familiar path from one place to another (van der Ham et al., 2017). Damage to different brain regions is associated with each of these different spatial deficits.

This is not to say that specific brain regions provide you with different "senses of locality." In some regions such as the entorhinal cortex, several different kinds of spatially sensitive neurons are present. Additionally, people with different patterns of damage may show similar symptoms, and individuals with damage to the same region may show different deficits. The range of spatial problems associated with different kinds of damage simply strengthens the idea that spatial navigation involves interactions between many parallel processes. Walking down a sidewalk to a restaurant may feel similar to walking across that restaurant to get to a bathroom, but the underlying mechanisms that enable you to do both things may differ substantially.

Links between Spatial Processing and Other Cognitive Processes

The hippocampus and medial temporal lobe (where the entorhinal cortex can be found) are not only associated with spatial navigation; they are also closely associated with explicit memory abilities, including memories of specific episodes like knowing what you had for lunch two days ago (see Chapter 8). This coincidence has led some researchers to propose that the kinds of coding you use to navigate space may also be useful for other cognitive processes (Bellmund et al., 2018). For instance, just as places can be mapped out in terms of physical distances between familiar landmarks, perhaps icons on a computer screen could be mapped out and used to guide mouse trajectories.

Researchers have also identified hippocampal "time cells" that fire at specific time points in a task sequence (Schiller et al., 2015), indicating that temporal patterns might be mapped in ways that parallel spatial patterns, with significant sequences tagged as "landmarks" (Rueckemann et al., 2021). This seems especially likely in species such as bats that use temporal patterns to navigate.

Chapter 5 describes a theory of category learning, the category-boundary model, which proposes that how a person categorizes an item depends on the shape and orientation of the border between different categories. If hippocampal border cells can detect physical boundaries, might there be other hippocampal or entorhinal neurons that fire when a perceived object is close to a category boundary? Neuroimaging studies in adult humans showing overlapping neural activation during both navigation through virtual spaces and during visual image classification tasks seem to support this possibility (Nau et al., 2018).

Rats in mazes are often used as a cartoonish symbol of psychological experiments; however, rats exploring space made the discovery of spatially selective neurons possible. Understanding how both external markers of space and internal cues to body position are integrated into percepts and concepts that guide actions in the world is likely key to understanding what people are seeking when they explore and how what they discover is incorporated into their ongoing impressions of the world.

Chemically-Induced Time Warping

Brain damage can derail your ability to spatially navigate, and in some cases, like hemispatial neglect, it can even reduce your ability to perceive space. Brain damage can also muck with your perception of time. The most extensively studied example is Parkinson's disease, an aging-related disorder in which abnormal functioning of the basal ganglia causes problems with motor control.

Temporal Distortion in Parkinson's Patients

Disruption of the basal ganglia in individuals with Parkinson's disease can cause them to move abnormally quickly or in slow motion. People with Parkinson's disease not only have problems timing their motor actions but also show a reduced ability to judge second-long intervals (Malapani et al., 1998). They do not exhibit the scalar property when judging longer intervals, mainly because their ability to judge shorter intervals is so variable (Jones et al., 2008).

Individuals who do not have Parkinson's disease but who do have damaged basal ganglia are able to time intervals (Coslett et al., 2010), so the effects of the disorder on time perception are not simply the result of a broken brain module. Instead, disordered temporal processing appears to result from abnormally low dopamine levels (Miyawaki, 2022). Dopamine is a neurochemical, distributed throughout your brain, that affects processing and plasticity, depending on how and when it is released. People with Parkinson's show severely depleted levels of dopamine in their basal ganglia. When individuals with Parkinson's disease are tested on levodopa, a drug that increases dopamine levels in the basal ganglia, their problems with judging intervals go away (Pastor et al., 1992).

Findings from people with Parkinson's suggest that modifying the chemical balance of your brain can change your capacity to time motor actions and your subjective perception of time. Further evidence supporting this idea comes from the effects of alcohol consumption. Alcohol, particularly in large doses, can greatly disrupt motor timing (which is why drunk drivers get into accidents) and distort time perception (Ogden et al., 2011). Intoxication generally leads to overestimates of duration and the feeling that time is passing more quickly than normal.

Where Are the Brain Clocks?

The effects of alcohol on motor timing probably come from its effects on the cerebellum. As noted in Chapter 2, the cerebellum is known to modulate the timing of many motor acts. This function led researchers to suspect that circuits in the cerebellum might act as timers (Paton & Buonomano, 2018), especially for intervals shorter than a second. It's less clear that a tanked cerebellum is the source of alcohol-related subjective time distortion because cerebellar damage doesn't affect subjective estimates of duration or interval timing. Effects of alcohol on subjective time may instead be a result of cortical changes.

Traditionally, internal clocks and timers have been thought to be located in evolutionarily old brain regions such as the cerebellum or basal ganglia. This assumption makes some intuitive sense given the fundamental role of time tracking in staying alive. Also, the one neural timekeeper that has been definitively identified is a small region of the brain in the hypothalamus, the suprachiasmatic nucleus, which controls circadian rhythms, consistent with the idea that older brain regions are associated with processing temporal information.

Modern research suggests that cortical regions are more involved in time perception than was previously thought (Harrington et al., 1998). Numerous neurons that fire selectively to specific durations have been found in the cortices of various animals (Hayashi et al., 2015). Duration-selective neurons have been recorded in the auditory and visual cortex. They are mostly selective for intervals of less than half a second.

Responding to specific durations is not the only way that cortical circuits can represent temporal intervals. Recordings from neurons in the frontal cortices of monkeys show sustained firing for intervals of three to twelve seconds when the monkeys are required to wait for these intervals before responding (Emmons et al., 2017). And a chemical disruption of firing by these cortical neurons made monkeys crash and burn at discriminating intervals (Wang et al., 2018).

When the specific firing patterns of different frontal neurons were analyzed, researchers discovered that they were not simply related to time, as might be expected of a ticking internal clock or of oscillators with regular rhythms. Instead, the firing patterns were temporally all over the place. But researchers found that the firing patterns during judgments of longer intervals were stretched out versions of the patterns during shorter intervals, like an accordion of neural activity. The speed at which cortical neurons were producing specific patterns was changing depending on the duration that monkeys had to wait during trials.

High Time

So, if waiting different durations can cause cortical neurons to produce their activity patterns faster or slower, might chemically causing cortical neurons to fire faster or slower make durations seem shorter or longer? As you might suspect (or know), alcohol is not the only drug that can alter the perception of time. Marijuana can, too. Individuals high on THC (the active agent in marijuana) also overestimate durations but report a subjective slowing of time. When they have to produce specific intervals, they typically produce shorter intervals than required (**Figure 6.19**). These effects are consistent with what you might expect if an internal clock were being sped up. Marijuana definitely affects activity in the frontal cortex (Prashad et al., 2018), but whether it literally compresses the firing patterns of cortical neurons is unknown.

Cortical firing patterns related to temporal intervals and timing are not only found in sensory cortices and the frontal cortex. They have been observed in the parietal cortex, motor cortex, and premotor cortex as well. Overall, perception of time and coordination of actions in relation to specific intervals at different time scales seem to depend on several different neural mechanisms distributed throughout multiple cortical and subcortical regions, as is the case for spatial processing. There seem to be multiple ways of timing and judging intervals, not all of which depend on internal clocks or "time cells," and some of which are affected by the distribution of neurochemicals or drug actions in the brain.

Various drugs can warp your subjective perception of time and your ability to judge intervals, but they don't necessarily affect your ability to track rhythms. Can you be drunk and high and still keep the beat? To put it another way, do you think professional rock percussionists are all teetotalers? Oddly, beat-based timing seems to depend on different neural mechanisms than those used for judging intervals, subjective time perception, or even the timing of motor actions. Apparently, judging relative time differences and synchronicity requires representing time in different ways from judging absolute durations.

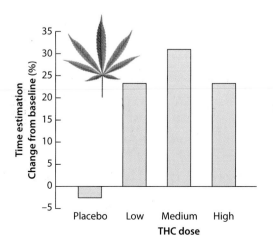

FIGURE 6.19. Effects of marijuana on temporal processing. People who were not frequent users of marijuana were given various doses of THC and then tested on a temporal perception task that involved estimating the time interval between two flashes on a computer screen. Participants consistently overestimated the durations of intervals ranging from five to thirty seconds, suggesting that participants' subjective perception of time was compressed relative to measured time, as might happen if their internal clocks were running fast (graph shows that effects were consistent across different doses). (Inset image: GeorgePeters; graph after Sewell et al., 2013)

SIGHT BITES

Neurons in the hippocampus and entorhinal cortex show multiple patterns of responsiveness to spatial cues that likely contribute to spatial navigation abilities.

Chemical imbalances in the brain can distort motor timing, interval discrimination, and an individual's subjective impressions of the passage of time.

APPLIED PERSPECTIVES

SNEAK PEEK: Poor math skills may come from dyscalculia—a developmental disorder—or from the reduced perception of numerosity. Perception and production of rhythmic patterns shape how time and space are represented from an early age.

The jobs that most psychologists commonly perform don't necessarily require much in the way of spatial or mathematical skills, and the ability to perceive differences in time aren't so critical either. Technology provides numerous crutches that can help people overcome many weaknesses in such skills, which might seem to make understanding spatial, temporal, and quantitative cognition processing not that useful. Can't perceive time? Set an alarm. Can't spatially navigate? Let your phone be your guide.

On the other hand, there are reasons to think that reduced abilities to perceive basic features of the world could have serious cognitive implications. This is, after all, part of why educational systems were developed—to increase the number of people who possess basic mathematical skills—and why such abilities are often used as a general indicator of cognitive prowess.

As long as the links between mechanisms of cognizing (including perception of time and space) and other cognitive abilities remain mysterious, it will be difficult to predict the possible consequences of technological aids on cognitive development or the pros and cons of different developmental trajectories. When should kids start depending on calculators? Does it matter? Does early practice with rhythm blocks enhance musical or cognitive proficiency later in life, or are such skills cognitively irrelevant? The following sections consider some of the possible implications that a better understanding of the cognitive mechanisms of "abstract" cognizing might have on educational practices for training children in math and music.

Mastering Math Skills

Math is infamous for being one of the most intimidating academic subjects. In the timeless words of Teen Talk Barbie, "Math class is tough." Many people dislike math, and for some, even thinking about calculating provokes severe anxiety (Dowker et al., 2016).

The calculations that make up mathematics depend on a complex mixture of cognitive abilities beyond just perceiving amounts, including language skills, memory manipulation, reasoning, and cognitive control (see Chapters 8, 9, and 10). Calculations also depend on the perception of visual space and representations of body movements, especially the fingers.

Predicting Intelligence from Numerosity Perception

Given the diverse cognitive processes that contribute to mathematical prowess, you might expect that the ability to perceive differences in numerosity would only minimally affect a person's proficiency at mathematics. After all, lots of species are able to judge differences in amounts, while only humans perform calculations using culturally constructed symbols.

Surprisingly, how well people judge approximate amounts predicts not only their performance on standardized math tests (Libertus et al., 2012) but also the likelihood that they will experience math anxiety (Lindskog et al., 2017). Why might your ability to perceive amounts affect your ability to solve a problem like 23 + 79 (or vice versa)? If you could change your ability to distinguish amounts, might that boost your mathematical abilities in the same sort of way that wearing glasses can increase your spatial resolution?

Psychologists have suggested three possibilities as to why the ability to distinguish between amounts is correlated with math skills. The most straightforward of these is that better numerical resolution early on makes math skills easier to learn. The reverse path is also possible. Maybe people who are good at math spend more time attending to amounts, and as a result, tend to be better than average at discriminating amounts.

The third possibility is what psychologists call the third variable problem. The **third variable problem** refers to the fact that any time two measures are correlated, it's always possible that an additional hidden factor is the source of the correlation. For example, in tests of numerosity discrimination participants are typically shown arrays of dots or other shapes and then asked to choose the option that contains more elements. The shapes within sets vary in size and spacing so that people don't choose based on nonnumerical properties like "pile size." This means that in order to judge numerosity, participants must not only discriminate number but they must also ignore features other than number.

The ability to selectively attend to one dimension of a visual percept while ignoring others (see Chapter 4) also varies across individuals. This makes individual differences in selective attention a possible third variable that could affect performance both in numerosity discrimination tasks and in math classes (Gilmore et al., 2013).

Why Counting on Your Fingers Makes Calculations Easier

Calculation abilities are widely viewed as a key indicator of cognitive capacity. Assessments of these abilities are usually a major component of intelligence and achievement tests at almost every level of academics. They are also often included in neuropsychological tests of mental abilities.

Calculating clearly depends on multiple concepts related to numbers, as well as specific symbolic skills and knowledge of procedures and "math facts" that can be acquired through practice. The diversity of processes involved predicts that many different brain regions and mental representations can come into play when you perform even the most basic arithmetical operations.

One concept that seems particularly important in the development of numerical skills is the "same-different" concept introduced in Chapter 5. When you learned to count, one of the first tasks you probably mastered was keeping track of things counted versus those remaining to be counted. You might have sequentially touched individual items (splitting them into two categories: touched or untouched) or moved them from one pile into another. In the end game, you compared the quantity with some memory of past quantities you had encountered to determine whether the current conditions matched ones familiar to you.

This approach to determining amounts by matching shows up early in human history in the form of notches, knots, and pebble piles used as physical records of quantities. Using your fingers to calculate is another example of using amount matching. All of these tricks provide external, **analog representations** of number; they are representations that match the properties of the thing being represented in some way. Use of symbols, such as Arabic numerals, rather than analog representations is a relatively modern shortcut for dealing with quantities.

Intuitively, you might imagine that analog representations of numbers might be more useful in calculating given that they retain direct indications of quantities. However, most advances in mathematical techniques were achieved only after symbols replaced pebble piles. Even in nonhumans, the use of symbolic number representations seems to expand the range of what's mentally possible. For instance, in numerosity comparisons, most animals are naturally drawn to larger amounts, finding it hard to attend to smaller sets when given a choice between more or less. But when the same amounts are represented symbolically, most animals have no problem learning to choose the lesser of two amounts (Boysen et al., 1996).

When Math Is More than Tough

Younger kids rarely become stressed when they first start working with numbers, despite the fact that they are learning strategies that took humans thousands of years to develop. Typically, they are most likely to start becoming uncomfortable with math in elementary school while being taught to add, subtract, multiply, and divide. Some kids run into bigger problems learning these skills than others and end up being diagnosed with **dyscalculia** or "mathematics disorder."

Dyscalculia is a developmental disorder that takes many forms. The main symptoms all relate to below-average abilities at solving math problems. The kinds of errors that are characteristic of dyscalculia include mistakes in organizing quantities spatially, problems writing numerals, errors in memory and reasoning, and so on. Kids with this disorder generally perform normally on matching numbers to quantities, identifying greater amounts, and counting, which seems odd given the correlations between nonverbal quantity estimation and math skills.

The perception of approximate quantities is widely thought to be foundational for math skills (Feigenson et al., 2004). Some recent tests of this idea show that having children practice discriminating numerosity improved their performance in arithmetic tests (Park & Brannon, 2013, 2014) (**Figure 6.20**). Other tests have failed to replicate this benefit of number sense training in children, however (Kim et al., 2018).

Traditional efforts to counteract dyscalculia (and math anxiety) focus more on developing cognitive workarounds than on fixing the main source of the problem, which is usually unknown. Treatments may involve extensive remedial training, the use of math-based learning games, and the use of imagery and musical stimuli.

Dyscalculia is often associated with other developmental disorders such as attention deficit hyperactivity disorder, raising further questions about whether the deficits are actually numerical in nature. Given the many different cognitive processes that potentially contribute to human mathematical skills, it seems likely that the disruption of any one of them could potentially lead to frustration and slower-than-normal cognitive skill acquisition.

Historically, mathematical techniques were invented by specialists to solve puzzles or practical problems they faced as adults. It has proven challenging to train young children to flexibly learn these same skills in contexts where the skills mainly serve to establish that a child can perform them. Knowing more specifically what cognitive processes limit a child's success in progressing mathematically can be important to developing more effective educational practices. Knowing the potential mental

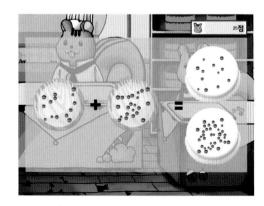

FIGURE 6.20. Sight math. Computerized math games based on visual perception of numerosity (here, amounts of small circles) are being developed in an attempt to improve children's arithmetic skills, with mixed results. What are some possible problems with trying to teach math using pictures? (Kim, et al. 2018, *Front Psychol Sec Cognition* 9, © 2018 Kim, Jang, and Cho [CC-BY])

costs and benefits of the early acquisition of math skills can similarly clarify how valuable this outcome is.

Rhythm Matters

Psychological studies of time, space, and number perception tend to emphasize the discrimination and tracking of environmental changes—sensed durations, positions of landmarks, or piles of pebbles. The role of voluntary and involuntary actions, emotions, and internal processes, when mentioned at all, are usually noted only as a way to collect additional environmental cues.

It seems natural to think of yourself as an agent operating in a world that is an encompassing space filled with quantities of objects that change over time. It's also easy to imagine that your mental representations of these properties are like biological versions of technological artifacts such as clocks, maps, or abacuses. There are signs, however, that this comforting portrayal of mental processing may be inadequate for understanding the cognitive mechanisms that underlie perception of time, space, and number.

Learning Mom Time

Imagine what your world was like when you were still in your mother's womb. Your space was limited, as were most sights and sounds. Navigation wasn't really an option. Your main sensations came from your mother's body or your own. Some of the earliest patterns that registered were likely rhythmic, from the fluctuating heartbeats and breathing rates that served as your "ground," to the swaying motions produced by your mother moving around, especially while walking. There's evidence that your mother's rhythm of speaking also made it through because newborns are sensitive to the cadence of the language their mother spoke and even to the patterns of a Dr. Suess book read multiple times pre-birth (DeCasper & Spence, 1986).

Babies do not always respect circadian rhythms as much as parents might want them to, but they do like moving periodically. Rocking chairs, baby swings, and bouncing moms are the norm. When infants hear rhythmic patterns, they often move their bodies rhythmically and sometimes even match the tempo they hear. And the more their movements match the beat, the happier they are (Zentner & Eerola, 2010). Infants seem to be geared toward oscillating.

Your bouncing-baby past may seem irrelevant to how you cognize space, time, or number now. Percept-matching actions may be more fundamental to the ways you experience the world than you might think, however (Wilson, 2001). Consider that skills such as counting and navigating start out depending heavily on your ability to match your movements to percepts of external objects. Self-motion cues are a major contributor to egocentric maps, and exploratory actions (like crawling) are often periodic. The rhythmic coordination of actions and percepts shows up a lot in cognitive development. Such coordination is fundamental to learning to produce speech—babies' first speech sounds often involve regularly timed repetitions (such as "mama" and "papa").

Using Rhythm to Counteract Cognitive Decline

The production and perception of rhythms are not only relevant to action coordination but also seem to play a key role in matching actions to perceived durations. Some evidence suggests that your ability to judge durations partly depends on your heart rate and/or respiration rate and the extent to which they fit the durations you are attempting to match (Wittmann, 2009, 2013). Similarly, typical musical tempos appear to be closely related to normal walking speeds (Styns et al., 2007). The perception of internal rhythms may thus play the role of internal clocks in shaping your perception of second-long intervals.

The perception and production of rhythmic patterns may also affect cognitive processing more generally. For instance, memory tests of college students and older adults performed while they were

FIGURE 6.21. Maintaining minds through motion. Moving your body to the beat in old age can potentially help to preserve your mental capacities. How might you test whether these benefits come from the external inputs that dance classes provide or from the production and perception of movements? (monkeybusinessimages)

walking on a treadmill revealed that walking while remembering degraded memory in older individuals but sometimes enhanced memory in college students (Verrel et al., 2009). The decrement in older individuals seems to arise because of their need to monitor their walking more carefully. Reduced balance (perception of body position in space) is often associated with aging, but the consequences for cognition are less obvious.

Age-related loss of visual and auditory sensitivities can obviously degrade various cognitive skills (for example, reading and comprehending speech), and numerous technologies exist to counteract such deficits. Vestibular and kinesthetic sensory abilities may also deteriorate with age and negatively affect cognitive capacities (such as memory and attention) in less obvious ways; currently, there are no technologies that directly counter such deficits.

Interestingly, there is evidence that having older individuals participate in dance classes does counteract cognitive decline in Parkinson's patients (de Natale et al., 2017) and older adults more generally (Coubard, et al., 2011; Kattenstroth et al., 2013) (**Figure 6.21**). Generally, researchers have assumed that the cognitive benefits of dance classes come from better health and more opportunities for social interaction. But systematic production and perception of rhythms might also help to preserve representational capacities.

If you think about text you have memorized throughout your life, you will discover that it's probably mostly music lyrics or text you produce with a particular rhythm, like the Pledge of Allegiance. There are some indications that rhythmic patterning of inputs can enhance retention, either by increasing dopamine production or by amplifying synchronous activity across brain regions. Neural activity is inherently rhythmic (Buzsaki, 2006), so it's perhaps not surprising that encouraging brains to do what they do best might have cognitive enhancing effects.

Relatively little is known about how rhythmic coordination of actions and percepts contribute to how humans and other animals represent the world or themselves. In part, this is a consequence of past emphasis on information processing models of cognition (computers don't dance). Increased interest in embodied cognition and dynamic systems models in recent decades is beginning to counteract this bias, opening up new opportunities for exploring how your innermost feelings and body parts contribute to your mental states and cognitive capacities.

CLOSURE

Sporting events admittedly are more about action and competition than they are about abstract concepts. Even so, they highlight the many ways that perceptual awareness of time, space, and number comes into play during daily activities. When the Berkeley football players began their last-ditch game of "hot potato" in the infamous Play, they didn't just toss the ball randomly.

Each player waited until just milliseconds before being taken down by an opponent before getting rid of the ball—a challenging timing task. Players attempting to move the ball closer to the goal were faced with a rapid numerosity discrimination—where are the fewest tacklers (an approximate number judgment)—combined with an assessment of open real estate—where is there room to run (a visual distance judgment). This dynamic navigational task is what professional athletes get paid the big bucks for successfully performing.

The invading Stanford band members operated on an entirely different perceptual scale, focusing mainly on the field as a landmark while simultaneously entraining their musical performance to the predictable rhythmic patterns produced by their drummers. The durations of musical sounds and silences, predetermined by whoever wrote the musical piece they were playing, also monopolized band members' temporal perception (a case of interval timing). The only numbers the trampled trombonist perceived prior to tasting grass were the score and time remaining (both symbolic number representations).

Athletes' movements were driven by visual-motor interactions on a millisecond time scale over distances of a few feet, while band members' actions were guided by auditory-motor synchronization at the level of seconds and by the distance from the stands to the football field. Both athletes and musicians were doing their thing within the same space and time, but their cognizance of space, time, and number differed dramatically.

For everyone involved, percepts of space and time played a major role in guiding both decisions and actions. What people saw and heard likely shared many elements, but how they incorporated their sensations into an organized experience likely differed greatly. Even percepts of self-motions produced by running fast or blowing hard may have affected how each person experienced the Play and thought about it later.

Unlike in physics, there is no specific time, space, or quantity psychologically. Even for a single individual, there may be, and usually are, multiple representations of all of these dimensions contributing to ongoing experiences or competing to do so. Your mental states can simultaneously represent time, space, and number within multiple time frames and across various distances. The cognitive processes that coordinate these representations engage several brain regions in parallel, sometimes in synchrony and sometimes in predictably patterned sequences.

Concepts of space and time have been a major focus of philosophical discussions for thousands of years and a component of the earliest experimental psychology research. Debate continues over how to best think about what mental impressions of space, time, and number reveal about their actual qualities, or about how percepts of these dimensions are neurally and cognitively represented.

Increasing recognition of the spooky similarities between these different domains, both in terms of psychophysics (how they all seem to bow to Weber's law) and in terms of the common brain regions that they engage, has raised awareness that there may be a common origin or representational element that binds them all together. At the same time, the wide variety of cues that organisms use to navigate through space suggests that the processes that determine how you represent these seemingly fundamental qualities of the world may come in all sorts of shapes and sizes and may even depend on how long you have lived and where! Identifying the forces that shape how humans cognize themselves and the world remains one of the greatest challenges faced by cognitive psychologists.

COGNITIVE LINGO

allothetic cue	internal clock	path integration
analog representation	interval timing	place cell
approximate number system	invariant cue	rubber hand illusion
beacon	landmark	scalar property
circadian timing	multisensory integration	spatial orientation
cognitive map	numerosity	synchronized
dyscalculia	object tracking system	third variable problem
entrainment	optic flow	
idiothetic cue	oscillator	

CHAPTER SUMMARY

Timing and Time Perception
Synchronizing actions with events requires different mechanisms from judging the duration of events. Some theories of time perception assume an internal clock makes timing possible while others suggest that no such clock is necessary.

Spatial Cognition
Spatial percepts vary over time as experience increases. Interpreting spatial cues often depends on using learned reference frames. Psychological models of spatial processing attempt to explain how dynamic sensations are transformed into stable representations of space.

Numerical Competence
Many organisms naturally judge the numerosity of objects, agents, and events, and do so using at least two different systems. Arithmetic operations can be performed without symbols or the ability to count, but symbols greatly increase the range of operations that one can perform.

Brain Substrates
Neurons in multiple brain regions show sensitivities to spatial cues and likely contribute to spatial navigation, as well as a broader range of cognitive processes. Like spatial processing, temporal processing depends on several mechanisms distributed throughout the brain.

Applied Perspectives
Basic mechanisms of numerosity perception may affect how easily children learn mathematical skills in school. Perception and production of rhythmic patterns can also affect cognitive processing in surprising ways.

REVIEW EXERCISES

Timing and Time Perception
• Describe the relationship between interval timing and internal clocks.
• How does circadian timing differ from interval timing?

Spatial Cognition
• Explain what the rubber hand illusion reveals about the perception of space.
• What are some of the different kinds of cues that you might use to navigate through Disney World?

Numerical Competence
• What are two systems that cognitive psychologists think toddlers use to judge amounts?

• What sorts of evidence suggest that perception of time, space, and number may work similarly?

Brain Substrates
• What sorts of "spatial neurons" have been discovered so far and how do they differ?
• Explain how different drugs can distort perception of time and timing.

Applied Perspectives
• Describe the third variable problem and explain why it can complicate the interpretation of experiments.

CRITICAL THINKING QUESTIONS

1. Ants are able to navigate through complex, novel environments on a daily basis without getting lost, while five- and six-year-old children commonly become disoriented in stores and thousands of adults get lost in parks annually while walking on nature trails. Why might humans have a harder time keeping track of their position and orientation than ants do (or might ants often get lost, too)?

2. Time flies when you're having fun, but not when you're waiting in a long line or staring at water until it boils. What mechanisms might account for these differences in your subjective impressions of durations?

3. Some people with autism spectrum disorder have the ability to calendar calculate, which means that they can tell you what day of the week almost any date falls on. Do such individuals represent time and/or number differently than most people do? How might you experimentally test your answer to the previous question?

4. It's often said that your whole life flashes before your eyes just before you're about to die or think you are. Aside from dying, in what other ways might a person be able to mentally compress long stretches of time into relatively brief subjective experiences?

5. Drivers in the United States increasingly rely on GPS systems to get around, and in the future, people may rely on self-driving cars for transportation. How might technology-dependent navigation affect cognitive maps or other spatial representations possessed by the next generation?

Memory

The starting point for many psychology textbooks (including this one) is perception. In *The Principles of Psychology*, however, William James kicks off his discussion of psychological phenomena with a chapter called "Habit." In that chapter, he lays out his first and most fundamental principle: "We may without hesitation lay down as our first proposition the following, that *the phenomena of habit in living beings are due to the plasticity of the organic materials of which their bodies are composed*" (James, 1890, v.1, p. 105). According to James, you and all the creatures you encounter are "bundles of habits," and anyone hoping to scientifically understand minds must start by identifying what the limits and nature of habits are.

Jamesian habits were not just routines people followed—like brushing their teeth—because their parents taught them to. He included any actions (including mental actions) that an individual frequently repeated. James hypothesized that habits form when neural transmissions "deepen old paths or make new ones," (James, 1890, v.1, p. 107) and more specifically that the modifications involved changes in the connections between neurons. In essence, James was arguing that what you learn changes your brain, and how it changes strongly determines the kinds of mental processes and physical actions you are likely to engage in.

Civilization's Major Mover

Let's assume for the moment that James was right and that you are, or soon will be, a walking bundle of habits. So what? At a personal level, the critical implication of this principle is that the activities you pursue daily are the architects of the future you. If your goal is to increase or maintain your current intellectual, musical, athletic, spiritual, social, or comedic abilities, your brain can be either a friend or foe depending on what you repeatedly do. The trick then is to gradually whittle your brain into the form you want it to be, through the situations you put yourself in and the actions you take in response to those situations.

For better or worse, the situations you can use to shape your mind are limited by the times you live in. One reason that James emphasized habits as the core issue that psychological scientists needed to work out was that he viewed habits as "the enormous flywheel of society," (James, 1890, v.1, p. 121) meaning that the collective habits of past and present humans determine what life is like and what everyone's lives could be like. When you "go with the flow," habits are the fount of the flow. Even if you rebel or strive to be the rolling stone that gathers no moss, how you roll will depend on the ruts that others have left before you. In this sense, your thoughts are not your own and your cognitive processes are the products of peers, parents, and teachers fostering repetitions across generations. This perspective may sound familiar. It has a lot in common with Piaget's proposals about constructivism and cognitive development. However, while Piaget argued that mind construction was largely complete by the time you hit high school, James claimed that habit formation in humans continued to progress until at least the age of thirty.

No modern psychology textbook includes a chapter on habits. The term rarely even appears in textbook indexes. How could phenomena that were featured so prominently and extensively in the first-ever psychology textbook disappear from modern discussions altogether? Partly, the demotion of habits happened when behaviorists rose to prominence and introduced their own jargon, replacing the general term "habits" with more refined labels like "conditioned responses." Then, when cognitive psychologists distanced themselves from the behaviorists and adopted information processing models, they largely left the learning behind. Computers didn't have habits and so many models of cognitive processes lacked them, too. Despite cognitive researchers' initial dismissal, habits continued to reveal their critical roles in new ways. For instance, the Stroop effect comes from the fact that reading habits trump color-labeling instructions and the word superiority effect is a consequence of readers' extensive practice recognizing words (see Chapter 4). The habits that have most thoroughly infiltrated cognitive research, however, are not those associated with reading or response conditioning, but those made famous by the self-studies of Hermann Ebbinghaus: the habits of memory.

Paintings of the Past

Most of your percepts seemingly pass into oblivion, but some leave remnants that you can consciously consider. Your subjective impressions of time, rhythms, and coincidences (discussed in Chapter 6) depend on your ability to maintain awareness of the "just was." James described these experiences as intuitions of time: a persistent feeling that there is more to life than the just now. Memories go a step further in that they give the impression of recurrence: like percepts that left for some time but then came back. Many psychological theories of memories describe them as if they were reactivated representations. James pointed out that this portrayal is insufficient. He described memories as mentally projected events, imagined in either the past or the future; experiences that were conceived not perceived. If percepts are actors and props on the stage of life, then from the Jamesian perspective, memories are the backdrop behind the stage. But, backdrops that you create yourself, such that memories are your mental paintings of the past, combined with a firm belief that recall provides a clear view from a former you.

What does this have to do with habits? If habits are what you do when repeated experiences change your brain, then how you construct your memories depends on your bundle of memory recall habits. In which case, how you repeatedly represent and retrieve memories may determine what memories you can have. For instance, your studying habits over many years will determine what you can possibly get out of studying for an exam next week. Both what you know (your existing brain ruts) and how you study (your memory "painting skills") matter more than momentary motivation or zealous effort. Ironically, the kinds of academic habits currently encouraged in children are exactly those likely to lead to the least enduring memories and the most problematic habits.

The following two chapters link learning, plasticity, and memory to your conceptions of the past and future. They follow the lead of James by viewing memory recall as a psychophysical phenomenon in which the physical component relates to changes in the structure and function of neural circuits (brain plasticity) and the psychological element involves experienced memories plus the belief that remembered events happened. Just as psychophysical studies of perception span several sensory modalities and dimensions of change, cognitive studies of memory encompass a wide range of experience-related changes in recollections, from memories of factual statements to vivid flashbacks, all of which connect to slow or rapid changes in the activity of neural circuits. Memory processes are currently one of the main targets of cognitive research and the topic of most pragmatic relevance to college students given that every course is an exercise in the acquisition and retention of new information and skills. Learning how to think about novel topics is arguably the rationale for taking any academic course, so understanding how brain plasticity, associative learning, and habits contribute to memory acquisition, retention, and construction is key to knowing how to best train your brain. The more you know, the more your recall skills can grow. Caffeine helps also.

Acquiring and Applying Memories

MikeDotta via Shutterstock

Ted's first run at getting an undergraduate degree did not go well. After two years of studying Chinese at the University of Washington, he dropped out. His girlfriend viewed this as a sign that Ted was too immature and carefree, so she dumped him soon after. Her rejection motivated him to get his act together. A couple of years later, he decided to re-enroll, this time as a psychology major. Ted excelled in psychology, becoming an honors student and impressing his professors enough that they happily recommended him to law schools. It seemed the girlfriend's action had set Ted on a new path (**Figure 7.1**).

Ted's ex was so amazed at the transformation that she eventually got back together with him. They even discussed getting married. Then, about six months into the renewed romance, Ted cut off all contact with his to-be fiancée. It turns out he just wanted her to see what it felt like to get jilted. This was around the same time that Ted assaulted a random 18-year-old in her basement apartment (she lived but was left with permanent injuries).

Over the next year, Ted perfected his technique of luring women by pretending to have an injury. He wore a sling when he approached young women on college campuses and asked them for help carrying a briefcase or books, then abducted and murdered the more helpful ones. Several women who did not fall for this trick described Ted to the police who worked up a sketch and broadcasted it on local television stations. Four different people who knew Ted reported him to the police as a possible suspect. But detectives thought it unlikely that a young law student with no criminal record was kidnapping and murdering college students. And there was no physical evidence of what happened to most of the women—they just disappeared.

Ted Bundy's girlfriend at the time of the murders, whom he had been with for about three years, was one of the people who reported him as a possible suspect. She kept on seeing him, even though more disappearances and murders piled up, and she repeatedly reported him as a possible suspect to

FIGURE 7.1. Deadly memories. Ted Bundy managed to murder at least thirty young women, mostly college students between the ages of seventeen and twenty-three, before being caught. How might learning processes have contributed to Ted's ability to avoid capture for so long? (GLArchive/Alamy Stock Photo)

various law enforcement agencies. In later interviews with police, she noted that she'd found odd items in her house and in Ted's apartment, like crutches, a meat cleaver, and surgical gloves. She also described him as a warm and loving man.

It's often difficult to predict how people will respond to any one event. Sometimes a single event can change an individual's behavior in ways that lead to a cascading chain of unintended consequences. Most of Ted Bundy's victims physically resembled the college girlfriend who dumped him. Repeated criminal acts that go unpunished not only can increase a person's motivation to go further but also can increase the criminal's skill at luring victims and evading detection. Ted may also have benefitted from his knowledge of psychology, exploiting empathetic tendencies in unsuspecting targets and sowing doubt in government officials.

Predicting what will happen in various circumstances is what acquiring and using memories is all about. Police initially failed to connect the dots because of their prior knowledge and beliefs about the kinds of things that law students typically do and about how criminals usually act. They *generalized* from past experiences in ways that led them to make mistakes. Ted Bundy may have generalized from his heartbreaking girlfriend to physically similar women whom he either consciously or unconsciously felt deserved to be punished.

The young women's actions, too, were likely guided by their memories. Perhaps they had been taught that kindness is a virtue. Or, maybe they had had enjoyable encounters with attractive strangers at parties or in other settings. Possibly, they failed to recall their parents' warnings about talking to strangers or felt that those rules were only relevant when they were younger.

Acquisition and application of memories is not just something that happens in classrooms when you want it to. The consequences of learning go far beyond determining your grades. Everything you know, everything you can do, and everything you think has been shaped by your past experiences. Many effects of memory happen without you ever noticing. Memories are what made a predator like Ted Bundy possible, and learning is what enabled police to finally stop him. This chapter focuses on identifying how people and other organisms acquire and apply memories and looks at how learned skills and knowledge can affect the ways that you think and behave.

BEHAVIORAL PROCESSES

If you are reading this chapter as part of a course you're taking, then probably either you or someone at your university hopes that you are learning something about cognitive psychology. You may have even been given a syllabus that lays out specific learning objectives, including things you should be able to do or know after successfully completing the course.

These kinds of predefined learning goals are meant to provide you with a mental roadmap for where the course should take you. But how will you get there? The standard path often includes assignments, discussions, exams, lectures, and a good bit of "studying," which, loosely defined, is any activity that might boost your performance whenever your knowledge or skills are evaluated.

But what exactly are your academic efforts doing for you (or to you)? Are you becoming a more skilled thinker? A better-organized fact receptacle? A more effective procrastinator? Or perhaps a sophisticated citizen of the world? How might you know whether you are achieving prescribed learning objectives? Will accomplishing those goals significantly affect your future cognitive activities or will they have no effect at all? You probably have no objective way of answering any of these questions. And yet you still learn, moving forward in life with only a vague sense of what is happening in your head as you acquire new memories.

Psychologists today know a lot more about learning and memory acquisition than they did a couple of centuries ago, but not so much that they can predict what effect a particular academic course will have on a specific individual's intellectual competence or behavior, much less what effect several courses taken over multiple years might have on a person's thought processes. At best, psychologists know what *can* happen, along with a few tricks for increasing the likelihood that certain desired outcomes *will* happen for motivated students.

Scientific studies of memory acquisition have typically focused on simpler situations than those that occur on college campuses. Laboratory research on learning and memory emphasizes scenarios in which behavioral changes associated with past experiences can be closely monitored and controlled (Kumar, 2021; Squire & Kandel, 2000). The ability of individuals to show what they know, both in familiar and novel contexts, is the main event in learning and memory studies, especially when participants learn about what's happening, what's about to happen, and how they should respond under the circumstances.

Learning to Predict Significant Events: Pavlovian Conditioning

SNEAK PEEK: Understanding how the world works requires learning to recognize events that occur in predictable sequences. How do repeated experiences contribute to memory acquisition and how important is effort in forming new associations?

Any experience can potentially lead to learning and memory formation, but the kinds of events that most consistently result in learning are events that happen repeatedly. Memory acquisition is a process of experiences generating changes, so perhaps it's not too surprising that more repetition can produce more of a change. It's not a given though that more is better—attempting to fly each morning by flapping your arms rapidly is unlikely to produce any progress.

You might have to try to learn how to fly, but many of the memories you acquire daily require no conscious effort. Several different modes of "learning by living" were presented in earlier chapters. Perceptual learning can happen when your repeated experiences increase your ability to make subtle distinctions between highly similar percepts (see Chapter 4) (Yang et al., 2020). Spatial learning, in which you become familiar with where things are located, simply requires you to look around while you're moving through an environment (see Chapter 6) (Peer et al., 2021). How you sort faces, scenes, objects, and sounds can also develop over time without any effort (described in Chapter 5)

(Abudarham et al., 2019). Lots of learning "just happens" when events proceed in predictable ways. Much of the research on memory acquisition is based on examining individuals' experiences with repeated sequences.

Recognizing Predictable Sequences

When an individual's behavior is gradually modified by repeated exposures to similar events, the process is referred to as **conditioning**. The process of conditioning studied by Russian physiologist Ivan Pavlov (1849–1936), often referred to as Pavlovian or classical conditioning, is probably the most well-known (and most misunderstood) example (Domjan, 2005; Pavlov, 1927). When you think of Pavlov, bells, dogs, and slobber may spring to mind. What Pavlov was really attempting to do, however, was to understand how individuals learn to predict the future (Honey et al., 2020).

When one event consistently predicts others—say a wasp on your hand predicts throbbing pain in the near future—the two events become mentally linked. The first time a child encounters a wasp, that child may perceive it as an exciting new source of entertainment (based on similar past experiences with fun new things). One unpleasant discovery may be enough to change that view, with no mental effort required. Similarly, pairing an unfamiliar object with a pleasant event can increase the attractiveness of that object (**Figure 7.2**).

Other less surprisingly painful or arousing encounters may take more repetitions to sink in, but the underlying mechanisms obey similar rules. The ease with which a particular event can be linked to others varies; some events are easier to associate than others. For instance, children can form the memory that a wasp stings more quickly than the memory that a curtain swings.

Pavlov developed experimental tasks in which dogs learned that random events (neutral stimuli) were predictive of acid or food going into their mouths (yes, acid). This enabled him to measure how rapidly conditioning happened in different circumstances and to identify what dogs learned from their experiences (Pavlov, 1927).

Pavlov discovered that dogs not only learned about the specific sights and sounds that he paired with the acid or food but also about the context and timing of relevant events and even the identities of specific trainers. The dogs didn't just use percepts of objects and agents to predict what would

FIGURE 7.2. Conditioning salivation post-Pavlov.
Advertisers pair images of their products with celebrities in an effort to condition customers' responses. The hope is that an image of the celebrity (an unconditioned stimulus or US) evokes arousal (an unconditioned response or UR) that occurs in association with the image of the product (a neutral stimulus). Any positive feelings associated with the celebrity can quickly become linked to the product through repeated exposures such that the product becomes associated with the US (making it a conditioned stimulus or CS). In this way, the product can generate feelings that might make it more attractive. How might you reveal any memories produced by this marketing technique? (Brad Pitt: Xinhua/Alamy Stock Photo; perfume bottle: PLAINVIEW)

Neutral stimulus

Arousal (UR)

Three weeks later while in store…

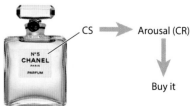

CS → Arousal (CR)

Buy it

happen next. They also learned about the **context**—the locations and conditions of the experiment—associating complex combinations of dynamic events with one particularly attention-grabbing experience that followed them. Similarly, a child stung by a wasp in a novel playground might learn not just to fear wasps but also to be wary of that specific playground or of parks with similar playgrounds.

Once Pavlov realized that dogs could learn all kinds of different associations relatively quickly, he began to explore the distinctions dogs made when they learned associations. For instance, if a dog learned that one person was in charge of running the food experiments and that another ran the acid experiments, what sort of features of trainers did the dog use to tell the people apart: height? smell? voice? facial differences?

To figure out the sorts of sensory cues that were easiest for dogs to associate, Pavlov ran countless experiments in which dogs experienced different contrasting events, some of which predicted important outcomes and others that predicted nothing. By examining which features dogs picked up on and how many repetitions it took for them to learn distinctions, Pavlov was able to rank which features within modalities (like shape versus color) dogs learned about the quickest. Essentially, Pavlov used learning as a way to discover what dogs noticed and which stimuli dogs were likely to link to other events (thereby making those stimuli conditioned stimuli or CSs, see Figure 7.2).

By identifying what dogs learned while being conditioned, Pavlov was also able to discover new information about how dogs represent their world, or what it's like to be a dog (see the discussion of *Umwelten* in Chapter 3). He used this knowledge to develop several novel hypotheses about the origins of mental disorders in humans (Pavlov, 1941). Pavlov's conditioning technique continues to be widely used today in developmental studies designed to reveal what infants learn and perceive (Ludwig & Welch, 2020; Sullivan et al., 1991).

What you learn about a sequence of events depends a lot on what you already know. For instance, in **blocking** experiments, two groups repeatedly experience multiple stimuli occurring just before some notable event—think rain, clouds, and lightning predicting thunder. Before conditioning with these combinations of stimuli, some participants first learn that a single cue presented alone predicts the notable event. The typical result of this procedure is that the participants who first learned about the single cue fail to learn that the additional cues presented in the second round of training also predict the event—the first cue blocks associations with later cues (Denton & Kruschke, 2006; Le Pelley et al., 2016).

If Pavlovian conditioning mainly involves learning when you fail to predict a notable event, then it makes sense that you'd be less likely to learn in situations where you already know what's about to happen. On the other hand, when your predictions are off, adjusting your expectations may be advantageous.

A child stung for the first time by a wasp in an unfamiliar yard at a birthday party is likely to associate the yard, the party paraphernalia, and the wasp with the painful outcome. However, if the child had been stung on a previous occasion, it's unlikely that any associations between stings and parties will form. In the second case, the child's earlier learning effectively blocks the formation of a new association to the new context. Similarly, your past experiences determine what you are likely to learn now from repeated experiences. If you find learning about a new topic difficult, feel free to blame your past conditioning.

Traditional analyses of conditioning often emphasize how repeated experiences with event sequences change how learners respond to future events. However, the effects of conditioning are not always obvious. **Latent learning** occurs when behavioral changes are not immediately apparent to anyone during or after conditioning (Tolman, 1948; Wang & Hayden, 2021). If you feel sick to your stomach whenever you see someone eat fried butter, but never mention it or otherwise give away your nausea, then your learned fried butter associations are latent (not evident to observers or you). Similarly, associations between a celebrity and a perfume might not show themselves until you are in a store and see the familiar perfume bottle.

Latent learning can occur when you learn to attend to specific stimuli in a familiar context. For instance, if you have a crush on someone, then every time you're in a place where they might show up, you may start thinking about them. This conditioned mental state may affect your perception of other events happening in that setting as well as your ability to learn from those events. For instance, you might find that fries are more flavorful in a club where your crush likes to hang out.

It's often not obvious what an individual is perceiving, attending to, or thinking about, making it trickier to detect conditioning-related changes in these kinds of cognitive processes. Past conditioning research has instead emphasized conditioned responses (CRs, see Figure 7.2) because they are more detectable and measurable (not because there is any evidence that behavioral responses are more likely to be modified by conditioning than hidden mental reactions).

Extinguishing Learned Associations

If you have read or thought about psychological research before, then there's a good chance that you've formed all sorts of psychology-related associations. There is a reason why when you hear "Pavlov" you think "bells." But, let's say you find out that Pavlov never conditioned any dogs to respond to bells (surprise! he never did). How are you going to get this Pavlov-bell association out of your head?

One approach might be to just avoid thinking about Pavlov so that eventually you forget about anything he ever supposedly did. Chapter 8 will reveal why attempting to avoid thinking about a topic is seldom an effective way of removing associations. Another option might be for me to repeat the factual statement, "Pavlov never used bells," over and over in this chapter and throughout the book. That strategy is unlikely to work either because you can easily find ten other textbooks that say he did. In general, getting rid of associations is a lot harder than forming them.

Some of the hardest associations to overcome are those that involve uniquely unpleasant experiences. A single instance of food poisoning after eating seafood can turn you off seafood for life and no amount of shrimp nibbling may erase that association. Associations formed during highly pleasant experiences can be equally difficult to shake, even if, later on, the cues that once predicted pleasantness (like the taste of alcohol or smell of smoke) no longer do.

One learning process that is often associated with the weakening of associations over time is **extinction**. During extinction, repeated presentations of a CS in the absence of any consequence weaken responses to the CS (**Figure 7.3**). If a child's parents force the child to go to birthday parties despite an earlier party-related wasp trauma, eventually the fear that festive balloons (a CS) trigger will likely fade. Behaviorally, it may seem as if the child has forgotten all about the painful episode or

FIGURE 7.3. Conditioning and extinction. Repeated pairings of a colored bottle with the image of a celebrity can, over time, cause an observer to respond to the bottle as if it were a celebrity (shown in the plot before the dashed line; CR=conditioned response). If after this conditioning experience the same visual stimulus is presented without the celebrity (Brad gone), the bottle image (CS) will quickly lose its power to produce the learned response. This does not mean that the association is gone, however. (Perfume bottle: PLAINVIEW)

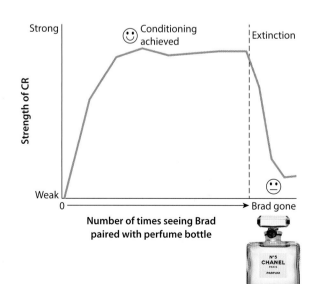

has gradually figured out that balloons aren't really great predictors of stings. However, looks can be deceiving.

Experimental studies of extinction have revealed that it doesn't take much for a "forgotten" association to reappear (Bouton et al., 2021). You can revive a child's balloon fears by randomly pinching the child while you both are at a balloon-infested party. The reactivated association can lead to renewed panic that will carry over to future parties.

This kind of memory rebirth can happen even after the child grows up and has no conscious memory of ever being stung by a wasp! Pavlov found that if he took a cue that a dog had previously associated with food and repeatedly presented it to the dog without providing any food (leading to extinction), the dog would quickly learn that the cue was no longer relevant. To his surprise, if he simply ignored the dog for a few months and then retested it, guess what happened? After the break, the dog would often respond to the conditioned cue the same way it had before the association was extinguished.

Rather than forgetting what the cue had once predicted, or remembering that the cue was no longer reliable, the dogs seemed to forget that the once predictive cue had become irrelevant. More recent relevant experiences affected behavior less than earlier, now irrelevant, associations. This is partly why you're going to continue associating Pavlov with bells no matter what I tell you.

The powerful effects of past associations on behavior have important practical implications for a variety of cognitive processes. Consider the case of someone who leaves home to go to college and then learns to be independent and self-sufficient, to study hard, and so on. That same person returning home to spend the holidays with family, upon encountering the situations and cues that they grew up with, may easily fall back into behavioral patterns more typical of their younger self, including actions they wouldn't be caught dead doing away from home. The return of a familiar context and all its emotional triggers can overcome years of new learning and extinction, a phenomenon known as the **renewal effect** (Broomer & Bouton, 2022).

The persistence of conditioned associations can be problematic, but you might have guessed that it also has some advantages. For one, lots of cues reliably predict what is about to happen over a lifetime, enabling you to better avoid unpleasant outcomes like parental criticism. Also, it's not easy to predict when a particular event sequence may occur again, so losing associations just because they haven't been useful recently could be counterproductive. Finally, it often takes time and multiple repetitions to form new associations. That's why studying is sometimes un-fun. Having the capacity to quickly revert to a previous state can enhance behavioral and mental flexibility (Braem & Egner, 2018). So, even if all the associations you formed at an earlier age seem to have faded into oblivion, you will still be able to relearn them more quickly than if you had never formed them.

Explicit versus Implicit Predictions

One issue that often comes up in discussions of conditioning is whether the person forming the memories actually knows what is happening during the process. You might guess that the wasp-stung child knows that wasps are bad news after the unpleasant experience. You might be a bit more skeptical that a dog knows that the sound of a can opener means food is on the way.

Perhaps, as suggested by the philosopher Descartes, dogs learn about food-predicting sounds the same way your phone learns to recognize your voice or passcode. Evidence of learning comes mainly from changes in behavior independently of whether any knowing is happening. Similarly, a child might show a learned fear response when confronted with a balloon without necessarily realizing that the balloon is what is making them skittish. Knowing implies awareness. Association only implies connections.

Throughout the history of conditioning research, researchers have argued about whether Pavlovian conditioning is a completely unconscious process, whether it only happens when an individual is aware that it is happening, whether awareness is a necessary prerequisite for conditioning to

FIGURE 7.4. Implicit learning.
Pavlovian conditioning can potentially occur with or without awareness. Repeated experiences could condition you to expect that the gorilla will make confusing statements in board meetings, an association you notice. You might also learn to expect the gorilla to always have a full glass of water that it never drinks, without explicitly noticing this. Which is more likely? (Paul Bradbury)

Implicit CS (water)   Explicit CS (gorilla suit)

succeed in all animals, and so on (Clark et al., 2002; Droege et al., 2021; Jensen et al., 2015; Weidemann et al., 2016; Wiens & Ohman, 2002). These issues have yet to be resolved.

It is clear that some people become aware during conditioning that one event predicts another. And it is clear that awareness of what is happening in an experiment can influence a participant's behavior (see the discussion of expectancy effects in Chapter 3). At a minimum, an individual is more likely to learn associations between events that he or she consciously perceives than between events that were never detected, suggesting that awareness is at least predictive of the effectiveness of conditioning (**Figure 7.4**).

However, many of the learning phenomena discovered by Pavlov and subsequent conditioning researchers can be replicated with connectionist models (Dawson, 2008; Moustafa et al., 2009). Recall from Chapter 5 that connectionist models are computer programs in which neuron-like elements interact with each other within networks. Chapter 5 describes how connectionist models store representations of sensed events in ways that preserve the associations between those events. The links formed by connectionist models are numerical and therefore implicit (unconscious) rather than explicit (conscious). Repeated experiences change the strengths of connections within networks to improve recognition of familiar patterns.

When associative learning is viewed as a kind of implicit, automatic rewiring of neural connections, it may seem entirely independent of cognition (Olson & Fazio, 2001). When it is instead viewed as a process of consciously searching for a more complete understanding of the world, it seems a lot more cognitive (Kirsch et al., 2004). The gap between these two views of conditioning has led psychologists to propose two distinct ways that individuals may learn associations: one involving implicit memory acquisition and another that depends on conscious consideration of ongoing events (explicit memory acquisition).

Your explicit forecasting abilities can make life less confusing. The implicit associations you form can also be useful. But they can sometimes be a weakness, especially when they lead you to act in ways that are not in your best interest. This is a weakness that advertisers and politicians are more than happy to exploit. For instance, lots of people watch the Super Bowl, and companies are eager to take advantage of this in an effort to increase their profits. Like most commercials, Super Bowl ads are designed to make a mark so that later on viewers' purchases may be guided by what they saw during the game. Marketers want people to want their stuff.

One way that advertisers attempt to instill desire for a product is by repeatedly pairing the product with sounds and images that trigger pleasant feelings (ogle Brad Pitt in Figure 7.2). In this way, companies can potentially form associations between their brand/product and happy mental states. Political ads often use the opposite strategy, broadcasting commercials that pair the competition's name and image with sounds and scenes that provoke anger, disgust, or mistrust.

There's no way subjectively to tell exactly how effective any of these conditioning attempts are on you or your neighbors—you are likely to feel that few if any ads are affecting your choices or behavior. Propaganda has been successfully weaponized, however. Companies and politicians continue spending insane amounts of money in attempts to condition people. Clearly, there are reasons to think that the intended associations are often being formed. Keep on believing that commercials aren't affecting your behavior if you want. Just don't be surprised if you're better at matching ads to companies than psychological terms to their meanings.

SIGHT BITES

Conditioning an individual by repeatedly exposing them to predictable sequences enables them to learn to associate the events in those sequences.

Extinction is a process of counteracting learned associations by repeatedly presenting stimuli or contexts in the absence of outcomes that they previously predicted.

Associative learning can be viewed as an active process of searching for a more complete understanding about how the world works.

Connectionist models can simulate the gradual learning of associations, suggesting that it may be possible for memory acquisition to occur implicitly.

Learning to Predict Consequences

SNEAK PEEK: The pleasant and unpleasant outcomes of actions powerfully affect memory acquisition, whether those outcomes are discovered through trial and error or through observations of others. Given that, what are some ways that teachers might boost learning inside or outside of classrooms?

Forming memories by repeatedly presenting paired events is not always the most effective way of changing behavior. A major limitation of this approach is that the predicted outcome occurs regardless of what the learner does—the events being learned about are not under the learner's control. So, if you are trying to condition someone to perform a particular action in response to a specific context, say to smile whenever they see you, then other types of conditioning will likely be more useful.

> *"The great thing, then, in all education, is to make our nervous system our ally instead of our enemy… For this we must make automatic and habitual, as early as possible, as many useful actions as we can."*
> James, 1890, p 122

Instrumental conditioning (sometimes referred to as operant conditioning) focuses on getting individuals to perform specific actions by providing incentives. In Pavlovian conditioning, learning increases an individual's ability to predict what will happen when. Instrumental conditioning, in contrast, increases the likelihood that the individual will perform a desired action and predict its consequences. If the individual doesn't do the right thing, the desired outcome might never happen.

For instrumental conditioning to be effective, the individual needs to be motivated to do something. Often this motivation comes from an individual's wants, needs, or likes. It can also come from

FIGURE 7.5. Creating incentives. Instrumental conditioning depends on voluntary actions as well as the motivation to act. Dog trainers use instrumental conditioning to get dogs to perform actions they normally would not. At the same time, dog trainers exist because getting dogs to perform unique tricks is a rewarding activity. What are the motivational consequences that both dog and trainer are learning to expect in this context? (Stanislaw Tokarski via Shutterstock)

Salient stimulus   Shaped behavior   Instrumental conditioner

fear, uncertainty, or anger. In classroom settings, the motivators that drive conditioning are often culturally constructed: high grades beget passed courses, which lead to better jobs that provide more money to spend on nicer prizes. Both desired outcomes and feared consequences can change an individual's actions over time. An individual's ability to increasingly produce actions that lead to desired consequences provides evidence that learning is occurring (**Figure 7.5**).

Schools often attempt to use motivators such as learning objectives or grades to condition students, which produces some awareness in students of what the potential prizes are. In contrast, plants will change their behavior to get access to more sunlight or water but probably do not "like" or "want" water or have any water-related goals. It's unclear whether plants can be instrumentally conditioned, although there is increasing evidence that they can learn associations through Pavlovian conditioning (Abramson & Chicas-Mosier, 2016; Baluska et al., 2018).

Highly accurate responses on objective exams is currently the goal behavior in many educational settings, leading many educators to structure classes in ways that increase students' proficiency at test taking. To motivate teachers to adopt a "teaching to the test" conditioning strategy, some state governments have begun grading teachers' performances based on how much they are able to increase their students' test scores; the grade is called a value-added measure (VAM). Teachers with high VAMs may get bonuses, while those with low VAMs may find themselves looking for another job. As you might expect, teachers, like their students, find all sorts of ways to ramp up their VAMs.

Reinforcement and Punishment

The consequences that increase the performance of a specific action during instrumental conditioning are called **reinforcers**. Almost anything can play the role of a reinforcer (Skinner, 1963; Timberlake, 1993). In laboratory experiments with animals, food and water are mainly used as reinforcers. Reinforcers like these that are necessary for survival are called primary reinforcers. Other nonnecessary or secondary reinforcers, such as money, are usually linked somewhere down the line to a primary reinforcer.

Punishers are the counterparts of reinforcers in that they are consequences that *decrease* the performance of specific actions during conditioning. B. F. Skinner, a giant in the field of instrumental conditioning (see Chapter 1), spent decades studying the effects of different kinds of reinforcement

WEIRD, TRUE, FREAKY

Plant School

The hallmark of learning is changes in behavior. But not every change in behavior qualifies as learning. When you're tired or starving, your behavior will change simply as a function of reduced resources. And in some cases, like with latent learning, if behavior has not changed, it does not necessarily mean that learning hasn't happened.

So, if no change does not prove that no learning has happened and some changes provide no evidence of learning, how can you tell when memory acquisition is happening? Detecting learning is particularly challenging in organisms like plants that usually don't behave in ways that are obvious to humans. You might assume, given their seemingly static nature, plants don't learn at all. Recent research challenges that assumption.

Scientists have been curious about the possibility of plants learning for over a century. Early experiments focused on plants such as the predatory Venus fly trap and touch sensitive plants like the *Mimosa* that move at rates visually detectable by human observers (Abramson & Calvo, 2018) (see figure).

Mimosa plants have the ability to close individual leaves when touched. Eventually, the leaves reopen and will close if touched again. When this procedure is repeated multiple times, the plant eventually stops closing its leaves (Abramson & Chicas-Mosier, 2016). Is this learning or just plant fatigue?

One way to test these different possibilities is to change how the leaves are touched to see if a new kind of touching reactivates the withdrawal response. If lack of energy were the issue, then the leaves shouldn't respond to any kind of touch. Some experiments suggest that nonresponsive leaves will respond to novel types of touches, consistent with a simple form of learning called habituation (Baluska & Levin, 2016). Other studies, however, have failed to replicate these findings (Segundo-Ortin & Calvo, 2019).

There are also signs that *Mimosa* plants may be able to learn through Pavlovian conditioning. When a light was turned on just prior to touching a plant over repeated trials, the plants responded more to the light than in other conditions when the light and touch were not paired (Abramson & Chicas-Mosier, 2016). Recent studies in pea plants showed that after they were conditioned with repeated pairings of a fan and a light source, the plants were more likely to grow in the direction of airflow (Segundo-Ortin & Calvo, 2019).

Most plant movements occur at timescales so slow that you are unlikely to notice them, much less detect if they vary depending on a plant's past experiences. As time-lapse imaging technologies and automated stimulus delivery systems become more widely available, conditioning studies with different kinds of plants will become more feasible. Plants may turn out to be more capable learners than you think. They may even be able to teach humans a few things about how learning works.

Mimosa plants recoil when touched. But can they learn? (AjayTvm via Shutterstock)

and punishment on learning rate and retention and concluded that, in general, punishers aren't as effective as reinforcers at changing behavior. Unlike reinforcers, repeated punishers have much less predictable effects on learning and behavior. Punishment can increase the variety of actions an individual performs, although most of the novel actions may be attempts at escape, cheating, or avoidance (Church, 1963). Swift and harsh punishments tend to be most effective, which may partly explain why many current systems for punishing criminals have such a poor track record at reducing crime rates or recidivism.

No consequence is inherently punishing or reinforcing. The ability of a consequence to increase or decrease the prevalence of an action depends on the state of the individual (Wu et al., 2022). If you're hungry, food will usually be reinforcing. If you're full or nauseated, it won't be reinforcing. One person's punishment is another's reward (**Figure 7.6**). The timing of the consequence relative to when the desired action was performed is also critical (Staddon et al., 1991). In most cases, the shorter the interval between the action and its consequence, the faster an individual will learn (Lattal, 2010).

FIGURE 7.6. Reinforcing "punishments." People use hot sauce on food despite the fact that the direct effect is often mouth pain. How might Pavlovian conditioning or instrumental conditioning contribute to the formation of such associations? What kinds of conditioned responses might a small red bottle provoke in this context? (Carlos Pereira M via Shutterstock)

Salient stimulus (CS)   Shaped behavior

Building Associations through Practice

Instrumental conditioning is a formalized version of what most people refer to as practicing. In laboratory settings, an animal can be encouraged to practice specific actions by repeatedly reinforcing those actions. In a college dorm, an undergraduate may be encouraged to practice guitar skills by the praise of peers and by the improving quality of the music produced.

Practicing actions requires commitment, effort, and time. Repetition combined with predictable consequences is key for any individual to learn by practicing. But just as important is choice. Forcing someone to repeatedly perform an action that they are not motivated to perform can be counterproductive and degrade learning.

In contexts where individuals have multiple options that can lead to reinforcers, they will tend to be more motivated when they engage in a self-selected option. Of course, choice can also be counterproductive to changing behavior in new directions, if for instance the selected activity invariably involves using a smartphone or playing video games.

Impulsivity and Self-Control

Daily life is basically a series of choices about which actions to perform. Any actions that are selected are in some sense practiced. Instrumental conditioning involves a kind of imposed, directed practice in that the aim is for an individual to act in ways that they were not acting before. Deliberate practice to improve a skill, like playing the guitar, is a kind of naturalistic, self-imposed instrumental conditioning.

Psychologists proposed the **law of effect** to explain why it is that you choose to perform the actions that you choose each day. The law of effect states that, within a given context, you will choose to perform the action that has been most reinforcing in the past (Herrnstein, 1970; Thorndike, 1933). This may seem like a fancy way of saying that you usually do things you need to do or like to do, but it does draw attention to the fact that many of your current choices are being driven by what you have learned through past repetitions from long ago (as noted in the quote by James above). The idea that choices are driven by past experiences implies that if you have different repeated experiences over the next few years, you might start making different choices in your daily life. It's almost as if life is brainwashing you.

The law of effect also partly explains why instant gratification is often more attractive than, say, putting aside money for a rainy day or giving it to a charity (Orduña, 2015). Because shorter intervals between an action and a consequence make the consequence more reinforcing or punishing, the effect of immediate gratification will be larger than outcomes that you imagine happening in the far future. Individuals who succumb to the temptations of instant gratification are said to be impulsive, while those who are willing and able to suffer now for the later good are described as having self-control.

Simple economics shows that investing money early and repeatedly (essentially taxing yourself) almost always leads to a greater total payoff. Similarly, deliberate, repetitive practice directed toward a particular outcome changes behavior in desired directions more consistently than just practicing (or studying) when it feels right.

Psychologists have increasingly turned to behavioral economics, which focuses on how individuals choose their actions, as a way of better understanding the learning processes that shape daily activities (Tagliabue et al., 2019). Behavioral economics considers issues like why drugs are more reinforcing than love for some but not others (Pickover et al., 2016), and when does punishing undesired actions change behavior more effectively than reinforcing desired actions.

The tricky part about reinforcers in instrumental conditioning and practicing is that the only way you can know something is reinforcing is if it increases performance of a specific action (Meehl, 1950); whether a given stimulus acts as a reinforcer varies from one person to the next. This means that you can only really know if you were reinforcing an action after the fact. That's a bit late!

One way around this limitation is to first explore what actions an individual prefers. For instance, you might give children the option of eating candy, watching videos, or playing on a playground. Once you identify what each child prefers, you could then use each child's preferred option as a reinforcer for less attractive desired actions (like cleaning up).

The idea that preferred actions can be used to reinforce other actions is called the **Premack principle** (Premack, 1959; Herrod et al., 2023). A spin-off from this idea is that you can make all kinds of actions reinforcing simply by taking away the option to perform those actions. Sitting down can become reinforcing if you're forced to stand for a long time, and standing up can be reinforcing after a long sit.

Changing actions in a desired direction requires more than just providing reinforcers or punishments, especially when the desired action is complex and requires precise movements or planning. Getting a rat to press a lever for food is relatively easy. Getting a rat to do a backflip for food is a different story. For organisms to learn to do the new, a bit of coaching is often helpful.

Shaping Novel Actions and Cognitive Processes

If you're taking a course, one goal you might have is to know and understand the material being taught in that course. How will you or others determine if you've met that goal? A determination is often made based on what you can do. It's not clear exactly how something like instrumental conditioning or practice might get you from not understanding a topic to understanding it, however. How can you reinforce an act of understanding that you've never performed before?

Part of what distinguishes instrumental conditioning from Pavlovian conditioning is that instrumental conditioning requires the learner to do things for a consequence to occur. That usually includes trying new things. Reading books and listening to lectures enables you to potentially think thoughts you have not thought before. If you think those thoughts multiple times—by reading, listening, studying, discussing, and answering questions on exams—you might just condition yourself to think them with minimal prompting. This often is easier said than done, though, especially if the topics are ones you have not thought much about before.

Promoting Behavioral Changes

A historically influential idea about what controls when conditioning (and memory acquisition more generally) will work and when it will not was proposed by the Russian psychologist Lev Vygotsky (1896–1934). He suggested that children, in particular, would tend to settle into stable (usually nonideal) patterns of behaving unless others helped them refine their thoughts and actions (Vygotsky, 1978).

Vygotsky felt that there was a set of skills that would be difficult for an individual to perform without the aid of someone more knowledgeable, but that the individual could perform with social guidance. Vygotsky called this set of potentially performable skills the **zone of proximal development**. The basic idea is that people can learn more effectively when they don't have to do all the heavy cognitive lifting themselves and they will benefit most from practice when the actions being practiced are neither too easy nor too hard (Eun, 2019).

In the context of academic coursework, the zone of proximal development is associated with course prerequisites. The thinking there is that learning some topics (the more advanced ones) will be difficult or impossible if you don't first master other topics. This kind of staircase of learning seems sensible, but it doesn't always reflect how learning happens. For instance, some children with autism spectrum disorder learn to read before they learn to speak (called hyperlexia), although most people would assume that learning to talk is a prerequisite for learning to read (Ostrolenk et al., 2017).

There is substantial evidence from laboratory studies that progressing from easier tasks (those performed quickly and accurately) to more difficult tasks often leads to more rapid learning (Church et al., 2013; Wisniewski et al., 2017). Many online educational programs attempt to take advantage of this phenomenon by first identifying which topics a student has mastered and then selecting instructional materials to match the individual's ability level, essentially mapping out the zone of proximal development for that student. Similar to Vygotsky's proposal, the rationale for such customized tutoring is that there is a "sweet spot" where instruction and practice will lead to the most rapid improvements in an individual's performance.

Beyond the specific actions you practice and the order in which you practice them, the timing of when you practice a skill can also make a big difference in terms of what benefits you gain from practicing (Benjamin & Tullis, 2010; Carpenter et al., 2022). **Massed practice**, which is continuous and rapidly paced (like cramming for an exam), generally leads to quicker learning. **Spaced practice**, spread out over time, takes longer but the amount of change per repeated experience tends to be greater, and the changes usually persist longer (**Figure 7.7**).

Unfortunately, because massed practice leads to more obvious gains, it tends to be more reinforcing. In contrast, the gains provided by spaced practice, which occur over longer intervals, are more difficult to perceive. Consequently, spaced practice is often more frustrating and more likely to be subjectively unpleasant, even though you're getting more bang for your buck.

It should come as no surprise that college students are much more likely to mass their studying than to space it, even when they have been repeatedly told that this is an inefficient strategy. It requires a good bit of self-control to consistently practice studying and thinking about a topic on a spaced

FIGURE 7.7. Benefits and costs of spaced practice.
Postal workers who practiced operating a new computerized sorting system (in the 1970s) just one hour a day (spaced practice) improved after fewer hours of total practice than other workers who practiced the same sorting skills more intensely (massed practice). However, workers in the spaced practice condition complained much more about the training because it took them more days to complete it. The group that was most satisfied with the training was the group that trained four hours per day. This was also the group that learned the least after practicing the most. (Graph after Baddeley & Longman, 1978, inset Emmily via Shutterstock)

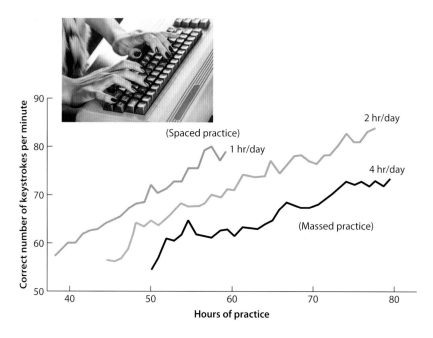

schedule when doing so may feel boring or pointless and when a slew of more entertaining actions are options.

Learning Guides

In most experimental studies of instrumental conditioning of laboratory animals, the rats, pigeons, or monkeys must discover what actions are the desired ones through trial and error. Laboratory studies of human memory acquisition, in contrast, almost always begin with an experimenter explaining to participants what they are supposed to do. Similarly, students in courses are usually told what they are supposed to do to get a good grade and how they are supposed to do it. How does this kind of instructional guidance affect learning? And does its use mean that people in classes are forming memories in ways that differ significantly from animals in a lab or in the wild?

Vygotsky thought that instructions boosted learning because they provided support for mental processes that were not quite ready to operate on their own—the mental equivalent of training wheels on a bicycle. However, he did not assume that teachers were engaging any mechanisms beyond those that might be involved in uninstructed learning. Other psychologists, including most famously Albert Bandura (b. 1925), suggested that people make extensive use of observational learning to acquire skills without the need for repeated experiences or any conditioning (Bandura, 1977).

Observational learning or social learning, discussed extensively in Chapter 11, generally refers to situations in which an individual learns how to do something by observing others doing it. When a person's actions are guided by instructions, this could be viewed as a case of observational learning in which an instructor's sentences provide the "demonstration" that leads to changes in the person's behavior. From this perspective, all teaching, coaching, or otherwise guiding how an individual performs or practices actions relies partly on observational learning. Animals other than humans rely less heavily on observational learning to modify their actions (Bandini & Tennie, 2020).

In laboratory experiments, animals are usually getting zero guidance from either observing others learn or from receiving instructions. Nevertheless, it is possible to guide learning of specific actions in nonhumans in specific directions with precisely timed reinforcers. It's how animal trainers get animals to perform various tasks and tricks (see Figure 7.5). This technique of trainer-guided conditioning, called **shaping**, requires selective, precisely timed reinforcement of actions that are closer to a desired action (Peterson, 2004; Skinner, 1975). In this way, a trainer can gradually nudge an individual to act in specific ways, such as encouraging a dog to catch a frisbee while flipping (Pryor, 2019). Like instructions, shaping leads to much faster learning than simply letting an animal flail around on its own in the hopes that it might randomly perform desired actions.

Shaping works with humans just as well as it does with other animals (Krueger & Dayan, 2009). And shaping may work in the same way that instructions do (**Figure 7.8**). Specifically, shaping narrows

FIGURE 7.8. Shaping with shapes.
Early interventions for children with autism spectrum disorder are designed to increase the prevalence of desired social behaviors. What kinds of actions might an adult be able to reinforce in face-to-face interactions with a child with autism? (Africa Studio via Shutterstock)

an individual's attention or preferences toward a small subset of possible actions, increasing the chances that the individual will select actions within that subset. Similarly, instructions (and demonstrations) constrain the range of possible actions a student can perform that the instructor is likely to reinforce, which usually increases the likelihood that the student will limit actions to those within the desired range.

Cognitive Skill Learning

The earliest studies of both Pavlovian and instrumental conditioning emphasized how animals learn to associate stimuli with specific motor responses. The rise of cognitive psychology shifted attention away from stimulus-response associations and more toward associations between ideas and concepts (see Chapters 1 and 5). At the same time, because most cognitive psychology studies were conducted with adult humans, there was a transition away from examining how nonhumans learn to predict events or consequences and toward exploring the different ways that adult humans use knowledge and skills (Bolhuis et al., 2023; Mandler, 2002).

The scientific leap from response-learning rats to concept-applying undergraduates, combined with Descartes's earlier ideas about the unique mental capacities of humans (discussed in Chapter 1), led many psychologists to think of mental acts as being driven by two separate processes: an unconscious, automatic associative process versus a conscious, voluntary reasoning process (Evans & Stanovich, 2013; Premack, 2007; Squire & Zola, 1996). This split is the foundation of most dual process models of thinking (see Chapters 3 and 10).

You might expect that, as with Pavlovian associations, there are two modes of instrumental conditioning. One is a consciously controllable scenario in which you intentionally gather information and consider what the things you know mean until eventually, you figure out what's what—a kind of Sherlockian wrestle with comprehension. And another is an unconscious whittling of neural circuits that gradually shifts the balance of power from one reflexive action pattern to another. Experimental studies described in the next section suggest otherwise.

The Path to Expertise

You practice an academic skill so that you become better at performing that skill. **Cognitive skills** include any ability you can improve through practice without necessarily changing your physical movements (Salvucci, 2013). Examples include time management, mathematical skills, understanding psychological theories, and so on.

Once you've mastered a cognitive skill, you will generally be able to perform it with minimal suffering and mistakes. As with most learning, the extent and type of practice you engage in plays a big part in determining which skills you master (VanLehn, 1996). Different individuals start out with different abilities, and the effects of practice also vary across individuals. So not everyone who extensively practices a skill will become an expert.

Many psychological studies of cognitive skill learning focus on academic tasks like solving math problems or reading. As people learn techniques for performing cognitive skills, they sometimes show periods of gradual improvement and other times show rapid jumps in performance.

There are several ways that practice can lead to improved performance of cognitive skills. More experiences may create more memories that can be compared against current circumstances to guide a response or strategy. Another possibility is that associative connections between the specifics of various problem types and their solutions (or techniques for finding solutions) are gradually strengthened through practice (**Figure 7.9**).

A third perspective on what happens during cognitive skill learning is that individuals progress through three separate stages (Tenison & Anderson, 2016). In the first stage of learning, participants run through a sequence of prescribed steps, like following a written recipe, until they achieve the desired outcome. After they have gained more experience with the task, they shift to using memories of past

FIGURE 7.9. Mastering cognitive skills in gaming. Chess experts spend thousands of hours practicing the cognitive skills required to defeat opponents. What experiments might you conduct to determine which actions expert chess players unconsciously perform differently from novices? (Check out the players' eyes...) (Xinhua/Alamy Stock Photo)

performances to guide their actions. Finally, after additional practice, they can perform the task without even thinking about it, the way you might know the answer to a simple multiplication problem like 2 × 1. This account of cognitive skill learning explains jumps in performance as shifts between stages.

Cognitive Plasticity

An individual's cognitive plasticity, or capacity to learn cognitive skills, can vary for many reasons. The large individual differences in cognitive plasticity across individuals and species suggest that similar experiences do not always lead to comparable memory acquisition (Mercado, 2008). In other words, the kinds of changes that conditioning and practice promote can vary quite a bit across individuals.

Just as some events are easier to associate than others, some cognitive skills are easier to learn than others. Most notably, humans seem to show an ability to learn languages that other species do not. This capacity may be age dependent (Kral et al., 2019). For instance, some evidence suggests that if a person fails to learn language skills by the time they become a teenager, then they may never be able to learn any language (see the discussion of sensitive periods in Chapters 2 and 12).

The variable effects of repeated experiences on cognitive skills have led to some confusion about what abilities people can actually improve through practice. For example, there is an ongoing debate about whether adults can improve their ability to maintain information temporarily in their working memory (see Chapters 1 and 8) by practicing (Morrison & Chein, 2011; Novick et al., 2019).

There is lots of evidence that people perform better on specific working memory tasks that they practice often, like remembering customers' orders while waiting tables. But the benefits of practice often do not carry over to other tasks thought to depend on working memory. For instance, someone who learns to keep multiple phone numbers and zip codes in mind simultaneously may be no better at waiting tables than someone with no training at keeping numbers and names in mind.

In general, the learning mechanisms that determine how and when you can improve your cognitive skills seems to operate similarly to the mechanisms that determine how conditioning affects other less cognitively demanding skills. In both cases, repetition, prediction, association, motivation, and consequences are critical to modifying both what you do and what you can do. These same factors also determine how you will respond when faced with novel challenges—how you apply the things you've learned and know.

SIGHT BITES

 Repetition combined with predictable consequences is key to instrumental conditioning; no consequence is inherently punishing or reinforcing.

 Trainers or teachers can nudge students to act in specific ways by selectively reinforcing actions that are moving in the direction of a desired behavior.

 How and when you can improve your cognitive skills depends on repetition, prediction, association, motivation, and the consequences of what you do.

 Learning of cognitive skills often progresses through multiple stages at a rate that depends on an individual's cognitive plasticity.

Generalization and Transfer

SNEAK PEEK: Memory acquisition is most valuable when the learner can flexibly apply memories in various contexts later in life. What determines how useful or problematic different learning experiences may be for a particular person?

You never encounter identical circumstances twice. Even if it were somehow possible to make all your sensory receptors fire in a pattern identical to one that occurred previously, you would still perceive that this was not your first exposure to the pattern. So, every instant you experience is "new," as is every action you perform.

You do recognize things, though, and that recognition is what enables you to respond in reasonable ways to all of those new experiences (see Chapter 4). In other words, your memories guide your actions. Subjectively, things often feel the same as earlier experiences when you recognize them. You find yourself in the "same" room when you wake up, even though your percepts when you awaken may differ significantly from those you experienced just before falling asleep.

Your past learning experiences similarly provide you with memories, some conscious (explicit) and some unconscious (implicit), that enable to you to predict what will happen and the likely consequences of actions you take when faced with novel circumstances. If a UPS delivery person comes to your door with a cardboard box, you are likely to open the door and accept the box. If a clown comes to your door with a chainsaw, you will probably be less likely to open the door (not that it will matter, because…chainsaw).

The similarity between past percepts and your current experiences provides clues that guide your thoughts and actions. When your current mental and physical responses are a consequence of your past experiences, which encompasses everything you do that is not reflexive, then you are generalizing or transferring what you have learned in the past. **Generalization**, or transfer of learning, affects almost everything you do (**Figure 7.10**). Figuring out when and how learning generalizes is one of the great challenges of cognitive research.

FIGURE 7.10. Generalizing to novel faces. It's almost impossible to see this cat and not think that it is grumpy or annoyed because you are familiar with what grumpy people's faces look like and automatically generalize your past learning to any face you see. In what other ways might generalization affect your responses to cat photos? (Jaguar/Alamy Stock Photo)

Generalizing to Novel Situations

Pavlov was the first researcher to systematically explore how conditioning generalizes (Pavlov, 1927). His explanation for why learning to salivate in response to a particular person might generalize to other people who physically resemble that person was that similar sensory patterns generate overlapping cortical activity patterns. Pavlov assumed that learning produced new links between cortical activity and reflexive responses, such that partially reactivating a cortical pattern would partially reactivate an associated reflexive response.

The American psychologist Edward Thorndike (1874–1949) proposed a similar scenario in which the number of shared features between a novel experience and a previous experience determines the extent to which learning will transfer to the novel experience, a proposal called **identical elements theory** (Thorndike & Woodworth, 1901). Both Thorndike's and Pavlov's explanations predict that the more similar two perceived events are, the more generalization should occur. In the case of cognitive skill learning, transfer from one cognitive task to a highly similar task is referred to as **near transfer**, while generalization to a very different task is called **far transfer** (Kassai et al., 2019). If learning to add single-digit numbers makes it easier for you to add double-digit numbers, then this would likely be described as near transfer. If learning how to add made it easier for you to solve chess problems, that would be an example of far transfer.

Generalization Gradients

Laboratory experiments have established several important features of generalization. One is if an individual learns to associate a specific stimulus with rewards or punishment, then if that stimulus is morphed along a single dimension, generalization tends to decrease symmetrically around the feature that was initially predictive of relevant outcomes (Ghirlanda & Enquist, 2003; Shepard, 1987). For example, if you repeatedly play a middle C on a piano right before giving a dog a treat, so it learns that middle Cs predict treats, then the dog will generalize as much to a note just above the middle C as it will to a note just below the middle C.

This symmetric pattern of generalization defines a **generalization gradient** for a learned response (**Figure 7.11**). A second key feature of generalization is that the shape of a generalization gradient changes as learning progresses. Surprisingly, the more an individual learns, the more generalization becomes limited to near transfer.

Identical elements theory predicts that you should generalize the most in situations that are the most similar to those that you experienced during learning. This seems like common sense, but it is

FIGURE 7.11. Generalizing learned pecking responses. Pigeons trained to peck a yellow key to receive food rewards will also peck keys of similar wavelengths the first time they see them. How much they respond to a novel color depends on its physical difference from the wavelength of the trained color. This generalization pattern (called a generalization gradient) provides an indirect estimate of how pigeons perceive similarities and differences between colors. The curve that describes response strength as a function of stimulus similarity (shown here) defines the generalization gradient for the conditioned response. (Graph after Gluck et al., 2016, based on data from Guttman & Kalish, 1956; inset image: Hank Morgan /Science Source)

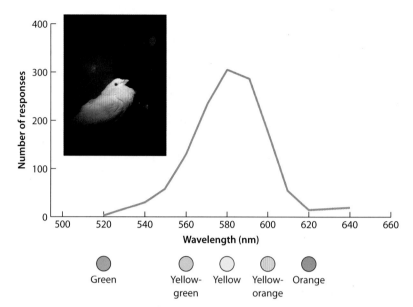

often not the case. Conditioning can cause you to respond more to situations that you have never experienced before than to the ones you originally learned about (Purtle, 1973; Wisniewski et al., 2009). This is particularly likely to happen if you learn that one scenario is rewarding while another highly similar scenario is not.

Say you go to a waterpark and learn through experience that a fifteen-foot-high waterslide there is boring, while a thirty-foot-high version of the same slide is actually pretty fun. If you are later given a choice between going on the specific thirty-foot slide you had fun on versus going on a forty-foot slide that looks similar, you will be more likely to choose the forty-foot slide, even though you've never been on it before. And you will be more likely to describe the taller slide as awesome than you would be if you'd never tried the fifteen-foot slide. This phenomenon is called the **peak shift effect** (**Figure 7.12**), a phenomenon in which learning to discriminate a favored stimulus from a less favored one results in the learner preferring an unfamiliar stimulus even more than the stimulus they learned to prefer during training (Livesey & McLaren, 2019).

Any kind of conditioning in which similar situations predict significantly different outcomes can shift the peak of a generalization gradient away from the specific conditions experienced during learning and toward novel conditions.

One implication of the peak shift effect is that, in some circumstances, you can enhance your performance more by practicing a skill that is not exactly the one you hope to master than you can by repeatedly practicing that exact skill. For instance, practicing a skill in slow motion may enhance your ability to perform that skill at faster speeds. Unfortunately, it's also why junk food and drinks keep being sold in larger and larger sizes. If your great-great-grandparents could have seen the current range of popcorn sizes and sodas sold at movie theaters, they probably would have considered them insane.

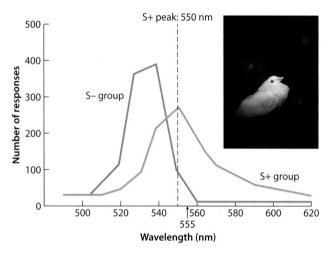

FIGURE 7.12. The peak shift effect. Pigeons trained to peck a green key (550 nm) to receive food rewards will respond most strongly to a green key (S+ control group). Pigeons trained to peck a green key to receive a food reward, while intermittently experiencing a yellow-green key (555 nm) that when pecked does nothing, respond much more strongly to novel shades of green than to the shade of green that they were trained to peck (the S−group). This phenomenon, called the peak shift effect, occurs in many species (including humans), and across many stimulus dimensions. (Graph after Gluck et al., 2016, based on data from Hanson, 1959; inset image: Hank Morgan/Science Source)

Increasing Generalization

If you are taking courses, then presumably you would prefer to get the most benefit possible from whatever effort you spend on learning the material in those courses. If you're an athlete, then the practice you put in may have some potential health benefits in addition to its value for honing your skills. Ideally, the time you spend studying, thinking, and problem-solving would have similar side benefits. But, as noted earlier, extensive practice can actually reduce generalization. So, should you study less to increase your chances of showing far transfer later in life?

Unfortunately, current theories of learning and generalization are not powerful enough to predict what types of practice will lead to the most generalization for all kinds of tasks and individuals. There are a few training regimens that have been discovered, however, that consistently lead to more generalization. One such technique is to gradually progress from practicing easier versions of a task to more difficult versions (Liu et al., 2008; Roads et al., 2018). In music or dance, practicing movements at both slow and fast tempos can increase the flexibility with which those movements can be performed in various situations.

Another path to enhanced generalization is to practice a variety of different skills using a range of materials and stimuli (Raviv et al., 2022; Yao et al., 2012). This kind of **variable practice**, like spaced practice, takes longer to yield benefits, but ultimately the skills you acquire can often be applied much more flexibly. Examples of this in music might include learning to play multiple scales or a variety of technical exercises. To a certain extent, the entire undergraduate experience could be viewed as a case of variable practice in which a mix of social, intellectual, and organizational skills are practiced in ways that can potentially increase the range of activities a graduate can successfully engage in after college.

Generalizing Skills

Prior to the 1900s, it was widely believed that training in formal intellectual domains—logic, mathematics, literature, philosophy—led to far transfer. Recitation of memorized poems was thought to refine students' minds and expand their intellectual potential. Thorndike's identical elements theory challenged this view by predicting that, by repeatedly memorizing poems, students only become better at memorizing poems.

Vestiges of this earlier view remain in modern academic institutions where students are often required to take courses in a broad range of topics, some of which have no clear links to any activities they plan to pursue in daily life. Educators have argued a lot about how certain cognitive skills should be taught. For instance, is it better to focus on rote memorization of basic skills or on helping children to understand more abstract, fundamental concepts? There has been less debate about the benefits of formally training children to perform a broad range of rarely used cognitive skills (like how to diagrammatically parse a sentence).

Learning Sets

Studies conducted by Harry Harlow (1905–1981) provided hints about how practicing a specific skill can potentially increase generalization. Harlow trained monkeys to perform visual discrimination tasks in which the monkeys were rewarded for choosing one specific item of a pair, but not the other (Harlow, 1949). Once a monkey mastered a particular pair, Harlow would switch to a new pair of images. He noticed that as monkeys became familiar with the task, they learned each new pair quicker than the last, until eventually, they were able to identify the rewarding image after a single trial. Harlow described this process as the formation of a **learning set**. In his view, the monkeys were not only learning to discriminate images but were also learning how to efficiently learn which image led to reinforcers.

Harlow argued that it was the formation of learning sets that enabled organisms to transform from automatons conditioned to implicitly associate stimuli with responses into thinkers that could consciously recognize similarities at a more abstract level. Comparably abstract learning might also occur in school settings. As children gain more experience working on problem sets, attending to teachers' instructions, or memorizing facts, they may form learning sets (study skills) that they can apply to a wide range of courses.

You can think of learning set formation as acquiring knowledge related to a particular task. Harlow's monkeys were learning a series of facts—image A is a better choice than image B, image C is better than D, and so on. They were also learning rules or strategies about how to tackle the problem—given two novel images, choose one and if you don't get a reward, switch to the other one, then keep on choosing the rewarded image.

The most famous examples of memory research involving learning sets in the history of psychology are the experiments of Hermann Ebbinghaus (1850–1909). Ebbinghaus's studies are widely acknowledged as the first serious quantitative assessments of human memory acquisition (Murdock, 1985; Murre & Chessa, 2023; Murre & Dros, 2015). In these experiments, Ebbinghaus learned ordered lists of nonsense words "by heart" by reading them aloud multiple times. Over the course of two years, Ebbinghaus learned thousands of different lists of varying lengths through tens of thousands of trials of practice and recorded how long it took him to learn to recite each list. His goal was to explore the relative difficulty of forming new associations and to identify how long associations lasted after a list was memorized (Ebbinghaus, 1885/1964).

Prior to quantifying his memorization capacities, Ebbinghaus spent a long time practicing the memorization of such lists so that his memory performance would not improve during the actual experiments. Like Harlow's monkeys, Ebbinghaus learned how to efficiently manage the experimental problem he faced. Just as the monkeys slowly figured out how to quickly identify rewarding images, Ebbinghaus gradually learned how to efficiently encode sequences of nonsense syllables so that he could later recite them from memory (**Figure 7.13**).

In college courses, you may have learned specific facts that you need to be able to recall later, and you may have also learned that when a professor underlines something, it means that it will probably be on an exam. The memorization rules you have learned may generalize to other courses, and the

FIGURE 7.13. Ebbinghaus's passion.
(A) Ebbinghaus trained himself to memorize serial lists of nonsense syllables. (B) By analyzing how long it took him to relearn old lists, he was able to show that "forgotten" lists could be memorized faster than totally novel lists. He found that longer gaps reduced the benefits of past learning in ways that were highly predictable. (A image: History and Art Collection/Alamy Stock Photo, B after Murre & Dros, 2015)

(A)

REK		HAZ
JID		BIX
MOJ		FAS
HEB		VIJ
QON		LEQ
GEP		TIB
		YUR
		JOF
		NOL

(B)

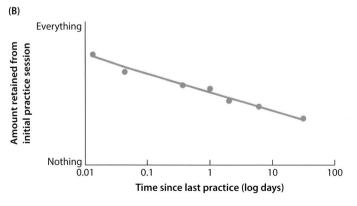

facts you have picked up may make it easier to learn or understand other related facts in more advanced courses. Although your learning set differs from Ebbinghaus's, you too have likely learned how to reproduce lists of nonsense.

Generalization from past learning can provide major benefits in that you can avoid the time and effort involved in learning a new skill from scratch. Your ability to recognize objects from different angles; categories of perceptually similar sensations; and relative differences in time, space, and number (discussed in Chapters 4 through 6) rests on your ability to generalize from past learning experiences.

On the other hand, generalization is not always beneficial. In some cases, you may experience negative transfer, where past learning interferes with later learning (Papini & Bitterman, 1990). You may also transfer learning to inappropriate situations. For instance, if you generalize from stereotypical portrayals of certain groups to individual members within those groups, there's a good chance that your predictions will be inaccurate.

Real-World Relevance

Perhaps the most widely and flexibly generalized cognitive skill you have mastered is the one you are using right now: language (discussed extensively in Chapter 12). You've likely practiced language use more than any other cognitive skill. Your practice has been variable, which likely contributes to your ability to flexibly use language. Having a conversation requires a particularly sophisticated ability to predict sequences and to flexibly produce words in response. When children are initially learning to use language, they often show evidence of generalizing word forms, producing novel word forms such as "bited" or "goed."

Early sentence production shows elements of learning set formation in that relatively fixed phrases, such as "I want _____," can be completed with a range of words that lead to reinforcing outcomes (Chater & Christiansen, 2018). Language development generally progresses from easier productions to more complex sequences, further enhancing the generalizability of the skills being learned.

Your ability to rapidly integrate terms like "learning set," "generalization gradient," or "cognitive plasticity" into your vocabulary and to understand (more or less) the meanings these terms are associated with is a direct consequence of your many past experiences with language. Like Harlow's monkeys, you have learned to rapidly form associative links in ways that help you minimize frustration.

Even language is limited in how flexibly it can be generalized to new contexts, however. For instance, the fact that you can read a recipe written by an expert chef does not imply that you will be able to cook food that is comparable to what the chef produces. Similarly, reading many different recipes written by a particularly innovative chef is probably not going to provide you with similarly innovative recipe creation skills. Such differences in performance are what people are referring to when they compare book learning to on-the-job training.

Some skills and knowledge can be learned and generalized by simply knowing what goes with what (as happens in Pavlovian conditioning). Others must be mastered more proactively through deliberate practice, trying out different actions to discover their consequences (as occurs during instrumental conditioning). In both cases, however, generalization after learning experiences seems to follow similar rules, a psychological convergence that several models of memory acquisition and generalization attempt to capture.

Modeling Generalization

As noted earlier, Pavlov's explanation for generalization relies heavily on assumptions about what happens in the cerebral cortex during and after conditioning. The model is qualitative—it does not numerically predict differences in the amount of saliva—and it is neurophysiological because it predicts that differences in cortical activity will produce differences in responding.

Pavlov developed similar explanations for why dogs trained to discriminate between similar stimuli might not show far transfer. In those cases, he proposed that the stimuli not predictive of food were also causing changes in cortical activity but in the opposite direction. Specifically, Pavlov suggested that stimuli predictive of rewards or punishment excited cortical neurons, increasing their activity, while similar stimuli presented in the same context that were not associated with relevant consequences inhibited cortical activity. Because there was overlap in the features of similar stimuli, cortical responses to either stimulus after conditioning would trigger a combination of excitatory and inhibitory cortical reactions (Lashley & Wade, 1946).

Pavlov's theories about how interacting cortical activation patterns lead to generalization after conditioning were largely ignored, but American behaviorists ran with the idea that different kinds of conditioning could lead to either excitatory or inhibitory effects on responding. They also agreed with Pavlov that these excitatory and inhibitory reactions could interact to generate some surprising patterns of generalization. In fact, early explanations of the peak shift effect proposed that it was the result of such interactions (Spence, 1937).

The nonintuitive prediction of theories of generalization that assume there is a competition between inhibitory and excitatory activity is that what you learn to ignore or avoid can affect how you will generalize when faced with novel situations. For instance, if you discover that you like Granny Smith apples, but are not a fan of McIntosh apples, then your favorite kind of apple will be different than if you have never tried a McIntosh apple. Or if you like rap music, but don't care for country music, then your favorite songs will likely be different than if you had never heard country music before. These scenarios may seem absurd. Nevertheless, laboratory studies have repeatedly confirmed the prediction (Riley, 1968). What you don't care about matters.

For some time, much of the research on generalization was restricted to studies of animals conditioned to prefer one stimulus compared with others. Then in the late 1950s, a researcher at Bell Labs named Roger Shepard began exploring generalization gradients in humans. Shepard (1929–2022) discovered that generalization gradients were highly similar across animals (including humans), modalities, and tasks, including the generalization of cognitive skills (Shepard, 1987). He argued that this uniformity, which he described as the Universal Law of Generalization, was due to the fact that all organisms were using the same process to evaluate how consistently novel events or scenarios led to consequences similar to those they had experienced during conditioning.

Shepard developed a mathematical model to describe various ways in which the probability of similar consequences could be estimated using different measures of similarity between perceived events and showed that his model of generalization could predict the shapes of generalization gradients.

This discovery greatly increased interest in the mechanisms of generalization. More theoretical models were developed and it was soon discovered that connectionist models could be conditioned in ways that produced generalization gradients similar to those seen experimentally (Shepard, 1990). The key innovation that made this possible was to have stimuli represented by overlapping sets of processing units rather than by individual feature detectors (**Figure 7.14**). Chapter 5 notes that these kinds of distributed representations are thought to be an important component of neural representations of categories and concepts.

When similar inputs are each represented as sets of multiple elements, some of which are shared, then connectionist models will show symmetric generalization gradients after being trained to respond to one of those inputs. Recall that this is exactly the scenario that both Pavlov and Thorndike proposed was the source of generalization—representations with overlapping features provide a subset of connections to associated outcomes.

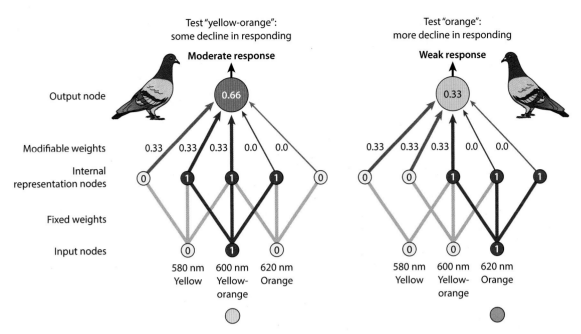

FIGURE 7.14. Generalization by a connectionist model. A connectionist model trained to respond strongly to presentations of a yellow-orange color will also respond to similar colors, but not as strongly. The key to getting a connectionist model to generalize in the ways observed experimentally is to represent each color as multiple elements. This is achieved by having each active node (red circle) for a stimulus trigger the activation of multiple internal representation nodes—the "fixed weights" in a connectionist model represent connections that can affect how strongly internal nodes are activated. Distributed internal representation nodes then act as stimuli that after learning can trigger a behavioral response. How strong that response is to a given color changes during learning based on how connections between the internal nodes and output nodes (the modifiable weights) change in strength. In this example, the strength of the response is calculated by multiplying each modifiable weight by the internal activity and then adding all the results together (for yellow-orange, this gives 0.33×1×0.33×1=0.66). (After Gluck et al., 2016)

SIGHT BITES

How learning generalizes depends not just on what was learned, but how it was learned, including the order, difficulty, and variety of practice.

Learning that events are not predictive of any relevant consequences can affect generalization of learned associations about events with relevant consequences.

Repeated learning of simpler tasks can lead to parallel learning of rules or strategies (learning set formation) that can be flexibly generalized across tasks.

Connectionist models generalize like conditioned individuals when they are trained with distributed representations.

BRAIN SUBSTRATES

SNEAK PEEK: Learning is associated with multiple changes in neural circuits through-out a brain. Changes in the levels and distribution of neurochemicals in the brain can strongly affect which brain regions change during learning as well as associated changes in behavior or cognitive abilities.

The three modes of memory acquisition discussed in this chapter—Pavlovian conditioning, instru-mental conditioning, and observational learning—do not exhaust the ways that individuals can learn and form memories. A host of different learning processes have been proposed. Despite the variety of ways in which experiences can change your mind, though, the physical mechanisms thought to make learning possible are basically the same for all types of learning. Specifically, when you learn, your neurons conform.

This way of thinking about learning has been popular since at least the late 1800s, when William James proposed that habits and associations gain strength as brain ruts deepen. Other researchers de-scribed learning as more like physical exercise, with different brain regions gaining strength in the same way that muscles do. Modern theories of learning mechanisms are mostly a combination of these two ideas: connections between neurons change in ways that facilitate or impede the flow of informa-tion, and the physical tissues that make this happen swell or shrink in size as learning progresses.

Neural and Synaptic Plasticity

Interactions between neurons make all known cognitive processes possible. Recall from Chapter 2 that the main channels through which most neurons in vertebrates interact are synapses, structures located in regions where parts of neurons are right next to each other and through which signals can be exchanged. Most interactions between neurons involve an exchange of chemicals called neu-rotransmitters. So, whenever learning leads to changes in your brain, there's a good chance that some-thing is shifting in the way that your neurotransmitters are moving between your synapses.

There are many physical changes that can happen in your neurons, and in the structures sur-rounding them, that can change how the neurons interact. Your neurons are constantly changing shape, size, composition, and activity levels in ways that affect how they function. The capacity of your neurons to change in these ways is called **neural plasticity**.

Many neural changes can happen without producing any noticeable effects in how the neurons interact. The changes most likely to affect neural interactions are changes to synapses. Like neurons, synapses can change in lots of different ways. The synaptic changes most often associated with learn-ing are changes that affect either the flow of neurotransmitters across synapses or the effects of neurotransmitters.

The capacity of neurons to adjust synaptic connections and interactions over time is called **synaptic plasticity**. Synaptic changes are widely believed to be the main way that conditioning and practice lead to changes in behavior. They are also thought to be a key neural substrate of memory acquisition.

Effects of Conditioning on Neural Activity

The strongest experimental evidence that repeated experiences change behavior by changing synapses comes from studies of Pavlovian conditioning in rodents and rabbits (Fanselow & LeDoux, 1999; Hu-meau & Choquet, 2019; Swain et al., 2011). In these experiments, animals typically learn to associate some neutral stimulus, like a brief tone or flash of light, with some type of reflex-generating event, like an electrical shock, air puff, loud noise—the kinds of infrequent events that would likely cause you to startle. By monitoring and manipulating neural activity during Pavlovian conditioning, researchers can observe and manipulate physical and electrical changes in animals' brains as they learn.

Any change in neural interactions can potentially lead to lots of changes in neural activity because all neurons are interacting with many other neurons. For instance, if something happens to your eyes that makes your vision blurry, then the signals transmitted from your eyes through your visual pathways and beyond will all change dramatically. This makes it tricky to figure out which changes in brain activity are the ones actually driving changes in behavior.

One brain region that is now known to be particularly critical for at least some types of Pavlovian conditioning is the cerebellum (**Figure 7.15**). Researchers have identified circuits within the cerebellum that link the detection of lights and tones and the startling events that they predict to reflexive motor responses that animals produce during conditioning (see Figure 7.15B). By monitoring learning-related changes in activity within these neural circuits, researchers can gain insights into which synapses change during learning and how much they change (Caligiore et al., 2019; Christian & Thompson, 2003; Medina, 2019). As predicted by Pavlov, learning leads to increases in neural activity in some circuits, while simultaneously producing decreases in the activity within other circuits.

Other brain regions that are less critical for Pavlovian conditioning seem to be crucial for instrumental conditioning. The basal ganglia, for instance, play a key role in learning to associate specific events with responses that lead to rewarding consequences (see Figure 7.15C). Basal ganglia circuits seem to become particularly important at later stages of learning when actions are becoming almost automatic (Balleine et al., 2009; Bouton et al., 2021).

While you are reading this text, you are most likely moving your eyes around in ways that sequentially direct your gaze to different locations where you expect readable words to be. You are doing this without consciously thinking about it in ways that you were instrumentally conditioned to

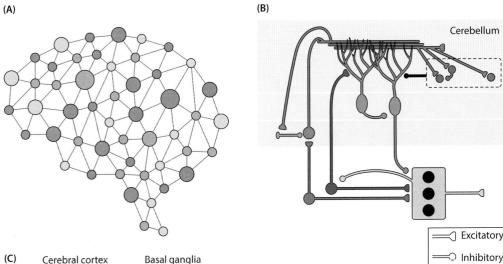

FIGURE 7.15. Multiple brain regions change during conditioning. (A) James proposed in the 1800s that all percepts, concepts, and thoughts depend on learned associations that he proposed were the mental consequences of physical connections between brain regions. He also thought that repeated mental and physical actions wore down physical pathways between brain regions, leading to stronger connections/associations. (B) Excitatory and inhibitory connections between neurons in the cerebellum change during conditioning in ways that affect when a conditioned stimulus (CS) triggers a specific response. Neurons in different layers (shaded regions) play different roles in the coordination of motor reactions to unconditioned and conditioned stimuli. (C) Neural circuits in the basal ganglia change their firing patterns as instrumental conditioning increases the likelihood that an individual performs a particular action in a particular context. Most learning experiences also lead to observable changes in activity and structure within the cerebral cortex, cerebellum, and brainstem. (B after Hwang et al., 2022, *Front Cell Neuroscience* © 2022 Hwang, Kim and Lee. [CC BY])

do when you first learned to read. Your eye movements are ultimately controlled by activity in your cerebellum and brainstem. Reading-relevant connections in your basal ganglia that have been refined over years are most likely making your ability to read possible by adjusting activity in these other brain regions.

Stages of Neural Change

One characteristic feature of learning is that behavior changes in a highly predictable pattern over time. Initial improvements are often rapid, followed by a period in which additional repeated experiences lead to smaller improvements (**Figure 7.16**). This pattern is so prevalent across species and tasks that it has been dubbed the **power law of practice**.

The "power" part of the law doesn't refer to how powerful the law is (although it does seem pretty powerful), but to the shape of the curve you get when you track learning-related improvements in performance over time—the so-called learning curve. This shape looks a lot like the curve associated with a mathematical equation called the power function. This coincidence has a lot of mathematically-oriented psychologists salivating over the possibility that there is an $E = mc^2$ type equation that relates the amount of practice to the number or size of changes that happen in neural circuits.

Encouragingly, some studies of changes in cortical circuits that have tracked the extent to which cortical activity changes as a function of practice seem to show that improvements in performance are correlated with changes in cortical activity (Durand-Ruel et al., 2023; Guigon et al., 1995; Karni et al., 1998). In other words, the initial large increases in performance seen during the early stages of learning are associated with large changes in cortical activity, and the smaller, more gradual improvements in performance are matched by smaller changes in cortical activity.

These findings suggest that the various stages of learning identified by researchers during the acquisition of cognitive skills are paralleled by changes in cortical activity. Different stages of learning may be associated with different kinds of changes that are occurring within a particular neural circuit (Luft & Buitrago, 2005; Murray & Escola, 2020).

Another possibility, however, is that different brain regions may be engaged at different stages of learning, so there are actually different circuits changing during each stage of learning. For instance, if early stages of learning depend more on voluntary control of actions, then cortical circuits associated with this kind of control might be more engaged in the earliest stages of learning. Later, action may shift to regions like the basal ganglia that are more involved in the automatization of familiar actions (Freedberg et al., 2020; Poldrack et al., 2001).

Given that most learning situations involve interpreting a broad array of multimodal sensations, relating them to past experiences, predicting what is going to happen next, and initiating relevant ac-

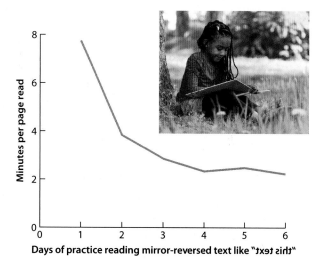

FIGURE 7.16. Power law of practice. Practice is most effective early on in learning. As practice progresses, the benefits gained from further practice shrink. This general principle applies to the learning of many different skills, including cognitive skills. Participants who practice reading mirror-reversed text are almost twice as fast after a day of practice but show much less improvement over five more days of practice. (Graph after Gluck et al., 2016, based on Singley & Anderson, 1989; inset: Samuel Borges Photography via Shutterstock)

Minutes per page read

Days of practice reading mirror-reversed text like "this text"

tions accordingly, it's likely that many neural circuits are continuously undergoing modifications during memory acquisition. That being said, there are definitely situations that lead brains to change more rapidly during conditioning and practice (Perich et al., 2018; Wang & Dragoi, 2015). Scenarios that consistently lead to pleasurable or frightening outcomes are near the top of the list of the most effective brain changers.

Neuromodulation and Metaplasticity

The previous section noted evidence of changes in neural interactions that happen in various parts of your brain as you learn. When you're actively attempting to learn and things are going slow, you might be wishing that your synapses would change a bit faster. Although neither the rate at which connections in your brain change nor the number of connections that change is under your direct control, there are things you can do to amplify learning-related changes. Similarly, there are things this book could do that would probably ramp up your learning rate—providing provocative, shocking, and/or offensive examples—but the textbook police say no.

Liking, Wanting, and Loathing

Conditioning experiments consistently show that individuals learn more rapidly when the benefits of learning, or the costs of not learning, are large (Ferrucci et al., 2019; Leff, 1969). One limit to this trend is that highly rewarding events rarely stay rewarding for long. If you reinforced yourself with a Hershey's kiss every time you finished a paragraph in this chapter, it wouldn't be long before the kisses stopped making it to your mouth and instead started collecting in a pile.

Many things that you find reinforcing get old if they keep coming. In the 1950s, however, a neuroscientist accidentally discovered a reinforcer that never gets old. This reinforcer was so powerful that participants would repeatedly choose it over food, water, sex, sleep, and even life. Rats given the reinforcer for pressing a lever would press it continuously for forty-eight hours or more until they keeled over (Milner, 1991).

The discovery was a complete surprise because the reinforcer was nothing more than a brief electrical current delivered inside the brain, just strong enough to cause some neurons to fire. Usually, this kind of electrical stimulation cannot be felt and provokes no response, but when the electrode was positioned in a particular spot in the brain, the electrical signal transformed into the most potent reinforcer ever seen.

Later it was discovered that stimulation of neurons in this special spot was causing a particular neurochemical called dopamine to be released (Wise, 2002). Dopamine can change the responsiveness of neurons in other brain regions that are sensitive to this neurochemical through a process called neuromodulation. It's now known that dopamine is released during many rewarding events (Lerner et al., 2021; Schultz, 2013).

Initially, researchers thought that dopamine was acting like a pleasure signal. Later research revealed that its effects were more like a "wanting" signal or internal motivational speaker (Davis et al., 2009). Patients with low levels of dopamine still reported liking treats like candy or kisses, but they were less motivated to make any effort to get them (Dagher & Robbins, 2009; Szczypiński & Gola, 2018). Rats that pressed levers ad infinitum for dopamine spurts were more like the ultimate hard workers than pleasure junkies.

No "bliss spot" within the human brain has been found that will enable you to electrically stimulate yourself into nirvana. There are signs that neurochemicals other than dopamine might act as pleasure signals, however (Berridge & Robinson, 2009). Endogenous (natural) opioids, in particular, sometimes produce feelings of euphoria when they are released in the brain. The drug heroin is thought to mimic the effects of endogenous opioids, which might explain why taking it produces such an intense high (Myers et al., 2017). Like dopamine, endogenous opioids are often released when reinforcing stimuli are encountered (Riters et al., 2019).

FIGURE 7.17. Brain systems of reward. (A) Studies with rodents have revealed different neural circuits that respond when an individual likes an outcome versus when they want a specific outcome to happen. Each set of circuits is modulated by specific regions within the brainstem. For instance, variations in levels of dopamine are controlled by the activity of neurons in the ventral tegmental area. (B) Similarities in facial expressions across species provide indications of what nonverbal individuals like or dislike; what individuals want is determined by what they will work to get. (A after, B from Berridge, 2018, *Front Psych* © 2018 Berridge. [CC-BY])

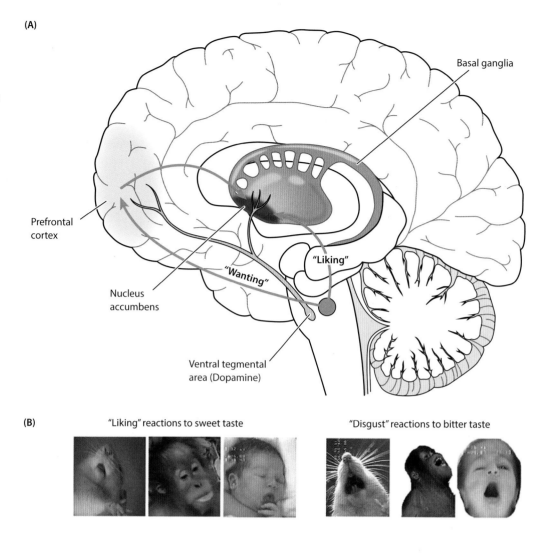

(A)

Basal ganglia

Prefrontal cortex

"Wanting"

"Liking"

Nucleus accumbens

Ventral tegmental area (Dopamine)

(B)

"Liking" reactions to sweet taste   "Disgust" reactions to bitter taste

Given that neurochemical surges are associated with changes in liking and wanting things, you might expect there are other neuromodulators that are released when you're angry or in pain (**Figure 7.17**). If there are such neuromodulators, they have yet to be identified. There are, however, neurons in a region of the cortex called the insula that consistently fire when bad things are happening and tend to fire more when things get worse (De Ridder et al., 2021; Schreckenberger et al., 2005). Also, people with a missing or heavily damaged insula seem to be punishment-proof. Or at least people with such damage don't respond to punishers by changing their actions (Holtmann et al., 2020).

In situations where outcomes fluctuate rapidly from being pleasant, to neutral, to unpleasant, and in which there is a strong motivation to reach a goal, there are likely to be many different electrochemical mechanisms competing to change synapses in one direction or another. When playing games, for instance, you might make a particularly devastating move, only to discover a short time later that you are the one being devastated. You want to win and like the action, so you are willing to take a bit of punishment to finally reach some threshold of success. Meanwhile, your brain is mixing cocktails of neurochemicals and refining your neural circuits to enhance your performance in future episodes.

Pavlov only got a glimpse of the complex processes contributing to learning in relatively simple conditioning tasks. He recognized that his dogs' brains were changing, but he was less aware of the chemical combos that were swirling around to make those changes possible. He also did not realize that there were fluctuating periods in which global shifts in internal states could determine when learning-related changes could happen.

Metaplasticity

In traditional conditioning studies, individuals are presented with various interrelated inputs and consequential outcomes. Many of the learning scenarios that humans experience, in contrast, involve social interaction with other individuals, typically instructors or peers. Recent research suggests that these kinds of social interactions can produce their own rewards (Lutz et al., 2020).

The rewarding effects of social interactions are associated with fluctuations of yet another neurochemical, oxytocin, that is quickly becoming known as a key modulator of how social encounters affect learning (Martins et al., 2020). Recent experiments with mice have shown that increasing levels of oxytocin can facilitate neural plasticity by ramping up the effects of other reward-related neuromodulators (Froemke & Young, 2021).

Brain mechanisms that globally regulate neural plasticity, including synaptic plasticity, are said to determine levels of **metaplasticity**. Metaplastic mechanisms have effects on synapses analogous to the effects of heat on wax (Abraham, 2008). One prominent example of this, discussed in Chapter 1, is the so-called sensitive period during which young individuals show heightened neural plasticity.

Oxytocin appears to have this effect on specific brain regions known to contribute to social interactions (Walsh et al., 2023). When oxytocin levels are high in these regions, changes in synapses are more prevalent. There is even some evidence that sensitive periods can be reactivated in adult mice by drug treatments that ramp up oxytocin levels (Nardou et al., 2019).

It's still a mystery how metaplastic mechanisms interact with the neurochemical correlates of liking, wanting, and other emotional states to determine what is learned and when. Fluctuations of these mechanisms across the lifespan, as well as across daily sleep-wake cycles, suggest that, like ocean tides, the potential for acquiring memories during learning may ebb and flow (Iyer et al., 2014; Phillips, 2017).

You could think of coffee as being a means of metaplastic regulation in that caffeine can increase your awareness of what's going on in ways that enhance the potential for forming associations. Alcohol at low doses may have similar metaplastic effects (Ostroumov & Dani, 2018). In larger doses, alcohol may globally degrade learning-related changes in neural circuits.

Understanding when and how synapses and other neural structures are most effectively changed by learning experiences is fundamental to figuring out more efficient ways of enhancing conditioning, practice, and intellectual development. When you are able to flexibly tweak your brain to change its ways, you will likely also be able to radically increase the rates at which you are able to achieve all your learning objectives.

SIGHT BITES

Neural circuits within subcortical regions, such as the cerebellum and basal ganglia, change during conditioning in ways that are correlated with behavioral changes.

During skill learning, cortical neurons gradually change their response properties in ways that parallel stage-like shifts in skill performance.

Surges in neurochemicals such as dopamine, endogenous opioids, and oxytocin occur during the delivery of reinforcers, while punishment increases activity in the insula; these changes modulate plasticity.

APPLIED PERSPECTIVES

> **SNEAK PEEK:** Social transfer of information can facilitate learning that would otherwise be unlikely or impossible. Learning does not always lead to desirable outcomes. Natural learning mechanisms can produce disorders, distort perception, and limit how learning generalizes.

You hopefully have realized while reading this chapter that what you perceive, think, feel, and do each day are all instances of generalization from earlier learning experiences. You've learned that sitting in buildings, staring at screens or text, is a relatively stress-free activity that sometimes brings benefits. People tend to associate memory acquisition with instruction and schools, but it's more about just being alive.

Psychologists run rodents through drills to explore the effects of different scenarios and to test hypotheses. The ultimate goal, however, is to know what makes people tick. Why does your behavior change some days but not others? What would it take to transform you into a world-class performer of some cognitive skill you have never attempted before? What are the limits on what you can do that is new?

Teaching Dolphins Sentences

People tend to assume that there are fundamental limits on what individuals can learn to do. There's little point in giving a dog piano lessons because they just don't have what it takes (fingers). This mindset is similar to the kind of thinking that led humans to believe that if you sailed too far across the ocean, you'd eventually fall off the edge of the world.

Neanderthals never learned algebra or how to play a piano, but not because of intrinsic limits on their cognitive capacities. They simply did not encounter appropriate configurations of experience, desires, and reinforcers (humans living alongside Neanderthals also failed to acquire these cognitive skills). Nonhumans, in the right circumstances, may be able to learn much more than people generally assume.

Learning Words

Before the 1940s, no sane scientist thought that dolphins were capable of learning a human vocabulary. In fact, many people questioned whether any animals other than humans could learn to understand words. Sure, you could get dogs to perform tricks in response to speech, or parrots to mimic a phrase, but that doesn't require any understanding and humans typically use language much more flexibly.

Then, a few psychologists and animal trainers studying captive dolphins began to suspect that dolphins were more capable learners than had been assumed. One of those psychologists, Donald Hebb (introduced in Chapter 2) put dolphins somewhere between a dog and a chimpanzee based on early observations of their behavior (McBride & Hebb, 1948). He never attempted to teach dolphins, though.

It wasn't until the 1960s that a few groovy scientists began attempting to teach dolphins more than acrobatic tricks. One, John Lilly (1915–2001), randomly discovered that dolphins could imitate sounds (Lilly, 1965). This discovery inspired him to begin a prolonged attempt at teaching dolphins to speak English. Ultimately, the effort did not pan out but it sparked a wave of interest in "delphinese" (a hypothetical dolphin language) that continues to inspire attempts to converse with whales and dolphins (Kohlsdorf et al., 2020; McCowan et al., 2023).

Later research in the 1970s revealed that dolphins were more intrigued by humans' arm-flailing abilities than they were by trainers' feeble attempts at making sounds (Herman et al., 1984). Once researchers switched from trying to communicate with sounds to using dynamic gestures, dolphins

FIGURE 7.18. Learning labels for actions and objects. Dolphins have learned to correctly interpret gestural instructions such as "LEFT FRISBEE BALL FETCH," meaning take a ball to the frisbee positioned on the left side of the trainer. What sorts of associations would a dolphin need to learn to do this? (Dolphin Inst./Science Source)

quickly learned signs for specific objects, actions, places, directions, and body parts (**Figure 7.18**). Dolphins also learned to pay attention to the order of gestures such that when the same symbols were presented in different orders, the dolphins interpreted them differently.

Like humans, dolphins showed an ability to learn not only from instrumental conditioning but also through observational learning. In particular, some dolphins surprised trainers by being able to perform complex sequences based only on their observations of other dolphins' training sessions (Pryor, 1975). Dolphins would also occasionally invent games with objects they were given, games like underwater ball dribbling while swimming (Kuczaj & Eskelinen, 2014). The most entertaining games quickly spread from one dolphin to others in the group.

Discoveries from studies of dolphins learning to use signed "words" revealed not only that dolphins had no problem learning to associate initially meaningless gestures with a wide variety of meanings but also that they could flexibly interpret sequences of symbols in novel contexts. These studies also highlighted the fact that the associability of events can differ considerably across species and that other animals can learn sophisticated cognitive skills when they find the skills interesting.

Psychologists quickly realized that dolphins who had been schooled in the interpretation of gestures could provide new clues not only about what cognitive skills nonhumans are able to learn but also about how they think and what they know.

Generalizing Concepts

What questions might you ask a dolphin, given that dolphins can currently only show what they know? How about what it's like to be a dolphin? For reasons discussed in Chapter 3, there is no way to know for sure whether being a dolphin is *like* anything. It is possible, however, to test how their responses to novel scenarios compare to yours.

In one series of experiments, dolphins were trained to repeat actions that they had just performed (Mercado et al., 1998). A dolphin gesturally instructed to "Do that again!" would be reinforced if the next action it performed matched the one it had just completed. This probably seems like an easy task, but for dolphins to learn to follow this instruction requires that they keep track of things they have recently been doing. And what exactly are dolphins keeping track of in their daily lives?

To explore this, researchers would ask the dolphins to do various actions before giving the repeat instruction to see what dolphins would do (Mercado et al., 1999). Sometimes the dolphins were initially instructed to perform an action with a specific object using a designated body part. Other times, the dolphins were instructed to perform multiple actions at the same time or to just do something wacky. To respond appropriately in these novel scenarios, the dolphins had to generalize from earlier experiences repeating recent actions to be able to correctly reenact complex actions they had never been asked to repeat before.

It's easy to think that the cognitive skills that you possess now are a kind of natural birthright. Actually, most of what you've learned are skills that humans have refined over thousands of years. A human without social supports would develop into an organism quite different from the ones you know. Many cognitive skills that you use routinely, including recalling things you were doing an hour ago, may not have ever been performed by your ancestors. And skills your ancestors were experts at you might have never performed.

The struggles that you have endured while learning piles of facts and skills in school may one day become unnecessary as researchers develop new technologies for changing brains. Currently, many companies are working to create computer programs that will customize experiences in ways that go beyond past pedagogical approaches. The goal is to construct a kind of online neuroeducation that controls your flow of neuromodulators to maximize learning-related brain changes.

Unfortunately, with no way to easily observe how brains change during learning in everyday life, and no way to reliably predict how any change will generalize in future contexts, it's difficult to say what the pros and cons of digital brain tweaking might be.

Like dolphins learning for the first time to treat flailing primate limbs as words, future humans may discover novel approaches for training brains, including hybrid brain-computer processing or direct inter-brain interfaces. If you glance around at people using their personal electronic devices, you might conclude that society has already accidentally discovered a way to keep people avidly engaged in repetitive learning episodes, but perhaps not in a way that is likely to enhance many cognitive abilities—more learning with greater reinforcement is not always a good thing.

Overcoming Bad Habits

Usually, when you learn, it's to your benefit. You get better at doing things you need to do or like to do and at avoiding things that might kill you or make you wish you were dead.

Sometimes though, learning can be too much of a good thing. Large numbers of psychologists work daily to help patients overcome the negative side effects of learning. Disorders like phobias, obsessive-compulsive disorder, anxiety disorders, and many more are all driven by learning mechanisms gone awry. About one in seven young adults (aged 18 to 25) in the United States has a substance abuse disorder. Deaths from drug overdoses are rising. Learning mechanisms can sometimes be killers.

Addiction

Few people intentionally develop a substance use disorder. Usually, they have good subjective reasons for initially taking the drugs that lead to addiction. Who doesn't want to feel better or have more fun? Las Vegas has created an entire economy to feed this natural desire.

The kind of reinforcers delivered by gambling can be particularly powerful and problematic because they come after unpredictable intervals. Receiving rewards at unpredictable times can boost your motivation to keep repeating an action (Haar, 2020). In some people, gambling can become a compulsion, one as powerful as an addictive drug.

The brain changes that lead to compulsive gambling overlap with the ones engaged during instrumental conditioning (Linnet, 2020). Dopamine is a prominent player. Remember the rats that pressed-to-the-death for neural stimulation that boosted dopamine? A similarly accidental discovery related to compulsive behavior was made regarding individuals with Parkinson's disease.

Older individuals with Parkinson's disease have less dopamine in their brains than normal. So early treatments of this disorder focused on boosting dopamine. In some individuals, the treatment led to compulsive gambling (Dodd et al., 2005). When the medication was stopped, the urge to gamble went away. This finding suggests not only that reinforcement-related increases in dopamine can contribute to compulsive actions but also that the same learning experiences can lead to significant individual differences in brain changes.

Many cases of substance use disorders also progress when drugs alter neuromodulator levels during learning experiences. But, since the drug-taking actions are the ones that the drugs help to reinforce, the learning cycle can be especially vicious. Pathological addictions are learned actions that cause harm to the learner. Part of the harm comes from the loss of control—the individual can no longer resist repeating the action, much like the electrically brain-stimulated rat cannot resist pressing the lever again. People with substance use disorders continue wanting drugs long after they stop liking their effects (**Figure 7.19**).

Actually, in later stages, the punishing consequences of withdrawal seem to maintain drug-taking more than reinforcement mechanisms. For some individuals addicted to smoking cigarettes, their addiction was "cured" when they had a stroke that destroyed their insula, the part of the brain most associated with the feelings of punishment (Naqvi et al., 2007).

Destroying brain regions is not the only way that addictions can be overcome. Many current treatments rely on the training of cognitive skills to counteract addiction. This often involves cognitive behavioral therapy combined with some type of collaborative learning designed to create contexts where drug-taking actions are reduced (think Alcoholics Anonymous).

The goal of all these behavioral techniques is to condition new actions and thought patterns that are incompatible with the actions that previously made drug taking easy or compulsory. Conditioning people with an addiction to seek reinforcement and avoid punishment through novel actions sets up a competition during action selection that can help some individuals fight internal compulsions related to drug use.

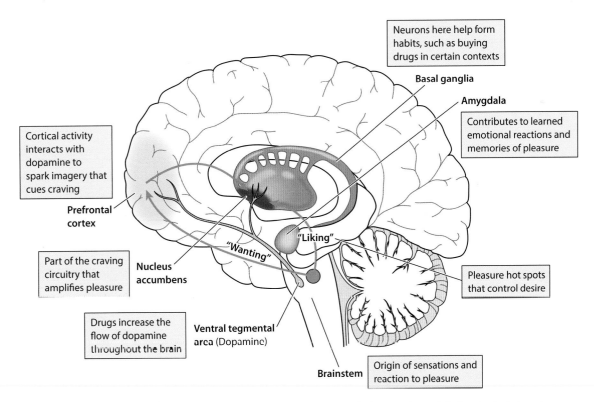

FIGURE 7.19. Craving and addiction in the brain. Modern methods for treating addiction try to take advantage of new knowledge about the neural substrates of instrumental conditioning. Several subcortical regions (amygdala, basal ganglia, brainstem, nucleus accumbens, and ventral tegmental area) contribute to the learning processes that lead to addiction, both through the formation of maladaptive habits and through thought processes that are more directly involved in action selection. Activity in the prefrontal cortex interacts with subcortical regions to create emotional experiences that contribute to craving and reactions to feelings of need. What strategies might doctors use to help them flexibly generalize their neuroknowledge when treating people with addictions?

Another way that people with substance use disorders can fight past learning is to avoid familiar situations that they have learned to associate with drug effects through Pavlovian conditioning. Sights, sounds, and smells that predict drug effects can revive cravings for those effects. Replacing familiar cues with novel situations can weaken learned associations and give new, less problematic associations a chance to form.

Stereotypes

Addiction is a case where the downside of learning is relatively obvious and the behavioral problems are related to specific, initially voluntary activities. Other problematic learning consequences can be more subtle. For instance, the way you categorize other people (see Chapter 5) depends on a lifetime of learning experiences, including both direct experiences, observational learning from various social channels, and implicit conditioning from daily social interactions.

You form stereotypes based on repeated experiences and generalize what you have learned daily in your social interactions and thoughts of others. Prejudice, social abuse, and terrorism are all born from such stereotypes. Not only do stereotypes affect how you and everyone else act but they also affect how you learn. This happens because your prior beliefs function as a filter for your ongoing experiences—you see and hear what you expect. This leads to confirmation bias, a tendency to ignore aspects of events that do not conform to your preexisting worldview. You will often learn less about events you ignore.

Societies are traditionally structured in ways that bolster existing stereotypes. In some, subgroups are explicitly divided up into different castes with differing rights and privileges. This kind of social segregation consistently has led to amplified antagonism between groups, hate crimes, and other deadly outcomes. This default organization is a consequence of learning and, like addictions, can potentially be counteracted by novel conditioning.

Online interactions, which have the potential to obscure racial and social differences, are one source of conditioning that can potentially overcome accumulated prejudices. Of course, these same types of interactions can also amplify existing stereotypes because confirmation bias will tend to steer people toward others with similar beliefs.

In principle, society could encourage interactions between people of different ages, orientations, and ethnicities, as was attempted in the United States when the desegregation of schools was mandated by law. Such approaches are most likely to be successful if actions that increase diverse interactions are explicitly and immediately reinforced. For instance, if participation in multicultural activities immediately entered the participants in a megamillion-dollar lottery, then such activities would quickly become more attractive to individuals who otherwise might never consider choosing such activities.

Reinforcing individuals for moving out of their comfort zone does not guarantee that they will overcome existing prejudices any more than existing treatments for substance use guarantee that individuals struggling with addiction will recover. Past laboratory studies of generalization show, however, that variable practice increases the flexibility with which individuals can respond to novel situations. Additionally, extinction of stereotypical associations between specific subgroups and certain traits or actions is more likely to happen after repeated instances in which those predictions do not pan out than if a person never encounters any events that contradict their preconceptions.

Probably the best strategy for dealing with addictions and negative stereotypes is to develop conditions where those problems are less likely to happen in the first place. This doesn't mean that everyone's behavior has to be tightly monitored and controlled. Environments can instead be shaped to encourage desired actions, like making trash cans and recycling cans easily available to reduce littering.

If young children are put in situations that avoid problematic learning either through observation or through conditioning, then they will learn to be less narrow-minded without even thinking about it. The trick is to understand learning mechanisms well enough to be able to create new opportunities for learning that counteract confirmation biases and that monitor learning trajectories in ways that better predict potentially problematic outcomes before they progress very far.

CLOSURE

A combination of stereotypes and confirmation bias is what made Ted Bundy's murder spree possible. Many of Bundy's victims generalized from learned social rules about when you should trust and help someone asking for assistance. The police generalized from acquired memories about how law students normally act and how criminals usually look.

Ted Bundy himself claimed to have practiced his techniques on many other women that he did not abduct and murder. When he turned deadly, he too was generalizing from past instrumental conditioning. And the physical similarities between many of his victims and the woman who broke up with him after he dropped out of college suggest that his selection of victims also was driven by generalization.

There are some indications that Bundy also generalized from what he learned as a psychology major. Of course, there are millions of psych majors who do not become serial killers. What students learn in college will vary greatly depending on what memories they've acquired before college and how that past learning affects what they attend to while learning new materials and skills.

The goal of educational institutions is to shape your cognitive skills in specific directions using techniques invented over centuries—books, lectures, homework, and exams are all cognitive crutches that have proven useful to past students. Although the use of these sorts of memory acquisition tools can lead to measurable changes in behavior, their effects on neural circuits and future flexibility remain largely unknown.

Forming new associations is relatively straightforward. Determining whether such an association is useful versus useless versus detrimental is a lot harder. Existing associations can affect new learning and interfere with the activation of other associations in ways that are difficult to predict. Chapter 8 reveals how these kinds of interactions can lead you to believe things have happened to you when they actually have not.

If you are having problems understanding someone's explanations of some cognitive phenomenon, who's to blame? The person providing the explanation? Or all the texts you've read and people you've interacted with and learned from in the past, which collectively have created a network of associations that may prevent you from comprehending the new explanation? Luckily, the fault is never yours.

Many of the most famous psychological laws identified by psychologists are laws of memory acquisition—the law of effect, the Universal law of Generalization, the power law of learning. It's not always obvious how such laws relate to cognitive processes of perception, attention, and problem-solving, but learned associations are fundamental to all cognition. All scientific research, including cognitive studies, can be viewed as an attempt to use one set of events to predict (and explain) another set of events, leading some psychologists (including Jean Piaget, introduced in Chapter 1) to describe young children as "little scientists," constantly forming and testing hypotheses about the world and themselves.

You may not think of yourself as a little scientist when you're reading about a new topic or learning new terminology, but each piece of information you experience has the potential to change the way you think. You see and hear (from educators) that what you're learning deserves your attention. What you perceive determines what you can remember. What you can remember, in turn, shapes how you think, what you are likely to say, and the kinds of problems you can solve. The entire scientific enterprise of cognitive psychology is an exercise in attempting to learn how minds work to better understand and predict what the consequences of future actions (such as the incessant monitoring of apps and social media) might be.

COGNITIVE LINGO

blocking

cognitive skills

conditioning

context

extinction

far transfer

generalization

generalization gradient

identical elements theory

instrumental conditioning

latent learning

law of effect

learning set

massed practice

metaplasticity

near transfer

neural plasticity

observational learning

peak shift effect

power law of practice

Premack principle

punisher

reinforcer

renewal effect

shaping

spaced practice

synaptic plasticity

variable practice

zone of proximal development

CHAPTER SUMMARY

Learning to Predict Significant Events: Pavlovian Conditioning

Memory acquisition often involves forming associations among facts, events, and experiences—conditioning, in which related events are repeatedly experienced can strengthen associations. Extinction can temporarily counteract such learned associations. Many learned associations are implicit, affecting behavior without the learner noticing that this is happening.

Learning to Predict Consequences

Actively modulating an individual's associative learning by reinforcing or punishing specific actions can facilitate improvements in intellectual abilities and other skills. Some training strategies are more effective than others. Cognitive skills can be improved through massed or spaced practice and through shaping and observational learning.

Generalization and Transfer

Associations formed during memory acquisition provide the foundation for reactions to ongoing events. Whether those reactions lead to desired outcomes or create problems depends on how learning generalizes. Similarities between a current situation and past experiences make it more likely that learned skills will transfer.

Brain Substrates

Circuits within brains are constantly changing in response to different experiences. Brain plasticity makes learning possible. Changes in the distribution and balance of chemicals throughout the brain determine when and where experience-dependent changes in brains happen.

Applied Perspectives

Learning experiences can dramatically change the range of cognitive acts that an individual can perform. In some cases, such as with addiction and negative stereotypes, those changes can reveal hidden talents while in others they can lead to a catastrophic deterioration of voluntary control.

REVIEW EXERCISES

Learning to Predict Significant Events: Pavlovian Conditioning

- Explain how conditioning can lead to latent learning or to blocking.
- Provide examples of extinction and explain how extinction differs from forgetting.
- How do explicit predictions differ from implicit predictions?

Learning to Predict Consequences

- Summarize the key differences between instrumental and Pavlovian conditioning.
- Define and provide examples of the law of effect.
- What is spaced practice and what are its benefits compared to massed practice?

Generalization and Transfer

- How does far transfer differ from near transfer? Which is easier to achieve?
- Explain the costs and benefits of variable practice.

Brain Substrates

- What is the power law of practice and how does it relate to brain plasticity?
- Describe some processes that are known to affect levels of metaplasticity.

Applied Perspectives

- How might teaching dolphins to interpret sentences relate to neuroeducation?
- What is the role of learning in addiction and stereotypes?

CRITICAL THINKING QUESTIONS

1. If visits to the dentist put you on edge, how might you condition yourself in ways that could reduce your learned fear?

2. Tipping your usual server is a good way to reinforce actions you like. Aside from tipping above-average amounts, how might you increase the impact of your tips on your server's behavior?

3. A primary goal of universities is to provide students with cognitive skills they can generalize outside of a school setting. What are some practices commonly used at universities that are likely to *decrease* the generalization of acquired cognitive skills in the "real world?"

4. How might the ability to directly stimulate specific brain regions either electrically or chemically be beneficial in educational settings? Are there any potential downsides to these kinds of invasive technologies?

5. Video games have become increasingly sophisticated and entertaining. Does the increasing realism of virtual environments in games have implications for what children learn from them? Might violent associations formed while playing games become increasingly generalized to everyday actions and interactions?

8 Remembering

Jeffrey Isaac Greenberg 18+/Alamy Stock Photo

The current Dalai Lama, Tenzin Gyatso, was identified at age two based on his memories of objects owned by his recently deceased predecessor (**Figure 8.1**). Tenzin was given a series of tests in which he was asked to choose from pairs of objects the one that seemed more familiar. In each case, he chose the object that belonged to the former Dalai Lama. Taken at face value, such objective memory tests are compelling because the odds of a toddler guessing the correct answer 100% of the time are low. If you passed a similar test by identifying your own possessions in a pile, no one would question that you recognize the things that belong to you. It's only because Tenzin Gyatso was two and chose objects owned by a man he had never met that his recognition of specific objects was considered to be noteworthy.

Recognizing a possession like your favorite shirt may seem trivial, but how people do this remains mysterious. It's clearly not the same as recognizing that what you're seeing is a shirt (discussed in Chapter 4)—it's not just any shirt, it's *your* shirt. Not only do you know your shirt when you see it, but you also know when you've identified it. If you're searching through a pile of laundry for the shirt, there is a distinctive feeling that happens when you discover it. A feeling that you have achieved your goal and that the shirt before you is the one you know and love. How did you know that your goal was to find that specific shirt? How did you keep that goal in mind while you were searching for the shirt? How did you recognize one shirt in particular as being the one that you were after? And how did that shirt gain its favored status in the first place? The answer to all of these questions is "memory," but that answer does little to explain what's really going on cognitively. Are your shirt memories different from the young Dalai Lama's "memories" of his predecessor's cane? If so, how are they different?

One distinctive feature of the memory processes you would likely engage during a shirt search is that many of the processes are voluntarily controlled or explicit. You know what you're doing and

FIGURE 8.1. The Dalai Lama. The most recent incarnation of the Dalai Lama was chosen based partly on his performance in a memory test. Specifically, elders tested whether the young Dalai Lama was a reincarnation of the preceding Dalai Lama by testing his ability to recognize objects that were owned by the recently deceased Dalai Lama. What kinds of memories might have guided the younger Dalai Lama's performance? (back: World History Archive/Alamy Stock Photo, front: Everett Collection Inc/Alamy Stock Photo)

can describe both what you're doing and why you're doing it. The specific skills you use while searching—pushing items aside, trying to remember if the shirt ever made it into the washer in the first place—are more implicit, happening almost automatically. These kinds of **implicit memories**, sometimes referred to as non-declarative memories, are the focus of Chapter 7. The current chapter is more concerned with **explicit memories**, things you know about and can voluntarily recall and express in words.

These two broad classes of memories have been divided into several different subtypes related to how long they persist and how personal they are. The longest-lasting memories are unimaginatively described as **long-term memories**. You can probably guess what the memories that last only a short time are called. Memories of events that you've personally experienced are called **episodic memories** and facts you know about are **semantic memories**. The fact that you know you have any memories at all is an example of metacognition, which you can think of as a kind of monitoring of recent thoughts (see Chapter 1).

The different kinds of memories noted above relate both to different things that you can remember (your parents versus math facts) and how it feels to actually remember them (memories of a past lover differ greatly from remembering the capital of a state which differs from remembering how to type). Cognitive psychologists tend to focus more on explaining variations in what people remember, and when they remember it, than on what the experience of remembering is like. Nevertheless, feelings related to certainty, conscious awareness, familiarity, and veracity during remembering play an important role in experimental studies of memory and metacognition, and it is these feelings that most clearly distinguish human memory from data storage and processing by computers.

Historically, much of the research on memory has focused on how memories are formed, stored, and later retrieved (Danziger, 2009). More recently, researchers have turned their attention to explaining how people use memories to guide their actions and thoughts (Benedek & Fink, 2019; Oberauer, 2019). For instance, you might use your memories of why you are taking a class to motivate yourself to work out time management or studying strategies to increase the chances that you pass the class. This may include recalling what has worked for you in the past and what has not or specific advice you've received from other students. Using memories in this way is an example of cognitive control (introduced in Chapter 1)—applying or manipulating cognitive processes to maintain or enhance their collective functionality.

Cognitive control mechanisms themselves are dependent on memory. You can't really control the time you spend reading this chapter without implicit memories for how to estimate time or how to read, and you need to be able to explicitly remember the meanings of words to understand this sentence. To the extent that cognitive processes depend on language skills (discussed in Chapter 12), they ultimately depend on the memories that make language use possible. Your powers of imagination, creativity, and reasoning (described in Chapters 9 and 10) are similarly dependent on memories of facts and experiences. Can you think of any cognitive process that does not in some way depend on memory mechanisms? On the flip side, all the memories you possess are constantly being shaped by how you cognize, problem-solve, and interact with the world. For instance, the memories you're forming right now will be shaped by your prior beliefs about cognition, reincarnation, and the science of minds, all of which you've formed through years of learning and thinking. To get the most out of this chapter, you will need to kick your metacognitive processing into high gear, because remembering what researchers know (or think they know) about how people remember is no mean feat.

BEHAVIORAL PROCESSES

Most psychologists would argue that a two-year-old could not possibly remember a specific object that he has never owned or seen, because recognition of a personal possession requires retrieval of one or more memories of the item, which in turn requires that those memories were acquired and stored. The Tibetans that discovered the current Dalai Lama would likely have agreed with this line of reasoning, noting that this is precisely why they used a memory test to screen possible candidates: only a child who had owned the objects in a previous life would recognize them, and if a child recognizes them, he must have owned them. From both perspectives, memories are first acquired and later retrieved. The main disagreement between these two viewpoints relates to how and where memories are stored.

Psychologists studying memory usually take it for granted that memories are stored by and in a person's brain so they focus their attention more on understanding how people acquire memories (especially explicit ones) and later retrieve them. Because it's difficult to monitor and control the personal experiences of individuals across years, most psychological studies of memory span much shorter intervals (minutes, hours, or days) and involve systematically controlled presentations of carefully selected items or events to be remembered (usually words or pictures).

Once experimental subjects have been placed in a situation where they are likely to have acquired some memories, they will then typically be tested on their ability to report on what they remember, either by asking them to recall details of what just happened or by presenting sets of items from which they must select recently experienced ones. In this way, researchers can explore the various factors that affect how reliably individuals remember (or forget) specific experiences.

The following sections explore some of the phenomena and principles that memory researchers have uncovered, starting with the only kinds of memories you are ever aware of and ending with recent discoveries about the kinds of memories that make it possible for you to realize that there are memories of which you are not aware.

Working Memory and Cognitive Control

SNEAK PEEK: Your conscious use of memory in daily life, both voluntary and involuntary, relies on a limited capacity to maintain recent events in mind. Your capacity to do this can increase or decrease over time.

Memories are naturally transient with death being the ultimate memory eraser. Humans have developed several technologies that enhance the persistence of some memories: sculptures, writing, painting, museums, selfies, audio recordings, and video. These memory aids have strongly shaped how researchers think about natural memory processes. Early on, human memory was viewed as similar to an imprint in wax or like the writing and images in books stored within a library. In the last century, computers have taken over as the foundation for explanations of memory, with the brain portrayed as a biological number cruncher that works by processing a continuous flow of electrical inputs and outputs symbolically representing information (**Figure 8.2**).

Viewing memory through the lens of computers makes it possible to think about memory at two distinct levels. On the one hand, you can focus on the physical systems that make memories possible. This **structural view** of memory emphasizes where and when different kinds of memories are stored and processed. But you can also investigate the processes that determine how information is represented and manipulated. This **proceduralist view** of memory is more concerned with principles that determine what will be remembered than the locations where memories are stored either temporarily or permanently (Surprenant & Neath, 2013).

Both viewpoints share the assumption that there are systems, like the microprocessor and long-term memory store in a computer, that control when memories are stored and retrieved as well as how they are used—that cognitive control is what makes memory processing possible. Both views also endorse the idea that "permanent" or long-term memories are processed in different ways from "temporary" or short-term memories. Finally, both views propose that more items can be stored long-term and that recently recalled memories tend to fade fast. Neither view really deals with the question of who (or what) controls the controllers in ways that would make recall explicit (voluntary and conscious) rather than implicit.

Recall of Recent Events

"To know... is to be able to perform, and to remember is to be able to reproduce a performance."
—Edelman, 1989, p 266

William James (1890) pointed out that what people usually think of as short-term memory is actually a component of current consciousness of ongoing experiences. For instance, if you are remembering the last time you had decent ice cream, then you are thinking about the ice cream *now*. James referred to such temporary memories as more like a state of mind (awareness of the just past) than as information re-

FIGURE 8.2. Computerish memory. In a typical laptop, computations are performed by a microprocessor (CPU) on numbers that are stored both temporarily in RAM (for fast access) and in a more permanent form (ROM). This basic computer architecture has been used as a model for how human memory works for decades. The diagram on the left is a graphic model of memory-related components in a computer and the diagram on the right is an early model of human memory, called the modal model. (After Atkinson & Shiffrin, 1968)

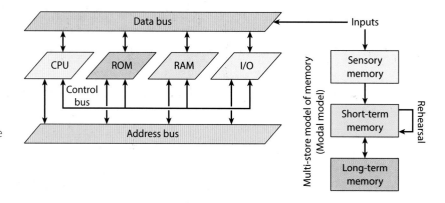

FIGURE 8.3. Motor memories.
Practice sessions on novel motor skills like CPR are intended to provide students with memories that can guide later actions. Would memories formed during such demos be more likely to be iconic, echoic, motor, or all of the above? (Pixel-Shot via Shutterstock)

trieved from storage. If you close your eyes (not yet), you will probably still be able to describe some elements of this page—the number of photos or figures on it and whether there are any larger-font headings present (try it). Although your **sensory memories** of what you were just perceiving rapidly fade, often lasting only fractions of a second, they clearly are related to what you were experiencing moments before (Nairne & Neath, 2013). Psychologists refer to sensory memories of sights as **iconic memories** and sensory memories of sounds as **echoic memories**. They serve as a sort of proof of concept that awareness can persist, even when the inputs that led to that awareness are gone, and that this after-consciousness is available for use by cognitive processes.

Just as your recent sights can persist even after you close your eyes, mental echoes of your recent acts, called **motor memories**, can persist after you've completed an action. Memories of recently performed actions can facilitate subsequent actions by making them quicker or more accurate (**Figure 8.3**), but they can also interfere with performance if, for instance, a sequence of repeating actions is suddenly altered (Lee & Schweighofer, 2009). Unlike sensory memories, motor memories are not usually consciously accessible, which is why you're less likely to notice them. Whenever recent activation of *any* kind of memory unconsciously affects an individual's later performance, the effect is called priming (see Chapter 3). Priming is often like prompting in that it can act as a reminder or can support ongoing thought processes (Tulving & Schachter, 1990), but it can also be a handicap, such as when a person's confidence is rattled by a recent failure.

Sensory memories persist for some time whether you want them to or not. Their natural tendency is to fade into subjective oblivion, however. Maintaining a "state of mind" beyond its natural expiration date usually requires some effort, and it is this aspect of retention in particular that has intrigued many psychologists (Kahneman & Wright, 1971; Oberaur & Souze, 2020; Postle et al., 2004). One way that a mental state can be extended is by repeating it, generally referred to as **rehearsal** (see Figure 8.2). This is the mental equivalent of a flashing safety sign, with each "flash" refreshing the ongoing mental state. The key difference is that only the first flash is experienced and the rest are imagined.

Controlling memory in this way involves manipulating attentional processes to preserve recent states of mind. The term working memory (introduced in Chapter 1) is often used to refer to systems that make such preservation possible. If you think of attention as guiding the selection of a subset of ongoing experiences for more extensive processing, then working memory is a way of expanding this selection beyond present percepts (Baddeley, 2012).

Experimental tests of working memory usually involve briefly presenting items and then measuring how a person's later behavior is affected by these earlier presentations. For example, in the ***n*-back task** (Figure 8.4) subjects are required to report when the current item is the same as the one that was presented *n* items ago (where *n* might be 1, 2, 3, or more). The bigger *n* is, the harder this monitoring task becomes. The task is similar to memory match card games, where players have to keep track of which images are at specific locations in order to find matching pairs (Owen et al., 2005).

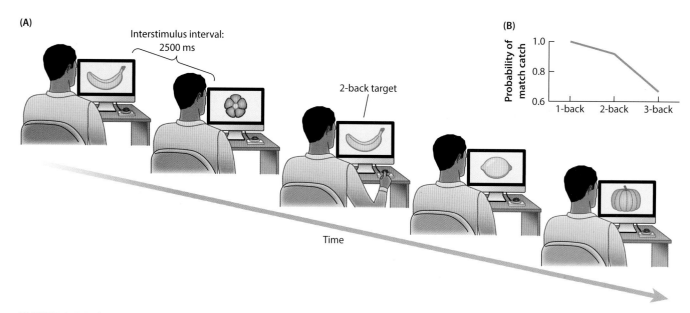

FIGURE 8.4. Using the *n*-back task to test working memory. (A) By having subjects continuously monitor sequences of images while they keep track of the last images recently seen (by requiring them to press a button when they detect matches of those images), researchers can systematically test variations in retention. (B) Typically, retention drops off rapidly when participants need to keep three or more images in mind. (B after Jaeggi et al., 2010)

Controlling Thoughts

The *n*-back task clearly requires not only some capacity to remember recent events but also some way to control what features of those events are retained and the goal of doing so. You need to keep the rules of the game in mind to know how many items to keep track of as well as when and what aspects of perceived events you should use to decide what responses to make and when. Working memory tasks test not only the persistence of memories but also the cognitive control of memory retention and use.

The importance of cognitive control for maintaining and recalling recent memories is on full display at memory competitions, where expert memorizers compete at tasks like rapidly memorizing sequences of thousands of ones and zeros; the order of cards in multiple decks; or lists of random words and random images, including faces (Dresler et al., 2017). By 2019, the record for recalling a series of numbers read out at one per second in the order they were said was 547! By contrast, most people are doing well if they can remember nine consecutive numbers in such memory tests.

How do these memory athletes do it? They're not born with "photographic memory" but have instead mastered special strategies for maintaining memories called mnemonics (introduced in Chapter 2). Basically, they've learned unique ways of cognitively controlling their mental states that greatly increase their working memory capacity over short periods (Wagner et al., 2021) (**Figure 8.5**).

Somewhat like gymnastics competitions, memory championships require competitors to perform feats that differ radically from more typical situations in which you might rely on working memory, such as if you're trying to remember where you put your phone or keys a few minutes ago. Sometimes remembering where you placed a personal item is trivial and other times not so much. You're more likely to lose track of your keys if something distracts you when you put them down or soon after; in other words, when you switch from one task to another. In general, most kinds of multitasking (discussed in Chapter 4) wreak havoc on working memory. However, as you will soon discover, there are some cases where multitasking during memory maintenance is no harder than uni-tasking, especially when multiple sensory modalities are involved.

If you've ever been stuck doing a chore you'd rather not be doing, then you might have discovered that listening to music while performing the task can make it more tolerable. But why? Potentially, background music could be a distraction that makes it harder to retrieve and maintain the memories necessary to perform the chore, but that's not what typically happens. Instead, you can

(A) **Making a memory palace**

(B) **Defining a path**

(C) **Encoding the list**

(D) **Recalling the list**

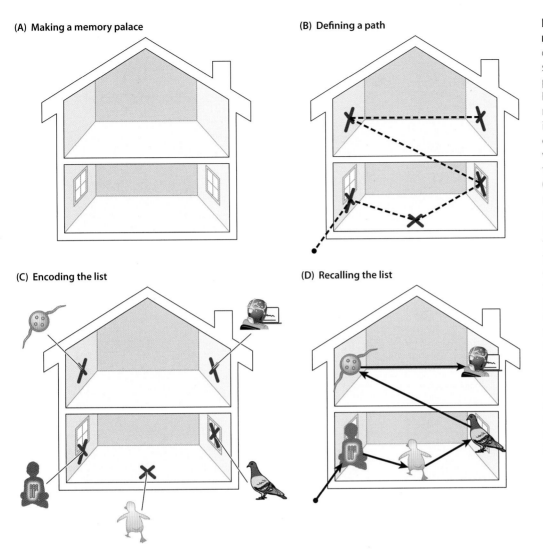

FIGURE 8.5. A walk down memory lane. Many memory champions use a mnemonic strategy known as the memory palace or method of loci to help them store and retrieve memories. (A) This involves first imagining a familiar place like one's home. (B) Then, they visualize navigating a path through that place, and (C) mentally place items to be remembered as occurring at particular spots along that path. (D) During recall, they then imagine walking along that same path and rediscovering the items in the locations where they mentally placed them earlier. It is a bit surprising that this mnemonic works so well given that it requires remembering more details than were actually included in the original list of items to be remembered. Adding details in this case makes retention and retrieval easier. (A–D after Sousa et al., 2021)

often listen and work in parallel without any problems. Such phenomena have led psychologists to hypothesize that there are multiple kinds of working memory just like there are separate sensory modalities. While sights and sounds can definitely interact, like when you see and hear a wasp getting close to your face or hand, there are lots of cases where they function independently, like when you talk on a phone while looking for your favorite shirt.

Most psychological studies of working memory focus on predicting which specific items people will or won't remember. Outside of the lab, however, working memory is more likely to come into play when you're thinking about what you were recently doing or what you will/should be doing in the near future. For instance, if a friend shows up and asks, "What's up?" you might respond by providing the latest on what you've recently been doing, thinking, witnessing, or planning. In this situation, you're more likely to be describing past personal experiences rather than factoids or lists that you've stored over the last few minutes. Do you think measuring how well you can remember a series of pictures can tell you anything about your working memory works in more naturalistic contexts? Put another way, does your ability to cognitively control your memories apply to all your memories or just some? And what limits your mental control?

Limits on Capacity

Measures of working memory capacity can be quantified based on how long memories are retained, how many items are remembered, or how accurately specific sequences of items are recalled (Shipstead et al., 2015). Some measures of working memory capacity are highly predictive of performance in other cognitive tasks, including intelligence tests (Engle et al., 1999). One interpretation of such correlations is that cognitive capacities are constrained by the limits of an individual's working memory capacity. However, this interpretation predicts that memory champions should be the most cognitively capable humans, which is not generally the case.

People generally show increases in working memory capacity during development, suggesting that either experience or maturity constrains capacity (Cowan, 2022). Nonverbal tests of working memory have made it possible not only to assess capacity limits in young children but also in other animals (**Figure 8.6**). Experiments with monkeys and other nonhumans have helped reveal some of the factors that limit working memory (Roberts & Santi, 2017; Wright et al., 2018). For example, one of the most famous findings of limits on list recall is the **serial position effect**, which is a measure of the likelihood an item will be remembered given the order in which it was encountered. The typical finding is that the first and last items in a list tend to be remembered better than items in the middle of the list.

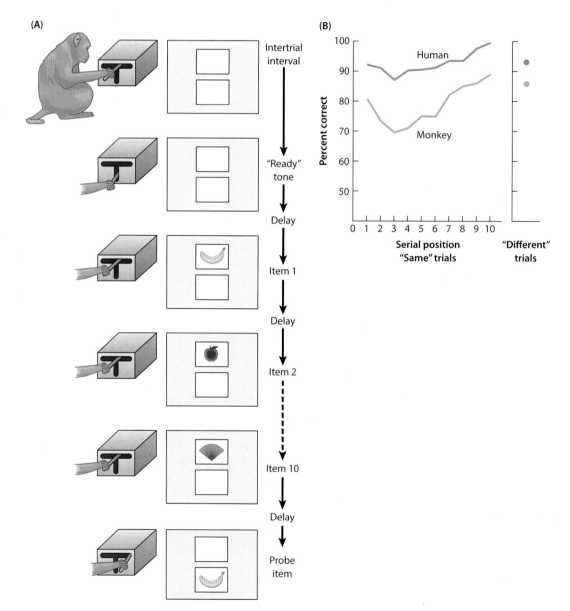

FIGURE 8.6. Memory tests to determine factors that limit working memory capacity. (A) Experiments in which monkeys identified objects they had recently seen revealed greater accuracy for items early and later in lists (B). This phenomenon, called the serial position effect, is also evident in humans. Studies involving large numbers of lists have revealed that interference between memories for different items constrains the memorability of items in the middle of lists. (A, B after Sands & Wright, 1980, *J Exp Psych: Anim Behav Proc* © 1980 American Psychological Association)

Initially, psychologists interpreted the serial position effect as evidence that more rehearsal (for early items) and less time for memories to fade from memory (for late items) both enhanced retention. Later experiments with monkeys, however, revealed that better memory for both early and late items can be explained as resulting from interference between items in the lists (Wright & Roediger, 2003). Items early in a list tend to make it harder to retrieve items later in a list, called **proactive interference**, and items later in a list make it harder to retrieve items from earlier in the list, called **retroactive interference**. So items in the middle are quashed from both ends of the list. Experiments on working memory in monkeys have the advantage that conditions can be more precisely controlled, hundreds of experiments can be conducted with the same individual, and brain activity can be more closely monitored and manipulated (as discussed in the Brain Substrates section).

Theories of Working Memory

Experimental studies of working memory have revealed numerous phenomena in addition to the serial position effect that provide important clues about the cognitive processes involved. Researchers continue to debate about how to best explain these findings. Most modern models of working memory are descendants of the **modal model** of memory, which consists of the temporary (sensory and short-term) and permanent (long-term) memory stores shown in Figure 8.2, plus a rehearsal mechanism to prolong temporary storage. The modal model was a major focus of most cognitive psychology textbooks written in the 1950s and 1960s. You can boost your recall of this classic model by viewing its name as an acronym: (**m**)odel (**o**)ld (**d**)udes (**a**)ll (**l**)oved. In some ways, the modal model is the model model for describing many cognitive processes.

One architectural feature of a computer that is missing from the modal model is the system for controlling which memories are kept in short-term memory. This controller is restored in an influential model of working memory popularized by Alan Baddeley and colleagues (Baddeley, 2000; Baddeley & Hitch, 1974). In this model (**Figure 8.7**), different kinds of memories are processed in separate short-term storage areas with a "central executive" system (memory controller) orchestrating the use of these different short-term stores.

Baddeley's working memory model beat out the modal model by explaining a number of findings it could not. Prominent among these is the **word length effect**—it's harder to remember a list of long words than to remember a list of short words. According to Baddeley's model, this is because your "inner voice"/phonological loop has less time to repeat each of the long words and less repetitions means less retention. Baddeley's model assumes that short-term memories will quickly fade if they're not refreshed by the central executive. Several experiments have challenged this assumption (Neath et al., 2019), and several alternative models of working memory have been proposed in the last three decades.

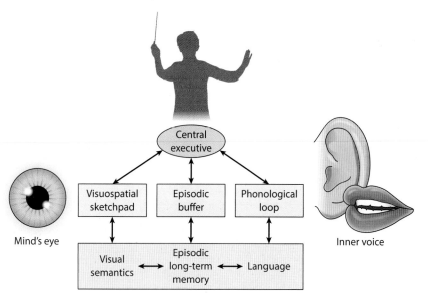

FIGURE 8.7. Baddeley's working memory model. In this model, memories of recently heard words are maintained by a phonological loop, active mental images are processed within a separate, visuospatial sketchpad, and personal events are maintained in a third episodic buffer. A central executive (memory controller) provides cognitive control of memory retrieval and maintenance. Memories maintained in the short term are supported by long-term visual, episodic, and linguistic memories. Subjectively, maintenance of word memories is like hearing an inner voice rehearse production of those words and retention of recently viewed scenes is like imaging them in the mind's eye. (After Baddeley, 2000)

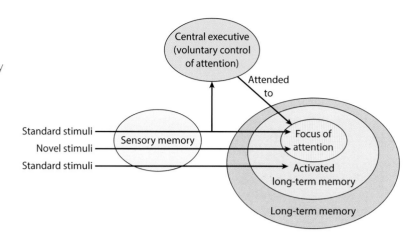

FIGURE 8.8. Cohen's working memory model. In this model, activated memories are long-term memories that have been promoted to being components of a current mental state based on current percepts (sensory memories triggered by incoming stimuli) that are associated with those memories as well as the current focus of attention. As in Baddeley's model, a central executive determines which stimuli an individual keeps in mind. (After Cowan & Schweppe, 1999)

Modern Models

Both the modal model and Baddeley's working memory model emphasize different system components that work together during the maintenance and retrieval of memories. A more recent variant of this approach suggests that there are not separate stores where memories are temporarily maintained for short intervals (Cowan, 1999, 2016), but that memories in current use are simply activated versions of long-term memories (**Figure 8.8**). If you think of long-term memory as being like this book, activated memories would be analogous to the pages you are currently reading—not separate from the book, but distinguished by the fact that you are currently seeing them as opposed to other pages you could be viewing.

Suppose you are uncertain about whether viewing short-term memories as active long-term memories is a better account of working memory than assuming that there are specialized systems for temporarily maintaining specific kinds of memories (as in Baddeley's working memory model). How might you decide which model is the best? As noted in Chapter 1, all models have strengths and weaknesses, so the goal is not really to identify the one model that rules them all. Modern models that treat short-term memories as activated long-term memories have some advantages when it comes to explaining how long-term memory can affect working memory capacity but may be less useful for explaining how memories become active or inactive and for understanding how a series of recently perceived events may disrupt recall of specific events in the series.

Managing Recall

So far, the main mechanism noted that can maintain memories in an active state is rehearsal initiated by a central executive process. Figure 8.8 suggests another way in which active memories might persist—attention to the contents of those memories might be maintained by making them the focus of sustained attention (as described in Chapter 4). Sustaining attention to current mental states is not always a good thing. Continued attention to negative mental states is called **rumination**, which in some cases can contribute to clinical disorders such as depression and anxiety (Joormann et al., 2011). Understanding how people maintain active memories can thus be important not only for clarifying the factors that constrain working memory but also for training people to control memory mechanisms in ways that can improve mental health (Beloe et al., 2020).

Many people think of memory abilities as more like height than strength in that you either find it easy to remember details of recent experiences (say a lecture in a class) or you don't. But how easily you can remember recent events is shaped as much by the ways in which you initially experienced those events as by any natural limitations on working memory capacity. Memory experts become memory champions by practicing effective strategies for organizing and maintaining their mental states, much like chess players or physicists (Ericsson et al., 2017).

In other words, keeping multiple things "in mind" is a cognitive skill (see Chapter 7). Like any other skill, you can potentially improve your ability to work with memories by practicing. Waiting

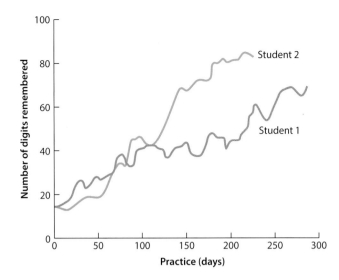

FIGURE 8.9. Boosting working memory capacity. College students who practiced using mnemonic strategies to quickly memorize random strings of digits more than doubled the number of digits that they could accurately recall in order, far exceeding the capacity to recall series of digits of most college students and other adults. (After Ericsson & Chase, 1982)

tables can gradually increase your ability to recall multiple strangers' orders and practicing recall of random lists of numbers can increase your ability to do that as well (**Figure 8.9**). However, ramping up your capacity to rapidly memorize number lists will not enhance your ability to remember people's dinner choices. Like other skills, expertise maintaining one class of memories generally does not transfer to other types (see the discussion of generalization and far transfer in Chapter 7).

This is one way that working memory and cognitive control in people differs significantly from temporary memory management by computers. Computers do not increase their temporary memory capacity through practice and how effectively a computer maintains and retrieves short-term memories does not depend on the content of those memories.

SIGHT BITES

Maintaining memories of recent events requires cognitive control to sustain specific mental states that would naturally dissipate over time.

Sensory and motor memories tend to last for only short intervals but continue to prime cognitive processes even after the memories fade from consciousness.

Limits on a person's capacity to recall recently experienced events, as seen in the serial position effect, provide clues about how working memory functions.

Theories of working memory focus on describing the separate systems involved (the structural view) as well as on how the systems operate (the proceduralist view).

Cognitive control of memory retention in the short term is a cognitive skill that can be improved through practice for specific memory tasks.

Memory for Facts and Events

SNEAK PEEK: Experiences are more memorable when they relate to things you know, provoke emotions, and are processed thoughtfully and in depth. Recall can fail not only through forgetting but also through recall of things that never happened (even when you are certain they did).

"Memory proper… is the knowledge of a former state of mind after it has already once dropped from consciousness; or rather it is the knowledge of an event or fact of which meantime we have not been thinking, with the additional consciousness that we have thought or experienced it before."
—James, 1890, p 648

Tests of memories for lists of recently perceived numbers or words are useful for exploring cognitive control and working memory, but they are not what most people are talking about when they say their memories are bad. They're more likely to mean that they have trouble remembering things they've read or heard people say or they often forget to perform tasks that needed doing. Similarly, people with "good memories" are often able to recall details of specific episodes that they experienced a long time ago with little effort or trivia that most people would rarely recall.

Such long-term, explicit memories have been a major focus of cognitive research, although not as well-studied as memories for lists of words and pictures (Eichenbaum, 2017). Explicit memories of life experiences and minutiae are special in the sense that they seem to be a specific talent of humans (Nelson & Fivush, 2020). In fact, some psychologists have argued that humans are the only organisms that can "mentally time travel" to the past to replay past episodes and probably are the only ones to care about trivia (Tulving, 2005). The following sections explore the unique (and not so unique) qualities of long-term memories for facts and events.

Kinds of Explicit Memories

Psychologists have lots of different ways of describing your memories. Remember the last time you rode in an elevator? That's an **episodic memory**, and an autobiographical memory, and an explicit memory, and a declarative memory (one you can convey verbally), and a memory for an event. Know what an elevator is? That's a semantic memory—a memory for a fact, or general knowledge, or an item in the category "things that move people"—as well as an explicit and declarative memory. Keeping track of all these labels is a memory task in and of itself!

Even worse, the distinctions between these kinds of memory are not always as clear cut as they might at first seem. Do you know your birthday? Is that an autobiographical memory or a semantic memory? Do you know what licorice tastes like? If so, is that a memory for a fact or an episode and is your memory of the taste explicit? If you're uncertain, join the club. Psychologists often debate about how to classify different memories and what criteria should be used.

In the case of episodic and semantic memories, there are a few features that most psychologists consider diagnostic. In humans, both kinds of memories can be communicated flexibly and are consciously accessible, which means you are aware of whether you remember the specific fact or event and can say "I don't remember" when you don't.

The main differences between episodic and semantic memories relate to the details of their contents and how you acquire them. Episodic memories are associated with a specific place, time, and person (you) and are unique in the same way that each moment of your life is unique. Semantic memories don't have to be associated with a specific place, time, or person (although like your birthday, they can be). More importantly, a fact is not unique—you can encounter the same fact many times and in many different forms and you can memorize a fact. A description of an episode consists of facts, assuming the description is accurate. And if you describe an episode many times you may end up simply recalling the description (facts) rather than the actual episode. In which case, your semantic memory would be behaviorally indistinguishable from an episodic memory.

In fact, some researchers argue that there is not a clear dividing line between semantic and episodic memories. Instead, these "kinds" of memories may represent two points along a continuum from high to low generality, with semantic memories being highly general and episodic memories being highly specific (Craik, 2002). Facts about "clothes" are more abstract and apply to many different objects (semantic memories), while facts about your favorite shirt, such as why there is a purple stain on the right sleeve, are more specific to that one shirt (episodic memories). The issue of whether there are unique kinds of explicit memories or simply differences in their content becomes important for understanding what physical memory traces might be and for how brains make memories happen, as discussed in the Brain Substrates section later in this chapter.

Origins of Memories

Both semantic and episodic memories are usually tested by instructing participants on how to perform a specific task that involves attempting to recall words, pictures, sentences, and so on. This approach doesn't really work with infants and nonhuman animals—it's generally tricky to determine whether any memories a baby or koala bear has qualify as explicit memories. Not impossible though! Testing semantic memory is a bit easier since this only requires that an individual show evidence of knowing what something is or what a symbol means.

For instance, rats can be trained that one specific arm in a radial maze (discussed in Chapter 6; see Figure 6.10B) is the free-food arm (Olton, 1979). If a rat that has repeatedly encountered food in a specific arm goes directly to the free-food arm when placed in an arm that it has never started from before, then it's reasonable to say that the rat knows where to find the food and can flexibly use this information (same as if you discovered a grocery store that frequently gives out free samples). The rat is likely responding based on its general knowledge (semantic memories) of a specific arm's contents. The rat might also have an episodic memory of the first time it was ever put in the maze, or the first time it found food in the arm, but there is no way to tell from this kind of memory test. Similar nonverbal tests show evidence of semantic memories in infants.

Evidence of episodic memories in babies or nonhuman animals is more controversial. In children, episodic memory abilities seem to mature more slowly than semantic memory abilities (Mullally and Maguire, 2014). Toddlers show evidence of remembering a single episode of interacting with a puppet, as revealed by a tendency to reenact movements that the puppet performed in the first encounter four months later (Myers et al., 1994). Dolphins in captivity also have demonstrated memories of single encounters with a diver in their tanks (an aquatic puppet?) by imitating the sounds the diver made while releasing bubbles at regular intervals, similar to the sounds produced by scuba equipment (Taylor & Saayman, 1973). Such performances do not show that either toddlers or dolphins reminisce about past experiences, but they do show that they are retaining specific details from unique episodes in their lives for relatively long periods, a hallmark of episodic memories.

Perhaps the most vivid explicit memories recalled by adults are memories of traumatic events. Memories formed during extreme emotion-provoking events are called **flashbulb memories** to capture their sudden onset and subjective vividness (Hirst & Phelps, 2016). Flashbulb memories can be associated with personal terrors such as those that lead to post-traumatic stress disorder as well as more public tragedies such as the unexpected death of a beloved celebrity (**Figure 8.10**).

Emotional states play a critical role in the formation of flashbulb memories. More generally, emotional events often lead to enhanced retention relative to memories of more mundane episodes (McGaugh, 2013). This is why you're more likely to remember the details of a particularly poignant movie than to recall a conversation you had with someone about how grass looks greener in the spring than in the summer.

Despite their vividness, flashbulb memories are as prone to being misremembered as other memories, a phenomenon discussed in more detail below.

FIGURE 8.10 Flashbulb memories. (A) Emotional memories of personal episodes can have long-lasting effects. (B) Cues that trigger flashbulb memories can also reawaken the associated emotions, which is why the phrase, "Remember the Alamo!" was used as a rallying cry by Texan soldiers. (A Spencer Grant/Science Source; B Brandon Seidel via Shutterstock)

(A)

(B)

Acquisition and Remembering

Forming a new episodic memory is literally as easy as falling down a flight of stairs. Adding a fact to your arsenal is not that much harder, though adding a lot of facts can be effortful. Repetitious rehearsal may be effective for keeping a list of words in mind, but it's not a great way to make recalling facts easier.

A better strategy for increasing retention is to link new facts to things you already know well. This is why super-fans find it easy to update their mental compendium of sports facts to include details of a team's most recent performance. Background knowledge about a topic provides a foundation for adding details. You will be better able to remember the details of this chapter if you've got a good handle on the material presented in earlier chapters. And if you've learned about memory from other sources before reading this book, your memories of those previously learned facts will further boost your capacity for recalling this chapter (even if your preexisting memories of memory studies and theories don't exactly match the ones you're reading about now!).

Part of the reason that being familiar with a topic can make it easier to recall additional facts related to the topic is that your existing knowledge supplements new facts with additional distinctive cues for later recall. As with mnemonics, elaborating on to-be-remembered material can actually make recall easier (Bartsch & Oberauer, 2021).

For instance, early experiments examining how well students could recall (through drawing) pairs of abstract pictures presented together revealed that students were able to recall more than twice as many pictures when a narrative description was provided in parallel with the paired images (**Figure 8.11**). Similarly, treating the first part of an unfamiliar term like "modal memory model" as an acronym about what old dudes all love can make the term easier to recall, even though it increases the number of words being stored.

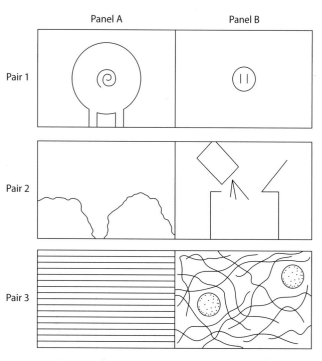

FIGURE 8.11. Embellishment can aid later recall. Students presented with pairs of abstract images proved better able to recall and draw the second of a pair of images when provided with a verbal narrative linking the images during initial exposure—Pair 2, for instance, was accompanied by the phrase, "piles of dirty clothes, then pouring detergent into the washing machine to wash the clothes." (From Bower et al., 1975)

WEIRD, TRUE, FREAKY

Accidental Memory Savants

Individuals with highly superior autobiographical memory (described in Chapter 1) are capable of recalling massive amounts of detail about most days of their life, a case of exceptional explicit memory capacity. Where these abilities come from remains a mystery. However, there are a few people that seem to have acquired similar recall abilities from either a blow to the head or as a result of developmental disorders like autism. Might this mean that mega-memory is an ice slip away for anyone?

Savant syndrome refers to instances in which a person with generally below-average mental abilities shows superior capacities in one specific area. For memory savants, that area is recall of past facts or experiences (Neumann et al., 2010). Unlike competitive memory performers, memory savants appear to gain their prodigious memory capacities with no effort, often at a young age (Brandt & Bakker, 2018). For example, Kim Peek who was identified as having mental disabilities quite young reportedly was memorizing books starting at the age of sixteen months (Treffert & Christensen, 2005). According to media reports, he'd memorized about 12,000 books by the time of his death, including many phonebooks and encyclopedias, and could accurately answer factual questions about their contents, suggesting he had flexible access to those memories.

Artist Stephen Wiltshire (diagnosed with autism) is famous for his ability to draw complex landscapes after having seen them once, which is about as close to "photographic memory" as humans have gotten so far (Treffert, 2007) (see figure). He began drawing at age three, two years before he began to speak. Based on his subjective reports, he continues to have access to memories of the visual scenes he has experienced for several days.

Even more startling are cases of acquired savant syndrome, in which a person with normal capacities suddenly gains exceptional abilities after experiencing a disease or accident (Treffert, 2021). Franco Magnani discovered a newfound ability to paint detailed images of scenes from the town where he grew up after a bout of delirium. Unlike Stephen Wiltshire, however, Franco's paintings were photorealistic and based on observations he had made more than a decade earlier!

Orlando Serrell gained the ability to remember the weather on every day after he was hit in the head with a baseball at the age of ten. You can tell him a specific month, date, and year any time after the date of his injury and he can instantly tell you what day of the week it was and what the weather was like throughout the day (Treffert, 2014). It's as if the baseball somehow turned on a memory booster in Orlando's brain, but mainly for weather-related events.

Cases such as these suggest that the human brain possesses hidden memory capacities that can potentially be released when the "standard" architecture is modified in specific ways. The tendency of natural memory savants to be developmentally disabled may mean there are cognitive costs associated with a phenomenal memory for facts and events, but perhaps in small doses, the benefit would offset those costs.

Stephen Wiltshire shows an uncanny ability to recreate detailed cityscapes from memory. (Xinhua/Alamy Stock Photo)

Early memory experiments showed that elaborating on the meanings of to-be-remembered words can also make them easier to recall, a phenomenon known as the **levels-of-processing effect**. The "levels" in this case relate to which features of words subjects are instructed to focus on: focusing on superficial features of a word such as how it sounds or what font was used is considered to be a shallow level of processing (like judging a book by its cover), whereas thinking about the meaning and "pleasantness" of a word involves processing the word at a deeper, more semantic level. In general, words processed more with respect to their meanings tend to be recalled more easily (Craik, 2002).

One complication of the levels-of-processing effect is that what counts as "deep" depends on the individual and context (Craik, 2020). Focusing on the font of this text could be shallow processing for you, but deep processing for a four-year-old. More generally, the kinds of processing that lead to superior recall depend on what will need to be recalled and how, as discussed in the next section.

Consolidation and Availability

How you think about events you've experienced or information you've obtained can affect your ability to use memories of those facts and events later on but this is not the only factor that determines what you remember. What happens after your initial experiences is equally important. A century of research shows that people's rates of forgetting are slower when they are sleeping than when they are awake (Ebbinghaus, 1885/1964). This is true for both undergraduates and cockroaches (Minami & Dallenbach, 1946). This phenomenon has been attributed to memory **consolidation**, a process in which memories gradually become more stably stored over time (Cowan et al., 2021).

As noted earlier in relation to serial position effects, items experienced later in a list can retroactively interfere with the recall of earlier items in a list. What you're experiencing now can potentially affect what you're able to recall from reading previous portions of this chapter. Ironically, this discussion of factors affecting how memorable facts and events are may actually reduce the memorability of preceding paragraphs! Perhaps you should stop reading now and cut your losses.

Another factor that can affect your ability to voluntarily recall past events is the scenario in which you make the attempt. If your mind is in a state similar to the one present when you encountered the to-be-remembered event or fact, then you will generally have more success recalling it (Godden & Baddeley, 1975). You can increase the mental match by controlling your external environment (being in the same place or context) or your internal environment (being in the same mood or focusing on the same features). Matching the conditions during recall to those of the original experience leads to **transfer appropriate processing**, which can enhance recall (Franks et al. 2000). In this case, you are "transferring" your mental states from the past to the present, a process made simpler when you engage the same cognitive processes in the same environment (just like when you generalize other cognitive skills; as described in Chapter 7).

One way to promote transfer appropriate processing is by providing specific prompts or cues to push a person's mental state in a particular direction. In psychology experiments, researchers do this by instructing participants about what they are supposed to do and providing "reminders" (cues) to specific facts or events. Some cues are less useful than others. For instance, a prompt like "recall as much as you can about the second figure shown in this chapter," gives you relatively few hints. Recall based on this kind of minimal guidance is called **free recall**. A request with a few more clues, "try and redraw the earlier figure showing how computers manage memory," called **cued recall**, is more likely to jog your memory (**Figure 8.12**). Cues that provoke specific mental states similar to those experienced in a previous episode increase the match between the two mental states, leading to more transfer-appropriate processing.

Cued recall is a breeze compared to free recall, but in the long run, practicing free recall leads to better retention. As with most abilities, some amount of struggling seems to be a necessary component of building memory prowess. This makes some intuitive sense because cues are like mental crutches—if you can voluntarily reconstruct a mental state from scratch once, then it will likely be easier to do so again in the future (say when you're taking a test). This **testing effect** is why many textbooks and courses include exercises where you can test your ability to freely recall the materials being covered (Roediger & Karpicke, 2006). Surprisingly, testing yourself can have benefits even when you aren't coming up with correct answers (Kang et al., 2011)!

Forgetting and False Memories

Probably the time when memories become most salient in a person's life is when someone close to them dies. There's a reason why funerals often include a memorial service. After a relative's death, memories are what's left and they often play a key role in enabling a person to come to grips with their loss. Cues become especially relevant: photos and stories enhance recall and symbols (coffins, flowers, headstones) act as reminders of the monumental event.

(A)

(B)

FIGURE 8.12. Cued recall in everyday life. (A) Providing yourself with specific external cues creates opportunities for cued recall in the future. If this dog's owner repeatedly uses this trick, what sorts of memories do you think the dog will recall whenever its owner plops a Post-it on it? (B) Headstones serve as cues to the past lives of individuals as well as a reminder of the inevitability of death. Do you think that the use of such monuments helps people to remember details of their loved one's life, hastens their forgetting of such details, or has no effect on episodic memories? (A Tuned_In; B Ed-Ni-Photo)

The phrase "gone but not forgotten," conveys the sense that one may live on in others' memories post-death. The grim reality is that most memories of the dead bear little resemblance to their actual past—"gone and misremembered" more accurately describes the norm. The unexpected death of an acquaintance or loved one can definitely lead to flashbulb memories. The associated grief and shock are more likely to distort any memories of the lost one than to engrain those memories.

If forgetting is defined as an inability to recognize or accurately recall a previously experienced fact or event, then on the whole, death of a loved one is a forgetting aid. In part this is because voluntary recall requires cognitive control and extreme emotional states tend to derail cognitive control.

Memory Deletion

If your memory really worked like that of a computer, you'd never need to study and could perfectly recall past encounters with dead relatives because once you'd stored those memories, retrieving them would simply be a process of moving old copies to new locations. Computers do not distort or delete memories unless they're damaged or instructed to do so. Biological memories, in contrast, are more like books in a burning house, volatile and prone to going up in smoke.

Although your memories are not as reliably retrievable as those of a computer, they do share one property: they can be voluntarily discarded. If you make an effort to forget specific facts, called **directed forgetting**, you will forget the facts faster than if you just let nature take its course (Anderson et al. 2004). This works for episodic memories too (Joslyn & Oakes, 2005). You just need to be instructed to forget whatever material you were just seeing or hearing (like if a friend lets you know that someone you just talked to at a party is a pathological liar).

Like memorizing, directed forgetting is imperfect. Some memories are harder to dislodge than others, and there is currently no way to verify that any memory is gone for good. This is partly what led Sigmund Freud to propose that people might automatically and unconsciously suppress painful memories and claim that such **repressed memories** could lead to mental disorders. Freud's idea was that although a patient might have no awareness that the painful event had ever occurred (100% forgotten), implicit memories of the event might still persist, negatively impacting ongoing mental states.

It's not clear how one might test this possibility, however, without secretly monitoring individuals their whole lives, intermittently probing their memories, and then documenting correlations between forgotten painful episodes and clinical outcomes. Even if someone suddenly remembers a horrific episode they'd forgotten, it's usually difficult or impossible to verify that the remembered event actually happened the way the person remembers it. And if the painful event did happen, this does not show that the previously hidden memory of the event was a source of deteriorated mental health.

This complication hasn't stopped some therapists (or religious groups such as Scientologists) from attempting to treat people by helping them to "recover" lost memories. Recovered memories have even been successfully used as evidence in court cases!

Modes of Memory Failure

For most people, purposeful forgetting is less of an issue than the more pernicious and frequently experienced variety that compels one to take notes, study them repeatedly, and generally wonder how early dementia might set in. Involuntary forgetting seems to be a basic feature of how memory works. One of the earliest and most consistently replicated experimental discoveries about memory is that involuntary forgetting often increases predictably over time (**Figure 8.13**). The consistent rate at which memories fade has led many memory researchers to portray forgetting as a kind of decay similar to what happens with neglected leftovers. **Memory decay** conceptually is like anti-consolidation—as time passes, the memory deteriorates. There's a major problem with this interpretation, however. The only behavioral evidence of memory decay is erroneous or absent recall. But an inability to consciously report a memory is not strong evidence that the memory is gone or rotting (as pointed out by Freud). Maybe the memory is just difficult to locate or access (Neath & Brown, 2012).

What if your memories don't decay over time but remain relatively stable like fossils in bedrock, waiting to be discovered? What then might explain your increasing tendency to forget as time passes? One possibility is that intervening experiences somehow interfere with recall. Just as proactive and retroactive interference can degrade recall of middle items in a list (leading to serial position effects, as noted earlier), they might also make recalling items in the list of life more difficult (Neath et al., 2019). This could occur if different mental states are directly competing for activation or if cognitive control processes are limited in their ability to inhibit distractions. In cases where interference is blocking recall, there is still hope that your "lost" memories might yet be found.

Some evidence of such memory rediscovery comes from **flashbacks**, personal experiences that are involuntarily recalled without warning. Flashbacks are relatively rare and can be triggered by relatively simple inputs like smells or sounds (so cued). They seem to occur more often in individuals who've experienced severe traumas such as soldiers returning from combat (Pillemer, 1984; Raw et al., 2023). Relatively little is known about how flashbacks work but they do seem in some cases to revive details of past episodes that were previously forgotten.

Not being able to recall a fact or event can be frustrating, but at least in that case, you know that you're failing to remember. A more insidious memory error occurs when you think you're remembering successfully, but you aren't. For instance, you might misremember that you heard a story reported in the news that you actually saw posted online. President Reagan often recalled the story of a B-17 bomber pilot who after ordering his crew to bail out of their damaged plane,

FIGURE 8.13. Forgetting after learning. Early theories of learning proposed that the rate of forgetting was determined by how well the original material was learned with higher levels of initial learning (higher points on the black curve) leading to slower rates of forgetting (blue curve). Note that the shape of each colored forgetting curve (tracking how much is retained as time passes) varies as one's level of learning goes up. (After Easley, 1937)

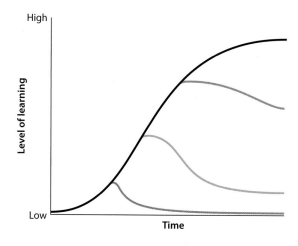

discovered that one crew member could not move. Reagan reported that the pilot told the soldier, "Never mind son, we'll ride it down together," and was later posthumously awarded the Medal of Honor. But no one ever received a medal for this particular scenario; the scene (and quote) actually came from a movie. President Reagan had recalled the story relatively accurately but misremembered its source. This kind of failure, known as a **source monitoring error**, is quite common and very difficult for the person making the error to detect (Mitchell & Johnson, 2009). It is a type of **false memory** in that the recalled content seems accurate to the person remembering it, despite the inaccuracies.

Source monitoring errors may seem like relatively harmless memory mistakes, but they can be particularly problematic when external sources are mistaken for personal experiences. For instance, some individuals who received therapy to help them recover painful memories ended up remembering fantastic scenarios involving satanic rituals and seemingly magical events (such as having a baby cut from their stomach, even though they had no scar and had never been pregnant). These false memories appear to have been prompted by questions that therapists were asking while the individuals were hypnotized (Loftus, 1993, 2003).

False memories can also be inadvertently "implanted" by police officers asking victims or witnesses about the details of what they experienced. Testimony from eyewitnesses can mean the difference between life and death in some trials, and there are an alarming number of cases where eyewitnesses who are convinced they are telling the truth have ended up convincing juries to convict innocent people (Loftus, 2019).

Given that emotional experiences like those associated with witnessing a crime tend to enhance recall, you can imagine how often inaccuracies show up in more mundane instances of remembering. And because false memories feel subjectively the same as accurate memories, the only way you can know which of your memories are false is if the event was recorded. Even asking your friends or family for confirmation is not a failsafe method, since their memories are also fallible and potentially they were the ones who involuntarily helped implant the false memory in the first place!

Many laboratory studies of false memories focus on tests of recall for words that were not present in a list of associated words (Roediger & McDermott, 1995). For instance, a participant might be shown a list of words such as "thread," "sewing," "point," "thimble," "haystack," etcetera, and then experimenters would observe how often a related word not on the list, such as "needle," was mistakenly recalled. Participants misremember having seen related words about 40% of the time, and generally were as confident about its presence as they were about words they actually studied.

If people are so prone to remembering things that never happened, what does this say about your everyday memories? First, it shows that memories are not like messages stored on your phone that you can search for at your leisure to retrieve information you previously experienced. Your impressions of your memories are like your impressions of the world more generally. You think you are seeing everything in front of your face, but you are not (review the findings on change blindness in Chapter 4). You think you are remembering what happened in your past, but many of the details are being filled in, not retrieved. In many respects, your memories may be like those of the young Dalai Lama, guiding your actions in functional ways regardless of their origins or accuracy.

Memory Loss

Daily forgetting and memory falsifying are so commonplace (and hidden) that they seldom provoke comment. Drastic loss of memory abilities, in contrast, can be quite frightening and attention grabbing. Memory loss after a blow to the head, for example, seems to almost erase a chunk of a person's life. On the other hand, such complete memory loss is more common than it might at first seem. Most adults experience four to six dreams every night, during which they may experience the kinds of fantastical scenes typically only seen in movie theatres. But most adults recall few or none of these experiences with no ill effect. Experiences you can recall, whether asleep or awake, are the exception, not the rule.

FIGURE 8.14. Lifespan changes in memory capacity. Many memory abilities gradually decrease throughout adulthood, while others such as knowledge about the world are more likely to be stable or improve. Interestingly, working memory abilities often show a similar decline to those shown for recall of events (long-term memories) suggesting a tight link between these two kinds of memory. (After Park & Bischof, 2022)

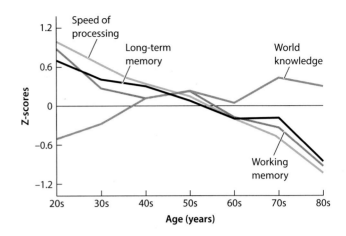

Memory loss becomes more of a problem when it begins to interfere with one's continuity of thought and capacity to socially interact (Jahn, 2022). Oddly, this can show up initially as a tendency to repetitively recall specific thoughts multiple times, such as when someone tells you the same funny anecdote twice in the same day. Typically, the repeater does not realize (remember) that they're delivering an encore performance, so the repeat is mainly awkward for the listener.

Memory loss is often associated with aging. You might be surprised at how early the deterioration can start for some (**Figure 8.14**). Not everyone shows a decline in memory abilities with age, but many do. Also, some memory capacities are more resilient than others. Working memory (short-term) and memories for past events (long-term memory) tend to decrease for most of a person's lifespan, while the ability to remember facts and vocabulary (world knowledge) is usually either stable or improving during this same period (Nyberg & Pudas, 2019).

Aging-related memory loss is not inevitable and researchers continue to explore ways to combat it. So far, the most effective preventative measure appears to be keeping physically fit (Erickson et al., 2011). Customized computer training also shows promise for combatting memory loss (Mahncke et al., 2006), although developing effective "mental exercise" routines has proven to be a challenge.

SIGHT BITES

 Explicit memories for facts and events (semantic and episodic memories) differ in their content and specificity but are similar in terms of how they are remembered.

 Emotional events are often easier to recall; however, the flashbulb memories associated with them can be inaccurate.

 Facts and events are more memorable when they relate to things you know; when you elaborate on the given information, processing it deeply; and when the conditions during recall match those during the original experience.

 Common memory failures include not only forgetting (which may result from interference) but also recall of false memories.

Monitoring Memory

SNEAK PEEK: Cognitive control involves not only the maintenance and retrieval of memories but also awareness of how your attempts at storing and recalling memories are working out. However, your impression of how you're doing often may not match reality.

People are often skeptical that they have multiple dreams every night because this claim does not jibe with their own experience. Or at least it does not match any experiences they can recall. A total lack of awareness of an event experienced in the past is called **amnesia**.

"I know that I know nothing."
—Socrates (supposedly)

Amnesia is often associated with brain disorders, but if you've ever zoned out in a class, then you've experienced it. You know you were awake because you're sitting upright, but no amount of cueing seems able to remind you of what you were seeing and hearing just a few minutes ago—there's just a non-memory, like the ones you have for dreams you don't recall. Believers in reincarnation, like the monks who tested the toddling Dalai Lama, would argue that the same lack of access to past experiences is why most people can't recall their prior lives. Believers in Freud's viewpoint would similarly argue that amnesia for early life experiences can contribute to many clinical disorders.

Models of working memory highlight how cognitive control mechanisms determine which memories are stored and manipulated, but they do not address how people evaluate these ongoing processes. How do you know when you've forgotten something? What makes you think that you're ever actually remembering anything? Your impressions and thoughts of your own remembering are collectively called **metamemory**, a metacognitive process that psychologists are actively exploring (McDonough et al., 2021; Rutishauser, 2021).

Assessing the Progress and Success of Recall

How can you tell the difference between something you've forgotten and something you never knew? Partly you can tell based on your familiarity with the cues that are prompting your recall attempt, but you can also judge this based on the subjective feelings you experience when attempting to recall an event or fact. You may feel quite certain that you have never heard or read the phrase "reduplicative paramnesia" before (or that you have). Such feelings of certainty are what make eyewitness testimony so compelling, even when the memories are false, and what makes people doubt claims that they have forty or so dreams a week.

Subjective impressions of certainty, or **feelings of knowing**, about when a memory is available (or ever was) occur rapidly and automatically. In fact, experiments that compared reaction times of people answering questions or saying whether they know the answers to the questions showed that people were generally faster at reporting whether they knew an answer (later verified) than they were at providing an answer (Reder & Ritter, 1992).

Occasionally, you may encounter situations where you "know you know" an answer, name, etcetera, but are unable to recall it. The tip-of-the-tongue phenomenon (discussed in Chapter 12) is a prime example of this. Attempts at voluntary recall in such cases may paradoxically be a less effective strategy than simply giving up—the answer may spontaneously pop into your head soon enough (or in some cases, right after you turn your test in). In this respect, successful memory recall is similar to successful problem-solving (discussed in Chapter 10) in that the most effective approach is not always the most direct or consciously controllable route (**Figure 8.15**).

As noted previously, feelings of knowing are not a reliable indicator of recall accuracy—a recalled memory may be false, or its origins may be misremembered, or it may not be a memory at all (Schacter, 1983), as in the case of déjà vu (O'Connor et al., 2021). With déjà vu, a person has a strong sensation that

FIGURE 8.15. Externally monitoring memory. New neurofeedback technologies make it possible to monitor neural correlates of successful and unsuccessful recall attempts. How might visual or auditory feedback about what your brain is doing during recall attempts supplement feelings of knowing or judgments of learning? (© 2023 Neuroelectrics. All rights reserved)

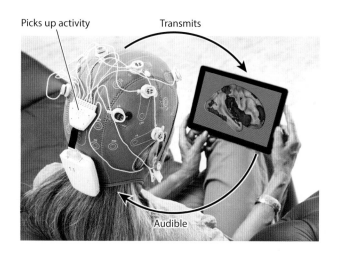

Picks up activity

Transmits

Audible

what they are experiencing at the moment is identical to an experience they have had before, even though in principle this can never happen. It can be an unnerving experience. The phenomenon is sometimes associated with disorders like epilepsy and can also be induced by electrical or pharmacological brain stimulation. The likelihood of déjà vu can also be increased when there are similarities between a current environment and one experienced previously but forgotten (Cleary et al., 2012).

Metamemory becomes particularly important when you're attempting to learn facts from a new domain (like now). If you feel like you've got a good handle on the material, or if you feel like your efforts to retain novel information are hopeless, then you'll probably spend less time and effort studying or thinking about the material. Alternatively, if you feel like your ability to recall details of the material is increasing over time, you may be motivated to keep plowing ahead.

Unfortunately, most research suggests that assessments of future abilities to recall facts recently encountered, called **judgments of learning**, tend to be way off the mark (Townsend & Heit, 2011). People who are significantly improving their probability of successful recall often report that they are not, and people who feel they have learned a lot often crash and burn when tested on their abilities to recall specific facts. Even worse, many of the strategies that people feel help them learn new facts either have no benefit or increase forgetting. How then are you supposed to know what to study if you can't trust your introspective assessment of what you will remember?

When Is Studying Worth the Effort?

Generally, you are likely to be more confident about your ability to recall facts and events that you are familiar with than those you are not. That is, if you've successfully recalled information in the past, then memories of those successes can drive confidence that you will be equally successful in the future. Testing yourself on material can thus provide a reality check that can supplement your subjective impressions of what you can remember (Roediger & Karpicke, 2006): for instance, can you explain what the word length effect is (if not, review p. 289)? Simply trying to answer such questions can improve later recall (called the testing effect, p. 296), but only in certain circumstances (**Figure 8.16**).

If you decide to try and increase your retention of the material presented in this chapter, there's no shortage of online pointers about ways to do this. But which strategies work? There's no recipe for optimal studying that applies in all scenarios. It really depends on how much time, interest, and background knowledge you have whether any particular strategy will be effective—and on whether your goal is to maximize your score on an upcoming test or to maximize your ability to recall the information over the next few decades.

Many of the memory strategies you've read about so far in this chapter—linking new facts to domains you already know a lot about, staying fit, and practicing free recall rather than cued recall (fill in the blank questions) or recognition (rereading the text or your notes)—can also enhance the benefits of studying.

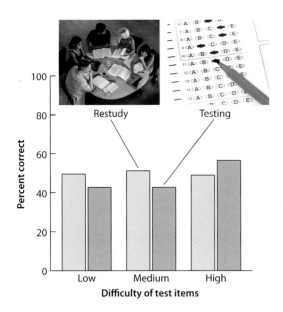

FIGURE 8.16. In-class effects of testing versus restudying for short-answer exam questions. Undergraduates in a cognitive psychology class were tested on short-answer questions (like "What is a source monitoring error?") a few months after they reviewed course materials by either studying summary statements (the restudy condition) or by attempting to answer related short-answer questions (the testing condition). A testing effect (relatively better performance after the testing condition) was evident only for question topics that students answered most accurately during review sessions, the high difficulty of test items condition. Interestingly, neither approach improved average performance much above 50%, raising questions about the efficacy of either approach! (Graph after Greving & Richter, 2018, insets Restudy: Jacob Ammentorp Lund; Testing: J.J. Gouin via Shutterstock)

Given that you now know (or think you know) that your feelings of knowing are not always reliable, you might consider recruiting an outside judge to assess what you can and cannot recall. There are large individual differences in recall prowess that can vary considerably across domains (poor spatial memory does not imply poor verbal memory), so objectively identifying your personal limitations and how they vary over time can potentially provide you with useful clues about what memory strategies will work best for you (Unsworth, 2019).

Of course, studying is not just about recall. Ideally, your goal should be to build and refine your concepts (as discussed in Chapter 5), to increase your capacity to solve future problems (see Chapters 9 and 10), and to flexibly convey and apply what you know in contexts beyond a classroom (through generalization processes detailed in Chapter 7).

Some approaches, like training yourself on the use of mnemonics (particularly ones that elaborate on key terms or that summarize lists or concepts, like acronyms), can pay off in the long run, especially for topic areas that require memorizing large numbers of facts or equations (Putnam, 2015).

Recently, cognitive-enhancing drugs have arisen as another possible study aid to amplify retention. Experimental evidence of the benefits of such drugs is relatively weak (Schifano et al., 2022). Clearly, some drugs like caffeine that extend the amount of time you can spend studying can potentially enhance recall relative to a scenario where you fall asleep before reviewing a specific topic. But you might be more likely to recall the material some other night when you're up late buzzing on caffeine than when you're trying to answer questions on an exam (think transfer appropriate processing).

Monitoring Uncertainty

Metacognition doesn't simply involve judging when you will or won't remember specific facts. You might also become aware that you're getting confused, bored, or intrigued, which can affect how you adjust cognitive control mechanisms, including voluntary attention, exploratory investigations, and recall attempts.

This kind of mental state monitoring historically was assumed to be something that only adult humans did. And at certain points in history, it was even questioned whether all genders, races, and social classes had this capacity. In the last two decades, however, evidence has accumulated that even young children and other species may attend to their cognitive status (Smith et al., 2014). Dolphins were some of the first animals to demonstrate the ability to report on their confidence levels when making perceptual distinctions (**Figure 8.17**). Given the choice, animals will often pass on making a decision in situations where the outcome is uncertain (Smith et al., 2003).

FIGURE 8.17. Uncertainty monitoring by dolphins.
(A) A dolphin making an easy visual discrimination will quickly and confidently choose a response. (B) When the dolphin is faced with a more difficult discrimination, it may choose more slowly and even switch its choice at the last moment. Dolphins can learn to opt out on difficult trials by pressing a response that skips the current trial, suggesting they recognize when they are uncertain. (C) Metacognitive monitoring of uncertainty, called uncertainty monitoring, can be viewed as a process of discrimination in which questions that lead to confident responses (outer regions of the two curves) are distinguished from those where evidence is consistent with both possibilities (gray shaded region in the middle). (A and B Dolphin Research Center, Inc.)

(A)

(B)

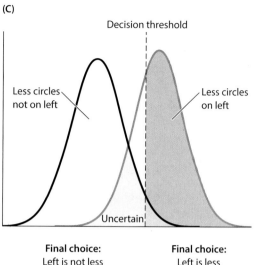

(C)

You can conceptualize someone's metacognitive judgments of their mental states as comparable to psychophysical comparisons between different percepts, as described in Chapter 4. One end of the continuum might represent evidence that an appropriate memory is available to guide a decision—the kind of evidence you might use to judge whether you are certain you know the answer to a question. The other end of the continuum could be evidence that you don't know the answer. Between these two extremes might fall evidence too ambiguous for you to decide one way or the other, leading to uncertainty (see Figure 8.17C). In this scenario, uncertainty monitoring might rely on cognitive mechanisms like those used to make perceptual decisions.

Metacognitive processes like uncertainty monitoring and metamemory are fundamentally introspective—they depend on your awareness and interpretations of your feelings and thoughts (Drigas et al., 2022). They also depend on your memories for how your current mental state relates to past states (Why is it that you are reading this? What goals motivate you to study?) and on your capacities for cognitive control (Can you attend more closely or effectively than you are now? Can you process the text more deeply?). All of the scientific constraints related to introspection apply to metacognitive reports, including the difficulty of telling when a nonverbal organism is introspecting or when those introspections accurately reflect what is being experienced.

Despite these limitations, much of what cognitive psychologists have to say about explicit memories is grounded in metacognitive assessments of what remembering is like, including the basic division between explicit and implicit memories. Explicit memories by definition are those that you can consciously reflect upon and report. Similarly, the distinction between episodic and semantic memories maps directly onto "things you remember happening" versus "things you know about," both of which are metacognitive distinctions between differing mental states. Flexible cognitive control of memory mechanisms (such as rehearsal, recall, or use of mnemonics) requires some awareness that there are things one can do to maintain or construct desired mental states. In other words, working memory depends on metamemory, as does the ability to recognize that a recently experienced event is what just happened versus what is happening now.

SIGHT BITES

Conscious monitoring and regulation of your memory processes (metamemory) is a key aspect of controlling and evaluating what you remember and know.

Feelings of knowing and judgments of learning provide clues that can guide how you study, but they are often not reliable indicators of what you will remember.

Judgments of uncertainty may reflect an attempt to perceptually discriminate between knowing that you know and knowing that you don't know.

BRAIN SUBSTRATES

SNEAK PEEK: For working memory to work, activity in prefrontal cortex is often critical. But maintenance and control of memories in the short term involves more than just keeping activity going. Memory traces that enable you to recall facts and events are distributed throughout multiple brain regions.

When it comes to neuroscience and memory, engrams currently reign supreme. **Engrams** were proposed in the early 1900s as "memory traces" within a brain that make recall possible—essentially the physical difference left from an experience that makes a difference (Josselyn et al., 2015). Chapter 7 describes evidence of engrams for implicit memories within cerebellar circuits. Less evidence exists of engrams for explicit memories, but few doubt their existence and most believe that they reside primarily in the hippocampus and the cerebral cortex.

Before considering why researchers believe this, it's worth taking a step back to review the zoo of memory categories described in this chapter and throughout the rest of this book (**Figure 8.18**).

The idea that the cerebral cortex might be where memories live has been around for thousands of years, while the proposal that the hippocampus is critical for memory only began gaining steam in the last century. Most neuroscientific studies of explicit memory have focused on localizing engrams, describing what they are, and explaining how experience constructs them. In the process, researchers have discovered new clues about the processes underlying both remembering and forgetting.

Cerebral Cortex and Memory Stores

Harvard psychologist Karl Lashley (1890–1958), introduced in Chapter 2, spent much of his career searching throughout the cerebral cortices of rats for engrams (Lashley, 1950). He never found any, leading him to suggest that engrams must be stored in widely distributed populations of cortical neurons. Lashley was partly right, only it turns out that he was too conservative in assuming that only cortical neurons were involved—multiple subcortical regions work in concert with cortex to make memories (**Figure 8.19**).

FIGURE 8.18. Kinds of memory and associated brain regions. Time (long-term versus short-term) and consciousness (explicit versus implicit) serve as initial dividing lines for the kinds of memories, followed by the specific content (such as facts versus events) and the form of recall outcomes (such as verbal reports versus emotional responses). Different kinds of behavioral evidence of retention have been used to link different memories to different brain structures. (After Eagleman & Downar, 2016)

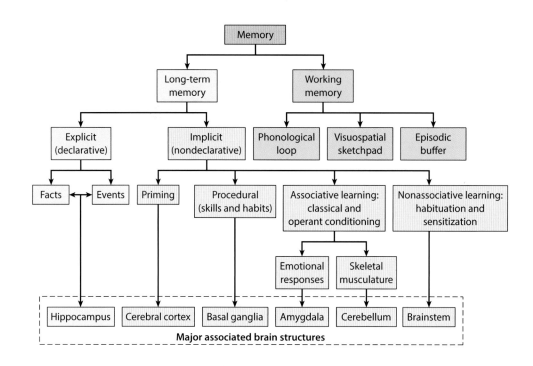

While Lashley was unable to discover any engrams in his laboratory rats, Wilder Penfield (1891–1976) was seemingly more successful in finding them in his human patients. Or at least, when he electrically stimulated specific spots in his patients' temporal lobes before surgery, some (about 5%) reported seeing and hearing detailed scenes of the sort that one would expect if a past episode or dream was being recalled (Penfield & Perot, 1963). Subsequent neurosurgical experiments, however, led to the counterclaim that temporal lobe stimulation was producing hallucinations rather than episodic memory recall (Horowitz & Adams, 1970). So, Penfield's attempts to locate the elusive engram ultimately met the same fate as Lashley's.

So far no one has definitively succeeded in artificially reactivating or removing an engram of a memory for a specific fact or event (check out the movie *Eternal Sunshine of the Spotless Mind* for an interesting take on how the availability of such technology might play out). But progress has been made in identifying which cortical and subcortical regions are most engaged during memory recall and in describing how different regions are involved. Now, I could tell you that the lateral parietal lobe is more engaged during the recall of past episodes, and the posterior hippocampus tends to be more active in recalling events that happened more than a year ago (just did), and so on. The most likely result of this, however, would be that you forget these details in less than ten minutes (many of these details are reviewed by Gluck et al., 2020, if you're curious). Additionally, knowing which regions are more or less active in a particular task might help you flesh out a parts list of memory mechanisms, but it probably won't give you much insight into what those parts actually do.

On the other hand, when your brain activity leads to memories that do not match your past experiences, then things get a bit more interesting. For instance, you now know that if you have false memories of events (you almost certainly have several), you're not going to be able to subjectively discriminate these faux memories from actual memories—frustrating but true. If en-

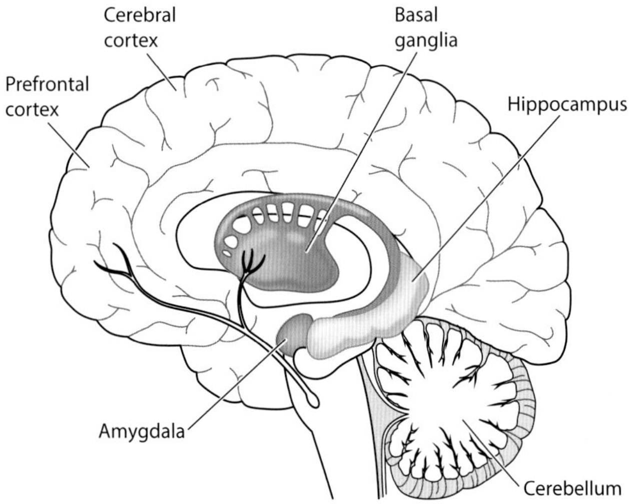

FIGURE 8.19. Multiple brain regions contribute to memory processing. Although the main regions contributing to explicit memory processing are the cerebral cortex and hippocampus, there is not one specific region where memories are located.

(A)

(B)

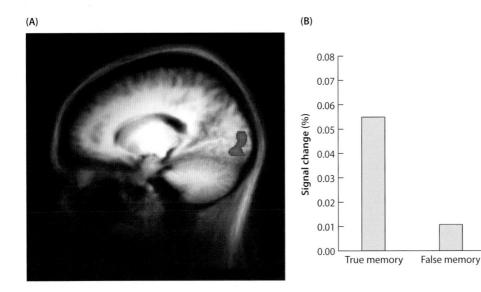

FIGURE 8.20. Neural signs of false memories. (A) The small red blob in this neuroimage shows a cortical region that responded less (B) when participants recalled false details of a previously witnessed episode. (A from, B after Karanian & Slotnick, 2017, *Cortex* 91, with permission from Elsevier)

grams are physical consequences of experience, though, then there must be some differences between memories you recall and memories you accidentally make up. Consistent with this intuition, there is neuroimaging evidence that your brain is doing different things when you recall false memories versus actual memories (**Figure 8.20**).

As you might guess, many of the brain regions engaged during the recall of false memories are the same ones engaged during the recall of the true ones (Dennis et al., 2014), including the hippocampus and various cortical regions. It turns out that false memories are more likely to occur when activity in these regions is reduced relative to what occurs when you recall an experience you actually had.

The discovery that cortical circuits respond differently during false memory recall suggests that cognitive control mechanisms "make do" with whatever neural activity they have. In short, recall of specific episodes appears to be a process of constructing mental states on the fly using available "ingredients" provided by multiple brain regions rather than a process of reactivating a specific engram stored at a unique time, place, or brain location—recalling episodic memories is not like flipping through a photo album.

Potential Modes of Storage

A major limitation of behavioral studies of memory is that they only provide indirect access to a small segment of what is happening mentally. Remembering normally requires no obvious behavioral response and neither does storing or maintaining memories for either short or long periods. Brain measurements provide ways of observing ongoing memory processes that are independent of behavior. One can get a better sense of what engrams might be like and how they relate to memory abilities by measuring how brains change during and after controlled events

Knowing which brain regions are involved in memory processes can help researchers begin to tease apart how those regions might contribute to remembering. Although this is what initially led researchers like Lashley and Penfield to focus on circuits in the cerebral cortex, more recent studies have focused on what's happening in hippocampal circuits, especially those in rodents (Brunec et al., 2020; Clark & Squire, 2013; Voss et al., 2017). Chapter 6 reviews early work looking specifically at hippocampal contributions to spatial memory.

Electrophysiological recordings from awake and asleep rats revealed that hippocampal neurons "replay" specific spiking patterns (often during sleep) that originally occurred as rats navigated through mazes (Panoz-Brown et al., 2018). This kind of replay has been interpreted as a reactivation

FIGURE 8.21. Action replays in rat brains. Electrophysiological studies have revealed that hippocampal neurons replay activity patterns generated during an initial experience such as a sequence of odors recently smelled. How might cognitive control mechanisms affect which experiences are replayed and when? (From Panoz-Brown et al., 2018)

of activity patterns that occurred during an initial experience, as might occur when a memory is being recalled (**Figure 8.21**). Because the hippocampus and the cerebral cortex are interconnected, such replay could also reactivate related cortical activity patterns.

Repeated reactivation of neural firing patterns conceivably could serve to "stamp in" a specific memory, providing a possible mechanism for memory consolidation (Pfeiffer, 2020). Interestingly, hippocampal replay is often sped up relative to the initial experience (the opposite of an instant replay in video) and sometimes reversed in time. So, the replays do not replicate the initial experience. Consolidation is generally portrayed as a drawn-out process happening in the background, like cement drying, whereas recall is a transient event, initiated by cognitive control mechanisms. But if consolidation consists of intermittently replaying experience-triggered brain patterns, then how exactly does consolidation differ from recall?

You may recall from Chapter 5 the proposal that the cerebral cortex and the hippocampus work as complementary learning systems to construct distributed representations of categories and concepts. Verbal knowledge of categories and concepts qualifies as semantic memories. The complementary learning systems proposal can also be applied to the consolidation of episodic memories and is sometimes called the **standard consolidation theory** (**Figure 8.22**). Standard consolidation theory suggests that the hippocampus initially binds all the elements of an experienced event together and then gradually trains the cerebral cortex to recreate the multimodal activity patterns on its own (Winocur & Moscovitch, 2011). From this perspective, hippocampal replay is like prompted practice while cortically-driven recall is the independent performance.

An alternative interpretation, however, is the hippocampus and the cerebral cortex are functioning in parallel, and every time an episodic memory is recalled a new duplicate memory is stored within both regions. As multiple versions of similar episodes pile up, their common features can be stored as a semantic memory in the cerebral cortex, but the event memories still are present in both cortical networks and the hippocampus. This **multiple trace theory** suggests that you should only see hippocampal replay in relation to memories for events, not for consolidation of semantic memories (Nadel et al., 2000).

Note that these two theories parallel the theories of category learning discussed in Chapter 5, with events taking the place of exemplars (each episode stored separately) and facts taking the place of prototypes (each summarizing a collection of experiences).

Modulators of Memory

Underlying all the talk of engrams, consolidation, and distributed representations is the idea that memory traces, whether of facts or events, are physical things. The exact form of engrams has been widely debated (Josselyn et al., 2015), but the current consensus is that they are composed of a constellation of synapses of varying strengths.

(A)   **(B)**   **(C)**

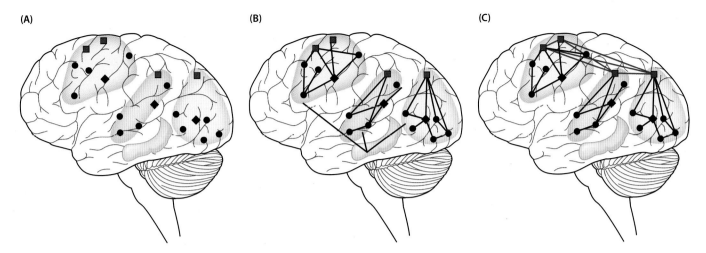

The idea that synaptic strength might be affected by repeated experiences was first popularized by Ramón y Cajal (introduced in Chapter 2). He generally viewed such changes as similar to the effects of physical exercise (DeFelipe, 2006). William James and Ivan Pavlov proposed similar mechanisms, though they did not specify synapses as the sites of the physical changes. The idea that changes in neural connection strengths might actually be memory traces did not really gain steam, however, until Donald Hebb (of Chapter 2 fame) reintroduced it within his theory of cell assemblies.

Once scientists began thinking more seriously about how synaptic memory traces might work, it was not long before they hypothesized that controlling the rate at which synapses change might affect how easily a memory trace could be recalled (Martin & Grimwood, 2000), ultimately leading to the hypothesis that neuromodulation—global changes in the neurochemicals present at synapses—might determine when and how engrams are formed (Atherton et al., 2015).

Why is it that emotional events are often easier to recall than neutral episodes? Part of the answer is that the amygdala, a subcortical region strongly engaged by emotion-triggering events, controls levels of norepinephrine (a neuromodulator). Increasing norepinephrine levels enhances recall and blocking its effects can erase the advantage in recall gained from emotional arousal (McGaugh, 2004). And increased norepinephrine levels facilitate synaptic changes (Tully & Bolshalov, 2010).

Norepinephrine is one of several neuromodulators (including dopamine and acetylcholine) that are now known to strongly affect memory formation and recall. These same neuromodulators can also affect memory deterioration. For instance, the memory loss associated with Alzheimer's disease is linked to reduced levels of acetylcholine, and several drugs used to treat the disease are designed to counteract this decrease. Unfortunately, artificially raising acetylcholine levels in the brain mainly has benefits during the early stages of the disease but does not appear to solve the cognitive problems in people with Alzheimer's disease.

Intriguingly, memories evoked by music seem to be preserved to a greater extent in people with Alzheimer's than other kinds of memories (Jacobsen et al., 2015), leading some to argue that there may be a musical memory system that is separate from other explicit memory systems, which is less affected by lower acetylcholine levels.

Finally, recent evidence shows that neuromodulator levels may affect synaptic plasticity not only directly but also indirectly by controlling the processes that drive long-term changes in synapses. For instance, levels of acetylcholine in the hippocampus can affect when replay of activity patterns occurs, as well as what form replay takes, and dopamine levels may determine which neurons are included in the replay (Atherton et al., 2015).

Collectively, these findings paint a picture in which the formation of engrams is substantially more complex than the storage of digital codes or the imprinting of wax (Roy et al., 2022).

FIGURE 8.22. Standard consolidation theory.
(A) A perceived event leads to distributed activity throughout the cerebral cortex. Here, various neural activity triggered by the event is depicted as circles, squares, and diamonds. (B) Early on, replay by hippocampal neurons serves to reactivate the same configuration of cortical activity that was originally triggered, leading to consolidation through the formation of stronger connections between co-active neurons (shown here as lines between shapes). (C) Over time, neurons that fire together, wire together, producing populations of cortical neurons that will tend to become coactive when a subset of their member regions are activated (an engram). In this case, newly formed connections between brain regions (red lines), make it possible for activity in one region to trigger specific patterns of activity in other regions, as might occur when you recall details of a specific episode (a particularly memorable lecture?).

Prefrontal Control of Memory Access

Studies of engrams emphasize potentially long-lasting structural changes in neural circuits, focusing especially on synapses in cortical and hippocampal regions where engrams for episodes and facts might be found—it's a classic structural view on memory.

Neuroscientific studies of working memory also often focus on identifying which brain regions contribute, but they additionally attempt to identify precisely how neural activity makes recall possible—a more proceduralist approach (Cai et al., 2021). Activity in the frontal lobes in particular has received the most scientific attention (Courtney et al., 1998; Ester et al., 2015).

In humans, the frontal lobes make up a third of the cerebral cortex. The front-most part of the frontal lobes, called the prefrontal cortex (PFC), is thought to be an evolutionary extension of the cortical circuits for motor control (including motor cortex) that make up the rest of the frontal lobes.

The PFC connects bidirectionally to many other brain regions, including the hippocampus, and sensory and motor cortical regions. These extensive connections are thought to facilitate links from perception to action circuits as well as the integration of multiple sources of information (Miller & Cohen, 2001).

Transcranial magnetic stimulation of certain PFC regions reliably degrades performance in working memory tasks (Mull & Seyal, 2001), as does damage to PFC in animal models (Curtis & D'esposito, 2004). But such disruptions reveal relatively little about what PFC neurons are doing. To get a better handle on that, neuroscientists have turned to electrophysiological methods.

Working Memory as Trace Maintenance

Knowing that experience can change the strengths of synaptic connections does not clarify how such variations will affect a person's ability to consciously recall recent events such as a recently read word list. Current ideas about the differences between working memory traces and those stored in synapses mostly come from the ways computers store memories. Long-lasting memory on a computer is often stored magnetically (on a hard drive) while temporary memories are stored as electrical charges that can dissipate if not continuously maintained. By analogy, synaptic engrams would act as your hard drive and your working memories would be ???? (your guess is as good as anyone's).

If brains implemented memory like digital computers, then working memory would use electrical copies of a subset of synaptic states. But for synapses to have any effects on neural activity, the presynaptic neurons that feed into them have to fire. Good luck trying to get only neurons that are connected to specific synapses to fire!

Most neuroscientists instead think that short-term memory traces in brains likely reflect either persistent firing by specific neurons or "round-robin" firing maintained by a small loop of interconnected neurons (Zylberberg & Strowbridge, 2017). It's also possible that synapses may temporarily change their strength (Santos et al., 2012).

Recordings from monkeys' PFC neurons showed early on that some neurons do persistently fire during the delay period in working memory tasks (**Figure 8.23**). This is exactly what you might expect if PFC neurons are acting to maintain temporary memory traces in a manner similar to digital computers. Consequently, researchers hypothesized that some PFC circuits might function like two of Baddeley's proposed working memory buffers: the phonological loop and visuospatial sketchpad (Petrides, 1996).

Understanding what the persistent activity of prefrontal "working memory cells" might mean in terms of memory processing requires knowing a bit more about the tasks that monkeys and humans were performing. In one commonly used task, called the delayed response task, an individual is briefly shown a sample such as an object or image. Next, the sample is removed from sight and nothing happens for a fixed interval (the delay). After the delay, the subject is given the opportunity to make a response on a multiple-choice test where the options include one correct choice and one or more incorrect choices. The correct choice depends on the identity or location of the sample, thus requiring the subject to remember the sample for that trial to perform accurately.

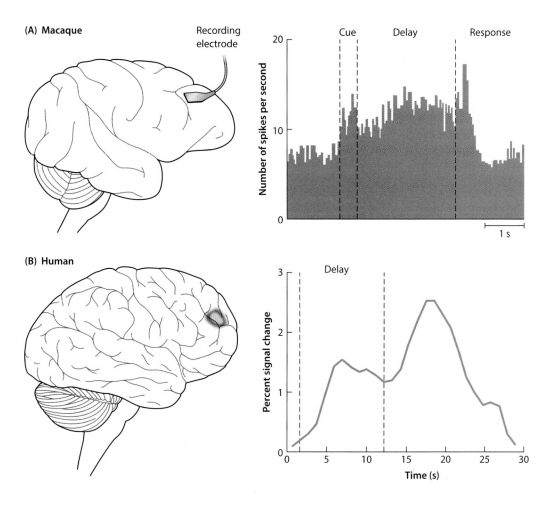

FIGURE 8.23. Persistent activity in PFC. (A) Single-cell recordings from neurons in the prefrontal cortices of monkeys collected while the monkeys performed working memory tasks revealed elevated responses to sample cues that persisted during the delay before recognition tests, when the cues were not present. The height of gray bars corresponds to the number of spikes produced by a PFC neuron. (B) Elevated activation in human PFC also persists during delays before a response is made. The height of the blue curve shows the relative increase in blood oxygenation during a trial (note the longer time scale). (A after Funahashi et al., 1989; B after Curtis & D'Esposito, 2003)

An obvious interpretation of what happens in the delayed response task is that subjects form a memory of the sample when it is presented, maintain this memory during the delay, and then use that memory to choose a response. However, there is a bit more going on than this. First, the subjects must know what they're supposed to be doing—that is, they have to keep in mind what the rules of the game are to make correct choices (much like the *n*-back task). Second, they need to have some motivation to do the task—so some memories of the costs or benefits of following/breaking the rules. Presentation of a sample may cue activation of any or all of these memories.

Even if you assume that PFC "memory cells" are specialized for storing information that is specific to each individual trial, this still does not tell you what is being stored or maintained. It could be a memory trace of the visual experience of seeing the sample. However, most experimental evidence suggests that for monkeys and other nonhumans, it's more likely to be a memory of the specific action that needs to be performed at the end of a trial (Roitblat & von Fersen, 1992), and for humans, it may additionally be labels that name the sample, or the correct response, or both. In other words, subjects may be predicting what they will need to do in the future while waiting rather than remembering what they saw in the past. Such action planning could happen unconsciously, in which case subjects wouldn't even know they're doing it!

Prefrontal Processing as Mental State Management

Before you buy into the idea that PFC neurons are Baddeley's memory buffers, you should probably know that animals (including humans) can successfully perform delayed response tasks with all their PFC neurons removed. This doesn't mean that PFC circuits don't store temporary memory traces, but clearly, they aren't necessary for achieving this capacity. For this reason, and several others, many researchers now hypothesize that PFC neurons implement the "central executive" postulated in working memory models (Funahasi & Andreau, 2013; Ott & Nieder, 2019).

You've probably figured out that the central executive is a member of the cognitive control team, in charge of keeping recently formed or recently activated memory traces in shape and where they need to be. Cognitive control mechanisms additionally are in charge of directing selective attention (discussed in Chapter 4) and monitoring how the central executive is faring, thereby making meta-cognition possible. How might persistently firing PFC neurons contribute to such sophisticated operations?

If you've ever worked in a large corporation, then you probably know that central executives succeed by directing employees to do things. In the case of cognitive control of memory, PFC may serve this role by recruiting other brain regions to contribute to memory-based cognitive processes.

Recent neurophysiological recordings in humans implicate prefrontal regions in the synchronization of cortical activity across multiple brain regions. Keeping physically separate cortical circuits "in synch" may facilitate dynamic coordination of cortical networks with capabilities appropriate for a given task. By encouraging cortical neurons to fire at specific frequencies (**Figure 8.24**), PFC may also be able to enhance processing in some cortical regions while suppressing activity in other regions (Rezayat et al., 2021).

If PFC neurons control which cortical regions act in concert and modulate cortical activity by ramping it up in some regions and damping it down in others, then perhaps it would be more accurate to think of PFC as an "orchestral conductor" of working memory. An orchestra can perform without a conductor, but different sections might find it difficult to flexibly adjust their relative contributions.

Overall, current neuroimaging and neurophysiological findings are consistent with Cohen's model of working memory in that the cortical and hippocampal regions engaged during recall of episodic and semantic memories largely overlap with those recruited during working memory tasks. Unlike computers, there do not seem to be separate "brain modules" devoted to each kind of memory.

Part of the reason that researchers originally hypothesized that the PFC might be important for working memory and cognitive control is that this region of the cerebral cortex evolved relatively recently. Given that humans excel at cognitive tasks that depend on working memory, the thinking was (is) that this brain region might be the source of humans' special intellectual talents.

Keep in mind, however, that neuromodulator levels ultimately control activity patterns in all cortical and subcortical regions, including the PFC. The neurons that control neuromodulator levels are mainly in the brainstem, an evolutionarily ancient system. So, if any part of your brain functions as a central executive or conductor, it's your brainstem.

Effects of Prefrontal Dysfunction on Memory

What do you think would happen to your working memory abilities if someone inserted an icepick through your eye socket and wiggled it back and forth a few times until most of the connections be-

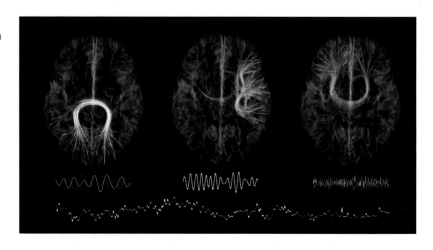

FIGURE 8.24. Synchronization of cortical regions. Cortical regions with activity that is synchronized at a particular rhythmic frequency may coordinate as a distributed network within your brain. Neurons in the prefrontal cortex may modulate or facilitate cross-cortical coordination. Colored lines in the top brain models depict coordinated brain regions both across and within hemispheres. The colored curves below each brain show the frequencies of synchronized activity (more squiggles means higher frequencies), and the white curve at the bottom shows the overall activity from these regions when combined—in other words what you would record from your scalp with electrodes. (Sébastien Dery, McConnell Brain Imaging Centre, Montreal, Neurological Institute)

tween your PFC and other cortical regions were severed? A version of this procedure—called a transorbital lobotomy—was implemented on thousands of patients in the 1940s as a "psychosurgical" treatment for schizophrenia and affective disorders (Terrier et al., 2019). It produced a wide range of not-great outcomes, including death, but memory loss was not one of them.

Frontal lobe syndrome, caused by damage to the frontal lobes, is associated with a variety of emotional, cognitive, motor, and social problems (Reber & Tranel, 2019). It can affect cognitive control by increasing distractibility, decreasing the ability to coordinate action sequences to achieve a goal, or reducing impulse control.

In adults, frontal lobe damage seems to only indirectly affect working memory abilities. Nevertheless, frontal lobe function may limit working memory capacities in undamaged brains. For instance, the PFC is one of the last regions of the brain to mature and working memory capacity seems to gradually increase in parallel with PFC maturity (Diamond, 2013). Similarly, age-related declines in working memory capacity are predicted by how rapidly an individual's PFC deteriorates (West, 1999). Developmental disorders that derail frontal function, like attention deficit hyperactivity disorder (ADHD), are also associated with reduced working memory capacity (Rogers et al., 2011).

Some of the differences between the minimal memory deficits seen after frontal lobe damage versus the more noticeable memory limitations linked to age or developmental disorders may come from the fact that brain damage is often limited to one hemisphere. Alternatively, it may be that having an inconsistent cortical "conductor" limits working memory capacity more than having no conductor at all.

Whenever cortical circuits are damaged, compensatory mechanisms kick in that, in some cases, can enable surrounding cortical regions to partially take over the functions of the damaged region. In situations where there is no brain damage, but the PFC may be dysfunctional, such as in ADHD or schizophrenia, such compensatory mechanisms are not likely to be triggered.

There may still be ways to provoke plasticity in these circuits, however. Electrophysiological recordings from monkeys revealed that training on a working memory task modifies the responses of PFC neurons (Spaak et al., 2017). The neurons become more selective for task-relevant cues and responses. Training-induced cortical plasticity may thus provide a way to modify PFC circuitry without the use of an ice pick. Plasticity of this sort may explain why cognitive training is sometimes effective as a treatment for ADHD (Jones et al., 2020; Weist et al., 2022).

SIGHT BITES

Engrams supporting memories for facts and events appear to be distributed throughout multiple brain regions, especially the hippocampus and cortex.

Unconscious replay of neural activity patterns may contribute to memory consolidation by strengthening synaptic connections throughout the brain.

Sustained firing by neurons in prefrontal cortex may contribute to working memory abilities by coordinating and adjusting activity in other cortical regions.

Dysfunctional activity in prefrontal cortex can degrade working memory capacities as much or more than physical damage to the frontal lobes.

APPLIED PERSPECTIVES

SNEAK PEEK: Human memories may seem impressive but there are others with memories far more expansive than ours. In principle, we might be able to modify human brains to expand our memory capacities. Permanent amnesia is relatively rare, but there are many conditions that can devastate one's capacity to recall events from specific periods.

There are varied opinions about the nature and extent of explicit memory capacities. Some psychologists argue that only humans experience episodic memories, and only after a certain age. Others suggest that at least a few birds and mammals can remember events in as much or more detail than humans and simply focus on different features of those events. One thing that all psychologists agree on, however, is that involuntary forgetting and perseverant remembering is often annoying.

Many people would prefer to avoid such frustrations (and spend less time studying), which is why stacks of "boost your memory" books continue to be sold. It's also why memory champions, people with highly superior autobiographical memory (described in Chapter 1), and memory savants are so impressive. They seem to have somehow broken the rules of the forgetting game.

Even these exceptional memorizers have failed to find the holy grail of memory mastery, however. Their abilities consistently are limited to a few fixed domains. Like professional chess players who only show advantages in remembering piece positions when tested on legal configurations (Lane & Change, 2018), memory experts are memory specialists.

What then would it take to create a brain/mind that excels at cognitive control for all kinds of memories? Such a brain/mind could flexibly retain and access many more details for as long as desired, without fear of omissions, distortions, fabrications, or unwanted intrusions for any experience it's possible to have or any fact that it's possible to know.

Are such advances possible? And if not, what improvements to memory abilities would be feasible? Scientists are moving closer to answering these questions by exploring the origins of naturally occurring individual differences in memory capacity as well as more artificial variations (Cooke & Bliss, 2003; Genon et al., 2022). Understanding the extremes of memory capacity and dysfunction can potentially reveal the keys to effectively enhancing everyone's remembering potential.

Mega-Memories

Humans tend to be more confident in their memory abilities than is warranted. The capacities of other species are usually assumed to be subpar by comparison. It's the same kind of mistake that was made in early studies of echolocation by bats. Other species can perceive things that humans can't and they may be able to remember things in ways that humans can't as well.

Animals with Stellar Memories

You may recall from Chapter 1 the chimpanzee Ayumu, whose working memory prowess makes most non-chimps look like chumps. If chimpanzees can beat out humans on a task made by humans for humans (Inoue & Matsuzawa, 2007), how do you think they might do on a test of memory for things chimpanzees actually care about given in a way that is better matched to the way chimpanzees normally operate?

Police officers train dogs to search out and follow the scent of specific individuals presented to them at the start of a chase (see Chapter 5). How can a dog maintain the memory of a unique scent while searching through a sea of odors? It seems unlikely that rehearsal is involved. Perhaps their smell memories are more like the eidetic visual memories of children (Remember these from Chapter 1? Probably you'd like to be able to).

FIGURE 8.25. Masters of memory. Some birds that hide seeds for the winter appear to be able to keep track of tens of thousands of hiding places every season. These memories need to last several months, but after that they are counterproductive. What would be a comparable situation that humans might face where they need to remember lots of details but only for a fixed duration? (YK via Shutterstock)

Animals' long-term memory abilities are as mysterious as their shorter-term capacities (**Figure 8.25**). What sort of memories enable sea turtles to return to the specific beach where they hatched years after the fact and from thousands of miles away? Are the memories similar to those humpback whales use when they migrate from Hawaii to Alaska after making the trip once or twice? Or are they more like the memories of young birds that imprint on a specific individual soon after birth? If an elephant encounters a remote watering hole once in its life, what sort of process enables it to recall and make use of that memory thirty years later?

Memories for these sorts of unique events seem more critical than the kinds of episodes that humans typically can recall, like what they had for breakfast or what they did last week. Might they be like flashbulb memories where the "flash" is much brighter?

Of course, memories for events critical to the survival and reproduction of a species might depend on evolutionary specialized systems of storage and recall (Vámos & Shaw, 2022). But those specialized systems are built from the same neurons that your brain is, so in principle, anything nonhuman brains can do, yours might be able to do too, assuming you make the proper adjustments…

Neuroengineering Better Memory

Modifying a human brain to try and increase an individual's memory capacity is a risky proposition. Lots could go wrong, as was learned from the lobotomy fiasco in the 1940s. Experiments with animal models currently provide the best option for working out such techniques. And animal experiments sometimes yield informative surprises. For instance, researchers studying the function of glia found that when they implanted human glia in the brains of mice, the "humice" showed faster learning-related changes in their synapses and developed above average learning and memory capacities (Han et al., 2013).

It's not necessary to install human brain parts to ramp up an animal's memory capacity. Researchers can achieve similar effects by introducing a digital memory controller that triggers learning trials based on what an animal's hippocampus is doing. Populations of hippocampal neurons spontaneously switch between different rhythmic firing patterns in awake animals. By monitoring hippocampal activity and only initiating trials when the hippocampal neurons are rhythmically firing at certain frequencies, researchers can greatly increase memory acquisition (Griffin et al., 2004). In humans, monitoring these same frequencies enables researchers to predict which words participants were most likely to remember (Düzel et al., 2010) and triggering word presentation when these frequencies were detected enhanced overall performance (Merkow et al., 2015). Imagine if you could halve the time you spend studying just by automatically limiting when you review specific facts to times when they are most likely to sink in!

FIGURE 8.26. Memory prosthetic to supplement natural memory. Monitoring ongoing cortical activity and using that information to electrically stimulate hippocampal activity using a device like the MIMO (multiple input, multiple output) model may make it possible for a person's brain to recall information that normally would be difficult to retrieve.

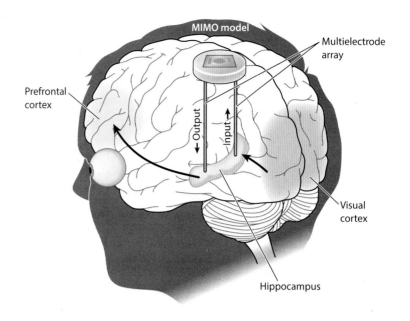

Timing your experiences so that they line up with times when you're most capable of storing memories is a clever way of making the most of what you've got, but it's sort of like making lemonade out of lemons. You're still at the mercy of whatever your brain naturally does. An alternative approach is to take more direct action by making your brain regions behave in ways they normally can't. Recall from Chapter 7 how neurostimulation of certain neuromodulatory neurons reinforces rats so much that they will starve themselves just to keep the stimulation coming. What if similar techniques could be used to push memory processing past its normal limits?

Several laboratories are working toward this goal, but mainly to rehabilitate deteriorating memory processes rather than to enable superhuman memory abilities (Jones et al., 2015; Ke et al., 2019). Current approaches focus on using implants to monitor patterns of cortical and hippocampal activity that make recall possible at relatively short delays and then using electrical stimulation of the hippocampus to mimic those patterns after longer delays (**Figure 8.26**). Using such **memory prostheses**, researchers have been able to increase retention by about 30% (Hampson et al., 2018). Whether such strategies might also help people without memory deficits to expand their retention remains to be seen.

Amnesia

Generally, when people want to change their memory they want to be able to know or remember more. There are cases, however, where people would prefer to remember less, such as after a traumatic experience. Although it's possible to reduce your likelihood of remembering specific incidents, as with directed forgetting, voluntary amnesia for specific time periods or events is not yet an option.

Temporary Memory Wipes

Controlled amnesia may sound like science fiction, but it's not outside the realm of possibility. In fact, there are known ways to "erase" memories, either temporarily or permanently. Surprisingly, one way to do this is by exercising a lot or swimming in cold water (Hodges & Warlow, 1990). Not a guaranteed technique, to be sure, but in some individuals this can trigger **transient global amnesia (TGA)**, a condition in which a person temporarily loses memories of the last decade or two, as well as the ability to keep track of recent events.

About 1 in 10,000 people experience transient global amnesia each year in the United States; mostly people over the age of sixty (Spiegel et al., 2017). The experience usually doesn't last more than about eight hours, during which the person might be unable to recall basic info like the date and where they live or work. The individual also might not realize that you had asked for this information three times in the last twenty minutes: so a temporary loss of some semantic, episodic, and working memories. Given that transient global amnesia goes away in a few hours, there aren't treatments for it and it's tricky to study. Although people with transient global amnesia regain their memory abilities, in some cases they remain unable to recall what was happening right before the onset of the episode, as if those memories were erased or never formed.

It's possible to produce a similar kind of amnesia by passing a strong electrical pulse through your brain, a technique called **electroconvulsive therapy (ECT)**. This technique works with numerous species, making it more scientifically (and clinically) useful. People who have undergone electroconvulsive therapy show a reduced ability to remember details of their own lives from the last few years, including details of television shows they watched (Vakil et al., 2000). The degree of memory loss seems to vary depending on the positions of the electrodes used and the form of electricity applied. In many cases, most of the lost memories return after about half a year, like a slow-motion version of transient global amnesia. As with transient global amnesia, the memories most likely to be lost forever are those that occurred just before the shock, although with electroconvulsive therapy, this period can be a week or more. About a million people receive electroconvulsive therapy each year, usually women seeking treatment for depression. Recent experiments with mice indicate that the benefits of electroconvulsive therapy (relief of depression) as well as the costs to memory both come from its effects on gene expression in the hippocampus (Chang et al., 2018).

Blackouts or "brownouts" (partial amnesia) caused by either excessive drinking or by head-butting hard things also typically involve short-lasting amnesia. About half of college students who drink alcohol report having experienced a blackout (Wetherill et al., 2016), which probably makes this one of the most prevalent forms of amnesia on the planet. Aside from studies of inebriated mice, there's scarce experimental evidence on the specific mechanisms causing blackouts, for reasons you can probably guess. As with electroconvulsive therapy, the source of the amnesia appears to be disruption of hippocampal activity and possibly also the frontal cortices. Paradoxically, although excessive alcohol can derail explicit memory abilities, it also can enhance implicit memories (Cui et al., 2013). This may partly explain why blackouts typically don't scare people off from excessive drinking. The positive, unconscious memories of fun times may override the more unnerving experience of not knowing what happened the next morning.

Amnesia doesn't always involve a loss of memories related to a specific time period. Sometimes memory loss can be more situation-specific, as when an actor experiencing a sudden bout of stage fright forgets the lines of the script. This is partly why lots of people fear public speaking—babbling nonsense or nothing at all when temporary memory loss sets in can be humiliating. The mechanisms of anxiety-related amnesia are thought to relate more to a breakdown of cognitive control than to a problem with memory processes per se (Eysenck et al., 2007)—the memory "conductor" may fail to cue part of the memory "orchestra" to begin performing, even though the memories would have been successfully retrieved if the right signals had been sent.

Unrecoverable Memories

The transient amnesias described above show that memories can be naturally "erased," but they don't really provide much insight into how one might purposefully achieve this goal without risking alcohol poisoning or brain damage. Unique cases of more permanent memory loss provide important clues about how intact memory systems work, as well as additional hints about how problematic memories might be overcome or erased.

Just as there are individuals with exceptional retention and recall capacities, there also are a few people with amazing memory disabilities—amnestic celebrities whose existence changed how researchers think about memory. Clive Wearing is one such person. A virus invaded his brain leading to extensive damage and massive memory loss (Wilson & Wearing, 1995). At age forty-six, he lost the ability to

FIGURE 8.27. Clive Wearing's diary. Clive Wearing's diary entries reveal what happens when the past is never present. How do you think his metacognitive processes might respond to this direct evidence that his current experience is not entirely accurate? (Consider the words that are repeatedly crossed out and replaced.) (Excerpt from the diary of Clive Wearing.)

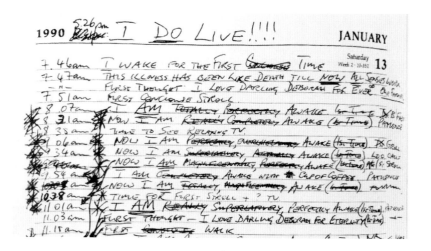

recognize most of his family, to name many common objects, and to access decades of musical knowledge (but not the ability to read music or play the piano). Even worse, Clive lost the ability to form new memories, experiencing each moment as if he had just become conscious seconds ago (**Figure 8.27**).

Interestingly, Clive's memory loss does not prevent him from engaging in conversations, including attempting to answer questions, suggesting that his comprehension of English is mostly intact, despite his difficulties naming things. Also, his window of memory has gradually expanded over time. In the first year of his disorder (1985), he was described as sometimes losing track of ongoing events after blinking. In 2008, his wife reported an incident in which he returned a lighter to a care assistant about ten to fifteen minutes after she mentioned losing it, asking her, "Is this your lighter?" (Sacks, 2008).

The virus that attacked Clive Wearing's brain wreaked havoc throughout his cerebral cortex causing damage in every lobe. You may have guessed that his hippocampus was demolished in both hemispheres. The extent of Clive's brain damage makes it difficult to identify the specific causes of his deficits, but loss of cortical and hippocampal networks are likely contributors. Clearer evidence of hippocampal damage as a source of extreme amnesia comes from perhaps the most famous amnesiac in psychology, Henry Molaison, commonly referred to in the scientific literature as H.M.

Unlike Clive, Henry's hippocampus in both hemispheres and surrounding cortical regions were surgically removed as part of an experimental treatment for epilepsy. Like Clive, Henry's memory loss after the surgery was extensive, wiping out many of his personal memories, as well as his ability to retain new information for more than a minute (Milner, 1972). His working memory abilities were more intact than Clive's. For example, Henry wrote himself notes to keep track of key facts he otherwise would forget. Semantic memories that Henry acquired before the surgery remained largely intact, but he was impaired at acquiring additional fact memories after the surgery. He was, however, still able to learn new perceptual-motor skills and his overall intellectual abilities (as measured by IQ) were unaffected. The spared working and procedural memory capacities that Henry possessed in combination with profound explicit memory deficits convinced many psychologists that there are multiple independent memory mechanisms (Corkin, 2002; Eichenbaum, 2013).

At this point, you may have the impression that amnesia is all about hippocampal damage, but that is not always the case. Korsakoff syndrome, a disorder associated with chronic alcohol abuse, leads to many of the same memory loss symptoms seen in Clive Wearing and Henry Molaison (Fama et al., 2012). Individuals with this disorder do not have hippocampal damage, but instead have damage to the thalamus, which you may recall from Chapter 2 is a subcortical region that transmits sensory and motor signals throughout the cerebral cortex. It's not clear why damage to the thalamus would produce amnesia comparable to that caused by hippocampal damage.

You might also have gotten the impression that permanent amnesia only happens when part of a person's brain is broken. Actually, most if not all adults are unable to recall episodes from their early lives, a phenomenon called **infantile amnesia** (Li et al., 2014). Despite the name, infantile amnesia

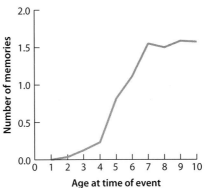

FIGURE 8.28. Infantile amnesia. Adults generally report no memories before the age of three and few memories before the age of seven. This same pattern is seen in twenty-year-olds and seventy-year-olds, suggesting that it is not just a function of general memory decay. (Image: Salty View/Alamy Stock Photo, graph after Josselyn & Frankland, 2012)

generally refers to your inability to recall episodes in your life before the age of around three, and the minimal memories you have of your first six or so years (**Figure 8.28**).

Given that emotional memories tend to be more memorable and that young children are soaking up all kinds of information early on, it is somewhat paradoxical that events like a birthday, holiday, trip to Disneyworld, death of a family member, etcetera, would leave no detectable mental mark. As noted earlier, Freud proposed that such notable events did leave traces, even though they were not normally accessible to consciousness.

Some psychologists have theorized that episodic memory capacities in particular take longer to develop in humans, requiring self-awareness, language abilities, or an understanding that others have minds (Howe & Courage, 1993). Extended cognitive development of such higher-order abilities could explain infantile amnesia. However, rats show similarly age-dependent forgetting of early events over shorter time periods, because they typically live only a couple of years (Alberini & Travaglia, 2017). It seems less likely that their improved memories for events that happened after early development are the result of accelerated self-discovery.

An alternative explanation for infantile amnesia is that the mental states experienced by adults are so different from those experienced by young children that adults never experience enough matching cues for recall to be possible—in other words, the memories are there, but there's no way to access or reactivate them, or to understand them if they were reactivated. If you did manage to reactivate a memory from when you were one, your experience might be more like having a mental breakdown than reminiscing about an earlier episode.

Infantile amnesia might seem like a "bug" or design flaw in that lots of potentially useful, or at least entertaining, memories are cast aside. Given the prevalence of forgetting throughout the lifespan, it seems more likely that infantile amnesia is a built-in feature of cognitive development. Understanding the pros and cons of retaining certain memories, as well as the ability to consciously access them, will be critical in efforts to augment human remembering and forgetting capacities beyond their natural constraints.

CLOSURE

Assume for the moment that the two-year-old Dalai Lama did remember people and items familiar to his deceased predecessor. There are several possible explanations for how something like this might happen. It could have been false memories that led to correct responses. Little is known about false memories in two-year-olds. But in general, young children are highly susceptible to false memories.

Another possibility consistent with the evidence is that most two-year-olds inherit memories from dead people (their former selves?), but because of infantile amnesia, no adults ever recall having those memories. Maybe this is not that likely, but how would you know? Much of what toddlers experience is obscure. The point here is not that you should accept claims of reincarnation, but that remembering a past episode (or not) comes with no guarantees. You can forget or make up all sorts of things with no awareness that you are doing so and high confidence that you aren't. Overestimating the consistency and veracity of your memories is the norm. Even your most vivid memories are potentially full of fallacies—there is no correlation between vividness and accuracy. Many people have been executed in the past based on someone's vivid memory of an event that never occurred.

Perhaps you'll feel nostalgic when you mentally travel back to an earlier, simpler time when describing your memories as being like a movie montage seemed sensible. Magic shows are still entertaining even when you know it's all illusions and sleight of hand. In the same way, theories that portray biological memory as like computer memory but wetter appear clever at first glance but aren't likely to give you many useful clues as to what's really happening in your head when you remember.

So what exactly is happening? William James (1890) argued that a person's ability to direct attention in a way that stabilizes a specific mental state was the essence of voluntary action. From this perspective, making conscious mental states persist beyond their natural "lifespan" is what makes some memories explicit. Maintaining mental states in either the short term (with working memory) or the long term (for episodic and semantic memories) depends on cognitive control mechanisms that engage multiple neural circuits distributed throughout your brain, as well as metacognitive mechanisms that evaluate how things are working out.

Pragmatically, you'll probably spend a lot of time learning facts that you'll have little ability to recall or use a year later. Based on typical forgetting rates, you'll be lucky to retain a quarter of them after a month. Stories you've seen, heard, or read about this year will fade into oblivion just as fast.

Echoes of those experiences will remain. You're likely to recognize at least parts of movies, videos, novels, or gossip if they come up again, but your ability to bring these memories to mind on the fly (a case of free recall) will be minimal to nonexistent.

You may even be able to recognize a few of the memory facts presented in this chapter a couple of years from now. Although, there's a decent chance that by then some of them may no longer be facts. Perhaps you'll even be able to recall a few that can help you to make yourself more memorable when it matters—last impressions often matter as much as first impressions (says the serial position effect). Old dudes rule!

COGNITIVE LINGO

amnesia	implicit memory	repressed memory
consolidation	infantile amnesia	retroactive interference
cued recall	judgment of learning	rumination
directed forgetting	levels-of-processing effect	semantic memory
echoic memory	long-term memory	sensory memory
electroconvulsive therapy (ECT)	memory decay	serial position effect
engram	memory prosthesis	source monitoring error
episodic memory	metamemory	standard consolidation theory
explicit memory	modal model	structural view
false memory	motor memory	testing effect
feelings of knowing	multiple trace theory	transfer appropriate processing
flashback	*n*-back task	transient global amnesia (TGA)
flashbulb memory	proactive interference	word length effect
free recall	proceduralist view	
iconic memory	rehearsal	

CHAPTER SUMMARY

Working Memory and Cognitive Control
Maintaining memories of recent experiences for seconds or minutes is a skill that determines many other cognitive capacities. Theories of working memory focus on both where memories are stored (the structural view) and how they are stored (the proceduralist view).

Memory for Facts and Events
Much of what you are capable of remembering persists for periods much longer than a few minutes, especially when the original events or facts are emotion-evoking. Feelings of trueness are, however, unreliable.

Monitoring Memory
Metamemory and judgments of uncertainty are key for controlling and assessing what you remember and know.

These introspective cognitive processes may depend on perceptual discrimination of internal states.

Brain Substrates
Memory traces (engrams) are thought to support long-term memories through distributed cortical and hippocampal networks. Prefrontal cortical networks are thought to make the cognitive control of short-term memories possible.

Applied Perspectives
Technologies for increasing memory capacity and accelerating forgetting of unpleasant incidents are emerging. Conscious recollection appears to be especially vulnerable to brain damage.

REVIEW EXERCISES

Working Memory and Cognitive Control
- What are some key differences between the modal model of memory and Baddeley's working memory model?
- What are the distinctive elements of Cowan's working memory model?
- What evidence suggests that working memory capacity depends on cognitive skills?

Memory for Facts and Events
- Explain some ways that semantic memories differ from episodic memories.
- How might you study the semantic memories of a goldfish?
- What sorts of evidence could you use to determine whether the memories of an eyewitness are false?

Monitoring Memory
- Why are judgments of learning not your friend when it comes to developing studying plans?
- In what ways might metacognition be similar to perceptual discrimination?

Brain Substrates
- How might "replay" of neural activity in hippocampal neurons contribute to the consolidation of memories?
- Why does dysfunctional activity in the prefrontal cortex commonly degrade working memory more than physical damage to this brain region?

Applied Perspectives
- What conditions can lead to amnesia other than damage to the hippocampus?
- How might neuroprosthetics affect the academic experiences of future students?

CRITICAL THINKING QUESTIONS

1. Children across the United States compete in spelling bees each year. What sorts of memories and metacognitive processes do you think the spelling bee champions are using to beat out the competition?

2. Artificial intelligence programs can answer a variety of questions, including in some cases, questions about how they work. Does this mean that they have explicit memories and metacognition? If not, why not?

3. Amnesiacs like Henry Molaison perform normally on standard intelligence tests despite severe memory deficits. What does this suggest about the relationship between memory and intelligence?

4. Some researchers think that cognitive control of memory involves precisely coordinating activity across multiple cortical regions. How might you test this hypothesis using the delayed response task and neurophysiological recordings from either monkeys or humans?

5. Infantile amnesia limits what adults can recall about their youth. Imagine that in the future it becomes possible to attach recording devices to infants and toddlers that record everything they see or hear. Would this approach make it possible to eradicate infantile amnesia?

Figuring

When people think about cognition, they often gravitate to thinking about thinking (following the lead of Descartes). As discussed in the last chapter, this is metacognition in action. Cognitive psychologists are essentially professional metacognizers. However, rather than taking the philosophical route of trying to explain the essential nature of minds, cognitive researchers focus on understanding how minds work. Identifying the principles of cognitive psychology means knowing more than what it feels like to remember and think. In the words of James, "We can ascend to knowledge *about* it by rallying our wits and proceeding to notice and analyze and think. What we are only acquainted with is only *present* to our mind; we *have* it, or the idea of it. But when we know about it, we do more than merely have it; we seem, as we think over its relations, to subject it to a sort of *treatment* and to *operate* upon it with our thought" (James, 1890, v.1, 222). At its core, cognitive psychology is about figuring stuff out, including figuring out how we figure stuff out.

In the history of studies of cognitive "figuring," two processes loom large: imagining and reasoning. These processes are typically juxtaposed against perception of external events. For instance, medieval scholars contrasted the five external senses (sight, hearing, touch, taste, and smell) with the five internal senses (common sense, imagination, logic, estimation, and memory). This split captures the subjective impression that pondering what you would do with a billion dollars has a certain feel to it that differs from seeing someone win a lottery. Much like perception, the different subjective experiences you have while thinking are not a reliable guide to identifying how thinking works.

Grasping Greater Things

How might one ascend to knowledge about thoughts and thinking? One way, discussed earlier in this book, involves learning new categories for describing things like space, time, and number as well as for comparing similarities and differences across concepts. In many respects, imagining is like perception with fewer external triggers to restrict possible interpretations. Another way to gain perspective about thoughts is through retrospective contemplation. If you cannot comprehend how someone might end up becoming a scientist, it might help to consider facts and past experiences that may yield insights. Reasoning involves remembering rules, relations, and consequences in ways that can lead to explanations or predictions that might not otherwise be noticed.

The capacity to gain insights is the reason why humans dubbed themselves *Homo sapiens*, "the wise man." From the perspective of Greek philosophers, this capacity involves escaping the constraints of perception and discovering the truths that are hidden beneath appearances. Psychology suggests that the grasping of greater things is not an ability limited to "man" and that the capacity to imagine the future and think about its implications are grounded in the ability to perceive. As discussed in previous chapters, your capacity to understand what is happening and respond effectively in ever-changing circumstances comes from your ability to generalize past learning and take advantage of memories of related experiences. Your potential for imagining new possibilities, solving challenging problems, and understanding unfamiliar theories of cognition, depends on the memories and skills you have acquired throughout your life. In this respect, your interpretation of the following discussion of imagery, planning, creativity, reasoning, and decision-making will arise from your current knowledge, beliefs, and feelings about perception and memory as well as from your existing cognitive skill set (as discussed in Chapter 7).

Exceptional thinkers and imagery architects (artists) have attained special status in modern society. Historical figures like Newton, Mozart, and Pavlov gained their notoriety from their facility at changing the way people think and explore. No doubt many other anonymous cognizers have radically shaped the trajectory of human civilizations. For these reasons, it is almost inevitable that both laypeople and cognitive researchers alike would hold the cognitive processes that make such progress possible in the highest esteem. One should not mistake impact for sophistication, however. Asteroids also have had a major impact on the development of human advancements, but not because of their complexity or uniqueness. In *The Principles of Psychology*, William James argued that instincts, reflexive processes that happen with minimal interference from planning or thought, were more important for human ingenuity than the ability to reason or imagine future possibilities.

Contemplating Cognition

How could instincts, which many (including Descartes) have viewed as being fundamentally opposed to rational thought be at the heart of human cognitive prowess? The key insight that James offered is that humans have a wide variety of impulses (driven by instinct) and actions performed in response to those impulses lead to learning and memory. Remnants of past experiences, in turn, affect responses to future impulses, such that later actions can become less "mindless." James argued that the variety of impulses that humans possess, some of which are contradictory (say curiosity versus a desire for security), increases the range of interactions between instincts in ways that promote a diversity of mental and physical actions. Importantly, he also noted that these impulses naturally vary over the course of a lifespan, such that the instincts that inspire infants and children to act and think certain thoughts can vary greatly from those that motivate adults.

From this perspective, instincts are the seeds from which your ideas grow, and reasoning is simply one cognitive process among many that can help you prune some thoughts while letting others run wild. Moving from such metaphors to mechanisms is one of the main ways that modern cognitive research has gone beyond early speculations about what thinking entails. Researchers can now directly observe brain activity associated with thinking versus remembering or with imagining versus perceiving. Through such studies, it has been confirmed that both imagery and problem-solving engage widely distributed networks of neurons, many of which overlap extensively with regions involved in memory and perception. Changes in the interactions between these regions can affect your ingenuity as well as the extent to which you consider pros versus cons when making a difficult decision.

One such decision you will face when reading the following two chapters is determining whether the cognitive mechanisms of creative thinking and problem-solving are unique to humans, involving highly specialized and sophisticated mental states, or whether they are a common feature of cognition in many species. Are the mental images you experience now more impressive than those you formed as a child? Perhaps they are simply different, or maybe your earlier images were more sophisticated and you have simply lost the capacity to appreciate (or remember) their brilliance. Some researchers, including Francis Galton, have suggested that the imagery abilities of younger humans (and perhaps nonhumans as well) far exceed those of highly educated adults. Others, like Albert Einstein, have suggested that imagistic thought processes can lead to insights beyond those one might achieve through image-less logic. It may be hard for you to imagine thinking about your thoughts or the cognitive processes underlying them in any way other than the ways that you normally think about mentality. Luckily, you don't need to imagine new thoughts to have them. The preceding chapters were designed to familiarize you with the building blocks of perception, memory, and cognition in general. The following two chapters will give you a chance to apply what you know to one of the most challenging topics in psychology: understanding how it is that you are able to think and what your thoughts and ideas really are.

9 Imagery, Planning, and Creativity

Reuters

hen you wish upon a star, makes no difference who you are, you will be imagining as dreamers do" (Washington and Harline, 1940). But how exactly do dreamers create the nightly dramas that play out inside their heads? And what is it that dreamers are creating?

You might think of dreams as visions—experiences like those that happen when you sense external events but without the sensations. Once upon a time, people put a lot of weight on reports of waking visions. Plus, people took vivid dreams seriously. René Descartes, introduced in Chapter 1, derived his main arguments about the nature of minds from interpretations of his own dreams.

Nowadays, dreams are more often associated with hopes and fantasy fulfillment than with deep insights into minds, at least in Western cultures. Consumers strive to find their dream home, paid for by their dream job, which they occasionally abandon to take a dream vacation, such as a journey to the place where dreams come true: Disneyland (**Figure 9.1**).

If you have ever made the trek to a Disney park, then you probably know that the best way to make sure the dream doesn't become a nightmare is to plan far ahead. To avoid going broke before you make it through the gate or standing in line for over an hour to get your picture taken with a fake princess, you will need to plot your course of action well in advance.

Attaining dreams in a non-dreamworld is more about long-term planning than it is about wishing and imagining. Even so, for something like a theme park to exist at all requires people to imagine and construct new sorts of plans that have never been thought of or attempted before—cue the entrance of the Imagineers. Dreams usually involve involuntary **mental images**, internal states that subjectively seem like percepts. But individuals can also voluntarily provoke mental images through the active process of constructing mental experiences, referred to as **imagination**.

Imagine if in the 1800s someone predicted that people would one day pay large sums of money to visit a kingdom reigned over by a five-foot-tall mouse. How long would it have taken for such a

FIGURE 9.1. Land of imagination.
Disney magic transforms fairytales into reality. But how was reality transformed into fairytales in the first place? What cognitive processes produce figments and why? (TJ22/Stockimo/Alamy Stock Photo)

visionary to end up in a madhouse? How exactly is it that *you* can imagine this scenario at all, given that your personal experiences do not include the 1800s or their madhouses? Somehow, you are able to think a novel thought simply by reading a sentence. You can also mentally roam nonexistent places or be saddened by the death of a two-dimensional, talking doe.

You do all of this not by perceiving, but by thinking. You think, "Now Bambi is motherless and all alone," even though there is no Bambi. Poor, nonexistent Bambi. You mentally create a tragedy where none exists and then later stand in line for the Bambi ride at Disneyland to reminisce.

Aside from making money, the main reason that Disney parks exist is for fun. What makes Disneyland more fun than a parking lot is partly its novelty. You can see and do things at Disneyland that you can't see and do elsewhere. And you can pretend you're somewhere you're not, bearing witness to a pirate adventure or exploring a haunted mansion.

The novelty of Disney comes from the creativity of the people who envisioned the park and designed its occupants. Artists, inventors, explorers, and Imagineers all rely on creativity to generate new thoughts in themselves and in others. Creative cognitive psychologists develop new methods and theories to solve scientific problems that earlier researchers didn't even recognize as problems.

Curiosity is a source of creativity not just in scientific investigations, but in all sorts of planning and problem-solving activities, from coming up with a new way to make burritos to brainstorming solutions to climate change. Exactly how curiosity can help you to generate new ideas or think about a problem in new ways remains a mystery.

The plan for this moderately creative chapter is to help you imagine the different mechanisms that enable you to imagine those mechanisms. The chapter provides a transition from thinking about the representations that underlie your everyday experiences—the people, places, things, and spaces that you're cognizant of—to thinking about how you use those representations. For example, how is it that you came to be reading this chapter right now as opposed to stuffing your face at a candy store? How is it that there is even such a thing as a candy store?

You could answer, "Cognition," and you'd be right. This chapter simply serves to flesh out that answer.

BEHAVIORAL PROCESSES

Thinking clearly lies at the core of cognition. Unfortunately, defining what exactly thinking entails is hard (Lewis & Smith, 1993). Descriptions such as mental activity, idea juggling, contemplation, or conscious consideration seem to capture elements of what happens when you think; however, these descriptions are just as cryptic as the term "thinking" itself, so they don't really help much.

Defining thinking as "things your brain does" is similarly useless since your brain does lots of things that don't qualify as thinking and there is currently no way of reliably discriminating a thinking brain from a nonthinking one.

Subjectively, it seems relatively easy to identify at least some specific instances when thinking is occurring, especially after someone has just presented you with a problem that they are expecting you to solve. Even then it can be tricky to describe what your ongoing thoughts are like, to know if your descriptions accurately convey your experience, and to know if your experiences provide reliable clues about what's actually happening. Maybe experiencing thought is more like watching a magic show.

Over the past few thousand years, two main camps have emerged that claim to have solved the problem of what thoughts are like. One camp believes that thoughts are like language: symbolic representations that act as a kind of internal communication (Fodor, 1975; Pylyshyn, 2002). Not silent speech exactly but structured in ways that are like an "inner voice."

The other camp pretty much accepts the claims of the thought-language camp, because if they didn't, how could they account for the ways in which individuals form or understand sentences? (Chapter 12 provides some possible answers.) But the second camp believes that there are also non-symbolic thoughts (Kosslyn et al., 2001; Paivio, 1971), such as those you might experience if you're silently envisioning a trip you took to Disneyland. Such thoughts, sometimes referred to as "the mind's eye," might guide an artist while painting a portrait or composing a song.

Internally constructing mental scenes or sentences clearly does not exhaust all the possible ways in which thinking might work. The following discussion focuses on experimental attempts to show that one or the other scenario is happening in certain conditions, mainly because this is how most psychologists have approached the problem to date.

Imagery

SNEAK PEEK: Creativity and imagery are highly prized elements of sophisticated problem-solving that can make the difference between a successful performance versus floundering.

Prior to entering school, many children (around 60%) regularly interact with imaginary companions. These companions are usually, but not always, invisible and often possess many of the same properties as the less-imaginary people with whom the children interact (Armah & Landers-Potts, 2021). A child's imaginary friend is (presumably) a product of the child's mental activity. Not exactly a hallucination, but equally unreal to outside observers. Whether or not children actually "see" these imaginary beings, they are definitely aware of what their companions are like and how they act. Children might not sense their creations, but they seem to know them.

Real versus Imagined Events

Most children eventually outgrow their invisible compadres. This doesn't mean that only delusional adults experience things that aren't there, however. Recall from Chapter 4 that amputees

FIGURE 9.2. Virtually replaced body parts. Phantom limbs are typically not under the control of their owners, which can lead to painful problems. Producing a visual surrogate of the missing part can in some cases help patients to move the phantom limb into a more comfortable position. (Pascal Goetgheluck/Science Source)

commonly report feeling their missing arms or legs; they have what's called a **phantom limb** (**Figure 9.2**). Postoperative transgender women sometimes have a phantom penis. Cat and dog amputees will initially attempt to use their missing paws, suggesting that they too feel their lost limbs, at least for a while.

People with phantom limbs often suffer from pain in that limb. The pain associated with phantom limbs is a real event, just as real as pain coming from any body part. The presence of the limb is spontaneously imagined; it is not just a side effect of cut nerves. Often, the imagined limb differs from its predecessor, being smaller than normal, for example, or in a distorted position (Schone et al., 2022).

Before the 1900s, amputees' reports of lost limbs sticking around were thought to be comparable to peoples' reports of seeing the shades (phantoms) of lost loved ones. Now, most researchers agree that phantom limbs are mental images of missing body parts. A piano player who has lost an arm may retain the ability to move their phantom fingers in practiced patterns and may even use invisible fingerings during the composition of new pieces (Tatu et al., 2014). Unlike a mirage, phantom limbs are akin to echoes of somatosensory percepts that refuse to fade away.

Afterimages

The idea that mental images often consist of persistent or revived percepts has been a core theme of psychological explanations of thinking for over a century (James, 1890). **Afterimages** are perceptual states that occur after the visual sensations from a perceived object end (**Figure 9.3**). They depend on what was originally seen and are a prime example of how "sense-less" awareness might happen. Afterimages are generally viewed as illusions since you are seeing something that is not actually present (Kirschfeld, 1999).

The close relationship between afterimages and the sensations that trigger them demonstrates the strong connections between perception and imagery. There is little question in this case that the afterimage you perceive is a continuation of your earlier sensory experience. In other cases, the link is not as clear-cut. For example, if you are woken up in the middle of a dream, you are likely to report having seen things happen. Dream imagery is hallucinatory in that there are usually no sensations driving perceived events (Waters et al., 2016). But dreams can also be viewed as delusional; the experiences can be quite bizarre, and external events can become incorporated into dream images in highly distorted forms.

Many of the methods researchers use to study mental imagery, including several described later in this chapter, rely on direct comparisons between peoples' responses when they directly perceive an external event and when they are instructed to imagine that the same event is occurring (Finke, 1985; Kosslyn et al., 1979; Waters et al., 2021). This approach treats mental images as internally generated percepts. These self-made percepts may lack the details available from percepts of external events, but they generally retain many of the same subjective qualities and may depend on similar underlying

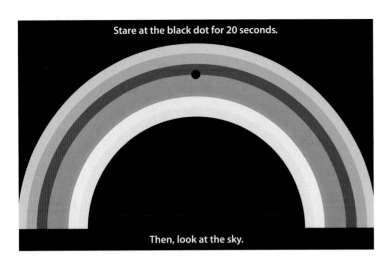

FIGURE 9.3. Afterimages. Of all the types of mental images, afterimages are probably the most straightforward to reproduce across individuals; this is because afterimages are a direct consequence of how sensory transduction by the eye works. These mental images are effectively side effects of seeing. Could other mental images similarly be side effects of how perception and thinking work? How might you test this hypothesis?

representational and cognitive mechanisms. In this scenario, everything you learned about perceptual representations in Chapter 4 would also apply to imaginal representations.

Individual Differences in Imaging Abilities

In extreme cases, visual imagery might simply be a visual percept that never entirely went away, kind of like a phantom limb. High-resolution perceptual persistence of this sort is called **eidetic imagery**. Maintaining eidetic images is not something most adults can do (Haber, 1979). You can test your own capacity for eidetic imagery by staring at a scene and then trying to imagine that same scene projected onto a blank wall. If you had tried this at a younger age, maybe six or younger, then you might have been able to describe detailed features of the scene for a few minutes after you stop seeing it based on your projected eidetic image.

This may sound a lot like a memory test. In fact, some researchers do refer to this phenomenon as eidetic memory (Cook & Wilson, 2010). If the original percept remains available throughout this kind of test, however, then the experience is more like staring than remembering. Note that in tests of eidetic imagery, the mental images that preserve recently observed scenes are projected onto an external surface. In contrast, when people are asked to visualize or imagine an object or scene (picture this—a cherry with tiny legs), they are more likely to report that the image is located somewhere in their head.

Imagined objects are revived memories of previous observations; perhaps in novel configurations, as with a legged cherry, but recalled nonetheless. Percepts, afterimages, eidetic images, and recalled images all have some subjective similarities as well as some distinctive features. Researchers are still debating about what distinguishes these phenomena at a representational level (Block, 2023; Dijkstra et al., 2019; Pearson, 2019). They could be related to different stages in the life span of a conscious experience, or they could be side effects of independent cognitive processes that just seem subjectively similar.

Most psychological studies of imagery focus on visual experiences. But the same sorts of phenomena show up in other modalities too. Studies of auditory imagery and audiation (imagining with the "mind's ear") tend to be limited to music cognition research or to the hallucinated voices that individuals with schizophrenia often hear (Hubbard & Ruppel, 2021; Pruitt et al., 2019). You can also feel the aftereffects of touching something hot or cold and can imagine what a puppy or a pinecone feels like or what it feels like to clap your hands (Schmidt & Blankenburg, 2019).

Odor imagery differs somewhat from mental images in other modalities. In particular, most people find it harder to reactivate a vivid odor image. There are a few people who can form eidetic images for odors, though. In fact, some individuals experience multimodal eidetic images that retain the sights, sounds, physical sensations, and odors of a recently perceived scene (Purdy, 1936). Interestingly, details of such eidetic images often transform over time. For example, objects in the image may move around or change shape. In this respect, both eidetic images and memory images are more dynamic than afterimages or percepts of photos.

FIGURE 9.4. Variations in visualizing. Aphantasia refers to a relatively rare condition in which a person apparently is missing a "mind's eye," lacking any ability to voluntarily visualize. People with hyperphantasia are at the opposite end of the spectrum, experiencing more intense and detailed imagery than the norm. (After Zeman et al., 2020; inset apple: Dimitris66)

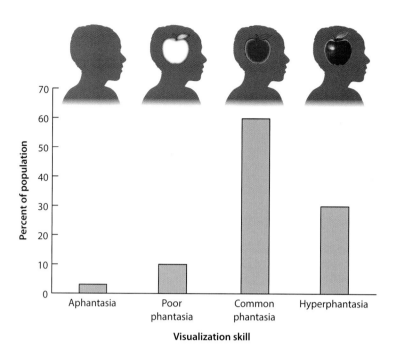

Some people seem to make greater use of mental images than others. Image vividness also seems to vary greatly across individuals (Gulyás et al., 2022; Keogh & Pearson, 2018) (**Figure 9.4**). Several standardized tests are available for measuring individual differences in visual imaging ability. Not only do different people report varied abilities to image but a single person's imaging capacity can also vary greatly over time, depending on what that person is attempting to image and the person's current mental state. As an extreme example, taking hallucinogenic drugs can radically alter a person's ability to voluntarily and involuntarily generate mental images.

The ability to manipulate mental images is what raises these mental experiences to the level of thought processes. When you are "thinking in pictures," it usually means you are not simply spectating as internal images fly by but are actively attempting to generate and use those images to gain insights, create new ideas, or discover solutions to problems (Grandin, 2009).

Manipulating Mental Images

Mental images that are constructed voluntarily through imagination and memory recall are clearly controlled; they are, in a sense, awakened from the unconscious. This sort of mental image control has been studied extensively over the last century (see Chapter 8). A more exotic form of mental image manipulation involves voluntarily morphing and controlling images experienced within lucid dreams.

In lucid dreams, the dreamer becomes aware that his or her experiences are not real—the sort of thing that might happen if you try pinching yourself to make sure you are not dreaming and then discover that you have the ability to pinch yourself to the bone with no ill effect. If you realize that you are experiencing a dream, you can sometimes obtain the godlike ability (within the dream) to change your subjective experience, like a virtual reality game where you control the action (Baird et al., 2019).

Lucid dreaming is a bit like eidetic imagery in that it is relatively rare, more common in young children, and often quite vivid. It's a bit trickier to test than eidetic imagery, though, because external observers can't really know what the dreamer is experiencing—a lucid dreamer just looks like someone lying in bed.

Experimenters work around this problem by tracking eye movements (Mota-Rolim, 2020). By comparing eye movements that occur during dreams to what a dreamer describes when woken up from the dream, it's possible to correlate eye tracks with subjective experiences. Lucid dreamers can be trained so that when they are "in the know and in control" within a dream, they move their eyes in pre-specified back-and-forth patterns. Eye-tracking methods can detect these dream-based eye movements, enabling researchers to correlate subsequent neural activity and eye movements with post-dream self-reports (Baird et al., 2022).

Lucid dreams illustrate the flexibility with which humans can, in principle, manipulate mental images. They also highlight one of the main problems with imagery research—it's hard to control events and measure outcomes. This is exactly the same issue that doomed early introspective approaches to cognitive psychology research (see Chapter 1). You can always question whether a person's reports of their inner experiences are reliable or accurate. You can even doubt your own subjective impressions!

Methods for Studying Imagery

Psychologists have attempted to increase the objectivity of imagery research by, you guessed it, simplifying the tasks that subjects are asked to perform. Modern imagery tasks usually involve imagining the movements of simple objects along a single dimension. Performance of imagery tasks is often then compared to performance on similar perceptual tasks. One of the main measures used in such comparisons is reaction time, the idea being that if a person's reported speeds for analyzing features of a mental image are comparable to the speeds at which they analyze features of a picture, then both tasks are probably engaging similar representations and mechanisms (Brochard et al., 2004; Cooper & Shepard, 1973; Kosslyn & Jolicoeur, 1980).

A famous example of this approach, developed by Roger Shepard and colleagues, required participants to inspect two shapes shown at different orientations and then decide whether the two shapes were identical (Shepard & Metzler, 1971). While participants' answers are usually correct in such tasks, the speed at which people make a decision depends on how different the two orientations are. It takes most people about four times longer to report that two complex images are identical when one of them is upside down, and it takes them about twice as long if one of the shapes is on its side.

In fact, the more an object is tilted relative to its partner, the longer it takes people to verify that both members of the pair are the same. This finding is widely viewed as evidence that to match two objects presented at different orientations, you need to rotate a mental image of one of the objects until it's at the same orientation as one of the directly perceived objects (**Figure 9.5**). At that point, you can "see" the match (or mismatch) mentally.

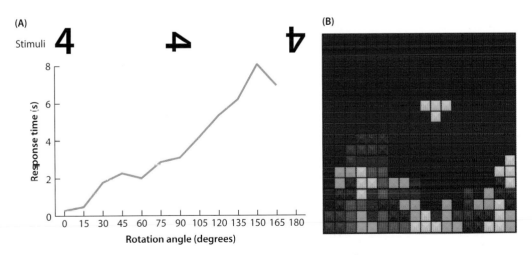

FIGURE 9.5. Mental rotation. (A) In laboratory tests, the farther a symbol is rotated, the longer it takes for people to determine whether it matches an upright version of the symbol, with the upside down image taking the longest to match. (B) The game Tetris requires players to imagine blocky shapes in different orientations and locations before adjusting how they fall. Or does it? What mechanisms other than mental rotation might enable you to successfully fit blocks together in this game? Might it take you longer to recognize a rotated symbol is a match because it takes you longer to recognize symbols in unfamiliar formats? (A after Flombaum, 2022, B Bobnevv via Shutterstock)

The task seems to require transforming a percept into a mental image and then manipulating that image to solve a specific visuospatial problem. For some objects, this task is trivial. For other more complex objects, it is almost impossible. **Mental rotation tasks** requiring such transformations are often included in tests of mental imagery abilities (Logie et al., 2011; Pearson et al., 2015).

Interestingly, men typically outperform women on standardized mental rotation tests. Specifically, men identify matches faster; it's one of the biggest cognitive differences that appear consistently between men and women (Collins & Kimura, 1997). Some researchers think that men and women may mentally rotate images in different ways, with men manipulating all parts of a mental image as a whole and women mentally rotating parts of objects individually (Bilge & Taylor, 2017). This is not to say that women cannot mentally rotate objects in the same ways as men, they just tend not to do so.

Another task often used to study visual imagery requires participants to scan a mental image of an object or scene. When people focus on a particular part of a mental image, it usually takes them some time to refocus their attention on a different part of the image. By having participants indicate how long it takes them to "see" different parts of a mental image, researchers can compare the timing of mental scans versus perceptual scans (Borst & Kosslyn, 2008). For example, if you are asked to imagine what the back of your body looks like, focus on your head, and then focus on either your butt or your right foot—indicating when you've done this—your response times may vary for different body parts. If you perform this same task while seeing a picture of the back of your body, the response times can also be measured and compared to how you responded when visualizing your back.

A common finding is that people take longer to focus on features that are physically farther from an initial imagined point. As in mental rotation tasks, farther translation seems to take more time. Findings from both tasks seem to suggest that mental images preserve the spatial relationships between features of perceived objects and scenes.

What Mental Images Are Like

Standard tests of visual imagery emphasize both the vividness of images and the ease with which images can spin and slide. Researchers draw distinctions between visualizing how things look versus how they are spatially or geometrically structured.

Distinctions between visual and spatial imagery are partly supported by neuropsychological studies showing that brain damage can selectively disrupt a person's ability to mentally rotate images (Farah et al., 1988), or alternatively may disrupt a patient's ability to construct certain elements of images (as in hemispatial neglect, discussed in Chapter 6). And an even bigger divide seems to separate mental images from verbalizable facts about the properties of those images.

The apparent differences between mental images and words have led to great debates about the nature of thinking. The argument centers on what thought is like. Does it involve language-like, symbolic **propositional representations** (see Chapter 10)? In that case, it's likely that only more mature humans are thinkers. Or might it be possible to "think in pictures," by manipulating mental images? In that case, many different animals probably think in some fashion.

For a long time, philosophers and researchers assumed that mental images were simply echoes of percepts, having little to do with actual thinking. One could think about these images, like you can think about a selfie you recently took, but the images were just an object of thought, not part of the thought process. Thinking was equated with reasoning, abstract concepts, and especially the ability to produce and understand sentences.

Some psychologists have gone a step further, arguing that even talking about mental images goes beyond science. This claim, championed most strongly by the behaviorists in the early 1900s, continued earlier arguments against depending on introspective reports as evidence of how thinking works (see Chapter 1).

More recent debates about mental imagery have focused less on whether mental images contribute to thinking and more on what mental images are like. On one side, researchers argue that mental images are a lot like drawings in that they map pretty directly onto perceived features (Kosslyn et al., 1979; Paivio, 1971). Skeptics counter that it's not necessary to assume that imagination involves mental drawings because symbolic representations are sufficient for generating images (Pylyshyn, 2002). For instance, computers display images just fine without needing to internally represent those images as tiny icons; instead, computers represent images symbolically as series of ones and zeros.

In principle, thinking could involve mentally juggling images, statements, and even more exotic representations of the world. The fact that computers don't do this does not mean that people don't. The savant Daniel Tammet, introduced in Chapter 4, claims to calculate by simply reporting on dynamic visual landscapes appearing in his mind, a situation in which the distinctions between symbols and imagery become a bit blurry. Such imaginative math would seem to qualify as thinking, even though the mental images experienced would be more like a drug-induced hallucination for anyone else.

It's unlikely that you have spent much time mentally rotating shapes or scanning mental images of maps or animals. You may, however, have caught yourself daydreaming about what it would be like to kiss someone you have a crush on, or stressing about what an upcoming final exam is going to be like. The following section considers the imagery mechanisms that contribute to these kinds of mental simulations of possible futures.

Imagining the Past and Future

Imagery is like "reperception," especially when you are trying to construct or keep in mind an image that contains specific information, as you might if you are trying to remember what a professor said about a specific topic in a lecture or if you are looking forward to a movie you plan to see in the near future. In such cases, forming mental images is effectively an act of controlling memory recall.

"Sensations, once experienced, modify the nervous organism, so that copies of them arise again in the mind after the original outward stimulus is gone. No mental copy, however, can arise in the mind, of any kind of sensation which has never been directly excited from without."
—James, 1890, p 44

Maintaining a memory of a recently observed picture for a few hundred milliseconds after it disappears requires keeping an image in mind, as does recalling its properties ten seconds later. Although different mechanisms are involved in preserving images for shorter or longer periods (see Chapter 8), both processes are thought to depend on a visual memory buffer that is consciously accessible and specialized for storing mental images.

Remembering is not synonymous with mental imaging. But thinking back to what it was like when you were lying in bed last night clearly has a lot in common with imagining what it's like to lie in a bed. And imagining what it's like to lie in a bed can easily trigger memories of past times you have been in a bed. More generally, imagery is often a key element of recall, both for good and for bad.

Mental Images as Memory Modulators

People have used mental images as memory aids for thousands of years. Most mnemonics either link images of scenes to words (like the method of loci described in Chapters 1 and 8) or auditory images to numbers. Interactive imagery, in which visual images associated with word pairs are combined, is a particularly effective approach to recalling word lists. For example, if you are trying to learn that the French word for tongue is *langue* (which sounds a bit like "lawn"), you might imagine that you're licking someone's lawn and then practice recalling that image whenever you're trying to translate the word tongue. When it comes to memorizing random facts, numbers, or lists, mental images are your friends (Blunt & VanArsdall, 2021).

Supplementing a word with imagined visual scenes may aid memory processing by increasing the number of sensory modalities involved (Wammes et al., 2019). Multisensory imagery has not been studied as much as visual imagery, but it is generally thought to engage mental representations above and beyond unisensory images. For instance, the cognitive maps described in Chapter 6 seem to incorporate information about visual cues, spatial relationships between those cues, and percepts of self-motion that drive transformations in percepts. Certainly, the dynamic audiovisual

FIGURE 9.6. Memorable images. Advertisers use imaginative, interactive images to enhance viewers' ability to remember their commercials. What sorts of multisensory sensations might a humorous commercial evoke that a boring ad would not? (Pixel Power/Alamy Stock Photo)

scenes that occur in vivid dreams can be particularly memorable (if you are woken up while experiencing them).

Mental images can enhance your memory (**Figure 9.6**), but they can also lead you astray (Strange & Takarangi, 2015). For instance, if you suffer from delusions of grandeur or paranoia, then the way you imagine the world to be can distort your memories of events. Similarly, if your perceptions of the world are shaped by negative statements about certain groups of people (for instance, by long-term exposure to racist stereotypes or propaganda), then your memories of an individual's actions may be clouded by your expectations. Some types of brain damage lead people to confabulate, meaning that their statements about themselves and the world may be totally divorced from reality (Schnider, 2003). In these atypical cases, "reperception" can lead to mental distortion.

Imagining Future Events

Just as you can construct images of yourself going to bed last night, you can also imagine what it will be like when you go to bed tonight. Looking to the future in this way, called **episodic future thinking**, engages many of the same cognitive mechanisms as recalling past episodes (Atance & O'Neill, 2001; Schacter & Madore, 2016). When older people begin showing cognitive decline in their ability to recall details of specific events, they also show similar deficits in the detail with which they can imagine future events (Schacter et al., 2017). Older individuals with such deficits also show a reduced ability to describe complex scenes that they have recently viewed, suggesting that their mental images are generally providing less information than those constructed by younger individuals.

Losing a bit of detail in your imagery capacities might not seem like that big of a deal. Consider, however, the case of an older person who has a stroke and loses the ability to speak or control a limb. That person's ability to recover those lost functions will depend heavily on their ability to imagine what it's like to perform the lost action. If the person's imagery abilities have deteriorated, then rehabilitation may be much more difficult or even impossible.

Motor imagery is probably most relevant to your daily life because mental images guide many of your actions. When you reach for your phone, you have likely not only imagined where your phone is located but also what will happen when your hand moves in a particular trajectory (it will eventually be on the phone) and what the phone will feel like when you grab it.

The rapidly formed and short-lasting mental images that enable you to make calls are in some ways less impressive than imagining a trip to Disneyland. In other respects, however, motor images are more impressive given that they are what make playing sports, eating pizza, and lawn licking possible.

Motor imagery is a bit unique among mental imaging abilities in that the events being imagined are internally driven. Specifically, motor images relate to kinesthetic sensations associated with move-

WEIRD, TRUE, FREAKY

Near-Death Experiences

Some people who almost die, or are clinically dead, before being brought back from the brink report having experienced a bright light, traveling through a tunnel, meeting with beings (including dead relatives), floating outside of their bodies, and feeling an otherworldly sense of inner peace (see figure). Such near-death experiences (NDEs) have been reported across cultures.

Surveys of individuals who flatlined during a heart attack reveal that 2% to 18% of people report NDEs. In these surveys, not all experiences count as NDEs; for instance, remembering a flash of light generally would not put you in the NDE club.

Because the people reporting NDEs were often face-to-face with death, the vivid memories they report are sometimes taken as evidence of an afterlife. Other popular explanations are that when a person's brain goes into panic mode, this may lead to specific types of hallucinations or mental defense mechanisms.

Regardless of the origins of these remembered otherworldly scenes, the ability to report them clearly depends on mental imagery abilities. Consequently, psychologists have tried to determine whether the vividness of mental imagery might be predictive of NDEs. In other words, people who are able to evoke vivid mental imagery could be more likely to have an NDE. Psychologists have also looked into whether people who are fantasy prone are also prone to NDEs. So far, there does not seem to be a strong link between any of these traits and the likelihood of having an NDE (Aleman & De Haan, 2014; Martial et al., 2018).

When NDEs are actually formed is not entirely clear. The fact that they can happen in scenarios where a person is technically never dead suggests that NDEs might arise just before the brain shuts down. Measurements of brain activity just prior to death show that there is a surge in the synchrony of cortical activity preceding brain death, which may be associated with highly vivid states of consciousness (Borjigin et al., 2013).

Abnormally heightened synchronous activity in cortical networks that occurs in association with epilepsy can also lead to hallucinations and religious visions (Devinsky & Lai, 2008), which is consistent with the idea that synchronized cortical activity promotes vivid imagery. It has even been suggested that some notable historical figures such as Joan of Arc and St. Paul might have experienced these kinds of vivid images due to partial seizures.

NDE-like scenes have also been reported by people who were never in danger of dying. These experiences can occur during extreme grief, while meditating, or after taking certain psychedelic drugs. The psychedelic drug DMT, which is one of the main active ingredients in ayahuasca—a drink used for spiritual enlightenment by ancient Amazonian tribes—produces subjective experiences that highly overlap with NDEs (Timmermann et al., 2019). DMT is known to affect the synchrony of cortical activity, but whether it leads to the kinds of patterns associated with dying is not yet known.

Both NDEs and experiences with drugs that produce NDE-like effects are reported to be potentially life changing. Apparently, extremely vivid imagery can radically change the way at least some people think!

Why do some people recall leaving their bodies during times when they are said to be clinically dead? (Frame Stock Footage via Shutterstock)

ments or what it feels like to move (Lotze & Halsband, 2006). Probably it would be more accurate to say that motor imagery is imagined feelings, but that sounds a bit too much like dreaming of being in love when you are not.

Although motor imagery may seem less vivid than visual imagery, it has become increasingly important over the last few decades. This is because some of the most effective interfaces between minds and machines, brain-computer interfaces (see Chapter 2), are technologies that transform imagined future movements into real-world actions (Kawala-Sterniuk et al., 2021). These technologies have enabled paralyzed individuals to navigate using motorized wheelchairs and move objects around using robotic arms (**Figure 9.7**). Even without knowing exactly how people mentally represent their actions or their consequences, engineers are learning how to translate thoughts into actions to solve problems. A future in which simply thinking about desired outcomes can make them happen may be closer than you might imagine.

FIGURE 9.7. Robotic motor imagery. Tracking neural activity and eye movement patterns associated with imagining specific movements of a robotic arm in a virtual environment can make it possible for a computer to transform those imagined movements into actual mechanical movements. (agefotostock/ Alamy Stock Photo)

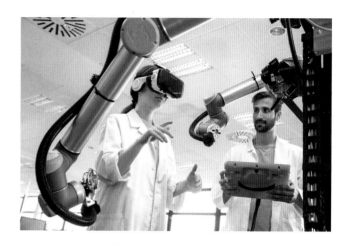

SIGHT BITES

Mental imagery contributes to thought processes by maintaining or repeating earlier experiences in ways that can be voluntarily controlled.

Imagery is closely related to both perception and memory and can vary considerably across individuals.

Debates about the nature of mental images center on whether they are like revived percepts or are represented more abstractly, like sentences.

Remembering the past and envisioning possible futures depends on constructing mental images from memories.

Planning

SNEAK PEEK: Effectively choosing future actions requires balancing verbalizable goals and strategies, imagined outcomes, and insistent emotional urges. Experimental studies of problem-solving make it possible to observe how these cognitive processes interact.

Imagery and imagination are often associated with off-kilter artists or carefree daydreaming. Mental imagery is not just about entertainment, though. As noted above, imagery can help you to reach out and touch someone (with a phone call). In principle, mental images could also help you to reach other goals. For instance, your ability to visualize a path to success might enable you to follow that path to a rewarding career. Psychologists have been skeptical about whether mental images ever play this sort of role, often favoring the hypothesis that linguistic thought processes run the show (Shaver et al., 1974).

The debate about what mental images are really good for is basically the same as the debate about whether mental images are represented as pictures or symbolic propositions. Do you think with a mental language or are you visualizing ideas? Does constructing a mental image of a cupcake compel you to make or buy one? Or does it trigger a chain of verbalizable thoughts that lead you to decide that obtaining a cupcake is the best path forward? Some psychologists have sidestepped this debate by focusing on a hybrid construct, the mental model, which rolls mental images and propositions all into one.

You can think of **mental models** as internal simulations of the properties of the actual world, including yourself. A mental model would include not only mental images of how things look, sound, or act but also your beliefs about how they work, why they are the way they are, what words you would use to describe properties of the things, and so on (Gentner & Stevens, 2014). Your mental model of a cupcakery would basically include everything you know or feel about them. Mental models are closely related to schemas (discussed in Chapter 11), mental summaries of your preconceptions about the world, since any simulations of events happening in the world necessarily depend on your knowledge of the world.

Your ability to think about cupcakeries doesn't say much about what mental models (or mental images) of cupcakeries are for. It's likely that your mental model of a cupcakery does, however, suggest pretty clearly what cupcakeries are for, which provides a big clue about a major cognitive role that mental models and imagery play. Cupcakeries exist because they solve (and simultaneously create) problems. How can I get people to give me their money? How can I make my mouth happy? In what scenario does having entire stores specializing in creating one kind of sugary monstrosity (say an oversized cinnamon roll) make any sense?

Your mental model of a cupcakery, which may include a cognitive map of how to find one, provides you with potential solutions if you ever find yourself in dire need of a cupcake—my apologies if that time is now. In other words, mental models are cognitive tools for solving future problems.

Looking to the Future

In cognitive psychology, **problem-solving** refers not just to working out numerical calculations or finding ways out of dilemmas. Any task that you do to achieve some goal counts as a "problem" to a cognitive psychologist. Making it into bed at night solves a problem from this perspective; so does digging in your bag to find a pen. Chapter 10 will focus on the various processes that enable you to solve different kinds of problems. This section focuses on one particular approach to solving problems you encounter daily: making plans for the future.

For a cognitive psychologist, **planning** refers to any process of selecting actions that will help to achieve a specific goal before implementing those actions; this can also involve selecting the specific goal. Planning includes not just the sort of convoluted, multi-day logistics you might have to endure to take a trip to Disneyland but also more mundane activities like deciding to read the next few sentences. Implementing a plan depends on a kind of memory called prospective memory—remembering to perform an action at a specific point in the future (Guynn et al., 1998)—and sometimes can involve future episodic thinking, as described above.

Some elements of both planning and problem-solving are verbalizable and consciously accessible. Researchers have sometimes had subjects "think aloud" as they work toward a solution or develop a plan to try and better understand the otherwise hidden steps in cognitive activities (Kaplan & Simon, 1990). This approach, called the **think-aloud protocol**, can clarify what elements of a task a person is focusing on, the different options they are considering, and the specific strategies they are using to achieve a particular goal or to generate and evaluate new ideas (**Figure 9.8**).

Other elements of planning are less accessible to consciousness. For instance, if subjects were told to think aloud while planning a party and also to think aloud about how they construct the sentences they are producing to describe their thoughts, those participants would probably be unable to comply. Constructing a sentence that describes what you are thinking requires both introspection in

FIGURE 9.8. The think-aloud protocol. Having a problem solver verbalize what's going on inside their head can provide insights into the cognitive processes that precede a problem's solution. Recorded and subjectively evaluated observations of a person's actions and facial expressions during a problem-solving task provide further clues to ongoing mental processes, including reactions to confusion. This same procedure is often used to test the intuitiveness of a new software interface. (After http://www.imarklab.com/wp -content/uploads/2014/07 /tests_utilisateurs.jpg)

real time and organizing sequences of speech production that capture your observations. Talking requires planning, but that planning is usually hidden from the speaker and everyone else, other than perhaps psycholinguists.

Preparing to Speak

You may not think that much planning is happening when you're talking to your friends, especially when you accidentally say something you probably shouldn't have, or when you lose track of a point you were trying to make. Creating sentences often feels like it "just happens." It's only when circumstances force you to tread carefully that a dramatic pause reveals that thinking is preceding your speaking.

Usually, planning-related gaps in speech are taken up by an "uh" here and a "like" there, making the flow of speech seem more seamless. Transcripts reveal that most conversational speech is nothing like the sentences you're reading now. They, uh, can…you know…be…it's hard to say. Recorded speech provides clear evidence that whole sentences are not being planned out completely before a person starts speaking, aside from monologues and public speeches (Turk & Shattuck, 2020).

Subjectively, though, it may often feel like you know what you want to convey before you open your mouth. There is often a goal that leads you to speak and the specific words you produce are attempts to achieve that goal. So, how do you do it?

Details of language production and comprehension are laid out in Chapter 12. Here, the focus is on how you jump from thought to vocal acts or any acts, and in particular the tradeoffs between planning everything in advance versus just-in-time planning. Observations of when and how long gaps occur between spoken words have revealed that phrases are often produced in bursts—people seem to produce chunks of words, meaning that they probably first plan a bit of what to say and then say it (Sedivy, 2014).

Planning what you want to say seems to happen separately from planning how you are going to say it. There is a sequence of processing, even if it's usually happening quite fast (Morsella & Miozzo, 2002). And sometimes you may know exactly what you want to convey without being able to find the words to express it. Even if you do know the words, producing them requires specific actions to make the right sounds, a fact that becomes painfully obvious when people are trying to produce words in a foreign language they are just beginning to learn or are speaking with their mouths full of food.

Each of these three speech acts—deciding what to say, choosing the words to say it, and physically producing the sounds—could happen partly in parallel and partly sequentially. Plans for each of these processes may also take differing amounts of time to construct and implement. One way that researchers tease apart what has been planned prior to speech production is by analyzing speech errors (Gauvin & Hartsuiker, 2020).

Speakers tend to make certain kinds of speech errors more often than others, such as exchanging words within sentences or sounds within words (Meyer, 1992). By looking at how far apart in time such switched speech usually occurs, psychologists can get a better feel for how far in advance the production of specific words or speech sounds was planned (generally only a few seconds). Errors in which parts of words are switched, such as "don't *pet* the *sweaty* things," reveal that people assemble parts of words on the fly rather than just selecting words as whole units. The best-laid plans of a good thought may end in disaster when word selection or construction fails. This is well illustrated by several infamous statements made by President George W. Bush, such as, "I know how hard it is to put food on your family," and, "You cannot lead if you send mexed messages."

By analyzing large numbers of natural speech errors and by developing methods for causing such errors in the lab, psychologists have gradually put together various models of how people plan out spoken sentences. The basic process plays out in stages: first, the message to be communicated is planned, then the ordering of words is selected, next specific words are chosen, and finally, motor plans for making the speech sounds within those words are initiated (Blackmer & Mitton, 1991). These separate stages may occur in sequence or in parallel. For example, you might start planning a new message before you have finished producing all the speech sounds that convey an earlier idea (Bock, 1995; Levelt, 1992).

It may seem odd that you would plan the order of words you are going to say before you even know what words you will be saying. It's helpful to keep in mind that there are often many words that mean the same thing, and you can replace such words in a sentence without changing its meaning. Also, the kind of sentence you plan to produce can often determine which words will be in it. For instance, questions typically start with certain words. Finally, think about how you might text a sentence instead of saying it. The constraints of texting determine how you are likely to structure your message as well as the kinds of "words" you are likely to include. Texting obviously includes different motor planning processes than speaking, but the other stages of message construction can proceed in much the same way as when you speak.

Planning out Solutions

Linguists and psycholinguists have spent decades attempting to understand the planning processes that enable people to speak. Unfortunately, there are still many gaps in that understanding. It's unclear how far in advance people start planning a sentence, whether this window of planning varies over time, or how much of the planning process is automated versus voluntary and attention-demanding.

Part of the difficulty in understanding how sentences are planned may be that there are just so many different things one can say. To simplify the problem of studying planning, researchers have turned to more constrained tasks, such as having participants move disks on sticks (Philips et al., 2021; Unterrainer et al., 2020). In the **Tower of London task**, for example, a person is challenged to move disks around on rods to match a specific target arrangement (**Figure 9.9**). The difficulty of this puzzle problem can be increased or decreased in terms of the number of steps required to move from one configuration to another. The advantage of this task is that it has well-defined starting points and ending points, along with a limited number of predefined steps that a person can take when attempting to find a solution.

The Tower of London task was developed as a way to test planning abilities in individuals with frontal lobe damage (Cockburn, 1995). Some people with this type of damage show distinct problems with planning daily activities. For instance, a female chef who had a large tumor removed from her

FIGURE 9.9. The Tower of London task. (A) By having participants mentally simulate (and count) the number of moves required to get from "their board" to match a set of target stacks, researchers can (B) quantify the number of steps required to solve the task by participants of different ages and can also assess the contributions of mental imagery to peoples' problem-solving abilities. College students usually perform such tasks more efficiently than other people. (B after Piper et al., 2012)

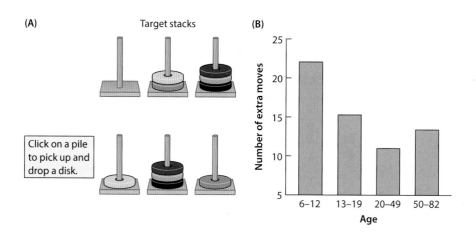

frontal cortex remained able to cook individual dishes after the surgery. But if she attempted to make more than one dish at a time, she was unable to switch between different tasks and ended up ruining all of them (Miller & Wallis, 2003).

There are a few rules to moving disks in the Tower of London task that make it a bit more challenging than it might at first look. Only disks without disks on top of them can be moved. There is also a physical limit to how many disks can be put on each stick. People with frontal lobe damage typically take more moves to solve the task than people without damage and may impulsively make moves before they have identified a solution to the problem (Unterrainer & Owen, 2006).

Your ability to solve a task like the Tower of London task may depend on your ability to imagine the possible configurations of disks that would result if you chose to move specific beads. In this case, your ability to consider, and perhaps visualize, different possible actions and their consequences can guide the sequence of actions that you select. These abilities develop gradually over time, such that the younger version of you would likely have found solving the task more difficult. Like patients with frontal lobe damage, young children's problem-solving capacities seem to be limited by their inability to resist moving disks before they have found a solution.

Interestingly, people who are instructed to solve a Tower of London puzzle in their minds before actually moving any disks solve significantly more of the problems than participants who are not given this instruction (Unterrainer et al., 2003), suggesting that peoples' default approaches to solving such problems are not always the most effective approach. Contrary to Nike's suggestion that people should "JUST DO IT," constructing a mental model of a plan before acting seems to provide some cognitive advantages.

Choice and Self-Control

Neuropsychological and developmental studies of peoples' performances in tasks like the Tower of London task show that your ability to self-monitor and control impulsive actions can greatly affect your ability to plan and solve problems, even insignificant ones like getting disks from one stick to another. **Impulsivity**, the tendency to act with minimal consideration of the consequences of acting, can also affect speech planning and production. Individuals with higher than typical impulsivity, such as people with attention deficit hyperactivity disorder, also show a reduced ability to stop talking (van den Wildenberg & Christoffels, 2010).

Your ability to mentally simulate future scenarios and consequences, basically imagining what things could be like, can be affected by ongoing pressing needs. Your plan of reading this chapter may be a step toward increasing your knowledge of thinking mechanisms so that you achieve a better understanding of cognition. However, if every few minutes you keep thinking, "I really do want a cupcake now," then your well-laid plans for mental improvement may be derailed. Monitoring your own actions during planning, and while you attempt to execute a plan, can be an important component of both planning and problem-solving. Sometimes you have to make adjustments; impulsive acts, thoughts, or feelings can be powerful plan disruptors.

Most of the daily choices you make don't require you to plan more than a few minutes into the future. Experiments examining the effects of impulsivity on choices often focus on this relatively short time frame and measure what an individual does when given the choice between one option that yields a small prize after a short interval and a second option that leads to a larger prize after a longer interval. Generally, subjects go for the short wait and are not too keen on waiting around for the larger prize (van Endert & Mohr, 2020).

One explanation for why most choose not to wait is that the value of a prize is discounted or viewed to be less valuable the longer you have to wait for it. Presumably, this is why lottery winners almost always chose the lump sum prize rather than yearly installments, even though winners who choose the "pile of cash now" option usually end up being bankrupt in a couple of years and always end up getting less free money. In a sense, such discounting is pragmatic since you never know when you might die. It's also irrational, though, since most prize-winners don't die immediately after winning.

A tricky thing about planning is that it's not always obvious when planning is happening. For instance, squirrels are famous for storing nuts during the fall so that they will have a food supply for the winter. This may seem like a straightforward case of the squirrel planning ahead for a winter food shortage; however, the squirrel doesn't necessarily have a goal. One way to test whether a squirrel's hoarding behavior is goal-driven is to consistently steal nuts from the squirrel's storage location (you can always return them later). Likely, the squirrel will keep putting more nuts there, as if oblivious to the fact that doing so is a waste of time.

People with addiction are like squirrels in that they end up repeating a behavior that ultimately does not lead to preferred outcomes. They usually know that their choices are leading to bad outcomes. The lack of self-control shown by those with an addiction suggests that their mechanisms of planning and choosing have become skewed relative to those without an addiction. Just as a prize can be discounted when it is far in the future, immediate gratification can also become exaggerated when it is right there for the taking. A cupcake in hand is worth ten in a cupcakery. Similarly, for a person with an addiction the effects of taking a drug in the present can easily outweigh any rewards in the more distant future that might be gained from not taking the drug.

Plans are one way of counteracting the powerful draw of immediate gratification (Liu et al., 2020). For example, if every morning the first thing a person with alcohol use disorder did was consume a substance that made the taste of alcohol provoke extreme pain and nausea, then it is unlikely that person would end up in a situation where taking a drink would be enticing. In that scenario, the execution of a deliberate plan effectively blocks future impulsive choices. This may sound like an extreme option, but there is a drug called Antabuse that, when taken, makes later consumption of alcohol extremely painful and unpleasant—basically it turns alcohol into poison.

Individuals vary in terms of how far in the future a reward can be delivered before it loses most of its subjective value (**Figure 9.10**). These individual differences can be experimentally measured by repeatedly offering a person a choice between smaller or larger rewards at varying delays (Holmes et al., 2016). Imagine something like a credit card that gives customers a choice between instant cash back on purchases versus reward points that after some time (weeks, months) can be exchanged for the same amount plus some bonus.

How big would a bonus prize need to be to convince people to wait for it? Someone who loves gambling may find the instant cash more attractive and so would need to be offered a larger bonus to prefer the delayed option. Adults or children with attention deficit hyperactivity disorder, who tend to be more impulsive, might also need a larger bonus.

This may make it seem like if you are impulsive, then you are doomed to be a poor planner. There are ways to counteract the cravings that lead to nonideal choices, however. One involves self-monitoring or keeping a close eye on the consequences of your actions. For instance, in one study of

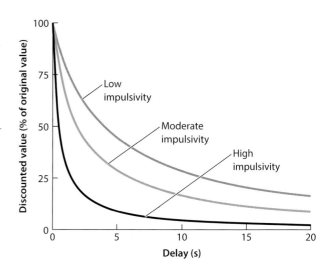

FIGURE 9.10. Individual differences in impulsivity. Everyone tends to view a rewarding outcome as less valuable the longer they have to wait for it, but people who are highly impulsive show a much stronger tendency to do this—they quickly discount the value of a future reward. (After McClure et al., 2014)

dieting, people were told to weigh themselves once a week and then to give away an amount of money equal to how much weight they lost that week. You might think this is a bad strategy because the best dieters end up being the poorest. As it turns out, this is a pretty effective way of getting people to lose weight (Castro & Rachlin, 1980). The reason why seems to be that giving away money amplifies the feedback given by the scale, making self-monitoring easier.

Of course, self-monitoring alone may not be enough to change the behavior of someone with a substance use disorder, especially in cases like compulsive gambling where the thrill of uncertainty is the driving force. Many states have taken advantage of this by offering lotteries for large sums of money as a way to capitalize on peoples' impulsive nature. In the case of lotteries, a mental image of what it would be like to be a megamillionaire in the near future is sufficient to convince many that spending a few dollars on a piece of cardboard is preferable to putting the money into a savings account.

Imagining a lottery win is a case of episodic future thinking that can lead to poor choices. There are other situations where this kind of daydreaming about possible futures can counteract impulsivity, however. In fact, the more vivid the imagery, the more attractive waiting for a later reward becomes (Peters & Büchel, 2010). For instance, women at an unhealthy weight who were first instructed to imagine possible future events at specified time points, and then later reminded of their visualizations using audio recordings while at a buffet of high-calorie foods, consumed fewer calories than women who instead were asked to imagine past episodes and given similar reminders (Daniel et al., 2013). So if you do end up heading to a cupcakery, perhaps you should stop on the way to buy a lottery ticket and then pull out the ticket while you're choosing which sugary treat to purchase. Your advance planning and future thinking may help you to avoid a sugar bomb later on!

Episodic future thinking is key to developing a plan as well as for choosing steps that are likely to be remembered and implemented at an appropriate point in the future. Using Post-it notes to remind a future you to complete some chore may not seem like much of a cognitive feat, but it likely requires thinking skills beyond what most organisms possess. You have to imagine the future you finding the reminder, which means knowing something about where you're likely to go, what you're likely to see, how you're likely to respond to a note from yourself, and so on.

Planning is more than just listing steps like in a recipe. Planning often requires a kind of personalized prospective memory that can guide specific sequences of actions designed to meet individualized goals in a designated time and place. Planning can also involve making conscious decisions and predicting their consequences, the topic of Chapter 10. Lots of plans don't require this level of deliberation, however, like when you make a sandwich or talk to your friends about how great your sandwich is.

SIGHT BITES

 Some plans are verbalizable while others that guide daily activities, like navigating and speaking, are not consciously accessible.

 Simple problem-solving tasks such as the Tower of London provide a window into the ways that mental images can enhance or degrade pre-planning of actions.

 Impulsivity can interfere with planning processes, biasing choices toward instant gratification and initiating actions before the consequences become clear.

Creativity

SNEAK PEEK: Understanding how people come up with new ideas and the relationship between insights, perception, and memory requires a variety of approaches that push the limits of cognitive psychological research.

The Imagineers employed by the Walt Disney Company are professional planners. Their job is to come up with new designs that "turn fantasy into reality"—to create plans for a future that diverges from the status quo.

Imagineering is a kind of inventing, and inventing is a creative cognitive process. You only need to glance at the world around you to encounter hundreds of creative products of imagineering. You are immersed in inventions: clothes, chairs, computers, schools, buildings, cities, and more. And you spend most of your waking hours interacting with the products of human creativity. Almost everything entertaining in your life comes from people's imaginative constructions: movies, art, music, comedy, sports, parks, games, and so on. Humans have collectively created your world.

When you think of creativity, you are likely to think of rock stars in areas you're familiar with, such as Oscar-winning directors, Nobel Prize-winning scientists, billionaire technologists from Silicon Valley, or actual Grammy-winning rock stars. These are the creators that pop out either in modern magazines or historical timelines—role models who inspire new humans to set their own creative goals. Because these larger-than-life icons of creativity are so widely idolized, it's easy to fall into the trap of thinking of creativity as a specialized talent that a few lucky individuals are born with, somewhat like genius-level intelligence.

Variations in Creative Potential

People definitely differ with respect to how much their creative products impact society and cultural development. It's unclear though how much peoples' genetic profiles or unique brain qualities contribute to their successes as artists, inventors, or scientists. Cultures also differ in terms of the creative acts they recognize and encourage (Niu & Kaufman, 2013).

Intelligence and personality are often linked to creativity (Barron & Harrington, 1981; Frith et al., 2021). Some minimal threshold of intelligence seems to be a prerequisite for creative acts and highly creative people tend to also be independent, unconventional, open to new experiences, and a bit mentally unstable (Furnham & Bachtiar, 2008). Undoubtedly, some children are more likely to construct imaginary social circles than others or to spend more time staring at clouds. But connections between such tendencies and later creative successes are not well established.

As with intelligence, several tests have been developed to quantify the relative creativity of different people. In the Remote Associates Test, for example, you would be presented with sets of three words (say, "room," "blood," "salts") and then asked to think of a fourth word that links to all three. This test rates creativity based on one's ability to rapidly come up with a correct solution. The Alternative Uses Task, in contrast, requires test takers to generate as many uses as possible when verbally presented with the name or picture of an object (like a spoon), and the number of plausible suggestions is used to gauge creativity. Like intelligence tests, there is debate about whether a person's creativity can be adequately measured using such standardized tests.

The idea that creativity is a resource or trait that a few special humans have at their disposal is increasingly being questioned by psychologists (Runco, 2009; Simonton, 2012). An alternative possibility is that creative processes are more the result of interactions between individuals and the circumstances they find themselves in. Although the idea that necessity is the mother of invention may have some truth in it, it's also the case that free time fosters flexible minds.

How you spend your time can affect your creative potential. Mental control practices, such as meditation, guided visualization, mindfulness training (see Chapter 3), or simply staring at waves on the beach, can affect the kinds of new ideas you are likely to have (Ding et al., 2014). Similarly, the expertise you acquire as you go through life strongly determines the kinds of innovations or inventions you are likely to create.

The importance of experience in creative cognitive processes is most clearly evident in problem-solving. Engineers go through years of training precisely because such experiences enable them to develop effective solutions to new problems. At one level, all the inventions that make modern life possible are tools designed to solve problems. Some are simply tools for avoiding boredom or unpleasantness, while others, like computers, are tools for making more tools.

Imagery also can be an important contributor to inventiveness (Palmiero et al., 2016). For example, students asked to use imagery to combine simple forms into interesting-looking novel "tools" (**Figure 9.11**), were subsequently able to assign potential functions to the created tools that others judged to be creative inventions (Finke et al., 1992). Similar processes may contribute to the unique contraptions that children construct using toys like Legos or Play-Doh.

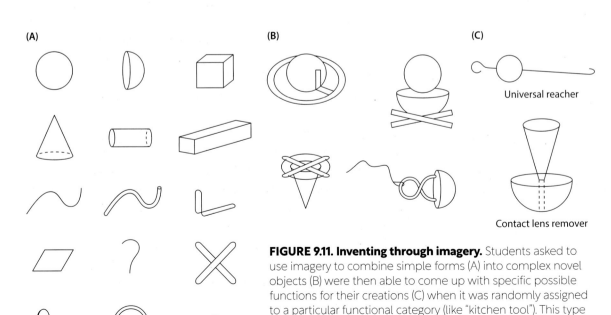

(A)   (B)   (C)

Universal reacher

Contact lens remover

FIGURE 9.11. Inventing through imagery. Students asked to use imagery to combine simple forms (A) into complex novel objects (B) were then able to come up with specific possible functions for their creations (C) when it was randomly assigned to a particular functional category (like "kitchen tool"). This type of pre-planned imagery exercise can potentially facilitate creative thinking. (A–C from Finke et al., 1992)

Producing new ideas, or creative thinking, is sometimes viewed as a magical process, based more on intuition or gifts from the gods than on reasoning, mental imagery, or logic. Many psychological studies of creative thinking focus on demystifying the mechanisms that let people think thoughts that few have thought before. A common theme among modern psychological studies of creativity is that creative thinking relies on pretty much the same mechanisms as all kinds of thinking, including the kinds of imagery and episodic future thinking processes described above (Beaty et al., 2016; Boden, 2004).

Part of the reason why creative solutions seem special, however, is that when a person encounters a solution to a problem that they did not foresee, there is often a unique emotional feeling of realization and understanding, where the pieces of a puzzle fall into place to create a coherent, understandable whole—the "Aha! Now I get it!" experience. Understanding this transition from the "I'm confused" state you feel when facing a difficult problem to the confident feeling of certainty you have after discovering a solution is a major focus of psychological studies of creative insight.

Creative Insight

Historically notable scientists are often described as having had flashes of inspiration that revealed a solution to a seemingly insurmountable problem. There's the tale of Isaac Newton spontaneously conceiving of gravity when a falling apple bonked him in the head, and the classic story of Archimedes streaking through the streets naked yelling "Eureka!" after suddenly realizing a way to tell whether a crown was made of pure gold. ("Eureka" is Greek for, "I found it.")

When solutions to problems are straightforward, finding them is usually described as knowing the answer. When solutions to difficult problems are discovered, however, the solutions are more likely to be described as creative insights. It's possible that someone could stumble onto the solution for a problem that they didn't even know was a problem, but most solutions are discovered by people actively attempting to solve a problem or who had been doing so at an earlier time.

Recognition that a problem exists is generally a conscious experience; so is the effortful task of trying to come up with a solution. The actual processes that produce a solution, in contrast, can often be unconscious. In fact, putting a problem aside (out of sight and out of mind), in a process called **incubation**, can make it easier to discover a solution (Hélie & Sun, 2010). Incubation can last from minutes to decades. The effectiveness of incubation can be affected by clues that are encountered during the incubation period. Misleading clues can reduce the likelihood of a solution being unconsciously discovered while informative clues can increase the probability of constructing a novel solution.

The odd thing about incubation is that when solutions to a problem are discovered, they seem to just pop into your head spontaneously, like if you had randomly found a one-hundred-dollar bill lying in the grass while walking in a park. This kind of rapid mental transition is what led such solutions to be called insights or illumination because it's as if someone suddenly flipped a light switch revealing a previously invisible scene. It also may be why the modern symbol of idea formation is a light bulb coming on over a person's head.

Cognitive psychologists have studied the processes that lead to insight by designing experiments in which participants are presented with relatively simple **insight problems** for which solutions are often suddenly discovered (Bowden et al., 2005). When thinking aloud about how close they feel to solving such problems (saying "cold" when they have no clue and then raising the temperature as they close in on the solution), participants attempting to solve insight problems usually report that they are "cold" up until the moment they realize the solution.

Some of the most famous insight problems have been studied in chimpanzees. Most notably, the German psychologist Wolfgang Köhler (1887–1967) conducted a series of experiments in which he would hang fruit from a ceiling and then provide a group of chimpanzees with various tools such as boxes and sticks that they could use to get to the fruit (Köhler, 1925). Initially, the chimpanzees would ignore the tools and simply try to jump to get the fruit, eventually giving up. After a relatively short incubation period, some chimpanzees would start glancing between the fruit and the tools in the

FIGURE 9.12. Chimpanzees' insightful solutions.
When faced with problems that cannot possibly be solved without using tools, chimpanzees sometimes discover unique ways of using objects as tools to achieve their goals. The novelty and usefulness of these solutions qualify them as creative, and the fact that they are impromptu identifies them as insights. (American Philosophical Society/Science Photo Library)

enclosure (visual clues to a solution), after which a chimpanzee might switch tactics and begin trying various ways of using the tools to get to the fruit (**Figure 9.12**).

The chimps' inventive solutions to obtaining high-hanging fruits were most impressive because they were novel and useful. These are probably the main qualities that distinguish any solution as being creative. Interestingly, like humans, chimpanzees showed distinct individual differences in their ability to come up with creative solutions to this problem. One chimpanzee in particular, named Sultan, appeared to be the Da Vinci of the group.

Note that the creative solutions discovered by Köhler's chimpanzees seem consistent with a combination of future episodic thinking and planning. Certainly, if adult humans came up with the exact same solutions in a similar context, it's likely that the thinking they engaged in while discovering these solutions would be described as involving both cognitive processes.

Current theories of creative problem-solving emphasize interactions between both deliberate attempts at conceptualizing problems and unconscious mechanisms for finding solutions. Most explanations of problem-solving assume some sort of search through a set of mental representations that are linked together by learned associations. The main differences among the different explanations relate to how the search is implemented and the mechanisms that determine when an option is identified as a solution.

Some creative thoughts are less about finding an answer that works and more about exploring what might be possible. For instance, a young child's crayon scribblings are less about solving a problem than they are about discovering what happens when you twirl your hand around while holding a colored wax stick. Nevertheless, these sorts of novel acts by children can be entertaining for them and can help them to discover new ways of creating images that they like. Creative improvisation of this sort can still lead to insights but seems to rely more on cognitive flexibility than on a mental search for an answer.

Improvisation

Improvisation is the process of acting creatively and on the spur of the moment (Lewis & Lovatt, 2013). What distinguishes improvisation from most other acts of creativity is that improvisational actions are spontaneous rather than planned out in advance; basically, improvisation is creativity in real time. In comedy, improvisation means trying to say something funny on the fly. In music, it means trying to create interesting music based on momentary inspirations.

To pull off an improvised creative act, the improviser must think in ways that are not totally predictable. Thinking in ways that deviate from the norm is called **divergent thinking**. Several standardized measures of divergent thinking exist, such as the Alternate Uses Task, described above. Divergent thinking is also associated with **cognitive flexibility**, which refers to the capacity to hold multiple thoughts in mind simultaneously or to rapidly switch between trains of thought.

Intuitively, you might expect that years of training might lock people into certain ways of thinking and performing that are dictated by the standards of their domain of expertise, with practice either making perfect or at least digging some deep mental ruts. If the training is in an area that specifically requires improvisation, however, such as playing chess or jazz music, increased expertise tends to increase improvisational skills as well as performance on divergent thinking tasks (Przysinda et al., 2017). There is also evidence that processes of forgetting can catalyze creativity (Storm & Patel, 2014), suggesting that perhaps accomplished improvisers are better able to live in the moment.

In most everyday contexts, divergent thinking is unwelcome. Conformity and convergent thinking are much more socially acceptable. Some amazingly creative individuals, such as Isaac Newton and Leonardo da Vinci, tend to confirm the stereotype of the creative genius as a social outcast (freaks and geeks). Surprisingly, this social bias also holds true within groups of geeks. Scientists in particular tend to dismiss novel interpretations of data, instead favoring those findings and explanations that mostly confirm their prior expectations.

Expertise does not immunize you from a bias toward convergent thinking, but it can give you an advantage in terms of discovering new solutions to difficult problems. Generally, the more expertise one has in a particular area, the easier it is to recognize the limitations of existing solutions to problems in that area. The more you learn, the more obvious gaps in existing knowledge become. Awareness of such knowledge "holes" can provide the clues and motivation necessary to develop new ways of thinking about a problem. Expertise can also provide you with the confidence and skills to explore new directions and to ask questions that others might find too overwhelming to even consider.

Ironically, extreme expertise can be a handicap. Albert Einstein's doctoral dissertation was initially rejected because his committee members could not follow his arguments. This is partly why he was working as a patent clerk when he made some of his most creative discoveries. Music critics initially described the Beatles' music as appallingly unmusical and hoarsely incoherent. Exceptional creativity seems to lie in the eye of the beholder.

On the other hand, most people encounter novel problems in their daily lives that they deal with handily. Spontaneity and creativity in everyday interactions are sometimes referred to as little-c creativity (Sternberg & Kaufman, 2018). Little-c creativity includes things like making a casserole out of unique combinations of leftovers or performing a comical reenactment of how different family members responded while eating said casserole. Little-c creativity is also what teachers tend to encourage in school when students work on an art project or writing assignment.

Current cognitive models of improvisation often assume that the mechanisms that make little-c creativity possible are the same ones underlying the thinking of creative giants like Frida Kahlo or Duke Ellington. This is partly pragmatic, since most cognitive studies of creativity involve experiments conducted with volunteer undergraduates. However, case studies of famous creative individuals provide some support for the idea that their creative thought processes are not radically different from the ones people engage in during everyday creative acts (Csikszentmihalyi, 1997).

Improvisation ultimately involves selecting and generating actions or thoughts in potentially novel combinations. To the extent that planning or memory searches are involved in spontaneous creative acts, they are necessarily very rapid. Learning to improvise seems more about free-styling than about gaining deep insights. In line with this view, other animals, such as dolphins, show the ability to flexibly improvise actions on command (Dudzkinski et al., 2018). Like jazz musicians, dolphins can

FIGURE 9.13. Creative cousins.
Surfing humans and dolphins rapidly adjust their wave-driven movements in ways that can vary greatly in terms of variety, difficulty, and novelty. What measures might a surfing judge use to compare the improvisational skills of humans versus dolphins? (muratart via Shutterstock)

even collaboratively improvise complex action sequences (Herman, 2002), suggesting that creative thinking may be a cognitive skill that is useful across a broad range of circumstances. And dolphins are not limited to collaborating with each other. They have also figured out ways to creatively collaborate with humans, as described in the Applied Perspectives section of this chapter (**Figure 9.13**).

Collaborative creativity works well for jazz and blues musicians improvising in a bar but may be less effective in other circumstances. For instance, brainstorming is a popular approach for enhancing creative idea generation by groups attempting to work together to solve some problem. During a brainstorming session, participants are supposed to engage in "blue-sky" thinking, ignoring practical constraints and not worrying about how unrealistic their ideas might sound or be. This approach often generates lots of ideas, most of which are worthless. Surprisingly, the number of ideas generated within such think tanks usually ends up being fewer than if individuals in the group tried to come up with as many ideas as possible on their own (Diehl & Stroebe, 1987). Additionally, if a few dominant individuals strongly support a particular idea, then this can lead to groupthink, such that the group members come to favor a mediocre idea over more creative or useful options (Turner & Pratkanis, 1998).

It should be clear by now that there is a strong relationship between creativity and imagination. Imagination involves constructing mental images, often in novel combinations. Consequently, you might imagine that a person's imagery capacities might be predictive of their creativity. And you would be right. Creative processes can be triggered by intensely vivid imagery—especially imagery that diverges from everyday perception (Chavez, 2016) and is controllable (like with lucid dreaming). In the last decade, research on creativity and imagination has begun to merge (Jankowska & Karwowski, 2015), providing new clues to the relationship between imagery and creativity that may soon awaken new insights within the minds of cognitive researchers.

SIGHT BITES

Creative thinking depends on the same cognitive mechanisms as everyday thought, some of which are consciously controlled and some of which are unconscious.

Insight problems—problems that are often solved in a flash of inspiration—have enabled psychologists to study how creativity contributes to such flashes.

Creativity is often about finding solutions to problems, but it can also be a way of exploring novel ways of acting or generating new problems.

BRAIN SUBSTRATES

SNEAK PEEK: Someday soon, it may become possible to detect when you are dreaming and identify what you are dreaming while you sleep. Maximizing your creative potential means more than just doing your best. Multiple regions of your brain must coordinate their activities in the right way.

At one time or another, you may have been encouraged to ramp up your creativity or imaginative efforts by expanding your horizons, freeing your mind, or letting some unspecified juices flow. These metaphors all relate to letting loose thought-wise.

It's not exactly clear, however, what sorts of cognitive processes such instructions might unleash. Do you let your attention run wild or do you search your memories more exhaustively? Are you actively breaking down preconceptions or are you throwing a mish-mash of mental ingredients together to see what comes out? Or maybe you are just doing the same thing you were doing before the encouragement but exerting a bit more mental effort.

Researchers are attempting to get a better handle on what happens when you tell a person to "be creative" or to "use your imagination" by monitoring how a person's brain activity changes when that person is presented with tasks thought to provoke creativity. By tracking brain changes as mental images arise or as creative ideas emerge, psychologists can gain objective evidence about how internally driven experiences differ from externally driven thoughts and percepts. They can also collect evidence about whether creative thinking and mental imaging might depend on unique patterns of brain activity.

It's impossible to see or measure what people are thinking by watching blood or electricity move through their brains. It may be possible, however, to predict when they are most likely to be experiencing vivid images or particularly original ideas. And knowing what your brain does when generating such mental experiences may make it possible to use new technologies to artificially increase your ability to think novel thoughts and to imagine fantastical scenarios.

Imaging of Imagery

The holodeck is a fictional virtual reality technology originally featured in *Star Trek* that allows users to see, hear, and feel objects, as well as artificially intelligent agents, in all sorts of complex scenarios. In essence, holodecks provide a way for people to dream while awake by immersing themselves in a technologically generated fantasy world. Modern day role-playing games and video games represent initial steps toward the kinds of experiences that holodecks make possible, as do lucid dreams and internet pornography.

"Come with me, and you'll be, in a world of pure imagination... living there you'll be free, if you truly wish to be."
—Gene Wilder as Willy Wonka, 1971

Dreams and hallucinations show that brains possess the capacity to simulate a wide range of experiences without external inputs, somewhat like an internalized holodeck. Not all modalities are equally likely to be featured in dreams, however, and even within a modality, some experiences occur less frequently than others. The content and quality of dreams vary considerably across life spans and across individuals. Why? To answer this question, you need to know a bit more about what happens inside your head when you construct mental images.

Visual Imagery

One question that has dominated many studies of mental imagery is whether the same brain regions that become active during perception are also active when you imagine the corresponding experience. William James noted that in awake states, people rarely mistake percepts for imagined events or vice-versa; this suggests that either sensations and imagined events are processed by different circuits,

FIGURE 9.14. Brain regions involved in visual imagery and perception. Cortical regions that are active during perception (green-blue) overlap with those engaged by visual imagery (orange) but tend to be focused in the occipital cortex. (From Dijkstra et al., 2017, and Wang et al. 2019, *J Neurosci* © 2019 by the authors [CC-BY-4.0])

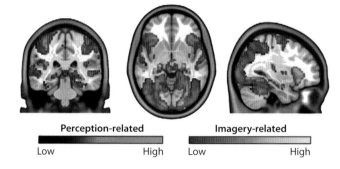

Perception-related
Low   High

Imagery-related
Low   High

or if both experiences arise from the same brain regions, then the brain activity associated with mental images and percepts must differ in some way.

Neuroimaging experiments suggest that both possibilities occur (Dijkstra et al., 2019; Xie et al., 2020). There is substantial overlap in the brain regions that become active when people perceive or imagine similar objects or events, but the overlap is not complete. And the cortical regions that are most active during perception differ from those that are most active during imagining (**Figure 9.14**).

People who report vivid visual imagery tend to show higher levels of brain activity in early processing in the visual cortex (Lee et al., 2012)). In addition, when both seeing and imagining certain objects generate similar brain activity in the visual cortex, the reports of the imagined object are more vivid. Some imagined "objects," such as faces, are consistently reported as being less vivid than others, such as letters or numbers. Overall, variation in vividness shows up as differences in activity throughout the cerebral cortex (Milton et al., 2021; Spagna et al., 2021).

Many different regions of the cerebral cortex become active when you see an object (see Chapters 2 and 4), including your occipital lobe followed by parts of your parietal, temporal, and frontal lobes. These same regions become active when you imagine an object but to a lesser degree. One of the main differences in cortical activation when you imagine seeing an object is that there is relatively more activity in later processing (in the parietal and frontal lobes) compared to activity in visual cortical pathways (see Figure 9.14). Consequently, the overlap between the processing of mental images and the processing of percepts grows as you move further away from the process of sensory transduction.

A neuroimaging technique called multivoxel pattern analysis (MVPA) has made it possible to more closely examine how cortical activity during perception differs from activity while imagining. This approach involves using computer programs to try and match high-resolution patterns of cortical activation (typically measured with fMRI) to subjectively experienced images. When MVPA works, this type of pattern analysis can identify the specific object a person has seen based on what their brain was doing while they saw it (Ragni et al., 2020). If the same pattern analysis program succeeds at identifying what object a person was imagining based on the brain activity that occurred while they imagined it, then this provides a good reason to believe that there are common patterns of cortical activity occurring during both visual perception and visual imagery that are specific to the object that was "seen" (Horikawa & Kamitani, 2017; Rakhimberdina et al., 2021).

MVPA results provide further evidence that seeing an object and imagining an object activate similar cortical circuits in similar ways. But seeing a photo definitely feels different from imagining what that photo shows, and mental images can be mentally transformed in ways that percepts of photos cannot. So, what is happening in your brain that distinguishes imagination from perception? Studies of motor imagery provide some clues.

Beyond Visions

Just as neuroimaging can be used to track brain activity during visual imagery, it can also be used to explore brain activity during motor imagery (Hétu et al., 2013). One unique aspect of motor imagery studies is that actions are often guided by expectations of what producing the actions will feel like (kinesthetic images), making it possible to study both automatic and intentional motor imagery. Percepts of actions often include consistent temporal patterning that visual percepts of objects do not, making it easier to compare mental images of action sequences to brain activity that occurs when a person either observes or performs those same sequences (Palmiero et al., 2019; Savaki & Raos, 2019).

The brain regions active during motor imagery have been more precisely identified than for visual imagery (**Figure 9.15**). As with visual imagery, cortical circuits in the frontal and parietal lobes are heavily involved in motor imagery. Unlike visual imagery, the motor cortex rarely becomes active during motor imagery while subcortical regions, including the cerebellum and basal ganglia, often do (Hétu et al., 2013). The specific constellation of brain regions involved in motor imagery depends on which body parts are used, how familiar the action is, and how precisely the movements need to be spatially controlled.

When you imagine performing an action, you are likely to not only imagine what it feels like to move in a certain way but also what it might look like and what the consequences of that movement will be. For instance, if you imagine jumping, you might also imagine how your visual inputs will change as you move up and down and the impact of your feet returning to the floor. This could involve a wide range of brain regions beyond just those needed to control your actions.

Learned consequences of specific motor sequences make it possible to study in greater detail what happens cortically during the imagination of sensory events. For instance, in one recent experiment, researchers placed an array of electrodes directly on the temporal lobe (where the auditory cortex is located) of a professional keyboard player who was undergoing a neurosurgical procedure (Martin et al., 2018). This approach to recording brain activity, called electrocorticography (ECoG), makes it possible to track neural activity much more precisely over time than is possible with fMRI.

The researchers asked the musician to play memorized classical pieces on a keyboard while he listened to himself play through headphones, creating a normal musical experience (well, as normal as it can be after someone has just removed part of your skull). Then they asked him to play the same pieces on the keyboard without listening to anything through the headphones but instead imagining what sounds his key presses would normally generate. This allowed the researchers to make sure that all physical actions were comparable and that the main difference was whether the musician was directly perceiving the music or constructing an auditory image of the music. The precise timing of key presses also made it possible to measure what the musician's brain was doing at the exact time when he was imagining specific chords, notes, or rhythms.

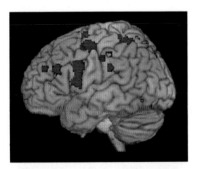
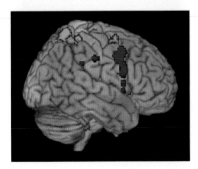

FIGURE 9.15. Cortical contributions to motor imagery.
Regions of the cortex shown in red are consistently activated during many motor imagery tasks. Activity is distributed rather than concentrated in a specialized motor imagery module. (From Hétu et al., *Neurosci & Biobehav Revs* 37, ©2013, with permission from Elsevier)

This ECoG experiment revealed that temporal lobe activity that occurred when the musician imagined his keystrokes was highly similar to the activity that occurred when he could actually hear the music. In fact, using an approach similar to MVPA, it was possible to identify individual notes that the musician was imagining from recordings of cortical activity alone. As observed in visual imagery studies, regions farther along in auditory processing showed relatively more activity for imagined sounds and more overlap with auditory perception. Importantly, how neurons in the auditory cortex responded to imagined sounds was basically the same as how they responded to sounds heard through the headphones, suggesting that differences in the intensity of responding across multiple brain regions are likely key factors that distinguish imagined experiences from percepts of events.

Dream Reading

Comparing percepts to intentional imagery provides a way to gain insights into neural activity common to both processes. This does not tell you what has to happen for an imagined experience to contribute to conscious thought processes, however. For example, if you wanted to check and see if a cat was imagining a missing toy and thought that you might be able to figure this out by monitoring the cat's brain activity, what exactly would you look for?

Researchers are beginning to identify the neural signatures of mental imagery by monitoring peoples' electroencephalogram (EEG) patterns while they sleep and by identifying what patterns are reliably associated with dreaming (Siclari et al., 2017). They have identified a "hot zone" in the back of the brain (where the occipital and parietal lobes meet) that can be monitored and used to determine when a person is dreaming with about 90% accuracy (**Figure 9.16**). In principle, there might be similar neural dream markers in other animals, though this has yet to be investigated. Interestingly, electrical stimulation of the hot zone while a person is awake can create the feeling of being in a parallel world (Koch et al., 2016).

In addition to being able to detect *when* sleepers are dreamers, researchers are beginning to be able to decipher *what* dreamers are seeing in their dreams. As noted earlier, it's possible to track people's eye movements as they dream, and in this way, gain some information about the internal images they are viewing. If you also record their EEG patterns in the hot zone, you can predict from the spatial distribution of activity across the scalp whether a person's dreams include faces, places, or movements. The patterns of cortical activity that predict these kinds of details match spatially the areas most activated during visual perception of these same features (see Chapters 4 and 5).

Dream content has also been predicted using neuroimages collected in fMRI studies (Horikawa et al., 2013). Specifically, MVPA was used to classify natural images in awake subjects and then applied to neuroimages collected while a person was sleeping. The image classifiers proved capable of predicting what a person would say they were dreaming about when woken up during a dream, again

FIGURE 9.16. A hot zone for dream detection. EEG patterns in the rear of the brain provide the best indicators of when a person is dreaming, serving as a neural signature of mental imagery during unconsciousness. (From Siclari et al., 2017, *Nat Neurosci* 20, reproduced with permission from SNCSC)

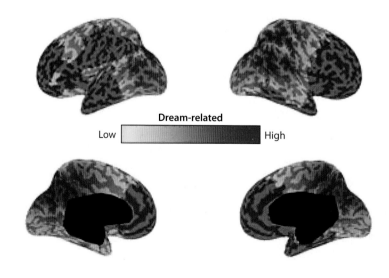

suggesting that the neural activity driving imagery within dreams is consistent with the activity that drives perception (and imagery) when people are awake.

Researchers studying imagery in dreamers have an advantage; there are effectively no ongoing external inputs (or motor acts) competing with imagery mechanisms. This lack of competition provides a relatively clear glimpse into the world of pure imagination. With a few more technological advances and an increasing understanding of how mental imagery mechanisms operate, it may one day be possible to automatically transcribe the contents of your dreams as easily as you can now record yourself speaking! And if you think you sound funny when you hear a recording of yourself talking, wait until you see all the bizarro scenarios happening in your dreams.

Stimulating Creativity

Kids in elementary school are often reprimanded for staring off into space. The thinking is that they should be paying attention to what's going on in the classroom instead of daydreaming about cupcakes. Researchers are becoming increasingly aware, however, that **mind wandering**, or involuntary streams of conscious thought, is key to creative thinking (Baird et al., 2012; Smith et al., 2022).

About half the time, when minds wander they are wandering toward the future. In other words, zoning out is often a case of spontaneous episodic future thinking (SEFT). As you might imagine, this occasionally happens when people are sitting (or lying) in a laboratory waiting for something to happen, which has made it possible for neuroimagers to observe what brains do when you're off in never-never land.

The Default Mode Network

The brain regions that become most active during mind wandering are called the **default mode network (DMN)**. The network consists of multiple brain regions in the frontal, parietal, and temporal lobes that show synchronous increases and decreases in activity (**Figure 9.17**). In addition to becoming active when you are imagining a trip to the beach, the default mode network also contributes to a host of other cognitive tasks, such as remembering past events, thinking about yourself and others,

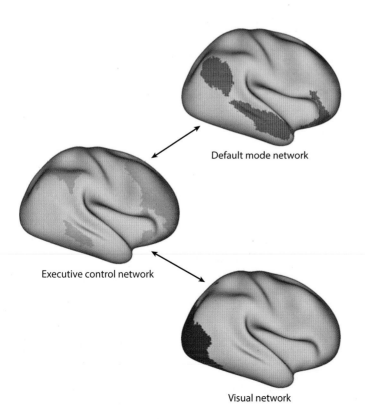

Default mode network

Executive control network

Visual network

FIGURE 9.17. Creativity networks. The default mode network and executive control network each contribute to creative thinking. The default mode network is linked to the generation of different possibilities while the executive control network is thought to contribute to the evaluation of the relative viability of different options. Visual imagery in a visual network also plays a role. (From Beaty et al., 2019, *Curr Opin Behav Sci* 27, © 2019, with permission from Elsevier)

imagining scenarios, and understanding stories (Smallwood et al., 2021). This network shuts down when people perform many laboratory tasks that involve focusing on simple visual or verbal stimuli across multiple trials, an experience that is arguably the opposite of imagining being on a beach.

When researchers monitored the default mode network as participants performed standardized divergent thinking tasks, they discovered that this network became increasingly active during tasks that required the generation and evaluation of creative ideas (Beaty et al., 2016). It is possible to predict how creative and open-minded people are based on how different brain regions in their default mode network are connected, both in terms of how synchronously the regions become active (Beaty et al., 2018) and how strongly they are physically connected (Beaty et al., 2019). Brain regions in the default mode network that fire together apparently inspire together.

Notably, many of the brain regions within the default mode network are also known to contribute to memory processing (see Chapter 8), which has led to the idea that guided memory retrieval is an important element of creative cognition. So, while mind wandering is mostly spontaneous, creativity is usually a bit more intentional. You're looking for a novel solution or source of entertainment, and a free-for-all may not get you there. Radical thinking or brainstorming may help you to generate options, but you need additional processes to judge whether any of those options are worth considering. Unicorns are nice; horses with a tentacle hanging off the side of their head, not so much.

The Executive Control Network

The **executive control network (ECN)** is a second set of brain regions that have been implicated in creative thought. The executive control network is thought to be the seat of cognitive control (see Chapters 8 and 10), making it possible for you to brush aside those generic ideas that most people come up with when trying to pick a Halloween costume so that you can find one that is truly and uniquely you. In the context of creative thought, cognitive control is a combination of selection and suppression. The regions associated with the executive control network are, again, mostly cortical and spread throughout the brain in the same lobes as the default mode network (see Figure 9.17).

You may have noticed that the role played by the executive control network is quite similar to the mechanisms of selective attention described in Chapter 4. In fact, thinking of the executive control network as a system for selectively attending to some thoughts and not to others is probably a good way to think about it. That could include attending to mental images of the sort described earlier.

The effectiveness of attempts at being creative seems to depend on tight coordination between the executive control network and default mode network, with the executive control network suppressing external inputs and dumb ideas while the default mode network activates, compares, and recombines various memory-based mental representations (Chrysikou, 2019). The implication of these neuroscientific findings is that specific patterns of cortical interactions can make creative thought easier or harder.

Coordination between cortical networks can be increased through practice and some research suggests that repeatedly engaging in creatively taxing tasks such as the Alternative Uses Task can change how these brain regions interact (**Figure 9.18**).

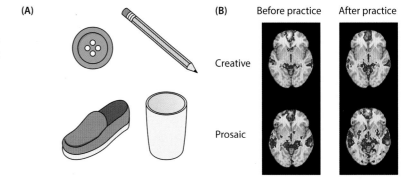

FIGURE 9.18. Creative brain changes. (A) Repeatedly performing the Alternative Uses Task in which you are asked to come up with many uses for everyday objects (like a cup) can lead to changes in the relative activation of frontal cortical regions (B), with changes being more prominent in individuals who initially show lower creativity. (A after, B from Wu et al., 2020)

Creative States

Coordinated activity within the default mode network and the executive control network is correlated with more effective divergent thinking and creativity. Might this mean that increasing synchronous activity in these networks can boost creative capacity? Some evidence consistent with this possibility comes from studies monitoring and manipulating brain activity in these regions.

For instance, it's possible to monitor EEG patterns (generated by cortical activity) that are present just before a person starts a divergent thinking task or as they are solving insight problems. By observing certain EEG patterns, researchers can predict whether the subject will come up with more ideas or find an insightful solution to a problem (Stevens & Zabelina, 2020), and certain mind-wandering activities and memory tasks can be used to promote such patterns (Baird et al., 2012). So in principle, you can put yourself in a particular state of mind (brain state) before attempting to think creatively, and that will potentially make the process easier and more effective.

Some of the brain states that are most conducive to creativity are not necessarily brain states you would want to experience, however. Links between creativity and mental disorders have been a major focus of psychological research over the past century, with a heavy emphasis on schizophrenia and bipolar disorder. In part, this is because these disorders are more common in artistic professions associated with creativity. The mentally imbalanced genius has also become a cliché, immortalized in such films as *A Beautiful Mind* in which a highly creative economist battles with paranoid delusions.

The connections between creativity and mental disorders are still unclear. There is increasing evidence that at least one factor associated with disordered thinking is also predictive of creativity, however: levels of dopamine in the brain (Zabelina et al., 2016). Chapters 2 and 7 note that dopamine is a neuromodulator often associated with pleasant experiences—increases in dopamine signify that the good times are rolling. Patients with lower levels of dopamine show greater impulsivity, especially with respect to repeating default actions, and also perform worse on divergent thinking tasks. Low dopamine levels in the executive control network can also lead to a creative block, and genetic profiles associated with reduced dopaminergic sensitivity are predictive of reduced creativity (Feist, 2019).

This relationship between dopamine and creativity may have sparked an insight within you that drugs that increase dopamine could potentially be used to boost creativity. You're not alone! Many companies are already marketing nootropics (smart drugs) as a way of increasing creativity, all of which work by changing the levels of neurochemicals, including dopamine, in your brain. However, while it is well established that having lower-than-average dopamine levels degrades some forms of creativity, there is no definitive evidence showing that having abnormally high levels enhances your creative thought processes. On the contrary, this can potentially disrupt your thinking (which may be why students sometimes think it's a clever idea to turn over cars and set them on fire when one of their teams wins a national championship).

Also, most drugs will affect activity throughout your brain. So while nootropics might conceivably ramp up coordinated activity in your executive control network or default mode network, they might also increase activity in other brain regions that could disrupt or counteract the contributions of your "creativity networks," leaving you no better off than you were before.

Overall, knowing more about what sorts of processes contribute to creative thinking increases the odds that someone will one day be able to discover new technologies that make it possible for you to amp up your own creative thoughts and imaginative abilities. Until then, your best bet is to invest in a thinking cap.

SIGHT BITES

 Many brain regions that contribute to perception overlap with those that are active during imaginative acts, but imagery seems less dependent on early sensory pathways.

 By monitoring patterns of neural activity it is now possible to know something about when a person is imagining and what they are imagining.

 Two main cortical networks composed of multiple brain regions appear to interact to make the generation and evaluation of creative thoughts possible.

 Changing activity in "creative networks," either through mental exercises or direct chemical interventions, can potentially increase or decrease a person's creativity.

APPLIED PERSPECTIVES

SNEAK PEEK: When are two heads better than one? The answer seems to depend on the kind of problem one is trying to solve and who is cooperating. Sometimes, mentally rehearsing future actions can be as effective as physical practice for improving performance.

Modern technological advances are driven by creative solutions to problems. This is why many "smart drugs" are marketed toward boosting creativity. But succeeding in the creative arts is often less about generating novelty than it is about developing highly refined expertise.

Creative ideas are like a treasure chest of possible futures. They do not determine how things will go; they expand the options. In the world of business, it is not creative ideas that CEOs rally around, it's the "vision" of a company, usually laid out in a carefully worded statement. IKEA's vision is "to create a better everyday life for the many people." Teach for America's is, "One day, all children in this nation will have the opportunity to attain an excellent education." Company visions are imagined futures, a kind of idealized groupthink that provides employees with a common goal.

Why do companies create vision statements? Thoughts of what a better future could be like provide a source of motivation that can, in principle, mobilize people to develop and implement plans that will potentially move things toward that imagined future.

It's a nice idea in concept. Whether shared mental images actually accelerate progress toward a better, brighter tomorrow is tricky to establish, though. Simpler situations, in which smaller groups attempt to implement joint actions to achieve a common goal, have allowed psychologists to more directly examine how shared imagery may contribute to planning and problem-solving.

Collective Problem-Solving

Joint action refers to multiple individuals coordinating their movements or activities (Brownell, 2011). Joint action is key to cooperative activities ranging from playing "patty cake" with a toddler, to having a conversation, to overthrowing a government.

Identifying when joint actions depend on shared thought processes is not easy. There are many ways two or more individuals' actions can become coordinated or synchronized that do not require any thought. Two people who accidentally fall out of a plane at the same time without parachutes may act in similar ways, but that would not imply that they are working together to achieve some goal. In contrast, if they intentionally jump out of a plane (with chutes) at different times, their actions might appear less coordinated, even if they share a common military goal.

In early experiments designed to try and get a handle on how one might separate joint actions based on shared thoughts from those that were mainly circumstantial, the American psychologist Robert Yerkes (1876–1956) began conducting experiments in which he tested young chimpanzees on their ability to cooperatively solve problems (Yerkes, 1937). In Köhler's studies of insight in chimpanzees, he reported a few instances of chimpanzees seeming to work together to gain access to hanging fruit (see Figure 9.12). Most psychologists have viewed such anecdotal evidence with skepticism. Circus and farm animals can be trained in ways that make it seem as if they are actively cooperating when they are really acting no differently than they would alone. By testing young, untrained chimpanzees, Yerkes wanted to see what would happen when the chimps were faced with problems that they could only solve by working together.

In a task now known as the cooperative pulling paradigm, two chimpanzees were presented with a heavy box outside their cage that had food on top of it. Connected to the box were two ropes. Only when both chimpanzees pulled on the ropes together were they able to move the box, a technique that they quickly figured out. Interestingly, when the chimps pulled the ropes together, they used a "heave-ho" strategy, not pulling continuously but at the same time at relatively fixed intervals. Also, when one of the two chimps lost interest in pulling, the other one would poke her or move her hand toward the second rope until she started pulling again. This simple pulling task has since been used with monkeys, birds, elephants, and even hyenas, all of which show some evidence of performing joint actions to achieve the common goal of getting food (de Waal, 2016).

Working together to reduce hunger obviously has advantages. So, it's not too surprising that different groups of animals might be able to do this. Nevertheless, some researchers have proposed that cooperative food gathering may have been a unique factor in the evolution of human cognition (Heyes, 2012). Cooperative foraging and hunting both can benefit from increasingly sophisticated mechanisms for coordinated planning of complex action sequences (**Figure 9.19**), as well as future episodic thinking.

A natural arms race between the hunters and the hunted may have helped to amplify capacities for joint actions not just in the present but also in an imagined future. Groups of male chimpanzees sometimes engage in complex strategies when hunting small monkeys, with certain individuals acting to channel panicked groups of monkeys into the arms of a hidden chimp waiting to ambush them (Mine et al., 2022).

FIGURE 9.19. Exceptional coordinators. Shepherds work with trained border collies to herd sheep in ways that other dogs seem less capable of learning. What kinds of differences in border collies might affect their capacity for joint herding actions with humans? (Edwin Remsberg/Alamy Stock Photo)

Human hunters sometimes coordinate their actions with those of dogs (for example, pointers, retrievers, etc.) that have been bred and trained to react to birds in specific ways to increase their usefulness to hunters. Hunting dogs coordinate their actions with humans, but it's mainly the humans that are orchestrating the hunt. Fishing cooperatives, in contrast, seem to be more truly collaborative operations.

Fishing cooperatives are situations in which human fishermen work together with wild dolphins to capture prey (Cantor et al., 2023). Much like groups of chimpanzees hunting monkeys, dolphins and humans play different roles in these efforts. For instance, a group of humans may stand in the water with fishing nets while the dolphins herd schools of fish closer to the fishermen. When the fish are in front of the fishermen, the dolphins may give a signal that triggers the fishermen to throw their nets, trapping the fish between the coordinated attacks. Killer whales once worked with human whalers in a similar way to trap humpback whales.

Cross-species cooperative hunting highlights some of the advantages that cognitive flexibility can provide for solving complicated problems. Although it's impossible to know if cooperative fishery participants share a vision, like "more fish better," their coordinated actions clearly achieve a common goal. To be successful, this kind of joint action requires some planning, such that the dolphins and humans are in the same places at the same times. Successful fishing cooperatives probably also require some ability to rapidly improvise actions, since schools of fish engage in their own sets of complex coordinated actions to avoid being herded and eaten.

The kinds of joint actions that humans started using as novel strategies to avoid hunger (and hungry predators) have since morphed into more entertaining endeavors. Specifically, all of the team sports that people spend hours watching and participating in are essentially ritualized joint actions that highlight people's imagery, planning, and little-c creativity skills. Teams make and execute detailed plans about what they will do when and where and participants rapidly improvise when things don't go quite as planned (see Chapter 6). Players try to imagine the different future actions that competitors and teammates might perform so that they can plan their own actions. As described in the following section, athletes may also visualize various scenarios to prepare themselves or think through past mistakes so that they can avoid repeating them.

Coaches are given lots of the credit or blame for the outcomes of most team competitions. Having the vision to guide the actions of players, basically to plan effective strategies that account for imagined possible scenarios, is the hallmark of a great coach. These are the same qualities associated with successful generals in the military, politicians in government, chefs in fancy restaurants, conductors of world-renowned orchestras, and directors of scientific laboratories. Understanding how creative thinking, mental imagery, and planning skills combine to make such achievements possible is a major challenge of cognitive psychology research, a complicated problem that groups of psychologists are working together to address (Moulton & Kosslyn, 2009).

New opportunities for joint actions are available in modern society that effectively merge collaboration with imagination. Specifically, it's now possible to go online and participate in multiplayer video games, including stimulated sports competitions, military missions, and much more. These games depend less on physical prowess and more on mental engagement. Multiplayer games are closer to imaginative play in that participants spend most of their time seated and staring at a screen, raising some concerns about whether extensive participation in such e-sports might have downsides for cognition and physical fitness.

In massively multiplayer online games, thousands of players may potentially interact in both competitive and cooperative tasks. Millions of subscribers participate in such games, some of whom spend more time acting in virtual worlds than in the natural world. Such platforms provide unprecedented access to people's naturalistic actions in imaginary worlds, but relatively little is known about what those actions might reveal about players' thought processes.

Are successful collaborators in such games more likely to be effective team members outside of games? Does early exposure to such gaming environments positively or negatively affect imagery and planning abilities later in life? Does gamification of academic or professional learning work any better than standard educational approaches?

It was once argued (by Plato) that storing knowledge in the form of writing would degrade the minds of humans, a claim that perhaps no modern, degraded mind can adequately assess. Understanding the mechanisms that underlie planning and imagery abilities will make it easier to predict the pros, cons, or irrelevance of multiplayer gaming and future virtual world experiences for different age groups and individuals. Then, people can make more informed decisions about whether these kinds of time and virtual character killers might also act as mind mucker-uppers.

Learning through Images

Physical images, illustrations, and diagrams are heavily used as educational supports. For example, children are introduced to reading through picture books. Counting and math are first taught by showing clusters of objects. Educational cartoons and video games also include fun animations to reward kids for paying attention to topics that they might not otherwise care much about. By associating visual images with symbols and concepts, teachers hope to provide students with new ways of representing and thinking about familiar events, and in effect, accelerate the learning process.

Although children are often encouraged to be imaginative when drawing and coming up with stories, seldom are they explicitly taught to use self-generated imagery as a way of solving problems. Psychologists studying the role of imagery in academic problem-solving in laboratory settings have shown that imagery can sometimes help students to discover solutions to a variety of problems (Roskos-Ewoldsen et al., 1993). In academics, however, this approach is generally emphasized much less than solving problems through the recall of relevant facts (either mentally or Google-style) and through mathematical calculations.

One area where mental imagery is increasingly being used as a tool to improve problem-solving is in sports. The main problems that athletes face relate to how to move their bodies in precise ways at appropriate times. And the main way they improve their ability to do this is through practice with feedback. Recently, however, mental practice through motor imagery has become an additional approach that some athletes are trying out (Di Rienzo et al., 2016).

The effectiveness of imagined practice compared to physical practice has been studied in numerous sports, as well as for surgical procedures and musical skills. Imagining practiced movements—basically recalling what performing an action is like without actually doing it or running through an action sequence in your head—can enhance movement accuracy, speed, and efficacy, thereby improving overall performance. Practicing motor imagery can also improve the form of performed actions, affecting specific trajectories of movements (**Figure 9.20**). For instance, high jumpers who practiced motor imagery improved movements associated with clearing a bar (Olsson et al., 2008).

FIGURE 9.20. Extreme motor imagery. In *The Matrix* movies, motor skills are constrained mainly by the character's ability to imagine practicing those skills. How might imagined fights differ from the real thing, and how might this affect the benefits of imagery practice? (Album/Alamy Stock Photo)

It might seem like practicing a sport by simply imagining performing the actions related to that sport wouldn't really work. If you are unable to execute the actions you're imagining, then that's probably true. However, performing a specific action requires not only moving muscles but also controlling when and how those muscles move. Recall that many of the brain regions that become active when you experience an event (including playing a sport) also become active when you imagine that same event occurring. Just as lifting weights can increase your physical strength in ways that can enhance your athletic skills, despite the many differences between moving metal around and most tasks in sports, mental exercises can increase your motor control capacities, even though it may look and feel like you're not really doing anything.

Something that is not yet known is what mix of imagined and actual practice will produce the most benefits. There is some evidence that motor imagery combined with physical execution, like a baseball player warming up before his turn at bat, may be more effective than either approach alone. Observing actions while both performing them and imagining performing them—which may occur when a dancer practices in front of a mirror—can also be highly effective.

The mental representations activated during motor imagery include not only kinesthetic images associated with mental simulations of movements but also the goals associated with specific actions. Several different ideas for how these representations relate to motor imagery and the benefits of mental practice have been proposed (Gentsch et al., 2016). Most of these accounts assume that representations of percepts, actions, and motor images overlap and that the representations are processed similarly when you observe, execute, or imagine a specific action or sequence of actions.

Theories about how motor imagery practice works differ in two main ways: they differ on how perceptual representations are organized and transformed during the control of actions and they differ on the types of thinking that accompany these cognitive processes. For instance, some theories suggest that motor imagery mainly engages cognitive processes involved in planning actions, such that practice affects a specific kind of future episodic thinking. Other theories argue instead that motor imagery activates most of the same processes as actually performing the imagined actions, just with the final motor outputs being suppressed.

Most theories of motor imagery assume that this process depends on a combination of sensory imaging (in particular, kinesthetic, visual, and spatial imagery) and intentional cognitive control processes. In other words, you decide to imagine what it would be like if you served a tennis ball, and then you roll the mental clip of serving based on your past experiences either seeing others play tennis or having hit a serve yourself. From this perspective, imagining an athletic action is basically a mental reenactment or simulation of a physical action occurring, along with some awareness that you are "pretending" to do the actions rather than physically attempting to do them. Practicing motor imagery then would consist of repeating mental reenactments.

Repeatedly activating neural circuits is a key ingredient for structurally changing those circuits, as discussed in Chapter 2. You should not be surprised then that both physical and mental practice can produce changes in cortical processing. Mental practice-related changes in sensory and motor cortices have been observed using a variety of neuroimaging and neurophysiological techniques. In general, the kinds of cortical changes that are observed after mental practice are similar to those seen after actual practice of motor skills. It's even possible to predict somewhat who will benefit the most from motor imagery practice by examining people's brain activity during such exercises (Herholz et al., 2016).

The people who can benefit the most from motor imagery practice are probably not athletes, but individuals who have lost the ability to perform any action. Brain-computer interfaces that link a paralyzed person's brain to computer systems with the ability to control cursors on a computer screen, movements of a robotic arm, or the steering of a motorized wheelchair (see Chapter 2) are making it possible for them to once again interact physically with the world. The way these systems work is that the individual practices thinking about how they want a device to move and then the computer system learns to recognize brain activity patterns that reliably occur when the person imagines that a specific outcome is happening.

People learn through trial and error what sorts of mental images of desired movements most effectively lead to those actions in the external world (through visual feedback), and the computers learn what patterns of cortical activity are most predictive of different "instructions." Currently, these technologies only monitor relatively small regions of motor cortex and relatively short windows of neural activity. As researchers find new ways to externally simulate what people internally imagine and gain more insight into the specific kinds of activity patterns that mental imagery generates in the brain, it seems likely that greater mental control of external events will become possible. In this way, regular people may soon begin to acquire telekinetic mental powers of the sort once only attributed to gods, demons, wizards, and aliens.

CLOSURE

A key lesson taught at the Disney Institute is, "The more a vision can be expressed in a vivid, imaginative way, the more it will motivate people to action in the present" (disneyinstitute.com). The official vision statement of the Walt Disney Company is "to be one of the world's leading producers and providers of entertainment and information." Just imagine it, a giant mouse as the world's leading producer of information.

To achieve that imaginative feat, you will probably need to enlist the aid of your default mode network and executive control network to get those creative juices flowing. Now, your intuition may lead you to believe that letting a pretend mouse be a major source of the world's information might not be the best plan of action. Preventing that possible future, however, will require you to join forces with like-minded individuals to develop novel solutions to counter impending mouse crusades.

The common processes underlying creative thought, planning, imagination, and perception set the stage for thinking about thinking. Some thinking just happens and other thoughts come only after an extended, effortful search. Thoughts build on memories of past experiences and mental transformations recombine past percepts to create new ways of cognizing and understanding.

One important lesson of mental imagery and creativity studies is that there is more than one way to think and people differ in the vividness and flexibility with which they can incorporate auditory, visual, and motor imagery into their ongoing thought processes. Walt Disney was sometimes described as an "odd guy." It's likely that his unique way of visualizing possibilities contributed to his creative achievements. Cognitive psychologists and neuroscientists are moving closer to developing new ways of directly observing the variety of thinking processes that organisms engage in as well as ways of amplifying creative potential.

While individual differences in the vividness with which mental images can be experienced clearly exist, it's less clear how these types of differences contribute to creative thinking in either artistic or scientific activities. Current thinking on creative cognition suggests that the mechanisms that make creativity possible are the same ones that make it possible to think. In other words, the metaphorical mental light bulb that flashes on in a moment of creative inspiration may not be much different from a sudden realization regarding the likely location of a missing phone or set of keys.

This is not to say that creative imagery cannot lead to impressively novel ideas. Some of the most surprising scientific realizations in history come from unexpected mental imagery, like the thought experiments of Albert Einstein in which he imagined chasing a beam of light or being inside a falling elevator pulled along by a god. Thinking in pictures can lead to insights and discoveries that might be difficult or impossible to achieve through logical reasoning (see Chapter 10) or calculations alone.

Simply having a vivid imagination is insufficient for solving most problems, however. Having expertise in the problem area appears to be critical. Athletes who benefit from practicing motor imagery are able to improve precisely because they have the skills necessary to implement imagined actions and the experience to distinguish between relatively subtle action trajectories. Grandmaster chess players are able to imagine and effectively plan for possible future scenarios within games because of their extensive knowledge of the various strategies that expert players have used in the past to create and exploit weaknesses.

At their core, scientific studies of cognition are an exercise in collective problem-solving and creative thinking that depends heavily on the imaginative efforts of numerous researchers and on their skills at planning experiments. The various technological and theoretical approaches that psychologists have developed in their attempts to better understand the cognitive processes that make thinking possible may not be as intriguing as Disney princesses or talking mice, but they may ultimately be what make your dreams (of understanding how minds work) come true.

COGNITIVE LINGO

afterimage	improvisation	mind wandering
cognitive flexibility	impulsivity	phantom limb
default mode network (DMN)	incubation	planning
divergent thinking	insight problem	problem-solving
eidetic imagery	joint action	propositional representations
episodic future thinking	mental image	think aloud protocol
executive control network (ECN)	mental model	Tower of London task
imagination	mental rotation task	

CHAPTER SUMMARY

Imagery
Imagery can vary a lot across individuals. Remembering the past and imagining the future depends on constructing mental images. Researchers continue to explore links between imagery and perception.

Planning
Planning for the future can mean creating mental models that combine mental imagery with propositional representations. Not all plans are verbalizable and some quickly go astray when impulsivity biases choices toward instant gratification.

Creativity
Creative thinking engages many of the same cognitive mechanisms as everyday cognition. Experimental studies of

people discovering solutions to problems through insight have provided insights on how creativity contributes to problem-solving.

Brain Substrates
Many of the brain regions that make perception possible are also involved in imagery. Multiple cortical regions contribute to creative thinking. Changing activity in these regions can change a person's creativity.

Applied Perspectives
Mechanisms of learning and plasticity are important for both imagery-based training programs and collective problem-solving.

REVIEW EXERCISES

Imagery
• Describe some evidence that suggests mental images are related to perception.
• Why do some researchers suggest that mental images are represented abstractly like sentences?

Planning
• Provide examples of how a mental model might combine both imagery and propositional representations.
• Why are tasks like the Tower of London useful for studying planning?

Creativity
• What are insight problems and how have researchers used them to study creativity?
• How might conscious and unconscious cognitive processes contribute to creative problem-solving?

Brain Substrates
• What can recordings of brain activity reveal about processes of imagery?

• Describe the default mode network and explain how it is thought to contribute to creativity.

Applied Perspectives
• How might cooperative problem-solving be combined with imagery-based training programs to improve the performance of an athletic team?

CRITICAL THINKING QUESTIONS

1. People with synesthesia naturally perceive extra modalities when presented with certain kinds of inputs; this might allow them to smell colors, for example. According to current models, what is likely to happen if someone with synesthesia imagines a visual stimulus that would normally activate a second modality when perceived?

2. Several developmental disorders are associated with atypically high levels of impulsivity. How might episodic future thinking develop differently in children with these disorders?

3. Highly creative individuals seem to be more susceptible to some mental disorders. But mental disorders are often defined in terms of behavior that deviates from the norm. Can you think of ways that might differentiate highly atypical creative thinking from mental processes that are dysfunctional?

4. Creativity depends on coordinated activity between multiple cortical networks of interconnected brain regions. If you wanted to genetically engineer people so that they can think more like a Da Vinci or Newton, what features of their brains would you change in order to do this?

5. Multimedia entertainment is becoming so immersive and mentally stimulating that, today, many children would choose to stare at a computer screen instead of going outside to play or interact with other children. In what ways (if any) might such entertaining experiences change the creative problem-solving abilities of future adults?

10 Reasoning and Decision-Making

FluxFactory

The difference between what we do and what we are capable of doing would suffice to solve most of the world's problems" (Gandhi). India was at a turning point when, in 1930, Gandhi and a few followers set out on a 240-mile march to protest Britain's policy of forbidding Indians from gathering or selling salt. Gandhi's goal: to gather salt left from evaporated seawater. By the time Gandhi arrived at his destination, tens of thousands of marchers had joined him. A month later, he was in jail.

Walking hundreds of miles to pick up some salt might seem like an odd solution to the problem of economic oppression by a foreign government. Some historians consider Gandhi's action, however, to have been an important first step (literally) to achieving India's independence seventeen years later.

Gandhi did not decide to march out of frustration. He made a calculated decision to attempt to spark mass, nonviolent civil disobedience as a way of counteracting what he perceived to be unfair policies (**Figure 10.1**). Others followed his lead, even when they were violently attacked for doing so. The deaths of peaceful demonstrators further amplified the political power of the protestors' civil disobedience.

Many Indians perceived the same problems as Gandhi but did not arrive at similarly effective solutions. Presumably, millions of people living in India at the time imagined what it would be like to not have to pay exorbitant prices for salt and openly questioned why they were being forced to do so. How did Gandhi move from imagining what a better India would be like to choosing a relatively simple action with the potential to move the country in a positive direction?

Most people would likely guess that Gandhi was extremely adept at political strategy, overcoming the reasoning abilities of his adversaries by playing a kind of three-dimensional political chess. **Reasoning**, which involves consciously thinking about an issue in a logical and systematic

FIGURE 10.1. Political problem-solver. Gandhi inspired millions of Indians to risk their lives by disobeying laws when they believed those laws were unfair. How might Gandhi's words have changed his audience's cognitive processing? (Dinodia Photos/ Alamy Stock Photo)

way, is widely viewed as the optimal option for making brilliant mental maneuvers. A distinctive feature of thinking by reasoning, at least for humans, is that the thoughts can be revealed and evaluated using **propositions**, symbolically represented statements that can be classified as being either true or false.

You are reading propositions about thinking and reasoning right now. You may also be reasoning and thinking about those propositions in an attempt to solve the problem of understanding what it is you are supposed to be learning from them. At some point, you may decide that reading propositions is less fun than texting and choose to stop reading.

Not yet? Reasoning has a special place in cognitive psychology because it is considered by many to be a cognitive feat that only humans can pull off. For philosophers like Descartes, reasoning was the defining feature of mentality and of humans—the primary evidence that thinking seriously about anything is reasonable.

Reasoning abilities are almost synonymous with intelligent thinking. Artificial intelligence (AI) mostly consists of computer programs attempting to simulate human reasoning by manipulating symbolic representations. Expert AI systems are successful when they can produce statements that provide solutions to problems. Technologists' obsession with developing computer programs that can dominate the brightest humans in strategy games like chess and Go came from the belief that strategic reasoning skills represent some of the most impressive cognitive capacities of any mind.

Now that computers are capable of beating humans at any challenging strategy game and writing essays that are comparable to those written by students in law school, researchers are beginning to step back and question whether those computers are really reasoning. If they are, then should reasoning be viewed as the be-all-end-all of thinking? Are the winningest AI systems doing anything significantly different from their less successful predecessors? Or are they just doing the same kind of number crunching, but faster?

This chapter rounds out the consideration of cognitive processes that contribute to problem-solving and thinking by reviewing modes of thinking that depend more on conscious manipulation of symbols and statements than on imagery. Such processes form the foundation for almost all academic enterprises, including learning about discoveries in psychological science. Attempting to understand reasoning and decision-making is a bit like walking through a mental hall of mirrors: the more you understand (or think you understand), the more problems you create that beg for a solution.

BEHAVIORAL PROCESSES

It is tempting to think of thinking as being a product of intelligence. The thoughts constructed by a highly intelligent person seem more likely to be solid and worth considering, while the "dumb ideas" of others are more likely to be viewed as a waste of time.

This apparent continuum of good-to-bad thinking is tightly linked to old ideas about the value of rational thought compared to ideas arising from emotions or intuition (irrational thought). **Rational thoughts** are thoughts that are logical and justified by valid principles and evidence. For many, rational thinking is the apex of human cognition (Kahneman, 2011; Pinker, 2022)

Chapter 9 introduced two main theoretical camps that most psychologists fall into when it comes to explaining how thoughts contribute to problem-solving: one camp emphasizes symbolic representations and while the other focuses on imagination, insight, and creativity. Spending billions on fake mouse kingdoms seems more about realizing a vision and less about logic, so maybe not so rational.

Rational thought implies symbolic representation because it requires some way for the thinker to provide evidence justifying the thought. The thought needs to fit with known facts, follow rules about how those facts can reasonably be interpreted (specifically, the rules of logic discussed below), and be communicable to anyone with comparable symbolic skills (through language, equations, or similar squiggles).

When it comes to solving problems, rational thought provides a source of potential solutions and a way to choose between alternative solutions. Cognitive psychologists have devised ingenious methods and theories in their efforts to identify the origins and mechanisms of rational thinking, a few of which are highlighted in the following discussion.

Solving Problems

SNEAK PEEK: Discovering solutions to daily challenges is a fundamental function of cognition. What makes some problems easier to solve than others? How important are language and rational thoughts to the search for solutions?

When you solve problems, you are transforming your experiences and the world around you into some preferable state, usually by any means necessary. The new state may be a familiar one, like when you organize a desk, or one you never expected (**Figure 10.2**), like when you accidentally discover a useful shortcut.

Cognitive studies have traditionally focused more on systematic problem-solving strategies of the sort you might engage in while trying to solve a riddle than on the more intuitive or situation-specific thought processes you might use when advising a friend about how to respond to a possible stalker (Ritter et al., 2019; VanLehn, 1991).

Setting and Pursuing Goals

Almost by definition, if you are thinking about a problem, it's because finding a solution to that problem is in some way advantageous. Your general goal in thinking about the problem might be to find a solution or to determine that there are no solutions. A more specific goal might be an imagined future in which the problem is no longer a problem. As in, a goal of being filthy rich might correspond to a possible future in which you have more freedom to do (or buy) whatever you want.

Representing Problems

Identifying goals may seem like the easy part of problem-solving. But goal setting raises many potential pitfalls that can derail a problem-solving process before it ever begins (Spellman & Holyoak,

FIGURE 10.2. Spontaneous problem-solving. Faced with an unexpected scenario, people often turn to conversation as a means of working out what actions to take next. What advantages does the use of language provide for solving problems that go beyond what might be achieved through imaginative thought? (tommaso79 via Shutterstock)

1996). For instance, if your goal to become rich comes from a belief that being rich will make you happier, then your goal may not actually be a viable solution to the problem.

How you structure a problem can determine the adequacy of any solutions you discover, as well as the likelihood you will discover any solutions (Gentner & Markman, 1997). In formalized problem-solving settings, the solution or conclusion corresponds to the goal state, such as when you discover the solution to a riddle or the answer to a math problem. There is a single valid solution, and your job is to find it.

Puzzles are **well-defined problems** because their solutions are predetermined (the puzzle is solved when the picture is complete). Getting rich, or happy, or both is a more **ill-defined problem** in that there is some ambiguity about when, or if, the goal state has or can be reached (how rich is rich enough?). Gandhi's goal was for Indians to be free from British rule; gaining freedom for Indians was a well-defined problem. Gandhi also hoped to make life better for Indians; how Indians might achieve a better life is a more ill-defined problem.

Moving Toward Solutions

The kinds of strategies that work for solving well-defined problems may be less effective for solving ill-defined problems (Schraw et al., 1995). In both cases, however, arriving at a conclusion or solution seems to involve some sort of mental search, first for possible options and then for the specific option that is most likely to successfully achieve the goal state.

If you conceive of problem-solving as a process of searching for solutions, then the process becomes comparable to both spatial navigation, with the goal state being like a destination (see Chapter 6), and categorization, in which different propositions or ideas are sorted (see Chapter 5) through until some combination is discovered that counts as a solution (Simon & Newell, 1962).

The "problem space" can be thought of as like a mental maze that you must navigate through to reach a specific goal location (Wang & Chiew, 2010). Like routes in physical space, paths through problem space are usually preferable when they move you closer to the goal. Unlike physical mazes, however, navigating through a problem space is not as constrained by your current state (**Figure 10.3**). In principle, you can "teleport" around to different starting points to try and find the most straightforward way of reaching the goal state.

Searching through a problem space is similar to exploring the natural world in that there are many ways of getting from point A to point B, and it is not always obvious which path is the best one to take. Following a familiar, well-worn path has the advantage of reliability, but it has the disadvantage that you may never know what you have missed by not exploring novel approaches. Additionally, becoming set in your problem-solving strategies can potentially make it harder for you to solve other kinds of problems later (McCaffrey, 2012). In problem-solving research, searching for a plausible path from A to B is called a divide-and-conquer approach or means-end analysis.

FIGURE 10.3. Figuring. Representing math problems symbolically provides a way to think about quantities without perceiving quantities. How might these propositional representations enhance your ability to solve math problems? (Lawrence Migdale/Science Source)

Exploring Alternatives: Behavioral Flexibility

Any time you intentionally attempt to solve a problem, you are likely to automatically engage several cognitive processes prior to resorting to reasoning, some of which may depend on propositional representations. For instance, in searching for solutions, you are likely to compare the current scenario to any similar problematic situations you've encountered in the past, relying on mechanisms of recognition (see Chapter 4) and recall (see Chapter 8).

The extent to which past scenarios aid in the identification of solutions depends on what you learned from the earlier episodes (Ohlsson, 1996), a topic discussed in detail in Chapter 7. The ease with which relevant precedents can be recalled also affects how one searches for solutions. If a possible solution to a problem comes quickly to mind, it tends to be more readily accepted as a correct solution. Ease of recall in turn depends on the types of cues available as well as the sequence in which you process cues. For instance, in court cases, a jury's verdict can be strongly affected by the order in which evidence is presented and by the way that the evidence is framed (Pennington & Hastie, 1990).

Solving Novel Problems

Problem-solving is a skill. Like most skills, your proficiency at solving a particular class of problem will depend on your past successes and failures in solving similar problems (Keen, 2011). When faced with a new and challenging problem, you are likely to experience elements of confusion and frustration. To solve a novel problem, you will likely have to invest greater time, effort, and attention. You are more likely to fail, to have to regroup, and to start from scratch several times. Highly familiar problems, in contrast, are ones you may be able to solve without much thinking.

Part of what makes novel problems hard problems is that you may not know how to select a point of attack. You probably will not know which factors are most relevant or how to think about the problem in a way that is appropriate (Schraagen, 1993). If you are ever in a car that won't start and know little about cars, then you may be hard pressed to start the problem-solving process, particularly if your phone battery is also dead. You may not get far beyond repeating steps that have already failed to solve the problem.

To solve novel problems, you either need to identify the relevant aspects of the problem or be really lucky. If you don't represent the problem or potential paths through the problem space in a relevant way, you will almost always fail to solve the problem.

Situated Cognition

Once you have encountered a particular class of problem a few times, you begin to recognize the scenarios and gain the ability to rapidly select actions that are more likely to yield good results. From the perspective of **situated cognition**, understanding how to solve a particular problem comes from familiarity with contextual factors and the effects of actions in specific contexts (Roth & Jornet, 2013; Vogel et al., 2020).

A familiar context affords certain actions that you are likely to repeat if they have proven effective in the past. Different actions might be initiated and abandoned on the fly as their success or failure adds to the situational context that drives them (which is why many attempts at solving novel problems end with things being banged).

Problem-Solving Strategies

Much of what is taught in schools, either directly or indirectly, are recipes for answering questions acceptably and efficiently. "I don't know" is a fine solution but not when it is the only option. Some academic recipes for solving problems come with the promise of 100% success when implemented correctly.

Algorithms are paths to solutions that simply require turning the crank to get to a desired goal state. They are the bread-and-butter of computer programs. Any problems you solve using a computer (including smart phones) are solved with algorithms. As artificially intelligent computer programs increase in sophistication, so too does the range of problems that can be solved automatically and algorithmically. All algorithms operate using symbolic representations.

Information processing models of cognition, which treat thinking as a computational process, effectively assume that all problem-solving is algorithmic (Suchow et al., 2017; Underwood, 2009). Since psychologists have so far failed to identify any algorithms that consistently replicate what humans do when they are attempting to solve problems, psychologists usually don't describe human strategies as algorithms. Instead, they call most of what humans do **heuristics**, which is a fancy way of saying "things people do when they are attempting to solve problems."

Heuristics might include strategies like "try stuff" or "copy people who seem like they know what they are doing." Like algorithms, heuristics are recipes. But they are recipes that don't always pan out, like a grandmother's recipe that she never wrote down.

Unlike algorithms, heuristics are more likely to lead to a "good enough" solution to a problem—one that works but that may not be the best (Gigerenzer, 2008). Psychologists like to use the heuristic "call it something obscure" when identifying commonly used heuristics. For instance, you might attack a problem using the **availability heuristic**, which is basically to try whatever solution pops into your head first.

Another commonly used heuristic, especially in mathematics and science, is the **means-end heuristic**, which involves breaking a problem into smaller, more manageable mini-problems, and then focusing on solving each of those mini-problems separately. The "means" to reach the desired "end" is to divide and conquer. If you are a college student, then you are probably solving the problem of getting a degree by applying a means-end heuristic and taking some classes each semester or quarter.

The upside to using heuristics is that they often provide a quick-and-dirty solution to all kinds of problems that you face each day. The downside is that a good number of those solutions are likely to be bad ones or fall into the "I don't know" category. Even worse, the solutions you come up with may feel right even when they are dramatically wrong, especially when the problems are ill-defined.

Mental Blocks

The final stage of any problem-solving effort involves selecting a solution, persisting in the search for a solution, or giving up. Deciding which of these outcomes to select is a key process in solving any problem (described in more detail in the Choosing Actions section below).

If you are stumped, this confused mental state is likely to provoke a peculiar feeling that clues you in to the fact that you are failing to find the solution that you seek. Metacognitive feelings of certainty or doubt (see Chapter 8) guide your search for solutions (Berardi-Coletta et al., 1995), but they don't always accurately reveal when you are close to finding a solution or when you have or haven't successfully solved a problem.

WEIRD, TRUE, FREAKY

Mental Health Chatbots

In the beginning (the 1960s), there was ELIZA, a computer program developed at MIT to simulate an interaction with a psychotherapist—specifically a psychotherapist that mainly just responded to statements with questions about those statements. User: "I think Josh's family is upset." ELIZA: "What caused you to feel that way?" User: "They yelled at me." ELIZA: "What other reasons might there be?" and so on.

ELIZA was designed mainly to respond to typed statements with plausible responses; not your most impressive AI. Surprisingly though, even this simple program was able to produce strong emotional responses. Users were automatically attributing intention and understanding to ELIZA, even when they knew it was a computer program generating the responses (Natale, 2019).

ELIZA is a primitive chatbot, a program that converses with humans. Modern chatbots often have the capacity to speak and may even include a visible avatar. Despite these fancy facades, the way that modern chatbots operate is essentially the same as ELIZA: they process statements to produce relevant responses or questions (Wollny et al., 2021) (see figure).

Chatbots have largely taken over the role of customer service representatives for most large companies where they methodically and persistently ask callers to choose from endless lists of numbers until the callers frantically press "0" to end the horror.

As annoying as customer service chatbots are, these kinds of computer programs are increasingly being explored as potential mental health service providers. You will have no trouble finding apps such as Woebot, a program designed to help with depression by "listening" and offering support to users (Sachan, 2018). The Woebot app can produce propositions of the sort a clinical psychologist might deliver in a therapy session. Unlike a traditional therapist, chatbots can be available twenty-four hours a day, seven days a week, providing an on-demand conversational partner and advisor.

As online technologies advance, the line between human interactions and simulated human interactions is likely to become increasingly blurred. For example, in online intervention programs designed to increase opportunities for youth to talk with counselors and to each other, chatbots can replace human moderators of online social groups (D'Alfonso et al., 2017).

Facebook, Microsoft, and Google have all invested significantly in developing therapeutic chatbots. Imagine a vocal search tool like Alexa that can not only answer random trivia questions but can also simulate empathetic responses to grief, frustration, or panic in order to prevent mental deterioration. ELIZA's responses to questions were all canned. Newer chatbots' responses are more likely to be selected by neural networks that have been trained how to respond using millions of actual conversational interactions.

AI programs are already better at playing strategy games than any human. Might they also be capable of becoming better conversationalists, advisors, or friends than is possible for any human (Thomas, 2023)? "Computers" used to be humans that performed complex calculations, until machines that were faster and more accurate made them obsolete. Might a similar fate await counselors?

Much of the recent focus on developing chatbots for mental healthcare centers on recognizing the emotional state of the person seeking treatment (Bilquise et al., 2022; Rathnayak et al.. 2022). If chatbots become adept at detecting and modulating the emotional states of users, then it is a short step from having a circle of online virtual advisors/friends to having a chatdate or chatspouse, a scenario already laid out in the science fiction movie *Her*. And once everyone finds or purchases their digital soulmate, then presumably counseling programs themselves will become obsolete.

Can computer programs achieve treatment results comparable to those of counseling psychologists? (Song_about_summer via Shutterstock)

Rigidity

One of the biggest roadblocks to solving problems occurs when someone gets locked into feeling that a certain solution should work (Ollinger et al., 2008). This scenario is a common consequence of relying on strategies like the availability heuristic. Perhaps the solution has worked several times in the past and seems like it should work in the current scenario, but for whatever reason, it is not working now.

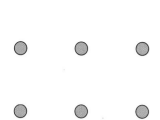

Draw four straight lines, passing through all nine of these dots, without lifting your pencil from the page.

FIGURE 10.4. The nine-dot problem. Brain teasers like this one are challenging because past experiences lead people astray in their search for possible solutions. Generally, this is because of incorrect assumptions that are part of a mental set.

When earlier experiences act like a mental magnet that keeps pulling you in the direction of a specific solution, you are said to be in a **mental set**. As in, you are set in your way of thinking and unlikely to consider other alternatives. Discovering insightful solutions to a problem often requires breaking free from a mental set. Scientific geniuses and inventors seem to have a knack for doing this.

As noted earlier, representing a problem in an appropriate way is key to finding solutions to the problem. Mental sets tend to steer people in the wrong direction with respect to how they represent certain problems. A classic example of this is the nine-dot problem, which most people find to be frustrating because of the mental set it commonly triggers (**Figure 10.4**). In this case, past experiences with connecting dots constrain the kinds of solutions that people typically come up with. There is a solution!

Surprisingly, the representations that people use to think through possible solutions can themselves lead to mental sets that affect the search for solutions. For instance, if you categorize cats as "pets," then you are less likely to consider them as an option when deciding what to have for lunch or what to throw at an intruder.

The way you label and conceptualize objects and events can interfere with your ability to discover novel solutions to problems or to recognize when a solution to a problem is right in front of you. This phenomenon is called **functional fixedness**. Mental sets and functional fixedness are examples of cognitive biases that can derail the search for potential solutions (Huang et al., 2019; Wiley, 1998).

Expert Problem Solvers Versus Novices

Your problem-solving skills in a particular domain can increase with practice as you gain familiarity with different kinds of problems, strategies for solving them, and specific solutions to well-defined problems (Patel et al., 2000).

When a problem first comes up, experts are more likely to rapidly diagnose the key issues and to more efficiently apply an appropriate means-end heuristic to develop a plan for resolving those issues (Hardiman et al., 1989). Experts also tend to be better at multitasking in their solution search, considering the pros and cons of multiple alternatives at the same time (**Figure 10.5**). Finally, ex-

FIGURE 10.5. Expert problem-solving. Pit crews continuously face two problems during races: (1) a car pushed to its limits will deteriorate rapidly and (2) every second spent fixing or maintaining the car puts the driver farther behind in the race. Are these problems well-defined or ill-defined? What sorts of heuristics might help a pit crew to perform successfully? How might expertise contribute to the search for solutions to problems in the pit? (Grindstone Media Group via Shutterstock)

perts are more tuned-in to how the problem-solving process is going, detecting and correcting missteps more quickly. This kind of mental monitoring and evaluation of thinking (thinking about thinking) depends on metacognitive skills (see Chapter 8) as well as memories of past failures and successes.

Although experts tend to be more proficient in their ability to solve familiar problems, they can still be defeated by mental sets and functional fixedness. Scientists, despite their love of objectivity, are notorious for being resistant to scientific discoveries and new theories (Campanario, 2010). Many scientific breakthroughs were initially viewed as worthless nonsense or heresy.

Nobel prize-winning physicist Max Planck once proclaimed, "A new scientific truth does not triumph by convincing its opponents and making them see the light, but rather because its opponents eventually die, and a new generation grows up that is familiar with it." In other words, scientific mindsets are often breakable only by death.

This claim seems to challenge the idea that logical problem-solving, the preferred approach of scientists, provides a clear path to factual conclusions. Do mental sets trump truth? Or can reason rise above the limitations of feelings and imagination in revealing superior solutions?

SIGHT BITES

 Problem-solving that involves propositional representations depends on setting goals, identifying strategies for reaching goals, and evaluating progress.

 Familiarity with a problem and strategies for solving it strongly affects which cognitive processes are likely to be engaged during the search for a solution.

 Past experiences can make solving some problems easier, but they can also produce mental sets that make it harder to see solutions to novel problems.

Reasoning

SNEAK PEEK: Reasoning often requires evaluating evidence or obeying rules. When does reasoning work best as a problem-solving strategy? Does logical reasoning always lead to the best possible solution?

The world is a complex and confusing place. In their attempts to deal with the blooming, buzzing confusion of life, Greek philosophers adopted reasoning as a heuristic for finding explanations for their experiences of the world and themselves.

As an explanatory strategy, reasoning has the advantage of moving beyond first impressions. Looks can be deceiving and Greek philosophers were not fans of misleading evidence. Mathematical relationships, in contrast, seemed to escape the confines of sensory inputs and everyday life more generally. Mathematics arose from the need to solve practical problems in economics, agriculture, and architecture. More specifically, mathematical techniques were developed by experts to solve specific problems, prior to becoming the playthings of curious philosophers (Netz, 2003).

Philosophers saw in mathematics a way to transform propositions that were practically useful into statements that were universally true. More importantly, the propositions suggested algorithms for how to generate more true statements. Mathematical reasoning shifted from being a practical tool to something more like a game.

The game of reasoning has only two rules and comes in two main varieties. Rule 1: Choose some aspects of experience that you want to reason about. Rule 2: Figure out some consequences of those selected aspects. The strategies you use to follow Rule 2 define the different types of reasoning.

If you treat the selected bits of experience as evidence and try to use them in combination to draw some conclusion, then you have entered the realm of **inductive reasoning**. If you represent the experience propositionally and use the selected proposition(s) as a seed to generate other valid propositions that follow from your initial propositions, then you've succumbed to **deductive reasoning**. These two major kinds of reasoning will be described in greater detail in the following sections.

In either case, the goal is to construct new propositions that are more trustworthy and useful than some statement you just spontaneously blurted out. The cognitive power of both modes of reasoning lies in their potential to guide thought processes in directions that reveal solutions that otherwise would remain undiscovered. This is the claim to fame for both science and mathematics—playing with propositions enables researchers and mathematicians to think new thoughts that can create new worlds.

Recognizing Relations

Like other modes of problem-solving, reasoning is a skill. One ability that expert reasoners possess that novices lack is the ability to select relevant features of a problem and substitute symbolic representations for those features.

So, if you are a student with a limited amount of time to spend studying for multiple courses, you might label or rank them in terms of their importance, difficulty, and number of assignments before attempting to construct a plan of action regarding how you might best manage the time you spend on each.

Because reasoning rests on propositional representations, the goal states will inevitably be verbalizable conclusions. Ideally, those conclusions would capture something factually relevant to solving a problem—"I'm going to need to schedule extra study time to pass this killer course"—rather than mere exasperation at the unfairness of it all.

Replacing the complexities of unique courses with relatively simplistic descriptors or numbers can make thinking about their implications more straightforward. Labeling complex situations can also make it easier to set aside emotional responses evoked by the original events (for example, fear, apprehension, or anxiety). It's easier to think about numbers without reacting emotionally than it is to think about all the meaningful experiences you will be missing out on while you sit at a desk staring at pages.

Simplifying complex situations by either quantifying or verbalizing them can also sometimes open up new ways of conceptualizing those situations by emphasizing subsets of features and suppressing attention to others. Reorganizing your thoughts into novel sequences and combinations can generate new insights and solutions (Bratman, 1992).

"Sometimes, it must be confessed, the conceiver's purpose falls short of reasoning and the only conclusion he cares to reach is the bare naming of the datum. 'What is that?' is our first question relative to any unknown thing. And the ease with which our curiosity is quenched as soon as we are supplied with any sort of name to call the object by, is ridiculous enough."
—James, 1890, p 339

Experts in a particular domain such as psychology can benefit from jargon that distinguishes many different qualities of phenomena precisely because this extended vocabulary expands the way scientists can think about and explain those phenomena. Similarly, qualitative and quantitative models of cognitive processes provide simplified symbolic representations that can be useful for figuring out how those processes work and for recognizing the implications of different explanations (Lee et al., 2019).

Inductive Reasoning

Inductive reasoning involves considering some number of observations and then attempting to use those observations to draw a conclusion. The conclusion could easily be wrong, but it is often more useful than no conclusion. Because the conclusions you make from past observations are always going to be tentative (**Figure 10.6**), you can think of inductive reasoning as a way of generating hypotheses—possible explanations or solutions that you can test and evaluate in various ways.

Solutions to problems arrived at through inductive reasoning are hypotheses about what might work in a particular context. For example, in the game *Twenty Questions* participants ask questions about the qualities of an object in order to collect evidence that narrows the scope of what the mystery object might be. If enough of the right kind of evidence is obtained, a player's confidence in their hypothesis about what the object is should increase.

One way that people typically reason inductively is by linking events that co-occur, especially when they are explaining why something happens. If every time you see a mail truck stop outside where you live you later find new mail in your mailbox, you might hypothesize that the person driving the truck is the source of the magically appearing mail. Repeated observations can lead you to believe that things occur together because one is causing the other.

On the other hand, what if you were never around when the mail truck came by? Checking your mailbox might still reveal that mail is sometimes in there. Should you then conclude that your checking of the mailbox is what makes mail appear? After all, these two things co-occur just as reliably as if you had witnessed a mail truck stopping by. Correlations provide clues, but other kinds of evidence provide more solid foundations for inductive reasoning.

Collecting and Considering Evidence

When you inductively reason in everyday life, you typically aren't going around with a magnifying glass looking for clues that will reveal what you should conclude. Instead, you are more likely to be considering facts you know and past circumstances you recall that are relevant to the current situation. Your current conclusions are thus likely to gravitate toward your past beliefs. This is why lawyers screen jurors—to try and get rid of individuals whose prior beliefs are likely to bias them against the conclusion the lawyer would like to prevail.

Because most of the evidence you consider when inductively reasoning comes from your memories, how you weigh evidence will depend heavily on which evidence you recall (Hawkins et al., 2016). Your dependence on memory will make you susceptible to reaching conclusions based on the availability heuristic. If your most vivid memories of encounters with statistics in the past are mostly

FIGURE 10.6. Odd swan out. A limitation of inductive reasoning based on past observations is that there is no number of observations that will guarantee that you have exhausted the possibilities. If you have only ever seen white swans, it always remains possible there are other colors of swans you have yet to encounter. (Darren Curzon)

unpleasant, then any conclusions you make about how fun statistics might be in the future will be driven by those memories. You might have had plenty of fun with statistics (or at least many more neutral experiences). And if you were able to recall all those less eventful episodes, inductive reasoning might lead you to a totally different conclusion.

A related issue with inductive reasoning is that it is relatively easy to remember evidence that is consistent with a conclusion you have already reached (Evans, 2006). This kind of rationalization of a solution or explanation after the fact may be difficult to differentiate from inductive reasoning since what you recall may be biased by a conclusion you would prefer to reach. Recall from Chapter 7 that the tendency to accept or notice evidence that is consistent with a prior belief or expectation is referred to as **confirmation bias**.

You can see evidence of confirmation bias in the superstitions people acquire. A hat becomes lucky after a few positive events happen while it is being worn, and a black cat becomes an omen due to a few random coincidences. Once an object's power is revealed, further evidence of its efficacy accumulates because the times when the object works its magic become more noticeable and memorable. Biased memories of confirmatory evidence can lead to **illusory correlations**—apparent links between events that are unrelated—which further confirm the observer's expectations (Costello & Watts, 2019).

You might think that this kind of superstitious thinking is irrational or based on naïve intuitions. But it is actually the kind of solution or explanation you would expect from inductive reasoning when you take into account the fact that the evidence driving the reasoning (memories of past episodes) is biased in ways that tip the scales.

Deductive Reasoning

Once you have a hypothesis, you can use deductive reasoning to come up with ways of testing the hypothesis. For instance, if you hypothesize that reasoning is a better approach to problem-solving than a trial-and-error heuristic, then you might predict (deduce) that individuals who exclusively reason when solving problems will tend to perform better in school than those who just wing it and learn from their mistakes.

It's often assumed that reasoning yields superior solutions than do most other kinds of thinking. Deductive reasoning, in particular, is thought to benefit from its reliance on logical principles that provide specific rules about what types of conclusions people should draw from "If…then…" statements.

Syllogisms

The role of propositions in deductive reasoning is most clearly evident in syllogisms, the haikus of deductive reasoning. A **syllogism** consists of two claims, followed by a third claim—the conclusion—which, based on the first two claims, is either logically valid or invalid. An easy-to-understand syllogism might be: all students love pizza, all pizza has cheese, therefore all students love cheese. Easy to understand, less easy to believe.

What you believe to be true, however, isn't factored into the logic of syllogisms. Sure, there are plenty of students who hate pizza, as well as some kinds of pizza with no cheese, and some students hate cheese. The rules of deductive logic couldn't care less. They are like the rules of the game *Simon Says*. If you are playing *Simon Says* and Simon says put your thumb on your tongue, you do it or you lose. If I say take your thumb off your tongue, and you do it, you lose. Making sense is not a goal of the game. Following rules is. The rules say: Do what Simon says and only what Simon says. Similarly, deductive reasoning is all about following rules.

Like in the game *Simon Says*, it's easy to make mistakes and break a rule when evaluating syllogisms. This is why philosophy departments offer semester-long courses in logic. How likely you are to reach the wrong conclusion depends, per usual, on your familiarity with the topics of the statements and the conclusion (Newstead et al., 2004; Šrol & De Neys, 2021).

If vowel, then even number.

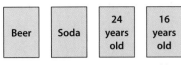

If drinking beer, then over 19 years old.

FIGURE 10.7. The Wason Four-Card Problem. Students evaluating the top rule often fail to turn over the 7 which is critical to evaluating whether the rule is being followed. Students evaluating the bottom rule, in contrast, often turned over the 16 years old card, which is logically what they should do in both cases. (Top row after Wason, 1966; bottom row after Griggs & Cox, 1982)

Historically, the goal of syllogisms was to provide a system for making conclusive factual statements by combining other statements about the world. The idea was that such a system would help people to avoid believing nonsense and to discover better solutions to intellectual problems.

The Wason Four-Card Problem

A more commonly encountered logical problem that can be solved through deductive reasoning relates to "If…then…" statements. These are the kinds of deductive processes that come into play when you are testing a hypothesis with a psychological experiment. For instance, if you hypothesize that most undergraduates are unlikely to be able to reliably detect valid syllogisms, then you would likely predict that they would perform poorly when asked to classify the pizza-love syllogism above as being either valid or invalid.

Experiments with a classic deductive reasoning task called the **Wason Four-Card Problem** show that undergraduates often run into trouble performing even simple deductive reasoning tasks (Ahn & Graham, 1999) (**Figure 10.7**). In this task, participants are asked to evaluate whether a set of four cards follows a particular rule. Participants are told that each card has a letter on one side and a number on the other side. Then they are asked to identify which cards they should turn over to decide whether cards with a vowel on one side have an even number on the other side. More than 90% of participants crash and burn when attempting to solve this problem (bad mental set anyone?).

Interestingly, 73% of participants successfully solved a different version of this task that sounded more like a drinking game (Griggs & Cox, 1982), suggesting again that the situation strongly affects how participants think when solving a problem (Kirby, 1994).

Dual Process Models

Modern views of thinking continue to portray deductive reasoning as the pinnacle of cognitive processing, a view illustrated by dual process models of thinking. There are several versions of **dual process models**, but they generally share the assumption that the two processes contributing to thoughts are unequal partners (Bago & De Neys, 2020; Evans & Stanovich, 2013).

In Daniel Kahneman's (2011) dual systems model of thinking, for example, one system (System 1) is described as intuitive, fast, unconscious, automatic, and prone to making mistakes, while the other system (System 2) is described as slow, deliberate, consciously controlled, and requiring attention (**Figure 10.8**). The underlying assumption of the dual systems model is that if people deployed their System 2 more often, they would make fewer errors when solving problems.

The division of labor in dual process models is reminiscent of Descartes's mind-body split but with the two problem-solving systems each taking on the prior roles of either the body or the mind. On the other hand, the different roles played by System 1 and System 2 also map onto differences seen between problem-solving by experts and novices, with System 2 reasoning corresponding to the slow effortful search for solutions typical of novices and System 1 processing being more characteristic of the accomplished expert.

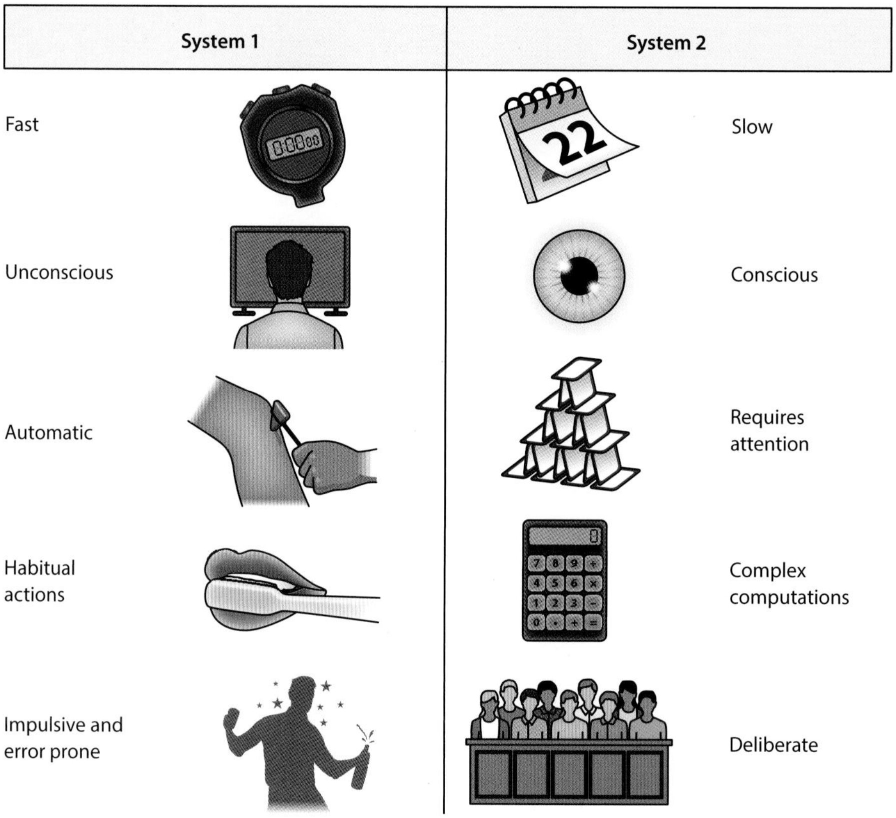

FIGURE 10.8. Two ways of thinking. Dual process models of reasoning propose that thinking and problem-solving tasks often initially trigger an automatic, unconscious mode of inductive processing (System 1), which only gives way to a slower, consciously controlled, more logical mode of processing (System 2) when the going gets tough.

FIGURE 10.8. Two ways of thinking. Dual process models of reasoning propose that thinking and problem-solving tasks often initially trigger an automatic, unconscious mode of inductive processing (System 1), which only gives way to a slower, consciously controlled, more logical mode of processing (System 2) when the going gets tough.

So, which is it? Is deliberative, conscious reasoning what you do when you are clueless? Or is it what you do when you engage the full force of your intellect?

As with the dualism of Descartes, some psychologists have argued that System 2 reasoning is what distinguishes humans from all other animals (Penn et al., 2008). But is there any evidence showing that human thought and human thought alone is of two minds?

Are Humans the Only Reasoning Animals?

There is no evidence that nonhuman animals naturally use symbolic languages or any other types of propositional representations. This lack of evidence is viewed by some to be a convincing case that only humans reason (Miller, 2013; Premack, 2007; Thorndike, 1949).

Animals other than humans clearly solve problems, however, and so they must possess some mechanisms for accomplishing these feats. The German philosopher Gottfried Leibniz (1646–1716) argued that animals solve complex problems through inductive reasoning (Frankish & Evans, 2009) and that this was how humans typically solved problems as well. But he also believed that humans additionally possessed a unique capacity for deductive reasoning, which arose from consciousness—a step toward modern dual process models.

Reasoning about Reasoning

Hypotheses about the kinds of reasoning processes that animals commonly engage in, or are capable of performing, come from observations and inductive reasoning (Völter & Call, 2017). The kinds of observations that lead people to believe that humans regularly solve problems deductively, but that other animals never do, are particularly likely to lead to questionable conclusions.

First, when you try to remember times when you've observed organisms reasoning deductively, you are guaranteed to come up with more examples of humans doing this than nonhumans. In other words, your use of the availability heuristic will push you toward the belief that only humans reason.

You might not be able to think of a single instance in which you've seen a nonhuman deductively reasoning. In this case, you are using what's known as a **representativeness heuristic** to search your memory. When you use this heuristic, you are basically trying to judge the probability of something being true based on how similar it is to something else you believe to be true (**Figure 10.9A**). You think you know what deductive reasoning in humans looks like (slow, logical, conscious, contemplative), and you search for things that look similar in other animals (Epley, 2007). Most likely, you fail. But why would you believe that deductive reasoning has to look the same across species?

Also, how many opportunities have you had to observe animals other than humans reasoning? People often assume that small samples are representative of a population when drawing conclusions about that population, a logical fallacy known as the **small-sample fallacy** (**Figure 10.9C**). The number of animals that you have observed in contexts where they might deductively reason is quite small relative to all animals behaving in all contexts.

Emphasizing the qualities of deductive reasoning that seem prototypical of human reflective thought also ignores the **base rate** of the phenomenon—how often the process actually occurs—which is unknown for any species of animal, including humans. People tend to ignore this gap in knowledge because of confirmation bias.

Consider the following syllogism: If nonhuman animals deductively reason, then someone would have seen evidence of it. I have not seen any nonhumans deductively reasoning. Therefore, animals do not deductively reason. Do you think this conclusion is logically valid? Do you think it is true?

(A) Representativeness heuristic

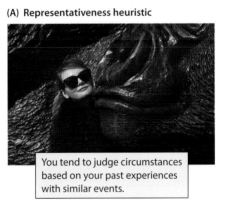

You tend to judge circumstances based on your past experiences with similar events.

(B) Belief bias

If a conclusion fits with your current beliefs, you'll accept information that supports it.

(C) Small sample fallacy

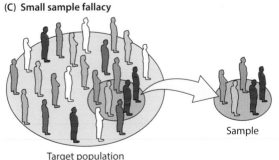

Target population

Sample

Your initial experience covers the full scope of possibilities.

FIGURE 10.9. Built-in biases. Cognitive biases such as (A) the representativeness heuristic, (B) the belief bias effect, and (C) the small sample fallacy affect how you evaluate evidence and the sorts of rules you consider when attempting to solve a problem. Such biases happen automatically when you think about a problem. Most likely, you are unaware of the effects such biases have on the conclusions you make as you go through the day. (A Sipa US/Alamy Stock Photo; B Picture Architect/Alamy Stock Photo; C Simonkr)

People tend to accept such arguments as both true and valid when they are neither. This tendency happens because the statements fit people's prior beliefs. When the rules of logical reasoning conflict with what a person believes, logic usually loses. This phenomenon, known as the **belief-bias effect (or belief bias)**, is common in politics where hard-core believers on the right or left often interpret any evidence as supportive of their original position (**Figure 10.9B**). Because beliefs vary across cultures, the belief-bias effect can also lead to differences in the conclusions people from different countries reach when faced with identical sets of evidence.

Thinking Animals

One argument commonly raised against the possibility of deductive reasoning in animals other than humans is that although nonhumans can think about percepts, they are incapable of thinking about abstract concepts (discussed in Chapter 5) like "redness" (Locke, 1690). The main assumptions underlying this claim are that language is a prerequisite for abstract thinking and that animals do not possess any language skills.

Experimental studies of animal cognition over the last century have laid to rest the idea that language skills are necessary for the formation and recognition of abstractions (Mercado & Scagel, 2023; Roitblat & Meyer, 1995). Language-less animals (including human infants) are capable of recognizing sameness, difference, aboveness, and similarly abstract properties (see Chapter 5).

There is even evidence that some nonhuman species (particularly chimpanzees) can use analogies to solve problems (Thompson & Oden, 1995). **Analogical reasoning** involves generalizing from one example to another. It's like inductive reasoning based on a single piece of evidence. Analogies lie at the heart of metaphors. Understanding an analogy requires recognizing that relationships between two events are comparable to relationships between other events. For instance, identical twins are similar in the same ways that cloned mice are similar, even though both pairs look and smell different.

Analogizing apes are not counter evidence to the claim that deductive reasoning is a human-only feat. Evidence of transitive inference in nonhumans, however, is (Gazes & Lazareva, 2021). **Transitive inference** is a form of deductive reasoning in which a relationship between item A and item B, and between item B and item C, is used to draw a conclusion about the relationship between A and C. For instance, if Bip is taller than Frogo, and Frogo is taller than Samsonite, then you can logically deduce what you will find when you compare the heights of Bip and Samsonite.

It is relatively easy to construct nonverbal versions of transitive inference tasks. Every species tested on transitive inference tasks, other than honeybees, have succeeded at performing these tasks (Lazareva, 2012); 16-month-old infants can also pass these tests (Mou et al., 2014). It seems that the processes required for at least some forms of deductive reasoning are neither language-dependent nor particularly sophisticated.

Reasoning about peoples' heights may seem rather trivial compared to the kinds of complex reasoning processes that an iconic figure like Gandhi used when developing strategies to achieve his political and ethical goals. Are nonhumans capable of identifying when a situation is fair or unfair or developing strategies for maintaining fairness? Some nonhuman primates do seem to think through these kinds of social problems. For instance, monkeys will work together to obtain food and then will share the prize (Bucher et al., 2021; Westergaard & Suomi, 1997), even when they could keep it all for themselves (**Figure 10.10**). And a monkey that sees another monkey getting larger rewards for performing a similar task will quickly become irate, suggesting some sensitivity to inequity (Brosnan & de Waal, 2003).

Such findings do not imply that animals other than humans reason in the same way that adult humans do. They do imply that current assumptions about what thought processes different species are capable of are often based on faulty reasoning rather than on scientific evidence.

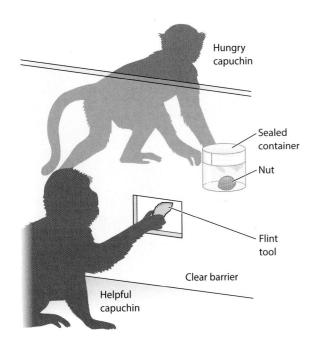

FIGURE 10.10. Fairness in monkeys.
Pairs of capuchin monkeys will work together to overcome obstacles in gaining treats. A monkey with access to a tool will provide it to a monkey who cannot get into a container without it. Once the worker monkey manages to break into the container, it often spontaneously shares the contents with the helper monkey. Similar actions in humans are interpreted as evidence of reciprocity or feelings of fairness.

SIGHT BITES

 Inductive reasoning focuses on collecting evidence, analyzing it, and then reaching a conclusion based on that evidence.

 Deductive reasoning depends on rules of logic and emphasizes evaluating whether conclusions follow from sequences of statements.

 Dual systems models of thinking propose that deliberative conscious processes compete with impulsive unconscious processes.

 Cognitive biases can lead to erroneous conclusions, even when people attempt to carefully and logically consider relevant evidence.

When Decisions Are Made

SNEAK PEEK: How much do hunches affect decision-making in comparison to thinking about pros and cons? Deciding what to do can depend on what options are available, who else is evaluating the decision, and memories of similar situations.

Finding a solution to a problem, either through reasoning or other means, is often not where thinking ends. In everyday situations, identifying solutions can be the beginning of a prolonged decision process, especially when there are multiple solutions to choose from.

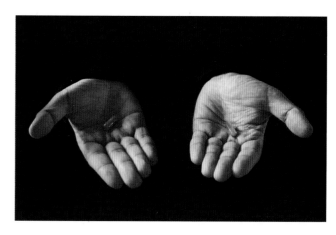

FIGURE 10.11. Difficulties of decision-making. "After this, there is no turning back. You take the blue pill—the story ends, you wake up in your bed and believe whatever you want to believe. You take the red pill—you stay in Wonderland, and I show you how deep the rabbit hole goes" (Morpheus, from *The Matrix*). How might your belief bias shape which pill you would choose? (diy13 via Shutterstock)

Decision-making is also a sort of problem-solving, the problem being how to choose an option that will lead to a favorable outcome or how to make the right choice (**Figure 10.11**). Making the right choice, or avoiding bad decisions, usually means comparing different options in terms of their potential future consequences in relation to your goals and the goals of others. Are the expected consequences a given or only wishful thinking? How certain are you about your fortune-telling skills? And are you sure you haven't missed something when thinking through the various options? You don't want to screw things up!

Choosing Actions

Early ideas about decision-making came from thinkers in religion, philosophy, and economics. Social groups established principles or rules for how to behave with consequences for noncompliance. Within these social frameworks, individuals were expected to select actions that would generally make themselves and others happy, content, or less afraid (Struck, 2016). The concept of **utility** eventually came to refer to the sum of all benefits of a particular action minus the downsides (Bossaerts & Murawski, 2017).

The commonsense foundation driving these ideas was that individuals generally avoid choosing against their best interests and avoid provoking others who might make their lives more difficult. From this perspective, when people make bad decisions, it's because they weren't paying attention, got bad information, or something is wrong with them. Otherwise, people are expected to rationally consider the consequences of their options and to choose one with greater utility, a view captured by **rational choice theory**.

Comparing Consequences

Evaluating possible consequences means not just identifying them but also estimating how likely they are to happen as well as the subjective experiences that are likely to occur if they do or don't happen. If you are considering asking someone out on a date, then the potential benefit of them saying yes is probably obvious. If the person is more likely to feel sorry for you or to laugh in your face than to say yes, then the possibility of humiliation might convince you to move on.

People are pretty good at estimating these kinds of probabilities. Sometimes, though, fears outweigh the odds. Everyone knows that flying in planes is safer than driving a car. And yet, people are still much more likely to panic at the thought of getting on a plane. Such fears are irrational but still affect people's choices.

Economists have mathematically modeled the kinds of calculations one might make when evaluating which options offer greater utility, taking into account both the probability of different outcomes and variations in the utility of each option. These models can often predict which options will be the most or least attractive, but the models are less able to explain the kinds of irrational, non-optimal decision-making that people exhibit (Dunn & Rao, 2019; Edwards, 1954).

Decision Distorters

Overestimates of the dangers of flying are partly due to the availability of memories of air tragedies broadcast on the news. Reporting on such events is more prolonged and dramatic than reports of accidental deaths of drivers, making them more memorable. The way that information relevant to making a decision is presented is called framing. Cognitive biases in decision-making that come from the way that information is framed, called **framing effects**, can dramatically affect decision-making (Mishra et al., 2012).

Con artists convince unsuspecting victims to make bad decisions by providing opportunities for actions with seemingly high utility. They then promote confirmation bias by providing small rewards when the "mark" makes desired choices. Finally, some fabricated crisis typically comes up that requires the victim to make an immediate choice. By framing a bad choice as a once-in-a-lifetime opportunity to win big, scammers exploit people's cognitive biases and limited reasoning abilities to rip them off (Perez et al., 2018).

Framing effects can also affect decisions at a societal level. People tend to go with the flow, especially when it requires little effort on their part. For instance, the Selective Service System (SSS) of the United States requires men between the ages of eighteen and twenty-five to register so that if the government decides to start drafting soldiers into the military, they have a list ready. Not many eighteen-year-olds would rationally choose to be forced to fight in a war, but more than 90% of young men register for the SSS.

The decision to register with the SSS (required by law) depends not only on awareness of potential costs and benefits but also on emotional responses to imagined consequences. Registering maintains the status quo unless a draft is implemented. Failing to register makes one a criminal, although the chances of being prosecuted for this crime are not much higher than the chances of being drafted. Nevertheless, the implicit threat of possible prosecution is sufficient to convince most young men to check off a box, which is, subjectively, a relatively painless option.

Framing effects also account for the tendency of gamblers to sometimes assume that if they have had a recent string of losses, then they are due for a win soon, or if a slot machine has not paid out in a while, then it is more likely to be "hot" (Takeuchi et al., 2020). In reality, the probability of a win does not depend on earlier games, and a losing streak means nothing.

One implication of the framing effect is that you can potentially change the decisions people will make by simply altering how you set the stage for the decision. For instance, if you present a choice as one in which there are potential gains as opposed to losses, people are more likely to choose the option that seems to deliver gains, even if numerically the outcomes are identical across the two scenarios (**Figure 10.12**). This cognitive bias comes from the fact that expected losses loom larger than gains, a phenomenon known as **loss aversion**.

All decision processes can be biased by the context within which the decision is made, whether that context is a series of unfortunate events, feelings of anxiety about what the future might bring, or statements that draw your attention to potential wins or losses (Sokol-Hessner & Rutledge, 2019).

Embodied Decisions

Humans and other animals often rely on rules of thumb (heuristics) when making decisions (Santos & Rosati, 2015). The specific heuristics that an individual applies when making a specific decision are context-dependent. In every context, there is a risk of making a poor choice. Every time you make a decision, you are doing so based on incomplete information about which alternatives you should consider and their potential outcomes.

Your decisions are shaped by the affordances of your current situation, including your physical features, emotional state, problem-solving skills, and living arrangements. You are continuously deciding what to do and you are continuously doing something.

FIGURE 10.12. Distorting decisions through framing. When two alternatives contrast how many people will be saved by each choice, people tend to favor the certain outcome. When the same outcomes are described in terms of who will die, people mostly avoid the outcome that guarantees that people will die. (After Eagleman & Downar, 2016, based on Tversky & Kahneman, 1991)

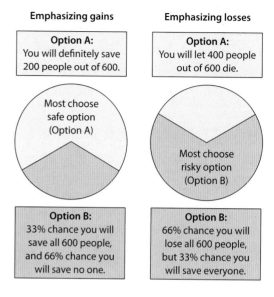

Traditionally, decision-making has been portrayed as a kind of logic problem that people solve by reasoning about possible futures. Newer studies in the field of embodied cognition are beginning to challenge this perspective, suggesting that decision-making may depend less on evaluating the value of different alternatives and more on dynamic interactions between organisms and their environments (Gordon et al., 2021; Raab & Araújo, 2019).

Survival of the Fittest

Making good choices is fundamental to surviving in the wild. Choosing when and where to search for food, a process that can expose an organism to predation or potential starvation, is particularly critical. When foraging, animals attempt to make choices that increase their chances of finding food relative to becoming food. As in rational choice theory, **optimal foraging theory** assumes that individuals select their actions so that they maximize utility (in this case, energy gained). The main difference is that ecologists do not assume that animals are consciously contemplating which action they should select next (Pyke, 2010).

Animal cognition researchers generally assume that evolution has produced adaptive specializations for decision-making that help match a particular species' decision-making capacities to its habitat and the physical constraints of its body (Kacelink et al., 2023). It's also possible, however, that different kinds of animals share some decision-making mechanisms, as proposed by Leibniz, the philosopher mentioned earlier who proposed that animals use inductive reasoning to solve complex problems.

Many of the cognitive biases that lead adults to make "irrational" decisions may reflect evolutionarily old adaptations that used to be advantageous for decision-making contexts that are no longer faced by modern humans. Individuals competing for food in the wild must consider multiple goals in parallel while foraging: minimize effort, avoid losing food to competitors, avoid being eaten, and so on. Heuristics that work well in natural foraging contexts might work less well in other contexts.

Decision-making in the wild requires rapid responses to dynamically fluctuating situations. The play-making NBA point guard may be making decisions closer to those that humans and other vertebrates evolved to resolve than are statisticians or shoppers deciding which of two pairs of shoes to purchase.

Weighty Decisions

Everyday decisions made on the fly may depend more on "gut feelings" than on the conscious consideration of possible futures. The **somatic marker hypothesis** proposes that subjective impressions of physiological changes, such as muscle tension or irregular heart rate, guide decisions about what ac-

FIGURE 10.13. Weighing right and wrong. Lady Justice uses a scale to weigh the evidence for and against a conclusion made by an accuser. The weight of a set of evidence is related to how persuasive or believable the evidence is. How might jurors in a case mentally weigh the evidence when making decisions? Are they more likely to use logical reasoning, gut feelings, or social guidance? (Brian A Jackson via Shutterstock)

tions are appropriate. Specifically, internal states correspond to expectations of future emotional states that can guide choices—you cringe before the catastrophe actually happens and perhaps duck and cover in preparation. Or you have a feeling of foreboding before all hell breaks loose. The somatic marker hypothesis was inspired by individuals with brain damage who showed both difficulties expressing and experiencing emotions as well as deficits in decision-making (Damasio, 1996).

One type of internal impression that is closely associated with decision-making, and unsolved problems in particular, is the feeling of weight. When troublesome problems are solved, people say that they feel as if a weight has been lifted from their shoulders. And when problems need to be solved immediately, they are said to be pressing. Are these just metaphors? Or might there be overlap between the physiological states associated with difficult choices and carrying heavy things?

Physical feelings of weight can influence the decisions people make (Jostmann et al., 2009), indicating that sensations of heaviness interact with the evaluation of alternative actions (**Figure 10.13**). Incidental emotional states, unrelated to an actual decision, can also affect how decisions are made— you are probably better off not going shopping while hungry. Collectively, links between basic physiology and decision-making suggest that the mechanisms involved may be more "primal" and irrational than philosophers and economists might lead you to believe (Angioletti et al., 2022; Balconi & Fronda, 2019).

The Bounds of Rationality

In the card game known as blackjack, or twenty-one, players have to decide on each turn whether they will "hit" (take another card) or "stand" (keep the cards they have). This decision will determine whether a player wins or loses. Psychologists have extensively studied how individuals behave in these kinds of two-choice tasks in which one choice has greater utility than the other, but the utility of either choice is uncertain (Smith & Ratcliff, 2004).

Generally, individuals will do better if they divide their choices between the two options. That's what most do. In fact, the way individuals divide up their choices is so predictable, it can be described mathematically with an equation known as the **matching law**. This law states that an individual's choice patterns will closely follow the relative rates of utility for each of the two possible options. In this way, the benefits of responding will be maximized (Killeen, 1972; McDowell, 2013).

The matching law doesn't just apply to choices in contrived laboratory experiments. It can also predict how college students will split up their time in group conversations (Borrero et al., 2007) and how college and professional basketball players will distribute their shot selection within games (Alferink et al., 2009).

Behavioral Economics

You make many complex decisions throughout your daily life so you may be skeptical that an equation or matching law can predict the choices you will make. How can an equation account for things

FIGURE 10.14. A utility curve. Utility curves describe the ways that perceived gains and losses interact to determine how valuable a specific action (choice) is. Loss aversion leads to stronger effects of perceived losses compared to gains. The framing of a problem, including the range of options available, determines the reference point (location of the vertical axis). For example, powerful politicians are less likely to pursue bold plans because they perceive them as more politically risky; their reference point for the value of the plan will be shifted to the right relative to a weaker politician.

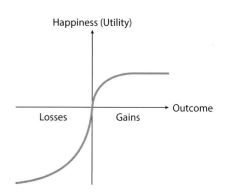

you decide to do on a whim or for choices you make that, in hindsight, you can't understand yourself?

Respecting the complexity of actual life, some researchers have turned to more ethological approaches to understanding choice behavior, observing how individuals make choices when, say, playing a video game. This approach, called **behavioral economics**, revealed that peoples' preferences for one choice over another can shift dynamically over time in odd ways (Camerer, 1999). For instance, if people were given a choice between buying a large or small soda at a movie theatre, they might choose the small size. But if the options were large, small, or insanely large, their likelihood of choosing the large soda would increase.

Rationally, the availability of a two-gallon jug of soda that most coherent individuals would never choose should not change the utility of other options on the menu. But it does. Rationally, charging $2.99 should not make the large soda any more attractive than if the cost were $3.00. But it does. Even more bizarrely, offering twelve different sizes of soda, rather than three, tends to make people bow out and choose not to get any soda.

These kinds of influences suggest that the choices themselves can distort how you decide to allocate your time, energy, and money, regardless of their objective utility (Peterson et al., 2021). Attempts to model these odd aspects of decision-making led to the development of utility curves (**Figure 10.14**). **Utility curves** attempt to capture how the attractiveness of a particular option can vary depending on an individual's subjective impressions of the costs and benefits of different options. From this perspective, your impressions of a situation can literally change how much utility you assign to each alternative.

Collective Decision-Making

Not only can the range of alternative actions affect how you make decisions but the people you are with also can shift the utilities you assign to different options (Mann, 2020). Sometimes referred to as peer pressure, the actions of others around you tend to promote a kind of group cohesion in choice making. This contributes to phenomena like **groupthink** in which attempts to reach a consensus end up pushing individuals toward bad decisions.

Collective decision-making is not always a bad thing. When choices are guided by an informed leader, the outcome can often be better than what individuals would have achieved making their own decisions (part of the rationale for having colleges and universities). Also, groups may have access to more information than would have been available to any individual within the group. Perhaps this is why brains evolved—to facilitate collective information processing by groups of cells (neurons).

In the 2001 film *A Beautiful Mind*, mathematician John Nash describes how a group of college guys can work together to increase their chances of picking up women at a bar, an idea that later inspires him to explore the benefits of group dynamics mathematically. According to Nash's model, an individual's choices can only be predicted by accounting for the social context within which they are made.

A group evaluating different options tends to converge on a reference point, like the one in utility curves, called the **Nash equilibrium**, which maximizes the utility for the group as a whole.

The mathematical approach developed by Nash has been used to analyze decision-making in a wide range of competitive situations where individual decisions interact to determine outcomes (Lee et al., 2005).

In certain contexts, particularly the worlds of politics and economics, collective decision-making can foster unethical choices. Often, the unethical acts of politicians and corporate leaders are attributed to the character of the individuals who were caught. Less attention is typically given to the specific social context or organizational systems within which the unethical choices were made.

Codes of conduct have little effect on choice when there is a minimal consequence of ignoring them. The actions of others, in contrast, can strongly affect decision-making. This is why con artists often make use of conspirators, or shills, who pretend to benefit from going along with the scammers' proposals. Not everyone will fall for a con or make unethical choices when given the chance, but the specific social settings within which such decisions are made can definitely increase the likelihood of a bad decision.

SIGHT BITES

 When individuals weigh the pros and cons of different options, their evaluations of the possible outcomes of each alternative will be affected by many factors.

 Decisions depend not only on objective costs and benefits or utility but also on how the decider feels when they are making a choice.

 Choice of actions is often evaluated based on the benefits they bring but can also be shaped by the options available and the social context of the decision.

BRAIN SUBSTRATES

SNEAK PEEK: Circuits within the frontal cortex integrate incoming signals from several other brain regions during decision-making processes. How those frontal circuits contribute to a choice depends on past experiences that shape how inputs are evaluated. Impressions of how pleasant or unpleasant different outcomes are likely to be can make it possible to compare alternatives before acting.

You've undoubtedly made decisions in your life that you later regretted, possibly even choices that, in retrospect, seem totally irrational or idiotic. How could your thinking have gone so wrong?

Psychological theories of problem-solving, reasoning, and decision-making tend to treat such mistakes as failures of self-control. Dual systems models, for example, assume that you could avoid making most mistakes if you spend more time thinking through the consequences of different options or if you collect more evidence before making a choice.

At the same time, by assuming that humans have a special faculty of reason that puts them ahead of the rest of the animal kingdom when it comes to decision-making, psychologists may overestimate how successful people's choices are relative to those of other animals. Psychologists' overconfidence about the superiority of human decision-making skills is consistent with a more general tendency for people to be overconfident in their conclusions.

So, are the bad decisions that you make a result of insufficient deliberation, a broken System 2 (the deliberative system), a lack of self-control, faulty reasoning, or just chance? Some "bad" decisions could be good decisions that simply did not pan out. Bad outcomes don't always imply mistakes.

On the other hand, you might be making decisions that are too risky for your own good. In which case, it might be useful for you to gain some insight into the mechanisms that are leading you to put yourself at risk.

Frontal Cortex and Decision-Making

The utility curve shown in Figure 10.14 reveals that expectations of losses affect utility more than expected gains. Studies of brain activity during risky decisions show that this difference is related to activity in distinct brain regions (Helfinstein et al., 2014; Korucuoglu et al., 2020). In other words, the neural circuits that you engage when considering the potential benefits of an alternative differ from the ones you use to evaluate the possible costs (**Figure 10.15**).

When you are considering a risky alternative in a positive light, regions associated with rewards, including regions of the basal ganglia (specifically, the nucleus accumbens) and frontal cortex, become more active (Tisdall et al., 2020). In contrast, if you are thinking about the potential downsides of a risky choice, neurons in your insula and amygdala become more active. The insula and amygdala are also key to experiencing the internal impressions that the somatic marker hypothesis points to as guiding decisions, suggesting that your "gut feelings" may be more responsive to perceived future losses.

FIGURE 10.15. Brain gains and losses. (A) Regions that become active when you consider the potential benefits of a future action, such as the frontal cortex and the nucleus accumbens (part of the basal ganglia), are distinct from the regions involved in assessing potential losses such as the amygdala and insula (B). This may partly explain why you do not weigh gains and losses equally when making decisions.

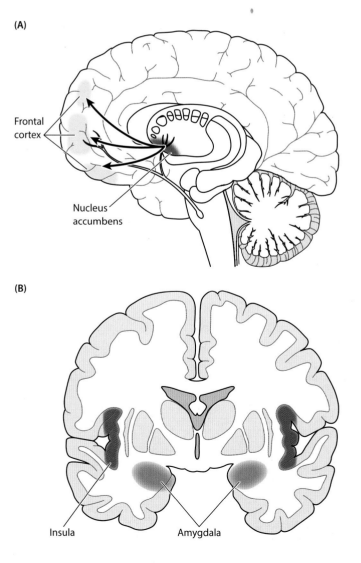

(A)

Frontal cortex

Nucleus accumbens

(B)

Insula   Amygdala

If you were able to directly monitor activity in someone's insula and compare it to the activity in their frontal cortex, you could probably predict when they would choose to make a purchase versus keep shopping (Knutson et al., 2007). If you wanted to let loose your inner gambler, you could probably achieve this by knocking out your insula, since this would likely wipe out your loss aversion. On the other hand, if you are willing to try this approach, perhaps your insula is already gone.

Evaluating Uncertainty

Identifying brain regions that contribute to the comparison of costs and benefits associated with different choices is only a small step toward understanding the cognitive processes involved in decision-making. There is considerable evidence from experimental and neuropsychological studies implicating interactions between the basal ganglia and circuits in the frontal cortex in decision-making (Clark et al., 2008; Cui et al., 2022), but what exactly those interactions are achieving is still being debated.

One idea is that frontal circuits are analyzing information about utility, computing how attractive each alternative is and how much effort it would involve—essentially performing a cost-benefit analysis (Tobler et al., 2009). Different subregions of the frontal cortex are thought to play different roles in this analysis. The outputs of this analysis would be transmitted to the basal ganglia where the information would then be used to control the selection of a particular response. Changes in response selection over time could then come from changes in frontal circuits, basal ganglia circuits, or connections between these regions.

Behavioral studies suggest that the context within which a decision is made and the subjective feelings of a decision maker can affect which alternative is selected. How does that play out in the interactions between different brain regions?

The differences between making decisions based on external sources of information versus internal feelings seem to boil down to which percepts are the focus of attention (**Figure 10.16**), which in turn depends on selective attention mechanisms discussed in Chapter 4. From this perspective, framing effects are the result of attention being channeled toward specific parts of problems. Consistent with this idea, participants who are most likely to change their decisions when a problem is reframed show the largest shifts in amygdala activity across conditions (De Martino et al., 2006).

Moral Dilemmas

Consequential decisions of the sort made by Gandhi and his followers, involving life-or-death actions, depend on many of the same processes and brain regions as more trivial decisions, such as deciding when to stop studying. When people are asked to think about their long-term hopes and dreams or goals for the future, circuits in the frontal cortex kick into gear (Badre & Nee, 2018). The relative weight of external motivators (money) versus internal drives (feelings of fairness) will vary from one hedonist to another saint, but the kinds of processing that use these values to guide actions will generally be comparable across individuals.

Your decision-making processes affect not just how you decide what to do but also your approaches to solving problems. Now that you know about heuristics and the potential cognitive biases associated with them, how might that affect your future deliberations? Will you admit that confirmation bias is clouding your conclusions and attempt to counteract this tendency by seeking out critics who will question your ideas? Or will you persist in your overconfidence that your current problem-solving strategies are "good enough" and live with the consequences?

In neuroimaging experiments that look at what happens when people are making hypothetical ethical decisions, participants are asked to choose from among multiple bad options (Fede & Kiehl, 2020; Young & Koenigs, 2007). For instance, what do you do if you are in a situation where your inaction will result in the deaths of multiple people, while your action would cause the death of a

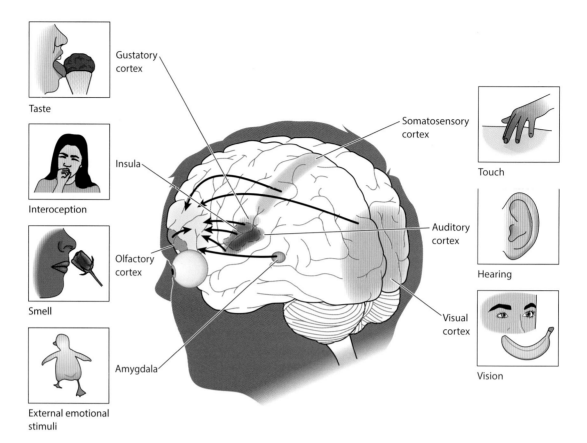

FIGURE 10.16. Integrating external and internal factors. The frontal cortex (light green) receives inputs from all sensory systems as well as from systems monitoring internal states (including the insula). The relative weight given to each source of information can vary depending on what elements of a situation are the focus of a decision maker's attention.

single person who would have been fine if you had not intervened (**Figure 10.17A**)? Would you end the life of a friend to provide life-saving organ transplants for five strangers?

Depending on how such problems are framed, the weight given to different options can shift. The activity in brain regions shifts in parallel (**Figure 10.17B**). When people's attention is focused on the downsides of choosing to end someone's life, regions associated with loss aversion dominate, and participants are more likely to select the option that involves them voluntarily ending someone's life (Sokol-Hessner & Rutledge, 2019).

When the emphasis is placed on the heroism and sacrifice required to make tough choices that save people's lives, activity shifts to a different set of brain regions less associated with feelings of angst. If participants are encouraged to closely consider which position is more morally defensible, then additional circuits in the frontal cortex (specifically, the prefrontal cortex) become active that may monitor activity across the competing regions (Riva et al., 2019).

Neurochemical Influences

Alcohol has been described as liquid courage because of its ability to increase feelings of confidence in situations where a person expects that the outcome of a choice may be unpleasant. How can a beverage tilt your internal scales toward performing an action that you might otherwise not?

Part of the answer comes from the role of neurochemicals in shaping neural activity. Alcohol is known to increase impulsivity, suggesting that it degrades processing by systems typically involved in conscious, deliberative reasoning—the kinds of processing sometimes attributed to System 2 (Herman & Duka, 2019).

(A)

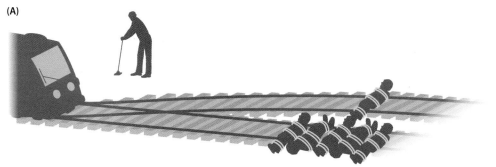

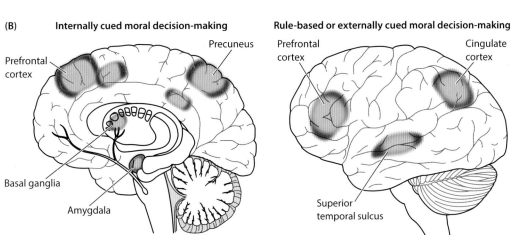

(B)
Internally cued moral decision-making

Precuneus

Prefrontal cortex

Basal ganglia

Amygdala

Rule-based or externally cued moral decision-making

Prefrontal cortex

Cingulate cortex

Superior temporal sulcus

FIGURE 10.17. Brain activation during moral contemplation. (A) A train is out of control and heading toward five innocents. Do you redirect the train to a track where it will kill Sally? (B) Focusing attention on internal cues (feelings of guilt, horror, etc.) engages multiple cortical and subcortical regions that differ from those evoked by external cues (the greater good). (After Eagleman & Downar, 2016)

Hormonal changes that occur when a person is stressed, such as increases in cortisol, can also increase impulsivity. So, you should probably avoid Las Vegas and motorcycles if you're stressed out.

Changing emotional states can shift how you make choices in ways that are similar to the effects of drugs or stressful situations. Less is known about the details of how emotions are influencing decisions—the somatic marker hypothesis is still being experimentally evaluated. But it is clear that deprivation of basic needs and desires, as well as prolonged states of depression or mania, can dramatically affect an individual's decision-making abilities.

Origins of Indecision: Neuroeconomics

Neuroeconomics is the neuroscientific counterpart to behavioral economics. A key assumption of neuroeconomics is that you make decisions based on the value you place on different outcomes. The amount of value you place on a particular outcome will depend on how motivated you are to obtain that outcome. But what happens when you are at a restaurant trying to decide what to order and cannot decide because all the options are enticing? What happens when your brain is faced with a tie?

Representing Subjective Value

In decision-making research, the subjective value of an alternative is the same as its utility. It can be tricky to control utility in experiments on human decision-making. With other animals, researchers can more precisely control the outcomes offered to subjects as well as the ways that outcomes vary over time (Chang et al., 2012).

Rats trained to press one lever to get sugar or a second lever to electrically stimulate a brain region known to reinforce behavioral responses provide an opportunity for researchers to vary rats' motivation to get either reward. In this way, researchers were able to equate the subjective value of the two options for individual rats (Schultz et al., 2015). Once researchers were able to equate utility across levers, they then showed that combining the two outcomes had the same behavioral effect as doubling

FIGURE 10.18. Money on the brain. (A) Impulsive individuals are less willing to wait a long time to get a money reward and more likely to accept a smaller amount now rather than wait (future money has a lower subjective value). (B) Brain regions in the prefrontal cortex, basal ganglia, and cingulate cortex show activity that corresponds to the subjective value of different money rewards, with higher values correlating with greater activity. (A, B after Kable & Glimcher, 2007)

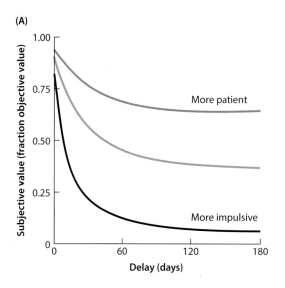

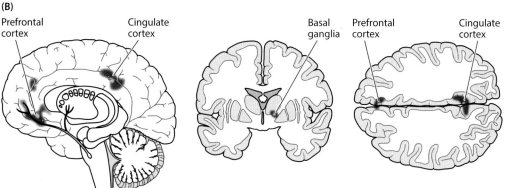

either of them. In other words, the rats' brains could combine different kinds of outcomes in ways that preserved their overall utility (Gallistel, 1994). This implies that there is something like an internal currency exchange for subjective value that facilitates comparisons between different options.

In human brains, there are brain regions in which activity seems to correlate with the subjective value of money (**Figure 10.18**). The same regions show a similar pattern of responding in relation to the attractiveness of snack foods (Chib et al., 2009; Kable & Glimcher, 2007).

Response Selection

In situations where your decisions can potentially affect the actions of others, decision-making processes quickly become complex. Consider the famous Battle of Wits from the classic movie *The Princess Bride*. After challenging the mastermind villain to guess which of two goblets contains an odorless poison, Vizzini (the challengee), proceeds to make his decision: "But it's so simple. All I have to do is divine from what I know of you: are you the sort of man who would put the poison into his own goblet or his enemy's? Now, a clever man would put the poison into his own goblet, because he would know that only a great fool would reach for what he was given. I am not a great fool, so I can clearly not choose the wine in front of you. But you must have known I was not a great fool. You would have counted on it, so I can clearly not choose the wine in front of me." And so begins an extended series of vacillations that ultimately ends with Vizzini making the wrong decision.

A somewhat less deathful game, called the **Ultimatum Game**, has been used in neuroimaging studies to examine brain activity during interactive decisions (**Figure 10.19**). In the Ultimatum Game, one person offers to split money with a second participant (the responder). If the responder rejects the offer, neither participant gets squat. Some offers sound reasonable: "We split the money 50/50." Others, not so much: "I take it all, you watch." In principle, the responder does not lose anything from

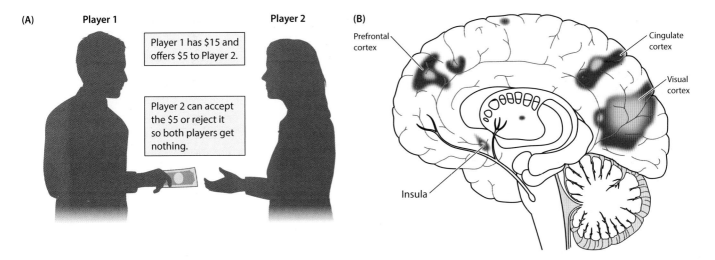

(A) Player 1   Player 2

Player 1 has $15 and offers $5 to Player 2.

Player 2 can accept the $5 or reject it so both players get nothing.

(B) Prefrontal cortex   Cingulate cortex   Visual cortex   Insula

FIGURE 10.19. The Ultimatum Game. (A) The funnest game you've likely never played. (B) Multiple brain regions activate as player 2 decides how to respond, including the usual suspects—the prefrontal cortex and the insula. Stronger activity in the insula, prefrontal region, cingulate cortex, and visual cortex predicts that the offer will be rejected. (A, B after Eagleman & Downar, 2016)

this second offer (since, if they reject the offer, they still get nothing), but they are unlikely to accept it, mainly because it seems wildly unfair. This goes on for about twenty rounds (Gabay et al., 2014).

Responders in this "game" (Player 2) typically rely on their internal feelings of fairness when deciding whether to accept or reject an offer, as well as their predictions about how their choices might affect the future actions of the dealmaker (Player 1). Rewarding a stingy splitter might encourage even worse deals down the road.

Experiments in which transcranial magnetic stimulation was used to disrupt activity in responders' frontal cortices as they played the Ultimatum Game revealed that this kind of interference in processing increased participants' willingness to accept unfair offers (Van't Wout et al., 2005).

Neuroimaging studies provide clues about what brain regions are active when you choose. They don't, however, provide the whole story about what's happening when you are having problems deciding whether to order the chocolate molten lava cake or the white chocolate raspberry swirl cheesecake (**Figure 10.20**).

Neurophysiological experiments point to the intensity of interactions between brain regions (or lack thereof) as a major source of indecision. When transcranial direct current stimulation was applied to regions between the frontal cortex and the parietal cortex as participants made decisions about food choices, the indecisiveness of participants' selections increased (Polania et al., 2015). It

FIGURE 10.20. Hidden preferences. Figuring out what music pets would choose to experience can be tricky when there are no obvious indicators like tail-wagging or fleeing. How might psychologists use neuroeconomics to identify which radio stations a dog loves, despises, or couldn't care less about? (©CSP_chalabala/Fotosearch LBRF/agefotostock)

seems that your brain regions need to keep in synch for your value-based decisions to be sure, at least when it comes to food choices.

SIGHT BITES

 Neuroimaging studies suggest that multiple brain systems interact during decision-making in ways that can be shaped by both internal and external events.

 Circuits in frontal cortex appear to use weighted inputs from sensory cortices and subcortical brain regions to direct response selection.

 The subjective values of different outcomes, as represented in the brain, provide the information necessary for comparing those outcomes.

 Variations in cortical responding during decision-making provide indications of what types of decisions an individual is likely to make.

APPLIED PERSPECTIVES

SNEAK PEEK: Prior beliefs about what is possible can limit the discovery of novel solutions to problems. In some circumstances, cooperative actions work better than any action that an individual might be able to choose on their own. Past emotional experiences can influence decision-making in negative ways, particularly when those experiences involve a lack of control or perceived lack of control.

Applied cognitive psychology as a field is mainly concerned with using findings from cognitive psychology research to solve problems. In educational contexts, the problem to be solved is often the problem of how one can increase students' problem-solving capacities in a particular domain.

Efforts to teach critical thinking skills, for instance, are geared toward enhancing peoples' abilities to reach more defensible conclusions and to identify when others have failed to do this.

The meta-goal of applied cognitive psychology is thus to help people help themselves in real-world contexts. This is also the explicit goal of clinical treatments such as cognitive behavioral therapy and an implicit goal of most other fields of psychological research.

Help comes in many forms, some more obvious than others. For those who have lost hope, it may come in the form of new techniques for overcoming old habits. For those lacking sight, it can come in the form of partnerships that provide new ways of solving basic problems in daily life.

Guide Dogs

For much of human history, blind babies were discarded and blind adults were denigrated. It has only been in the last two centuries that inventors and educators have developed new solutions and technologies that enable blind individuals to operate in environments designed for the sighted.

Blindness raises a host of problems in everyday life, both social and spatial. Those problems affect all other lifetime opportunities. Initial efforts to improve the situation for blind people focused on making information more socially accessible to blind children (through technologies such as Braille) and "vocational rehabilitation," aimed at increasing employable skills, particularly for blind veterans. The consensus view, as recently as the 1940s, was that blind people were essentially helpless and incapable of engaging in normal life.

Exceeding Expectations

A German shepherd initiated the effort to employ trained dogs as assistants for the blind. One day while making the rounds at a military hospital during World War I, a German doctor went to tend to another patient and left his dog with a patient who had been blinded in battle (Ostermeier, 2010). When the doctor came back to retrieve his German shepherd, he noticed that it appeared to be helping the blinded soldier. This episode inspired the doctor to explore whether this kind of behavior might be encouraged in dogs, eventually leading him to open the first guide dog school.

The doctor's recognition of a novel solution to a difficult problem points to the power of deductive reasoning in thinking. If one dog can help one blind soldier, then additional dogs can help multiple blind soldiers. But what prompted the dog to help the soldier? Was the dog responding to cues that accidentally led it to act in ways that were to the soldier's benefit? Or could the dog have recognized that its actions could potentially affect the soldier's capacity to achieve some goal?

Dogs and wolves, close cousins to dogs, are known to naturally possess the capacity to cooperate with others to achieve a goal (Marshall-Pescini et al., 2017). These tendencies have been amplified in some breeds like border collies to enhance their ability to work with humans. German shepherds were selected as the breed of choice for military work within the German army precisely because they excelled at working cooperatively with humans (see Applied Perspectives in Chapter 9). A German shepherd wouldn't need to know that a soldier was blind to feel the urge to provide some help.

As more people became aware of ongoing efforts to train dogs to serve as aides for blinded veterans, the more the problem switched from being one of training dogs to the problem of convincing skeptics that such a solution was feasible. Many in the public doubted the capabilities of the dogs, leading them to worry about the safety of the veterans. Others thought the dogs might interfere with ongoing activities in public spaces. In a way, the problem of public skepticism was a consequence of functional fixedness—dogs were viewed as pets (or pests) and blind people were viewed as invalids.

Eventually, the problems associated with public distrust of guide dogs were solved through demonstration. For instance, in the United States, a charismatic, blinded veteran in his twenties named Morris Frank joined forces with guide dog trainers and began to tour military hospitals as a kind of living example of what guide dogs could make possible.

Today, there are thousands of guide dogs assisting blind people. Training facilities spend years working with dogs to prepare them. Dogs are specifically bred to serve as potential guides, with their lives orchestrated from birth toward that purpose. Despite this selective breeding and years of specialized training, only about 70% of candidates end up qualifying to serve as guide dogs.

Guide dogs are trained on how to walk in straight lines, avoid obstacles, turn at appropriate locations, stop at curbs, respond appropriately to traffic patterns, ignore distractions, follow verbal instructions, assess which overhead obstacles might not be over their owner's head, and so on. In short, guide dogs are trained to solve the problems of navigation for the person they are guiding and to stay the course despite unexpected challenges (squirrels, cats, or kids) they might encounter. Guide dogs have to learn to make embodied decisions for their owner's body.

Collaborative Problem-Solving

It's easy to think of a guide dog as like a fancy cane—a tool that helps a blind person avoid running into things. Guide dogs do provide mobility support but their role is closer to that of a personal care worker than it is to a stick.

Guide dogs can greatly increase a blind person's independence, activity level, and confidence. The roles that guide dogs play in navigation can vary depending on their owners and the circumstances. Blind owners of guide dogs are often not dog trainers and may think of their dogs more as

FIGURE 10.21. Sightless navigation. Some individuals born blind have discovered ways of navigating by actively producing click sounds—a form of human echolocation. How might the decision-making of a blind bicyclist be similar to that of a person assisted by a guide dog? (PopTech, CC BY-SA 2.0, via Wikimedia Commons)

helpful pets than as tools. The owner may initiate travel and then dynamically exchange roles with the dog as they move along, with the dog initiating movements to avoid obstacles or navigate intersections and the owner initiating movements after social interactions or if the dog gets distracted.

Traveling with a guide dog appears to require collective decision-making about who will be in charge of leading when. Both partners have incomplete information about how to achieve specific goals. The dog may have limited awareness that there is a long-term goal, and the owner may have limited awareness of physical obstacles that stand in the way of reaching that goal.

Blind owners generally prefer that a guide dog be confident and able to act independently during navigation, especially when the dog disagrees with the owner about the best path to take and when to take it (Craigon et al., 2017). On the other hand, owners are not fond of being pulled around in ways that are unpredictable or uncomfortable. Unpredictable, disobedient, inattentive, or indecisive guide dogs cause anxiety. High certainty increases the subjective value of navigating with a guide dog (**Figure 10.21**).

One practical issue with the use of guide dogs is figuring out which dogs will be most competent at serving this role and what sorts of training will maximize a dog's likelihood of success. Recent studies suggest that problem-solving abilities and boldness at a young age are good predictors of which dogs will succeed. And somewhat surprisingly, how much mothers pamper their puppies seems to be predictive of the puppies' problem-solving prowess. Specifically, more attentive mothers produce less capable problem-solvers and less successful guide dogs.

This seems to be a general trend as pet dogs show less motivation and problem-solving abilities when faced with novel problems than do many wild birds or wolves (Udell, 2015). Instead, most pet dogs tend to try and recruit humans to solve problems for them (Ostojic & Clayton, 2014). The tendency for pampered pooches to pass the buck when it comes to problem-solving may also be an issue for other animals, including humans.

When modern humans are faced with a problem, they are less likely to crank up their reasoning processes than to just ask Alexa or Google it. Why reason when you can just ask? It remains to be seen what the effects of persistent reliance on prepackaged solutions will be for the problem-solving skills of future generations, but the phrase "use it or lose it" seems pertinent.

Overcoming Learned Helplessness

The inability to solve a problem or confidently make a decision can lead to feelings of helplessness and hopelessness. In some circumstances, these feelings are warranted, but in many others, they are pointless.

As noted earlier, people tend to assume that mental mistakes happen when people do not think through a problem long enough or are deficient thinkers. The deer frozen in headlights is emblematic of poor decision-making in the face of an oncoming disaster.

In the late 1960s, psychologists studying dogs discovered **learned helplessness**, a phenomenon in which individuals faced with continuous electrical shock simply sat there and took it rather than attempting to escape. Learned helplessness occurred when dogs had previously experienced sessions in which shocks were inescapable. It seemed that the dogs had learned that getting shocked is just what happens in laboratories.

Follow-up experiments revealed that learned helplessness was not specific to dogs and could also be observed in rats, fish, cats, mice, and humans (Seligman, 1972). The kinds of passive responses to suffering observed in human studies were similar to the symptoms of depression, leading some psychologists to suspect that this mental disorder might be a natural case of learned helplessness (Seligman, 1978).

Over the last fifty years, thousands of studies of learned helplessness have provided new clues about the circumstances and mechanisms that lead to this kind of irrational opting out, as well as ways that it can potentially be avoided (Maier & Seligman, 2016).

Failed Efforts

The original studies of learned helplessness in dogs were actually designed to show the opposite phenomenon. Researchers expected that if dogs were initially given shocks paired with warning signals while immobilized in a hammock (so that they would rapidly learn that the signal predicted an impending shock; see Chapter 7), and then they were placed in an enclosure where these kinds of painful shocks were predicted by this same signal, that the hammock-trained dogs would learn to jump out of the enclosure more quickly than dogs that had never experienced the signal paired with shock (since presumably, the trained dogs would "run for cover" once the shock alarm came on, while the naïve dogs would be oblivious to what the alarm meant). This did not happen, and in many cases (about 100) the pre-shocked dogs never learned to jump out of the enclosure to escape the shock. Dogs that had not learned about the alarm in shocking hammocks, in contrast, learned to jump out of the enclosure after relatively few shocks, the opposite outcome from what experimenters had expected.

Most intriguingly, dogs that were pre-shocked in the hammock but given a way to cut the alarm and shock off while in the hammock (say by pressing a button with their nose) learned to escape from the shock chamber just as quickly as naïve dogs. These findings were interpreted as evidence that dogs shocked in situations where there was nothing they could do about it became passive and unable to learn that their actions could reduce their suffering (in other words, they were taught that they were helpless).

Learned helplessness in humans is a bit more complex. Participants in experiments tended to come up with explanations for why their efforts were a waste of time (excuses for their passivity). In some cases, these explanations portrayed the sources of helplessness as temporary. In others, the proposed causes were more permanent. These different explanations were predictive of how long the effects of learned helplessness lasted. People also drew distinctions between personal failures versus problems that were simply unsolvable.

Studies with human participants suggested that the experience of inescapable suffering was less critical to producing learned helplessness than was the person's beliefs about why the specific negative experiences were unavoidable. When people expected that a problem should be solvable, they were more likely to break free from learned helplessness. Similar hypotheses about how children's beliefs sometimes lead to feelings of helplessness have increasingly been emphasized in educational settings.

Fixed Mindsets

A **growth mindset** is the belief that human problem-solving capacities are not genetically predetermined but can be improved through practice. The counterpoint, a **fixed mindset**, is the view that problem-solving and reasoning abilities are a talent that some people are born with and others are not (Haimovitz & Dweck, 2017).

Mindset researchers argue that children who explain their academic performances from a fixed mindset are less motivated to learn and more likely to experience a kind of helplessness or "wilting" in the face of poor academic performance. They suggest that the specific goals that children select (the outcomes they expect) can determine whether they will persist in attempting to escape from poor performance or simply settle for failing.

The idea that a child's mindset might determine what they learn quickly caught fire. It provided a potential explanation for why different children exposed to similar academic challenges might come out of those experiences with dramatically different outcomes—specifically, why some individuals might rise to a challenge while others might crash and burn. Evidence also suggested that children's views about the causes of academic success were themselves learned, implying that children could be taught to have either a growth mindset or a fixed mindset. In that case, shaping a child's beliefs could potentially free them from the risks of academic learned helplessness.

Recent attempts at developing interventions to foster growth mindsets in young children have focused on teaching children about brain plasticity and how learning can change connections to form "stronger" networks. There is also an effort to construct "growth mindset cultures" that promote the idea of growth mindset in a more immersive way. These kinds of interventions have been implemented in classrooms around the world.

It's difficult to know how the "punishment" of performing poorly in an academic setting compares with the physical pain produced by a strong electrical shock, or whether the passive experience of being repeatedly shocked in a hammock leads to similar expectations as intermittently getting incorrect solutions to math problems in a classroom. Consequently, any negative academic outcomes associated with a fixed mindset might involve different mechanisms than those that lead to learned helplessness.

Relatedly, the benefits of interventions designed to increase the number of children with growth mindsets could come from learned industriousness, which can be increased when effort is consistently rewarded, rather than from any reduction in learned helplessness (Eisenberger, 1992).

Regardless of the origins of learned helplessness, the negative consequences of giving up prematurely, either in school or in life, are clearly a problem worth solving. Luckily, some headway is being made toward this goal.

Mental Interventions

Coaches are infamous for hating on quitters. Experimental studies provide little indication that this is an effective strategy for reducing learned helplessness, however. One strategy that was found to be preventative in animal experiments was initial exposure to escapable shocks, a process called immunization. This kind of behavioral immunization seems to erase the soul-killing effects of later inescapable shocks (Greenwood & Fleshner, 2008). It's almost as if knowing that escape is possible keeps a glimmer of hope alive.

The protective power of immunization suggests that knowledge of what is possible can go a long way toward preventing learned helplessness. In cases like clinical depression, however, the sufferer presumably knows that it is possible to not be depressed and yet is still unable to break free from bleakness. Experiencing a successful escape from a painful state may be more important than awareness that this is sometimes possible. It's neither practical nor ethical to purposefully make people depressed so they have the opportunity to break out of depression. Furthermore, such depressive immunization might make recovery even more difficult because people diagnosed with depression are prone to relapse.

An alternative strategy for combatting learned helplessness is to identify what processes in the brain are contributing to this phenomenon and to explore whether they can be controlled. At this point, you will hopefully not be surprised to learn that interactions between the frontal cortex and basal ganglia are key players in learned helplessness (Maier & Seligman, 2016).

Prolonged aversive events like repeated hammock shocks lead to long-lasting increases in the delivery of neurochemicals, such as serotonin, throughout the brain. This change in neurochemical balance increases passivity and emotional responses to unpleasant events. Immunization experiences and other experiences in which animals can shut down a painful stimulus enable frontal circuits to counteract these neurochemical changes (Fallon et al., 2020).

Learned helplessness seems to result when circuits in frontal cortex are not inhibiting the increased release of neurochemicals. When frontal circuits are inhibiting passivity and anxiety, individuals can make better choices and learning proceeds quickly. The same kinds of processing that enable frontal circuits to monitor ongoing cortical utility evaluation and response selection by the basal ganglia seem to also be involved in counteracting learned helplessness.

From this perspective, individuals do not learn that they are powerless after repeated inescapable punishments (**Figure 10.22**), but they CAN learn that there are ways that they can control outcomes by selecting appropriate actions. Apparently, memories of successful problem-solving in similar contexts make the suppression of less helpful neurochemical states possible. Overcoming learned helplessness in this context means shutting down reflexive internal reactions that would otherwise make learning (or escape) difficult or impossible.

FIGURE 10.22. Learned helplessness. Elephants that learn from a young age that ropes prevent them from moving around freely will continue to behave as if this is still true long after they could easily break the rope. How many early educational experiences play a similar role in human behavior? (Anka Agency International/Alamy Stock Photo)

CLOSURE

Gandhi was undoubtedly a successful political strategist. His strategies worked because they changed people's decisions. He convinced Indians to choose to protest nonviolently, which contributed to the decision of British politicians to exit India.

Were the same cognitive processes driving the decisions made by all of the actors in this political drama? Probably not. British politicians may have been relying on deductive reasoning focused on maximizing economic costs and benefits, effectively playing the Ultimatum Game on a larger scale. Gandhi's followers might have been persuaded by inductive reasoning after seeing the positive effects of his civil disobedience. Gandhi rejected utility as a criterion for making decisions, instead arguing that the choice itself was all that mattered, regardless of the outcome.

Problem-solving, reasoning, and decision-making are clearly intertwined cognitive processes that together form the core of thinking, whether that thinking has global implications or simply affects what you decide to do next. Overthinking is warned against (except by proponents of dual systems models), but underthinking is just as problematic. And even the "right amount" of thinking can lead to poor choices when cognitive biases take over.

Modern theories of thinking focus heavily on information-based computations performed using algorithms that act on symbolic representations. The recent successes of artificial intelligence show that this is a powerful approach to solving problems. But the role such processes play in human thinking and in the problem-solving skills of other animals is still up for debate. Thought-provoking statements can change a person's mental set, but this does not imply that most of the thinking that people do each day depends on internalized conversations or the conscious evaluation of propositions.

When someone makes a decision based on a gut feeling, they are still making that choice for a "reason," even if that reason is a somatic feeling rather than a verbalizable proposition. Proponents of embodied cognition argue that much of thinking and action selection involves this sort of percept-driven decision-making. Gandhi's focus on choices rather than outcomes also highlights the importance of moral feelings versus explicit goals in making decisions—feelings that drive one to do what's right, come what may.

Right now, you are thinking about thinking. You may also be reasoning about thinking or deciding what you think about the propositions that you are reading. You might even be wondering if the propositions are valid. From the perspective of cognitive psychology, your decisions about what thinking is, how it works, when it works, and who does it should all be based on objective evidence. This is a somewhat different perspective from philosophy, in which thinking should work itself out, or from religion, in which right thinking should be revelatory. The challenges for psychologists are to decide what sorts of evidence will provide the clearest views on thinking, to develop methods for collecting relevant evidence, and trickiest of all, to figure out what the collected evidence means.

COGNITIVE LINGO

algorithm	heuristics	rational thought
analogical reasoning	ill-defined problem	reasoning
availability heuristic	illusory correlation	representativeness heuristic
base rate	inductive reasoning	situated cognition
behavioral economics	learned helplessness	small-sample fallacy
belief-bias effect (or belief bias)	loss aversion	somatic marker hypothesis
confirmation bias	matching law	syllogism
deductive reasoning	means-end heuristic	transitive inference
dual process model	mental set	Ultimatum Game
fixed mindset	Nash equilibrium	utility
framing effect	neuroeconomics	utility curve
functional fixedness	optimal foraging theory	Wason Four-Card Problem
groupthink	proposition	well-defined problem
growth mindset	rational choice theory	

CHAPTER SUMMARY

Solving Problems

Problems can be well-defined, ill-defined, or your relatives. Problem-solving often involves setting goals, applying heuristics, and assessing outcomes. Recognition of the essential qualities of a problem guides the cognitive processes used to solve it.

Reasoning

Combining evidence to draw a conclusion, inductive reasoning, is often contrasted with logically selecting propositions, deductive reasoning. Reasoning does not always produce correct solutions because of factors like confirmation bias and illusory correlations. Reasoning about the reasoning of others can also be influenced by logical fallacies.

When Decisions are Made

Decisions depend not just on what information is available but also on how the information is presented or framed. The feelings one experiences, including the perceived utility of different options and internal sensations of unease, can affect decisions and action selection as much as objective facts.

Brain Substrates

Different brain regions become active depending on whether you are considering the pros or cons of a particular choice. As considerations of consequences shift, so does the activity in frontal cortical circuits. The intensity of interactions between different regions determines feelings of indecision.

Applied Perspectives

Limitations related to disabilities or depression can lead to an inability to select better options. Strategies that take into account these roadblocks to problem-solving can provide ways of overcoming such limitations.

REVIEW EXERCISES

Solving Problems
• Explain how algorithms differ from heuristics.
• Provide examples of how a mental set can affect attempts at solving a problem.
• Outline how functional fixedness might help or hurt an expert solve problems.

Reasoning
• Summarize the key elements of inductive reasoning.
• Define and provide examples of syllogisms.
• How have psychologists studied the reasoning abilities of nonhumans?

When Decisions Are Made
• What are framing effects and how can they lead to poor decisions?

• Explain how the matching law is related to decision-making.

Brain Substrates
• What role does the frontal cortex play in decision-making?
• Describe the relationship between neuroeconomics and behavioral economics.

Applied Perspectives
• Provide an example of collaborative problem-solving in a real-world context.
• What conditions contribute to learned helplessness and what interventions are used to avoid this outcome?

CRITICAL THINKING QUESTIONS

1. Mathematics problems are often well-defined but difficult to solve while choosing what to eat for lunch is an ill-defined problem that is easy to solve. What makes math problems harder to solve than selecting a meal?

2. Hypotheses are typically arrived at through inductive reasoning. How might one come up with a hypothesis using deductive reasoning?

3. When the Wason Four-Card Problem is presented using meaningful words instead of letters and numbers, students are better able to logically evaluate the validity of statements about the cards. What does this suggest about how symbolic representations affect deductive reasoning?

4. Framing effects can influence the decisions that you make. How might the framing of a critical thinking question influence the answers that you come up with for it or how you attempt to answer it?

5. The brain regions that contribute to decision-making in adult humans overlap with those that other animals use to make decisions. If damaging a specific brain region in two different species leads to similar cognitive biases, what can you conclude about the role that this region plays in reasoning?

Knowing That

I f someone were to accost you after you have read most of this book and ask you, "What do you really know now that you didn't know before?" you might respond by saying something like, "I know who William James is." If you're feeling generous, you might even elaborate by explaining what you now know about one of the many esoteric theories or experiments you've read about. Most modern standards of "knowing" are based on what you can convey to others through speech or writing. If you claim to have learned lots of new things but are unable to say what any of those things are, people will most likely be unconvinced. Actions may speak louder than words when it comes to following through on a promise, but words remain the gold standard for demonstrating knowledge both in everyday life and in scientific fields like cognitive psychology.

Knowing that William James was a famous American psychologist implies more than simply being aware of that fact. It implies some ability to share this knowledge with others. Doing so requires some ability to communicate complex information, which, in turn, requires some ability to detect what others are likely to understand. You will be hard-pressed to convince a dog that you know something about William James, regardless of how sophisticated your communication skills are. Of course, you may know secrets that you'd never share with anyone, but even then you have the capacity to do so. Many psychologists believe that it is this capacity that makes sophisticated human cognition possible, specifically the capacity to represent and share knowledge in ways that persist longer than any individual knowers.

Communal Knowing

Much of what you know about cognition, and every other aspect of your life, you have gained from both direct and indirect social interactions (including reading this book!). Certainly, most of the words and communicative gestures you use daily are either borrowed from others or derived from words you have heard in the past. This is not the case for most other species, which has led many to suspect that the ability of humans to share knowledge in this way is what makes humans cognitively special. Language, imitation, culture, and intuitions about others' thoughts and feelings all contribute to (and benefit from) interactive social processes of knowledge sharing.

But, how special are these social knowledge generators? Are social cognitive processes the special sauce that makes human minds possible? And if so, do those processes rely on genetically-specialized circuitry that is only available to humans? Philosophical, religious, and scientific answers to these questions have fluctuated over time. James argued that the seeming specialness of human cognition was a mirage, and the basic principles of cognition and consciousness that lead to abilities such as concept formation, memory, and reasoning applied to all minds, not just those of adult humans. Whether his interpretations are insights or mistakes remains to be seen. Psychologists were once convinced that face recognition was a specialized human capacity, a "reasonable" belief that has since been completely debunked. Not only is face recognition not unique to humans but it also is not even unique to vertebrates. The capacity of cognitive experiments to challenge intuitive assumptions about how human cognition works (and about its unique qualities) is one of its primary strengths. Research exploring the role of social interactions and communication in cognition can potentially shed light on the value of formal schooling versus on-the-job training ("knowing that" or "knowing how") in a variety of social contexts both at schools and in careers.

Superficially, most cognitive research might seem to be asocial. Participants sit in a lab and are asked to perform tasks on their own, with minimal feedback from peers or experimenters. Experiments are designed to minimize direct social influences aside from conversations before and after task performance and instructions given during some tasks. At a deeper level, however, all cognitive experiments are steeped in social cognitive performances. No amount of isolation can make participants unaware that their performance is being motivated by and evaluated by others. In most cognitive tasks, participants are given instructions about what they should attempt to do while in the lab, and those who cannot understand (or follow) those instructions, for whatever reason, are excluded from consideration when interpreting experimental results. Instructions, whether spoken or written, depend on socially-acquired knowledge, and thus ground task performance within the context of past social interactions. In this respect, every cognitive experiment could be viewed as a test of each participant's capacity to generalize socially-acquired knowledge and skills to a novel context.

Intercourse

Beliefs about the modularity of cognitive mechanisms (especially the circuits that make language learning and imitation possible) have motivated large numbers of cognitive neuroscience studies over the last half-century. Some textbooks even attribute the rise of cognitive psychology to Noam Chomsky's claims about the special status of language. Cognitive psychologists effectively shifted scientific conversations away from questions like "What determines how organisms behave?" toward questions like "How do people know?" And a seemingly straightforward way of finding out how people know is to ask others (or yourself), "What do people know?" Someone following in the footsteps of Chomsky might reply that people know whatever their cognitive modules have evolved to enable them to know. That follower might further suggest that the best way to know what (and how) people know is to pay attention to what they say and do in response to instructions.

Participants' language skills can potentially provide a window into their ongoing mental processes. In fact, James argued that "large tracts of human speech are nothing but signs of direction in thought" (James, 1890, v. 1, p. 253) However, just as rose-colored glasses may distort one's view of the world, scientific attempts to understand minds through the lens of language may provide an incomplete picture. For instance, early studies of individuals with brain damage who also had language problems suggested that certain regions in a human's left hemisphere were specialized language modules. Only later, when new brain-imaging technologies became available, was it discovered that language use engaged widely distributed regions and that nonlinguistic tasks often engaged these same regions. James actively protested against overreliance on language as a means of understanding cognition, noting that "language is the most imperfect and expensive means yet discovered for communicating thought," and suggesting that "language works against our perception of the truth" (James, 1890, v. 1, p. 241). Of course, he was stuck with the reality that the only way he could convey his frustration and warnings to others was through language.

Like James, you are currently stuck with language as the main social tool for knowing about cognition (including the strengths and limits of sentences). Understanding how your main tool for knowing works (or at least for revealing your knowledge) can potentially help you think more deeply about a wide range of cognitive processes, from the development of abstract concepts to the storage and retrieval of narratives describing what your childhood was like. The following chapters will give you a chance to apply what you know to better understand how you can know, as well as how you can reveal your knowledge to others through intercourse.

11 Social Cognition

© Streets United Entertainment

Ryan was everything. Her first thought in the morning and her last every night. The reason for spending $100 on that new makeup. The reason for taking an 8 a.m. course on a topic no one would ever voluntarily think about. He knew she existed, but that was all she knew about what he knew. That was all she needed to know. He had looked into her eyes (twice!) and he knew her name—success beyond her wildest imagination. One time, he had even brushed up against her as they were leaving class. She had almost lost it.

Ryan was a player. He'd figured out early on that he had a gift for seduction and the looks to back it up. He naturally conveyed an aura of disinterest with flashes of beguiling adoration that he could unleash when the need arose. Ryan assumed, mostly accurately, that there were four or more women pining for him at any given moment, and possibly a couple of guys as well. He considered them to be like a set of golf clubs, waiting to be used when the moment to strike was right.

She knew she was lovesick and she was sick of it. The whole thing seemed idiotic. Ryan wasn't even her type, so why couldn't she stop thinking about him? Her friends had told her he was bad news—didn't matter. The heart wants what the mind can't grasp, or something like that. It was literally painful to sit behind him. She wasn't sure how much more she could take or how she could see him more often without looking as pathetic as she felt.

How was Ryan able to annihilate bright minds left and right by simply grinning? What sort of evolutionary process produces a brain that can be brought to its knees by a u-shaped orifice revealing teeth? Love conquers all, which is not necessarily a good thing since intense lovesickness can churn out obsessive stalkers, suicidal teens, and bouts of depression. What's good for the species may not be so good for the lovelorn.

Few events produce more intense experiences than those that lead to infatuation or romantic love (**Figure 11.1**). The mix of anticipation, craving, anxiety, caring, and obsessive thinking not only

405

FIGURE 11.1. Lovelorn. Lovesickness is like a mental virus that seizes control of a person's attention and ability to think straight. How might simply seeing another person unleash such a dramatic shift in cognitive processing? What does this phenomenon suggest about computational models of minds? (Mukhina1)

changes how a person feels but it can also change how that person sees the world, imagines the future, and conceives of themself. Social interactions need not be as intense as love at first sight to affect the way you think, however. Simply attending classes and talking with friends can do the trick. Social cognition refers to all the mental processes that determine how people think and feel about social interactions, as well as the consequences of such interactions on people's knowledge and beliefs.

Studies of social cognition attempt to explain social behavior in terms of cognitive processes and clarify the consequences of cognition on social interactions. The kinds of social interactions researchers are interested in are not just face-to-face encounters between individuals. They also include interactions within and between groups as well as individuals' interactions with themselves.

Self-contemplation lies at the heart of cognitive research. From René Descartes to William James, thinkers throughout history agree that the most conclusive evidence that cognizing happens comes from one's awareness that it happens (Metcalfe & Son, 2012; Rosenthal, 2000). Navel-gazing may seem totally different from people watching, but the cognitive processes that make both possible turn out to be more similar than you might think. Self-cognizing and social cognition are kissing cousins.

Much of what you know, including whatever you are gleaning from this book, comes from "others." Similarly, the cognitive skills you possess have been shaped either directly or indirectly by an extended community of thinkers. Given that how you think and what you know is strongly shaped by social forces, your understanding of cognition cannot be complete without taking those phenomena into account.

"The most peculiar social self which one is apt to have is in the mind of the person one is in love with."
—James, 1890, p 294

This chapter reconsiders many of the cognitive processes presented in earlier chapters but through a social lens. The goal of this approach is to evaluate whether there might be elements of social cognition that are "special" in terms of how they function and when they come online.

BEHAVIORAL PROCESSES

A commonsense view on thinking is that it is a kind of internal chatter or silent self-talk. If you are talking to yourself when you think, then what's the point? Surely telling yourself something you already know cannot change what you know.

The fact that this sort of internal dialogue is what most people would call thinking suggests that perhaps this is what thinking is really like—a conversation. Perhaps when you think, you really are conversing, like a child might talk to an invisible friend. If that's the case, then your thought processes would be a special case of social interaction, and the cognitive mechanisms involved in social interactions would presumably overlap quite a bit with thinking.

Why stop there? If your deliberative thought processes are like verbal social interactions, maybe your unconscious thought processes are like your nonverbal social interactions—the subtle glance, the giggle, the kiss. Could your experience of yourself simply be an extension of your experience of others? And if you value the opinions of others, how much of your sense of self is coming from you versus them?

The following sections evaluate more closely how your social interactions (and those of your ancestors) affect how you think and how you perceive the world. Throughout your life, your experiences have consistently been with others and of others. Those experiences have shaped your categories and concepts, what attracts your attention, and what you ignore—in short, what you cognize. As discussed in previous chapters, how you attend to, sort, and recognize things determines how you think and what you know. Consequently, no aspect of your mind is free from the influence of your social past.

Social Cognizance

SNEAK PEEK: Understanding the world of social interactions starts with the ability to recognize social agents and the implications of their movements. How do people quickly assess social situations and the intentions of others?

Most days, you are aware of yourself and other people. Your impressions of the social world, and your place in it, likely drive many of the actions you select, the thoughts you think, and the events you notice. Whether you are looking for entertainment, solutions to problems, or a deeper understanding of the universe, you are likely to turn to others.

When you're watching the action in a movie theater or hearing it from an audiobook, the events that keep you riveted are the social dramas. These events maintain interest because they involve interactions. And not just any interactions like, say, raindrops hitting a puddle, but social interactions that engage mental representations of agents with minds.

Detecting Animacy

Sensitivity to biological motion, the movements of animals, shows up quite early in development (Simion et al., 2008). Infants prefer visually perceived biological motion to other movements in the first few days after birth, and they probably learn to detect the tactile rhythms of their moving mother long before that (Greiner et al., 2022). Biological motion is an attentional magnet that facilitates social perception. As development progresses, the complexity of social information that infants perceive from watching the movements of agents gradually increases (Sifre et al., 2018).

Perception of Animacy

Biological motions include a wide variety of movement patterns—all the actions that living organisms can perform. At a detailed level, the motions may vary greatly across species and an individual's life span. Nevertheless, there do seem to be common elements that may serve as markers of biological control.

Animacy refers to the state of being alive and mobile. Organisms need not be sophisticated to provoke impressions of animacy. All that is needed is for certain trajectories and styles of movement to occur. The dynamically structured patterns of moving dots that are characteristic of point-light displays (discussed in Chapter 4) suggest animacy but so can a single dot if it moves in the right way.

Perception of animacy becomes even more likely when there are interactions between moving objects. For instance, if you were to observe a large silver disk hovering high above you everywhere you went, the correlation between your movements and the disk's would likely convince you something biological is controlling the disk's movements and whoever or whatever was in control of the disk was interested in you.

FIGURE 11.2. Animate shapes. Depending on how they move relative to one another, (A) a large triangle may be perceived as chasing other shapes around a box or (B) attempting to break into a room to get to a ball. (C) When their movements are coordinated, a smaller triangle can also seem to be trying to convince a larger triangle to leave a box. (After Gao & Scholl, 2011, *J Exp Psychol Hum Percept Perform* 37, Used with permission of American Psychological Association)

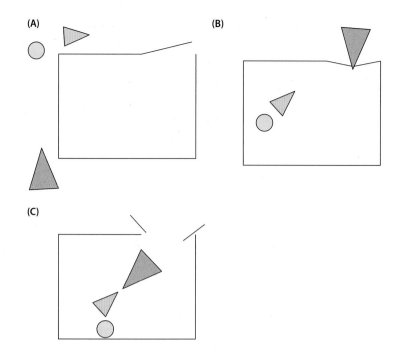

In laboratory experiments, simple shapes, such as triangles and squares, can be perceived as being alive (or as representing living agents) if they interact in socially interpretable ways (**Figure 11.2**). Cartoons capitalize on this phenomenon.

Perception of animacy in moving objects or agents occurs rapidly and automatically. The fact that you know shapes are not alive has no effect on your perception of their movements. The immediacy with which you can recognize point-light displays as walking agents, or that an animated lamp is "playing with a ball" (in *Luxo Jr.* by Pixar), is consistent with the idea that perception of animacy is an intrinsic property of seeing (Edwards & Shafer, 2022). You don't decide that cartoons look like real social interactions. Perceptually, they *are* real social interactions.

In children, the perception of biological motion and animacy are tightly linked to social cognitive abilities (Pavlova, 2012). For instance, a child's lack of sensitivity to biological motion is predictive of whether they will be diagnosed with autism spectrum disorder, a developmental disorder associated with deficits in social skills (Federici et al., 2020). And the level of the diagnosis (level 1 being the mildest form and level 3 being the most severe) is correlated with how insensitive a child is to biological motion. Evidence of abnormal processing of biological motion in toddlers who were later diagnosed with autism suggests that insensitivity to animacy may contribute to the reduced social abilities associated with this disorder (Todorova et al., 2019).

Behavior Contagion

Much of the research on animacy detection and perception has focused on how people attend to or interpret movements. However, perceiving biological motion also increases the likelihood that the observer will replicate aspects of those movements, a phenomenon known as **behavior contagion** or automatic imitation.

Behavior contagion can happen automatically and unconsciously. Even if an observer does not physically perform movements that correspond to those being observed, the observer may be primed to execute those actions, showing faster reaction times if they are instructed to move similarly, or they may be less able to perform actions that are inconsistent with the ones they observed (Heyes, 2011).

Some researchers interpret the strong links between the perception of biological motion and the production of similar motion as evidence of cross-modal mental representations of action, referred to as the **ideomotor theory** of action control (Moeller & Pfister, 2022; Shin et al., 2010). The ideomotor theory assumes that actions are represented in terms of the perceivable effects that they cause (visual and kinesthetic). In other words, you represent actions that you can recognize the same way you represent actions that you can perform, a view considered more closely in the discussion of mirror neurons in the Brain Substrates section of this chapter.

Person Perception and Social Judgment

Some of the most salient biological motions for a newborn are facial expressions. Chapter 3 discussed the importance of such movements for emotion perception, and Chapter 4 considered the possibility that there are modules in the human brain that are specialized for extracting information from faces. Although facial features clearly attract attention, not all faces are created equal. Familiar faces are processed more effectively than the faces of strangers (Ramon & Gobbini, 2018).

Generally, perception of facial movements and biological motion becomes more precise after repeated experiences, a phenomenon called **perceptual narrowing**. Perceptual narrowing occurs not just in human infants but also in other social species. Social interactions are part of what determines how facial processing narrows during development (Maurer & Werker, 2014).

Social Vision

Adults apprehend a lot from a face in only a few hundred milliseconds. Gender, race, age, and other socially-relevant qualities are almost immediately available. Basic emotions, such as anger or happiness, can be identified in even quicker glimpses.

Participants asked to describe faces based on brief presentations often describe them in terms of qualities associated with emotional and social traits: unhappy, caring, weird, mean, dominant, confident, sociable, attractive, stable, responsible, aggressive, or trustworthy (Todorov et al., 2008). Specific facial configurations tend to be associated with each of these traits. Some individuals are born with skull shapes that lead to facial features associated with one of these categories so that by default, the person looks more aggressive or responsible than they are. If you hang around with such individuals long enough, behavior contagion might end up causing you to unconsciously mimic their inborn expressions.

The different traits that you automatically attribute to people at first glance are partly a consequence of social categories that you've learned through experience. Although a few categories may come immediately to mind when you see a face, numerous other categories are simultaneously activated. In some cases, these secondary activations may be so weak that you are unaware of them. Even so, they can still affect how you perceive the person.

Evidence of covert, social-category activation has come from studies where participants move a mouse to choose a category for a particular face (Stillman et al., 2018). Interactions between categories can lead to deviations in mouse movements that provide evidence of competing categories. Additional evidence that unconscious categories can influence your subjective impressions comes from tests of implicit bias, such as the **implicit association test** in which reaction times are used as indirect measures of interference between social categories.

Perceiving Social Dimensions

The labels that you assign to briefly viewed individuals (which include not only humans but also other animals) are a function of both the visual features that enable you to recognize the image and the various learned social categories you have formed (especially categories related to age, race, and gender). Many of those labels correspond to endpoints along social dimensions like mean versus nice or aggressive versus docile. These dimensions are often interdependent (for example, a mean person is likely to also be aggressive).

Spontaneous first impressions of others based on their faces, clothes, or actions can have surprisingly strong effects on how you judge a person and may lead to erroneous assumptions. Attributing qualities like trustworthiness to individuals based only on their facial features, aside from being a

(A)

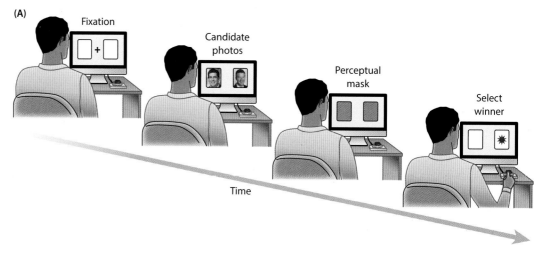

Time

(B)

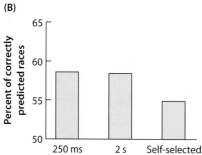

FIGURE 11.3. Flash politics. (A) Participants were given 250 milliseconds, 2 seconds, or a self-selected duration to view pairs of unfamiliar congressional candidates, followed by images that perceptually masked the photos. (B) When asked to judge which candidate looked more competent, their answers corresponded to the candidate who won close to 60% of the time. Good thing candidates spend millions of dollars trying to sway voters. (A both inset images: aastock via Shutterstock; B after Ballew & Todorov, 2007)

questionable method of identifying honest people, suggests that relatively sophisticated conceptualizations of the minds and intentions of others come into play at the earliest stages of perceptual processing.

As noted in Chapter 4, people can predict with about 70% accuracy who will win elections after viewing the candidates' publicity photos for about 100 milliseconds and then ranking the photos in terms of competence (**Figure 11.3**). Presumably, the participants were not psychic, which means that many voters' decisions also are likely to have been swayed by similar visual impressions.

Participants rapidly judging politicians on whether they look competent likely do so based either on memories of politicians they perceive to be competent or on some general qualities of attractiveness (Olivola et al., 2014). Optimistically, we can hope that winning an election may sometime lead to a self-fulfilling prophecy if a candidate feels pressure to live up to voters' opinions of the candidate's competence. At the same time, as the number of dishonest politicians that are elected increases, the more likely it becomes that people will begin to view physical indicators of dishonesty as markers of political competence.

Gaze Allocation

Social interactions generally do not consist of people simply looking at each other and making judgments. Interactions are usually dynamic, with multiple actors dividing their time between participants and choosing their actions and reactions on the fly. What exactly do people experience in such fluid social contexts?

Studies examining where people fixate, called **gaze allocation**, show that people spend most of their time in social contexts looking at other people (surprise), and they tend to spend more time gazing at people they perceive as socially dominant (Foulsham et al., 2010). This bias in gaze allocation was present even when the dominant individual was not the person doing most of the talking. Attention appears to be dynamically distributed depending on where socially interacting individuals expect the most relevant events to occur (Foulsham et al., 2011).

People spend a lot of time looking at the eyes of interacting individuals, a pattern that also shows up in people watching movies for entertainment. Eye-tracking studies provide an objective measure of whom observers focus on (and when) in social interactions. This approach has been expanded to studies of chimpanzees interacting with humans, providing new insights into how apes view each other (and humans) in social interactions, as well as insights into what apes' impressions are of others' knowledge about what's happening and what's about to happen (Lewis & Krupenye, 2022). These impressions reveal a kind of social savviness in chimpanzees that goes beyond social perception and into the realm of social thinking.

SIGHT BITES

Perceptual and attentional mechanisms for identifying and interpreting animacy and biological motion provide the experiences that ground social cognitive processes.

Individuals rapidly extrapolate from minimal visual information about a person's face and movements to classify the possible status, states, and traits of that person.

Social Thinking

SNEAK PEEK: Although many social interactions happen effortlessly and automatically, they can also be influenced by conscious consideration of the social situation. Natural impulses to empathize or cooperate can be suppressed by decision-making processes that take into account past experiences or possible future outcomes.

There are a couple of ideas about why human cognition is what it is. One, called the **social brain hypothesis**, is that when social interactions increased in complexity over evolutionary time scales, new demands were placed on information processing and memory capacities, providing a selective advantage for individuals with larger brains and greater cognitive capacity (Dunbar, 2009). In this scenario, human cognition is what evolves when successful navigation of complex social scenes is adaptive.

A second proposal, compatible with the social brain hypothesis but distinct from it, is that at some point in the evolution of humans, there was a mutation that made it possible for humans to learn language (or symbolically represented facts), and the appearance of this new ability radically changed what humans could achieve cognitively (Deacon, 1997). Language acquisition and use is inherently a socially interactive process (see Chapter 12), so here again the force driving the evolution of human thought is presumed to be social interactions.

Why might living in groups lead to any sort of complex thinking? After all, cows and ants live in groups and they don't seem to require sophisticated thinking abilities. Most attempts to answer this question have focused on the potential advantages of being able to precisely predict how specific individuals will behave in a wide variety of circumstances. The assumptions underlying these proposed explanations for human cognition are: (1) understanding why others behave the way they do can help you to socially interact in more productive ways, and (2) to achieve this kind of understanding of others' actions you need a theory of mind.

Understanding Theory of Mind

Recall from Chapter 3 that your **theory of mind** includes your ideas not just about others' mental states—their feelings, thoughts, beliefs, and desires—but also your thoughts about your own mind. Theory of mind refers to a type of metacognition (see Chapter 8) in which you think about or recognize what minds are like and how mental states can potentially affect people's behavior (Kloo et al., 2021). The field of cognitive psychology is essentially a collaborative, stylized theory of mind constructed by scientists based on methodically collected evidence.

Most people's theory of mind is more improvised than that of a cognitive psychologist; it is based on their personal experiences and word of mouth (or the Internet). Your theory of mind is what enables you to make social inferences.

Social Inference

Social inferences are conclusions you reach about other minds—what they are like and why. These conclusions can include split-second guesses about a person's qualities based on appearance, but they also can include more nuanced evaluations that take personal histories into account. The popular sport of "people watching" usually involves social inferencing based on overheard dialogue and behavioral clues. Social inferences often include elements of inductive and deductive reasoning (see Chapter 10) as well as generalization (see Chapter 7) and a bit of imagination (discussed in Chapter 9).

Social inferences allow you to explain people's behavior. Typically, explanations of others' actions center on their mental states, their traits, or on the specific situations they are in. Situational details are often given much less weight in explanations than inferred personality traits, which is a bias referred to as the **fundamental attribution error**. Observers with this bias tend to infer that people behave the way they do because of the way they are. The fundamental attribution error suggests that many people's theory of mind (at least in the United States) tends toward nativism (see Chapter 1).

The sorts of explanations of behavior associated with fundamental attribution errors—"He's getting another cookie because he's greedy"—emphasize internal mental states over situational factors. Explaining others' actions in terms of how they think about the world provides a way of predicting what they will do in the future. If someone is evil, then that person will likely choose actions in the future that will cause social problems. **Mental attribution**, explaining actions as being caused by preceding mental states, is what folk psychology and common sense are all about (Goldman, 1993).

When you explain someone's actions in terms of goals, desires, and wants—"He really wanted that cookie"—you are inferring that intentions drive decision-making and cause observed actions. This social inference is what distinguishes voluntary actions from reflexes. Somewhat like the fundamental attribution error, the default social inference in most contexts is that people's actions are "on purpose," guided by conscious goals that reflect a person's general character. Even organisms like ticks or mosquitos may be reflexively regarded as evil vampires that some unholy demon created to terrorize innocent victims.

Mentalism

Early psychological research focused heavily on attempts to understand mental states until the behaviorists convinced many psychologists that this kind of intuitive mentalism was a scientific dead end. Cognitivism can be seen as a return to mentalism but with the emphasis placed on the minds of others instead of introspective self-reports. Rather than constructing a theory of mind from the inside out, modern cognitive psychologists focus more on predicting what minds do in different circumstances (mostly nonsocial).

One of the simplest theories of mind, a **perceptual theory of mind**, focuses on learned associations between intentions and social cues, especially eye gazes and finger points. Infants and nonhuman animals can quickly guess trajectories of biological motions based on eye or body orientations

(Bugnyar et al., 2016), and their attention can easily be attracted to a particular location or object when a person looks at it, points at it, or moves toward it.

These kinds of predictable sequences can be learned and recognized without making any social inferences or mental attributions (see Chapter 7). The face of a politician can in principle be perceived without making any judgments about their character. Nevertheless, percepts of competence come to mind automatically and quickly. Attribution of intentions can be just as quick and automatic.

You are not only able to pick up on social cues that reveal where others are attending. You can also infer something about their current mental experiences, especially when those experiences are emotional in nature. Your **emotional theory of mind** enables you to make inferences about ongoing emotional experiences such as confusion, happiness, sadness, and so on (Tager-Flusberg & Sullivan, 2000). For instance, if you are having a conversation with someone and notice that their eyes are glazing over, you're likely to infer that the person is either uninterested in the topic of conversation or is not comprehending what it is that you are trying to convey (**Figure 11.4**). Behaviorally, your conversational partner is not revealing their intentions or producing cues that specifically predict a future action (other than perhaps leaving), but you can nevertheless infer something about how attentive they are to your statements.

When an observer interprets shapes moving in coordinated patterns as one shape chasing others (the foundation of many video games; think *Pac-Man*), the observer is attributing goals to both the chaser and its targets. Detection of these kinds of goal-directed actions, called goal attribution, is evident in six-month-old infants (Csibra, 2008). Like the social judgment of faces and the perception of animacy, goal attribution often happens spontaneously. You don't need to decide or consciously infer that the ghosts are attempting to kill Pac-Man. You just see it.

Inferences about the intentions, emotions, and goals of others that you derive from your theory of mind can clearly happen spontaneously and effortlessly, making them seem less like conclusions that you've worked out and more like intuitions or feelings that you reflexively experience. The apparent automaticity of social inferences has led some psychologists to distinguish between social inferences that are more irrational, associative, and inflexible versus inferences that are rational, verbally expressible, and more actively thought through (Kruglanski & Orehek, 2007), a division similar to the ones in dual process models of thinking (see Chapter 10).

Per usual, components of your theory of mind that involve conscious, deliberative processing are considered by many to be cognitively elite processes that only moderately mature humans possess. Researchers are willing to grant that infants and animals other than humans may be able to predict what will happen in social interactions (Gredebäck & Melinder, 2010; Waller et al., 2016). But the default assumption is that they don't really understand what's happening. So, for instance, a dog may be able to predict that you are about to throw a ball and where you are going to throw the ball. And the

FIGURE 11.4. Inferring mental activity. Your perception of this woman's "boredom eyes" makes it possible for you to infer (perhaps using an emotional theory of mind) that she is not contemplating going to a party. Does your ability to infer what her mental state is depend on your theory of mind? How might your inference be affected by knowing that she is a paid model? (Prostock-Studio)

dog might even infer that you're happy when it fetches it (Albuquerque et al., 2022). But the dog can make these kinds of inferences without having a clue as to why you're throwing a ball.

Perspective Taking

For a dog to understand why you might take time out of your busy schedule to repeatedly throw a ball in the same direction, it would need to understand something about what the world is like for you. This kind of **perspective taking** depends not only on attributing mental states to other individuals but also on imagining what those mental states are like.

The study of gaze following, mentioned earlier, in which observers focused most of their attention on dominant individuals within the group provides an example of how researchers have studied perspective taking in laboratory settings. By monitoring where members of a group attend, it's possible to infer something about what those individuals are seeing and also potentially what they are thinking (Capozzi & Ristic, 2022).

If you notice Julie keeps looking in Ryan's direction, for instance, and when she does so she seems to be in a daze, then you might be able to infer that she is madly in love with Ryan. If you also notice that when Ryan notices Julie's stares, he turns and smirks, you might then infer that he knows she has a crush on him and finds it amusing. Based on your observations, you might conclude Ryan is likely to take advantage of Julie and she is not going to like the outcome (you imagine her perspective), and as a result, decide to warn her. If so, you've understood the social situation and have chosen how to act based on the narrative you have inferred from what you've seen and what you know.

Children's abilities to perform these types of complex social inferences have been studied extensively using tasks such as the Sally-Anne task (Baron-Cohen et al., 1985), in which children have to keep track of what different characters know and then answer questions about the characters' actions or beliefs to reveal their understanding of what's happening (**Figure 11.5**). Such experiments show that children's theory of mind becomes progressively more sophisticated as they grow older.

Tasks like the Sally-Anne task illustrate the range of cognitive processes that people may use when making social inferences and interpreting social interactions, including perception, recognition, attention, categorization, memory, and reasoning processes. Theory of mind as applied in the land of adult social interactions involves a kind of cognitive cooking where many different cognitive

FIGURE 11.5. The Sally-Anne task. In this task, a child is presented with a simulated social interaction involving a sequence of bizarre events and then is questioned about what the characters in the doll soap opera will do when confronted with a problem. Sally stores an object and then heads out on a mission. Anne then proceeds to take the object and hide it. When Sally comes back to retrieve the object, there is a mismatch between her expectations and reality. The goal of the task is to see whether children understand what others believe, how well children can adopt the perspective of someone else, and when children can detect that a character will believe something that is not true. (After Baron-Cohen et al., 1985)

1. Sally has a ball. She puts the ball into her basket.

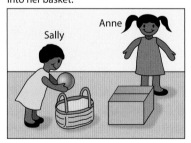

2. Sally goes out for a walk.

3. Anne takes the ball out of the basket and puts it into the box.

4. Now Sally comes back. She wants to play with her ball. Where will Sally look for her ball?

ingredients are brought into play. The fact that people make such cognitive commitments each day in their social interactions is a testament to the power of prosocial behavior.

Prosocial Behavior

Prosocial behavior, actions that benefit a group such as sharing or cooperating, is the glue that makes social interactions beneficial. Arguably, the main advantage of having a theory of mind, beyond being able to predict what is likely to happen next in social interactions, is the opportunities such a theory affords for successful participation in social interactions.

If you can correctly infer what other people are thinking and correctly recognize what their intentions and feelings are, then you can potentially act in ways that reinforce those mental states or counteract them if they are problematic. For instance, in the Sally-Anne task, a child might decide to tell Sally where to look for the ball, especially if the story is presented as a puppet show with multiple kids observing the action. Or if you want other people to attribute certain qualities to you that will affect their future actions, then you might act in ways that encourage observers to view you in a favorable light.

Social Preferences

People's concepts of right and wrong are closely related to their perception of prosocial versus antisocial behavior. Preverbal children show hints of preferring characters who consistently help others versus those that act in ways that seem to counter the goals of others (**Figure 11.6**). When familiarized with shapes that repeatedly either helped other shapes move along or that blocked shapes from moving, infants consistently showed a preference for the helpers (Hamlin et al., 2007). Infants not only appear to be attracted to the prosocial shapes but also to be repelled by the more obnoxious shapes. The precocious nature of social preferences suggests that they play important roles in social inferences and how people apply their theory of mind to specific individuals.

The preference of infants for helpers points toward a psychological disposition to notice movement patterns associated with social interactions (a special class of joint biological motions) and take pleasure in positive social interactions. Either participating in positive social interactions or observing such interactions seems to be rewarding. Social scenes are not only attention-grabbing but also pleasant to watch (which is why movies make money).

"A man's Social Self is the recognition which he gets from his mates. We are not only gregarious animals, liking to be in sight of our fellows, but we have an innate propensity to get ourselves noticed, and noticed favorably by our kind. No more fiendish punishment could be devised, were such a thing physically possible, than that one should be turned loose in society and remain absolutely unnoticed by all the members thereof."
—James, 1890, p 294

The rewarding aspects of social interactions are likely what motivate people to seek out such interactions and participate in them for extended periods. A side effect of social motivation, which can be either positive or negative, is that people want to be viewed as attractive, interesting, likable, and reliable. This concern for having a positive reputation shows up prominently in social media and in the behavior of teenagers attempting to fit into specific social groups.

Failure to accurately understand or attend to social interactions, or be consistently rewarded by social experiences, can lead to degraded social cognitive skills, producing a vicious cycle of social

(A)

(B)

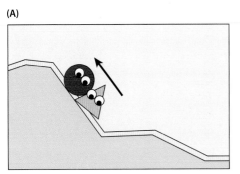
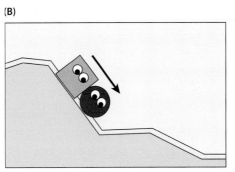

FIGURE 11.6. Social interactions of shapes. (A) Consistent helpers (yellow triangle) were preferred by infants over (B) consistent bullies (blue square), suggesting that prosocial behavior is attractive from a young age. (A, B after Hamlin et al., 2007)

failure that can be difficult to break (Dawson et al., 2004). Techniques that boost social attention or reward (such as early interventions) may help to avoid such behavioral pitfalls.

Cooperation

Sharing, helping, and comforting are prosocial behaviors in which there are givers and receivers. In cooperative actions, multiple participants play both roles to achieve a common goal. Many of the impressive accomplishments of humans, including scientific advances, depend on cooperation, and yet relatively little is known about what cognitive processes contribute to successful cooperation.

Keeping track of the actions of others and detecting "cheaters" is obviously relevant to maintaining social cohesion. Intuitively, theory of mind could be relevant to cooperating, but social insects are capable of impressive cooperative acts without taking into consideration the mental states of others. So, the relevance of mental attribution to cooperation may be more apparent than real.

Social facilitation refers to phenomena in which individuals working together can achieve more than is possible through individual effort. Simply performing in the presence of others who are producing similar actions can sometimes boost performance (Bond & Titus, 1983). Action enhancement in groups could happen because of increased attention to possible social evaluation (participants don't want to look bad). However, audience effects can just as easily degrade performance.

Chimpanzees that are prone to sharing show more openness to cooperating, providing some support for the idea that prosocial behavior can facilitate cooperation (Melis & Warneken, 2016). Relatedly, bonobos are more likely to share food and engage in cooperative behavior than chimpanzees. Behavioral experiments with a variety of primates, including humans, show they are sensitive to fairness and willing to self-punish if they feel mistreated, for example, by choosing no reward over a smaller reward, a phenomenon referred to as **inequity aversion** (Shaw et al., 2016; Verspeek & Stevens, 2023).

The factors that drive cooperation are not always straightforward (**Figure 11.7**). For instance, in studies of a game called the **Prisoner's Dilemma**, two participants pretend to be prisoners and each must decide whether to cooperate with the jailers. If both parties keep their mouths shut, then they both get a year in prison. If they both squeal, then they both get two years. Finally, if one talks but the other does not, then the one that talks goes free, while the other person gets three years. The decision about what to do is made in isolation by both participants at the same time. The rational option is to avoid potentially spending three years in prison and talk to the jailers. Participants nevertheless tend to be biased toward not talking, effectively choosing to cooperate (potentially) with their fellow criminal rather than their jailers.

The Prisoner's Dilemma may seem a bit hokey, but it maps pretty well onto cooperative dilemmas that groups of people face in everyday life (Lee & Harris, 2013). For instance, all countries are likely to be negatively affected by climate change. The benefits of cooperating to minimize or counteract these negative effects will be globally greatest if every nation pitches in. But if one country opts

FIGURE 11.7. Cooperative competition. Cooperation by team members in competitive games is a theme seen throughout sports. What sorts of social rewards might have led to the emergence of seemingly functionless cooperative actions such as pulling on two sides of a rope? (wavebreakmedia via Shutterstock)

out, then that country is likely to benefit (economically) while other countries will bear an even larger burden. If every country cheated though, then every country would pay the price. This last scenario is sometimes referred to as the **tragedy of the commons**.

Social Influence

Cooperation sounds like a good thing—people working together to achieve a greater good. But that is not always the case. Suicide bombers cooperate with their handlers to achieve maximum carnage. In the infamous Milgram study on the power of authority, participants cooperated with lab-coated experimenters to shock random victims into silence (don't worry, the victims were simulated). Chapter 10 reviewed several cognitive biases that nudge reasoning processes in the wrong direction. Social influence practically shoves reasoning processes out of the way.

Persuasion and Coercion

Social influence works its magic through social feelings. In particular, it depends on empathy, the capacity to appreciate what others are feeling. Empathy looms large in an individual's emotional theory of mind and can be viewed as an extension of it. Not only can you understand what someone feels, but you can directly experience how they feel, at least partially. Your understanding of someone's loss leads to feelings of compassion or sympathy. Seeing someone being treated unfairly makes you angry. Empathy serves as an emotional communication channel, one which can sway your decisions in ways you might not necessarily choose.

Emotional states can affect thinking in numerous ways, and social interactions can often play those states like a piano. In some cases, emotional states can enhance cognition, such as when tragic stories lead to more durable memories (see Chapter 8). In others, emotions may cloud your judgment, like when you have a crush on someone who is likely to crush you. Emotions can affect your confidence in your thinking, a phenomenon that works against you when someone attempts to persuade you to act or think in ways that you would not have otherwise considered.

In a case like the Milgram experiment, uncertainty apparently led participants to hand over the reins of decision-making to authority figures. For suicide bombers, certainty about the kind of strategy that is likely to lead to change has a similar effect.

Social feelings of certainty and uncertainty that modulate decision-making are relevant not only to daily social interactions but also to beliefs more generally (Feldmanhall & Shenhav, 2019). Trust determines which sources of information one takes into account when thinking, conversing, and even when perceiving. Attempts to study the impact of trust on decision-making and belief formation have focused on simple social interactions such as the Prisoner's Dilemma, noted earlier in this chapter, and the Trust Game (Frith & Singer, 2008).

In the **Trust Game**, one person is assigned the role of investor and the other takes on the role of money handler or trustee. The investor chooses how much money to give the trustee. The trustee then gets triple the amount received and can decide how much of that windfall to return to the investor (**Figure 11.8**).

When players of the Trust Game are time constrained, they tend to make prosocial decisions, cooperating to maximize mutual rewards. When they have more time to think things through, the trustee tends to be more exploitative (Van Lange et al., 2017). Contemplated self-gain thus can override natural tendencies toward prosocial, cooperative actions. Ironically, prolonged social thinking tends to promote antisocial actions.

Some researchers interpret this tendency to first act prosocially as evidence that prosocial behavior is what people do when cognitive control has not yet reared its ugly head. A similar trend is seen in cognitive development, where younger children are initially brutally honest but then later discover that lying can be advantageous. In fact, an arms race between cheaters and cooperators is partly what the social brain hypothesis suggests led to the evolution of flexible cognition in humans and other great apes, as well as the appearance of sophisticated theories of mind.

FIGURE 11.8. The Trust Game.
(A) In the Trust Game, a trustee's willingness to share the spoils with an investor can affect the investor's decisions about how much money to give to the trustee. Monitoring consecutive interactions in this game makes it possible to explore the dynamics of trust when the trustee is not reliably delivering the rewards. (B) Generally, the probability a person will entrust another with more money (proportion of investments) can be predicted based on what they get back (probability of reciprocation). (A after Eagleman & Downar, 2016; B after Ma et al., 2020)

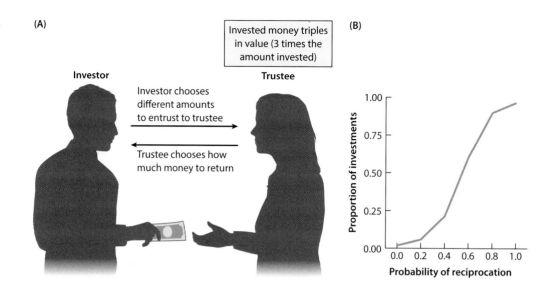

Deception arises from the recognition that others don't always have access to the same experiences and the awareness that such differences in mental states can often be fruitfully exploited. Once the capacity for deception develops, the thought processes required to decide when lying might be the right option increase in complexity. In some cases, the benefits of going with the flow, even when such actions do not match your beliefs (a form of deception), may outweigh any costs of potentially being revealed as a faker. It could even be argued that this sort of deception is a requirement of successful social interactions, since if everyone said what they really thought, prosocial behavior might become much rarer.

Compliance

The complement of persuasion is compliance, succumbing to the persuader's intent. Compliance in social interactions serves as a signal that the complier understands what is desired and required. Several strategies have been discovered that boost compliance. These strategies are known as disrupt-then-reframe techniques (Cialdini & Goldstein, 2004). The techniques work through a kind of cognitive misdirection in which the processing of an initial persuasion attempt is interrupted and then presented in a different way that seems to sweeten the deal. Confuse and conquer is a tactic that works well for marketing: "But wait! There's more! If you act now, you will also get to think that what I just told you is even more amazing than it really is!"

A second strategy that reliably leads to compliance involves the **foot-in-the-door phenomenon**. If you comply with an initial small request (say, letting someone borrow a dollar), then you are more likely to comply with a somewhat larger request later on (perhaps a request to borrow twenty dollars). This phenomenon is why people often advocate nipping a problem in the bud. Complying with seemingly harmless requests may be the first step toward a seriously bad option.

Social rewards come to those who conform. Punishments await those who deviate. So if you want someone to comply with your requests, a good way to go about it is to do the following: (1) make resistors feel incompetent or insecure; (2) make the request in the context of a compliant group that includes no other dissenters; (3) make the group popular or elite; and (4) make sure the response to the request is public.

Now, consider when social norms are represented by someone who is appointed to make sure that people comply with those norms, which can include guidelines, instructions, laws, policies, or rules. Compliance in this scenario can be quite high. In Milgram's experiments, more than 60% of participants were willing to shock someone into apparent unconsciousness. The more prestigious the institution the authority figure represents, the greater the compliance. Also, compliance increases when empathetic responses are less likely, such as when the consequences of actions are not directly perceived.

Situations in which complying with social demands requires choosing actions other than those one would normally choose can lead to **cognitive dissonance**, an uncomfortable emotional state similar to unease or guilt. Cognitive dissonance seems to be triggered by inconsistencies between alternative actions (Harmon-Jones & Mills, 2019). It does not seem to require a sophisticated theory of mind because nonhuman animals show similar responses as humans to conflicting choices (Egan et al., 2007). For instance, Pavlov found that when he attempted to train dogs to respond differentially to a circle versus a highly similar ellipse, the dogs would grow increasingly agitated, until eventually, they ripped their way out of the training apparatus, a phenomenon he described as experimental neurosis (Pavlov, 1927).

The social motivation to conform, combined with the unpleasantness of cognitive dissonance, can lead to greater consistency in action selection. This can, in turn, foster the kinds of mental habits described as mental sets in cognitive psychology (see Chapter 10) and as attitudes in social psychology

WEIRD, TRUE, FREAKY

Social Robots

The birth of social robotics began with tortoises in the 1940s (Fong et al., 2003). The robotortoises interacted with each other using light signals. They had little interest in their human creators. Early studies of social robots focused more on understanding self-organization of actions within groups than on possible human applications.

Modern efforts to develop socially interactive robots are geared more toward constructing machines that: (1) produce and recognize emotions; (2) communicate using spoken sentences; (3) learn from experience; (4) form social relationships; (5) use nonverbal social cues; and (6) have distinctive personalities (think C-3PO from the *Star Wars* franchise). Social robots that need to interact with humans must also follow social norms.

Social robots do not need to look like a human to interact successfully with a human, although the capacity to simulate biological motions can help facilitate social interactions. Similarly, robots do not need to feel emotions to make use of an emotional theory of mind when interacting with a human.

Initially, roboticists focused on developing programs that simulated human behavior by reacting to internal scripts. More recently, there has been increased interest in developing systems with social learning mechanisms, including the ability to copy others' actions and to learn from teachers (de Greeff & Belpaeme, 2015).

Social robots can be viewed as physical models of human cognition. They often incorporate processing strategies borrowed from humans, such as directional visual sensors, separate channels for processing different kinds of energy, selective filtering of inputs, and so on. Some social robots that simulate human infants (Infanoid, Cog) were specifically designed to test current theories of social cognitive development and social learning (Oudeyer, 2017).

Social robots are not limited to being metal guinea pigs for psychological experiments. They can also potentially play functional roles in society, such as assisting with elder care or patient care. Social robots are also beginning to be used as public guides through exhibits and as children's toys (mostly using animatronics).

Cute robotic dolls (see figure) and dogs create the impression that social robots can be a fun source of entertainment for children. But might prolonged interactions with such devices affect social thinking in unpredictable ways? For instance, what happens when social toys become so adorable that children prefer their company to the company of other humans?

The potential for social robots to shift social norms and social thinking is not just an issue for developing children. Concerns are also growing about the implications for adults. Lawmakers in several countries, including the United States, have proposed or passed new laws banning sexbots, particularly those that look like young children.

One concern about sexbots is that they replace natural social interactions with artificial situations that may reduce users' ability to separate fantasy from reality. The newest models of sexbots are socially interactive and capable of social learning, further clouding their distinctiveness from human partners. Sexbots may also promote the objectification of others, encouraging aggressive, antisocial actions.

Similar concerns could be raised about the use of social robots for jobs like elder care. How ethical is it to hand over the care of someone with dementia to a machine that will pretend to care about them? Would it be fine to have robotic prison guards as well? Understanding how social interactions with atypical or artificial social partners can affect social learning and social decision-making would go a long way toward making it possible to assess the potential costs and benefits of welcoming social robots into human societies.

Social robots. Your digital friends of the future? (QTrobot, CC BY-SA 4.0, via Wikimedia Commons)

research. The mental sets that you apply when participating in or interpreting social interactions are a function of knowledge and beliefs that you have accumulated throughout your life, including the societal rules that separate right from wrong.

Your understanding of morality is a prime example of a mental set you have accumulated that biases your social behavior and your interpretations of people's intentions. Feelings about whether another's actions are bad or good, or decisions about what an appropriate reaction might be to those actions, vary from one generation and geographical location to the next. The suicide bomber is both murderer and martyr.

Moral reasoning is an extension of social feelings and social influences that contribute to cognitive development from a young age. Whether a particular scenario is perceived as immoral depends on the rules and norms one has encountered growing up. Norms that define the boundaries of what is socially acceptable also determine the types of social thinking that are likely to happen. In this respect, families embedded in societies construct the cognitive processes that determine how people will choose to act in their daily lives, as well as how people will perceive their actions and the actions of others. Social cognition, perhaps more than any other domain of cognition, is a consequence of what individuals learn, remember, and know.

SIGHT BITES

Using a theory of mind, individuals can interpret goal-directed actions, take the perspectives of others, and better understand others' intentions and likely actions.

Participants in social interactions have a bias toward helping and cooperating that can be quickly overridden by deliberative thought processes.

People are rewarded for acting in ways that both fit with their prior beliefs and that comply with the wishes of those observing their actions.

Social Knowledge

SNEAK PEEK: Human culture arises from the social transmission of information through language, imitation, and other interactive mechanisms. The knowledge gained through such interactions can change not only how individuals behave but also how they think about themselves.

Where do your social inclinations come from? Day in and day out, you are checking messages or posts either sent to you specifically or put out into the world for anyone to see. You favor some individuals' ponderings over others. Some messages resonate, while others fall flat.

You care about people's verbalized thoughts and social actions because you are human and because of what you've learned over many years. **Social learning**, which happens when you attend to the actions of others and use memories of those actions to guide your own decisions, has enabled you to keep in contact with those around you and keep track of what's happening in the social world. Exposure to the rules of the social game has provided you with examples of ways to act and ways of thinking about yourself and others. Perhaps you have also observed actions that did not work out so well. Either way, your actions and thoughts have been gradually tweaked to make you who you are today.

Social Learning and Imitation

It's often difficult to predict what individuals will learn from observing the actions of others. You can watch all kinds of events without changing your behavior in any obvious way. Much of what you learn from watching others is latent learning (see Chapter 7). You may not even realize it's happening.

Unlike Pavlovian and instrumental conditioning (also discussed in Chapter 7), social learning doesn't always include clear rewards for noticing correlated events or punishments for not noticing them. It's also not clear how extensively different animals learn from observing others' actions. Some psychologists argue that only humans can learn in this way, hypothesizing that it requires especially sophisticated cognitive mechanisms for representing and understanding events and their consequences (Heyes, 2023).

The various methods that humans have developed for communicating and gathering information, such as by writing or reading a textbook, make it possible for them to socially learn in ways that no other animal can. The many impressive ways that modern humans learn through directly or indirectly observing others tend to confirm researchers' beliefs about the special nature of social learning. Unfortunately, the complexity of situations in which people might socially learn makes it quite difficult to detect when learning is really happening.

Social Transmission

The effects of mass media and social media on cognitive development have been hot topics in social learning research since the time of the Greeks. Plato argued (through a story) that "writing" would make people forgetful because they would learn to rely on the writing rather than their memories, becoming dependent on external triggers for their thoughts. He also argued that while these kinds of visually triggered ideas might make people feel wise, reading would only generate the illusion of knowledge and leave people incapable of thinking on their own. Similar concerns have been raised about the ease with which people can now access and distribute information using the Internet.

Worries have been especially widespread about the negative effects of violent entertainment on mental development in children. There is extensive evidence of correlations between the amount of violent imagery observed by youth and their likelihood of engaging in violent acts (Bushman & Huesmann, 2006). This evidence, combined with a few widely publicized cases of school shooters who entertained themselves by playing violent video games, has convinced many that extended experiences observing acts of violence and virtually committing them can "poison" the mental sets that guide children's social and moral decision-making processes.

The consensus view is that extensive exposure to virtual violence is likely to increase aggressive feelings, thoughts, and actions. Violent experiences can increase a child's capacity for violent acts, as evidenced by child soldiers in Africa who are forcibly recruited to act as deadly mercenaries. But this does not imply that witnessing such acts in games or movies will lead to violent actions. Experimental studies of social learning of aggressive acts more typically show that the effects of social observations on later behavior are dependent on many different factors.

A famous experiment that explored imitation and observational learning of violent actions is Albert Bandura's (1925–2021) Bobo doll experiment in which children observed a film of an adult beating up an inflatable clown in highly inventive ways (Bandura et al., 1961). Later, when the children were in a room with the clown, some of them replicated the aggressive actions that they observed. The implication of this experiment was that children can learn specific violent acts modeled by adults, even if they are not explicitly reinforced for copying adults (Bandura et al., 1963).

FIGURE 11.9. Model mom.
Children are thought to acquire much of their social knowledge from observing and copying adults. What might toddlers learn about computer use by staring at and tapping on a toy computer after watching their mothers do this? (Prostock-studio via Shutterstock)

The Bobo doll experiments clearly showed that the children remembered the bizarre film that they had been shown, and these observations caused them to be more likely to perform similar actions in certain situations. However, only children who were provoked were likely to pummel the clown in the ways that an adult modeled. Other children were actually less likely to beat up Bobo after seeing the adult's actions than were children shown control videos. Perhaps the less aggrieved children felt that Bobo had already suffered enough.

Discovering actions that one can potentially perform may enable an observer to think about performing (or avoiding) that action in ways that would not be possible if the observer had remained ignorant (**Figure 11.9**). Such observations do not compel the observer to copy the acts, however. The knowledge gained from watching something like cartoons might have no effect on how similar the observer's actions are to those that were viewed, even if the viewer watched these cartoons many times and can answer any question you like about what the characters do in various situations.

Attentional Cues and Reenactments

Studies like the Bobo doll experiment reinforce the idea that children can learn how to act by imitating adults' actions. But imitation is just one way that observations of others can lead to social learning. Using cues to determine another individual's attentional focus can make an observer aware of features that they might not notice or focus on otherwise. For instance, it was noted earlier that observers who see a lovesick admirer gazing intently at the object of their affection can potentially use this information to discover something about the admirer.

Directing an individual's attention toward specific objects, events, locations, or individuals within an environment is called **stimulus enhancement**. This can happen involuntarily, as in the case of the dreamy-eyed student, or voluntarily, like when someone yells your name to get your attention (**Figure 11.10**). Joint attention in a social interaction can strongly shape what participants learn from that interaction. Stimulus enhancement is similar to social facilitation in that the mere presence of another individual attending to relevant events in the world can enhance learning (Heyes et al., 2000).

In addition to redirecting an individual's attention to a specific person, place, or thing, stimulus enhancement can also increase an individual's curiosity or interest in that object, enabling the individual to discover potential ways that the attended-to object might be used. For instance, a child who has never seen playdough before might observe another child playing with the substance by squashing it into various shapes. These observations can help the first child to gain new insights into the plasticity of the material and its fun potential, even if that child does not recall the specific shapes or squashing actions they observed. The discovery of possible uses and functions of objects through social observations is called **affordance learning**.

Affordance learning is just one process within the broadly studied form of social learning referred to as emulation. **Emulation** involves observing someone else achieve a goal, adopting that

FIGURE 11.10. Shared vision. Pointing draws the attention of others to a particular location or stimulus, increasing the odds that other observers will share the pointer's perspective. Does this mean that socially learning from a pointing gesture requires perspective-taking by members of a group? (Hero Images Inc./Alamy Stock Photo)

goal, and then performing some actions aimed at achieving the same goal. Unlike stimulus enhancement, emulation requires understanding that there are such things as goal-directed actions (Whiten et al., 2009). If you saw someone climb a tree, pick an apple, and eat it, and then later you went to that same tree, shook it, and picked up an apple off the ground before eating it, then you would be emulating the first apple fetcher.

Imitation is a specialized kind of emulation in which you copy the specific goal-directed actions that you observed. So, if you saw someone use a ladder to get apples out of the tree, and then you used a ladder in the same way to get apples out of the tree, then you are imitating. Traditionally, imitation is viewed as the most impressive form of social learning and one that can only be convincingly demonstrated if the observer copies a novel action, such as hitting a Bobo doll with a hammer.

For a long time, it was thought that humans were born endowed with a special ability to imitate. Some studies with infants in the 1970s seemed to show that even newborn humans would imitate actions such as an adult sticking out their tongue (Meltzoff & Moore, 1977). More recent studies failed to replicate these findings, however, and revealed that the actions that newborns "imitate" most often are reflexive reactions to any exciting event (Heyes, 2016). So, yes, an infant might stick their tongue out at you if you stick your tongue out at them, but they would also probably stick their tongue out at you if you just shoved your whole hand in your mouth. Studying imitation is tricky because many actions that look imitative are not!

Imitation has often been pointed to as the key form of social learning that enables humans to think like humans because it is critical for language learning; learning the social tricks and norms passed down from one generation to the next; and learning the various cognitive skills taught in schools, including reading, writing, and memorizing. The specific role that imitation plays in cognitive development relative to other forms of social learning, or to other learning processes like instrumental conditioning, has yet to be nailed down, however.

Learning while other people are present, as young children often do, is not the same as socially learning from the actions and goals of those people. And the fact that a parent punishes a child for throwing rocks at people—teaching them a social norm—does not imply that the learning mechanism that enables the child to follow this rule requires social learning. Much of the learning that produces social knowledge does not require the learner to imitate or emulate other people's actions or goals.

Teaching

In modern societies, many learning experiences, a subset of which depend on social learning, happen in schools. Teachers may demonstrate the correct way to perform certain skills or use academic tools and then provide opportunities for students to practice doing the same. Teachers may also provide social rewards, such as praise or high grades, when students perform well.

When teachers with expertise provide students with demonstrations or instructions about how to accomplish specific tasks, they are organizing a **didactic learning experience**, passing their knowledge on to others. When students with comparable levels of knowledge work together to share ideas and discover knowledge on their own, they create **cooperative learning experiences**, teaching each other.

Teachers arranging didactic learning experiences often make use of **scaffolding**, in which subcomponents or simpler versions of a skill are presented to gradually ease the student into performing the final skill. Effective use of scaffolding requires a student-specific theory of mind; the teacher needs to recognize what the student does not understand or what skills the student lacks in order to break the task up in a useful way, and the teacher must recognize what information should be socially transmitted.

Teaching involves social interactions specifically designed to boost the cognitive skills and knowledge of students. The contrived situations that teachers create provide novel opportunities for "stimulus enhancement" where the attended-to stimuli are often ideas. Teachers also model novel affordances by presenting new labels that students can use to sort events into more precise conceptual categories. And teachers demonstrate mastery of certain topics, potentially encouraging students to aspire to a similar or higher level of understanding, or at least to comply with prescribed educational activities and assignments.

Teaching is just one way in which others can potentially shape your thinking. **Cognitive socialization** includes learning from teachers, as well as all other social influences, in a way that leads to changes in your cognitive skills (Greenfield, 2009). This includes interactions with friends and family and things you pick up on the job or from the Internet. For teenagers and college students, social interactions with peers, including discussions and group activities, strongly determine the sophistication of thinking skills that emerge. Social environments that encourage critical thinking produce more skillful thinkers, while environments that encourage deceptive self-promotion produce skilled pretenders.

Schemas and Scripts

Cognitive socialization includes the acquisition of **social knowledge**, which is information you have learned both consciously and unconsciously that enables you to interpret and participate in social interactions. Social knowledge includes what you learn about specific individuals, their relationships to one another, their likes and dislikes, and so on. Your social knowledge includes specific episodes that you can recall, as well as more general knowledge about the ways of the world (Landau et al., 2010).

General Social Knowledge

Your daily life largely consists of routines that you have performed many times before—routines so predictable you might call them rituals. Your social knowledge supports many of these rituals. When you brush your teeth or get dressed in the morning, you are complying with social norms regarding hygiene and appearance. What you eat, when you eat, and how you eat are also all socially prescribed. These daily rituals require a relatively sophisticated synthesis of memory and attention that enables you to know what's supposed to happen as you move from one situation to the next.

When these sorts of rituals are consistent within a social group, but less so across social groups, the phenomenon is described as culture. Culture is a product of social learning because the details of the rituals are a consequence of what group members learn from observing and interacting with others in their community. Language use, which varies across social groups, is probably the most obvious case of a culturally-driven cognitive skill. But many other nonlinguistic traditions of cognition may come from socially transmitted information and other social learning processes (**Figure 11.11**).

Culture includes systems of beliefs, values, and rules—a kind of institutional social knowledge. The cognitive skills that a society values and promotes are culturally-dependent. Scientific under-

FIGURE 11.11. Whale culture? Humpback whales appear to learn their complex songs by copying novel songs that they hear other whales singing, a phenomenon that some scientists have described as an example of culture. What kinds of evidence might establish that whale songs are cultural? (Marie-Elizabeth Mali)

standing of cognition is similarly determined by cultural factors. For instance, the bulk of cognitive experiments are performed on undergraduates living in the United States or Europe. This may bias scientists toward assuming that mental processing by young adults from WEIRD (Western, educated, industrialized, rich, and democratic) societies is representative of cognition more generally (Henrich et al., 2010).

Using such biased examples may paint a misleading picture of what humans know and how they come to know what they know. Cross-cultural studies provide one way that scientists can test the generality of cognitive theories and measure the contributions of culture to individual variations in cognitive processes and social cognition, in particular (Barrett, 2020).

As noted earlier in this chapter, extensive exposure to violent media is thought by many to increase the aggressive, and perhaps criminal, behavior of viewers through social learning mechanisms. On the other hand, social learning is also thought to be key to promoting prosocial behavior or "building character," which is why sharing and helping are often heavily emphasized in preschools. The idea is, if children see adults model kind behavior and are given many reminders of the importance of kindness, then their daily routines will be more likely to include acts of kindness. Of course, this also implies that, if children are repeatedly exposed to hypocrisy, they are also more likely to learn to be hypocrites.

Regardless of whether the cumulative social experiences of children are to their benefit or detriment, it is clear that humans learn a lot about how to accomplish goals and how to function in societies by observing events and gradually building up an arsenal of social knowledge. The weapons of thought that they acquire are called schemas.

Schemas and Memory

The term **schema** refers to general knowledge about things that are associated with a familiar context, such as things that people usually see and do at a party or ways that people act when they fall in love. Piaget popularized the term, using it to describe what children learned about repeated encounters with objects and events. For instance, a child's schema for stuffed animals might include their sensory qualities, affordances, specific ones that are favorites, things adults do with them, where they are likely to be found, and so on. Schemas are like concepts with all the extras.

Your theory of mind is basically a social schema that guides both your social interactions and your thoughts about minds. Schemas are closely related to the idea of mental models, which are hypothetical mental simulations of things that can happen in the world (see Chapter 9). If you imagine what it would be like to become romantically involved with someone you have a crush on, then you are using your schema of love to construct a mental model of what your experience will be like when you and your crush finally get together.

FIGURE 11.12. Scripted social schema. Teddy-bear tea parties once were reenactments of adult activities that children observed from afar. Now that adult tea parties are rare, what social learning mechanisms might help keep this cultural tradition alive? (kryzhov via Shutterstock)

The effects of schemas on cognition have been studied most extensively in relation to memory (Gilboa & Mariatte, 2017; Tse et al., 2007). When you recall an experience that happened in a familiar situation like a party, your schema for parties is likely to influence what you remember about a specific party that you attended recently. Your party schema may make you more likely to recall details that did not actually happen (a kind of false memory; discussed in Chapter 8), and less likely to recall details that do not fit into your schema. The longer it's been since you experienced the event, the more likely it is that your schemas will interfere with your ability to accurately recall specific episodes.

Memories for details that don't quite fit what you expected can be replaced by more agreeable or understandable versions of events. This property of memory is why two people who can potentially be blamed for a problem, say a car wreck, often recall what happened differently. As you are reading this book, your social knowledge and psychology-related schemas will cause you to recall more details from chapters that fit your preconceptions. If you read statements that challenge your views, there's a good chance you will either forget them or will warp them in your mind later on to better fit with ideas that you believed before you read the book.

Your social schemas often include **scripts**, mental representations of sequences of events that typically occur in a predictable order in relation to a familiar situation. A script for a party might include arriving, socially interacting, hanging out, and listening to music (**Figure 11.12**). A script for a romantic encounter could include a one-on-one conservation, prolonged eye contact, close spatial proximity, smiling, and heart fluttering. Scripts can include things you expect to see, like in a wedding, as well as things you expect to do, like get popcorn and find a seat at a movie theater. Scripts are often normative, meaning that they lay out not just what is likely to happen but also what is supposed to happen according to social norms (Schank & Abelson, 2013). Deviations from scripts can cause cognitive chaos.

Stereotypes

Given what you know about how rapidly people make social inferences when seeing a person's image and the distorting effects schemas can have on the recall of specific episodes, you can probably predict the effects your social knowledge has on the social inferences you make. Historically, for instance, **gender stereotypes**—beliefs about prototypical characteristics of men and women—have influenced the outcomes of elections such that women are underrepresented in most political organizations.

Stereotypes are schemas that lead to cognitive biases. These biases can influence decision-making and social inferences in a wide variety of social situations (Greenwald & Banaji, 1995; Koch et al., 2015).

People tend to think of themselves as fair and unbiased in social interactions. However, because biases associated with stereotypes tend to form early on and accumulate over time, they often kick in automatically and unconsciously; sometimes, they are even undetectable. People are unlikely to describe themselves (or to think of themselves) as racist, sexist, ageist, ableist, or xenophobic. Such labels imply a tendency toward socially discouraged prejudice and unfair actions that relatively few would include in a personal profile.

As noted earlier, implicit association tests may reveal features of schemas that are consciously inaccessible (Schimmack, 2021). These tests consistently reveal that responses to stereotype-consistent pairings of images are made more rapidly than stereotype-inconsistent pairings. By tracing the relative speeds of different pairings of images and text, it's possible to map out unconscious cognitive biases that arise from an individual's social schemas.

Stereotypes can have significant effects in legal settings when witnesses' memories of events are morphed by their social knowledge. People will generally construct a narrative description that better fits their expectations rather than provide undistorted details, filling in blanks about what motivated the people performing the actions and adding details that support their social inferences. The tendency of people to recall details that better match an idealized (schema-driven) portrayal of an observed episode or scene is called **boundary extension**.

Boundary extension inevitably distorts recalled events, leading to a caricature of what was seen (Bernecker, 2017; Kim et al., 2015). Boundary extension effectively inserts one's own learned scripts into descriptions, making them more proscriptive (for instance, condemning specific acts that were observed or inferred) than descriptive (providing an objective record of what was experienced). These kinds of "revisionist history" accounts can be especially problematic when social interactions contribute to reports of recalled events, as when witnesses are questioned.

Collaborative Recall

The sharing of memories has held a prominent place in societies for a long time. **Collective memories**, including facts and events recalled similarly by members of a group, are often related to notable events experienced or discussed by many individuals in parallel (Hirst et al., 2018). Like diaries, collective memories can be viewed within the context of extended mind theory, which, as discussed in Chapter 1, is the idea that mental processes involve elements outside of an individual's brain.

Collective memories can be shared within small groups, such as a family, or by larger groups, such as citizens of a country. Collective memories can include popular myths, fairy tales, or nursery rhymes that have persisted for a long time. Because collective memories depend in part on conversations between individuals, studies of this phenomenon have often focused on how communication affects the formation and maintenance of such memories. Interactions between pairs of individuals can lead to convergence, with memories becoming more consistent within a group (Hirst & Coman, 2018), if the number of members is not too large (fewer than thirty individuals). Convergence of collective memories may be a consequence of shared social schemas that preserve those features of a story that fit with most people's expectations of what seems right.

Not all collective memories consist of historically notable events, facts, or stories. For instance, memories of cultural fads can persist far beyond the fads themselves. You may know of a dance associated with a specific song called "Macarena" without recalling (or ever knowing) that it was popularized by Los del Río or that it rose to fame in 1995. Cultural phenomena that strike a chord in a critical mass of people, such as the birth of a new dance or an iconic movie scene, can become part of cultural consciousness just as effectively as a national tragedy.

It's easy to think of collective memory as just being what happens when a group of individuals all remember the same thing. There are some features of collaborative recall that provide evidence against this interpretation, however. Intuitively, you might expect that recalling an event in a group might lead to social facilitation, with details recalled by one person cueing others to recall aspects that they had forgotten; this, in turn, could facilitate their ability to recall further details in a sort of memory chain reaction. A more common finding is that groups show **collaborative inhibition**, whereby the amount of information being retrieved by a group tends to be less than the sum of what all the members come up with when recalling information individually (Weldon et al., 2000). Collaborative inhibition increases as the group size grows larger.

The availability of on-demand mass media has led to the rapid spread of memes, viral videos, and socially-endorsed lies, which may change the nature of collective memories for future generations. In the past, word of mouth was the main medium for passing on cultural narratives, and allusions to Bible verses or famous quotes connected generations. Now, students are more likely to reference catchphrases of fictional characters or remember notable marketing campaigns than to remember whatever it is that they are supposed to remember about the Alamo. Today's cartoons constantly reference famous scenes from films, taglines from celebrities, and popularized news stories in ways that make them less likely to be understandable even a decade into the future, ensuring that they will have less longevity than classic fairy tales or nursery rhymes. Will replacing Jack and Jill with Itchy and Scratchy have any lasting effects on the schemas shared by humans? If so, then "D'oh!"

Self-Awareness

One percept that you can never escape, at least while you are aware, is your sense of self. It is ever-present. This sensed self has its own schema (or schemas)—basically, everything you know about yourself—as well as a distinctive feeling that distinguishes you from everything else. Your experience of yourself as separate from the rest of the world and other people is referred to as **self-awareness**.

Though one of the most revered phenomena in psychology, self-awareness has received relatively little attention from cognitive psychologists in the last few decades, with the possible exception of a few researchers studying cognitive development or animal cognition (Baciadonna et al., 2021; Rochat, 2003). Partly, this is because it is difficult to control percepts of the self in the same way that sights, sounds, and memory cues can be controlled. Experimental studies of self-awareness, instead, depend on indirect measures that provide clues about what self-observers are observing and what internal representations of selves are like.

Self-Recognition

One of William James's most enduring and widely doubted quotes is that a baby, upon being born, "assailed by eyes, ears, nose, skin, and entrails at once, feels it all as one great blooming, buzzing confusion." James was emphasizing the role of experience in organizing percepts. His quote implies that, for newborns, experiences of the self, environment, and others are all lumped together.

Numerous experiments have since provided evidence that newborns actually can discriminate lots of sensory events, even before they leave the womb. Nevertheless, there is also evidence confirming that newborns don't know that there are hands attached to them, much less that there is a "them" that could have hands. Even two-year-old toddlers sometimes seem oblivious to the fact that their bodies are physical objects in the world that can affect the movements of other objects (Moore et al., 2007). Body self-awareness in humans only develops slowly and may depend on years of kinesthetic and visual experiences.

Toddlers are not the only individuals who lack body self-awareness (**Figure 11.13**). A few adults suffer from body integrity identity disorder, which basically means they do not recognize one of their limbs as belonging on their body (Sedda, 2011). Some go so far as to amputate a functional limb so that their actual body matches their perceived body. Adults with this condition seem to have acquired an incomplete or inaccurate "body schema" (anorexia might be a more familiar case of this). This

FIGURE 11.13. Self obliviousness. Snakes occasionally fail to recognize their own body and may even attack themselves, sometimes resulting in death. How might luckier snakes represent themselves in such a way that they can avoid this embarrassing mistake? (Piotr Velixar via Shutterstock)

disorder is similar to the experience of phantom limbs (see Chapter 4), but in reverse, and could be viewed as an extreme case of alien hand syndrome (see Chapter 3).

Even after toddlers discover that they are stuck with their bodies, it still takes them a couple more years to come to grips with the fact that their experiences are not shared by others. This phenomenon, called **egocentrism**, shows up in both their statements and actions. If they can't see other people, the idea that someone else might still be able to see them does not occur to an egocentric toddler—a case of perceptual egocentrism. If a three-year-old knows there are cookies in a box, everyone they encounter is presumed to also possess this important knowledge. The default social schema for toddlers is one in which everyone's percepts and thoughts are whatever the child observer experiences.

Before children can engage in any sort of perspective taking, they need to overcome their "me-and-only-me" schema. This requires not only recognizing their body as "me" but also their percepts and thoughts. Overcoming egocentric schemas is a lifelong process that many people may never complete.

Egocentrism in young children might seem to suggest that social cognition is relatively minimal at first and that children are aware of themselves primarily. But how can you tell if a child is conscious of themselves as a person? What evidence counts as a sign of self-awareness?

The gold standard for evidence of self-awareness, other than just stating that you experience it, is some indication of visual self-recognition (Nielsen et al., 2006). In the **mark test**, an individual secretly has a mark made on their body that they can only see with the help of a mirror. If the individual discovers the mark and reacts to that discovery, then they pass the test. Toddlers often pass this test at around eighteen months if they grew up in homes with mirrors. Adults of many other species never pass it.

Although the mark test provides clear evidence that toddlers can detect a mark on their head using a mirror, there are various ways that toddlers could do this that do not require self-awareness. All that is necessary is the ability to recognize that mirror images correspond to things that are not inside or on the mirror and the capacity to match how actions look to how they feel (Mitchell, 1992). Unaware robots are able to recognize themselves in mirrors using this kind of information.

Most likely, children are self-aware long before they can pass the mark test, in the sense that they perceive themselves. What is probably lacking, and that may depend on social feedback, is the thought that a subset of what they sense is themselves. Separating out this part of experience requires attentional processes to turn in on themselves—a mode of thinking that might require more flexible processing than the processing needed to learn how mirrors work.

Self-Reflection

Philosophical and religious concepts of "self" have dominated for thousands of years. The earliest socially-endorsed schemas of self emphasized reflecting on feelings, particularly feelings about authority figures. Self-concepts of this sort depend on social cognition and on compliance with socially prescribed standards: social rituals, norms of behavior, culpability, social cognizance, and so on. Reflection on one's own feelings is like self-empathy or meta-emotion.

Self-awareness in the context of emotional self-reflection becomes the experience that is contemplated, evaluated, and used to draw social inferences. Because the main focus of attention is on "feelings" (visceral sensations), this kind of self-reflection is likely a case of thinking about percepts. This would make emotional self-reflection what happens when you apply your emotional theory of mind to yourself.

Historically, cognitive psychologists have focused more on cognitive self-reflection (surprise), starting with the introspective measures of Wundt, or possibly the philosophical self-reflections of Descartes. As with emotional self-reflection, the starting point of cognitive self-reflection is self-awareness. The main difference is what elements of self-awareness are attentionally selected as the subject of extended consideration.

Experimental studies of metacognition, problem-solving, and cognitive development are where issues of cognitive self-reflection appear most prominently in cognitive psychology. But cognitive self-reflection is also related to constructs like episodic memory, prospective memory, autobiographical memory, visual illusions, and decision-making, where conscious reflection on what is going on cognitively is an inherent feature of the cognitive construct (Goupil & Kouider, 2019).

Cognitive self-reflection is also prominent in self-evaluations, which are basically social evaluations you make about your own behavior or qualities. If you ever compare yourself to others in terms of your looks, intellectual abilities, or life successes, you are cognitively self-reflecting in ways that draw attention to components of your concept of yourself as an individual—your self-concept.

Finally, cognitive self-reflection plays a critical, if sometimes hidden, role in the development of cognitive psychology theories. The psychologist's fallacy (see Chapter 3) happens when someone projects their own mental models of cognition onto the cognitive phenomena that they are studying. Researchers create "cognition" schemas that they use to explain why and how people's minds work. This can affect how they interpret the results of cognitive experiments and even how they design them.

For instance, most cognitive experiments use a fixed set of materials to control for the possibility that differences in stimuli might contribute to differences in participants' responses across conditions. From the perspective of the experimenter, each participant is being given the "same" treatment because the materials aren't varying.

Like a Rorschach inkblot test, however, each participant may experience the experimental stimuli in their own way based on their personal categories and schemas, which may lead to percepts and thoughts that are quite different from what the experimenter intended and that can vary substantially across participants. This complication is why results from experiments with participants from WEIRD populations may predict little about the responses of participants from other societies and may explain why subtle changes in experimental protocols across laboratories can cause a psychological phenomenon to disappear (making it difficult to replicate experimental findings).

The psychologist's fallacy is a case of egocentrism combined with cognitive self-reflection, leading to a skewed view of cognitive processing in other minds. It's cute when toddlers think you can't see them because they are covering their eyes. It's not so cute when scientists think they understand something about how minds work because they project their schema of how things seem to them onto others.

SIGHT BITES

 Various modes of social learning, such as stimulus enhancement, emulation, imitation, and teaching, contribute to cognitive socialization.

 The routines and beliefs that enable societies to function are embedded in schemas and scripts that lay out what is normally supposed to happen.

 Self-recognition and self-contemplation depend on similar cognitive mechanisms as those used to develop a theory of mind.

BRAIN SUBSTRATES

SNEAK PEEK: Understanding how scenes can be mentally transformed into actions is key to understanding the role of cognition in social interactions. Although social decision-making is typically guided by social norms and empathetic feelings, individual differences in cortical processes can lead to divergent social thinking and choices.

Language, imitation, and self-consciousness, which are all rooted in social cognition, are commonly noted as what makes humans unique in the universe. Imitative skills are thought to be the source of cultural advances, while language and self-consciousness make it possible for humans to know that there are such things as cultural advances. The apparent uniqueness of these cognitive competencies in humans has made them a special target of both scientific researchers and technologists attempting to create artificial minds with computer hardware and software.

The "cognitive revolution" sparked by Chomsky's critique of Skinner (see Chapter 1) was based on the idea that special cognitive skills demand special scientific explanations. If humans are the only animals that naturally learn languages, then it must be because they have some seed of knowledge or cognitive power that other animals don't. Similar arguments have been made for imitation and self-awareness.

For some, such as Descartes, that seed can be found in the soul. For others, there is not one seed, but several, and they can all be found in unique structures within the human brain. You just need to dig them out with MRI scanners and related technologies.

The first attempts at mapping out cognitive processes in human brains, led by phrenologists and physicians such as Broca and Wernicke (discussed in Chapter 12), spawned the field of neuropsychology. More recently, neurophysiologists have joined the fray by identifying neurons with properties that seem capable of explaining everything from empathy to imitation—mirror neurons.

Mirror Neurons

Mirror neurons were accidentally discovered by European neurophysiologists in the 1990s (di Pellegrino et al., 1992). These neurons were found not in humans, but in the cerebral cortices of monkeys, specifically in macaques. The neurons caught the attention of researchers because the neurons were supposed to function mainly in controlling the movements of monkeys' arms, but they also

FIGURE 11.14. Monkey mirror neuron hot spots. Mirror neurons are most commonly found in a monkey's frontal lobe (Area F5), which is associated with the control of actions, and in a region in the temporal lobe (the superior temporal sulcus region) known to contribute to the visual perception of complex actions. (After Eagleman & Downar, 2016)

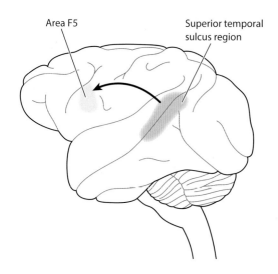

responded similarly when monkeys observed a human moving in ways that were similar to how the monkeys moved during experiments (Rizzolatti et al., 2001).

In monkey brains, neurons with this kind of cross-modal responding, called **mirror neurons**, were found in two main cortical regions (**Figure 11.14**), regions that are now known to play an important role in social perception as well as in action perception. The monkeys' mirror neurons showed several interesting response patterns. The neurons would respond to observed actions even when parts of the action happened out of the monkey's view. In some cases, mirror neurons also responded to the sound of the action. Mirror neurons responded most strongly to goal-directed actions, as opposed to movements with no obvious purpose.

Neuroimaging studies later found that similarly located cortical regions in humans also showed consistent responding during both the performance and perception of actions (Chong et al., 2008). These cortical regions are often collectively referred to as **mirror systems** because neuroimaging methods do not directly measure the activity of individual neurons. The mirror systems of humans also become active when people are imitating movements.

Mirror systems respond in different ways to different goal-directed actions. So in principle, activity in mirror systems could make it possible for an observer to identify a person's specific goals in producing the movements. As noted earlier, recognizing that others have goals is an important part of social perception and in developing a theory of mind.

Possible Functional Roles of Mirror Neurons

Researchers have hypothesized that mirror neurons might be involved in a variety of cognitive processes that involve understanding the mental states of others (Heyes & Catmur, 2022). In the case of empathy, for example, it's easy to imagine that if seeing someone in pain makes you cringe, then perhaps it's because of cross-modal matching between your visceral sensations and the visual cues that suggest suffering in another. If you had mirror neurons that matched self-generated emotions to emotions observed in others, then this might explain the origins of empathy.

There is little experimental support for the existence of emotional mirror neurons, however (Lamm & Majdanžić, 2015). There are brain regions, such as the insula (see Chapter 9), that respond similarly when someone is either feeling disgusted or visually observing another person who is disgusted (Wicker et al., 2003) and when someone is either feeling pain or seeing another person in pain (Singer & Lamm, 2009). Activation of the insula is also implicated in empathy. Such correlational evidence is consistent with what you might expect if there are mirror neurons in the insula, but it is also consistent with the insula being a source of unpleasant subjective experiences. The kinds of mirror neuron systems involved in action observation have also been speculated to contribute to empathy

(Iacoboni, 2009). How this system might interact with other brain systems linked to empathy has yet to be worked out.

Mirror neurons provide a link between actions you've seen and actions you can perform. You might suspect then that they are likely to play a role in social learning mechanisms, like emulation and imitation, that require you to do exactly this kind of cross-modal matching. If seeing someone eat an oyster activates the motor circuits you would need to replicate that action, then presumably you could use those same circuits to reenact the technique (Fabbri-Destro & Rizzolatti, 2008). One complication in this hypothesis is that macaques, despite all the mirror neurons that they possess, show little if any ability to imitate or emulate the actions of others.

There are cortical regions in the mirror systems of humans that are active during the execution, observation, and imitation of actions. Given that you do not imitate every action you observe, there must be some additional circuitry involved in imitative acts, especially voluntary ones. There is some evidence that mirror systems might be involved in **automatic imitation**, in which perceiving another person's actions leads to involuntary copying (Southgate & Hamilton, 2008). Automatic imitation is not only involuntary but also unconscious. You automatically imitate people you interact with every day without knowing it, especially when you engage in face-to-face conversations.

Some individuals with frontal lobe damage are prone to involuntarily imitating other people's actions, even when those actions differ from the ones they intended to perform (Brass et al., 2003). People with reduced frontal activity, which might occur during a major depressive episode, also show this tendency (Lhermitte, 1993). These deficits indicate that the extent to which you automatically imitate your friends is much less than it would be if your frontal circuits weren't suppressing your imitative tendencies.

Finally, researchers have proposed that mirror systems might be important for understanding others' actions, enabling you to construct a theory of mind (Gallese & Goldman, 1998). Given that mirror neurons can potentially reveal others' intentions, it seems reasonable to think that they might also contribute to the formation of schemas about the mental states and beliefs driving those intentions. Mirror systems in humans do overlap somewhat with brain regions that become active as people engage in tasks thought to depend on a theory of mind (**Figure 11.15**).

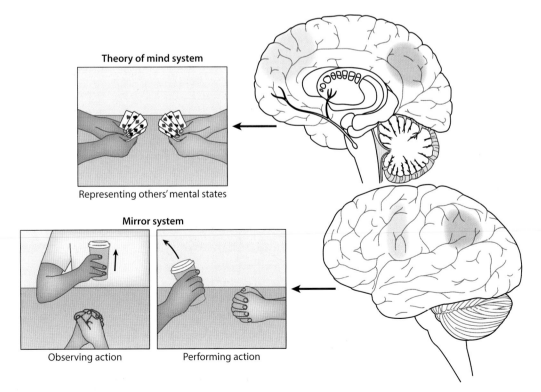

Theory of mind system

Representing others' mental states

Mirror system

Observing action   Performing action

FIGURE 11.15. Brain systems for interpreting others. Mirror systems are localized in cortical regions that are similar in location to a "theory of mind system," except that the theory of mind system engages more frontal regions and can become active when a person just imagines the mental states of others. The top brain shows cortical regions activated when people are representing other's mental states (using their theory of mind) and the bottom brain shows regions (the mirror system) activated when they are observing or performing a specific action. (After Eagleman & Downar, 2016)

It's important to keep in mind that overlapping activity in cortical regions across different tasks does not imply uniformity in what neural circuits are doing in those tasks. Artificially changing firing patterns of mirror neurons to examine how this affects various cognitive functions is one way to clarify the specific functional roles that mirror neurons play.

Effects of Mirror Neuron Deficits

If mirror systems play a major functional role in empathy, imitation, or theory of mind, then you might expect that damage to these cortical regions would disrupt one or more of those functions. Somewhat surprisingly, neuropsychological studies of patients with damage to these regions make no mention of such deficits (Hickok, 2009). Either brains have ways of compensating for damage to these regions or the functional roles that mirror systems play differ from what researchers have proposed so far.

Functional features of a damaged brain may not always reveal how the intact brain functions. An alternative approach to investigating the role of mirror systems on cognition is to systematically alter activity in those systems using technologies like transcranial magnetic stimulation (TMS) or transcranial direct current stimulation (tDCS). Both TMS and tDCS can either amplify or interfere with neural activity depending on how they are applied.

Studies that use either TMS or tDCS to modulate activity in the mirror system have found that disrupting activity in this system impairs people's capacity to distinguish goal-directed actions as well as their ability to predict upcoming actions within time frames of less than a second (Keysers et al., 2018). Changing activity in mirror systems does seem to disrupt rapid evaluation of goal-directed actions, even if it does not show clear effects on a person's understanding of those actions.

Although neuroscientific research has clarified some of the ways in which neural processing might contribute to social perception and social learning, it has not revealed any specialized structures within the brain that provide humans with social cognition superpowers. All of the brain regions where mirror neurons are found are present in most mammals; mirror neurons have also been found in birds, who have no cerebral cortex.

In the case of imitation, the basic representational problem is matching visual percepts to action plans. Those action plans may be represented in terms of the sequences of kinesthetic sensations they would normally produce, in which case the problem becomes one of matching images to feelings. Recall that these are the same kinds of cross-modal matches necessary for mirror recognition of body parts. Mirror neurons may play a role in detecting these kinds of matching events. On the other hand, almost any associative learning mechanism (including those described in Chapter 7) is equally capable of establishing such connections (Cook et al., 2014), so it's not clear that mirror neurons provide any special functional advantages. When it comes to mechanisms of social cognition, mirror neurons may just be more neurons.

Brains of the Antisocial

Modern notions of justice emphasize the idea of fairness, a construct that depends on a collective theory of mind, social norms, and schemas that support an understanding of others' intentions. Retribution provides a way to counteract unfair actions and to express feelings of sympathy. What happens, though, when socially shared theories of mind do not match reality? What counts as fair in that scenario?

Studies of memory have challenged the long-held assumption that eyewitness testimony is the most reliable source of evidence as well as the idea that intensive interrogation is the best way to squeeze details out of witnesses. Similarly, studies of social cognition are beginning to raise questions about how guilt should be assigned to wrongdoers, especially when a perpetrator's cognitive mechanisms are dysfunctional.

Disinhibition and Frontal Dysregulation

Individuals who are often antisocial, irresponsible, impulsive, egocentric, and unlikely to engage in prosocial behavior are commonly described as sociopaths, psychopaths, or persons with antisocial personality disorder. The public tends to associate these traits with criminality, but there are plenty of noncriminal psychopaths; psychopaths who have not committed crimes are sometimes referred to as successful psychopaths (Pemment, 2013).

There is increasing interest in systematic differences between the brains of criminal psychopaths relative to more typical individuals. Neuroimaging studies found that individuals diagnosed with antisocial personality disorder have less gray matter in frontal regions (Yang & Raine, 2009), and individuals classified as psychopaths show the same pattern but with more extensive structural differences (**Figure 11.16**). Deficits in these same regions are associated with reduced empathy and lower sensitivity to social norms (Tiihonen et al., 2008).

Individuals showing sociopathic behavior show reduced physiological responses to stimuli that would normally evoke empathetic emotional responses in most people (Damasio et al., 1990). This difference suggests that sociopathy doesn't just provoke people to behave in antisocial ways or think about social rules differently but may instead fundamentally alter how they perceive or experience the emotional states of others.

The brains of antisocial individuals differ structurally from those of their prosocial counterparts, but this doesn't necessarily mean that these individuals are less functional. They perform normally in theory of mind tasks, showing an understanding of others' intentions and actions (Richell et al., 2003). Their social perceptual abilities are also on par with those of typical adults. Successful psychopaths show executive control capacities that are comparable to or greater than those of prosocial peers (Gao & Raine, 2010).

Although many past studies have focused on the empathetic limitations of individuals with antisocial tendencies, psychologists have also considered the possibility that problems with attentional control might be a source of many of their behavioral issues. This hypothesis arose when it was

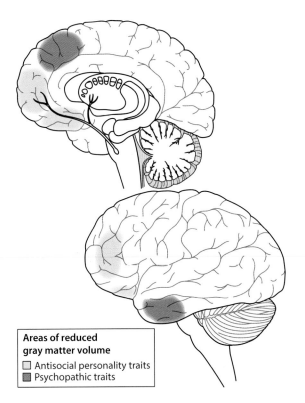

Areas of reduced gray matter volume
☐ Antisocial personality traits
■ Psychopathic traits

FIGURE 11.16. Brain differences associated with psychopathy. Colored blobs indicate cortical regions where gray matter was reduced in individuals identified as having antisocial personality disorder or psychopathy. Note that all shaded regions were reduced in the individuals with psychopathy. Reduced gray matter is presumed to be correlated with dysfunction in these regions. (After Eagleman & Downar, 2016)

FIGURE 11.17. Possible cognitive origins of psychopathy. Problems of attention such as an inability to bind perceptual features (see Chapter 4) may impair an individual's ability to integrate perceptual representations of complex events, which may then degrade the formation of associative neural networks underlying typical social schemas, leading to psychopathic deficits and antisocial behavior. In this model, the symptoms of psychopathy come not from an individual's "heartlessness," but from seeing the world differently. Environmental factors shape what one perceives so in this model they can strongly contribute to the development of the antisocial acts associated with psychopathy. (After Hamilton et al., 2015)

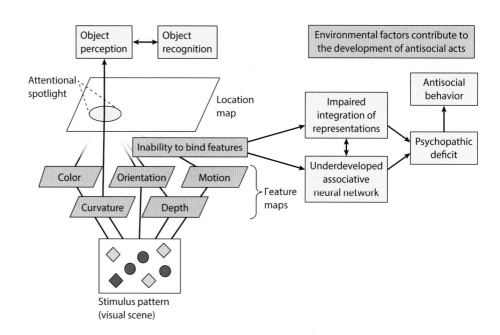

discovered that psychopaths showed more typical performance when their attention was drawn to relevant features of the tasks (Hamilton et al., 2015).

How might attentional deficits lead to psychopathy? What a person attends to determines what they perceive and also what categories they learn (see Chapters 4 and 5). If your ability to attend to multiple aspects of complex events (like social interactions) is limited, then what you learn about those events may also be limited. Psychologists hypothesize that starting at a young age, the attentional constraints of children with psychopathy reduce their ability to effectively integrate complex perceptual information (Hamilton et al., 2015). This, in turn, affects interactions within cortical networks, leading to antisocial behavior and reduced empathy (**Figure 11.17**).

Unsuccessful psychopaths who end up in the criminal system seem to differ from successful psychopaths not because they are more extreme in their lack of empathy, but because either they have reduced cognitive control capacities (Sifferd & Hirstein, 2013) or because they experienced environments growing up that led them to develop antisocial mental sets and schemas.

Cognitive interpretations of what is happening in unsuccessful psychopaths raise questions about how their actions should be judged. Children are judged differently in criminal courts because adults understand that their mental processes often operate differently from those of adults. If the cognitive capacities of individuals with psychopathy also differ from those of mentally healthy adults, should they also be held to a different standard?

Criminal Culpability

Many individuals with psychopathy show symptoms from a young age. Some, however, only develop symptoms after suffering brain damage, a condition known as acquired sociopathy. Acquired sociopathy typically happens when the cortical regions shown in Figure 11.16 are damaged. This cortical damage can lead to a dramatic increase in antisocial behavior, including crimes (de Oliveira-Souza et al., 2019).

Individuals with acquired sociopathy, often older individuals who have had a stroke, understand that their actions are wrong and can describe why the consequences of those actions are bad for everyone involved. Even so, they do not appear to feel guilty about the antisocial acts or show any remorse (Mendez et al., 2011). If one of your older relatives had a stroke and soon after that went on a crime spree, would you think that it is fair to send them to prison?

Incarcerating people because they've had a stroke seems like adding insult to injury. On the other hand, people are reluctant to let someone off the hook simply because the person claims that their brain made them break the law. Current structural neuroimaging methods are insufficient for sorting people based on whether they have good or bad brains. The brains of successful psychopaths are not noticeably different from the brains of unsuccessful psychopaths in MRI scans (Johanson et al., 2019).

There is a long history of trying to use a person's physiology to determine what their "true" mental state is, starting with the development of lie detection tests in the early 1900s. Current approaches to technological mind reading are called cognitive biometrics. The most sensitive technique for detecting lies involves repeated fMRI measures. If you are scanned while telling lies and while telling the truth, it is possible to develop classifiers that can detect when you are lying with high accuracy (Langleben et al., 2005). However, there are ways of defeating such lie-detection technologies and so far their results are not admissible in courts.

A rising number of criminal defendants are including brain-based arguments, or neuroforensics, as part of their defense. There is also increasing discussion of what an appropriate response to crimes might be (or how they might best be prevented before they happen) when a person's brain or schemas are leading them to make poor decisions or act antisocially. This issue of who is culpable comes up not just for individuals with psychopathy but also for people with addiction, victims of abuse, and others.

Children's vision and hearing capacities are systematically tested from a young age because it is recognized that deficits in either can significantly degrade a child's ability to learn and succeed. Behavioral tests could, in principle, be developed to quickly assess attentional control, perceptual integration of complex information, or empathetic responses, which would facilitate earlier interventions. There may not yet be "empathy aids" that can enhance social processing the way that hearing aids do, but if part of the problem is attentional or perceptual, then perhaps there are interventions that could help fix people's feelings.

SIGHT BITES

Mirror neurons and mirror systems respond similarly when an action is performed and when that same action is observed.

Modulating the activity of mirror systems can affect the perception of goal-directed actions, but the role these systems play in social cognition is uncertain.

Variations in frontal and temporal circuitry are correlated with antisocial behavior and a lack of empathy.

Cortical deficits can lead to changes in social decision-making that diverge from current social norms and schemas.

APPLIED PERSPECTIVES

SNEAK PEEK: In many social interactions that lead to learning, there is a leader who guides the process. At a cultural level, peoples' social learning may deviate from the processes studied in laboratories. What additional factors may account for the polarization of thought processes in modern societies?

The human capacity for perspective taking likely arose because it helped individuals navigate social environments. Perspective taking integrates processes of memory, attention, perception, imagination, and reasoning. It may be what makes mirror self-recognition possible and surely is what enables humans to introspect.

Perspective taking involves making social inferences about others' thoughts, beliefs, and cognitive skills. Perspective taking is particularly important when one person is trying to change the minds of others.

Humans have become master mind changers. From religious institutions to social media influencers, techniques for persuading and reinforcing compliance have become a staple of modern societies. The perspectives you take are hardly yours. Social shaping of minds is the norm.

College students cooperatively participate in societal efforts to shape their thoughts by attending colleges and universities, jumping through the hoops set up for them by administrators and faculty, and intermittently listening to lectures and reading textbooks. How might perspective taking help or hinder this sort of mental intervention?

Natural Teaching

As noted earlier in this chapter, teaching in educational institutions makes use of a combination of social learning mechanisms and other training tricks to help students reach some learning objectives. Teaching groups of students is a historically recent innovation, however. Long before there were classrooms, one-on-one teaching dominated.

Apprenticeships

Although you may associate teaching with classrooms, plenty of teaching happens in more natural settings. Many animals, both young and old, engage in play behavior, providing opportunities for cooperative learning experiences. In the case of apes (including humans), more experienced members of a social group often monitor play sessions to make sure that things don't get out of hand.

Apes are also known to provide more direct mentoring in the learning of specific foraging skills, although this is not as common as many people suppose (Boesch et al., 2019). Wild chimpanzees in Africa use stone anvils to crack open hard nuts, a skill that takes several years to master. Not all groups of chimpanzees do this, suggesting that the technique has been socially transmitted within groups across generations. Such transmission could happen through mechanisms of stimulus enhancement. However, ethologists have observed mothers occasionally modifying their actions in ways that seem to guide the actions of their offspring (Estienne et al., 2019).

Orcas show clearer evidence of actively shaping youngsters' foraging skills (Hoppitt et al., 2008). Groups of orcas often participate in hunting activities that sometimes include younger orcas (**Figure 11.18A**). Mother orcas have been seen performing hunting maneuvers in synchrony with their young and wearing out prey before handing it over to their calves. In other cases, groups of orca play with their prey while accompanied by calves, capturing and releasing it multiple times before killing it in order to provide opportunities for their young to practice.

Meerkats are another mammal that provides its young with novel learning opportunities (**Figure 11.18B**). Adult meerkats will capture scorpions and bring them to where pups are located, sometimes disabling the scorpions before presenting the crippled prey to the pups. Meerkats also ap-

(A)

(B)

FIGURE 11.18. Mother tutors.
Several species, including (A) orcas and (B) meerkats, use scaffolding with their young to enhance their ability to learn how to hunt. What social learning mechanisms may contribute to the effectiveness of this technique? (A BIOSPHOTO/Alamy Stock Photo; B ©Francois Gohier—ardea.com/Mary Evans Picture Library Ltd/agefotostock)

pear to monitor the progress of pups as they manipulate prey, retrieving the prey when it escapes from pups and injuring the prey when pups are flailing and failing (Thornton & McAuliffe, 2006).

Note that in these natural teaching contexts, the intentions of the teacher and students are unknown. There may be no learning objectives. Whether teaching is intentional or not, its main role is to solve problems. The main difference between teaching in the wild and most cases of teaching by humans is that humans rely heavily on language as a tool for directing attention more precisely, flexibly, and proactively. Human teachers don't just provide opportunities for simplified skill learning, they direct students' thoughts and actions while providing evaluative feedback.

Human teachers can use their theories of mind to select what needs to be taught and to organize the learning experiences. Ideally, teaching is a cooperative activity in which the students' goals align with those of the teacher. However, students may also view teachers as unreliable partners seeking to influence their actions in ways that produce more costs than benefits. In that case, the social interaction becomes more competitive than cooperative.

Within indigenous communities, social norms can establish a culture of learning that is part of the fabric of society (Rogoff et al., 2015). This can be viewed as a form of learning-by-doing in which scaffolding is integrated into the division of labor and communal activities. By working together to achieve a common goal, such as collecting food, younger members of a community can not only learn adults' goals but also become familiar with various scripts and heuristics for accomplishing those goals. At the same time, working collaboratively may help indigenous children to form social schemas that are integrated with the mastery of cognitive and physical skills.

This more ancient, community-based mode of teaching combines elements of didactic learning and cooperative learning because expert adults are initiating goal-directed activities in a way that is more participatory than instructive. Parallels to this approach can be seen in on-the-job training within companies, where newbies have to pick up on norms and skills on the fly while working with colleagues who may be at various stages of mastering the relevant skills.

Some children in middle schools and high schools may also have spontaneously adopted this mode of teaching and learning. But instead of mastering the academic material promoted in their classes, they're acquiring and modeling the skills needed to participate effectively in social activities. Ironically, socially-constructed academic institutions may have created learning environments that are more effective for teaching nonacademic skills than for increasing the mental skills and knowledge that they were designed to boost.

Teaching with Multimedia

Modern approaches to teaching emphasize technological tools. For instance, online teaching may include recorded instructional videos or computer programs that run users through series of problem sets meant to build academic skills. This type of techno-teaching relies heavily on observational learning mechanisms, self-directed instrumental conditioning, and social transmission of information.

Some online learning platforms also incorporate lessons from cognitive psychology related to how materials should be presented to maximize learning: spacing learning episodes over time, interleaving exercises and worked out examples, combining diagrams with verbal information, quizzing, and so on (Pashler et al., 2007). The basic premise underlying this approach is that there are general principles of learning and cognitive processing that determine how any student will optimally learn.

Critics of digital teaching argue that a one-style-fits-all delivery of content ignores both the unique strategies relevant to teaching skills in different domains and the conditions necessary for learned skills to generalize. For instance, the strategies that work best in teaching mathematical skills might differ substantially from those that would lead students to become better creative writers, historians, or horseback riders.

Skeptics of online educational initiatives like Coursera and Khan Academy also point out that opportunities for social evaluation, customized shaping of behavior, and interactive learning mechanisms are less likely to contribute to learning when the main interface between the teaching media and the student involves mostly one-way information transmission, a critique that also applies to large lecture classes at universities. However, new online approaches that integrate and organize peer interactions are beginning to overcome these limitations (Hwang et al., 2021).

Some of the most effective technological advances in teaching involve using simulators to train complex skills like piloting. Simulators facilitate scaffolding and increase the likelihood of transfer of training. Training with robotic surgery simulators, for instance, can help bring medical students up to speed more rapidly and give them more opportunities to practice under different conditions (MacCraith et al., 2019).

If they are given adequate tools and motivation, people can learn complex skills without being explicitly taught. Self-education, or autodidacticism, usually depends on socially-generated materials and technologies; as such, it still depends on observational learning mechanisms to a certain extent. Learning with multimedia has elements of self-teaching, but with the specific content selected by outside parties.

The success of self-teaching depends on the learner's motivation, persistence, and metacognitive capacities. Currently, there are no objective criteria for predicting what teaching approach is most likely to produce the desired outcome for any given student. Consequently, it is difficult to know under which circumstances a specific student will benefit more from instruction by a teacher, from opportunities to learn on their own, or by working to solve problems cooperatively with peers. So for now, students can either do what they are told to by authorities, or wing it and see what happens. Either option has its risks.

Climate Change Risk Perceptions

You may think that your social knowledge and social schemas only affect how you interact with others or how you interpret what's going on inside their heads. In reality, your social worldview can affect most of your cognitive processes in ways you might not predict or detect. Similarly, other people's worldviews can shape your thought processes and mental skills in ways that you would not necessarily choose. You don't have to join a cult to end up thinking things that a younger version of yourself would view as irrational or even insane.

Current social views on climate change—what it is and what should be done about it—illustrate how social schemas can shape people's percepts and reasoning processes. Viewed by some as an existential crisis and by others as a hoax designed to shift the balance of economic and political power, climate change seems like the kind of high-stakes problem that human cognition was made to solve (or create). And yet, it seems that a substantial number of coherent adults cannot even agree on what the problem is, much less how, or if, the problem might be solved.

Societal Perceptions

In college sports, there are clearly tribal views about which teams are the best. Such debates can usually be objectively resolved on the field, at least for a day, despite the fact that a win could depend on any number of factors that neither team has any control over and that have nothing to do with which team is actually better.

It's a bit unnerving that decisions about athletic contests are so straightforward while arguments about variations in the temperature of the planet, a phenomenon that can be precisely measured with something as simple as a thermometer, seem to be perpetually debated. Why is it that fans will bow to points on a scoreboard as irrefutable evidence of who should be called the victors, but then may also interpret graphs of temperature measurements that gradually increase over time as meaningless propaganda or as uninteresting trivia?

Scientists have reached a consensus view that climate change is happening. Globally, the governments of most nations have publicly heeded the reports of scientists. Governmental actions do not match their proclamations, however, leading environmentalists to doubt their conviction and sincerity (**Figure 11.19**). In the United States, there is significant political resistance to even accepting climate scientists' reports as being reliable. Following in the footsteps of this political divide, many citizens also give little weight to the scientific consensus or its implications. Why?

One interpretation of what is happening, likely to be endorsed by climate scientists, is that citizens discounting the scientific evidence are being irrational. The idea is that climate skeptics are either ignoring the evidence or are not using it to inductively reason in ways that would lead them to a conclusion consistent with that of scientists. From this perspective, climate change deniers must either not know what is happening or must be incapable of thinking about the issue logically.

An alternative possibility, partly supported by scientific evidence (Druckman & McGrath, 2019), is that climate change denial is based on logical reasoning, but it is a kind of deductive reasoning that challenges some of the basic assumptions of scientists. Specifically, if someone doubts that the scientists' reports are objective and impartial, then they are likely to discount any measurements that those scientists present, and as a consequence, not believe either the scientists' data or their conclusions. These climate change skeptics do not perceive a risk to themselves or others because they doubt the source of the data.

When these skeptics see other likeminded individuals from their political group reaching a similar conclusion, this provides social rewards for maintaining their beliefs. Their conclusions become part of their social schema, which makes challenges to their beliefs a challenge to their identity.

In this social context, trying to convince climate change deniers or climate scientists to change their minds is not much different from trying to convince fans of rival football teams that they should

FIGURE 11.19. The Greta effect. Environmental crusader Greta Thunberg has made it her mission to persuade the public that climate change is a major problem. What social cognitive processes might explain why this effort has only been moderately successful? (Liv Oeian via Shutterstock)

switch to cheering for the other team mid-game. That option, for most, will seem more irrational than sticking with whatever their original reasoning process led them to believe. Reasoning that serves to maintain status within, or the coherence of, a specific group, is called identity-protective cognition.

At a societal level, reasoning about climate change seems to be more about tribalism and less about weighing scientific evidence. Similarly, the lackluster efforts of nations to address the economic and ecological problems associated with climate change may have more to do with political power plays than with consideration of any long-term consequences of inaction. Decisions that are rational for an individual at a personal level within a short time frame can easily be self-destructive or socially harmful over longer time frames.

When scientists want to solve a problem, their go-to heuristic is to collect more data that can be used to test hypotheses and resolve ambiguities. In the case of the climate change debate, the amount of data seems to be moot. There is more data available now, including personal experiences with natural disasters, than there was a decade ago. This extra data has led to little political or societal movement.

This seemingly irrational societal debate is reminiscent of earlier findings from sociological studies of cults. In several doomsday cults, a charismatic leader prophesized that the world would end on a specific date (or that aliens would stop by to pick up the true believers, or some other similarly monumental event), only to be faced with the reality that nothing happened on that date. Contrary to what you might expect, followers don't kick themselves for being so gullible or turn on their dear leader. Instead, they become even more fervent in their beliefs (Balch et al., 1983).

As in the case of climate change debaters, the favored explanation for such persistence of prior beliefs in the face of counterevidence is that switching gears would create cognitive dissonance that is so extreme that most people never go there.

Making a decision about whether the climate is changing as a consequence of earlier human decisions and actions, from a scientific perspective, is not much different from trying to decide whether the Earth travels around the sun. That historical debate, too, was shaped by social schema.

Specifically, collective religious beliefs about the special status of the Earth led to lots of skeptics of heliocentrism in high places. In that case, the decision about what to believe only affected what humans could learn and discover about physics and space. In the case of climate change, the decision and reactions to it can directly affect the future of the Earth and its inhabitants. Hopefully, future generations of teachers and cognitive psychologists will figure out less self-destructive strategies for constructing social schemas, so that these kinds of global problems can be avoided.

CLOSURE

Ryan was a dog. And he was possibly a sociopath. He felt no guilt or pity when he left women crying on their sofas. To him, it seemed like a reasonable thing for them to do. Plus, it was not like he was forcing anyone to do anything that they didn't want to do, that they didn't dream of doing. They just hadn't thought things through to their logical conclusion.

You may think that Ryan was a jerk. If so, you have your social schemas and emotional theory of mind to thank for that. Maybe you can empathize with his conquests, imagining what their subjective experiences were like—the loss, the unfairness, the betrayal, the death of a dream. Or maybe you think Ryan is just a guy, and his groupies should have known better. A little bit of reasoning might have gone a long way toward avoiding all the melodrama.

Either way, your brain has automatically engaged your full inventory of cognitive processes in making a judgment. You've linked names (or pronouns) to imagined people having imagined thoughts about others and themselves in order to make social inferences about future imagined outcomes. And you've done it without even trying. These convoluted extrapolations happen so effortlessly that they hardly seem to involve thinking at all, just like walking doesn't seem to require much balancing, until you're dizzy.

Much of the social knowledge that you use when thinking through what various events mean is hidden from you. So are many of the heuristics you use in your attempts to understand the actions, intentions, and minds of others and yourself. You are an expert social thinker, and the cognitive skills you use when thinking about minds in everyday life have become automatized. Now, you just do it. This hidden social knowledge doesn't just help you to understand social interactions, it affects how you perceive and think about everything.

"There are these two young fish swimming along and they happen to meet an older fish swimming the other way, who nods at them and says, 'Morning, boys. How's the water?' And the two young fish swim on for a bit, and then eventually one of them looks over at the other and goes, 'What the hell is water?'" (Wallace & Kenyon College, 2009). Social knowledge, skills, and tricks acquired through social learning are the water within which your thoughts swim.

Some killjoy philosophers have argued that all knowledge, scientific or otherwise, is a product of social conventions, a position referred to as relativism. From the perspective of relativists, everything you believe you know about minds and their operations—your theory of mind writ large—is only "true" to the extent that sociocultural norms have led you to believe that your ideas are correct. How many times in the past have humans been certain that they had a firm grip on reality only to be later posthumously chastised by their ancestors for their wrong-headed assumptions and beliefs? Without a clearer grasp of the role that social cognitive processes play in the development of theories of mind—both the personal and scientific varieties—claims about how minds work will continue to be questionable.

COGNITIVE LINGO

affordance learning	fundamental attribution error	prosocial behavior
animacy	gaze allocation	scaffolding
automatic imitation	gender stereotype	schema
behavior contagion	ideomotor theory	script
boundary extension	imitation	self-awareness
cognitive dissonance	implicit association test	social brain hypothesis
cognitive socialization	inequity aversion	social facilitation
collaborative inhibition	mark test	social inference
collective memory	mental attribution	social knowledge
cooperative learning experience	mirror neuron	social learning
didactic learning experience	mirror system	stimulus enhancement
egocentrism	perceptual narrowing	theory of mind
emotional theory of mind	perceptual theory of mind	tragedy of the commons
emulation	perspective taking	Trust Game
foot-in-the-door phenomenon	Prisoner's Dilemma	

CHAPTER SUMMARY

Social Cognizance

Perception of animacy and biological motion provide the foundation for social cognitive processes. Rapid classification of faces based on past associations also can strongly influence expectations about others' future actions.

Social Thinking

Thinking about others' actions depends on the ability to imagine what others' thoughts and goals might be. Young children naturally attend to social interactions that involve cooperation and helping. Over time, feelings of compassion and empathy can give way to strategies of coercion and deception.

Social Knowledge

Cognitive skill learning often depends on both indirect and direct social guidance, including modeling acts to be copied and feedback from teachers. Social experiences promote the acquisition of schemas and scripts that guide later selection of actions. One of the most enduring pieces of social knowledge acquired by humans is the distinction between self and others.

Brain Substrates

The circuits that make social cognition possible overlap extensively with those that contribute to cognitive processing in other domains. Changes in frontal circuits can disrupt some forms of imitation as well as the capacity to take others' feelings into account.

Applied Perspectives

Academic approaches to promoting social learning build on natural teaching tendencies. Social knowledge gained from competing authorities can lead to incompatible interpretations of reality.

REVIEW EXERCISES

Social Cognizance

- Explain how perception of animacy can be shown in young children.
- What have implicit association tests revealed about social categories?
- How can eye tracking be used to better understand social cognition?

Social Thinking

- How does perspective taking relate to mental attribution?
- What is prosocial behavior? In what ways can prosocial behavior be rewarding?
- Describe the phenomenon of inequity aversion and explain how it might lead to cognitive dissonance.

Social Knowledge

- What is the difference between social learning and imitation?
- How do schemas differ from mental models?
- Describe key elements that distinguish collective memory from other kinds of memory.

Brain Substrates

- Explain how mirror neurons might contribute to social learning.
- Describe some cognitive processes that are thought to differ in people that are antisocial.

Applied Perspectives

- How might scaffolding contribute to teaching?
- In what ways have social schema contributed to public perception of climate change?

CRITICAL THINKING QUESTIONS

1. People can predict with decent accuracy which of two prisoners will be executed on death row by examining images of their faces for less than half a second, suggesting that factors other than guilt may determine who will get the death penalty. How might such social biases be counteracted in court?

2. Children attribute mental states to invisible playmates soon after they show the first clear signs of having a theory of mind. What does this suggest about the cognitive processes that contribute to your theory of mind?

3. Social insects show complex coordinated behavior in a variety of different contexts. Is this behavior cooperative? Is it prosocial?

4. Infants are thought to learn both communicative and social skills from imitating their parents. However, recent studies suggest that parents are more likely to imitate their infants than infants are to imitate their parents. How might imitation by parents contribute to social learning?

5. Dysfunctional mirror neurons have been hypothesized to be a contributing factor to the social deficits that are symptomatic of autism spectrum disorder. How might problems in mirror systems degrade the ability of people with autism to interact socially?

12 Communication and Language

athenaphotography

Speech is A-KEH-DI-GLINI NE-AHS-JAH TKIN MOASI DZEH LHA-CHA-EH, but not always clearly 🔊. Sometimes, obfuscation can be advantageous, such as when military commanders need to direct their troops' movements from afar and eavesdroppers may be listening. The outcome of World War II was determined, in part, by the ability of cryptographers on both sides to decipher encoded messages. The German military relied heavily on encryption by a machine known as Enigma to protect their private communications, while the U.S. military took advantage of the unique linguistic skills of Native Americans to transmit their secrets. "A-KEH-DI-GLINI" is Navajo for "victor," which in the U.S. military alphabet signifies the letter "v." Because only speakers of Navajo knew the meaning of these words, intercepted messages provided little information to foreign agents (**Figure 12.1**).

Deciphering unfamiliar languages is hard. Before the discovery of the Rosetta Stone, an artifact with a single decree inscribed in three different languages, many researchers had failed in their attempts to translate Egyptian hieroglyphs. By contrast, human infants learn whatever languages are used around them with ease, despite not only being unfamiliar with the meanings conveyed by those languages but also with the very fact that languages exist.

Infants and toddlers learn languages so effortlessly that it is hard to imagine how this could possibly be a challenging task. Yet, no other organisms appear to naturally possess this ability and even adult humans often run into problems learning new languages without diligent practice and coaching. If you've ever taken a foreign language course, you might be familiar with this phenomenon.

Language use is the most obvious way that humans communicate, but it is not the only way. Sometimes a simple glance, smile, or eye roll can convey as much meaning as any sentence. But how? Has any animal, other than a human, ever rolled its eyes (or tentacles?) in response to actions or

FIGURE 12.1. Navajo code. Navajo code talkers used words familiar to any speaker of Navajo to send secret messages for the U.S. military. Why do you think codes based on natural languages are so tricky to decipher? (Everett Collection Inc/Alamy Stock Photo)

messages it observes? Where is the meaning coming from and how is meaningful communication related to the way people think?

Some philosophers and psychologists argue that without language, thought is impossible. Others suggest that spoken and written languages are simply technological tools that facilitate thought—much like clothes help humans to stay warm—and that most animals (including humans) naturally communicate and think in similar ways and for similar reasons.

Language clearly has unique and complex features, such that cognitive psychologists specializing in language research, called **psycholinguists**, continue to make new discoveries each year, even after decades of experiments.

In this final chapter, after having learned about the many different mechanisms that enable you to cognize, you should be able to re-cognize the complexities of language that are hidden in plain sight. You should also be able to understand why the encoded messages of the Navajo code talkers, which were impossible for expert German linguists to interpret, are relatively easy for most Navajo children to learn to understand.

BEHAVIORAL PROCESSES

The Navajo code that U.S. military personnel used to transmit secret messages was not normal speech in that the sequences of words produced would never happen in a typical conversation. Even so, it shared many features with natural ways of communicating. First, there was a **sender**, an agent who generated the message.

Actually, more than one agent was often involved when transmitting messages. For instance, a general might decide to move some troops and ask a Navajo code talker to transmit his commands into the field. In that case, both the general and the code talker cooperated to generate a **signal**, which consisted of an encrypted message. In this case, the signal is not a single event, as it includes both the speech of the general and the radio transmissions sent by the code talker.

The signal travels out into the world through a physical process of **transmission**—it's literally moving through space. As the signal travels, it may be noticed and interpreted by multiple agents, or **receivers** (Figure 12.2). For those receivers who know the code, the signal serves as a message. Eavesdroppers can guess that the signal is conveying something to other recipients, but that's about it. This process of producing, transmitting, receiving, and interpreting signals is an act of **communication**.

If you've read the chapters preceding this one, then you know that cognitive processes contribute to each of the elements of communication: producing, transmitting, receiving, and interpreting. For

Perceptual processing   Signal deployment

Receiver response

Signal form

FIGURE 12.2. Communicating with signals. Communication involves the coordinated production and perception of signals. A sender can deploy and transmit signals in multiple forms at the same time and receivers may perceive and respond to several cues in parallel as they decode the message being sent. (Bazilfoto)

receivers to correctly interpret signals, they must perceive and recognize not only the signal but also the context within which the signal is sent (processes involved in recognizing speech and visual stimuli are reviewed in Chapters 2 and 4).

Native Navajo speakers might easily recognize the words being said by a code talker, but they may still be confused about what the particular sequence of words means unless they know that each word stands for a letter of the alphabet (**Table 12.1**). The effective transmission of a message often requires knowledge of where potential or targeted recipients are located, like when you yell to get a friend's attention at a party or whisper to them in class. And of course, produced signals, whether they are text, music, barks, eye rolls, or emojis, are the clearest evidence of cognition (or of its absence) that you are likely to encounter.

The following sections consider the broader picture of how communication makes cognitive interactions between agents possible, the unique features of language as a component of communication and cognition, and the processes that make it possible for humans to acquire language skills.

TABLE 12.1 Navajo Alphabet Cipher

Navajo	English	Letter
MOASI	Cat	C
LHA-CHA-EH	Dog	D
DZEH	Elk	E
TKIN	Ice	I
NE-AHS-JAH	Owl	O
A-KEH-DI-GLINI	Victor	V

Producing and Comprehending Messages

SNEAK PEEK: Communication involves more than just saying what you think. Sometimes actions speak louder, especially when you are attempting to coordinate your actions with those of other minds.

Communication does not always require cognition. Circuits in your phone continuously send and receive signals in the absence of any cognizing, as do individual neurons in your brain. Nevertheless, communication and cognition are intimately connected.

Your ability to understand claims about the relationship between cognition and communication depends on your ability to understand the messages you're receiving right now from this chapter. Those messages are mostly language based, but the various fonts, images, and punctuation also serve as signals that can potentially affect how you interpret the images you see on each page. The kinds of messages that any individual can send depend heavily on the types of signals that a sender can produce.

Types of Communicative Signals

"Nonverbal communication is an elaborate secret code that is written nowhere, known by none, and understood by all."
—Sapir, 1927

You might think of signaling as the kind of thing you do when you're about to turn while driving or give a thumbs-up in response to someone's suggestion. Signaling includes these things and much more.

When you smile, talk, sigh, text, vote, clap, make a purchase, sing in the shower, raise your hand, wear perfume or cologne, offer someone a doughnut, come to class late, or mail your mom a card on Mother's Day, you are acting as a sender. Every act you perform, voluntary or not, is a potential signal. Like notes in bottles that are cast into the sea or comments on popular YouTube videos, many of the signals you produce will never be received. Others may be sent and received against your will, like when you invite mosquitoes to dine on you by breathing.

Signals come in many forms. Some, like speech sounds, are perceptible, while others, like the digital signals your phone uses to transmit texts, are not. The form that a signal takes often limits how it can be used for both communication and cognition, so understanding how senders produce signals can provide important clues about how signals are used.

Discrete and Graded Signals

Every sender has a **signal repertoire** that consists of the full set of signals that the sender produces. Signals that are clearly distinguishable, like the turn signals on a car, are called **discrete signals**, while signals that vary continuously along a spectrum, like smiles, are called **graded signals** (Green & Marler, 1979).

You can send graded signals with your car horn by controlling how long you press it. Speech signals contain both discrete elements—such as unique voice qualities that identify you—as well as graded elements, including features that can reveal how stressed or tired you are.

Discrete signals work well when the goal is to avoid miscommunication because they facilitate the sorting of signals by receivers into specific categories (see Chapter 5). Animals often use discrete signals to clearly communicate their emotional state (**Figure 12.3**). An advantage of graded signals is that they can convey subtle nuances that supplement the main message.

A common approach to categorizing communication signals is to create a taxonomy of the different kinds of signals that a sender produces, as well as an organizational framework for labeling

FIGURE 12.3. Canine communication. Dogs use discrete visual signals to communicate their emotional state. By using discrete signals, such as clear, distinguishable body postures, dogs increase the likelihood that receivers will be able to reliably sort perceived signals into appropriate categories. (After Doggone Safe, 2017)

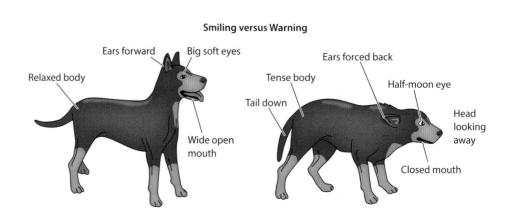

Smiling versus Warning

Ears forward   Big soft eyes

Relaxed body

Wide open mouth

Ears forced back

Tense body   Half-moon eye

Tail down   Head looking away

Closed mouth

different signal components. For instance, you might break up the text printed in this chapter into paragraphs composed of sentences that consist of sequences of words made up of individual letters. You could sort those letters into vowels versus consonants, and sort the words into verbs, nouns, conjunctions, etcetera. Describing communicative signals in this way makes it possible to carefully examine different parts of messages.

Symbolic and Iconic Signals

As noted earlier, signals need not be intentionally produced to be communicative. Professional psychics use a strategy whereby they provide clients with ambiguous cues. These cues lead the client to provide critical details or produce subtle facial expressions that help the psychics know when their interpretations and guesses are moving in the right direction.

Psychics pick up on signals that their clients typically have no awareness of sending. And it's not just psychics that do this. Most people engaged in a conversation automatically and unconsciously begin adjusting their speech patterns so that they are similar to those of the person they are speaking with (Garrod & Pickering, 2009; Miller et al., 2010). The fact that people mimic conversational partners' speech patterns without being aware this is happening suggests that they automatically perceive and respond to subtle cues. Failure to automatically imitate a speaker can degrade a conversation. These types of inadvertent communicative acts show that signaling involves more than just delivering preconceived messages.

Psychics not only read body language to construct their mystical narratives they also interpret less personal signals, such as the patterns tea leaves make in the bottom of a teacup. In tea-based divination (called tasseography), visual patterns formed by clumps of tea leaves are interpreted as signals that reveal an individual's future; a similar strategy is used when reading Tarot cards.

Signals that are related to their meanings in arbitrary ways (in tasseography, tea leaves clumped in triangles signal good luck) are called **symbols**. Signals that correspond more directly to what they stand for, like when your friend texts you 💀💀💀💀 after you tell her that your tea leaves said you're about to have some good luck, are **iconic** rather than symbolic; "LMAO" would be the symbolic version of this same signal.

Iconic communication signals need not look physically similar to what they stand for. For instance, honeybees send each other signals by performing elaborate dances in which the distance, angle, and intensity of their movements convey the quality and location of food sources (**Figure 12.4**).

Symbolic signals are generally viewed as being more cognitively complex than iconic signals. This is because symbolic signals make it possible to communicate about abstract qualities, categories, and concepts that cannot be directly perceived, like "justice" and "absurdity." For this reason, symbolic communication is, in principle, more flexible than iconic communication. Ways that symbols can catalyze cognition are discussed in detail in the section below on The Power of Symbols.

FIGURE 12.4. Iconic bee dancing.
Bees "dance" to communicate about food discoveries. Senders move in specific patterns that provide signals to receivers about where they might fly to find food. The extent and direction of the dance change with the direction and distance of the food, providing an iconic signal that stands for the food's location. (ZU_09)

FIGURE 12.5. Symbolic warnings. Vervet monkeys use symbolic vocalizations to signal the presence of specific predators. Senders produce one kind of sound when they see an eagle, another kind of sound when they see a snake, and a third kind of sound when they see a leopard. These different vocal signals are shown iconically as colored rectangles in which more red depicts more sound at particular times (horizontal axis) and pitches (vertical axis). The monkeys also produce different visual signals in parallel with these vocal signals. The visual signals are iconic in that they directly reveal what monkeys do upon encountering each predator (such as looking up when there is an eagle and looking down when there is a snake). A young monkey calling "Snake!" while looking up in the sky might provoke less of a response from other monkeys. (After Gillam, 2011, spectrograms courtesy E. Mercado III)

On the other hand, there is truth behind the saying that a picture is worth a thousand words. Symbolic signals are only as good as the knowledge that supports them, which is why some systems of symbolic communication, such as the system of glyphs discovered on Easter Island known as "rongorongo," are no longer interpretable.

The use of symbolic signals appears to be relatively rare in nature, which has further driven speculation that the use of such signals might require particularly sophisticated cognitive abilities (Deacon, 1997). Among nonhuman mammals, vervet monkeys use different alarm calls that specify types of predators (Seyfarth et al., 1980). These alarm calls are symbolic in that they don't resemble any sounds produced by the predators they stand for, and they also aren't similar to the sounds a monkey makes while being bitten by one of these predators (**Figure 12.5**).

The type of signal, whether it's discrete, graded, symbolic, or iconic, determines its communicative potential. But signal qualities do not determine how signals function or the kinds of cognitive processes needed to interpret them.

Consider the lilies of the field. For insects, these flowers signal food. When exchanged by people, they signal devotion. For other nearby plants, lily flowers signal nothing. Handwritten text varies as a function of language, generation, and penmanship, but for someone who is illiterate, all these variations are irrelevant.

Knowing a sender's repertoire of signals provides some clues about what a sender might be communicating. However, it's ultimately a receiver's perception of the signals along with comprehension of what the signals mean that determines whether any communication occurs or how cognitively sophisticated that communication might be. This is especially obvious in the earliest stages of signal production and comprehension by children.

Theories of Communication

Many psychological theories of communication propose that communication involves breaking down communication signals into parts that are processed in separate stages before being recom-

WEIRD, TRUE, FREAKY

Captain Cyborg

Telepathic communication has a long history in both parapsychology and science fiction. The concept is simple in practice—skip signal production and reception, and just allow brains to interface directly. While there is no definitive evidence that telepathic communication exists in nature, technological advances are edging ever closer to making such communication a reality.

Direct inter-brain communication has been a goal of Kevin Warwick's for a long time. In the late nineties, Professor Warwick decided to take matters into his own hands, literally, by implanting a silicon transponder that enabled him to control electronic systems using electrical signals from nerve activity in his arm (see figure). Implanting electronics that add functionality to an existing nervous system is often referred to as biohacking, an approach that has been successfully applied in humans and other animals (Moorjani, 2016; Talwar et al., 2002).

Several labs are experimenting with systems that enable people with paraplegia to move cursors, wheelchairs, and robotic arms through electrodes implanted in their cortical circuits (Bates, 2017). Most of these involve neurofeedback training, in which a computer adaptively learns to identify neural signals that precede thoughts about the movement of a targeted object. A patient learns to consistently generate such signals by thinking about where they want the target to move. The patient and computer are effectively learning a novel communication system.

Brain-computer interfaces are an exciting new mode of communicating, but the kind of "mind reading" typically

associated with telepathy is quite different. Professor Warwick's wife volunteered to be cyborg #2 in his study and had a chip implanted in her as well. The two-way connection enabled Professor Warwick to detect the activation of touch receptors in his wife's hand, which may be the first case of shared sensation outside of conjoined twins. Arm reading is still not mind reading but sharing sensations over a distance is not too far from sharing percepts or ideas.

Today, the limits of direct brain-to-brain communication are not so much technological as they are pragmatic (who wants to volunteer for brain surgery?) and limited by how little we know. Without knowing exactly how people neurally represent sentences, it is difficult to pinpoint which brain regions from different individuals should be directly linked (or how) in order to make conscious, voluntary, inter-brain conversations ("telepathy") possible.

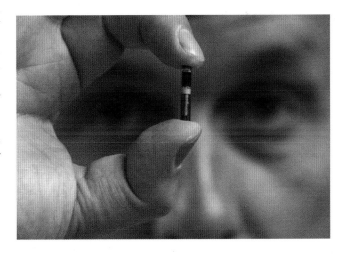

Kevin Warwick uses electronics implanted in his body to monitor his neural activity. He then can use measures of that activity to control computerized systems. (REUTERS/Alamy Stock Photo)b

---

bined and interpreted as a message. For instance, as you scan this page, your eyes repeatedly fixate on small clusters of words. Yet, you can interpret whole sentences, suggesting that something in your head is combining all those separate clusters to make the whole sentence understandable.

Traditional models of communication often portray the process as a tête-à-tête between two, turn-taking individuals—one the sender and the other the receiver (**Figure 12.6**). However, the kinds of social communicative interactions that are most prevalent in nature often involve more complex configurations.

Certain kinds of animal communication, for example, may be influenced by the communicative interactions of others (McGregor & Dabelsteen, 1996; Snijders et al., 2017)—commonly referred to as **eavesdropping**—or simply by the presence of other individuals.

In some ways, these multi-agent **communication networks** can be compared to modern ways of communicating with sites like Facebook and Twitter. In such networks, eavesdroppers can use communication signals not specifically sent to them to guide their own comprehension and signal production, leading to the emergence of memes, viral videos, and FOMO (fear of missing out). Later in this chapter, you will discover how communication networks can also strongly influence the development and use of language by toddlers.

FIGURE 12.6. Assembling messages. Communication is often portrayed as the exchange of parts of signals. The sender produces complex, continuous signals by assembling combinations of simpler, discrete signals. These signal "building blocks" can include sounds, gestures, facial expressions, moving flags (in semaphore), pictures, flashing lights (in Morse Code), and just about any other event that is perceivable. The receiver then collects parts of signals and recombines them into something meaningful.

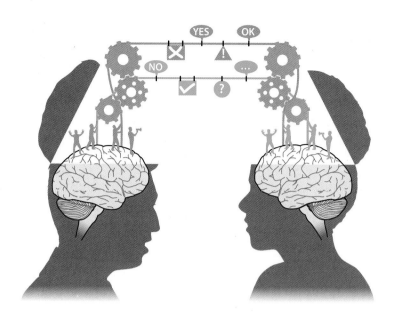

Communication as Information Processing

The idea that communication involves a sender transmitting signals to receivers has had a tremendous impact not only on how cognitive psychologists attempt to understand human communication but also on how they think about cognition more generally. For instance, the theory that mental representations encode information about the world, introduced in Chapter 1, in effect claims that objects and agents in a person's environment generate signals that are received, encoded, and distributed by the brain before being interpreted by higher-level processes.

Sound familiar? This process is essentially the same one used by Navajo code talkers—receive some information, represent it in a new way, and pass it on to interpreters, who give it to the commanders who act on the information. The **information processing approach** to communication (and cognition) focuses on the exchange of signals that move information from one place to another.

The conceptual foundation of this approach comes from techniques developed by engineers and mathematicians to efficiently and reliably transmit electrical signals (such as radio-transmitted codes). From this perspective, "the fundamental problem of communication is that of reproducing at one point, either exactly or approximately, a message selected at another point,"(Shannon, 1948). In other words, the presumed goal of communication is to replicate and relocate chunks of information, and theories of communication are meant to describe and explain how this happens.

One complication with the information processing approach is that it's not always clear what counts as a signal. Consider infants learning their first words. Is the information being communicated to the babies through the sounds made by the parents or through the context within which the sounds are produced? Perhaps the information is communicated through the parents' facial expressions, through the predictability of certain sound combinations, or by the emotional states that the babies are experiencing while hearing certain sounds.

You might be inclined to say all of the above and maybe more contribute to communicative information processing by babies. The information processing approach is not great at dealing with this kind of multifaceted communication because it treats signals as "things" that can be isolated, measured, and quantified.

Communication as Body Language

Some researchers have proposed that rather than trying to explain communication between people as an exchange of signals, it might be simpler to think of communication as a joint action between two individuals, analogous to dancing (Rendall et al., 2009). Just as two people dancing together perform

FIGURE 12.7. Multimodal transmission. Communication can include dynamic combinations of speech, images, facial expressions, postures, and hand gestures. Such actions may serve to collectively coordinate cognition during social interactions. (©Jon Feingersh/Blend Images/agefotostock)

similar movements, a parent who talks to their infant may be increasing the similarities between the internal states they both experience.

This portrayal, sometimes described as **embodied communication**, focuses less on the sequential encoding and decoding of messages and more on the coordination of activities within social interactions (Cook & Tanenhaus, 2009). Just as hearing music, holding hands, and staring at each other can potentially enhance the synchrony of a dancing couple, tracking multimodal events might also enhance coordinated communication between a sender and receiver (**Figure 12.7**). Embodied approaches to understanding communication have been most influential in studies related to gesturing during social interactions.

From the perspective of embodied communication, the communicative signals produced by a dancing bee might be similar to a floodlight encountered by moths. The light alters the actions of nearby moths, but not because the bulb is broadcasting information to them.

Moths approach lights because they are compelled to do so not because the light is sending out messages to moths. Similarly, if a tree branch fell on your head, you probably would not assume that the tree is attempting to communicate with you. Honeybee dances are a type of embodied communication, but one that is not as cooperative as a conversation between adults.

What then distinguishes communication that involves the sharing of meaningful messages from communication that serves mainly as a means of manipulating or coordinating actions with others? Put another way, when is communication at its most cognitive? For most cognitive scientists, the answer lies in language.

SIGHT BITES

Communication involves transmitting signals from a sender to one or more receivers.

The signal repertoire used during communication can include both icons and symbols produced alone or in sequences.

Communication can be viewed either as the exchange of information (the information processing approach) or as a way to coordinate actions (embodied communication).

The Nature of Language

SNEAK PEEK: Much of what psychologists know about language comes from studies of sentence production. The flexibility with which you can communicate your thoughts comes from the ways in which language enables you to take advantage of symbols.

For most people, talking is as natural and effortless as walking. Even so, scientists and philosophers argue that talking is one of the most cognitively sophisticated acts in the world. What's so fancy about talking? Is it really so different from the ways that birds, bees, and monkeys communicate?

Talking is the dominant mode of communication used by humans and the most obvious example of language use. **Language** includes all the combinations of words, phrases, and sentences that people use, along with their meanings. Thousands of different languages exist, most of which have been developed over centuries. The main function of language is communication, but it also plays important roles in the development and application of concepts and in thinking more generally (Lupyan et al., 2007).

As noted earlier, psycholinguists specialize in studying language processing. Their work is closely tied to that of linguists, who typically study the origins and qualities of languages. Cognitive researchers who don't explicitly study language often study language processes indirectly. For instance, in most cognitive experiments, participants are given verbal instructions that strongly shape how they behave in the experiment.

Many memory studies use written or spoken words or word-like speech sounds as stimuli, including the earliest studies by Ebbinghaus, described in Chapter 7. Additionally, findings from cognitive studies are shared through written or verbal reports. The scientific study of cognition is infected by language from beginning to end.

And yet, most toddlers learn to talk long before they show anything like the cognitive sophistication of adults, suggesting that language might involve relatively simple processes. In fact, classic models of language processing (**Figure 12.8**) are hardly more complex than the basic information processing models of communication described above in which a sender transmits a signal to a receiver. The "magic" of language happens when sent signals spark interpretations and new ideas in receivers. Nowhere is this more evident than in communication via written text.

Writing

You've probably communicated with your friends by texting without thinking too much about how you're doing it. But how are you doing it? Are the processes the same as those involved in talking, but with your fingers replacing your vocal organs and your eyes doing the job normally done by your ears? This doesn't seem likely because millions of people who use speech from an early age never learn to write or read.

The timing and ordering of text production are also often quite different from speech. For instance, I constructed this sentence over several years, tweaking it repeatedly based on comments from colleagues and editors, to create the fantastic monstrosity that you see before you. Imagine if someone you were talking with was still working on producing a sentence three or more years after starting it!

Writing also persists. In other words, it's possible for a written message to be revisited and redistributed by both senders and receivers without it changing. If talking is like walking, then writing is like pole vaulting—it's a specialized cognitive skill that can develop from conversational skills but goes beyond them.

Although writing differs from spoken language in many ways, the cognitive processes underlying the ability to write and speak—attention, long-term memory, working memory, etcetera—clearly overlap.

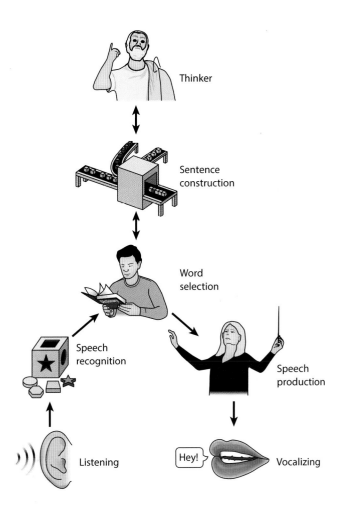

Thinker

Sentence
construction

Word
selection

Speech
recognition

Speech
production

Listening

Hey!

Vocalizing

FIGURE 12.8. An information processing approach to understanding language use. Classical studies of language focus on sequential processes that make communication with speech possible, including recognition, thought, and production. It's basically an inside-the-head version of the classic sender-transmission-receiver model. But in language processing, there is a hypothetical assembly line of internal senders and receivers: some are specialized for recognizing speech sounds, some for recognizing words, and others for constructing or deconstructing sentences.

Writing as Information Processing

While writing can engage a wide range of cognitive processes, there are cases where generating text is less complex than speaking. When you take notes during a lecture, for example, you're mainly trying to record key statements, like an amateur stenographer.

Notetaking can be viewed as a sequential process in which you organize speech sounds into representations of spoken words that trigger memories of the visual patterns of letters used to spell those words, which are then used to guide motor acts that make those visual patterns appear (**Figure 12.9**).

The first stage of note-taking is basically the same as for talking—you need to recognize the language to transcribe it. What happens next depends on your past training. You could "translate" the heard words into your own words or an abbreviated form like the shorthand used by court stenographers. You might alternatively focus on exactly copying phrases or use guessed spellings for names or jargon that you've never heard before. Each of these different options is thought to engage different but overlapping cognitive processes; some are the same ones you use when chatting or texting.

Evidence of these overlapping processes comes from the spelling errors of children, from individuals who have lost specific writing skills due to localized brain damage, and from measurements of the speed with which college students can recognize words (Harley, 2008).

Writing skills are often a key ingredient for academic success and are the best predictor of whether someone will do well in their first year of college (Kellogg & Raulerson, 2007). So how might you ramp up your writing skills? Practice is critical but identifying the right way to practice is tricky. You have to hone your memory, language, and thinking abilities in an integrated way and you may also need to gain a deep knowledge of the topic you are writing about.

FIGURE 12.9. Multiple routes to notetaking. Note-taking starts the same as most listening tasks, with perception and speech pattern recognition. How it progresses next depends on the goals and skills of the notetaker. Text may be transcribed directly by converting speech sounds into familiar letter combos, by replacing recognized words with abstract representations of those words, or by extracting meaning from sequences of words (retrieving semantic memories) and producing new text that summarizes key elements of what was heard.

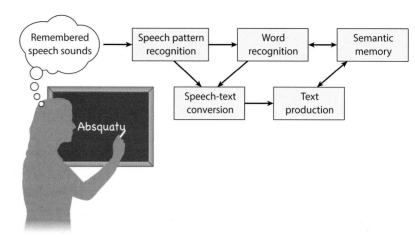

Writing as Embodied Communication

Surprisingly, as a communication signal, text can be even more embodied than speech. For example, let's say that I tell you the next sentence you read will be unbelievably great! I'm clearly trying to increase your excitement about this admittedly mundane sentence.

The act of writing can also affect the writer. Describing upsetting experiences in a diary can improve a person's mental and physical health and in some cases even their grade point average (GPA) (Pennebaker et al., 2003)! How is it that writing sentences can change the person who constructed them?

According to classical information processing models of communication, a sender that transmits a signal to itself has accomplished nothing because no new information has been received or transmitted to a new location. Alternatively, if you view writing as a kind of thinking aloud (see Chapter 10), then written text may act like a working memory aid (see Chapter 8), helping you to consider more complicated possibilities or increasing your capacity for metacognitive problem-solving.

In children, mastering basic writing skills, including the movements required to generate script or text, seems to free up resources for more complex text production. Professional writers have typically spent thousands of hours writing about topics they are deeply interested in, much like professional musicians spend many years playing music they like. The core skill underlying writing is, of course, constructing sentences worth reading. Understanding exactly how people do this has been a major focus of cognitive research.

Producing Words and Sentences

The ease with which people can produce a continuous flow of language signals is highlighted by the diarrhea of the mouth seen in some gossips. Streaming language of this sort is referred to as **discourse**, as are conversations, storytelling, polemics, pontificating, sermons, and monologues.

Pragmatics and Propositions

Discourse is most effective when all participants know and follow the rules and customs of the language communication game—the **pragmatics** of language. These rules of language production enable listeners (receivers) to make accurate inferences and avoid confusion.

For instance, spoken sentences will ideally be accurate, informative, relevant, and clear (Grice, 1975). Any violation of these expectations, such as sarcasm, insinuation, or comedy, achieves its goal precisely because it blatantly deviates from the norm. The phrase, "That's what she said," is rarely accurate, informative, relevant, or clear. Nevertheless, interpreting it in context is not too hard.

Typical goals of speech also help listeners to interpret sentences. A speech act might describe the world ("It's hot"), express a feeling ("I'm bored"), declare a change ("I'm single"), persuade a listener to do something ("Eat it"), or request information ("How long?"). Encoding meaning within streams of sentences, phrases, and words is sometimes described as a process of making propositions—statements that are either true or false—although clearly, not all statements fit this description ("Long enough").

Part of the reason that being familiar with a topic can make it easier to recall additional facts related to the topic is that your existing knowledge supplements new information with additional distinctive cues for later recall. As with mnemonics, elaborating on to-be-remembered material can make recall easier.

For instance, early experiments examining how well students could recall (through drawing) pairs of abstract pictures presented together found that students were able to recall more than twice as many pictures when a narrative description was provided in parallel with the paired images (see Figure 8.11). Treating the first part of an unfamiliar term like "modal memory model" as an acronym about what old dudes all love can also make the term easier to recall, even though it increases the number of words being stored.

Syntax and Lexicons

The "rules" of language include not only general customs of conversation but also more specific recipes for the right way to make sentences—the kinds of speech laws commonly enforced by the "grammar police." Foremost among these are the rules of **syntax**, or how sentences should be structured, especially how words should be ordered.

If you speak, then you generally know what the syntactical rules of your language are, even if you can't recite them. When these rules are broken—say when Yoda from the *Star Wars* movies notes, "Always in motion is the future"—the oddity of the word ordering intriguing is.

On the other hand, if an older person were to tell you, "Oh well it influence the football right here like cause it comes in see the end of it see," then you might become alarmed and begin to wonder whether you should call a doctor.

For English, the typical structure of sentences (and conversations) can be described hierarchically (**Figure 12.10**). In this framework, clusters of phonemes (see Chapter 4) are combined into sequences of discrete words. Individual words and clusters of words can be viewed as signals conveying specific messages depending on how both the words and clusters are ordered. An obvious question raised by this hierarchical portrayal of sentence structure is: How are such signal streams constructed?

If you want to say something, you need to put that "something" into words and then produce those words: a three-stage process of conceptualization, formulation, and execution (Harley, 2008). Syntactical rules shape how you formulate sentences—that is, how you put words together. Such rules are worthless, however, if you don't have words to put together, and so another key element of formulating a sentence involves selecting the words that you want to say.

Choosing a word is called **lexicalization** and the vocabulary of words you have to choose from is your **lexicon**, sometimes described as a mental dictionary. If you've never heard the term lexicon before, then you're one step closer to adding it to your lexicon.

There are competing views about how many lexicons an individual may possess. If you're multilingual, you might have a separate lexicon for each language. If you're literate in at least one language, you might have an additional lexicon that is specialized for visual representations of words.

The **tip-of-the-tongue** phenomenon, in which the word you want to select is just out of reach, is often seen as a failed attempt at lexicalization. Such failures occur more often for words that you rarely use, suggesting that not all words in a lexicon are equal. In general, the accessibility of any given word depends on the frequency with which it is used and how similar it sounds to other words (Citraro et al., 2023).

(A)

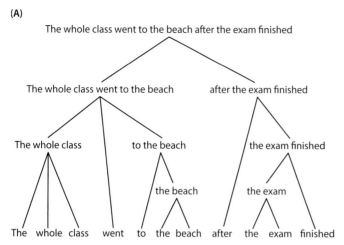

(B)

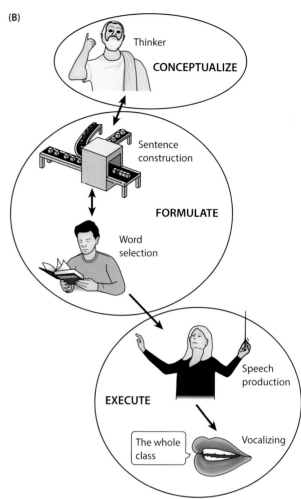

FIGURE 12.10. Structure of a sentence. (A) Spoken and written sentences can be segmented into parts, each of which is composed of smaller elements. (B) Predictable patterns of word ordering within sentences provide evidence that sentence production follows certain rules in terms of how sentences are conceptualized, formulated, and executed. The syntax of a language is the set of rules that people use when constructing sentences. (A from https://languagetools.info/grammarpedia /concepts.htm)

Phonetics

Once a word has been selected, it still needs to be physically produced to be communicated. This part of the sentence production process is often viewed as the least cognitive aspect of talking, in part because it is relatively easy to generate sentences by broadcasting a recording with a speaker. However, the biological production of speech is more complex than it might seem and only a handful of species possess the ability to do it.

Speaking is physically challenging because it requires the relatively precise, voluntary control of airflow, the flexible shaping of vocal organs, and sophisticated vocal learning mechanisms. The acoustic details, or **phonetics**, of spoken words, including the consonants and vowels within those words, reveal a greater level of complexity of vocal motor control than you might expect based on the way speech sounds.

Children typically master speech recognition well before they master the ability to speak. The fact that speech production is tricky becomes especially clear if you try to produce words in a language you don't know. The words you attempt to make may sound fine to you, but to native speakers, they often sound hilarious.

The last stages of processing before words spill from your mouth is often described as **phonetic encoding**, a process in which abstract word representations are transformed into the motor commands necessary for producing speech.

Beyond writing and speaking, people can also produce sentences using hand gestures, eye movements (tracked by a computer), whistles, graphic symbols that depict ideas or objects (like emojis), and more. Other animals, including apes, parrots, and dolphins, also have the ability to produce sentence-like streams of signals, showing that they have somewhat comparable motor and vocal control (Deacon, 1997). However, nonhumans do not naturally converse using sentences, a fact that some view as evidence that humans have a unique cognitive capacity for developing and using language.

Of course, not all humans naturally talk in sentences; deaf individuals never exposed to sign language and some people with autism spectrum disorder don't, for example. One question that psycholinguists and other cognitive psychologists are still trying to answer is: What cognitive abilities must an individual have in order to successfully learn to use a language? Models of lexical selection and phonetic encoding represent an attempt to answer this question.

Models of Language Production

Many cognitive models of sentence production describe word selection as a multistage process. During this process, a message moves from an abstract level into ordered sets of words, which initiate the motor instructions needed to control the production of specific speech signals, similar to the writing process described earlier. Most of these models assume that the representations of individual words make up the lexicon and that message senders engage in a search process before selecting which of those representations become sequentially activated.

Typically, the three stages—conceptualization, formulation, and execution—are modeled as levels of processing, with thinking occurring at the highest level and physical movements representing the lowest level (similar to the levels-of-processing effect discussed in Chapter 8).

Models of lexical processing and representation tend to be highly abstract. The models mainly attempt to explain how the lexicon is organized, how words are accessed, and how different levels of processing interact during word selection.

Lexicons can vary substantially across languages, especially in terms of how meanings are mapped to different words. Consequently, a model constructed to explain lexical processing in English might not be applicable to other languages.

Words within lexicons have been modeled as being either discrete mental representations or distributed representations (see Chapter 5). For models with discrete representations, each word is stored separately. Distributed representations, in contrast, involve interconnected, overlapping networks—like the connectionist models described in previous chapters—that become active when each word is selected.

In both cases, the search process is often described as a competition in which the winner is the selected word. Similarly, the search for the best model of lexical processing is a scientific competition in which the "winners" are the models that best predict the speed at which a person can access specific words and the slips of the tongue that a speaker is most likely to make.

Speech Errors

It may seem odd that scientists use language flubs to figure out how speech production works, but there is a method to the madness. If you say a different word from what you mean to, or accidentally switch the order of words, this can provide a glimpse at a "second place" winner in the sentence construction competition.

Knowing what these runner-up words are can shed light on how the selection process works. For instance, if you accidentally say "bet" when you meant to say "bed," then a competition involving sound similarity is probably happening.

Adults rarely make speech errors, but the ones they do make are consistent enough that researchers can use them to test their models. When words or sounds interfere with each other—like in tongue twisters—it shows that the processing of certain words can affect the selection and production of other words occurring before or after them. Difficulties in speech production, such as stuttering, can provide clues about how control mechanisms normally function.

Unlike adults, young children rarely produce error-free speech. Researchers study the frequency and sequential emergence of different types of errors made by children to better understand how sentence construction skills develop. If you hear a child say "Gi me my bay baa" (Give me my baby back), then you have some evidence that her word representations emphasize first syllables and that her basic syntactical ordering skills are more developed.

Aphasia

Observations of speech errors have strongly shaped how scientists think about language processes, but it is not the everyday blunders of children or adults that have had the biggest impact. Instead, the rare errors produced by adults with brain damage have had the most influence.

First among these are the unusual speech patterns produced by the patient Tan (discussed later in the Brain Substrates section), which consisted exclusively of the phrase "tan tan." Damage-induced disruption of speech production, called **aphasia**, can potentially provide clues about the separate contributions of different levels of language processing—how they are organized and how they interact.

For instance, individuals with aphasia may find it easier to produce some words, or specific classes of words like nouns or verbs, than others (Kemmerer, 2015). These differences can reveal the relative accessibility of different kinds of words in a person's lexicon.

Some aphasias strongly impair the selection and production of words, while others cause the patient to produce an incomprehensible word salad. It's tricky to infer how language production works from studying people in whom it doesn't, but the variety of speaking problems people with brain damage experience provides additional ways to test cognitive models.

Listening and Comprehension

"Every impression that comes in from without, be it a sentence which we hear, an object of vision, or an effluvium which assails our nose, no sooner enters our consciousness than it is drafted off in some determinate direction or other, making connection with the other materials already there, and finally producing what we call our reaction."
—James, 2008, p 123

Early models of language often described its use as more like a bucket brigade than like walking (**Figure 12.11**). In bucket brigades, firefighters formed a line in which multiple water-filled buckets were rapidly transported from a well before being used to douse a fire. Similarly, talking (or writing) may be described as a process in which a sender transmits a volley of information packaged into separate buckets (words) that are ultimately dumped into a receiver's mind.

While this simple model accurately describes successful communication in electronic systems, including computers, and possibly in some plants and animals, it fails to capture a key aspect of language processing in humans. As noted earlier in the quote by William James, when words are perceived by a listener, they do not simply arrive as a replica of information provided by a sender.

How the words are perceived and how they are interpreted are strongly affected by the past experiences of the receiver, as well as by the specific context within which they are received. To a certain

FIGURE 12.11. Passing it on.
A bucket brigade fighting a fire is similar to language-based communication. How is the fire like listening? (Sergey Nezhinkiy/ Alamy Stock Photo)

extent, the message delivered by the word "fire" is not so much in the signal that is transmitted as it is in the reaction (including memories and emotions) that the word triggers in the listener.

While reactions to the words "water" and "fire" are predictable and consistent, a listener's reaction to a full sentence may differ greatly depending on who the listener is and when the listener perceives the signal. Even recognizing signals as words can be tricky if you are unfamiliar with a language.

Speech signals received by someone without the right learning experiences are effectively noise—this is why Navajo code talkers were so effective at shielding secret messages. The key to understanding sentences and language more generally is closely tied to understanding how speech, writing, and related signals activate memories that affect ongoing cognitive processes.

Semantics

The foundation for understanding sentences comes from identifying the **semantics**, or meanings, of words. In Chapters 5 and 8, you were introduced to some of the models that cognitive psychologists have developed to explain how people organize and access hypothetical semantic networks, and how semantic memories for facts and events shape recall and thinking. If a lexicon is like a dictionary, then semantic representations are similar to the definitions and examples indexed by words in the dictionary.

Words that serve as labels are closely linked to categories; sometimes the label is linked to a very specific category (like your name). The meanings of words are also dependent on those preceding them, which is why you understood what I meant when I used the word "them" in this sentence.

Semantic processing is usually associated with accessing long-term memories but also depends on the availability of recent memories. So, when I write here that you probably don't want to end up like Tan, you can probably agree.

Models of Language Comprehension

Many cognitive models of sentence comprehension are simply the reverse of sentence construction (**Figure 12.12**). This symmetry of processing might seem to imply that learning to produce and understand speech occurs in parallel. However, as you will soon discover, learning to comprehend language typically precedes the ability to produce even single words, suggesting that these two processes are distinct.

A typical undergraduate student knows about 10,000 nouns. How exactly each noun is represented is hotly debated. At one point, it was thought that words are essentially abstract symbols that catalog lists of features: pizza = hot, cheesy, food.

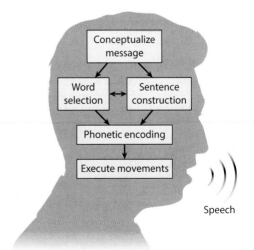
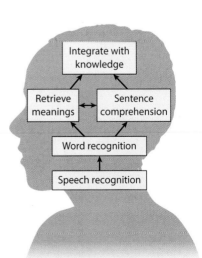

Speech

FIGURE 12.12. Speech reception as reversed speech production. Sentence comprehension, like production, involves recognizing speech sounds as words, linking words to their meanings, and conceptualizing/interpreting groups of words as a message.

An alternative view was that words serve as cues to associated memories—when you hear or read "pizza," it may remind you of some of the better pizzas you recently ate, rather than a list of their ingredients, and may even evoke imagery (see Chapter 9) associated with past pizza encounters. But it is unlikely that this happens every time you see the word pizza.

In fact, what "pizza" means can vary over time. Say the word "pizza" a hundred times in a row and it will likely cease to even seem like a word. See "pizza" flash by in a commercial and you might not even realize you read it. Even such unconscious processing can affect how you interpret subsequent words you see or hear, leading to priming of the sort discussed in Chapter 3.

The meaning of some labels is less definitional than others. If I say, "That turtle is toast," then you can assume that a turtle is about to meet its demise. "That turtle is f***ed," conveys the same basic information, but in a way that some would find unacceptable (like those who required the asterisks). These turtle descriptors on their own might evoke different meanings and emotional states.

In short, extracting meaning from words is not simply a matter of looking them up in a mental dictionary. Interpreting words is often more like interpreting a wink and a nod as a gestural sign of shared knowledge that is left unsaid.

Parsing and Prosody

Thinking of sentence understanding as a process of searching for word meanings ignores the fact that word order matters. Some linguists, such as Chomsky, have argued that the structural organization of sentences is what makes language cognitively unique and enables children to learn to use language (Pinker & Jackendoff, 2005). From this perspective, the deconstruction of sentences in terms of grammatical rules, or **parsing** of sentences, is critical to comprehending and using language.

The importance of parsing for comprehending sentences varies across languages. Even within a language, parsing may be more or less important when processing particular sentences. Psycholinguists who study parsing man desks, where they attempt to identify odd syntactic (but grammatically "legal") structures that derail sentence understanding of the undergraduates. Studies of how people process such off sentences (like the one you just read) can reveal cognitive biases that shape sentence parsing and understanding.

Deconstructing sentences requires not only paying attention to the order of words but also noting variations in how the words are said, especially in speech processing. These variations are important in comprehending speech, and they also play a role in interpreting written sentences.

For instance, my use of punctuation, can simulate, variations in, the timing of word production…Or shifts in vocal pitch, right? Variations in the **prosodic features** of a sentence, such as pauses or pitch shifts, can convey information beyond that revealed by the syntax and semantics of sentences. Sometimes, prosody can even change the meaning of a sentence entirely: "Let's eat, mom" versus "Let's eat mom."

Prosody processing may also provide a foundation for learning speech patterns. Recent studies have shown that babies learn about prosody even before they're born and can recognize the rhythms of sentences from specific books read to them pre-birth (Abboub et al., 2016). Prosody also contributes to your ability to recognize when someone is joking, exaggerating, or being sarcastic: assuming you can (**Figure 12.13**).

Models of Sentence Processing

Contemporary models of sentence comprehension propose that receivers make use of multiple representations when trying to ex-

FIGURE 12.13. Pictured prosody. In early film posters, the prosodic features of speech were often indicated by modifying the font, size, boldness, or other qualities of words to simulate variations in the stress given to specific words. Punctuation marks also symbolically indicate variations…in prosody! (Pictorial Press Ltd/Alamy Stock Photo)

tract meaning from received signals (Van Gompel, 2013). Representations of words, rhythms, and phrases are recognized, integrated, and categorized in terms of their semantic and syntactic properties to identify what the sender means.

All of these models assume that successful interpretations rely heavily on the past experiences of the listener—sentence comprehension is a cognitive skill that continues to change even after decades of practice. Disagreements about how sentences are cognitively processed mainly relate to the form of the representations, how they are activated, and how they are acquired.

Structuralist approaches to explaining sentence comprehension tend to focus on mechanisms of transforming signals into recognizable propositions. **Emergentist** approaches, instead, emphasize how receivers construct, organize, and use representations of inputs and how they access relevant knowledge.

Increasingly, researchers are considering how individual differences in non-language-specific processes (like working memory capacity) may influence sentence comprehension abilities. All modern approaches to sentence comprehension explain it as a chain reaction sparked by sensory inputs in which multiple cognitive processes interact through both coordination and competition. In this respect, current models of language processing retain many features of the earlier associationist models of knowledge acquisition (see Chapter 7).

Understanding Language in the Real World

Situations where a listener is hearing multiple sentences simultaneously—the norm at most parties—are seldom considered in modern language theory. If sentence comprehension is a chain reaction to received words, then how can anyone have a conversation in a restaurant or in front of a TV?

Reception and recognition of overlapping speech sounds should lead to a garbled mess (**Figure 12.14**), which can happen if two people are trying to talk to you at the same time. Selective attention (see Chapter 4) and auditory scene analysis (see Chapter 6) are clearly important, but exactly how they make comprehension possible when many competing signals are present is less clear. It is not simply a matter of tuning out other speakers because if someone yells your name out at a party, you will recognize it.

Most theoretical models of language processing treat sentences as if they are excerpts from a soliloquy, but sentence comprehension in natural contexts is more catch-as-catch-can. The difficulties of speech stream segregation and the separation of words within speech streams (see Chapter 4 for more information on speech segmentation) highlight the fact that speech comprehension is as much about successful social interaction and monitoring of specific senders as it is about extracting meaning from sentences.

Hordes of sentences have been constructed about language production and comprehension throughout the history of cognitive psychology. What is it about linguistic skills that attracts so much

FIGURE 12.14. A garbled mess?
On the trading floor of the New York stock exchange, speech processing is rarely a monologue. The ability to extract individual speech streams from overlapping ones is critical to communication in many social contexts. (Randy Duchaine/Alamy Stock Photo)

attention? Does clumping words together really increase the kinds of information that you can transmit, comprehend, or think about? Or is talking just the preferred way that humans convey messages? Understanding the contribution of symbols to language is key to answering these questions and explaining how language affects thought processes.

The Power of Symbols

What is a symbol? It is easy to think of examples, but it's less straightforward to say what those examples have in common.

Symbols have long been thought to possess special powers, but historically those powers were more mystical than intellectual. It's only been recently, with the rise of computers, that symbols became linked to computing power. From the perspective of the computational theory of mind (described in Chapter 1), computing power translates into cognitive capacity within human minds.

Physical Symbol Systems

Two computer scientists, Allen Newell and Herbert Simon, popularized the idea that symbols are a source of cognition with their **physical symbol system (PSS)** hypothesis: "A physical symbol system has the necessary and sufficient means for general intelligent action." For them, the special powers of symbols came from the fact that symbols could represent all kinds of computations (Newell, 1980; Newell & Simon, 1972).

The physical symbol system hypothesis explains everything that computers can do. It builds on the successes of mathematicians and logicians in using symbolic notation as a conceptual tool. A computer is a physical symbol system, and so is a person. Really, all that is required for something to be a physical symbol system is that it uses symbols in predictable ways.

In computers, all symbols ultimately correspond to numbers, and the computer programming languages that make software work are essentially recipes for how to maintain or change these numbers over time (**Figure 12.15**). Executing a computer program is similar to sentence comprehension in the sense that word-like inputs initiate chain reactions that affect what the program does.

Symbols as Signs

The sounds and images of human language are not numerical, but they still count as symbols because they are signs that, by convention, mean something to people that perceive them. You might have thought that symbols exist independently of their interpreters, but nope.

Symbols are just one kind of sign. Other types of signs, like emojis, tend to be less arbitrary and less abstract. The physical symbol system hypothesis proposes that symbols are part of a physical system, which means that, like the sounds and letters of languages, you can observe and measure them.

The arbitrariness of symbols is part of what makes them flexible communicative signals. By combining sounds (or letters) into words and then combining words into sequences, one can create an unending string of varying signals. We don't take full advantage of these possibilities, however. People

FIGURE 12.15. Source code. Computer programming languages often use ordered sequences of "words" similar to those in sentences; however, unlike symbols that label objects, actions, or agents, the words and symbols in computer languages encode numbers. (Yurich84)

use a relatively small set of speech sounds and letters, and about 50,000 words, on average; most sentences contain 20 words or less.

Additionally, associations between words and the things that they refer to are not always arbitrary. Some spoken words, like "moo," actually have qualities related to what they signify (and so don't really qualify as symbols!). Some nonwords, like "bouba" and "kiki" seem to naturally pair up with certain kinds of images (**Figure 12.16**), even for people who speak different languages (Bremner et al., 2013).

Constructed Languages and Grammars

Computer programming languages differ from natural languages not only because their symbols and "words" represent numbers and computational instructions but also because they are physical symbol systems designed to mimic some features of natural languages or **constructed languages**. Constructed languages typically have extensive vocabularies, as well as syntactical rules. Consequently, the learning and use of constructed languages can engage natural language processing mechanisms.

Some simple constructed languages have been designed specifically to investigate language processes. Symbols in these constructed languages consist of initially meaningless symbols (like "bouba") organized using simplified syntactic rules that participants gradually learn through trial and error. In this way, psychologists can assess how learnable different sets of syntactical rules are.

Other constructed languages were developed as part of fictional storylines, such as the Klingon language used by an alien race in *Star Trek* and the Elvish language used in J.R.R. Tolkien's *Lord of the Rings*. The overlap in form and function between constructed languages and natural languages has led some to suggest that natural languages may simply be what you get when you haphazardly construct languages over multiple generations.

In some rare cases, a group of people may construct a new natural language in a single generation. Researchers recorded an instance of this in the early 2000s, in which deaf children in Nicaragua developed their own sign language, independently of spoken languages and without the guidance of adults (Senghas et al., 2004). The children collectively chose the gestures that would be used as words, and developed the rules for using the gestures, effectively giving them a secret system for communicating (**Figure 12.17**).

FIGURE 12.16. Which image is the "kiki" and which is the "bouba?" People tend to agree about which labels best fit each shape, which is not what you might expect if speech sounds are arbitrarily mapped onto things. Most people think "kikis" are pointy. Did you?

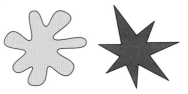

FIGURE 12.17. Nicaraguan sign language. Children attending a school for the deaf in Nicaragua independently developed their own sign language to make communicating easier. Do you think it is more likely that the signs they developed were iconic or symbolic? (Rebecca Ore/Alamy Stock Photo)

For both natural and constructed languages, words can, in principle, be combined to produce an infinite number of combinations; researchers frequently point to this as "the difference that makes a difference." The syntactic rule systems that allow for such endless combos are called **grammars**. The grammar you learn in school is just one example of such a system.

The complexity of a grammar affects how flexibly sequences can be used to symbolically encode messages. Early on, psychologists established that people learn grammatical symbol sequences more rapidly than random sequences, an ability also seen in birds and monkeys.

When adults learn to recognize novel grammatical sequences, they often do so without realizing that they are learning anything. They may detect that the sequences are not random, but they often have trouble identifying the rules or patterns that are guiding their detections—the learning is implicit, as described in Chapter 7.

Symbolic Reference

Beyond grammar, the symbolic properties of languages make it possible for you to express new ideas, receive new information (like you're doing now), and talk about things beyond what you are currently experiencing. Part of the power of language comes from the wide variety of categories, objects, agents, and actions that are linked to symbolic labels.

Reference, the relationship between a symbol and what it stands for, is what seems to give words and sentences their meaning. For instance, natives of Easter Island inscribed sequences of figures (called rongorongo) onto various artifacts (**Figure 12.18**). The "writing" appears similar to other ancient examples of early writing. But there aren't any natives from the island that can verify what these etchings are. Are they names? Letters? Words? Or stylized pictures? Without knowing what rongorongo refers to, it is impossible to extract any meaning from it, or to even know if rongorongo contains any symbols!

Symbolic reference is not limited to human languages. Recall from the discussion above that the calls of some monkeys refer to specific predators. These natural symbols are highly limited in terms of what they can convey. In contrast, the kinds of things that the spoken, gestured, and written symbols used by humans can refer to are effectively limitless. You can even call spiky shapes "boubas," assuming you can find enough people willing to go along with your unconventional lexicon.

Language and Thought

If someone asks you, "What's on your mind?" there's a good chance that they are expecting you to verbalize your thoughts. And most likely you'd make an attempt at answering the question, which implies that you are at least willing to go along with the idea that your thoughts are verbalizable. This is a core assumption of many studies of metacognition reviewed in Chapter 8, the thinking-out-loud methodology discussed in Chapter 10, and pretty much all exit interviews for psychology experiments that require self-reports.

Some philosophers and cognitive scientists have gone one step further, arguing that the use of symbolic communication by humans reveals the core features of thought (Fodor, 2008). The idea is that natural language reflects the organization of internal symbolic representations that, like sentences,

FIGURE 12.18. Hidden meaning.
Rongorongo, constructed by natives of Eastern Island is likely symbolic communication, but without knowing what the images refer to, any meaning with the sequences remains hidden.

can be described as sequences of referential propositions that are systematically organized according to certain rules.

In this framework, the human mind is essentially a physical symbol system, like your computer, and mental representations (at least those that are verbalizable) are organized in terms of sequences of symbols—a kind of mental language that works like computer software. This matches common-sense views about thinking being like self-talk by an inner voice, except that the voice is generated by something akin to a Siri-in-your-head rather than by "you."

A different view of the relationship between language and thought is that language is a tool that increases your capacity to coordinate with or manipulate others (Reboul, 2015). Just as Arabic numerals and mathematical notation make it easier to perform calculations and to think about numbers in new ways, spoken and written words might make it easier for you to form concepts and communicate thoughts.

It may seem odd to think of something as natural and basic as language as being an invention comparable to clothes or hammers. But consider how you use language when you stub your toe or discover your lunch is on fire, even if no one else is around. Are you attempting to communicate with unseen entities by yelling obscenities? How about when you try to motivate yourself not to procrastinate? Wouldn't it be easier to just think the words rather than to say them?

Somehow, putting words out into the world just works better. Cursing from pain or frustration might not seem like a way to amplify your intellect, but the point is that language can affect your mental state in ways that go beyond just adding or sharing information. If using language is more like using a paintbrush than like running a computer program, then it's a bit easier to imagine how someone (perhaps a poet or a rapper) could create new and surprising imagery or thoughts with words. Rather than being the foundation of thought, symbolic communication may simply be an upgrade.

Multilingualism

Language development is typically thought of as a cumulative process of acquiring speech production, reception, and interpretation capacities. As noted above, theories of sentence production, like other models of action generation, generally start with some high-level idea creation and a delivery process that guides the coordination of word selection, ordering, and physical speech production.

The later acquisition of additional language skills—foreign language learning—is generally viewed as following the same basic process with a few additional complications related to interference from existing language skills and reduced language learning capacity at older ages.

Young children have little difficulty learning multiple languages despite receiving almost no instructional guidance. Meanwhile, adults typically struggle at learning a new language, even with expert instruction and diligent practice. This outcome seems paradoxical given that infants and toddlers are otherwise cognitively incompetent relative to adults.

Toddlers possess less attentional, memory, and problem-solving abilities than adults, all of which predict that learning a skill as complex as language should be much more difficult for them. Adding multiple languages into the mix should make learning even harder. Some view the relative ease of language learning by youngsters as evidence of built-in language learning mechanisms.

From the perspective of dynamic systems (discussed in Chapter 3), however, no such genetically endowed language competencies are necessary. Instead, the construction of words and sentences is viewed as a behavioral pattern that emerges from interactions between simpler mental and external events.

One implication of dynamic systems models of language learning, or the acquisition of other complex cognitive skills, is that the initial conditions of pattern formation can have a persistent effect on later learning. Just as the geometry at the core of a snowflake strongly constrains how later structures will develop, initial conditions during language learning have ripple effects throughout a person's life.

Toddlers exposed to multiple languages simultaneously may benefit from the fact that their neural circuits are not predisposed to organize different languages in a specific way, facilitating self-organizing processes that can accommodate multiple languages at the same time. The unsupervised language learning of a toddler may thus be more effective than the supervised learning of an adult because there are fewer habitual responses interacting with incoming sensations (de Bot et al., 2007).

Many cognitive studies of multilingualism in the last century have focused on determining whether acquiring multiple languages degrades or enhances other cognitive abilities. Identifying such effects is not as simple as comparing the performance of multilingual participants to that of monolinguals because differences in language exposure and learning are almost always con-founded with cultural differences. Much of the current debate focuses on whether multilingualism might enhance cognitive control skills, including working memory processes (discussed in Chapter 8), or may affect brain connectivity (Bialystok, 2017). Past focus on understanding how learn-ing multiple languages might drive individual differences in thought processes and knowledge organization is paralleled by research on whether the specific language you learn might shape how you cognize.

Linguistic Relativity and Determinism

Some researchers distinguish language—a system of symbolic communication that most people learn from a young age—from the faculty of language, which you can think of as all the represen-tational and control mechanisms that you use to produce and comprehend sentences. So, infants that grow up in different communities may learn different languages, but they might all use the same cognitive mechanisms to do this. The hardware is shared, but the apps are culturally determined.

Most cognitive studies of the faculty of language have tested English-speaking undergraduates on the assumption that whatever is learned from them about the faculty of language would apply to all humans. However, English is widely considered to be a somewhat odd language, because in English, changes in pitch don't differentiate speech sounds and many words are weirdly spelled. Stud-ies focused exclusively on English speakers may provide an incomplete view of how languages are normally processed.

Variations in the lexicons used by different cultures can potentially affect not only how people communicate but also how they think about the world (Bowers & Pleydell-Pearce, 2011), a possibility formally known as **linguistic relativity**. For instance, if from a very young age, you often hear, or are engaged in, conversations about ch'i (qi) and the need to keep it balanced, then the way you think about disease may differ greatly from someone who grew up in a culture that has no concept of ch'i. The meaning transmitted by this word would be lost in translation.

An extreme version of this idea, called **linguistic determinism**, suggests that most of your cognitive processes—how you categorize, remember, and think about your experiences—are a direct function of the specific language(s) you have learned. According to this view, if you've never learned a language, then how you represent the world and think should differ greatly from language learners. As noted in Chapter 3, the labels you assign to images can strongly affect what you perceive in those images, enabling past experiences to drive your current perception. Many researchers believe that language skills can affect the development of perceptual expertise (dis-cussed in Chapter 4) and the mental organization of knowledge and abstract concepts (Lupyan et al., 2020).

In that case, how is it that humans ever became able to learn languages? And how might cogni-tion in language-less individuals differ from those that possess language skills? One way to answer these questions is by studying youngsters.

SIGHT BITES

Language is a multifunctional communication system with organizational features that are revealed by written sentences.

Sentence construction, whether written or spoken, involves conceptualization, formulation, and execution.

The selection of words for speech production is a competitive process that can sometimes lead to informative errors.

Much of the flexibility and utility of language, both in communication and in thought, comes from symbols.

Language Development

SNEAK PEEK: Humans are biologically prepared to learn language, but much remains unknown about how they do this or why other species do not. Social interactions involving imitation may be critical to language acquisition.

Watching toddlers is often entertaining because of their crude attempts at sending signals. Crying babies on a long flight are less entertaining for the same reason. The vocal signals produced by wailing infants are involuntary and have many genetically predetermined qualities; these are considered to be prototypical **innate signals**.

The somewhat garbled phrases produced by toddlers, in contrast, seem to be voluntary and dependent on a toddler's specific experiences with language. These attempted phrases are typically classified as **learned signals**. All behavior is shaped by gene-environment interactions (see Chapter 2), so classifying signals as either learned or innate mainly serves to highlight the importance of experience in shaping how signals are formed and used.

Researchers cannot experiment on infants and young children in the ways that are needed to nail down the mechanisms that make language learning and development possible. Consequently, scientists have turned to studies of animal models to try and better understand how various cognitive processes might contribute to the development of flexible communication systems.

Learning to Communicate

Psychologists, neuroscientists, and ethologists study songbirds to understand the ways in which genetics and experience can contribute to the diversity of an individual's repertoire of signals (Wohlgemuth et al., 2014). Birds clearly differ from people in how they communicate, but the mechanisms they engage when they sing are more similar to those of speaking humans than you might suspect.

The techniques used to study singing birds are extremely powerful as a way of revealing how genes and experience contribute to the development of communication. For instance, by deafening birds at a young age, putting them under the care of a species other than their own, or monitoring every sound they make from the time they hatch, researchers have found evidence of sensitive periods of development. During these periods, young birds have an increased ability to store memories of specific songs that they've heard only a few times (Marler, 1997).

Researchers also have found evidence of genetically determined, internal templates that enable young birds to focus on species-specific features of songs, even when those songs are heard within a cacophony of songs produced by other species.

Such studies make it clear that complex communication signals are often automatically processed in ways that differ from other sensed events. Studies of developing birds also demonstrate that how a receiver perceives signals very early in life can significantly shape how that receiver produces communicative signals later in life.

How Learnable Is Language?

The idea that genes determine communicative signal types played a pivotal role in the history of cognitive psychology. When American psychology was dominated by behaviorist researchers (see Chapter 1), B. F. Skinner argued that humans learn to communicate with words the same way that they learned to do everything else, through practice motivated by the rewards of success (Skinner, 1957).

American linguist Noam Chomsky (introduced in Chapter 2) strongly criticized Skinner's view. He argued that "verbal behavior" was radically different from other kinds of behavior and that there was no way that young children could learn to use words correctly in so little time. Instead, he suggested that there were innate processes that guided children's acquisition of language skills.

Chomsky's critique of Skinner's learning-based account of language is commonly cited as a driving force in the emergence of cognitive psychology (Mandler, 2002). Chomsky's claims aligned with many peoples' intuitions that languages were simply too complex for toddlers to figure out on their own and provided support for the widespread belief that humans possess cognitive capacities far exceeding those of other animals.

Does language really involve communicative signals so complex that no child could hope to learn them without genetic cheats? One way to evaluate this possibility is to consider cases in which children have learned to communicate using a constructed language consisting of signals that they were explicitly taught.

One of the most famous such cases is that of Helen Keller (**Figure 12.19**). Helen became deaf and blind before she was two years old, which severely limited most common methods of human communication (Keller, 1905). Unable to successfully communicate with her family, Helen became prone to extreme tantrums.

FIGURE 12.19. Constructed communication. Helen Keller with her teacher Anne Sullivan who trained her to associate the feel of different hand configurations with events in her surroundings and to use those signals as a means of communicating with others. (Everett Collection Inc/Alamy Stock Photo)

A young teacher, Anne Sullivan, was recruited by Helen's parents to help solve the problem. She initially trained Helen to recognize felt sequences of gesturally signed letters and to repeat those sequences. The gestural sequences spelled out words, but Helen initially had no way of knowing this.

Eventually, Helen discovered that the sequences were matched to specific events, after which she rapidly learned to use the gestural sequences to label things and to read using raised letters.

Ultimately, Helen Keller learned to speak, completed a college degree, and became a national celebrity. It is clear in Helen's case that repetitive training and practice enabled her to acquire the language skills that she used, because the palm is not a channel that naturally plays a major role in language development and because humans do not naturally communicate through spelling.

Learning Words from Hearing Words

Most children do not need to be taught how to interpret and use communicative signals; instead, they acquire these abilities simply by being immersed in environments where they frequently interact with signal users. Detailed analyses of early exposure to speech have revealed that toddlers initially produce an increasing number of words, up until around their eighteenth month, and then show a drop in how quickly they pick up new words (**Figure 12.20A**). It's as if they first collect a lot of words and then reach a point where they have enough to get by.

You might guess that the first words infants or toddlers learn to say are the words they hear being used the most often. However, it turns out that, on average, the words that toddlers produce first are words that they experience in very specific contexts, for example, at night in their bedroom (Roy et al., 2015). This suggests that a youngster's ability to learn to produce specific words is affected not only by experience with the word but also by memories of when and where the speech is typically produced (**Figure 12.20B**).

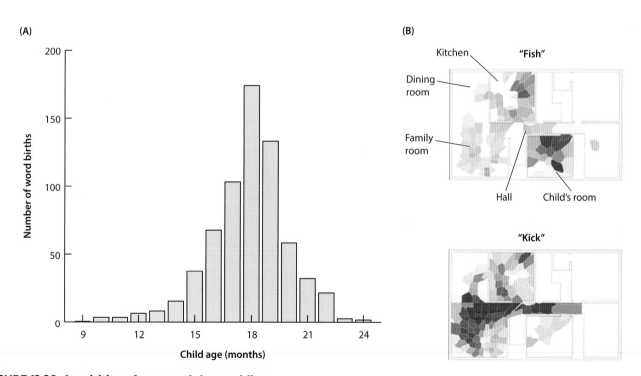

FIGURE 12.20. Acquisition of new words by a toddler.
(A) Up to the age of eighteen months, a toddler produces an increasing number of new words (a word is "born" the first time a toddler produces it) but then shows a drop in the number of new words produced. (B) Mapping every time a toddler hears or uses a specific word based on the location in the house where the word was said or heard reveals that certain words are more likely to occur in specific rooms in the house (red = occurs more often). Because specific rooms often are used at predictable times (for example, a dining room is more likely to be used at meal times), word usage in different locations is also linked to different times within daily cycles. Words that show specificity in terms of when and where they are used tend to be produced at a younger age than words that are produced in many different contexts, suggesting that the context within which speech signals are used may help toddlers learn to use them. (A after, B from Roy et al., 2015)

Experimental results from parrots show that social aspects of signal production are also likely to play a big role in developing communication skills. Parrots exposed to recordings of other birds communicating are much less likely to learn to produce similar signals than parrots directly exposed to birds making those sounds (Pepperberg, 1988).

A child that grows up in isolation, hearing speech sounds but never seeing or interacting with the speaking adults, might similarly fail to learn to produce speech. Unfortunately, there are several famous cases of children who grew up in socially deprived environments where they had few opportunities to interact with other speakers (Rymer, 1993). Such children generally show language deficits consistent with the idea that social communication is a key component of language learning.

Of course, any time an individual develops in such deprived contexts, many other factors could explain why language might not develop normally. There are numerous species of animals other than humans that can be raised in social isolation and still grow up to produce typical communicative signals. So, it's not a given that social deprivation will always derail communicative abilities.

Statistical Learning

It may seem odd that toddlers would slow down in producing new words after only eighteen months when they have barely even begun learning the thousands of words that adults typically use. But it is important to keep in mind that learning to communicate with speech signals involves more than just learning to speak.

Learning to recognize words is perhaps more important, and toddlers can recognize many more words than they can produce. In fact, infants show evidence of discriminating words from nonwords as early as twelve months (Jusczyk & Aslin, 1995).

Most songbirds, like infants, also learn to recognize communication signals prior to producing them. Obviously, it is much trickier to tell that an infant (or bird) has learned to recognize specific signals it has heard but never produced.

Researchers have tested infants' abilities to recognize words by comparing how long they show interest in familiar words versus unfamiliar words. They've used this same strategy to test how quickly infants can learn to recognize new words (Saffran et al., 1996). After about two minutes of repeating speech sounds in a specific order, most infants start treating the combo like a word.

An infant's ability to learn to recognize consistently ordered phonemes is called **statistical learning** because the sound orders in actual words are encountered more often than other combinations of speech sounds. You would tend to interpret thsi as a typo rather than a word, in part because you've probably never observed "this" being used as a word before. Infants don't treat less frequent orders of speech sounds as "speechos," but they do notice and use them to segregate words from within continuous streams of speech.

Recognizing speech sounds that occur in familiar orders is just one way that young children learn about language. Just as important is learning what different words mean. Chapter 5 introduced the phenomenon of fast mapping in which children (and some dogs) rapidly learn to associate novel words with novel things. Learning what words mean becomes especially tricky when words from different languages are being used to refer to the same things.

Multilingualism

If you've ever been around people speaking a foreign language, then you can relate to the situation that infants face when adults are conversing either near or at them. It's probably about as close to James's infamous "blooming, buzzing confusion" as you can get.

Additionally, when adults talk to babies (or to dogs wearing baby clothes), they often exaggerate their speech in odd ways that might seem counterproductive if the goal is to teach the babies how to speak normally. Some studies suggest that "baby talk," or **child-directed speech**, makes it easier for babies to learn words (Dave et al., 2018), and it may even work for adults attempting to learn new languages (Ingvalson et al., 2017).

FIGURE 12.21. Signing before speaking. Babies who are not deaf and who learn to communicate with sign language prior to speaking show no delays in learning speech and may even learn spoken words faster. (SDI Productions)

Why would distorting communicative signals from their normal form make learning easier? The discussion of perceptual learning in Chapter 5 provides some clues. For now, just know that learning how to properly produce and interpret communication signals is more complicated than simply memorizing and copying what you hear and see others doing.

Developing the ability to communicate using speech is a challenging task, so imagine how much more difficult this task must be for a young human who is exposed to multiple languages simultaneously. And yet, many children seem to have no problem learning to use multiple languages—called **multilingualism**—or switching between languages that they experience early on (Poarch & Bialystok, 2015).

Intuition suggests that learning two or more languages at the same time should be at least twice as hard as learning one, but this is not the case. In fact, some researchers who observed babies trained to use a "baby sign language" prior to producing any spoken words found that the babies tend to learn words faster than babies who had no experience with sign language (Goodwyn & Acredolo, 1998) (**Figure 12.21**).

Recall that one way infants learn about words is through statistical learning—identifying speech sounds that consistently occur in specific orders. For instance, an infant growing up in the United States might often hear "hun" followed by "gry" or "cry" followed by "ing," but that infant probably would never hear "hun" followed by "ing" or "cry" followed by "gry." Consistent ordering of syllables gives infants clues as to what sounds are words, but what happens when infants hear multiple speakers at once, possibly speaking different languages?

Statistical learning works not just for isolated words but also for continuous, overlapping speech streams, like those an infant might hear when eavesdropping on adults' conversations. Paradoxically, the differences in speech sounds used within different languages may make it easier for infants to separate streams of conversations being produced simultaneously by different individuals in different languages.

The ease with which children learn multiple languages and novel communication systems implies that many people may have untapped potential for learning to communicate using a wide range of signal repertoires and communicative systems.

Cross-Species Communication

Preschoolers typically are able to learn one or more languages with minimal effort. Comparable language development does not occur in any other species. This is just one of the ways in which languages differ from the communication signals and systems used by most other animals (Rendall et al., 2009).

The seemingly arbitrary speech sounds, gestures, and squiggles that people use to send symbolic messages as well as the flexible ways in which people combine these symbols to construct novel thoughts, together, make language unique. Some have argued that these features of language are what make human cognition possible. This section explores past attempts, most designed to clarify how humans learn language, to encourage other species to develop language skills.

Animal Talk

You wouldn't have to look too hard online to find videos of dogs that seem to say phrases like "I love you," and you may have occasionally found yourself speaking to an annoying insect or pet. These faux, one-way conversations provide little reason to think that any animals other than humans have the capacity to understand language. The signals may be there, but either the messages aren't received, or the message the listener receives differs from the one that was sent.

One famous case of this, involving a clever horse, changed the way researchers have studied and thought about communication for over a century. Clever Hans was an Orlov Trotter horse, famous for his ability to solve math problems. His German owner would present the horse with a math problem, after which Hans would tap out the answer on the floor with his hoof (**Figure 12.22**).

At first, experts thought this was a trick, but they soon discovered that Hans could correctly answer math questions even when his owner was not present. Scientists were incredulous that a horse could do math and puzzled over how the horse could figure out the correct answer.

Finally, a psychologist named Oskar Pfungst discovered that Hans could only respond correctly if the person asking the question knew the correct answer. For instance, if someone who did not know German asked Hans a question in German, he would give the wrong answer.

Hans had learned to clop until he detected subtle physical movements made by the questioner, and then to stop clopping—the questioners were sending signals without even knowing it!

As a result of this discovery, an aura of skepticism surrounded later claims about animals' abilities to understand language (Sebeok & Rosenthal, 1981); once burnt, twice shy. The key lesson learned from controlled experiments with Hans was that it's a mistake to assume that appropriate responses to verbal instructions (or the ability to produce speech) are reliable evidence of language comprehension. This is just as true for young children as it is for horses!

Learning Symbolic Communication

Horse trainers sometimes do use vocal commands to direct horses' actions, so horses clearly have some ability to recognize and distinguish among spoken words. However, the main way riders communicate

FIGURE 12.22. Horse sense. Clever Hans, the horse who was once thought to be able to answer mathematics questions asked to him in German.

with horses is by using trained, tactile signals. These signals may have semantics like spoken words, but they might also simply be conditioned stimuli (see Chapter 7) that provoke specific actions.

Strong evidence of semantic processing comes from studies of symbolic communication with parrots, dolphins, and chimpanzees (Roitblat et al., 1993). With enough training, animals can reveal what they understand about the meaning of specific symbols by using them to label objects, answer questions, and select actions.

Experimenters have learned to design experiments so that subjects cannot see anyone who knows what their responses should be and to insure that any observers judging responses don't know what the subjects see or hear during trials—a **double-blind research design**. These methods eliminate the subject's ability to use cues like the ones Clever Hans did. Controlled experiments using this approach have shown that animals can learn symbols that refer not only to objects and actions but also to abstract concepts and perceptual dimensions, like an object's shape or color (Wasserman, 1997).

Attempts to symbolically communicate with animals—mainly apes, dolphins, and parrots—are usually based on human language systems. Visual or gestural symbols might be used as "words" presented in sentence-like sequences. The vocabularies used in such "animal language" experiments may consist of a few hundred words referring mainly to objects, agents, or actions.

As in human languages, the symbols used are mostly arbitrary and come to be meaningful through repeated experiences. Early on, some researchers tried to teach animals to actually produce speech, but this approach really only worked with birds.

Apes picked up on using hand gestures as symbols and even passed some of their skills down to their young. But signing apes have never approached the proficiency and flexibility of human signers.

So far, the bonobo Kanzi has achieved the most advanced use of spoken human language by proving to be able to understand simple sentences spoken in English. Kanzi's speech comprehension abilities are particularly interesting because he apparently learned these skills at a young age mainly through observations of social interactions between humans and his mother (Savage-Rumbaugh et al., 1993).

Simply being around humans who are having conversations will not allow an animal to learn a language, so it is unlikely that any pets you have would pass even a basic vocabulary test. Many animals can learn that a specific sound or word precedes a reward or punishment, however, through basic associative conditioning (see Chapter 7).

The fact that a dog runs to its bowl when it hears the word "dinnertime" does not provide clear evidence that it understands its owner's speech as an attempt to communicate. The best evidence that dogs can, with training, learn to treat spoken words as symbolic labels, comes from studies in which dogs learned to recognize labels for large numbers of objects or actions and then responded correctly to those labels given in new combinations.

After three years of daily training, a border collie named Chaser learned the names of over 1,000 toys (Pilley & Reid, 2011). Because no one has attempted similar speech recognition training with cats or hamsters, it's hard to know if dogs are especially adept at learning words, more tolerant of the odd vocal "games" that their owners choose to play, or no better than most animals at learning words. Researchers also don't know for sure what aspects of the toys Chaser actually associated with their names. Maybe the words came to stand for certain smells and textures rather than the visual shape and color features that humans would find most distinctive.

Of course, dogs and other animals can communicate with each other and with humans without needing to use language, symbols, or even a shared set of signals. Skeptics of animal language studies often view the actions of trained subjects as more like a parody of language use than the real deal because animals are invariably more limited in how they can learn and use symbolic communication.

Some scientists are willing to accept that other species can learn to use symbol sequences, but they don't believe that any nonhuman species can use symbols to transmit messages that are even remotely comparable to the ones that humans send and receive. Other scientists argue that animals generally aren't that interested in communicating with humans.

There are a few cases, however, of wild animals developing their own systems for communicating with humans. Honeyguides, for example, are birds that lead humans to honey-filled beehives so they can munch on the leftovers after the humans take the honey. Such interactions are not symbolic, but they show that animals are not always limited to communicating only with members of their own species. In some cases, animals may even be naturally motivated or compelled to attend to communication signals from multiple species, especially those animals (including humans) that learn to vocally produce their signals from listening to others.

Vocal Imitation

Many psychologists believe that **vocal imitation**—the vocal reenactment of previously heard sounds—is what makes language learning possible for infants. In fact, some researchers describe vocal imitation in humans as a specialized capacity to learn how to speak (Pinker & Jackendoff, 2005).

Vocal imitation is not limited to babies learning to talk, however. Adults do it, too. And vocal imitation by adults is not something that only celebrity impersonators do. When adults have a conversation, they automatically and unknowingly imitate the people they're speaking with. Interestingly, parents are more likely to vocally imitate their infants' speech-like sounds than the other way around (Jones, 2006). So, vocal imitation could serve as a way for parents to indirectly communicate their approval of specific vocal acts, which might increase the odds that a baby repeats those acts in the future.

Animals that Imitate Sounds

A few animals, including some birds and dolphins, also imitate the vocalizations of other individuals that they grow up with, including sounds produced by other species (Mercado et al., 2014). Belugas (a type of whale) sometimes imitate human speech and dolphins can learn to imitate random sounds on command. How well a person or dolphin imitates sounds, either voluntarily or involuntarily, can provide clues about how the imitator represents those sounds, just as a child's drawings can provide hints about how that child represents objects and agents.

Studies of vocal imitation are advantageous in that they can be conducted with several different species, making it possible to measure and manipulate subjects' auditory experiences. For instance, the development of vocal communication by zebra finches (**Figure 12.23**) can be continuously monitored from birth until adulthood while tightly controlling when and how long the birds hear specific sounds in various social contexts (Tchernichovski et al., 2001). Such studies can not only reveal sensitive periods when learners are more likely to learn different types of signals but also make it possible to track every instance of vocal production. Large data sets of this kind are critical for evaluating vocal imitation models and how vocal imitation contributes to the development of signal repertoires.

FIGURE 12.23. Zebra finches.
The vocal imitation performances of zebra finches can be closely monitored for their entire life span and their experiences (and neural circuits) can be tightly controlled to test hypotheses. (Slowmotiongli)

Stages of Vocal Development

A key distinction between most animal communication systems and human language is that the signals used by many animals are genetically predetermined and unconsciously produced. Words and hand signs, in contrast, are socially learned and voluntarily produced.

As noted earlier in this chapter, vocal imitations can be either voluntarily or unconsciously produced. So, are parrots imitating speech voluntarily, automatically, or both?

Psychologist Jean Piaget (introduced in Chapter 1) mapped out vocal development in his children and concluded that at first "imitations" were unconsciously triggered. For instance, when one crying baby on an airplane sparks a chorus of crying babies, this is a kind of reflexive **vocal contagion**, which is also common in howling wolves and dogs.

Later, babies engage in gestural and vocal babbling during social interactions. Babbling happens regardless of what the babies hear or see, so is still mainly reflexive. However, soon after this, babies begin producing repetitive series of speech-like sounds, which could be viewed as a kind of self-imitation.

Eventually, infants start copying novel sounds and producing them in different combinations. So, it seems that vocal imitation may develop in stages. While starting off as an involuntary communicative process, it gradually transforms into a flexible way of generating sequences of sounds that are later combined and used as symbolic references to things in the world. Both within and across species, vocal imitation seems to facilitate communication in a variety of ways.

Increasingly detailed studies of vocal imitation in young and old humans, birds, and marine mammals have made it possible to develop detailed computational models of the mechanisms that make vocal imitation possible. Learning and social interactions are key elements of these models.

Computational models of vocal imitation and speech production can help explain why speech sounds and other vocal signals vary across development and across individuals. Similar models can also be applied to learned, nonvocal signals like those used in sign language and in the gestural communication systems of social insects, such as bees and ants. These models can also provide a way to integrate what is known about communicative behaviors with what is known about the neural mechanisms that make such behaviors possible (described in the following section).

SIGHT BITES

Some signals are genetically predetermined, while others, like spoken words, are learned in ways that can be context dependent.

Studies of language learning and vocal imitation by other species provide unique opportunities for exploring how language abilities develop.

BRAIN SUBSTRATES

SNEAK PEEK: Individuals with brain damage have provided clues about which regions are important for successful language use. Your two hemispheres show some specializations for processing language. Children with specific genetic differences use languages in ways that are atypical. However, the deficits may be caused by the disruption of general learning mechanisms

Communicative acts often depend on senders producing complex vocal or manual movements, some of which are learned through decades of practice. A receiver's ability to extract information

FIGURE 12.24. Brain regions known to contribute to human communication. Different cortical regions are specialized for producing speech signals versus receiving them. In both cases, the regions of the cerebral cortex associated with language processing are distinct and relatively small. What's happening in the opposite hemispheres during these processes? Read on to find out.

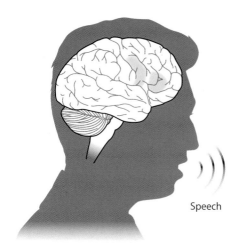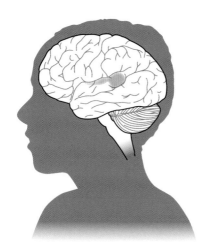

Speech

from signals may also depend on thousands of hours of experience. In other cases, however, complex communication requires no learning at all. Given the versatility with which different organisms communicate, you should not be surprised to find that the underlying mechanisms that make communication possible are also quite diverse. And yet, when it comes to language, most research has focused on a relatively small set of cortical regions that are thought to be both critical and exclusive to humans (**Figure 12.24**).

Neurolinguistics

A popular idea among some linguists and psychologists is that human language is so complex that the only way a baby could successfully develop language skills in two years or less is if they were born pre-wired for learning language. This hypothesis, known as **linguistic nativism**, essentially argues that humans have evolved specialized language learning and processing brain regions that endow them with unique abilities to recognize and learn about words and sentences (Fitch et al., 2005; Pinker & Jackendoff, 2005).

There are lots of theories about which features of babies' brains might help them learn to use language, most of which point to specialized cortical regions. Research focused on identifying brain substrates of language production, comprehension, and acquisition is called **neurolinguistics**. Evidence supporting the idea that humans have "special brain parts" for language comes from cases in which brain damage has led to language deficits (usually aphasias) and from neuroimaging data showing hotspots of activation associated with language comprehension tasks (Kemmerer, 2015).

As discussed in Chapter 2, the idea that specific parts of the brain might be specialized for specific, complex cognitive functions was first popularized by Franz Gall. Gall proposed, in the early 1800s, that the faculty of language was located in symmetric brain regions just behind the eyeballs. Since then, the proposed locale of a "language organ" has migrated, but the idea that it is positioned somewhere in (or perhaps spread throughout) the cortex has persisted.

Lateralization

Perhaps the biggest shift in thinking about where language processing happens occurred in the late 1800s when several physicians reported that damage to the left side of the brain was especially likely to cause language deficits. Such **lateralization** of function was initially surprising, given the symmetrical properties of brains; it was, however, consistent with the fact that people favor the use of one hand over the other. In fact, right-handed people are much more likely to show greater activation of left hemisphere regions during language tasks than left-handed people. Structural neuroimaging data show that cortical regions that activate asymmetrically during language tasks are also physically asymmetric and generally larger in the dominant hemisphere (**Figure 12.25**).

FIGURE 12.25. Lateralization of cortical structures involved in language processing. Individuals whose left hemisphere is particularly active during language processing tasks show structural asymmetries between the two hemispheres, with the more active region (often in the left hemisphere) typically being larger.

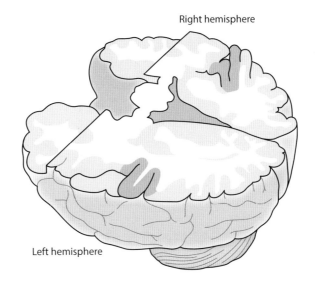

Right hemisphere

Left hemisphere

Remember Tan, the patient with aphasia who could only say "tan tan?" His physician, Paul Broca, preserved Tan's brain so that researchers could continue to examine it (**Figure 12.26**). Descriptions of Tan's brain and behavior had such a big impact on how people thought about language processing that the damaged region of cortex in the left frontal lobe of Tan's brain is now referred to as **Broca's area.**

Patients with damage to Broca's area often lose the ability to produce normal sentences (a condition called Broca's aphasia). They usually are not as impaired as Tan, however. In neuroimaging studies, Broca's area becomes active during sentence production, but so do a number of other cortical regions, particularly in the frontal cortex. So, perhaps Gall was on the right track after all!

Damage to Broca's area can also impair speech processing, and this region becomes more active during some language comprehension tasks. The region also shows increased activation during tasks that do not seem to require language processing, raising questions about what exactly this region might be doing during speech production and perception.

Some evidence suggests that Broca's area may contribute to imitative capacities, and it even seems to somehow help people to recognize shadow puppets (Fadiga et al., 2006). Cortical regions that are structurally similar to Broca's area are present in other primates, but their functional roles are unknown.

Around the same time that Broca was studying Tan's language deficits, a physician named Carl Wernicke was studying a separate group of individuals with brain damage who had somewhat different communicative difficulties. These people could produce streams of speech, but their "sentences" were uninterpretable. For example, they might say something like, "You know that smoodle pinkered

FIGURE 12.26. Lesions to the left hemisphere that impair language abilities. (A) Due to damage in his left hemisphere, Tan was able to produce only one phrase: "tan tan." This cortical region, known as Broca's area, contributes to many functions, including sentence production. (B) Damage to Wernicke's area can also disrupt language use, but the associated deficits differ from those caused by damage to Broca's area. (C) Broca's area and Wernicke's area are separate from each other and from the auditory cortex, consistent with the hypothesis that localized regions of the cerebral cortex are specialized for either producing or perceiving language. (A from Dronkers et al., 2007, by permission of Oxford University Press; B from Sheehy & Haines, 2004, *Brain and Language*, 89, with permission from Elsevier)

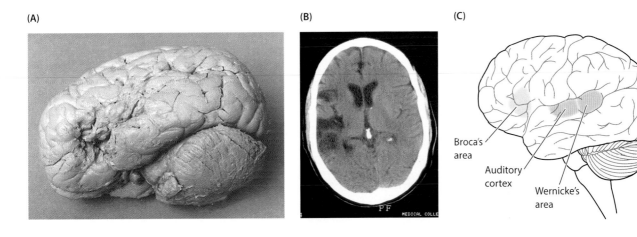

(A)

(B)

(C)

Broca's area

Auditory cortex

Wernicke's area

and that I want to get him round and take care of him like you want before," to indicate that their dog needs to go for a walk (National Institutes of Health, 1997); this condition is called Wernicke's aphasia.

Postmortem examinations revealed that damage in such individuals was mainly in the left temporal lobe, just behind Broca's area, in a region of cortex now called **Wernicke's area** (see Figure 12.26). The people Wernicke studies not only produced odd word combinations they also had problems comprehending sentences. People with damage to Wernicke's area appear to have problems accessing their lexicon and identifying parts of words (Howard & Franklin, 1988). Interestingly, they also often create unique nonwords, like "smoodle" when naming things.

As with Broca's area, language processing activates Wernicke's area, and the involvement of this region is usually lateralized. Damage to Broca's and Wernicke's areas doesn't just affect speech processing, it also affects the ability to write, and in the case of deaf individuals, their ability to sign.

Further support for the idea that language skills were mainly the domain of the left hemisphere came from studies of **split-brain individuals** in the 1960s (Sperry, 1961). Split-brain individuals have had their two hemispheres disconnected by a surgeon, usually to reduce the severity of epileptic seizures. By cutting through the corpus callosum, the major connection between the two hemispheres, doctors can prevent a seizure from spreading throughout the whole brain. This split also blocks all other transmissions across hemispheres.

Disconnecting a person's left and right hemispheres does not affect the individual's language skills in any obvious way. However, it was discovered that some split-brain individuals were able to name an object when they held it in their right hand but were unable to name that same object when they held it in their left hand (Gazzaniga, 2005). Similarly, these individuals seemed unable to name objects shown only off to their left. In both cases, the sensory inputs traveled to the right hemisphere, which seemed incapable of verbally identifying their source. These findings were widely interpreted as definitive evidence that cortical regions in the left hemisphere were specialized language organs.

Brain-Based Models of Language Processing

Based on evidence from patients with brain damage, early models of language processing included three major modules localized in the left hemisphere: (1) a lexicon that was used to sort incoming speech sounds, direct speech production, and access conceptual information; (2) a system for transforming words into vocal acts; and (3) a knowledge store of organized conceptual information. These hypothetical modules were assumed to reside in Wernicke's area, Broca's area, and associative cortical regions respectively. This view of language processing was summarized in the 1800s with a model now known as the Wernicke-Geschwind model, which effectively designated the left hemisphere as the language side of the brain.

You might have noticed that none of these modules is specifically devoted to language learning, which is a key aspect of linguistic nativism. The Wernicke-Geschwind model is more a model of what adults' brains do when they have conversations than it is a model of how adults become able to converse in the first place. The model, though obsolete now, provides a foundation for most contemporary theories of language processing in the brain.

Case studies and neuroimaging data provide compelling correlational evidence that certain brain regions are more critical for language processing than others, but they are less useful for teasing apart how different brain regions interact during the production and comprehension of communicative signals. Understanding these interactions requires researchers to track processes over short intervals because of the rapid pace at which people process words and sentences. By monitoring electrical or magnetic activity at the scalp, researchers can observe cortical changes that are correlated with understanding sentences and detecting errors in sentences (**Figure 12.27**).

In infants, oscillations in cortical activity patterns can be used to predict which babies are likely to have problems with language, long before these problems become obvious (Gou et al., 2011). Inter-

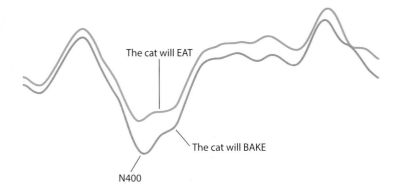

The cat will EAT

The cat will BAKE

N400

FIGURE 12.27. Brain activity shows signs that "wrong" sentences are processed differently. Four hundred milliseconds after you hear a word that doesn't quite fit in a sentence, your cortical neurons will respond more strongly to the unexpected word (a response called the N400). (After Osterhout & Nicol, 1999)

fering with cortical activity by electrically or magnetically stimulating the brain through either transcranial direct current stimulation or transcranial magnetic stimulation (see Chapter 11) makes it possible to create virtual lesions during task performance. These lesions, which simulate damage in certain areas of the brain, allow researchers to test hypotheses about how and when different regions affect processing.

Experimental studies using these neurophysiological methods have led to some revisions of the Wernicke-Geschwind model (Kemmerer, 2015). First, both neuroimaging and neurophysiological studies show that a much broader range of brain regions contribute to language processing than researchers originally assumed. These regions include not only the cerebral cortex but also several subcortical regions, such as the basal ganglia, hippocampus, and cerebellum. Such findings weakened the idea that there is a specialized "module" for language that evolved in humans.

Second, the idea that most language functions are performed by cortical circuits in the left hemisphere has also become less plausible. Today, the general view is that both hemispheres of the brain contribute to language abilities, but different sides play different roles and most of the regions involved also contribute to many other nonlinguistic skills.

Hemispheres are asymmetric in their processing, but this may relate more to how they sort inputs than to any functional specialization. A modernized version of the Wernicke-Geschwind model, called the **dual-stream model** (**Figure 12.28**), proposes that separate circuits in both hemispheres of the cortex process heard words in parallel, with some regions focusing on speech-based representations and others focusing on identifying the meaning of words (Poeppel & Hickok, 2004). The dual-stream model, like the Wernicke-Geschwind model, focuses mainly on the use of spoken languages by adults and has little to say about how languages are learned.

Plasticity in Language Circuits

Surprisingly, studies of brain damage in children have provided some of the strongest evidence to date against the idea that left hemisphere cortical regions are innately specialized for language processing. Some children with extreme seizures undergo a surgical procedure in which an entire hemisphere of their brain is removed. Children who have had their left hemisphere removed usually mature to have good conversational skills (Liegeois et al., 2008).

Additional evidence that the right brain can handle language comes from studies of left-handed individuals, many of whom show asymmetric processing in which their right hemisphere is more active in language tasks. Perhaps most surprisingly, some individuals who are missing most of both their left and right hemispheres (including the remarkable French man described in Chapter 2) are still able to converse normally (Feuillet et al., 2007)!

Unique cases of language competence in individuals with abnormal brain circuits have raised awareness of the importance of neural circuit reorganization during language learning. Recent studies of cortical connections, or connectomes (see Chapter 2), are beginning to reveal how individual differences arise in language development, and new connectionists models (see Chapter 3) of speech

(A)

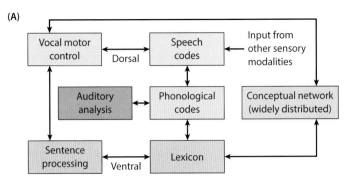

FIGURE 12.28. The dual-stream model of speech processing.
(A) Schematic of the dual-stream model. (B) The two streams of processing in this model flow across the top (dorsal) and through the temporal lobe (ventral). The dorsal stream is more lateralized and involved in speech production, while the ventral stream involves both hemispheres and is more engaged during speech comprehension. (A, B after Hickok & Poeppel, 2007)

(B)

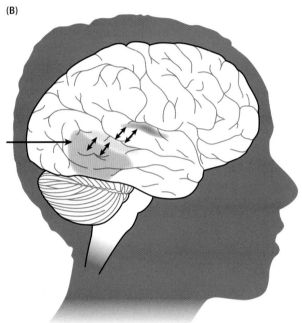 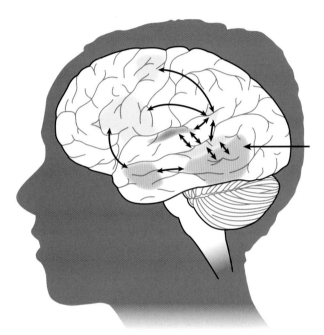

processing are starting to reveal how sophisticated processing of speech sounds can emerge from circuits with few if any mechanisms customized for learning languages.

The quest to locate a specialized language acquisition module in the human cortex has instead revealed that language use depends on a broad network of circuits spread throughout the brain, including circuits that vary substantially across individuals. This has led some researchers to focus more on identifying genetic mechanisms that drive the formation and organization of language-related brain circuits as the key to understanding how language differs from the communication systems used by other species.

"There is no 'organ' of Speech in the brain any more than there is a 'Faculty' of Speech in the mind. The entire mind and the entire brain are more or less at work in a man who uses language."
—James, 1890, p 56

Circuits and Genes Specialized for Communication

You are a proven language learner. Possibly you've learned multiple languages. If you know more than five, you're a polyglot (like Chris Taylor, from Chapter 2). If you know eleven or more languages, you're a hyperpolyglot (and quite rare).

Some hyperpolygots have learned more than thirty languages (Erard, 2012). Do you think their brains might be doing things differently from yours? It's possible that you are just less linguistically motivated, but such large individual differences in communicative repertoires hint at the possibility of genetic predispositions to learn languages—an extreme case of a gift for gab. No genes for multilingual talents have been discovered so far, but researchers have found genes that can negatively affect a person's language competence.

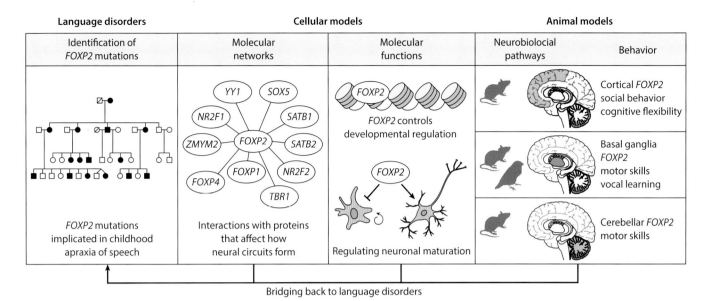

FIGURE 12.29. **Identifying genetic contributions to language skills.** By combining studies across multiple disciplines scientists are beginning to identify networks of genes that can lead to language disorders or atypical language acquisition. Comparing the genetics of individuals with and without specific language disorders makes it possible to identify specific mutations (like *FOXP2* mutations) that negatively affect language skills. Once such genes have been identified, detailed studies of cellular models can reveal specific ways that these mutations may lead to language disorders, such as by derailing the development of neural circuits. Hypotheses about the effects of genetic mutations on communicative abilities can then be tested in animal models to see if disrupting targeted genes in particular brain regions leads to behavioral deficits analogous to those seen in people with language disorders. (After Den Hoed & Fisher, 2020)

Inheritable Language Disorders

There are several developmental disorders that lead to delays in the acquisition of language skills. The disorder that receives the most attention in the context of language specializations is **specific language impairment**, a disorder in which children who hear normally are delayed in learning language skills. The deficits leading to this diagnosis appear to be limited to language skills. Children with specific language impairment may learn to talk later than normal and may not be understood when they do speak—they have lots of trouble with verbs, saying things like, "She drink the milk," even after they are five years old.

Specific language impairment often runs in families. Identical twins generally have more similar diagnoses than fraternal twins, pointing toward strong genetic influences. Initially, researchers thought this might mean there are specific "language genes" that need to be functional for language development to progress normally.

A different, strongly genetic developmental disorder, called Williams syndrome, reinforced this idea. Children with **Williams syndrome** show impaired cognitive abilities but can achieve relatively normal language skills, although at later ages than is typical. They are often hyperverbal, talking to everyone they encounter, and they may use more descriptive and prosodic language than is seen in other children with comparable cognitive deficits. A wide range of genes has been implicated in both Williams syndrome and specific language impairment (**Figure 12.29**), but none seem to be solely responsible for determining the functionality of language circuits (Logan et al., 2011). Instead, studies of both disorders suggest that various constellations of neural dysfunction can affect language development in unique ways.

While there is little evidence of specific genes devoted to language function in humans, there is clear evidence that the neural circuits most other species use for communication are largely genetically predetermined. For instance, researchers have transplanted sections of a baby quail's brain into the brain of a developing chicken. These "Frankenchicks" are called "quickens," and they vocalize in ways that are quail-like when they grow up (Balaban et al., 1988).

This doesn't mean that every individual of a species will communicate in a fixed way. Most species can learn to modify even innate signals to better match the communicative signals they experience others using (Tyack, 2008). They can also modify their communicative signals based on histories of rewards and punishments associated with certain signals. Ants and bees will even adjust their signals to accommodate the forms of signals used by other insect species that they frequently encounter (Ryabko & Reznikova, 2009).

Language Genes

Earlier comparisons between innate and learned signals in this chapter may have given you the mis-impression that innate signals are more genetically controlled than learned signals. Both signal types are strongly influenced by genes, but in different ways. In the case of birds that learn their songs, genetic programs affect the sequence and timing of learning, the kinds of signals that birds are most likely to attend to and learn about, the kinds of sounds they are able to make, and the rate at which they learn to produce and use sounds (Marler, 1997).

A couple of decades ago, a gene was discovered in humans—*FOXP2*—that was found to be critical for normal language development. Interfering with a comparable gene in zebra finches degrades song development, and mice with mutations of this gene produce abnormal vocal sequences, all of which suggested that *FOXP2* might be a "learned vocal communication" gene.

Additional studies revealed, however, that *FOXP2* regulates a host of other genes as well (see Figure 12.29). These genes affect several different brain plasticity mechanisms that determine trajectories of circuit development throughout the brains of many different species. Although *FOXP2* is not the sort of language system blueprint that linguistic nativists might have hoped to find, its study does highlight the many ways in which genes can shape neurodevelopment to either degrade or potentially enhance the learning and flexible use of communication systems.

Past attempts to identify specific cortical regions or individual genes responsible for human language skills are an example of the ongoing search for cognitive modules in specific brain regions (see Chapters 1 and 2).

The reality is that combinations of genes promote the development of complex neural circuits that work collectively to make the learning and use of language possible. Given that humans, even those with language disorders, are more proficient at learning language skills than other animals, there must be some underlying differences that account for why not all brains can do this.

But these differences do not have to be language-specific. Humans can achieve skills with a piano keyboard that no other animal can match, but this does not mean there are "piano genes" or a "keyboard learning module" in the brain. The neural circuits that enable humans to precisely and voluntarily control their vocal organs and finger movements are probably key to acquiring speech and sign language. And cognitive control mechanisms within the frontal lobes (see Chapter 10) certainly help people learn to organize and plan combinations of words.

Potentially, the combination of multiple cognitive systems operating in parallel within your brain is what makes it possible for you to talk about language, somewhat like mixing eggs, flour, sugar, and bean paste drops in certain combinations can lead to the magic of chocolate chip cookies.

SIGHT BITES

 Language deficits in patients with cortical damage led researchers to conclude that language modules in the cortex were located in small regions in the left hemisphere.

 The dual-stream model of language processing proposes that the meaning and form of speech is processed in parallel in both cerebral hemispheres.

 Children with specific language impairment and Williams syndrome show that genetic changes can selectively impair or preserve a person's ability to learn and use languages.

APPLIED PERSPECTIVES

SNEAK PEEK: Much of what researchers have learned about language processing also applies to the production and perception of music. Musical training may even be able to enhance your language skills. Reading is a multimodal process that can vary considerably in terms of the ease with which different individuals can learn to do it.

Chomsky (a linguist) threw down the gauntlet to psychologists by arguing that psychological theories based on learning experiments with pigeons had no hope of explaining human language. Psychologists responded to this challenge by promoting a new brand of research: cognitive psychology. For most people, debates about how language works and about how it differs from other kinds of communication are just one example of the kind of specificity that academics love. Does it really matter to you if the words you use are embodied constructs rather than informational representations?

It's true that people will keep on babbling, regardless of whether such conflicts are resolved, but there are advantages to better understanding how language and other communication systems work.

Obviously, knowing how brain systems implement language skills could be useful for developing new treatments for children and patients with language deficits, but understanding how language works can also be important for other reasons, including helping people to develop new ways of learning. After all, texts such as this one have only been widely applied as teaching tools in the last few centuries.

All of the "three Rs" that form the foundation of modern educational systems—reading writing, and arithmetic—focus on symbolic communication systems, based on the assumption that these systems are fundamental to building cognitive skills and capacity. Why else would we spend decades training people to use them?

Without knowing exactly what such training does, though, it is hard to tell whether the intended goals are really being achieved. People used to think that memorizing Latin poems increased intellect. And before that, Plato argued that teaching children to write and read was a good way of destroying their minds—"they will be hearers of many things and will have learned nothing; they will appear to be omniscient and will generally know nothing" (Phaedrus). Understanding how different modes of communication operate can potentially reveal new ways of understanding and enhancing cognition more generally.

Making Meaningful Music

Language is not the only communicative system that humans seem to have a monopoly on. Music can also lay claim to that title. Sure, there are other animals that sing and make percussive sounds. But as with language, there are several qualities of music made by humans that seem to be unique, not the least of which is that music can be merged with language to convey specific messages.

Language-Like Properties of Music

Like language, musical signals can be divided into sequences of arbitrary symbols (notes) that can be transmitted through writing. Unlike language, the individual signals of music generally are not associated with specific meanings—there is not a semantics of notes or chords. Instead, combinations of sounds can affect the way a listener feels; sort of like the effect of prosodic variations!! Or an emoji 😩. The similarities between language and music are so striking that some researchers (including Darwin) have proposed that they are sibling communication systems (Patel, 2003).

Music clearly possesses sequential structure and there are parallels between musical form and the syntax of language. A child's ability to perceive rhythms is predictive of that child's syntactic abilities (Gordon et al., 2015). In addition, neural activity in Broca's area in response to tone sequences is

FIGURE 12.30. Speech and music evoke similar responses in Broca's area. Measures of electrical activity originating from Broca's area as individuals listen to grammatical errors or to musical incongruities. The green line shows how people's brains responded when they heard musical sequences that violated their expectations. (After Patel et al., 1998)

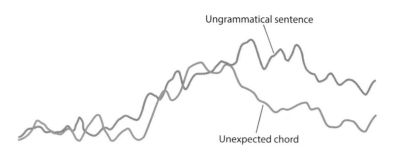

similar to the activity generated by hearing speech. You can even generate an error-related N400 response by breaking musical rules, just like those generated by implausible sentences (Patel et al., 1998) (**Figure 12.30**).

Musical aptitude is predictive of several language skills, including phonological processing, proficiency with multiple languages, sensitivity to prosody, and reading abilities (Anvari et al., 2002; Strait et al., 2012).

This is not to say that the brain substrates of language and music processing are identical. They definitely are not. And appreciating music doesn't seem to depend on recognizing relationships between individual elements in the same way as language—there are no musical equivalents to nouns, verbs, and adjectives.

There are similarities between the prosodic features of speech and music, however. Recall that prosody relates mainly to the timing and pitches used during speech, making it possible for you to convey emotions through sentences. Variations in the acoustic features of speech that are associated with feelings of happiness or sadness are also present in melodies that evoke these emotions. In a way, music shapes listeners' emotional states much like cursing can, but a bit more subtly.

Not only can music lead to shared emotional states among listeners but it can also lead to more synchronous neural activity in both listeners' and performers' brains (**Figure 12.31**). Guitarists playing in an ensemble show higher cortical synchrony, and singers in a choir synchronize their breathing and heart rates (Lindenberger et al., 2009; Muller & Lindenberger, 2011).

Dancers in a club synchronize their movements to music, which undoubtedly increases the synchrony of their auditory and motor cortical patterns. People's ability to drum in synchrony varies significantly across their life span, with mature adults showing the highest ability to synchronize. Most animals show little ability to synchronize either their vocalizations or movements in rhythmic patterns, further suggesting that this type of coordination is not easy.

If communication is viewed as a means of coordinating thoughts and emotions across individuals (as in, I'm trying to generate sentences that will guide how you are thinking about musical communication right now), then music may be the ultimate, real-time homogenizer of brain activity within a group. It's no wonder then that music is so prevalent in social contexts where unity is paramount, such as religious gatherings, parties, and revolutions!

Changing Minds with Music

As with language, some individuals are born with musical deficits, a condition called **amusia**. Similar to specific language impairment, amusia is often found in children who show no other comparable cognitive deficits. One common form of amusia involves a degraded ability to detect out-of-tune singing.

Perhaps you have encountered such individuals at a birthday party? If not, you may have amusia. People with amusia are still appreciative of music and may even be audiophiles. In fact, their brains often respond to music in ways that match those of much better singers. Nevertheless, they remain oblivious to wrong notes. Current hypotheses about the problems that lead to amusia focus on atypical connections between frontal regions and the auditory cortex, rather than dysfunction in a localizable pitch processing module (Peretz & Hyde, 2003).

FIGURE 12.31. Musical brain waves. Musicians playing together in ensembles show increased synchrony in cortical activity patterns. But is this increased brain coordination a prerequisite for successful music coordination, or is it a consequence of shared sensory inputs? Is communication between players important, or is good timing sufficient? (LIVELab. https://livelab.mcmaster.ca/gallery/)

Developmental disorders can sometimes disrupt musical abilities. But oddly, they can also sometimes enhance them, as can brain damage. As a result of a massive concussion from diving into a pool while catching a football, Derek Amato gained savant-like abilities at playing the piano and other instruments, with no training and little practice! Some children with autism spectrum disorder become surprisingly adept at playing the piano, becoming prodigies despite their other cognitive deficits.

Musical savantism points toward hidden capacities in the brain that can be potentially unlocked by depriving it of more typical functional patterns. The idea that brain dysfunction might actually enhance specific cognitive abilities may seem odd, but such effects are now well documented (Treffert, 2014). And there is some evidence that enhanced musical abilities can, in turn, facilitate the development of other modes of communication and cognition more generally.

There once was a study that reported that people who listened to music by Mozart just before taking an IQ test scored better than those who didn't. This phenomenon came to be known as the Mozart effect (Bangerter & Heath, 2004), although later work suggested that similar effects could be produced with all sorts of engaging performances (Schellenberg, 2012). The effect was temporary, but that didn't stop some people from proclaiming that Mozart's music was a cognitive enhancer. At one point the governor of Georgia was looking to send every child born in the state a Mozart CD. Listening to classical music is unlikely to up your IQ. But is it possible that more extensive musical training might do the trick?

There is evidence suggesting that musical training, in particular, can increase performance in standardized cognitive tasks—art lessons, sadly, do not (Moreno et al., 2011; Schellenberg, 2004). Musical training seems to be effective at improving reading skills and verbal memory. Singing is also sometimes used as a technique for rehabilitating stroke patients who have lost the ability to speak. These patients may be able to sing sentences that they cannot say. In some cases, practicing singing or chanting helps patients to recover speech function (Johansson, 2011). It appears music can change minds in more ways than one.

Musical Education and Creativity

Music educators have argued for decades that musical experiences can play an important role in cognitive development. But there are still many questions about how musical training might improve performance. Is just listening sufficient? Would beating on drums give the same kinds of benefits as singing or playing a stringed instrument? Can all students benefit from training, or just a select few? Does directly practicing specific cognitive skills lead to the same or greater benefits?

FIGURE 12.32. Improvisational jazz engages "language" regions of cortex. Comparisons of activity during the performance of memorized pieces and activity during the performance of improvisational pieces requiring interactions between players show that interactive improvisation activates many of the same regions of the cortex that contribute during spoken conversations. Red areas show regions that are more active during improvisation and blue regions show areas that are less active: the top row shows activity during improvisation while producing scales and the bottom row shows activity associated with spontaneous improvisation during the performance of memorized jazz compositions. (From Donnay et al., 2014, PloS ONE 9, ©2014 Donnay et al. [CC-BY])

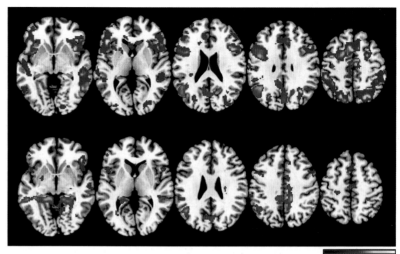

Low   High

Without understanding how the mechanisms of musical processing and language abilities interact, it is difficult to answer such questions. The discovery that language processing recruits broad cortical networks that overlap with those engaged by musical skills provides hints at how learning in one domain might transfer over to the other.

Music provides a way for composers and performers to communicate with an audience, but it also provides ways for them to communicate with each other; ways that are analogous to texting. Interactive musical performances, common in genres such as jazz, are conversational in the sense that ideas are exchanged and emergent (Donnay et al., 2014; Limb & Braun, 2008).

Neuroimaging studies of jazz musicians improvising show that many of the same regions involved in sentence comprehension and production are also active during interactive improvisation (**Figure 12.32**). Such overlap strengthens the idea that these cortical regions are not specialized for language but contribute to many kinds of communication.

Both improvisation and conversation require people to creatively construct sequences on the fly, an aspect of symbolic communication that has received relatively little scientific attention so far. If educational systems seek to increase peoples' capacity for innovation, then understanding how people gradually learn to converse, either musically or linguistically, could provide important clues about how to do this.

Even in contexts where language and music skills might be expected to show the most overlap, they differ in important ways. Like spoken communication, music can be transcribed using visual symbols so that the message can be extracted by experienced readers. The symbols that represent musical sequences are much more constrained than the lexicon of any language. With every note corresponding to one specific pitch and duration, there is little room for any ambiguity. Yet, even experienced musicians can run into difficulties reading music they have never seen before.

Why is the seemingly straightforward task of converting musical symbols to sounds more difficult than reading words that frequently provide incompatible cues, like "pour" and "sour"? Reading and writing are relatively recent innovations, so there's no chance you have an innate reading module to help you out. Instead, there must be some aspects of reading words that do not apply to reading musical notes.

Perhaps the complexity of language relative to music, which Chomsky argued makes language nearly impossible to learn without innate cheats, somehow makes reading text easier than reading music. Psychologists are just beginning to discover how reading relates to language and symbolic communication, even though a good chunk of what is known about language processing comes from experiments that require subjects to read words!

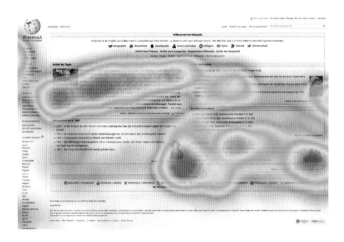

FIGURE 12.33. Reader hot spots. By representing a reader's fixation durations as "hot spots," one can gain insights into what aspects of the text are receiving more sustained processing versus those that are being glossed over or ignored. Sustained attention might indicate either interest or confusion.

How Fundamental Is Reading?

As you read this, you may have the impression that you are engulfing each word as you see it like a Pac-man consuming dots. If you could track how your eyes are focusing on this page, though, you'd see that they flick around (saccade) in an almost frantic way—sometimes jumping over one or two words, other times jumping back to previous words, or even to pictures, personal devices, or your thumb.

Eye-tracking technologies have revealed parts of the hidden world of reading (**Figure 12.33**). Eye tracks can reveal not only where you are fixating (essentially, micro-staring) but also when you are having trouble comprehending what you are reading. Companies like Google and Facebook are using eye-tracking data to better control what users perceive and absorb while using a website.

Modern eye trackers often use video streams to monitor saccades and fixations. If reading text was simply a matter of sequentially recognizing visual patterns, then you might expect that a musician's eyes might show similar patterns whether they are reading music or reading text. Both will definitely include fixations and saccades, but the movement patterns are distinctive for each mode of reading. The data collected so far suggests that the complexity of movements during music reading is higher (Wurtz et al., 2009). Although moving your eyes around might seem to be the least cognitive aspect of reading, eye tracks currently provide one of the most precise ways of testing cognitive models of reading and language processing more generally.

Routes to Reading

As with speech, the basic processing of pattern recognition, word identification, and meaning recall are critical to reading. Some minimal attentional control to keep your eyes moving here and then here and later to here, is also key.

Like writing, reading requires the coordination of multiple cognitive processes in parallel. Unlike writing, reading (by experts) seems more closely related to listening with respect to how words and sentences are sequentially processed. Nevertheless, reading presents some unique challenges, including: (1) requiring additional spatial processing; (2) focusing on unimodal signals, with less contextual information or social interaction; and (3) requiring more practice to master. These features of reading require more complicated cognitive processing than is typically needed to understand speech. Specifically, readers often engage two modes of word processing in parallel—one in which words are recognized by "sounding out" their parts, and another in which words are recognized through sight alone (**Figure 12.34**).

This multimodal processing of text is called the **dual route approach to reading**. The route based on sight alone is thought to directly activate representations of words within your lexicon. The second route basically maps letter combos onto speech sounds, indirectly activating speech recognition processes. Why do researchers think there are two routes? Well, for one, you can tell the

FIGURE 12.34. Two routes to reading. Text that is recognized can be read either by sounding out word parts and matching them to their corresponding speech sounds, or by mapping whole words in a text to the words they represent (sometimes called sight reading). These parallel paths explain why you can correctly read aloud weird words like "crypt," and also why you can read words you don't know, like "prixipooter" (a robot that makes sounds from random holes) or "absquatulate" (stop). Memories for both words (the lexicon) and their meanings (semantic memory) shape how reading progresses.

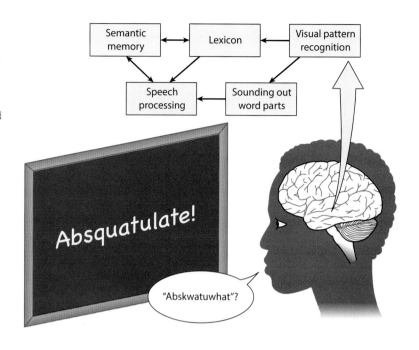

difference between eating a steak versus eating a stake. If you were simply mapping visual words to spoken word representations when you read, the words "steak" and "stake" would activate the same representation.

On the other hand, reading slows down considerably if you are reading a tongue twister, such as pad kid poured curd pulled cod. If you were simply responding to visual inputs, then such phrases should be just as easy to read as any other.

The two routes to reading have led to some anxiety about how one might best teach children to read. The debate surrounds which of the two routes should be the main focus, with some educators favoring teaching kids to identify whole words and others convinced that sounding out words is the way to go.

The argument is more of an issue in learning to read English than other languages because there are so many exceptions to general rules about how different letter combinations should be pronounced in English. A further complication comes from the fact that children are learning to read not only familiar words but also some new ones (like names of characters, places, and exotic creatures). In most educational settings, children face the challenge of mastering all these elements in parallel. For a few children, however, the apparent complexities of learning to read are a nonissue.

Reading "Disabilities"

Children generally learn to read and write with instruction, but there are children that seem to break this rule. Children with **hyperlexia** may learn to read even before they learn to speak, at ages younger than two years old, without being explicitly taught by others (Ostrolenk et al., 2017). Parents of such children are often startled to discover their otherwise nonverbal children reading on their own.

Surprisingly, hyperlexia is most common in children with developmental disorders, particularly autism spectrum disorder, who otherwise tend to show degraded communicative and social abilities (Newman et al., 2007). One of the most famous cases of hyperlexia is that of Kim Peek. Not only did Kim learn to read at a very early age but he learned to read independently with each eye so that he was able to read the left and right pages of a book simultaneously! As the result of a congenital birth defect, the two hemispheres of Kim's brain were disconnected (like in split-brain individuals), which may have made it possible for him to achieve this unique reading feat.

The social deficits associated with autism often interfere with the typical development of speech, and it may be that reading, which can be performed without direct social engagement, fills this vacuum. Even so, it is amazing that toddlers can sometimes teach themselves to read, especially given the difficulties that older children and illiterate adults often have learning to read proficiently. Apparently, the fact that most typically developing humans usually learn spoken language doesn't mean that this type of communication is inherently easier for all young children to learn.

Much more common than precocious, self-taught readers are children with developmental disorders that impede their progress when learning to read. Generally referred to as **dyslexia**, disorders of reading abilities are trickier to evaluate than conditions like amusia. There are many reasons why a child's reading skills might be delayed, some of which may have little to do with dysfunctional language processing systems.

Deficits in visual or auditory processing can be a factor, as can inadequate practice or instruction. There are large individual differences in the ease with which different children learn to read aside from any disorders, making it difficult to use delays in reading proficiency as a criterion for diagnosis.

In children, dyslexia is often viewed as a learning disorder; however, some adults can acquire dyslexic symptoms through brain damage. Several studies point to problems with phonological processing as a major contributor to dyslexia for some children. Others may be affected more by limitations in visual processing.

Training programs aimed at increasing children's capacity to distinguish speech sounds have shown some ability to normalize brain activity during reading and improve performance (Temple et al., 2003). However, there are not yet solid interventions that reliably "cure" dyslexia. Some successful individuals diagnosed with dyslexia, including movie director Steven Spielberg and entrepreneur Richard Branson, have argued that the challenges associated with dyslexia that they overcame contributed to their later successes. This line of reasoning suggests that dyslexia is not a condition that needs to be cured.

Reading as Cognitive Enhancement

If you've made it through this chapter, you've read tens of thousands of words. Do you think that's sufficient for you to know more about how language and communication work or think in ways you haven't thought before? If so, how long do you think that's likely to last?

Reading is often described as an essential skill for functioning in modern society. While it is definitely true that avid readers on the whole attain more impressive verbal skills, it is less clear that more reading yields more knowledge or greater cognitive aptitude.

The belief that reading improves cognition is widespread. And yet, there is relatively little scientific evidence supporting (or contradicting) this belief. Most studies of reading focus on how accurately readers answer questions immediately after having read a block of text rather than attempting to track any long-term effects or reading-driven changes in abilities that do not depend on reading.

Reading can lead to false feelings of knowing (see Chapter 8), as well as cryptomnesia, when you come up with a great new idea that in reality you unknowingly stole from someone else. In short, you can't trust your gut (or metacognition) on this one.

Reading a lot can change connections within your brain, but whether this has any long-term cognitive consequences is unknown. Amazingly, there is more evidence that musical training can improve general intellectual abilities than there is evidence that literacy training can. It's nice to think that text has powers of enlightenment that go beyond bar banter or daydreaming, but it's worth considering the possibility that there may be better ways than books or websites for maximizing your cognitive potential.

In *The Salmon of Doubt*, novelist Douglas Adams writes, "I've come up with a set of rules that describe our reactions to technologies: 1. Anything that is in the world when you're born is normal and ordinary and is just a natural part of the way the world works. 2. Anything that's invented between when you're fifteen and thirty-five is new and exciting and revolutionary and you can probably get a career in it. 3. Anything invented after you're thirty-five is against the natural order of things."

Written text is a technology that clearly falls into Adams's first category, and as such, it seems to be near the top of human cognitive achievements, especially as they relate to communication systems and the transmission of knowledge.

When considering what cognition is, how it works, and how you might put your understanding of cognition to good use, it is important to keep in mind that modern modes of cognizing are what happens after you continuously bombard children with written words. It's not the sort of environment any primate brain evolved to deal with, so you shouldn't be surprised if the way your mind works seems weird.

CLOSURE

Secret languages like Navajo code talk, Pig Latin, and possibly rongorongo, make it easy to imagine that there might be all sorts of hidden messages being sent and received by people (telepaths?) and other animals. Much of cognitive psychology can be viewed as the study of hidden messages transmitted within a person's mind.

Representations can be viewed as codes for actions and events, or even as symbols, as proposed by the physical symbol system hypothesis. Information processing models of cognition assume that internal representations are exchanged by distinct cognitive systems for perception, attention, memory, and reasoning, each of which sends and receives information from other systems.

Communication is more than just a biological postal system, however. At its core, communication is interactive. Communicative interactions are often social, but not always. Communication can provide participants with useful information, but this is also not necessary. Acknowledging the wide variety of contexts within which people construct and interpret signals is critical to understanding the many cognitive mechanisms that they use when doing so.

Language dominates thought in most modern humans and has been a major focus of cognitive research because of its unique properties. The more researchers learn about language, the clearer it becomes that its function is closely tied to many other communication systems and cognitive skills. Many brain regions contribute to language abilities, most of which are present in lots of other vertebrates. Some birds, apes, and dogs can learn to recognize spoken words and phrases, as well as their meanings, at levels that were once thought to only be achievable by humans. Language use is clearly special, but perhaps not in the ways that Chomsky and others originally thought.

Now that you know a bit more about how language relates to communication, and the different ways that psychologists think cognition contributes to everyday social interactions, hopefully you can better appreciate the importance that your own use of symbols plays in how you think about the world.

Perhaps you've occasionally struggled in a class and wondered why that class was harder than others. Might it be because your lexicon wasn't sufficient for you to fully extract the meaning from the messages you were receiving during lectures or when reading a text? Or maybe there is something about your existing network of knowledge that is resistant to intrusions by newcomers, as when knowing one language makes it harder to learn a new one.

If you really want to gain some cognitive benefit from listening to lectures, participating in coursework, or reading textbooks, then pay attention to what communicating brains do and think and act more like a baby.

COGNITIVE LINGO

amusia	iconic signal	psycholinguist
aphasia	information processing approach	receiver
Broca's area	innate signal	reference
child-directed speech	language	semantics
communication	lateralization	sender
communication network	learned signal	signal
constructed language	lexicalization	signal repertoire
discourse	lexicon	specific language impairment
discrete signal	linguistic determinism	split-brain individual
double blind research design	linguistic nativism	statistical learning
dual route approach to reading	linguistic relativity	structuralist
dual-stream model	multilingualism	symbol
dyslexia	neurolinguistics	syntax
eavesdropping	parsing	tip-of-the-tongue
embodied communication	phonetic encoding	transmission
emergentist	phonetics	vocal contagion
graded signal	physical symbol system (PSS)	vocal imitation
grammar	pragmatics	Wernicke's area
hyperlexia	prosodic feature	Williams syndrome

CHAPTER SUMMARY

Producing and Comprehending Messages
Communicating involves selecting signals from a repertoire and exchanging them to share information. A successful transaction requires coordinated actions as well as recognition of icons and symbols.

The Nature of Language
Symbolic communication systems like language provide new ways of organizing ideas through the conceptualization, formulation, and execution of sentences. Production of sentences engages hidden competitive processes.

Language Development
Acquisition of new words and language skills depends on some specialized abilities like vocal imitation and recognition of specific contexts within which predictable sequences of words are frequently heard.

Brain Substrates
Early reports of brain damage leading to language deficits seemed to point to the existence of "language modules," but more recent neuroimaging and genetic research suggests that general plasticity mechanisms may determine when and how language develops.

Applied Perspectives
The cognitive processes that make music and language possible are tightly coupled and involve overlapping brain systems. Studies of reading have revealed a wide range of hidden differences between individual readers.

REVIEW EXERCISES

Producing and Comprehending Messages
- List some examples of graded signals that you have used to communicate with others in the past week.
- What distinguishes symbolic communication from communicating with icons?
- How does embodied communication differ from information processing models of communication?

The Nature of Language
- Explain the different routes of language processing that likely occur when you take notes.
- Describe some of the key differences between syntax and semantics.
- What are some examples of physical symbol systems and what if anything makes them special?

Language Development
- How does context affect which words a toddler is likely to learn?
- Explain how statistical learning might be studied in infants.
- Compare and contrast the kinds of language learning processes that can be studied in birds, apes, and dolphins.

Brain Substrates

• What scientific findings made researchers think that there were language organs in the left hemisphere? What findings question this belief?

• Why was *FOXP2* thought to be specialized for language learning?

• How have studies of developmental disorders contributed to the scientific understanding of language?

Applied Perspectives

• In what ways are prosody and singing related?

• Explain the difference between hyperlexia and dyslexia.

CRITICAL THINKING QUESTIONS

1. In the 2016 movie *Arrival*, humans attempt to develop ways of communicating with aliens that do not vocally communicate. Given the difficulties that researchers have translating ancient writing and understanding animal communication, how likely would it be that humans would be able to decipher the communication systems of an alien race? Assuming that the aliens are attempting to communicate, how might researchers test to see whether or not aliens are using symbolic communication?

2. People engaged in conversations unknowingly imitate one another. How might vocal imitation during discourse affect communication? Do you think this phenomenon would be more or less obvious if one of the speakers has a heavy accent?

3. Helen Keller initially learned language through a unique channel: sensations in her palm. Later, however, she was able to produce spoken English and write. If it were possible to go back in time and study her brain activity using tools such as fMRI or EEG, do you think the brain regions that became active when Helen spoke or wrote would be the same as the ones you use? If not, how might they be different?

4. Some researchers argue that similar processes are engaged during both speech production and listening. They maintain that when you hear speech, you automatically transform it into representations of the actions that would be required to produce that speech. How might you test this hypothesis using a technique like transcranial magnetic stimulation?

5. Scientists are attempting to develop electronic systems that would make two-way acoustic communication between humans and dolphins possible. What are some factors that these scientists will need to consider when designing such a system?

Glossary

A

absolute threshold The minimum change in energy required for sensations to affect a perceptual representation. [123]

abstract concept Concepts that depend less on percepts and instead seem to transcend specific sensations of objects. [167]

active perception A form of perception in which the perceiver is generating the energy that drives the sensation; occurs during tactile object recognition. [120]

ADHD See *attention deficit hyperactivity disorder*.

affordance Describes the ways an object may be used. [120]

affordance learning Discovery of the possible uses and functions of objects through social observations. [422]

afterimage Perceptual states that occur after the visual sensations from a perceived object end. [328]

algorithm Paths to solutions that simply require turning the crank to get to a desired goal state. [370]

alien hand syndrome A condition in which a person's hand seems to have an agenda that differs from the one reported by its owner. [67]

allothetic cue An external cue that is seen, heard, smelled, or touched. [211]

amnesia A total lack of awareness of an event experienced in the past. [301]

amusia Condition in which an individual is born with musical deficits such as an inability to detect out-of-tune singing. [486]

analog Representations that match the properties of the thing being represented in some way. [231]

analogical reasoning Reasoning that involves generalizing from one example to another. [380]

animacy The state of being alive and mobile. [407]

animal model Nonhuman species that have been studied to try and answer scientific or medical questions. [61]

aphasia A damage-induced disruption of speech production. [460]

approximate number system A nonverbal system for judging numerosity that estimates larger amounts based on sensation patterns. [220]

artificial intelligence Computer programs specifically designed to behave like humans. [8]

associationist model A model of mind in which cumulative experiences shape how you think. [7]

associative learning A form of learning that can be explained as a process of linking percepts, actions, and outcomes. [176]

attention Process or processes that strongly affect what you sense, perceive, and think. [112]

attention deficit hyperactivity disorder (ADHD) A developmental disorder associated not just with inattention but also with impulsivity and constant moving or fidgeting. [135]

attention span How long you can maintain your focus without becoming distracted or bored. [135]

attentional blink Occurs when a person fails to detect a salient target object that occurs between 200 and 500 milliseconds after a target was just detected. [148]

attentional reweighting A model of selective attention in which target features come to be considered more or less important over time. [139]

auditory scene analysis A process of interpreting sounds coming from multiple places at once. [118]

auditory stream A series of related sounds occurring within an auditory scene. [119]

automatic imitation A process in which perceiving another person's actions leads to involuntary copying. [433]

automaton Machines that operate with no perceptual awareness. [100]

availability heuristic A strategy involving trying whatever solution pops into your head first. [370]

axon The main output of a neuron. [51]

B

basal ganglia Clusters of neurons deep inside the brain that receive many different, highly processed sensory inputs and send out signals that help to control movements. [186]

base rate How often a process or phenomenon actually occurs. [379]

basic level category What you think of first when describing a picture of an object. [174]

BCI See *brain-computer interface*.

beacon Stationary sources that tell you where you are going. [213]

behavior contagion A phenomenon in which perceiving biological motion increases the likelihood that the observer will replicate aspects of those movements. [408]

behavioral economics A system of thought that focuses on how individuals choose their actions as a way of better understanding the learning processes that shape daily activities. [386]

belief-bias effect Occurs when rules of logical reasoning conflict with what a person believes but beliefs are still maintained. [380]

binocular cues Sensations from both eyes that are integrated to generate three-dimensional visual representations of the world. [127]

biological motion The movements of animals. [121]

blindsight A condition, usually caused by brain injury, in which a person reports having extensive blind spots but sometimes acts as if they can actually see fine. [74]

blocking An experimental effect in which learning about an initial cue can prevent learning about later cues. [245]

bottom-up processing Externally provoked perception, with your sense organs being at the bottom and your perceptual awareness being the ultimate outcome or top. [111]

boundary extension The tendency of people to recall details that better match an idealized (schema-driven) portrayal of an observed episode or scene. [427]

brain plasticity The brain's ability to change its structure or function. [54]

brain-computer interface (BCI) System in which computers monitor brain activity. [62]

Broca's area Region of the left frontal lobe which if damaged can lead to defects in speech production. [479]

C

categorical perception A phenomenon that occurs during perception of speech when sounds that are similar are described as being from different categories. [176]

categorize The cognitive act of sorting entities in the world. [160]

category A set of things or events that share at least one characteristic. [160]

category-boundary model A model suggesting that what people compare when categorizing items is where each item falls relative to internally represented borders between categories. [169]

category-specific neuron Neurons that respond selectively to items in a category, like those in the inferotemporal cortex. [184]

cerebellum Subcortical region of the brain, located under the occipital lobe, which plays a role in learning new cognitive skills. [45]

cerebral cortex The outer layer of the mammalian brain, divided into two hemispheres and multiple lobes. [45]

change blindness A phenomenon in which people are unable to detect differences between percepts that should be way above their thresholds for detection. [117]

child-directed speech "Baby talk" involving exaggerated speech. [472]

circadian timing Daily predictable temporal cycles. [200]

cocktail party effect When the speech by an individual is voluntarily selected by the perceiver and everything else is designated as the ground or noise. [118]

cognitive behavioral therapy A strategy for treating patients with mental health issues that focuses on changing how a person thinks about ongoing emotional experiences. [88]

cognitive bias An unconscious tendency to mentally act in certain ways. [98]

cognitive dissonance An uncomfortable emotional state similar to unease or guilt triggered by inconsistencies between alternative actions. [419]

cognitive flexibility The capacity to hold multiple thoughts in mind simultaneously or to rapidly switch between trains of thought. [347]

cognitive map Hypothetical internal maps reflecting spatial relationships between locations. [211]

cognitive module A cognitive system in which specific kinds of computations are automatically performed. [39]

cognitive neuroscience A field of study focused on investigating brain function in order to better understand cognition. [44]

cognitive plasticity The capacity of individuals to modify their cognitive abilities through practice. [59]

cognitive prosthetic A device that replaces or augments cognitive processes. [62]

cognitive skills Any ability you can improve through practice without necessarily changing your physical movements. [256]

cognitive socialization Interactions with teachers, as well as all other social influences, in a way that leads to changes in your cognitive skills. [424]

cognize To be consciously aware of ongoing events, both internal and external. [6]

collaborative inhibition When the amount of information being retrieved by a group tends to be less than the sum of what all the members come up with individually. [428]

collective memory Facts and events recalled similarly by members of a group. [427]

communication An act of producing, transmitting, receiving, and interpreting signals. [446]

communication network Flow and transmission of information between individuals in a group. [451]

complementary learning systems A model of category learning in which the hippocampus rapidly stores exemplars, while the cerebral cortex gradually constructs new concepts. [188]

computational theory of mind The "mind-as-machine" model proposing that brains are biological computers and that minds are information processing systems. [8]

concept A mental representation that summarizes or tags percepts, categories, or relationships between them. [160]

conditioning The gradual modification of an individual's behavior by repeated exposures to similar events. [244]

confirmation bias The tendency to accept or notice evidence that is consistent with a prior belief or expectation. [376]

conjunction search A search task in which the target is identified by two or more features. [137]

connectionist model A model of the mind in which a cognitive activity results from a distributed network of interconnected neurons. [189]

connectome Maps of connections between different neurons or brain regions. [47]

conscious A state of being alert, awake, and capable of responding to sensed events. [69]

consolidation Process in which memories gradually become more stably stored over time. [296]

constructed language An artificial language specifically designed for some purpose. [465]

constructivism He idea that perceptual representations are built out of repeated experiences. [119]

context The locations and conditions in which an experiment is performed. [245]

cooperative learning experience When students with comparable levels of knowledge work together to share ideas and discover knowledge on their own. [424]

covert spatial attention A type of attention in which viewers can attend to locations other than where their eyes are fixated. [133]

cued recall A form of recall in which clues are given to provoke specific mental states similar to those experienced in a previous episode. [296]

D

deductive reasoning Reasoning in which the experience is represented propositionally and then used to generate other valid propositions that follow from initial propositions. [374]

deep net Computer programs that work by searching for lots of different features and lots of different patterns; short for deep learning neural network. [145]

default mode network (DMN) The brain regions that become most active during mind wandering. [353]

dendrite Rootlike structures that extend out from the cell body of a neuron. [49]

dendritic spine Protrusion present on dendrites where the axon of another neuron synapses. [52]

dichotic listening task A task in which participants are instructed to focus on one of the two speakers/ears and are later asked questions about what the two people said. [131]

didactic learning experience When teachers with expertise pass on their knowledge to students with demonstrations or instructions about how to accomplish specific tasks. [424]

directed forgetting When an effort is made to forget specific facts. [297]

discourse A continuous flow of language signals, such as occurs during conversations, storytelling, polemics, pontificating, sermons, and monologues. [456]

discrete signals Signals that are clearly distinguishable. [448]

discrimination The ability to distinguish percepts. [160]

displacement activity Behaviors performed during cognitive activities that drawing serve to draw your attention away from conscious thought processes. [101]

distributed representation Representations that are spread out across many separate neurons. [189]

divergent thinking Thinking in ways that deviate from the norm. [347]

divided attention Perceptual multitasking, or the ability to attend to more than one stimulus or task at the same time. [132]

DMN See *default mode network*.

domain specificity The idea that each cognitive ability depends on one or more innately specialized brain regions. [38]

double-blind research design Experimental design in which neither subjects nor observers have information about the experimental conditions. [475]

dual process model Model to explain thinking in which two systems contribute to thought, often unequally. [377]

dual route approach to reading Multimodal processing of text requiring recognition by both sight and speech sounds. [489]

dual-stream model A model of language processing in which circuits in both hemispheres process heard words in parallel, with some regions focusing on speech and others on meaning. [481]

duplex theory of sound localization Model of perception in which differences in the timing and intensity of sounds at each ear are used to represent the direction from which a sound came. [125]

dynamic system A model that portrays action selection and production as an interactive process leading to movement patterns without requiring a top-down command. [82]

dyscalculia Developmental disorder defined by below-average abilities at solving math problems. [232]

dyslexia Developmental disorder resulting in impairment of reading ability. [491]

E

early-selection model A model of attention in which unattended auditory signals are eliminated early in processing. [136]

eavesdropping A type of animal communication in which an individual is influenced by the communicative interactions of others. [451]

echoic memory Sensory memory of sounds. [285]

ECN See *executive control network*.

ECT See *electroconvulsive therapy*.

EEG See *electroencephalogram*.

egocentrism Developmental phase during which children are unable to understand that their experiences are not shared by others. [429]

eidetic imagery High-resolution persistence of a percept for relatively extended periods. [329]

electroconvulsive therapy (ECT) Administration of a strong electrical pulse through the brain. [317]

electroencephalogram (EEG) A recording of brain electrical activity from electrodes placed on the scalp. [48]

embodied communication A framework in which communication is viewed as a joint action between two individuals, focusing on the coordination of activities within social interactions. [453]

emergent pattern A pattern that arises from interactions between control mechanisms and new environmental conditions. [83]

emergentist An approach to explaining sentence comprehension that emphasizes how receivers construct, organize, and use representations of inputs and how they access relevant knowledge. [463]

emotion A combination of neurophysiological processes, behavior, and subjective feelings. [86]

emotional regulation The controlled reaction to ongoing emotional states. [88]

emotional theory of mind A theory of mind in which inferences are made about ongoing emotional experiences such as happiness, sadness, and confusion. [413]

empathy Experience of identifying the emotional state of another individual by understanding their feelings and having some capacity to share that experience. [88]

empiricist A person who argues that everything that humans perceive and know comes from experience. [19]

emulation The act of observing someone else achieve a goal, adopting that goal, and then performing some actions aimed at achieving the same goal. [422]

engram Proposed memory traces within a brain that make recall possible. [305]

entrainment The process of adjusting your actions to match a temporal pattern. [199]

episodic future thinking The process of imagining experiences that might occur in the future. [334]

episodic memory Memory of an event that you've personally experienced. [292]

equivalence class Functional category in which all category members are equal. [164]

eugenics Selective breeding with the goal of improving humans. [40]

executive control network (ECN) A set of brain regions that have been implicated in creative thought and cognitive control. [354]

executive function Processes that provide cognitive control. [23]

exemplar A specific percept that falls into a particular category and can be used to recognize and categorize percepts in the future. [167]

exemplar model A model of categorization that proposes that people categorize items by comparing them to representations of previously experienced items (exemplars). [170]

expectancy effect A kind of cognitive bias that occurs when participants know or suspect what it is that an experimenter is attempting to show. [98]

explicit cognition Conscious thoughts and experiences. [73]

explicit memory Something you know about and can voluntarily recall and express in words. [282]

extended mind thesis The proposal that minds are not things trapped inside one's head, but include any tools that you use to support your thinking. [9]

extinction A learning process in which conditioned responses decrease over time. [246]

F

face-selective brain region A region of the cerebral cortex that is especially involved in processing visually perceived faces. [141]

facial microexpression A slight facial movement that is usually subliminal and that is correlated with a person attempting to hide that they are lying, afraid, or excited. [88]

false memory A memory for which the recalled content seems accurate to the person remembering it, despite inaccuracies. [299]

family resemblance The relationship between category items that are perceptually similar. [161]

far transfer When an individual generalizes learned performance of one cognitive task to a task that is not similar to the originally practiced task. [259]

fast mapping A rapid increase in a child's ability to classify all kinds of objects that begins soon after children start learning the names of different objects. [179]

feature analysis model A model of perception in which representations are formed by sorting sensations into sets of features and then sorting combinations of features to identify their source. [116]

feature A perceived property of an object, agent, or scene. [50]

feature detector A conceptualization of a neuron that responds most strongly to a specific set of sensory patterns. [50]

feature integration theory A model of visual processing proposing that attention combines sensed features into unified percepts of objects. [137]

feature-based attention A process of searching for patterns with certain properties. [135]

feelings of knowing Subjective impressions of certainty. [301]

fixed mindset The view that problem-solving and reasoning abilities are a talent that some people are born with and others are not. [397]

flashback A personal experience that is involuntarily recalled without warning. [298]

flashbulb memory A vivid memory of a situation that led to an extreme emotional reaction. [293]

fMRI See *functional magnetic resonance imaging*.

foot-in-the-door phenomenon A phenomenon in which a person who complies with an initial small request becomes more likely to comply with a somewhat larger request later. [418]

framing effect A cognitive bias in decision-making resulting from the way that information is verbally presented. [383]

free recall Memory recall based on minimal guidance from external cues. [296]

frontal lobe A region of your brain near the back of your head. [45]

functional fixedness A phenomenon in which the way you conceptualize objects and events can interfere with your ability to discover solutions to problems. [372]

functional magnetic resonance imaging (fMRI) A neuroimaging method that tracks changes in how blood is being used throughout a brain. [49]

fundamental attribution error A cognitive bias in which situational explanations for behavior are given less weight than inferred personality traits. [412]

fusiform face area A region of the cerebral cortex involved in processing visually perceived faces. [142]

G

gaze allocation Where people focus their eyes when viewing a scene. [410]

gender stereotype A belief about prototypical characteristics of men, women, or others. [426]

generalization A process of responding to novel events based on their similarity to other events you have experienced in the past; sometimes called the transfer of learning. [258]

generalization gradient A curve that describes response strength as a function of the similarity between conditioned stimuli and novel stimuli. [259]

genetic engineering Artificially removing, adding, or replacing specific genes. [42]

Gestaltism An approach to understanding perception that emphasizes fundamental principles that lead some forms to stand out as figures. [125]

glia Cells in a brain that are not neurons, but that function in ways that strongly determine how neurons interact and function. [50]

graded signal Signals that vary continuously along a series of similar forms. [448]

grammar The syntactic rule systems that allow for different combinations of words to convey meaning. [466]

grandmother cell hypothesis This hypothesis proposes that there is a neuron somewhere in your head that responds any time you perceive or think about a specific person. [183]

groupthink A phenomenon in which attempts to reach a consensus end up pushing individuals toward bad decisions. [386]

growth mindset The belief that human problem-solving capacities are not genetically predetermined but can be improved through practice. [397]

H

hemispatial neglect An extreme form of inattentional blindness in which a person behaves as if they are unaware of anything existing in one half of their environment (usually the left side). [133]

herding effect A socially induced cognitive bias that leads one to conform to others' actions. [93]

heredity The genetic transmission of traits. [37]

heritability A quantitative measure that estimates how much genetic variation contributes to variations in traits or performances seen within a group. [41]

heuristic A general strategy that people use when attempting to solve a problem. [370]

hierarchical model A model of cognition and action in which instructions are delivered from an "executive" process that directs movements and thoughts; see also top-down processing. [78]

highly superior autobiographical memory (HSAM) An exceptional capacity to recall details about personal past events, based on the date and time the event occurred. [4]

hippocampus A subcortical structure in the temporal lobe that is critical for memory processes. [187]

hyperlexia A phenomenon in which children learn to read at ages younger than two years old, without being explicitly taught by others. [490]

I

iconic memory A sensory memory of something recently seen. [285]

iconic signal A signal that more directly depicts the message that it is meant to communicate. [449]

identical elements theory A model in which the number of shared features between a novel experience and a previous experience determines when learning will transfer. [259]

ideomotor theory A model proposing that actions are represented in terms of the perceivable effects that they cause (visual and kinesthetic). [408]

idiothetic cue An internally generated cue, such as a kinesthetic percept generated by one's own actions or changes in orientation that reveals changes in an organism's location. [211]

ill-defined problem A problem in which there is some ambiguity about when, or if, the goal state or solution has or can be reached. [368]

illusory conjunction Incorrectly combined perceptual representations that may occur when attention is overloaded and items are physically close together. [137]

illusory contour Perceived edges that appear to outline objects that are not actually present. [116]

illusory correlation An apparent link between events that are unrelated. [376]

imagination The capacity to voluntarily evoke mental images through the active process of constructing mental experiences. [325]

imitation A specialized kind of emulation in which you copy the specific goal-directed actions that you have observed. [423]

implicit association test A task in which reaction times are used to find evidence that unconscious categories (implicit biases) can influence your subjective impressions. [409]

implicit cognition Processes that affect your cognitive performance without your awareness. [73]

implicit memory A memory retrieved automatically and unconsciously; sometimes referred to as non-declarative memories. [282]

improvisation The process of acting creatively and on the spur of the moment. [346]

impulsivity The tendency to act with minimal consideration of the consequences of acting. [340]

inattentional blindness A kind of obliviousness in which even large changes that seemingly should be obvious can occur without an observer being perceptually aware of the changes. [133]

incubation Putting a problem aside (out of sight and out of mind) in way that eventually facilitates the discovery of a solution. [345]

inductive reasoning Considering some number of observations and then attempting to use those observations to draw a conclusion. [374]

inequity aversion A sensitivity to fairness shown by a willingness to self-punish in response to unfair circumstances, for example, by choosing no reward over a smaller reward. [416]

infantile amnesia The phenomenon that most if not all adults are unable to recall episodes from their early lives. [318]

inferotemporal cortex A part of the visual cortex that is important for recognizing complex shapes. [184]

information integration The proposal that learning label-less perceptual categories depends on the perceptual merging of features or dimensions. [187]

information processing approach A framework for understanding cognition and communication that focuses on the exchange of signals that move information from one place to another. [452]

innate signal A signal that is produced involuntarily and that has many genetically predetermined properties. [469]

insight problem A task in which solutions are often suddenly discovered. [345]

instrumental conditioning A training technique that focuses on getting individuals to perform specific actions by providing incentives; sometimes referred to as operant conditioning. [249]

internal clock A hypothetical biological mechanism that functions like a mechanical clock by repeatedly and reliably measuring out fixed intervals of time. [204]

interval timing Subjective estimates of duration. [201]

introspection Objective reports on inner experiences made by experts during the performance of tightly controlled experimental tasks. [28]

invariant cue Patterns of sensation that change the least regardless of the structure of the environment, the energy available, and the movements of sensory receptors. [217]

J

joint action Multiple individuals coordinating their movements or activities. [356]

judgment of learning An assessment of one's own future ability to recall facts recently encountered. [302]

just noticeable difference (JND) The smallest perceivable difference between two similar sensory events for a particular individual. [123]

L

landmark Any stationary sources of information about where in space you are. [213]

language All the combinations of words, phrases, and sentences that people use, along with their meanings. [454]

late-selection models A model of attention in which percepts are interpreted before an attentional gatekeeper selects those that deserve to be brought into consciousness. [136]

latent learning Learning that is not immediately evident from the learner's actions. [245]

lateralization When a particular function depends more on one cerebral hemisphere than the other. [478]

law of effect A principle proposing that, within a given context, you will choose to perform the action that has been most reinforcing in the past. [252]

learned helplessness A phenomenon in which individuals faced with avoidable punishment simply do not attempt to escape from the punishment. [397]

learned signal A signal that can be produced voluntarily and only occurs if the sender has had specific experiences with that signal. [469]

learning set A set of learned associations that enables the learner to rapidly recognize an appropriate response when faced with novel stimuli. [261]

levels-of-processing effect A phenomenon in which elaborating on the meanings of to-be-remembered words can make them easier to recall. [295]

lexicalization Choosing a word to produce. [457]

lexicon The vocabulary of words you have learned. [457]

linguistic determinism The proposal that most of your cognitive processes—how you categorize, remember, and think about your experiences—are a direct function of the languages you know. [468]

linguistic nativism The idea that human language is so complex that a baby could only develop language skills in two years or less is if they are born pre-wired for learning language. [478]

linguistic relativity The possibility that variations in the lexicons used by different cultures can potentially affect not only how people communicate but also how they think about the world. [468]

local representation A neural representation of a perceived event that can be localized to a particular neuron or a small number of neurons. [183]

locked-in syndrome A condition in which a person is conscious but cannot physically respond to events. [71]

long-term memory The longest-lasting memories. [282]

loss aversion A cognitive bias in which expected losses loom larger than gains. [383]

M

mark test A test of self-awareness in which a mark is secretly placed in a location that can only be seen with the help of a mirror; discoverers of the mark pass the test. [429]

massed practice Practice that is continuous and rapidly paced, which generally leads to quicker learning but less retention. [254]

matching law A principle proposing that an individual's choice patterns will closely follow the relative rates of utility for each of multiple options. [385]

McGurk effect A video showing a person producing one speech sound when paired with the audio recording of a different speech sound causes observers to hear a third speech sound. [122]

means-end heuristic An approach to problem-solving that involves breaking a problem into smaller mini-problems and then focusing on solving each of those mini-problems separately. [370]

media multitasking Using multiple information sources in parallel. [151]

memory decay A hypothetical process in which the passage of time leads to the deterioration of a memory. [298]

memory prosthesis A technological intervention designed to restore lost memory capacity or to push memory processing past its normal limits. [316]

mental attribution Explaining actions as being caused by preceding mental states. [412]

mental image An internal state that subjectively is similar to a percept. [325]

mental model A hypothetical internal simulation of the properties of the actual world, including yourself. [337]

mental representation A hypothetical substitute for, or pointer to, concepts, memories, percepts, sensations, or thoughts that capture important aspects of experiences. [114]

mental rotation task A task that seems to require transforming a percept into a mental image and then manipulating that image to solve a specific visuospatial problem. [332]

mental set When earlier experiences bias your attention toward specific solutions to a problem. [372]

metacognition Monitoring of recent thoughts or mental states. [19]

metamemory Your impressions and thoughts of your own remembering. [301]

metaplasticity The capacity to globally regulate levels of neural plasticity. [271]

mind wandering Involuntary streams of conscious thought. [353]

mindfulness An approach to channeling awareness that involves voluntarily controlling what you attend to with "now" typically being the main target. [70]

mirror neuron Neurons that respond similarly when an agent is producing or perceiving an action. [432]

mirror system Cortical regions in humans that show consistent activation during both the performance and perception of actions. [432]

mnemonic A method that you can use to increase your ability to recall specific facts or events. [58]

modal model A model of memory consisting of temporary and permanent (long-term) memory stores plus a rehearsal mechanism to prolong temporary storage. [289]

motivation The ongoing internal states that lead you to act in certain ways, either physically or mentally. [23]

motor memory A short-term memory of a recently performed action. [285]

motor theory of speech perception A model proposing that when you hear words you represent them by recognizing the vocal actions you would use to reproduce the word. [128]

multilingualism Use of multiple languages. [473]

multimodal Involving some combination of sights, sounds, and actions. [122]

multiple trace theory A model of memory in which the hippocampus and cerebral cortex function in parallel, with a new memory stored in both regions every time an episodic memory is recalled. [308]

multiple-object tracking Monitoring the movements of objects (typically four to five maximum) at the same time. [133]

multisensory integration A process of combining inputs from multiple sensory modalities. [216]

N

n-back task In this working memory task, subjects are required to report when the current item is the same as the one that was presented *n* items ago (where *n* might be 1, 2, 3, or more). [285]

Nash equilibrium A reference point that maximizes the utility of actions for a group as a whole when they are collectively and cooperatively evaluating different options. [386]

nativist Someone who claims that experiences mainly are determined by the innate properties of the mind and brain, which effectively determine what one's percepts and thoughts are like. [19]

near transfer When an individual generalizes learned performance of one cognitive task to a highly similar task. [259]

nervous system Specialized tissues that continuously work to maintain all of your organs so that you stay alive. [45]

network In neuroscience, sets of neurons (populations) that interact during the performance of a particular function (including all cognitive functions). [51]

neural correlates of consciousness The minimal conditions or structures that can produce conscious states. [71]

neural plasticity The capacity of neurons to change their shape, size, composition, and activity levels in ways that affect how they function. [266]

neuroeconomics The neuroscientific counterpart to behavioral economics which focuses on monitoring brain systems engaged during decision-making. [391]

neurolinguistics A field of research focused on identifying brain substrates of language production, comprehension, and acquisition. [478]

neuron A cell within the nervous system with dendrites and an axon that transmits electrical impulses. [49]

numerosity The approximate number of items. [219]

O

object tracking system A system for judging numerosity that automatically specifies the number of items in a small set based on how many items are being tracked. [220]

object-based attention A process of selectively attending to specific objects. [133]

observational learning Learning that happens when you attend to the actions of others and use memories of those actions to guide your own actions or decisions. [255]

occipital lobe A region of your brain near the back of your head. [45]

optic flow Patterns of motion that occur whenever a viewer moves through an environment. [214]

optimal foraging theory A model of decision-making during food-finding that assumes individuals select their actions so that they maximize utility (energy gained from food). [384]

oscillator A regularly repeating system. [200]

P

parietal lobe A region of your brain near the peak of your head. [45]

parsing The deconstruction of sentences in terms of grammatical rules. [462]

path integration Keeping track of where you are by continuously monitoring the movements you are making (through self-motion cues). [213]

pattern recognition A process in which incoming sensations are identified using sets of feature detectors. [126]

peak shift effect A phenomenon in which learning to discriminate a preferred stimulus leads the learner to prefer certain novel stimuli more than the one they learned to prefer. [260]

percept The mental consequence of sensations. [111]

perceptual awareness Your first-person subjective experience or *Umwelt* during awake states. [114]

perceptual binding Combining sensory features to create a unified perceptual awareness. [127]

perceptual category A category composed of perceptually similar items. [161]

perceptual constancy The preservation of perceived qualities regardless of sensory fluctuations. [117]

perceptual expertise The ability to rapidly discriminate and recognize complex percepts. [181]

perceptual learning Relatively long-lasting changes in your ability to discriminate percepts gained through experience. [181]

perceptual narrowing A phenomenon in which perception of facial movements and biological motion becomes more precise after repeated experiences. [409]

perceptual representation Mental representation that organizes and preserves aspects of experienced events. [114]

perceptual similarity The perceived overlap between two experiences. [161]

perceptual theory of mind This model of social cognition focuses on learned associations between intentions and social cues, especially eye gazes and finger points. [412]

perspective taking A process in which one attributes mental states to other individuals or imagines what others' mental states are like. [414]

PFC See *prefrontal cortex*.

phantom limb A phenomenon in which amputees commonly report feeling their missing arms, hands, or legs. [328]

phoneme A variation in a speech sound that changes the meanings of words. [154]

phonetic encoding A process in which abstract word representations are transformed into the motor commands necessary for producing speech. [458]

phonetics The acoustic details of spoken words, including the consonants and vowels within those words. [458]

physical symbol system (PSS) Any system that uses symbols in predictable ways to perform computations. [464]

place cell Neurons in the hippocampus that tend to fire whenever an individual arrives at a particular locale. [226]

planning Any process of selecting actions that will help to achieve a specific goal before implementing those actions. [337]

point-light display Recorded movements of an agent made in ways that only show changes in the positions of small lights attached to the agent. [121]

power law of practice Initial improvements after practicing a task are often rapid, followed by a period in which additional repeated experiences lead to smaller improvements. [268]

pragmatics The rules and customs of language-based communication. [456]

prefrontal cortex (PFC) A region of the cerebral cortex near your forehead. [185]

Premack principle Preferred actions can be used to reinforce other actions. [253]

priming When a recent percept or activated memory unconsciously affects an individual's later performance. [75]

Prisoner's Dilemma Two "prisoners" must decide whether to cooperate with their jailers in a situation where their choices determine how long each will be imprisoned. [416]

proactive interference A hypothesized mechanism that explains why items earlier in a list make it harder to retrieve items from later in the list. [289]

probabilistic category A category in which items tend to be linked to specific outcomes, but not 100% of the time. [186]

problem-solving Processes that you use when attempting to achieve some goal. [337]

proceduralist view A framework for explaining memory that focuses on principles that determine what will be remembered. [284]

proposition Symbolically represented statements that can be classified as being either true or false. [366]

propositional representation A hypothetical language-like, symbolic, mental representation that underlies conscious thinking. [332]

prosocial behavior Actions that benefit a group such as sharing or cooperating. [415]

prosodic feature A feature of a sentence, such as a pause or pitch shift, that can convey information beyond that revealed by the syntax and semantics. [462]

prototype An item that is the best example for a category, capturing common qualities associated with many members of that category. [163]

prototype model A model that describes categorization as a search for similarities between current percepts and stored representations of prototypes. [170]

pseudocategory A category in which items are randomly included regardless of their perceptual or functional similarities. [177]

PSS See *physical symbol system.*

psycholinguist A cognitive psychologist specializing in language research. [446]

psychologist's fallacy A conceptual error that occurs when one attributes some quality to a cognitive phenomenon based on one's subjective impressions of the phenomenon. [97]

psychophysical methods Experimental methods that relate internal experiences to external events. [122]

punisher Consequences that decrease the performance of specific actions during conditioning. [250]

Q

qualia Your personal subjective experiences of what it is like to be conscious. [100]

R

rational choice theory A model of decision-making in which people are expected to rationally consider the consequences of their options and to choose one with greater utility. [382]

rational thought Thoughts that are logical and justified by valid principles and evidence. [367]

readiness potential Changes in brain activity that precede voluntary acts. [79]

reasoning Consciously thinking about an issue in a logical and systematic way. [365]

receiver An agent that notices and interprets a transmitted signal. [446]

recognition The matching of a current experience to a prior one combined with a feeling of familiarity. [112]

recognition-by-components theory A model of object recognition proposing that the components (templates) used to represent objects are simple three-dimensional shapes called geons. [127]

reductionism A common scientific tactic of trying to understand a complex phenomenon by breaking it down into its most basic elements. [27]

reference The relationship between a symbol and what it stands for. [466]

rehearsal Extending the persistence of a mental state by repeating it. [285]

reinforcer Consequences that increase the performance of a specific action during instrumental conditioning. [250]

relational category A category in which items are included based on relationships or comparisons between events rather than sensible properties of individual objects or agents. [167]

reminiscence bump The finding that older adults are generally more likely to recall episodes in their life when they were younger (around twenty). [91]

renewal effect A phenomenon in which the return of a familiar context and all its emotional triggers can overcome years of new learning and extinction. [247]

representativeness heuristic When one attempts to judge the probability of something being true based on how similar it is to something else believed to be true. [379]

repressed memories Hypothetical unpleasant memories that are automatically and unconsciously suppressed. [297]

response What you do after detecting and recognizing a stimulus. [122]

retroactive interference A hypothesized mechanism that explains why items later in a list make it harder to retrieve items from earlier in the list. [289]

rubber hand illusion An illusion in which a fake hand is stroked while a person's real hand is stroked in the same way out of sight causing the person to feel as though the fake hand is theirs. [207]

rule-based model A model that explains categorization as a process of sorting items by testing whether they fulfill a specific set of conditions. [171]

rumination Continued attention to negative mental states. [290]

S

saliency map A hypothetical perceptual representation that identifies regions of interest within a specific scene. [145]

scaffolding A teaching technique in which subcomponents or simpler versions of a skill are presented to gradually ease the student into performing the final skill. [424]

scalar property The phenomenon that your ability to resolve different durations decreases at a predictable rate as intervals grow longer. [203]

schema General knowledge about things that are associated with a familiar context. [425]

script Mental representations of sequences of events that typically occur in a predictable order in relation to a familiar situation. [426]

selective attention Favoring of a specific source of sensory patterns. [131]

self-awareness Your experience of yourself as separate from the rest of the world and other people. [428]

self-organize Patterns that emerge spontaneously within dynamic systems. [83]

self-regulated learning Learning that requires one to be aware of emotions and strategically plan activities in a way that takes likely future emotional states into account. [94]

semantic memory Memory for a fact or general knowledge. [282]

semantics The meanings of words and sentences. [461]

sender An agent who generates a message used to communicate. [446]

sensitive period A window of time during which neural circuits are especially plastic, with connections between neurons being strongly determined by sensory and social inputs. [54]

sensorimotor stage A stage of development proposed by Piaget when infants become aware that the movements of their limbs are under their control. [119]

sensory cue A feature that is particularly important for isolating or identifying specific objects or agents within a scene. [127]

sensory memory Remnants of what you were recently perceiving that rapidly fade, often lasting only fractions of a second. [285]

sentient Having the capacity to feel pain and/or be aware of the world, including oneself and others. [100]

serial position effect The phenomenon that first and last items in a list tend to be remembered better than items in the middle of a list. [288]

shape constancy Perceptually stability of the shape of objects and agents that persists despite variations in the angle from which they are viewed. [117]

shaping A type of instrumental conditioning in which a trainer gradually guides an individual to perform specific actions. [255]

signal A message used to communicate information that is produced by a sender. [446]

signal detection theory A mathematical approach that describes how relevant evidence (a signal) might be distinguished from irrelevant details (noise). [129]

signal repertoire The full set of signals that a sender produces when communicating. [448]

situated cognition A framework suggesting that understanding how to solve a particular problem comes from familiarity with contextual factors and the effects of actions in specific contexts. [369]

size constancy Seen objects appear to be the same size even when you are moving toward or away from them. [117]

small-sample fallacy A logical fallacy in which one assumes that small samples are representative of a population when drawing conclusions about that population. [379]

social brain hypothesis The proposal that increasing social complexity produced new demands on cognition, favoring the evolution of larger brains and greater cognitive capacity. [411]

social facilitation A phenomenon in which individuals working together can achieve more than is possible through individual effort. [416]

social inference Conclusions you reach about other minds—about what individuals are like and why. [412]

social knowledge Information you have learned both consciously and unconsciously that enables you to interpret and participate in social interactions. [424]

social learning Learning that happens when you attend to the actions of others and use memories of those actions to guide your own actions or decisions. [420]

somatic marker hypothesis The proposal that subjective impressions of physiological changes, such as muscle tension or irregular heart rate, guide decisions about what actions are appropriate. [384]

source monitoring error A memory recall error in which the information is retrieved relatively accurately but the origins of the information are misremembered. [299]

spaced practice Practice that is spread out over time, which takes longer but typically leads to more change per repeated experience that persists longer. [254]

sparse representation Representation that consists of only a few elements. [121]

spatial attention A process of attending to increase the clarity of sensations coming from a particular location. [133]

spatial orientation The process of monitoring and controlling one's movements (or positioning the body) in a particular direction. [210]

specific language impairment A disorder in which children who hear normally are delayed in learning language skills. [483]

split-brain individual A person who has had their two hemispheres disconnected by a surgeon, usually to reduce the severity of epileptic seizures. [480]

standard consolidation theory A proposal that the cerebral cortex and the hippocampus work together to construct representations of categories, concepts, and memories of events. [308]

statistical learning The ability to learn to recognize consistently ordered stimuli. [472]

stimuli External events that evoke reactions in your nervous system. [122]

stimulus enhancement When an individual's attention is directed toward specific objects, events, locations, or individuals within an environment by another individual's actions. [422]

stimulus generalization When responses to novel objects or events are a consequence of associative-learning experiences with other similar events. [176]

Stroop effect Delayed color naming caused by label-color-mismatches. [132]

structural view A conceptualization of memory that emphasizes where and when different kinds of memories are stored and processed. [284]

structuralist An approach to explaining sentence comprehension that focuses on mechanisms of transforming signals into recognizable propositions. [463]

structure-from-motion A phenomenon in which you can recognize objects from motion cues alone. [120]

subliminal perception Unconscious processing of perceptual events. [75]

syllogism Two claims, followed by a third claim—the conclusion—which, based on the first two claims, is either logically valid or invalid. [376]

symbol Signals that are related to their meanings in arbitrary ways. [449]

synapse A structure located in regions where parts of neurons are next to each other through which signals can be exchanged. [51]

synaptic plasticity The capacity of neurons to adjust synaptic connections and interactions over time. [266]

synchronized A state in which actions or events are produced at times that exactly match the timing of other events. [199]

synesthesia A condition in which images, sounds, tastes, or touches trigger additional unrelated sensory experiences. [111]

syntax How sentences are structured, especially how words are ordered. [457]

T

template theory A model of object recognition in which stored representations of perceptual patterns (templates) are compared to inputs to detect the template that is most similar. [127]

temporal lobe The part of your brain that is by your temple and closest to your dimple. [45]

testing effect A phenomenon in which practicing free recall leads to better retention than re-reading information. [296]

theory of mind Your ideas about others' mental states—their feelings, thoughts, beliefs, and desires—and your thoughts about your own mind. [412]

theory-based model A model of categorization which proposes that people categorize items based on their general understanding of ongoing events. [172]

think-aloud protocol A method of observing thought processes by having participants say what they are doing as they work toward a solution or develop a plan. [337]

third variable problem The fact that any time two measures are correlated, it's always possible that an additional hidden factor is the source of the correlation. [231]

tip-of-the-tongue When the word you want to recall or say is just out of reach. [457]

top-down processing A type of information processing model of cognitive processes in which predictions, goals, or ongoing mental states shape reactions to external inputs. [78]

Tower of London task A task in which a person is challenged to move disks around on rods to match a specific target arrangement. [339]

tragedy of the commons A scenario in which many members of a social contract cheat leading to the destruction of a shared resource. [417]

transfer appropriate processing When conditions during recall match those of the original experience. [296]

transient global amnesia A condition in which a person temporarily loses memories of the last decade or two, as well as the ability to keep track of recent events. [316]

transitive inference A form of deductive reasoning in which knowing how items A and B are related, and how items B and C are related, implies how items A and C are related. [380]

transmission A physical process in which a signal travels out into the world. [446]

Trust Game A task in which an "investor" chooses how much money to give a "trustee," after which the trustee gets triple the amount received and decides how much to return to the investor. [417]

typicality A measure of how likely people are to mention an item as being in a specific category. [164]

U

Ultimatum Game A task in which one person offers to split money with a second participant who can accept or rejects the offer; if the offer is rejected, neither participant gets any money. [392]

Umwelt The subjective world of an organism, including ongoing percepts and unconscious internal representations that guide actions. [99]

utility The sum of all benefits of a particular action minus the downsides. [382]

utility curve A graph that describes how the attractiveness of a choice varies depending on your impressions of the costs and benefits of different options. [386]

V

variable practice Practicing a variety of different skills using a range of materials and stimuli. [261]

visual search A voluntary attentional process in which you attempt to experience a specific kind of percept. [134]

vocal contagion Unconsciously triggered repetitions of heard sounds. [477]

vocal imitation The vocal reenactment of previously heard sounds. [476]

volition A cognitive process that enables you to consciously choose when and how to act. [23]

W

Wason Four-Card Problem A task in which participants must decide if a set of four cards follows a particular rule; they are asked to state which cards they would turn over to decide. [377]

Weber's Law Mathematically describes the principle that to strengthen a perceived event by a fixed amount, you need to increase sensory inputs by a specific percentage. [123]

well-defined problem Problems with predetermined solutions. [368]

Wernicke's area A cortical region in the left temporal lobe, just behind Broca's area, that when damaged leads to problems constructing and comprehending sentences. [480]

Williams syndrome Children with this syndrome show impaired cognitive abilities but achieve relatively typical language skills; they are often hyperverbal. [483]

word length effect Remembering a list of long words is harder than remembering a list of short words. [289]

word superiority effect Recognizing a rapidly flashed word is easier than recognizing isolated letters. [132]

working memory The capacity to store, temporarily maintain, and manipulate recent thoughts in mind. [17]

Z

zone of proximal development A set of potentially performable skills that would be difficult for an individual to perform without the aid of someone more knowledgeable, but that the individual could perform with social guidance. [254]

REFERENCES

A

Abboub, N., Nazzi, T., & Gervain, J. (2016). Prosodic grouping at birth. *Brain Lang, 162,* 46–59. https://doi.org/10.1016/j.bandl.2016.08.002

Abe, Y., Ushirogawa, H., & Tomioka, K. (1997). Circadian locomotor rhythms in the cricket, *Gryllodes sigillatus*. I. Localization of the pacemaker and the photoreceptor. *Zoolog Sci, 14*(5), 719–727. https://doi.org/10.2108/zsj.14.719

Abraham, W. C. (2008). Metaplasticity: Tuning synapses and networks for plasticity. *Nat Rev Neurosci, 9*(5), 387. https://doi.org/10.1038/nrn2356

Abramson, C. I., & Calvo, P. (2018). General issues in the cognitive analysis of plant learning and intelligence. In F. Baluska, M. Gagliano, & G. Witzany (Eds.), *Memory and learning in plants* (pp. 35–49). Germany: Springer International Publishing.

Abramson, C. I., & Chicas-Mosier, A. M. (2016). Learning in plants: Lessons from *Mimosa pudica. Front Psychol, 7,* 417. https://doi.org/10.3389/fpsyg.2016.00417

Abudarham, N., Shkiller, L., & Yovel, G. (2019). Critical features for face recognition. *Cognition, 182,* 73–83. https://doi.org/10.1016/j.cognition.2018.09.002

Addyman, C., French, R. M., & Thomas, E. (2016). Computational models of interval timing. *Curr Opin Behav Sci, 8,* 140–146.

Adesnik, H., & Abdeladim, L. (2021). Probing neural codes with two-photon holographic optogenetics. *Nat Neurosci, 24*(10), 1356–1366. https://doi.org/10.1038/s41593-021-00902-9

Adler, M. J. (1967). *The difference of man and the difference it makes.* New York, NY: Holt Rhinehart.

Afrasiabi, M., Redinbaugh, M. J., Phillips, J. M., Kambi, N. A., Mohanta, S., Raz, A.,… Saalmann, Y. B. (2021). Consciousness depends on integration between parietal cortex, striatum, and thalamus. *Cell Syst, 12*(4), 363–373 e311. https://doi.org/10.1016/j.cels.2021.02.003

Agrillo, C., Parrish, A. E., & Beran, M. J. (2014). Do rhesus monkeys (*Macaca mulatta*) perceive the Zollner illusion? *Psychon Bull Rev, 21*(4), 986–994. https://doi.org/10.3758/s13423-013-0573-2

Ahn, W.-K., & Graham, L. M. (1999). The impact of necessity and sufficiency in the Wason four-card selection task. *Psychol Sci, 10,* 237–242.

Alaerts, K., Nackaerts, E., Meyns, P., Swinnen, S. P., & Wenderoth, N. (2011). Action and emotion recognition from point light displays: an investigation of gender differences. *PLoS One, 6*(6), e20989. https://doi.org/10.1371/journal.pone.0020989

Alais, D., & Burr, D. (2004). The ventriloquist effect results from near-optimal bimodal integration. *Curr Biol, 14*(3), 257–262. https://doi.org/10.1016/j.cub.2004.01.029

Alberini, C. M., & Travaglia, A. (2017). Infantile amnesia: A critical period of learning to learn and remember. *J Neurosci, 37*(24), 5783–5795. https://doi.org/10.1523/JNEUROSCI.0324-17.2017

Alberts, N. M., Law, E. F., Chen, A. T., Ritterband, L. M., & Palermo, T. M. (2018). Treatment engagement in an internet-delivered cognitive behavioral program for pediatric chronic pain. *Internet Interv, 13,* 67–72. https://doi.org/10.1016/j.invent.2018.07.005

Albuquerque, N., Mills, D. S., Guo, K., Wilkinson, A., & Resende, B. (2022). Dogs can infer implicit information from human emotional expressions. *Anim Cogn, 25*(2), 231–240. https://doi.org/10.1007/s10071-021-01544-x

Aleman, A., & de Haan, E. H. F. (2004). Fantasy proneness, mental imagery and reality monitoring. *Pers Individ Dif, 36,* 1747–1754.

Alexander, R. M. (2003). *Principles of Animal Locomotion.* NJ: Princeton University Press.

Alferink, L. A., Critchfield, T. S., Hitt, J. L., & Higgins, W. J. (2009). Generality of the matching law as a descriptor of shot selection in basketball. *J Appl Behav Anal, 42*(3), 595–608. https://doi.org/10.1901/jaba.2009.42-595

Allen, C. (2014). Umwelt or Umwelten? How should shared representation be understood given such diversity? *Semiotica, 198,* 137–158.

Allen, T. A., & Fortin, N. J. (2013). The evolution of episodic memory. *Proc Natl Acad Sci U S A, 110*(supplement 2), 10379–10386. https://doi.org/10.1073/pnas.1301199110

Allman, M. J., Teki, S., Griffiths, T. D., & Meck, W. H. (2014). Properties of the internal clock: first- and second-order principles of subjective time. *Annu Rev Psychol, 65,* 743–771. https://doi.org/10.1146/annurev-psych-010213-115117

Alzahabi, R., & Becker, M. W. (2013). The association between media multitasking, task-switching, and dual-task performance. *J Exp Psychol Hum Percept Perform, 39*(5), 1485–1495. https://doi.org/10.1037/a0031208

Andersen, R. A., & Bradley, D. C. (1998). Perception of three-dimensional structure from motion. *Trends Cogn Sci, 2*(6), 222–228. https://doi.org/10.1016/s1364-6613(98)01181-4

Andersen, R. A., Hwang, E. J., & Mulliken, G. H. (2010). Cognitive neural prosthetics. *Annu Rev Psychol, 61,* 169–190, C161–163. https://doi.org/10.1146/annurev.psych.093008.100503

Anderson, J. M., Clegg, T. M., Veras, L., & Holland, K. N. (2017). Insight into shark magnetic field perception from empirical observations. *Sci Rep, 7*(1), 11042. https://doi.org/10.1038/s41598-017-11459-8

Anderson, M. (1992). *Intelligence and development: A cognitive theory.* Hoboken, NJ: Blackwell.

Anderson, M. C., Ochsner, K. N., Kuhl, B., Cooper, J., Robertson, E., Gabrieli, S. W., Glover, G. H., & Gabrieli, J. D. (2004). Neural systems underlying the suppression of unwanted memories. *Science, 303*(5655), 232–235. https://doi.org/10.1126/science.1089504

Andrews, K. (2020a). *The animal mind: An introduction to the philosophy of animal cognition.* Routledge.

Andrews, K. (2020b). *How to study animal minds.* UK: Cambridge University Press.

Angell, J. R. (1909). The influence of Darwin on psychology. *Psychol Rev, 16,* 152–169.

Angioletti, L., Tormen, F., & Balconi, M. (2022). Judgment and embodied cognition of lawyers. Moral decision-making and interoceptive physiology in the legal field. *Front Psychol, 13,* 853342. https://doi.org/10.3389/fpsyg.2022.853342

Anvari, S. H., Trainor, L. J., Woodside, J., & Levy, B. A. (2002). Relations among musical skills, phonological processing, and early reading ability in preschool children. *J Exp Child Psychol, 83*(2), 111–130. https://www.ncbi.nlm.nih.gov/pubmed/12408958

Arbilly, M., & Laland, K. N. (2017). The magnitude of innovation and its evolution in social animals. *Proc R Soc B, 284*. https://doi.org/10.1098/rspb.2016.2385

Armah, A., & Landers-Potts, M. (2021). A review of imaginary companions and their implications for development. *Imagin Cogn Person, 41*, 31–53.

Ashby, F. G., & Maddox, W. T. (2011). Human category learning 2.0. *Ann N Y Acad Sci, 1224*, 147–161. https://doi.org/10.1111/j.1749-6632.2010.05874.x

Ashby, F. G., & Rosedahl, L. (2017). A neural interpretation of exemplar theory. *Psychol Rev, 124*(4), 472–482. https://doi.org/10.1037/rev0000064

Ashby, F. G., Alfonso-Reese, L. A., Turken, A. U., & Waldron, E. M. (1998). A neuropsychological theory of multiple systems in category learning. *Psychol Rev, 105*(3), 442–481. http://www.ncbi.nlm.nih.gov/pubmed/9697427

Atance, C. M., & O'Neill, D. K. (2001). Episodic future thinking. *Trends Cogn Sci, 5*(12), 533–539. https://doi.org/10.1016/s1364-6613(00)01804-0

Atherton, L. A., Dupret, D., & Mellor, J. R. (2015). Memory trace replay: The shaping of memory consolidation by neuromodulation. *Trends Neurosci, 38*(9), 560–570. https://doi.org/10.1016/j.tins.2015.07.004

Atkinson, R. C., & Shiffrin, R. M. (1968). Human memory: A proposed system and its control processes. In K. W. Spence & J. T. Spence (Eds.), *The psychology of learning and motivation* (Vol. 2, pp. 89–195). Cambridge, MA: Academic Press.

Aubin, T., & Jouventin. (2002). How to vocally identify kin in a crowd: The penguin model. *Adv Study Behav, 31*, 243–277.

Aubin, T., Jouventin, P., & Hildebrand, C. (2000). Penguins use the two-voice system to recognize each other. *Proc Biol Sci, 267*(1448), 1081–1087. https://doi.org/10.1098/rspb.2000.1112

Ayzenberg, V., & Behrmann, M. (2022). Does the brain's ventral visual pathway compute object shape? *Trends Cogn Sci, 26*(12), 1119–1132. https://doi.org/10.1016/j.tics.2022.09.019

Baciadonna, L., Cornero, F. M., Emery, N. J., & Clayton, N. S. (2021). Convergent evolution of complex cognition: Insights from the field of avian cognition into the study of self-awareness. *Learn Behav, 49*(1), 9–22. https://doi.org/10.3758/s13420-020-00434-5

B

Baddeley, A. (2000). The episodic buffer: a new component of working memory? *Trends Cogn Sci, 4*(11), 417–423. http://www.ncbi.nlm.nih.gov/pubmed/11058819

Baddeley, A. (2012). Working memory: theories, models, and controversies. *Annu Rev Psychol, 63*, 1–29. https://doi.org/10.1146/annurev-psych-120710-100422

Baddeley, A. D., & Longman, J. A. (1978). The influence of length and frequency of training session on the rate of learning to type. *Ergonomics, 21*, 627–635.

Baddeley, A., & Hitch, G. (1974). Working memory. *Psycho Learn Motiv, 8*, 47–89.

Badre, D., & Nee, D. E. (2018). Frontal cortex and the hierarchical control of behavior. *Trends Cogn Sci, 22*(2), 170–188. https://doi.org/10.1016/j.tics.2017.11.005

Bago, B., & De Neys, W. (2020). Advancing the specification of dual process models of higher cognition: a critical test of the hybrid model view. *Think Reason, 26*, 2020.

Baillargeon, R., Li, J., Gertner, Y., & Wu, D. (2011). How do infants reason about physical events? In U. Goswami (Ed.), *The Wiley-Blackwell handbook of childhood cognitive development* (pp. 11–48). Hoboken, NJ: Wiley Blackwell.

Baird, B., Mota-Rolim, S. A., & Dresler, M. (2019). The cognitive neuroscience of lucid dreaming. *Neurosci Biobehav Rev, 100*, 305–323. https://doi.org/10.1016/j.neubiorev.2019.03.008

Baird, B., Smallwood, J., Mrazek, M. D., Kam, J. W., Franklin, M. S., & Schooler, J. W. (2012). Inspired by distraction: mind wandering facilitates creative incubation. *Psychol Sci, 23*(10), 1117–1122. https://doi.org/10.1177/0956797612446024

Baird, B., Tononi, G., & LaBerge, S. (2022). Lucid dreaming occurs in activated rapid eye movement sleep, not a mixture of sleep and wakefulness. *Sleep, 45*(4). https://doi.org/10.1093/sleep/zsab294

Balaban, E., Teillet, M. A., & Le Douarin, N. (1988). Application of the quail-chick chimera system to the study of brain development and behavior. *Science, 241*(4871), 1339–1342. https://www.ncbi.nlm.nih.gov/pubmed/3413496

Balci, F. (2015). Interval timing behavior: Comparative and integrative approaches. *Int J Comp Psychol, 28*, 510.

Balconi, M., & Fronda, G. (2019). Physiological correlates of moral decision-making in the professional domain. *Brain Sci, 9*(9). https://doi.org/10.3390/brainsci9090229

Bale, T. L., Abel, T., Akil, H., Carlezon, W. A., Jr., Moghaddam, B., Nestler, E. J.,…Thompson, S. M. (2019). The critical importance of basic animal research for neuropsychiatric disorders. *Neuropsychopharmacology, 44*(8), 1349–1353. https://doi.org/10.1038/s41386-019-0405-9

Balleine, B. W., & Dezfouli, A. (2019). Hierarchical action control: Adaptive collaboration between actions and habits. *Front Psychol, 10*, 2735. https://doi.org/10.3389/fpsyg.2019.02735

Balleine, B. W., Liljeholm, M., & Ostlund, S. B. (2009). The integrative function of the basal ganglia in instrumental conditioning. *Behav Brain Res, 199*(1), 43–52. https://doi.org/10.1016/j.bbr.2008.10.034

Ballew, C. C., 2nd, & Todorov, A. (2007). Predicting political elections from rapid and unreflective face judgments. *Proc Natl Acad Sci U S A, 104*(46), 17948–17953. https://doi.org/10.1073/pnas.0705435104

Baluska, F., Gagliano, M., & Witzany, G. (Eds.). (2018). *Memory and learning in plants.* Springer International Publishing.

Baluska, F., & Levin, M. (2016). On having no head: Cognition throughout biological systems. *Front Psychol, 7*, 902. https://doi.org/10.3389/fpsyg.2016.00902

Bandini, E., & Tennie, C. (2020). Exploring the role of individual learning in animal tool-use. *PeerJ, 8*, e9877. https://doi.org/10.7717/peerj.9877

Bandura, A. (1977). *Social learning theory.* Prentice Hall.

Bandura, A., Ross, D., & Ross, S. A. (1961). Transmission of aggression through imitation of aggressive models. *J Abnorm Soc Psychol, 63*, 575–582. https://doi.org/10.1037/h0045925

Bandura, A., Ross, D., & Ross, S. A. (1963). Imitation of film-mediated aggressive models. *J Abnorm Soc Psychol, 66*, 3–11. https://doi.org/10.1037/h0048687

Bangerter, A., & Heath, C. (2004). The Mozart effect: Tracking the evolution of a scientific legend. *Br J Soc Psychol, 43*(Pt 4), 605–623. https://doi.org/10.1348/0144666042565353

Banich, M. T., & Compton, R. J. (2018). *Cognitive neuroscience.* UK: Cambridge University Press.

Barahona-Correa, J. B., Camacho, M., Castro-Rodrigues, P., Costa, R., & Oliveira-Maia, A. J. (2015). From thought to action: How the interplay between neuroscience and phenomenology changed our understanding of obsessive-compulsive disorder. *Front Psychol, 6*, 1798. https://doi.org/10.3389/fpsyg.2015.01798

Barnes, J. (1971). Aristotle's concept of mind. *Proc Aristot Soc, 72*, 101–114.

Baron-Cohen, S., Bor, D., Billington, J., Asher, J., Wheelwright, S., & Ashwin, C. (2007). Savant memory in a man with colour form-number synaesthesia and Asperger syndrome. *J Conscious Stud, 14*(9–10), 237–251.

Baron-Cohen, S., Burt, L., Smith-Laittan, F., Harrison, J., & Bolton, P. (1996). Synaesthesia: Prevalence and familiality. *Perception, 25*, 1073–1079.

Baron-Cohen, S., Leslie, A. M., & Frith, U. (1985). Does the autistic child have a "theory of mind"? *Cognition, 21*(1), 37–46. https://doi.org/10.1016/0010-0277(85)90022-8

Barrett, H. C. (2020). Towards a cognitive science of the human: Cross-cultural approaches and their urgency. *Trends Cogn Sci, 24*(8), 620–638. https://doi.org/10.1016/j.tics.2020.05.007

Barron, F., & Harrington, D. M. (1981). Creativity, intelligence, and personality. *Annu Rev Psychol, 32*, 439–476.

Bartsch, L. M., & Oberauer, K. (2021). The effects of elaboration on working memory and long-term memory across age. *J Mem Lang, 118*, 104215.

Bates, M. (2017). From brain to body: New technologies improve paralyzed patients? Quality of life. *IEEE Pulse, 8*(5), 22–26. https://doi.org/10.1109/MPUL.2017.2729411

Bateson, P. (2000). What must be known in order to understand imprinting? In C. Heyes & L. Huber (Eds.), *The evolution of cognition* (pp. 85–102). Cambridge, MA: MIT Press.

Beaty, R. E., Benedek, M., Silvia, P. J., & Schacter, D. L. (2016). Creative cognition and brain network dynamics. *Trends Cogn Sci, 20*(2), 87–95. https://doi.org/10.1016/j.tics.2015.10.004

Beaty, R. E., Kenett, Y. N., Christensen, A. P., Rosenberg, M. D., Benedek, M., Chen, Q.,... Silvia, P. J. (2018). Robust prediction of individual creative ability from brain functional connectivity. *Proc Natl Acad Sci U S A, 115*(5), 1087–1092. https://doi.org/10.1073/pnas.1713532115

Beaty, R. E., Seli, P., & Schacter, D. L. (2019). Network neuroscience of creative cognition: Mapping cognitive mechanisms and individual differences in the creative brain. *Curr Opin Behav Sci, 27*, 22–30. https://doi.org/10.1016/j.cobeha.2018.08.013

Bellmund, J. L. S., Gardenfors, P., Moser, E. I., & Doeller, C. F. (2010). Navigating cognition: Spatial codes for human thinking. *Science, 362*. https://doi.org/10.1126/science.aat6766

Beloe, P., & Derakshan, N. (2020). Adaptive working memory training can reduce anxiety and depression vulnerability in adolescents. *Dev Sci, 23*(4), e12831. https://doi.org/10.1111/desc.12831

Benedek, M., & Fink, A. (2019). Toward a neurocognitive framework of creative cognition: the role of memory, attention, and cognitive control. *Curr Opin Behav Sci, 27*, 116–122.

Benhamou, S. (2010). Orientation and navigation. *Encyclopedia of Behavioral Neuroscience, 2*, 497–503.

Benjamin, A. S., & Tullis, J. (2010). What makes distributed practice effective? *Cogn Psychol, 61*(3), 228–247. https://doi.org/10.1016/j.cogpsych.2010.05.004

Beran, M. J., & Beran, M. M. (2004). Chimpanzees remember the results of one-by-one addition of food items to sets over extended time periods. *Psychol Sci, 15*, 94–99. https://doi.org/10.1111/j.0963-7214.2004.01502004.x

Beran, M. J., Brandl, J. L., Perner, J., & Proust, J. (Eds.). (2012). *Foundations of metacognition.* New York, NY: Oxford University Press.

Beran, M. J., Menzel, C. R., Parrish, A. E., Perdue, B. M., Sayers, K., Smith, J. D., & Washburn, D. A. (2016). Primate cognition: Attention, episodic memory, prospective memory, self-control, and metacognition as examples of cognitive control in nonhuman primates. *Wiley Interdiscip Rev Cogn Sci, 7*(5), 294–316. https://doi.org/10.1002/wcs.1397

Berardi-Coletta, B., Buyer, L. S., Dominowski, R. L., & Rellinger, E. R. (1995). Metacognition and problem solving: A process-oriented approach. *J Exp Psychol: Learn Mem Cogn, 21*, 205–223.

Berent, I. (2021). Can we get human nature right? *Proc Natl Acad Sci U S A, 118*(39). https://doi.org/10.1073/pnas.2108274118

Berliere, M., Roelants, F., Watremez, C., Docquier, M. A., Piette, N., Lamerant, S., Megevand, V.,...Duhoux, F. P. (2018). The advantages of hypnosis intervention on breast cancer surgery and adjuvant therapy. *Breast, 37*, 114–118. https://doi.org/10.1016/j.breast.2017.10.017

Berlingeri, M., Magnani, F. G., Salvato, G., Rosanova, M., & Bottini, G. (2019). Neuroimaging studies on disorders of consciousness: A meta-analytic evaluation. *J Clin Med, 8*(4). https://doi.org/10.3390/jcm8040516

Bernecker, S. (2017). A causal theory of mnemonic confabulation. *Front Psychol, 8*, 1207. https://doi.org/10.3389/fpsyg.2017.01207

Bernstein, J. G., & Boyden, E. S. (2011). Optogenetic tools for analyzing the neural circuits of behavior. *Trends Cogn Sci, 15*(12), 592–600. https://doi.org/10.1016/j.tics.2011.10.003

Berridge, K. C. (2018). Evolving concepts of emotion and motivation. *Front Psychol, 9*, 1647. https://doi.org/10.3389/fpsyg.2018.01647

Berridge, K. C., Robinson, T. E., & Aldridge, J. W. (2009). Dissecting components of reward: 'liking', 'wanting', and learning. *Curr Opin Pharmacol, 9*(1), 65–73. https://doi.org/10.1016/j.coph.2008.12.014

Bhatt, R. S., & Wasserman, E. A. (1989). Secondary generalization and categorization in pigeons. *J Exp Anal Behav, 52*(3), 213–224. http://www.ncbi.nlm.nih.gov/pubmed/16812595

Bialystok, E. (2017). The bilingual adaptation: How minds accommodate experience. *Psychol Bull, 143*(3), 233–262. https://doi.org/10.1037/bul0000099

Biasiucci, A., Franceschiello, B., & Murray, M. M. (2019). Electroencephalography. *Curr Biol, 29*(3), R80-R85. https://doi.org/10.1016/j.cub.2018.11.052

Biederman, I. (1987). Recognition-by-components: A theory of human image understanding. *Psychol Rev, 94*(2), 115–147. https://doi.org/10.1037/0033-295X.94.2.115

Bilge, A. R., & Taylor, H. A. (2017). Framing the figure: Mental rotation revisited in light of cognitive strategies. *Mem Cognit, 45*(1), 63–80. https://doi.org/10.3758/s13421-016-0648-1

Billock, V. A., & Tsou, B. H. (2010). Seeing forbidden colors. *Sci Am, 302*(2), 72–77. https://doi.org/10.1038/scientific american0210-72

Bilquise, G., Ibrahim, S., & Shaalan, K. (2022). Emotionally intelligent chatbots: A systematic literature review. *Hum Behav Emerg Technol, 2022*, 9601630.

Birch, J., Schnell, A. K., & Clayton, N. S. (2020). Dimensions of Animal Consciousness. *Trends Cogn Sci, 24*(10), 789–801. https://doi.org /10.1016/j.tics.2020.07.007

Bishop, D. V. (2009). Genes, cognition, and communication: Insights from neurodevelopmental disorders. *Ann N Y Acad Sci, 1156*(1), 1–18. https://doi.org/10.1111/j.1749-6632.2009.04419.x

Blach, R. W., Farnsworht, G., & Wilkins, S. (1983). When the bombs drop: Reactions to disconfirmed prophecy in a millenial sect. *Sociological perspectives, 26*, 137–158.

Blackmer, E. R., & Mitton, J. L. (1991). Theories of monitoring and the timing of repairs in spontaneous speech. *Cognition, 39*(3), 173–194. https://doi.org/10.1016/0010 -0277(91)90052-6

Blake, A. (2017). TSA failed to detect 95 percent of prohibited items at Minneapolis airport: Report. *The Washington Times*.

Blakemore, C., Movshon, J. A., & Van Sluyters, R. C. (1978). Modifica-tion of the kitten's visual cortex by exposure to spatially periodic patterns. *Exp Brain Res, 31*(4), 561–572. https://doi.org /10.1007/BF00239812

Blanch, A. (2020). *Chess and individual differences*. UK: Cambridge University Press.

Block, N. (2023). *The border between seeing and thinking*. New York, NY: New York, NY: Oxford University Press.

Block, R. A., & Gruber, R. P. (2014). Time perception, attention, and memory: A selective review. *Acta Psychol (Amst), 149*, 129–133. https://doi.org/10.1016/j.actpsy.2013.11.003

Bludau, A., Royer, M., Meister, G., Neumann, I. D., & Menon, R. (2019). Epigenetic Regulation of the Social Brain. *Trends Neurosci, 42*(7), 471–484. https://doi.org/10.1016/j.tins.2019.04.001

Blunt, J. R., & VanArsdall, J. E. (2021). Animacy and animate imagery improve retention in the method of loci among novice users. *Mem Cognit, 49*(7), 1360–1369. https://doi.org/10.3758/s13421 -021-01175-0

Bock, K. (1995). *Sentence production: From mind to mouth*. Cambridge, MA: Academic Press.

Boden, M. A. (2004). *The creative mind: Myths and mechanisms*. London, UK: Psychology Press.

Boekaerts, M. (1995). Self-regulated learning: Bridging the gap between metacognitive and metamotivation theories. *Educational Psychologist, 30*, 195–200.

Boesch, C., Bombjakova, D., Meier, A., & Mundry, R. (2019). Learning curves and teaching when acquiring nut-cracking in humans and chimpanzees. *Sci Rep, 9*(1), 1515. https://doi.org/10.1038 /s41598-018-38392-8

Bolhuis, J. J., Brown, G. R., Richardson, R. C., & Laland, K. N. (2011). Darwin in mind: New opportunities for evolutionary psychol-ogy. *PLoS Biol, 9*(7), e1001109. https://doi.org/10.1371/journal .pbio.1001109

Bolhuis, J. J., Crain, S., & Roberts, I. (2023). Language and learning: The cognitive revolution at 60-odd. *Biol Rev Camb Philos Soc*. https://doi.org/10.1111/brv.12936

Bond, C. F., Jr., & Titus, L. J. (1983). Social facilitation: A meta-analysis of 241 studies. *Psychol Bull, 94*(2), 265–292. https://www.ncbi .nlm.nih.gov/pubmed/6356198

Bookbinder, J., & Osman, E. (1979). Attentional strategies in dichotic listening. *Memory & Cognition, 7*, 511–520.

Borghi, A. M., Binkofski, F., Castelfranchi, C., Cimatti, F., Scorolli, C., & Tummolini, L. (2017). The challenge of abstract concepts. *Psychol Bull, 143*(3), 263–292. https://doi.org/10.1037 /bul0000089

Boring, E. G. (1953). A history of introspection. *Psychol Bull, 50*(3), 169–189. https://doi.org/10.1037/h0090793

Borjigin, J., Lee, U., Liu, T., Pal, D., Huff, S., Klarr, D., … Mashour, G. A. (2013). Surge of neurophysiological coherence and connectivity in the dying brain. *Proc Natl Acad Sci U S A, 110*(35), 14432– 14437. https://doi.org/10.1073/pnas.1308285110

Borrero, J. C., Crisolo, S. S., Tu, Q., Rieland, W. A., Ross, N. A., Francisco, M. T., & Yamamoto, K. Y. (2007). An application of the matching law to social dynamics. *J Appl Behav Anal, 40*(4), 589–601. https://doi.org/10.1901/jaba.2007.589-601

Borst, G., & Kosslyn, S. M. (2008). Visual mental imagery and visual perception: Structural equivalence revealed by scanning processes. *Mem Cognit, 36*(4), 849–862. https://doi.org/10.3758 /mc.36.4.849

Bos, A. P. (2009). Aristotle on the soul and soul-'parts' in semen (GA 2.1 735a4–22). *Mnemosyne, 62*, 378–400.

Bossaerts, P., & Murawski, C. (2017). Computational complexity and human decision-making. *Trends Cogn Sci, 21*(12), 917–929. https://doi.org/10.1016/j.tics.2017.09.005

Botvinick, M., & Braver, T. (2015). Motivation and cognitive control: From behavior to neural mechanism. *Annu Rev Psychol, 66*, 83–113. https://doi.org/10.1146/annurev-psych -010814-015044

Bouchard, T. J. (2013). The Wilson Effect: The increase in heritability of IQ with age. *Twin Res Hum Genet, 16*(5), 923–930. https://doi .org/10.1017/thg.2013.54

Bouton, M. E., Maren, S., & McNally, G. P. (2021). Behavioral and neurobiological mechanisms of Pavlovian and instrumental extinction learning. *Physiol Rev, 101*(2), 611–681. https://doi.org /10.1152/physrev.00016.2020

Bowden, E. M., Jung-Beeman, M., Fleck, J., & Kounios, J. (2005). New approaches to demystifying insight. *Trends Cogn Sci, 9*(7), 322–328. https://doi.org/10.1016/j.tics.2005.05.012

Bower, G. H. (1981). Mood and memory. *Am Psychol, 36*(2), 129–148. http://www.ncbi.nlm.nih.gov/pubmed/7224324

Bower, G. H., Karlin, M. B., & Dueck, A. (1975). Comprehension and memory for pictures. *Mem Cognit, 3*(2), 216–220. https://doi.org /10.3758/BF03212900

Bowers, J. S., & Pleydell-Pearce, C. W. (2011). Swearing, euphemisms, and linguistic relativity. *PLoS One, 6*(7), e22341. https://doi.org /10.1371/journal.pone.0022341

Boyer, J. L., Harrison, S., & Ro, T. (2005). Unconscious processing of orientation and color without primary visual cortex. *Proc Natl Acad Sci U S A, 102*(46), 16875–16879. https://doi.org/10.1073 /pnas.0505332102

Boysen, S. T., Bernston, G. G., Hannan, M. B., & Cacioppo, J. T. (1996). Quantity-based interference and symbolic representations in chimpanzees (*Pan troglodytes*). *J Exp Psychol Anim Behav Process, 22*, 76–86.

Braem, S., & Egner, T. (2018). Getting a grip on cognitive flexibility. *Curr Dir Psychol Sci, 27*(6), 470–476. https://doi.org/10.1177/0963721418787475

Braithwaite, D. W., & Goldstone, R. L. (2015). Effects of variation and prior knowledge on abstract concept learning. *Cognition and Instruction, 33*, 3.

Branch, C. L., Semenov, G. A., Wagner, D. N., Sonnenberg, B. R., Pitera, A. M., Bridge, E. S.,…Pravosudov, V. V. (2022). The genetic basis of spatial cognitive variation in a food-caching bird. *Curr Biol, 32*(1), 210–219 e214. https://doi.org/10.1016/j.cub.2021.10.036

Brandt, J., & Bakker, A. (2018). Neuropsychological investigation of "the amazing memory man." *Neuropsychology, 32*(3), 304–316. https://doi.org/10.1037/neu0000410

Branstetter, B. K., Finneran, J. J., Fletcher, E. A., Weisman, B. C., & Ridgway, S. H. (2012). Dolphins can maintain vigilant behavior through echolocation for 15 days without interruption or cognitive impairment. *PLoS One, 7*(10), e47478. https://doi.org/10.1371/journal.pone.0047478

Brass, M., Derrfuss, J., Matthes-von Cramon, G., & von Cramon, D. Y. (2003). Imitative response tendencies in patients with frontal brain lesions. *Neuropsychology, 17*(2), 265–271. https://doi.org/10.1037/0894-4105.17.2.265

Bratman, M. E. (1992). Practical reasoning and acceptance in context. *Mind, 101*, 1–15.

Braver, T. S. (2012). The variable nature of cognitive control: A dual mechanisms framework. *Trends Cogn Sci, 16*(2), 106–113. https://doi.org/10.1016/j.tics.2011.12.010

Bregman, A. S. (1994). *Auditory scene analysis: The perceptual organization of sound.* Cambridge, MA: MIT Press.

Bremner, A. J., Caparos, S., Davidoff, J., de Fockert, J., Linnell, K. J., & Spence, C. (2013). "Bouba" and "Kiki" in Namibia? A remote culture make similar shape-sound matches, but different shape-taste matches to Westerners. *Cognition, 126*(2), 165–172. https://doi.org/10.1016/j.cognition.2012.09.007

Bressler, S. L., & Kelso, J. A. (2001). Cortical coordination dynamics and cognition. *Trends Cogn Sci, 5*(1), 26–36. https://doi.org/10.1016/s1364-6613(00)01564-3

Broadbent, D. E. (1958). *Perception and communication.* Pergamon Press.

Brochard, R., Dufour, A., & Despres, O. (2004). Effect of musical expertise on visuospatial abilities: Evidence from reaction times and mental imagery. *Brain Cogn, 54*(2), 103–109. https://doi.org/10.1016/S0278-2626(03)00264-1

Broomer, M. C., & Bouton, M. E. (2022). A comparison of renewal, spontaneous recovery, and reacquisition after punishment and extinction. *Learn Behav.* https://doi.org/10.3758/s13420-022-00552-2

Brosnan, S. F., & De Waal, F. B. (2003). Monkeys reject unequal pay. *Nature, 425*(6955), 297–299. https://doi.org/10.1038/nature01963

Brown, R. E. (2020). Donald O. Hebb and the Organization of Behavior: 17 years in the writing. *Mol Brain, 13*(1), 55. https://doi.org/10.1186/s13041-020-00567-8

Brown, R. E., & Milner, P. M. (2003). The legacy of Donald O. Hebb: More than the Hebb synapse. *Nat Rev Neurosci, 4*(12), 1013–1019. https://doi.org/10.1038/nrn1257

Brownell, C. A. (2011). Early developments in joint action. *Rev Philos Psychol, 2*(2), 193–211. https://doi.org/10.1007/s13164-011-0056-1

Bruce, V., & Young, A. (1986). Understanding face recognition. *Br J Psychol, 77 (Pt 3)*, 305–327. https://doi.org/10.1111/j.2044-8295.1986.tb02199.x

Brunec, I. K., Robin, J., Olsen, R. K., Moscovitch, M., & Barense, M. D. (2020). Integration and differentiation of hippocampal memory traces. *Neurosci Biobehav Rev, 118*, 196–208. https://doi.org/10.1016/j.neubiorev.2020.07.024

Bruner, J. S. (1965). The growth of mind. *Am Psychol, 20*(12), 1007–1017. https://doi.org/10.1037/h0023276

Bucher, B., Kuroshima, H., Anderson, J. R., & Fujita, K. (2021). On experimental tests for studying altruism in capuchin monkeys. *Behav Processes, 189*, 104424. https://doi.org/10.1016/j.beproc.2021.104424

Bugnyar, T., Reber, S. A., & Buckner, C. (2016). Ravens attribute visual access to unseen competitors. *Nat Commun, 7*, 10506. https://doi.org/10.1038/ncomms10506

Buhusi, C. V., & Meck, W. H. (2005). What makes us tick? Functional and neural mechanisms of interval timing. *Nat Rev Neurosci, 6*(10), 755–765. https://doi.org/10.1038/nrn1764

Buolamwini, J., & Gebru, T. (2018). Gender shades: Intersectional accuracy disparities in commercial gender classification. In *Conference on fairness, accountability, and transparency*, pp 77–91.

Burgess, N., Maguire, E. A., & O'Keefe, J. (2002). The human hippocampus and spatial and episodic memory. *Neuron, 35*(4), 625–641. https://doi.org/10.1016/s0896-6273(02)00830-9

Bushman, B. J., & Huesmann, L. R. (2006). Short-term and long-term effects of violent media on aggression in children and adults. *Arch Pediatr Adolesc Med, 160*(4), 348–352. https://doi.org/10.1001/archpedi.160.4.348

Buxbaum, L. J., Ferraro, M. K., Veramonti, T., Farne, A., Whyte, J., Ladavas, E., Frassinetti, F., & Coslett, H. B. (2004). Hemispatial neglect: Subtypes, neuroanatomy, and disability. *Neurology, 62*(5), 749–756. https://doi.org/10.1212/01.wnl.0000113730.73031.f4

Buzsaki, G. (2006). *Rhythms of the brain.* New York, NY: Oxford University Press.

C

Cai, W., Ryali, S., Pasumarthy, R., Talasila, V., & Menon, V. (2021). Dynamic causal brain circuits during working memory and their functional controllability. *Nat Commun, 12*(1), 3314. https://doi.org/10.1038/s41467-021-23509-x

Caird, J. K., Johnston, K. A., Willness, C. R., Asbridge, M., & Steel, P. (2014). A meta-analysis of the effects of texting on driving. *Accid Anal Prev, 71*, 311–318. https://doi.org/10.1016/j.aap.2014.06.005

Caligiore, D., Arbib, M. A., Miall, R. C., & Baldassarre, G. (2019). The super-learning hypothesis: Integrating learning processes across cortex, cerebellum and basal ganglia. *Neurosci Biobehav Rev, 100*, 19–34. https://doi.org/10.1016/j.neubiorev.2019.02.008

Calvo-Merino, B., Grezes, J., Glaser, D. E., Passingham, R. E., & Haggard, P. (2006). Seeing or doing? Influence of visual and motor familiarity in action observation. *Curr Biol, 16*(19), 1905–1910. https://doi.org/10.1016/j.cub.2006.07.065

Camerer, C. (1999). Behavioral economics: Reunifying psychology and economics. *Proc Natl Acad Sci U S A, 96*(19), 10575–10577. https://doi.org/10.1073/pnas.96.19.10575

Campanario, J. M. (2010). The parallelism between scientists' and students' resistance to new scientific ideas. *Intl J Sci Educ, 24*, 1095–1110.

Cannon, W. B. (1931). Against the James-Lange and the thalamic theories of emotion. *Psychol Rev, 38*, 281–295.

Cantor, M., Farine, D. R., & Daura-Jorge, F. G. (2023). Foraging synchrony drives resilience in human-dolphin mutualism. *Proc Natl Acad Sci U S A, 120*(6), e2207739120. https://doi.org/10.1073/pnas.2207739120

Capozzi, F., & Ristic, J. (2022). Attentional gaze dynamics in group interactions. *Visual Cognition, 30*, 135–150.

Cardoso-Leite, P., & Bavelier, D. (2014). Video game play, attention, and learning: How to shape the development of attention and influence learning? *Curr Opin Neurol, 27*(2), 185–191. https://doi.org/10.1097/WCO.0000000000000077

Carey, S., & Barner, D. (2019). Ontogenetic origins of human integer representations. *Trends Cogn Sci, 23*(10), 823–835. https://doi.org/10.1016/j.tics.2019.07.004

Carey, S., & Bartlett, E. (1978). Acquiring a single new word. *Proc Stanford Child Lang Conf, 15*, 17–29.

Carey, S., & Gelman, R. (Eds.). (1991). *The epigenesis of mind: Essays on biology and cognition.* Mahwah, NJ: Lawrence Erlbaum.

Carlile, S. (2014). The plastic ear and perceptual relearning in auditory spatial perception. *Front Neurosci, 8*, 237. https://doi.org/10.3389/fnins.2014.00237

Carpenter, S. K., Pan, S. C., & Butler, A. C. (2022). The science of effective learning with spacing and retrieval practice. *Nat Rev Psychol, 1*, 496–511.

Carruthers, P. (2002). The cognitive functions of language. *Behav Brain Sci, 25*(6), 657–674; discussion 674–725. https://doi.org/10.1017/s0140525x02000122

Carruthers, P. (2005). The case for massively modular models of mind. In R. Stainton (Ed.), *Contemporary debates in cognitive science* (pp. 205–225). Hoboken, NJ: Blackwell.

Carruthers, P. (2013). Animal minds are real (distinctively), human minds are not. *Am Philos Q, 50*, 233–248.

Castro, L., & Rachlin, H. (1980). Self-reward, self-monitoring, and self-punishment as feedback in weight control. *Behav Ther, 11*, 38–48.

Castro, L., Savic, O., Navarro, V., Sloutsky, V. M., & Wasserman, E. A. (2020). Selective and distributed attention in human and pigeon category learning. *Cognition, 204*, 104350. https://doi.org/10.1016/j.cognition.2020.104350

Cavanagh, P., & Alvarez, G. A. (2005). Tracking multiple targets with multifocal attention. *Trends Cogn Sci, 9*(7), 349–354. https://doi.org/10.1016/j.tics.2005.05.009

Celeghin, A., Diano, M., Bagnis, A., Viola, M., & Tamietto, M. (2017). Basic emotions in human neuroscience: Neuroimaging and beyond. *Front Psychol, 8*, 1432. https://doi.org/10.3389/fpsyg.2017.01432

Chang, A. D., Vaidya, P. V., Retzbach, E. P., Chung, S. J., Kim, U., Baselice, K.,... Reti, I. M. (2018). Narp mediates

antidepressant-like effects of electroconvulsive seizures. *Neuropsychopharmacology, 43*, 1088–1098. https://doi.org/10.1038/npp.2017.252

Chang, D. H., Harris, L. R., & Troje, N. F. (2010). Frames of reference for biological motion and face perception. *J Vis, 10*(6), 22. https://doi.org/10.1167/10.6.22

Chang, E., Kim, H. T., & Yoo, B. (2020). Virtual reality sickness: A review of causes and measurements. *Int J Hum Comput Interact, 36*, 1658–1682.

Chang, S. W., Barack, D. L., & Platt, M. L. (2012). Mechanistic classification of neural circuit dysfunctions: Insights from neuroeconomics research in animals. *Biol Psychiatry, 72*(2), 101–106. https://doi.org/10.1016/j.biopsych.2012.02.017

Charness, N., Tuffiash, M., Krampe, R., Reingold, E., & Vasyukova, E. (2005). The role of deliberate practice in chess expertise. *Appl Cogn Psychol, 19*, 151–165.

Chater, N., & Christiansen, M. H. (2018). Language acquisition as skill learning. *Curr Opin Behav Sci, 21*, 205–208.

Chater, N., Oaksford, M., Hahn, U., & Heit, E. (2010). Bayesian models of cognition. *Wiley Interdiscip Rev Cogn Sci, 1*(6), 811–823. https://doi.org/10.1002/wcs.79

Chavez, R. A. (2016). Imagery as a core process in the creativity of successful and awarded artists and scientists and its neurobiological correlates. *Front Psychol, 7*, 351. https://doi.org/10.3389/fpsyg.2016.00351

Chen, P. J., Awata, H., Matsushita, A., Yang, E. C., & Arikawa, K. (2016). Extreme spectral richness in the eye of the common bluebottle butterfly, *Graphium sarpedon. Front Ecol Evol, 4*, 18.

Cherry, E. C. (1953). Experiments on the recognition of speech with one and two ears. *J Acoust Soc Am, 25*, 975.

Chib, V. S., Rangel, A., Shimojo, S., & O'Doherty, J. P. (2009). Evidence for a common representation of decision values for dissimilar goods in human ventromedial prefrontal cortex. *J Neurosci, 29*(39), 12315–12320. https://doi.org/10.1523/JNEUROSCI.2575-09.2009

Chiesa, A., Calati, R., & Serretti, A. (2011). Does mindfulness training improve cognitive abilities? A systematic review of neuropsychological findings. *Clin Psychol Rev, 31*(3), 449–464. https://doi.org/10.1016/j.cpr.2010.11.003

Chomsky, N. (1959). Review of B. F. Skinner, Verbal Behavior. *Language, 32*, 26–58.

Chomsky, N. (1975). *Reflections on language.* New York, NY: Random House.

Chomsky, N. (2002). *On nature and language.* UK: Cambridge University Press.

Chomsky, N. (2017). The language capacity: Architecture and evolution. *Psychon Bull Rev, 24*(1), 200–203. https://doi.org/10.3758/s13423-016-1078-6

Chong, T. T., Cunnington, R., Williams, M. A., Kanwisher, N., & Mattingley, J. B. (2008). fMRI adaptation reveals mirror neurons in human inferior parietal cortex. *Curr Biol, 18*(20), 1576–1580. https://doi.org/10.1016/j.cub.2008.08.068

Christian, K. M., & Thompson, R. F. (2003). Neural substrates of eyeblink conditioning: Acquisition and retention. *Learn Mem, 10*(6), 427–455. https://doi.org/10.1101/lm.59603

Chrysikou, E. G. (2019). Creativity in and out of (cognitive) control. *Curr Opin Behav Sci, 27*, 94–99.

Chu, J., & Schulz, L. E. (2020). Play, curiosity, and cognition. *Annu Rev Dev Psychol, 2*, 317–343.

Chung, C., Shin, W., & Kim, E. (2022). Early and late corrections in mouse models of autism spectrum disorder. *Biol Psychiatry, 91*(11), 934–944. https://doi.org/10.1016/j.biopsych.2021.07.021

Church, B. A., Krauss, M. S., Lopata, C., Toomey, J. A., Thomeer, M. L., Coutinho, M. V.,…Mercado, E., 3rd. (2010). Atypical categorization in children with high-functioning autism spectrum disorder. *Psychon Bull Rev, 17*(6), 862–868. https://doi.org/10.3758/PBR.17.6.862

Church, B. A., Mercado, E., Wisniewski, M. G., & Liu, E. H. (2013). Temporal dynamics in auditory perceptual learning: Impact of sequencing and incidental learning. *J Exp Psychol Learn Mem Cogn, 39*(1), 270–276. https://doi.org/10.1037/a0028647

Church, R. M. (1963). The varied effects of punishment on behavior. *Psychol Rev, 70*, 369–402. https://doi.org/10.1037/h0046499

Churchland, P. S., & Sejnowski, T. J. (1992). *The computational brain.* Cambridge, MA: MIT Press.

Cialdini, R. B., & Goldstein, N. J. (2004). Social influence: Compliance and conformity. *Annu Rev Psychol, 55*, 591–621. https://doi.org/10.1146/annurev.psych.55.090902.142015

Cienki, A. (2022). The study of gesture in cognitive linguistics: How it could inform and inspire other research in cognitive science. *Wiley Interdiscip Rev Cogn Sci, 13*(6), e1623. https://doi.org/10.1002/wcs.1623

Citraro, S., Vitevitch, M. S., Stella, M., & Rossetti, G. (2023). Feature-rich multiplex lexical networks reveal mental strategies of early language learning. *Sci Rep, 13*(1), 1474. https://doi.org/10.1038/s41598-022-27029-6

Clark, A., & Chalmers, D. (1998). The extended mind. *Analysis, 58*, 7–19.

Clark, L., Bechara, A., Damasio, H., Aitken, M. R., Sahakian, B. J., & Robbins, T. W. (2008). Differential effects of insular and ventromedial prefrontal cortex lesions on risky decision-making. *Brain, 131*(Pt 5), 1311–1322. https://doi.org/10.1093/brain/awn066

Clark, R. E., Manns, J. R., & Squire, L. R. (2002). Classical conditioning, awareness, and brain systems. *Trends Cogn Sci, 6*(12), 524–531. https://doi.org/10.1016/s1364-6613(02)02041-7

Clark, R. E., & Squire, L. R. (2013). Similarity in form and function of the hippocampus in rodents, monkeys, and humans. *Proc Natl Acad Sci U S A, 110* (supplement 2), 10365–10370. https://doi.org/10.1073/pnas.1301225110

Clayton, M. (2012). What is entrainment? Definition and applications in musical research. *Empir Musicol Rev, 7*, 49–56.

Cleary, A. M., Brown, A. S., Sawyer, B. D., Nomi, J. S., Ajoku, A. C., & Ryals, A. J. (2012). Familiarity from the configuration of objects in 3-dimensional space and its relation to deja vu: A virtual reality investigation. *Conscious Cogn, 21*(2), 969–975. https://doi.org/10.1016/j.concog.2011.12.010

Clerkin, E. M., Hart, E., Rehg, J. M., Yu, C., & Smith, L. B. (2017). Real-world visual statistics and infants' first-learned object names. *Philos Trans R Soc Lond B Biol Sci, 372*(1711), https://doi.org/10.1098/rstb.2016.0055

Cocchi, L., Zalesky, A., Fornito, A., & Mattingley, J. B. (2013). Dynamic cooperation and competition between brain systems during cognitive control. *Trends Cogn Sci, 17*(10), 493–501. https://doi.org/10.1016/j.tics.2013.08.006

Cockburn, J. (1995). Performance on the Tower of London test after severe head injury. *J Int Neuropsychol Soc, 1*(6), 537–544. https://doi.org/10.1017/s1355617700000667

Cohen, L. B., Chaput, H. H., & Cashon, C. H. (2002). A constructivist model of infant cognition. *Cognitive Development, 17*, 132–1343.

Cohen, M. R., & Maunsell, J. H. (2009). Attention improves performance primarily by reducing interneuronal correlations. *Nat Neurosci, 12*(12), 1594–1600. https://doi.org/10.1038/nn.2439

Coll, S. Y., Glauser, A., & Grandjean, D. (2019). Timing is crucial for the integration of angry facial expressions with motor responses: Investigation of subliminal and supraliminal emotion-action bindings. *Emotion, 19*(3), 543–557. https://doi.org/10.1037/emo0000457

Collinger, J. L., Kryger, M. A., Barbara, R., Betler, T., Bowsher, K., Brown, E. H.,…Boninger, M. L. (2014). Collaborative approach in the development of high-performance brain-computer interfaces for a neuroprosthetic arm: Translation from animal models to human control. *Clin Transl Sci, 7*(1), 52–59. https://doi.org/10.1111/cts.12086

Collins, A. M., & Qulillian, M. R. (1969). Retrieval time from semantic memory. *J Verbal Learning Verbal Behav, 8*, 240–247.

Collins, D. W., & Kimura, D. (1997). A large sex difference on a two-dimensional mental rotation task. *Behav Neurosci, 111*(4), 845–849. https://doi.org/10.1037//0735-7044.111.4.845

Coltheart, M. (1999). Modularity and cognition. *Trends Cogn Sci, 3*(3), 115–120. https://doi.org/10.1016/s1364-6613(99)01289-9

Conway, A. R., Kane, M. J., & Engle, R. W. (2003). Working memory capacity and its relation to general intelligence. *Trends Cogn Sci, 7*(12), 547–552. https://doi.org/10.1016/j.tics.2003.10.005

Cook, P., & Wilson, M. (2010). Do young chimpanzees have extraordinary working memory? *Psychon Bull Rev, 17*(4), 599–600. https://doi.org/10.3758/PBR.17.4.599

Cook, R., Bird, G., Catmur, C., Press, C., & Heyes, C. (2014). Mirror neurons: From origin to function. *Behav Brain Sci, 37*(2), 177–192. https://doi.org/10.1017/S0140525×13000903

Cook, S. W., & Tanenhaus, M. K. (2009). Embodied communication: Speakers' gestures affect listeners' actions. *Cognition, 113*(1), 98–104. https://doi.org/10.1016/j.cognition.2009.06.006

Cooke, S. F., & Bliss, T. V. (2003). The genetic enhancement of memory. *Cell Mol Life Sci, 60*(1), 1–5. https://doi.org/10.1007/s000180300000

Cooper, L. A., & Shepard, R. N. (1973). Chronometric studies of the rotation of mental images. In W. G. Chase (Ed.), *Visual information processing* (pp. 75–176). Cambridge, MA: Academic Press.

Corbetta, M. (2014). Hemispatial neglect: Clinic, pathogenesis, and treatment. *Semin Neurol, 34*(5), 514–523. https://doi.org/10.1055/s-0034-1396005

Corbetta, M., & Shulman, G. L. (2011). Spatial neglect and attention networks. *Annu Rev Neurosci, 34*, 569–599. https://doi.org/10.1146/annurev-neuro-061010-113731

Corkin, S. (2002). What's new with the amnesic patient H.M.? *Nat Rev Neurosci, 3*(2), 153–160. https://doi.org/10.1038/nrn726

Coslett, H. B., Wiener, M., & Chatterjee, A. (2010). Dissociable neural systems for timing: Evidence from subjects with basal ganglia lesions. *PLoS One, 5*, e10324. https://doi.org/10.1371/journal.pone.0010324

Cosmides, L., & Tooby, J. (1997). *Evolutionary psychology: A primer.* Santa Barbara, CA: Center for Evolutionary Psychology.

Costello, F., & Watts, P. (2019). The rationality of illusory correlation. *Psychol Rev, 126*(3), 437–450. https://doi.org/10.1037/rev0000130

Coubard, O. A., Duretz, S., Lefebvre, V., Lapalus, P., & Ferrufino, L. (2011). Practice of contemporary dance improves cognitive flexibility in aging. *Front Aging Neurosci, 3*, 13. https://doi.org/10.3389/fnagi.2011.00013

Courtney, S. M., Petit, L., Maisog, J. M., Ungerleider, L. G., & Haxby, J. V. (1998). An area specialized for spatial working memory in human frontal cortex. *Science, 279*(5355), 1347–1351. https://doi.org/10.1126/science.279.5355.1347

Cowan, E. T., Schapiro, A. C., Dunsmoor, J. E., & Murty, V. P. (2021). Memory consolidation as an adaptive process. *Psychon Bull Rev, 28*(6), 1796–1810. https://doi.org/10.3758/s13423-021-01978-x

Cowan, N. (1999). An embedded-process model of working memory. In A. Miyake & P. Shah (Eds.), *Models of working memory* (pp. 62–101). UK: Cambridge University Press.

Cowan, N. (2017). The many faces of working memory and short-term storage. *Psychon Bull Rev, 24*, 1158–1170. https://doi.org/10.3758/s13423-016-1191-6

Cowan, N. (2022). Working memory development: A 50-year assessment of research and underlying theories. *Cognition, 224*, 105075. https://doi.org/10.1016/j.cognition.2022.105075

Cowen, A. S., & Keltner, D. (2017). Self-report captures 27 distinct categories of emotion bridged by continuous gradients. *Proc Natl Acad Sci U S A, 114*(38), E7900-E7909. https://doi.org/10.1073/pnas.1702247114

Cox, J. R., & Griggs, R. A. (1982). The effects of experience on performance in Wason's selection task. *Mem Cognit, 10*(5), 496–502. https://doi.org/10.3758/bf03197653

Craigon, P. J., Hobson-West, P., England, G. C. W., Whelan, C., Lethbridge, E., & Asher, L. (2017). "She's a dog at the end of the day": Guide dog owners' perspectives on the behaviour of their guide dog. *PLoS One, 12*(4), e0176018. https://doi.org/10.1371/journal.pone.0176018

Craik, F.I.M. (2002). Levels of processing: Past, present. and future? *Memory, 10*(5–6), 305–318. https://doi.org/10.1080/09658210244000135

Craik, F.I.M. (2020). Remembering: An activity of mind and brain. *Annu Rev Psychol, 71*, 1–24. https://doi.org/10.1146/annurev-psych-010419-051027

Crawley, J. N. (2012). Translational animal models of autism and neurodevelopmental disorders. *Dialogues Clin Neurosci, 14*(3), 293–305. https://doi.org/10.31887/DCNS.2012.14.3/jcrawley

Crews, F. T., & Boettiger, C. A. (2009). Impulsivity, frontal lobes and risk for addiction. *Pharmacol Biochem Behav, 93*(3), 237–247. https://doi.org/10.1016/j.pbb.2009.04.018

Crick, F., & Koch, C. (1990). Some reflections on visual awareness. *Cold Spring Harb Symp Quant Biol, 55*, 953–962. https://doi.org/10.1101/sqb.1990.055.01.089

Crist, E. (2002). The inner life of earthworms: Darwin's argument and its implications. In M. Bekoff & C. Allen (Eds.), *The cognitive animal: Empirical and theoretical perspectives on animal cognition* (pp. 3–8). Cambridge, MA: MIT Press.

Csibra, G. (2008). Goal attribution to inanimate agents by 6.5-month-old infants. *Cognition, 107*(2), 705–717. https://doi.org/10.1016/j.cognition.2007.08.001

Csikszentmihalyi, M. (1996). *Creativity.* New York, NY: HarperCollins.

Csikszentmihalyi, M. (1997). *Creativity: Flow and the psychology of discovery and invention.* New York, NY: HarperCollins.

Cui, C., Noronha, A., Morikawa, H., Alvarez, V. A., Stuber, G. D., Szumlinski, K. K.,...Wilcox, M. V. (2013). New insights on neuro-biological mechanisms underlying alcohol addiction. *Neuropharmacology, 67*, 223–232. https://doi.org/10.1016/j.neuropharm.2012.09.022

Cui, L., Ye, M., Sun, L., Zhang, S., & He, G. (2022). Common and distinct neural correlates of intertemporal and risky decision-making: Meta-analytical evidence for the dual-system theory. *Neurosci Biobehav Rev, 141*, 104851. https://doi.org/10.1016/j.neubiorev.2022.104851

Curtis, C. E., & D'Esposito, M. (2003). Persistent activity in the prefrontal cortex during working memory. *Trends Cogn Sci, 7*(9), 415–423. https://doi.org/10.1016/s1364-6613(03)00197-9

Curtis, C. E., & D'Esposito, M. (2004). The effects of prefrontal lesions on working memory performance and theory. *Cogn Affect Behav Neurosci, 4*(4), 528–539. https://doi.org/10.3758/cabn.4.4.528

D

D'Alfonso, S., Santesteban-Echarri, O., Rice, S., Wadley, G., Lederman, R., Miles, C.,...Alvarez-Jimenez, M. (2017). Artificial intelligence-assisted online social therapy for youth mental health. *Front Psychol, 8*, 796. https://doi.org/10.3389/fpsyg.2017.00796

Dacke, M., Baird, E., Byrne, M., Scholtz, C. H., & Warrant, E. J. (2013). Dung beetles use the Milky Way for orientation. *Curr Biol, 23*, 298–300. https://doi.org/10.1016/j.cub.2012.12.034

Dagher, A., & Robbins, T. W. (2009). Personality, addiction, dopamine: Insights from Parkinson's disease. *Neuron, 61*(4), 502–510. https://doi.org/10.1016/j.neuron.2009.01.031

Damasio, A. R. (1996). The somatic marker hypothesis and the possible functions of the prefrontal cortex. *Philos Trans R Soc Lond B Biol Sci, 351*(1346), 1413–1420. https://doi.org/10.1098/rstb.1996.0125

Damasio, A. R., Damasio, H., & Van Hoesen, G. W. (1982). Prosopag-nosia: Anatomic basis and behavioral mechanisms. *Neurology, 32*(4), 331–341. https://doi.org/10.1212/wnl.32.4.331

Damasio, A. R., Tranel, D., & Damasio, H. (1990). Individuals with sociopathic behavior caused by frontal damage fail to respond autonomically to social stimuli. *Behav Brain Res, 41*(2), 81–94. https://doi.org/10.1016/0166-4328(90)90144-4

Damasio, H., Grabowski, T., Frank, R., Galaburda, A. M., & Damasio, A. R. (1994). The return of Phineas Gage: Clues about the brain from the skull of a famous patient. *Science, 264*(5162), 1102–1105. https://doi.org/10.1126/science.8178168

Daniel, T. O., Stanton, C. M., & Epstein, L. H. (2013). The future is now: Comparing the effect of episodic future thinking on impulsivity in lean and obese individuals. *Appetite, 71*, 120–125. https://doi.org/10.1016/j.appet.2013.07.010

Danziger, K. (1980). The history of introspection reconsidered. *J Hist Behav Sci, 16*, 241–262.

Danziger, K. (2009). *Marking the mind: A history of memory.* UK: Cambridge University Press.

Daou, A., & Margoliash, D. (2021). Intrinsic plasticity and birdsong learning. *Neurobiol Learn Mem, 180*, 107407. https://doi.org/10.1016/j.nlm.2021.107407

Darwin, C. (1859). *On the origin of species by means of natural selection, or the preservation of favoured races in the struggle for life.* London, UK: John Murray.

Darwin, C. (1871). *The descent of man and selection in relation to sex.* London, UK: John Murray.

Darwin, C. (1881). *The formation of vegetable mould, through the action of worms, with observations on their habits.* London, UK: John Murray.

Dave, S., Mastergeorge, A. M., & Olswang, L. B. (2018). Motherese, affect, and vocabulary development: Dyadic communicative interactions in infants and toddlers. *J Child Lang*, 1–22. https://doi.org/10.1017/S0305000917000551

Davis, C. A., Levitan, R. D., Reid, C., Carter, J. C., Kaplan, A. S., Patte, K. A.,... Kennedy, J. L. (2009). Dopamine for "wanting" and opioids for "liking": A comparison of obese adults with and without binge eating. *Obesity (Silver Spring), 17*(6), 1220–1225. https://doi.org/10.1038/oby.2009.52

Dawson, G., Toth, K., Abbott, R., Osterling, J., Munson, J., Estes, A., & Liaw, J. (2004). Early social attention impairments in autism: Social orienting, joint attention, and attention to distress. *Dev Psychol, 40*(2), 271–283. https://doi.org/10.1037/0012-1649.40.2.271

Dawson, M. R. W. (2008). Connectionism and classical conditioning. *Comp Cogni Behav Rev, 3*, 1–115.

Day, J. J., & Sweatt, J. D. (2011). Epigenetic mechanisms in cognition. *Neuron, 70*(5), 813–829. https://doi.org/10.1016/j.neuron.2011.05.019

De Bot, K., Lowie, W., & Verspoor, M. (2007). A dynamic system theory approach to second language acquisition. *Biling Lang Cogn, 10*, 7–21.

De Carlos, J. A., & Borrell, J. (2007). A historical reflection of the contributions of Cajal and Golgi to the foundations of neuroscience. *Brain Res Rev, 55*(1), 8–16. https://doi.org/10.1016/j.brainresrev.2007.03.010

De Gelder, B. (2010). Uncanny sight in the blind. *Sci Am, 302*(5), 60–65. https://doi.org/10.1038/scientificamerican0510-60

de Graaf, T. A., Hsieh, P. J., & Sack, A. T. (2012). The 'correlates' in neural correlates of consciousness. *Neurosci Biobehav Rev, 36*(1), 191–197. https://doi.org/10.1016/j.neubiorev.2011.05.012

de Greeff, J., & Belpaeme, T. (2015). Why robots should be social: Enhancing machine learning through social human-robot interaction. *PLoS One, 10*(9), e0138061. https://doi.org/10.1371/journal.pone.0138061

de Hevia, M. D., Izard, V., Coubart, A., Spelke, E. S., & Streri, A. (2014). Representations of space, time, and number in neonates. *Proc Natl Acad Sci U S A, 111*(13), 4809–4813. https://doi.org/10.1073/pnas.1323628111

De Jaegher, H., Di Paolo, E., & Gallagher, S. (2010). Can social interaction constitute social cognition? *Trends Cogn Sci, 14*, 441–447.

De Kock, R., Gladhill, K. A., Ali, M. N., Joiner, W. M., & Wiener, M. (2021). How movements shape the perception of time. *Trends Cogn Sci, 25*(11), 950–963. https://doi.org/10.1016/j.tics.2021.08.002

De Martino, B., Kumaran, D., Seymour, B., & Dolan, R. J. (2006). Frames, biases, and rational decision-making in the human brain. *Science, 313*(5787), 684–687. https://doi.org/10.1126/science.1128356

de Natale, E. R., Paulus, K. S., Aiello, E., Sanna, B., Manca, A., Sotgiu, G.,... Deriu, F. (2017). Dance therapy improves motor and cognitive functions in patients with Parkinson's disease. *NeuroRehabilitation, 40*(1), 141–144. https://doi.org/10.3233/NRE-161399

de Oliveira-Souza, R., Paranhos, T., Moll, J., & Grafman, J. (2019). Gender and hemispheric asymmetries in acquired sociopathy. *Front Psychol, 10*, 346. https://doi.org/10.3389/fpsyg.2019.00346

De Ridder, D., Adhia, D., & Vanneste, S. (2021). The anatomy of pain and suffering in the brain and its clinical implications. *Neurosci Biobehav Rev, 130*, 125–146. https://doi.org/10.1016/j.neubiorev.2021.08.013

De Waal, F. (2016). *Are we smart enough to know how smart animals are?* New York, NY: W. W. Norton.

de Waal, F. B., & Ferrari, P. F. (2010). Towards a bottom-up perspective on animal and human cognition. *Trends Cogn Sci, 14*(5), 201–207. https://doi.org/10.1016/j.tics.2010.03.003

Deacon, T. W. (1997). *The symbolic species: The co-evolution of language and the brain.* New York, NY: W. W. Norton.

Deary, I. J., Cox, S. R., & Hill, W. D. (2022). Genetic variation, brain, and intelligence differences. *Mol Psychiatry, 27*(1), 335–353. https://doi.org/10.1038/s41380-021-01027-y

Deary, I. J., Penke, L., & Johnson, W. (2010). The neuroscience of human intelligence differences. *Nat Rev Neurosci, 11*, 201–211. https://doi.org/10.1038/nrn2793

DeCasper, A., & Spence, M. (1986). Prenatal maternal speech influences newborns' perception of speech sounds. *Infant Behav Dev, 9*, 133–150.

DeFelipe, J. (2006). Brain plasticity and mental processes: Cajal again. *Nat Rev Neurosci, 7*(10), 811–817. https://doi.org/10.1038/nrn2005

Dehaene, S. (1997). *The number sense.* New York, NY: Oxford University Press.

Dehaene, S., Changeux, J. P., Naccache, L., Sackur, J., & Sergent, C. (2006). Conscious, preconscious, and subliminal processing: A testable taxonomy. *Trends Cogn Sci, 10*(5), 204–211. https://doi.org/10.1016/j.tics.2006.03.007

den Hoed, J., & Fisher, S. E. (2020). Genetic pathways involved in human speech disorders. *Curr Opin Genet Dev, 65*, 103–111. https://doi.org/10.1016/j.gde.2020.05.012

Dennis, N. A., Johnson, C. E., & Peterson, K. M. (2014). Neural correlates underlying true and false associative memories. *Brain Cogn, 88*, 65–72. https://doi.org/10.1016/j.bandc.2014.04.009

Denton, S. E., & Kruschke, J. K. (2006). Attention and salience in associative blocking. *Learn Behav, 34*(3), 285–304. https://doi.org/10.3758/bf03192884

Der, R., & Martius, G. (2015). Novel plasticity rule can explain the development of sensorimotor intelligence. *Proc Natl Acad Sci U S A, 112*(45), E6224–6232. https://doi.org/10.1073/pnas.1508400112

Descartes, R. (1644/1984). *Principles of philosophy, translated with explanatory notes by V. R. Miller and R. P. Miller.* Kluwer Academic.

Descartes, R. (1662/1972). *Treatise of man: French text with translation and Commentary, trans. Thomas Steele Hall.* Cambridge, MA: Harvard University Press.

Desimone, R. (1991). Face-selective cells in the temporal cortex of monkeys. *J Cogn Neurosci, 3*(1), 1–8. https://doi.org/10.1162/jocn.1991.3.1.1

Devinsky, O., & Lai, G. (2008). Spirituality and religion in epilepsy. *Epilepsy Behav, 12*(4), 636–643. https://doi.org/10.1016/j.yebeh.2007.11.011

Dezecache, G., Allen, J. M., von Zimmermann, J., & Richardson, D. C. (2021). We predict a riot: Inequity, relative deprivation and collective destruction in the laboratory. *Proc Biol Sci, 288*(1959), 20203091. https://doi.org/10.1098/rspb.2020.3091

Dhein, K. (2021). Karl von Frisch and the discipline of ethology. *J Hist Biol, 54*(4), 739–767. https://doi.org/10.1007/s10739-021-09660-7

di Pellegrino, G., Fadiga, L., Fogassi, L., Gallese, V., & Rizzolatti, G. (1992). Understanding motor events: A neurophysiological study. *Exp Brain Res, 91*(1), 176–180. https://doi.org/10.1007/BF00230027

Di Rienzo, F., Debarnot, U., Daligault, S., Saruco, E., Delpuech, C., Doyon, J.,…Guillot, A. (2016). Online and offline performance gains following motor imagery practice: A comprehensive review of behavioral and neuroimaging studies. *Front Hum Neurosci, 10*, 315. https://doi.org/10.3389/fnhum.2016.00315

Diamond, A. (2013). Executive functions. *Annu Rev Psychol, 64*, 135–168. https://doi.org/10.1146/annurev-psych-113011-143750

Diamond, M. (1988). *Enriching heredity*. New York, NY: Free Press.

Diamond, M. C. (1988). *Enriching heredity: The impact of the environment on the anatomy of the brain*. New York, NY: Free Press.

Diehl, M., & Stroebe, W. (1987). Productivity loss in brainstorming groups: Toward the solution of a riddle. *J Pers Soc Psychol, 53*, 497–509.

Dijkstra, N., Bosch, S. E., & van Gerven, M. A. (2017). Vividness of visual imagery depends on the neural overlap with perception in visual areas. *J Neurosci, 37*(5), 1367–1373. https://doi.org/10.1523/JNEUROSCI.3022-16.2016

Dijkstra, N., Bosch, S. E., & van Gerven, M. A. J. (2019). Shared neural mechanisms of visual perception and imagery. *Trends Cogn Sci, 23*(5), 423–434. https://doi.org/10.1016/j.tics.2019.02.004

Ding, X., Tang, Y. Y., Tang, R., & Posner, M. I. (2014). Improving creativity performance by short-term meditation. *Behav Brain Funct, 10*, 9. https://doi.org/10.1186/1744-9081-10-9

Dodd, M. L., Klos, K. J., Bower, J. H., Geda, Y. E., Josephs, K. A., & Ahlskog, J. E. (2005). Pathological gambling caused by drugs used to treat Parkinson disease. *Arch Neurol, 62*(9), 1377–1381. https://doi.org/10.1001/archneur.62.9.noc50009

Doelling, K. B., Assaneo, M. F., Bevilacqua, D., Pesaran, B., & Poeppel, D. (2019). An oscillator model better predicts cortical entrainment to music. *Proc Natl Acad Sci U S A, 116*(20), 10113–10121. https://doi.org/10.1073/pnas.1816414116

Domjan, M. (2005). Pavlovian conditioning: A functional perspective. *Annu Rev Psychol, 56*, 179–206. https://doi.org/10.1146/annurev.psych.55.090902.141409

Dong, Z., Wang, G., Lu, S., Li, J., Yan, W., & Wang, S. J. (2021). Spontaneous facial expressions and micro-expressions coding: From brain to face. *Front Psychol, 12*, 784834. https://doi.org/10.3389/fpsyg.2021.784834

Donnay, G. F., Rankin, S. K., Lopez-Gonzalez, M., Jiradejvong, P., & Limb, C. J. (2014). Neural substrates of interactive musical improvisation: An FMRI study of 'trading fours' in jazz. *PLoS One, 9*(2), e88665. https://doi.org/10.1371/journal.pone.0088665

Dotson, V. M., McClintock, S. M., Verhaeghen, P., Kim, J. U., Draheim, A. A., Syzmkowicz, S.,…Wit, L. (2020). Depression and cognitive control across the lifespan: A systematic review and meta-analysis. *Neuropsychol Rev, 30*(4), 461–476. https://doi.org/10.1007/s11065-020-09436-6

Dowker, A., Sarkar, A., & Looi, C. Y. (2016). Mathematics anxiety: What have we learned in 60 years? *Front Psychol, 7*, 508. https://doi.org/10.3389/fpsyg.2016.00508

Draheim, C., Pak, R., Draheim, A. A., & Engle, R. W. (2022). The role of attention control in complex real-world tasks. *Psychon Bull Rev, 29*(4), 1143–1197. https://doi.org/10.3758/s13423-021-02052-2

Dresler, M., Shirer, W. R., Konrad, B. N., Muller, N.C.J., Wagner, I. C., Fernandez, G.,…Greicius, M. D. (2017). Mnemonic training reshapes brain networks to support superior memory. *Neuron, 93*(5), 1227–1235 e1226. https://doi.org/10.1016/j.neuron.2017.02.003

Drigas, A., Mitsea, E., & Skianis, C. (2022). Metamemory: Metacognitive strategies for improved memory operations and the role of VR and mobiles. *Behav Sci (Basel), 12*(11). https://doi.org/10.3390/bs12110450

Droege, P., Weiss, D. J., Schwob, N., & Braithwaite, V. (2021). Trace conditioning as a test for animal consciousness: A new approach. *Anim Cogn, 24*(6), 1299–1304. https://doi.org/10.1007/s10071-021-01522-3

Dronkers, N. F., Plaisant, O., Iba-Zizen, M. T., & Cabanis, E. A. (2007). Paul Broca's historic cases: High resolution MR imaging of the brains of Leborgne and Lelong. *Brain, 130*(Pt 5), 1432–1441. https://doi.org/10.1093/brain/awm042

Druckman, J. N., & McGrath, M. C. (2019). The evidence for motivated reasoning in climate change preference formation. *Nat Clim Chang, 9*, 111–119.

Dudzinski, K. M., Yeater, D., Bolton, T., Eskelinen, H., & Hill, H. (2018). Defining creativity and confirming understanding of the concept in dolphins: Research and training perspectives. *Aquat Mamm, 44*, 426–437.

Dunbar, R. I. (2009). The social brain hypothesis and its implications for social evolution. *Ann Hum Biol, 36*(5), 562–572. https://doi.org/10.1080/03014460902960289

Dunbar, R. I. (2012). The social brain meets neuroimaging. *Trends Cogn Sci, 16*(2), 101–102. https://doi.org/10.1016/j.tics.2011.11.013

Duncan, J., & Humphreys, G. W. (1989). Visual search and stimulus similarity. *Psychol Rev, 96*(3), 433–458. https://doi.org/10.1037/0033-295x.96.3.433

Dunlosky, J., & Metcalfe, J. (2009). *Metacognition: A textbook for cognitive, educational, lifespan and applied psychology*. Sage.

Dunn, J. C., & Rao, L.-L. (2019). Models of risky choice: A state-trace and signed difference analysis. *J Math Psychol, 90*, 61–75.

Durand-Ruel, M., Park, C. H., Moyne, M., Maceira-Elvira, P., Morishita, T., & Hummel, F. C. (2023). Early motor skill acquisition in healthy older adults: Brain correlates of the learning process. *Cereb Cortex*. https://doi.org/10.1093/cercor/bhad044

Duzel, E., Penny, W. D., & Burgess, N. (2010). Brain oscillations and memory. *Curr Opin Neurobiol, 20*(2), 143–149. https://doi.org/10.1016/j.conb.2010.01.004

E

Eagleman, D. M. (2008). Human time perception and its illusions. *Curr Opin Neurobiol, 18*(2), 131–136. https://doi.org/10.1016/j.conb.2008.06.002

Eagleman, D., & Downar, J. (2015). *Brain and behavior: A cognitive neuroscience perspective.* New York, NY: Oxford University Press.

Eagleman, D., & Downar, J. (2016). *Brain and behavior: A cognitive neuroscience perspective.* New York, NY: Oxford University Press.

Easley, H. (1937). The curve of forgetting and the distribution of practice. *J Educ Psychol, 28*, 474–478.

Ebbinghaus, H. (1885/1964). *Memory: A contribution to experimental psychology* (H. A. Ruger & C. E. Bussenius, Trans.). Mineola, NY: Dover.

Edelman, G. M. (1989). *The remembered present: A biological theory of consciousness.* New York, NY: Basic Books.

Edelman, S., & Poggio, T. (1991). Models of object recognition. *Curr Opin Neurobiol, 1*(2), 270–273. https://doi.org/10.1016/0959-4388(91)90089-p

Edwards, A. D., & Shafer, D. M. (2022). When lamps have feelings: Empathy and anthropomorphism toward inanimate objects in animated films. *Projections, 16*, 27–52.

Edwards, K. S., & Shin, M. (2017). Media multitasking and implicit learning. *Atten Percept Psychophys, 79*(5), 1535–1549. https://doi.org/10.3758/s13414-017-1319-4

Edwards, W. (1954). The theory of decision making. *Psychol Bull, 51*(4), 380–417. https://doi.org/10.1037/h0053870

Egan, L. C., Santos, L. R., & Bloom, P. (2007). The origins of cognitive dissonance: Evidence from children and monkeys. *Psychol Sci, 18*(11), 978–983. https://doi.org/10.1111/j.1467-9280.2007.02012.x

Ehrsson, H. H., Holmes, N. P., & Passingham, R. E. (2005). Touching a rubber hand: Feeling of body ownership is associated with activity in multisensory brain areas. *J Neurosci, 25*(45), 10564–10573. https://doi.org/10.1523/JNEUROSCI.0800-05.2005

Eibl-Eibesfeldt, I. (1979). Human ethology: Concepts and implications for the sciences of man. *Behav Brain Sci, 2*, 1–26.

Eichenbaum, H. (2013). What H.M. taught us. *J Cogn Neurosci, 25*(1), 14–21. https://doi.org/10.1162/jocn_a_00285

Eichenbaum, H. (2017). Memory: Organization and control. *Annu Rev Psychol, 68*, 19–45. https://doi.org/10.1146/annurev-psych-010416-044131

Eimas, P. D., & Miller, J. L. (1978). Effects of selective adaptation on the perception of speech and visual patterns. In R. D. Walk & H. L. Pick (Eds.), *Perception and experience: Perception and perceptual development, Vol. 1.* New York, NY: Springer.

Eimer, M. (2000). Effects of face inversion on the structural encoding and recognition of faces. Evidence from event-related brain potentials. *Brain Res Cogn Brain Res, 10*(1–2), 145–158. https://doi.org/10.1016/s0926-6410(00)00038-0

Eisenberger, R. (1992). Learned industriousness. *Psychol Rev, 99*(2), 248–267. https://doi.org/10.1037/0033-295x.99.2.248

El Jundi, B., Foster, J. J., Khaldy, L., Byrne, M. J., Dacke, M., & Baird, E. (2016). A snapshot-based mechanism for celestial orientation. *Curr Biol, 26*, 1456–1462. https://doi.org/10.1016/j.cub.2016.03.030

El-Shamayleh, Y., & Horwitz, G. D. (2019). Primate optogenetics: Progress and prognosis. *Proc Natl Acad Sci U S A, 116*(52), 26195–26203. https://doi.org/10.1073/pnas.1902284116

Elvik, R. (2013). Risk of road accident associated with the use of drugs: A systematic review and meta-analysis of evidence from epidemiological studies. *Accid Anal Prev, 60*, 254–267. https://doi.org/10.1016/j.aap.2012.06.017

Emmons, E. B., De Corte, B. J., Kim, Y., Parker, K. L., Matell, M. S., & Narayanan, N. S. (2017). Rodent medial frontal control of temporal processing in the dorsomedial striatum. *J Neurosci, 37*, 8718–8733. https://doi.org/10.1523/JNEUROSCI.1376-17.2017

Endersby, J. (2009). Lumpers and splitters: Darwin, Hooker, and the search for order. *Science, 326*(5959), 1496–1499. https://doi.org/10.1126/science.1165915

Engle, R. W., Tuholski, S. W., Laughlin, J. E., & Conway, A. R. A. (1999). Working memory, short-term memory, and general fluid intelligence: A latent-variable approach. *J Exp Psychol Gen, 128*(3), 309–331. https://doi.org/10.1037//0096-3445.128.3.309

Epley, N., Waytz, A., & Cacioppo, J. T. (2007). On seeing human: a three-factor theory of anthropomorphism. *Psychol Rev, 114*(4), 864–886. https://doi.org/10.1037/0033-295X.114.4.864

Erard, M. (2012). *Babel no more: Search for the world's most extraordinary language learners.* New York, NY: Free Press.

Erickson, K. I., Voss, M. W., Prakash, R. S., Basak, C., Szabo, A., Chaddock, L., … Kramer, A. F. (2011). Exercise training increases size of hippocampus and improves memory. *Proc Natl Acad Sci U S A, 108*(7), 3017–3022. https://doi.org/10.1073/pnas.1015950108

Ericsson, K. A., & Chase, W. G. (1982). Exceptional memory. *Am Sci, 70*(6), 607–615. https://www.ncbi.nlm.nih.gov/pubmed/7181217

Ericsson, K. A., Cheng, X., Pan, Y., Ku, Y., Ge, Y., & Hu, Y. (2017). Memory skills mediating superior memory in a world-class memorist. *Memory, 25*(9), 1294–1302. https://doi.org/10.1080/09658211.2017.1296164

Ericsson, K. A., & Fox, M. C. (2011). Thinking aloud is not a form of introspection but a qualitatively different methodology: Reply to Schooler (2011). *Psychol Bull, 137*(2), 351–354. https://doi.org/10.1037/a0022388

Ericsson, K. A., Nandagopal, K., & Roring, R. W. (2009). Toward a science of exceptional achievement: Attaining superior performance through deliberate practice. *Ann N Y Acad Sci, 1172*, 199–217. https://doi.org/10.1196/annals.1393.001

Ester, E. F., Sprague, T. C., & Serences, J. T. (2015). Parietal and frontal cortex encode stimulus-specific mnemonic representations during visual working memory. *Neuron, 87*(4), 893–905. https://doi.org/10.1016/j.neuron.2015.07.013

Estienne, V., Cohen, H., Wittig, R. M., & Boesch, C. (2019). Maternal influence on the development of nut-cracking skills in the chimpanzees of the Tai forest, Cote d'Ivoire (Pan troglodytes verus). *Am J Primatol, 81*(7), e23022. https://doi.org/10.1002/ajp.23022

Eun, B. (2019). The zone of proximal development as an overarching concept: A framework for synthesizing Vygotsky's theories. *Educ Philos Theory, 51*, 18–30.

Evans, J. S. (2006). The heuristic-analytic theory of reasoning: Extension and evaluation. *Psychon Bull Rev, 13*(3), 378–395. https://doi.org/10.3758/bf03193858

Evans, J. S., & Stanovich, K. E. (2013). Dual-process theories of higher cognition: Advancing the debate. *Perspect Psychol Sci, 8*(3), 223–241. https://doi.org/10.1177/1745691612460685

Eysenck, M. W., Derakshan, N., Santos, R., & Calvo, M. G. (2007). Anxiety and cognitive performance: Attentional control theory. *Emotion, 7*, 336–353. https://doi.org/10.1037/1528-3542.7.2.336

F

Fabbri-Destro, M., & Rizzolatti, G. (2008). Mirror neurons and mirror systems in monkeys and humans. *Physiology (Bethesda), 23*, 171–179. https://doi.org/10.1152/physiol.00004.2008

Facchin, A., Folegatti, A., Rossetti, Y., & Farne, A. (2019). The half of the story we did not know about prism adaptation. *Cortex, 119*, 141–157. https://doi.org/10.1016/j.cortex.2019.04.012

Fadiga, L., Craighero, L., Destro, M. F., Finos, L., Cotillon-Williams, N., Smith, A. T., & Castiello, U. (2006). Language in shadow. *Soc Neurosci, 1*, 77–89.

Fallon, I. P., Tanner, M. K., Greenwood, B. N., & Baratta, M. V. (2020). Sex differences in resilience: Experiential factors and their mechanisms. *Eur J Neurosci, 52*(1), 2530–2547. https://doi.org/10.1111/ejn.14639

Fama, R., Pitel, A. L., & Sullivan, E. V. (2012). Anterograde episodic memory in Korsakoff syndrome. *Neuropsychol Rev, 22*(2), 93–104. https://doi.org/10.1007/s11065-012-9207-0

Fanselow, M. S., & LeDoux, J. E. (1999). Why we think plasticity underlying Pavlovian fear conditioning occurs in the basolateral amygdala. *Neuron, 23*(2), 229–232. https://doi.org/10.1016/s0896-6273(00)80775-8

Farah, M. J. (2004). *Visual agnosia*. Cambridge, MA: MIT Press.

Farah, M. J., Hammond, K. M., Levine, D. N., & Calvanio, R. (1988). Visual and spatial mental imagery: Dissociable systems of representation. *Cog Psychol, 20*, 439–462.

Farrell, S., & Lewandowsky, S. (2018). *Computational modeling of cognition and behavior*. UK: Cambridge University Press.

Faymonville, M. E., Meurisse, M., & Fissette, J. (1999). Hypnosedation: A valuable alternative to traditional anaesthetic techniques. *Acta Chir Belg, 99*(4), 141–146. https://www.ncbi.nlm.nih.gov/pubmed/10499382

Fede, S. J., & Kiehl, K. A. (2020). Meta-analysis of the moral brain: Patterns of neural engagement assessed using multilevel kernel density analysis. *Brain Imaging Behav, 14*(2), 534–547. https://doi.org/10.1007/s11682-019-00035-5

Federici, A., Parma, V., Vicovaro, M., Radassao, L., Casartelli, L., & Ronconi, L. (2020). Anomalous perception of biological motion in autism: A conceptual review and meta-analysis. *Sci Rep, 10*(1), 4576. https://doi.org/10.1038/s41598-020-61252-3

Feigenson, L., Carey, S., & Spelke, E. (2002). Infants' discrimination of number vs. continuous extent. *Cogn Psychol, 44*(1), 33–66. https://doi.org/10.1006/cogp.2001.0760

Feigenson, L., Dehaene, S., & Spelke, E. (2004). Core systems of number. *Trends Cogn Sci, 8*, 307–314. https://doi.org/10.1016/j.tics.2004.05.002

Feist, G. J. (2019). Creativity and the Big Two model of personality. *Curr Opin Behav Sci, 27*, 31–35.

FeldmanHall, O., & Shenhav, A. (2019). Resolving uncertainty in a social world. *Nat Hum Behav, 3*(5), 426–435. https://doi.org/10.1038/s41562-019-0590-x

Fernandez-Duque, D., & & Johnson, M. L. (1999). Attention metaphors: How metaphors guide the cognitive psychology of attention. *Cogn Sci, 23*, 83–116.

Ferrucci, L., Nougaret, S., Brunamonti, E., & Genovesio, A. (2019). Effects of reward size and context on learning in macaque monkeys. *Behav Brain Res, 372*, 111983. https://doi.org/10.1016/j.bbr.2019.111983

Feuillet, L., Dufour, H., & Pelletier, J. (2007). Brain of a white-collar worker. *Lancet, 370*(9583), 262. https://doi.org/10.1016/S0140-6736(07)61127-1

Finke, R. A. (1985). Theories relating mental imagery to perception. *Psychol Bull, 98*(2), 236–259. https://www.ncbi.nlm.nih.gov/pubmed/3901061

Finke, R. A., Ward, T. B., & Smith, S. M. (1992). *Creative cognition: Theory, research, and applications*. Cambridge, MA: MIT Press.

Finn, A. S., Kraft, M. A., West, M. R., Leonard, J. A., Bish, C. E., Martin, R. E.,... Gabrieli, J. D. (2014). Cognitive skills, student achievement tests, and schools. *Psychol Sci, 25*(3), 736–744. https://doi.org/10.1177/0956797613516008

Firestone, C., & Scholl, B. J. (2016). Cognition does not affect perception: Evaluating the evidence for "top-down" effects. *Behav Brain Sci, 39*, e229. https://doi.org/10.1017/S0140525×15000965

Fischi-Gomez, E., Vasung, L., Meskaldji, D. E., Lazeyras, F., Borradori-Tolsa, C., Hagmann, P.,... Huppi, P. S. (2015). Structural brain connectivity in school-age preterm infants provides evidence for impaired networks relevant for higher order cognitive skills and social cognition. *Cereb Cortex, 25*(9), 2793–2805. https://doi.org/10.1093/cercor/bhu073

Fisher, M., Loewy, R., Carter, C., Lee, A., Ragland, J. D., Niendam, T.,... Vinogradov, S. (2015). Neuroplasticity-based auditory training via laptop computer improves cognition in young individuals with recent onset schizophrenia. *Schizophr Bull, 41*(1), 250–258. https://doi.org/10.1093/schbul/sbt232

Fitch, W. T. (2020). Animal cognition and the evolution of human language: Why we cannot focus solely on communication. *Philos Trans R Soc Lond B Biol Sci, 375*(1789), 20190046. https://doi.org/10.1098/rstb.2019.0046

Fitch, W. T., Hauser, M. D., & Chomsky, N. (2005). The evolution of the language faculty: Clarifications and implications. *Cognition, 97*(2), 179–210; discussion 211–125. https://doi.org/10.1016/j.cognition.2005.02.005

Flombaum, J. (2022). *JoVE Science Education Database. Cognitive Psychology. Mental Rotation*.

Flynn, J. R. (2000). IQ gains and fluid g. *Am Psychol, 55*(5), 543. https://doi.org/10.1037/0003-066x.55.5.543

Fodor, J. (2008). *LOT2: The language of thought revisited*. New York, NY: Oxford University Press.

Fodor, J. A. (1975). *The language of thought*. Cambridge, MA: Harvard University Press.

Fodor, J. A. (1983). *The modularity of mind*. Cambridge, MA: MIT Press.

Fodor, J. A. (1998). *Concepts: Where cognitive science went wrong*. New York, NY: Oxford University Press.

Fodor, J. A., & Pylyshyn, Z. W. (1988). Connectionism and cognitive architecture: A critical analysis. *Cognition, 28*(1–2), 3–71. https://doi.org/10.1016/0010-0277(88)90031-5

Foell, J., Bekrater-Bodmann, R., Diers, M., & Flor, H. (2014). Mirror therapy for phantom limb pain: Brain changes and the role of body representation. *Eur J Pain, 18*(5), 729–739. https://doi.org/10.1002/j.1532-2149.2013.00433.x

Foerde, K., & Shohamy, D. (2011). The role of the basal ganglia in learning and memory: Insight from Parkinson's disease. *Neurobiol Learn Mem, 96*(4), 624–636. https://doi.org/10.1016/j.nlm.2011.08.006

Folstein, J. R., Gauthier, I., & Palmeri, T. J. (2012). How category learning affects object representations: Not all morphspaces stretch alike. *J Exp Psychol Learn Mem Cogn, 38*(4), 807–820. https://doi.org/10.1037/a0025836

Fong, T., Nourbakhsh, I., & Dautenhahn, K. (2003). A survey of socially interactive robots. *Rob Auton Syst, 42*(143–166).

Fossette, S., Gleiss, A. C., Chalumeau, J., Bastian, T., Armstrong, C. D., Vandenabeele, S.,... Hays, G. C. (2015). Current-oriented swimming by jellyfish and its role in bloom maintenance. *Curr Biol, 25*, 342–347. https://doi.org/10.1016/j.cub.2014.11.050

Foulsham, T., Cheng, J. T., Tracy, J. L., Henrich, J., & Kingstone, A. (2010). Gaze allocation in a dynamic situation: Effects of social status and speaking. *Cognition, 117*(3), 319–331. https://doi.org/10.1016/j.cognition.2010.09.003

Foulsham, T., Walker, E., & Kingstone, A. (2011). The where, what and when of gaze allocation in the lab and the natural environment. *Vision Res, 51*(17), 1920–1931. https://doi.org/10.1016/j.visres.2011.07.002

Frank, M. C., Everett, D. L., Fedorenko, E., & Gibson, E. (2008). Number as a cognitive technology: Evidence from Piraha language and cognition. *Cognition, 108*, 819–824. https://doi.org/10.1016/j.cognition.2008.04.007

Frankish, K., & Evans, J. S. B. T. (2009). The duality of mind: An historical perspective. In J. S. B. T. Evans & K. Frankish (Eds.), *In two minds: Dual processes and beyond*. New York, NY: Oxford University Press.

Franks, J. J., Bilbrey, C. W., Lien, K. G., & McNamara, T. P. (2000). Transfer-appropriate processing (TAP) and repetition priming. *Mem Cognit, 28*(7), 1140–1151. https://doi.org/10.3758/bf03211815

Freedberg, M., Toader, A. C., Wassermann, E. M., & Voss, J. L. (2020). Competitive and cooperative interactions between medial temporal and striatal learning systems. *Neuropsychologia, 136*, 107257. https://doi.org/10.1016/j.neuropsychologia.2019.107257

Freud, S. (1920). *A general introduction to psychoanalysis*. Stanley Hall.

Fridriksson, J., Yourganov, G., Bonilha, L., Basilakos, A., Den Ouden, D. B., & Rorden, C. (2016). Revealing the dual streams of speech processing. *Proc Natl Acad Sci U S A, 113*(52), 15108–15113. https://doi.org/10.1073/pnas.1614038114

Fries, P., Reynolds, J. H., Rorie, A. E., & Desimone, R. (2001). Modulation of oscillatory neuronal synchronization by selective visual attention. *Science, 291*(5508), 1560–1563. https://doi.org/10.1126/science.1055465

Friese, U., Daume, J., Goschl, F., Konig, P., Wang, P., & Engel, A. K. (2016). Oscillatory brain activity during multisensory attention reflects activation, disinhibition, and cognitive control. *Sci Rep, 6*, 32775. https://doi.org/10.1038/srep32775

Frith, C. D., & Singer, T. (2008). The role of social cognition in decision making. *Philos Trans R Soc Lond B Biol Sci, 363*(1511), 3875–3886. https://doi.org/10.1098/rstb.2008.0156

Frith, E., Elbich, D. B., Christensen, A. P., Rosenberg, M. D., Chen, Q., Kane, M. J.,...Beaty, R. E. (2021). Intelligence and creativity share a common cognitive and neural basis. *J Exp Psychol Gen, 150*(4), 609–632. https://doi.org/10.1037/xge0000958

Fritz, J. B., Elhilali, M., David, S. V., & Shamma, S. A. (2007). Auditory attention—Focusing the searchlight on sound. *Curr Opin Neurobiol, 17*(4), 437–455. https://doi.org/10.1016/j.conb.2007.07.011

Froemke, R. C., & Young, L. J. (2021). Oxytocin, neural plasticity, and social behavior. *Annu Rev Neurosci, 44*, 359–381. https://doi.org/10.1146/annurev-neuro-102320-102847

Fu, J., Liu, J., Jiang, J., Li, Y., Bao, Y., & Lu, H. (2021). Scene segmentation with dual relation-aware attention network. *IEEE Trans Neural Netw Learn Syst, 32*(6), 2547–2560. https://doi.org/10.1109/TNNLS.2020.3006524

Fu, Q. J., & Galvin, J. J., 3rd. (2007). Perceptual learning and auditory training in cochlear implant recipients. *Trends Amplif, 11*(3), 193–205. https://doi.org/10.1177/1084713807301379

Fuchs, T. (2017). *Ecology of the brain: The phenomenology and biology of the embodied mind*. New York, NY: New York, NY: Oxford University Press.

Funahashi, S., & Andreau, J. M. (2013). Prefrontal cortex and neural mechanisms of executive function. *J Physiol Paris, 107*(6), 471–482. https://doi.org/10.1016/j.jphysparis.2013.05.001

Funahashi, S., Bruce, C. J., & Goldman-Rakic, P. S. (1989). Mnemonic coding of visual space in the monkey's dorsolateral prefrontal cortex. *J Neurophysiol, 61*(2), 331–349. https://doi.org/10.1152/jn.1989.61.2.331

Furnham, A., & Bachtiar, V. (2008). Personality and intelligence as predictors of creativity. *Pers Individ Differ, 45*, 613–617.

G

Gabard-Durnam, L., & McLaughlin, K. A. (2020). Sensitive periods in human development: Charting a course for the future. *Curr Opin Behav Sci, 36*, 120–128.

Gabay, A. S., Radua, J., Kempton, M. J., & Mehta, M. A. (2014). The Ultimatum Game and the brain: A meta-analysis of neuroimaging studies. *Neurosci Biobehav Rev, 47*, 549–558. https://doi.org/10.1016/j.neubiorev.2014.10.014

Gaffan, D., & Heywood, C. A. (1993). A spurious category-specific visual agnosia for living things in normal human and nonhuman primates. *J Cogn Neurosci, 5*(1), 118–128. https://doi.org/10.1162/jocn.1993.5.1.118

Gallese, V., & Goldman, A. (1998). Mirror neurons and the simulation theory of mind-reading. *Trends Cogn Sci, 2*(12), 493–501. https://doi.org/10.1016/s1364-6613(98)01262-5

Gallistel, C. R. (1994). Foraging for brain stimulation: Toward a neurobiology of computation. *Cognition, 50*(1–3), 151–170. https://doi.org/10.1016/0010-0277(94)90026-4

Gallistel, C. R., & Gelman, I. I. (2000). Non-verbal numerical cognition: From reals to integers. *Trends Cogn Sci, 4*, 59–65.

Gallistel, C. R., & Gibbon, J. (2000). Time, rate, and conditioning. *Psychol Rev, 107*(2), 289–344. https://doi.org/10.1037/0033-295x.107.2.289

Galton, F. (1869). *Hereditary genius and inquiry into its laws and consequences*. New York, NY: Macmillan.

Gao, T., & Scholl, B. J. (2011). Chasing vs. stalking: Interrupting the perception of animacy. *J Exp Psychol Hum Percept Perform*, *37*(3), 669–684. https://doi.org/10.1037/a0020735

Gao, Y., & Raine, A. (2010). Successful and unsuccessful psychopaths: A neurobiological model. *Behav Sci Law*, *28*(2), 194–210. https://doi.org/10.1002/bsl.924

Garrod, S., & Pickering, M. J. (2009). Joint action, interactive alignment, and dialog. *Top Cogn Sci*, *1*, 292–304. https://doi.org/10.1111/j.1756-8765.2009.01020.x

Gauthier, I., & Logothetis, N. K. (2000). Is face recognition not so unique after all? *Cogn Neuropsychol*, *17*(1), 125–142. https://doi.org/10.1080/026432900380535

Gauthier, I., & Tarr, M. J. (2016). Visual object recognition: Do we (finally) know more now than we did? *Annu Rev Vis Sci*, *2*, 377–396. https://doi.org/10.1146/annurev-vision-111815-114621

Gauthier, I., Tarr, M. J., Anderson, A. W., Skudlarski, P., & Gore, J. C. (1999). Activation of the middle fusiform 'face area' increases with expertise in recognizing novel objects. *Nat Neurosci*, *2*(6), 568–573. https://doi.org/10.1038/9224

Gauvin, H. S., & Hartsuiker, R. J. (2020). Towards a new model of verbal monitoring. *J Cogn*, *3*(1), 17. https://doi.org/10.5334/joc.81

Gazes, R. P., & Lazareva, O. F. (2021). Does cognition differ across species, and how do we know? Lessons from research in transitive inference. *J Exp Psychol Anim Learn Cogn*, *47*(3), 223–233. https://doi.org/10.1037/xan0000301

Gazova, I., Laczo, J., Rubinova, E., Mokrisova, I., Hyncicova, E., Andel, R.,…Hort, J. (2013). Spatial navigation in young versus older adults. *Front Aging Neurosci*, *5*, 94. https://doi.org/10.3389/fnagi.2013.00094

Gazzaniga, M. S. (2005). Forty-five years of split-brain research and still going strong. *Nat Rev Neurosci*, *6*(8), 653–659. https://doi.org/10.1038/nrn1723

Gazzaniga, M. S. (Ed.). (2009). *The cognitive neurosciences* (4th ed.). Cambridge, MA: MIT Press.

Gelman, R., & Gallistel, C. R. (1978). *The child's understanding of number*. Cambridge, MA: Harvard University Press.

Genevsky, A., Garrett, C. T., Alexander, P. P., & Vinogradov, S. (2010). Cognitive training in schizophrenia: A neuroscience-based approach. *Dialogues Clin Neurosci*, *12*(3), 416–421. https://doi.org/10.31887/DCNS.2010.12.3/agenevsky

Genon, S., Eickhoff, S. B., & Kharabian, S. (2022). Linking interindividual variability in brain structure to behaviour. *Nat Rev Neurosci*, *23*(5), 307–318. https://doi.org/10.1038/s41583-022-00584-7

Gentner, D., & Goldin-Meadow, S. (Eds.). (2003). *Language in mind: Advances in the study of language and thought*. Cambridge, MA: MIT Press.

Gentner, D., & Markman, A. B. (1997). Structure mapping in analogy and similarity. *Amer Psychol*, *52*, 45–56.

Gentner, D., & Stevens, A. L. (Eds.). (2014). *Mental models*. London, UK: Psychology Press.

Gentsch, A., Weber, A., Synofzik, M., Vosgerau, G., & Schutz-Bosbach, S. (2016). Towards a common framework of grounded action cognition: Relating motor control, perception and cognition. *Cognition*, *146*, 81–89. https://doi.org/10.1016/j.cognition.2015.09.010

Geranmayeh, F., Wise, R. J., Mehta, A., & Leech, R. (2014). Overlapping networks engaged during spoken language production and its cognitive control. *J Neurosci*, *34*(26), 8728–8740. https://doi.org/10.1523/JNEUROSCI.0428-14.2014

Gerbella, M., Caruana, F., & Rizzolatti, G. (2019). Pathways for smiling, disgust and fear recognition in blindsight patients. *Neuropsychologia*, *128*, 6–13. https://doi.org/10.1016/j.neuropsychologia.2017.08.028

Gershman, S. J., & Niv, Y. (2010). Learning latent structure: Carving nature at its joints. *Curr Opin Neurobiol*, *20*(2), 251–256. https://doi.org/10.1016/j.conb.2010.02.008

Gershon, M. D. (1999). The enteric nervous system: A second brain. *Hosp Pract*, *34*, 31–52.

Geva-Sagiv, M., Las, L., Yovel, Y., & Ulanovsky, N. (2015). Spatial cognition in bats and rats: From sensory acquisition to multiscale maps and navigation. *Nat Rev Neurosci*, *16*(2), 94–108. https://doi.org/10.1038/nrn3888

Ghirlanda, S., & Enquist, M. (2003). A century of generalization. *Anim Behav*, *66*, 15–36.

Gibson, J. J. (1977). The theory of affordances. In R. Shaw & J. Bransford (Eds.), *Perceiving, acting, and knowing: Toward an ecological psychology* (pp. 67–82). Erlbaum.

Gibson, J. J. (1979). *The ecological approach to visual perception*. Boston, MA: Houghton Mifflin.

Gibson, J. J. (1986). *The ecological approach to visual perception*. Boston, MA: Houghton Mifflin.

Gigerenzer, G. (1991). From tools to theories: A heuristic of discovery in cognitive psychology. *Psychol Rev*, *98*, 254–267.

Gigerenzer, G. (2008). Why Heuristics Work. *Perspect Psychol Sci*, *3*(1), 20–29. https://doi.org/10.1111/j.1745-6916.2008.00058.x

Gilboa, A., & Marlatte, H. (2017). Neurobiology of Schemas and Schema-Mediated Memory. *Trends Cogn Sci*, *21*(8), 618–631. https://doi.org/10.1016/j.tics.2017.04.013

Gill, L. N., Renault, R., Campbell, E., Rainville, P., & Khoury, B. (2020). Mindfulness induction and cognition: A systematic review and meta-analysis. *Conscious Cogn*, *84*, 102991. https://doi.org/10.1016/j.concog.2020.102991

Gillam, E. (2011). An introduction to animal communication. *Nat Educ Knowl*, *3*, 70.

Gillham, N. W. (2009). Cousins: Charles Darwin, Sir Francis Galton, and the birth of eugenics. *Significance*, *6*, 132–135.

Gilmore, C., Attridge, N., Clayton, S., Cragg, L., Johnson, S., Marlow, N.,…Inglis, M. (2013). Individual differences in inhibitory control, not non-verbal number acuity, correlate with mathematics achievement. *PLoS One*, *8*, e67374. https://doi.org/10.1371/journal.pone.0067374

Gino, F., Sharek, Z., & Moore, D. A. (2011). Keeping the illusion of control under control: Ceilings, floors, and imperfect calibration. *Organ Behavr Hum Decis Process*, *114*, 104–114.

Giray, E. F., Altkin, W. M., Vaught, G. M., & Roodin, P. A. (1976). The incidence of eidetic imagery as a function of age. *Child Dev*, *47*, 1207–1210. https://www.ncbi.nlm.nih.gov/pubmed/1001094

Giurfa, M. (2019). An insect's sense of number. *Trends Cogn Sci*, *23*(9), 720–722. https://doi.org/10.1016/j.tics.2019.06.010

Giurfa, M., Zhang, S., Jenett, A., Menzel, R., & Srinivasan, M. V. (2001). The concepts of 'sameness' and 'difference' in an insect. *Nature*, *410*(6831), 930–933. https://doi.org/10.1038/35073582

Glanzman, D. L. (2005). Associative learning: Hebbian flies. *Curr Biol, 15*(11), R416–419. https://doi.org/10.1016/j.cub.2005.05.028

Glaser, R. (1981). The future of testing: A research agenda for cognitive psychology and psychometrics. *Am Psychol, 36*, 923–936.

Glenberg, A. M., Witt, J. K., & Metcalfe, J. (2013). From the revolution to embodiment: 25 years of cognitive psychology. *Perspect Psychol Sci, 8*(5), 573–585. https://doi.org/10.1177/1745691613498098

Glickstein, M. (2006). Golgi and Cajal: The neuron doctrine and the 100th anniversary of the 1906 Nobel Prize. *Curr Biol, 16*(5), R147–151. https://doi.org/10.1016/j.cub.2006.02.053

Gluck, M. A., & Myers, C. E. (1993). Hippocampal mediation of stimulus representation: A computational theory. *Hippocampus, 3*(4), 491–516. https://doi.org/10.1002/hipo.450030410

Gluck, M. A., Mercado, E., & Myers, C. E. (2016). *Learning and memory: From brain to behavior.* New York, NY: Worth.

Gluck, M. A., Mercado, E., & Myers, C. E. (2020). *Learning and memory: From brain to behavior.* New York, NY: Worth.

Godden, D., & Baddeley, A. (1975). Context-dependent memory in two natural environments: On land and under water. *Br J Psychol, 66*, 325–331.

Goldhill, O. (2018). French hospital used hypnosis to block pain in 150 cancer surgeries. *Quartz.* https://qz.com/1298753/a-french-hospital-used-hypnosis-to-block-pain-in-150-cancer-surgeries

Goldman, A. I. (1993). The psychology of folk psychology. *Behav Brain Sci, 16*, 15–28.

Goldstone, R. L. (1998). Perceptual learning. *Annu Rev Psychol, 49*, 585–612. https://doi.org/10.1146/annurev.psych.49.1.585

Goldstone, R. L., & Kersten, A. (2003). Concepts and categorization. *Handbook of Psychology. Eight, 22*, 597–621.

Goldstone, R. L., Kersten, A., & Carvalho, P. F. (2017). Categorization and concepts. In J. Wixted (Ed.), *Stevens' handbook of experimental psychology and cognitive neuroscience, 4 ed, Vol 3: Language & thought* (pp. 275–317).

Gonzalez-Castillo, J., Kam, J. W. Y., Hoy, C. W., & Bandettini, P. A. (2021). How to interpret resting-state fMRI: Ask your participants. *J Neurosci, 41*(6), 1130–1141. https://doi.org/10.1523/JNEUROSCI.1786-20.2020

Goodall, J. (1964). Tool-using and aimed throwing in a community of free-living chimpanzees. *Nature, 201*, 1264–1266. https://doi.org/10.1038/2011264a0

Goodwyn, S. W., & Acredolo, L. P. (1998). Encouraging symbolic gestures: A new perspective on the relationship between gesture and speech. *New Dir Child Dev*(79), 61–73. https://www.ncbi.nlm.nih.gov/pubmed/9507704

Goolkasian, P., & Woodberry, C. (2010). Priming effects with ambiguous figures. *Atten Percept Psychophys, 72*(1), 168–178. https://doi.org/10.3758/APP.72.1.168

Gordon, J., Maselli, A., Lancia, G. L., Thiery, T., Cisek, P., & Pezzulo, G. (2021). The road towards understanding embodied decisions. *Neurosci Biobehav Rev, 131*, 722–736. https://doi.org/10.1016/j.neubiorev.2021.09.034

Gordon, R. L., Jacobs, M. S., Schuele, C. M., & McAuley, J. D. (2015). Perspectives on the rhythm-grammar link and its implications for typical and atypical language development. *Ann N Y Acad Sci, 1337*, 16–25. https://doi.org/10.1111/nyas.12683

Gou, Z., Choudhury, N., & Benasich, A. A. (2011). Resting frontal gamma power at 16, 24 and 36 months predicts individual differences in language and cognition at 4 and 5 years. *Behav Brain Res, 220*(2), 263–270. https://doi.org/10.1016/j.bbr.2011.01.048

Goulas, A., Majka, P., Rosa, M. G. P., & Hilgetag, C. C. (2019). A blueprint of mammalian cortical connectomes. *PLoS Biol, 17*(3), e2005346. https://doi.org/10.1371/journal.pbio.2005346

Goupil, L., & Kouider, S. (2019). Developing a reflective mind: From core metacognition to explicit self-reflection. *Curr Dir Psychol Sci, 28*, 403–408.

Grahek, I., Shenhav, A., Musslick, S., Krebs, R. M., & Koster, E. H. W. (2019). Motivation and cognitive control in depression. *Neurosci Biobehav Rev, 102*, 371–381. https://doi.org/10.1016/j.neubiorev.2019.04.011

Grandin, T. (2009). How does visual thinking work in the mind of a person with autism? A personal account. *Philos Trans R Soc Lond B Biol Sci, 364*(1522), 1437–1442. https://doi.org/10.1098/rstb.2008.0297

Grant, J. E., & Chamberlain, S. R. (2014). Impulsive action and impulsive choice across substance and behavioral addictions: Cause or consequence? *Addict Behav, 39*(11), 1632–1639. https://doi.org/10.1016/j.addbeh.2014.04.022

Gray, J. R., & Thompson, P. M. (2004). Neurobiology of intelligence: Science and ethics. *Nat Rev Neurosci, 5*(6), 471–482. https://doi.org/10.1038/nrn1405

Gredeback, G., & Melinder, A. (2010). Infants' understanding of everyday social interactions: A dual process account. *Cognition, 114*(2), 197–206. https://doi.org/10.1016/j.cognition.2009.09.004

Green, C. S., & Bavelier, D. (2003). Action video game modifies visual selective attention. *Nature, 423*(6939), 534–537. https://doi.org/10.1038/nature01647

Green, S., & Marler, P. (1979). The analysis of animal communication. In P. Marler & J. G. Vandenbergh (Eds.), *Social behavior and communication* (pp. 73–158). Springer.

Greenfield, P. M. (2009). Technology and informal education: What is taught, what is learned. *Science, 323*(5910), 69–71. https://doi.org/10.1126/science.1167190

Greenspan, N. S. (2022). Genes, heritability, 'race', and intelligence: Misapprehensions and implications. *Genes (Basel), 13*(2). https://doi.org/10.3390/genes13020346

Greenwald, A. G., & Banaji, M. R. (1995). Implicit social cognition: Attitudes, self-esteem, and stereotypes. *Psychol Rev, 102*(1), 4–27. https://doi.org/10.1037/0033-295x.102.1.4

Greenwald, A. G., Spangenberg, E. R., Pratkanis, A. R., & Eskenazi, J. (1991). Doubleblind tests of subliminal self-help audiotapes. *Psychol Sci, 2*, 119–122.

Greenwood, B. N., & Fleshner, M. (2008). Exercise, learned helplessness, and the stress-resistant brain. *Neuromolecular Med, 10*(2), 81–98. https://doi.org/10.1007/s12017-008-8029-y

Gregory, R. L. (2009). *Seeing through illusions.* New York, NY: Oxford University Press.

Greiner, P., Houdek, P., Sladek, M., & Sumova, A. (2022). Early rhythmicity in the fetal suprachiasmatic nuclei in response to maternal signals detected by omics approach. *PLoS Biol, 20*(5), e3001637. https://doi.org/10.1371/journal.pbio.3001637

Greving, S., & Richter, T. (2018). Examining the testing effect in university teaching: Retrievability and question format matter. *Front Psychol, 9*, 2412. https://doi.org/10.3389/fpsyg.2018.02412

Grice, H. P. (1975). Logic and conversation. In P. Cole & J. Morgan (Eds.), *Syntax and Semantics: Vol. 3 Speech Acts*. Cambridge, MA: Academic Press.

Griffin, A. L., Asaka, Y., Darling, R. D., & Berry, S. D. (2004). Theta-contingent trial presentation accelerates learning rate and enhances hippocampal plasticity during trace eyeblink conditioning. *Behav Neurosci, 118*, 403–411. https://doi.org/10.1037/0735-7044.118.2.403

Griffiths, S. (2014, 2/16/23). Dogs see us move in SLOW MOTION: Animal's brain processes visual information faster than humans, study finds. *Daily Mail online.*

Griffiths, T. L. (2015). Manifesto for a new (computational) cognitive revolution. *Cognition, 135*, 21–23. https://doi.org/10.1016/j.cognition.2014.11.026

Griffiths, T. L., & Tenenbaum, J. B. (2006). Optimal predictions in everyday cognition. *Psychol Sci, 17*(9), 767–773. https://doi.org/10.1111/j.1467-9280.2006.01780.x

Grondin, S. (2010). Timing and time perception: A review of recent behavioral and neuroscience findings and theoretical directions. *Atten Percept Psychophys, 72*(3), 561–582. https://doi.org/10.3758/APP.72.3.561

Gross, C. G. (1995). Aristotle on the brain. *Neuroscientist, 1*, 245–250.

Gross, J. (2019). Magnetoencephalography in cognitive neuroscience: A primer. *Neuron, 104*(2), 189–204. https://doi.org/10.1016/j.neuron.2019.07.001

Gross, J., Baillet, S., Barnes, G. R., Henson, R. N., Hillebrand, A., Jensen, O.,…Schoffelen, J. M. (2013). Good practice for conducting and reporting MEG research. *Neuroimage, 65*, 349–363. https://doi.org/10.1016/j.neuroimage.2012.10.001

Grothe, B., Pecka, M., & McAlpine, D. (2010). Mechanisms of sound localization in mammals. *Physiol Rev, 90*(3), 983–1012. https://doi.org/10.1152/physrev.00026.2009

Groussard, M., Viader, F., Landeau, B., Desgranges, B., Eustache, F., & Platel, H. (2014). The effects of musical practice on structural plasticity: The dynamics of grey matter changes. *Brain Cogn, 90*, 174–180. https://doi.org/10.1016/j.bandc.2014.06.013

Gruber, M. J., & Fandakova, Y. (2021). Curiosity in childhood and adolescence—What can we learn from the brain. *Curr Opin Behav Sci, 39*, 178–184. https://doi.org/10.1016/j.cobeha.2021.03.031

Grush, R. (2004). The emulation theory of representation: Motor control, imagery, and perception. *Behav Brain Sci, 27*(3), 377–396; discussion 396–442. https://doi.org/10.1017/s0140525×04000093

Gu, B. M., van Rijn, H., & Meck, W. H. (2015). Oscillatory multiplexing of neural population codes for interval timing and working memory. *Neurosci Biobehav Rev, 48*, 160–185. https://doi.org/10.1016/j.neubiorev.2014.10.008

Guigon, E., Dorizzi, B., Burnod, Y., & Schultz, W. (1995). Neural correlates of learning in the prefrontal cortex of the monkey: A predictive model. *Cereb Cortex, 5*(2), 135–147. https://doi.org/10.1093/cercor/5.2.135

Gulyas, E., Gombos, F., Sutori, S., Lovas, A., Ziman, G., & Kovacs, I. (2022). Visual imagery vividness declines across the lifespan. *Cortex, 154*, 365–374. https://doi.org/10.1016/j.cortex.2022.06.011

Guttman, N., & Kalish, H. I. (1956). Discriminability and stimulus generalization. *J Exp Psychol, 51*(1), 79–88. https://doi.org/10.1037/h0046219

Guynn, M. J., McDaniel, M. A., & Einstein, G. O. (1998). Prospective memory: When reminders fail. *Mem Cognit, 26*(2), 287–298. https://doi.org/10.3758/bf03201140

Gyurak, A., Gross, J. J., & Etkin, A. (2011). Explicit and implicit emotion regulation: A dual-process framework. *Cogn Emot, 25*(3), 400–412. https://doi.org/10.1080/02699931.2010.544160

H

Haar, C. V. (2020). Challenges and opportunities in animal models of gambling behavior. *Curr Opin Behav Sci, 31*, 42–47.

Haber, R. N. (1979). Twenty years of haunting eidetic imagery: Where's the ghost? *Behav Brain Sci, 2*, 583–594.

Hacques, G., Komar, J., Dicks, M., & Seifert, L. (2021). Exploring to learn and learning to explore. *Psychol Res, 85*(4), 1367–1379. https://doi.org/10.1007/s00426-020-01352-x

Haggard, P. (2019). The neurocognitive bases of human volition. *Annu Rev Psychol, 70*, 9–28. https://doi.org/10.1146/annurev-psych-010418-103348

Haier, R. J. (2016). *The neuroscience of intelligence*. UK: Cambridge University Press.

Haimovitz, K., & Dweck, C. S. (2017). The origins of children's growth and fixed mindsets: New research and a new proposal. *Child Dev, 88*(6), 1849–1859. https://doi.org/10.1111/cdev.12955

Hamilton, P. J., & Nestler, E. J. (2019). Epigenetics and addiction. *Curr Opin Neurobiol, 59*, 128–136. https://doi.org/10.1016/j.conb.2019.05.005

Hamilton, R. K., Hiatt Racer, K., & Newman, J. P. (2015). Impaired integration in psychopathy: A unified theory of psychopathic dysfunction. *Psychol Rev, 122*(4), 770–791. https://doi.org/10.1037/a0039703

Hamlin, J. K., Wynn, K., & Bloom, P. (2007). Social evaluation by preverbal infants. *Nature, 450*(7169), 557–559. https://doi.org/10.1038/nature06288

Hammond, K. R., & Summers, D. A. (1972). Cognitive control. *Psychol Rev, 79*, 58–67.

Hampson, R. E., Song, D., Robinson, B. S., Fetterhoff, D., Dakos, A. S., Roeder, B. M.,…Deadwyler, S. A. (2018). Developing a hippocampal neural prosthetic to facilitate human memory encoding and recall. *J Neural Eng, 15*(3), 036014. https://doi.org/10.1088/1741-2552/aaaed7

Han, X., Chen, M., Wang, F., Windrem, M., Wang, S., Shanz, S.,…Nedergaard, M. (2013). Forebrain engraftment by human glial progenitor cells enhances synaptic plasticity and learning in adult mice. *Cell Stem Cell, 12*(3), 342–353. https://doi.org/10.1016/j.stem.2012.12.015

Hanson, H. M. (1959). Effects of discrimination training on stimulus generalization. *J Exp Psychol, 58*, 321–334. https://doi.org/10.1037/h0042606

Hardiman, P. T., Dufresne, R., & Mestre, J. P. (1989). The relation between problem categorization and problem solving among experts and novices. *Mem Cognit, 17*(5), 627–638. https://doi.org/10.3758/bf03197085

Hare, B., Plyusnina, I., Ignacio, N., Schepina, O., Stepika, A., Wrangham, R., & Trut, L. (2005). Social cognitive evolution in captive foxes is a correlated by-product of experimental domestication. *Curr Biol, 15*(3), 226–230. https://doi.org/10.1016/j.cub.2005.01.040

Hariri, A. R., Goldberg, T. E., Mattay, V. S., Kolachana, B. S., Callicott, J. H., Egan, M. F., & Weinberger, D. R. (2003). Brain-derived neurotrophic factor val66met polymorphism affects human memory-related hippocampal activity and predicts memory performance. *J Neurosci, 23*(17), 6690–6694. https://doi.org/10.1523/JNEUROSCI.23-17-06690.2003

Harley, T. A. (2008). *The psychology of language: From data to theory.* London, UK: Psychology Press.

Harlow, H. F. (1949). The formation of learning sets. *Psychol Rev, 56*(1), 51–65. https://doi.org/10.1037/h0062474

Harmon-Jones, E., & Mills, J. (2019). An introduction to cognitive dissonance theory and an overview of current perspectives on the theory. In E. Harmon-Jones (Ed.), *Cognitive dissonance: Reexamining a pivotal theory in psychology* (pp. 3–24). Washington, DC: American Psychological Association.

Harnad, S. (2016). Animal sentience: The other-minds problem. *Animal Sentience, 1*, 1–11.

Harrington, D. L., Haaland, K. Y., & Knight, R. T. (1998). Cortical networks underlying mechanisms of time perception. *J Neurosci, 18*(3), 1085–1095. https://doi.org/10.1523/JNEUROSCI.18-03-01085.1998

Harris, C. S. (1965). Perceptual adaptation to inverted, reversed, and displaced vision. *Psychol Rev, 72*, 419–444.

Hassan, A., & Josephs, K. A. (2016). Alien hand syndrome. *Curr Neurol Neurosci Rep, 16*(8), 73. https://doi.org/10.1007/s11910-016-0676-z

Hastings, M. H., Maywood, E. S., & Brancaccio, M. (2019). The mammalian circadian timing system and the suprachiasmatic nucleus as its pacemaker. *Biology (Basel), 8*(1). https://doi.org/10.3390/biology8010013

Hawkins, G. E., Hayes, B. K., & Heit, E. (2016). A dynamic model of reasoning and memory. *J Exp Psychol Gen, 145*(2), 155–180. https://doi.org/10.1037/xge0000113

Hayashi, M. J., Ditye, T., Harada, T., Hashiguchi, M., Sadato, N., Carlson, S.,… Kanai, R. (2015). Time adaptation shows duration selectivity in the human parietal cortex. *PLoS Biol, 13*(9), e1002262. https://doi.org/10.1371/journal.pbio.1002262

Hebb, D. O. (1949). *The organization of behavior: A neuropsychological theory.* New York, NY: Wiley.

Hebb, D. O. (1949). *The organization of behavior: A psychological theory.* New York, NY: Wiley.

Hecht, E. E., Kukekova, A. V., Gutman, D. A., Acland, G. M., Preuss, T. M., & Trut, L. N. (2021). Neuromorphological changes following selection for tameness and aggression in the Russian fox farm experiment. *J Neurosci, 41*(28), 6144–6156. https://doi.org/10.1523/JNEUROSCI.3114-20.2021

Heidelberger, M. (2004). *Nature from within: Gustav Theodor Fechner and his psychophysical worldview.* PA: University of Pittsburgh Press.

Helfinstein, S. M., Schonberg, T., Congdon, E., Karlsgodt, K. H., Mumford, J. A., Sabb, F. W.,… Poldrack, R. A. (2014). Predicting risky choices from brain activity patterns. *Proc Natl Acad Sci U S A, 111*(7), 2470–2475. https://doi.org/10.1073/pnas.1321728111

Helie, S., & Sun, R. (2010). Incubation, insight, and creative problem solving: A unified theory and a connectionist model. *Psychol Rev, 117*(3), 994–1024. https://doi.org/10.1037/a0019532

Helmholtz, H. v. (1878/1971). The facts of perception. In R. Kahl (Ed.), *Selected writings of Hermann von Helmholtz.* Middletown, CT: Wesleyan University Press.

Henrich, J., Heine, S. J., & Norenzayan, A. (2010). Most people are not WEIRD. *Nature, 466*(7302), 29. https://doi.org/10.1038/466029a

Henrich, J., Heine, S. J., & Norenzayan, A. (2010). The weirdest people in the world? *Behav Brain Sci, 33*, 61–83. https://doi.org/10.1017/S0140525×0999152X

Herdman, C. M., & Friedman, A. (1985). Multiple resources in divided attention: A cross-modal test of the independence of hemispheric resources. *J Exp Psychol Hum Percept Perform, 11*(1), 40–49. https://doi.org/10.1037//0096-1523.11.1.40

Herholz, S. C., Coffey, E. B., Pantev, C., & Zatorre, R. J. (2016). Dissociation of neural networks for predisposition and for training-related plasticity in auditory-motor learning. *Cereb Cortex, 26*(7), 3125–3134. https://doi.org/10.1093/cercor/bhv138

Herman, A. M., & Duka, T. (2019). Facets of impulsivity and alcohol use: What role do emotions play? *Neurosci Biobehav Rev, 106*, 202–216. https://doi.org/10.1016/j.neubiorev.2018.08.011

Herman, L. M., Richards, D. G., & Wolz, J. P. (1984). Comprehension of sentences by bottlenosed dolphins. *Cognition, 16*(2), 129–219. https://doi.org/10.1016/0010-0277(84)90003-9

Herman., L. M. (2002). Vocal, social, and self-imitation by bottle-nosed dolphins. In K. Dautenhahn & C. L. Nehaniv (Eds.), *Imitation in animals and artifacts.* Cambridge, MA: MIT Press.

Herrnstein, R. J. (1970). On the law of effect. *J Exp Anal Behav, 13*(2), 243–266. https://doi.org/10.1901/jeab.1970.13-243

Herrod, J. L., Snyder, S. K., Hart, J. B., Frantz, S. J., & Ayres, K. M. (2023). Applications of the Premack principle: A review of the literature. *Behav Modif, 47*(1), 219–246. https://doi.org/10.1177/01454455221085249

Hess, U., & Thibault, P. (2009). Darwin and emotion expression. *Am Psychol, 64*(2), 120–128. https://doi.org/10.1037/a0013386

Hessels, R. S., & Hooge, I. T. C. (2019). Eye tracking in developmental cognitive neuroscience—The good, the bad and the ugly. *Dev Cogn Neurosci, 40*, 100710. https://doi.org/10.1016/j.dcn.2019.100710

Hetu, S., Gregoire, M., Saimpont, A., Coll, M. P., Eugene, F., Michon, P. E., & Jackson, P. L. (2013). The neural network of motor imagery: An ALE meta-analysis. *Neurosci Biobehav Rev, 37*(5), 930–949. https://doi.org/10.1016/j.neubiorev.2013.03.017

Hewitt, J. K. (2020). Twin studies of brain, cognition, and behavior. *Neurosci Biobehav Rev, 115*, 64–67. https://doi.org/10.1016/j.neubiorev.2020.04.009

Heyes, C. (2011). Automatic imitation. *Psychol Bull, 137*(3), 463–483. https://doi.org/10.1037/a0022288

Heyes, C. (2012). New thinking: The evolution of human cognition. *Philos Trans R Soc Lond B Biol Sci, 367*(1599), 2091–2096. https://doi.org/10.1098/rstb.2012.0111

Heyes, C. (2016). Imitation: Not in our genes. *Curr Biol, 26*(10), R412–414. https://doi.org/10.1016/j.cub.2016.03.060

Heyes, C. (2023). Imitation and culture: What gives? *Mind Lang, 38*, 42–63.

Heyes, C. M., Ray, E. D., Mitchell, C. J., & Nokes, T. (2000). Stimulus enhancement: Controls for social facilitation and local enhancement. *Learn Motiv, 31*, 83–98.

Heyes, C., & Catmur, C. (2022). What happened to mirror neurons? *Perspect Psychol Sci, 17*(1), 153–168. https://doi.org/10.1177/1745691621990638

Hickok, G. (2009). Eight problems for the mirror neuron theory of action understanding in monkeys and humans. *J Cogn Neurosci, 21*(7), 1229–1243. https://doi.org/10.1162/jocn.2009.21189

Hickok, G., & Poeppel, D. (2007). The cortical organization of speech processing. *Nat Rev Neurosci, 8*(5), 393–402. https://doi.org/10.1038/nrn2113

Hirst, W., & Coman, A. (2018). Building a collective memory: The case for collective forgetting. *Curr Opin Psychol, 23*, 88–92. https://doi.org/10.1016/j.copsyc.2018.02.002

Hirst, W., & Phelps, E. A. (2016). Flashbulb memories. *Curr Dir Psychol Sci, 25*(1), 36–41. https://doi.org/10.1177/0963721415622487

Hirst, W., Yamashiro, J. K., & Coman, A. (2018). Collective memory from a psychological perspective. *Trends Cogn Sci, 22*(5), 438–451. https://doi.org/10.1016/j.tics.2018.06.001

Hiver, P., Al-Hoorie, A. H., & Evans, R. (2021). Complex dynamic systems theory in language learning: A scoping review of 25 years of research. *Stud Second Lang Acquis*, 1–29.

Hodges, J. R., & Warlow, C. P. (1990). Syndromes of transient amnesia: Towards a classification. A study of 153 cases. *J Neurol Neurosurg Psychiatry, 53*, 834–843. http://www.ncbi.nlm.nih.gov/pubmed/2266362

Hofman, P. M., Van Riswick, J. G., & Van Opstal, A. J. (1998). Relearning sound localization with new ears. *Nat Neurosci, 1*(5), 417–421. https://doi.org/10.1038/1633

Holmes, A. J., Hollinshead, M. O., Roffman, J. L., Smoller, J. W., & Buckner, R. L. (2016). Individual differences in cognitive control circuit anatomy link sensation seeking, impulsivity, and substance use. *J Neurosci, 36*(14), 4038–4049. https://doi.org/10.1523/JNEUROSCI.3206-15.2016

Holtmann, O., Bruchmann, M., Monig, C., Schwindt, W., Melzer, N., Miltner, W. H. R., & Straube, T. (2020). Lateralized deficits of disgust processing after insula-basal ganglia damage. *Front Psychol, 11*, 1429. https://doi.org/10.3389/fpsyg.2020.01429

Honey, R. C., Dwyer, D. M., & Iliescu, A. F. (2020). HeiDI: A model for Pavlovian learning and performance with reciprocal associations. *Psychol Rev, 127*(5), 829–852. https://doi.org/10.1037/rev0000196

Hooks, B. M., & Chen, C. (2007). Critical periods in the visual system: Changing views for a model of experience-dependent plasticity. *Neuron, 56*(2), 312–326. https://doi.org/10.1016/j.neuron.2007.10.003

Hoppitt, W. J., Brown, G. R., Kendal, R., Rendell, L., Thornton, A., Webster, M. M., & Laland, K. N. (2008). Lessons from animal teaching. *Trends Ecol Evol, 23*(9), 486–493. https://doi.org/10.1016/j.tree.2008.05.008

Horikawa, T., & Kamitani, Y. (2017). Generic decoding of seen and imagined objects using hierarchical visual features. *Nat Commun, 8*, 15037. https://doi.org/10.1038/ncomms15037

Horikawa, T., Tamaki, M., Miyawaki, Y., & Kamitani, Y. (2013). Neural decoding of visual imagery during sleep. *Science, 340*(6132), 639–642. https://doi.org/10.1126/science.1234330

Horn, J. L. (1968). Organization of abilities and the development of intelligence. *Psychol Rev, 75*(3), 242–259. https://doi.org/10.1037/h0025662

Horowitz, M. J., Adams, J. E., & Rutkin, B. B. (1968). Visual imagery on brain stimulation. *Arch Gen Psychiatry, 19*(4), 469–486. http://www.ncbi.nlm.nih.gov/pubmed/4876804

Horvath, G., Andersson, H., & Paulsson, G. (2010). Characteristic odour in the blood reveals ovarian carcinoma. *BMC Cancer, 10*, 643. https://doi.org/10.1186/1471-2407-10-643

Howard, D., & Franklin, S. (1988). *Missing the meaning*. Cambridge, MA: MIT Press.

Howard, R. W. (2009). Individual differences in expertise development over decades in a complex intellectual domain. *Mem Cognit, 37*, 194–209. https://doi.org/10.3758/MC.37.2.194

Howe, M. L., & Courage, M. L. (1993). On resolving the enigma of infantile amnesia. *Psychol Bull, 113*(2), 305–326. https://doi.org/10.1037/0033-2909.113.2.305

Hu, Q., & Zhang, M. (2019). The development of symmetry concept in preschool children. *Cognition, 189*, 131–140. https://doi.org/10.1016/j.cognition.2019.03.022

Huang, F., Han, L., Jiang, Y., Li, F., & Luo, J. (2019). Neural adaptation and cognitive inflexibility in repeated problem-solving behaviors. *Cortex, 119*, 470–479. https://doi.org/10.1016/j.cortex.2019.08.001

Hubbard, T. L., & Ruppel, S. E. (2021). Vividness, clarity, and control in auditory imagery. *Imagin Cogn Pers, 41*, 207–221.

Hubel, D. H., & Wiesel, T. N. (1970). The period of susceptibility to the physiological effects of unilateral eye closure in kittens. *J Physiol, 206*(2), 419–436. https://doi.org/10.1113/jphysiol.1970.sp009022

Hubel, D. H., & Wiesel, T. N. (1979). Brain mechanisms of vision. *Sci Am, 241*(3), 150–162. https://doi.org/10.1038/scientificamerican0979-150

Hull, C. L. (1943). *Principles of behavior*. Appleton-Century-Crofts.

Humeau, Y., & Choquet, D. (2019). The next generation of approaches to investigate the link between synaptic plasticity and learning. *Nat Neurosci, 22*(10), 1536–1543. https://doi.org/10.1038/s41593-019-0480-6

Hurme, M., Koivisto, M., Revonsuo, A., & Railo, H. (2017). Early processing in primary visual cortex is necessary for conscious and unconscious vision while late processing is necessary only for conscious vision in neurologically healthy humans. *Neuroimage, 150*, 230–238. https://doi.org/10.1016/j.neuroimage.2017.02.060

Husband, R. W. (1929). A comparison of human adults and white rats in maze learning. *J Comp Psychol, 9*, 361–377.

Hwang, G. J., Wang, S. Y., & Lai, C. L. (2021). Effects of a social regulation-based online learning framework on students' learning achievements and behaviors in mathematics. *Comput Educ, 160*, 104031.

Hwang, K. D., Kim, S. J., & Lee, Y. S. (2022). Cerebellar circuits for classical fear conditioning. *Front Cell Neurosci, 16*, 836948. https://doi.org/10.3389/fncel.2022.836948

I

Iacoboni, M. (2009). Imitation, empathy, and mirror neurons. *Annu Rev Psychol, 60*, 653–670. https://doi.org/10.1146/annurev.psych.60.110707.163604

Ingusci, S., Verlengia, G., Soukupova, M., Zucchini, S., & Simonato, M. (2019). Gene therapy tools for brain diseases. *Front Pharmacol, 10*, 724. https://doi.org/10.3389/fphar.2019.00724

Ingvalson, E. M., Nowicki, C., Zong, A., & Wong, P. C. (2017). Non-native speech learning in older adults. *Front Psychol, 8*, 148. https://doi.org/10.3389/fpsyg.2017.00148

Innis, N. K. (1992). Tolman and Tryon. Early research on the inheritance of the ability to learn. *Am Psychol, 47*(2), 190–197. https://doi.org/10.1037//0003-066x.47.2.190

Inoue, S., & Matsuzawa, T. (2007). Working memory of numerals in chimpanzees. *Curr Biol, 17*, R1004–1005. https://doi.org/10.1016/j.cub.2007.10.027

Iordan, M. C., Greene, M. R., Beck, D. M., & Fei-Fei, L. (2015). Basic level category structure emerges gradually across human ventral visual cortex. *J Cogn Neurosci, 27*(7), 1427–1446. https://doi.org/10.1162/jocn_a_00790

Iskra, A., & Tomc, H. G. (2016). Eye-tracking analysis of face observing and face recognition. *J Graph Eng Des, 7*, 5–11.

Itti, L., & Koch, C. (2000). A saliency-based search mechanism for overt and covert shifts of visual attention. *Vision Res, 40*(10–12), 1489–1506. https://doi.org/Doi 10.1016/S0042-6989(99)00163-7

Iverson, P., & Kuhl, P. K. (2000). Perceptual magnet and phoneme boundary effects in speech perception: Do they arise from a common mechanism? *Percept Psychophys, 62*(4), 874–886. http://www.ncbi.nlm.nih.gov/pubmed/10883591

Ivry, R. B., & Schlerf, J. E. (2008). Dedicated and intrinsic models of time perception. *Trends Cogn Sci, 12*(7), 273–280. https://doi.org/10.1016/j.tics.2008.04.002

Iyer, R., Wang, T. A., & Gillette, M. U. (2014). Circadian gating of neuronal functionality: A basis for iterative metaplasticity. *Front Syst Neurosci, 8*, 164. https://doi.org/10.3389/fnsys.2014.00164

J

Jaaskelainen, I. P., Sams, M., Glerean, E., & Ahveninen, J. (2021). Movies and narratives as naturalistic stimuli in neuroimaging. *Neuroimage, 224*, 117445. https://doi.org/10.1016/j.neuroimage.2020.117445

Jacobs, J., Weidemann, C. T., Miller, J. F., Solway, A., Burke, J. F., Wei, X. X.,…Kahana, M. J. (2013). Direct recordings of grid-like neuronal activity in human spatial navigation. *Nat Neurosci, 16*(9), 1188–1190. https://doi.org/10.1038/nn.3466

Jacobsen, J. H., Stelzer, J., Fritz, T. H., Chetelat, G., La Joie, R., & Turner, R. (2015). Why musical memory can be preserved in advanced Alzheimer's disease. *Brain, 138*(Pt 8), 2438–2450. https://doi.org/10.1093/brain/awv135

Jaeggi, S. M., Buschkuehl, M., Perrig, W. J., & Meier, B. (2010). The concurrent validity of the N-back task as a working memory measure. *Memory, 18*(4), 394–412. https://doi.org/10.1080/09658211003702171

Jahn, H. (2022). Memory loss in Alzheimer's disease. *Dialogues Clin Neurosci, 15*, 445–454.

James, W. (1890). *The principles of psychology*. New York, NY: H. Holt.

James, W. (1962). *Psychology: Briefer course*. New York, NY: Collier.

James, W. (2008). *Talks to teachers on psychology: And to students on some of life's ideals*. Rockville, MD: Arc Manor.

Jameson, K. A., Joe, K. C., Satalich, T. A., Bochko, V. A., Atilano, S. R., & Kenney, M. C. (2019). Color perception in observers with varying photopigment opsin genotypes. *J Vis, 19*, 29.

Jankowska, D. M., & Karwowski, M. (2015). Measuring creative imagery abilities. *Front Psychol, 6*, 1591. https://doi.org/10.3389/fpsyg.2015.01591

Jansson, G., & Johansson, G. (1973). Visual perception of bending motion. *Perception, 2*(3), 321–326. https://doi.org/10.1068/p020321

Jardim-Messeder, D., Lambert, K., Noctor, S., Pestana, F. M., de Castro Leal, M. E., Bertelsen, M. F.,…Herculano-Houzel, S. (2017). Dogs have the most neurons, though not the largest brain: Trade-off between body mass and number of neurons in the cerebral cortex of large carnivoran species. *Front Neuroanat, 11*, 118. https://doi.org/10.3389/fnana.2017.00118

Jeffery, K. J. (2007). Integration of the sensory inputs to place cells: What, where, why, and how? *Hippocampus, 17*, 775–785. https://doi.org/10.1002/hipo.20322

Jensen, K., Kirsch, I., Odmalm, S., Kaptchuk, T. J., & Ingvar, M. (2015). Classical conditioning of analgesic and hyperalgesic pain responses without conscious awareness. *Proc Natl Acad Sci U S A, 112*(25), 7863–7867. https://doi.org/10.1073/pnas.1504567112

Jensen, M. S., Yao, R., Street, W. N., & Simons, D. J. (2011). Change blindness and inattentional blindness. *Wiley Interdiscip Rev Cogn Sci, 2*(5), 529–546. https://doi.org/10.1002/wcs.130

Jiang, X., Bradley, E., Rini, R. A., Zeffiro, T., Vanmeter, J., & Riesenhuber, M. (2007). Categorization training results in shape- and category-selective human neural plasticity. *Neuron, 53*(6), 891–903. https://doi.org/10.1016/j.neuron.2007.02.015

Johanson, M., Vaurio, O., Tiihonen, J., & Lahteenvuo, M. (2019). A systematic literature review of neuroimaging of psychopathic traits. *Front Psychiatry, 10*, 1027. https://doi.org/10.3389/fpsyt.2019.01027

Johansson, B. B. (2011). Current trends in stroke rehabilitation. A review with focus on brain plasticity. *Acta Neurol Scand, 123*(3), 147–159. https://doi.org/10.1111/j.1600-0404.2010.01417.x

Jones, C. R., Malone, T. J., Dirnberger, G., Edwards, M., & Jahanshahi, M. (2008). Basal ganglia, dopamine and temporal processing: Performance on three timing tasks on and off medication in Parkinson's disease. *Brain Cogn, 68*(1), 30–41. https://doi.org/10.1016/j.bandc.2008.02.121

Jones, G. (2005). Echolocation. *Curr Biol, 15*(13), R484–488. https://doi.org/10.1016/j.cub.2005.06.051

Jones, K. T., Stephens, J. A., Alam, M., Bikson, M., & Berryhill, M. E. (2015). Longitudinal neurostimulation in older adults improves working memory. *PLoS One, 10*(4), e0121904. https://doi.org/10.1371/journal.pone.0121904

Jones, M. R., Katz, B., Buschkuehl, M., Jaeggi, S. M., & Shah, P. (2020). Exploring *N*-back cognitive training for children with ADHD. *J Atten Disord, 24*(5), 704–719. https://doi.org/10.1177/1087054718779230

Jones, S. S. (2006). Infants learn to imitate by being imitated. In C. Yu, L. B. Smith, & O. Sporns (Eds.), *Proccedings of the International Conference on Development and Learning*. Indiana University.

Joormann, J., Levens, S. M., & Gotlib, I. H. (2011). Sticky thoughts: Depression and rumination are associated with difficulties manipulating emotional material in working memory. *Psychol Sci, 22*(8), 979–983. https://doi.org/10.1177/0956797611415539

Joslyn, S. L., & Oakes, M. A. (2005). Directed forgetting of autobiographical events. *Mem Cognit, 33*, 577–587.

Josselyn, S. A., & Frankland, P. W. (2012). Infantile amnesia: A neurogenic hypothesis. *Learn Mem, 19*(9), 423–433. https://doi .org/10.1101/lm.021311.110

Josselyn, S. A., Kohler, S., & Frankland, P. W. (2015). Finding the engram. *Nat Rev Neurosci, 16*(9), 521–534. https://doi.org/10 .1038/nrn4000

Jostmann, N. B., Lakens, D., & Schubert, T. W. (2009). Weight as an embodiment of importance. *Psychol Sci, 20*(9), 1169–1174. https://doi.org/10.1111/j.1467-9280.2009.02426.x

Jozefowiez, J., Gaudichon, C., Mekkass, F., & Machado, A. (2018). Log versus linear timing in human temporal bisection: A signal detection theory study. *J Exp Psychol Anim Learn Cogn, 44*(4), 396–408. https://doi.org/10.1037/xan0000184

Jusczyk, P. W., & Aslin, R. N. (1995). Infants' detection of the sound patterns of words in fluent speech. *Cogn Psychol, 29*(1), 1–23. https://doi.org/10.1006/cogp.1995.1010

Just, M. A., & Carpenter, P. A. (1976). Eye fixations and cognitive processes. *Cogn Psychol, 8*, 441–480.

K

Kable, J. W., & Glimcher, P. W. (2007). The neural correlates of subjective value during intertemporal choice. *Nat Neurosci, 10*(12), 1625–1633. https://doi.org/10.1038/nn2007

Kacelnik, A., Vasconcelos, M., & Monteiro, T. (2023). Testing cognitive models of decision-making: Selected studies with starlings. *Anim Cogn, 26*(1), 117–127. https://doi.org/10.1007/s10071-022 -01723-4

Kahneman, D. (2011). *Thinking fast and slow.* New York, NY: Farrar, Strauss, and Giroux.

Kahneman, D., & Wright, P. (1971). Changes of pupil size and rehearsal strategies in a short-term memory task. *Q J Exp Psychol, 23*(2), 187–196. https://doi.org/10.1080/1464074710 8400239

Kaminski, J., Call, J., & Fischer, J. (2004). Word learning in a domestic dog: Evidence for "fast mapping." *Science, 304*(5677), 1682–1683. https://doi.org/10.1126/science.1097859

Kanai, R., Paffen, C. L., Hogendoorn, H., & Verstraten, F. A. (2006). Time dilation in dynamic visual display. *J Vis, 6*(12), 1421–1430. https://doi.org/10.1167/6.12.8

Kanan, C., Bseiso, D. N., Ray, N. A., Hsiao, J. H., & Cottrell, G. W. (2015). Humans have idiosyncratic and task-specific scanpaths for judging faces. *Vision Res, 108*, 67–76. https://doi.org/10.1016/j .visres.2015.01.013

Kang, S. H. K., Pashler, H., Cepeda, N. J., Rohrer, D., Carpenter, S. K., & Mozer, M. C. (2011). Does incorrect guessing impair fact learning? *J Educ Psychol, 103*, 48–59.

Kanwisher, N. (2000). Domain specificity in face perception. *Nat Neurosci, 3*(8), 759–763. https://doi.org/10.1038/77664

Kanwisher, N., McDermott, J., & Chun, M. M. (1997). The fusiform face area: A module in human extrastriate cortex specialized for face perception. *J Neurosci, 17*(11), 4302–4311. https://doi.org/10 .1523/JNEUROSCI.17-11-04302.1997

Kaplan, C., & Simon, H. A. (1990). In search of insight. *Cogn Psychol, 22*, 374–419.

Kaplan, H. S., Salazar Thula, O., Khoss, N., & Zimmer, M. (2020). Nested neuronal dynamics orchestrate a behavioral hierarchy across timescales. *Neuron, 105*(3), 562–576 e569. https://doi.org /10.1016/j.neuron.2019.10.037

Kaplan, R. (2000). *The nothing that is: A natural history of zero.* New York, NY: Oxford University Press.

Kapur, N. (1996). Paradoxical functional facilitation in brain-behaviour research. A critical review. *Brain, 119 (Pt 5)*, 1775–1790. https://doi.org/10.1093/brain/119.5.1775

Karanian, J. M., & Slotnick, S. D. (2017). False memory for context and true memory for context similarly activate the parahippocampal cortex. *Cortex, 91*, 79–88. https://doi.org/10.1016/j.cortex .2017.02.007

Karmarkar, U. R., & Buonomano, D. V. (2007). Timing in the absence of clocks: Encoding time in neural network states. *Neuron, 53*(3), 427–438. https://doi.org/10.1016/j.neuron .2007.01.006

Karni, A., Meyer, G., Rey-Hipolito, C., Jezzard, P., Adams, M. M., Turner, R., & Ungerleider, L. G. (1998). The acquisition of skilled motor performance: Fast and slow experience-driven changes in primary motor cortex. *Proc Natl Acad Sci U S A, 95*(3), 861–868. https://doi.org/10.1073/pnas.95.3.861

Kassai, R., Futo, J., Demetrovics, Z., & Takacs, Z. K. (2019). A meta-analysis of the experimental evidence on the near- and far-transfer effects among children's executive function skills. *Psychol Bull, 145*(2), 165–188. https://doi.org/10.1037 /bul0000180

Katsyri, J., Forger, K., Makarainen, M., & Takala, T. (2015). A review of empirical evidence on different uncanny valley hypotheses: Support for perceptual mismatch as one road to the valley of eeriness. *Front Psychol, 6*, 390. https://doi.org/10.3389/fpsyg .2015.00390

Kattenstroth, J. C., Kalisch, T., Holt, S., Tegenthoff, M., & Dinse, H. R. (2013). Six months of dance intervention enhances postural, sensorimotor, and cognitive performance in elderly without affecting cardio-respiratory functions. *Front Aging Neurosci, 5*, 5. https://doi.org/10.3389/fnagi.2013.00005

Katz, J. S., Wright, A. A., & Bodily, K. D. (2007). Issues in the comparative cognition of abstract-concept learning. *Comp Cogn Rev, 2*, 79–92.

Kawala-Sterniuk, A., Browarska, N., Al-Bakri, A., Pelc, M., Zygarlicki, J., Sidikova, M.,… Gorzelanczyk, E. J. (2021). Summary of over fifty years with brain-computer interfaces—A review. *Brain Sci, 11*(1). https://doi.org/10.3390/brainsci11010043

Ke, Y., Wang, N., Du, J., Kong, L., Liu, S., Xu, M., An, X., & Ming, D. (2019). The effects of transcranial direct current stimulation (tDCS) on working memory training in healthy young adults. *Front Hum Neurosci, 13*, 19. https://doi.org/10.3389/fnhum.2019.00019

Keen, R. (2011). The development of problem solving in young children: A critical cognitive skill. *Annu Rev Psychol, 62*, 1–21. https://doi.org/10.1146/annurev.psych.031809.130730

Keller, H. (1905). *The story of my life.* New York, NY: Doubleday.

Kellogg, R. T., & Raulerson, B. A., 3rd. (2007). Improving the writing skills of college students. *Psychon Bull Rev, 14*(2), 237–242. https://www.ncbi.nlm.nih.gov/pubmed/17694907

Kemmerer. (2015). *Cognitive neuroscience of language.* London, UK: Psychology Press.

Kenny, D. (2011). *The psychology of performance anxiety.* New York, NY: Oxford University Press.

Keogh, R., & Pearson, J. (2018). The blind mind: No sensory visual imagery in aphantasia. *Cortex, 105*, 53–60. https://doi.org/10 .1016/j.cortex.2017.10.012

Keuroghlian, A. S., & Knudsen, E. I. (2007). Adaptive auditory plasticity in developing and adult animals. *Prog Neurobiol, 82*(3), 109–121. https://doi.org/10.1016/j.pneurobio.2007.03.005

Keysers, C., Paracampo, R., & Gazzola, V. (2018). What neuromodulation and lesion studies tell us about the function of the mirror neuron system and embodied cognition. *Curr Opin Psychol, 24*, 35–40. https://doi.org/10.1016/j.copsyc.2018.04.001

Killeen, P. (1972). The matching law. *J Exp Anal Behav, 17*(3), 489–495. https://doi.org/10.1901/jeab.1972.17-489

Killeen, P. R. (2023). Trace theory of perception for temporal bisection. *Timing Time Percept, 1*, 1–13.

Killeen, P. R., & Fetterman, J. G. (1988). A behavioral theory of timing. *Psychol Rev, 95*(2), 274–295. https://doi.org/10.1037/0033-295x.95.2.274

Killeen, P. R., & Grondin, S. (2022). A trace theory of time perception. *Psychol Rev, 129*(4), 603–639. https://doi.org/10.1037/rev0000308

Killingly, C., & Lacherez, P. (2023). The song that never ends: The effect of repeated exposure on the development of an earworm. *Q J Exp Psychol (Hove)*, 17470218231152368. https://doi.org/10.1177/17470218231152368

Kim, N., Jang, S., & Cho, S. (2018). Testing the efficacy of training basic numerical cognition and transfer effects to improvement in children's math ability. *Front Psychol, 9*, 1775. https://doi.org/10.3389/fpsyg.2018.01775

Kim, S., Dede, A. J., Hopkins, R. O., & Squire, L. R. (2015). Memory, scene construction, and the human hippocampus. *Proc Natl Acad Sci U S A, 112*(15), 4767–4772. https://doi.org/10.1073/pnas.1503863112

Kingstone, A. (2020). Everyday human cognition and behaviour. *Can J Exp Psychol, 74*(4), 267–274. https://doi.org/10.1037/cep0000244

Kirby, K. N. (1994). Probabilities and utilities of fictional outcomes in Wason's four-card selection task. *Cognition, 51*(1), 1–28. https://doi.org/10.1016/0010-0277(94)90007-8

Kirsch, I., Lynn, S. J., Vigorito, M., & Miller, R. R. (2004). The role of cognition in classical and operant conditioning. *J Clin Psychol, 60*(4), 369–392. https://doi.org/10.1002/jclp.10251

Kirschfeld, K. (1999). Afterimages: A tool for defining the neural correlate of visual consciousness. *Conscious Cogn, 8*(4), 462–483. https://doi.org/10.1006/ccog.1999.0388

Kloo, D., Sodian, B., Kristen-Antonow, S., Kim, S., & Paulus, M. (2021). Knowing minds: Linking early perspective taking and later metacognitive insight. *Br J Dev Psychol, 39*(1), 39–53. https://doi.org/10.1111/bjdp.12359

Knudsen, E. I. (2004). Sensitive periods in the development of the brain and behavior. *J Cogn Neurosci, 16*(8), 1412–1425. https://doi.org/10.1162/0898929042304796

Knutson, B., Rick, S., Wimmer, G. E., Prelec, D., & Loewenstein, G. (2007). Neural predictors of purchases. *Neuron, 53*(1), 147–156. https://doi.org/10.1016/j.neuron.2006.11.010

Koch, A. J., D'Mello, S. D., & Sackett, P. R. (2015). A meta-analysis of gender stereotypes and bias in experimental simulations of employment decision making. *J Appl Psychol, 100*(1), 128–161. https://doi.org/10.1037/a0036734

Koch, C., Massimini, M., Boly, M., & Tononi, G. (2016). Neural correlates of consciousness: Progress and problems. *Nat Rev Neurosci, 17*(5), 307–321. https://doi.org/10.1038/nrn.2016.22

Köhler, W. (1925). *The mentality of apes* (E. Winter, Trans.). Kegan, Trench.

Köhler, W. (1925). *The mentality of apes*. San Diego, CA: Harcourt Brace.

Kohlsdorf, D., Herzing, D., & Starner, T. (2020). An auto encoder for audio dolphin communication. *2020 International Joint Conference on Neural Networks*, Glasgow, UK.

Koppel, J., & Rubin, D. C. (2016). Recent advances in understanding the reminiscence bump: The importance of cues in guiding recall from autobiographical memory. *Curr Dir Psychol Sci, 25*(2), 135–149. https://doi.org/10.1177/0963721416631955

Korucuoglu, O., Harms, M. P., Kennedy, J. T., Golosheykin, S., Astafiev, S. V., Barch, D. M., & Anokhin, A. P. (2020). Adolescent decision-making under risk: Neural correlates and sex differences. *Cereb Cortex, 30*(4), 2690–2706. https://doi.org/10.1093/cercor/bhz269

Kosslyn, S. M., Ganis, G., & Thompson, W. L. (2001). Neural foundations of imagery. *Nat Rev Neurosci, 2*(9), 635–642. https://doi.org/10.1038/35090055

Kosslyn, S. M., & Jolicoeur, P. (2021). A theory-based approach to the study of individual differences in mental imagery. In R. E. Snow, P.-A. Fredrico, & W. E. Montague (Eds.), *Aptitude, learning, and instruction* (pp. 139–175). Erlbaum.

Kosslyn, S. M., Pinker, S., Smith, G. E., & Shwartz, S. P. (1979). On the demystification of mental imagery. *Behav Brain Sci, 2*, 535–548.

Köster, M., Kayhan, E., Langeloh, M., & Hoehl, S. (2020). Making sense of the world: Infant learning from a predictive processing perspective. *Perspect Psychol Sci, 15*(3), 562–571. https://doi.org/10.1177/1745691619895071

Kral, A., Dorman, M. F., & Wilson, B. S. (2019). Neuronal development of hearing and language: Cochlear implants and critical periods. *Annu Rev Neurosci, 42*, 47–65. https://doi.org/10.1146/annurev-neuro-080317-061513

Krechevsky, I. (1932). "Hypotheses" in rats. *Psychol Rev, 39*, 516–532.

Kret, M. E., & Tomonaga, M. (2016). Getting to the bottom of face processing. Species-specific inversion effects for faces and behinds in humans and chimpanzees (*Pan Troglodytes*). *PLoS One, 11*(11), e0165357. https://doi.org/10.1371/journal.pone.0165357

Kriegeskorte, N. (2015). Deep neural networks: A new framework for modeling biological vision and brain information processing. *Annu Rev Vis Sci, 1*, 417–446. https://doi.org/10.1146/annurev-vision-082114-035447

Kristjansson, A., & Draschkow, D. (2021). Keeping it real: Looking beyond capacity limits in visual cognition. *Atten Percept Psychophys, 83*(4), 1375–1390. https://doi.org/10.3758/s13414-021-02256-7

Krueger, K. A., & Dayan, P. (2009). Flexible shaping: How learning in small steps helps. *Cognition, 110*(3), 380–394. https://doi.org/10.1016/j.cognition.2008.11.014

Kruglanski, A. W., & Orehek, E. (2007). Partitioning the domain of social inference: Dual mode and systems models and their alternatives. *Annu Rev Psychol, 58*, 291–316. https://doi.org/10.1146/annurev.psych.58.110405.085629

Kruschke, J. K. (2003). Attention in learning. *Curr Dir Psychol Sci, 12*, 171–175.

Kuczaj, S. A., & Eskelinen, H. C. (2014). Why do dolphins play. *Anim Behav Cogn, 1*, 113–127.

Kuhl, P. K. (2004). Early language acquisition: Cracking the speech code. *Nat Rev Neurosci, 5*(11), 831–843. https://doi.org/10.1038/nrn1533

Kuhl, P. K., Williams, K. A., Lacerda, F., Stevens, K. N., & Lindblom, B. (1992). Linguistic experience alters phonetic perception in infants by 6 months of age. *Science, 255*(5044), 606–608. http://www.ncbi.nlm.nih.gov/pubmed/1736364

Kumar, A. A. (2021). Semantic memory: A review of methods, models, and current challenges. *Psychon Bull Rev, 28*(1), 40–80. https://doi.org/10.3758/s13423-020-01792-x

Kumaran, D., Hassabis, D., & McClelland, J. L. (2016). What learning systems do intelligent agents need? Complementary learning systems theory updated. *Trends Cogn Sci, 20*(7), 512–534. https://doi.org/10.1016/j.tics.2016.05.004

Kwakkel, G., Veerbeek, J. M., van Wegen, E. E., & Wolf, S. L. (2015). Constraint-induced movement therapy after stroke. *Lancet Neurol, 14*(2), 224–234. https://doi.org/10.1016/S1474-4422(14)70160-7

L

Lakatos, P., Musacchia, G., O'Connel, M. N., Falchier, A. Y., Javitt, D. C., & Schroeder, C. E. (2013). The spectrotemporal filter mechanism of auditory selective attention. *Neuron, 77*(4), 750–761. https://doi.org/10.1016/j.neuron.2012.11.034

Laland, K., & Seed, A. (2021). Understanding human cognitive uniqueness. *Annu Rev Psychol, 72*, 689–716. https://doi.org/10.1146/annurev-psych-062220-051256

Lalanne, C., & Lorenceau, J. (2004). Crossmodal integration for perception and action. *J Physiol Paris, 98*(1–3), 265–279. https://doi.org/10.1016/j.jphysparis.2004.06.001

Lamm, C., & Majdandzic, J. (2015). The role of shared neural activations, mirror neurons, and morality in empathy—A critical comment. *Neurosci Res, 90*, 15–24. https://doi.org/10.1016/j.neures.2014.10.008

Landy, D., & Goldstone, R. L. (2005). How we learn about things we don't already understand. *J Exp Theor Artif Intell, 17*, 343–369.

Lane, D. M., & Chang, Y. A. (2018). Chess knowledge predicts chess memory even after controlling for chess experience: Evidence for the role of high-level processes. *Mem Cognit, 46*(3), 337–348. https://doi.org/10.3758/s13421-017-0768-2

Langleben, D. D., Loughead, J. W., Bilker, W. B., Ruparel, K., Childress, A. R., Busch, S. I., & Gur, R. C. (2005). Telling truth from lie in individual subjects with fast event-related fMRI. *Hum Brain Mapp, 26*(4), 262–272. https://doi.org/10.1002/hbm.20191

Lashley, K. (1950). In search of the engram. *Symp. Soc. Exp. Biol., 4*, 454–482.

Lashley, K. S. (1950). In search of the engram. In J. F. Danielli & R. Brown (Eds.), *Society of Experimental Biology Symposium, No. 4: Psychological mechanisms in animal behavior* (pp. 454–482). Cambridge, MA: Academic Press.

Lashley, K. S., & Wade, M. (1946). The Pavlovian theory of generalization. *Psychol Rev, 53*, 72–87. https://doi.org/10.1037/h0059999

Lattal, K. A. (2010). Delayed reinforcement of operant behavior. *J Exp Anal Behav, 93*(1), 129–139. https://doi.org/10.1901/jeab.2010.93-129

Lawrence, S., & Margolis, E. (2002). Radical concept nativism. *Cognition, 86*, 25–55.

Lazareva, O. F. (2012). Transitive inference in nonhuman animals. In E. A. Wasserman & T. R. Zentall (Eds.), *The Oxford handbook of comparative cognition* (2nd ed.) (pp. 718–735). New York, NY: Oxford University Press.

Lazareva, O. F., Castro, L., Vecera, S. P., & Wasserman, E. A. (2006). Figure-ground assignment in pigeons: Evidence for a figural benefit. *Percept Psychophys, 68*(5), 711–724. https://doi.org/10.3758/bf03193695

Lazarus, R. S. (1991). Cognition and motivation in emotion. *Am Psychol, 46*(4), 352–367. https://doi.org/10.1037//0003-066x.46.4.352

Le Pelley, M. E., Mitchell, C. J., Beesley, T., George, D. N., & Wills, A. J. (2016). Attention and associative learning in humans: An integrative review. *Psychol Bull, 142*(10), 1111–1140. https://doi.org/10.1037/bul0000064

Leber, A. B., Kawahara, J., & Gabari, Y. (2009). Long-term abstract learning of attentional set. *J Exp Psychol Hum Percept Perform, 35*(5), 1385–1397. https://doi.org/10.1037/a0016470

LeDoux, J. E. (2012). Evolution of human emotion: A view through fear. *Prog Brain Res, 195*, 431–442. https://doi.org/10.1016/B978-0-444-53860-4.00021-0

Lee, D., McGreevy, B. P., & Barraclough, D. J. (2005). Learning and decision making in monkeys during a rock-paper-scissors game. *Brain Res Cogn Brain Res, 25*(2), 416–430. https://doi.org/10.1016/j.cogbrainres.2005.07.003

Lee, G. Y., & Kisilevsky, B. S. (2014). Fetuses respond to father's voice but prefer mother's voice after birth. *Dev Psychobiol, 56*(1), 1–11. https://doi.org/10.1002/dev.21084

Lee, J. Y., & Schweighofer, N. (2009). Dual adaptation supports a parallel architecture of motor memory. *J Neurosci, 29*(33), 10396–10404. https://doi.org/10.1523/JNEUROSCI.1294-09.2009

Lee, M. D., Criss, A. H., Devezer, B., Donkin, C., Etz, A., Leite, F. P., … Vandekerckhove, J. (2019). Robust modeling in cognitive science. *Comp Brain Behav, 2*, 141–153.

Lee, S. H., Kravitz, D. J., & Baker, C. I. (2012). Disentangling visual imagery and perception of real-world objects. *Neuroimage, 59*(4), 4064–4073. https://doi.org/10.1016/j.neuroimage.2011.10.055

Lee, S., Kim, J., & Tak, S. (2020). Effects of autonomous sensory meridian response on the functional connectivity as measured by functional magnetic resonance imaging. *Front Behav Neurosci, 14*, 154. https://doi.org/10.3389/fnbeh.2020.00154

Lee, V. K., & Harris, L. T. (2013). How social cognition can inform social decision making. *Front Neurosci, 7*, 259. https://doi.org/10.3389/fnins.2013.00259

Lee, Y.-S. (2014). Genes and signaling pathways involved in memory enhancement in mutant mice. *Mol Brain, 7*, 43.

Leff, R. (1969). Effects of punishment intensity and consistency on the internalization of behavioral suppression in children. *Dev Psychol, 1*, 345–356.

Lehrman, D. S. (1953). A critique of Konrad Lorenz's theory of instinctive behavior. *Q Rev Biol, 28*(4), 337–363. https://doi.org/10.1086/399858

Leibovich, T., Katzin, N., Harel, M., & Henik, A. (2017). From "sense of number" to "sense of magnitude": The role of continuous magnitudes in numerical cognition. *Behav Brain Sci, 40*, e164. https://doi.org/10.1017/S0140525×16000960

Leisman, G., Moustafa, A. A., & Shafir, T. (2016). Thinking, walking, talking: Integratory motor and cognitive brain function. *Front Public Health, 4*, 94. https://doi.org/10.3389/fpubh.2016.00094

Lejeune, H., & Wearden, J. H. (2006). Scalar properties in animal timing: Conformity and violations. *Q J Exp Psychol (Hove), 59*(11), 1875–1908. https://doi.org/10.1080/17470210600784649

Lenc, T., Merchant, H., Keller, P. E., Honing, H., Varlet, M., & Nozaradan, S. (2021). Mapping between sound, brain and behaviour: Four-level framework for understanding rhythm processing in humans and non-human primates. *Philos Trans R Soc Lond B Biol Sci, 376*(1835), 20200325. https://doi.org/10.1098/rstb.2020.0325

Lepora, N. F. (2016). Biomimetic active touch with fingertips and whiskers. *IEEE Trans Haptics, 9*(2), 170–183. https://doi.org/10.1109/TOH.2016.2558180

LePort, A. K., Mattfeld, A. T., Dickinson-Anson, H., Fallon, J. H., Stark, C. E., Kruggel, F., … McGaugh, J. L. (2012). Behavioral and neuroanatomical investigation of highly superior autobiographical memory (HSAM). *Neurobiol Learn Mem, 98*, 78–92. https://doi.org/10.1016/j.nlm.2012.05.002

LePort, A. K., Stark, S. M., McGaugh, J. L., & Stark, C. E. (2015). Highly superior autobiographical memory: Quality and quantity of retention over time. *Front Psychol, 6*, 2017. https://doi.org/10.3389/fpsyg.2015.02017

LePort, A. K., Stark, S. M., McGaugh, J. L., & Stark, C. E. (2017). A cognitive assessment of highly superior autobiographical memory. *Memory, 25*, 276–288. https://doi.org/10.1080/09658211.2016.1160126

Lerner, T. N., Holloway, A. L., & Seiler, J. L. (2021). Dopamine, updated: Reward prediction error and beyond. *Curr Opin Neurobiol, 67*, 123–130. https://doi.org/10.1016/j.conb.2020.10.012

Leslie, A. M., Gelman, R., & Gallistel, C. R. (2008). The generative basis of natural number concepts. *Trends Cogn Sci, 12*(6), 213–218. https://doi.org/10.1016/j.tics.2008.03.004

Leslie, A. M., & Thaiss, L. (1992). Domain specificity in conceptual development: Neuropsychological evidence from autism. *Cognition, 43*(3), 225–251. https://doi.org/10.1016/0010-0277(92)90013-8

Leung, B., & Waddell, S. (2004). Four-dimensional gene expression control: Memories on the fly. *Trends Neurosci, 27*(9), 511–513. https://doi.org/10.1016/j.tins.2004.06.013

Levelt, W. J. (1992). Accessing words in speech production: Stages, processes and representations. *Cognition, 42*(1–3), 1–22. https://doi.org/10.1016/0010-0277(92)90038-j

Lewin, R. (1980). Is your brain really necessary? *Science, 210*(4475), 1232–1234. https://www.ncbi.nlm.nih.gov/pubmed/7434023

Lewis, A., & Smith, D. (1993). Defining higher order thinking. *Theory Pract, 32*, 131–137.

Lewis, C., & LOvatt, P. J. (2013). Breaking away from set patterns of thinking: Improvisation and divergent thinking. *Think Ski Creat, 9*, 46–58.

Lewis, L. S., & Krupenye, C. (2022). Eye-tracking as a window into primate social cognition. *Am J Primatol, 84*(10), e23393. https://doi.org/10.1002/ajp.23393

Lhermitte, F. (1993). [Imitation and utilization behavior in major depressive states]. *Bull Acad Natl Med, 177*(6), 883–890; discussion 890–882. https://www.ncbi.nlm.nih.gov/pubmed /8221188 (Les comportements d'imitation et d'utilisation dans les etats depressifs majeurs.)

Li, S., Callaghan, B. L., & Richardson, R. (2014). Infantile amnesia: Forgotten but not gone. *Learn Mem, 21*(3), 135–139. https://doi.org/10.1101/lm.031096.113

Liberman, A. M., & Mattingly, I. G. (1985). The motor theory of speech perception revised. *Cognition, 21*(1), 1–36. https://doi.org/10.1016/0010-0277(85)90021-6

Libertus, M. E., Odic, D., & Halberda, J. (2012). Intuitive sense of number correlates with math scores on college-entrance examination. *Acta Psychologica, 141*, 373–379. https://doi.org/10.1016/j.actpsy.2012.09.009

Libet, B., Gleason, C. A., Wright, E. W., & Pearl, D. K. (1983). Time of conscious intention to act in relation to onset of cerebral activity (readiness-potential). The unconscious initiation of a freely voluntary act. *Brain, 106 (Pt 3)*, 623–642. https://doi.org/10.1093/brain/106.3.623

Liegeois, F., Cross, J. H., Polkey, C., Harkness, W., & Vargha-Khadem, F. (2008). Language after hemispherectomy in childhood: Contributions from memory and intelligence. *Neuropsychologia, 46*(13), 3101–3107. https://doi.org/10.1016/j.neuropsychologia.2008.07.001

Lilly, J. C. (1965). Vocal mimicry in tursiops: Ability to match numbers and durations of human vocal bursts. *Science, 147*(3655), 300–301. https://doi.org/10.1126/science.147.3655.300

Limb, C. J., & Braun, A. R. (2008). Neural substrates of spontaneous musical performance: An FMRI study of jazz improvisation. *PLoS One, 3*(2), e1679. https://doi.org/10.1371/journal.pone.0001679

Lin, Q., Dong, Z., Zheng, Q., & Wang, S. J. (2022). The effect of facial attractiveness on micro-expression recognition. *Front Psychol, 13*, 959124. https://doi.org/10.3389/fpsyg.2022.959124

Lindenberger, U., Li, S. C., Gruber, W., & Muller, V. (2009). Brains swinging in concert: Cortical phase synchronization while playing guitar. *BMC Neurosci, 10*, 22. https://doi.org/10.1186/1471-2202-10-22

Lindskog, M., Winman, A., & Poom, L. (2017). Individual differences in nonverbal number skills predict math anxiety. *Cognition, 159*, 156–162. https://doi.org/10.1016/j.cognition.2016.11.014

Linnet, J. (2020). The anticipatory dopamine response in addiction: A common neurobiological underpinning of gambling disorder and substance use disorder? *Prog Neuropsychopharmacol Biol Psychiatry, 98*, 109802. https://doi.org/10.1016/j.pnpbp.2019.109802

Litwin, P. (2020). Extending Bayesian models of the rubber hand illusion. *Multisens Res, 33*, 127–160.

Liu, E. H., Mercado, E., 3rd, Church, B. A., & Orduna, I. (2008). The easy-to-hard effect in human (Homo sapiens) and rat (Rattus norvegicus) auditory identification. *J Comp Psychol, 122*(2), 132–145. https://doi.org/10.1037/0735-7036.122.2.132

Liu, M., Argyriou, E., & Cyders, M. A. (2020). Developmental Considerations for Assessment and Treatment of Impulsivity in Older Adults. *Curr Top Behav Neurosci, 47*, 165–177. https://doi.org/10.1007/7854_2019_124

Lively, S. E., Logan, J. S., & Pisoni, D. B. (1993). Training Japanese listeners to identify English /r/ and /l/. II: The role of phonetic environment and talker variability in learning new perceptual categories. *J Acoust Soc Am, 94*(3 Pt 1), 1242–1255. http://www.ncbi.nlm.nih.gov/pubmed/8408964

Livesey, E. J., & McLaren, I. P. (2019). Revisiting peak shift on an artificial dimension: Effects of stimulus variability on generalisation. *Q J Exp Psychol (Hove)*, *72*(2), 132–150. https://doi.org/10.1177/1747021817739832

Lobo, L., Heras-Escribano, M., & Travieso, D. (2018). The History and Philosophy of Ecological Psychology. *Front Psychol*, *9*, 2228. https://doi.org/10.3389/fpsyg.2018.02228

Locke, J. (1690). *An essay concerning human understanding*. UK: Thomas Basset.

Locke, J. (1693). *An essay concerning human understanding*. UK: Thomas Bassett.

Loewenstein, G., Rick, S., & Cohen, J. D. (2008). Neuroeconomics. *Annu Rev Psychol*, *59*, 647–672. https://doi.org/10.1146/annurev.psych.59.103006.093710

Loftus, E. F. (1993). The reality of repressed memories. *Am Psychol*, *48*(5), 518–537. http://www.ncbi.nlm.nih.gov/pubmed/8507050

Loftus, E. F. (2003). Our changeable memories: Legal and practical implications. *Nat Rev Neurosci*, *4*(3), 231–234. https://doi.org/10.1038/nrn1054

Loftus, E. F. (2019). Eyewitness testimony. *Appl Cogn Psychol*, *33*, 498–503.

Logan, J., Petrill, S. A., Flax, J., Justice, L. M., Hou, L., Bassett, A. S.,... Bartlett, C. W. (2011). Genetic covariation underlying reading, language and related measures in a sample selected for specific language impairment. *Behav Genet*, *41*(5), 651–659. https://doi.org/10.1007/s10519-010-9435-0

Logie, R. H., Pernet, C. R., Buonocore, A., & Della Sala, S. (2011). Low and high imagers activate networks differentially in mental rotation. *Neuropsychologia*, *49*(11), 3071–3077. https://doi.org/10.1016/j.neuropsychologia.2011.07.011

Loh, K. K., & Kanai, R. (2014). Higher media multi-tasking activity is associated with smaller gray-matter density in the anterior cingulate cortex. *PLoS One*, *9*(9), e106698. https://doi.org/10.1371/journal.pone.0106698

Longo, M. R., & Haggard, P. (2010). An implicit body representation underlying human position sense. *Proc Natl Acad Sci U S A*, *107*, 11727–11732. https://doi.org/10.1073/pnas.1003483107

Longo, M. R., & Haggard, P. (2011). Weber's illusion and body shape: Anisotropy of tactile size perception on the hand. *J Exp Psychol Hum Percept Perform*, *37*(3), 720–726. https://doi.org/10.1037/a0021921

Lorenz, K. Z. (1978). *The foundations of ethology*. Springer-Verlag.

Lotze, M., & Halsband, U. (2006). Motor imagery. *J Physiol Paris*, *99*(4–6), 386–395. https://doi.org/10.1016/j.jphysparis.2006.03.012

Lowenstein, P. R., & Castro, M. G. (2001). Genetic engineering within the adult brain: Implications for molecular approaches to behavioral neuroscience. *Physiol Behav*, *73*(5), 833–839. https://doi.org/10.1016/s0031-9384(01)00520-0

Lubinski, D., & Benbow, C. P. (2021). Intellectual precocity: What have we learned since Terman? *Gift Child Q, 65*, 3–28.

Ludwig, R. J., & Welch, M. G. (2020). How babies learn: The autonomic socioemotional reflex. *Early Hum Dev*, *151*, 105183. https://doi.org/10.1016/j.earlhumdev.2020.105183

Luft, A. R., & Buitrago, M. M. (2005). Stages of motor skill learning. *Mol Neurobiol*, *32*(3), 205–216. https://doi.org/10.1385/MN:32:3:205

Lupyan, G., Abdel Rahman, R., Boroditsky, L., & Clark, A. (2020). Effects of Language on Visual Perception. *Trends Cogn Sci*, *24*(11), 930–944. https://doi.org/10.1016/j.tics.2020.08.005

Lupyan, G., Rakison, D. H., & McClelland, J. L. (2007). Language is not just for talking: Redundant labels facilitate learning of novel categories. *Psychol Sci*, *18*(12), 1077–1083. https://doi.org/10.1111/j.1467-9280.2007.02028.x

Luria, A. R. (1968). *The mind of a mnemonist: A little book about a vast memory*. Cambridge. MA: Harvard University Press.

Lutz, P.-E., Courtet, P., & Calati, R. (2020). The opiod system and the social brain: Implications for depression and suicide. *J Neurosci Res*, *98*, 588–600.

Lynn, S. J., Kirsch, I., Terhune, D. B., & Green, J. P. (2020). Myths and misconceptions about hypnosis and suggestion: Separating fact and fiction. *Appl Cogn Psychol*, *34*, 1253–1264.

Lyons, J. (1978). *Noam Chomsky*. London, UK: Penguin.

M

Ma, I., Sanfey, A. G., & Ma, W. J. (2020). The social cost of gathering information for trust decisions. *Sci Rep*, *10*(1), 14073. https://doi.org/10.1038/s41598-020-69766-6

MacCraith, E., Forde, J. C., & Davis, N. F. (2019). Robotic simulation training for urological trainees: A comprehensive review on cost, merits and challenges. *J Robot Surg*, *13*(3), 371–377. https://doi.org/10.1007/s11701-019-00934-1

MacDonald, A. A., Naci, L., MacDonald, P. A., & Owen, A. M. (2015). Anesthesia and neuroimaging: Investigating the neural correlates of unconsciousness. *Trends Cogn Sci*, *19*(2), 100–107. https://doi.org/10.1016/j.tics.2014.12.005

Mackenzie, B. D. (1977). *Behaviourism and the limits of the scientific method*. NJ: Humanities Press.

Mackintosh, N. J. (1965). Selective attention in animal discrimination learning. *Psychol Bull*, *64*, 124–150. https://doi.org/10.1037/h0022347

Macknik, S. L., King, M., Randi, J., Robbins, A., Teller, Thompson, J., & Martinez-Conde, S. (2008). Attention and awareness in stage magic: Turning tricks into research. *Nat Rev Neurosci*, *9*(11), 871–879. https://doi.org/10.1038/nrn2473

MacLean, K. A., Ferrer, E., Aichele, S. R., Bridwell, D. A., Zanesco, A. P., Jacobs, T. L.,... Saron, C. D. (2010). Intensive meditation training improves perceptual discrimination and sustained attention. *Psychol Sci*, *21*(6), 829–839. https://doi.org/10.1177/0956797610371339

MacLeod, C. M. (1991). Half a century of research on the Stroop effect: An integrative review. *Psychol Bull*, *109*(2), 163–203. https://doi.org/10.1037/0033-2909.109.2.163

Macpherson, E. A., & Middlebrooks, J. C. (2002). Listener weighting of cues for lateral angle: The duplex theory of sound localization revisited. *J Acoust Soc Am*, *111*(5 Pt 1), 2219–2236. https://doi.org/10.1121/1.1471898

Mahncke, H. W., Connor, B. B., Appelman, J., Ahsanuddin, O. N., Hardy, J. L., Wood, R. A.,... Merzenich, M. M. (2006). Memory enhancement in healthy older adults using a brain plasticity-based training program: A randomized, controlled study. *Proc Natl Acad Sci U S A*, *103*(33), 12523–12528. https://doi.org/10.1073/pnas.0605194103

Maier, S. F., & Seligman, M. E. (2016). Learned helplessness at fifty: Insights from neuroscience. *Psychol Rev, 123*(4), 349–367. https://doi.org/10.1037/rev0000033

Malapani, C., Rakitin, B., Levy, R., Meck, W. H., Deweer, B., Dubois, B., & Gibbon, J. (1998). Coupled temporal memories in Parkinson's disease: A dopamine-related dysfunction. *J Cogn Neurosci, 10,* 316–331.

Maloney, L. T., & Zhang, H. (2010). Decision-theoretic models of visual perception and action. *Vision Res, 50*(23), 2362–2374. https://doi.org/10.1016/j.visres.2010.09.031

Mandler, G. (2002). Origins of the cognitive (r)evolution. *J Hist Behav Sci, 38*(4), 339–353. https://doi.org/10.1002/jhbs.10066

Mann, R. P. (2020). Collective decision-making by rational agents with differing preferences. *Proc Natl Acad Sci U S A, 117*(19), 10388–10396. https://doi.org/10.1073/pnas.2000840117

Marchetti, S. (Ed.). (2021). *The Jamesian mind.* Routledge.

Marler, P. (1997). Three models of song learning: Evidence from behavior. *J Neurobiol, 33*(5), 501–516. http://www.ncbi.nlm.nih.gov/pubmed/9369456

Marr, D. (1971). Simple memory: A theory for archicortex. *Philos Trans R Soc Lond B Biol Sci, 262*(841), 23–81. http://www.ncbi.nlm.nih.gov/pubmed/4399412

Marr, D. (1982). *Vision: A computational investigation into the human representation and processing of visual information.* W. H. Freeman.

Marshall-Pescini, S., Schwarz, J. F. L., Kostelnik, I., Viranyi, Z., & Range, F. (2017). Importance of a species' socioecology: Wolves outperform dogs in a conspecific cooperation task. *Proc Natl Acad Sci U S A, 114*(44), 11793–11798. https://doi.org/10.1073/pnas.1709027114

Martial, C., Cassol, H., Laureys, S., & Gosseries, O. (2020). Near-death experience as a probe to explore (disconnected) consciousness. *Trends Cogn Sci, 24*(3), 173–183. https://doi.org/10.1016/j.tics.2019.12.010

Martin, S. J., Grimwood, P. D., & Morris, R. G. (2000). Synaptic plasticity and memory: An evaluation of the hypothesis. *Annu Rev Neurosci, 23,* 649–711. https://doi.org/10.1146/annurev.neuro.23.1.649

Martin, S., Mikutta, C., Leonard, M. K., Hungate, D., Koelsch, S., Shamma, S., Chang, E. F.,…Pasley, B. N. (2018). Neural encoding of auditory features during music perception and imagery. *Cereb Cortex, 28*(12), 4222–4233. https://doi.org/10.1093/cercor/bhx277

Martins, D., Lockwood, P., Cutler, J., Moran, R., & Paloyelis, Y. (2022). Oxytocin modulates neurocomputational mechanisms underlying prosocial reinforcement learning. *Prog Neurobiol, 213,* 102253. https://doi.org/10.1016/j.pneurobio.2022.102253

Mathur, M. B., Reichling, D. B., Lunardini, F., Geminiani, A., Antonietti, A., Ruijten, P. A.,…Aczel, B. (2020). Uncanny but not confusing: Multisite study of perceptual category confusion in the uncanny valley. *Comput Human Behav, 103,* 21–30.

Matthews, W. J., & Meck, W. H. (2016). Temporal cognition: Connecting subjective time to perception, attention, and memory. *Psychol Bull, 142*(8), 865–907. https://doi.org/10.1037/bul0000045

Maurer, D., & Werker, J. F. (2014). Perceptual narrowing during infancy: A comparison of language and faces. *Dev Psychobiol, 56*(2), 154–178. https://doi.org/10.1002/dev.21177

Mayer, E. A. (2011). Gut feelings: The emerging biology of gut-brain communication. *Nat Rev Neurosci, 12*(8), 453–466. https://doi.org/10.1038/nrn3071

Mazzoni, G., Clark, A., De Bartolo, A., Guerrini, C., Nahouli, Z., Duzzi, D.,…Venneri, A. (2019). Brain activation in highly superior autobiographical memory: The role of the precuneus in the autobiographical memory retrieval network. *Cortex, 120,* 588–602. https://doi.org/10.1016/j.cortex.2019.02.020

McAuley, J. D., & Jones, M. R. (2003). Modeling effects of rhythmic context on perceived duration: A comparison of interval and entrainment approaches to short-interval timing. *J Exp Psychol Hum Percept Perform, 29*(6), 1102–1125. https://doi.org/10.1037/0096-1523.29.6.1102

McBride, A. F., & Hebb, D. O. (1948). Behavior of the captive bottle-nose dolphin, *Tursiops truncatus. J Comp Physiol Psychol, 41*(2), 111–123. https://doi.org/10.1037/h0057927

McCaffrey, T. (2012). Innovation relies on the obscure: A key to overcoming the classic problem of functional fixedness. *Psychol Sci, 23*(3), 215–218. https://doi.org/10.1177/0956797611429580

McClelland, J. L., McNaughton, B. L., & O'Reilly, R. C. (1995). Why there are complementary learning systems in the hippocampus and neocortex: Insights from the successes and failures of connectionist models of learning and memory. *Psychol Rev, 102*(3), 419–457. http://www.ncbi.nlm.nih.gov/pubmed/7624455

McClelland, J. L., Rumelhart, D. E., & The_PDP_Research_Group (Eds.). (1986). *Parallel distributed processing: Vol. 1.* Cambridge, MA: MIT Press.

McClure, J., Podos, J., & Richardson, H. N. (2014). Isolating the delay component of impulsive choice in adolescent rats. *Front Integr Neurosci, 8,* 3. https://doi.org/10.3389/fnint.2014.00003

McCowan, B., Hubbard, J., Walker, L., Sharpe, F., Frediani, J., & Doyle, L. (2023). Interactive bioacoustic playback as a tool for detecting and exploring nonhuman intelligence: Conversing with an Alaskan humpback whale. *bioRxiv, 2023–02.*

McCoy, M. B. (2009). Alidamas, Isocrates, and Plato on speech, writing, and philosophical rhetoric. *Anc Philos, 29,* 45–66.

McCue, L. M., Cioffi, W. R., Heithaus, M. R., Barrè, L., & Connor, R. C. (2020). Synchrony, leadership, and association in male Indo-pacific bottlenose dolphins (*Tursiops aduncus*). *Ethology, 126,* 741–750.

McDonough, I. M., Enam, T., Kraemer, K. R., Eakin, D. K., & Kim, M. (2021). Is there more to metamemory? An argument for two specialized monitoring abilities. *Psychon Bull Rev, 28*(5), 1657–1667. https://doi.org/10.3758/s13423-021-01930-z

McDowell, J. J. (2013). On the theoretical and empirical status of the matching law and matching theory. *Psychol Bull, 139*(5), 1000–1028. https://doi.org/10.1037/a0029924

McGaugh, J. L. (2004). The amygdala modulates the consolidation of memories of emotionally arousing experiences. *Annu Rev Neurosci, 27,* 1–28. https://doi.org/10.1146/annurev.neuro.27.070203.144157

McGaugh, J. L. (2013). Making lasting memories: Remembering the significant. *Proc Natl Acad Sci U S A, 110*(supplement 2), 10402–10407. https://doi.org/10.1073/pnas.1301209110

McGregor, P. K., & Dabelsteen, T. (1996). Communication networks. In D. E. Kroodsma & E. H. Miller (Eds.), *Ecology and evolution of acoustic communication in birds* (pp. 409–425). Ithaca, NY: Cornell University Press.

Medin, D. L., & Schafer, M. M. (1978). Context theory of classification learning. *Psychol Rev, 85*, 207–238.

Medina, J. F. (2019). Teaching the cerebellum about reward. *Nat Neurosci, 22*(6), 846–848. https://doi.org/10.1038/s41593-019-0409-0

Meehl, P. E. (1950). On the circularity of the law of effect. *Psychol Bull, 47*, 52–75.

Melis, A. P., & Warneken, F. (2016). The psychology of cooperation: Insights from chimpanzees and children. *Evol Anthropol, 25*(6), 297–305. https://doi.org/10.1002/evan.21507

Meltzoff, A. N., & Moore, M. K. (1977). Imitation of facial and manual gestures by human neonates. *Science, 198*(4312), 75–78. https://doi.org/10.1126/science.198.4312.75

Menary, R. (Ed.). (2010). *The extended mind*. Cambridge, MA: MIT Press.

Mendez, M. F., Shapira, J. S., & Saul, R. E. (2011). The spectrum of sociopathy in dementia. *J Neuropsychiatry Clin Neurosci, 23*(2), 132–140. https://doi.org/10.1176/jnp.23.2.jnp132

Mercado, E., 3rd, & Scagel, A. (2023). Second verse, same as the first: Learning generalizable relational concepts through functional repetition. *Anim Cogn, 26*(1), 141–151. https://doi.org/10.1007/s10071-022-01702-9

Mercado, E., 3rd, Chow, K., Church, B. A., & Lopata, C. (2020). Perceptual category learning in autism spectrum disorder: Truth and consequences. *Neurosci Biobehav Rev, 118*, 689–703. https://doi.org/10.1016/j.neubiorev.2020.08.016

Mercado, E., 3rd, Orduña, I., & Nowak, J. M. (2005). Auditory categorization of complex sounds by rats (*Rattus norvegicus*). *J Comp Psychol, 119*(1), 90–98. https://doi.org/10.1037/0735-7036.119.1.90

Mercado, E., III. (2008). Neural and cognitive plasticity: From maps to minds. *Psychol Bull, 134*(1), 109–137. https://doi.org/10.1037/0033-2909.134.1.109

Mercado, E., III, Mantell, J. T., & Pfordresher, P. Q. (2014). Imitating sounds: A cognitive approach to understanding vocal imitation. *Comp Cogni Behav Rev, 9*, 17–74.

Mercado, E., III, Uyeyama, R. K., Pack, A. A., & Herman, L. M. (1999). Memory for action events in the bottlenosed dolphin. *Anim Cogn, 2*, 17–25.

Mercado, E., Murray, S. O., Uyeyama, R. K., Pack, A. A., & Herman, L. M. (1998). Memory for recent actions in the bottlenosed dolphin (*Tursiops truncatus*): Repetition of arbitrary behaviors using an abstract rule. *Anim Learn Behav, 26*, 210–218.

Merchant, H., Zarco, W., & Prado, L. (2008). Do we have a common mechanism for measuring time in the hundreds of millisecond range? Evidence from multiple-interval timing tasks. *J Neurophysiol, 99*(2), 939–949. https://doi.org/10.1152/jn.01225.2007

Merkley, R., & Ansari, D. (2010). Using eye tracking to study numerical cognition: The case of the ratio effect. *Exp Brain Res, 206*(4), 455–460. https://doi.org/10.1007/s00221-010-2419-8

Merkow, M. B., Burke, J. F., & Kahana, M. J. (2015). The human hippocampus contributes to both the recollection and familiarity components of recognition memory. *Proc Natl Acad Sci U S A, 112*(46), 14378–14383. https://doi.org/10.1073/pnas.1513145112

Mervis, C. B., & Rosch, E. (1981). Categorization of natural objects. *Annu Rev Psychol, 32*, 89–115.

Merzenich, M. M., Jenkins, W. M., Johnston, P., Schreiner, C., Miller, S. L., & Tallal, P. (1996). Temporal processing deficits of language-learning impaired children ameliorated by training. *Science, 271*(5245), 77–81. https://doi.org/10.1126/science.271.5245.77

Mesaros. (2014). Aristotle and animal mind. *Procedia Soc Behav Sci, 163*, 185–192.

Mesgarani, N., Cheung, C., Johnson, K., & Chang, E. F. (2014). Phonetic feature encoding in human superior temporal gyrus. *Science, 343*(6174), 1006–1010. https://doi.org/10.1126/science.1245994

Metcalfe, J., & Son, L. K. (2012). Anoetic, noetic, and autonoetic metacognition. In M. Beran, J. R. Brandl, J. Perner, & J. Proust (Eds.), *Foundations of Metacognition* (pp. 289–301). New York, NY: Oxford University Press.

Meyer, A. S. (1992). Investigation of phonological encoding through speech error analyses: Achievements, limitations, and alternatives. *Cognition, 42*(1–3), 181–211. https://doi.org/10.1016/0010-0277(92)90043-h

Michael, J., Sebanz, N., & Knoblich, G. (2016). Observing joint action: Coordination creates commitment. *Cognition, 157*, 106–113. https://doi.org/10.1016/j.cognition.2016.08.024

Michel, C. (2021). Overcoming the modal/amodal dichotomy of concepts. *Phenomenol Cogne Sci, 20*, 655–677.

Miletto Petrazzini, M. E., Sovrano, V. A., Vallortigara, G., & Messina, A. (2020). Brain and Behavioral Asymmetry: A Lesson From Fish. *Front Neuroanat, 14*, 11. https://doi.org/10.3389/fnana.2020.00011

Miller, E. K. (2000). The prefrontal cortex and cognitive control. *Nat Rev Neurosci, 1*(1), 59–65. https://doi.org/10.1038/35036228

Miller, E. K., & Cohen, J. D. (2001). An integrative theory of prefrontal cortex function. *Annu Rev Neurosci, 24*, 167–202. https://doi.org/10.1146/annurev.neuro.24.1.167

Miller, E. K., Freedman, D. J., & Wallis, J. D. (2002). The prefrontal cortex: Categories, concepts and cognition. *Philos Trans R Soc Lond B Biol Sci, 357*(1424), 1123–1136. https://doi.org/10.1098/rstb.2002.1099

Miller, E. K., & Wallis, J. D. (2003). The prefrontal cortex and executive brain functions. In L. R. Squire, F. E. Bloom, J. L. Roberts, M. J. Zigmond, S. K. McConnell, & N. C. Spitzer (Eds.), *Fundamental neuroscience* (pp. 1353–1376). Cambridge, MA: Academic Press.

Miller, G. A. (2003). The cognitive revolution: A historical perspective. *Trends Cogn Sci, 7*, 141–144. https://www.ncbi.nlm.nih.gov/pubmed/12639696

Miller, M. R. (2013). Descartes on animals revisited. *J Philosl Res, 38*, 89–114.

Miller, R., Sanchez, K., & Rosenblum, L. (2010). Alignment to visual speech information. *Atten Percept Psychophys, 72*, 1614–1625. https://doi.org/10.3758/APP.72.6.1614

Milner, B. (1972). Disorders of learning and memory after temporal lobe lesions in man. *Clin Neurosurg, 19*, 421–446. https://doi.org/10.1093/neurosurgery/19.cn_suppl_1.421

Milner, P. M. (1991). Brain-stimulation reward: A review. *Can J Psychol, 45*(1), 1–36. https://doi.org/10.1037/h0084275

Milton, F., Fulford, J., Dance, C., Gaddum, J., Heuerman-Williamson, B., Jones, K.,…Zeman, A. (2021). Behavioral and neural signatures of visual imagery vividness extremes: Aphantasia versus hyperphantasia. *Cereb Cortex Commun, 2*(2), tgab035. https://doi.org/10.1093/texcom/tgab035

Minami, H., & Dallenbach, K. M. (1946). The effect of activity upon learning and retention in the cockroach, *Periplaneta americana*. *Am J Psychol, 59*, 1–58. http://www.ncbi.nlm.nih.gov/pubmed/21015312

Mine, J. G., Slocombe, K. E., Willems, E. P., Gilby, I. C., Yu, M., Thompson, M. E.,…Machanda, Z. P. (2022). Vocal signals facilitate cooperative hunting in wild chimpanzees. *Sci Adv, 8*(30), eabo5553. https://doi.org/10.1126/sciadv.abo5553

Minsky, M. (1986). *The society of mind*. New York, NY: Simon and Schuster.

Mishra, S., Gregson, M., & Lalumiere, M. L. (2012). Framing effects and risk-sensitive decision making. *Br J Psychol, 103*(1), 83–97. https://doi.org/10.1111/j.2044-8295.2011.02047.x

Mitchell, D. B., Kelly, C. L., & Brown, A. S. (2018). Replication and extension of long-term implicit memory: Perceptual priming but conceptual cessation. *Conscious Cogn, 58*, 1–9. https://doi.org/10.1016/j.concog.2017.12.002

Mitchell, K. J., & Johnson, M. K. (2009). Source monitoring 15 years later: What have we learned from fMRI about the neural mechanisms of source memory? *Psychol Bull, 135*(4), 638–677. https://doi.org/10.1037/a0015849

Mitchell, R. W. (1992). Developing concepts in infancy: Animals, self-perception, and two theories of mirror self-recognition. *Psychol Inq, 3*, 127–130.

Miyawaki, E. K. (2022). Review: Subjective time perception, dopamine signaling, and parkinsonian slowness. *Front Neurol, 13*, 927160. https://doi.org/10.3389/fneur.2022.927160

Moeller, B., & Pfister, R. (2022). Ideomotor learning: Time to generalize a longstanding principle. *Neurosci Biobehav Rev, 140*, 104782. https://doi.org/10.1016/j.neubiorev.2022.104782

Molnar, Z., & Brown, R. E. (2010). Insights into the life and work of Sir Charles Sherrington. *Nat Rev Neurosci, 11*(6), 429–436. https://doi.org/10.1038/nrn2835

Monahan, J. L., Murphy, S. T., & Zajonc, R. B. (2000). Subliminal mere exposure: Specific, general, and diffuse effects. *Psychol Sci, 11*(6), 462–466. https://doi.org/10.1111/1467-9280.00289

Monti, M. M., Vanhaudenhuyse, A., Coleman, M. R., Boly, M., Pickard, J. D., Tshibanda, L.,…Laureys, S. (2010). Willful modulation of brain activity in disorders of consciousness. *N Engl J Med, 362*, 579–589.

Moore, C., Mealiea, J., Garon, N., & Povinelli, D. J. (2007). The development of body self-awareness. *Infancy*, 157–174.

Moorjani, S. (2016). Miniaturized Technologies for Enhancement of Motor Plasticity. *Front Bioeng Biotechnol, 4*, 30. https://doi.org/10.3389/fbioe.2016.00030

Moran, J., & Desimone, R. (1985). Selective attention gates visual processing in the extrastriate cortex. *Science, 229*(4715), 782–784. https://doi.org/10.1126/science.4023713

Moray, N. (1959). Attention in dichotic listening: Affective cues and the influence of instructions. *Q J Exp Psychol, 11*, 56–60.

Moreno, S., Bialystok, E., Barac, R., Schellenberg, E. G., Cepeda, N. J., & Chau, T. (2011). Short-term music training enhances verbal intelligence and executive function. *Psychol Sci, 22*(11), 1425–1433. https://doi.org/10.1177/0956797611416999

Mori, M. (1970). Bukimi no tani [the uncanny valley]. *Energy, 7*, 33–35.

Morrison, A. B., & Chein, J. M. (2011). Does working memory training work? The promise and challenges of enhancing cognition by training working memory. *Psychon Bull Rev, 18*(1), 46–60. https://doi.org/10.3758/s13423-010-0034-0

Morsella, E., & Miozzo, M. (2002). Evidence for a cascade model of lexical access in speech production. *J Exp Psychol Learn Mem Cogn, 28*(3), 555–563. https://www.ncbi.nlm.nih.gov/pubmed/12018507

Mota-Rolim, S. A. (2020). On moving the eyes to flag lucid dreaming. *Front Neurosci, 14*, 361. https://doi.org/10.3389/fnins.2020.00361

Mou, Y., Province, J. M., & Luo, Y. (2014). Can infants make transitive inferences? *Cogn Psychol, 68*, 98–112. https://doi.org/10.1016/j.cogpsych.2013.11.003

Moulton, S. T., & Kosslyn, S. M. (2009). Imagining predictions: Mental imagery as mental emulation. *Philos Trans R Soc Lond B Biol Sci, 364*(1521), 1273–1280. https://doi.org/10.1098/rstb.2008.0314

Moustafa, A. A., Morris, A. N., & ElHaj, M. (2018). A review on future episodic thinking in mood and anxiety disorders. *Rev Neurosci, 30*(1), 85–94. https://doi.org/10.1515/revneuro-2017-0055

Moustafa, A. A., Myers, C. E., & Gluck, M. A. (2009). A neurocomputational model of classical conditioning phenomena: A putative role for the hippocampal region in associative learning. *Brain Res, 1276*, 180–195. https://doi.org/10.1016/j.brainres.2009.04.020

Moxon, K., Saez, I., & Ditterich, J. (2019). Mind over matter: Cognitive neuroengineering. *Cerebrum, 2019*. https://www.ncbi.nlm.nih.gov/pubmed/32206166

Muchnik, L., Aral, S., & Taylor, S. J. (2013). Social influence bias: A randomized experiment. *Science, 341*(6146), 647–651. https://doi.org/10.1126/science.1240466

Mull, B. R., & Seyal, M. (2001). Transcranial magnetic stimulation of left prefrontal cortex impairs working memory. *Clin Neurophysiol, 112*(9), 1672–1675. https://doi.org/10.1016/s1388-2457(01)00606-x

Mullally, S. L., & Maguire, E. A. (2014). Learning to remember: The early ontogeny of episodic memory. *Dev Cogn Neurosci, 9*, 12–29. https://doi.org/10.1016/j.dcn.2013.12.006

Muller, V., & Lindenberger, U. (2011). Cardiac and respiratory patterns synchronize between persons during choir singing. *PLoS One, 6*(9), e24893. https://doi.org/10.1371/journal.pone.0024893

Munakata, Y., Snyder, H. R., & Chatham, C. H. (2012). Developing cognitive control: Three key transitions. *Curr Dir Psychol Sci, 21*(2), 71–77. https://doi.org/10.1177/0963721412436807

Murdock, B. B. (1985). The contributions of Hermann Ebbinghaus. *J Exp Psychol Learn Mem Cogn, 11*, 469–471.

Murphy, G. L., & Medin, D. L. (1985). The role of theories in conceptual coherence. *Psychol Rev, 92*(3), 289–316. http://www.ncbi.nlm.nih.gov/pubmed/4023146

Murray, J. M., & Escola, G. S. (2020). Remembrance of things practiced with fast and slow learning in cortical and subcortical pathways. *Nat Commun, 11*(1), 6441. https://doi.org/10.1038/s41467-020-19788-5

Murre, J.M.J., & Chessa, A. G. (2023). Why Ebbinghaus' savings method from 1885 is a very 'pure' measure of memory performance. *Psychon Bull Rev, 30*(1), 303–307. https://doi.org/10.3758/s13423-022-02172-3

Murre, J. M., & Dros, J. (2015). Replication and analysis of Ebbinghaus' forgetting curve. *PLoS One, 10*(7), e0120644. https://doi.org/10.1371/journal.pone.0120644

Myers, C. E., Rego, J., Haber, P., Morley, K., Beck, K. D., Hogarth, L., & Moustafa, A. A. (2017). Learning and generalization from reward and punishment in opioid addiction. *Behav Brain Res, 317*, 122–131. https://doi.org/10.1016/j.bbr.2016.09.033

Myers, N. A., Perris, E. E., & Speaker, C. J. (1994). Fifty months of memory: A longitudinal study in early childhood. *Memory, 2*, 383–415. https://doi.org/10.1080/09658219408258956

N

Nadel, L., Samsonovich, A., Ryan, L., & Moscovitch, M. (2000). Multiple trace theory of human memory: Computational, neuroimaging, and neuropsychological results. *Hippocampus, 10*(4), 352–368. https://doi.org/10.1002/1098-1063(2000)10:4<352::AID-HIPO2>3.0.CO;2-D

Nagel, T. (1974). What is it like to be a bat? *Philos Rev, 83*, 435–450.

Nahorna, O., Berthommier, F., & Schwartz, J. L. (2012). Binding and unbinding the auditory and visual streams in the McGurk effect. *J Acoust Soc Am, 132*(2), 1061–1077. https://doi.org/10.1121/1.4728187

Nairne, J. S., & Neath, I. (2013). Sensory and working memory. In A. F. Healy, R. W. Proctor, & I. B. Weiner (Eds.), *Handbook of psychology: Experimental psychology* (pp. 419–445). Hoboken, NJ: John Wiley & Sons.

Naqvi, N. H., Rudrauf, D., Damasio, H., & Bechara, A. (2007). Damage to the insula disrupts addiction to cigarette smoking. *Science, 315*(5811), 531–534. https://doi.org/10.1126/science.1135926

Nardou, R., Lewis, E. M., Rothhaas, R., Xu, R., Yang, A., Boyden, E., & Dolen, G. (2019). Oxytocin-dependent reopening of a social reward learning critical period with MDMA. *Nature, 569*(7754), 116–120. https://doi.org/10.1038/s41586-019-1075-9

Natale, S. (2019). If software is narrative: Joseph Weizenbaum, artificial intelligence and the biographies of ELIZA. *New Media Soc, 21*, 712–728.

National Institutes of Health, N. I. o. D. a. D. (1997). *Aphasia* NIH pub no. 97-4257.

Nau, M., Julian, J. B., & Doeller, C. F. (2018). How the brain's navigation system shapes our visual experience. *Trends Cogn Sci, 22*(9), 810–825. https://doi.org/10.1016/j.tics.2018.06.008

Neath, I., & Brown, G. D. (2012). Arguments against memory trace decay: A SIMPLE account of Baddeley and Scott. *Front Psychol, 3*, 35. https://doi.org/10.3389/fpsyg.2012.00035

Neath, I., Saint-Aubin, J., Bireta, T. J., Gabel, A. J., Hudson, C. G., & Surprenant, A. M. (2019). Short- and long-term memory tasks predict working memory performance, and vice versa. *Can J Exp Psychol, 73*(2), 79–93. https://doi.org/10.1037/cep0000157

Neisser, U. (1967). *Cognitive psychology*. Appleton-Century-Crofts.

Neitz, M., & Neitz, J. (2014). Curing color blindness—Mice and nonhuman primates. *Cold Spring Harb Perspect Med, 4*(11), a017418. https://doi.org/10.1101/cshperspect.a017418

Nelson, C. A. (2001). The development and neural bases of face recognition. *Infant Child Dev, 10*, 3–18.

Nelson, K., & Fivush, R. (2020). The development of autobiographical memory, autobiographical narratives, and autobiographical consciousness. *Psychol Rep, 123*(1), 71–96. https://doi.org/10.1177/0033294119852574

Netz, R. (2003). *The shaping of deduction in Greek mathematics: A study in cognitive history*. UK: Cambridge University Press.

Neumann, N., Dubischar-Krivec, A. M., Braun, C., Low, A., Poustka, F., Bolte, S., & Birbaumer, N. (2010). The mind of the mnemonists: An MEG and neuropsychological study of autistic memory savants. *Behav Brain Res, 215*(1), 114–121. https://doi.org/10.1016/j.bbr.2010.07.008

Newell, A. (1980). Physical symbol systems. *Cogn Sci, 4*, 135–183.

Newell, A., & Simon, H. A. (1972). *Human problem solving*. Hoboken, NJ: Prentice-Hall.

Newman, R. S. (2005). The cocktail party effect in infants revisited: Listening to one's name in noise. *Dev Psychol, 41*(2), 352–362. https://doi.org/10.1037/0012-1649.41.2.352

Newman, T. M., Macomber, D., Naples, A. J., Babitz, T., Volkmar, F., & Grigorenko, E. L. (2007). Hyperlexia in children with autism spectrum disorders. *J Autism Dev Disord, 37*(4), 760–774. https://doi.org/10.1007/s10803-006-0206-y

Newstead, S. E., Handley, S. J., Harley, C., Wright, H., & Farrelly, D. (2004). Individual differences in deductive reasoning. *Q J Exp Psychol A, 57*(1), 33–60. https://doi.org/10.1080/02724980343000116

Newton, I. (1972). *Of colour*. New York, NY: Oxford University Press.

Nguyen, L., Murphy, K., & Andrews, G. (2019). Immediate and long-term efficacy of executive functions cognitive training in older adults: A systematic review and meta-analysis. *Psychol Bull, 145*(7), 698–733. https://doi.org/10.1037/bul0000196

Nielsen, M., Suddendorf, T., & Slaughter, V. (2006). Mirror self-recognition beyond the face. *Child Dev, 77*(1), 176–185. https://doi.org/10.1111/j.1467-8624.2006.00863.x

Niessing, J., & Friedrich, R. W. (2010). Olfactory pattern classification by discrete neuronal network states. *Nature, 465*(7294), 47–52. https://doi.org/10.1038/nature08961

Nilsson, M., Perfilieva, E., Johansson, U., Orwar, O., & Eriksson, P. S. (1999). Enriched environment increases neurogenesis in the adult rat dentate gyrus and improves spatial memory. *J Neurobiol, 39*(4), 569–578. https://doi.org/10.1002/(sici)1097-4695(19990615)39:4<569::aid-neu10>3.0.co;2-f

Nisbett, R. E., & Miyamoto, Y. (2005). The influence of culture: Holistic versus analytic perception. *Trends Cogn Sci, 9*(10), 467–473. https://doi.org/10.1016/j.tics.2005.08.004

Niu, W., & Kaufman, J. C. (2013). Creativity of Chinese and American cultures: A synthetic analysis. *J Creat Behav, 47*, 77–87.

Noë, A., & Noë, A. (2004). *Action in perception*. Cambridge, MA: MIT Press.

Nordeen, K. W., & Nordeen, E. J. (2004). Synaptic and molecular mechanisms regulating plasticity during early learning. *Ann N Y Acad Sci, 1016*, 416–437. https://doi.org/10.1196/annals.1298.018

Nosek, B. A., Hardwicke, T. E., Moshontz, H., Allard, A., Corker, K. S., Dreber, A., ... Vazire, S. (2022). Replicability, robustness, and reproducibility in psychological science. *Annu Rev Psychol, 73*, 719–748. https://doi.org/10.1146/annurev-psych-020821-114157

Nosofsky, R. M., Palmeri, T. J., & McKinley, S. C. (1994). Rule-plus-exception model of classification learning. *Psychol Rev, 101*(1), 53–79. http://www.ncbi.nlm.nih.gov/pubmed/8121960

Notter, M. P., Hanke, M., Murray, M. M., & Geiser, E. (2019). Encoding of auditory temporal gestalt in the human brain. *Cereb Cortex, 29*(2), 475–484. https://doi.org/10.1093/cercor/bhx328

Novick, J. M., Bunting, M. F., Dougherty, M. R., & Engle, R. W. (Eds.). (2019). *Cognitive and working memory training: Perspectives from psychology, neuroscience, and human development.* New York, NY: Oxford University Press.

Nunez, R., & Cooperrider, K. (2013). The tangle of space and time in human cognition. *Trends Cogn Sci, 17*, 220–229. https://doi.org/10.1016/j.tics.2013.03.008

Nunn, J. A., Gregory, L. J., Brammer, M., Williams, S.C.R., Parslow, D. M., Morgan, M. J.,…Gray, J. A. (2002). Functional magnetic resonance imaging of synesthesia: Activation of V4/V8 by spoken words. *Nat Neurosci, 5*(4), 371–375. https://doi.org/10.1038/nn818

Nyberg, L., & Pudas, S. (2019). Successful memory aging. *Annu Rev Psychol, 70*, 219–243. https://doi.org/10.1146/annurev-psych-010418-103052

O

O'Connor, A. R., Wells, C., & Moulin, C. J. A. (2021). Deja vu and other dissociative states in memory. *Memory, 29*(7), 835–842. https://doi.org/10.1080/09658211.2021.1911197

O'Dowd, A., & Newell, F. N. (2020). The rubber hand illusion is influenced by self-recognition. *Neurosci Lett, 720*, 134756. https://doi.org/10.1016/j.neulet.2020.134756

O'Keefe, J., & Nadel, L. (1978). *The hippocampus as a cognitive map.* New York, NY: Oxford University Press.

O'Keeffe, K. P., Hong, H., & Strogatz, S. H. (2017). Oscillators that sync and swarm. *Nat Commun, 8*(1), 1504. https://doi.org/10.1038/s41467-017-01190-3

O'Reilly, R. C. (2006). Biologically based computational models of high-level cognition. *Science, 314*(5796), 91–94. https://doi.org/10.1126/science.1127242

O'Reilly, R. C., Herd, S. A., & Pauli, W. M. (2010). Computational models of cognitive control. *Curr Opin Neurobiol, 20*(2), 257–261. https://doi.org/10.1016/j.conb.2010.01.008

Oakes, L. M., & Rakison, D. H. (2020). *Developmental cascades: Building the infant mind.* New York, NY: Oxford University Press.

Oberauer, K. (2019). Working memory and attention—A conceptual analysis and review. *J Cogn, 2*(1), 36. https://doi.org/10.5334/joc.58

Oberauer, K., & Souza, A. S. (2020). How fast can people refresh and rehearse information in working memory? *Mem Cognit, 48*(8), 1442–1459. https://doi.org/10.3758/s13421-020-01062-0

Ogden, R. S., Wearden, J. H., Gallagher, D. T., & Montgomery, C. (2011). The effect of alcohol administration on human timing: A comparison of prospective timing, retrospective timing and passage of time judgements. *Acta Psychologica, 138*, 254–262. https://doi.org/10.1016/j.actpsy.2011.07.002

Ohlsson, S. (1996). Learning from performance errors. *Psychol Rev, 103*, 241–262.

Okruszek, L., & Chrustowicz, M. (2020). Social perception and interaction database—A novel tool to study social cognitive processes with point-light displays. *Front Psychiatry, 11*, 123. https://doi.org/10.3389/fpsyt.2020.00123

Olasagasti, I., Bouton, S., & Giraud, A. L. (2015). Prediction across sensory modalities: A neurocomputational model of the McGurk effect. *Cortex, 68*, 61–75. https://doi.org/10.1016/j.cortex.2015.04.008

Oliveira, A. L. (2022). A blueprint for conscious machines. *Proc Natl Acad Sci U S A, 119*(23), e2205971119. https://doi.org/10.1073/pnas.2205971119

Olivola, C. Y., Funk, F., & Todorov, A. (2014). Social attributions from faces bias human choices. *Trends Cogn Sci, 18*(11), 566–570. https://doi.org/10.1016/j.tics.2014.09.007

Ollinger, M., Jones, G., & Knoblich, G. (2008). Investigating the effect of mental set on insight problem solving. *Exp Psychol, 55*(4), 269–282. https://doi.org/10.1027/1618-3169.55.4.269

Olmstead, M. C., & Kuhlmeier, V. A. (2015). *Comparative cognition.* UK: Cambridge University Press.

Olson, M. A., & Fazio, R. H. (2001). Implicit attitude formation through classical conditioning. *Psychol Sci, 12*(5), 413–417. https://doi.org/10.1111/1467-9280.00376

Olsson, C. J., Jonsson, B., Larsson, A., & Nyberg, L. (2008). Motor representations and practice affect brain systems underlying imagery: An FMRI study of internal imagery in novices and active high jumpers. *Open Neuroimag J, 2*, 5–13. https://doi.org/10.2174/1874440000802010005

Olton, D. S. (1979). Mazes, maps, and memory. *Am Psychol, 34*(7), 583–596. https://doi.org/10.1037/0003-066x.34.7.583

Ongaro, G., Hardman, D., & Deschenaux, I. (2022). Why the extended mind is nothing special but central. *Phenomenol Cogn Sci, 1–23.*

Ophir, E., Nass, C., & Wagner, A. D. (2009). Cognitive control in media multitaskers. *Proc Natl Acad Sci U S A, 106*(37), 15583–15587. https://doi.org/10.1073/pnas.0903620106

Orduna, V. (2015). Impulsivity and sensitivity to amount and delay of reinforcement in an animal model of ADHD. *Behav Brain Res, 294*, 62–71. https://doi.org/10.1016/j.bbr.2015.07.046

Osherson, D. N., & Smith, E. E. (1981). On the adequacy of prototype theory as a theory of concepts. *Cognition, 9*(1), 35–58. http://www.ncbi.nlm.nih.gov/pubmed/7196818

Osterhout, L., & Nicol, J. (1999). On the distinctiveness, independence, and time course of the brain responses to syntactic and semantic anomalies. *Lang Cognitive Proc, 14*, 283–317.

Ostermeier, M. (2010). History of guide dog use by veterans. *Mil Med, 175*(8), 587–593. https://doi.org/10.7205/milmed-d-10-00082

Ostojic, L., & Clayton, N. S. (2014). Behavioural coordination of dogs in a cooperative problem-solving task with a conspecific and a human partner. *Anim Cogn, 17*(2), 445–459. https://doi.org/10.1007/s10071-013-0676-1

Ostrolenk, A., Forgeot d'Arc, B., Jelenic, P., Samson, F., & Mottron, L. (2017). Hyperlexia: Systematic review, neurocognitive modelling, and outcome. *Neurosci Biobehav Rev, 79*, 134–149. https://doi.org/10.1016/j.neubiorev.2017.04.029

Ostroumov, A., & Dani, J. A. (2018). Convergent Neuronal Plasticity and Metaplasticity Mechanisms of Stress, Nicotine, and Alcohol. *Annu Rev Pharmacol Toxicol, 58*, 547–566. https://doi.org/10.1146/annurev-pharmtox-010617-052735

Ott, T., & Nieder, A. (2019). Dopamine and Cognitive Control in Prefrontal Cortex. *Trends Cogn Sci, 23*(3), 213–234. https://doi.org/10.1016/j.tics.2018.12.006

Oudeyer, P. Y. (2017). What do we learn about development from baby robots? *Wiley Interdiscip Rev Cogn Sci, 8*(1–2). https://doi.org/10.1002/wcs.1395

Owen, A. M., McMillan, K. M., Laird, A. R., & Bullmore, E. (2005). N-back working memory paradigm: A meta-analysis of normative functional neuroimaging studies. *Hum Brain Mapp, 25*(1), 46–59. https://doi.org/10.1002/hbm.20131

Owen, A. M., Roberts, A. C., Hodges, J. R., Summers, B. A., Polkey, C. E., & Robbins, T. W. (1993). Contrasting mechanisms of impaired attentional set-shifting in patients with frontal lobe damage or Parkinson's disease. *Brain, 116(Pt 5)*, 1159–1175. http://www.ncbi.nlm.nih.gov/pubmed/8221053

Owens, J. M., McLaughlin, S. B., & Sudweeks, J. (2011). Driver performance while text messaging using handheld and in-vehicle systems. *Accid Anal Prev, 43*(3), 939–947. https://doi.org/10.1016/j.aap.2010.11.019

Ozcaliskan, S., & Goldin-Meadow, S. (2005). Gesture is at the cutting edge of early language development. *Cognition, 96*(3), B101–113. https://doi.org/10.1016/j.cognition.2005.01.001

P

Pagnoni, G., & Cekic, M. (2007). Age effects on gray matter volume and attentional performance in Zen meditation. *Neurobiol Aging, 28*(10), 1623–1627. https://doi.org/10.1016/j.neurobiolaging.2007.06.008

Paivio. (1971). *Imagery and verbal processes*. New York, NY: Holt, Reinhert, & Winston.

Palmeri, T. J., & Cottrell, G. W. (2010). Modeling perceptual expertise. In I. Gauthier, M. J. Tarr, & D. Bub (Eds.), *Perceptual expertise: Bridging brain and behavior* (pp. 197–244). New York, NY: Oxford University Press.

Palmiero, M., Piccardi, L., Giancola, M., Nori, R., D'Amico, S., & Olivetti Belardinelli, M. (2019). The format of mental imagery: From a critical review to an integrated embodied representation approach. *Cogn Process, 20*(3), 277–289. https://doi.org/10.1007/s10339-019-00908-z

Palmiero, M., Piccardi, L., Nori, R., Palermo, L., Salvi, C., & Guariglia, C. (2016). Editorial: Creativity and mental imagery. *Front Psychol, 7*, 1280. https://doi.org/10.3389/fpsyg.2016.01280

Panksepp, J. (2003). At the interface of the affective, behavioral, and cognitive neurosciences: Decoding the emotional feelings of the brain. *Brain Cogn, 52*(1), 4–14. https://doi.org/10.1016/s0278-2626(03)00003-4

Panoz-Brown, D., Iyer, V., Carey, L. M., Sluka, C. M., Rajic, G., Kestenman, J.,… Crystal, J. D. (2018). Replay of episodic memories in the rat. *Curr Biol, 28*(10), 1628–1634 e1627. https://doi.org/10.1016/j.cub.2018.04.006

Papassotiropoulos, A., & de Quervain, D. J. (2011). Genetics of human episodic memory: Dealing with complexity. *Trends Cogn Sci, 15*(9), 381–387. https://doi.org/10.1016/j.tics.2011.07.005

Papesh, M. H. (2018). Photo ID verification remains challenging despite years of practice. *Cogn Res Princ Implic, 3*, 19. https://doi.org/10.1186/s41235-018-0110-y

Papini, M. R., & Bitterman, M. E. (1990). The role of contingency in classical conditioning. *Psychol Rev, 97*(3), 396–403. https://doi.org/10.1037/0033-295x.97.3.396

Paraskevoudi, N., Balci, F., & Vatakis, A. (2018). "Walking" through the sensory, cognitive, and temporal degradations of healthy aging. *Ann N Y Acad Sci*. https://doi.org/10.1111/nyas.13734

Park, D. C., & Bischof, G. N. (2013). The aging mind: Neuroplasticity in response to cognitive training. *Dialogues Clin Neurosci, 15*, 109–119.

Park, J. E., & Silva, A. C. (2019). Generation of genetically engineered non-human primate models of brain function and neurological disorders. *Am J Primatol, 81*(2), e22931. https://doi.org/10.1002/ajp.22931

Park, J., & Brannon, E. M. (2013). Training the approximate number system improves math proficiency. *Psychol Sci, 24*, 2013–2019. https://doi.org/10.1177/0956797613482944

Park, J., & Brannon, E. M. (2014). Improving arithmetic performance with number sense training: An investigation of underlying mechanism. *Cognition, 133*, 188–200. https://doi.org/10.1016/j.cognition.2014.06.011

Pashler, H., Rohrer, D., Cepeda, N. J., & Carpenter, S. K. (2007). Enhancing learning and retarding forgetting: Choices and consequences. *Psychon Bull Rev, 14*(2), 187–193. https://doi.org/10.3758/bf03194050

Pastor, M. A., Artieda, J., Jahanshahi, M., & Obeso, J. A. (1992). Time estimation and reproduction is abnormal in Parkinson's disease. *Brain, 115 Pt 1*, 211–225. https://doi.org/10.1093/brain/115.1.211

Patel, A. D. (2003). Language, music, syntax and the brain. *Nat Neurosci, 6*(7), 674–681. https://doi.org/10.1038/nn1082

Patel, A. D., Gibson, E., Ratner, J., Besson, M., & Holcomb, P. J. (1998). Processing syntactic relations in language and music: An event-related potential study. *J Cogn Neurosci, 10*(6), 717–733. https://www.ncbi.nlm.nih.gov/pubmed/9831740

Patel, V. L., Glaser, R., & Arocha, J. F. (2000). Cognition and expertise: Acquisition of medical competence. *Clin Invest Med, 23*(4), 256–260. https://www.ncbi.nlm.nih.gov/pubmed/10981537

Patke, A., Young, M. W., & Axelrod, S. (2020). Molecular mechanisms and physiological importance of circadian rhythms. *Nat Rev Mol Cell Biol, 21*(2), 67–84. https://doi.org/10.1038/s41580-019-0179-2

Paton, J. J., & Buonomano, D. V. (2018). The neural basis of timing: Distributed mechanisms for diverse functions. *Neuron, 98*(4), 687–705. https://doi.org/10.1016/j.neuron.2018.03.045

Pavlov, I. P. (1927). *Conditioned reflexes: An investigation of the physiological activity of the cerebral cortex*. London, UK: Oxford University Press.

Pavlov, I. P. (1941). *Conditioned relfexes and psychiatry*. New York, NY: International Publishers.

Pavlova, M. A. (2012). Biological motion processing as a hallmark of social cognition. *Cereb Cortex, 22*(5), 981–995. https://doi.org/10.1093/cercor/bhr156

Pavlova, M., Krageloh-Mann, I., Sokolov, A., & Birbaumer, N. (2001). Recognition of point-light biological motion displays by young children. *Perception, 30*(8), 925–933. https://doi.org/10.1068/p3157

Pazzani, M. J. (1991). Influence of prior knowledge on concept acquisition: Experimental and computational results. *J Exp Psychol Learn Mem Cogn, 17*, 416–432.

Pearson, J. (2019). The human imagination: The cognitive neuroscience of visual mental imagery. *Nat Rev Neurosci, 20*(10), 624–634. https://doi.org/10.1038/s41583-019-0202-9

Pearson, J., Naselaris, T., Holmes, E. A., & Kosslyn, S. M. (2015). Mental imagery: Functional mechanisms and clinical applications. *Trends Cogn Sci, 19*(10), 590–602. https://doi.org/10.1016/j.tics.2015.08.003

Peer, M., Brunec, I. K., Newcombe, N. S., & Epstein, R. A. (2021). Structuring knowledge with cognitive maps and cognitive graphs. *Trends Cogn Sci, 25*(1), 37–54. https://doi.org/10.1016/j.tics.2020.10.004

Pemment, J. (2013). The neurobiology of antisocial personality disorder: The quest for rehabilitation and treatment. *Aggress Violent Behav, 18*, 79–82.

Penfield, W., & Perot, P. (1963). The brain's record of auditory and visual experience. A final summary and discussion. *Brain, 86,* 595–696. https://doi.org/10.1093/brain/86.4.595

Penn, D. C., Holyoak, K. J., & Povinelli, D. J. (2008). Darwin's mistake: Explaining the discontinuity between human and nonhuman minds. *Behav Brain Sci, 31*(2), 109–130; discussion 130–178. https://doi.org/10.1017/S0140525×08003543

Penn, D. C., & Povinelli, D. J. (2007). Causal cognition in human and nonhuman animals: A comparative, critical review. *Annu Rev Psychol, 58,* 97–118. https://doi.org/10.1146/annurev.psych.58.110405.085555

Pennebaker, J. W., Mehl, M. R., & Niederhoffer, K. G. (2003). Psychological aspects of natural language use: Our words, our selves. *Annu Rev Psychol, 54,* 547–577. https://doi.org/10.1146/annurev.psych.54.101601.145041

Pennington, N., & Hastie, R. (1990). Practical implications of psychological research on juror and jury decision making. *Pers Soc Psychol Bull, 16,* 90–105.

Pepperberg, I. M. (1988). The importance of social interaction and observation in the acquisition of communicative competence: Possible parallels between avian and human learning. In T. R. Zentall & B. G. Galef (Eds.), *Social learning: Psychological and biological perspectives* (pp. 279–299). Hillsdale, NJ: Lawrence Erlbaum Associates.

Pepperberg, I. M. (2013). Abstract concepts: Data from a Grey parrot. *Behav Processes, 93,* 82–90. https://doi.org/10.1016/j.beproc.2012.09.016

Pepperberg, I. M. (2021). Nonhuman and nonhuman-human communication: Some issues and questions. *Front Psychol, 12,* 647841. https://doi.org/10.3389/fpsyg.2021.647841

Peretz, I. (2010). Towards a neurobiology of musical emotions. In P. N. Juslin & J. A. Sloboda (Eds.), *Handbook of music and emotion: Theory, research, applications* (pp. 99–126). New York, NY: Oxford University Press.

Peretz, I., & Hyde, K. L. (2003). What is specific to music processing? Insights from congenital amusia. *Trends Cogn Sci, 7*(8), 362–367. https://www.ncbi.nlm.nih.gov/pubmed/12907232

Perez, A. M., Spence, J. S., Kiel, L. D., Venza, E. E., & Chapman, S. B. (2018). Influential cognitive processes on framing biases in aging. *Front Psychol, 9,* 661. https://doi.org/10.3389/fpsyg.2018.00661

Perich, M. G., Gallego, J. A., & Miller, L. E. (2018). A neural population mechanism for rapid learning. *Neuron, 100*(4), 964–976 e967. https://doi.org/10.1016/j.neuron.2018.09.030

Peters, J., & Buchel, C. (2010). Neural representations of subjective reward value. *Behav Brain Res, 213*(2), 135–141. https://doi.org/10.1016/j.bbr.2010.04.031

Peterson, G. B. (2004). A day of great illumination: B. F. Skinner's discovery of shaping. *J Exp Anal Behav, 82*(3), 317–328. https://doi.org/10.1901/jeab.2004.82-317

Peterson, J. C., Bourgin, D. D., Agrawal, M., Reichman, D., & Griffiths, T. L. (2021). Using large-scale experiments and machine learning to discover theories of human decision-making. *Science, 372*(6547), 1209–1214. https://doi.org/10.1126/science.abe2629

Petrides, M. (1996). Specialized systems for the processing of mnemonic information within the primate frontal cortex. *Philos Trans R Soc Lond B Biol Sci, 351*(1346), 1455–1461; discussion 1461–1452. https://doi.org/10.1098/rstb.1996.0130

Pfeiffer, B. E. (2020). The content of hippocampal "replay." *Hippocampus, 30*(1), 6–18. https://doi.org/10.1002/hipo.22824

Phillips, C. (2017). Physical activity modulates common neuroplasticity substrates in major depressive and bipolar disorder. *Neural Plast, 2017,* 7014146. https://doi.org/10.1155/2017/7014146

Phillips, L. H., Lawrie, L., Schaefer, A., Tan, C. Y., & Yong, M. H. (2021). The effects of adult ageing and culture on the tower of london task. *Front Psychol, 12,* 631458. https://doi.org/10.3389/fpsyg.2021.631458

Piaget, J. (1952). *The child's conception of number.* London, UK: Humanities Press.

Piaget, J. (1952). *The origins of intelligence in children.* New York, NY: International Universities Press.

Piaget, J. (1964). Cognitive development in children. *J Res Sci Teach, 2,* 176–186.

Piaget, J., & Inhelder, B. (1956). *The child's conception of space.* UK: Routledge & Kegan Paul.

Pickover, A. M., Messina, B. G., Correia, C. J., Garza, K. B., & Murphy, J. G. (2016). A behavioral economic analysis of the nonmedical use of prescription drugs among young adults. *Exp Clin Psychopharmacol, 24*(1), 38–47. https://doi.org/10.1037/pha0000052

Pierce, J. E., Thomasson, M., Voruz, P., Selosse, G., & Peron, J. (2022). Explicit and implicit emotion processing in the cerebellum: A meta-analysis and systematic review. *Cerebellum.* https://doi.org/10.1007/s12311-022-01459-4

Pillemer, D. B. (1984). Flashbulb memories of the assassination attempt on President Reagan. *Cognition, 16*(1), 63–80. https://doi.org/10.1016/0010-0277(84)90036-2

Pilley, J. W., & Reid, A. K. (2011). Border collie comprehends object names as verbal referents. *Behav Processes, 86,* 184–195. https://doi.org/10.1016/j.beproc.2010.11.007

Pinker, S. (1994). *The language instinct: How the mind creates language.* New York, NY: William Morrow.

Pinker, S. (2022). *Rationality: What it is, why it seems scarce, why it matters.* New York, NY: Penguin.

Pinker, S., & Jackendoff, R. (2005). The faculty of language: What's special about it? *Cognition, 95*(2), 201–236. https://doi.org/10.1016/j.cognition.2004.08.004

Piper, B. J., Li, V., Eiwaz, M. A., Kobel, Y. V., Benice, T. S., Chu, A. M., … Raber, J. (2012). Executive function on the Psychology Experiment Building Language tests. *Behav Res Methods, 44*(1), 110–123. https://doi.org/10.3758/s13428-011-0096-6

Pirrone, F., & Albertini, M. (2017). Olfactory detection of cancer by trained sniffer dogs: A systematic review of the literature. *J Vet Behav, 19,* 105–117.

Pitcher, D., Walsh, V., Yovel, G., & Duchaine, B. (2007). TMS evidence for the involvement of the right occipital face area in early face processing. *Curr Biol, 17*(18), 1568–1573. https://doi.org/10.1016/j.cub.2007.07.063

Pléh, C. (2019). The inspirational role of Chomsky in the cognitive turn of psychology. *Acta Linguist Acad, 66,* 397–428.

Plomin, R., & Deary, I. J. (2015). Genetics and intelligence differences: Five special findings. *Mol Psychiatry, 20*(1), 98–108. https://doi.org/10.1038/mp.2014.105

Plomin, R., & von Stumm, S. (2018). The new genetics of intelligence. *Nat Rev Genet, 19*(3), 148–159. https://doi.org/10.1038/nrg.2017.104

Poarch, G. J., & Bialystok, E. (2015). Bilingualism as a Model for Multitasking. *Dev Rev, 35*, 113–124. https://doi.org/10.1016/j.dr.2014.12.003

Poeppel, D., & Hickok, G. (2004). Towards a new functional anatomy of language. *Cognition, 92*(1–2), 1–12. https://doi.org/10.1016/j.cognition.2003.11.001

Polania, R., Moisa, M., Opitz, A., Grueschow, M., & Ruff, C. C. (2015). The precision of value-based choices depends causally on fronto-parietal phase coupling. *Nat Commun, 6*, 8090. https://doi.org/10.1038/ncomms9090

Poldrack, R. A., Clark, J., Pare-Blagoev, E. J., Shohamy, D., Creso Moyano, J., Myers, C., & Gluck, M. A. (2001). Interactive memory systems in the human brain. *Nature, 414*(6863), 546–550. https://doi.org/10.1038/35107080

Posner, M. I., & Dehaene, S. (1994). Attentional networks. *Trends Neurosci, 17*(2), 75–79. https://doi.org/10.1016/0166-2236(94)90078-7

Posner, M. I., Goldsmith, R., & Welton, K. E. (1967). Perceived distance and the classification of distorted patterns. *J Exper Psychol, 73*, 28–38.

Posner, M. I., Nissen, M. J., & Ogden, W. C. (1978). Attended and unattended processing modes: The role of set for spatial location. In H. L. Pick & I. J. Saltzman (Eds.), *Modes of perceiving and processing information* (pp. 137–157). Erlbaum.

Posner, M. I., Synder, C. R., & Solso, R. (2004). Attention and cognitive control. *Cogn Psychol Key Readings, 205*, 55–85.

Postle, B. R., Awh, E., Jonides, J., Smith, E. E., & D'Esposito, M. (2004). The where and how of attention-based rehearsal in spatial working memory. *Brain Res Cogn Brain Res, 20*(2), 194–205. https://doi.org/10.1016/j.cogbrainres.2004.02.008

Pozuelos, J. P., Combita, L. M., Abundis, A., Paz-Alonso, P. M., Conejero, A., Guerra, S., & Rueda, M. R. (2019). Metacognitive scaffolding boosts cognitive and neural benefits following executive attention training in children. *Dev Sci, 22*(2), e12756. https://doi.org/10.1111/desc.12756

Prashad, S., Dedrick, E. S., & Filbey, F. M. (2018). Cannabis users exhibit increased cortical activation during resting state compared to non-users. *Neuroimage, 179*, 176–186. https://doi.org/10.1016/j.neuroimage.2018.06.031

Premack, D. (1959). Toward empirical behavior laws. I. positive reinforcement. *Psychol Rev, 66*(4), 219–233. https://doi.org/10.1037/h0040891

Premack, D. (1983). The codes of man and beasts. *Behav Brain Sci, 6*, 125–167.

Premack, D. (2007). Human and animal cognition: Continuity and discontinuity. *Proc Natl Acad Sci U S A, 104*(35), 13861–13867. https://doi.org/10.1073/pnas.0706147104

Press, C., Kok, P., & Yon, D. (2020). The perceptual prediction paradox. *Trends Cogn Sci, 24*(1), 13–24. https://doi.org/10.1016/j.tics.2019.11.003

Pruitt, T. A., Halpern, A. R., & Pfordresher, P. Q. (2019). Covert singing in anticipatory auditory imagery. *Psychophysiology, 56*(3), e13297. https://doi.org/10.1111/psyp.13297

Pryor, K. (1975). *Lads before the wind: Adventures in porpoise training.* New York, NY: Harper Row.

Pryor, K. (2019). *Don't shoot the dog: The art of teaching and training.* New York, NY: Simon & Schuster.

Przysinda, E., Zeng, T., Maves, K., Arkin, C., & Loui, P. (2017). Jazz musicians reveal role of expectancy in human creativity. *Brain Cogn, 119*, 45–53. https://doi.org/10.1016/j.bandc.2017.09.008

Pulsifer, M. B., Brandt, J., Salorio, C. F., Vining, E. P., Carson, B. S., & Freeman, J. M. (2004). The cognitive outcome of hemispherectomy in 71 children. *Epilepsia, 45*(3), 243–254. https://doi.org/10.1111/j.0013-9580.2004.15303.x

Purdy, D. M. (1936). Eidetic imagery and plasticity of perception. *J Gen Psychol, 15*, 437–454.

Purtle, R. B. (1973). Peak shift: A review. *Psychol Bull, 80*, 408–421.

Purves, D., Wojtach, W. T., & Lotto, R. B. (2011). Understanding vision in wholly empirical terms. *Proc Natl Acad Sci U S A, 108*, 15588–15595. https://doi.org/10.1073/pnas.1012178108

Putnam, A. L. (2015). Mnemonics in education: Current research and applications. *Trans Issues Psychol Sci, 1*, 130–139.

Putnam, H. (1960). Minds and machines. In S. Hook (Ed.), *Dimensions of mind: A symposium* (pp. 20–33). New York University Press.

Pyke, G. H. (2010). Optimal foraging theory: Introduction. In M. D. Breed & J. Moore (Eds.), *Encyclopedia of animal behavior.* Cambridge, MA: Academic Press.

Pylyshyn, Z. W. (2002). Mental imagery: In search of a theory. *Behav Brain Sci, 25*(2), 157–182; discussion 182–237. https://doi.org/10.1017/s0140525×02000043

Q

Quartz, S. R. (1999). The constructivist brain. *Trends Cogn Sci, 3*(2), 48–57. https://doi.org/10.1016/s1364-6613(98)01270-4

Quinlan, P. T. (2003). Visual feature integration theory: Past, present, and future. *Psychol Bull, 129*(5), 643–673. https://doi.org/10.1037/0033-2909.129.5.643

Quiroga, R. Q., Reddy, L., Kreiman, G., Koch, C., & Fried, I. (2005). Invariant visual representation by single neurons in the human brain. *Nature, 435*(7045), 1102–1107. https://doi.org/10.1038/nature03687

R

Raab, M., & Araujo, D. (2019). Embodied cognition with and without mental representations: The case of embodied choices in sports. *Front Psychol, 10*, 1825. https://doi.org/10.3389/fpsyg.2019.01825

Rabi, R., & Minda, J. P. (2016). Category learning in older adulthood: A study of the Shepard, Hovland, and Jenkins (1961) tasks. *Psychol Aging, 31*(2), 185–197. https://doi.org/10.1037/pag0000071

Ragni, F., Tucciarelli, R., Andersson, P., & Lingnau, A. (2020). Decoding stimulus identity in occipital, parietal and inferotemporal cortices during visual mental imagery. *Cortex, 127*, 371–387. https://doi.org/10.1016/j.cortex.2020.02.020

Rakhimberdina, Z., Jodelet, Q., Liu, X., & Murata, T. (2021). Natural image reconstruction from fMRI using deep learning: A survey. *Front Neurosci, 15*, 795488. https://doi.org/10.3389/fnins.2021.795488

Rakison, D. H., & Poulin-Dubois, D. (2001). Developmental origin of the animate-inanimate distinction. *Psychol Bull, 127*(2), 209–228. http://www.ncbi.nlm.nih.gov/pubmed/11316011

Rakitin, B. C., Gibbon, J., Penney, T. B., Malapani, C., Hinton, S. C., & Meck, W. H. (1998). Scalar expectancy theory and peak-interval timing in humans. *J Exp Psychol Anim Behav Process, 24*(1), 15–33. https://doi.org/10.1037//0097-7403.24.1.15

Ralph, B. C., Thomson, D. R., Cheyne, J. A., & Smilek, D. (2014). Media multitasking and failures of attention in everyday life. *Psychol Res, 78*(5), 661–669. https://doi.org/10.1007/s00426-013-0523-7

Ramon, M., & Gobbini, M. I. (2018). Familiarity matters: A review on prioritized processing of personally familiar faces. *Vis Cogn, 26*, 179–195.

Rathbone, C. J., Moulin, C. J., & Conway, M. A. (2008). Self-centered memories: The reminiscence bump and the self. *Mem Cognit, 36*(8), 1403–1414. https://doi.org/10.3758/MC.36.8.1403

Rathnayaka, P., Mills, N., Burnett, D., De Silva, D., Alahakoon, D., & Gray, R. (2022). A mental health chatbot with cognitive skills for personalised behavioural activation and remote health monitoring. *Sensors (Basel), 22*(10). https://doi.org/10.3390/s22103653

Raviv, L., Lupyan, G., & Green, S. C. (2022). How variability shapes learning and generalization. *Trends Cogn Sci, 26*(6), 462–483. https://doi.org/10.1016/j.tics.2022.03.007

Raw, J., Rorke, A., Ellis, J., Murayama, K., & Sakaki, M. (2023). Memory of the U.K.'s 2016 EU referendum: The effects of valence on the long-term measures of a public event. *Emotion, 23*(1), 52–74. https://doi.org/10.1037/emo0000788

Reber, J., & Tranel, D. (2019). Frontal lobe syndromes. *Handb Clin Neurol, 163*, 147–164. https://doi.org/10.1016/B978-0-12-804281-6.00008-2

Reboul, A. C. (2015). Why language really is not a communication system: A cognitive view of language evolution. *Front Psychol, 6*, 1434. https://doi.org/10.3389/fpsyg.2015.01434

Reder, L. M., & Ritter, F. E. (1992). What determines initial feeling of knowing? Familiarity with question terms, not with the answer. *J Exp Psychol Learn Mem Cogn, 18*, 435–451.

Reicher, G. M. (1969). Perceptual recognition as a function of meaningfulness of stimulus material. *J Exp Psychol, 81*(2), 275–280. https://doi.org/10.1037/h0027768

Rendall, D., Owren, M. J., & Ryan, M. J. (2009). What do animal signals mean? *Anim Behav, 78*, 233–240.

Reppert, S. M., & Weaver, D. R. (2002). Coordination of circadian timing in mammals. *Nature, 418*(6901), 935–941. https://doi.org/10.1038/nature00965

Rey, H. G., Gori, B., Chaure, F. J., Collavini, S., Blenkmann, A. O., Seoane, P.,... Quian Quiroga, R. (2020). Single neuron coding of identity in the human hippocampal formation. *Curr Biol, 30*(6), 1152–1159 e1153. https://doi.org/10.1016/j.cub.2020.01.035

Reynolds, C. R., Altmann, R. A., & Allen, D. N. (2021). The problem of bias in psychological assessment. In C. R. Reynolds, R. A. Altmann, & D. N. Allen (Eds.), *Mastering modern psychological testing* (pp. 573–613). New York, NY: Springer.

Reynolds, J. H., & Chelazzi, L. (2004). Attentional modulation of visual processing. *Annu Rev Neurosci, 27*, 611–647. https://doi.org/10.1146/annurev.neuro.26.041002.131039

Rezayat, E., Dehaqani, M. A., Clark, K., Bahmani, Z., Moore, T., & Noudoost, B. (2021). Frontotemporal coordination predicts working memory performance and its local neural signatures. *Nat Commun, 12*(1), 1103. https://doi.org/10.1038/s41467-021-21151-1

Rhodes, G., Brake, S., & Atkinson, A. P. (1993). What's lost in inverted faces? *Cognition, 47*(1), 25–57. https://doi.org/10.1016/0010-0277(93)90061-y

Richell, R. A., Mitchell, D. G., Newman, C., Leonard, A., Baron-Cohen, S., & Blair, R. J. (2003). Theory of mind and psychopathy: Can psychopathic individuals read the 'language of the eyes'? *Neuropsychologia, 41*(5), 523–526. https://doi.org/10.1016/s0028-3932(02)00175-6

Richler, J. J., & Palmeri, T. J. (2014). Visual category learning. *Wiley Interdiscip Rev Cogn Sci, 5*(1), 75–94. https://doi.org/10.1002/wcs.1268

Riemer, M., Trojan, J., Beauchamp, M., & Fuchs, X. (2019). The rubber hand universe: On the impact of methodological differences in the rubber hand illusion. *Neurosci Biobehav Rev, 104*, 268–280. https://doi.org/10.1016/j.neubiorev.2019.07.008

Riley, D. A. (1968). *Discrimination learning.* Allyn and Bacon.

Riters, L. V., Kelm-Nelson, C. A., & Spool, J. A. (2019). Why Do Birds Flock? A Role for Opioids in the Reinforcement of Gregarious Social Interactions. *Front Physiol, 10*, 421. https://doi.org/10.3389/fphys.2019.00421

Ritter, F. E., Tehranchi, F., & Oury, J. D. (2019). ACT-R: A cognitive architecture for modeling cognition. *Wiley Interdiscip Rev Cogn Sci, 10*(3), e1488. https://doi.org/10.1002/wcs.1488

Riva, P., Manfrinati, A., Sacchi, S., Pisoni, A., & Romero Lauro, L. J. (2019). Selective changes in moral judgment by noninvasive brain stimulation of the medial prefrontal cortex. *Cogn Affect Behav Neurosci, 19*(4), 797–810. https://doi.org/10.3758/s13415-018-00664-1

Rizzolatti, G., Fogassi, L., & Gallese, V. (2001). Neurophysiological mechanisms underlying the understanding and imitation of action. *Nat Rev Neurosci, 2*(9), 661–670. https://doi.org/10.1038/35090060

Rizzuto, D. S., Madsen, J. R., Bromfield, E. B., Schulze-Bonhage, A., Seelig, D., Aschenbrenner-Scheibe, R., & Kahana, M. J. (2003). Reset of human neocortical oscillations during a working memory task. *Proc Natl Acad Sci U S A, 100*(13), 7931–7936. https://doi.org/10.1073/pnas.0732061100

Roads, B. D., Xu, B., Robinson, J. K., & Tanaka, J. W. (2018). The easy-to-hard training advantage with real-world medical images. *Cogn Res Princ Implic, 3*(1), 38. https://doi.org/10.1186/s41235-018-0131-6

Roberson, D., Davies, I., & Davidoff, J. (2000). Color categories are not universal: Replications and new evidence from a stone-age culture. *J Exp Psychol Gen, 129*(3), 369–398. https://doi.org/10.1037//0096-3445.129.3.369

Roberts, W. A., & Santi, A. (2017). The comparative study of working memory. In J. Call, G. M. Burghardt, I. M. Pepperberg, C. T. Snowdon, & T. Zentall (Eds.), *APA handbook of comparative psychology: Perception, learning, and cognition* (pp. 203–225). Washington, DC: American Psychological Association.

Robertson, L. C. (2003). Binding, spatial attention and perceptual awareness. *Nat Rev Neurosci, 4*(2), 93–102. https://doi.org/10.1038/nrn1030

Rochat, P. (2003). Five levels of self-awareness as they unfold early in life. *Conscious Cogn, 12*(4), 717–731. https://doi.org/10.1016/s1053-8100(03)00081-3

Roediger, H. L., & Karpicke, J. D. (2006). Test-enhanced learning: Taking memory tests improves long-term retention. *Psychol Sci, 17*(3), 249–255. https://doi.org/10.1111/j.1467-9280.2006.01693.x

Roediger, H. L., & McDermott, K. B. (1995). Creating false memories: Remembering words not presented in lists. *J Exp Psychol Learn Mem Cogn, 21*, 803–814.

Roediger, H. L., III. (1980). Memory metaphors in cognitive psychology. *Mem Cognit, 8*(3), 231–246. https://doi.org/10.3758/bf03197611

Roediger, H. L., III., & Karpicke, J. D. (2006). The power of testing memory: Basic research and implications for educational practice. *Perspect Psychol Sci, 1*, 181–210. https://doi.org/10.1111/j.1745-6916.2006.00012.x

Rogers, M., Hwang, H., Toplak, M., Weiss, M., & Tannock, R. (2011). Inattention, working memory, and academic achievement in adolescents referred for attention deficit/hyperactivity disorder (ADHD). *Child Neuropsychol, 17*(5), 444–458. https://doi.org/10.1080/09297049.2010.544648

Rogers, T. T., & McClelland, J. L. (2008). Précis of semantic cognition: A parallel distributed processing approach. *Behav Brain Sci, 31*, 689–714.

Rogoff, B., Moore, L. C., Correa-Chávez, M., & Dexter, A. L. (2015). Children develop cultural repertoires through engaging in everyday routines and practices. In J. E. Grusec & P. D. Hastings (Eds.), *Handbook of socialization* (2nd ed.) (pp. 472–498). New York, NY: Guliford Press.

Roitblat, H. L., Herman, L. M., & Nachtigall, P. E. (1993). *Language and communication: Comparative perspectives.* London, UK: Psychology Press.

Roitblat, H. L., & Myers, J.-A. (Eds.). (1995). *Comparative approaches to cognitive science.* Cambridge, MA: MIT Press.

Roitblat, H. L., & von Fersen, L. (1992). Comparative cognition: Representations and processes in learning and memory. *Annu Rev Psychol, 43*, 671–710. https://doi.org/10.1146/annurev.ps.43.020192.003323

Rosch, E., & Mervis, C. B. (1975). Family resemblances: Studies in the internal structure of categories. *Cogn Psychol, 7*, 573–605.

Rosch, E., Mervis, C. B., Gray, W., Johnson, D., & Boyes-Braem, P. (1976). Basic objects in natural categories. *Cogn Psychol, 8*, 382–439.

Roseboom, W., Fountas, Z., Nikiforou, K., Bhowmik, D., Shanahan, M., & Seth, A. K. (2019). Activity in perceptual classification networks as a basis for human subjective time perception. *Nat Commun, 10*(1), 267. https://doi.org/10.1038/s41467-018-08194-7

Rosenthal, D. M. (2000). Consciousness, content, and metacognitive judgments. *Conscious Cogn, 9*(2 Pt 1), 203–214. https://doi.org/10.1006/ccog.2000.0437

Roskos-Ewoldsen, B., Intons-Peterson, M. J., & Anderson, R. E. (Eds.). (1993). *Imagery, creativity, and discovery: A cognitive perspective.* Elsevier.

Ross, H. E. (1995). Weber then and now. *Perception, 24*(6), 599–602. https://doi.org/10.1068/p240599

Rossion, B. (2022). Twenty years of investigation with the case of prosopagnosia PS to understand human face identity recognition. Part I: Function. *Neuropsychologia, 173*, 108278. https://doi.org/10.1016/j.neuropsychologia.2022.108278

Rossmeisl, J. H., Jr., Rohleder, J. J., Pickett, J. P., Duncan, R., & Herring, I. P. (2007). Presumed and confirmed striatocapsular brain infarctions in six dogs. *Vet Ophthalmol, 10*(1), 23–36. https://doi.org/10.1111/j.1463-5224.2007.00487.x

Roth, W. M., & Jornet, A. (2013). Situated cognition. *Wiley Interdiscip Rev Cogn Sci, 4*(5), 463–478. https://doi.org/10.1002/wcs.1242

Rouder, J. N., & Ratcliff, R. (2004). Comparing categorization models. *J Exp Psychol Gen, 133*(1), 63–82. https://doi.org/10.1037/0096-3445.133.1.63

Roy, B. C., Frank, M. C., DeCamp, P., Miller, M., & Roy, D. (2015). Predicting the birth of a spoken word. *Proc Natl Acad Sci U S A, 112*(41), 12663–12668. https://doi.org/10.1073/pnas.1419773112

Roy, D. S., Park, Y. G., Kim, M. E., Zhang, Y., Ogawa, S. K., DiNapoli, N.,... Tonegawa, S. (2022). Brain-wide mapping reveals that engrams for a single memory are distributed across multiple brain regions. *Nat Commun, 13*(1), 1799. https://doi.org/10.1038/s41467-022-29384-4

Ruben, R. J. (1999). A time frame of critical/sensitive periods of language development. *Indian J Otolaryngol Head Neck Surg, 51*(3), 85–89. https://doi.org/10.1007/BF02996542

Rueckemann, J. W., Sosa, M., Giocomo, L. M., & Buffalo, E. A. (2021). The grid code for ordered experience. *Nat Rev Neurosci, 22*(10), 637–649. https://doi.org/10.1038/s41583-021-00499-9

Runco, M. A. (2009). Simplifying theories of creativity and revisiting the criterion problem: A comment on Simonton's (2009) hierarchical model of domain-specific disposition, development, and achievement. *Perspect Psychol Sci, 4*(5), 462–465. https://doi.org/10.1111/j.1745-6924.2009.01156.x

Russell, R., Duchaine, B., & Nakayama, K. (2009). Super-recognizers: People with extraordinary face recognition ability. *Psychon Bull Rev, 16*(2), 252–257. https://doi.org/10.3758/PBR.16.2.252

Rutherford, A. (2021). A cautionary history of eugenics. *Science, 373*(6562), 1419. https://doi.org/10.1126/science.abm4415

Rutherford, A. (2021). Race, eugenics, and the canceling of great scientists. *Am J Phys Anthropol, 175*(2), 448–452. https://doi.org/10.1002/ajpa.24192

Rutishauser, U. (2021). Metamemory: Rats know the strength of their memory. *Curr Biol, 31*(21), R1432-R1434. https://doi.org/10.1016/j.cub.2021.09.062

Ryabko, B., & Reznikova, Z. (2009). The use of information theory for studying "language" and intelligence in ants. *Entropy, 11*, 836–853.

Rymer, R. (1993). *Genie: A scientific tragedy.* New York, NY: Harper Collins.

S

Sachan, D. (2018). Self-help robots drive blues away. *Lancet Psychiatry, 5*(7), 547. https://doi.org/10.1016/S2215-0366(18)30230-X

Sacks, O. (1970). *The man who mistook his wife for a hat and other clinical tales.* Summit Books.

Sacks, O. (2008). *Musicophilia: Tales of music and the brain.* Toronto, ON: Vintage Canada.

Safe, D. (2017). *Learning to speak dog!* https://doggonesafe.com/Dog-Detective

Saffran, J. R., Aslin, R. N., & Newport, E. L. (1996). Statistical learning by 8-month-old infants. *Science, 274*(5294), 1926–1928. https://www.ncbi.nlm.nih.gov/pubmed/8943209

Sakata, H., Tsutsui, K., & Taira, M. (2005). Toward an understanding of the neural processing for 3D shape perception. *Neuropsychologia, 43*(2), 151–161. https://doi.org/10.1016/j.neuropsychologia.2004.11.003

Salvucci, D. D. (2013). Integration and reuse in cognitive skill acquisition. *Cogn Sci, 37*(5), 829–860. https://doi.org/10.1111/cogs.12032

Sands, S. F., & Wright, A. A. (1980). Serial probe recognition performance by a rhesus monkey and a human with 10- and 20-item lists. *J Exp Psychol Anim Behav Process, 6*, 386–396.

Santos, L. R., & Rosati, A. G. (2015). The evolutionary roots of human decision making. *Annu Rev Psychol, 66*, 321–347. https://doi.org/10.1146/annurev-psych-010814-015310

Santos, M. D., Mohammadi, M. H., Yang, S., Liang, C. W., Kao, J. P., Alger, B. E.,…Tang, C. M. (2012). Dendritic hold and read: A gated mechanism for short term information storage and retrieval. *PLoS One, 7*(5), e37542. https://doi.org/10.1371/journal.pone.0037542

Sapir, E. (1927). The unconscious patterning of behavior in society. In D. G. Mandelbaum (Ed.), *Selected writings of Edward Sapir* (pp. 544–559). Oakland: University of California Press.

Sartori, G., Scarpazza, C., Codognotto, S., & Pietrini, P. (2016). An unusual case of acquired pedophilic behavior following compression of orbitofrontal cortex and hypothalamus by a Clivus Chordoma. *J Neurol, 263*(7), 1454–1455. https://doi.org/10.1007/s00415-016-8143-y

Satori, R. M., & Job. (1988). The oyster with four legs: A neuropsychological study on the interaction of visual and semantic information. *Cogn Neuropsychol, 5*, 105–132.

Savage-Rumbaugh, E. S., Murphy, J., Sevcik, R. A., Brakke, K. E., Williams, S. L., & Rumbaugh, D. M. (1993). Language comprehension in ape and child. *Monogr Soc Res Child Dev, 58*(3–4), 1–222. https://www.ncbi.nlm.nih.gov/pubmed/8366872

Savaki, H. E., & Raos, V. (2019). Action perception and motor imagery: Mental practice of action. *Prog Neurobiol, 175*, 107–125. https://doi.org/10.1016/j.pneurobio.2019.01.007

Saxena, A., Khanna, A., & Gupta, D. (2020). Emotion recognition and detection methods: A comprehensive survey. *J Artif Intell Syst, 2*, 53–79.

Schacter, D. L. (1983). Feeling of knowing in episodic memory. *J Exp Psychol Learn Mem Cogn, 9*, 39–54.

Schacter, D. L., Benoit, R. G., & Szpunar, K. K. (2017). Episodic future thinking: Mechanisms and functions. *Curr Opin Behav Sci, 17*, 41–50. https://doi.org/10.1016/j.cobeha.2017.06.002

Schacter, D. L., & Buckner, R. L. (1998). Priming and the brain. *Neuron, 20*(2), 185–195. https://doi.org/10.1016/s0896-6273(00)80448-1

Schacter, D. L., Chiu, C. Y., & Ochsner, K. N. (1993). Implicit memory: A selective review. *Annu Rev Neurosci, 16*, 159–182. https://doi.org/10.1146/annurev.ne.16.030193.001111

Schacter, D. L., & Madore, K. P. (2016). Remembering the past and imagining the future: Identifying and enhancing the contribution of episodic memory. *Mem Stud, 9*(3), 245–255. https://doi.org/10.1177/1750698016645230

Schafer, W. R. (2018). The worm connectome: Back to the future. *Trends Neurosci, 41*(11), 763–765. https://doi.org/10.1016/j.tins.2018.09.002

Schalk, G., Kapeller, C., Guger, C., Ogawa, H., Hiroshima, S., Lafer-Sousa, R.,…Kanwisher, N. (2017). Facephenes and rainbows: Causal evidence for functional and anatomical specificity of face and color processing in the human brain. *Proc Natl Acad Sci U S A, 114*(46), 12285–12290. https://doi.org/10.1073/pnas.1713447114

Schank, R. C., & Abelson, R. P. (2013). *Scripts, plans, goals, and understanding.* London, UK: Psychology Press.

Schellenberg, E. G. (2004). Music lessons enhance IQ. *Psychol Sci, 15*(8), 511–514. https://doi.org/10.1111/j.0956-7976.2004.00711.x

Schellenberg, E. G. (2012). Cognitive performance after music listening: A review of the Mozart effect. In G. MacDonald, G. Kreutz, & L. A. Mitchell (Eds.), *Music, health, and wellbeing* (pp. 324–338). New York, NY: Oxford University Press.

Schifano, F., Catalani, V., Sharif, S., Napoletano, F., Corkery, J. M., Arillotta, D.,…Guirguis, A. (2022). Benefits and harms of 'smart drugs' (nootropics) in healthy individuals. *Drugs, 82*(6), 633–647. https://doi.org/10.1007/s40265-022-01701-7

Schiller, D., Eichenbaum, H., Buffalo, E. A., Davachi, L., Foster, D. J., Leutgeb, S., & Ranganath, C. (2015). Memory and space: Towards an understanding of the cognitive map. *J Neurosci, 35*, 13904–13911. https://doi.org/10.1523/JNEUROSCI.2618-15.2015

Schimmack, U. (2021). The implicit association test: A method in search of a construct. *Perspect Psychol Sci, 16*(2), 396–414. https://doi.org/10.1177/1745691619863798

Schmahmann, J. D. (2019). The cerebellum and cognition. *Neurosci Lett, 688*, 62–75. https://doi.org/10.1016/j.neulet.2018.07.005

Schmidt, T. T., & Blankenburg, F. (2019). The somatotopy of mental tactile imagery. *Front Hum Neurosci, 13*, 10. https://doi.org/10.3389/fnhum.2019.00010

Schnider, A. (2003). Spontaneous confabulation and the adaptation of thought to ongoing reality. *Nat Rev Neurosci, 4*(8), 662–671. https://doi.org/10.1038/nrn1179

Schnyer, D. M., Maddox, W. T., Ell, S., Davis, S., Pacheco, J., & Verfaellie, M. (2009). Prefrontal contributions to rule-based and information-integration category learning. *Neuropsychologia, 47*(13), 2995–3006. https://doi.org/10.1016/j.neuropsychologia.2009.07.011

Schone, H. R., Baker, C. I., Katz, J., Nikolajsen, L., Limakatso, K., Flor, H., & Makin, T. R. (2022). Making sense of phantom limb pain. *J Neurol Neurosurg Psychiatry, 93*(8), 833–843. https://doi.org/10.1136/jnnp-2021-328428

Schraagen, J. M. (1993). How experts solve a novel problem in experimental design. *Cogn Sci, 17*, 285–309.

Schraw, G., Dunkle, M. E., & Bendixen, L. D. (1995). Cognitive processes in well-defined and ill-defined problem solving. *Appl Cogn Psychol, 9*, 523–538.

Schreckenberger, M., Siessmeier, T., Viertmann, A., Landvogt, C., Buchholz, H. G., Rolke, R.,…Birklein, F. (2005). The unpleasantness of tonic pain is encoded by the insular cortex. *Neurology, 64*(7), 1175–1183. https://doi.org/10.1212/01.WNL.0000156353.17305.52

Schreiner, C. E., & Polley, D. B. (2014). Auditory map plasticity: Diversity in causes and consequences. *Curr Opin Neurobiol, 24*(1), 143–156. https://doi.org/10.1016/j.conb.2013.11.009

Schultz, W. (2013). Updating dopamine reward systems. *Curr Opin Neurobiol, 23*, 229–238.

Schultz, W., Carelli, R. M., & Wightman, R. M. (2015). Phasic dopamine signals: From subjective reward value to formal economic utility. *Curr Opin Behav Sci, 5*, 147–154. https://doi.org/10.1016/j.cobeha.2015.09.006

Schusterman, R. J., Reichmuth, C. J., & Kastak, D. (2000). How animals classify friends and foes. *Curr Dir Psychol Sci, 9*, 1–6.

Schweppe, J., & Rummer, R. (2014). Attention, working memory, and long-term memory in multimedia learning: An integrated perspective based on process models of working memory. *Edu Psychol Rev, 26*, 285–306.

Sebanz, N., Knoblich, G., & Humphreys, G. W. (2008). Cognitive ethology for humans: Inconvenient truth or attentional deficit? *Br J Psychol, 99*(Pt 3), 347–350; discussion 355–349. https://doi.org/10.1348/000712608×297080

Sebeok, T. A., & Rosenthal, R. E. (1981). The Clever Hans phenomenon: Communication with horses, whales, apes, and people. *Ann N Y Acad Sci, 364*, 1–311. https://www.ncbi.nlm.nih.gov/pubmed/6942738

Sedda, A. (2011). Body integrity identity disorder: From a psychological to a neurological syndrome. *Neuropsychol Rev, 21*(4), 334–336. https://doi.org/10.1007/s11065-011-9186-6

Sedivy, J. (2014). *Language in mind: An introduction to psycholinguistics.* New York, NY: Sinauer Associates, an imprint of New York, NY: Oxford University Press.

Seed, A., & Byrne, R. (2010). Animal tool-use. *Curr Biol, 20*, R1032–1039. https://doi.org/10.1016/j.cub.2010.09.042

Seelig, J. D., & Jayaraman, V. (2015). Neural dynamics for landmark orientation and angular path integration. *Nature, 521*, 186–191. https://doi.org/10.1038/nature14446

Seger, C. A., & Miller, E. K. (2010). Category learning in the brain. *Annu Rev Neurosci, 33*, 203–219. https://doi.org/10.1146/annurev.neuro.051508.135546

Seger, C. A., & Peterson, E. J. (2013). Categorization=decision making+generalization. *Neurosci Biobehav Rev, 37*, 1187–1200.

Segundo-Ortin, M., & Calvo, P. (2019). Are plants cognitive? A reply to Adams. *Stud Hist Philos Sci, 73*, 64–71. https://doi.org/10.1016/j.shpsa.2018.12.001

Seitz, A. R. (2017). Perceptual learning. *Curr Biol, 27*(13), R631-R636. https://doi.org/10.1016/j.cub.2017.05.053

Selfridge, O. G., & Neisser, U. (1960). Pattern recognition by machine. *Sci Am, 203*, 60–69.

Seligman, M. E. (1972). Learned helplessness. *Annu Rev Med, 23*, 407–412. https://doi.org/10.1146/annurev.me.23.020172.002203

Seligman, M. E. (1978). Learned helplessness as a model of depression. Comment and integration. *J Abnorm Psychol, 87*(1), 165–179. https://www.ncbi.nlm.nih.gov/pubmed/649850

Senghas, A., Kita, S., & Ozyurek, A. (2004). Children creating core properties of language: Evidence from an emerging sign language in Nicaragua. *Science, 305*(5691), 1779–1782. https://doi.org/10.1126/science.1100199

Serino, A., Angeli, V., Frassinetti, F., & Ladavas, E. (2006). Mechanisms underlying neglect recovery after prism adaptation. *Neuropsychologia, 44*, 1068–1078. https://doi.org/10.1016/j.neuropsychologia.2005.10.024

Serre, T. (2016). Models of visual categorization. *Wiley Interdiscip Rev Cogn Sci, 7*(3), 197–213. https://doi.org/10.1002/wcs.1385

Sevdalis, V., & Keller, P. E. (2010). Cues for self-recognition in point-light displays of actions performed in synchrony with music. *Conscious Cogn, 19*(2), 617–626. https://doi.org/10.1016/j.concog.2010.03.017

Sewell, R. A., Schnakenberg, A., Elander, J., Radhakrishnan, R., Williams, A., Skosnik, P. D.,…D'Souza, D. C. (2013). Acute effects of THC on time perception in frequent and infrequent cannabis users. *Psychopharmacology (Berl), 226*(2), 401–413. https://doi.org/10.1007/s00213-012-2915-6

Seyfarth, R. M., Cheney, D. L., & Marler, P. (1980). Monkey responses to three different alarm calls: Evidence of predator classification and semantic communication. *Science, 210*(4471), 801–803. https://www.ncbi.nlm.nih.gov/pubmed/7433999

Shamay-Tsoory, S. G. (2011). The neural bases for empathy. *Neuroscientist, 17*(1), 18–24. https://doi.org/10.1177/1073858410379268

Shannon, C. E. (1948). A mathematical theory of communication. *Bell Syst Tech J, 27*, 379–423.

Shapiro, K. L., Raymond, J. E., & Arnell, K. M. (1997). The attentional blink. *Trends Cogn Sci, 1*(8), 291–296. https://doi.org/10.1016/S1364-6613(97)01094-2

Shapiro, P. N., & Penrod, S. D. (1986). Meta-analysis of face identification studies. *Psychol Bull, 100*, 139–156.

Sharma, J., Angelucci, A., & Sur, M. (2000). Induction of visual orientation modules in auditory cortex. *Nature, 404*(6780), 841–847. https://doi.org/10.1038/35009043

Shaver, P., Pierson, L., & Lang, S. (1974). Converging evidence for the functional significance of imagery in problem solving. *Cognition, 3*, 359–375.

Shaw, A., Choshen-Hillel, S., & Caruso, E. M. (2016). The Development of inequity aversion. *Psychol Sci, 27*(10), 1352–1359. https://doi.org/10.1177/0956797616660548

Shaw, R. C. (2021). Animal tool use: Many tools make light work for wild parrots. *Curr Biol, 31*(20), R1383-R1385. https://doi.org/10.1016/j.cub.2021.08.036

Sheehan, M. J., & Tibbetts, E. A. (2011). Specialized face learning is associated with individual recognition in paper wasps. *Science, 334*(6060), 1272–1275. https://doi.org/10.1126/science.1211334

Sheehy, L. M., & Haines, M. E. (2004). Crossed Wernicke's aphasia: A case report. *Brain Lang, 89*(1), 203–206. https://doi.org/10.1016/S0093-934X(03)00365-1

Sheinberg, D. L., & Logothetis, N. K. (2001). Noticing familiar objects in real world scenes: The role of temporal cortical neurons in natural vision. *J Neurosci, 21*(4), 1340–1350. https://doi.org/10.1523/JNEUROSCI.21-04-01340.2001

Shepard, R. (1968). Cognitive psychology. *Am J Psychol, 8*, 285–289.

Shepard, R. N. (1987). Toward a universal law of generalization for psychological science. *Science, 237*(4820), 1317–1323. https://doi.org/10.1126/science.3629243

Shepard, R. N. (1990). Neural nets for generalization and classification: Comment on Staddon and Reid (1990). *Psychol Rev, 97*(4), 579–580. https://doi.org/10.1037/0033-295x.97.4.579

Shepard, R. N., Hovland, C. I., & Jenkins, H. M. (1961). Learning and memorization of classifications. *Psychol Mono Gen Appl, 75*, 1–42.

Shepard, R. N., & Metzler, J. (1971). Mental rotation of three-dimensional objects. *Science, 171*(3972), 701–703. https://doi.org/10.1126/science.171.3972.701

Shettleworth, S. J. (2010). *Cognitive, evolution, and behavior* (2nd ed). New York, NY: Oxford University Press.

Shin, Y. K., Proctor, R. W., & Capaldi, E. J. (2010). A review of contemporary ideomotor theory. *Psychol Bull, 136*(6), 943–974. https://doi.org/10.1037/a0020541

Shipstead, Z., Harrison, T. L., & Engle, R. W. (2015). Working memory capacity and the scope and control of attention. *Atten Percept Psychophys, 77*(6), 1863–1880. https://doi.org/10.3758/s13414-015-0899-0

Shomstein, S., Zhang, X., & Dubbelde, D. (2023). Attention and platypuses. *Wiley Interdiscip Rev Cogn Sci, 14*(1), e1600. https://doi.org/10.1002/wcs.1600

Siclari, F., Baird, B., Perogamvros, L., Bernardi, G., LaRocque, J. J., Riedner, B.,…Tononi, G. (2017). The neural correlates of dreaming. *Nat Neurosci, 20*(6), 872–878. https://doi.org/10.1038/nn.4545

Sidman, M. (1994). *Equivalence relations and behavior: A research story.* Authors Cooperative.

Sifferd, K. L., & Hirstein, W. (2013). On the criminal culpability of successful and unsuccessful psychopaths. *Neuroethics, 6,* 129–140.

Sifre, R., Olson, L., Gillespie, S., Klin, A., Jones, W., & Shultz, S. (2018). A Longitudinal Investigation of Preferential Attention to Biological Motion in 2- to 24-Month-Old Infants. *Sci Rep, 8*(1), 2527. https://doi.org/10.1038/s41598-018-20808-0

Sigala, N., & Logothetis, N. K. (2002). Visual categorization shapes feature selectivity in the primate temporal cortex. *Nature, 415*(6869), 318–320. https://doi.org/10.1038/415318a

Silbert, L. C., Nelson, C., Howieson, D. B., Moore, M. M., & Kaye, J. A. (2008). Impact of white matter hyperintensity volume progression on rate of cognitive and motor decline. *Neurology, 71*(2), 108–113. https://doi.org/10.1212/01.wnl.0000316799.86917.37

Simion, F., Regolin, L., & Bulf, H. (2008). A predisposition for biological motion in the newborn baby. *Proc Natl Acad Sci U S A, 105*(2), 809–813. https://doi.org/10.1073/pnas.0707021105

Simon, H. A., & Newell, A. (1962). Computer simulation of human thinking and problem solving. *Monogr Soc Res Child Dev, 27*(2), 137–150. https://www.ncbi.nlm.nih.gov/pubmed/13913103

Simons, D. J., & Chabris, C. F. (1999). Gorillas in our midst: Sustained inattentional blindness for dynamic events. *Perception, 28*(9), 1059–1074. https://doi.org/10.1068/p281059

Simonton, D. K. (2009). *Origins of genius: Darwinian perspectives on creativity.* New York, NY: Oxford University Press.

Simonton, D. K. (2012). Quantifying creativity: Can measures span the spectrum? *Dialogues Clin Neurosci, 14*(1), 100–104. https://doi.org/10.31887/DCNS.2012.14.1/dsimonton

Singer, T., & Lamm, C. (2009). The social neuroscience of empathy. *Ann N Y Acad Sci, 1156,* 81–96. https://doi.org/10.1111/j.1749-6632.2009.04418.x

Singer, T., Lindenberger, U., & Baltes, P. B. (2003). Plasticity of memory for new learning in very old age: A story of major loss? *Psychol Aging, 18*(2), 306–317. https://www.ncbi.nlm.nih.gov/pubmed/12825778

Singley, M. K. (1989). *Transfer of cognitive skill.* Cambridge, MA: Harvard University Press.

Sinnett, S., Jager, J., Singer, S. M., & Antonini Philippe, R. (2020). Flow states and associated changes in spatial and temporal processing. *Front Psychol, 11,* 381. https://doi.org/10.3389/fpsyg.2020.00381

Skeels, S., von der Emde, G., & Burt de Perera, T. (2023). Mormyrid fish as models for investigating sensory-motor integration: A behavioral perspective. *J Zool,* Early view.

Skinner, B. F. (1938). *The behavior of organisms: An experimental analysis.* Norwalk, CT: Appleton-Century-Crofts.

Skinner, B. F. (1953). *Science and human behavior.* New York, NY: Free Press.

Skinner, B. F. (1957). *Verbal behavior.* Acton, MA: Copley Publishing Group.

Skinner, B. F. (1963). Operant behavior. *Am Psycholt, 8,* 503–515.

Skinner, B. F. (1975). The shaping of phylogenic behavior. *J Exp Anal Behav, 24*(1), 117–120. https://doi.org/10.1901/jeab.1975.24-117

Smallwood, J., Bernhardt, B. C., Leech, R., Bzdok, D., Jefferies, E., & Margulies, D. S. (2021). The default mode network in cognition: A topographical perspective. *Nat Rev Neurosci, 22*(8), 503–513. https://doi.org/10.1038/s41583-021-00474-4

Smith, A. P., Brosowsky, N., Murray, S., Daniel, R., Meier, M. E., & Seli, P. (2022). Fixation, flexibility, and creativity: The dynamics of mind wandering. *J Exp Psychol Hum Percept Perform, 48*(7), 689–710. https://doi.org/10.1037/xhp0001012

Smith, D. M., & Mizumori, S. J. (2006). Hippocampal place cells, context, and episodic memory. *Hippocampus, 16,* 716–729. https://doi.org/10.1002/hipo.20208

Smith, E. E. (1989). Concepts and induction. In M. I. Posner (Ed.), *Foundations of cognitive science* (pp. 501–526). Cambridge, MA: MIT Press.

Smith, G. E., Housen, P., Yaffe, K., Ruff, R., Kennison, R. F., Mahncke, H. W., & Zelinski, E. M. (2009). A cognitive training program based on principles of brain plasticity: Results from the improvement in memory with plasticity-based adaptive cognitive training (IMPACT) study. *J Am Geriatr Soc, 57*(4), 594–603. https://doi.org/10.1111/j.1532-5415.2008.02167.x

Smith, J. D., Couchman, J. J., & Beran, M. J. (2014). Animal metacognition: A tale of two comparative psychologies. *J Comp Psychol, 128*(2), 115–131. https://doi.org/10.1037/a0033105

Smith, J. D., Minda, J. P., & Washburn, D. A. (2004). Category learning in rhesus monkeys: A study of the Shepard, Hovland, and Jenkins (1961) tasks. *J Exp Psychol Gen, 133*(3), 398–414. https://doi.org/10.1037/0096-3445.133.3.398

Smith, J. D., Redford, J. S., Washburn, D. A., & Taglialatela, L. A. (2005). Specific-token effects in screening tasks: Possible implications for aviation security. *J Exp Psychol Learn Mem Cogn, 31*(6), 1171–1185. https://doi.org/10.1037/0278-7393.31.6.1171

Smith, J. D., Shields, W. E., & Washburn, D. A. (2003). The comparative psychology of uncertainty monitoring and metacognition. *Behav Brain Sci, 26*(3), 317–339; discussion 340–373. http://www.ncbi.nlm.nih.gov/pubmed/14968691

Smith, J. D., Zakrewski, A. C., Johnson, J. M., Valleau, J. C., & Church, B. A. (2016). Categorization: The view from animal cognition. *Behav Sci, 6,* 12.

Smith, L. B., & Slone, L. K. (2017). A Developmental Approach to Machine Learning? *Front Psychol, 8,* 2124. https://doi.org/10.3389/fpsyg.2017.02124

Smith, N., Tsimpli, I., Morgan, G., & Woll, B. (2011). *The signs of a savant.* UK: Cambridge University Press.

Smith, P. L., & Ratcliff, R. (2004). Psychology and neurobiology of simple decisions. *Trends Neurosci, 27*(3), 161–168. https://doi.org/10.1016/j.tins.2004.01.006

Snyder, A. W., Stavenga, D. G., & Laughlin, S. B. (1977). Spatial information capacity of compound eyes. *J Comp Physiol A, 116,* 183–207.

Sobel, D. M., & Kushnir, T. (2013). Knowledge matters: How children evaluate the reliability of testimony as a process of rational inference. *Psychol Rev, 120*(4), 779–797. https://doi.org/10.1037/a0034191

Sokol-Hessner, P., & Rutledge, R. B. (2019). The psychological and neural basis of loss aversion. *Curr Dir Psychol Sci, 28*, 20–27.

Solms, M. (1997). What is consciousness? *J Am Psychoanal Assoc, 45*(3), 681–703; discussion 704–678. https://doi.org/10.1177/00030651970450031201

Solms, M. (2004). Freud returns. *Sci Am, 290*(5), 82–88. https://doi.org/10.1038/scientificamerican0504-82

Soon, C. S., Brass, M., Heinze, H. J., & Haynes, J. D. (2008). Unconscious determinants of free decisions in the human brain. *Nat Neurosci, 11*(5), 543–545. https://doi.org/10.1038/nn.2112

Sousa, A. E., Mahdid, Y., Brodeur, M., & Lepage, M. (2021). A feasibility study on the use of the method of loci for improving episodic memory performance in schizophrenia and non-clinical subjects. *Front Psychol, 12*, 612681. https://doi.org/10.3389/fpsyg.2021.612681

Southgate, V., & Hamilton, A. F. (2008). Unbroken mirrors: Challenging a theory of autism. *Trends Cogn Sci, 12*(6), 225–229. https://doi.org/10.1016/j.tics.2008.03.005

Spaak, E., Watanabe, K., Funahashi, S., & Stokes, M. G. (2017). Stable and dynamic coding for working memory in primate prefrontal cortex. *J Neurosci, 37*, 6503–6516. https://doi.org/10.1523/JNEUROSCI.3364-16.2017

Spagna, A. (2022). Visual mental imagery: Inside the mind's eyes. *Handb Clin Neurol, 187*, 145–160. https://doi.org/10.1016/B978-0-12-823493-8.00010-9

Spalding, T. L., & Murphy, G. L. (1999). What is learned in knowledge-related categories? Evidence from typicality and feature frequency judgments. *Mem Cognit, 27*(5), 856–867. http://www.ncbi.nlm.nih.gov/pubmed/10540814

Spearman, C. (1904). 'General intelligence,' objectively determined and measured. *Am J Psychol, 15*, 201–293.

Spelke, E. S. (1998). Nativism, empiricism, and the origins of knowledge. *Infant Behav Dev, 21*, 181–200.

Spelke, E. S., & Newport, E. L. (1998). Nativism, empiricism, and the development of knowledge. In W. Damon & R. M. Lerner (Eds.), *Handbook of child psychology: Theoretical models of human development*. Hoboken, NJ: John Wiley & Sons.

Spellman, B. A., & Holyoak, K. J. (1996). Pragmatics in analogical mapping. *Cogn Psychol, 31*(3), 307–346. https://doi.org/10.1006/cogp.1996.0019

Spence, C. (2011). Crossmodal correspondences: A tutorial review. *Atten Percept Psychophys, 73*(4), 971–995. https://doi.org/10.3758/s13414-010-0073-7

Spence, K. W. (1937). The differential response in animals to stimuli varying within a single dimension. *Psychol Rev, 44*, 430–444.

Spencer, J. P., Austin, A., & Schutte, A. R. (2012). Contributions of dynamic systems theory to cognitive development. *Cogn Dev, 27*(4), 401–418. https://doi.org/10.1016/j.cogdev.2012.07.006

Sperry, R. W. (1961). Cerebral organization and behavior: The split brain behaves in many respects like two separate brains, providing new research possibilities. *Science, 133*(3466), 1749–1757. https://doi.org/10.1126/science.133.3466.1749

Spiegel, D. R., Smith, J., Wade, R. R., Cherukuru, N., Ursani, A., Dobruskina, Y., … Dreyer, N. (2017). Transient global amnesia: Current perspectives. *Neuropsychiatr Dis Treat, 13*, 2691–2703. https://doi.org/10.2147/NDT.S130710

Squire, L. R., & Kandel, E. R. (2000). *Memory: From minds to molecules*. Scientific American Library.

Squire, L. R., & Zola, S. M. (1996). Structure and function of declarative and nondeclarative memory systems. *Proc Natl Acad Sci U S A, 93*(24), 13515–13522. https://doi.org/10.1073/pnas.93.24.13515

Šrol, J., & De Neys, W. (2021). Predicting individual differences in conflict detection and bias susceptibility during reasoning. *Think Reason, 27*, 38–68.

Staddon, J.E.R. (1991). The role of timing in reinforcement schedule performance. *Learn Motiv, 22*, 200–225.

Stebbins, W. C. (1970). *Animal psychophysics: The design and conduct of sensory experiments*. Springer.

Steckenfinger, S. A., & Ghazanfar, A. A. (2009). Monkey visual behavior falls into the uncanny valley. *Proc Natl Acad Sci U S A, 106*(43), 18362–18366. https://doi.org/10.1073/pnas.0910063106

Stefanidou, M., Sola, C., Kouvelas, E., del Cerro, M., & Triarhou, L. C. (2007). Cajal's brief experimentation with hypnotic suggestion. *J Hist Neurosci, 16*(4), 351–361. https://doi.org/10.1080/09647040600653915

Sternberg, R. J. (2018). Evaluating merit among scientists. *J Appl Res Mem Cogn, 7*, 209–216.

Sternberg, R. J. (Ed.). (2020). *Human intelligence: An introduction*. UK: Cambridge University Press.

Sternberg, R. J., & Kaufman, J. C. (2018). *The nature of human creativity*. UK: Cambridge University Press.

Stevens, C. E., Jr., & Zabelina, D. L. (2020). Classifying creativity: Applying machine learning techniques to divergent thinking EEG data. *Neuroimage, 219*, 116990. https://doi.org/10.1016/j.neuroimage.2020.116990

Stevenson, R. A., Ghose, D., Fister, J. K., Sarko, D. K., Altieri, N. A., Nidiffer, A. R., … Wallace, M. T. (2014). Identifying and quantifying multisensory integration: A tutorial review. *Brain Topogr, 27*(6), 707–730. https://doi.org/10.1007/s10548-014-0365-7

Stich, S., & Ravenscroft, I. (1994). What is folk psychology? *Cognition, 50*(1–3), 447–468. https://doi.org/10.1016/0010-0277(94)90040-x

Stillman, P. E., Shen, X., & Ferguson, M. J. (2018). How mouse-tracking can advance social cognitive theory. *Trends Cogn Sci, 22*(6), 531–543. https://doi.org/10.1016/j.tics.2018.03.012

Storm, B. C., & Patel, T. (2014). Forgetting as a consequence and enabler of creative thinking. *J Exp Psychol Learn Mem Cogn, 40*, 1594–1609.

Strait, D. L., Parbery-Clark, A., Hittner, E., & Kraus, N. (2012). Musical training during early childhood enhances the neural encoding of speech in noise. *Brain Lang, 123*(3), 191–201. https://doi.org/10.1016/j.bandl.2012.09.001

Strange, D., & Takarangi, M. K. (2015). Memory distortion for traumatic events: The role of mental imagery. *Front Psychiatry, 6*, 27. https://doi.org/10.3389/fpsyt.2015.00027

Stroop, J. R. (1938). Factors affecting speed in serial verbal reactions. *Psychol Monogr, 50*, 38–48.

Struck, P. T. (2016). *Divination and human nature: A cognitive history of intuition in classical antiquity.* NJ: Princeton University Press.

Styns, F., van Noorden, L., Moelants, D., & Leman, M. (2007). Walking on music. *Hum Mov Sci, 26,* 769–785. https://doi.org/10.1016/j.humov.2007.07.007

Su, F., & Xu, W. (2020). Enhancing brain plasticity to promote stroke recovery. *Front Neurol, 11,* 554089. https://doi.org/10.3389/fneur.2020.554089

Suchow, J. W., Bourgin, D. D., & Griffiths, T. L. (2017). Evolution in mind: Evolutionary dynamics, cognitive processes, and bayesian inference. *Trends Cogn Sci, 21*(7), 522–530. https://doi.org/10.1016/j.tics.2017.04.005

Sullivan, R. M., Taborsky-Barba, S., Mendoza, R., Itano, A., Leon, M., Cotman, C. W., … Lott, I. (1991). Olfactory classical conditioning in neonates. *Pediatrics, 87*(4), 511–518. https://www.ncbi.nlm.nih.gov/pubmed/2011429

Sun, H., Fu, S., Cui, S., Yin, X., Sun, X., Qi, X., … Wan, Y. (2020). Development of a CRISPR-SaCas9 system for projection- and function-specific gene editing in the rat brain. *Sci Adv, 6*(12), eaay6687. https://doi.org/10.1126/sciadv.aay6687

Surprenant, A. M., & Neath, I. (2013). *Principles of memory.* London, UK: Psychology Press.

Swain, R. A., Kerr, A. L., & Thompson, R. F. (2011). The cerebellum: A neural system for the study of reinforcement learning. *Front Behav Neurosci, 5,* 8. https://doi.org/10.3389/fnbeh.2011.00008

Szczypinski, J. J., & Gola, M. (2018). Dopamine dysregulation hypothesis: The common basis for motivational anhedonia in major depressive disorder and schizophrenia? *Rev Neurosci, 29*(7), 727–744. https://doi.org/10.1515/revneuro-2017-0091

T

Tager-Flusberg, H., & Sullivan, K. (2000). A componential view of theory of mind: Evidence from Williams syndrome. *Cognition, 76*(1), 59–90. https://doi.org/10.1016/s0010-0277(00)00069-x

Tagliabue, M., Squatrito, V., & Presti, G. (2019). Models of cognition and their applications in behavioral economics: A conceptual framework for nudging derived from behavior analysis and relational frame theory. *Front Psychol, 10,* 2418. https://doi.org/10.3389/fpsyg.2019.02418

Takeuchi, H., Tsurumi, K., Murao, T., Mizuta, H., Kawada, R., Murai, T., & Takahashi, H. (2020). Framing effects on financial and health problems in gambling disorder. *Addict Behav, 110,* 106502. https://doi.org/10.1016/j.addbeh.2020.106502

Tallal, P., & Gaab, N. (2006). Dynamic auditory processing, musical experience and language development. *Trends Neurosci, 29*(7), 382–390. https://doi.org/10.1016/j.tins.2006.06.003

Tallal, P., Miller, S. L., Bedi, G., Byma, G., Wang, X., Nagarajan, S. S., … Merzenich, M. M. (1996). Language comprehension in language-learning impaired children improved with acoustically modified speech. *Science, 271*(5245), 81–84. https://doi.org/10.1126/science.271.5245.81

Talwar, S. K., Xu, S., Hawley, E. S., Weiss, S. A., Moxon, K. A., & Chapin, J. K. (2002). Rat navigation guided by remote control. *Nature, 417*(6884), 37–38. https://doi.org/10.1038/417037a

Tanaka, J. W., & Taylor, M. (1991). Object categories and expertise: Is the basic level in the eye of the beholder. *Cogn Psychol, 23,* 457–482.

Tanaka, J. W., Curran, T., & Sheinberg, D. L. (2005). The training and transfer of real-world perceptual expertise. *Psychol Sci, 16*(2), 145–151. https://doi.org/10.1111/j.0956-7976.2005.00795.x

Tanaka, K., Saito, H., Fukada, Y., & Moriya, M. (1991). Coding visual images of objects in the inferotemporal cortex of the macaque monkey. *J Neurophysiol, 66*(1), 170–189. http://www.ncbi.nlm.nih.gov/pubmed/1919665

Tang, Y. P., Shimizu, E., Dube, G. R., Rampon, C., Kerchner, G. A., Zhuo, M., … Tsien, J. Z. (1999). Genetic enhancement of learning and memory in mice. *Nature, 401*(6748), 63–69. https://doi.org/10.1038/43432

Tatu, L., Bogousslavsky, J., & Boller, F. (2014). Phantoms in artists: The lost limbs of Blaise Cendrars, Arthur Rimbaud, and Paul Wittgenstein. *J Hist Neurosci, 23*(4), 355–366. https://doi.org/10.1080/0964704X.2014.881168

Taylor, C. K., & Saayman, G. (1973). Imitative behavior by Indian Ocean bottlenose dolphins (*Tursiops aduncus*) in captivity. *Behaviour, 44,* 286–298.

Tchernichovski, O., Mitra, P. P., Lints, T., & Nottebohm, F. (2001). Dynamics of the vocal imitation process: How a zebra finch learns its song. *Science, 291*(5513), 2564–2569. https://doi.org/10.1126/science.1058522

Teachman, B. A., Clerkin, E. M., Cunningham, W. A., Dreyer-Oren, S., & Werntz, A. (2019). Implicit cognition and psychopathology: Looking back and looking forward. *Annu Rev Clin Psychol, 15,* 123–148. https://doi.org/10.1146/annurev-clinpsy-050718-095718

Temple, E., Deutsch, G. K., Poldrack, R. A., Miller, S. L., Tallal, P., Merzenich, M. M., & Gabrieli, J. D. (2003). Neural deficits in children with dyslexia ameliorated by behavioral remediation: Evidence from functional MRI. *Proc Natl Acad Sci U S A, 100*(5), 2860–2865. https://doi.org/10.1073/pnas.0030098100

Tenison, C., & Anderson, J. R. (2016). Modeling the distinct phases of skill acquisition. *J Exp Psychol Learn Mem Cogn, 42*(5), 749–767. https://doi.org/10.1037/xlm0000204

Terman, L. M. (1940). Psychological approaches to the biography of genius. *Science, 92,* 293–301. https://doi.org/10.1126/science.92.2388.293

Terrier, L. M., Leveque, M., & Amelot, A. (2019). Brain lobotomy: A historical and moral dilemma with no alternative? *World Neurosurg, 132,* 211–218. https://doi.org/10.1016/j.wneu.2019.08.254

Thaler, L., & Goodale, M. A. (2016). Echolocation in humans: An overview. *Wiley Interdiscip Rev Cogn Sci, 7*(6), 382–393. https://doi.org/10.1002/wcs.1408

Thelen, E., & Smith, L. B. (1994). *A dynamic systems approach to the development of cognition and action.* Cambridge, MA: MIT Press.

Thelen, E., & Ulrich, B. D. (1991). Hidden skills: A dynamic systems analysis of treadmill stepping during the first year. *Monogr Soc Res Child Dev, 56*(1), 1–98; discussion 99–104. http://www.ncbi.nlm.nih.gov/pubmed/1922136

Thivierge, J. P., & Marcus, G. F. (2007). The topographic brain: From neural connectivity to cognition. *Trends Neurosci, 30*(6), 251–259. https://doi.org/10.1016/j.tins.2007.04.004

Thomas, E., & French, R. (2017). Grandmother cells: Much ado about nothing. *Lang Cogn Neurosci, 32,* 342–349.

Thomas, S. P. (2023). Grappling with the Implications of ChatGPT for Researchers, Clinicians, and Educators. *Issues Ment Health Nurs, 44*(3), 141–142. https://doi.org/10.1080/01612840.2023 .2180982

Thompson, R. K., & Oden, D. L. (1995). A profound disparity revisited: Perception and judgment of abstract identity relations by chimpanzees, human infants, and monkeys. *Behav Processes, 35*(1–3), 149–161. https://doi.org/10.1016/0376-6357(95)00048-8

Thomson, D. R., Besner, D., & Smilek, D. (2016). A critical examination of the evidence for sensitivity loss in modern vigilance tasks. *Psychol Rev, 123*(1), 70–83. https://doi.org/10.1037/rev0000021

Thomson, E. E., Zea, I., Windham, W., Thenaisie, Y., Walker, C., Pedowitz, J.,… Nicolelis, M.A.L. (2017). Cortical neuroprosthesis merges visible and invisible light without impairing native sensory function. *eNeuro, 4*(6). https://doi.org/10.1523/ENEURO .0262-17.2017

Thorndike, E. L. (1932). *The fundamentals of learning.* New York, NY: Teachers College, Columbia University.

Thorndike, E. L. (1933). A proof of the law of effect. *Science, 77*(1989), 173–175. https://doi.org/10.1126/science.77.1989.173-a

Thorndike, E. L. (1949). Do animals reason? In W. Dennis (Ed.), *Readings in general psychology* (pp. 289–301). Hoboken, NJ: Prentice Hall.

Thorndike, E. L. (1949). *Selected writings from a connectionist's psychology.* Norwalk, CT: Appleton-Century-Crofts.

Thorndike, E. L., & Woodworth, R. S. (1901). The influence of improvement in one mental function upon the efficiency of other functions. *Psychol Rev, 8*, 247–261.

Thornton, A., & McAuliffe, K. (2006). Teaching in wild meerkats. *Science, 313*(5784), 227–229. https://doi.org/10.1126/science .1128727

Tiihonen, J., Rossi, R., Laakso, M. P., Hodgins, S., Testa, C., Perez, J.,… Frisoni, G. B. (2008). Brain anatomy of persistent violent offenders: More rather than less. *Psychiatry Res, 163*(3), 201–212. https://doi.org/10.1016/j.pscychresns.2007.08.012

Timberlake, W. (1993). Behavior systems and reinforcement: An integrative approach. *J Exp Anal Behav, 60*(1), 105–128. https://doi.org/10.1901/jeab.1993.60-105

Timberlake, W., & Farmer-Dougan, V. A. (1991). Reinforcement in applied settings: Figuring out ahead of time what will work. *Psychol Bull, 110*(3), 379–391. https://doi.org/10.1037/0033-2909 .110.3.379

Timmermann, C., Roseman, L., Schartner, M., Milliere, R., Williams, L.T.J., Erritzoe, D.,… Carhart-Harris, R. L. (2019). Neural correlates of the DMT experience assessed with multivariate EEG. *Sci Rep, 9*(1), 16324. https://doi.org/10.1038/s41598-019-51974-4

Tinbergen, N. (1972). *The animal in its world.* Cambridge, MA: Harvard University Press.

Tisdall, L., Frey, R., Horn, A., Ostwald, D., Horvath, L., Pedroni, A.,… Mata, R. (2020). Brain-behavior associations for risk taking depend on the measures used to capture individual differences. *Front Behav Neurosci, 14*, 587152. https://doi.org/10.3389 /fnbeh.2020.587152

Tizard, B. (1959). Theories of brain localization from Flourens to Lashley. *Med Hist, 3*(2), 132–145. https://doi.org/10.1017 /s0025727300024418

Tobler, P. N., Christopoulos, G. I., O'Doherty, J. P., Dolan, R. J., & Schultz, W. (2009). Risk-dependent reward value signal in

human prefrontal cortex. *Proc Natl Acad Sci U S A, 106*(17), 7185–7190. https://doi.org/10.1073/pnas.0809599106

Todd, N. P., & Lee, C. S. (2015). The sensory-motor theory of rhythm and beat induction 20 years on: A new synthesis and future perspectives. *Front Hum Neurosci, 9*, 444. https://doi.org/10 .3389/fnhum.2015.00444

Todorov, A., Said, C. P., Engell, A. D., & Oosterhof, N. N. (2008). Understanding evaluation of faces on social dimensions. *Trends Cogn Sci, 12*(12), 455–460. https://doi.org/10.1016/j.tics .2008.10.001

Todorova, G. K., Hatton, R. E. M., & Pollick, F. E. (2019). Biological motion perception in autism spectrum disorder: A meta-analysis. *Mol Autism, 10*, 49. https://doi.org/10.1186/s13229-019 -0299-8

Toga, A. W., & Thompson, P. M. (2005). Genetics of brain structure and intelligence. *Annu Rev Neurosci, 28*, 1–23. https://doi.org/10 .1146/annurev.neuro.28.061604.135655

Tolin, D. F., Abramowitz, J. S., Przeworski, A., & Foa, E. B. (2002). Thought suppression in obsessive-compulsive disorder. *Behav Res Ther, 40*(11), 1255–1274. https://doi.org/10.1016/s0005 -7967(01)00095-x

Tolman, E. C. (1925). Purpose and cognition: The determiners of animal learning. *Psychol Rev, 32*, 285–297.

Tolman, E. C. (1932). *Purposive behavior in animals and men.* Post Falls, ID: Century.

Tolman, E. C. (1948). Cognitive maps in rats and men. *Psychol Rev, 55*(4), 189–208. https://doi.org/10.1037/h0061626

Tomasello, M., & Call, J. (2011). Methodological challenges in the study of primate cognition. *Science, 334*(6060), 1227–1228. https://doi.org/10.1126/science.1213443

Tong, F., Meng, M., & Blake, R. (2006). Neural bases of binocular rivalry. *Trends Cogn Sci, 10*(11), 502–511. https://doi.org/10.1016/j .tics.2006.09.003

Townsend, C. L., & Heit, E. (2011). Judgments of learning and improvement. *Mem Cognit, 39*(2), 204–216. https://doi.org/10 .3758/s13421-010-0019-2

Traetta, L. (2020). At the beginning of learning studies there was the maze. *Open J Med Psychol, 9*, 168–183.

Trainor, L. J., Chang, A., Cairney, J., & Li, Y. C. (2018). Is auditory perceptual timing a core deficit of developmental coordination disorder? *Ann N Y Acad Sci, 1423*(1), 30–39. https://doi.org /10.1111/nyas.13701

Treffert, D. A. (2007). The autistic artist, "special faculties," and savant syndrome. *Arch Pediatr Adolesc Med, 161*, 323.

Treffert, D. A. (2014). Accidental genius. *Sci Am, 311*(2), 52–57. https://doi.org/10.1038/scientificamerican0814-52

Treffert, D. A. (2014). Savant syndrome: Realities, myths and misconceptions. *J Autism Dev Disord, 44*(3), 564–571. https:// doi.org/10.1007/s10803-013-1906-8

Treffert, D. A. (2021). The sudden savant: A new form of extraordinary abilities. *WMJ, 120*(1), 69–73. https://www.ncbi.nlm.nih.gov /pubmed/33974770

Treffert, D. A., & Christensen, D. D. (2005). Inside the mind of a savant. *Sci Am, 293*(6), 108–113. https://doi.org/10.1038 /scientificamerican1205-108

Treffert, D. A., & Ries, H. J. (2021). The sudden savant: A new form of extraordinary abilities. *WMJ, 114*, E1-E5.

Treisman, A. (1999). Solutions to the binding problem: Progress through controversy and convergence. *Neuron, 24*, 105–110.

Treisman, A. M., & Gelade, G. (1980). A feature-integration theory of attention. *Cogn Psychol, 12*(1), 97–136. https://doi.org/10.1016/0010-0285(80)90005-5

Treisman, A., & Sato, S. (1990). Conjunction search revisited. *J Exp Psychol Hum Percept Perform, 16*(3), 459–478. https://doi.org/10.1037//0096-1523.16.3.459

Treisman, A., & Schmidt, H. (1982). Illusory conjunctions in the perception of objects. *Cogn Psychol, 14*(1), 107–141. https://doi.org/10.1016/0010-0285(82)90006-8

Trevethan, C. T., Sahraie, A., & Weiskrantz, L. (2007). Form discrimination in a case of blindsight. *Neuropsychologia, 45*(9), 2092–2103. https://doi.org/10.1016/j.neuropsychologia.2007.01.022

Triki, Z., Granell-Ruiz, M., Fong, S., Amcoff, M., & Kolm, N. (2022). Brain morphology correlates of learning and cognitive flexibility in a fish species (*Poecilia reticulata*). *Proc Biol Sci, 289*(1978), 20220844. https://doi.org/10.1098/rspb.2022.0844

Tromp, D., Dufour, A., Lithfous, S., Pebayle, T., & Despres, O. (2015). Episodic memory in normal aging and Alzheimer disease: Insights from imaging and behavioral studies. *Ageing Res Rev, 24*(Pt B), 232–262. https://doi.org/10.1016/j.arr.2015.08.006

Tryon, R. (1940). Studies in individual differences in maze ability. VII. The specific components of maze ability, and a general theory of psychological components. *J Comp Psychol, 30*, 283–335.

Tryon, R. C. (1940). Genetic differences in maze-learning abilities in rats. *Yearbk Natl Soc Stud Educ, 39*, 111–119.

Tse, D., Langston, R. F., Kakeyama, M., Bethus, I., Spooner, P. A., Wood, E. R.,…Morris, R. G. (2007). Schemas and memory consolidation. *Science, 316*(5821), 76–82. https://doi.org/10.1126/science.1135935

Tully, K., & Bolshakov, V. Y. (2010). Emotional enhancement of memory: How norepinephrine enables synaptic plasticity. *Mol Brain, 3*, 15. https://doi.org/10.1186/1756-6606-3-15

Tulving, E. (1985). Memory and consciousness. *Can Psychol, 26*, 1–12.

Tulving, E. (2002). Episodic memory: From mind to brain. *Annu Rev Psychol, 53*, 1–25. https://doi.org/10.1146/annurev.psych.53.100901.135114

Tulving, E. (2005). Episodic memory and autonoesis: Uniquely human? In H. S. Terrace & J. Metcalfe (Eds.), *The missing link in cognition: Origins of self-reflective consciousness* (pp. 3–56). New York, NY: Oxford University Press.

Tulving, E., & Schacter, D. L. (1990). Priming and human memory systems. *Science, 247*(4940), 301–306. https://doi.org/10.1126/science.2296719

Turk, A., & Shattuck-Hufnagel, S. (2020). *Speech timing: Implications for theories of phonology, phonetics, and speech motor control.* New York, NY: Oxford University Press.

Turner, M. E., & Pratkanis, A. R. (1998). Twenty-five years of groupthink theory and research: Lessons from the evaluation of a theory. *Organ Behav Hum Decis Process, 73*(2/3), 105–115. https://doi.org/10.1006/obhd.1998.2756

Tyack, P. L. (2008). Convergence of calls as animals form social bonds, active compensation for noisy communication channels, and the evolution of vocal learning in mammals. *J Comp Psychol, 122*(3), 319–331. https://doi.org/10.1037/a0013087

U

Uddin, L. Q. (2011). Brain connectivity and the self: The case of cerebral disconnection. *Conscious Cogn, 20*(1), 94–98. https://doi.org/10.1016/j.concog.2010.09.009

Udell, M. A. (2015). When dogs look back: Inhibition of independent problem-solving behaviour in domestic dogs (*Canis lupus familiaris*) compared with wolves (*Canis lupus*). *Biol Lett, 11*(9), 20150489. https://doi.org/10.1098/rsbl.2015.0489

Underwood, G. (2009). Cognitive processes in eye guidance: Algorithms for attention in image processing. *Cogn Comp, 1*, 64–76.

Unsworth, N. (2019). Individual differences in long-term memory. *Psychol Bull, 145*(1), 79–139. https://doi.org/10.1037/bul0000176

Unterrainer, J. M., & Owen, A. M. (2006). Planning and problem solving: From neuropsychology to functional neuroimaging. *J Physiol Paris, 99*(4–6), 308–317. https://doi.org/10.1016/j.jphysparis.2006.03.014

Unterrainer, J. M., Rahm, B., Leonhart, R., Ruff, C. C., & Halsband, U. (2003). The Tower of London: The impact of instructions, cueing, and learning on planning abilities. *Brain Res Cogn Brain Res, 17*(3), 675–683. https://doi.org/10.1016/s0926-6410(03)00191-5

Unterrainer, J. M., Rahm, B., Loosli, S. V., Rauh, R., Schumacher, L. V., Biscaldi, M., & Kaller, C. P. (2020). Psychometric analyses of the Tower of London planning task reveal high reliability and feasibility in typically developing children and child patients with ASD and ADHD. *Child Neuropsychol, 26*(2), 257–273. https://doi.org/10.1080/09297049.2019.1642317

Urban, E. (2018). On matters of mind and body: Regarding Descartes. *J Anal Psychol, 63*(2), 228–240. https://doi.org/10.1111/1468-5922.12395

V

Vagnoli, L., Caprilli, S., Vernucci, C., Zagni, S., Mugnai, F., & Messeri, A. (2015). Can presence of a dog reduce pain and distress in children during venipuncture? *Pain Manag Nurs, 16*(2), 89–95. https://doi.org/10.1016/j.pmn.2014.04.004

Vakil, E., Grunhaus, L., Nagar, I., Ben-Chaim, E., Dolberg, O. T., Dannon, P. N., & Schreiber, S. (2000). The effect of electroconvulsive therapy (ECT) on implicit memory: Skill learning and perceptual priming in patients with major depression. *Neuropsychologia, 38*, 1405–1414. http://www.ncbi.nlm.nih.gov/pubmed/10869584

Valentine, T. (1991). A unified account of the effects of distinctiveness, inversion, and race in face recognition. *Q J Exp Psychol A, 43*(2), 161–204. http://www.ncbi.nlm.nih.gov/pubmed/1866456

Vámos, T.I.F., & Shaw, R. C. (2022). How does selection shape spatial memory in the wild. *Curr Opin Behav Sci, 45*, 101117.

van 't Wout, M., Kahn, R. S., Sanfey, A. G., & Aleman, A. (2005). Repetitive transcranial magnetic stimulation over the right dorsolateral prefrontal cortex affects strategic decision-making. *Neuroreport, 16*(16), 1849–1852. https://doi.org/10.1097/01.wnr.0000183907.08149.14

van den Wildenberg, W. P., & Christoffels, I. K. (2010). STOP TALKING! Inhibition of speech is affected by word frequency and dysfunctional impulsivity. *Front Psychol, 1*, 145. https://doi.org/10.3389/fpsyg.2010.00145

van der Ham, I.J.M., Martens, M.A.G., Claessen, M.H.G., & van den Berg, E. (2017). Landmark agnosia: Evaluating the definition of landmark-based navigation impairment. *Arch Clin Neuropsychol, 32*, 472–482. https://doi.org/10.1093/arclin/acx013

van der Schuur, W. A., Baumgartner, S. E., Sumter, S. R., & Valkenburg, P. M. (2018). Media multitasking and sleep problems: A longitudinal study among adolescents. *Comput Human Behav, 81*, 316–324.

van Endert, T. S., & Mohr, P. N. C. (2020). Likes and impulsivity: Investigating the relationship between actual smartphone use and delay discounting. *PLoS One, 15*(11), e0241383. https://doi.org/10.1371/journal.pone.0241383

Van Gompel, R.P.G. (2013). *Sentence processing.* London, UK: Psychology Press.

Van Lange, P.A.M., Rockenbach, B., & Yamagishi, T. (2017). *Trust in social dilemmas.* New York, NY: Oxford University Press.

van Marle, K., Chu, F. W., Mou, Y., Seok, J. H., Rouder, J., & Geary, D. C. (2018). Attaching meaning to the number words: Contributions of the object tracking and approximate number systems. *Dev Sci, 21.* https://doi.org/10.1111/desc.12495

Van Overwalle, F., Manto, M., Cattaneo, Z., Clausi, S., Ferrari, C., Gabrieli, J.D.E., … Leggio, M. (2020). Consensus paper: Cerebellum and social cognition. *Cerebellum, 19*(6), 833–868. https://doi.org/10.1007/s12311-020-01155-1

van Someren, M. W., Barnard, Y. F., & Sandberg, J. A. C. (1994). *The think aloud method: A practical guide to modelling cognitive processes.* Cambridge, MA: Academic Press.

VanLehn, K. (1991). Rule acquisition events in the discovery of problem-solving strategies. *Cogn Sci, 15*, 1–47.

VanLehn, K. (1996). Cognitive skill acquisition. *Annu Rev Psychol, 47*, 513–539. https://doi.org/10.1146/annurev.psych.47.1.513

Velliste, M., Perel, S., Spalding, M. C., Whitford, A. S., & Schwartz, A. B. (2008). Cortical control of a prosthetic arm for self-feeding. *Nature, 453*(7198), 1098–1101. https://doi.org/10.1038/nature06996

Verrel, J., Lovden, M., Schellenbach, M., Schaefer, S., & Lindenberger, U. (2009). Interacting effects of cognitive load and adult age on the regularity of whole-body motion during treadmill walking. *Psychol Aging, 24*, 75–81. https://doi.org/10.1037/a0014272

Verspeek, J., & Stevens, J. M. G. (2023). Behavioral and physiological response to inequity in bonobos (Pan paniscus). *Am J Primatol, 85*(1), e23455. https://doi.org/10.1002/ajp.23455

Vigo, R., Evans, S. W., & Owens, J. S. (2015). Categorization behaviour in adults, adolescents, and attention-deficit/hyperactivity disorder adolescents: A comparative investigation. *Q J Exp Psychol (Hove), 68*(6), 1058–1072. https://doi.org/10.1080/17470218.2014.974625

Viskontas, I. V., Quiroga, R. Q., & Fried, I. (2009). Human medial temporal lobe neurons respond preferentially to personally relevant images. *Proc Natl Acad Sci U S A, 106*(50), 21329–21334. https://doi.org/10.1073/pnas.0902319106

Vogel, D.H.V., Jording, M., Kupke, C., & Vogeley, K. (2020). The Temporality of Situated Cognition. *Front Psychol, 11*, 546212. https://doi.org/10.3389/fpsyg.2020.546212

Vogels, R. (1999). Categorization of complex visual images by rhesus monkeys. Part 2: Single-cell study. *Eur J Neurosci, 11*(4), 1239–1255. http://www.ncbi.nlm.nih.gov/pubmed/10103119

Völter, C. J., & Call, J. (2017). Causal and inferential reasoning in animals. In J. Call (Ed.), *APA handbook of comparative psychology vol. 2: Perception, learning, and cognition*

(pp. 643–671). Washington, DC: American Psychological Association.

Volz, L. J., & Gazzaniga, M. S. (2017). Interaction in isolation: 50 years of insights from split-brain research. *Brain, 140*(7), 2051–2060. https://doi.org/10.1093/brain/awx139

Voss, J. L., Bridge, D. J., Cohen, N. J., & Walker, J. A. (2017). A closer look at the hippocampus and memory. *Trends Cogn Sci, 21*(8), 577–588. https://doi.org/10.1016/j.tics.2017.05.008

Voss, P. (2013). Sensitive and critical periods in visual sensory deprivation. *Front Psychol, 4*, 664. https://doi.org/10.3389/fpsyg.2013.00664

Vygotsky, L. S. (1978). *Mind in society: The development of higher psychological processes.* Cambridge, MA: Harvard University Press.

Vygotsky, L. S., & Cole, M. (1978). *Mind in society: Development of higher psychological processes.* Cambridge, MA: Harvard University Press.

W

Wagemans, J., Feldman, J., Gepshtein, S., Kimchi, R., Pomerantz, J. R., van der Helm, P. A., & van Leeuwen, C. (2012). A century of Gestalt psychology in visual perception: II. Conceptual and theoretical foundations. *Psychol Bull, 138*(6), 1218–1252. https://doi.org/10.1037/a0029334

Wagner, I. C., Konrad, B. N., Schuster, P., Weisig, S., Repantis, D., Ohla, K., … Dresler, M. (2021). Durable memories and efficient neural coding through mnemonic training using the method of loci. *Sci Adv, 7*(10). https://doi.org/10.1126/sciadv.abc7606

Waller, B. M., Whitehouse, J., & Micheletta, J. (2016). Macaques can predict social outcomes from facial expressions. *Anim Cogn, 19*(5), 1031–1036. https://doi.org/10.1007/s10071-016-0992-3

Walsh, J. J., Christoffel, D. J., & Malenka, R. C. (2023). Neural circuits regulating prosocial behaviors. *Neuropsychopharmacology, 48*(1), 79–89. https://doi.org/10.1038/s41386-022-01348-8

Walsh, V. (2003). A theory of magnitude: Common cortical metrics of time, space and quantity. *Trends Cogn Sci, 7*(11), 483–488. https://doi.org/10.1016/j.tics.2003.09.002

Wammes, J. D., Jonker, T. R., & Fernandes, M. A. (2019). Drawing improves memory: The importance of multimodal encoding context. *Cognition, 191*, 103955. https://doi.org/10.1016/j.cognition.2019.04.024

Wang, C., Xu, T., Geng, F., Hu, Y., Wang, Y., Liu, H., & Chen, F. (2019). Training on abacus-based mental calculation enhances visuospatial working memory in children. *J Neurosci, 39*(33), 6439–6448. https://doi.org/10.1523/JNEUROSCI.3195-18.2019

Wang, J., Narain, D., Hosseini, E. A., & Jazayeri, M. (2018). Flexible timing by temporal scaling of cortical responses. *Nat Neurosci, 21*, 102–110. https://doi.org/10.1038/s41593-017-0028-6

Wang, M. Z., & Hayden, B. Y. (2021). Latent learning, cognitive maps, and curiosity. *Curr Opin Behav Sci, 38*, 1–7. https://doi.org/10.1016/j.cobeha.2020.06.003

Wang, Y., & Chiew, V. (2010). On the cognitive processes of human problem solving. *Cogn Syst Res, 11*, 81–92.

Wang, Y., & Dragoi, V. (2015). Rapid learning in visual cortical networks. *Elife, 4.* https://doi.org/10.7554/eLife.08417

Warren, W. H. (2012). Does this computational theory solve the right problem? Marr, Gibson, and the goal of vision. *Perception, 41*(9), 1053–1060. https://doi.org/10.1068/p7327

Warrington, E. K., & Shallice, T. (1984). Category specific semantic impairments. *Brain, 107*(Pt 3), 829–854. http://www.ncbi.nlm .nih.gov/pubmed/6206910

Washburn, M. F. (1926). *The animal mind: A text-book of comparative psychology.* New York, NY: Macmillan.

Wason, P. C. (1966). Reasoning. In B. Foss (Ed.), *New horizons in psychology* (pp. 135–151). New York, NY: Penguin.

Wasserman, E. A. (1997). The science of animal cognition: Past, present, and future. *J Exp Psychol Anim Behav Process, 23*(2), 123–135. https://www.ncbi.nlm.nih.gov/pubmed /9095537

Wasserman, E. A., Kiedinger, R. E., & Bhatt, R. S. (1988). Conceptual behavior in pigeons: Categories, subcategories, and pseudo-categories. *J Exp Psychol Anim Behav Process, 14*, 235–246.

Wasserman, J. D. (2018). A history of intelligence assessment: The unfinished legacy. In D. P. Flanagan & E. M. McDonough (Eds.), *Contemporary intellectual assessment: Theories, tests, and issues* (pp. 3–55). New York, NY: Guilford Press.

Waters, F., Barnby, J. M., & Blom, J. D. (2021). Hallucination, imagery, dreaming: Reassembling stimulus-independent perceptions based on Edmund Parish's classic misperception framework. *Philos Trans R Soc Lond B Biol Sci, 376*(1817), 20190701. https://doi.org/10.1098/rstb.2019.0701

Waters, F., Blom, J. D., Dang-Vu, T. T., Cheyne, A. J., Alderson-Day, B., Woodruff, P., & Collerton, D. (2016). What is the link between hallucinations, dreams, and hypnagogic-hypnopompic experiences? *Schizophr Bull, 42*(5), 1098–1109. https://doi.org/10 .1093/schbul/sbw076

Watrin, J. P., & Darwich, R. (2012). On behaviorism in the cognitive revolution: Myth and reactions. *Rev Gen Psychol, 16*, 269–282.

Watson, J. B. (1924). *Behaviorism.* New York, NY: W. W. Norton.

Watson, J., & Rayner, R. (1920). Conditioned emotional reactions. *J Exp Psychol, 3*, 1–14.

Weidemann, G., Satkunarajah, M., & Lovibond, P. F. (2016). I think, therefore eyeblink: The importance of contingency awareness in conditioning. *Psychol Sci, 27*(4), 467–475. https://doi.org/10 .1177/0956797615625973

Weiskrantz, L. (2004). Roots of blindsight. *Prog Brain Res, 144*, 229–241. http://www.ncbi.nlm.nih.gov/pubmed/14650852

Weldon, M. S., Blair, C., & Huebsch, P. D. (2000). Group remembering: Does social loafing underlie collaborative inhibition? *J Exp Psychol Learn Mem Cogn, 26*(6), 1568–1577. https://doi.org/10 .1037//0278-7393.26.6.1568

Wenger, M. J., & Townsend, J. T. (2000). Basic response time tools for studying general processing capacity in attention, perception, and cognition. *J Gen Psychol, 127*(1), 67–99. https://doi.org/10 .1080/00221300009598571

Werner, A., Sturzl, W., & Zanker, J. (2016). Object recognition in flight: How do bees distinguish between 3D shapes? *PLoS One, 11*(2), e0147106. https://doi.org/10.1371/journal.pone.0147106

West, R. (1999). Visual distraction, working memory, and aging. *Mem Cognit, 27*(6), 1064–1072. https://doi.org/10.3758/bf03201235

Westbrook, A., van den Bosch, R., Maatta, J. I., Hofmans, L., Papado-petraki, D., Cools, R., & Frank, M. J. (2020). Dopamine promotes cognitive effort by biasing the benefits versus costs of cognitive work. *Science, 367*(6484), 1362–1366. https://doi.org/10.1126 /science.aaz5891

Westergaard, G. C., & Suomi, S. J. (1997). Transfer of tools and food between groups of tufted capuchins (Cebus apella). *Am J Primatol, 43*(1), 33–41. https://doi.org/10.1002/(SICI)1098 -2345(1997)43:1<33::AID-AJP2>3.0.CO;2-Z

Wetherill, R. R., & Fromme, K. (2016). Alcohol-induced blackouts: A review of recent clinical research with practical implications and recommendations for future studies. *Alcohol Clin Exp Res, 40*, 922–935. https://doi.org/10.1111/acer.13051

Whishaw, I. Q., & Brooks, B. L. (1999). Calibrating space: Exploration is important for allothetic and idiothetic navigation. *Hippocampus, 9*, 659–667. https://doi.org/10.1002/(SICI)1098 -1063(1999)9:6<659::AID-HIPO7>3.0.CO;2-E

Whiten, A., McGuigan, N., Marshall-Pescini, S., & Hopper, L. M. (2009). Emulation, imitation, over-imitation and the scope of culture for child and chimpanzee. *Philos Trans R Soc Lond B Biol Sci, 364*(1528), 2417–2428. https://doi.org/10.1098/rstb.2009.0069

Wicker, B., Keysers, C., Plailly, J., Royet, J. P., Gallese, V., & Rizzolatti, G. (2003). Both of us disgusted in my insula: The common neural basis of seeing and feeling disgust. *Neuron, 40*(3), 655–664. https://doi.org/10.1016/s0896-6273(03)00679-2

Wiens, S., & Ohman, A. (2002). Unawareness is more than a chance event: Comment on Lovibond and Shanks (2002). *J Exp Psychol Anim Behav Process, 28*(1), 27–31. https://www.ncbi .nlm.nih.gov/pubmed/11868230

Wiest, G. M., Rosales, K. P., Looney, L., Wong, E. H., & Wiest, D. J. (2022). Utilizing cognitive training to improve working memory, attention, and impulsivity in school-aged children with ADHD and SLD. *Brain Sci, 12*(2). https://doi.org/10.3390 /brainsci12020141

Wiley, J. (1998). Expertise as mental set: The effects of domain knowledge in creative problem solving. *Mem Cognit, 26*(4), 716–730. https://doi.org/10.3758/bf03211392

Williams, N., & Henson, R. N. (2018). Recent advances in functional neuroimaging analysis for cognitive neuroscience. *Brain Neurosci Adv, 2*, 2398212817752727. https://doi.org/10.1177 /2398212817752727

Willner, P., & Lindsay, W. R. (2016). Cognitive behavioral therapy. In N. N. Singh (Ed.), *Handbook of evidence-based practices in intellectual and developmental disabilities* (pp. 283–310). New York, NY: Springer.

Wilson, B. A., & Wearing, D. (1995). Prisoner of consciousness: A state of just awakening following herpes simplex encephalitis. In R. Campbell & M. A. Conway (Eds.), *Broken memories: Case studies in memory impairment* (pp. 14–30). Hoboken, NJ: Blackwell.

Wilson, J. P., & Rule, N. O. (2015). Facial Trustworthiness predicts extreme criminal-sentencing outcomes. *Psychol Sci, 26*(8), 1325–1331. https://doi.org/10.1177/0956797615590992

Wilson, M. (2001). Perceiving imitatible stimuli: Consequences of isomorphism between input and output. *Psychol Bull, 127*, 543–553.

Wilson, M. A., & McNaughton, B. L. (1994). Reactivation of hippocampal ensemble memories during sleep. *Science, 265*(5172), 676–679. http://www.ncbi.nlm.nih.gov/pubmed/8036517

Windholz, G. (1986). A comparative analysis of the conditional reflex discoveries of Pavlov and Twitmyer, and the birth of a paradigm. *Pavlov J Biol Sci, 21*(4), 141–147. https://doi.org/10.1007/BF02734512

Winocur, G., & Moscovitch, M. (2011). Memory transformation and systems consolidation. *J Int Neuropsychol Soc, 17*(5), 766–780. https://doi.org/10.1017/S1355617711000683

Winter, B., Marghetis, T., & Matlock, T. (2015). Of magnitudes and metaphors: Explaining cognitive interactions between space, time, and number. *Cortex, 64*, 209–224. https://doi.org/10.1016/j.cortex.2014.10.015

Wintler, T., Schoch, H., Frank, M. G., & Peixoto, L. (2020). Sleep, brain development, and autism spectrum disorders: Insights from animal models. *J Neurosci Res, 98*(6), 1137–1149. https://doi.org/10.1002/jnr.24619

Wiradhany, W., van Vugt, M. K., & Nieuwenstein, M. R. (2020). Media multitasking, mind-wandering, and distractibility: A large-scale study. *Atten Percept Psychophys, 82*(3), 1112–1124. https://doi.org/10.3758/s13414-019-01842-0

Wise, R. A. (2002). Brain reward circuitry: Insights from unsensed incentives. *Neuron, 36*(2), 229–240. https://doi.org/10.1016/s0896-6273(02)00965-0

Wisniewski, M. G., Church, B. A., & Mercado, E., 3rd. (2009). Learning-related shifts in generalization gradients for complex sounds. *Learn Behav, 37*(4), 325–335. https://doi.org/10.3758/LB.37.4.325

Wisniewski, M. G., Radell, M. L., Church, B. A., & Mercado, E., 3rd. (2017). Benefits of fading in perceptual learning are driven by more than dimensional attention. *PLoS One, 12*(7), e0180959. https://doi.org/10.1371/journal.pone.0180959

Wittgenstein, L. (1953). *Philosophical investigations*. Hoboken, NJ: Blackwell.

Wittmann, M. (2009). The inner experience of time. *Philos Trans R Soc Lond B Biol Sci, 364*, 1955–1967. https://doi.org/10.1098/rstb.2009.0003

Wittmann, M. (2011). Moments in time. *Front Integr Neurosci, 5*, 66. https://doi.org/10.3389/fnint.2011.00066

Wittmann, M. (2013). The inner sense of time: How the brain creates a representation of duration. *Nat Rev Neurosci, 14*, 217–223. https://doi.org/10.1038/nrn3452

Wohlgemuth, S., Adam, I., & Scharff, C. (2014). FoxP2 in songbirds. *Curr Opin Neurobiol, 28*, 86–93. https://doi.org/10.1016/j.conb.2014.06.009

Wolfe, J. M. (2020). Forty years after feature integration theory: An introduction to the special issue in honor of the contributions of Anne Treisman. *Atten Percept Psychophys, 82*(1), 1–6. https://doi.org/10.3758/s13414-019-01966-3

Wolfe, J. M. (2021). Guided Search 6.0: An updated model of visual search. *Psychon Bull Rev, 28*(4), 1060–1092. https://doi.org/10.3758/s13423-020-01859-9

Wollny, S., Schneider, J., Di Mitri, D., Weidlich, J., Rittberger, M., & Drachsler, H. (2021). Are We There Yet?—A Systematic Literature Review on Chatbots in Education. *Front Artif Intell, 4*, 654924. https://doi.org/10.3389/frai.2021.654924

Wong, B. (2010). Points of view: Gestalt principles (part 1). *Nat Methods, 7*(11), 863. https://doi.org/10.1038/nmeth1110-863

Wong, N.H.L., & Chang, D.H.F. (2018). Attentional advantages in video-game experts are not related to perceptual tendencies. *Sci Rep, 8*(1), 5528. https://doi.org/10.1038/s41598-018-23819-z

Wood, C. C., Allison, T., Goff, W. R., Williamson, P. D., & Spencer, D. D. (1980). On the neural origin of P300 in man. *Prog Brain Res, 54*, 51–56. https://doi.org/10.1016/S0079-6123(08)61605-2

Workman, L., & Reader, W. (2021). *Evolutionary psychology: An introduction*. UK: Cambridge University Press.

Worrell, F. C., Subotnik, R. F., Olszewski-Kubilius, P., & Dixson, D. D. (2019). Gifted students. *Annu Rev Psychol, 70*, 551–576. https://doi.org/10.1146/annurev-psych-010418-102846

Wright, A. A., & Roediger, H. L., 3rd. (2003). Interference processes in monkey auditory list memory. *Psychon Bull Rev, 10*(3), 696–702. http://www.ncbi.nlm.nih.gov/pubmed/14620366

Wright, A. A., Kelly, D. M., & Katz, J. S. (2018). Comparing cognition by integrating concept learning, proactive interference, and list memory. *Learn Behav, 46*, 107–123.

Wu, H. Y., Kuo, B. C., Huang, C. M., Tsai, P. J., Hsu, A. L., Hsu, L. M., Liu, C. Y.,…Wu, C. W. (2020). Think hard or think smart: Network reconfigurations after divergent thinking associate with creativity performance. *Front Hum Neurosci, 14*, 571118. https://doi.org/10.3389/fnhum.2020.571118

Wu, J., Luan, S., & Raihani, N. (2022). Reward, punishment, and prosocial behavior: Recent developments and implications. *Curr Opin Psychol, 44*, 117–123. https://doi.org/10.1016/j.copsyc.2021.09.003

Wundt, W. M. (1912). *An introduction to psychology*. New York, NY: Macmillan.

Wurtz, P., Mueri, R. M., & Wiesendanger, M. (2009). Sight-reading of violinists: Eye movements anticipate the musical flow. *Exp Brain Res, 194*(3), 445–450. https://doi.org/10.1007/s00221-009-1719-3

Wynn, K. (1992). Evidence against empiricist accounts of the origins of numerical knowledge. *Mind Lang, 7*, 315–332.

Wyttenbach, R. A., May, M. L., & Hoy, R. R. (1996). Categorical perception of sound frequency by crickets. *Science, 273*(5281), 1542–1544. https://doi.org/10.1126/science.273.5281.1542

X

Xie, S., Kaiser, D., & Cichy, R. M. (2020). Visual imagery and perception share neural representations in the alpha frequency band. *Curr Biol, 30*(15), 3062. https://doi.org/10.1016/j.cub.2020.07.023

Xing, L., Kubik-Zahorodna, A., Namba, T., Pinson, A., Florio, M., Prochazka, J.,… Huttner, W. B. (2021). Expression of human-specific ARHGAP11B in mice leads to neocortex expansion and increased memory flexibility. *EMBO J, 40*(13), e107093. https://doi.org/10.15252/embj.2020107093

Xu, R., Bichot, N. P., Takahashi, A., & Desimone, R. (2022). The cortical connectome of primate lateral prefrontal cortex. *Neuron, 110*(2), 312–327 e317. https://doi.org/10.1016/j.neuron.2021.10.018

Y

Yamada, Y., Kawabe, T., & Ihaya, K. (2013). Categorization difficulty is associated with negative evaluation in the "uncanny valley" phenomenon. *Jpn Psychol Res, 55*, 20–32.

Yang, J., Yan, F. F., Chen, L., Xi, J., Fan, S., Zhang, P.,… Huang, C. B. (2020). General learning ability in perceptual learning. *Proc Natl Acad Sci U S A, 117*(32), 19092–19100. https://doi.org/10.1073/pnas.2002903117

Yang, Y., & Raine, A. (2009). Prefrontal structural and functional brain imaging findings in antisocial, violent, and psychopathic individuals: A meta-analysis. *Psychiatry Res, 174*(2), 81–88. https://doi.org/10.1016/j.pscychresns.2009.03.012

Yao, W. X., Cordova, A., De Sola, W., Hart, C., & Yan, A. F. (2012). The effect of variable practice on wheelchair propulsive efficiency and propulsive timing. *Eur J Phys Rehabil Med, 48*(2), 209–216. https://www.ncbi.nlm.nih.gov/pubmed/22071502

Yee, D. M., & Braver, T. S. (2018). Interactions of motivation and cognitive control. *Curr Opin Behav Sci, 19*, 83–90. https://doi.org/10.1016/j.cobeha.2017.11.009

Yerkes, R. M. (1937). Primate cooperation and intelligence. *Am J Psychol, 50*, 254–270.

Yin, P., Fritz, J. B., & Shamma, S. A. (2014). Rapid spectrotemporal plasticity in primary auditory cortex during behavior. *J Neurosci, 34*(12), 4396–4408. https://doi.org/10.1523/JNEUROSCI.2799-13.2014

Yost, W. A. (2017). History of sound source localization: 1850–1950. *Proc Meet Acoust, 30*, 050002.

Young, L., & Koenigs, M. (2007). Investigating emotion in moral cognition: A review of evidence from functional neuroimaging and neuropsychology. *Br Med Bull, 84*, 69–79. https://doi.org/10.1093/bmb/ldm031

Yovel, G. (2016). Neural and cognitive face-selective markers: An integrative review. *Neuropsychologia, 83*, 5–13. https://doi.org/10.1016/j.neuropsychologia.2015.09.026

Yu, F., Jiang, Q. J., Sun, X. Y., & Zhang, R. W. (2015). A new case of complete primary cerebellar agenesis: Clinical and imaging findings in a living patient. *Brain, 138*(Pt 6), e353. https://doi.org/10.1093/brain/awu239

Z

Zabelina, D. L., Colzato, L., Beeman, M., & Hommel, B. (2016). Dopamine and the creative mind: Individual differences in creativity are predicted by interactions between dopamine genes DAT and COMT. *PLoS One, 11*(1), e0146768. https://doi.org/10.1371/journal.pone.0146768

Zadra, J. R., & Clore, G. L. (2011). Emotion and perception: The role of affective information. *Wiley Interdiscip Rev Cogn Sci, 2*(6), 676–685. https://doi.org/10.1002/wcs.147

Zeithamova, D., Mack, M. L., Braunlich, K., Davis, T., Seger, C. A., van Kesteren, M.T.R., & Wutz, A. (2019). Brain mechanisms of concept learning. *J Neurosci, 39*(42), 8259–8266. https://doi.org/10.1523/JNEUROSCI.1166-19.2019

Zeman, A., Milton, F., Della Sala, S., Dewar, M., Frayling, T., Gaddum, J., … Winlove, C. (2020). Phantasia—The psychological significance of lifelong visual imagery vividness extremes. *Cortex, 130*, 426–440. https://doi.org/10.1016/j.cortex.2020.04.003

Zentall, T. R. (2005). Selective and divided attention in animals. *Behav Processes, 69*(1), 1–15. https://doi.org/10.1016/j.beproc.2005.01.004

Zentner, M., & Eerola, T. (2010). Rhythmic engagement with music in infancy. *Proc Natl Acad Sci U S A, 107*, 5768–5773. https://doi.org/10.1073/pnas.1000121107

Zhao, T. C., & Kuhl, P. K. (2022). Development of infants' neural speech processing and its relation to later language skills: A MEG study. *Neuroimage, 256*, 119242. https://doi.org/10.1016/j.neuroimage.2022.119242

Zola-Morgan, S. (1995). Localization of brain function: The legacy of Franz Joseph Gall (1758–1828). *Annu Rev Neurosci, 18*, 359–383. https://doi.org/10.1146/annurev.ne.18.030195.002043

Zylberberg, J., & Strowbridge, B. W. (2017). Mechanisms of persistent activity in cortical circuits: Possible neural substrates for working memory. *Annu Rev Neurosci, 40*, 603–627. https://doi.org/10.1146/annurev-neuro-070815-014006

INDEX

Page references in italics indicate figures.